NEET TEST SERIES

30+ TESTS

PHYSICS

Latest Solved Papers
with Complete Explanations

NEET TEST SERIES

30+ TESTS

PHYSICS

Latest Solved Papers
with Complete Explanations

Author
Mukesh Kumar
B.Tech (Electrical) from MNIT, Jaipur

ARIHANT PRAKASHAN (SERIES), MEERUT

ARIHANT PRAKASHAN (SERIES), MEERUT

ADMINISTRATIVE & PRODUCTION OFFICES

Regd. Office
'Ramchhaya' 4577/15, Agarwal Road, Darya Ganj, New Delhi -110002
Tele: 011- 47630600, 43518550

Head Office
Kalindi, TP Nagar, Meerut (UP) - 250002, Tel: 0121-7156203, 7156204

SALES & SUPPORT OFFICES
Agra, Ahmedabad, Bengaluru, Bareilly, Chennai, Delhi, Guwahati, Hyderabad, Jaipur, Jhansi, Kolkata, Lucknow, Nagpur & Pune.

ISBN 978-93-27194-12-8

PRICE ₹295.00

PO No.: TXT-59-T051377-1-23

Published By Arihant Publications (India) Ltd.

For further information about the books published by Arihant, log on to www.arihantbooks.com or e-mail at info@arihantbooks.com

Follow us on   

Contents

Syllabus

CLASS 11th

UNIT I Physical World and Measurement

Physics : Scope and excitement, nature of physical laws; Physics, technology and society.

Need for measurement: Units of measurement, systems of units, SI units, fundamental and derived units. Length, mass and time measurements, accuracy and precision of measuring instruments, errors in measurement, significant figures.

Dimensions of physical quantities, dimensional analysis and its applications.

UNIT II Kinematics

Frame of reference, Motion in a straight line, Position-time graph, speed and velocity. Uniform and non-uniform motion, average speed and instantaneous velocity. Uniformly accelerated motion, velocity-time and position-time graphs, for uniformly accelerated motion (graphical treatment).

Elementary concepts of differentiation and integration for describing motion. Scalar and vector quantities: Position and displacement vectors, general vectors, general vectors and notation, equality of vectors, multiplication of vectors by a real number, addition and subtraction of vectors. Relative velocity.

Unit vectors. Resolution of a vector in a plane-rectangular components.

Scalar and Vector products of Vectors. Motion in a plane. Cases of uniform velocity and uniform acceleration-projectile motion. Uniform circular motion.

UNIT III Laws of Motion

Intuitive concept of force. Inertia, Newton's first law of motion; momentum and Newton's second law of motion, impulse, Newton's third law of motion. Law of conservation of linear momentum and its applications.

Equilibrium of concurrent forces. Static and Kinetic friction, laws of friction, rolling friction, lubrication.
Dynamics of uniform circular motion. Centripetal force, examples of circular motion (vehicle on level circular road, vehicle on banked road).

UNIT IV Work, Energy and Power

Work done by a constant force and variable force, kinetic energy, work-energy theorem, power. Notion of potential energy, potential energy of a spring, conservative forces, conservation of mechanical energy (kinetic and potential energies), non-conservative forces, motion in a vertical circle, elastic and inelastic collisions in one and two dimensions.

UNIT V Motion of System of Particles and Rigid Body

Centre of mass of a two-particle system, momentum conservation and centre of mass motion. Centre of mass of a rigid body, centre of mass of uniform rod.
Moment of a force, torque, angular momentum, conservation of angular momentum with some examples.
Equilibrium of rigid bodies, rigid body rotation and equation of rotational motion, comparison of linear and rotational motions, moment of inertia, radius of gyration. Values of MI for simple geometrical objects (no derivation). Statement of parallel and perpendicular axes theorems and their applications.

UNIT VI Gravitation

Kepler's laws of planetary motion. The universal law of gravitation. Acceleration due to gravity and its variation with altitude and depth.

Gravitational potential energy, gravitational potential. Escape velocity, orbital velocity of a satellite. Geostationary satellites.

UNIT VII Properties of Bulk Matter

Elastic behavior, Stress-strain relationship. Hooke's law, Young's modulus, bulk modulus, shear, modulus of rigidity, poisson's ratio; elastic energy.

Viscosity, Stokes' law, terminal velocity, Reynold's number, streamline and turbulent flow. Critical velocity, Bernoulli's theorem and its applications.

Surface energy and surface tension, angle of contact, excess of pressure, application of surface tension ideas to drops, bubbles and capillary rise.

Heat, temperature, thermal expansion, thermal expansion of solids, liquids and gases. Anomalous expansion. Specific heat capacity, C_P, C_V-calorimetry; change of state – latent heat.

Heat transfer- conduction and thermal conductivity, convection and radiation. Qualitative ideas of Black Body Radiation, Wein's displacement law and Green House effect.

Newton's law of cooling and Stefan's law.

UNIT VIII Thermodynamics

Thermal equilibrium and definition of temperature (zeroth law of Thermodynamics). Heat, work and internal energy. First law of thermodynamics: Isothermal and adiabatic processes.

Second law of the thermodynamics: Reversible and irreversible processes. Heat engines and refrigerators.

UNIT IX Behaviour of Perfect Gas and Kinetic Theory

Equation of state of a perfect gas, work done on compressing a gas.

Kinetic theory of gases: Assumptions, concept of pressure. Kinetic energy and temperature, degrees of freedom, law of equipartition of energy (statement only) and application to specific heat capacities of gases, concept of mean free path.

UNIT X Oscillations and Waves

Periodic motion-period, frequency, displacement as a function of time. Periodic functions. Simple harmonic motion(SHM) and its equation, phase, oscillations of a spring-restoring force and force constant, energy in SHM–kinetic and potential energies, simple pendulum-derivation of expression for its time period, free, forced and damped oscillations (qualitative ideas only), resonance.

Wave motion. Longitudinal and transverse waves, speed of wave motion. Displacement relation for a progressive wave. Principle of superposition of waves, reflection of waves, standing waves in strings and organ pipes, fundamental mode and harmonics. Beats, Doppler effect.

Class 12th

UNIT I Electrostatics

Electric charges and their conservation. Coulomb's law-force between two point charges, forces between multiple charges, superposition principle and continuous charge distribution.

Electric field, electric field due to a point charge, electric field lines, electric dipole, electric field due to a dipole, torque on a dipole in a uniform electric field.

Electric flux, statement of Gauss's theorem and its applications to find field due to infinitely long straight wire, uniformly charged infinite plane sheet and uniformly charged thin spherical shell (field inside and outside).

Electric potential, potential difference, electric potential due to a point charge, a dipole and system of charges, equipotential surfaces, electrical potential energy of a system of two point charges and of electric diploes in an electrostatic field.

Conductors and insulators, free charges and bound charges inside a conductor, Dielectrics and electric polarization, capacitors and capacitance, combination of capacitors in series and in parallel, capacitance of a parallel plate capacitor with and without dielectric medium between the plates, energy stored in a capacitor, Van de Graaff generator.

UNIT II Current Electricity

Electric current, flow of electric charges in a metallic conductor, drift velocity and mobility and their relation with electric current, Ohm's law, electrical resistance, V-I characteristics (linear and non-linear), electrical energy and power, electrical resistivity and conductivity.

Carbon resistors, colour code for carbon resistors, series and parallel combinations of resistors, temperature dependence of resistance.

Internal resistance of a cell, potential difference and emf of a cell, combination of cells in series and in parallel.

Kirchhoff's laws and simple applications. Wheatstone bridge, metre bridge.

Potentiometer-principle and applications to measure potential difference, and for comparing emf of two cells, measurement of internal resistance of a cell.

UNIT III Magnetic Effects of Current and Magnetism

Concept of magnetic field, Oersted's experiment. Biot-Savart's law and its application to current carrying circular loop.

Ampere's law and its applications to infinitely long straight wire, straight and toroidal solenoids. Force on a moving charge in uniform magnetic and electric fields. Cyclotron.

Force on a current-carrying conductor in a uniform magnetic field. Force between two parallel current-carrying conductors-definition of ampere. Torque experienced by a current loop in a magnetic field, moving coil galvanometer-its current sensitivity and conversion to ammeter and voltmeter.

Current loop as a magnetic dipole and its magnetic dipole moment. Magnetic dipole moment of a revolving electron. Magnetic field intensity due to a magnetic dipole (bar magnet) along its axis and perpendicular to its axis. Torque on a magnetic dipole (bar magnet) in a uniform magnetic field, bar magnet as an equivalent solenoid, magnetic field lines, Earth's magnetic field and magnetic elements.

Para-, dia-and ferro-magnetic substances with examples.

Electromagnetic and factors affecting their strengths. Permanent magnets.

UNIT IV Electromagnetic Induction and Alternating Currents

Electromagnetic induction: Faraday's law, induced emf and current, Lenz's Law, Eddy currents. Self and mutual inductance.

Alternating currents, peak and rms value of alternating current/ voltage, reactance and impedance, LC oscillations (qualitative treatment only), LCR series circuit, resonance, power in AC circuits, wattles current.

AC generator and transformer.

UNIT V Electromagnetic Waves

Need for displacement current.

Electromagnetic waves and their characteristics (qualitative ideas only). Transverse nature of electromagnetic waves.

Electromagnetic spectrum (radiowaves, microwaves, infrared, visible, ultraviolet, X-rays, gamma rays) including elementary facts about their uses.

UNIT VI Optics

Reflection of light, spherical mirrors, mirror formula. Refraction of light, total internal reflection and its applications optical fibres, refraction at spherical surfaces, lenses, thin lens formula, lens-maker's formula. Magnification, power of a lens, combination of thin lenses in contact combination of a lens and a mirror. Refraction and dispersion of light through a prism.

Scattering of light- blue colour of the sky and reddish appearance of the sun at sunrise and sunset.

Optical instruments Human eye, image formation and accommodation, correction of eye defects (myopia and hypermetropia) using lenses.

Microscopes and astronomical telescopes (reflecting and refracting) and their magnifying powers.

Wave optics: Wavefront and Huygens' principle, reflection and refraction of plane wave at a plane surface using wavefronts.

Proof of laws of reflection and refraction using Huygens' principle.

Interference, Young's double hole experiment and expression for fringe width, coherent sources and sustained interference of light.

Diffraction due to a single slit, width of central maximum.

Resolving power of microscopes and astronomical telescopes. Polarisation, plane polarised light, Brewster's law, uses of plane polarised light and Polaroids.

UNIT VII Dual Nature of Matter and Radiation

Photoelectric effect, Hertz and Lenard's observations, Einstein's photoelectric equation- particle nature of light.

Matter waves- wave nature of particles, de-Broglie relation. Davisson-Germer experiment (experimental details should be omitted, only conclusion should be explained).

UNIT VIII Atoms and Nuclei

Alpha- particle scattering experiments, Rutherford's model of atom, Bohr model, energy levels, hydrogen spectrum. Composition and size of nucleus, atomic masses, isotopes, isobars, isotones.

Radioactivity- α, β and γ particles/ rays and their properties decay law. Mass-energy relation, mass defect, binding energy per nucleon and its variation with mass number, nuclear fission and fusion.

UNIT IX Electronic Devices

Energy bands in solids (qualitative ideas only), conductors, insulators and semiconductors, semiconductor diode- I-V characteristics in forward and reverse bias, diode as a rectifier, I-V characteristics of LED, photodiode, solar cell and Zener diode, Zener diode as a voltage regulator. Junction transistor, transistor action, characteristics of a transistor, transistor as an amplifier
(common emitter configuration) and oscillator. Logic gates (OR, AND, NOT, NAND and NOR).
Transistor as a switch.

Revisiting the Concepts

Complete Revision Notes for NEET Physics

This section has complete Revision Notes to revise all the concepts of Physics quickly before attempting the tests.

Revision Notes

1. Units and Measurement

- **Physical quantities** All the quantities which are used to describe the laws of physics are called physical quantities. e.g. Length, mass, volume, etc.
- To express the measurement of a physical quantity, we need to know two things as given below
  (i) The unit in which the quantity is measured.
  (ii) The numerical value or the magnitude of the quantity.
  i.e. The number of times that unit is contained in the given physical quantity $= nu$

$$\therefore \quad n \propto \frac{1}{u}$$

$$\Rightarrow \quad nu = \text{constant}$$

where, n = numerical value of the physical quantity,
u = size of unit.

- **Physical units** The standard amount of a physical quantity chosen to measure the physical quantity of same kind is called a physical unit.
- **Fundamental quantities and fundamental units** Those physical quantities which are independent from other physical quantities and are not defined in terms of other physical quantities, are called **fundamental** or **base quantities.** The units of these quantities are called **fundamental** or **base units.** The table below gives the seven fundamental quantities and their SI units.

Base quantity	SI Units		
	Name	Symbol	Definition
Length	Metre	m	The metre is the length of the path travelled by light in vacuum during a time interval of 1/299792458 of a second.
Mass	Kilogram	kg	The kilogram is equal to the mass of the international prototype of the kilogram (a platinum-iridium alloy cylinder) kept at international Bureau of Weights and Measures at Sevres, near Paris, France.
Time	Second	s	The second is the duration of 9192631770 periods of the radiation corresponding to the transition between the two hyperfine levels of the ground state of the cesium-133 atom.
Electric current	Ampere	A	The ampere is that constant current which if maintained in two straight parallel conductors of infinite length, of negligible circular cross-section and placed 1 m apart in vacuum, would produce a force between these conductors equal to 2×10^{-7} N/m of length.
Thermodynamic temperature	Kelvin	K	The kelvin is the fraction 1/273.16 of the thermodynamic temperature of the triple point of water.
Amount of substance	Mole	mol	The mole is the amount of substance of a system which contains as many elementary entities as there are atoms in 0.012 kg of carbon-12.
Luminous intensity	Candela	cd	The candela is the luminous intensity in a given direction of a source that emits monochromatic radiation of frequency 540×10^{12} Hz and that has a radiant intensity in that direction of 1/683 watt/steradian.

- **Derived quantities and derived units** The quantities which can be expressed in terms of the fundamental quantities are called **derived quantities**. The units of these quantities are called **derived units.**
  e.g. Unit of speed = ms^{-1} can be derived from fundamental unit, i.e. unit of length and time as

$$\text{Speed} = \frac{\text{Distance}}{\text{Time}} = \frac{m}{s} = ms^{-1}$$

- **System of units** A complete set of units which is used to measure all kinds of fundamental and derived quantities is called a system of units.
  Some of the commonly used systems of units are as follows
  - **CGS system** In this system, the units of length, mass and time are measured in centimetre (cm), gram (g) and second (s) respectively. In this system of units, the unit of force is dyne and unit of work or energy is erg.
  - **FPS system** In this system, the units of length, mass and time are measured in foot, pound and second, respectively. The unit of force in this system is poundal.
  - **MKS system** In this system, the units of length, mass and time are measured in metre (m), kilogram (kg) and second (s), respectively. In this system of units, the unit of force is newton (N) and unit of work or energy is joule (J).

- **International system (SI) of units** This system of units helps in revolutionary changes over the MKS system and is known as **rationalised MKS system.** It is helpful to obtain all the physical quantities in physics.

- **Error** The difference between the true value and the measured value of a quantity is called a error.

Some mathematical terms used for error calculation are given below

- **Absolute error** The difference between the true value and the measured value of a quantity is called absolute error.

  i.e. $\Delta a_n = a_m - a_n$

  where, $a_m = \sum_{i=1}^{n} \frac{a_i}{n}$

- **Mean absolute error** The arithmetic mean of the magnitude of absolute errors in all the measurement is called mean absolute error.

$$\overline{\Delta a} = \frac{|\Delta a_1| + |\Delta a_2| + \ldots + |\Delta a_n|}{n}$$

- **Relative error** or **fractional error** The ratio of mean absolute error to the true value is called relative error.

$$\text{Relative error} = \frac{\text{Mean absolute error}}{\text{True value}} = \frac{\overline{\Delta a}}{a_m}$$

- **Percentage error** The relative error expressed in percentage is called percentage error.

$$\text{Percentage error} = \frac{\overline{\Delta a}}{a_m} \times 100\%$$

- **Combination of errors**

- **Error in addition** or **subtraction** Let $x = a + b$ or $x = a - b$

  If the measured values of two quantities a and b are $(a \pm \Delta a)$ and $(b \pm \Delta b)$, where Δa and Δb are the absolute errors in the measurement of a and b, then maximum absolute error in their addition or subtraction is $\Delta x = \pm (\Delta a + \Delta b)$.

- **Error in multiplication** or **division** Let $x = a \times b$ or $x = a/b$

  If the measured values of a and b are $(a \pm \Delta a)$ and $(b \pm \Delta b)$, then maximum relative error,

$$\frac{\Delta x}{x} = \pm \left(\frac{\Delta a}{a} + \frac{\Delta b}{b} \right)$$

- **Error in a quantity raised to a power** Let $z = a^p b^q / c^r$

  If the measured values of a, b and c are $(a \pm \Delta a)$, $(b \pm \Delta b)$ and $(c \pm \Delta c)$, then maximum error,

$$\frac{\Delta z}{z} = \pm \left[p\left(\frac{\Delta a}{a}\right) + q\left(\frac{\Delta b}{b}\right) + r\left(\frac{\Delta c}{c}\right) \right]$$

- **Significant figures are the digits about the correction of which we are sure, plus the last digits which is doubtful.**
  Larger the number of significant figures obtained in a measurement, greater is the accuracy of the measurement.

- The order of magnitude of a quantity means its value (in suitable power of 10) nearest to the actual value of the quantity.

- **Rounding off** The process of omitting the non-significant digits and retaining only the desired number of significant digits, incorporating the required modifications to the last significant digit is called rounding off the number.

- **Order of magnitude** Any physical quantity can be expressed in the form of $a \times 10^b$ (in terms of magnitude), where a is a number lying between 1 and 10 and b is any negative or positive exponent of 10, then the exponent b is called the **order of magnitude** of the physical quantity and the expression of a quantity as $a \times 10^b$ is called **scientific notation.**

- **Dimensions of physical quantities** The dimensions of a physical quantity are the powers (or exponents) to which the fundamental quantities must be raised to represent that quantity.

  e.g. $\text{Density} = \frac{\text{Mass}}{\text{Volume}} = \frac{\text{Mass}}{(\text{Length})^3}$

  or $\text{Density} = (\text{Mass})\,(\text{Length})^{-3}$

  Thus, the dimensions of density are 1 in mass and – 3 in length.

- The expression of a physical quantity in terms of its dimensions is called its **dimensional formula.**

- **Principle of homogeneity** This principle states that, the dimensions of each term on both sides of an equation must be the same.

- **Dimensional analysis and its applications** The method of studying a physical phenomenon on the basis of dimensions is called **dimensional analysis.** The following are the three main uses of dimensional analysis

  (i) To convert a physical quantity from one system of units to another.

  (ii) To check the correctness of a given physical relation.

  (iii) To derive a relationship between different physical quantities.

2. Motion in a Straight Line

- **Rest** If the position of an object does not change w.r.t. its surroundings or with the passage of time, it is said to be at rest. e.g. Book lying on the table, a person sitting on a chair, etc.

- **Motion** If the position of an object is continuously changing w.r.t. its surroundings, then it is said to be in the **state of motion.**

- On the basis of the number of co-ordinates required to specify the motion of object can be classified as

  (i) One-dimensional motion

  (ii) Two-dimensional motion

  (iii) Three-dimensional motion

- **Scalar and vector quantities** Physical quantities are studied under two heads, scalars and vectors. Both types of quantity can be defined as follows
  - (i) **Scalar quantity** If only the magnitude is required to specify a physical quantity, that physical quantity is known as **scalar quantity**. e.g. Mass, length, time, speed, etc.
  - (ii) **Vector quantity** If magnitude as well as direction both are required to specify a physical quantity, that physical quantity is known as vector quantity.
    e.g. Displacement, velocity, acceleration, etc.
- **Distance** The total length of the path covered by the object in a given time interval is known as its **distance** or **path length travelled.** It is a scalar quantity. Its SI unit is metre (m).
- **Displacement** The change in position of an object in a particular direction is termed as displacement, i.e. the minimum difference between the final and initial positions of the object in a given time. It is denoted by Δx. Mathematically, it is represented by

$$\text{Displacement, } \Delta x = x_2 - x_1$$

where, x_1 and x_2 are the initial and final positions of the object, respectively. It is a vector quantity. Its SI unit is metre.

  - Displacement of a motion may be zero or negative but path length or distance can never be zero or negative. i.e., displacement may be positive, negative or zero.

- **Uniform motion in a straight line**

A body is said to be in a uniform motion, if it travels equal distances in equal interval of time along a straight line.

- **Non-uniform motion in a straight line**
  - A body is said to be in non-uniform motion, if it travels unequal displacement in equal intervals of time.
  - During the non-uniform motion, the speed of the body or its direction of motion or both change with time.
- **Speed** The path length or the distance covered by an object divided by the time taken by the object to cover that distance is called the speed of that object.

$$\text{Speed} = \frac{\text{Distance travelled}}{\text{Time taken}}$$

Speed is a scalar quantity. Its SI unit is ms^{-1}.

- **Average speed** Average speed of an object is defined as the total distance travelled divided by the total time taken.

$$\text{Average speed, } v_{av} = \frac{\text{Total distance travelled}}{\text{Total time taken}}$$

- **Instantaneous speed** Speed at an instant is defined as the limit of the average speed as the time interval (Δt) becomes infinitesimally small or approaches to zero.
- Mathematically, instantaneous speed at any instant of time t is expressed as

$$\text{Instantaneous speed, } s_{\text{inst}} = \lim_{\Delta t \to 0} \frac{\Delta s}{\Delta t} \quad \text{or } s_{\text{inst}} = \frac{ds}{dt}$$

where, ds is the distance covered in time dt.

- **Velocity** The rate of change in displacement of an object is called the velocity of that object.

$$\text{Velocity} = \frac{\text{Displacement}}{\text{Time}}$$

It is a vector quantity. Its SI unit is ms^{-1}.

- **Average velocity** Average velocity of a body is defined as the change in displacement ($\Delta \mathbf{x}$) divided by the time interval (Δt) in which that displacement occurs.

Average velocity of a body is given by

$$\mathbf{v}_{av} = \frac{\Delta \mathbf{x}}{\Delta t} = \frac{\mathbf{x}_2 - \mathbf{x}_1}{t_2 - t_1}$$

- **Instantaneous velocity** Velocity at an instant is defined as the limit of average velocity as the time interval (Δt) becomes infinitesimally small or approaches to zero.
- Mathematically, instantaneous velocity at an instant of time t is given by

$$\mathbf{v}_{\text{inst}} = \lim_{\Delta t \to 0} \frac{\Delta \mathbf{x}}{\Delta t} \quad \text{or} \quad \mathbf{v}_{\text{inst}} = \frac{dx}{dt}$$

where, dx is displacement for time dt.

- **Acceleration** The rate of change of velocity is known as acceleration.

$$\text{Acceleration} = \frac{\text{Change in velocity}}{\text{Time taken}}$$

It is a vector quantity. Its SI unit is ms^{-2}.

- **Average acceleration** The average acceleration is the ratio of the change in velocity to the time taken to undergo this change.

$$\mathbf{a}_{av} = \frac{\mathbf{v}(t_2) - \mathbf{v}(t_1)}{t_2 - t_1} = \frac{\Delta \mathbf{v}}{\Delta t}$$

- **Instantaneous acceleration** Instantaneous acceleration is the acceleration at any instant of time or at any given point.

$$\mathbf{a} = \lim_{\Delta t \to 0} \frac{\Delta \mathbf{v}}{\Delta t} = \frac{dv}{dt}$$

- **Equations of uniformly accelerated motion** Motion of a body moving with constant acceleration can be expressed by the following equations
  - (i) $\mathbf{v} = \mathbf{u} + \mathbf{a}t$ (Velocity-time equation)
  - (ii) $\mathbf{s} = \mathbf{u}t + \frac{1}{2}\mathbf{a}t^2$ (Displacement-time equation)
  - (iii) $\mathbf{v}^2 = \mathbf{u}^2 + 2\mathbf{as}$ (Displacement-velocity equation)
  - (iv) $\mathbf{s}_{nth} = \mathbf{u} + \frac{\mathbf{a}}{2}(2n - 1)$ (Displacement in nth second)

where, $\mathbf{v}$ = final velocity,
$\mathbf{u}$ = initial velocity,
$\mathbf{a}$ = acceleration,
t = time and $\mathbf{s}$ = displacement.

- **Equations of motion for object falling under gravity** When the object falls under the influence of gravity, its motion is uniformly accelerated motion. Hence, equations of motion are applicable in this case also.

- For upward motion, i.e. an object is thrown vertically upwards

$$v = u - gt,\ h = ut - \frac{1}{2}gt^2$$

and $v^2 = u^2 - 2gh.$

– **Note** In upward motion, g is taken as negative.

- For downward motion, i.e., an object is thrown vertically downwards

$$v = u + gt,\ h = ut + \frac{1}{2}gt^2$$

and $v^2 = u^2 + 2gh.$

– **Note** In downward motion, g is taken as positive.

- If an object is dropped (from some height), then $u = 0$, hence

$$v = gt$$

$$h = \frac{1}{2}gt^2$$

$$v^2 = 2gh$$

– **Note** If an object is dropped from some height, then initial velocity is taken as zero.

- For fast calculations of objective problems, remember the following results
  (i) Maximum height attained by a particle thrown upward from ground, $h = \frac{u^2}{2g}$
  (ii) Velocity of a particle at the time of striking the ground, when released ($u = 0$) from a height h, $v = \sqrt{2gh}$
  (iii) Time of collision with ground, $t = \sqrt{\frac{2h}{g}}$

- **Non-uniformly accelerated motion** When a particle is not uniformly accelerated, i.e. acceleration of particle is not constant or acceleration is a function of time, then the following relations hold for one-dimensional motion.
  (i) $v = \frac{ds}{dt}$
  (ii) $a = \frac{dv}{dt} = \frac{dv}{ds} \times \frac{ds}{dt} = v\frac{dv}{ds}$
  (iii) $ds = vdt$
  (iv) $dv = adt$
  or $vdv = ads$

Graphs in one-dimensional motion There are three types of graphs representing motion in one dimension as given below
(i) Position-time graph (s-t)
(ii) Velocity-time graph (v-t)
(iii) Acceleration-time graph (a-t)

The tabular forms of s-t, v-t and a-t graphs are given for one-dimensional motion with a uniform velocity or with constant acceleration.

Note – Area under v-t graph gives the value at displacement covered in given time.
– Area under the acceleration-time (a - t) graph between t_1 to t_2 gives the change in velocity, i.e.

$$v_2 - v_1 = \text{Area under } a\text{ - }t \text{ graph} = \int_{t_1}^{t_2} a\,dt$$

Different cases	s-t Graph	v-t Graph	a-t Graph	Slope of v-t Graph
At rest	s, O, t	—	—	—
Uniform motion	s, $s = vt$, O, t	v, v = constant, O, t	a, O, t	Slope is zero.
Uniformly accelerated motion with $u = 0$, $s = 0$ at $t = 0$.	s, $s = \frac{1}{2}at^2$, O, t	v, $v = at$, O, t	a, a = constant, O, t	Slope is positive.
Uniformly accelerated motion with $u \neq 0$ but $s = 0$ at $t = 0$.	s, $s = ut + \frac{1}{2}at^2$, O, t	v, u, $v = u + at$, O, t	a, O, t	Slope is positive.
Uniformly retarded motion	s, $s = ut - \frac{1}{2}at^2$, O, t_0, t	v, $v = u - at$, O, t_0, t	a, O, t	Slope is negative.

Different cases	s-t Graph	v-t Graph	a-t Graph	Slope of v-t Graph
Non-uniform accelerated motion	—		—	Slope is positive.
Non-uniform decelerated motion	—		—	Slope is first increase, then decreases.
A body falling freely under gravity				Slope is negative.
A body is projected vertically upwards				Slope is negative.

3. Motion in a Plane

- **A vector** can have only two rectangular components in plane and only three rectangular components in space.
- Parallelogram law of vector addition.

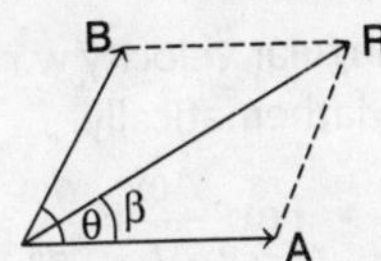

$$R = \sqrt{A^2 + B^2 + 2AB\cos\theta}$$

and $\tan\beta = \dfrac{B\sin\theta}{(A + B\cos\theta)}$

where, A and B are magnitude of vectors,

R = magnitude of resultant vectors,

θ = angle between vectors **A** and **B**,

β = angle between resultant vector **R** and vector **A**.

- If $\mathbf{A} + \mathbf{B} = \mathbf{C}$ or if $\mathbf{A} + \mathbf{B} + \mathbf{C} = 0$, then **A**, **B** and **C** lies on one plane.
- If $\mathbf{A} \times \mathbf{B} = \mathbf{C}$, then **C** is perpendicular to **A** as well as **B**.
- A vector can be expressed as, $\mathbf{A} = A_x\hat{\mathbf{i}} + A_y\hat{\mathbf{j}}$

where, A_x and A_y are its components along X and Y-axes. If vector **A** makes an angle θ with the X-axis, then

$$A_x = A\cos\theta \quad \text{and} \quad A_y = A\sin\theta$$

$$A = |\mathbf{A}| = \sqrt{{A_x}^2 + {A_y}^2}$$

and $\tan\theta = \dfrac{A_y}{A_x}$

- The dot product of two vectors,

$$\mathbf{A}\cdot\mathbf{B} = AB\cos\theta \text{ and } \cos\theta = \frac{\mathbf{A}\cdot\mathbf{B}}{|\mathbf{A}||\mathbf{B}|}$$

where, θ = angle between vector **A** and vector **B**.

- Projection of vector **B** in the direction of vector,

$$B\cos\theta = \frac{\mathbf{A}\cdot\mathbf{B}}{|\mathbf{A}|}$$

- Scalar or dot product of unit vectors,

$$\hat{\mathbf{i}}\cdot\hat{\mathbf{i}} = \hat{\mathbf{j}}\cdot\hat{\mathbf{j}} = \hat{\mathbf{k}}\cdot\hat{\mathbf{k}} = 1$$

$$\hat{\mathbf{i}}\cdot\hat{\mathbf{j}} = \hat{\mathbf{j}}\cdot\hat{\mathbf{k}} = \hat{\mathbf{k}}\cdot\hat{\mathbf{i}} = 0$$

where, $\hat{\mathbf{i}}$, $\hat{\mathbf{j}}$ and $\hat{\mathbf{k}}$ are orthogonal unit vectors.

- The cross product of two vectors,

$$\mathbf{A}\times\mathbf{B} = AB\sin\theta\,\hat{\mathbf{n}}$$

where, $\hat{\mathbf{n}}$ is a unit vector perpendicular to both **A** and **B**.

- Vector product or cross product of unit vectors

$$\hat{\mathbf{i}}\times\hat{\mathbf{i}} = \hat{\mathbf{j}}\times\hat{\mathbf{j}} = \hat{\mathbf{k}}\times\hat{\mathbf{k}} = 0$$

$$\hat{\mathbf{i}}\times\hat{\mathbf{j}} = \hat{\mathbf{k}},\ \hat{\mathbf{j}}\times\hat{\mathbf{k}} = \hat{\mathbf{i}},\ \hat{\mathbf{k}}\times\hat{\mathbf{i}} = \hat{\mathbf{j}}$$

- **Relative velocity** It is the rate of change of relative position of one object with respect to another.
- Relative velocity of object A w.r.t. B, when both are moving in same direction is $v_{AB} = v_A - v_B$ and when they are moving in opposite direction, then $v_{AB} = v_A + v_B$.
- To cross the river over shortest distance, the velocity of swimmer w.r.t. river is

$$v_{SR} = \sqrt{v_S^2 - v_R^2}$$

and time taken, $t = \dfrac{d}{\sqrt{v_S^2 - v_R^2}}$

where, d = width of river.

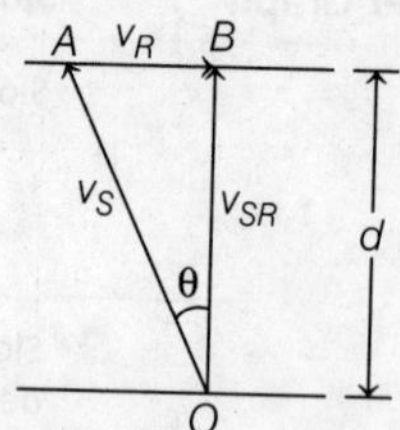

- To cross the river in possible shortest time, the velocity of swimmer w.r.t. river is

$$v_{SR} = \sqrt{v_S^2 - v_R^2}$$

and time taken, $t = \dfrac{\sqrt{x^2 + d^2}}{\sqrt{v_S^2 + v_R^2}}$

A←x→B, v_R, v_S, v_{SR}, d, θ, O Downstream

- **Projectile motion** It is an example of motion in a plane, where we have to analyse the motion separately in X and Y-direction
- Suppose, a particle is projected from ground with a velocity u at angle θ from the horizontal. Then, trajectory of the projectile,

$$y = x \tan\theta - \frac{gx^2}{2u^2 \cos^2\theta}$$

Time of flight, $T = \dfrac{2u \sin\theta}{g}$

Range, $R = \dfrac{u^2 \sin 2\theta}{g}$

$\Rightarrow R_{max} = \dfrac{u^2}{g}$ (where, θ = 45°)

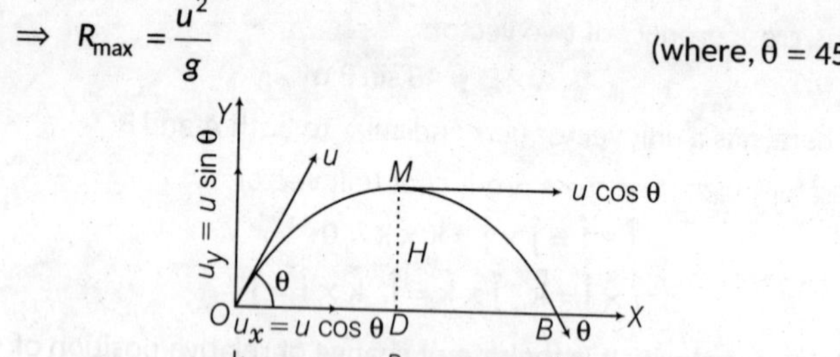

Maximum height attained, $H = \dfrac{u^2 \sin^2\theta}{2g}$

When the particle goes from O to M, the following changes take place

- Change in speed $= u\,(1 - \cos\theta) = 2u \sin^2\dfrac{\theta}{2}$
- Change in momentum in Y- direction $= mu \sin\theta$
- Change (loss) in kinetic energy $= \dfrac{1}{2} mu^2 \sin^2\theta$
- Change (gain) in potential energy $= \dfrac{1}{2} mu^2 \sin^2\theta$

- On return to the ground, i.e. in going from M to B, the following changes take place.
  - Change in momentum in Y- direction $= 2\,mu \sin\theta$
  - Change in kinetic energy = zero
  - Change in potential energy = zero
- When a body moves along the circumference of a circle with constant speed, then motion of the body is known as uniform circular motion.
- When a body moves along the circumference of a circle with variable speed, then motion of the body is known as non-uniform circular motion.
- The angle traced by the particle moving in a circular path in a certain interval of time is called the angular displacement.

Angular displacement, $\theta = \dfrac{\text{Length of the arc } (l)}{\text{Radius } (r)}$

- **Angular velocity** It is defined as the rate of change of angular displacement of a body. Mathematically,

$$\text{Angular velocity, } \omega = \frac{\delta\theta}{\delta t}$$

- If a body makes n revolution in t second, then its angular velocity, $\omega = 2\pi n$ rad/s.
- Angular velocity and linear velocity are related as,

$$\mathbf{v} = \boldsymbol{\omega} \times \mathbf{r}$$

- The rate of change of angular velocity w.r.t. time is known as **angular acceleration.** Mathematically,

Angular acceleration, $\alpha = \lim\limits_{\Delta t \to 0} \dfrac{\Delta\omega}{\Delta t} = \dfrac{d\omega}{dt}$

- Radial acceleration of a particle in a uniform circular motion is given by $a_r = \dfrac{v^2}{r} = r\omega^2$

where, ω = angular velocity,
v = linear velocity of the particle,
r = radius of circular path.

- Linear acceleration and angular acceleration are related as, $a = r\alpha$
- **Equations of motion of a body in a circular motion** When a body rotates in a circular motion, it can have three equations of motion as given below

$\omega = \omega_0 + \alpha t$ (analogous to $v = u + at$)

$\theta = \omega_0 t + \dfrac{1}{2}\alpha t^2$ (analogous to $s = ut + \dfrac{1}{2}at^2$)

$\omega^2 = \omega_0^2 + 2\alpha\theta$ (analogous to $v^2 - u^2 = 2as$)

where, α = uniform angular acceleration of a body,
ω_0 = initial angular velocity,
ω = final angular velocity,
θ = angular displacement.

- The radial force acting on a body in a uniform circular motion which is directed towards the centre of circular path and which maintain the circular motion of the body is known as **centripetal force.**

  Centripetal force = Mass × Centripetal acceleration

  $$\Rightarrow \quad F = \frac{mv^2}{r}$$

- The radial force acting on the particle performing a uniform circular motion which is directed away from the centre of circular path known as **centrifugal force**. The magnitude of a centrifugal force is equal to that of centripetal force, i.e.

  $$F = \frac{mv^2}{r} = mr\omega^2$$

- When a vehicle negotiates a circular path, its maximum speed will be

  $$v_{max} = \sqrt{\mu rg}$$

  where, r = radius of circular path, μ = coefficient of friction.

- When a cyclist goes round to a circular track, the angle made by him with the vertical is

  $$\theta = \tan^{-1}\left(\frac{v^2}{rg}\right)$$

- For safe journey on a curved road, it is banked at an angle θ from the horizontal on outer end. So, the moving speed of vehicle becomes

  $$v_{max} = \sqrt{\frac{r_g(\mu_s + \tan\theta)}{(1 - \mu_p \tan\theta)}}$$

4. Laws of Motion

- Force is that external agent (a push or pull) which changes or tends to change the state of rest or of uniform motion of a body in a straight line.
- **Newton's first law** A body continues in the state of rest or of uniform motion along a straight line unless acted upon by an external force.
- **Newton's second law** The rate of change of momentum of a body is equal to the external force applied on it. Thus,

  $$F_{ext} = \frac{\Delta p}{\Delta t} = ma$$

- **Newton's third law** Every action has an equal and opposite reaction.
- **Law of conservation of momentum** The total linear momentum of a system of particles is conserved, provided external force is zero.
- **Impulse** Impulse is the product of a force F and time t, for which it acts. Mathematically,

  Impulse $= F \times t$

  The acceleration of the wedge and the block is

  $$a = \frac{F}{(M + m)}$$

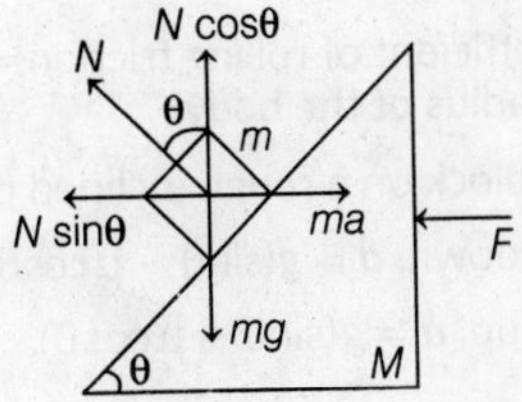

Force of block, $F = (M + m)\,a = (M + m)g\tan\theta$

- **Lami's theorem** For three concurrent forces in equilibrium position, it is written as given below.

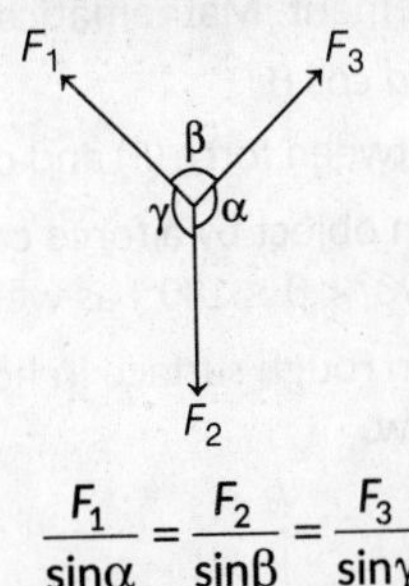

$$\frac{F_1}{\sin\alpha} = \frac{F_2}{\sin\beta} = \frac{F_3}{\sin\gamma}$$

- **Pulleys** If two unequal masses $(m_1 > m_2)$ suspended from a pulley, then

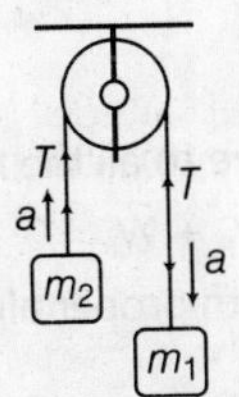

(i) Acceleration, $a = \left(\dfrac{m_1 - m_2}{m_1 + m_2}\right)g$

(ii) Tension, $T = \left(\dfrac{2m_1m_2}{m_1 + m_2}\right)g$

- Consider the motion on a smooth inclined plane,

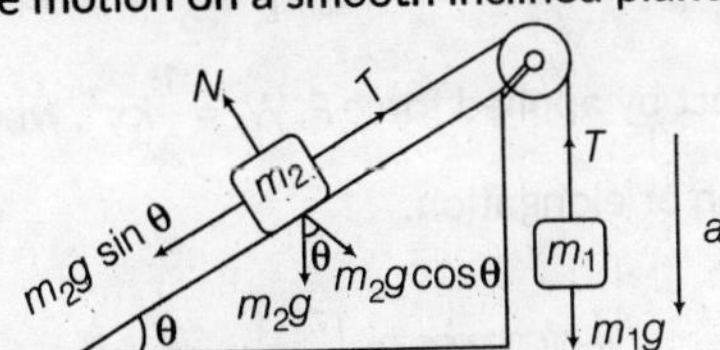

The expression for a and T can be given as

(i) $a = \left(\dfrac{m_1 - m_2\sin\theta}{m_1 + m_2}\right)g$

(ii) $T = \dfrac{m_1m_2(1 + \sin\theta)g}{(m_1 + m_2)}$

- **Friction coefficient** Coefficient of friction, $\mu = \dfrac{F}{R}$

  where, F = force of friction and R = normal reaction.

  The coefficient of friction may be static (μ_s) or kinetic (μ_K).

  Angle of friction, $\tan\theta = \mu_s$

  In case of rolling friction, $F_{rolling} = \mu_r \dfrac{R}{r}$

where, μ_r = coefficient of rolling friction,
r = radius of the body.

- Acceleration of a block on a rough inclined plane
  (i) When sliding down, $a = g(\sin\theta - \mu\cos\theta)$
  (ii) When sliding up, $a = g(\sin\theta + \mu\cos\theta)$.

5. Work, Energy and Power

- Work done by a force on a body is equal to the scalar product of force and displacement. Mathematically,
  Work, $\mathbf{W} = \mathbf{F} \cdot \mathbf{d} = Fd\cos\theta$
  where, θ = angle between force (F) and displacement (d).
- The work done on an object by a force can be positive, ($\theta < 90°$), negative ($90° < \theta \le 180°$) as well as zero ($\theta = 90°$).
- If an object moves on rough surface in horizontal direction as shown in figure below.

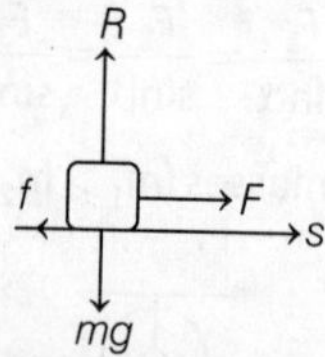

Then, net work done due to all the forces,

$$W_{net} = W_R + W_F + W_f = 0 + Fs - fs = (F - f)s$$

Area under F-s curve with proper algebraic sign represents work done by the force.

So, $W = \int \mathbf{F} \cdot d\mathbf{s} = \int dA$ = Area under F-s curve.

- **Work done by a spring force**
  - Spring force, $F_s = -kx$, where k is a force constant and x is the extension or compression in the length of spring. If $x = 0$, then $F_s = 0$.
  - Work done by spring force, $W_{spring} = \frac{1}{2}kx^2$ and work done on the object by applied force F, $W_F = \frac{1}{2}kx^2$, where x is compression or elongation.

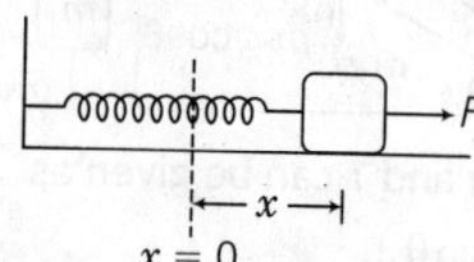

- **Energy** Energy is defined as capacity of doing work. It is a scalar quantity. It has dimensions $[ML^2T^{-2}]$ and its SI unit is joule (J).
  - **Kinetic energy** It is given by the formula $KE = \frac{1}{2}mv^2$
    where, m = mass of the body and v = velocity of the body.
  - **Potential energy** The energy stored in a body by virtue of its configuration or its position is called potential energy.
    (i) Elastic potential energy, $U = \frac{1}{2}kx^2$
    where, k = spring constant,
    x = compression or expansion in spring.
    (ii) Gravitational potential energy, $U = mgh$
- **Work-energy theorem** Work done by all the forces (conservative or non-conservative, external or internal) acting on a particle or on an object is equal to the change in kinetic energy (ΔK) of it.
  i.e. $U_i + K_i = U_f + K_f$
- **Law of conservation of mechanical energy** Total mechanical energy of a system remains constant if only conservative forces are acting on the system and work done by all other forces is zero.
- **Power** It is defined as the rate of doing work. It is equivalent to an amount of energy consumed per unit time.
  Also, average power, $P_{av} = \frac{\text{Total work done}}{\text{Total time taken}} = \frac{W_{total}}{t}$
- **Instantaneous power,** $P_{inst} = \frac{dW}{dt} = \frac{\mathbf{F} \cdot d\mathbf{s}}{dt} = \mathbf{F} \cdot \mathbf{v}$
  Some important units of power are
  (i) 1 kW = 10^3 W
  (ii) 1 MW = 10^6 W
  (iii) 1 HP = 746 W
- **Collision** When the two bodies of masses m_1 and m_2 collide with each other, then

$$m_1u_1 + m_2u_2 = m_1v_1 + m_2v_2$$

(linear momentum is conserved)

where, u_1 = initial velocity of body of mass m_1,
u_2 = initial velocity of body of mass m_2,
v_1 = final velocity of body of mass m_1,
v_2 = final velocity of body of mass m_2.

  - **Elastic collision** In elastic collision, the following conditions take place.
    (i) $\frac{1}{2}m_1u_1^2 + \frac{1}{2}m_2u_2^2 = \frac{1}{2}m_1v_1^2 + \frac{1}{2}m_2v_2^2$
    (ii) $v_1 = \frac{(m_1 - m_2)u_1}{m_1 + m_2} + \frac{2m_2u_2}{m_1 + m_2}$
    (iii) $v_2 = \frac{2m_1u_1}{m_1 + m_2} + \frac{(m_2 - m_1)u_2}{m_1 + m_2}$
  - **Inelastic collision** In inelastic collision, the velocities of the bodies after collision are
    (i) $v_1 = \left(\frac{m_1 - em_2}{m_1 + m_2}\right)u_1 + \left(\frac{(1+e)m_2}{m_1 + m_2}\right)u_2$
    (ii) $v_2 = \left(\frac{(1+e)m_1}{m_1 + m_2}\right)u_1 + \left(\frac{m_2 - em_1}{m_1 + m_2}\right)u_2$
- **Coefficient of restitution** When two bodies collide with each other, the coefficient of restitution is given by

$$e = \frac{|\mathbf{v}_2 - \mathbf{v}_1|}{|\mathbf{u}_1 - \mathbf{u}_2|}$$

In general $0 \le e \le 1$, $e = 0$ for completely inelastic collision, $e = 1$ for perfectly elastic collision.

- **Energy loss in collision** Elastic collision for first (incident) particle,

$$\frac{K_f}{K_i} = \left(\frac{m_1 - m_2}{m_1 + m_2}\right)^2$$

$$\Rightarrow \quad \frac{\Delta K_{loss}}{K_i} = \frac{4m_1m_2}{(m_1 + m_2)^2}$$

Inelastic collision, loss in kinetic energy

$$\Delta K_{loss} = K_i - K_f = \frac{1}{2}\frac{m_1m_2}{m_1 + m_2}(u_1 - u_2)^2(1 - e^2)$$

- **Rebounding of ball on collision with floor**

Speed of ball after nth rebound,

$$v_n = e^n\sqrt{2gh_0}$$

Height covered, $h_n = e^{2n}h_0$

Total distance covered, $H = h_0\left(\frac{1 + e^2}{1 - e^2}\right)$

Total time taken, $T = \sqrt{\frac{2h_0}{g}}\left(\frac{1 + e}{1 - e}\right)$

6. System of Particles and Rotational Motion

- The point at which whole mass of a body is supposed to be concentrated known as a centre of mass of body.
- **Some useful relations for centre of mass**
  - Centre of mass of N particle system,

$$x_{CM} = \frac{m_1x_1 + m_2x_2 + \cdots + m_nx_n}{m_1 + m_2 + \cdots + m_n}$$

where, $x_1, x_2, \ldots, x_n$ are the positions of the centre of masses of $m_1, m_2, \ldots, m_n$, respectively.

  - Velocity of centre of mass,

$$\mathbf{v}_{CM} = \frac{m_1\mathbf{v}_1 + m_2\mathbf{v}_2 + \cdots + m_n\mathbf{v}_n}{m_1 + m_2 + \cdots + m_n}$$

where, $\mathbf{v}_1, \mathbf{v}_2, \ldots, \mathbf{v}_n$ are velocities of the particles having masses $m_1, m_2, \ldots, m_n$.

  - Acceleration of the centre of mass of the body,

$$\mathbf{a}_{CM} = \frac{m_1\mathbf{a}_1 + m_2\mathbf{a}_2 + \cdots + m_n\mathbf{a}_n}{m_1 + m_2 + \cdots + m_n}$$

where, $a_1, a_2, \ldots, a_n$ are acceleration of the particles having masses $m_1, m_2, \ldots, m_n$ respectively.

- **Moment of inertia** The moment of inertia of the body about given axis is the sum of products of the masses of the particles and squares of their perpendicular distances from axis of rotation. If a body consists of n number of particles having masses $m_1, m_2, \ldots, m_n$ and $r_1, r_2, \ldots, r_n$ be their perpendicular distances from axis of rotation, then moment of inertia of body.

$$I = m_1r_1^2 + m_2r_2^2 + \cdots + m_nr_n^2 = \sum_{i=1}^{n} m_ir_i^2$$

- **Radius of gyration** The radius of gyration of the body about given axis of rotation is the distance of the axis of rotation and the point at which the whole of the mass of the body is supposed to be concentrated, so as to have same moment of inertia.

Mathematically, $I = mK^2$ or $K = \sqrt{\frac{I}{m}}$

- **Perpendicular axes theorem** It states that the moment of inertia of a planar body (lamina) about an axis perpendicular to its plane is equal to the sum of its moments of inertia about two perpendicular axes concurrent with perpendicular axes and lying in the plane of the body.

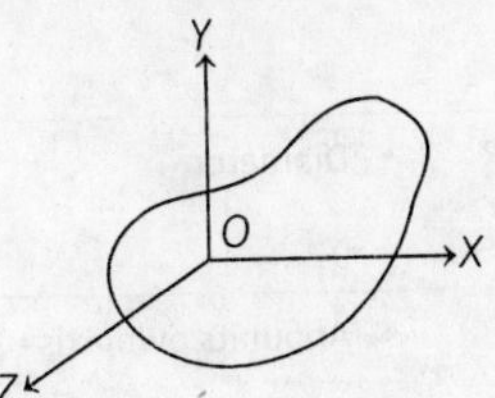

Thus, $I_Z = I_X + I_Y$

where, I_Z = moment of inertia of the body about axis perpendicular to the plane of lamina.

I_X and I_Y = moment of inertia of the lamina about two mutually perpendicular axes in the plane of lamina.

- **Parallel axes theorem** It states that the moment of inertia of a body about a parallel axis is equal to the sum of the moment of inertia about an axis passing through its centre of mass and the product of its mass and the square of distance between the two parallel axes.

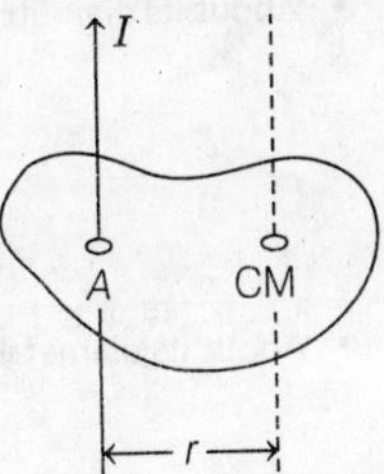

According to parallel axes theorem,

$$I_0 = I_{CM} + Mr^2$$

where, I_0 = moment of inertia of the body about an axis passing through any point A,

I_{CM} = moment of inertia of the body about an axis passing through centre of mass of the body,

r = distance between two parallel axes.

Moment of inertia in some standard cases

Body	Axis of rotation	Figure	Moment of inertia	Radius of gyration
A thin circular ring of radius R	• About an axis passing through CG and perpendicular to its plane		MR^2	R
Thin circular ring of radius R	• About its diameter		$\frac{1}{2}MR^2$	$\frac{R}{\sqrt{2}}$
Thin rod of length, L	• Perpendicular to rod at mid-point		$\frac{1}{12}ML^2$	$\frac{L}{\sqrt{12}}$
Circular disc of radius R	• Perpendicular to disc at centre		$\frac{1}{2}MR^2$	$\frac{R}{\sqrt{2}}$
Circular disc of radius R	• Diameter		$\frac{1}{4}MR^2$	$\frac{R}{\sqrt{4}}$
Hollow cylinder of Radius R	• About its own axis		MR^2	R
Solid cylinder of radius R	• About its own axis		$\frac{MR^2}{2}$	$\frac{R}{\sqrt{2}}$
Solid sphere of radius R	• About its diametric axis		$\frac{2}{5}MR^2$	$\sqrt{\frac{2}{5}}R$
Hollow sphere of radius R	• About its diametric axis		$\frac{2}{3}MR^2$	$\sqrt{\frac{2}{3}}R$

- **Torque** or **moment of force** on a system of n particles about the origin is $\tau = \Sigma \mathbf{r}_i \times \mathbf{F}_i$, where $\mathbf{r}_i$ is the position vector of ith particle on which force $\mathbf{F}_i$ acts.
- **Angular momentum** of a system of n particles about the origin is $\mathbf{L} = \sum_{i=1}^{n} \mathbf{r}_i \times \mathbf{p}_i = I\omega$, where $\mathbf{r}_i$ is the position vector of ith particle having linear momentum $\mathbf{p}_i$.
- If a system having angular momentum L and external torque acting on the system is τ_{ext}, then $\tau_{ext} = dL/dt$. For $\tau_{ext} \times t = 0$, $L = I\omega =$ constant called conservation of angular momentum.

- **Work done** When a body is in the rotational motion, the work done by torque τ acting on it is, $W = \tau \cdot d\theta$ where, $d\theta$ = angular displacement.
- Kinetic energy of rotation can be given as, $K_R = \frac{1}{2} I\omega^2$

  where, ω = angular velocity and I = moment of inertia.

  For combined rotation and translation motions, total energy is given by

$$E_{total} = \frac{1}{2} mv^2 \left(1 + \frac{K^2}{r^2}\right)$$

  For pure rolling motion $v = \omega r$, otherwise $v \neq \omega r$

7. Gravitation

- **Newton's law of gravitation** According to this law, the attractive force between two bodies of masses m_1 and m_2 can be given as, $F = \frac{Gm_1m_2}{r^2}$

  where, G = gravitational constant $= 6.67 \times 10^{-11}$ N-m^2 kg^{-2}.
- The force of attraction exerted by the earth on a body is called **gravitational pull**. The acceleration produced in the motion of a body under the effect of gravity is called acceleration due to gravity and given by, $g = \frac{GM}{R^2}$

  where, M = mass of the earth,

  R = radius of the earth.
- At a height h above the earth's surface,

$$g' = \frac{GM}{(R+h)^2} \quad \text{(exact)}$$

  Also, variation at depth d, $g' = g\left(1 - \frac{d}{R}\right) \Rightarrow \left(\frac{g - g'}{g}\right) = \frac{d}{R}$
- Intensity of gravitational field of mass M at distance r,

$$E = \frac{GM}{r^2}$$

- Gravitational potential due to a mass M at a distance r is given by,

$$V = -\frac{GM}{r}$$

- **For a solid sphere**

  At a point inside the sphere, $V = -\frac{GM}{2R^3}(3R^2 - r^2)$

  At the centre of sphere, $V = -\frac{3GM}{2R} = \frac{3}{2} V_{surface}$
- **For spherical shell**

  At a point inside or on the surface,

$$V = -\frac{GM}{R} = V_{surface}$$

- If m_1, m_2 are two masses separated by infinite distance, then gravitational potential energy of the system when they are brought to a separation of r is given by,

$$U = -\frac{Gm_1m_2}{r}$$

  Here, the negative sign indicates that the two bodies are attracting each other.
- **Kepler's laws of planetary motion**
  - **First law** All planets move around the sun in elliptical orbits with the sun at one focus.
  - **Second law** The area swept by the line joining the sun and the planet per unit time is constant.
  - **Third law** The square of the time taken to complete the orbit (time period T) is proportional to the cube of the semi-major axis (r) of the elliptical orbit.

    Mathematically, $T^2 \propto r^3$
- **Velocity of satellite**
  - Orbital velocity of satellite,

$$v_o = \sqrt{gR} = \sqrt{\frac{GM}{R}}$$

  - Orbital angular velocity of satellite,

$$\omega_o = \sqrt{\frac{g}{R}} = \sqrt{\frac{GM}{R^3}}$$

- **Time period of satellite** Period of satellite,

$$T = \frac{2\pi (R+h)}{v_o} = 2\pi \sqrt{\frac{(R+h)^3}{GM}}$$

- The minimum velocity with which a projected body from the surface of the earth, escapes (becomes free) from the earth's gravitational field is called **escape velocity** of that body, i.e.

$$v_e = \sqrt{2gR} = \sqrt{\frac{2GM}{R}} = \sqrt{\frac{8}{3}\pi GR^2 d}$$

  On the surface of the earth, $(v_e)_E = 11200 \text{ ms}^{-1} = 11.2 \text{ km s}^{-1}$

  On the surface of the moon, $(v_e)_M = 2370 \text{ ms}^{-1}$
- Escape velocity $= \sqrt{2} \times$ Orbital velocity

$$\Rightarrow v_e = \sqrt{2}\, v_o$$

- When a satellite is revolving round the earth in stable circular orbit at height h, then
  - Potential energy of satellite above the earth's surface,

$$U = -\frac{GMm}{R+h}$$

    If $h << R$, then $U = -\frac{GMm}{R} = -mgR$
  - Kinetic energy of satellite, $K = \frac{GMm}{2(R+h)}$

    If $h << R$, then $K = \frac{GMm}{2R} = \frac{mgR}{2}$
  - Total energy of satellite, $E = U + K = -\frac{GMm}{2(R+h)}$

If $h << R$, then $E = -\frac{GMm}{2R} = -\frac{mgR}{2}$

The negative sign indicates that the satellite is bound to the earth.

- Binding energy of satellite, $E_B = \frac{GMm}{2(R+h)}$

8. Mechanical Properties of Solids

- The restoring force per unit cross-sectional area set up within the body is called **stress.**

$$\text{Stress} = \frac{\text{Restoring force}}{\text{Area of cross-section}} = \frac{F}{A}$$

$$\text{Longitudinal or Tensile stress} = \frac{F_{\text{perpendicular}}}{A}$$

$$\text{Shearing stress} = \frac{F_{\text{tangential}}}{A}$$

- The change in dimension per unit original dimension is called as **strain.**

$$\text{Strain} = \frac{\text{Change in dimension}}{\text{Original dimension}}$$

$$\text{Longitudinal strain} = \frac{\text{Change in length}}{\text{Original length}} = \frac{\Delta l}{L}$$

$$\text{Bulk or Volumetric strain} = \frac{\text{Change in volume}}{\text{Original volume}} = \frac{\Delta V}{V}$$

$$\text{Shearing strain} = \frac{\text{Relative displacement of a layer}}{\text{Distance between the layers}} = \tan\theta$$

Also, Shearing strain = 2 × Longitudinal strain

Volumetric strain = 3 × Longitudinal strain

- The maximum stress to which body can be subjected without permanent deformation is called **elastic limit.**
- **Hooke's law** Within the elastic limit, the stress developed is proportional to the strain produced in the body, which is called hooke's law, i.e. stress ∝ strain

$\frac{\text{Stress}}{\text{Strain}} = E$ = modulus of elasticity of the material of the body.

As there are three types of stresses and strains, therefore, there are three moduli of elasticity, i.e. Young's modulus, bulk modulus and modulus of rigidity. All are described here.

- Young's modulus, $Y = \frac{\text{Longitudinal stress}}{\text{Longitudinal strain}} = \frac{FL}{Al}$
- Bulk modulus, $K = \frac{\text{Normal stress}}{\text{Volumetric strain}} = V\frac{dp}{dV}$
- Modulus of rigidity, $\eta = \frac{\text{Shearing stress}}{\text{Shearing strain}} \Rightarrow \eta = \frac{F}{A\theta}$

- Compressibility $= \frac{1}{\text{Bulk modulus }(K)} = \frac{dV}{Vdp}$
- Poisson's ratio, $\sigma = \frac{\text{Lateral strain}}{\text{Longitudinal strain}} = \frac{-d/D}{l/L}$

where, d = change in diameter, D = original diameter, l = change in length and L = original length.

Theoretical limits of Poisson's ratio are – 1 and 0.5, while the practical limits are 0.2 and 0.5.

- **Relations between Y, K, η and σ**

$$K = \frac{Y}{3(1-2\sigma)},\quad \eta = \frac{Y}{2(1+\sigma)},\quad \sigma = \frac{3K-2\eta}{2(3K+\eta)}$$

and $Y = \frac{9\eta K}{3K+\eta}$

$$\Rightarrow \frac{9}{Y} = \frac{3}{\eta} + \frac{1}{K}$$

- **Work done in a stretched wire** Strain energy or work done per unit volume, $W = \frac{1}{2} \times \text{Stress} \times \text{Strain}$
- Breaking stress $= \frac{\text{Breaking force}}{\text{Area of cross-section}}$
- Thermal stress $= Y\alpha\Delta\theta$

Thermal strain $= \frac{\Delta l}{l} = \alpha\Delta\theta$

where, α = coefficient of linear expansion.

9. Mechanical Properties of Fluids

- If two liquids of densities ρ_1 and ρ_2 having masses m_1 and m_2 are mixed together, then the density of mixture,

$$\rho = \frac{m_1 + m_2}{\left(\frac{m_1}{\rho_1} + \frac{m_2}{\rho_2}\right)} \quad \left[\because \rho = \frac{\text{Mass }(m)}{\text{Volume }(V)}\right]$$

- **Relative density** $= \frac{\text{Density of substance}}{\text{Density of water at } 4°\text{C}}$
- **Pressure** of liquid at a point is the thrust (or normal force) exerted by the liquid at rest per unit area around that point. The unit of pressure is N/m^2 (pascal) in SI system. Pressure due to a liquid column (density ρ) of height h is $p = \rho g h$. Pressure at all points lying on same horizontal level in a liquid at rest is same.
- **Pascal's law** states that the external pressure applied on any part of a fluid contained in a vessel, transmitted undiminished and equally in all directions.
- **Archimedes' principle** states that when a body is immersed fully or partially in a liquid at rest, it experiences an upthrust, equal to the weight of the liquid displaced by the immersed part of the body.

Apparent weight of body = Weight of body – Upthrust or weight of liquid displaced

Volume of body outside the liquid, $V_o = V\left(1 - \frac{\rho}{\sigma}\right)$

where, ρ = density of liquid and σ = density of body.

Buoyant force, $F = h\rho g A = mg$

(i) When $\rho > \sigma$, the body will sink in liquid.

(ii) When $\rho = \sigma$, the body will float fully submerged in liquid.

(iii) When $\rho < \sigma$, the body will float partially immersed in liquid.

- **Equation of continuity** states that rate of flow of non-viscous and incompressible fluid through a cross-section area (*A*) of a tube of flow is constant.
- **Bernoulli's theorem** According to this theorem, the sum of pressure energy (*p*), kinetic energy $\left(\frac{1}{2}\rho v^2\right)$ and potential energy per unit volume (ρgh) of an incompressible, non-viscous fluid in a streamlined irrotational flow remains constant at every cross-section throughout the liquid flow.

$$p + \frac{1}{2}\rho v^2 + \rho gh = \text{constant}$$

- **Velocity of efflux** $v = \sqrt{2gh}$

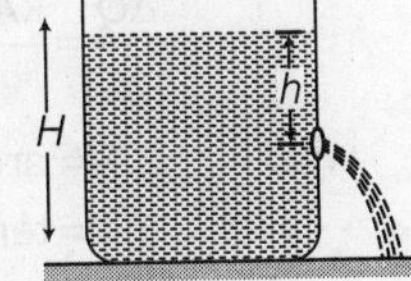

where, *h* = depth of the hole. The time taken by the liquid to reach the base level in above case,

$$t = \sqrt{\frac{2(H - h)}{g}}$$

where, *H* = height of water in the vessel.

- Range of flowing liquid, $R = 2\sqrt{h(H - h)}$

It will be maximum, when $h = \frac{H}{2}$, i.e. $R_{max} = H$

- **Stoke's law** According to this law, the viscous drag force *F* on a sphere of radius *a*, moving with velocity *v*, through a fluid of viscosity η can be given as,

$$F = -6\pi\eta a v$$

- **Viscous force** between two liquid layers is proportional to velocity gradient between the layers.

$$F = -\eta A \frac{dv}{dr}$$

- **Reynold's number** $R_e = \rho v d/\eta$

If $0 < R_e < 2000$, then liquid flow is streamline or laminar.

If $R_e > 3000$, then liquid flow is turbulent.

If $2000 < R_e < 3000$, then the flow is unstable.

- **Poiseuille's formula** $Q = \frac{dv}{dt} = \frac{\pi p R^4}{8\eta L}$

where, *Q* = rate of volume flow,
L = length of the capillary tube,
R = radius of the capillary tube,
p = pressure difference across the tube.

- **Terminal velocity** It is defined as the maximum constant velocity acquired by a body while falling through a viscous fluid.

Mathematically, $v_T = \frac{2}{9}\frac{r^2(\rho - \sigma)g}{\eta}$

where, *r* = radius of the body,
ρ = density of material of the body,
σ = density of fluid,
η = coefficient of viscosity.

- **Surface tension** $T = \frac{F}{L}$

where, *F* = total force acting perpendicularly on length *L* of a line drawn on the liquid length.

- Work done to increase the area of surface film by *A*,

$$W = T \times A$$

- Work done in blowing a liquid drop,

$$W = T \times 4\pi(r_2^2 - r_1^2)$$

- Work done in blowing a soap bubble,

$$W = T \times 8\pi(r_2^2 - r_1^2)$$

- Work done in splitting a bigger drop into *n* smaller droplets,

$$W = T \times 4\pi R^2(n^{1/3} - 1)$$

- Energy released in coalescing of drops,

$$\Delta U = T \times 4\pi r^2 n(1 - n^{-1/3})$$

- **Excess pressure**

Inside a drop bubble of radius *R*, $p = \frac{2T}{R}$

Inside a soap bubble of radius *R*, $p = \frac{4T}{R}$

- **Capillary rise or fall** of a liquid, $h = \frac{2T\cos\theta}{r\rho g}$

where, *T* = surface tension of the liquid,
g = acceleration due to gravity,
θ = angle of contact,
r = radius of the capillary bore,
ρ = density of the liquid.

For pure liquid, $\theta = 0°$, $h = \frac{2T}{r\rho g}$ $(\because \cos 0° = 1)$

- If $\theta < 90°$, then there will be a capillary rise.
- If $\theta = 90°$, then there will be neither a rise nor fall.
- If $\theta > 90°$, then there will be a capillary depression.

- If capillary tube dipped in a liquid is tilted at an angle α, the length of liquid column in tube is

$$l = \frac{h}{\cos\alpha}$$

10. Thermal Properties of Matter

- Temperature is the property of a state of matter by virtue of which we predict its hotness or coldness, relative to somebody.
- The devices which are used to measure the temperature are termed as **thermometers**, while the science related to measurement of temperature is termed as **thermometry**.

- Three most common scales are celsius scale or centigrade scale, fahrenheit scale and kelvin scale (absolute scale).

Ice and steam points of three scales of temperature

Scale	Ice point	Steam point	Unit
Celsius	0	100	°C
Fahrenheit	32	212	°F
Kelvin	273.15	373.15	K

- Relation between C, F and K scales is given by

$$\frac{C}{5}=\frac{F-32}{9}=\frac{K-273.15}{5}$$

- In general, for two scales X and Y.

$$\frac{\text{Temperature on } X - \text{Ice point of } X}{\text{Steam point of } X - \text{Ice point of } X}$$
$$=\frac{\text{Temperature on } Y - \text{Ice point of } Y}{\text{Steam point of } Y - \text{Ice point of } Y}$$

- If a rod is having length l_0 at temperature T, then elongation in length of rod due to rise in temperature by ΔT is,

$$\Delta l = l_0 \alpha \, \Delta T$$

where, α is the coefficient of linear expansion whose value depends on the nature of the material.

Final length, $l_f = l_0 + l_0 \, \alpha \Delta T = l_0(1+\alpha \Delta T)$

- Superficial expansion is valid only for solids

$$A_f = A_0(1+\beta \Delta T)$$

where, A_0 is the area of body at temperature T, β is the coefficient of superficial expansion and A_f is the area of body when temperature has been changed by ΔT.

- Volume after expansion, $V = V_0(1+\gamma \Delta T)$, where symbols have their usual meanings. γ is the coefficient of cubical expansion.
- **Anomalous behaviour of water** Water contracts on heating between temperature 0°C to 4°C.
- $\gamma_{gas} > \gamma_{liquid} > \gamma_{solid}$ as molecules in gases are more mobile than that of liquids and solids. The quantity of heat Q required to change the temperature of a mass m of certain material by ΔT, is approximately proportional to product of m and ΔT. The expression for heat can be given as

$$Q \propto m\Delta T \text{ or } Q = ms\,\Delta T$$

where, s is the specific heat capacity of the material.

- Specific heat capacity can have any value from 0 to ∞. For some substances under particular situations, it can have negative values also. Specific heat of ice is 500 cal/kg °C and that of water is 1000 cal/kg°C.
- The amount of heat required to change the temperature of unit mole of substance by 1°C is termed as its **molar heat capacity.** Mathematically, $C = \frac{Q}{n\Delta T}$

where, n = number of moles $= \frac{m}{M}$.

- The heat required to change the state of a system is proportional to mass of system, i.e. $Q \propto m$

$$Q = mL$$

where, L = latent heat.

- Latent heat for melting is termed as **latent heat of fusion L_f**. In case of ice, latent heat of fusion is 80 cal/g.
- Latent heat for vaporisation process is termed as **latent heat of vaporisation L_v**. In case of water, latent heat of vaporisation is 536 cal/g.
- According to principle of calorimetry, heat supplied by few bodies = heat consumed by remaining bodies,

i.e. Heat lost = Heat gained.

- The rate of transmission of heat by conduction is given by,

$$\frac{\Delta Q}{\Delta t}=\frac{KA\Delta T}{l}$$

where, A = area of cross-section,
ΔT = temperature difference,
Δt = time elapsed,
K = thermal conductivity.

The unit of thermal conductivity is $Wm^{-1}K^{-1}$.

- The term $\frac{l}{KA}$ is generally called the thermal resistance.
- In a series combination of two metal rods, thermal conductivity,

$$\Rightarrow \quad K_s = \frac{2K_1K_2}{K_1+K_2} \quad (\text{if } l_1 = l_2)$$

- In a parallel combination of two metal rods, thermal conductivity, $K_p = \frac{K_1A_1 + K_2A_2}{A_1 + A_2}$
- When radiant energy Q is incident on a body, a part of it Q_a is absorbed, another part Q_r is reflected back and yet another part Q_t is transmitted such that,

$$Q = Q_a + Q_r + Q_t$$

$$\Rightarrow \quad \frac{Q_a}{Q}+\frac{Q_r}{Q}+\frac{Q_t}{Q} = a + r + t = 1$$

- **Kirchhoff's law of radiation** This law states that the ratio of emissive power to absorptive power is same for all surfaces at the same temperature and is equal to the emissive power of a perfectly black body at that temperature.

Mathematically, $\frac{e_1}{a_1}=\frac{e_2}{a_2}=\dots=E$ (Black body)

where, a = spectral absorptive power

$$=\frac{\text{Energy absorbed}}{\text{Energy incident}}$$

and e = emissive power $= \frac{1}{A}\frac{\Delta Q}{\Delta t}$

- **Stefan's law** The emissive power of a perfectly black body (energy emitted by black body per unit surface area per unit time) is directly proportional to the fourth power of its absolute temperature.

  Mathematically, $E \propto T^4$ or $E = \sigma T^4$

  where, σ is a constant known as the Stefan's constant. Value of σ is 5.67×10^{-8} Wm^{-2} K^{-4}.
- **Newton's law of cooling** The rate of cooling of a body is directly proportional to the temperature difference between the body and the surroundings provided that the temperature difference is small.

  Mathematically, $\frac{dT}{dt} \propto (T - T_0)$ or $-\frac{dT}{dt} = k(T - T_0)$

  where, k is a constant.
- **Wien's displacement law** This law states that, as temperature of black body T increases, the wavelength λ_m corresponding to maximum emission decreases such that,

  $$\lambda_m \propto \frac{1}{T} \text{ or } \lambda_m T = \text{constant} = b$$

  where, b is known as Wien's constant and its value is 2.89×10^{-3} m-K.

11. Thermodynamics

- **Zeroth law of thermodynamics** If two thermodynamical systems (A and B) are in the thermal equilibrium with the third one (C), then both the thermodynamical systems (A and B) will be in equilibrium with each other.
- **First law of thermodynamics** According to this law,

  $$\Delta Q = \Delta U + \Delta W$$

  where, ΔQ is the heat supplied to the system, ΔU is the increase in internal energy and ΔW is the work done by the system on the surroundings.
- Specific heat capacity, $s = \frac{1}{m} \frac{\Delta Q}{\Delta t}$
- Molar specific heat capacity, $C = \frac{1}{n} \frac{\Delta Q}{\Delta t}$

  where, n is the number of moles of the substance.
- For an ideal gas, the molar specific heat capacities at constant pressure and volume satisfy the relation, $C_p - C_V = R$, called Mayer's formula.
- **Isothermal process** In this process, temperature of the system is kept constant during the changes of state.

  As, $Q = nC_{iso}dT \Rightarrow C_{iso} = \frac{Q}{ndT} = \infty$ $\quad (\because dT = 0)$
  - From $dU = nC_V\,dT$ as $dT = 0$, so $dU = 0$, i.e. internal energy is constant. Process equation is pV= constant.
  - From first law of thermodynamics, $dQ = dW$, i.e. heat given to the system is equal to the work done by system on surroundings.
  - Work done, $W = nRT \ln\left(\frac{V_f}{V_i}\right) = nRT \ln\left(\frac{p_i}{p_f}\right)$
- **Adiabatic process** In this process, no heat exchange takes place between the system and surroundings, i.e. $dQ = 0$ or Q = constant.
  - From $dQ = nCdT$, $C_{adi} = 0$ as $dQ = 0$, i.e. molar heat capacity for adiabatic process is zero.
  - From first law, $dU = -dW$, i.e. work done by the system is equal to the decrease in internal energy.
  - Process equation is pV^γ = constant. Process equation can be written in an other ways as $TV^{\gamma-1}$ = constant or $p^{1-\gamma}T^\gamma$ = constant, where $\gamma = \frac{C_p}{C_V}$
  - Work done in an adiabatic process is,

    $$W = \frac{nR(T_1 - T_2)}{\gamma - 1} = \frac{p_1V_1 - p_2V_2}{\gamma - 1}$$
- **Isobaric process** This is the process in which pressure is kept constant.
  - Molar heat capacities of the process,

    $$dQ = nC_p dT \quad \text{and} \quad dU = nC_V\,dT$$
  - Work done $dW = pdV = nRdT$
  - Process equation is $\frac{V}{T}$ = constant.
- **Isochoric process** This is the process in which volume is kept constant. Volume is constant, so $dW = 0$. $dQ = nC_V\,dT$, molar heat capacity for isochoric process is C_V.
  - From first law of thermodynamics, $dQ = dU$. As, heat is supplied to the system, internal energy increases and hence the temperature increases.
  - Process equation is $\frac{p}{T}$ = constant.
- **Cyclic process** In a cyclic process the system returns to its initial state. As, initial and final states are the same, so $dU = 0$ for a cyclic process.

  Efficiency of the cycle is given by, $\eta = \frac{\text{Work done}}{\text{Heat supplied}}$
- **Second law of thermodynamics**
  - **Kelvin-Planck statement** No process is possible whose sole result is the absorption of heat from a reservoir and the complete conversion of the heat into work.
  - **Clausius statement** No process is possible whose sole result is the transfer of heat from a colder object to a hotter object without doing work.
  - **Heat engine** It is a device by which a system is made to undergo a cyclic process, results in conversions of heat to work . Its thermal efficiency, $\eta = 1 - \frac{Q_2}{Q_1}$

    where, Q_1 = heat absorbed and Q_2 = heat released.
  - **Carnot engine** It is a reversible engine which operates between two temperature of source (T_1) and sink (T_2). Its thermal efficiency $\eta = 1 - \frac{T_2}{T_1}$. It has the maximum possible efficiency.

- **Refrigerator or heat pump** It is basically a heat engine which runs in reverse directions.
- **Coefficient of performance** It is the ratio of heat extracted from the cold body to the work needed to transfer it to the hot body.

$$B = \frac{Q_2}{Q_1 - Q_2} = \frac{1-\eta}{\eta}$$

12. Kinetic Theory of Gases

- **Boyle's law** For a given mass of an ideal gas at constant temperature, the volume of a gas is inversely proportional to its pressure,

i.e. $V \propto \frac{1}{p}$ or $pV = \text{constant}$

- **Charles' law** For the pressure remaining constant, the volume of the given mass of a gas is directly proportional to its absolute temperature,

i.e. $V \propto T$ or $\frac{V}{T} = \text{constant}$

- **Graham's law of diffusion** When two gases at the same temperature and pressure are allowed to diffuse, then rate of diffusion of each gas is inversely proportional to the square root of density of the gas.
- Ideal gas obeys the gas equation, $pV = nRT$.
- Real gases do not obey the gas equation, $pV = nRT$. On the other hand, they obey the van der Waals' equation

$$\left(p + \frac{an}{V^2}\right)(V - nb) = nRT$$

where, n = number of moles and a, b are constants called **van der Waals' constants.**

- rms velocity is related to density (ρ) or molar mass (M) by the relation, $v_{\text{rms}} = \sqrt{\frac{3p}{\rho}} = \sqrt{\frac{3RT}{M}} = \sqrt{\frac{3k_bT}{M}}$

where, p = pressure,
T = temperature,
R = universal gas constant,
k_b = Boltzmann constant.

- For two different gases, $\frac{v_{\text{rms}_1}}{v_{\text{rms}_2}} = \sqrt{\frac{T_1M_2}{T_2M_1}}$
- Average speed of n molecules moving with speeds $v_1, v_2, \ldots, v_n$ is, $\bar{v} = \frac{v_1 + v_2 + \ldots + v_n}{n} = \sqrt{\frac{8RT}{\pi M}}$
- Most probable speed, $v_{\text{mp}} = \sqrt{\frac{2RT}{M}}$
- Kinetic energy of gas per unit volume, $E = \frac{1}{2}\frac{M}{V}v_{\text{rms}}^2$
- The average kinetic energy of one mole of ideal gas is,

$$E = \frac{3}{2}RT$$

- The mean kinetic energy of the molecule of an ideal gas is, $E_{(\text{molecule})} = \frac{3}{2}k_bT$
- Molar specific heat at constant pressure,

$$C_p = C_V + R \quad \text{or} \quad C_p = \left(\frac{f}{2} + 1\right)R$$

- The relation between degree of freedom (f) of gas and ratio of specific heats (γ) is $\gamma = 1 + \frac{2}{f}$,
- **Ratio of specific heat**

$$\gamma = 1 + \frac{2}{f} \begin{cases} \xrightarrow{\text{Monoatomic}} 1 + \frac{2}{3} = \frac{5}{3} \\ \xrightarrow{\text{Diatomic}} 1 + \frac{2}{5} = \frac{7}{5} \\ \xrightarrow{\text{Triatomic}} 1 + \frac{2}{7} = \frac{9}{7} \end{cases}$$

- **Law of equipartition of energy** According to Maxwell, the total energy of the gas is shared equally among various degrees of freedom. The energy per molecule per degree of freedom $= \frac{1}{2}kT$.

where, k = Boltzmann constant.

- The mean free path of a gas molecules is given by,

$$\lambda = \frac{1}{\sqrt{2}\pi d^2 n}$$

where, d = diameter of molecule,
n = number of molecules per unit volume.

- **Avogadro's number** According to Avogadro's hypothesis, gram atomic masses of all element contain the same number of atoms and this number is given by

$$N_A = 6.02 \times 10^{23}$$

13. Oscillations

- A motion which repeats itself over and over again after a regular interval of time is called a **periodic motion.**
- A motion in which a body moves back and forth repeatedly about a fixed point (called mean position) is called oscillatory or vibratory motion.
- **Simple harmonic motion** (SHM) is that type of oscillatory motion in which the particle moves to and fro about a fixed point under a restoring force whose magnitude is directly proportional to its displacement, i.e. $F = -kx$

where, k is a positive constant called force constant or spring factor.

- The displacement of a particle executing SHM is in general expressed as, $y = A\sin(\omega t + \phi)$

where, A is amplitude of SHM, ω the angular frequency $\left(\text{where, } \omega = \frac{2\pi}{T} = 2\pi\nu\right)$ and ϕ the initial phase of SHM.

- The velocity of particle executing SHM is, $v = \omega\sqrt{A^2 - y^2}$

  At mean position, (i.e. $y = 0$) during its motion

  $$v = A\omega = v_{max}$$

  and at extreme positions (i.e. $y = \pm A$) $v = 0$.
- The acceleration of a SHM at an instant is, $a = -\omega^2 y$

  The acceleration is also variable. At mean position (i.e. $y = 0$) acceleration $a = 0$ and at extreme position (i.e. $y = \pm A$) the acceleration is maximum and given as, $a_{max} = \mp A\omega^2$.
- Time period of SHM,

  $$T = \frac{2\pi}{\omega} = 2\pi\sqrt{\frac{|y|}{|a|}} = 2\pi\sqrt{\frac{\text{Displacement}}{\text{Acceleration}}}$$
- At any displacement x,

  Potential energy, $U = \frac{1}{2}m\omega^2x^2 = \frac{1}{2}kx^2$

  Kinetic energy, $K = \frac{1}{2}m\omega^2(A^2 - x^2) = \frac{1}{2}k(A^2 - x^2)$

  Total energy, $E = U + K = \frac{1}{2}m\omega^2A^2 = 2\pi^2 m v^2 A^2$
- **A simple pendulum** The motion of a simple pendulum is simple harmonic motion whose time period and frequency are given by

  $$T = 2\pi\sqrt{\frac{l}{g}} \text{ and } \nu = \frac{1}{2\pi}\sqrt{\frac{g}{l}}$$
- A second's pendulum is a pendulum whose time period is 2 s. At a place where $g = 9.8 \text{ ms}^{-2}$, the length of a second's pendulum is 0.9929 m (or 1 m approx).
- The spring pendulum oscillates simple harmonically having time period and frequency,

  $$T = 2\pi\sqrt{\frac{m}{k}} \text{ and } \nu = \frac{1}{2\pi}\sqrt{\frac{k}{m}}$$

  For combination of springs, $T = 2\pi\sqrt{\frac{m}{k_{eq}}}$, for series combination $k_{eq} = \frac{k_1k_2}{k_1 + k_2}$ and for parallel combination $k_{eq} = k_1 + k_2$.
- The oscillations in which amplitude decreases gradually with the passage of time are called **damped vibrations.**

  Damping force, $F_d = -bv$

  where, v is the velocity of the oscillator and b is a damping constant.
- The vibrations in which a body oscillates under the effect of an external periodic force, whose frequency is different from the natural frequency of oscillating body, are called **forced vibrations.**
- The forced vibrations in which frequency of external force is exactly same as the natural frequency of oscillator are called **resonant vibrations.** Resonant vibrations play a very important role in music and tuning of station/channel in a radio/TV.

14. Waves

- The equation of a **plane progressive** simple harmonic wave travelling along positive direction of X-axis is

  $$y = a\sin(\omega t - kx) = a\sin\frac{2\pi}{\lambda}(vt - x)$$

  – Velocity, v = Frequency (ν) × Wavelength (λ)

  – Angular speed, $\omega = 2\pi\nu = \frac{2\pi}{T} = \frac{2\pi v}{\lambda}$
- Angular wave number, $k = \frac{2\pi}{\lambda}$
- Relation between phase difference, path difference and time difference

  Phase difference (ϕ) $= \frac{2\pi}{\lambda} \times$ Path difference (x)

  $= 2\frac{\pi}{T} \times$ Time difference (t)
- When two waves of same frequency (or same wavelength) travelling along same path superimpose, then after superposition, intensity of resultant wave is maximum at some points and minimum at another points. This phenomena is called **interference of waves.** If at a given position (suppose at origin) displacements due to two waves be, $y_1 = a_1\sin\omega t$ and $y_2 = a_2\sin(\omega t + \phi)$

  Then, resultant displacement,

  $$y = y_1 + y_2 = a\sin(\omega t + \phi)$$

  where, $a = \sqrt{a_1^2 + a_2^2 + 2a_1a_2\cos\phi}$

  and $\tan\theta = \frac{a_2\sin\phi}{a_1 + a_2\cos\phi}$

  where, ϕ is the phase difference between two waves and θ is the angle made by resultant with the direction of first wave.

  – At those points where phase difference $\phi = 0°$ or $2n\pi$, i.e. an integral multiple of 2π ($n = 1, 2, 3, \ldots$), $a = a_1 + a_2 = a_{max}$. This is known as **constructive interference.**

  – At those points where $\phi = (2n - 1)\pi$, i.e. phase difference is an odd multiple of π and hence

  $$a = a_1 - a_2 = a_{min}.$$

  This is known as **destructive interference.**
- If I_1 and I_2 be the intensities due to two waves, then resultant intensity

  $$I = I_1 + I_2 + 2\sqrt{I_1I_2}\cos\phi$$

  For maximum intensity, $\phi = 0°$

  $\therefore$ $I_{max} = I_1 + I_2 + 2\sqrt{I_1I_2}$

  For minimum intensity, $\phi = 180°$

  $\therefore$ $I_{min} = I_1 + I_2 - 2\sqrt{I_1I_2}$

If P is the power of source, then intensity follows inverse square law of distance d,

$$I = \frac{P}{4\pi d^2}$$

- **Stationary waves on a string** Transverse wave is set up on the string whose speed is given by, $v = \sqrt{\frac{T}{\mu}}$
- **Vibration of string fixed at both ends**
  - Let only one anti-node A is formed at the centre and string vibrates in one segment only, then $l = \frac{\lambda_1}{2}$

  $\therefore$ Frequency of vibration in fundamental mode,

  $$\nu_1 = \frac{v}{\lambda_1} = \frac{1}{2l}\sqrt{\frac{T}{\mu}}$$

  It is known as the fundamental frequency or first harmonic.
  - If string vibrates in two segments, then

  $$l = \lambda_2 \text{ and } \nu_2 = \frac{v}{\lambda_2} = \frac{1}{l}\sqrt{\frac{T}{\mu}} = 2\nu_1$$

  It is known as **first overtone** or **second harmonic.**
  - In general, if a string vibrates in p segments [i.e. have $(p+1)$ nodes and p anti-nodes].

  Then, $\nu_{pth} = \frac{p}{2l}\sqrt{\frac{T}{\mu}} = p\nu_1$ and it is known as pth **harmonic** or **$(p-1)$ th overtone.**
- In vibration of a string **fixed at one end**, only odd harmonics are present having fundamental frequency

  $$= \frac{1}{4L}\sqrt{\frac{T}{\mu}}$$
- Mechanical waves in air having a frequency ranging from 20 Hz to 20 kHz are known as **audio waves** or **sound waves.**
- The frequencies below 20 Hz are called infrasonics and that above 20 kHz are called ultrasonics or supersonics.
- **Velocity of sound** The velocity of sound can be determined by using Newton's formula,

  $$v = \sqrt{\frac{E}{\rho}}$$

  where, E denotes modulus of elasticity and ρ denotes density of medium.
- **Laplace's correction**
  - **For gases** $v = \sqrt{\frac{\gamma p}{\rho}}$, where $\gamma = \frac{C_p}{C_V}$
  - **For solids** $v = \sqrt{\frac{Y}{\rho}}$.
  - **For liquids** $v = \sqrt{\frac{K}{\rho}}$

  where, Y = Young's modulus of elasticity,
  K = bulk modulus of elasticity.
- Although, $\rho_{solid} > \rho_{liquid} > \rho_{gas}$ but

  $$v_{solid} >> v_{liquid} >> v_{gas}$$

  As a result, it is observed that speed of sound is maximum in solids, lesser in liquids and least in gases.

  e.g. $v_{steel} = 5941 \text{ ms}^{-1}$,

  $v_{water} = 1482 \text{ ms}^{-1}$ (at 20°C)

  and $v_{air} = 332 \text{ ms}^{-1}$ (at 0°C)
- With rise in temperature, the velocity of sound increases as

  $$v = \sqrt{\frac{\gamma RT}{M}} \text{ i.e. } v \propto \sqrt{T}$$
- **Open organ pipe** In this pipe, anti-nodes of sound wave are formed at both the open ends of pipe and one or more nodes are formed in between the open ends. The number of nodes is less than the number of anti-nodes.

  In fundamental mode (1st harmonic) only one node is formed at the centre of pipe and so,

  $$l = \frac{\lambda_1}{2} \text{ and } \nu_1 = \frac{v}{\lambda_1} = \frac{v}{2l}$$

  All harmonics are present in open pipe with their frequencies in the ratio 1 : 2 : 3 : 4 . . . .
- **Closed organ pipe** Longitudinal stationary waves are formed such that open end of pipe behaves as an anti-node and a node is formed at the closed end.

  In fundamental mode, $l = \frac{\lambda_1}{4}$ or $\lambda_1 = 4l$

  $\therefore$ Fundamental (1st harmonic) frequency, $\nu_1 = \frac{v}{\lambda_1} = \frac{v}{4l}$

  only odd harmonics are present in closed organ pipe with their frequencies in the ratio 1 : 3 : 5 : 7. . . .
- When two sound waves of nearly equal (but never equal) or slightly different frequencies and equal or nearly equal amplitudes travelling along the same direction superimpose at a given point, the resultant sound intensity alternately rises and falls. This alternate rise and fall of sound at a given position is called **beats.**
- Number of beats formed per second is called the **frequency of beats.** If two sound waves of frequencies ν_1 and ν_2 superimpose, then frequency of beats $= (\nu_1 \sim \nu_2)$, i.e. either $(\nu_1 - \nu_2)$ or $(\nu_2 - \nu_1)$.
- **Doppler's effect** The Doppler's effect is a change in the observed frequency of a wave when either the source S of wave or the observer O or both move relative to the medium.

  S → v   O
  → v_S → v_O

  For sound waves, if v be the velocity of sound in given medium, v_s the velocity of source relative to the medium and v_o the velocity of observer relative to the medium, then the observed frequency is given by, $\nu = \nu_o\left[\frac{v \pm v_o}{v \pm v_s}\right]$

where, v_o = true frequency. In the formula given above, v_s and v_o are taken with negative sign, if motion is along source to observer and positive if motion is along observer to source.

- Our perception of loudness is better correlated with the sound level measured in decibel (dB) and defined as follows

$$\beta = 10\log_{10}\left(\frac{I}{I_0}\right)$$

where, $I_0 = 10^{-12}$ W/m^2 at 1 kHz.

15. Electric Charges and Fields

- Electric charge is quantised. The minimum unit of charge, which may reside independently is the electronic charge e having a value 1.60×10^{-19} C. Charge on any other body is $q = \pm ne$, where n is any integer.
- If q_1 and q_2 be two stationary point charges in free space separated by a distance r, then force of attraction/repulsion between them is

$$F = k\frac{q_1 q_2}{r^2} = \frac{1}{4\pi\varepsilon_0}\cdot\frac{q_1 q_2}{r^2}$$

- Electric field vector **E** (also known as electric field intensity) at any point is given by, $\mathbf{E} = \lim_{q_0 \to 0}\left(\frac{\mathbf{F}}{q_0}\right)$

  where, q_0 is a small positive test charge which experiences a force **F** at given point.

  Electric field at a distance r from a point charge q is

$$E = \frac{1}{4\pi\varepsilon_0}\cdot\frac{q}{r^2}$$

- Electric field due to infinitely long uniformly charged wire is

$$E = \frac{\lambda}{2\pi\varepsilon_0 r} \quad \left(\text{where, } \lambda = \text{linear charge density} = \frac{q}{L}\right)$$

- Electric field due to a uniformly charged infinite plane sheet is

$$E = \frac{\sigma}{2\varepsilon_0} \quad \left(\text{where, } \sigma = \text{surface charge density} = \frac{q}{A}\right)$$

- Electric field due to a uniformly charged thin spherical shell is

$$E = \frac{Q}{4\pi\varepsilon_0 r^2} \text{ and } E = 0 \quad \text{(inside the shell)}$$

- Electric flux is a measure of flow of electric field through a surface.

  i.e. $\phi_E = \int E\, dS\cos\theta = \int \mathbf{E}\cdot d\mathbf{S} = \int \mathbf{E}\cdot\hat{\mathbf{n}}\, dS$

  where, $\hat{\mathbf{n}}$ is the unit vector normal to area element dS.

  Electric flux is a scalar quantity having SI unit N-m^{2}C^{-1} or V-m.

- According to Gauss' law in electrostatics, the total electric flux linked with a closed surface is equal to $\frac{1}{\varepsilon_0}$ times the net charge enclosed by that surface.

  Mathematically, $\phi_E = \oint_S \mathbf{E}\cdot d\mathbf{S} = \frac{1}{\varepsilon_0}(q_{\text{enclosed}})$

- The dipole moment of a dipole is defined as the product of the magnitude of either charge and distance between them. Thus, dipole moment, $p = q(2a) \Rightarrow |\mathbf{p}| = q(2a)$

  It is a vector quantity directed from negative to positive charge having unit C-m.

- Electric field at a point distant r from a short dipole along a line inclined at an angle θ with dipole axis,

$$E = \frac{1}{4\pi\varepsilon_0}\cdot\frac{p}{r^3}\sqrt{3\cos^2\theta + 1}$$

  For axial point put $\theta = 0°$,

  For equatorial point put $\theta = 90°$.

- When a dipole is placed at an angle θ from the direction of a uniform electric field E, it experiences a torque given by, $\tau = pE\sin\theta$ or $\boldsymbol{\tau} = \mathbf{p}\times\mathbf{E}$
- The potential energy is the amount of work done in rotating an electric dipole from a direction perpendicular to electric field to the given direction. Hence,

$$U = -pE\cos\theta$$

  or $U = -\mathbf{p}\cdot\mathbf{E}$

16. Electrostatic Potential and Capacitance

- Electric potential is a state function and does not depend on the path followed. For a point charge q at a distance r,

$$V = \frac{1}{4\pi\varepsilon_0}\frac{q}{r}$$

- If n number of charges $q_1, q_2, q_3, \ldots q_n$ are present in space, then electric potential, $V = \frac{1}{4\pi\varepsilon_0}\sum_{i=1}^{n}\left(\frac{q_i}{r_i}\right)$
- Electric potential due to an electric dipole,

$$V = \frac{1}{4\pi\varepsilon_0}\frac{p\cos\theta}{r^2}$$

  At axial position, $\theta = 0°$, $V = \frac{1}{4\pi\varepsilon_0}\frac{p}{r^2}$

  At equatorial axis, $\theta = 90°$. So, $V = 0$

- Electric potential due to a charged conducting sphere/shell

$$V = \frac{q}{4\pi\varepsilon_0 R}, \text{ for } r \le R$$

  For a charged non-conducting sphere,

$$V = \frac{q}{4\pi\varepsilon_0 r}, \text{ for } r > R$$

  or $$V = \frac{q}{4\pi\varepsilon_0}\left(\frac{3R^2 - r^2}{2R^3}\right), \text{ for } r \le R$$

- **Equipotential surface** is an imaginary surface joining the points of same potential in a electric field. Electric field is normal at each point of an equipotential surface.

- For a system of two point charges q_1 and q_2 separated by a distance r, electrostatic potential energy,

$$U = \frac{1}{4\pi\varepsilon_0}\frac{q_1 q_2}{r}$$

- Capacity of a conductor, $C = \frac{\text{Charge}}{\text{Potential}} = \frac{q}{V}$

In SI system, the unit of capacity is farad.

- **Parallel plate capacitor**
  - Capacity of the parallel plate air capacitor, $C_0 = \frac{q}{V} = \frac{\varepsilon_0 A}{d}$
  - If the gap between plates is filled with dielectric media of dielectric constant K, then $C = \frac{K\varepsilon_0 A}{d} = K\varepsilon_0$
  - Force between the plates, $F = \frac{1}{2}\frac{q^2}{A\varepsilon_0}$
  - If dielectric slab of thickness t is introduced in a parallel plate air capacitor whose plates are separated by a distance d, then capacity of the capacitor increases and will be given by,

$$C = \frac{\varepsilon_0 A}{d - t + \frac{t}{K}} \quad \text{(dielectric slab)}$$

If a metal is inserted, put $K = \infty$

- **Series combination of capacitors** If n number of capacitors are connected in series, then the equivalent capacity of the combination is,

$$\frac{1}{C_s} = \frac{1}{C_1} + \frac{1}{C_2} + \cdots + \frac{1}{C_n}$$

- **Parallel combination of capacitors** If n number of capacitors are connected in parallel, then the equivalent capacity of the combination is,

$$C_p = C_1 + C_2 + C_3 + \cdots + C_n$$

- If dielectric mediums of constants K_1 and K_2 are filled in between the plates of the capacitor as shown in the figure, then

$$C = \frac{\varepsilon_0 A(K_1 + K_2)}{2d}$$

If the dielectric substances of dielectric constants K_1 and K_2 are filled in between the plates of a capacitor as shown in the figure, then

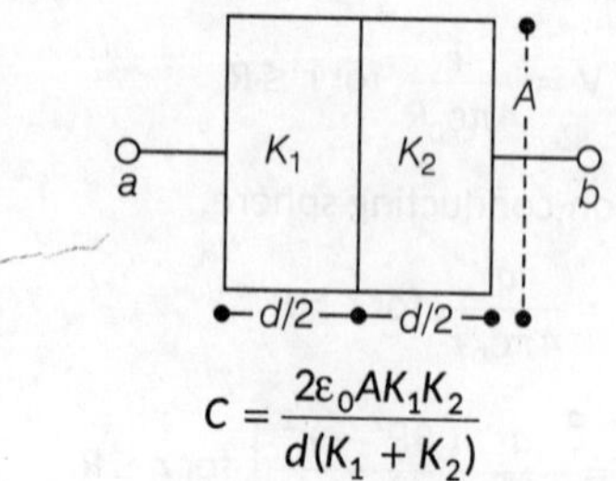

$$C = \frac{2\varepsilon_0 A K_1 K_2}{d(K_1 + K_2)}$$

- Capacity of a capacitor with n parallel plates is given,

$$C = \frac{(n-1)\varepsilon_0 K A}{d}$$

where, K = dielectric constant of the medium.

In the case of air or vacuum, $C = \frac{(n-1)\varepsilon_0 A}{d}$

Since, work done is stored as potential energy in capacitor, therefore energy of a charged capacitor,

$$W = E = \frac{1}{2}\frac{q^2}{C} = \frac{1}{2}CV^2 \quad [\because q = CV]$$

where, q = amount of charge stored,

C = capacity of the capacitor.

- Loss of energy in sharing charges between two conductors at potential V_1 and V_2 and having capacities C_1 and C_2,

$$E = \frac{1}{2}\frac{C_1 C_2}{(C_1 + C_2)} \times (V_1 - V_2)^2$$

- Common potential, $V = \frac{C_1 V_1 + C_2 V_2}{C_1 + C_2}$
- Energy density between the plates, $u = \frac{1}{2}\varepsilon_0 E^2$

17. Current Electricity

- Electric current is defined as the time rate of flow of electric charge through a cross-section of the conductor.

Instantaneous value of current at any instant is given by,

$$I_{inst} = \lim_{\Delta t \to 0}\left(\frac{\Delta q}{\Delta t}\right) = \frac{dq}{dt}$$

The SI unit of electric current is ampere (A).

- Current density, $J = \frac{I}{A}\,\text{Am}^{-2}$
- The drift velocity is given by the relation, $v_d = -\frac{eE}{m}\tau$

where, τ is known as relaxation time and is the mean value of time between two successive collisions of an electron with ions in the conductor.

- Drift velocity per unit electric field is called the **mobility** of the electrons. In terms of drift speed, electric current flowing through a conductor is expressed as, $I = nAev_d$

where, A = cross-section area of conductor

n = number of conduction electrons per unit volume.

- According to Ohm's law, if the physical conditions (temperature, mechanical strain, etc) remaining unchanged, then the current flowing through a conductor is directly proportional to the potential difference across its ends. Thus, $I \propto V \Rightarrow V = IR$

where, R is a constant known as the electrical resistance of given conductor.

- In terms of free electron density n and relaxation time τ, the resistance of a conductor is given by,

$$R = \frac{m}{ne^2\tau}\cdot\frac{l}{A} = \frac{\rho l}{A}$$

where, ρ is resistivity and l is a length of the conductor.

- Resistance and resistivity of metallic conductors increases with increase in temperature. The relation is written as

$$R = R_0(1 + \alpha T) \quad \text{and} \quad \rho = \rho_0(1 + \beta T)$$

where, R_0 and ρ_0 are the values of resistance and resistivity at 0°C and R and ρ at T°C, α and β are two constants whose value vary from metal to metal.

- High resistances used are usually carbon resistances and the values of such resistances are marked on them according to a colour codes which are in bracket with colours, i.e. Black (0), Brown (1), Red (2), Orange (3), Green (5), Blue (6), Violet (7), Grey (8) and White (9). **Tolerances** are Gold (5%), Silver (10%) and no colour (20%).
- **Series grouping of resistances** In series grouping of resistances, same current I flows through all the resistances but potential difference across each resistor is different.

  Total equivalent resistance in series grouping is

$$R_s = R_1 + R_2 + R_3 + \cdots R_n$$

  where, $R_1, R_2, R_3, \ldots, R_n$ are the resistances connected in series.
- **Parallel grouping of resistances** In parallel grouping of resistances, same potential difference V appears across each resistance but currents flowing through each resistors are different.

  Equivalent resistance R_p in parallel grouping is

$$\frac{1}{R_p} = \frac{1}{R_1} + \frac{1}{R_2} + \frac{1}{R_3} + \cdots + \frac{1}{R_n}$$

  where, $R_1, R_2, R_3, \ldots, R_n$ are the resistances connected in parallel.
- If E be the emf and r the internal resistance of a cell and a resistance R is joined with it, then current in the circuit,

$$I = \frac{E}{R + r}$$

  and terminal potential difference, $V = IR = \dfrac{ER}{(R + r)}$
- **Series grouping of cells** In series grouping if all the cells are joined, so as to supply current in the same direction, then resultant emf

$$E_{eq} = E_1 + E_2 + E_3 + \cdots$$

Positive E_1 r_1 E_2 r_2 E_3 r_3 Negative

  The equivalent internal resistance of cell,

$$r_{eq} = r_1 + r_2 + r_3 + \ldots$$

- **Parallel grouping of cells** In parallel grouping if positive terminals of all cells have been joined at one point and all negative terminals at another point, then

$$\frac{1}{r_{eq}} = \frac{1}{r_1} + \frac{1}{r_2} + \frac{1}{r_3} + \cdots$$

Positive E_1 r_1 E_2 r_2 E_3 r_3 Negative

  The equivalent emf of the parallel grouping is given by

$$\frac{E_{eq}}{r_{eq}} = \frac{E_1}{r_1} + \frac{E_2}{r_2} + \frac{E_3}{r_3} + \cdots$$

- Electric energy in a conductor changes to heat energy and is given by

$$H = I^2Rt \text{ joule} = \frac{I^2Rt}{4.18} \text{ cal}$$

- Power is the rate at which work is done by the energy source to maintain current in a circuit and is given by

$$p = VI = I^2R = \frac{V^2}{R}$$

- **Kirchhoff's laws** Kirchhoff gave two laws, which are as follows:
  - **First law** The algebraic sum of the currents flowing into any junction is zero.

  Thus, $$\sum_{\text{junction}} I = 0$$

  Kirchhoff's first law is based on conservation law of electric charge.
  - **Second law** This law states that the algebraic sum of changes in potential around any closed loop involving resistors and cells in the loop is zero.
- The Wheatstone bridge is an arrangement of four resistances P, Q, R and S.

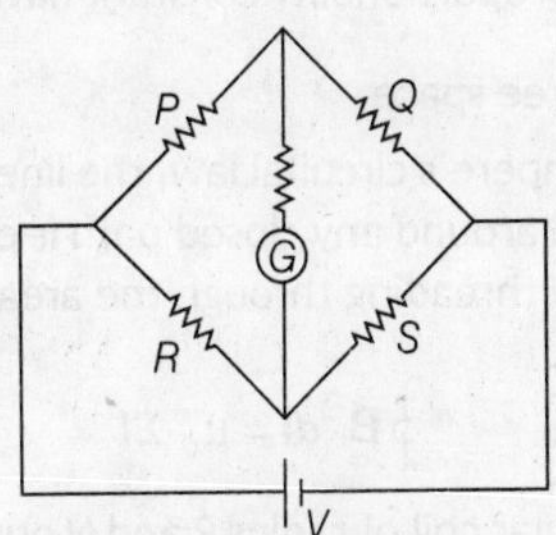

The null point condition is given by, $\dfrac{P}{Q} = \dfrac{R}{S}$

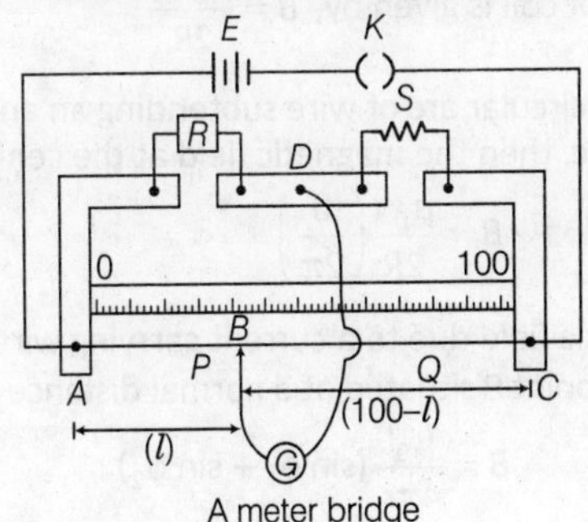

A meter bridge

At balancing situation of bridge,

$$\frac{P}{Q} = \frac{R}{S} \Rightarrow \frac{l}{100 - l} = \frac{R}{S}$$

- **Potentiometer** is an ideal device to measure the potential difference between two points.

  Potential gradient, $K = \dfrac{\text{Potential difference across wire}}{\text{Total length of wire}}$

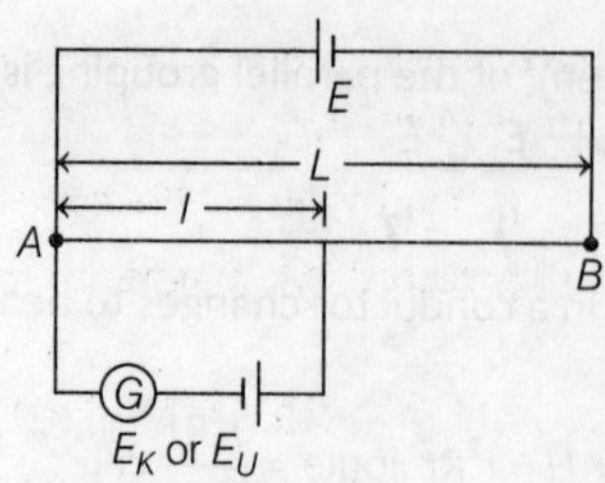

(i) The emf of an unknown battery can be found as

$$E_U = \left(\frac{l_2}{l_1}\right)E$$

(ii) The internal resistance of cell can be found as

$$r = \left(\frac{l_1}{l_2} - 1\right)R$$

18. Moving Charges and Magnetism

- According to Biot-Savart's law, the magnetic field dB at a point P due to a current element Idl is given by

$$d\mathbf{B} = \frac{\mu_0}{4\pi}\frac{I\,(d\mathbf{l}\times\mathbf{r})}{r^3}$$

where, $\frac{\mu_0}{4\pi}$ is a proportionality constant having a value of 10^{-7} T-mA^{-1} in free space.

- According to Ampere's circuital law, the line integral of the magnetic field **B** around any closed path is equal to μ_0 times the net current I threading through the area enclosed by the closed path.

Mathematically, $\oint \mathbf{B}\cdot d\mathbf{l} = \mu_0\,\Sigma I$

- If there is a circular coil of radius R and N number of turns, carrying a current I through the turns, then magnetic field at the centre of coil is given by, $B = \frac{\mu_0 NI}{2R}$
- If there is a circular arc of wire subtending an angle θ at the centre of arc, then the magnetic field at the centre point,

$$B = \frac{\mu_0 I}{2R}\left(\frac{\theta}{2\pi}\right)$$

- The magnetic field due to a current carrying wire of finite length at a point P situated at a normal distance r is

$$B = \frac{\mu_0 I}{4\pi r}(\sin\phi_1 + \sin\phi_2)$$

where, ϕ_1 and ϕ_2 are angles made by ends of wire.

- The magnetic field due to a thick wire at a point P at a normal distance r is $B = \frac{\mu_0 I}{2\pi r}$.

Magnetic field inside a hollow current carrying conductor is zero.

- The magnetic force $\mathbf{F}_m$ acting on a charge q moving with a velocity **v** in a magnetic field **B** is given by,

$$\mathbf{F}_m = q\,(\mathbf{v}\times\mathbf{B})$$

where, θ is angle between **v** and **B**. The direction of force $\mathbf{F}_m$ is given by rule of vector product.

- If a charged particle enters a uniform magnetic field B with a velocity v in a direction perpendicular to that of B (i.e. $\theta = 90°$), then the charged particle experiences a force $F_m = qvB$. Under its influence, the particle describes a circular path such as
  - Radius of circular path, $r = \frac{mv}{qB}$
  - The period of revolution of charged particle, $T = \frac{2\pi m}{qB}$ and $f = \frac{Bq}{2\pi m}$.
- Period of revolution and frequency of charged particle is independent of its velocity.
- If the charged partice is moving at an angle θ to the magnetic field, then it will follow helical path, such as
  - Radius of helical path, $r = \frac{mv\sin\theta}{qB}$
  - Pitch of helical path, $P = \frac{2\pi mv\cos\theta}{qB}$
- The positive ions of charge q and mass m in cyclotron attains maximum energy which is given by,

$$E_{\max} = \frac{1}{2}mv^2 = \frac{1}{2}\cdot\frac{B^2q^2r^2}{m}$$

- If two infinitely long parallel conductors carry currents I_1 and I_2 respectively, and are separated by a distance r, then magnetic force experienced by l length of any one conductor due to the other current carrying conductor is

$$F = \frac{\mu_0}{4\pi}\frac{2I_1I_2}{r}l$$

Like parallel currents attract and anti parallel currents repel each other.

- A current carrying loop (of any shape) behaves as a magnetic dipole whose magnetic moment is given by

$$\mathbf{M} = I\mathbf{A}$$

- When a coil of area A having N turns and carrying current I is suspended inside a magnetic field of strength B, then torque on the coil is given by, $\tau = NIBA\sin\theta$
- **Magnetic field of a solenoid** Inside the solenoid magnetic field is uniform and parallel to the solenoid axis. Outside the solenoid magnetic field is assumed to be zero.

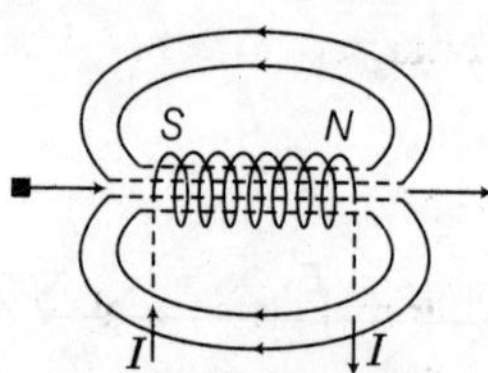

$$B = \mu_0\,nI$$

where, n = number of turns per unit length.

An endless solenoid in the form of a ring is called a toroid.

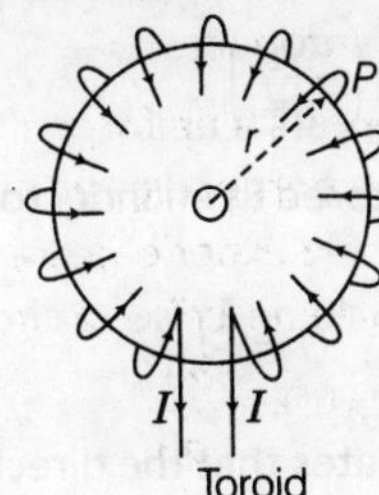

Toroid

If the toroid is a material cored of relative permeability μ_r, then $B = \mu_0 \mu_r nI$

where, n = number of turns per unit length.

- **A moving coil galvanometer** is used to measure the current upto nanometres.

An ammeter is made by connecting a low resistance S in parallel to galvanometer G, whose value is given by

$$S = \left(\frac{I_g}{I - I_g}\right)G$$

- A voltmeter is made by connecting a high resistance R in series with galvanometer G, whose value is given by

$$R = \frac{V}{I_g} - G$$

- Current and voltage sensitivity of a galvanometer are as

$$S_I = \frac{NBA}{K} \text{ and } S_V = \frac{NBA}{RK}$$

where, K = galvanometer constant.

19. Magnetism and Matter

- **Magnetic moment** is a vector whose direction is from S pole to N pole. SI unit of magnetic pole strength (m) is ampere metre (A-m) and that of magnetic dipole moment ($\mathbf{M}$) is ampere metre^2 (A-m^2).
- When a bar magnet is placed along the magnetic meridian with its North pole pointing towards geographic North, two neutral points are obtained on either side of the magnet along its equatorial line. If r be the distance of neutral point, then

$$B_H = \frac{\mu_0}{4\pi} \cdot \frac{M}{r^3}$$

- When a bar magnet is placed along the magnetic meridian with its North pole pointing towards geographic South, two neutral points are obtained on either side of the magnet along its axial line.

Hence, we have, $B_H = \frac{\mu_0}{4\pi} \cdot \frac{2M}{r^3}$

- When a bar magnet is making an angle θ with the magnetic axis, the magnetic field is given by

$$B = \frac{\mu_0}{4\pi} \frac{M}{r^3} \sqrt{3\cos^2\theta + 1}$$

- A magnetic dipole when placed in a uniform magnetic field, it experiences a torque given by

$$\tau = \mathbf{M} \times \mathbf{B} = MB\sin\theta$$

- The potential energy stored in a magnetic dipole by rotating it is given by

$$U = -\mathbf{M} \cdot \mathbf{B} = -MB\cos\theta$$

- The time period of a magnetic compass oscillating in a magnetic field is

$$T = 2\pi\sqrt{\frac{I}{MB}}$$

- **Angle of declination (α)** At a given place, the acute angle between the magnetic meridian and the geographical meridian is called the angle of declination (or magnetic declination) α at that place.
- **Angle of inclination or Dip (δ)** The angle of dip δ at a place is the angle which the direction of the earth's total magnetic field B_E subtends with the horizontal direction.
- **Horizontal component of the earth's magnetic field (B_H)** As earth's magnetic field, in general is inclined at an angle δ with the horizontal direction, it may be resolved into horizontal component B_H and a vertical component B_V, where

$$B_H = B_E \cos\delta \text{ and}$$

$$B_V = B_E \sin\delta$$

$$\Rightarrow \quad B_E = \sqrt{B_H^2 + B_V^2}$$

and $\tan\delta = \dfrac{B_V}{B_H}$

- If $\mathbf{B}_0$ be the magnetic field in free space, then on placing the given magnetic substance, the magnetic field changes from $\mathbf{B}_0$ to $\mathbf{B}$, where $\mathbf{B} = \mu_r \cdot \mathbf{B}_0$

$\mu_r = \mathbf{B}/\mathbf{B}_0$ = relative magnetic permeability of that substance.

Relative magnetic permeability μ_r is a unitless and dimensionless term. For magnetic substance like iron, $\mu_r > 1000$.

- Intensity of magnetisation of a substance is defined as the magnetic moment induced in the substance per unit volume when placed in the magnetising field.

Thus, $\mathbf{I} = \dfrac{\mathbf{M}}{V}$

It is a vector quantity and its SI unit is Am^{-1}.

- **Magnetic intensity** It is the measure of the capability of external magnetising field to magnetise the given substance and is mathematically defined as,

$$H = \frac{B_0}{\mu_0}$$

Magnetic intensity H is a vector quantity and its SI unit is Am^{-1}.

- Magnetic susceptibility of a substance is the ratio of intensity of magnetisation I induced in the substance to the magnetic intensity H.

Thus, $\chi_m = \dfrac{I}{H}$. It is a scalar term and has no unit or dimensions.

- **Useful relations**
 (i) $B = \mu_0(H + I)$
 (ii) $\mu_r = 1 + \chi_m$
- The materials which show a very small decrease in magnetic flux when placed in a strong magnetising field, are called **diamagnetic materials.**
- The relative permeability of diamagnetic substance is slightly less than 1 (i.e. $\mu_r < 1$) but it can never be negative, i.e. $0 < \mu_r < 1$ and susceptibility has a small negative value.
- The materials which show a small increase in magnetic flux when placed in a magnetising field are called **paramagnetic materials.**
- The relative permeability μ_r of a paramagnetic material is slightly greater than one ($\mu_r > 1$). Magnetic susceptibility χ_m of paramagnetic materials is positive.
- Paramagnetism is a temperature dependent. According to **Curie's law,** the magnetic susceptibility of a paramagnetic substance is inversely proportional to its temperature T.
 Mathematically, $\chi_m = \frac{C}{T}$
 where, C is a constant known as Curie constant.
- The materials which are strongly attracted by a magnetic field and can themselves be magnetised even in a weak magnetising field are called **ferromagnetic materials.**
 These materials show a large increase in magnetic flux, when placed in a magnetic field. Thus, for them, $\mu_r >> 1$. Accordingly, χ_m is positive and large.
- Above curie temperature T_c, the magnetic susceptibility of ferromagnetic material varies as

$$\chi_m = \frac{C}{(T - T_c)}$$

20. Electromagnetic Induction

- The magnetic flux (ϕ) linked with a given surface area is defined as the total number of magnetic field lines (lines of induction) passing normally through the given area.
 Mathematically, $\phi = \oint \mathbf{B} \cdot d\mathbf{S}$
 It is a scalar quantity having unit weber (Wb).
- **Faraday's law** An emf is induced in a circuit when the magnetic flux linked with the circuit changes with time. It is given by

$$e = -N\frac{d\phi}{dt} = -L\frac{dI}{dt}$$

 From this relation, self-inductance (L) of a coil/circuit is the magnitude of induced emf per unit rate of change of current in the circuit. N is number of turns.
- If a circuit having resistance R is closed, then due to induced emf, induced current, $I = -\frac{N}{R}\frac{d\phi_B}{dt}$
 Induced charge, $dq = -\frac{N}{R}d\phi_B$
 Induced power, $P = \frac{N^2}{R}\left(\frac{d\phi_B}{dt}\right)$
- The magnetic energy stored in an inductor is the work done by the emf of the source.

$$U = \frac{1}{2}LI^2$$

- **Lenz's law** This law states that the direction of induced emf/current in a circuit is such that it opposes the change in magnetic field that produced it. Lenz's law is strictly in accordance with the law of conservation of energy.
- If a conducting rod of length l be moving with a uniform velocity $\mathbf{v}$ perpendicular to a uniform magnetic field $\mathbf{B}$, then an induced emf is set up. The magnitude of induced emf will be $|e| = Blv$
- Induced current, $|I| = \frac{Blv}{R}$
- Magnetic force, $F_m = BIl = \frac{B^2l^2v}{R}$
- Let a conducting rod of length l rotates about an axis passing through one of its ends (that end may be fixed) with an angular velocity ω in a plane perpendicular to the magnetic field $\mathbf{B}$. Then, an induced emf is set up between the ends of rod, whose magnitude is given by

$$|e| = \frac{1}{2}Bl^2\omega$$

- Induced emf due to mutual inductance,

$$e_2 = -N\frac{d\phi_{B_2}}{dt} = -M\frac{dI_1}{dt}$$

 Hence, mutual inductance (M) for a pair of coils is numerically equal to the magnitude of induced emf in one coil when current in the other coil changes at a rate of 1 As^{-1}.
- For a pair of two magnetically coupled coils of self-inductances L_1 and L_2 respectively, the mutual inductance is $M_{12} = M_{21} = K\sqrt{L_1L_2}$, where K = coupling coefficient.
- If two coils of self-inductances L_1 and L_2 are arranged in series, then their equivalent inductance is

$$L_s = L_1 + L_2$$

- If two coils of inductances L_1 and L_2 are arranged in parallel, then their equivalent inductance is

$$L_p = \frac{L_1L_2}{L_1 + L_2}$$

- **Eddy currents** are the currents induced in the body of bulk conductor due to changing magnetic flux linked to them.

21. Alternating Current

- The common alternating current varying as sine function of time is given by, $I = I_0 \sin\omega t = I_0 \sin\frac{2\pi t}{T}$

and $$V = V_0 \sin\omega t = V_0 \sin\frac{2\pi t}{T}$$

Here, I_0 and V_0 are the maximum or peak values of current and voltage, ω the angular frequency and T the period of given AC.

- In our domestic circuits, the frequency of AC is 50 Hz. Thus, it changes its direction after every $\frac{1}{100}$ s.
- The average value of an AC for one complete cycle is zero and for half cycle its value is 63.6% of its peak value.
- The rms value of an AC is defined as

$$I_{rms} = \frac{I_0}{\sqrt{2}} \text{ and } V_{rms} = \frac{V_0}{\sqrt{2}}$$

- **Pure resistive circuit** Let an alternating voltage $V = V_0 \sin\omega t$ be applied across a pure resistance R. Then,

Current, $I = \frac{V}{R}$ or $I_{rms} = \frac{V_{rms}}{R}$

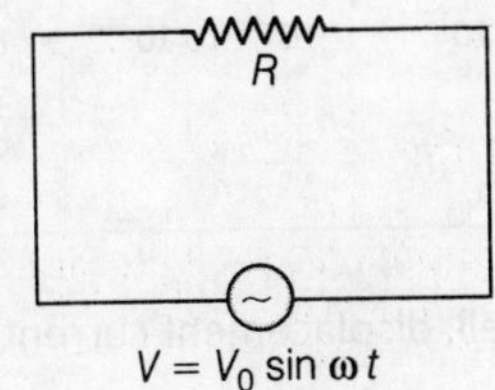

$V = V_0 \sin \omega t$

Current and voltage are in same phase, i.e. current is given by $I = I_0 \sin\omega t$ and $V = V_0 \sin\omega t$

- **Pure inductive circuit** Let an alternating voltage $V = V_0 \sin\omega t$ be applied across a pure inductance L. Then, average power $= V_{rms} I_{rms} \cos\frac{\pi}{2} = 0$

Such a current, for which average power as well as power factor is zero is called the **wattless current.**

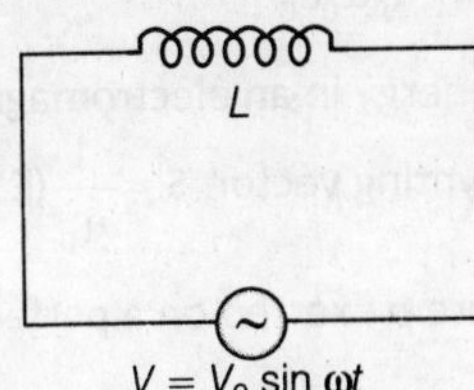

$V = V_0 \sin \omega t$

The inductance offers some opposition for the flow of AC. It is known as **inductive reactance** $X_L = 2\pi\nu L = L\omega$.

Thus, a pure inductance does not oppose flow of DC ($\omega = 0$) but opposes flow of AC.

Current flowing, $I = \frac{V}{X_L}$

The current decreases with increase in frequency. The current lags behind the voltage by $\frac{\pi}{2}$.

(or voltage leads the current by $\frac{\pi}{2}$) and is thus given by,

$$I = I_0 \sin\left(\omega t - \frac{\pi}{2}\right)$$

- **Pure capacitive circuit** Let an alternating voltage $V = V_0 \sin\omega t$ be applied across a pure capacitance C.

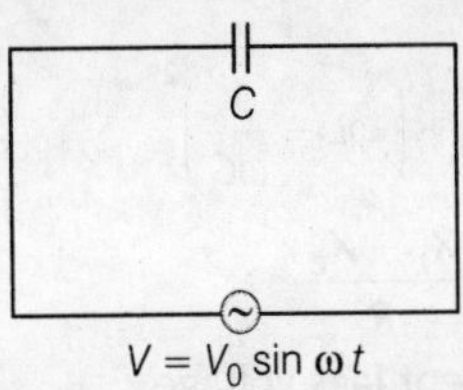

$V = V_0 \sin \omega t$

The capacitance offers some opposition for flow of current but allows AC to pass through it. The opposition offered is known as **capacitive reactance.**

$$X_C = \frac{1}{C\omega} = \frac{1}{C \cdot 2\pi\nu}$$

$\Rightarrow$ Current flowing, $I = \frac{V}{X_C}$

The current increases with increase in frequency. The current leads the voltage by $\frac{\pi}{2}$ (or voltage is behind the current by $\frac{\pi}{2}$)

and is thus given by, $I = I_0 \sin\left(\omega t + \frac{\pi}{2}\right)$

- Total opposition offered by an AC circuit to flow through it is called its **impedance** Z. Its unit is ohm (Ω) and dimensional formula is $[ML^2T^{-3}A^{-2}]$. For a circuit,

$$Z = \sqrt{X^2 + R^2} = \sqrt{(X_L - X_C)^2 + R^2}$$

- The term $\cos\phi$ is known as **power factor** of given circuit.

Thus, $\cos\phi = \frac{R}{Z}$ = Power factor = $\frac{\text{True power}}{\text{Apparent power}}$

For a pure resistive circuit V and I are in phase $\phi = 0°$. Hence, $\cos\phi = 1$ and average power = $V_{rms} I_{rms}$

- For a pure inductive or a pure capacitive circuit current and voltage differ in phase by $\frac{\pi}{2}\left(\phi = \frac{\pi}{2}\right)$.
- If current is leading the voltage by ϕ, then $V^2 = V_R^2 + V_C^2$ and if current is lagging the voltage by ϕ, then $V^2 = V_R^2 + V_L^2$

where, V = net voltage, V_R = voltage across the resistor, V_C = voltage across the capacitor and V_L = voltage across the inductor.

- **Series *L-C-R* circuit** Consider a series *L-C-R* circuit as shown in figure.

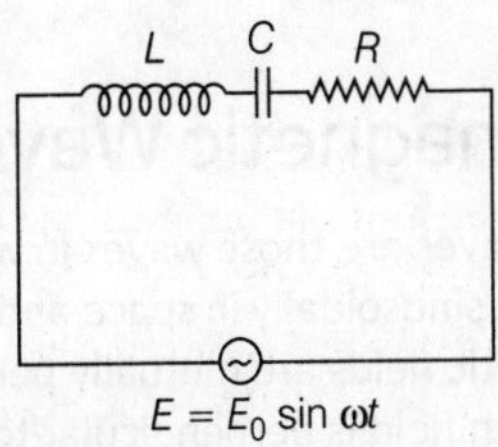

$E = E_0 \sin \omega t$

– For $E = E_0 \sin\omega t$,

Current, $I = \frac{E_0}{Z}\sin(\omega t - \phi)$

where, impedance

$$Z = \sqrt{R^2 + \left(\omega L - \frac{1}{\omega C}\right)^2}$$

and $\tan\phi = \frac{X}{R} = \frac{X_L - X_C}{R}$

- For $X_L > X_C$ current lags voltage,
  $X_L < X_C$ current leads voltage
  and $X_L = X_C$ current and voltage are in phase.
- If $X_L = X_C \Rightarrow \omega_0 = \frac{1}{\sqrt{LC}}$, i.e. the natural frequency of the circuit is equal to applied frequency, then the circuit is said to be in resonance.
- At resonance, current in the circuit is maximum and impedance is minimum.

At resonance, $I_0 = \frac{E_0}{R}$

and $V_L = I_0 X_L = V_C = I_0 X_C = QE_0$

where, $Q = \frac{\omega L}{R} = \frac{1}{\omega RC} = \frac{1}{R}\sqrt{\frac{L}{C}}$, is termed as **quality factor.** It determines the sharpness of resonance. Higher the value of Q, sharper is the resonance.

- Instantaneous power in AC circuit,
  $P_{inst} = VI = V_0 I_0 \sin\omega t \sin(\omega t - \phi)$
  Average power, $P_{av} = V_{rms} I_{rms} \cos\phi = \frac{1}{2} V_0 I_0 \cos\phi$
- **AC generator** or dynamo is a device used to produce electrical energy at the expense of mechanical energy. It works on the principle of electromagnetic induction.
  The induced emf is given by
  $e = e_0 \sin\omega t = NBA\omega \sin\omega t$
- **Transformer** is a device which works on the principle of electromagnetic induction. It is used to increase or decrease the voltage in an AC circuit.
  For an ideal transformer, transformer ratio,
  $$K = \frac{e_s}{e_p} = \frac{V_s}{V_p} = \frac{N_s}{N_p} = \frac{I_p}{I_s}$$
- For step-up transformer, $K > 1$ and for step-down transformer, $K < 1$.
  Efficiency, $\eta = \frac{V_s I_s}{V_p I_p}$

22. Electromagnetic Waves

- Electromagnetic waves are those waves in which electric and magnetic field vary sinusoidally in space and time in it. The electric and magnetic fields are mutually perpendicular to each other and each field is perpendicular to the direction of propagation of the wave.

Electromagnetic spectrum

Name	Frequency range (Hz)	Wavelength range (m)	Source
Radio waves	10^4 to 10^8	0.1 to 600	• Oscillating electric circuits
Microwaves	10^9 to 10^{12}	10^{-3} to 0.3	• Oscillating current in special vacuum tubes
Infrared	10^{11} to 5×10^{14}	10^{-6} to 5×10^{-3}	• Outer electrons in atoms and molecules
Visible light	4×10^{14} to 7×10^{14}	4×10^{-7} to 8×10^{-7}	• Outer electrons in atoms
Ultraviolet	10^{15} to 10^{17}	1.5×10^{-7} to 3.5×10^{-7}	• Outer electrons in atoms
X-rays	10^{18} to 10^{20}	10^{-11} to 10^{-8}	• Inner electrons in atoms and sudden deceleration of high energy free electrons
Gamma rays	10^{19} to 10^{14}	10^{-16} to 10^{-13}	• Nuclei of atoms and sudden deceleration of high energy free electrons

- According to Maxwell, displacement current is given by, $i_d = \varepsilon_0 \frac{d\phi_E}{dt}$. The generalised form of Ampere's law is
  $$\oint \mathbf{B} \cdot dl = \mu_0(i + i_d) = \mu_0\left(i + \varepsilon_0 \frac{d\phi_E}{dt}\right)$$
- Maxwell's theory predicted that the electromagnetic waves of all frequencies (and hence all wavelengths) propagate in vacuum with speed of light given by,
  $$c = \frac{1}{\sqrt{\mu_0 \varepsilon_0}} = 3 \times 10^8 \text{ m/s}$$
- The rate of flow of energy in an electromagnetic wave is described by the poynting vector, $\mathbf{S} = \frac{1}{\mu_0}(\mathbf{E} \times \mathbf{B})$
- The radiation pressure p exerted on a perfectly absorbing surface, $p = \frac{S}{c}$.
- If the surface is a perfect reflector and incidence is normal, then the momentum transported to the surface in a time t is given by, $p = \frac{2u}{c}$ and the radiation pressure will be, $p = \frac{2S}{c}$.
- Energy density of electromagnetic wave,
  $$u_e = \frac{1}{2}\varepsilon_0 E^2_{u_B} = \frac{1}{2}\frac{B^2}{\mu_0}$$
- Momentum delivered, $p = \frac{u}{c}$ (absorbing surface)
  $p = \frac{2u}{c}$ (reflecting surface)
- Energy of wave $= \frac{hc}{\lambda} = h\nu$

23. Ray Optics and Optical Instruments

- According to the laws of reflection,
  - The incident ray, reflected ray and the normal drawn on reflecting surface at the point of incidence lie in the same plane.
  - The angle of incidence $\angle i$ = angle of reflection $\angle r$.
- The focal length of a spherical mirror is half of its radius of curvature, i.e. $f = \frac{R}{2}$.
- The mirror formula is given by, $\frac{1}{v} + \frac{1}{u} = \frac{1}{f}$
- The power of a mirror is given by, $P = \frac{1}{f}$
- If a thin object of linear height h is placed perpendicular to the principal axis of a mirror and the linear height of its image be h', then linear (also known as transverse) or lateral magnification is given by

$$m = \frac{h'}{h} = -\frac{v}{u} = \frac{f}{f-u} = \frac{f-v}{f}$$

- Refraction of light is the phenomenon of bending of a ray of light while passing from one transparent medium to another.
- According to the laws of refraction,
  - The incident ray, the refracted ray and the normal to the refracting surface at the point of incidence all lie in the same plane.
  - The ratio of the sine of the angle of incidence to the sine of the angle of refraction is constant for the two given medium, i.e. $(\sin i / \sin r) = (\mu_2 / \mu_1) = {}^1\mu_2$, where $({}^1\mu_2)$ is refractive index of second medium with respect to first.
- The refractive index of a medium w.r.t. vacuum in terms of speed of light is

$$\mu = \frac{c}{v}$$

- When an object in a denser medium is viewed from a rarer medium, then refractive index of danser medium is

$${}^1\mu_2 = \frac{\text{Real depth } (h)}{\text{Apparent depth } (h')}$$

Shift, $y = \left(1 - \frac{1}{{}^1\mu_2}\right)h$

- **Total internal reflection** When a ray of light goes from a denser to a rarer medium, it bends away from the normal. For a certain angle of incidence i_C, the angle of refraction in rarer medium becomes 90°, the angle i_C called critical angle.

$$\sin i_c = \frac{n_1}{n_2}$$

For angle of incidence in denser medium even greater than the critical angle $(i > i_C)$, the light ray is totally internally reflected back into the denser medium itself.

- A refracting surface which forms a part of a sphere of transparent refracting material is called a spherical refracting surface

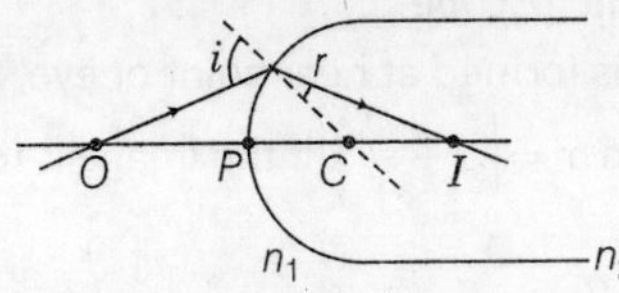

$$\frac{n_2}{v} - \frac{n_1}{u} = \frac{n_2 - n_1}{R}$$

- The lens formula is given by, $\frac{1}{v} - \frac{1}{u} = \frac{1}{f}$

The linear magnification m is given by,

$$m = \frac{h'}{h} = \frac{v}{u} = \frac{f}{f+u} = \frac{f-v}{f}$$

- **Lens maker's formula** According to this formula, the magnifying power can be given as,

$$P = \frac{1}{f} = ({}_1n_2 - 1)\left(\frac{1}{R_1} - \frac{1}{R_2}\right)$$

- The equivalent focal length of co-axial combination of two lenses is

$$\frac{1}{F} = \frac{1}{f_1} + \frac{1}{f_2} - \frac{d}{f_1 f_2}$$

where, d = distance between two lenses.
If a number of lenses are in contact, then

$$\frac{1}{F} = \frac{1}{f_1} + \frac{1}{f_2} + \ldots$$

and power of combination of lenses is

$$P = P_1 + P_2 + \ldots$$

- Angle of minimum deviation through a prism,

$$\delta_m = i + e - A$$

where, i is the angle of incidence, e the angle of emergence and A the angle of prism.

- Refractive index of a prism material, $n = \frac{\sin\left(\frac{A + \delta_m}{2}\right)}{\sin\left(\frac{A}{2}\right)}$
- Angular dispersion in a prism is given by

$$\delta = \delta_v - \delta_r = (n_v - n_r)A$$

- Dispersive power, $\omega = \frac{n_v - n_r}{n - 1}$, where $n = \frac{n_v + n_r}{2}$
- When two prisms with angles A and A' and refractive indices n and n' are combined, then

(i) Dispersion without deviation, $A' = -\frac{(n-1)}{(n'-1)}A$

(ii) Deviation without dispersion, $A' = -\left[\frac{n_v - n_r}{n'_v - n'_r}\right]A$

- Scattering of light is the phenomenon of absorption of light by molecules of medium and their emission in all directions.

For rayleigh scattering, intensity $\propto \frac{1}{\lambda^4}$

- In the **simple microscope,**
  - If the image is formed at near point of eye, then magnification $m = \left(1 + \frac{D}{f}\right)$. If the image is formed at infinity, then $m = \frac{D}{f}$.
- In the **compound microscope,**
  - If final image is formed at the near point (D) of eye, then, $m = -\frac{v_o}{u_o}\left(1 + \frac{D}{f_e}\right)$
  - If final image is formed at infinity, then $m = \frac{-v_o}{u_o} \cdot \frac{D}{f_e}$
- In the **astronomical telescope,**
  - If final image is formed at infinity, $m = \frac{-f_o}{f_e}$
  - If the final image is formed at near point of the observer's eye, then $m = -\frac{f_o}{f_e}\left(1 + \frac{f_e}{D}\right)$
- **Resolving power of a microscope** The least distance (d) between two points, whose images are just seen distinctly by a microscope is given by, $d = \frac{1.22\lambda}{2 n_m \sin\theta}$

  where, n_m is refractive index of the medium between the object and objective lens.
- The resolving power of microscope, $R_P = \frac{1}{d} = \frac{n_m \sin\theta}{0.61\lambda}$

  The terms $n_m \sin\theta$ is called the numerical aperture of the microscope.
- Resolving power of telescope, $R_P = \frac{1}{d\theta} = \frac{D}{1.22\lambda}$

24. Wave Optics

- **Huygen's principle** Every point on a given wavefront acts as secondary source of light and emits secondary wavelets which travel in all directions with the speed of light in the medium. A surface touching all these secondary wavelets tangentially, in the forward direction, gives the new wavefront at that instant of time.
- **Interference of light** It is the phenomenon of redistribution of light energy in space when two light waves of same frequency (or same wavelength) emitted by two coherent sources, travelling in a given direction, superimpose on each other.
- If a_1 and a_2 be the amplitudes of two light waves of same frequency and ϕ be the phase difference between them, then the amplitude of resultant wave is given by,

$$A_R = \sqrt{a_1^2 + a_2^2 + 2a_1 a_2 \cos\phi}$$

and in terms of intensity of light

$$I_R = I_1 + I_2 + 2\sqrt{I_1 \cdot I_2} \cdot \cos\phi$$

- The ratio of maximum and minimum intensities,

$$\frac{I_{max}}{I_{min}} = \frac{I_1 + I_2 + 2\sqrt{I_1 I_2}}{I_1 + I_2 - 2\sqrt{I_1 I_2}} = \left[\frac{\sqrt{I_1} + \sqrt{I_2}}{\sqrt{I_1} - \sqrt{I_2}}\right]^2 = \left[\frac{a_1 + a_2}{a_1 - a_2}\right]^2$$

- **Young's double slit experiment** The arrangement is shown in figure given below. In this monochromatic light of one wavelength is used.

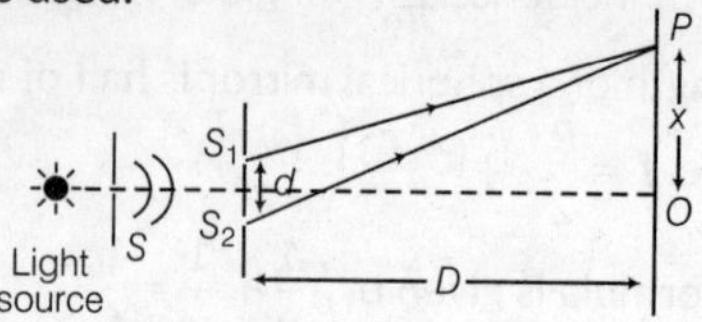

For light waves reaching a point P, situated at a distance x from central point O, the path difference

$$\Delta x = S_2P - S_1P = \frac{xd}{D}$$

- If $\frac{xd}{D} = n\lambda$, then we get **nth bright fringe.** Here, position of bright fringes on the screen are given by x.
- If $\frac{xd}{D} = (2n-1)\frac{\lambda}{2}$, then we get **nth dark fringe.**

Hence, for nth dark fringe, $x = \frac{(2n-1)D\lambda}{2d}$

- **Fringe width** β The separation between any two consecutive bright and dark fringes is called **fringe width** β and is given by, $\beta = \frac{D\lambda}{d}$.
- When a thin transparent plate of thickness t and refractive index μ is introduced in the path of one of interfering wave, then the path difference becomes $= \frac{xd}{D} - t(\mu - 1)$

  Extra path $= (\mu - 1)t$
- Fraunhofer's arrangement for studying diffraction at a single slit is shown below.

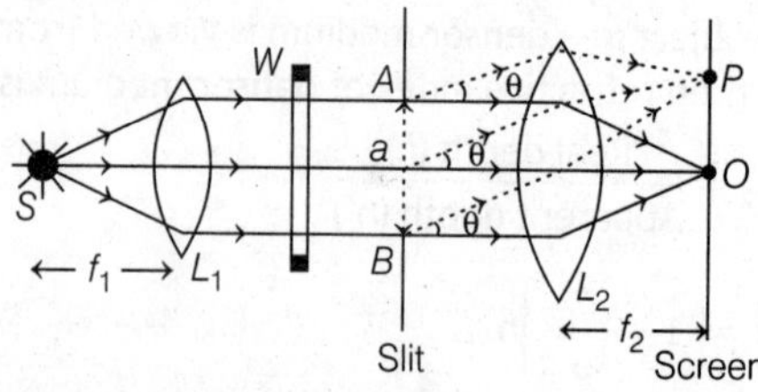

- For diffraction minima, $a\sin\theta = n\lambda$

  and for secondary maxima, $a\sin\theta = (2n+1)\frac{\lambda}{2}$
- The angular position of nth secondary minima is $\theta = \frac{n\lambda}{a}$

  and for nth maxima, it is $\theta = \frac{(2n+1)\lambda}{2a}$.
- The angular width of central maxima $= 2\theta = \frac{2\lambda}{a}$

- According to Malus' law, the intensity of emergent light out of analyser varies as, $I \propto \cos^2\theta$ or $I = I_0 \cos^2\theta$,

where, θ is the angle between the planes of transmission axis of polariser and analyser.
According to **Brewster's law**, $\tan i_p = n$
Moreover, in such an event, the reflected and transmitted rays are mutually perpendicular. Thus, angle of refraction $r = (90° - i_p)$.

25. Dual Nature of Radiation and Matter

- The minimum energy of incident radiation needed to eject the electrons from metal surface is known as **work function** (ϕ_0) of that surface. Work function is related to threshold frequency as, $\phi_0 = h\nu_0 = \dfrac{hc}{\lambda_0}$

where, λ_0 = threshold wavelength.

In electron volt units, $\phi(\text{eV}) = \dfrac{hc}{e\lambda_0} = \dfrac{12400}{\lambda(\text{Å})}$

- According to Einstein's photoelectric equation,
$h\nu = \phi_0 + K_{max}$
where, $K_{max} = \dfrac{1}{2}mv^2_{max}$ = maximum kinetic energy of ejected photoelectron and ν is the frequency of incident light photon.
As, $\phi_0 = h\nu_0$, hence Einstein's equation may be written as,
$h(\nu - \nu_0) = K_{max} = \dfrac{1}{2}mv^2{}_{max}$

- If in a photoelectric tube we apply a negative potential, then for a certain minimum negative potential, the photoelectric current becomes zero. This negative potential is known as **stopping potential** (V_0). It is thus a measure of maximum kinetic energy of photoelectrons.

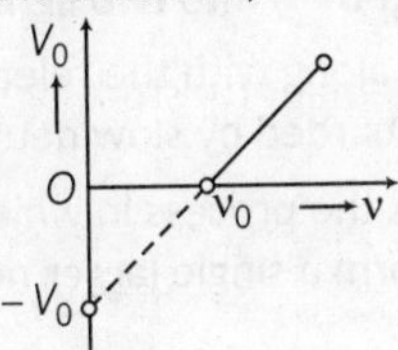

i.e. $eV_0 = K_{max} = \dfrac{1}{2}mv^2{}_{max}$

$eV_0 = h(\nu - \nu_0) = h\nu - \phi_0$ (Einstein's photoelectric equation)

$\Rightarrow \quad V_0 = \dfrac{h}{e}\nu - \dfrac{\phi_0}{e}$

- The kinetic mass of photon, $m = \dfrac{h}{c\lambda}$

and the momentum of photon, $p = \dfrac{h}{\lambda}$

- The de-Broglie wavelength of a particle of mass m and moving with velocity v is given by, $\lambda = \dfrac{h}{mv}$

- The de-Broglie wavelength of a particle of mass m and kinetic energy K is given by, $\lambda = \dfrac{h}{\sqrt{2mK}}$

- The de-Broglie wavelength associated with a charged particle is given by, $\lambda = \dfrac{h}{\sqrt{2mqV}}$

- The de-Broglie wavelength of a gas molecule at temperature T is given by, $\lambda = \dfrac{h}{\sqrt{3mkT}}$

where, k = Boltzmann constant = 1.38×10^{-23} J/K

26. Atoms and Nuclei

- In α-particle scattering experiment, the number of α-particles scattered through angle θ is given by

$$N(\theta) \propto \frac{Z^2}{\sin^4\left(\frac{\theta}{2}\right)(\text{KE})^2}$$

- The distance of closest approach for a nucleus is

$$r_0 = \frac{4(\text{KE})Ze^2}{mv^2}$$

- The diameter of the nucleus is of the order of 10^{-14} m.

- The electrons revolve around the nucleus only in certain permitted orbits, in which the angular momentum of the electrons is an integral multiple of $h/2\pi$, where h is the Planck's constant.

- If energy of the electron in nth and mth orbits be E_n and E_m respectively, and the electron jumps from nth to mth orbit, the radiation frequency ν is emitted, such that,

$$E_n - E_m = h\nu$$

The orbital radius of the electron is,

$$r_n = 4\pi\varepsilon_0 \frac{n^2h^2}{4\pi^2 Zme^2} = 0.53\frac{n^2}{Z}\ \text{Å}$$

- The orbital velocity of electron is, $v_n = \dfrac{1}{4\pi\varepsilon_0} \cdot \dfrac{2Z\pi e^2}{nh}$

- Orbital frequency is given by,

$$f = \frac{1}{T} = \frac{v}{2\pi r} = \frac{mZ^2e^4}{4\varepsilon_0^2 n^3h^3}$$

- The total energy of the orbital electron is

$$E = -\left(\frac{1}{4\pi\varepsilon_0}\right)^2 \left[\frac{2\pi^2 mZ^2e^4}{h^2}\right]\left[\frac{1}{n^2}\right] = 13.6\frac{Z^2}{n^2}\ \text{eV}$$

$$\text{KE} = \frac{me^4Z^2}{8n^2h^2\varepsilon_0^2} \text{ and } \text{PE} = \frac{-me^4Z^2}{4n^2h^2\varepsilon_0^2}$$

- **Hydrogen spectrum** Hydrogen spectrum consists of spectral lines classified to five spectral series of hydrogen atom.

- **Lyman series** Spectral lines of Lyman series correspond to transition of electron from higher energy levels (orbits) $n_i = 2, 3, 4, \ldots$ to ground energy level (1st orbit) $n_f = 1$.

For Lyman series

$$\frac{1}{\lambda} = \bar{\nu} = R\left[\frac{1}{(1)^2} - \frac{1}{n^2}\right]$$

where, $n = 2, 3, 4, \ldots$

- **Balmer series** Electronic transition from $n_i = 3, 4, 5, \ldots$ to $n_f = 2$ give rise to spectral lines of Balmer series. Thus, for a Balmer series

$$\frac{1}{\lambda} = \bar{\nu} = R\left[\frac{1}{(2)^2} - \frac{1}{n^2}\right],$$

where, $n = 3, 4, 5, \ldots$

- **Paschen series** Lines of this series lie in infrared region and correspond to electronic transition from $n_i = 4, 5, 6, \ldots$ to $n_f = 3$.

Thus, $$\frac{1}{\lambda} = \bar{\nu} = R\left[\frac{1}{(3)^2} - \frac{1}{n^2}\right],$$

where, $n = 4, 5, 6, \ldots$

- **Brackett series** It too lies in infrared region and corresponds to transition from $n_i = 5, 6, 7, \ldots$ to $n_f = 4$.

Thus, for Brackett series, $\frac{1}{\lambda} = \bar{\nu} = R\left[\frac{1}{(4)^2} - \frac{1}{n^2}\right],$

where, $n = 5, 6, 7, \ldots$

- **Pfund series** It lies in far infrared region of spectrum and corresponds to electronic transition from higher orbits to orbit having $n_i = 6, 7, 8, \ldots$ to $n_f = 5$. Thus, we have

$$\frac{1}{\lambda} = \bar{\nu} = R\left[\frac{1}{(5)^2} - \frac{1}{n^2}\right],$$

where, $n = 6, 7, 8, \ldots$

- Ionisation energy of an atom is defined as the energy required to ionise it, i.e. to make the electron jump from its present orbit to infinite orbit.

Thus, ionisation energy of hydrogen atom in the ground state $= E_\infty - E_1 = 0 - (-13.6\text{ eV}) = +13.6\text{ eV}$

- For a neutral atom, number of protons = number of electrons = atomic number (Z)
- Mass number (A) = number of protons + number of neutrons
- The size of the nucleus is of the order of fermi (10^{-15}m).
- The radius of nucleus is given by, $R = R_0 (A)^{1/3}$.
- **Isotopes** of an element are nuclides having same atomic number Z but different mass number A (or different neutron number N).

$_1H^1$, $_1H^2$, $_1H^3$ and $_6C^{11}$, $_6C^{12}$, $_6C^{14}$ etc are isotopes.

- Nuclides having same mass number A but different atomic number Z are called **isobars**. Isobars represent different chemical properties.

$_1H^3$, $_2He^3$ and $_6C^{14}$, $_7C^{14}$ are isobars.

- Nuclides with different atomic number Z and different mass number A, but same neutron number are called isotones.

^3_1H, ^4_2He are examples of **isotones**.

- The difference in mass of a nucleus and its constituent nucleons is called the **mass defect** of that nucleus. Thus, mass defect, $\Delta M = ZM_p + (A - Z) M_n - M$

where, M is the mass of given nucleus.

- The energy equivalent of the mass defect of a nucleus is called its binding energy.

Thus, binding energy,

$$\Delta E_b = \Delta Mc^2 = [ZM_p + (A - Z) M_n - M] c^2$$

- The rate of a radioactive material at any instant is proportional to the quantity of that material actually present at that time.

i.e. $-\frac{dN}{dt} \propto \lambda$ or $\frac{dN}{dt} = -\lambda N$

and $N = N_0 e^{-\lambda t}$

- Half-life period of a radioactive sample is the time in which half of the quantity of the sample initially present gets disintegrated. The half-life period is related to decay constant λ as, $T_{1/2} = \frac{0.693}{\lambda}$
- After n half-lives the quantity of a radioactive substance left intact (undecayed) is given by,

$$N = N_0 \cdot \left(\frac{1}{2}\right)^n = N_0 \left(\frac{1}{2}\right)^{\frac{t}{T_{1/2}}}$$

- The half-life and mean life of a radioactive sample are related as, $T_{1/2} = 0.693\,\tau$ or $\tau = 1.44\,T_{1/2}$
- The activity of a radioactive substance is the rate of disintegration and is given by

$$R = -\frac{dN}{dt} = R_0 e^{-\lambda t}$$

- **Nuclear fission** It is the process of splitting of a heavy nucleus ($_{92}U^{235}$ or $_{94}Pu^{239}$) into two lighter nuclei of comparable masses along with the release of a large amount of energy after bombarded by slow neutrons.
- **Nuclear fusion** It is the process in which two or more light nuclei combine to form a single larger nucleus.

27. Semiconductors and Electronic Devices

- A pure semiconductor in which no impurity of any sort has been mixed is called **intrinsic semiconductor**. Germanium ($E_g = 0.72$ eV) and silicon ($E_g = 1.1$eV) are intrinsic semiconductors.
- At 0 K, these behave as 100% insulators. But at any other temperature, they have thermally generated charge carriers and thus behave as semiconductor.
- In an intrinsic semiconductor, the number of free electrons in conduction band n_e is exactly equal to the number of holes n_h in valence band. Thus, $n_e = n_h = n_i$, where n_i is called the number density of intrinsic carriers.

- μ_e and μ_h are their respective mobilities (i.e. mobility of electrons and holes). Electrical conductivity of pure semiconductor is very small.
- To prepare a ***n*-type semiconductor**, a pentavalent impurity, e.g. P, As, Sb is used as a dopant with Si or Ge. Such an impurity is called donor impurity because each dopant atom provides one free electron.
  In *n*-type semiconductor $n_e >> n_h$, i.e. electrons are majority charge carriers and the holes are minority charge carriers such that $n_e \cdot n_h = n_i^2$.
- **A *p-n* junction diode** is obtained by joining a small *p*-type crystal with a small *n*-type crystal.
  Due to diffusion of electrons and holes across function a potential barriers is created.
- The conductivity of a semiconductor is given by

$$\sigma = \frac{y}{E} = e(n_e \mu_e + n_h \mu_n)$$

- A *p-n* junction diode acts as a voltage controlled switch. In forward biasing, it acts like ON switch and in reverse biasing, its acts like OFF switch.
- In half wave rectifier, only one diode is used.
- The ripple factor $= \dfrac{\text{Effective AC component of voltage}}{\text{Effective DC component of voltage}}$
- In full wave rectifier, two *p-n* junction diodes have been joined in complimentary modes. In this rectifier, we obtain a continuous unidirectional current through the load resistor, R_L.
- Ripple factor in full wave rectifier,

$$\frac{V_{AC}}{V_{DC}} = 0.48 = 48\%$$

- **Zener diode** is a highly doped *p-n* junction diode which is not damaged by high reverse current. It is always used in reverse bias in breakdown voltage region and is chiefly used as a voltage regulator.

- **Light emitting diode (LED)** is a specially designed diode made from GaAsP, GaP, etc. When is forward biased, it emits light in visible region of spectrum.
- **Photodiode** is used in reverse bias, which conducts only when a light of suitable wavelength falls on the junction.
- **Solar cell** is a diode which directly converts solar energy into electrical energy.
- **A transistor** is a combination of two *p-n* junctions joined in series. A junction transistor is known as **bipolar junction** transistor (BJT). Transistors are of two types, i.e. *n-p-n* transistor and *p-n-p* transistor.
- A transistor has three regions, i.e. emitter, base and collector. All are described here
  - An **emitter** (E) which is most heavily doped and is of moderate size. It supplies large number of charge carriers, which are free electrons in a *n-p-n* transistor and holes in a *p-n-p* transistor.
  - A **base** (B) which is very lightly doped and is very thin (thickness $\simeq 10^{-5}$ m).
  - A **collector** (C) which is moderately doped and is thickest. A transistor is symbolically represented as shown in figures.

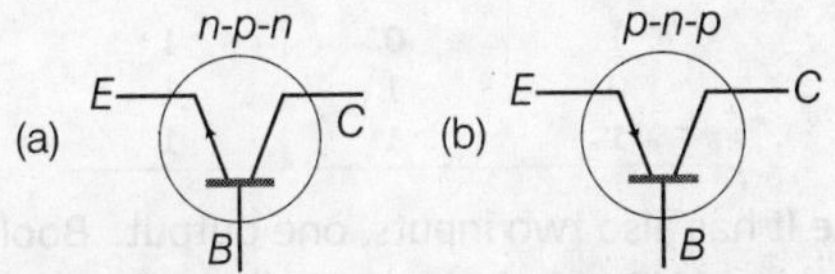

- In a *n-p-n* transistor, electrons flow from emitter towards the base and constitute a current I_E. Due to larger reverse bias at base-collector junction, most of these electrons further pass into the collector, constituting a collector current I_C. But a small percentage of electrons (less than 5%) may combine with holes present in base. These electrons constitute a base current I_B. It is self evident that, $I_E = I_C + I_B$
- A transistor can be connected in either of the following three configurations :
  - Common Emitter (CE) configuration
  - Common Base (CB) configuration
  - Collector (CC) configuration
- Characteristics of a transistor in CE configuration are given below.
- Input resistance, $r_i = \left(\dfrac{\Delta V_{BE}}{\Delta I_B}\right)_{V_B = \text{constant}}$
- Output resistance, $r_o = \left(\dfrac{\Delta V_{CE}}{\Delta I_C}\right)_{I_B = \text{constant}}$
- AC current gain, $\beta = \left(\dfrac{\Delta I_C}{\Delta I_B}\right)_{V_{CE} = \text{constant}}$
- Voltage gain of amplifier, $A_V = \dfrac{V_o}{V_i} = \beta \dfrac{R_C}{R_B}$
- In CB configuration, AC current gain, $\alpha = \left(\dfrac{\Delta I_C}{\Delta I_E}\right)_{V_{CE} = \text{constant}}$
- Power gain $= \beta_{AC}^2 \times$ resistance gain
- Currents gains α and β are correlated as,

$$\beta = \frac{\alpha}{1-\alpha}$$

or

$$\alpha = \frac{\beta}{1+\beta}$$

- A logic gate is a digital electronic circuit which follows a logical relationship between its input and output. A logic gate may have one or more inputs but has only one output.
- Logic gates follow Boolean algebra, which consists of three basic operations, namely AND ($A \cdot B = Y$) OR ($A + B = Y$) and NOT ($\overline{A} = Y$).
- **OR gate** It has two inputs, one output. Logic symbol of OR gate is shown in figure. Its Boolean expression is $Y = A + B$ (being read as Y equals A or B).

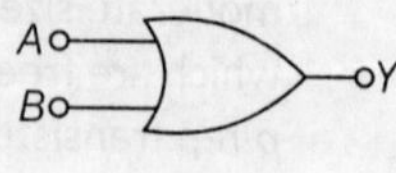

The truth table of OR gate is

A	B	Y
0	0	0
1	0	1
0	1	1
1	1	1

- **AND gate** It has also two inputs, one output. Boolean expression of AND gate is $Y = A \cdot B$ (being read as, Y equals A and B).

The truth table of AND gate is

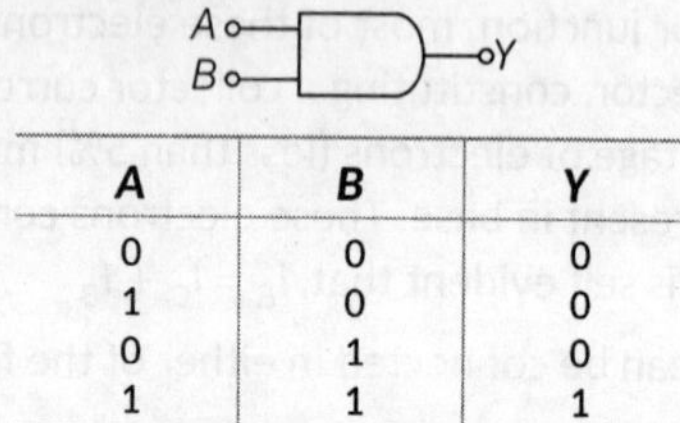

A	B	Y
0	0	0
1	0	0
0	1	0
1	1	1

- **NOT gate** It has one input and one output. Boolean expression of NOT gate $\overline{A} = Y$ (being read as A negated equals Y).

The truth table of NOT gate is

A	Y
0	1
1	0

- **NAND gate** If the output of AND gate is joined to input of a NOT gate, the combination is a NAND gate.

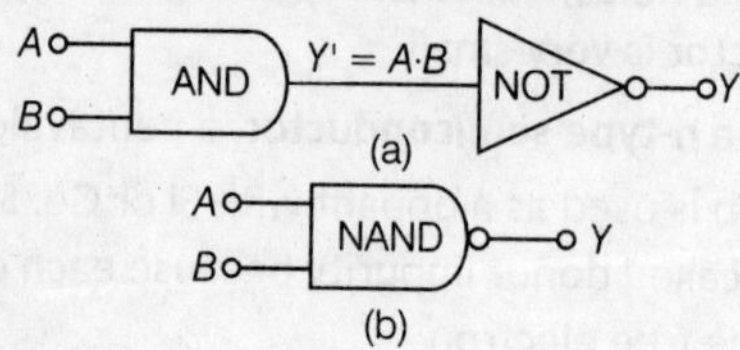

(a)

(b)

- Boolean expression of NAND gate is $\overline{A \cdot B} = Y$. Its logic symbol is shown in the following figure.

The truth table of NAND gate is

A	B	Y
0	0	1
1	0	1
0	1	1
1	1	0

- **NOR gate** If the output of OR gate is joined to input of a NOT gate, the combination is a NOR gate. Boolean expression of NOR gate is $\overline{A + B} = Y$. Its logic symbol is shown in the following figure.

(a)

(b)

The truth table of NOR gate is

A	B	Y
0	0	1
1	0	0
0	1	0
1	1	0

The Qualifiers

One Test for each Unit of NEET Physics

To ensure good score in NEET, You must be sure of the good understanding of each unit of NEET Syllabus. You must complete these tests with atleast 75% score, then only move to the next section.

QUALIFIER 01

Physical World & Measurement

1. Dimensional formula of luminous flux is

(a) $[MLT^{-2}]$ (b) $[ML^2T^{-1}]$

(c) $[ML^2T^{-3}]$ (d) $[ML^2T^{-2}]$

2. Which of the following relation of physical quantities has same unit as ohm?

(a) $\frac{h}{e}$ (b) $\frac{h^2}{e}$ (c) $\frac{h}{e^2}$ (d) $\frac{h^2}{e^2}$

(where, h is Planck's constant and e is electronic charge)

3. The dimensional formula of α in $e^{\alpha x}$ is (where, x is distance)

(a) $[M^0L^0T^0]$ (b) $[M^0LT^0]$

(c) $[M^0L^{-1}T^0]$ (d) $[M^{-1}L^0T^{-1}]$

4. An enclosed ideal gas has its pressure as a function of its volume V as $p = p_0 - \alpha V^2$, where p_0 is initial pressure and α is constant. The physical dimensions of α are

(a) $[M^{-1}L^7T^2]$ (b) $[L^{-6}]$

(c) $[ML^{-1}T^{-2}]$ (d) $[ML^{-7}T^{-2}]$

5. If area (A), velocity (v) and density (ρ) are taken as fundamental units, then correct dimensional formula of force is represented by

(a) $A^2v\rho$ (b) $Av\rho^2$

(c) $Av^2\rho$ (d) $\frac{Av}{\rho}$

6. Force F and density ρ are related as $F = \frac{\alpha}{\beta + \sqrt{\rho}}$, then dimensional formula of α and β, respectively is

(a) $[M^{\frac{1}{2}}L^{\frac{1}{2}}T^{-2}]$ & $[M^{\frac{1}{2}}L^{\frac{3}{2}}]$

(b) $[M^{\frac{3}{2}}L^{-\frac{1}{2}}T^{-2}]$ & $[M^{\frac{1}{2}}L^{-\frac{3}{2}}]$

(c) $[M^{\frac{3}{2}}L^{-\frac{1}{2}}T^{-1}]$ & $[M^{\frac{1}{2}}L^{-\frac{3}{2}}]$

(d) Cannot be calculated

7. Assertion (A) In vander Waals' equation of state, $\left(p + \frac{a}{V^2}\right)(V - b) =$ a constant; Unit of ab is N-m^7.

Reason (R) We can add, subtract, multiply or divide physical quantities having same dimensions.

Choose most appropriate answer from options given below

(a) Both A and R are true but R is not the correct explanation of A.

(b) A is true but R is false.

(c) A is false but R is true.

(d) Both A and R are true and R is the correct explanation of A.

8. If K represents kinetic energy, v is velocity and T is time are taken as the fundamental quantities, then dimensional formula of surface tension in terms of K, v and T is

(a) $[Kv^{-2}T^{-1}]$ (b) $[Kv^2T^{-1}]$

(c) $[Kv^{-2}T^{-2}]$ (d) $[Kv^2T^2]$

9. If P and Q are two physical quantities having different dimensional formulae, then which of the following can represent a new physical quantity?

(a) $P + Q$ (b) $e^{P/Q}$

(c) $\frac{P}{Q}$ (d) $\sin\left(\frac{P}{Q}\right)$

10. A massive star of mass m is in a uniform circular orbit around a supermassive black hole of mass M_b. Initially, the radius and angular frequency of the orbit are R and ω, respectively. According to the Einstein's theory of general relativity, the space around the two objects is distorted and gravitational waves are radiated. The power radiated through gravitational wave by this star is given by $P = kc^xG^yM^2R^4\omega^6$, where c = speed of light.

Using dimensional analysis, the sum of values of x and y are

(a) 6 (b) – 4

(c) – 7 (d) – 6

11. A quantity X is given by $\varepsilon_0 L \frac{\Delta V}{\Delta t}$, where ε_0 is the permittivity of free space, L is length, ΔV is the potential difference and Δt is the time interval, then dimensional formula of X is the same as that of

(a) resistance (b) charge

(c) voltage (d) current

12. The pair of physical quantities that have different dimensional formulae is

(a) Reynolds' number and coefficient of friction

(b) latent heat and gravitational potential

(c) activity and frequency of sound wave

(d) Planck's constant and torque

13. Let speed of light (c), gravitational constant (G) and Planck's constant (h) are taken as fundamental quantities in a system of units.

Now, match physical quantities in Column I with its dimensions in Column II.

	Column I		Column II
A.	Density	P.	$[c^{\frac{1}{2}} G^{-\frac{1}{2}} h^{\frac{1}{2}}]$
B.	Mass	Q.	$[c^{-\frac{5}{2}} G^{\frac{1}{2}} h^{\frac{1}{2}}]$
C.	Time	R.	$[c^{-\frac{3}{2}} G^{\frac{1}{2}} h^{\frac{1}{2}}]$
D.	Length	S.	$[c^5 G^{-2} h^{-1}]$

Choose the correct answer from options given below
(a) A→P, B→Q, C→R, D→S
(b) A→S, B→R, C→Q, D→P
(c) A→S, B→P, C→Q, D→R
(d) A→S, B→Q, C→P, D→R

14. Match combination of physical quantities in Column I with their dimensions in Column II.

	Column I		Column II
A.	$\frac{1}{\sqrt{LC}}$	P.	$[MLT^{-2}]$
B.	$\eta A\left(\frac{\Delta v}{\Delta x}\right)$	Q.	$[M^0LT^{-1}]$
C.	$\frac{1}{\sqrt{\varepsilon_0 \mu_0}}$	R.	$[ML^2T^{-2}]$
D.	CV^2	S.	$[M^0L^0T^{-1}]$

Here, C = capacitance, V = potential difference
L = inductance, η = coefficient of viscosity
A = area, $\frac{\Delta v}{\Delta x}$ = velocity gradient,
ε_0 = permittivity and μ_0 = permeability.
Choose the correct answer from options given below
(a) A→S, B→P, C→Q, D→R
(b) A→S, B→R, C→Q, D→P
(c) A→S, B→R, C→P, D→Q
(d) A→P, B→Q, C→R, D→S

15. Which of the following statements regarding precision and accuracy is true?
(a) A most precise measurement will necessarily be most accurate.
(b) A most precise measurement may be most accurate.
(c) A most accurate measurement will necessarily be most precise.
(d) A most precise measurement will be less accurate.

16. If a physical quantity x depends on two other quantities a and b such that $x = \frac{a^m}{b^n}$, then relative error in the measurement of x is given as $\frac{\Delta x}{x} = m\left(\pm \frac{\Delta a}{a}\right) + n\left(\pm \frac{\Delta b}{b}\right)$.
The expression is true, when
(a) m and n both are positive
(b) both Δa and Δb are very small compared to their respective quantities
(c) Δa and Δb both have positive value
(d) There is no condition at given expression

17. In an experiment, four quantities a, b, c and d are measured with percentage errors of 2%, 3%, 1% and 0.5%, respectively.
A quantity x is defined as $x = \frac{a\sqrt{b}}{c^{3/2}d^4}$. The maximum percentage error in the measurement of x will be
(a) 5%
(b) 6%
(c) 7%
(d) 9%

18. A student performs an experiment in lab in order to measure a physical quantity and takes 100 observations. He repeats the same experiment and takes 400 observations. By doing so, the possible error
(a) remains same
(b) is doubled
(c) is halved
(d) is reduced to one-fourth

19. A physical quantity X can be calculated by using experiment. It is dependent of three other physical quantities A, B and C such that the percentage error occurred in the measurement of these quantities are 1%, 1.5% and 3%, respectively. If the maximum percentage error in the measurement of X is 6%, then which of the following expression can be true for X?
(a) $\frac{A^2B}{\sqrt{C}}$
(b) $\frac{A^2\sqrt{B}}{C^3}$
(c) $\frac{A\sqrt{A}}{BC}$
(d) $\frac{AB^2}{C}$

20. The number of significant digits in 20.000 and 6.23×10^1 are, respectively
(a) 2, 3
(b) 5, 3
(c) 2, 4
(d) 1, 3

21. Study the following statements.
Statement I The length of a state highway when expressed in km is 65.2 km, where it has 3 significant figures.
Statement II The same length when expressed in metres as 65200 m, has five significant figures.
In light of above statements, choose the most appropriate answer from the options given below :
(a) Both Statement I and Statement II are incorrect.
(b) Statement I is correct and Statement II is incorrect.
(c) Statement I is incorrect and Statement II is correct.
(d) Both Statement I and Statement II are correct.

22. The initial and final temperatures of water as recorded by a student are (30.4 ± 0.2)°C and (51.5 ± 0.4)°C. The rise in temperature is
(a) (21.1 ± 0.2)°C
(b) (21.1 ± 0.6)°C
(c) (19.9 ± 0.6)°C
(d) (19.9 ± 0.8)°C

23. A student measures two quantities as $A = (1.0 \pm 0.2)$ m and $B = (2.0 \pm 0.2)$m. The correct value of $(AB)^{1/2}$ is

(a) (1.4 ± 0.4) m
(b) (1.41 ± 0.15)m
(c) (1.4 ± 0.3) m
(d) (1.4 ± 0.2)m

24. In the following figure, vernier and main scale of vernier calliper has been shown. If each main scale division is of 1 mm and 4th division of vernier scale coincides with a main scale division, then the zero correction is

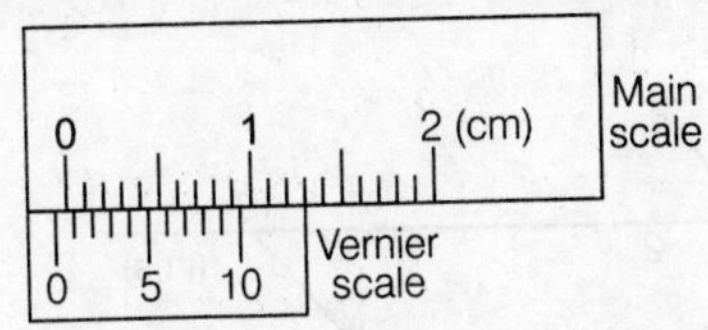

(a) 0.6 mm (b) – 0.6 mm (c) + 0.4 mm (d) – 0.4 mm

25. While measuring the thickness of a thin sheet, by using a micrometer, screw gauge and the readings of scale has been shown. So, the thickness of the sheet will be

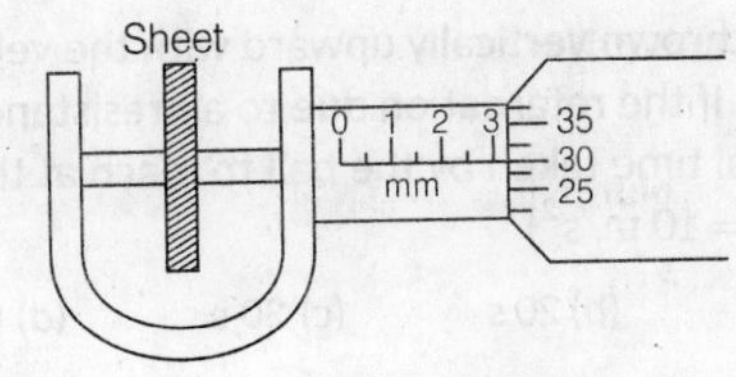

(a) 3.29 mm
(b) 3.30 mm
(c) 3.36 mm
(d) 3.41 mm

Answers

1 (c)	2 (c)	3 (c)	4 (d)	5 (c)
6 (b)	7 (b)	8 (c)	9 (c)	10 (b)
11 (d)	12 (d)	13 (c)	14 (a)	15 (b)
16 (b)	17 (c)	18 (d)	19 (c)	20 (b)
21 (b)	22 (b)	23 (d)	24 (a)	25 (b)

See detailed explanations on page no. 173

QUALIFIER **02**

Kinematics

1. A particle starts motion from point *O*. It follows the path $O \rightarrow A \rightarrow B \rightarrow C$ as shown in the figure. The displacement of the particle from point O to point C is

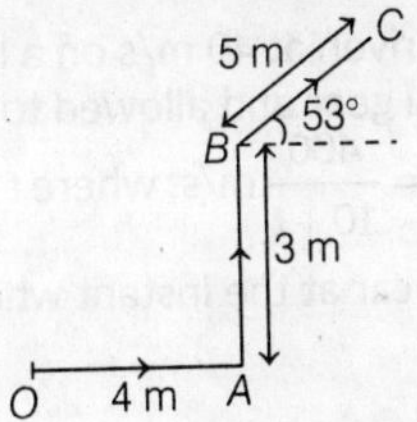

(a) 10 m
(b) 12 m
(c) $7\sqrt{2}$ m
(d) None of these

2. An aeroplane is flying in horizontal direction at some height from the ground. At certain instant of time when its velocity is 30 m/s and acceleration is 10 m/s^2, a packet is released from it. The velocity and acceleration of the packet at t = 3 s, are

(a) 30 m/s, $10\sqrt{2}$ m/s^2
(b) 40 m/s, $10\sqrt{2}$ m/s^2
(c) 50 m/s, $10\sqrt{2}$ m/s^2
(d) 50 m/s, 10 m/s^2

3. Assertion (A) Path of a projectile seen from another projectile is parabolic, if both are thrown at different angles of projection.

Reason (R) Relative acceleration of first projectile with respect to second projectile is zero.

Choose most appropriate answer from options given below

(a) Both A and R are true but R is not the correct explanation of A.
(b) A is true but R is false.
(c) A is false but R is true.
(d) Both A and R are true and R is the correct explanation of A.

4. A ball is thrown vertically upward with some velocity. During its motion, it passes through a point at t = 4 s and then again at t = 9 s, the height of this point from the ground is

(a) 190 m
(b) 180 m
(c) 90 m
(d) 80 m

5. A ball is thrown vertically upward with the velocity of 120 m/s. If the retardation due to air resistance is 2 m/s^2, then total time taken by the ball to reach at the ground is (Take, $g = 10$ m/s^2)

(a) 25 s (b) 20 s (c) 30 s (d) $(10+5\sqrt{6})$ s

6. Two persons named Peter and Nitro, are standing at distance of 10 m from each other. Nitro wants to catch Peter and for this, Nitro moves with constant velocity of 4.5 m/s and at the same instant, Peter starts to move with acceleration 1 m/s^2 from rest in same direction of motion of Nitro. At what instant, Nitro will catch Peter?

(a) 4 s (b) 5 s (c) 10.85 s (d) Never catch

7. A ball is released from a height of 10 m. After some time, it strikes to the ground and rebounds with a speed of 7 m/s. The graph between distance travelled by ball and time taken when it is about to strike the ground again is (Take, $g = 9.8$ m/s^2)

(a)
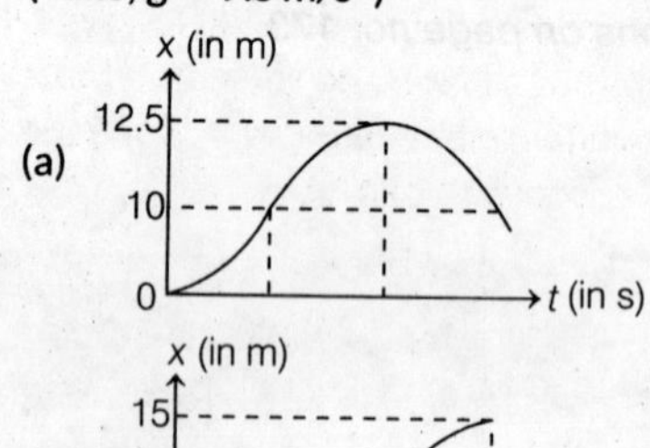

(b)
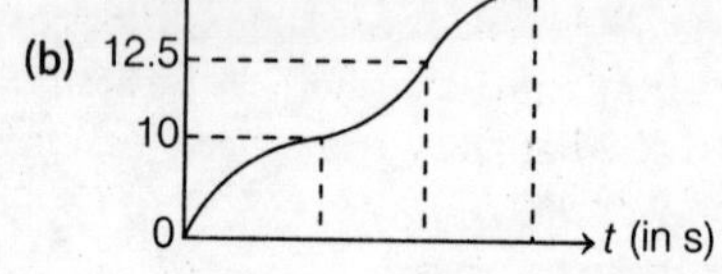

(c)
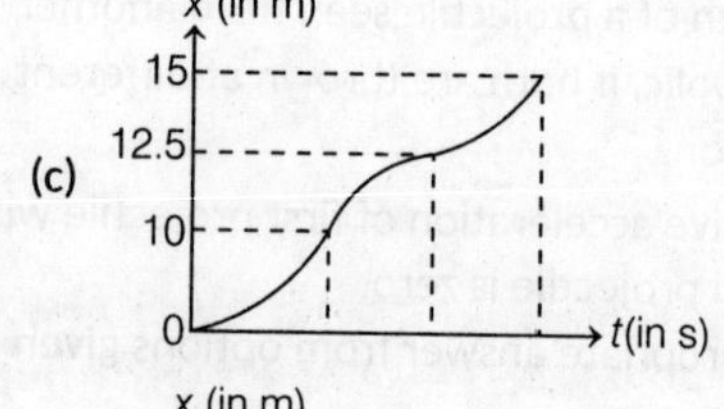

(d)
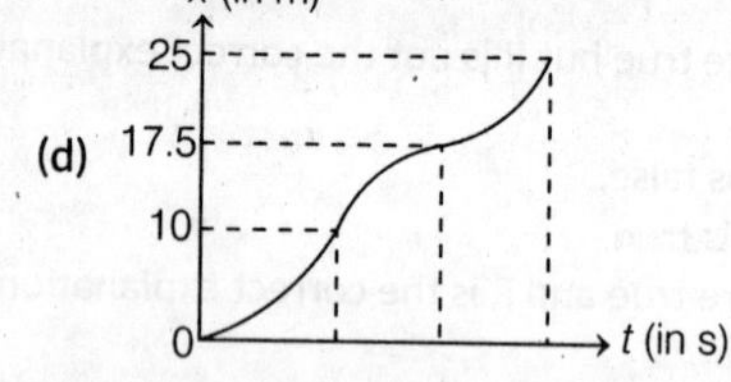

8. The velocity-time graph of a car moving on a straight road is shown below in the following figure. The correct representation of acceleration-time graph of motion of car is

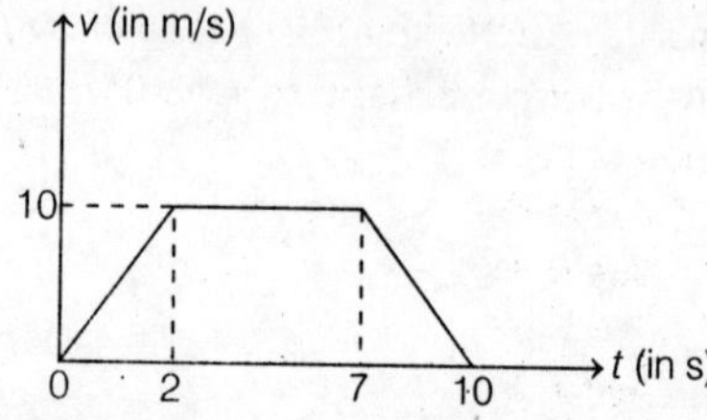

(a)
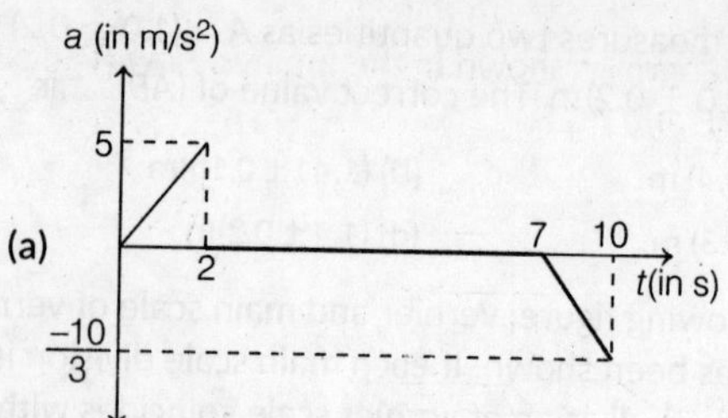

(b)
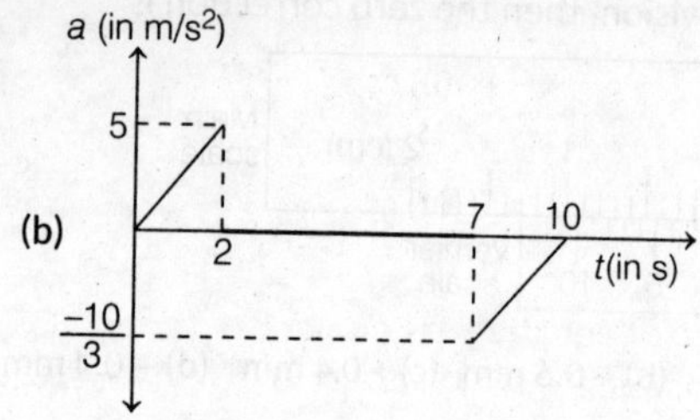

(c)
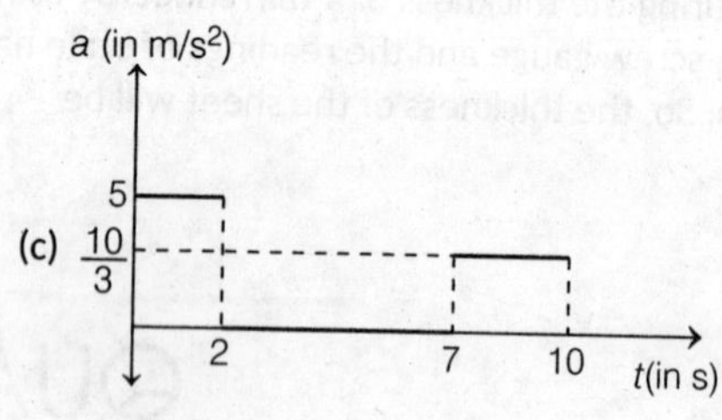

(d)
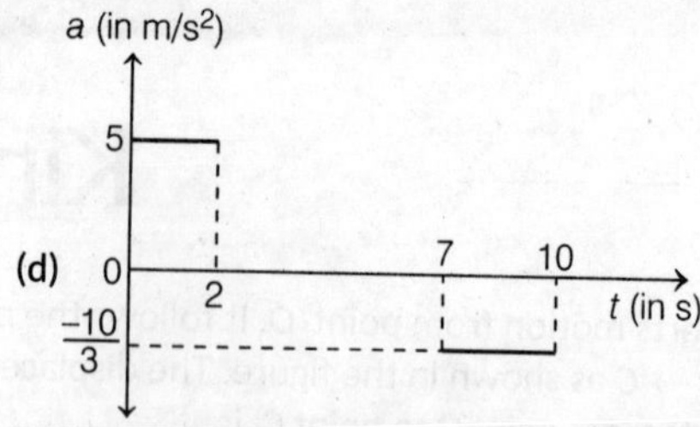

9. A car is being driven at 40 m/s on a level road is suddenly put into neutral gear and allowed to coast, the velocity decreases as $v = \dfrac{400}{10+t}$ m/s, where t is in second. The acceleration of car at the instant when its speed is 5 m/s, is

(a) $-\dfrac{1}{16}$ m/s^2

(b) $-\dfrac{1}{8}$ m/s^2

(c) $-\dfrac{1}{4}$ m/s^2

(d) $-\dfrac{1}{20}$ m/s^2

10. If $\mathbf{a} = 3\hat{\mathbf{i}} + 4\hat{\mathbf{j}}$ and $\mathbf{b} = 7\hat{\mathbf{i}} + 24\hat{\mathbf{j}}$, then vector having the same magnitude as $\mathbf{b}$ and direction opposite to $\mathbf{a}$ is $x\hat{\mathbf{i}} + y\hat{\mathbf{j}}$, then value of $\dfrac{x+y}{5}$ is

(a) 7 (b) 14
(c) −7 (d) −4

11. A cube of length l is shown in the figure below. The angle between AE and AG is

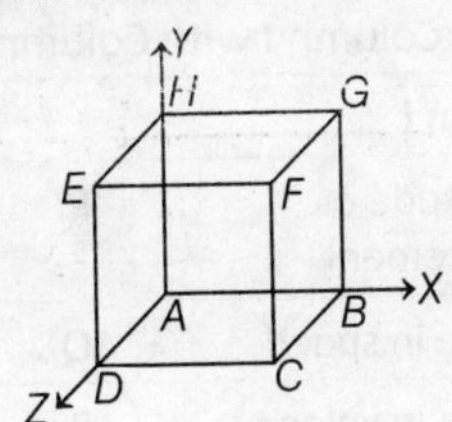

(a) 60° (b) $\cos^{-1}\left(\frac{1}{3}\right)$

(c) $\cos^{-1}\left(\frac{1}{\sqrt{3}}\right)$ (d) $\cos^{-1}\left(\sqrt{\frac{2}{3}}\right)$

12. Match the vector equation in Column II with vector diagram in Column I.

Column I		Column II
A. (triangle with sides c, b, a)	(i)	$\mathbf{a}-(\mathbf{b}+\mathbf{c})=0$
B. (vectors a, b, c)	(ii)	$\mathbf{b}-\mathbf{c}=\mathbf{a}$
C. (triangle with sides a, b, c)	(iii)	$\mathbf{a}+\mathbf{b}=-\mathbf{c}$
D. (vectors b, a, c)	(iv)	$\mathbf{a}+\mathbf{b}=\mathbf{c}$

Choose the correct answer from the options given below

	A	B	C	D		A	B	C	D
(a)	(i)	(iii)	(ii)	(iv)	(b)	(iii)	(iv)	(i)	(ii)
(c)	(iv)	(i)	(iii)	(ii)	(d)	(iii)	(ii)	(iv)	(i)

13. Statement I Vector addition of two vectors is always greater than their vector subtraction.

Statement II Magnitude of resultant of two vectors may be less than the magnitude of either vector.

In light of above statements, choose the most appropriate answer from the options given below :

(a) Both Statement I and Statement II are incorrect.
(b) Statement I is correct and Statement II is incorrect.
(c) Statement I is incorrect and Statement II is correct.
(d) Both Statement I and Statement II are correct.

14. Resultant of two vectors **a** and **b** (shown) is of magnitude $\sqrt{7}b$. The value of b/a is

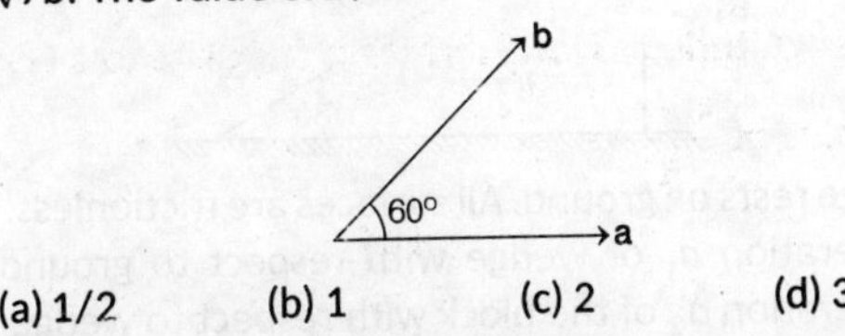

(a) 1/2 (b) 1 (c) 2 (d) 3

15. Position of a particle moving in space is given by

$$\mathbf{r}=6t\hat{i}-2t^2\hat{j}+4\hat{k}$$

Ratio of magnitudes of velocity and acceleration at $t=2$ s is

(a) $\frac{5}{2}$ (b) $\frac{2}{7}$

(c) $\frac{3}{5}$ (d) $\frac{7}{9}$

16. A boy is riding a bike with a speed of 5 m/s towards East direction observes rain drops falling vertically downward. On increasing the speed to 15 m/s, rain appears to fall making an angle of 45° of the vertical. The magnitude of velocity of rain w.r.t. ground is

(a) 5 m/s (b) $5\sqrt{5}$ m/s
(c) 25 m/s (d) 10 m/s

17. Peter and Nitro can swim with a speed of 8 m/s in still water. Both start from the middle of a river of width 200 m and move in opposite directions and always swim at an angle 37° with the banks. If the velocity of water in river is 2 m/s, then distance between them along the river when they reach the opposite banks is

(a) 128 m (b) 100 m
(c) $\frac{800}{3}$ m (d) None of these

18. A man can cross the 400 m wide river in least possible time of 80 s. If he wants to reach exactly opposite point to starting point, then at what angle from the direction of flow in river he should swim?
(Take, river flow velocity = 3 m/s)

(a) 37°
(b) 53°
(c) 127°
(d) 143°

19. A man wants to reach a point on the other bank of a river that is directly opposite to his starting point. River flows at the rate of 8 km/h and swimming speed of the man relative to water is 6 km/h. Then, to reach to the desired point, he should start swimming at an angle of

(a) $\cos^{-1}\left(\frac{0}{4}\right)$ with stream
(b) $\cos^{-1}\left(-\frac{3}{4}\right)$ with stream
(c) $\cos^{-1}\left(\frac{4}{3}\right)$ with stream
(d) He cannot reach the desired point directly by swimming.

20. A car travelling due North at the speed of $20\sqrt{2}$ m/s turn towards right (without changing speed) by 90° in 2 s. Acceleration of car is

(a) 10 ms^{-2} due N-E
(b) 10 ms^{-2} due N-W
(c) 10 ms^{-2} due S-W
(d) 10 ms^{-2} due S-E

21. Just after firing, a bullet is found to be moving at an angle of 37° to the horizontal. Its acceleration is 10 m/s^2 downwards. The component of its acceleration in the direction of its velocity is

(a) – 8 m/s^2 (b) +8 m/s^2
(c) – 6 m/s^2 (d) Need value of v

22. A ball is projected with initial velocity of 25 m/s at angle 53° with horizontal from the ground. During the motion, it passes through points A and B which are 15 m high from ground. The time taken by the ball from A to B is (Take, $g = 10$ m/s^2)

(a) 4 s (b) 2 s (c) 3 s (d) $2\sqrt{3}$ s

23. A ball is projected from a point O with some velocity at an angle 60° with the horizontal. A target is placed at point B ($10\sqrt{3}$ m, 15 m). With what velocity, the ball must be projected so that it can hit the target? Take point of projection as origin and $g = 10$ m/s^2.

(a) 20 m/s (b) 10 m/s (c) $10\sqrt{2}$ m/s (d) $10\sqrt{3}$ m/s

24. A particle is moving uniformly in a circular path of radius r. When it moves through an angular displacement θ, the magnitude of the corresponding linear displacement will be

(a) $2r\cos(\theta/2)$ (b) $2r\cot(\theta/2)$
(c) $2r\tan(\theta/2)$ (d) $2r\sin(\theta/2)$

25. A particle moves over a circular path of radius $r = 10$ m with a constant speed of 10 ms^{-1}. Particle turns over path by 60°. Match Column I with Column II.

	Column I		Column II
A.	Magnitude of displacement	P.	$\frac{10}{3}\pi$
B.	Change in speed	Q.	10
C.	Change in velocity	R.	zero
D.	Distance covered	S.	Non-zero

Choose the correct answer from the options given below:

	A	B	C	D		A	B	C	D
(a)	P	Q	R	S	(b)	Q	P	R	S
(c)	Q, S	R	Q, S	P, S	(d)	Q	R	Q	P

Answers

1 (c)	2 (d)	3 (c)	4 (b)	5 (d)
6 (a)	7 (c)	8 (d)	9 (a)	10 (c)
11 (a)	12 (b)	13 (c)	14 (a)	15 (a)
16 (b)	17 (c)	18 (c)	19 (d)	20 (d)
21 (c)	22 (b)	23 (a)	24 (d)	25 (c)

See detailed explanations on page no. 175

QUALIFIER 03

Laws of Motion

1. A bullet of mass 0.1 kg stops by 50 cm of a wooden block. Velocity of bullet before entering the block is 10 m/s. Magnitude of retarding force on bullet is nearly

(a) 10 N (b) 11 N
(c) 12 N (d) 13 N

2. Position x of a body of mass 4 kg varies with time as

$$x = \begin{cases} 0; t < 0 \\ \frac{3}{4}t; 0 \le t \le 4\text{ s} \\ 3; t > 4\text{ s} \end{cases}$$

Impulse given to body is

(a) –3 N-s at $t = 0$s.
(b) 3 N-s at $t = 0$s and –3 N-s at $t = 4$s.
(c) –3 N-s at $t = 0$s and 3 N-s at $t = 4$s.
(d) No impulse is given to body.

3. Statement I Same force applied for the same time causes same change in momentum for different bodies.

Statement II Direction of momentum and direction of change of momentum are always same.

In light of above statements, choose the most appropriate answer from the options given below:

(a) Both Statement I and Statement II are incorrect.
(b) Statement I is correct and Statement II is incorrect.
(c) Statement I is incorrect and Statement II is correct.
(d) Both Statement I and Statement II are correct.

4. A block of mass 8 kg is placed on a wedge which is of mass 16 kg.

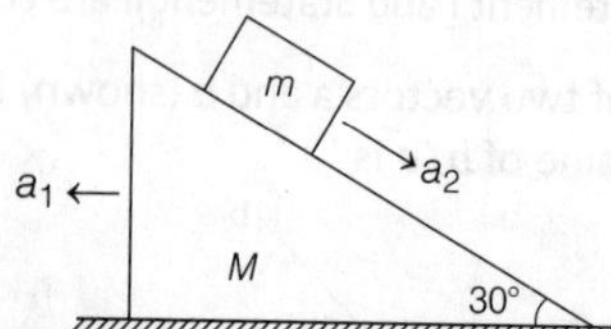

Wedge rests on ground. All surfaces are frictionless. Ratio of acceleration a_1 of wedge with respect to ground and of acceleration a_2 of the block with respect to wedge will be

(a) $\frac{1}{2\sqrt{3}}$ (b) $\frac{2}{\sqrt{3}}$ (c) $\frac{3\sqrt{3}}{2}$ (d) $\frac{1}{5\sqrt{6}}$

5. A person of mass 60 kg is in an elevator.

Match the entries of Column I with Column II.

	Column I		Column II
A.	Elevator moving with constant speed	P.	Force on floor by person = 600 N
B.	Elevator accelerates upward at 3 ms^{-2}	Q.	Force on floor by person = 780 N
C.	Elevator accelerates downward at 3 ms^{-2}	R.	Force on floor by person = 420 N
D.	Cable breaks and elevator falls freely	S.	Force on floor by person = 0

Choose the correct answer from the options given below:

(a) A → Q, B → R, C → S, D → P
(b) A → P, B → Q, C → S, D → R
(c) A → P, B → Q, C → R, D → S
(d) None of the above

6. A boy of mass 45 kg is standing stationary with respect to a horizontal conveyor belt that is accelerating with 2 m/s^2. The net force acting on the man is

(a) 45 N (b) between 45 N to 90 N
(c) 90 N (d) zero

7. A point mass m is in uniform circular motion with a tangential speed of 1 ms^{-1}. Change in momentum of body when it describes a quarter (one-fourth) circle is

(a) zero (b) m (c) $\sqrt{2}\,m$ (d) $\frac{m}{\sqrt{2}}$

8. A bullet moving with a velocity of $30\sqrt{2}$ m/s is fired into a fixed target. It penetrated into the target to the extent of s metre. If the same bullet is fired into a target of thickness $\frac{s}{2}$ m and of the same material with the same velocity, then bullet comes out of the target with velocity

(a) 20 m/s (b) 30 m/s (c) $20\sqrt{2}$ m/s (d) $10\sqrt{2}$ m/s

9. A person is driving a vehicle at a uniform speed of 5 ms^{-1} on a level curved track of radius 5 m. The coefficient of static friction between tyres and road is 0.1. Will the person slip while taking the turn with the same speed? (Take, g = 10 ms^{-2}).

(a) A person will slip, if $v^2 = 5\ m^2s^{-2}$
(b) A person will slip, if $v^2 > 5\ m^2s^{-2}$
(c) A person will slip, if $v^2 < 5\ m^2s^{-2}$
(d) A person will not slip, if $v^2 > 5\ m^2s^{-2}$

10. A block of mass 5 kg is placed in XZ-plane on a rough horizontal surface with coefficient of friction 0.5. If it is given a velocity $(15\hat{i} + 20\hat{k})$ m/s, then friction force acting on the block at this instant is

(a) $(-6\hat{i} - 8\hat{j})$ N (b) $(-8\hat{i} - 6\hat{j})$ N
(c) $(6\hat{i} - 8\hat{k})$ N (d) $(-6\hat{i} - 8\hat{k})$ N

11. A block of mass m resting on a wedge of angle θ is shown in the following figure. The wedge is given acceleration a in horizontal direction. The minimum value of a, so that the mass m falls freely is

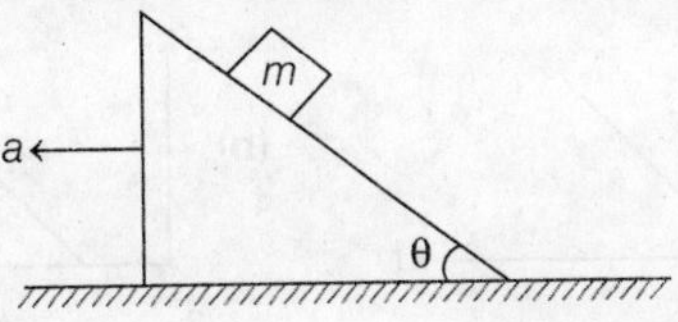

(a) $g\cos\theta$ (b) $g\tan\theta$
(c) $g\cot\theta$ (d) g

12. A balloon with mass m is descending down with an acceleration a (where, $a < g$). How much mass should be removed from it, so that it starts moving up with an acceleration a?

(a) $\frac{2ma}{g+a}$ (b) $\frac{2ma}{g-a}$ (c) $\frac{ma}{g+a}$ (d) $\frac{ma}{g-a}$

13. A man of mass M is standing on a weighing machine placed in cabin of negligible mass. The cabin is joined by a string with a block of mass m placed on smooth horizontal surface. The measured mass of man is

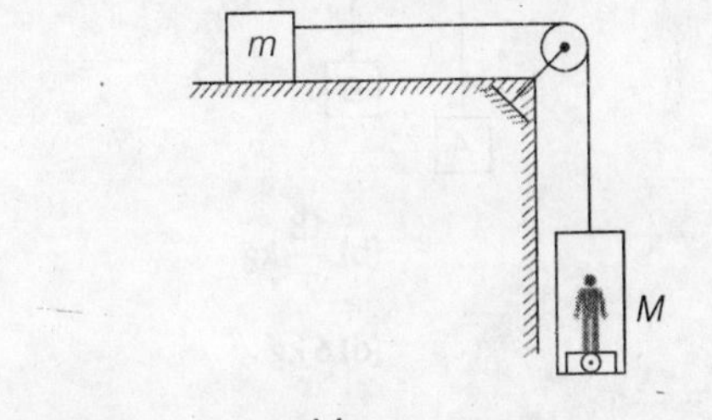

(a) $\frac{Mm}{M+m}$ (b) $\frac{Mm}{M-m}$ (c) M (d) $\frac{M-m}{M+m}$

14. Three blocks of masses 2 kg, 3 kg and 7 kg are placed on a smooth horizontal surface as shown in the following figure. The ratio of contact force between (2 kg and 3 kg) block and (3 kg and 7 kg) block is

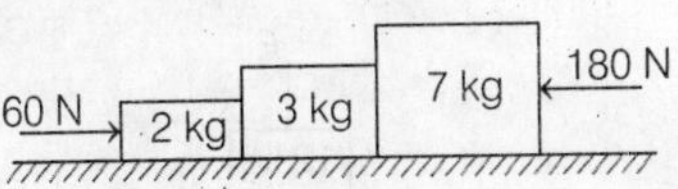

(a) 1 : 3 (b) 8 : 11 (c) 5 : 7 (d) 2 : 7

15. Assertion (A) Spring force is always negative.

Reason (R) Spring force F and displacement x are related as

$$F = -kx$$

where, k = spring constant

In the light of the above statemens, choose the most appropriate answer from the options given below:

(a) Both A and R are true but R is not the correct explanation of A.
(b) A is true but R is false.
(c) A is false but R is true.
(d) Both A and R are true and R is the correct explanation of A.

16. A block of mass 4 kg is resting over a rough horizontal floor, which have coefficients of friction μ_s and μ_k ($<\mu_s$). A time dependent force $F = 2t$ is applied at $t = 0$. The variation of acceleration of block is best represented as

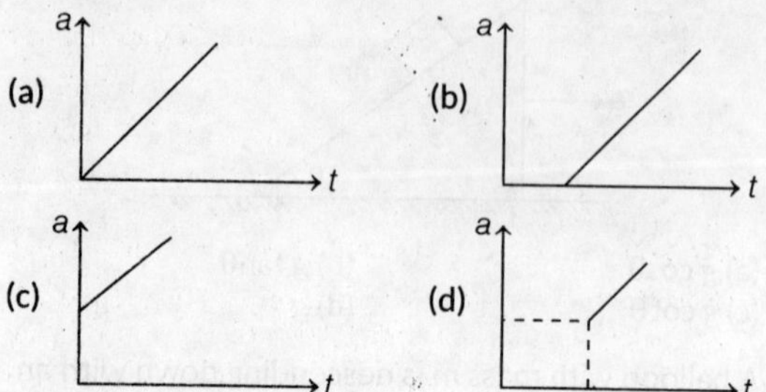

17. Two blocks A and B of masses 2 kg and M kg respectively are hanging on a string passing over a fixed frictionless pulley as shown in the following figure. When the system is released from the rest, then block A covers a distance 2.5 m in 2 s. Mass of block B is

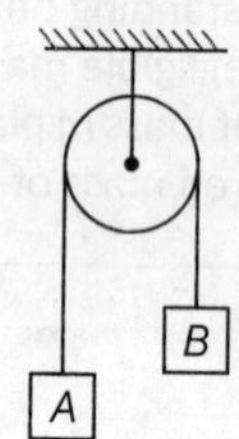

(a) $\frac{4}{7}$ kg (b) $\frac{18}{7}$ kg
(c) $\frac{14}{9}$ kg (d) 6 kg

18. Consider the arrangement of three blocks of masses 12 kg, 8 kg and M are connected by two ideal strings and the system is pulled by a force F as shown in the figure alongside. If the difference of tension in string 1 and string 2 is 80 N and ratio is 3 : 1, then force F and mass M are (Take, $g = 10\ m/s^2$)

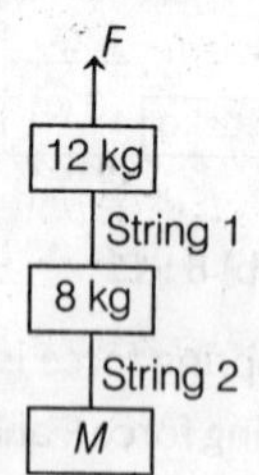

(a) 220 N, 2 kg
(b) 240 N, 4 kg
(c) 280 N, 8 kg
(d) None of these

19. The system shown in the figure is released from rest. Pulley and string are massless and friction is absent everywhere. Assuming that string is sufficiently long. The time after which block B reaches to ground is (Take, $g = 10\ m/s^2$)

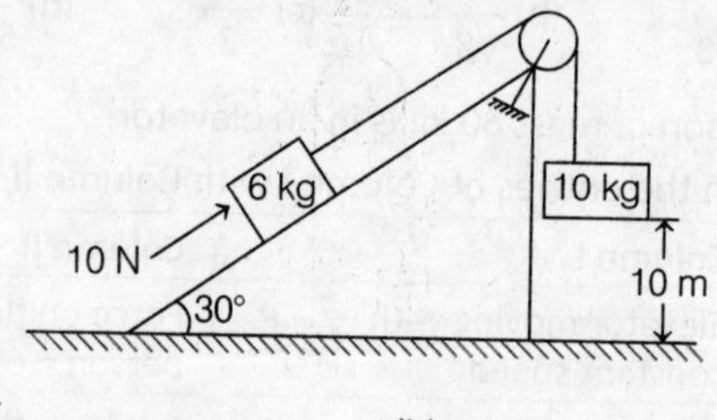

(a) $\sqrt{2}$ s (b) 2 s
(c) $\sqrt{3}$ s (d) 2.35 s

20. Two rectangular blocks are placed on a rough inclined plane as shown in figure. The system is released from rest. If the accelerations of blocks are a_A and a_B respectively, then

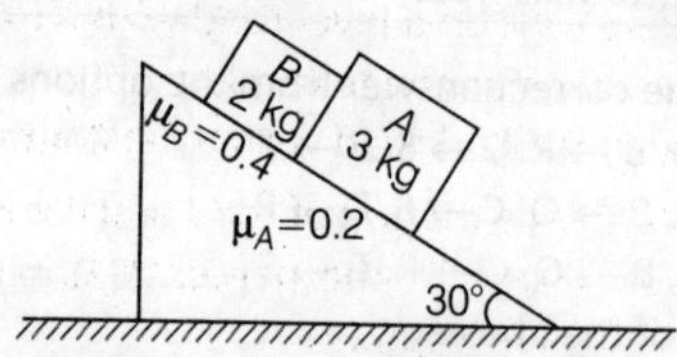

(a) $a_A = 0, a_B = 0$ (b) $a_A \neq 0, a_B = 0$
(c) $a_A > a_B > 0$ (d) $a_A = a_B > 0$

21. A block of mass m is placed on a rough inclined plane of inclination θ. As the angle θ is gradually increased from 0° to 90°, the correct variation of the contact force (F_c) between the block and the plane *versus* inclination angle θ is best represented as

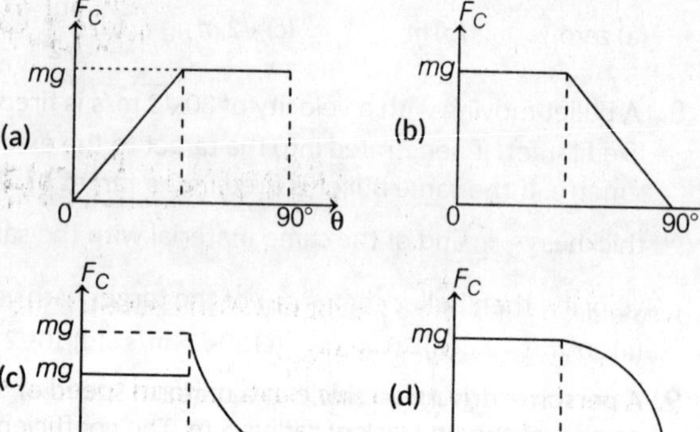

22. A horizontal smooth flat plank is rotated with an angular speed of 0.5 rad/s. Ratio of normal reaction force on a block of wood which is kept on plank at angular positions of 45° and 30° of plank is

(a) $\sqrt{6}$ (b) $\frac{1}{\sqrt{6}}$
(c) $\frac{\sqrt{2}}{\sqrt{3}}$ (d) $\frac{\sqrt{3}}{\sqrt{2}}$

23. Two blocks A and B of masses m and $2m$ respectively are held at rest such that the spring is in natural length. The accelerations of both blocks A and B just after release are respectively

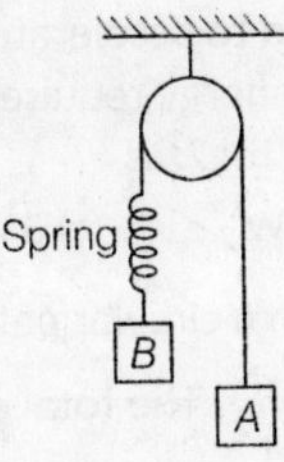

(a) 0, 0
(b) g downward, 0
(c) g downward, g downward
(d) $\frac{g}{3}$ downward, $\frac{g}{3}$ upward

24. A car can take a turn on a level road with a maximum speed v_1 and same car can take a turn on a similar (same type of surface) banked road with a maximum speed v_2. If coefficient of static friction of road and car is $\mu_s = 0.2$ and banking angle is $\theta = 30°$, the percentage increase in safe turning speed will be around
(a) 13%
(b) 29%
(c) 31%
(d) 17%

25. Consider the arrangement of blocks shown in the following figure.The horizontal surface is a rough and have coefficient of friction 0.5. The minimum value of M, so that system remains at rest is

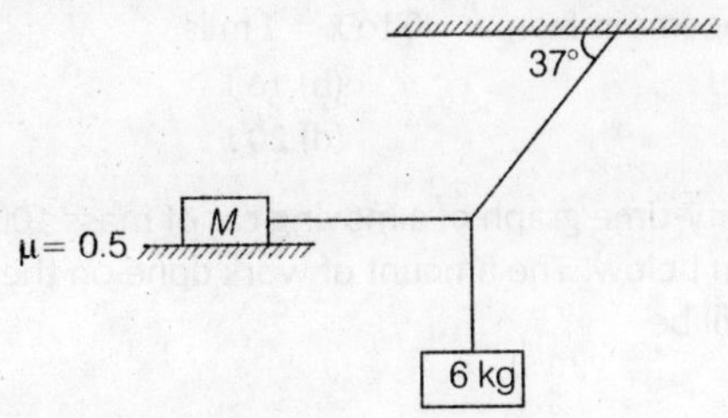

(a) 9.6 kg (b) 12 kg (c) 9 kg (d) 16 kg

Answers

1 (a)	2 (b)	3 (b)	4 (a)	5 (c)
6 (c)	7 (c)	8 (b)	9 (b)	10 (d)
11 (c)	12 (a)	13 (a)	14 (b)	15 (c)
16 (d)	17 (c)	18 (b)	19 (b)	20 (c)
21 (d)	22 (c)	23 (c)	24 (b)	25 (d)

See detailed explanations on page no. 179

QUALIFIER 04

Work, Energy and Power

1. A rain drop falls from a height of 500 m above the ground. Choose the correct statement.
(a) Work done by gravitational force is equal to change in kinetic energy.
(b) Acceleration of drop decreases with time.
(c) Velocity of drop keeps on increasing with time.
(d) Work done by gravitational force in first half of journey is more than that of second half.

2. Statement I Work done by centripetal force in a uniform circular motion is zero.

Statement II When a body moves on circular path with a uniform speed, then its kinetic energy remains constant.

In light of above statements, choose the most appropriate answer from the options given below:
(a) Both Statements I and Statement II are incorrect.
(b) Statement I is correct and Statement II is incorrect.
(c) Statement I is incorrect and Statement II is correct.
(d) Both Statement I and Statement II are correct.

3. A particle moves along Y-axis from $y = 0$ to $y = 4$ m under the influence of a force given by $F = 3y^2 - 4y + 5$. The amount of work done (in J) is
(a) 52 (b) 42 (c) 46 (d) 108

4. A body of mass 1 kg is displaced from a position of $(\hat{i} + \hat{j} - \hat{k})$ m to $(2\hat{i} - \hat{j} + 2\hat{k})$ m by applying a force of $(3\hat{i} - \hat{j} + \hat{k})$ N. The work done by the force on the body is
(a) 6 J (b) 9 J (c) 8 J (d) 12 J

5. A force acting on a body varies with distance x as shown below. The work done by the force on moving the body from $x = 0$ to $x = 8$ m is

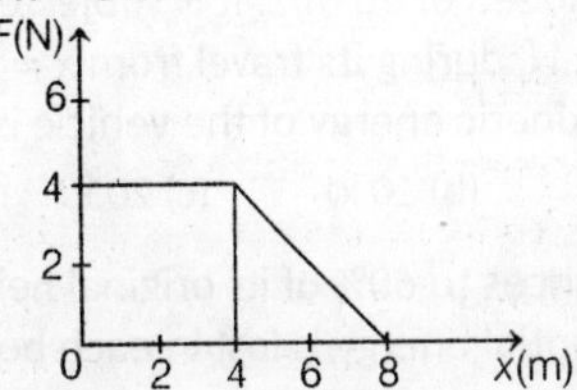

(a) 40 J (b) 32 J (c) 16 J (d) 24 J

6. A massive particle of mass 1 kg moves in a straight line with velocity $v = ax^{3/2}$, where $a = 4\ m/s^2$. The work done by the net force on the massive particle during its displacement from $x = 0$ to $x = 1$ m is

(a) 12 J (b) 16 J
(c) 8 J (d) 20 J

7. Velocity-time graph of a moving car of mass 100 kg is shown below. The amount of work done on the moving car will be

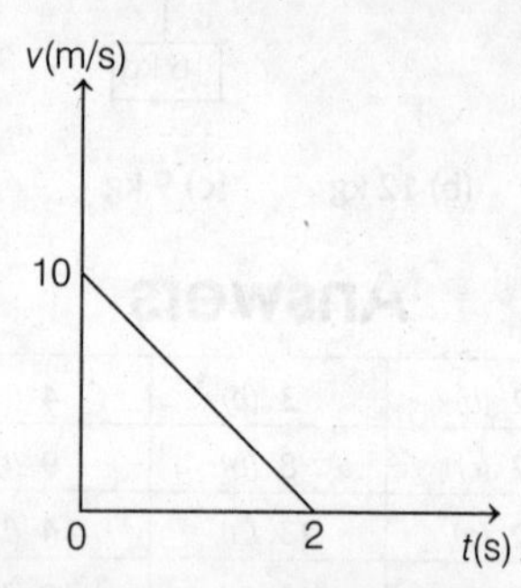

(a) -10^4 J (b) 10^4 J
(c) -5×10^3 J (d) 5×10^3 J

8. A ball of mass 8 kg and another ball of mass 4 kg are dropped together from a 40 m tall building. After a fall of 20 m each towards the earth, their respective kinetic energies will be in the ratio of

(a) 2 : 1 (b) 4 : 1
(c) 1 : 2 (d) 1 : 4

9. A car needs an engine of 5000 W to keep it moving with a constant velocity of 25 ms^{-1} on a levelled road. The force resisting the motion is

(a) 200 N (b) 100 N
(c) 150 N (d) 50 N

10. If the kinetic energy of a moving body is increased to four times, then percentage increase in its momentum will be

(a) 50% (b) 100%
(c) 200% (d) 150%

11. Displacement of a moving body with time t is related as, $x = 2t^3 + 5t + 2$. If the mass of the body is 4 kg, then increase in kinetic energy one second after the instant of motion will be

(a) 192 J (b) 96 J
(c) 56 J (d) 112 J

12. A vehicle of mass 75 kg is moving in x-direction with a constant speed of 20 m/s. It is subjected to retarding force $F = -0.2x$ N, during its travel from $x = 10$ m to $x = 20$ m. The final kinetic energy of the vehicle is

(a) 15 kJ (b) 10 kJ (c) 20 kJ (d) 25 kJ

13. A ball bounces to 60% of its original height. What fraction of its potential energy is lost in each bounce?

(a) 0.8 (b) 0.6 (c) 0.4 (d) 0.2

14. The energy required to accelerate a car from rest to 10 ms^{-1} is W. The energy required to accelerate the car from 10 ms^{-1} to 20 ms^{-1} is

(a) W (b) $2W$ (c) $3W$ (d) $4W$

15. A body is moving on a circular path of radius r under the influence of a force $\frac{k}{r^2}$. The total energy of the particle is

(a) $\frac{k}{2r}$ (b) $\frac{k}{r}$ (c) $\frac{-k}{r}$ (d) $\frac{-k}{2r}$

16. The power of a water pump is 5 kW. The amount of water it can raise in 2 min to a height of 20 m is
(Take, $g = 10\ m/s^2$)

(a) 1000 kg (b) 2000 kg (c) 3000 kg (d) 4000 kg

17. A motor drives a body along a straight line with a constant force. The power P developed by the motor must vary with time t as

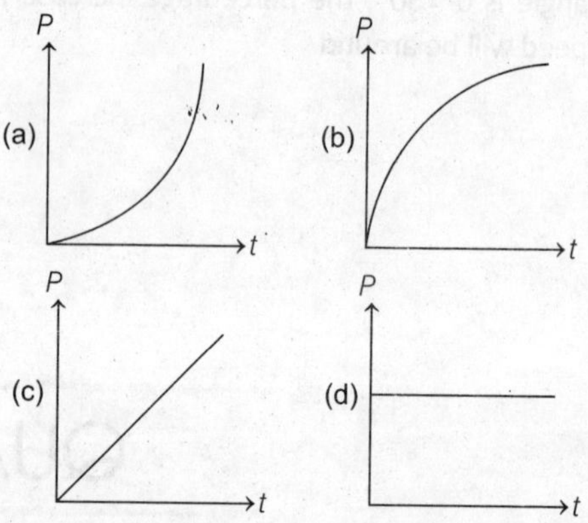

18. A force F acting on a body depends on its displacement s as $F \propto s^{-1/3}$. The power delivered by F will depend on displacement s as

(a) $s^{2/3}$ (b) $s^{-5/3}$
(c) s^0 (d) $s^{1/2}$

19. Assertion (A) A bulb of 1000 W can glows for a duration of 1.5 month, if a mass of 1 pico-kilogram is converted into energy.

Reason (R) Mass can neither be created nor destroyed in a chemical reaction.

In the light of the above statements, choose the most appropriate answer from the options given below:

(a) Both A and R are true but R is not the correct explanation of A.
(b) A is true but R is false.
(c) A is false but R is true.
(d) Both A and R are true and R is the correct explanation of A.

20. A moving block of mass M collides with another stationary block of mass $4M$. The lighter block comes to rest after collision. When the initial velocity of lighter block is v, the value of coefficient of restitution (e) will be

(a) 0.50 (b) -0.25
(c) 0.75 (d) 1

21. A particle of mass m is attached to a string of length L and given velocity is $\sqrt{10gL}$ in the horizontal direction at the lowest point. Column I represents the position of the particle and Column II represents tensions at different situation of the particle. Match Column I with Column II.

	Column I		Column II
A.	Tension in the string when the particle is at lowest position	P.	$\frac{13}{2}mg$
B.	Tension in the string when the particle is at highest position	Q.	$\frac{19}{2}mg$
C.	Tension in the string, when the string makes an angle 60° with lower vertical	R.	5 mg
D.	Tension in the string when the string makes an angle 60° with upper vertical	S.	11 mg

Choose the correct answer from the options given below:

(a) A $\rightarrow$ S, B $\rightarrow$ R, C $\rightarrow$ Q, D $\rightarrow$ P
(b) A $\rightarrow$ S, B $\rightarrow$ R, C $\rightarrow$ P, D $\rightarrow$ Q
(c) A $\rightarrow$ S, B $\rightarrow$ P, C $\rightarrow$ R, D $\rightarrow$ Q
(d) A $\rightarrow$ S, B $\rightarrow$ Q, C $\rightarrow$ R, D $\rightarrow$ P

22. A 0.5 kg block is pushed with an initial speed of 3 m/s towards a spring over a track *ABCD*. The spring (k = 4 N/m) is of length 1 m with one of end rigidly fixed to a support at point *D*.

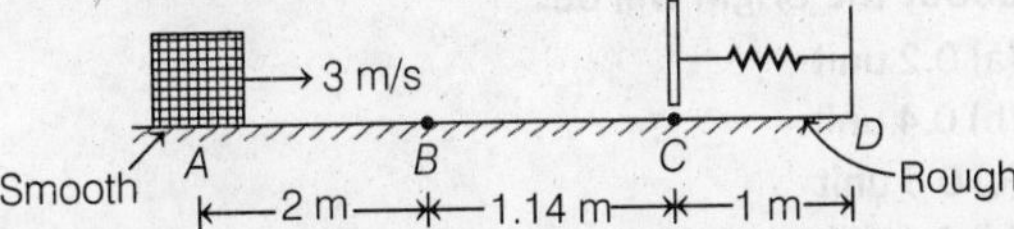

Part *AB* is smooth. For *BD*, $\mu_s = 0.22$ and $\mu_k = 0.2$. Total distance moved by the block before coming to rest for the first time is (Take, $g = 10\text{ ms}^{-2}$)

(a) 3.44 m (b) 4.14 m (c) 3.14 m (d) 8.28 cm

23. Statement I In an elastic collision of two billiard balls, the total kinetic energy is conserved during short time of collision when balls are in contact.

Statement II Energy lost due to friction does not follow the law of conservation of energy.

In light of above statements, choose the most appropriate answer from the options given below:

(a) Both Statement I and Statement II are incorrect.
(b) Statement I is correct and Statement II is incorrect.
(c) Statement I is incorrect and Statement II is correct.
(d) Both Statement I and Statement II are correct.

24. A bullet (m = 10 g) strikes a hanging block of wood (m = 10 g) and get embedded in it.

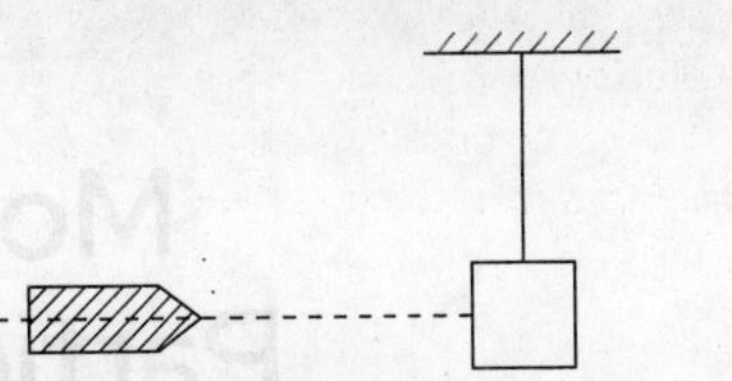

Loss of energy in this process is

(a) 0% (b) 50%
(c) 75% (d) 100%

25. Potential energy curve of a particle is shown. Match Column I with Column II by observing this PE curve.

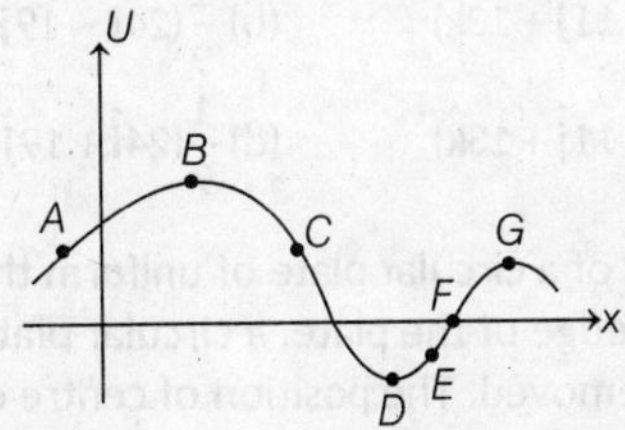

	Column I		Column II
A.	Force is maximum	P.	At G
B.	Force acting towards left	Q.	At F
C.	Force acting towards right	R.	At E
D.	Stable equilibrium	S.	At C
		T.	At D

Choose the correct answer from the options given below:

(a) A $\rightarrow$ Q, B $\rightarrow$ P & S, C $\rightarrow$ P & Q, D $\rightarrow$ P
(b) A $\rightarrow$ P & S, B $\rightarrow$ Q & R, C $\rightarrow$ T, D $\rightarrow$ R & Q
(c) A $\rightarrow$ S, B $\rightarrow$ Q & R, C $\rightarrow$ T, D $\rightarrow$ P
(d) A $\rightarrow$ P, B $\rightarrow$ Q, C $\rightarrow$ R & S, D $\rightarrow$ T

Answers

1 *(b)*	2 *(d)*	3 *(a)*	4 *(c)*	5 *(d)*
6 *(c)*	7 *(c)*	8 *(a)*	9 *(a)*	10 *(b)*
11 *(a)*	12 *(a)*	13 *(c)*	14 *(c)*	15 *(d)*
16 *(c)*	17 *(c)*	18 *(c)*	19 *(c)*	20 *(b)*
21 *(a)*	22 *(a)*	23 *(b)*	24 *(b)*	25 *(c)*

See detailed explanations on page no. 183

QUALIFIER 05

Motion of System of Particles and Rigid Body

1. Two bodies of masses 4 kg and 5 kg are kept at fixed locations having position vectors $-\hat{i}+\hat{j}+2\hat{k}$ and $4\hat{i}-3\hat{j}+\hat{k}$, respectively. The position vector of centre of mass of this system is

(a) $\frac{1}{9}(16\hat{i}+11\hat{j}+13\hat{k})$ (b) $\frac{1}{9}(24\hat{i}-19\hat{j}+13\hat{k})$

(c) $\frac{1}{9}(16\hat{i}-11\hat{j}+13\hat{k})$ (d) $\frac{1}{9}(24\hat{i}+19\hat{j}+13\hat{k})$

2. The radius of a circular plate of uniform thickness is 28 cm. From one edge of the plate, a circular plate of radius 21 cm is removed. The position of centre of mass from the centre of circular plate is

(a) 12 cm b) 6 cm

(c) 9 cm (d) 3 cm

3. The radius of wheel of a bicycle is 1 m. It moves with angular velocity of $\omega = 1 + t$, where t is in seconds and ω in rad s^{-1}. The distance moved by the bicycle from $t = 1$ s to 2 s is

(a) 2 m (b) 4 m (c) 3.5 m (d) 2.5 m

4. A rotating wheel changes angular speed from 1500 rpm to 2400 rpm in 6 s. The uniform angular acceleration of the rotating wheel is

(a) 4π rad/s^2 (b) 6π rad/s^2

(c) 5π rad/s^2 (d) 10π rad/s^2

5. A ball tied to a string takes 8 s to complete one revolution along a horizontal circle. If by pulling the cord, the radius of the circle is reduced to one-fourth of the previous value, then how much time the ball will take in one revolution?

(a) 1 s (b) 2 s (c) 0.5 s (d) 2.5 s

6. The graph between angular velocity *versus* time of a flywheel is shown below. The angle (in rad) through which the flywheel turns during 30 s is

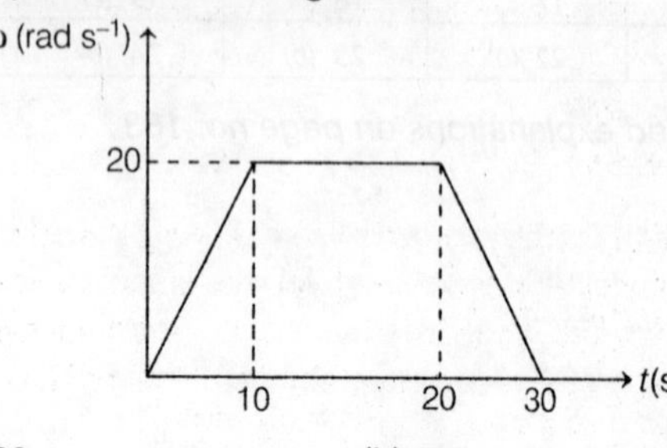

(a) 300 (b) 400

(c) 200 (d) 100

7. Assertion (A) Without any external torque, kinetic energy of a system of particles rotating around an axis remains constant with time.

Reason (R) Without any external torque, angular momentum of system remains constant.

In the light of the above statements, choose the most appropriate answer from the options given below:

(a) Both A and R are true but R is not the correct explanation of A.

(b) A is true but R is false.

(c) A is false but R is true.

(d) Both A and R are true and R is the correct explanation of A.

8. A body of mass 2 kg is moving with a uniform speed $v = \frac{1}{\sqrt{5}}$ in *XOY*-plane along the line $y = 2x + 2$. The magnitude of the angular momentum of the particle about the origin will be

(a) 0.2 unit

(b) 0.4 unit

(c) 0.8 unit

(d) 0.6 unit

9. The instantaneous angular position of a point on a rotating wheel is given by the equation $\theta(t) = 3t^3 - 3t^2 + 6t + 1$. The torque on the wheel becomes zero at

(a) $\frac{3}{2}$ s (b) $\frac{3}{4}$ s

(c) $\frac{4}{3}$ s (d) $\frac{1}{3}$ s

10. A thin meter scale is kept vertical by placing its one end in contact stationary, when it is allowed to fall. The velocity of its upper end when it hit the floor is

(a) $\sqrt{gl}$ (b) $\sqrt{5gl}$

(c) $\sqrt{2gl}$ (d) $\sqrt{3gl}$

11. Match the items of Column I with the items of Column II.

	Column I		Column II
A.	Moment of inertia of spherical shell about its diameter having mass M and radius R	P.	$\frac{7}{5}MR^2$
B.	Moment of inertia of spherical shell about a tangential axis having mass M and radius R	Q.	$\frac{2}{5}MR^2$

C.	Moment of inertia of solid sphere about its diametric axis having mass M and radius R	R.	$\frac{5}{3}MR^2$
D.	Moment of inertia of solid sphere about its tangential axis having mass M and radius R	S.	$\frac{2}{3}MR^2$

Choose the correct answer from the options given below

	A	B	C	D		A	B	C	D
(a)	S	R	P	Q	(b)	S	R	Q	P
(c)	R	S	Q	P	(d)	S	Q	R	P

12. Three hollow spheres of mass m and radius r each are kept as shown below. The moment of inertia of the system about YY'-axis is

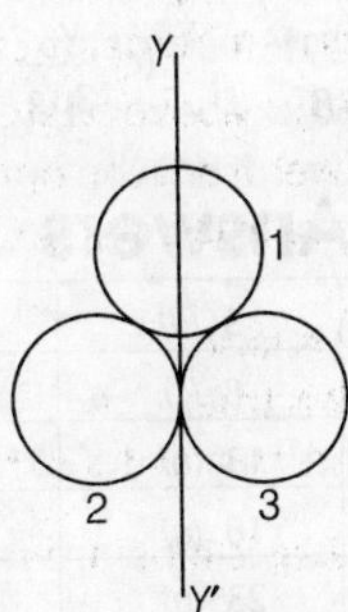

(a) $\frac{8}{3}mr^2$ (b) $2mr^2$
(c) $4mr^2$ (d) $\frac{16}{3}mr^2$

13. Two identical rods A and B of mass M and length l each are joined as shown below. The moment of inertia about an axis passing through point O and perpendicular to the plane of rods is

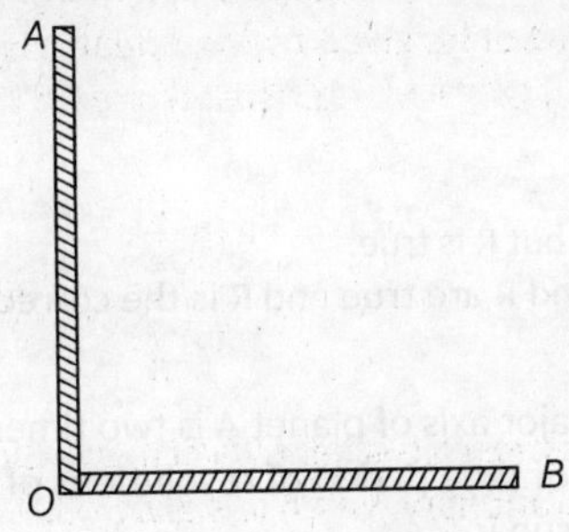

(a) $\frac{ML^2}{3}$ (b) $\frac{2ML^2}{3}$
(c) ML^2 (d) $\frac{2}{7}ML^2$

14. A flywheel having a radius of gyration of 1 m and mass 2 kg rotates at an angular speed of 4 rad/s about an axis perpendicular to it and passing through its centre. The kinetic energy of rotation is

(a) 32 J
(b) 16 J
(c) 4 J
(d) 8 J

15. The moment of inertia of a body about a given axis is 0.2 kg-m^2. Initially, the body is at rest. In order to produce a rotational kinetic energy of 1000 J, an angular acceleration of 10 rad/s^2 must be applied about that axis for a duration of

(a) 20 s (b) 15 s (c) 5 s (d) 10 s

16. If the rotational kinetic energy of a body is increased by 300%, then percentage increase in its angular momentum will be

(a) 50% (b) 100%
(c) 150% (d) 200%

17. A pulley of diameter 4 m is rotated about its axis by a force $F = (20t - 5t^2)$ N applied tangentially. If the moment of inertia of the pulley about its axis of rotation is 10 kg-m^2, the number of rotations made by the pulley before its direction of motion is reversed, is

(a) more than 3 but less than 6
(b) more than 3 but less than 9
(c) more than 6 but less than 9
(d) more than 9

18. A rigid body is rolling without slipping on a horizontal surface. Then, match Column I with Column II.

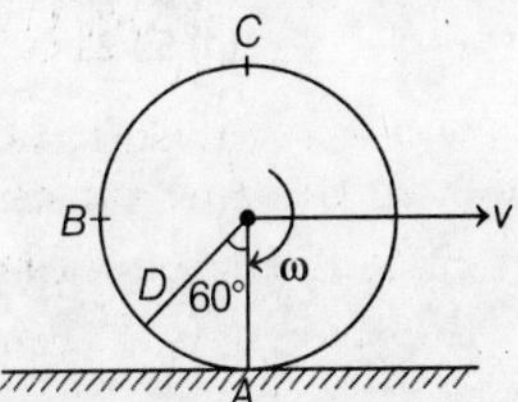

	Column I		Column II
A.	Velocity at point A (v_A)	P.	$v\sqrt{2}$
B.	Velocity at point B (v_B)	Q.	Zero
C.	Velocity at point C (v_C)	R.	v
D.	Velocity at point D (v_D)	S.	2v

Choose the correct answer from the option given below.

	A	B	C	D		A	B	C	D
(a)	Q	P	S	R	(b)	Q	P	R	S
(c)	Q	S	P	R	(d)	P	Q	S	R

19. A flywheel of moment of inertia 5 kg-m^2 is rotating at 40 rad/s. How much power is required to bring it at rest in 5 s?

(a) 856 W (b) 1225 W
(c) 625 W (d) 800 W

20. A cylindrical roller of mass m is being pulled on horizontal surface with force F parallel to the surface and applied at its centre. If the acceleration of the cylinder is a and it is rolling without slipping, then the value of F is

(a) $\frac{ma}{2}$ (b) $\frac{3ma}{2}$
(c) ma (d) $2ma$

21. **Statement I** A disc rolls down on an inclined plane faster than a ring of same outer radius, material and thickness.

Statement II Radius of gyration of disc is greater than that of ring.

In light of above statements, choose the most appropriate answer from the options given below

(a) Both Statement I and Statement II are incorrect.
(b) Statement I is correct and Statement II is incorrect.
(c) Statement I is incorrect and Statement II is correct.
(d) Both Statement I and Statement II are correct.

22. A hollow sphere is rolling down on an inclined plane of inclination 60° without slipping. Its linear acceleration along the inclined plane will be

(a) $\frac{3\sqrt{3}}{10}g$ (b) $\frac{\sqrt{3}}{10}g$ (c) $\frac{\sqrt{3}}{2}g$ (d) $\frac{\sqrt{3}}{5}g$

23. A ring of mass m and radius r is rotating about its diameter. A solid sphere of same mass and radius $\frac{r}{2}$ is also rotating about its geometrical axis with an angular speed twice that of the sphere. The ratio of their kinetic energy of rotation will be

(a) 16 : 9 (b) 5 : 16
(c) 9 : 16 (d) 5 : 21

24. When a body is under pure rolling, the fraction of its total kinetic energy which is purely rotational is $\frac{2}{5}$. The body is a

(a) cylinder (b) hollow sphere
(c) solid sphere (d) ring

25. A uniform disc of mass m, radius R is projected horizontally on a surface with speed v_0. After time t, it acquires pure rolling. Surface has coefficient of friction μ_0.

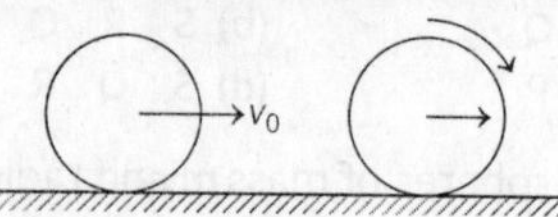

Then, value of t is

(a) $\frac{v_0}{\mu g}$ (b) $\frac{2v_0}{\mu g}$ (c) $\frac{v_0}{3\mu g}$ (d) $\frac{3v_0}{2\mu g}$

Answers

1 (c)	2 (c)	3 (d)	4 (c)	5 (c)
6 (b)	7 (c)	8 (c)	9 (d)	10 (d)
11 (b)	12 (c)	13 (b)	14 (b)	15 (d)
16 (b)	17 (a)	18 (a)	19 (d)	20 (b)
21 (b)	22 (a)	23 (b)	24 (b)	25 (c)

See detailed explanations on page no. 186

QUALIFIER **06**

Gravitation

1. **Statement I** Gravitational force has longest range among all known forces.

Statement II Gravitational force is very larger than other field forces.

In light of above statements, choose the most appropriate answer from the options given below:

(a) Both Statement I and Statement II are incorrect.
(b) Statement I is correct and Statement II is incorrect.
(c) Statement I is incorrect and Statement II is correct.
(d) Both Statement I and Statement II are correct.

2. **Assertion (A)** While a planet moves around sun in an elliptical orbit, its areal speed remains constant.

Reason (R) Gravitation is a central force.

In the light of the above statements, choose the most appropriate answer from the options given below:

(a) Both A and R are true but R is not the correct explanation of A.
(b) A is true but R is false.
(c) A is false but R is true.
(d) Both A and R are true and R is the correct explanation of A.

3. The semi-major axis of planet A is two times of the planet B. The ratio of time period of revolutions of planets around the sun is

(a) 4 : 1 (b) 2 : 1 (c) $\sqrt{2}$: 1 (d) $2\sqrt{2}$: 1

4. Three identical point masses each of mass 2 kg lie in the XY-plane at points (0, 0), (0, 0.2 m) and (0.2 m, 0). The gravitational force on the mass at the origin is

(a) $6.67 \times 10^{-11} (\hat{i} + \hat{j})$N (b) $3.34 \times 10^{-10} (\hat{i} + \hat{j})$N
(c) $6.67 \times 10^{-9} (\hat{i} + \hat{j})$N (d) $3.34 \times 10^{-10} (\hat{i} - \hat{j})$N

5. Four particles each of mass m are located at the vertices of an square of side a. At what speed must they move if they all revolve under the influence of their gravitational force of attraction in a circular orbit circumscribing the square while still preserving the square?

(a) $2\sqrt{\frac{Gm}{a}}$ (b) $\sqrt{\frac{Gm}{a}\left(\sqrt{2}+\frac{1}{2}\right)}$

(c) $\sqrt{\frac{Gm}{a}\left(\sqrt{2}+\frac{1}{\sqrt{2}}\right)}$ (d) $\sqrt{\frac{Gm}{a}\left(1+\frac{1}{2\sqrt{2}}\right)}$

6. Suppose that gravitational force F between two point masses is directly proportional to r^n where, n is a constant. If a satellite of mass m is revolving around the planet of mass m in circular orbit of radius r, then time period of satellite is directly proportional to

(a) $r^{\frac{1+n}{2}}$ (b) $r^{\frac{1-n}{2}}$ (c) $r^{\frac{2n-1}{2}}$ (d) $r^{\frac{1-2n}{2}}$

7. If both mass and radius of earth decrease by 1%, then the value of

I. acceleration due to gravity would increase by 1%.
II. acceleration due to gravity would decrease by 1%.
III. escape velocity from earth's surface would decrease by 1%.
IV. the gravitational potential energy of a body on earth's surface will remain unchanged.

(a) I and III (b) I and IV (c) II and IV (d) III and IV

8. A solid sphere of mass M and radius R has a spherical cavity of radius $R/2$ such that the centre of cavity is at a distance $R/2$ from the centre of the sphere. A point mass m is placed inside the cavity at a distance $R/4$ from the centre of sphere. The gravitational pull between the sphere and the point mass m is

(a) $\frac{11GMm}{R^2}$ (b) $\frac{14GMm}{R^2}$ (c) $\frac{GMm}{2R^2}$ (d) $\frac{GMm}{R^2}$

9. An object weighs 50 N at an altitude equal to the radius of earth. The ratio of weight of object on earth's surface to that at depth of half of radius of earth is

(a) 1 : 1 (b) 1 : 4 (c) 3 : 1 (d) 2 : 1

10. As we move from centre of earth to a height h above the surface such that ($h >> R$), then change in acceleration due to gravity with distance r from the centre of the earth is best represented by

(a)
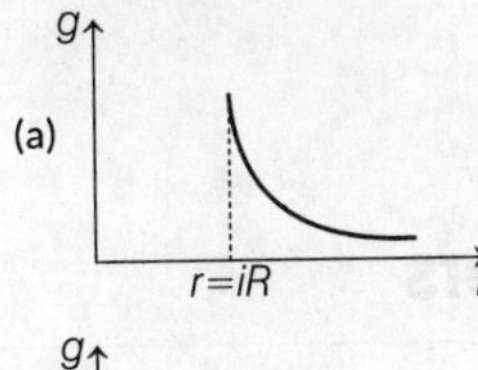

(b) g, r=R, r

(c)
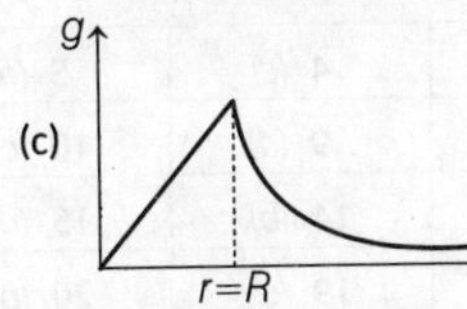

(d) g, r=R, r

11. The planets with radii R_1 and R_2 have densities ρ_1, ρ_2 respectively. Their atmospheric pressures are p_1 and p_2 respectively. Therefore, the ratio of masses of their atmospheres, neglecting variation of g within the limits of atmosphere is

(a) $\frac{\rho_1 R_2 p_1}{\rho_2 R_1 p_2}$ (b) $\frac{p_1 R_2 \rho_2}{p_2 R_1 \rho_1}$ (c) $\frac{p_1 R_1 \rho_1}{p_2 R_2 \rho_2}$ (d) $\frac{p_1 R_1 \rho_2}{p_2 R_2 \rho_1}$

12. The mass of a planet is M and radius is R. An object of mass 2 kg is taken from the surface to a height $4R$ very slowly, then work done is

(a) $\frac{8GM}{5R}$ (b) $\frac{2GM}{R}$ (c) $\frac{5GM}{R}$ (d) $\frac{4GM}{3R}$

13. Gravitational potential difference between a point on surface of planet and another point 20 m above is 4 J/kg. If gravitational field is considered nearly uniform, then work done in moving a mass of 2 kg from the surface to a point 5 m above the surface is

(a) 4 J (b) 2 J
(c) 8 J (d) 0.2 J

14. The gravitational potential energy of a body at a distance $2R$ from the centre of earth is -90×10^7 J. Its weight at a distance $3R$ from the centre of earth is

(a) 15.625 N (b) 31.25 N
(c) 62.5 N (d) None of these

15. An object of mass m is projected from the surface of the earth at 60° with initial velocity $\sqrt{\frac{GM}{R}}$, where M is mass of earth and R is radius of earth. The maximum distance of object from the centre of earth is

(a) $\frac{R}{4}$ (b) $\frac{3}{4}R$
(c) $\frac{5R}{4}$ (d) $\frac{3R}{2}$

16. A planet is moving around the sun in an elliptical orbit as shown in figure. As the planet moves from P to Q ,then its

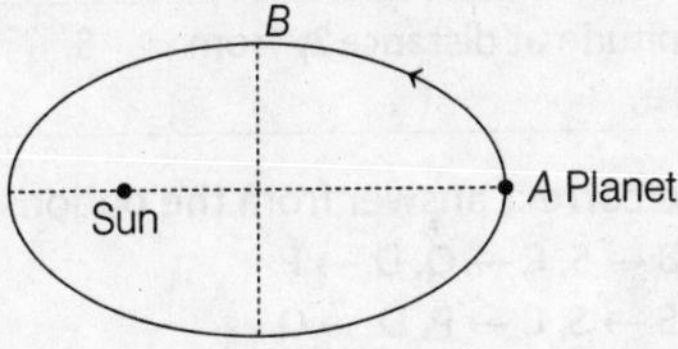

(a) total energy decreases
(b) kinetic energy remains same
(c) angular momentum about centre of sun will remain unchanged
(d) magnitude of linear momentum remains unchanged

17. While revolving around the earth, a satellite has kinetic energy K, potential energy U and total energy E. If the value of $\frac{E}{K}$ is x and $\frac{E}{U}$ is y, then ratio $\left|\frac{x}{y}\right|$ is

(a) 2 : 3 (b) 2 : 1
(c) 3 : 1 (d) 3 : 2

18. A satellite of mass m is in a circular orbit of radius $2R$ about the earth. It is transferred to a circular orbit of radius $4R$. Then, change in kinetic energy of satellite is
(R is the radius of earth, E is total energy of satellite)

(a) E (b) E (c) $\frac{E}{4}$ (d) $-\frac{E}{2}$

19. The binding energy of a system of earth and its satellite orbiting around the earth in a circular orbit is 4×10^6 J. If mass of the satellite is 800 kg, then linear speed in that orbit is

(a) 1414 m/s (b) 707 m/s
(c) 100 m/s (d) 500 m/s

20. Two stars of mass m and $2m$ are initially d_o distance apart. They come closer to each other due to gravitational pull. When the separation between them becomes $\frac{d_o}{2}$, they move towards each other with velocities v_1 and v_2, then velocity of mass $2m$ is

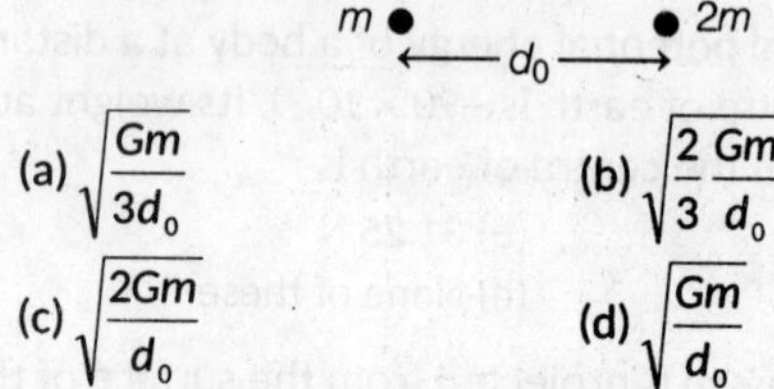

(a) $\sqrt{\frac{Gm}{3d_o}}$ (b) $\sqrt{\frac{2\,Gm}{3\,d_o}}$
(c) $\sqrt{\frac{2Gm}{d_o}}$ (d) $\sqrt{\frac{Gm}{d_o}}$

21. The magnitude of gravitational potential on surface of a solid sphere is x and radius is y. Match Column I with Column II.

	Column I		Column II
A.	Field strength at distance $2y$ from centre	P.	$\frac{x}{2y}$
B.	Magnitude of potential at distance $y/2$ from centre	Q.	$\frac{x}{2}$
C.	Field strength at distance $y/2$ from centre	R.	$\frac{x}{4y}$
D.	Magnitude at distance $2y$ from centre	S.	$\frac{11}{8}x$

Choose the correct answer from the options given below:
(a) A $\to$ R, B $\to$ S, C $\to$ Q, D $\to$ P
(b) A $\to$ R, B $\to$ S, C $\to$ P, D $\to$ Q
(c) A $\to$ P, B $\to$ Q, C $\to$ R, D $\to$ S
(d) A $\to$ P, B $\to$ S, C $\to$ R, D $\to$ Q

22. The potential energy, kinetic energy and total energy of moving satellite around the earth are U, K and E respectively. The graph of these energies with distance r from the centre of earth has been plotted.

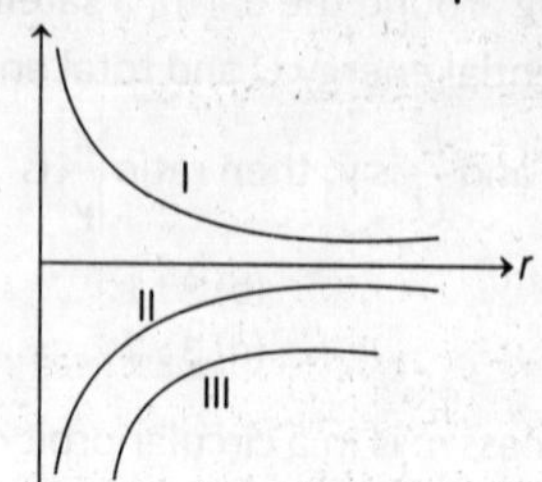

Then, I, II and III denote
(a) K, E, U, respectively (b) K, U, E, respectively
(c) $K-E, E, U$, respectively (d) $E+K, U, K$ respectively

23. The time period of a planet revolving around the sun in an elliptical path of mean radius r is T, then which of the following graph is correct?

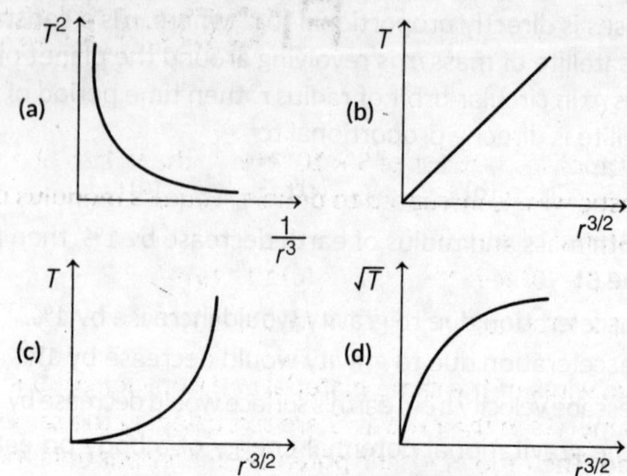

24. A smooth tunnel is dug along the diameter of planet and then a particle is projected with velocity v from its centre such that it can just overcome the gravitational pull of earth. The change in potential energy is

(a) $\frac{1}{2}mv^2$ (b) mv^2 (c) $\sqrt{\frac{3}{2}}mv^2$ (d) $\frac{3}{2}mv^2$

25. Match the values of quantities of Column II with the quantity given in Column I for a geostationary satellite.

	Column I		Column II
A.	Time period in seconds	P.	3070
B.	Height above earth's surface (in km)	Q.	36000
C.	Orbital velocity (in m/s)	R.	86400

Choose the correct answer from the options given below:
(a) A $\to$ P, B $\to$ Q, C $\to$ R
(b) A $\to$ R, B $\to$ P, C $\to$ Q
(c) A $\to$ Q, B $\to$ P, C $\to$ R
(d) A $\to$ R, B $\to$ Q, C $\to$ P

Answers

1 (b)	2 (a)	3 (d)	4 (c)	5 (d)
6 (b)	7 (b)	8 (b)	9 (d)	10 (c)
11 (d)	12 (a)	13 (b)	14 (b)	15 (d)
16 (c)	17 (b)	18 (c)	19 (c)	20 (b)
21 (b)	22 (a)	23 (b)	24 (a)	25 (d)

See detailed explanations on page no. 189

QUALIFIER 07

Properties of Bulk Matter

1. On applying a stress of 5×10^9 N/m^2, the length of a elastic wire is increased to double. Young's modulus of the material of wire is

(a) 2.5×10^9 N/m^2 (b) 10^{10} N/m^2
(c) 5×10^9 N/m^2 (d) 5×10^8 N/m^2

2. Two wires of the same material and same length but diameters in the ratio 1 : 2 are stretched by the same load. The ratio of elastic potential energy per unit volume for the two wires is

(a) 1 : 1 (b) 2 : 1
(c) 4 : 1 (d) 16 : 1

3. Poisson's ratio for a material is 0.2. A load is applied on it due to which it suffers the longitudinal strain of 3×10^{-3}, then percentage change in its volume is

(a) 0.12% (b) 0.18%
(c) 0.24% (d) 1.5%

4. A steel rod is 5 cm longer than a brass rod. If this difference in their lengths is to remain the same at all temperatures, then the length of brass rod is (Take, coefficients of linear expansion for steel and brass rod 12×10^{-6}/°C and 18×10^{-6}/°C, respectively)

(a) 15 cm (b) 10 cm
(c) 20 cm (d) 12 cm

5. Two equal drops of water are falling through air with a steady velocity v. If the drops are coalesced, then new velocity of the combination of drops will be

(a) $2^{1/3}$v (b) $4^{2/3}$v
(c) $4^{1/3}$v (d) $-2^{2/3}$v

6. A cylinder of height 45 m is completely filled with water. The velocity of efflux of water through a small hole on the side wall of the cylinder near its bottom is (Take, $g = 10$ m/s^2)

(a) 20 m/s (b) 30 m/s
(c) 45 m/s (d) 10 m/s

7. Two liquids of densities ρ and 4ρ having volumes $2V$ and V are mixed together. The density of the mixture is

(a) $\frac{\rho}{2}$ (b) $\frac{3\rho}{2}$
(c) 2ρ (d) $\frac{5\rho}{2}$

8. A liquid filled in cylindrical vessel (radius = r) is rotated about its axis (angular speed = ω).

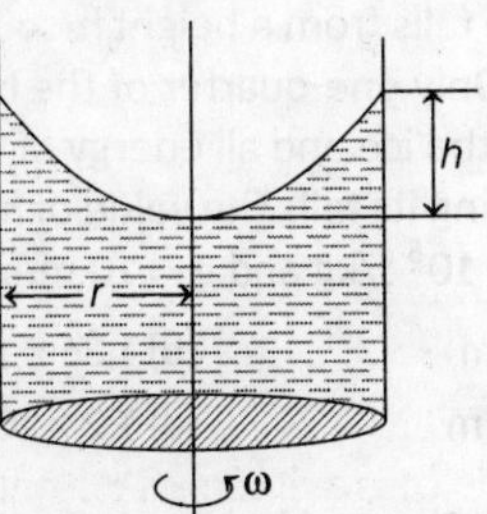

Then, height h of fluid above centre of vessel is

(a) $\frac{r\omega}{2g}$ (b) $\frac{r^2\omega^2}{2g}$ (c) $\sqrt{2gr\omega}$ (d) $\frac{\omega^2}{2gr^2}$

9. A rectangular liquid film is extended from 10 cm × 20 cm to (20 cm ×25 cm). If the work done in this process is 5×10^{-3}J, then the value of surface tension of the liquid is

(a) 0.012 N/m (b) 0.045 N/m
(c) 0.083 N/m (d) 0.063 N/m

10. Statement I For liquids, which wet the walls of a vessel, the angle of contact is acute.

Statement II The liquid that wets the solid surface has convex meniscus.

In light of above statements choose the most appropriate answer from the options given below:

(a) Both Statement I and Statement II are incorrect.
(b) Statement I is correct and Statement II is incorrect.
(c) Statement I is incorrect and Statement II is correct.
(d) Both Statement I and Statement II are correct.

11. Water rises in a capillary tube to a height of 2 cm. In another capillary tube whose radius is half of it, how much the water will rise?

(a) 2 cm (b) 3 cm
(c) 4 cm (d) 5 cm

12. A capillary tube is attached horizontally to a constant pressure head arrangement. If the radius of the capillary tube is increased by 10%, then the rate of flow of liquid will change nearly by

(a) 10% (b) 46%
(c) – 10% (d) – 40%

13. The pressure inside a small air bubble of 0.1 mm radius situated just below the water surface is (Take, surface tension of water, $T = 7.2 \times 10^{-2}$ N/m and atmospheric pressure, $p_0 = 1.013 \times 10^5$ N/m^2)

(a) 10^4 N/m^2 (b) 10^5 N/m^2
(c) 10^6 N/m^2 (d) 10^7 N/m^2

14. In steady state, the temperature at the ends *A* and *B* of a long rod *AB* of 20 cm are 120°C and 0°C, respectively. The temperature at a point 10 cm from end *A* is

(a) 45°C (b) 55°C (c) 50°C (d) 60°C

15. A piece of ice falls from a height *h*, so that it melts completely. Only one-quarter of the heat produced is absorbed by the ice and all energy of ice gets converted into heat during its fall. The value of *h* is (Take, latent heat of ice = 3.4×10^5 J/kg and $g = 10$ m/s^2)

(a) 1.86×10^5 m (b) 1.36×10^5 m
(c) 2.46×10^4 m (d) 1.2×10^6 m

16. Assertion (A) Slope of heating curve (ΔT *versus* ΔQ) when temperature is changing in inversely proportional to specific heat.

Reason (R) Slope of heating curve is zero when there is a change of phase.

In the light of the above statements, choose the most appropriate answer from the options given below:

(a) Both A and R are true but R is not the correct explanation of A.
(b) A is true but R is false.
(c) A is false but R is true.
(d) Both A and R are true and R is the correct explanation of A.

17. Three liquids *X*, *Y* and *Z* having same specific heat and masses *m*, 2*m* and 3*m* have temperatures 20°C, 40°C and 60°C, respectively. Match Column I with Column II.

	Column I (Temperature of the mixture when)		Column II
A.	*X* and *Y* are mixed	P.	40°C
B.	*X* and *Z* are mixed	Q.	52°C
C.	*Y* and *Z* are mixed	R.	33.3°C
D.	*X*, *Y* and *Z* all are mixed	S.	50°C

Choose the correct answer from the options given below:

(a) A → R, B → S, C → Q, D → P
(b) A → R, B → S, C → P, D → Q
(c) A → S, B → R, C → Q, D → P
(d) A → R, B → Q, C → S, D → P

18. A black body at 227°C radiates heat at the rate of 8 cal cm^{-2} s^{-1}. At the temperature of 527°C, the rate of heat radiated in the same unit will be

(a) $\frac{1}{8}\left(\frac{8}{5}\right)^4$ (b) $8\left(\frac{8}{5}\right)^4$ (c) $\left(\frac{8}{5}\right)^4$ (d) $8\left(\frac{5}{8}\right)^4$

19. 5 g ice at 0° C is mixed with 10 g steam at 100°C. The final temperature of the composition of the mixture is (For ice, $L_f = 80$ cal/g and for steam, $L_v = 54$ cal/g)

(a) 40°C (b) 60°C
(c) 50°C (d) 45°C

20. In the following figure, the distribution of energy density of the radiation emitted by a black body at a given temperature is shown. The possible temperature of the black body at $\lambda_m = 2.8\,\mu$m is (Take, $b = 2.8 \times 10^{-3}$ m-K)

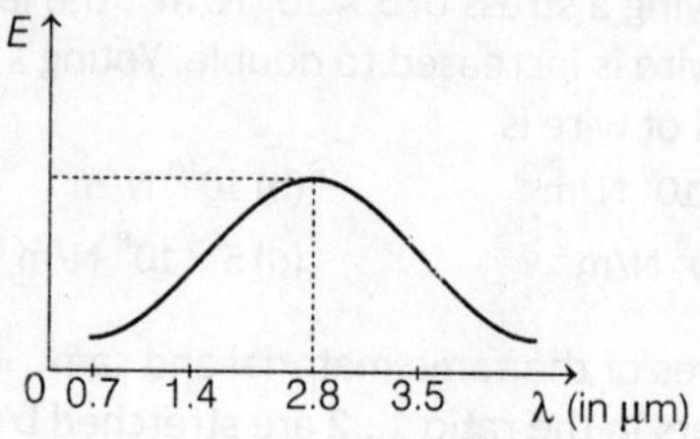

(a) 1000 K (b) 2000 K
(c) 500 K (d) 1500 K

21. Three identical rods are connected as shown below and one of end of each rod is kept at a constant temperature given below.

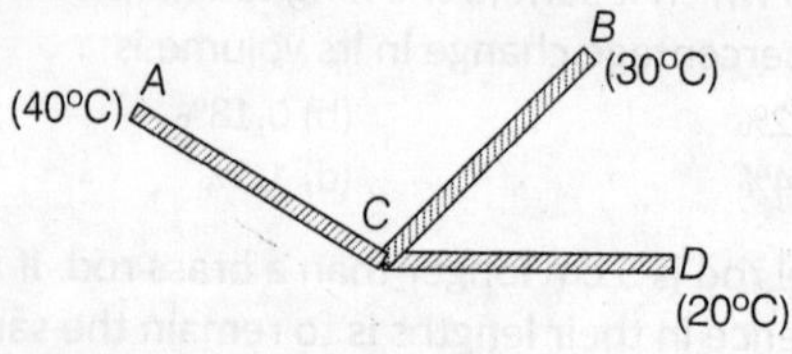

Now, choose correct statement.

(a) No heat flow between A and C.
(b) No heat flow between B and C.
(c) No heat flow between C and D.
(d) No heat flow between B and D.

22. The initial temperature of a body is 80°C. If its temperature falls to 64°C in 5 min and to 52°C in next 10 min, then the temperature of the surroundings will be

(a) 44.5°C
(b) 49.5°C
(c) 35.5°C
(d) 32.5°C

23. The ratio of energy radiated by two metallic spheres of radii *R* and 2*R*, which are at temperatures 2*T* and *T* respectively, is

(a) 1 : 1
(b) 2 : 1
(c) 9 : 1
(d) 4 : 1

24. Statement I A blue star is hotter than a red star.

Statement II Wavelength of emitted radiation is inversely proportional to temperature.

In light of above statements, choose the most appropriate answer from the options given below:
(a) Both Statement I and Statement II are incorrect.
(b) Statement I is correct and Statement II is not incorrect.
(c) Statement I is incorrect and Statement II is correct.
(d) Both Statement I and Statement II are correct.

25. Match entries of Column I with Column II.

Column I		Column II
A. Conduction in solids at low and moderate temperatures	P.	Phenon vibration
B. Conduction in solids at high temperatures	Q.	Drift of electrons
C. Conduction in gases	R.	Molecular collisions
D. Conduction in liquids		

Choose the correct answer from the options given below.
(a) A → P ; B → P ; C → Q ; D → R
(b) A → P ; B → R ; C → R ; D → Q
(c) A → Q ; B → Q ; C → P ; D → R
(d) A → P ; B → P,Q; C →R; D → Q,R

Answers

1 (c)	2 (d)	3 (b)	4 (b)	5 (c)
6 (b)	7 (c)	8 (b)	9 (c)	10 (b)
11 (c)	12 (b)	13 (b)	14 (d)	15 (b)
16 (a)	17 (a)	18 (b)	19 (a)	20 (a)
21 (b)	22 (b)	23 (d)	24 (d)	25 (d)

See detailed explanations on page no. 192

QUALIFIER 08

Thermodynamics

1. Assertion (A) Temperature of a system is directly proportional to kinetic energy of its particles.

Reason (R) Heat given to a matter sample is absorbed in form of kinetic energy only.

In the light of the above statements, choose the most appropriate answer from the options given below:
(a) Both A and R are true but R is not the correct explanation of A.
(b) A is true but R is false.
(c) A is false but R is true.
(d) Both A and R are true and R is the correct explanation of A.

2. If a system is in thermodynamic equilibrium with its surroundings, it means
(a) temperature of system and surroundings must be same
(b) pressure and volume of system and surroundings must be same
(c) pressure, volume and temperature of system and surroundings may be different
(d) None of the above

3. Statement I The extensive variables of thermodynamic state indicate the size of the system.

Statement II Pressure and temperature are intensive variables for a thermodynamic state.

In light of above statements choose the most appropriate answer from the options given below:
(a) Both Statement I and Statement II are incorrect.
(b) Statement I is correct and Statement II is incorrect.
(c) Statement I is incorrect and Statement II is correct.
(d) Both Statement I and Statement II are correct.

4. If the change in internal energy in a non-cyclic process of an ideal gas is zero, then process
(a) may be isobaric
(b) may be isochoric
(c) may be isothermal
(d) must be isothermal

5. The figures given below show different process for a given amount for an ideal gas. For which of the following processes, work done on a system is positive?

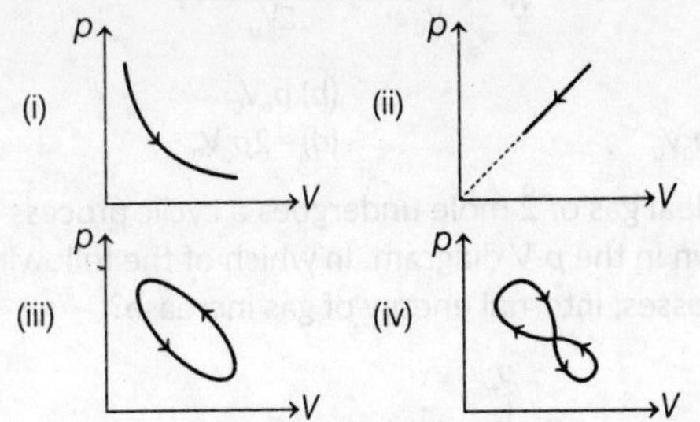

(a) only (iv) (b) only (iii) (c) (i), (ii), (iv) (d) (ii), (iv)

6. An ideal gas is allowed to expand keeping pressure constant. During this process,
(a) heat exchange from surroundings is zero
(b) internal energy of gas decreases
(c) work done by the gas is positive
(d) molar heat capacity is zero

7. Choose the correct statement.
(a) In adiabatic process, work is independent of path.
(b) In adiabatic expansion, temperature of gas remains constant.
(c) In adiabatic process, only two thermodynamic variables change and third variable remains same.
(d) All of the above are true

8. A closed system of an ideal gas is taken through a process in which the initial pressure and volume is equal to the final pressure and volume, then
(a) entropy of the system increases
(b) initial internal energy must be equal to the final internal energy
(c) work done by the system must be zero
(d) heat must be given to the system

9. An ideal gas has initial volume V and pressure p. If volume of the gas is doubled, then in which of the following processes work done will be minimum?
(a) Isothermal (b) Isobaric
(c) Adiabatic (d) Same in all given processes

10. A certain amount of heat energy is supplied to a diatomic ideal gas which expands at constant pressure. The fraction of heat energy converted into work is
(a) $\frac{2}{5}$ (b) $\frac{3}{5}$
(c) $\frac{5}{7}$ (d) $\frac{2}{7}$

11. p-V diagram of an ideal gas for a process ABC has been shown in the figure below. The change in internal energy of the gas during process ABC is

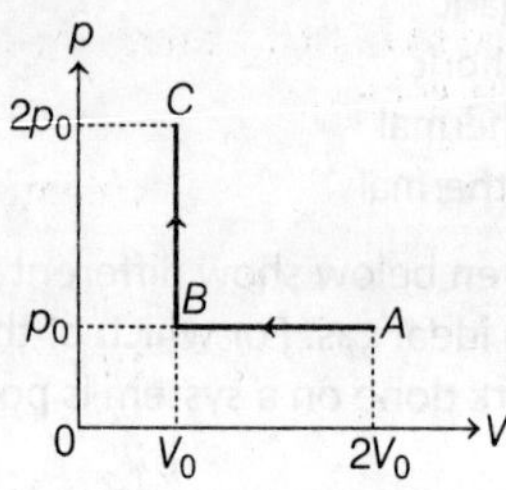

(a) 0 (b) p_0V_0
(c) $2p_0V_0$ (d) $-2p_0V_0$

12. An ideal gas of 2 mole undergoes a cyclic process as shown in the p-V diagram. In which of the following processes, internal energy of gas increase?

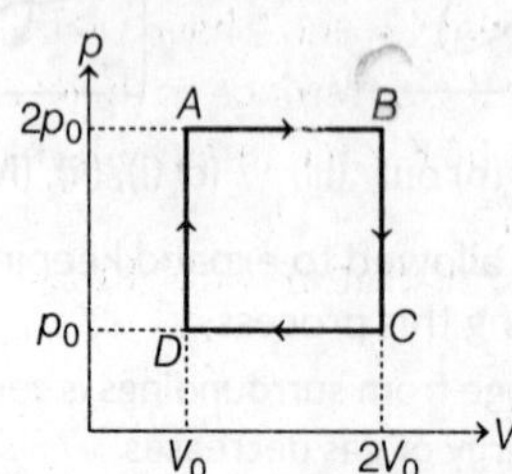

(a) AB and BC (b) AB and CD
(c) AB and DA (d) BC and DA

13. The graph for an ideal gas between p and V of a polytropic process pV^α = constant has been shown below. The value of α is

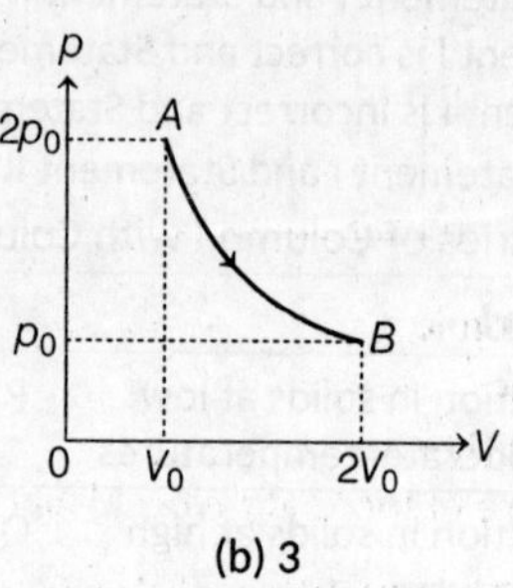

(a) 2 (b) 3
(c) 1 (d) 5

14. Temperature of a monoatomic gas is increased from T_0 to $2T_0$ in three different processes, i.e. isochoric, isobaric and adiabatic. If the heat given to the gas in these three processes are Q_1, Q_2 and Q_3 respectively, then which of the following is correct?
(a) $Q_3 > Q_1$ (b) $Q_1 > Q_2$
(c) $Q_2 > Q_3$ (d) All are correct

15. A gas undergoes an adiabatic process in which pressure becomes 8 times and volume becomes $\frac{3}{4}$ of initial volume. If initial absolute temperature is T, then final temperature is
(a) $\frac{3\sqrt{3}}{8}T$ (b) $6T$
(c) $\frac{\sqrt{3}}{2}T$ (d) $\frac{32}{3}T$

16. 2 mole of an ideal gas undergo from an initial state A to final state B *via* two different processes. If during first, it undergoes isothermal expansion from volume V_0 to $2V_0$ and then its volume is decreased from $2V_0$ to V_0 at constant pressure. The correct p-V diagram representing two processes is

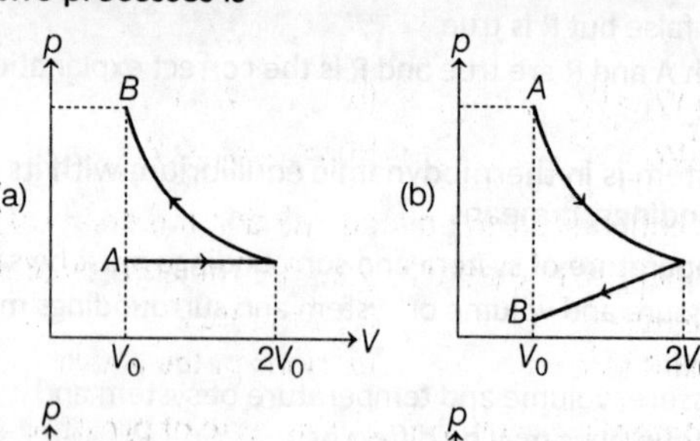

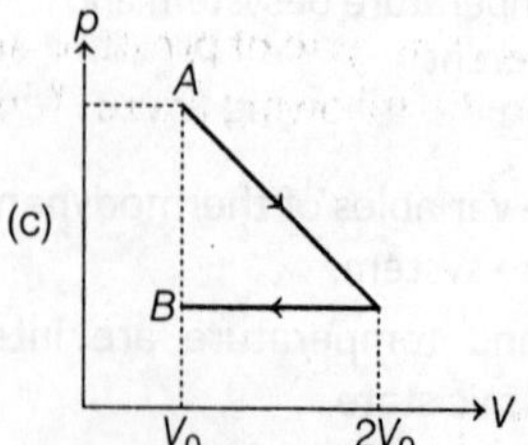

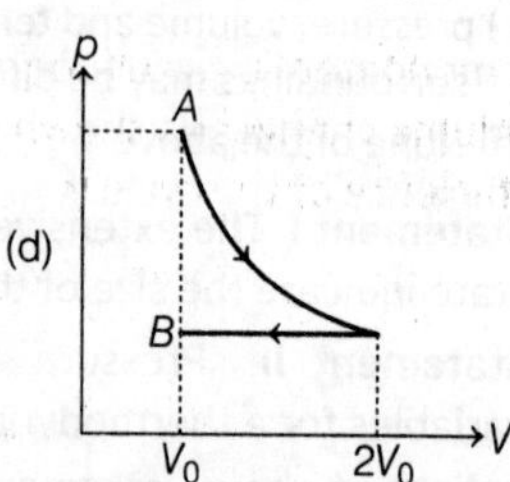

17. For an ideal gas, the graph between $\log T$ and $\log V$ for an adiabatic process has been shown in the following figure. The gas is (where, T and V are in the SI unit)

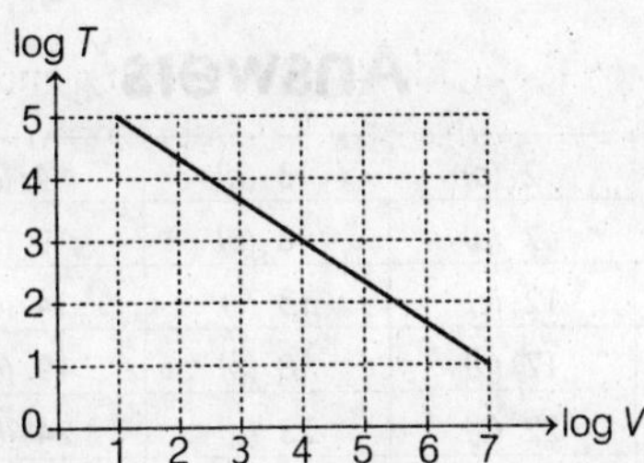

(a) monoatomic
(b) diatomic
(c) triatomic linear
(d) a mixture of monoatomic and diatomic

18. 1 mole of a monoatomic ideal gas is taken through process $pT =$ constant. On increasing temperature from T_0 to $2T_0$, the work done by gas is W_0. The work done by gas if temperature is increased further $2T_0$ to $3T_0$, is

(a) $\frac{2}{3}W_0$ (b) W_0 (c) $\frac{3}{2}W_0$ (d) $(\sqrt{3}-\sqrt{2})W_0$

19. The cyclic processes for 1 mole of an ideal gas on three different pV diagrams have been shown below. The work done are W_1, W_2 and W_3 respectively, then

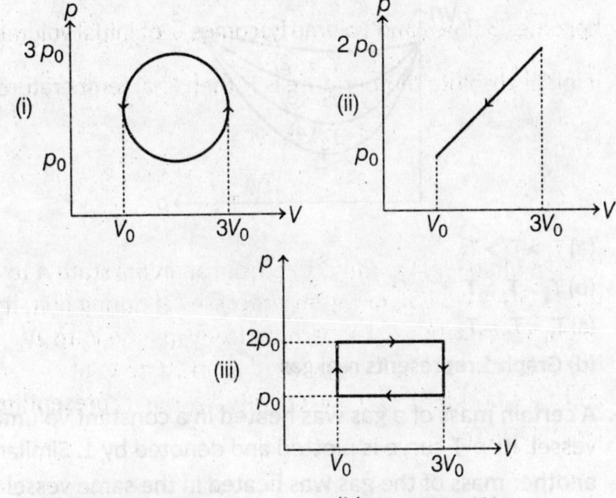

(a) $W_1 > W_2 > W_3$ (b) $W_2 > W_1 > W_3$
(c) $W_3 > W_2 > W_1$ (d) $W_2 > W_3 > W_1$

20. A gas is confined to an isolated cylinder. It is compressed adiabatically to one-third its volume. The entropy of the gas

(a) increases (b) decreases
(c) remains same (d) None of the above

21. A monoatomic gas undergoes the cycle of pressure and volume changes as shown in the following figure. The efficiency of the cycle is

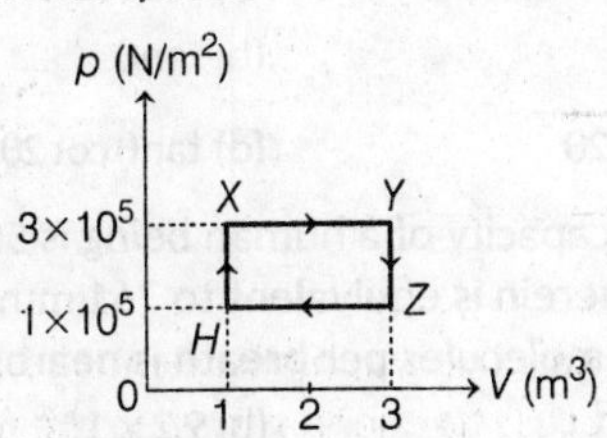

(a) 36.6% (b) 20%
(c) 22.2% (d) Data insufficient

22. Match process which undergoes by a gas listed in Column I with the value of specific heat listed in Column II.

	Column I (Process)		Column II (Specific heat)
A.	Gas is suddenly compressed in an insulated cylinder	P.	$C < 0$
B.	Gas is heated in a cylinder with a movable piston	Q.	$C > 0$
C.	Gas is expanded forcibly while heat is supplied	R.	$C = \infty$
		S.	$C = 0$

Choose the correct answer from the options given below

(a) A → S, B → R, C → P
(b) A → P, B → Q, C → R
(c) A → S, B → Q, C → P
(d) A → R, B → P, C → Q

23. A gas is subjected to three different processes. (All values are in SI unit).

Process	ΔQ	ΔW	ΔU
1.	35	− 15	Z
2.	− 15	Y	− 20
3.	X	− 20	20

Use above table to match Column I with the Column II (All values are in SI unit).

	Column I		Column II
A.	X	P.	5
B.	Y	Q.	50
C.	Z	R.	0

Choose the correct answer from the options given below:

(a) A → R, B → P, C → Q
(b) A → P, B → Q, C → R
(c) A → R, B → Q, C → P
(d) A → Q, B → R, C → P

24. Two carnot engines A and B have their efficiency in the ratio of 3 : 2. If the difference of their working temperature is 50 K, then temperatures of engines A and B respectively, are
(Assume sink temperature = 300 K)

(a) 400 K, 450 K
(b) 450 K, 400 K
(c) 150 K, 200 K
(d) 450K, 500 K

25. A refrigerator takes heat from water at 5°C and transfers it to room at 27°C. If 50 kg of water is converted into ice at 0°C, then work done by refrigerator is ($L_f = 3.4 \times 10^5$ J/kg, $s_w = 4.2 \times 10^3$ J/kg-°C)
(a) 1.24×10^6 J
(b) 1.32×10^6 J
(c) 1.8×10^7 J
(d) 1.24×10^7 J

Answers

1 (b)	2 (a)	3 (d)	4 (d)	5 (b)
6 (c)	7 (a)	8 (b)	9 (c)	10 (d)
11 (a)	12 (c)	13 (c)	14 (c)	15 (b)
16 (d)	17 (a)	18 (b)	19 (a)	20 (c)
21 (c)	22 (a)	23 (a)	24 (b)	25 (b)

See detailed explanations on page no. 194

QUALIFIER 09

Behaviour of Perfect Gas & Kinetic Theory

1. Match Column I with Column II for ideal gas and choose the correct answer from the options given below.

Column I	Column II
A. (graph)	P. Charles' law
B. (graph)	Q. Boyle's law
C. (graph)	R. Gay Lussac's law

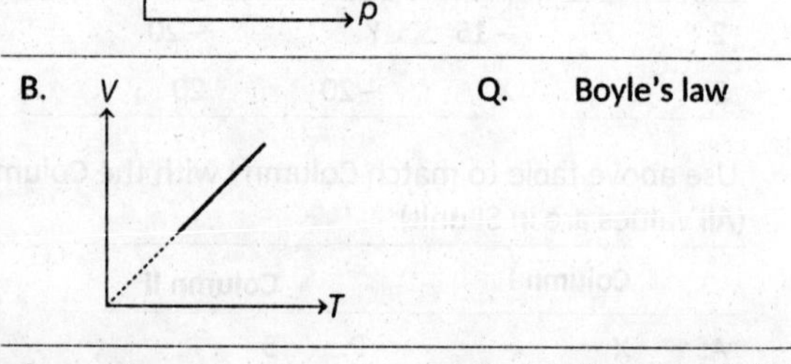

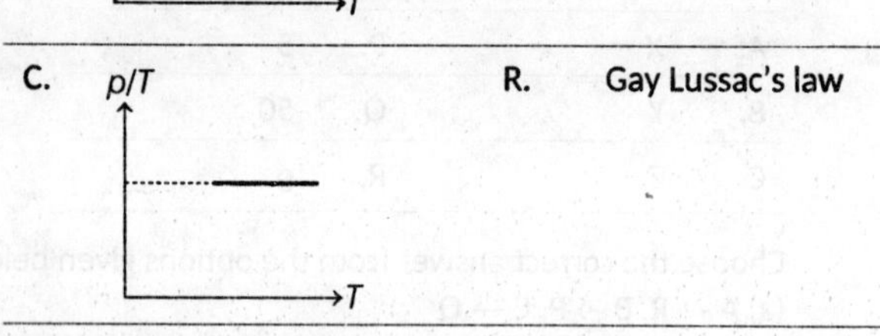

(a) A → R, B → P, C → Q
(b) A → P, B → R, C → Q
(c) A → Q, B → P, C → R
(d) A → R, B → Q, C → P

2. Two vessels separately contain two ideal gases *A* and *B* at the same temperature, the pressure of *A* being twice that of *B*. Under such conditions, the density of *A* is found to be 1.5 times the density of *B*. The ratio of molecular weight of *A* and *B* is
(a) $\frac{2}{3}$
(b) $\frac{3}{4}$
(c) 2
(d) $\frac{1}{2}$

3. The behaviour of real gases at different temperatures is shown in the figure given below. So,

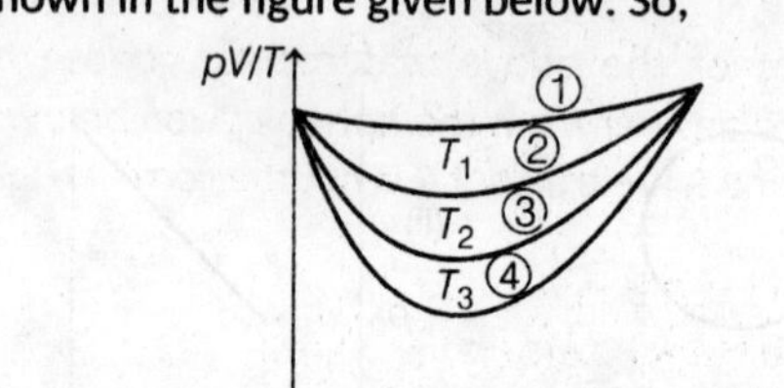

(a) $T_1 > T_2 > T_3$
(b) $T_3 > T_2 > T_1$
(c) $T_1 = T_2 = T_3$
(d) Graph 1 represents real gas

4. A certain mass of a gas was heated in a constant volume vessel. Its *p-T* curve is plotted and denoted by 1. Similarly, another mass of the gas was heated in the same vessel and its *p-T* curve is represented by 2. The ratio of masses of the gas in the two experiment is

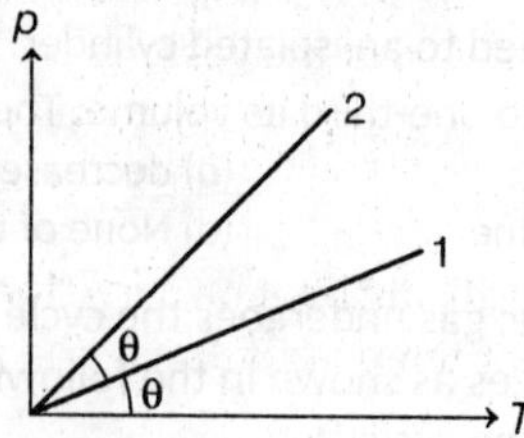

(a) $\frac{\sin\theta}{\cos 2\theta}$
(b) $\tan\theta$
(c) $\tan\theta \tan 2\theta$
(d) $\tan\theta \cot 2\theta$

5. If the lung capacity of a human being is 500 cm^3 and pressure therein is equivalent to 761 mm of Hg, then number of molecules per breath is nearby
(a) 1.2×10^{22}
(b) 9.2×10^{20}
(c) 9.2×10^{14}
(d) Need more information

6. A cylindrical vessel contains two non-reactive gases helium (monoatomic) and nitrogen (diatomic). The ratio of their partial pressure is 5 : 3. The ratio of number of molecules is

(a) 2 : 3 (b) 5 : 3
(c) 1 : 1 (d) 1 : 2

7. Statement I At constant temperature, the pressure of saturated vapour is independent of volume.

Statement II Unsaturated vapour obeys gas law, while saturated vapour does not.

In light of above statements, choose the most appropriate answer from the options given below:

(a) Both statement I and statement II are incorrect.
(b) Statement I is correct and statement II is incorrect.
(c) Statement I is incorrect and statement II is correct.
(d) Both statement I and statement II are correct.

8. Assertion (A) When temperature of a gas is increased 3 times, its pressure also increases 3 times.

Reason (R) Pressure of N-molecules of an ideal gas contained in a volume V is $p = \frac{2}{3}\frac{N}{V}\left(\frac{1}{2}m\bar{v}^2\right)$

In the light of the above statements, choose the most appropriate answer from the options given below:

(a) Both A and R are true but R is not the correct explanation of A.
(b) A is true but R is false.
(c) A is false but R is true.
(d) Both A and R are true and R is the correct explanation of A.

9. 1 kg of a diatomic gas is at a pressure of 8×10^4 Nm^{-2} and the density of the gas is 4 kgm^{-3}. What is the energy of the gas due to its thermal motion?

(a) 3×10^4 J (b) 5×10^4 J
(c) 6×10^4 J (d) 7×10^4 J

10. A cubical vessel contains 1 g molecule atoms of argon at a pressure of 2 atm and temperature 27°C. Assume that atoms are moving with rms velocity, then the number of collisions per unit area per second, which the molecules make with the wall of the vessel is

(a) 1.17×10^{-29} (b) 1.05×10^{29}
(c) 1.17×10^{29} (d) 3.7×10^{27}

11. Maxwell velocity distribution curve for a gas is given at three different temperatures. For the given curves,

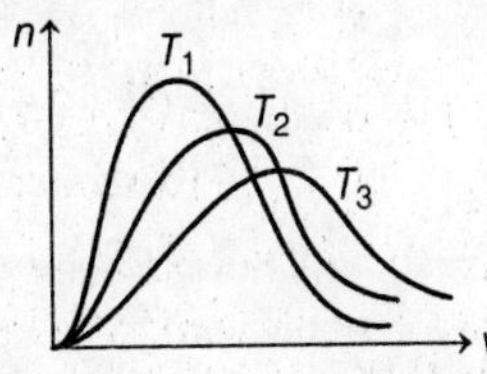

(a) $T_1 > T_2 > T_3$ (b) $T_3 > T_2 > T_1$
(c) $T_2 > T_1 > T_3$ (d) $T_3 > T_1 > T_2$

12. When atomicity of gases increases, then

(a) C_p, C_V and γ increase
(b) C_p, C_V increase but γ remains constant
(c) C_p, C_V remain constant but γ decreases
(d) C_p, C_V increase but γ decreases

13. A cylinder of fixed capacity of 67.2 L helium gas is at standard temperature and pressure. The amount of heat required to raise the temperature of the gas in the cylinder by 30°C, will be (Take, $R = 8.31$ J mol^{-1} K^{-1})

(a) 374 J (b) 1121.85 J (c) 247 J (d) 474 J

14. For gas CO, the ratio of molar specific heat capacities $\frac{C_p}{C_V}$ can be

(a) 1.33 (b) 1.40
(c) 1.29 (d) Data insufficient

15. For a given gas at 1 atm pressure, rms speed of the molecules is 200 m/s at 127°C. At 2 atm pressure and at 227°C temperature, the rms speed of the molecules will be

(a) $100\sqrt{5}$ m/s (b) 80 m/s
(c) 100 m/s (d) $80\sqrt{5}$ m/s

16. The mean free path for a gas molecule with average speed 74 m/s at STP is (radius of molecule, $r = 10^{-10}$ m and number of molecules per unit volume is 2.7×10^{25} m^{-3})

(a) 3.5×10^{-7} m (b) 4×10^{-7} m
(c) 2.05×10^{-7} m (d) 5×10^{-7} m

17. For constant volume, the correct variation of free mean path of a molecule is

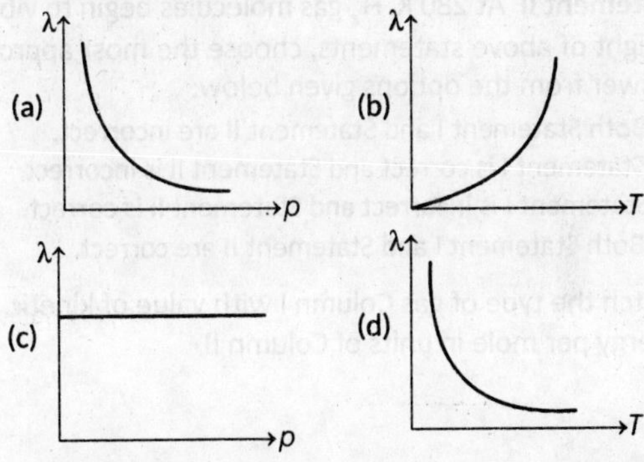

18. Which one of the following graphs shows the correct variation of heat capacity (C) with temperature (T) of solids?

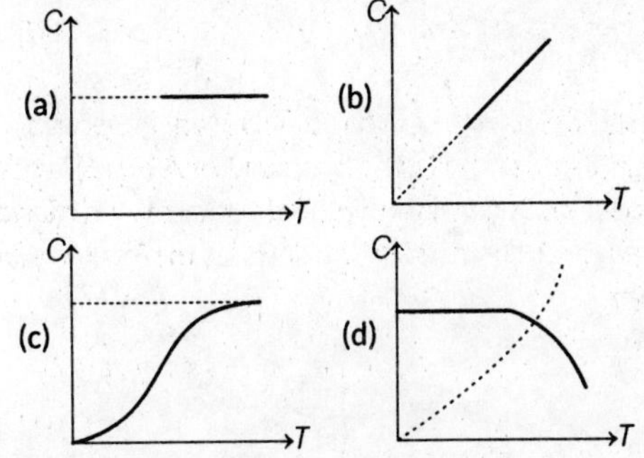

19. For an ideal diatomic gas at room temperature T, the ratio of translational kinetic energy to potential energy is
(a) 3 : 5
(b) 3 : 2
(c) 3 : 5
(d) None of these

20. The specific heat of an unknown monoatomic gas X at constant volume is 0.15 kcal kg^{-1}-K^{-1}. The atomic weight of gas X is
(a) 40 g/mol
(b) 20 g/mol
(c) 33.3 g/mol
(d) 26.6 g/mol

21. The specific heats, C_p and C_V of a gas of diatomic molecules A, are given (in units of J mol^{-1} K^{-1}) by 29 and 22, respectively. Another gas of diatomic molecules B, has the corresponding values 30 and 21. If they are treated as ideal gases, then
(a) A has a vibrational mode but B has none
(b) both A and B have a vibrational mode each
(c) A has one vibrational mode and B has two
(d) A is rigid but B has a vibrational mode

22. **Statement I** Below 50 K temperature for H_2 gas, value of specific heat (C_V) is $\frac{3}{2}R$ and above 250 K, its value of specific heat (C_V) becomes $\frac{5}{2}R$.

Statement II At 280 K, H_2 gas molecules begin to vibrate.
In light of above statements, choose the most appropriate answer from the options given below:
(a) Both Statement I and Statement II are incorrect.
(b) Statement I is correct and Statement II is incorrect.
(c) Statement I is incorrect and Statement II is correct.
(d) Both Statement I and Statement II are correct.

23. Match the type of gas Column I with value of kinetic energy per mole in units of Column II.

	Column I		Column II
A.	Monoatomic	P.	3.5 RT
B.	Diatomic	Q.	3 RT
C.	Triatomic non-linear	R.	2.5 RT
D.	Triatomic linear	S.	1.5 RT

Choose the correct answer from the options given below:
(a) $A \to P$, $B \to Q$, $C \to R$, $D \to S$
(b) $A \to P$, $B \to Q$, $C \to S$, $D \to R$
(c) $A \to S$, $B \to R$, $C \to Q$, $D \to P$
(d) $A \to S$, $B \to R$, $C \to P$, $D \to Q$

24. Consider a sample of gas that contains only 12 molecules with speeds (in cms^{-1}), 6, 2, 4, 6, 6, 4, 1, 8, 5, 3, 7 and 8, respectively. This sample is contained in a box of size 1 cm × 1 cm × 1 cm. The ratio of rms to mean speed of molecules is
(a) 2.05 (b) 1.09
(c) 1.54 (d) 2.05

25. If the pressure of CO_2 gas (real gas) in a container is $p = \frac{RT}{\frac{V}{2} - b} - \frac{a}{4b^2}$, where a and b have positive values, then mass of the gas in container is
(a) 11 g (b) 22 g
(c) 44 g (d) 88 g

Answers

1 (c)	2 (b)	3 (a)	4 (c)	5 (a)
6 (b)	7 (d)	8 (a)	9 (b)	10 (d)
11 (d)	12 (d)	13 (b)	14 (b)	15 (a)
16 (c)	17 (c)	18 (c)	19 (d)	20 (b)
21 (a)	22 (b)	23 (c)	24 (b)	25 (b)

See detailed explanations on page no. 198

QUALIFIER 10

Oscillations and Waves

1. **Assertion (A)** If displacement of particle is $x = A\sin(\omega t + \phi)$, then force on particle is $F = -m\omega^2 A \cdot \sin(\omega t + \phi)$.

Reason (R) Force on a particle executing simple harmonic motion is periodic in nature.

In the light of the above statements, choose the most appropriate answer from the options given below:

(a) Both A and R are true but R is not the correct explanation of A.
(b) A is true but R is false.
(c) A is false but R is true.
(d) Both A and R are true and R is the correct explanation of A.

2. For a particle executing simple harmonic motion, its displacement equation is $x = (\sin\omega t - \cos\omega t)$, then the initial phase and amplitude of the particle respectively, are

(a) zero, 1 m (b) $\frac{\pi}{4}, \sqrt{2}$ m (c) $-\frac{\pi}{4}, \sqrt{2}$ m (d) $\frac{\pi}{2}, \sqrt{2}$ m

3. A block is attached to a spring and executing simple harmonic motion with amplitude A on smooth horizontal surface. At what value of x, average potential energy and average kinetic energy are equal for one time period?

(a) $\frac{A}{2}$ (b) $\frac{A}{\sqrt{2}}$
(c) At all values of x (d) for no value of x

4. The bob of a pendulum having relative density 4 is made to oscillate in a non-viscous fluid of relative density 2. If the length of simple pendulum is 1 m, then time period for small oscillations is nearly (Take, $g = 9.8\,m/s^2$)

(a) 2.83 s (b) 1.41 s (c) 2 s (d) 1.72 s

5. Five massless springs of equal force constant k are connected as shown in the figure. The period of SHM of the block is

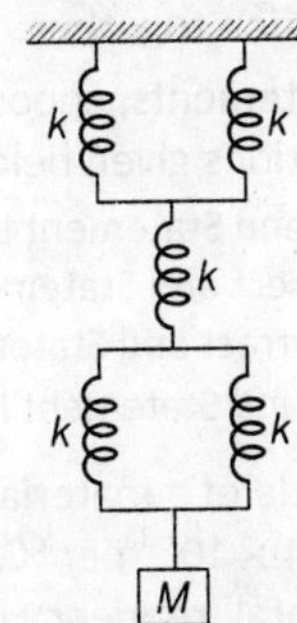

(a) $\sqrt{2}\,\pi\sqrt{\frac{M}{k}}$ (b) $2\sqrt{2}\,\pi\sqrt{\frac{M}{k}}$ (c) $2\pi\sqrt{\frac{M}{2k}}$ (d) $2\pi\sqrt{\frac{3M}{2k}}$

6. Time period of a spring-block system is T_0. Now, the spring is cut into two parts in the ratio 3 : 5. The time period of same block with the smaller part of the spring is

(a) $\sqrt{\frac{3}{5}}T_0$ (b) $\sqrt{\frac{5}{3}}T_0$ (c) $\sqrt{\frac{3}{8}}T_0$ (d) $\sqrt{\frac{8}{3}}T_0$

7. A block executes SHM of time period 2 s and amplitude 8 cm. The time taken by it to travel 3 cm from negative extremity of oscillation is

$\left[\text{Use } \sin^{-1}\left(\frac{5}{8}\right) = 0.435,\ \cos^{-1}\left(\frac{5}{8}\right) = 0.9\right]$

(a) 0.467 s (b) 0.534 s
(c) 0.286 s (d) 0.7 s

8. A man of mass 60 kg is standing on a platform executing SHM in the vertical plane. The displacement from the mean position varies as $y = 5\sin\omega t$ metre. The maximum value of ω, for which man always keep in touch with platform is nearly

(a) 1.4 rad/s (b) 0.14 rad/s
(c) 14 rad/s (d) 1.96 rad/s

9. A block of mass 2.5 kg attached to a spring of stiffness 100 N/m is executing SHM with an amplitude of 100 cm. When the block is passing through its mean position, a piece of mass 0.5 kg from block gets detached from it and immediately come to rest. However, the other part continues SHM, then its maximum velocity is

(a) 7.9 m/s (b) 2.5 m/s
(c) 0.632 m/s (d) 6.32 m/s

10. The displacement equation of a particle performing SHM along X-axis is $x(t) = 20\sin\frac{\pi}{3}(15t + 0.5)$ cm and the displacement of another particle performing SHM along Y-axis is $y(t) = 8\,[\sin 10\pi t + 0.75\cos 10\pi t]$ cm. The ratio of their amplitudes and time periods are respectively.

(a) $\frac{A_x}{A_y} = \frac{2}{1}, \frac{T_x}{T_y} = \frac{2}{1}$ (b) $\frac{A_x}{A_y} = 1, \frac{T_x}{T_y} = 2$
(c) $\frac{A_x}{A_y} = 2, \frac{T_x}{T_y} = 1$ (d) $\frac{A_x}{A_y} = 1, \frac{T_x}{T_y} = 1$

11. Potential energy of a particle in SHM along X-axis is given by $U = 4 + (x - 1)^2$ J, here U is in joule and x is in metre. If the mass of particle is 2 kg and total mechanical energy is 20 J, then amplitude of oscillation is

(a) 2 m (b) 4 m
(c) $2\sqrt{3}$ m (d) $4\sqrt{5}$ m

12. Four oscillating systems are shown in Column I and their small oscillation's time period is given in Column II. Match the following columns correctly. (Symbols have their usual meaning.)

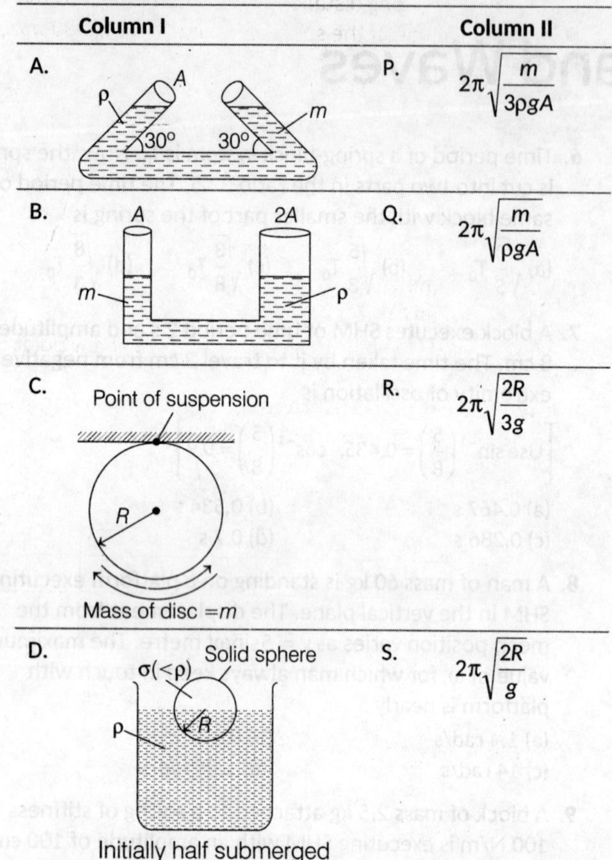

Choose the correct answer from the options given below:

(a) A → Q, B → P, C → R, D → S

(b) A → Q, B → P, C → S, D → R

(c) A → P, B → Q, C → R, D → S

(d) A → P, C → Q, C → S, D → R

13. The displacement-time wave function of a wave pulse is given as $y = \frac{20}{3 + (x + 2t)^2}$, where x is in metre and t in second, then

(a) wave pulse is travelling along positive x-direction

(b) propagating speed of wave pulse is 2 cm/s

(c) the amplitude of pulse is $\frac{20}{3}$ m

(d) All are correct

14. Equation of a transverse wave travelling along a rope is given by $y = 10\sin(At - Bx)$, where x and y are expressed in cm and time in seconds. If maximum velocity of the particle and wave velocity are 40 cm/s and 2m/s, respectively, then value of A and B respectively are

(a) $4\ s^{-1}$, 2 m/s (b) 20 cm/s, $4\ s^{-1}$

(c) $400\ s^{-1}$, 2 m/s (d) $4\ s^{-1}$, 0.2 m/s

15. The displacement equation of a travelling wave is as follows $y = 4\cos 2\pi(5t - 0.0040x + 0.25)$, where x and y are in cm and t in seconds. The phase difference between oscillatory motion of two points separated by a distance of 2m is

(a) $16\pi \times 10^{-3}$ rad (b) 1.6π rad

(c) 1.6×10^{-3} rad (d) $1.6\pi \times 10^{-3}$ rad

16. The transverse displacement of a string (clamped at its both ends) is given by $y = 0.04 \sin\left(\frac{\pi}{3}x\right)\cos(60\pi t)$, where x and y are in metres and t is in seconds. If the length of the string is 2.0 m and its mass is 2×10^{-2} kg, then tension in the string is

(a) 648 N (b) 324 N

(c) 216 N (d) 162 N

17. A steel rod 200 cm long is clamped at its middle. The fundamental frequency of longitudinal vibrations of the rod is given as 2 kHz, the speed of sound in steel is

(a) 800 km/s (b) 400 km/s

(c) 4 km/s (d) 8 km/s

18. A pipe, 20 cm long, is open at both ends. Then, which harmonic mode of the pipe resonates at 1650 Hz ? (Speed of sound in air is 330 m/s.)

(a) Third harmonic (b) First harmonic

(c) Fourth harmonic (d) Second harmonic

19. Two sound waves of wavelengths 4 m and 4.5 m produce 9 beats/s, the speed of sound is

(a) 324 m/s (b) 0.25 m/s

(c) 4.5 m/s (d) 85.5 m/s

20. The air columns in two identical pipes vibrate at frequency of 300 Hz. The percentage of change needed in the length of one of the pipes to produce 3 beats/s is

(a) 1% (b) 2%

(c) 3% (d) 4%

21. Consider the following statements.

Statement I Velocity of particles, while crossing mean position in case of stationary waves varies from maximum at anti-nodes to zero at nodes.

Statement II All particles between two successive nodes cross the mean position together.

In light of above statements, choose the most appropriate answer from the options given below:

(a) Both Statement I and Statement II are incorrect.

(b) Statement I is correct and Statement II is incorrect.

(c) Statement I is incorrect and Statement II is correct.

(d) Both Statement I and Statement II are correct.

22. An organ pipe is made of a material which has coefficient of linear expansion 4×10^{-3} per °C. The temperature at which the fundamental frequency of an organ pipe is independent of small variation in the temperature, is

(a) 125 K (b) 125°C (c) 62.5°C (d) 250°C

23. Consider a source *S* and an observer O on a straight line.

Let source is emitting a sound of frequency 500 Hz.

Given, speed of source is $v_s = 30$ m/s, speed of observer = 30 m/s and speed of sound is 330 m/s.

Now, match entries of Column I with the change in frequency values given in Column II.

	Column I		Column II
A.	Source is moving away from observer, while observer is at rest.	P.	100 Hz
B.	Source and observer both are moving towards each other.	Q.	83 Hz
C.	Source and observer both are moving away from each other.	R.	42 Hz

Choose the correct answer from the options given below:

(a) A → R, B → Q, C → P
(b) A → R, B → P, C → Q
(c) A → P, B → Q, C → R
(d) A → Q, B → R, C → P

24. A stationary source of sound emitting a certain frequency that appears 540 Hz, when the observer is approaching the source with speed 25 m/s and when the observer recedes from the source, then observed frequency is 420 Hz. The frequency of source is

(a) 500 Hz
(b) 475 Hz
(c) 509.1 Hz
(d) 480 Hz

25. A source of sound with frequency 400 Hz rotates in a circle of radius 3 m at a linear speed of 20 m/s. An observer is standing at a long distance away, with respect to the centre of circle. If the speed of sound in air is 330 m/s, then

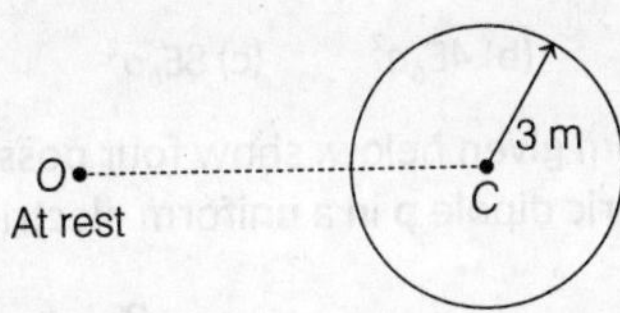

(a) Minimum frequency observed by observer is 377.1 Hz
(b) Maximum frequency observed by observer is 488.9 Hz
(c) Observed frequency can never be equal at any point on circle
(d) If radius of circle is increased, then minimum frequency decreases and maximum frequency increases

Answers

1 *(a)*	2 *(c)*	3 *(c)*	4 *(a)*	5 *(b)*
6 *(c)*	7 *(c)*	8 *(a)*	9 *(a)*	10 *(a)*
11 *(b)*	12 *(b)*	13 *(c)*	14 *(a)*	15 *(b)*
16 *(b)*	17 *(d)*	18 *(d)*	19 *(a)*	20 *(a)*
21 *(d)*	22 *(b)*	23 *(b)*	24 *(d)*	25 *(a)*

See detailed explanations on page no. 200

QUALIFIER 11

Electrostatics

1. The magnitude of electrostatic force between two point charges in air is 100 N. If a medium of dielectric constant *K* is filled between them, then net electrostatic force is reduced by 20 N. The value of dielectric constant is

(a) 1.2
(b) 1.25
(c) 5
(d) 4

2. The electric field due to an electric dipole *r* distance away along the axis is **E**. The electric field at distance 2*r* along the perpendicular bisector is

(a) $\frac{-\mathbf{E}}{4}$
(b) $\frac{\mathbf{E}}{4}$
(c) $\frac{\mathbf{E}}{8}$
(d) $\frac{\mathbf{E}}{16}$

3. Two statements are given below.

Statement I Gauss' law is true for any closed surface, irrespective of its shape and size.

Statement II Gauss' law is based on the inverse square dependence on distance contained in the Coulomb's law.

In light of above statements choose the most appropriate answer from the options given below :

(a) Both Statement I and Statement II are incorrect.
(b) Statement I is correct and Statement II is incorrect.
(c) Statement I is incorrect and Statement II is correct.
(d) Both Statement I and Statement II are correct.

4. A cube is placed in an electric field, $\mathbf{E} = \frac{E_0 x}{a}\hat{\mathbf{i}}$. The electric flux passing through the shaded surface of a cube is

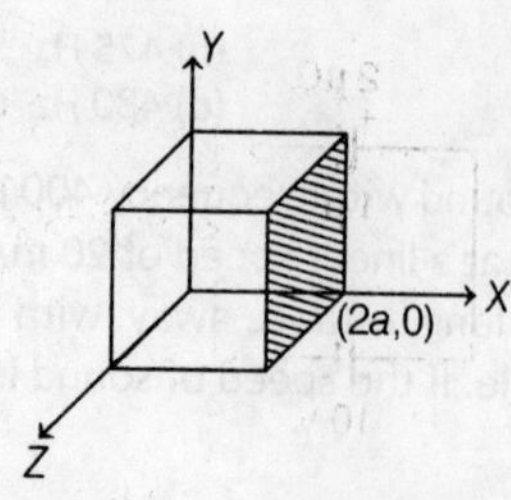

(a) $2E_0a^2$ (b) $4E_0a^2$ (c) $8E_0a^2$ (d) zero

5. The diagram given below, show four possible orientations of an electric dipole **p** in a uniform electric field **E**.

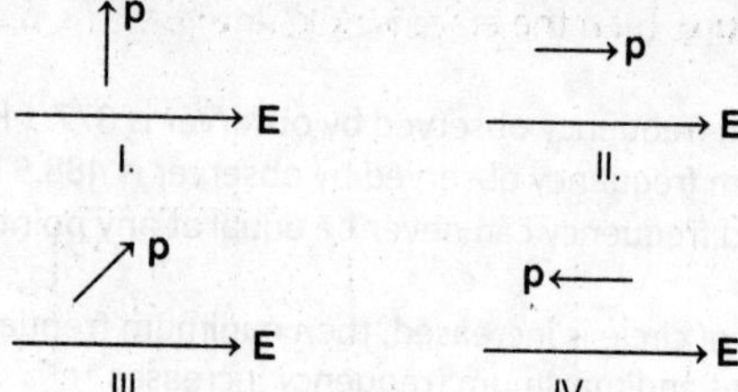

The correct order of magnitude of torque on the dipole, is

(a) $\tau_{IV} > \tau_I > \tau_{III} > \tau_{II}$ (b) $\tau_I > \tau_{III} > \tau_{IV} > \tau_{II}$
(c) $\tau_I > \tau_{III} > \tau_{II} = \tau_{IV}$ (d) $\tau_{II} > \tau_{III} > \tau_I > \tau_{IV}$

6. The variation of electric field due to a uniformly charged insulating sphere having volume charge density ρ and radius R at distance r from centre has been shown below. The value of ρ is

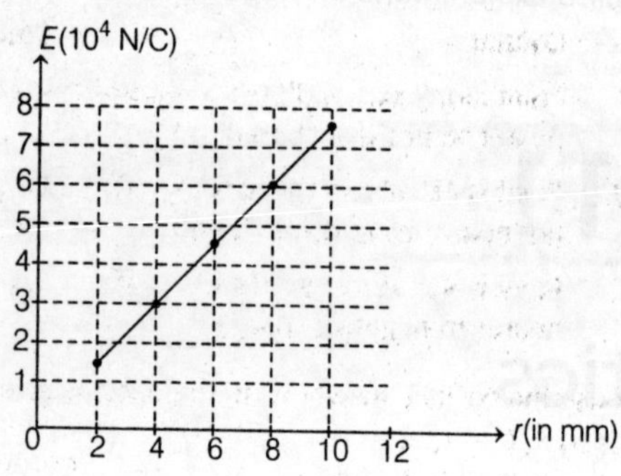

(a) 3.54×10^{-18} C / m³ (b) 18×10^{-18} C / m³
(c) 2×10^{-4} C / m³ (d) 2×10^{-6} C / m³

7. An electric dipole of length l has been placed in a uniform electric field E making an angle θ as shown in the following figure. The potential energy of the system is

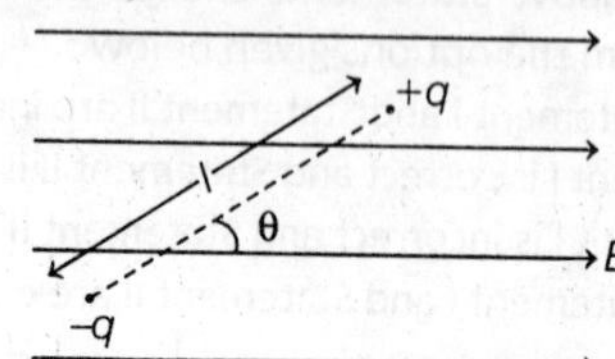

(a) $-pE\cos\theta$ (b) $-pE\sin\theta$
(c) $+pE\cos\theta$ (d) $-pE\cos\theta - \frac{kq^2}{l}$

8. An electric dipole of dipole moment **p** is placed in its stable equilibrium position in uniform electric field **E**, the work done in rotating it to its unstable equilibrium position very slowly

(a) zero (b) pE
(c) $2pE$ (d) $-2pE$

9. Two infinite long conducting charged sheets are placed parallel to each other and perpendicular to the plane of paper as shown in the following figure. The electric field at point P will

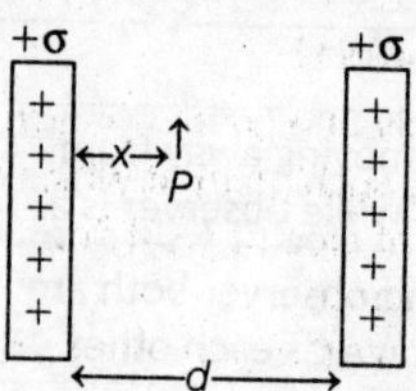

(a) depend only on x and σ (b) depend on x, σ, and d
(c) depend only on σ (d) not depend on x, σ and d

10. A pendulum bob of mass m carrying a charge q is at rest with its string making an angle θ with the vertical in a uniform horizontal electric field. The electric field is directly proportional to

(a) $\sin\theta$ (b) $\cos\theta$ (c) $\tan\theta$ (d) $\cot\theta$

11. Few drops of same size are charged to a potential of 1 V each. If they coalesce to form a single drop, its potential becomes 100 V. Required number of drops is

(a) 10 (b) 100 (c) 1000 (d) $100\sqrt{10}$

12. Two point charges 9 μC and 16 μC are placed 1 m apart in vacuum. The electric potential between the two charges is minimum at a distance of

(a) $\frac{2}{7}$ m from 9 μC

(b) $\frac{3}{7}$ m from 9 μC

(c) $\frac{4}{7}$ m from 9 μC

(d) minimum potential point doesn't exist.

13. Consider two concentric conducting shells. The potential of outer shell is 20 V and that of inner shell is 30 V. If the outer shell is grounded, the potential of inner shell is

(a) 50 V (b) 30 V (c) 20 V (d) 10 V

14. A charge of 8 μC experiences a force 480 dyne, when placed in a uniform electric field. The potential difference between two points separated by a distance of 3.2 cm along the electric field lines is

(a) 1.86 V (b) 18.6 V (c) 186 V (d) 0 V

15. Assertion (A) Force between plates of a parallel plate capacitor is, $F = \frac{1}{2}\left(\frac{Q^2}{\varepsilon_0 A}\right)$

Reason (R) Force is given by $F = Q \cdot E$

In the light of the above statements, choose the most appropriate answer from the options given below:

(a) Both A and R are true but R is not the correct explanation of A.
(b) A is true but R is false.
(c) A is false but R is true.
(d) Both A and R are true and R is the correct explanation of A.

16. The potential function of an electrostatic field is given by $V = 3x^2 + (y^3 - 1)$. Then, which of the following statements is correct?

(a) There exist only one point at which potential is zero.
(b) There exist no such point at which electric field is zero.
(c) The direction of electric field does not change through out the points of space.
(d) The charge $2\sqrt{2}\ \mu C$ experiences a force of $24\ \mu N$ at point $(1\text{ m}, \sqrt{2}\text{ m})$.

17. Three capacitors of capacitance C_1, C_2 and C_3 are connected in series with a battery of emf E as shown below. The graph of electric potential V from point X to point Y has been also shown in figure. The correct relation is

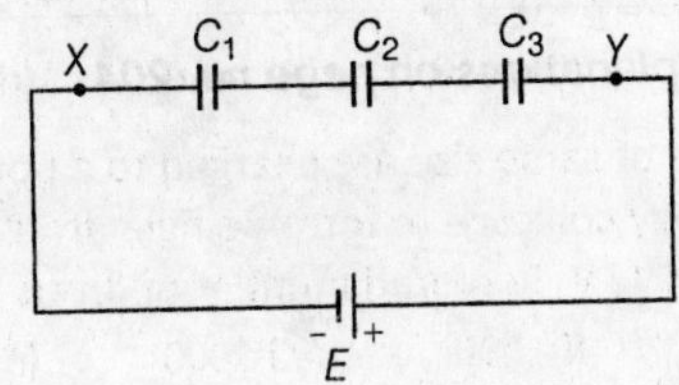

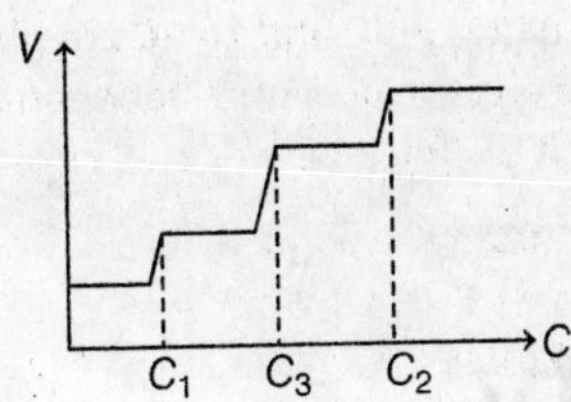

(a) $C_1 > C_2 > C_3$
(b) $C_2 > C_3 > C_1$
(c) $C_3 > C_2 > C_1$
(d) $C_1 > C_3 > C_2$

18. The charge on surface A, as shown in figure, is

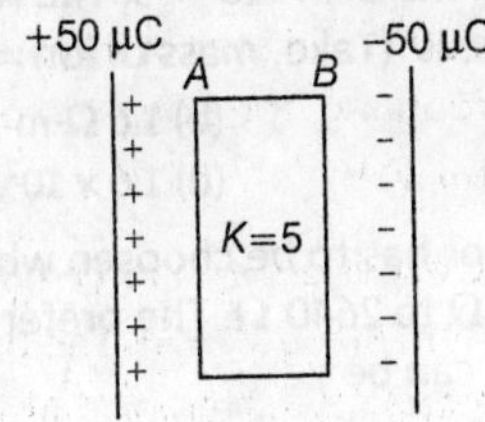

(a) $-50\ \mu C$
(b) $-10\ \mu C$
(c) $-40\ \mu C$
(d) depends on thickness of dielectric slab

19. A capacitor of capacitance $1\ \mu F$ initially, has charge $2\ \mu C$. It is connected to a battery of emf 10 V as shown in figure. The work done by battery is

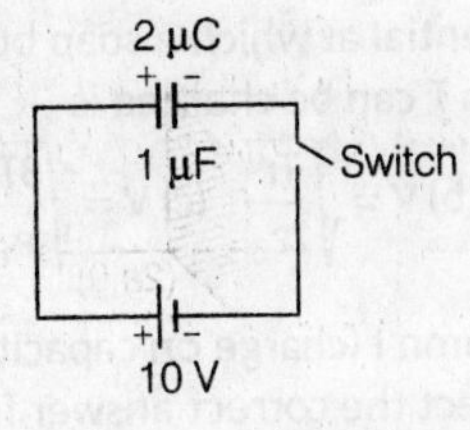

(a) $20\ \mu J$
(b) $30\ \mu J$
(c) $40\ \mu J$
(d) $80\ \mu J$

20. If a block of mass M is required to keep the right side charged plate of parallel plate capacitor stationary as shown in figure, then the electric field between the plates is

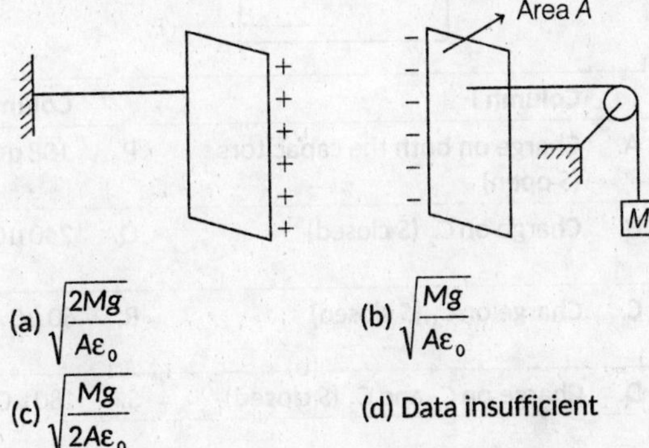

(a) $\sqrt{\dfrac{2Mg}{A\varepsilon_0}}$
(b) $\sqrt{\dfrac{Mg}{A\varepsilon_0}}$
(c) $\sqrt{\dfrac{Mg}{2A\varepsilon_0}}$
(d) Data insufficient

21. A point P lies at a distance of 4.1×10^{-9} m from the centre of a dipole of dipole moment 4.8×10^{-30} Cm. Match items of Column I with the items of Column II.

	Column I		Column II
A.	Point along axis of dipole nearer to positive charge	P.	-1.8×10^{-3} V
B.	Point is 45° above the axis but nearer to positive charge	Q.	1.8×10^{-3} V
C.	Point is 45° above axis but nearer to negative charge	R.	2.6×10^{-3} V

Choose the correct answer from the options given below:

(a) A → R, B → Q, C → P
(b) A → P, B → Q, C → R
(c) A → R, B → P, C → Q
(d) A → Q, B → P, C → R

22. A small dipole (dipole moment **p**) is placed at a distance x $(x > r)$ from a charged sphere having a charge Q and of radius r.

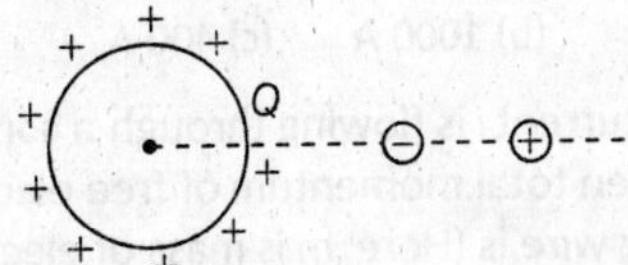

Force on the dipole is $(K = 1/4\pi\varepsilon_0)$

(a) $\dfrac{2KQp}{x^3}$
(b) $\dfrac{KQp}{x^3}$
(c) $\dfrac{4KQp}{3x^3}$
(d) $\dfrac{KQp}{2x^3}$

23. Maximum potential at which a soap bubble of radius r and surface tension T can be charged is

(a) $V = \sqrt{\frac{8Tr}{\varepsilon_0}}$ (b) $V = \sqrt{\frac{Tr}{2\varepsilon_0}}$ (c) $V = \sqrt{\frac{3Tr}{\varepsilon_0}}$ (d) $V = \sqrt{\frac{2Tr}{3\varepsilon_0}}$

24. Match the Column I (charge on capacitor) with Column II (value) and select the correct answer from the codes given below.

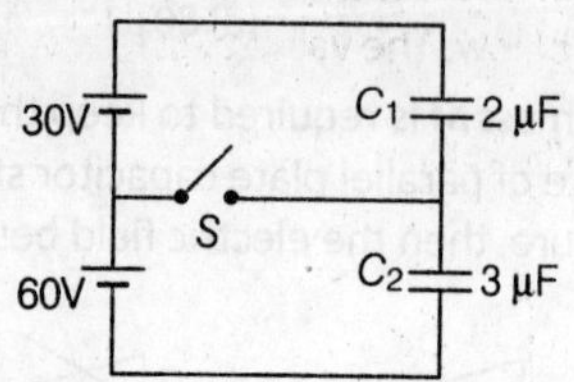

	Column I		Column II
A.	Charge on both the capacitors (S open)	P.	108 µC
B.	Charge on C_2 (S closed)	Q.	240 µC
C.	Charge on C_1 (S closed)	R.	60 µC
D.	Charge on C_1 and C_2 (S closed)	S.	180 µC

Choose the correct answer from the options given below:

(a) A→P, B→Q, C→R, D→S
(b) A→S, B→R, C→Q, D→P
(c) A→P, B→S, C→R, D→Q
(d) A→P, B→R, C→Q, D→S

25. A parallel plate capacitor plate area A, distance between plates d is filled with a dielectric ($K = 3$) slab of thickness t, ($t < d$). If energy stored in dielectric is half of energy stored in capacitor, then t will be

(a) $\frac{d}{4}$ (b) $\frac{d}{2}$
(c) $\frac{3d}{4}$ (d) $\frac{4d}{5}$

Answers

1 (b)	2 (d)	3 (d)	4 (c)	5 (c)
6 (c)	7 (d)	8 (c)	9 (d)	10 (c)
11 (c)	12 (b)	13 (d)	14 (b)	15 (b)
16 (d)	17 (d)	18 (c)	19 (d)	20 (a)
21 (a)	22 (a)	23 (a)	24 (c)	25 (c)

See detailed explanations on page no. 204

QUALIFIER 12

Current Electricity

1. The relaxation time for collision of electron with ions in a conducting wire is 16.2×10^{-12}s. The mobility of electron inside the conductor is

(a) $4.82\ m^2V^{-1}s^{-1}$ (b) $2.84\ m^2V^{-1}s^{-1}$
(c) $2.84 \times 10^{-2}\ m^2V^{-1}s^{-1}$ (d) $56.8\ m^2V^{-1}s^{-1}$

2. A current through a wire varies with time as $I = 100 + 8t$, where t is in second and I is in ampere. The average value of current across the wire in first 10 s is

(a) 140 A (b) 1000 A (c) 400 A (d) 1400 A

3. If electric current i is flowing through a conducting wire of length l, then total momentum of free electrons in conducting wire is (Here, m is mass of electron, e is charge on electron)

(a) $\frac{mil^2}{2e}$ (b) $\frac{mil}{e}$
(c) $\frac{mil}{2e}$ (d) $\frac{mi^2l^2}{e}$

4. A conducting wire has an electron density of $8 \times 10^{22}\ m^{-3}$. The average time interval between successive collision of electrons with ions is 4×10^{-11} s. The resistivity of the conducting wire is (Take, mass of ion $= 2.56 \times 10^{-26}$ kg)

(a) 3.2 Ω-m (b) 1.6 Ω-m
(c) 3.2×10^2 Ω-m (d) 1.6×10^2 Ω-m

5. A carbon resistor has to be choosen whose resistance is between 1760 Ω to 2640 Ω. The preferable colour code for the resistor can be

(a) Brown, Red, Brown, No colour
(b) Red, Red, Black, No colour
(c) Red, Black, Red, No colour
(d) Red, Red, Red, No colour

6. Temperature coefficient of resistance of two different materials are α_1 and α_2, respectively. If a new material is made by combining these two materials such that the resistivity of the material does not change with temperature, then

(a) Both α_1 and α_2 are positive
(b) Both α_1 and α_2 are negative
(c) α_1 and α_2 are of opposite sign
(d) α_1 and α_2 must have equal value but opposite sign

7. A set of n resistor, each of resistance R are connected in parallel to a battery of emf E and internal resistance R. The current drawn from battery is I. Now, these n resistors are connected in series to the same battery. Then, the current drawn from the battery becomes $\frac{I}{6}$. The value of n is

(a) 3 (b) 6
(c) 9 (d) 18

8. In the given circuit, the percentage change in potential drop across resistor of resistance 200 Ω in presence of voltmeter of resistance 200 Ω, is

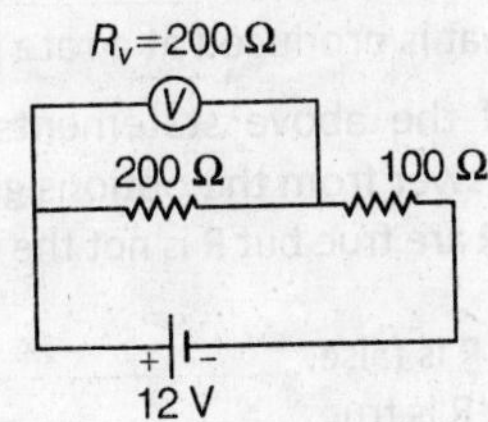

(a) 25% (b) 50%
(c) 12.5% (d) 33.3%

9. For the circuit shown in figure.

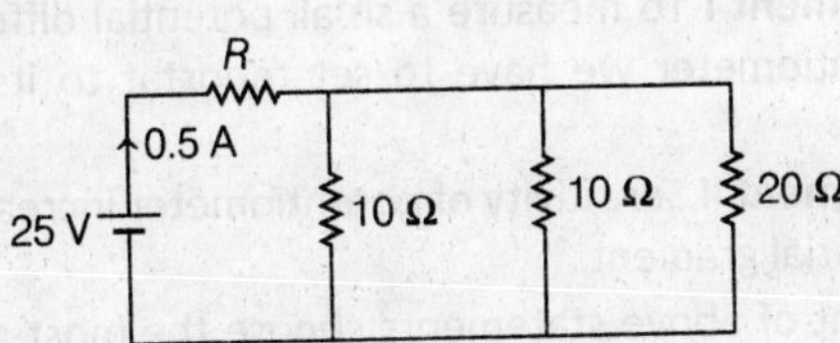

(a) Current through 20 Ω resistance is 0.1 A.
(b) Potential difference across the middle resistance is 2 V.
(c) R is equal to 46 Ω.
(d) All of the above

10. Consider the following circuit shown in the figure.

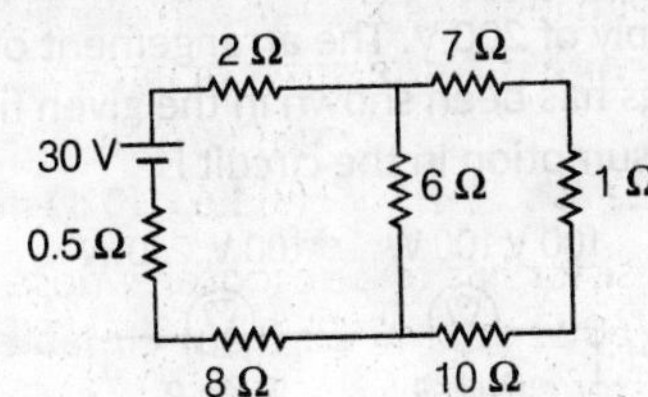

The power consumed or supplied by resistors or battery are given in Column II. Match the Column I with Column II.

	Column I		Column II
A.	Battery of emf 30 V	P.	8 W
B.	2 Ω resistor	Q.	1.75 W
C.	7 Ω resistor	R.	13.5 W
D.	6 Ω resistor	S.	None of the above

Choose the correct answers from the options given below:
(a) A→S; B→P; C→Q; D→R
(b) A→R; B→P; C→S; D→Q
(c) A→S; B→P; C→Q; D→R
(d) A→R; B→Q; C→P; D→S

11. A battery is used in discharging mode, i.e., it is connected in series with an external resistance. The graph between terminal potential difference V and current I through it has been shown below. The value of internal resistance of cell is

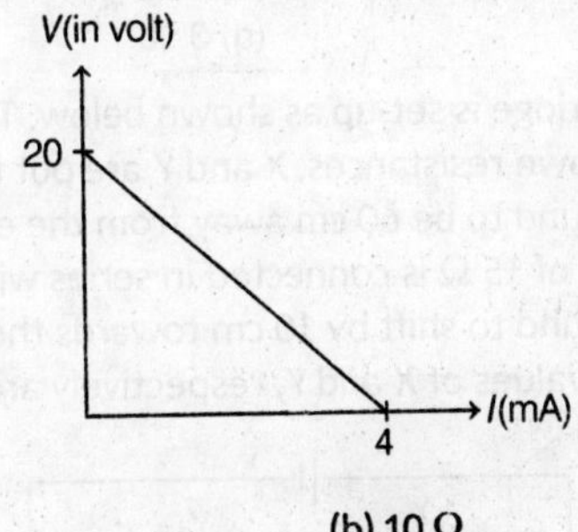

(a) 5 Ω (b) 10 Ω
(c) 100 Ω (d) 4 Ω

12. 24 identical electrical cells each of internal resistance 0.5 Ω are used for an arrangement such that maximum current is to be obtained through external resistance of 3 Ω, then number of rows and number of cells in each row are respectively

(a) 12, 2 (b) 2, 12
(c) 6, 4 (d) 4, 6

13. When current of 4 A is drawn from a cell, its terminal voltage is 20 V. If current of 1 A is given to same cell, then terminal voltage of cell is 25 V. The internal resistance and emf of cell is

(a) 1 Ω, 22.5 V (b) 2 Ω, 21 V
(c) 1 Ω, 24 V (d) 1 Ω, 22.5 V

14. A 1.5 V dry cell is tested by connecting it to a low resistance ammeter. The ammeter reads 25 A. Potential drop across ammeter is

(a) 1.5 V (b) 0.5 V
(c) 1.0 V (d) 0

15. An ideal cell of emf 10 V is connected in circuit shown in the following figure. Each resistance is 2 Ω. The potential difference (in V) across the capacitor when it is fully charged is

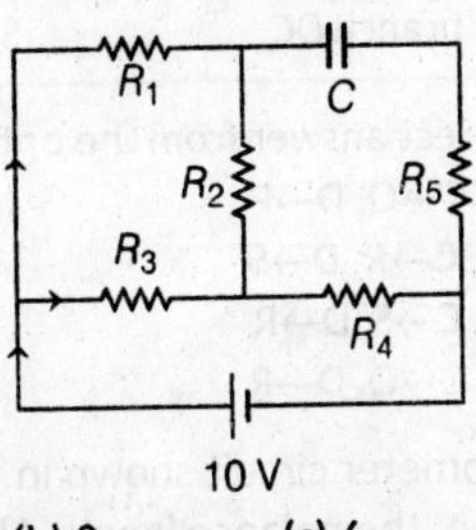

(a) 4 (b) 8 (c) 6 (d) 10

16. Find the ratio of currents I_1 and I_2 for the circuit shown below.

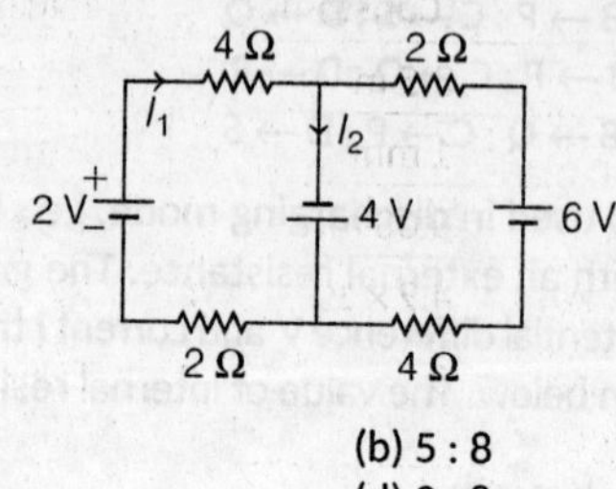

(a) 1 : 3
(b) 5 : 8
(c) 5 : 3
(d) 3 : 8

17. A meter bridge is set-up as shown below. To determine two unknown resistances, X and Y are put in gap. The null point is found to be 60 cm away from the end A, a resistance of 15 Ω is connected in series with Y, then null point is found to shift by 10 cm towards the end A of the wire. The values of X and Y, respectively are

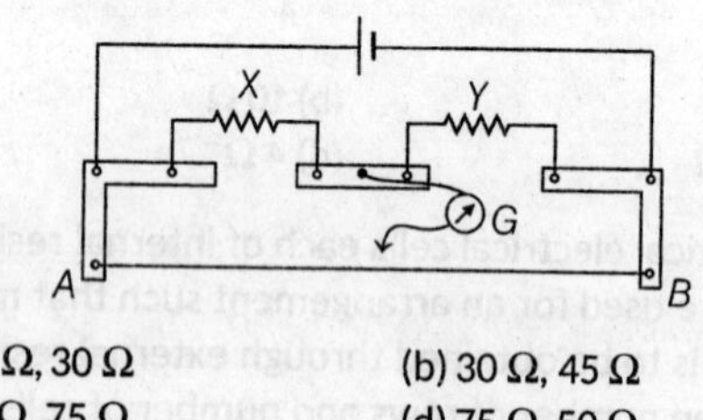

(a) 45 Ω, 30 Ω
(b) 30 Ω, 45 Ω
(c) 50 Ω, 75 Ω
(d) 75 Ω, 50 Ω

18. In given circuit, current in branch AD is I_2. Now match Column I with Column II.

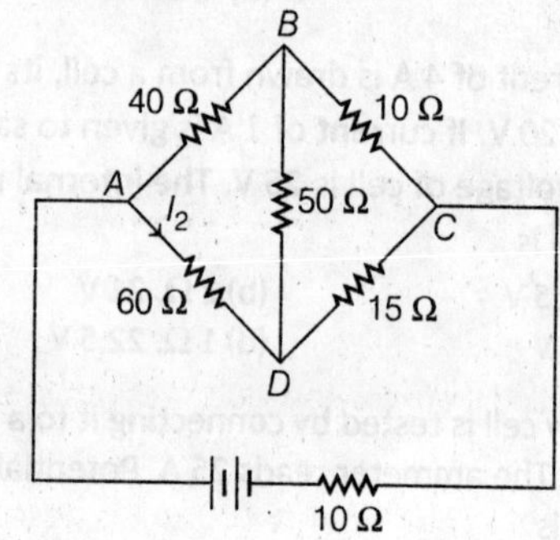

	Column I		Column II
A.	Power branch AB	P.	$15 I_2^2$
B.	Power branch BC	Q.	$60 I_2^2$
C.	Power branch AD	R.	$22.5 I_2^2$
D.	Power branch DC	S.	$90 I_2^2$

Choose the correct answer from the options given below:
(a) A→S, B→R, C→Q, D→P
(b) A→P, B→Q, C→R, D→S
(c) A→P, B→Q, C→S, D→R
(d) A→S, B→P, C→Q, D→R

19. In the potentiometer circuit shown in the figure, when switch S is open, the balance length AP = 70 cm. But when switch S is closed and the value of R is 6 Ω, the balance length AQ = 60 cm. The internal resistance of the cell of emf ε_2 is

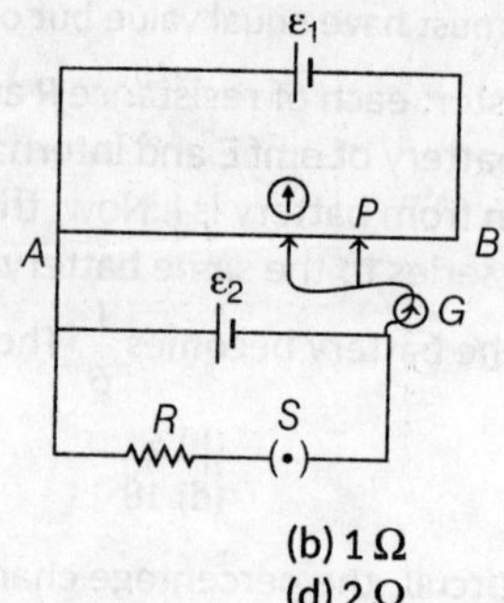

(a) 0.5 Ω
(b) 1 Ω
(c) 1.5 Ω
(d) 2 Ω

20. Assertion (A) To speed up the heating process, resistance of coil of a room heater is increased.

Reason (R) Heat is produced at a rate given by $H = I^2R$.

In the light of the above statements, choose the most appropriate answer from the options given below:
(a) Both A and R are true but R is not the correct explanation of A.
(b) A is true but R is false.
(c) A is false but R is true.
(d) Both A and R are true and R is the correct explanation of A.

21. Given below are two statements.

Statement I To measure a small potential difference by a potentiometer we have to set rehostat to its maximum value.

Statement II Sensitivity of potentiometer increases with its potential gradient.

In light of above statements choose the most appropriate answer from the options given below.
(a) Both Statement I and Statement II are incorrect.
(b) Statement I is correct and Statement II is incorrect.
(c) Statement I is incorrect and Statement II is correct.
(d) Both Statement I and Statement II are correct.

22. Two bulbs are connected in series with each other to a power supply of 200 V. The arrangement of bulbs and their ratings has been shown in the given figure. The total power consumption in the circuit is

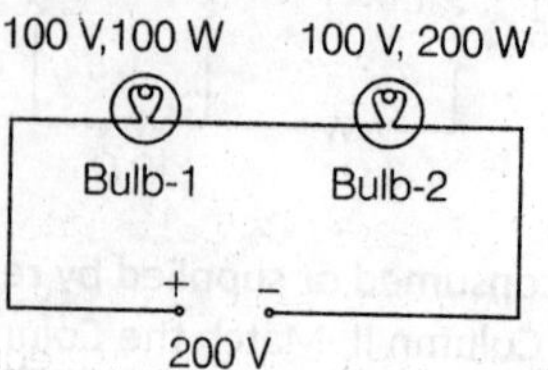

(a) zero
(b) $\frac{800}{3}$ W
(c) 150 W
(d) 300 W

23. Four identical bulbs are connected as shown in the following figure. Assume that no bulb get fused, when the voltage is supplied, then correct order of brightness for the bulbs is

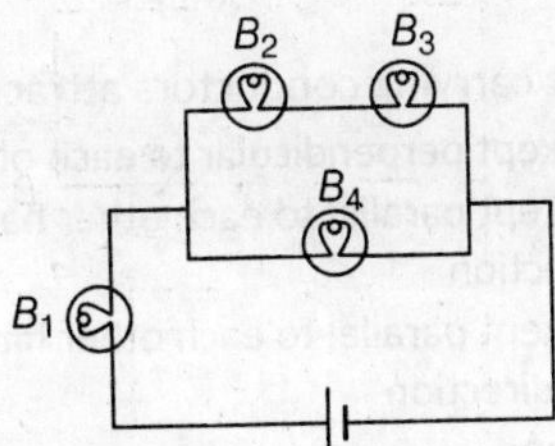

(a) $B_1 > B_2 = B_3 > B_4$
(b) $B_2 = B_3 > B_1 > B_4$
(c) $B_1 > B_3 > B_2 > B_4$
(d) $B_1 > B_4 > B_2 = B_3$

24. Power rating of an appliance of 20 Ω resistance is 2 kW. It cannot be used with a 300 V DC source because
(a) current drawn is very large and it can blow the fuse
(b) current drawn is very less and appliance does not operate
(c) appliance may melt
(d) Both (a) and (c)

25. Two fuses A and B have following specifications :

Specification	Fuse A (Constantan)	Fuse B (Nichrome)
Length	8.5 m	4.2 m
Width	1 mm	2 mm
Thickness	0.03 mm	0.06 mm
Resistivity	4.9×10^{-7} Ω-m	11×10^{-7} Ω-m
Temperature coefficient	0	0

If you require a more sensitive fuse, then
(a) A is better option
(b) B is better option
(c) Both A and B are same in use
(d) Both A and B are used together

Answers

1 (b)	2 (a)	3 (b)	4 (a)	5 (d)
6 (c)	7 (b)	8 (a)	9 (d)	10 (c)
11 (a)	12 (b)	13 (c)	14 (d)	15 (b)
16 (d)	17 (a)	18 (a)	19 (b)	20 (c)
21 (b)	22 (a)	23 (d)	24 (c)	25 (b)

See detailed explanations on page no. 207

QUALIFIER 13

Magnetic Effects of Current and Magnetism

1. An electron is moving on a circular path of radius 20 cm in a magnetic field of 2×10^{-3} T. The speed of electron is
(a) 1.5×10^5 m/s
(b) 1.6×10^6 m/s
(c) 7×10^7 m/s
(d) 8×10^8 m/s

2. A charge particle of charge q enters into a magnetic field B with velocity v perpendicular to it. The energy gained by the charge particle in magnetic field when it moves on a circular path of radius r is
(a) $\frac{q^2Br^2}{2m}$
(b) $\frac{q^2B^2r^2}{2m}$
(c) $\frac{q^2B^2r}{m}$
(d) $\frac{q^2B^2r^2}{m}$

3. Assertion (A) Magnetic dipole moment of a toroid is zero.
Reason (R) Magnetic field intensity of a solenoid and a toroid made from that solenoid are equal.
In the light of the above statements, choose the most appropriate answer from the options given below:
(a) Both A and R are true but R is not the correct explanation of A.
(b) A is true but R is false.
(c) A is false but R is true.
(d) Both A and R are true and R is the correct explanation of A.

4. A deutron of kinetic energy 100 keV is describing a circular orbit of radius 1 m in a plane perpendicular to magnetic field of 2T. The kinetic energy of the proton that describes a circular orbit of radius 2 m in the same plane with the same magnetic field is
(a) 200 keV
(b) 400 keV
(c) 800 keV
(d) 600 keV

5. The ratio of angular momentum of electron moving in Bohr's orbit to magnetic dipole moment of electron in Bohr's orbit in terms of mass (m) of electrons and its charge (e) is given as
(a) $\frac{m}{e}$
(b) $\frac{m}{2e}$
(c) $\frac{e}{2m}$
(d) $\frac{2m}{e}$

6. Consider the following statements (I) and (II) and identify the correct answer.

I. When a charged particle enters into a uniform magnetic field perpendicular to it, it moves on a circular path.

II. Intensity of magnetisation of a bulk material is given by magnetic dipole moment developed per unit area when it is placed inside the external magnetic field.

(a) Both I and II are correct
(b) Both I and II are incorrect
(c) I is correct and II is incorrect
(d) I is incorrect but II is correct

7. Match the following pairs of magnetic field in Column II according to the given figure in Column I.

Column I		Column II	
A.	(figure: i, $3r$, $8r$, P)	P.	$\frac{\sqrt{2}\mu_0 i}{\pi r}$
B.	(figure: P, i, $2r$)	Q.	$\frac{\mu_0 i}{4r}$
C.	(figure: ∞, i, r, P, i, ∞)	R.	$\frac{2}{15}\frac{\mu_0 i}{\pi r}$
D.	(figure: r, P, i, i)	S.	$\frac{\mu_0 i}{2\pi r}(1+\pi)$

Choose the correct answer from the options given below:

(a) A → P, B → R, C → Q, D → S
(b) A → R, B → P, C → Q, D → S
(c) A → R, B → Q, C → S, D → P
(d) A → S, B → Q, C → P, D → R

8. Two long straight current carrying parallel wires are arranged as shown in the following figure

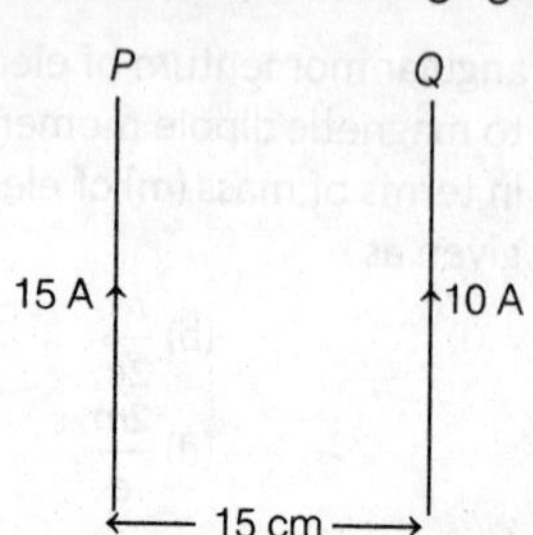

Where should a third wire (R) having current of 50 A be placed from wire P, so that it may not experience any force.

(a) 12 cm (b) 9 cm
(c) 10 cm (d) 7 cm

9. Two current carrying conductors attract to each other, if

(a) they are kept perpendicular to each other
(b) they are kept parallel to each other having currents in same direction
(c) they are kept parallel to each other having currents in opposite direction
(d) Both (b) and (c)

10. Resistance of galvanometer coil is 12 Ω. It shows full scale deflection for a current of 2.5 mA. The ratio of net resistance of an ammeter of range 0 to 7.5 A and a voltmeter of range 0 to 10 V is

(a) 10^{-6} (b) 10^{-8} (c) 10^{-10} (d) 10^{-12}

11. The core of a toroid having 1000 turns has inner and outer radii 11 cm and 12 cm, respectively. The magnetic field in the core for a current of 0.70 A is 2.5 T. The relative permeability of the core is

(a) 2055 (b) 685 (c) 1370 (d) 1095

12. A rectangular coil of 500 turns carrying a current of 2mA. Its plane is making an angle of 30° with the direction of magnetic field intensity of strength $\sqrt{3}$ T. If the length and width of the coil are 2 cm and 1 cm respectively, then torque on the rectangular coil will be

(a) 3×10^{-4} N-m (b) $\sqrt{3}\times10^{-4}$ N-m
(c) 5×10^{-5} N-m (d) 10^{-4} N-m

13. An ammeter of resistance 0.8 Ω can measure currents upto 1 A. What must be the value of shunt resistance to enable the ammeter to measure current upto 5 A?

(a) 0.5 Ω (b) 0.2 Ω (c) 0.4 Ω (d) 0.6 Ω

14. Sensitivity of a moving coil galvanometer is increased by increasing the

(a) number of turns in the coil
(b) strength of the magnetic field
(c) the area of the coil
(d) All of the above

15. Match the following magnetic material (Column I) with their plot of susceptibility *vs* temperature graph (Column II).

Column I		Column II	
A.	Diamagnetic	P.	(graph: χ vs T, origin O)

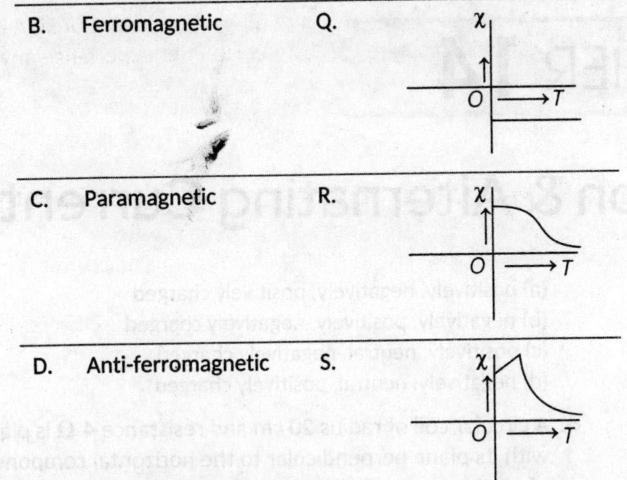

Choose the correct answer from the options given below:

(a) A → Q, B → R, C → P, D → S
(b) A → S, B → R, C → Q, D → P
(c) A → Q, B → P, C → R, D → S
(d) A → R, B → S, C → Q, D → P

16. On increasing temperature of a diamagnetic substance, its magnetic susceptibility

(a) increases
(b) decreases
(c) remains same
(d) None of these

17. Statement I Above Curie temperature, a ferromagnetic substance becomes paramagnetic substance.

Statement II On increasing the temperature of a ferromagnetic material, its magnetisation increases.

In light of above statements, choose the most appropriate answer from the options given below.

(a) Both Statement I and Statement II are incorrect.
(b) Statement I is correct and Statement II is incorrect.
(c) Statement I is incorrect and Statement II is correct.
(d) Both Statement I and Statement II are correct.

18. Two bar magnets having magnetic dipole moment M each are kept in such a way that the angle between their axis is 60° and their unlike poles are touching each other as shown below. The magnetic dipole moment of the system is

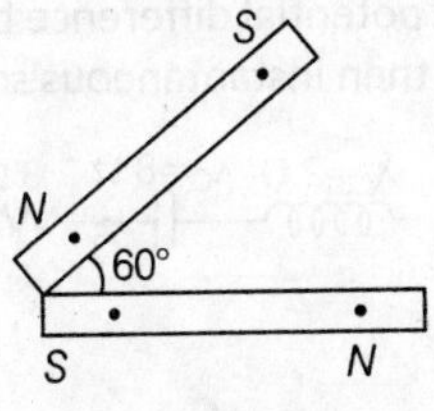

(a) $\frac{M}{\sqrt{2}}$ (b) M
(c) $\sqrt{2}M$ (d) $\sqrt{3}M$

19. If a long thin magnet of magnetic dipole moment M is bent into a semicircle, then new value of magnetic dipole moment of the magnet will be

(a) $\frac{M}{2\pi}$ (b) $\frac{2M}{\pi}$ (c) $\frac{3M}{2\pi}$ (d) $\frac{M}{3\pi}$

20. The work done in turning a magnet of magnetic dipole moment M by an angle of 90° from the meridian is n times the corresponding work done to turn it through an angle of 60°. The value of n is given by

(a) 1 (b) 2 (c) 1.5 (d) 0.5

21. A vibrational magnetometer placed in magnetic meridian has a small bar magnet. The magnet executes oscillations with a time period of 4 s in earth's horizontal magnetic field of 12 mT. When a horizontal field of 9 mT is produced opposite to the earth's field by placing current carrying wire, then new time period of the magnet will be

(a) $\frac{8}{\sqrt{3}}$ s (b) $8\sqrt{3}$ s (c) $2\sqrt{2}$ s (d) $\frac{4}{\sqrt{3}}$ s

22. At a place in magnetic meridian, horizontal and vertical component of earth's magnetic field are equal. The angle of dip at this place will be

(a) 0° (b) 90°
(c) 30° (d) 45°

23. In the magnetic meridian of a certain place, the horizontal component of earth's magnetic field is 0.8 G and dip angle is 60°. The value of magnetic field of the earth at this location is

(a) 0.4 G (b) 0.8 G
(c) 1.2 G (d) 1.6 G

24. A paramagnetic sample shows a net magnetism of 6 A/m when it is placed in a magnetic field of 0.4 T at 4K temperature. When sample placed in a magnetic field of 0.3 T at a temperature of 24K, then magnetism will be

(a) 4 A/m (b) 0.75 A/m
(c) 0.35 A/m (d) 2.25 A/m

25. Area of B - H curve signifies

(a) Strength of magnetic field
(b) Induced magnetic dipole moment
(c) Heat loss per cycle of magnetisation and demagnetisation
(d) Net magnetic dipole moment per unit volume

Answers

1 (c)	2 (b)	3 (a)	4 (c)	5 (d)
6 (c)	7 (b)	8 (b)	9 (b)	10 (a)
11 (a)	12 (a)	13 (b)	14 (d)	15 (a)
16 (c)	17 (b)	18 (b)	19 (b)	20 (b)
21 (a)	22 (d)	23 (d)	24 (b)	25 (c)

See detailed explanations on page no. 210

QUALIFIER 14

Electromagnetic Induction & Alternating Current

1. The magnetic flux passing through a coil of 40 number of turns varies as $\phi = (6t^3 - 18t^2)$ mT. If the total resistance of the coil is $5\,\Omega$, then maximum current induced in the coil is

(a) 0.0036 A (b) 0.0288 A
(c) 0.144 A (d) 0.288 A

2. Consider the following two statements.

Statement I A hot wire ammeter reads the rms value of AC current.

Statement II Ammeter to measure AC can be made using a galvanometer.

In light of above statements, choose the most appropriate answer from the options given below :

(a) Both Statement I and Statement II are incorrect.
(b) Statement I is correct and Statement II is incorrect.
(c) Statement I is incorrect and Statement II is correct.
(d) Both Statement I and Statement II are correct.

3. A square loop is placed to the right of large current carrying straight wire as shown in the following figure. The current flowing through wire varies with time as $I = (t^2 - 1)$ A. The direction of induced current in the square loop is

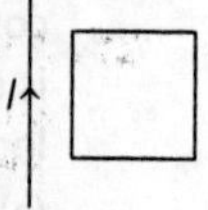

(a) clockwise
(b) anti-clockwise
(c) first clockwise, then anti-clockwise
(d) first anti-clockwise, then clockwise

4. An AC generator's coil has 3000 turns and is rotated with angular speed of 400 rad/s. The area of the coil is 20 cm^2. If the peak voltage in the coil of 100 V is to be produced, then required magnetic field is

(a) 28 mT (b) 41 mT
(c) 57.98 mT (d) 28.49 mT

5. A conducting rod is rotating with a constant angular velocity ω about point O (its centre) in a magnetic field B which is directed into the plane of paper as shown in figure. Due to the rotation, the points of rod, i.e. P, O, Q, respectively are

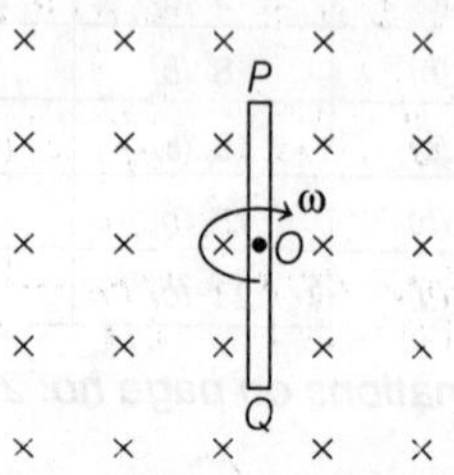

(a) positively, negatively, positively charged
(b) negatively, positively, negatively charged
(c) positively, neutral, negatively charged
(d) negatively, neutral, positively charged

6. A circular coil of radius 20 cm and resistance $4\,\Omega$ is placed with its plane perpendicular to the horizontal component of earth's magnetic field. It is rotated about its vertical diameter through 180° in 0.5 s. The magnitude of emf induced in the coil is ($B_H = 3 \times 10^{-5}$ T)

(a) $1.2\,\pi\mu$ V (b) $2.4\,\pi\mu$ V (c) $3.6\,\pi\mu$ V (d) $4.8\,\pi\mu$ V

7. Assertion (A) Induced emf in a coil opposes motion of a magnet moving towards it.

Reason (R) Work done against opposing force appears as electrical energy of induced current.

In the light of the above statements, choose the most appropriate answer from the options given below:

(a) Both A and R are true but R is not the correct explanation of A.
(b) A is true but R is false.
(c) A is false but R is true.
(d) Both A and R are true and R is the correct explanation of A.

8. The current in a self-inductance $L = 40$ mH is to be increased uniformly from 1 A to 11 A in 4 ms. The induced emf in the inductor during the process is

(a) 100 V (b) 0.4 V (c) 40 V (d) 440 V

9. Two coils of self-inductances 2 mH and 8 mH are placed, so close together that the effective flux in one coil is completely linked with the other. The mutual inductance between these coils is

(a) 10 mH (b) 6 mH (c) 4 mH (d) 16 mH

10. Consider the electrical circuit shown in the following figure. The source voltage is $V = 100\sin(314t)$ V. If the instantaneous potential difference between P and Q points is 30 V, then instantaneous source voltage is

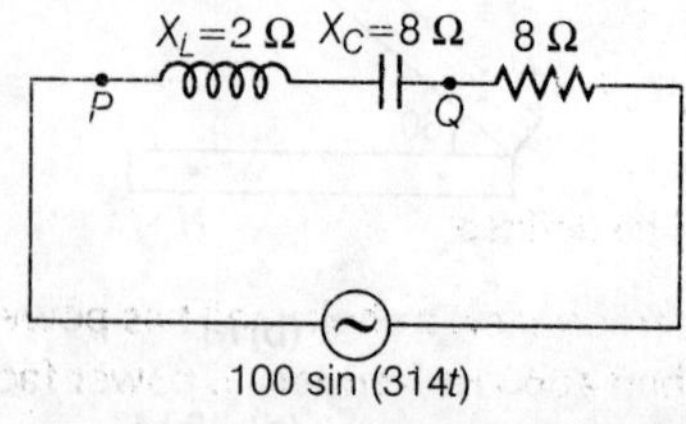

(a) 50 V (b) 40 V (c) 30 V (d) 20 V

11. The voltage applied to a purely inductive coil of self inductance 31.8 mH is given by the equation

$$V = 50 + 100\sin 157t + 75\sin 942t$$

The equation of current wave is given as

(a) $20\sin(157t) + 2.5\sin(942t)$ A

(b) $20\sin\left(157t - \frac{15}{2}\right) + 2.5\sin\left(942t - \frac{\pi}{2}\right)$A

(c) $20\sin\left(157t + \frac{\pi}{2}\right) + 2.5\sin\left(942t + \frac{15}{2}\right)$A

(d) None of the above

12. The potential difference across a 0.6 H inductor as a function of time is shown in the following figure. If the initial current flowing through the inductor is zero, then current at $t = 3$ s is

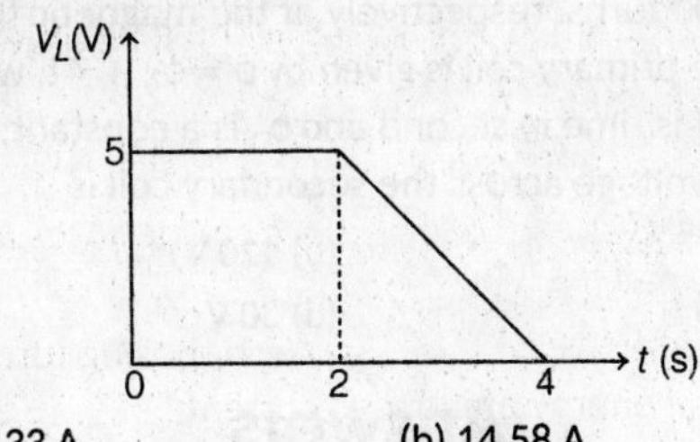

(a) 33.33 A (b) 14.58 A
(c) 21.5 A (d) None of these

13. If a lamp rated at 60 V and 10 W is to be operated at AC source of 100 V and 50 Hz, then required value of inductance is

(a) 2.28 H (b) 0.76 H
(c) 1.52 H (d) 3.04 H

14. In a series *L-C-R* circuit, at resonance, the bandwidth frequency can be represented as

(a) $\frac{R}{LC}$ (b) $\frac{R}{C}$
(c) $\frac{RL}{2\pi}$ (d) $\frac{R}{2\pi L}$

15. The quality factor of the circuit shown in the figure is

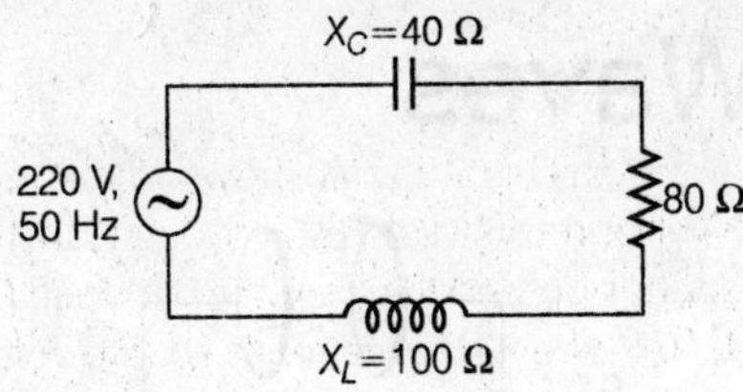

(a) 0.019
(b) 0.0079
(c) 126.49
(d) Cannot be defined

16. At 180 Hz frequency, a choke coil has power factor of 0.5 lagging, then at 60 Hz frequency, power factor of same choke coil is

(a) 0.6 (b) 0.8
(c) 0.866 (d) 0.707

17. In an AC circuit when applied voltage is $V = 200\sin\left(\omega t + \frac{\pi}{3}\right)$V, current flowing through it, is $I = 5\sqrt{2}\cos\left(\omega t - \frac{\pi}{6}\right)$A, then power consumption by it will be

(a) 0 W (b) 500 W (c) 1000 W (d) $500\sqrt{2}$ W

18. For a circuit with inductor *L* and capacitor connected in series with an alternating potential. The correct variation of impedance *Z* with angular frequency ω can be shown best by which of the following graph?

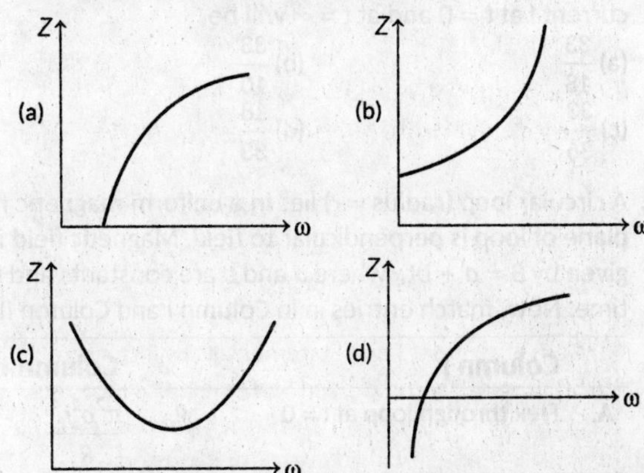

19. A full charged capacitor of capacitance C is connected to an uncharged inductor of inductance at t = 0. The time when the energy in both capacitor and inductor is equal, is

(a) $\frac{\pi\sqrt{LC}}{3}$ (b) $\frac{\pi\sqrt{LC}}{2}$ (c) $\frac{5\pi\sqrt{LC}}{4}$ (d) $\frac{5\pi\sqrt{LC}}{2}$

20. Match circuit given in Column I with their respective phase differences given in Column II.

	Column I (Circuit)		Column II (Phase difference)
A.	Resistive AC circuit	P.	30°
B.	Inductive AC circuit	Q.	90°
C.	Series *L-C-R* circuit when $X_L = 2X_C$ and $R = X_C$	R.	0
D.	Series *L-C-R* circuit when $X_L = 2X_C$ and $R = \sqrt{3}X_C$	S.	45°

Choose the correct answer from the options given below.

(a) A - P, B - Q, C - R, D - S (b) A - S, B - R, C - Q, D - P
(c) A - R, B - Q, C - S, D - P (d) A - R, B - Q, C - P, D - S

21.

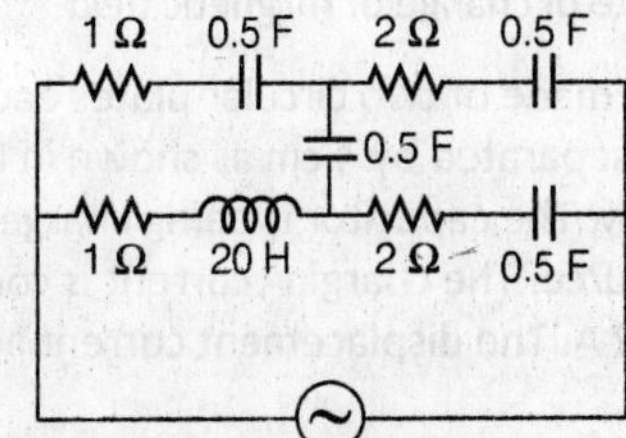

At very high frequencies, impedence of above circuit will be

(a) 2 Ω (b) 1 Ω (c) 4 Ω (d) ∞

22. 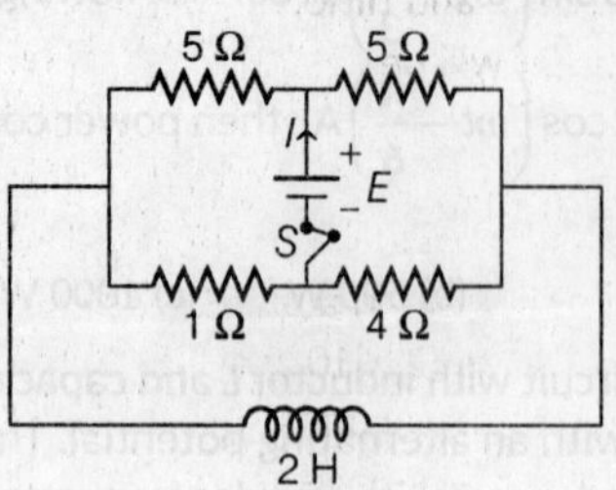

In above circuit switch S is closed at $t = 0$. Ratio of values of current I at $t = 0$ and at $t = \infty$ will be

(a) $\frac{33}{18}$ (b) $\frac{33}{10}$

(c) $\frac{33}{36}$ (d) $\frac{18}{33}$

23. A circular loop (radius = r) lies in a uniform magnetic field, plane of loop is perpendicular to field. Magnetic field is given by $B = a + bt$, where a and b are constants and t is time. Now, match entries in in Column I and Column II.

	Column I		Column II
A.	Flux through loop at $t = 0$	P.	$\frac{\pi^2 b^2 r^4}{R}$
B.	Emf induced in loop	Q.	$-\frac{\pi b r^2}{R}$
C.	Induced current in loop (resistance of loop in RΩ)	R.	$-\pi b r^2$
D.	Energy dissipation rate of loop	S.	$\pi a r^2$

Choose the correct answer from the options given below.

(a) A - S, B - R, C - Q, D - P
(b) A - P, B - Q, C - R, D - S
(c) A - S, B - Q, C - P, D - R
(d) A - P, B - R, C - S, D - Q

24. A transformer of 100% efficiency has 200 turns in the primary and 40000 turns in secondary. It is connected to a 220 V main supply and secondary feeds to a 100 kΩ resistance. The potential difference per turn is

(a) 1.1 V
(b) 25 V
(c) 18 V
(d) 11 V

25. The primary and secondary coils of transformer have 50 and 1500 turns, respectively. If the magnetic flux ϕ linked with the primary coil is given by $\phi = \phi_0 + 4t$, where ϕ is in weber, t is time in second and ϕ_0 is a constant, then the output voltage across the secondary coil is

(a) 90 V (b) 120 V
(c) 220 V (d) 30 V

Answers

1 (c)	2 (b)	3 (b)	4 (b)	5 (a)
6 (d)	7 (d)	8 (a)	9 (c)	10 (c)
11 (d)	12 (b)	13 (c)	14 (d)	15 (d)
16 (c)	17 (d)	18 (d)	19 (c)	20 (c)
21 (a)	22 (c)	23 (a)	24 (a)	25 (b)

See detailed explanations on page no. 213

QUALIFIER 15

Electromagnetic Waves

1. Displacement current between the two plates of the capacitor during charging or discharging, arises due to

(a) time rate of change of electric field
(b) time rate of change of magnetic field
(c) space rate of change of electric field
(d) space rate of change of magnetic field

2. A capacitor made of two circular plates each of radius 10 cm and separated by 4 cm as shown in the following figure below. The capacitor is being charged by an external source. The charging current is constant and is equal to 0.2 A. The displacement current across the plates, is

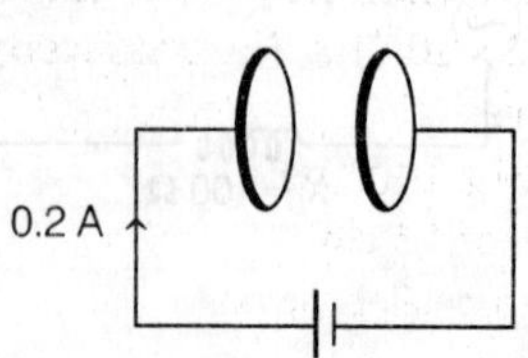

(a) 0 A (b) 0.2 A (c) 0.4 A (d) 0.3 A

3. Conducting plates of a parallel plate capacitor having plate area 10^{-12} m^2 are separated by a short distance. If the displacement current between the plates is 15 A, then rate of change in electric field w.r.t. time between the capacitor plates, is

(a) 1.69×10^{12} V / m (b) 1.69×10^{13} V / m
(c) 1.69×10^{14} V / m (d) 1.69×10^{15} V / m

4. A capacitor is made of two square shaped conducting plates each of side 8 cm and separated by a distance of 2 cm. If the capacitor is being charged by an external source and the charging current is equals to 0.5 A, then the rate of change of potential difference between the plates is
(a) 17.65×10^{10} V/s (b) 17.65×10^{11} V/s
(c) 3.53×10^{11} V/s (d) 3.53×10^{12} V/s

5. Match the Column I with Column II and mark the correct option from the codes given below.

	Column I		Column II
A.	$\oint \mathbf{B}\cdot d\mathbf{l}=\mu_0 I$	P.	Gauss' law
B.	$\oint \mathbf{B}\cdot d\mathbf{l}=\mu_0\left(I+\varepsilon_0\frac{d\phi_E}{dt}\right)$	Q.	Faraday's laws of electromagnetic induction
C.	$\oint \mathbf{E}\cdot d\mathbf{l}=-\frac{d}{dt}\oint_s \mathbf{B}\cdot d\mathbf{s}$	R.	Ampere-Maxwell's law
D.	$\oint \mathbf{E}\cdot d\mathbf{s}=\frac{1}{\varepsilon_0}\oint_s \rho\, ds$	S.	Ampere's circuital law

Choose the correct answer from the options given below.
(a) A→P, B→Q, C→R, D→S
(b) A→S, B→R, C→Q, D→P
(c) A→S, B→Q, C→P, D→R
(d) A→R, B→P, C→Q, D→S

6. An *L-C* resonant circuit contains a 80 pF capacitor and a 500 μH inductor. It is used as an oscillator to produce electromagnetic waves. The angular frequency of the circuit is
(a) 5×10^7 rad/s (b) 5×10^8 rad/s
(c) 7.96×10^7 rad/s (d) 7.96×10^8 rad/s

7. Consider an electromagnetic wave which is travelling in a medium with a speed of 6×10^7 m/s. The relative magnetic permeability of the medium is 5. The relative electrical permittivity of the medium, is
(a) 2.25 (b) 4 (c) 4.67 (d) 5

8. A charge particle oscillates about its mean position with a frequency of 2×10^{10} Hz. The produced electromagnetic waves will have
(a) frequency of 2×10^{16} Hz
(b) wavelength of 1.5 cm
(c) fall in the ultravoilet region
(d) All are correct

9. An electromagnetic wave going through vacuum is described by electric field $E=E_0\sin(px+qt)$ and magnetic field $B=B_0\sin(px+qt)$, then which of the following relation is true?
(a) $E_{rms}p=B_0 q$ (b) $qE_0=pB_0$
(c) $pE_{rms}=qB_{rms}$ (d) None of these

10. The plane electromagnetic wave of frequency 6 MHz travels in free space along the *Y*-direction. At a particular point in space and time, $E=8\hat{k}$ V/m. The magnetic field **B** at that point will be
(a) $2\times10^{-8}(\hat{i})$ T (b) $2.33\times10^{-8}(-\hat{i})$T
(c) $2.33\times10^{-8}\hat{i}$T (d) $3\times10^{-8}\hat{i}$T

11. The magnetic field in a plane EM wave is given by $B_x=6\times10^{-8}\sin(2\times10^3y-3\times10^{10}t)$ T, where *y* is in metre and *t* is in seconds. The expression of the electric field for the given wave is
(a) $2\times10^{-8}\sin(2\times10^3y-3\times10^{10}t)$ V/m
(b) $2\times10^{-8}\sin(2\times10^3y+3\times10^{10}t)$ V/m
(c) $18\sin(2\times10^3y-3\times10^{10}t)$ V/m
(d) $12.73\sin(2\times10^3y-3\times10^{10}t)$ V/m

12. An electromagnetic wave enters from air in a non-magnetic material medium . The electric field in air is $E_1=E_{01}\sin\left[\pi v\left(\frac{x}{c}-t\right)\right]$ and in medium is $E_2=E_{02}\sin[k(2x-ct)]$, where *k*, and *v* represent wave number and frequency in air. The relative permeability of the medium, is
(a) 2 (b) 3 (c) 4 (d) 6

13. Travelling in *x*-direction, the equation of electric field component of a light beam is given as $E_y=200\sin\omega\left(t-\frac{x}{c}\right)$ V/m. A charge of 2 μC is constrained to move along the *Y*-direction with speed 400 m/s. The maximum magnetic force on charge, is
(a) 5.33×10^{-10} N (b) 5.33×10^{-11} N
(c) 3.77×10^{-10} N (d) 3.77×10^{-11} N

14. A linearly polarised EM wave given as $\mathbf{E}=\hat{k}\ 40\cos(kx-6\times10^8t)$ V/m is incident normally on a perfectly reflecting infinite wall at $x=a$. Assuming that the material of the wall is optically inactive, the reflected wave $\mathbf{E}_r$ is given as
(a) $\mathbf{E}_r=\hat{k}\ 40\sin(kx-6\times10^8t)$ V/m
(b) $\mathbf{E}_r=-\hat{k}\ 40\sin(kx-6\times10^8t)$ V/m
(c) $\mathbf{E}_r=\hat{k}\ 40\cos(kx+6\times10^8t)$ V/m
(d) $\mathbf{E}_r=-\hat{k}\ 40\cos(kx+6\times10^8t)$ V/m

15. A plane EM wave is propagating along the direction $\hat{i}-2\hat{j}+5\hat{k}$. If the electric field component of this wave is in the direction $3\hat{i}-\hat{j}-\hat{k}$, then which of the following is the direction of the magnetic field component?
(a) $7\hat{i}-16\hat{j}+5\hat{k}$ (b) $-7\hat{i}+16\hat{j}-5\hat{k}$
(c) $-7\hat{i}-16\hat{j}+5\hat{k}$ (d) $7\hat{i}+16\hat{j}+5\hat{k}$

16. If an electromagnetic wave is travelling through a material medium, then its wavelength can never be equal to
(a) 0.5 m (b) 1.2 m (c) 2 m (d) 8.5 m

17. An electromagnetic wave is travelling in positive x-direction where amplitude of electric field is $E_0 = 80$ N/C and frequency is 30 MHz. The expression of magnetic field is

(a) $2.67 \times 10^{-8} \sin\{6\pi \times 10^7 (\text{rad/s})t - 0.4 (\text{cm}^{-1}) x\}$ T
(b) $2.67 \times 10^{-7} \sin\{6\pi \times 10^7 (\text{rad/s})t - 0.4 (\text{cm}^{-1}) x\}$ T
(c) $2.67 \times 10^{-8} \sin\{6\pi \times 10^7 (\text{rad/s})t - 0.6 (\text{m}^{-1}) x\}$ T
(d) $2.67 \times 10^{-7} \sin\{6\pi \times 10^7 (\text{rad/s})t - 0.6 (\text{m}^{-1}) x\}$ T

18. An electromagnetic wave is travelling in a material medium whose oscillating electric field is described by the equation $E(x,t) = 0.1\sin\pi\,(3 \times 10^4 x - 7.5 \times 10^{14} t)$ V/m, where x is in cm and t is in seconds. The refractive index of medium is

(a) 1 (b) 1.2
(c) 1.25 (d) 1.33

19. The maximum value of electric field produced by the radiation coming from a 60 W bulb at a distance of 3 m is (Take efficiency of bulb 5% and is a point source)

(a) 3.16 V/m (b) 4.46 V/m (c) 2.23 V/m (d) 6.30 V/m

20. The intensity of a plane electromagnetic wave travelling in space is $5.9 \times 10^{-4}\, \text{W/m}^2$. Then, rms value of component of electric field, is

(a) 0.235 V/m (b) 0.333 V/m (c) 0.471 V/m (d) 0.667 V/m

21. Assertion (A) Both electric field and magnetic field component of electromagnetic wave vibrate parallel to the direction of propogation of electromagnetic wave.

Reason (R) Electromagnetic radiations exert pressure.

In the light of the above statements, choose the most appropriate answer from the options given below:

(a) Both A and R are true but R is not the correct explanation of A.
(b) A is true but R is false.
(c) A is false but R is true.
(d) Both A and R are true and R is the correct explanation of A.

22. An electromagnetic wave is represented by the electric field $\mathbf{E} = E_0 \hat{n} \sin[\omega t + (6y - 8z)]$. Taking unit vectors in x, y and z-directions to be $\hat{\mathbf{i}}, \hat{\mathbf{j}}, \hat{\mathbf{k}}$, the direction of propagation $\hat{\mathbf{s}}$ is

(a) $\hat{\mathbf{s}} = \dfrac{3\hat{\mathbf{i}} - 4\hat{\mathbf{j}}}{5}$ (b) $\hat{\mathbf{s}} = \dfrac{-4\hat{\mathbf{k}} + 3\hat{\mathbf{j}}}{5}$

(c) $\hat{\mathbf{s}} = \left(\dfrac{-3\hat{\mathbf{j}} + 4\hat{\mathbf{k}}}{5}\right)$ (d) $\hat{\mathbf{s}} = \dfrac{4\hat{\mathbf{j}} - 3\hat{\mathbf{k}}}{5}$

23. Statement I In a microwave oven, a magnetron produces radiations of nearly 3 GHz to heat food items.

Statement II Water molecules absorbs microwaves and emits infrared radiations or heat waves.

In light of above statements, choose the most appropriate answer from the options given below :

(a) Both Statement I and Statement II are incorrect.
(b) Statement I is correct and Statement II is incorrect.
(c) Statement I is incorrect and Statement II is correct.
(d) Both Statement I and Statement II are correct.

24. Match Column I (electromagnetic wave type) with Column II (its application) and select the correct option from the choices given below the columns.

	Column I		Column II
A.	Microwave	P.	ground wave propagation
B.	Radiowave	Q.	for measurement of speed of vehicle
C.	Infrared	R.	Sterilise surgical instruments
D.	Ultraviolet	S.	military purpose

Choose the correct answer from the options given below

(a) A - P, B - Q, C - S, D - R (b) A - Q, B - P, C - R, D - S
(c) A - Q, B - P, C - S, D - R (d) A - S, B - Q, C - P, D - R

25. Electric vector of a light beam is $E = 800 \sin\left(\omega t - \dfrac{x}{c}\right)$ V/m.

An electron is projected perpendicular to direction of propagation of light beam with speed of 3×10^7 m/s. What is the maximum force experienced by electron due to light beam?

(a) 1.28×10^{-16} N (b) 1.28×10^{-17} N
(c) 1.28×10^{-19} N (d) Zero

Answers

1 (a)	2 (b)	3 (c)	4 (a)	5 (b)
6 (a)	7 (d)	8 (b)	9 (c)	10 (c)
11 (c)	12 (c)	13 (a)	14 (c)	15 (d)
16 (a)	17 (d)	18 (b)	19 (b)	20 (c)
21 (c)	22 (c)	23 (b)	24 (c)	25 (a)

See detailed explanations on page no. 216

QUALIFIER 16

Optics

1. A bulb is hanging centrally in front of a mirror wall of length $L = 5$ m. A man walks in front of mirror wall with a speed of 0.5 m/s. Distance of bulb and mirror is d and distance of man and mirror is $2d$ (as shown).

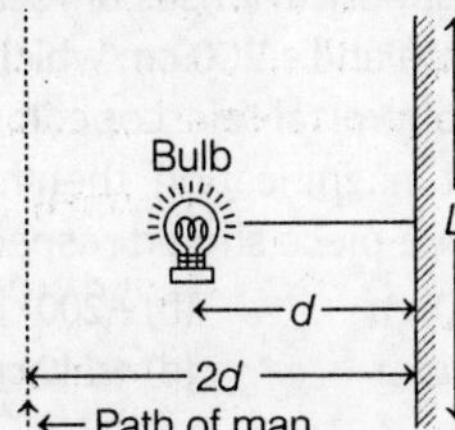

Time for which man can see image of bulb is

(a) 5 s (b) 10 s (c) 20 s (d) 25 s

2. **Assertion (A)** A small angled prism is not able to produce a clear spectrum.

Reason (R) Angular dispersion produced by a prism depends on refractive indices of different colours.

In the light of the above statements, choose the most appropriate answer from the options given below:

(a) Both A and R are true but R is not the correct explanation of A.

(b) A is true but R is false.

(c) A is false but R is true.

(d) Both A and R are true and R is the correct explanation of A

3. An object of length 1 cm lies along the axis of a concave mirror of focal length 4 cm at a distance 6 cm from the pole of the mirror. The size of the image is approximately equal to

(a) $\frac{1}{\sqrt{2}}$ cm (b) $\frac{1}{4}$ cm (c) $\sqrt{2}$ cm (d) 4 cm

4. The apparent depth of water in cylindrical water tank of diameter $2R$ cm is reducing at the rate of x cm/min when water is being drained out at a constant rate. The amount of water drained in cc per minute is

(μ_1 = refractive index of air, μ_2 = refractive index of water)

(a) $x\pi R^2 \mu_1 / \mu_2$ (b) $x\pi R^2 \mu_2 / \mu_1$

(c) $2\pi R \mu_1 / \mu_2$ (d) $\pi R^2 x$

5. If refractive indices of core and cladding of optical fibre are μ_1 and μ_2 respectively, then the maximum value of incidence angle for which light can be propagated through the fibre is

(a) $\sin^{-1}(\sqrt{\mu_1^2 - \mu_2^2})$ (b) $\cos^{-1}(\sqrt{\mu_1^2 - \mu_2^2})$

(c) $\sin^{-1}\left(\sqrt{1 - \frac{\mu_2^2}{\mu_1^2}}\right)$ (d) $\cos^{-1}\left(\sqrt{1 - \frac{\mu_2^2}{\mu_1^2}}\right)$

6. A layer of ice $(n = 4/3)$ lies on a glass plate $(n = 3/2)$. A ray of light makes an angle of incidence 60° on the surface of ice as shown in the figure below.

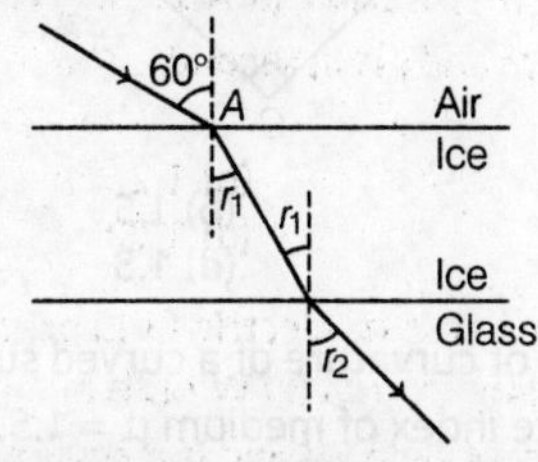

With reference to the above figure, match the Column I (parameter) with Column II (value).

Column I		Column II	
A.	$\sin r_1$	P.	$1/\sqrt{3}$
B.	$\sin r_2$	Q.	$3\sqrt{3}/8$
C.	Refractive index of ice w.r.t. glass	R.	8/9

Choose the correct answer from the options given below

(a) A - P, B - Q, C - R (b) A - Q, B - P, C - R

(c) A - Q, B - R, C - P (d) A - P, B - R, C - Q

7. A converging beam of light is incident on a concave lens of focal length 40 cm. In the absence of lens, the beam converges at a point 20 cm behind the lens. After refraction, the beam

(a) converges to 10 cm behind the lens

(b) diverges to 20 cm behind the lens

(c) converges to 12 cm

(d) converges to 40 cm behind the lens

8. A small air bubble is inside a glass cube of side 12 cm. When looking the top face, the bubble appears to be at a distance of 3 cm. However, when it is seen from the opposite face, it appears to be at a distance of 5 cm. The bubble distance from the top face of cube and refractive index of the glass respectively are

(a) 7.5 cm, 1.4 (b) 7.5 cm, 1.5

(c) 4.5 cm, 1.4 (d) 4.5 cm, 1.5

9. A concave mirror of radius 15 cm is kept on a horizontal surface. A transparent liquid is poured in it upto a height of 3 cm. When the distance of object from the surface of liquid is 9 cm, it is seen that image of object is formed on itself, and the refractive index of liquid is

(a) 1.2 (b) 1.33 (c) 1.5 (d) 1.6

10. A right prism is made by suitable material and the angle α and β ($\beta < \alpha$) is as shown in the following figure. It is desired that a ray of light incident on the face AB emerges parallel to the incident direction after two internal reflection. The minimum refractive index (μ) for this to be possible is

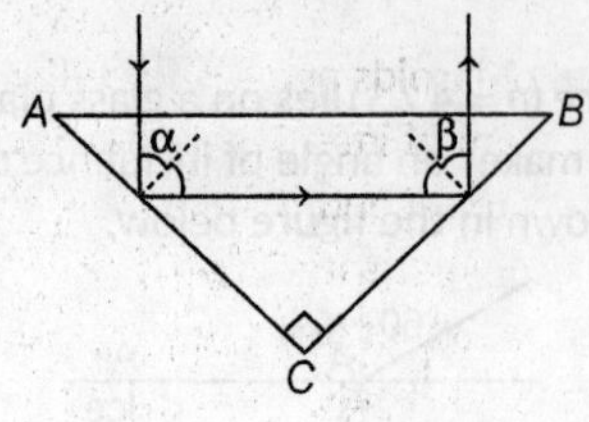

(a) $\sqrt{3}$ (b) 1.5
(c) $\sqrt{2}$ (d) 1.8

11. Given radius of curvature of a curved surface is $R = 30$ cm and refractive index of medium $\mu = 1.5$. Now, match Column I (type of lens) with Column II (focal length).

Column I	Column II
A. Convex	P. -30 cm
B. Concave	Q. 30 cm
C. Plano-convex	R. 60 cm
D. Plano-concave	S. -60 cm

Choose the correct answer from the options given below:
(a) A - Q, B - P, C - S, D - R (b) A - Q, B - P, C - R, D - S
(c) A - P, B - Q, C - R, D - S (d) A - Q, B - R, C - S, D - P

12. Moon is observed by an astronomical refracting telescope having an objective of focal length 12 m and an eye-piece of focal length of 1.5 cm. The incorrect statement is
(a) The distance between the objective and the eye piece is 12.015 m.
(b) The angular magnification of the planet is 800.
(c) The image of the planet is erect.
(d) The objective is larger than the eye-piece.

13. A simple telescope, consisting of an objective of focal length 50 cm and a single eye-piece of focal length 4 cm is focused on a distant object in such a way that parallel rays comes out from the eye-piece. If the object subtends an angle 2° at the objective, then angular width of the images is
(a) 8° (b) 25° (c) $\frac{4^\circ}{25}$ (d) 50°

14. In a compound microscope, the focal lengths of the objective and the eye-piece are 4 cm and 5 cm, respectively. The distance between the objective and eye-piece is 200 cm. The final image formed by the eye-piece is at infinity. The distances of the object and the image produced by the objective measured from the objective lens are respectively
(a) 5.33 cm, 16 cm
(b) 5.33 cm, 20 cm
(c) 5 cm, 16 cm
(d) 5 cm, 20 cm

15. There are four spherical lenses of focal lengths +10 cm, +20 cm, +140 cm and +200 cm which are available for making an astronomical telescope. If someone wants to produce largest magnification, then focal length of objective and eye-piece should respectively be
(a) +10 cm, +200 cm (b) +200 cm, +15 cm
(c) +20 cm, +140 cm (d) +140 cm, +20 cm

16. Two coherent waves having amplitude in ratio of 2 : 1 interfere. The value of $\frac{I_{max} - I_{min}}{I_{max} + I_{min}}$ is
(a) 1 : 1 (b) 3 : 2
(c) 4 : 5 (d) 4 : 1

17. YDSE is performed in a medium whose refractive index μ can be varied. Which among the following graph best represent the variation of angular width θ with μ ?

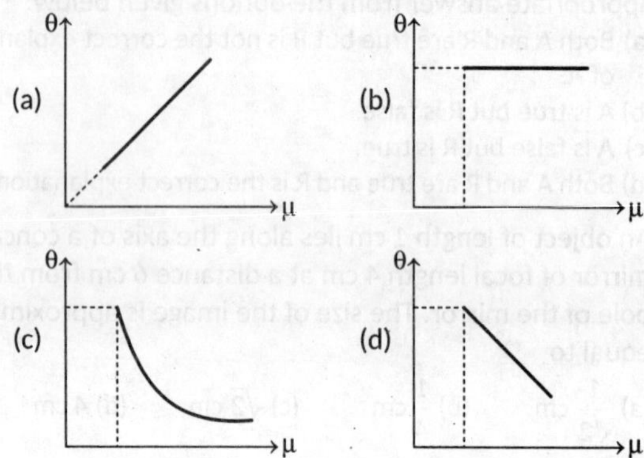

18. In YDSE, laser light of wavelength 5800 Å incident on pair of identical slits, produces an interference pattern where dark fringes are separated by 7.25 mm. If another laser light produces interference pattern where bright fringes are separated by 5.075 mm, then wavelength of second light is
(a) 4060 Å (b) 5075 Å
(c) 6090 Å (d) None of these

19. The slits are 0.24 mm apart from each other and illuminated with a light of wavelength λ. If the distance of screen from slits plane is 0.8 m, then the distance between ninth dark fringe to sixth bright fringe is obtained to be 5.4 mm, then value of λ is
(a) 4628 Å (b) 5490 Å
(c) 6480 Å (d) None of these

20. In Young's double slit experiment, the intensity of light at a point on the screen where path difference λ is I. If intensity at a point is $\frac{I}{4}$, then possible path differences at this point are

(a) $\frac{\lambda}{2}, \frac{\lambda}{3}$
(b) $\frac{\lambda}{3}, \frac{2\lambda}{3}$
(c) $\frac{\lambda}{3}, \frac{\lambda}{4}$
(d) $\frac{2\lambda}{3}, \frac{\lambda}{4}$

21. A parallel beam of monochromatic light of wavelength 6000 Å passes through a slit of width 0.24 mm and diffraction pattern is observed on screen 1 m away from slit. The width of central maxima and first secondary maxima, respectively are

(a) 0.25 cm, 0.25 cm
(b) 0.5 cm, 0.25 cm
(c) 0.25 cm, 0.5 cm
(d) 0.5 cm, 0.5 cm

22. Diffraction pattern due to a single slit has been shown in the following figure.

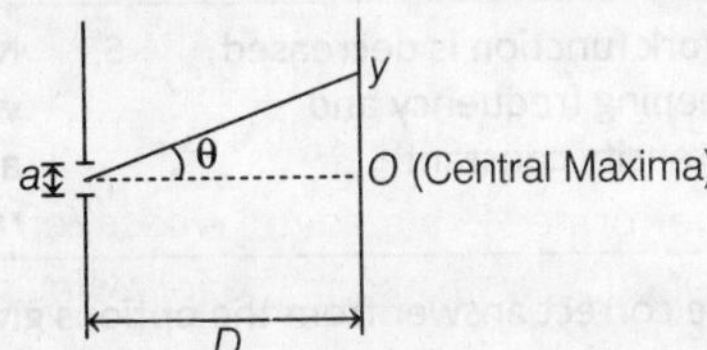

Which among the following graph best represents the intensity I variation with $\sin\theta$?

(a)
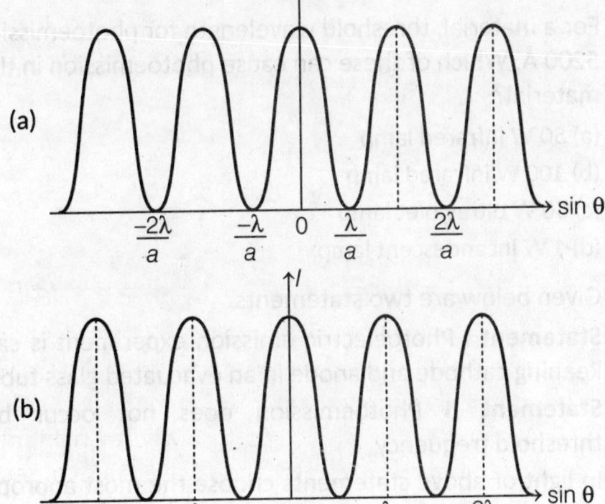

(b)

(c)
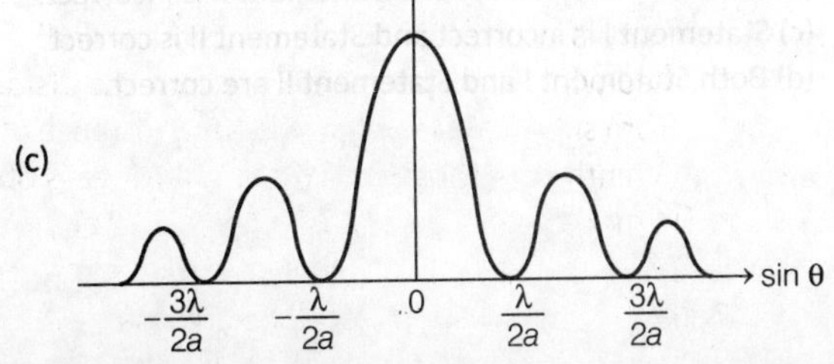

(d)
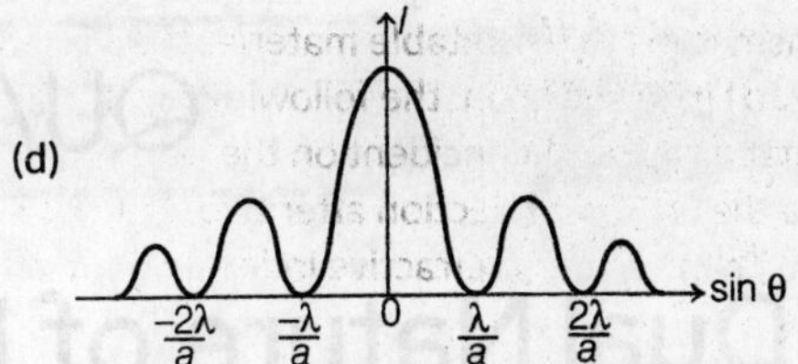

23. Two identical polaroids are placed in the path of unpolarised beam of intensity I such that no light is emitted from the second polaroid. If a third identical polaroid whose polarisation axis makes an angle θ with the polarisation axis of first polaroid, is placed between between these polaroids, then the intensity of light emerging from the last polaroid is

(a) $\left(\frac{I}{8}\right)\sin^2 2\theta$ (b) $\left(\frac{I}{4}\right)\sin^2 2\theta$ (c) $\left(\frac{I}{2}\right)\cos^4\theta$ (d) $I\cos^4\theta$

24. A beam of light is incident on the surface of transparent medium as shown in following figure. In which of following option, the angle between reflected rays and refracted rays is $\frac{\pi}{2}$?

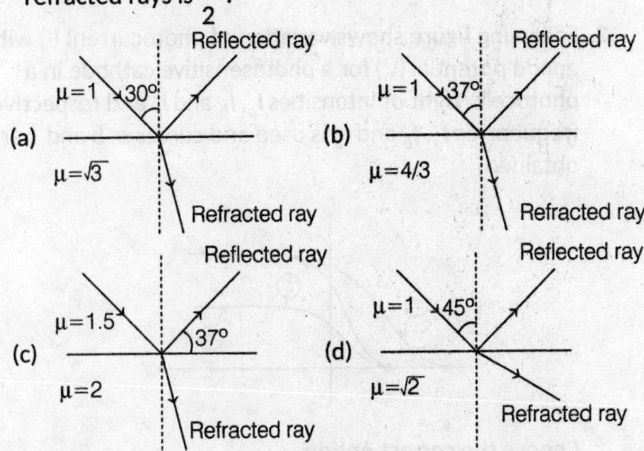

25. Given below are two statements.

Statement I For sustained interference, the interfering waves should be in the same state of polarisation.

Statement II In sustained interference, the positions of maxima and minima of intensity on the observation screen slightly changes with time.

(a) Both Statement I and Statement II are incorrect.
(b) Statement I is correct and Statement II is incorrect.
(c) Statement I is incorrect and Statement II is correct.
(d) Both Statement I and Statement II are correct.

Answers

1 *(c)*	2 *(a)*	3 *(d)*	4 *(b)*	5 *(a)*
6 *(b)*	7 *(d)*	8 *(d)*	9 *(b)*	10 *(c)*
11 *(b)*	12 *(c)*	13 *(b)*	14 *(a)*	15 *(a)*
16 *(d)*	17 *(c)*	18 *(a)*	19 *(c)*	20 *(b)*
21 *(b)*	22 *(d)*	23 *(a)*	24 *(c)*	25 *(b)*

See detailed explanations on page no. 219

QUALIFIER 17

Dual Nature of Matter and Radiation

1. **Assertion (A)** Angular momentum of an electron in Bohr's atom is quantised.

   Reason (R) In a stationary state, the circumference of a circular orbit contains integral number of de-Broglie wavelengths.

   In the light of the above statements, choose the most appropriate answer from the options given below.

   (a) Both A and R are true but R is not the correct explanation of A.
   (b) A is true but R is false.
   (c) A is false but R is true.
   (d) Both A and R are true and R is the correct explanation of A.

2. Following figure shows variation of photocurrent (I) with anode potential (V) for a photosensitive cathode in a photocell. Light of intensities I_a, I_b and I_c and respective frequencies f_a, f_b and f_c is used and curves a, b and c are obtained.

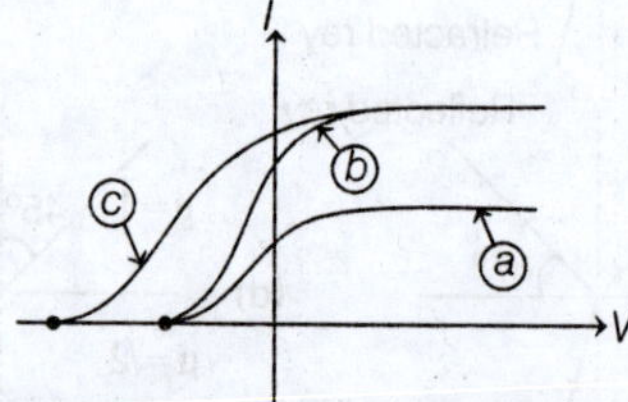

   Choose the correct option.

   (a) $f_a = f_b$ and $I_a \neq I_b$
   (b) $f_a = f_c$ and $I_a = I_c$
   (c) $f_a = f_b$ and $I_a = I_b$
   (d) $f_a = f_b$ and $I_b = I_c$

3. Consider the photoelectric experiment.

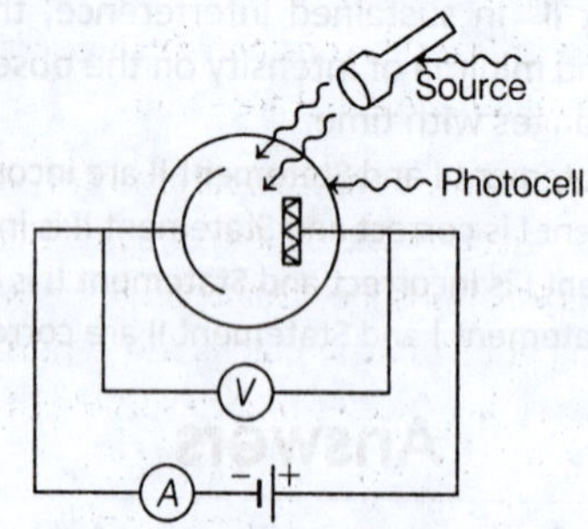

   Now match Column I with Column II.

	Column I		Column II
A.	Frequency of radiation is increased keeping work function and intensity constant	P.	Stopping potential increases
B.	Intensity is increased keeping frequency and work function constant	Q.	Saturation current increases
C.	Distance of anode and cathode is decreased	R.	KE of emitted electrons increases
D.	Work function is decreased keeping frequency and intensity constant	S.	No change in voltmeter or ammeter reading

   Choose the correct answer from the options given below

   (a) A - P, B - Q, C - R, D - S
   (b) A - Q, B - R, C - S, D - P
   (c) A - P, B - Q, C - S, D - R
   (d) A - Q, B - S, C - P, D - R

4. For a material, threshold wavelength for photoemission is 5200 Å. Which of these can cause photoemission in this material?

   (a) 50 W infrared lamp
   (b) 100 W infrared lamp
   (c) 50 W ultraviolet lamp
   (d) 1 W incandescent lamp

5. Given below are two statements.

   Statement I Photoelectric emission experiment is carried keeping cathode and anode in an evacuated glass tube.

   Statement II Photoemission does not occur below threshold frequency

   In light of above statements choose the most appropriate answer from the options given below :

   (a) Both Statement I and Statement II are incorrect.
   (b) Statement I is correct and Statement II is incorrect.
   (c) Statement I is incorrect and Statement II is correct.
   (d) Both Statement I and Statement II are correct.

6. The stopping potential in the experimental set-up shown in the following figure is

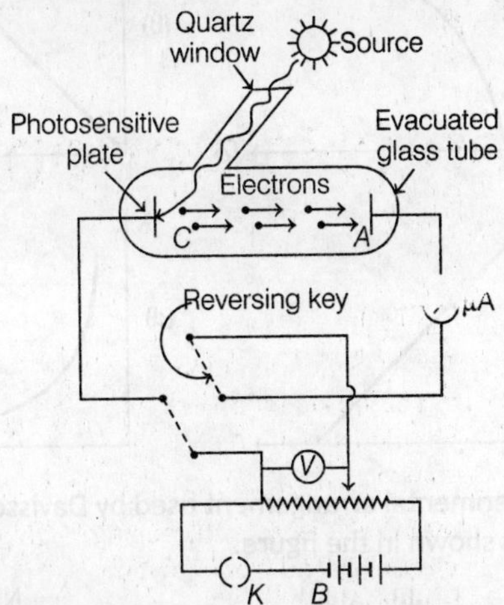

(a) positive potential (V_0) given to the plate A for which the photocurrent saturates
(b) positive potential (V_0) given to the plate A for which the photocurrent stops
(c) positive potential (V_0) given to the plate A for which the photocurrent stops increasing
(d) negative potential (V_0) given to the plate A for which the photocurrent becomes zero

7. The work function of metals is in the range of 1.5 eV to 2.5 eV. Which of the following wavelength of light cannot be used for photoelectric effect?

(a) 410 nm (b) 500 nm (c) 650 nm (d) 850 nm

8. A light beam of wavelength 600 nm is incident on surface at angle of incidence 60° which reflects 40% light. If the beam exerts a force of 10^{-6}N, then number of photons striking to the surface per second is

(a) 1.29×10^{20} (b) 1.29×10^{21}
(c) 1.13×10^{20} (d) 1.13×10^{21}

9. The following figure shows few data points in a photoelectric effect experiment for a certain metal. The minimum energy for the ejection of electron from its surface is (Take, Planck's constant, $h = 6.62 \times 10^{-34}$ J-s)

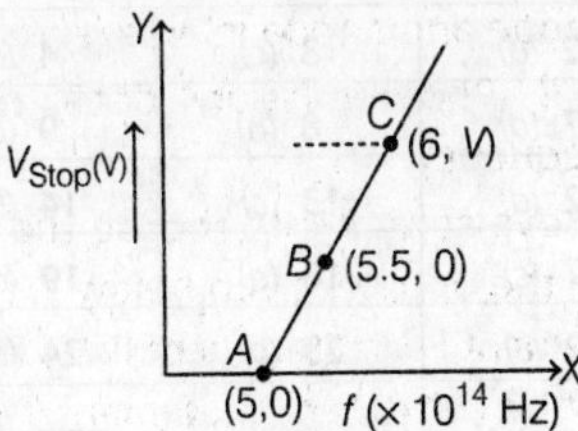

(a) 1.93 eV (b) 2.59 eV (c) 2.27 eV (d) 2.10 eV

10. When the energy of the incident radiation is increased by 40%, the kinetic energy of the photoelectrons emitted from a metal surface increases from 0.8 eV to 1.2 eV. The work function of the metal is

(a) 2 eV (b) 0.2 eV (c) 0.4 eV (d) 5.8 eV

11. The momentum of photon of electromagnetic radiation is 1.65×10^{-29} kg ms^{-1}. The frequency of the wave associated with it, is

(a) 7.47×10^{12} Hz (b) 7.47×10^{11} Hz
(c) 7.47×10^{6} Hz (d) 7.47×10^{9} Hz

12. An electromagnetic wave has electric field equation $200 \sin(1.5 \times 10^{15}\, t - 1257\, x]$ V/m, where x is in metre and t is in second. It is incident on metal surface which has work function 1.8 eV. The maximum kinetic energy of emitted electrons is

(a) 3.27 eV (b) 2.85 eV
(c) 0.974 eV (d) None of these

13. An electromagnetic wave is passing through vacuum. The wavelength of wave is 520 nm. The associated energy and effective mass of each photons are respectively. (Planck's constant $= 6.62 \times 10^{-34}$ J-s)

(a) 2.387 eV, 4.24×10^{-35} kg (b) 23.87 eV, 4.24×10^{-35} kg
(c) 2.387 eV, 4.24×10^{-36} kg (d) 0.238 eV, 4.24×10^{-36} kg

14. A student performs an experiment on photoelectric effect, using two materials A and B. The graph between stopping potential V_s and incident frequency ν has been shown below.

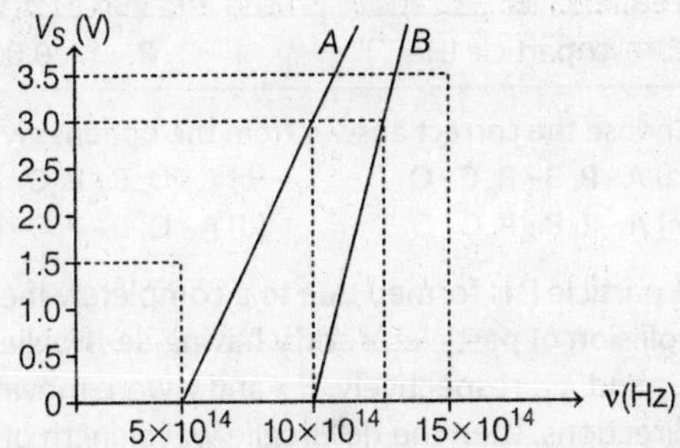

(a) Material A has greater work function.
(b) Material B has greater work function.
(c) The value of Planck's constant obtained from experiment for material A is higher.
(d) The value of Planck's constant obtained from experiment for both material A and B are same.

15. A 60 W bulb radiates energy uniformly in all directions. The bulb is placed at the centre of a metallic sphere that absorbs all radiations incident on it. If the wavelength of light coming out from the bulb is 662 nm, then the rate at which photons are incidenting to surface of metal, is

(a) 2×10^{19} (b) 2×10^{20}
(c) 3×10^{19} (d) 3.2×10^{20}

16. In an experiment on photoelectric effect, the slope of the cut-off voltage *versus* frequency of incident light, is found to be 4.13×10^{-15} V-s. The value of Planck's constant is

(a) 6.59×10^{-34} J-s (b) 6.58×10^{-34} J-s
(c) 6.61×10^{-34} J-s (d) 6.62×10^{-34} J-s

17. A photocell converts
(a) heat energy into electrical energy
(b) thermal energy into mechanical energy
(c) light energy into electrical energy
(d) electrical energy into light energy

18. The maximum frequency of X-rays produced by 41.4 kV electrons, is
(a) 1.5×10^{18} Hz (b) 6.2×10^{17} Hz
(c) 6×10^{8} Hz (d) 1×10^{19} Hz

19. If the de-Broglie wavelength associated with a moving electron is changed by 0.25%, then its momentum changes by *P*. The initial momentum of electron is
(a) $\frac{p}{400}$ (b) $\frac{p}{100}$
(c) 200 *p* (d) 400 *p*

20. Three positively charged particles : Deutron ion, Helium ion and α-particle are accelerated through a potential difference of 64 V from rest. The corresponding de-Broglie wavelengths has been mentioned in Column II.

	Column I		Column II
A.	Helium ion (He^{+})	P.	0.0126 Å
B.	Deutron ion (H^{+})	Q.	0.0178 Å
C.	α-particle (He^{++})	R.	0.0252 Å

Choose the correct answer from the options given below:
(a) A - P, B - R, C - Q (b) A - Q, B - R, C - P
(c) A - R, B - P, C - Q (d) A - Q, B - P, C - R

21. A particle *P* is formed due to a completely inelastic collision of particles *x* and *y* having de-Broglie wavelengths λ_x and λ_y, respectively. If *x* and *y* were moving in opposite directions, then the de-Broglie wavelength of *P* is
(a) $\lambda_x - \lambda_y$ (b) $\frac{\lambda_x \lambda_y}{\lambda_x - \lambda_y}$
(c) $\frac{\lambda_x \lambda_y}{\lambda_x + \lambda_y}$ (d) $\lambda_x + \lambda_y$

22. When the de-Broglie wavelength of a particle is to be reduced from 1.2×10^{-10} m to 0.6×10^{-10} m, the required percentage of initial energy to be added, will be
(a) 50% (b) 100%
(c) 300% (d) 400%

23. An object of mass *m* is moving with same velocity, has momentum *p* and kinetic energy *E*. The correct variation of de-Broglie wavelength λ associated with *p* and *E* is

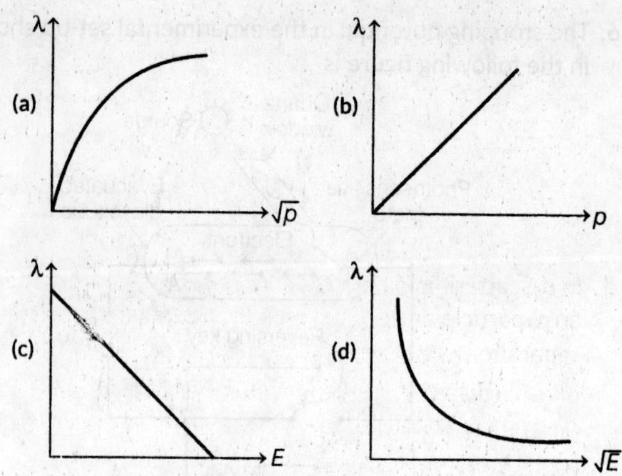

24. Experimental arrangement used by Davisson and Germer is as shown in the figure.

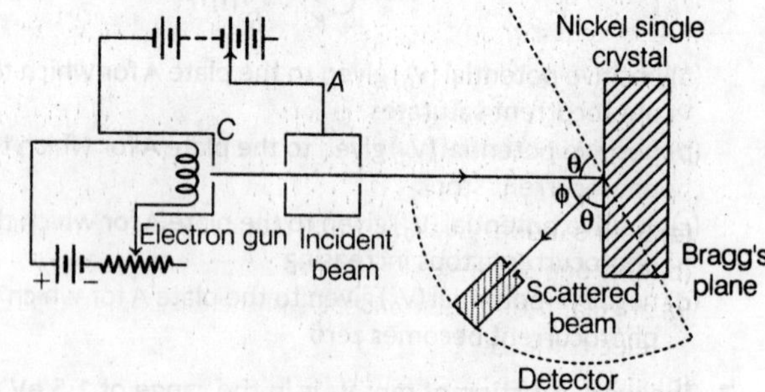

When angle of scattering is φ, then intensity of scattered beam of electrons is found to be maximum. From the figure, the values of φ and θ respectively are
(a) 50°, 54° (b) 54°, 50°
(c) 54°, 65° (d) 50°, 65°

25. In Davisson and Germer experiment, electron beam of wavelength 1.2 Å is incident on a N_1 crystal of lattice spacing 2.4 Å. The incident angle for second maxima, is
(a) 30° (b) 60°
(c) $\sin^{-1}\left(\frac{1}{4}\right)$ (d) $\sin^{-1}\left(\frac{2}{3}\right)$

Answers

1 (d)	2 (d)	3 (c)	4 (c)	5 (d)
6 (d)	7 (d)	8 (b)	9 (c)	10 (b)
11 (a)	12 (d)	13 (c)	14 (b)	15 (b)
16 (c)	17 (c)	18 (d)	19 (d)	20 (b)
21 (b)	22 (c)	23 (d)	24 (d)	25 (a)

See detailed explanations on page no. 222

QUALIFIER 18

Atoms and Nuclei

1. **In α-scattering experiment, in a head-on-collision between an α-particle and a gold nucleus, the minimum distance of separation or closest approach is 4×10^{-14} m. The energy of α-particle is (take, atomic number of gold = 79)**

(a) 5.68 MeV (b) 8 MeV
(c) 4.47 MeV (d) 7.24 MeV

2. **According to Bohr's model, for the electron in the ground state of hydrogen atom angular momentum is equals to $\frac{h}{2\pi}$. Angular momentum is a vector and hence, there will be infinitely many orbits with the vector pointing in all possible directions. However in actual, this is not true, because**

(a) Bohr's model gives incorrect values of angular momentum
(b) only one of these would have a minimum energy
(c) angular momentum must be in the direction of spin of electron
(d) electrons go around only in horizontal orbits

3. **In hydrogen and hydrogen like atoms, if the principal quantum number *n* is increased, then choose the correct option regarding variation in quantities like total energy, time period and angular speed.**

	Total energy	Time period	Angular speed
(a)	Increases	Decreases	Decreases
(b)	Decreases	Increases	Decreases
(c)	Decreases	Decreases	Increases
(d)	Increases	Increases	Decreases

4. **The expression of the energy associated with energy levels of a hypothetical one electron atom is given by $E_n = -\frac{20}{n^2}$ eV, where $n = 1, 2, 3 \ldots$ For this atom, the excitation potential of the second excited state, is**

(a) 15 V (b) 17.78 V (c) 5 V (d) 2.22 V

5. **The potential energy of electron in He^+ ion in first excited state to be zero. The total energy of electron in ground state, is**

(a) + 27.2 eV (b) – 27.2 eV (c) – 54.4 eV (d) – 81.6 eV

6. **For a hydrogen like monoelectronic species, the energy required to separate atom into proton and an electron from its first excited state to infinity is 30.6 eV. The orbital radius of the electron in this species in ground state, is**

(a) 2.12 Å (b) 0.706 Å (c) 1.06 Å (d) None of these

7. **If *r*, *v* and *E* represent the radius of the orbit, speed of electron and total energy of electron, respectively in Bohr model of the hydrogen atom, then which of the following quantities are directly proportional to the principal number *n*?**

(a) v^2r (b) rE (c) $\frac{v}{E}$ (d) $\frac{r}{E}$

8. **Match laws/processes of Column I with emission observed in Column II.**

	Column I		Column II
A.	Transition of electron between two energy levels.	P.	Positrons
B.	Photons absorbed by a metal surface.	Q.	X-rays
C.	Scattering of a fast electron by an atom.	R.	Electrons
D.	A proton is converted into a neutron.	S.	Infrared light

Choose the correct answer from the options given below:

(a) A → S, B → R, C → P, D → Q
(b) A → S, B → R, C → Q, D → P
(c) A → R, B → S, C → P, D → Q
(d) A → Q, B → P, C → S, D → R

9. **The figure shown below represents the energy level diagram of helium ion (He^+) and the origin of eight spectral lines in emission spectra. The total number of spectral lines that occurs in the absorption spectrum is**

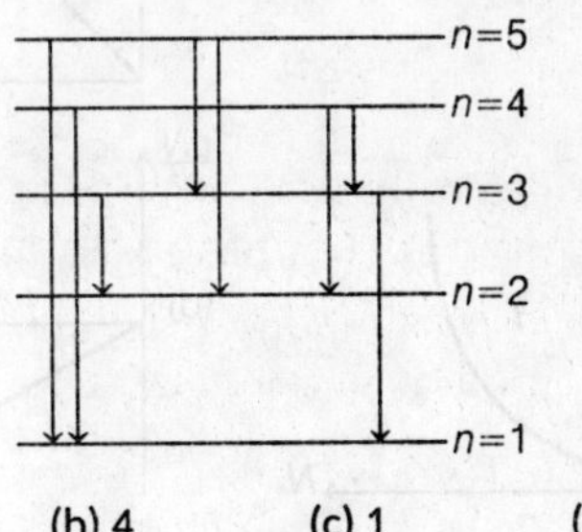

(a) 3 (b) 4 (c) 1 (d) 8

10. **The filament current in the electron gun of a coolidge tube is increased while the potential difference used to accelerate the electrons is decreased. As a result, in the emitted radiation.**

(a) intensity decreases while minimum wavelength increases
(b) intensity increases while minimum wavelength decreases
(c) intensity and minimum wavelength both increase
(d) intensity and minimum wavelength both decrease

11. The ratio of minimum frequency of Paschen series to the minimum frequency of Brackett series will be

(a) $\frac{160}{81}$ (b) $\frac{175}{81}$ (c) $\frac{175}{27}$ (d) $\frac{160}{27}$

12. The shortest wavelength of Balmer series of the He^+ ion, is (R = Rydberg constant)

(a) $\frac{1}{R}$ (b) $\frac{3}{7R}$ (c) $\frac{2}{R}$ (d) $\frac{4}{3R}$

13. The binding energy per nucleon of iron nucleus ($^{56}_{26}Fe$) is 8.6 MeV. If mass of proton and neutron are 1.007 amu and 1.008 amu respectively, then mass of iron nucleus is

$\left(1\ \text{amu} = \frac{931.5\ \text{meV}}{c^2}\right)^2$

(a) 56.939 amu (b) 56.431 amu
(c) 55.905 amu (d) 56.412 amu

14. Assertion (A) An electron of H-atom in its ground state cannot absorbs energy greater than 13.6 eV.

Reason (R) When an electron of H-atom absorbs an energy of 13.6 eV in ground state, atom becomes ionised.

In the light of the above statements, choose the most appropriate answer from the options given below.

(a) Both A and R are true but R is not the correct explanation of A.
(b) A is true but R is false.
(c) A is false but R is true.
(d) Both A and R are true and R is the correct explanation of A.

15. Among the given graphs, which one shows the correct variation of decay rate $\frac{dN}{dt}$ with number of active nuclei N?

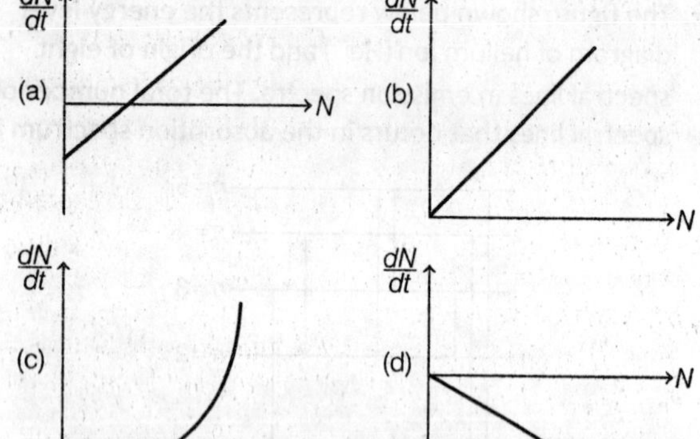

16. Consider the following nuclear reactions.

I. $^{6}_{3}Li + X \longrightarrow {}^{7}_{4}Be + {}^{1}_{0}n$

II. $^{35}_{17}Cl + Y \longrightarrow {}^{32}_{16}S + {}^{4}_{2}He$

III. $^{79}_{35}Br + {}^{2}_{1}H \longrightarrow Z + 2{}^{1}_{0}n$

The X, Y and Z respectively are

(a) $^{2}_{1}H$, $^{1}_{1}H$ and $^{79}_{36}Kr$ (b) $^{2}_{1}H$, $^{2}_{1}H$ and $^{79}_{36}Kr$
(c) $^{1}_{1}H$, $^{1}_{1}H$ and $^{79}_{36}Kr$ (d) $^{2}_{1}H$, $^{1}_{1}H$ and $^{77}_{36}Kr$

17. A nuclear reaction is given as

$^{176}Lu \longrightarrow {}^{176}Hf + e + \bar{\nu}$

If atomic mass of ^{176}Lu is 175.942694 u and that of ^{176}Hf is 175.941420 u, then maximum energy that a β-particle can have, is

(a) 11.82 MeV (b) 1.182 MeV
(c) 0.591 MeV (d) 1.182 MeV

18. The activity of a sample is measured as N_0 counts per second initially. The counts per second at $t = 10$ s is $\frac{N_0}{e^2}$. The time at which the activity reduces to half its value is

(a) $5\log_e 2$ s (b) $\frac{5\log_e 2}{2}$ s
(c) $5\log_{10} 2$ s (d) $\frac{\log_{10} 2}{5}$ s

19. A radioactive sample of a nucleus is kept in a container. Its radioactivity at time t is R and at time $3t$ is R_2. If the half-life of the sample is T, then in time duration t to $3t$, the number of decayed atoms is equal to

(a) $t(3R_1 - R_2)$ (b) $(R_1 - R_2)T$
(c) $\frac{t(3R_1 - R_2)}{\ln 2}$ (d) $\frac{(R_1 - R_2)T}{\ln 2}$

20. A stationary nucleus of mass 48 amu emits a gamma photon. The energy of the emitted photon is 7 MeV. The recoil energy of the nucleus is

(a) 1.1 keV (b) 0.55 keV
(c) 1.55 keV (d) 11 keV

21. Two radioactive substances A and B have decay constant 4λ and λ, respectively. Initially, they have same number of nuclei. After a time interval of $\frac{2}{3\lambda}$, the ratio of number of nuclei of A to those of B, is

(a) $\frac{1}{e}$ (b) $\frac{1}{e^2}$ (c) $\frac{1}{e^{10/3}}$ (d) $\frac{1}{e^{5/3}}$

22. Two statements are given below.

Statement I Any substance with large specific heat can be used as a moderator.

Statement II Moderator carries energy in form of heat to heat exchanger.

In light of above statements, choose the most appropriate answer from the options given below.

(a) Both Statement I and Statement II are incorrect.
(b) Statement I is correct and Statement II is incorrect.
(c) Statement I is incorrect and Statement II is correct.
(d) Both Statement I and Statement II are correct.

23. If t_A is half-life of sample A and t_B is the half-life of sample B. The graph between rate of decay $\left(\frac{dN}{dt}\right)$ and time t has been shown in figure, which of the following is correct?

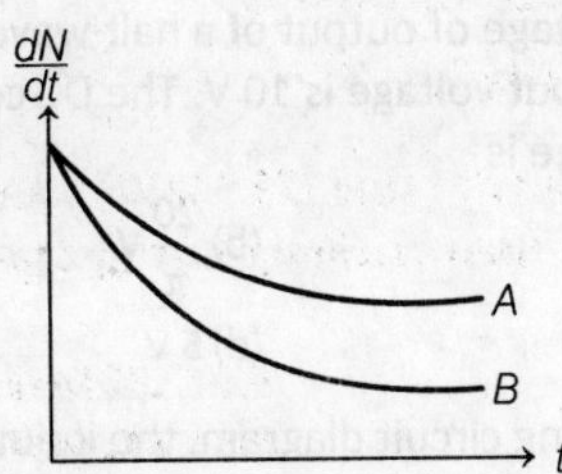

(a) $t_A = t_B$
(b) $t_A < t_B$
(c) $t_A > t_B$
(d) Data insufficient

24. Nucleus A is transformed into C through the following nuclear reactions by releasing α and β particles.

$$A \longrightarrow B + m\alpha$$
$$B \longrightarrow C + n\beta$$

(a) If $m = 1$ and $n = 1$, then A and C are isotopes
(b) If $m = 1$ and $n = 2$, then A and C are isotopes
(c) If $m = 1$ and $n = 1$, then A and C are isobars
(d) If $m = 2$ and $n = 1$, then A and B are isotones

25. Match Column I (Reaction) with Column II (Products).

	Column I		Column II
A.	${}_1^1H + {}_6^{12}C$	P.	${}_7^{15}N + {}_{-1}\beta^0$
B.	${}_8^{15}O$	Q.	${}_6^{12}C + {}_2^4He$
C.	${}_1^1H + {}_7^{15}N$	R.	${}_{94}^{239}Pu + {}_{-1}^{0}\beta + \nu$
D.	${}_{93}^{239}NP$	S.	${}_7^{13}N + \gamma$

Choose the correct answer from the options given below.
(a) A→R, B→S, C→Q, D→P
(b) A→P, B→Q, C→R, D→S
(c) A→S, B→P, C→Q, D→R
(d) A→Q, B→R, C→P, D→S

Answers

1 *(a)*	2 *(a)*	3 *(d)*	4 *(b)*	5 *(b)*
6 *(b)*	7 *(c)*	8 *(b)*	9 *(a)*	10 *(c)*
11 *(b)*	12 *(a)*	13 *(c)*	14 *(c)*	15 *(d)*
16 *(a)*	17 *(b)*	18 *(a)*	19 *(b)*	20 *(b)*
21 *(b)*	22 *(a)*	23 *(c)*	24 *(b)*	25 *(c)*

See detailed explanations on page no. 225

QUALIFIER 19

Electronic Devices

1. According to the classification of solids on the basis of energy bands, a solid is classified as a semiconductor if the energy gap (E_g) between the valence band and conduction band

(a) lies between 0 to 1 eV
(b) less than 3 eV
(c) lies between 3 to 6 eV
(d) greater than 3 eV

2. A pure semiconductor crystal has 2×10^{27} atoms/m^3. It is doped by 4 ppm concentration of pentavalent atom. The number of holes in crystal per metre cube is
(Take $n_i = 10^{16}$ per m^3)

(a) 2×10^{11} per m^3 (b) 2×10^{9} per m^3
(c) 2×10^{10} per m^3 (d) 2×10^{8} per m^3

3. The width of depletion layer of a *p-n* junction is

(a) less with light doping
(b) more with heavy doping
(c) independent of applied voltage
(d) increased under reverse bias

4. Assertion (A) A *p-n* junction rectifier conducts in forward bias and no heat is produced during the process.
Reason (R) In forward bias, current flows from *p* to *n*-side.
In the light of the above statements, choose the most appropriate answer from the options given below:

(a) Both A and R are true but R is not the correct explanation of A.
(b) A is true but R is false.
(c) A is false but R is true.
(d) Both A and R are true and R is the correct explanation of A.

5. Without applying biasing across a *p-n* junction, the variation of electric field in depletion region is best represented by which of the following graph?

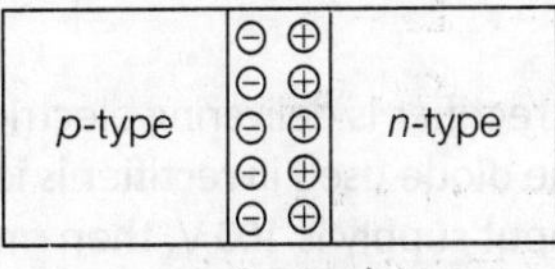

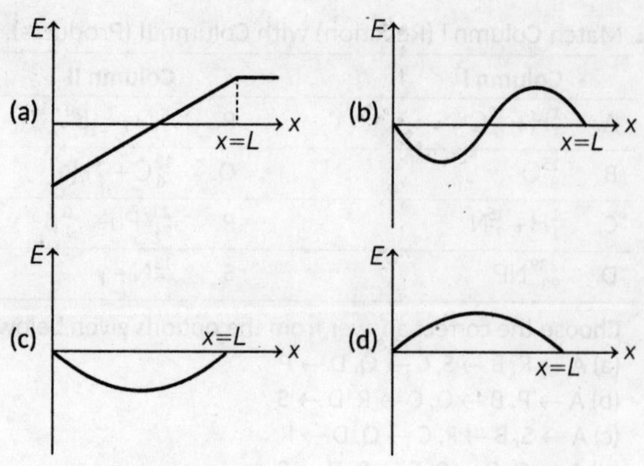

6. In a board practical examination, a student was given a diode to find potential barrier in forward biasing. For this purpose, he used some apparatus and arranged in following manner.

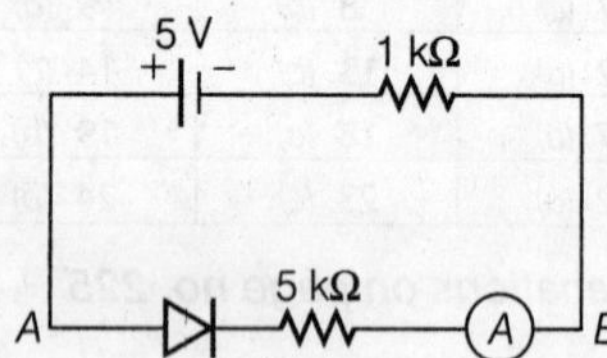

If the reading of an ideal ammeter is 0.8 mA, then potential barrier of the diode used is

(a) 0.2 V (b) 0.1 V
(c) 0.5 V (d) 0.7 V

7. In the circuit shown below, the diodes are ideal. The output waveform for the circuit shown in the following figure is

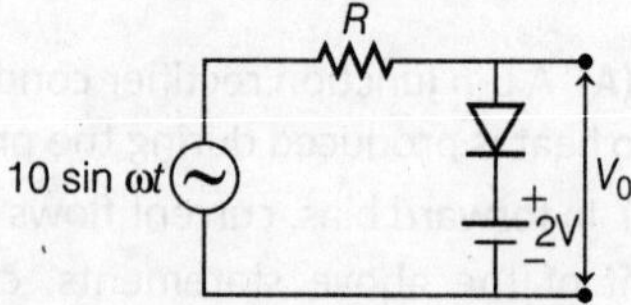

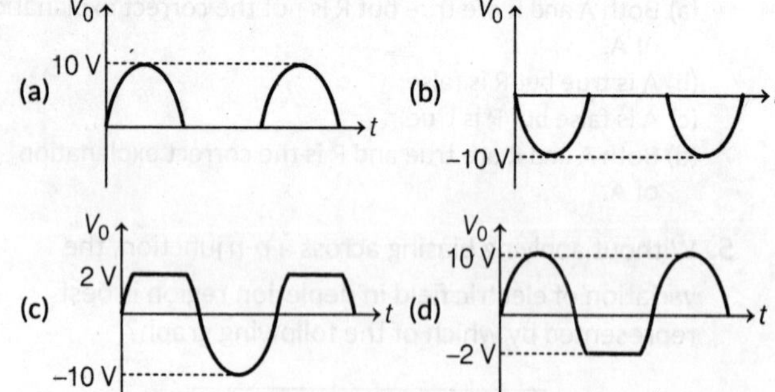

8. A half-wave rectifier is delivering electric power to a load of 2 kΩ. If the diode used in rectifier is ideal and peak voltage of input supply is 100 V, then rms value of ripple voltage is

(a) 38.5 V (b) 77 V
(c) 15.34 V (d) 30.7 V

9. The peak voltage of output of a half-wave rectifier with a sinusoidal input voltage is 10 V. The DC component of the output voltage is

(a) $\frac{10}{\pi}$ V (b) $\frac{20}{\pi}$ V
(c) $5\sqrt{2}$ V (d) 5 V

10. In the following circuit diagram, the input is applied across terminals *A* and *C* and the output is taken across *B* and *D*. Then, the output is

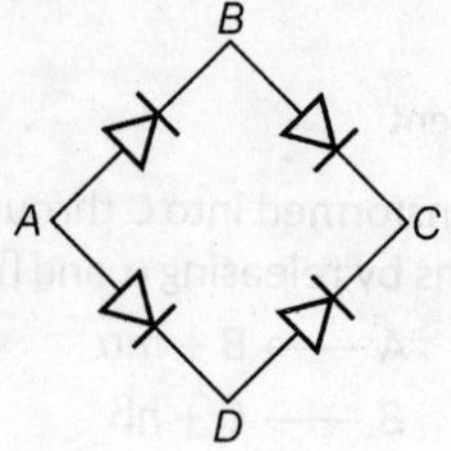

(a) always zero
(b) same as the input
(c) same as that of half-wave rectifier
(d) same as that of full wave rectifier

11. In the circuit shown in figure, if each diode has a forward bias resistance of 25 Ω and infinite resistance in reverse bias. The value of emf of battery ε is

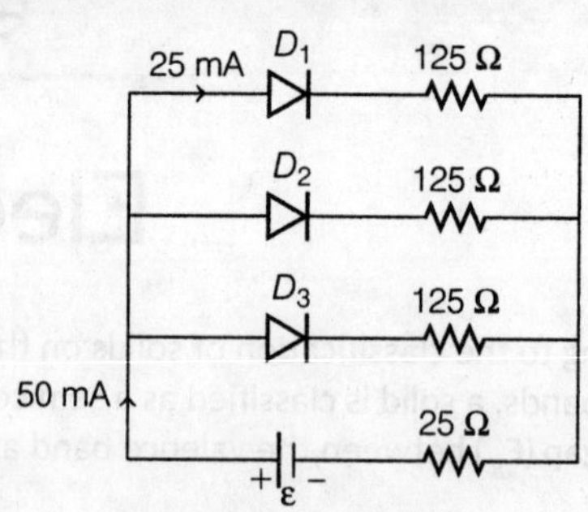

(a) 5 V (b) 10 V
(c) 3.75 V (d) 4.375 V

12. Statement I A photodetector diode is used in reverse bias.

Statement II Fractional change in reverse bias current (due to change in intensity of light) is easily measurable.

In light of above statements choose the most appropriate answer from the options given below :

(a) Both Statement I and Statement II are incorrect.
(b) Statement I is correct and Statement II is incorrect.
(c) Statement I is incorrect and Statement II is correct.
(d) Both Statement I and Statement II are correct.

13. The breakdown voltage of a zener diode used for voltage regulation is 12 V. The load current is 12 mA and the unregulated input is 20 V. If the maximum current through the zener diode is 25 mA, then value of series resistance *R* is

(a) 21.62 Ω (b) 216.2 Ω
(c) 864.86 Ω (d) 86.48 Ω

14. The transfer characteristics of common emitter amplifier has been shown in figure. Which statement is incorrect?

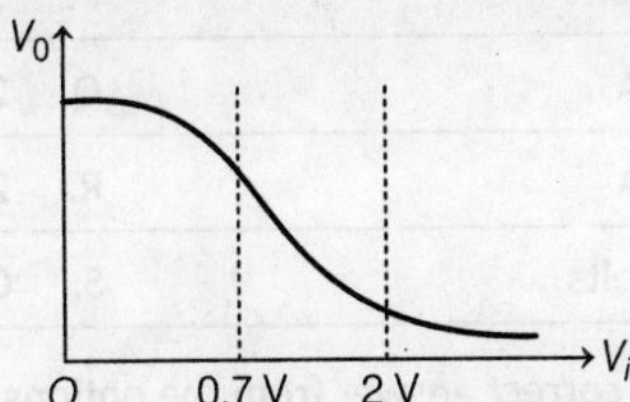

(a) At $V_i = 0.4$ V, transistor is in cut-off mode.
(b) At $V_i = 1$ V, transistor is in active region.
(c) At $V_i = 0.5$ V, transistor is in active state.
(d) At $V_i = 3$ V, transistor can be used as a switch turned on.

15. A *n-p-n* transistor is connected in common emitter configuration in a given amplifier. A load resistance of 800 Ω is connected in the collector circuit and the voltage drop across it is 0.8 V. If the current amplification factor is 0.96 and the input resistance of the circuits is 192 Ω, then the voltage gain and the power gain of the amplifier respectively are

(a) 3.69, 3.84 (b) 4, 4
(c) 4, 3.69 (d) 4, 3.84

16. For the circuit shown in the figure, if $V_{CE} = 7$ V, $R_C = 2\,k\Omega$, $V_{BE} = 0$ and collector current to base current ratio is 100, then base current is

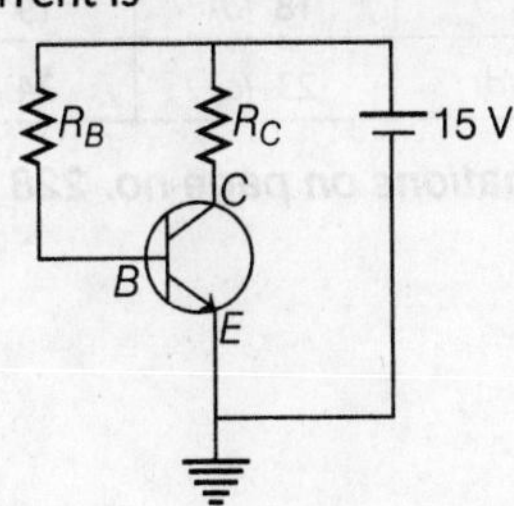

(a) 40 μA (b) 40 mA
(c) 4 mA (d) 0.02 mA

17. Match Column I (type of diode) with Column II (energy gap of semiconductor used).

Column I		Column II	
A.	Photodiode for optical link to detect wavelength of 1240 nm.	P.	1.1 to 1.5 eV
B.	Solar cell	Q.	1.8 to 2.8 eV
C.	LED	R.	0.75 to 1.1 eV
D.	Rectifier diode	S.	1 eV

Choose the correct answer from the options given below:
(a) A → S, B → P, C → Q, D → R
(b) A → P, B → S, C → R, D → Q
(c) A → R, B → S, C → P, D → Q
(d) A → Q, B → R, C → S, D → P

18. In the circuit shown in figure, if the value of resistance R_1 is increased, then readings of ammeter and voltmeter

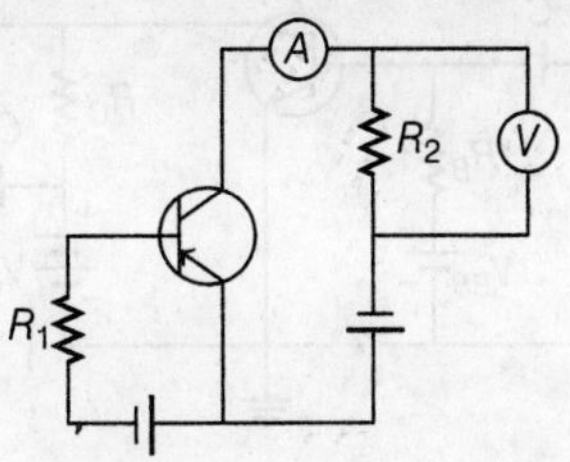

(a) increase, increase (b) increase, decrease
(c) decrease, increase (d) decrease, decrease

19. The input voltage, in the circuit shown in figure is 20 V. For *n-p-n* transistor $V_{BE} = 0$, $V_{CE} = 0$ and $\beta = 125$. The value of I_B and I_C respectively are

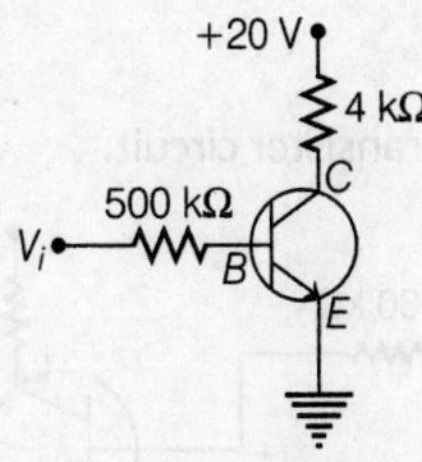

(a) 40 μA, 5 mA (b) 5 μA, 40 mA
(c) 40 μA, 10 mA (d) 20 μA, 10 mA

20. Two transistor amplifiers are connected in series (cascaded). The output voltage gain of first amplifier is 20 dB and that of second is 20 dB. The over all voltage gain of amplifier is

(a) 1 dB (b) 10 dB (c) 40 dB (d) 400 dB

21. The following voltage waveforms shows the two inputs *A* and *B* of a logic gate and output *Y*.

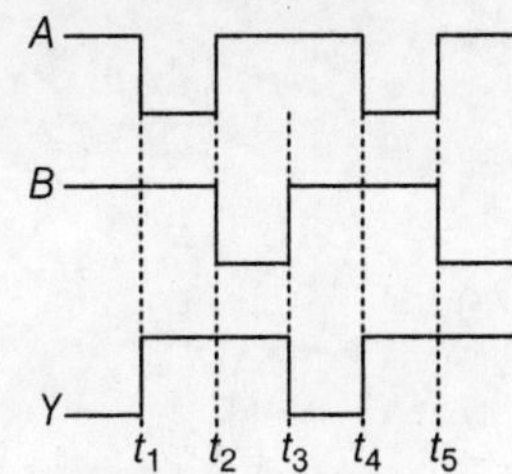

The logic gate can be
(a) AND (b) NAND (c) OR (d) NOR

22. The given logic circuit is equivalent to

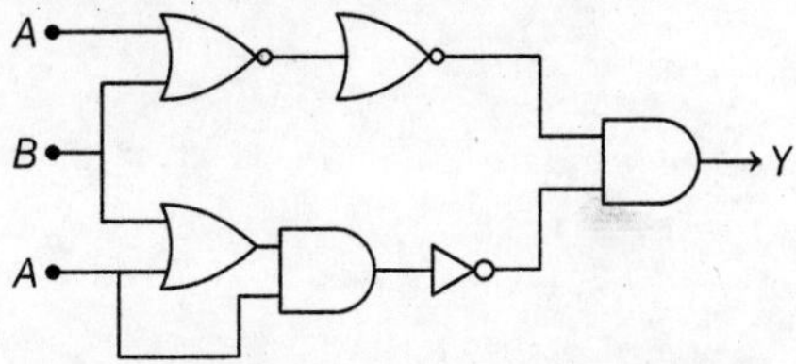

(a) OR gate (b) AND gate (c) NAND gate (d) None of these

23. In given amplifier circuit,

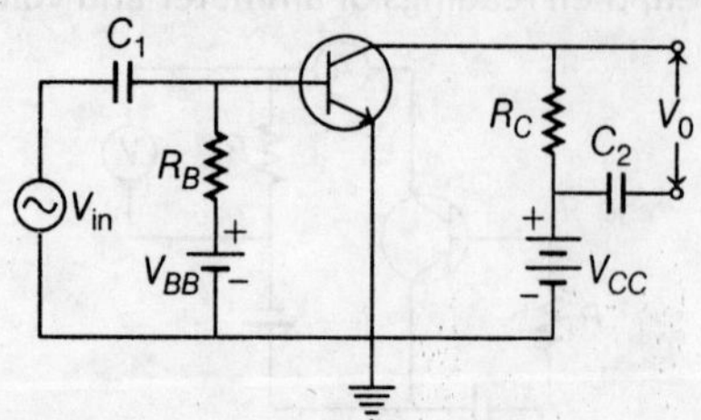

Phase difference between input (V_i) and output (V_0) voltage is of

(a) π rad
(b) $\frac{\pi}{2}$ rad
(c) 2π rad
(d) zero rad

24. Consider given transistor circuit.

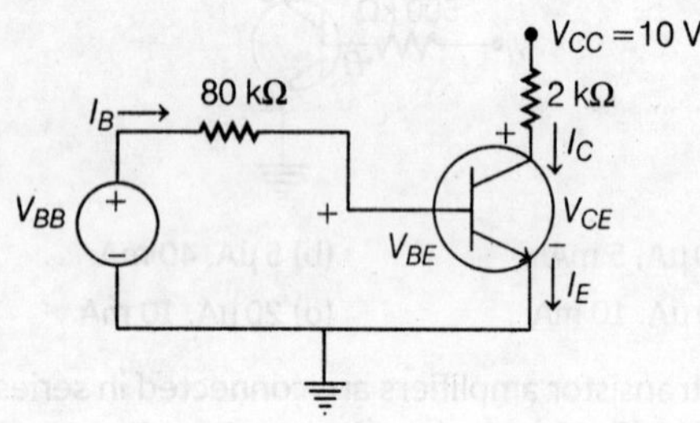

It is a *n-p-n*, CE configuration. Given, $\beta = 100$ and $V_{BB} = 2.7$ V. Now, match Column I with Column II.

Column I	Column II
A. V_{BE} in volts	P. 5.0
B. I_B in mA	Q. 2.5
C. I_C in mA	R. 2.5×10^{-3}
D. V_{CE} in volts	S. 0.7

Choose the correct answer from the options given below:

(a) A → S, B → R, C → Q, D → P
(b) A → P, B → Q, C → R, D → S
(c) A → R, B → S, C → P, D → Q
(d) A → Q, B → P, C → R, D → S

25. *n-p-n* transistor can be used as oscillator. Frequency of output voltage depends on

(a) input frequency
(b) voltage gain of transistor
(c) amplification of transistor
(d) tank circuit

Answers

1 (b)	2 (a)	3 (d)	4 (c)	5 (c)
6 (a)	7 (c)	8 (a)	9 (a)	10 (a)
11 (a)	12 (d)	13 (b)	14 (c)	15 (d)
16 (a)	17 (a)	18 (d)	19 (a)	20 (c)
21 (b)	22 (d)	23 (a)	24 (a)	25 (d)

See detailed explanations on page no. 228

Part Tests

Based on Complete Syllabus of Class 11th & 12th

This section will check your overall understanding of complete syllabus of class 11 and class 12 respectively.

Part Test 01

(Based on Complete Class 11th Syllabus)

NEET

PHYSICS

Instructions

1. This question paper contains 50 Multiple Choice Questions of Physics, divided into two Sections; **Section I** and **Section II**.
2. Section I contains **35 questions** and all questions are compulsory.
3. Section II contains **15 questions** out of which **only 10 questions** are to be attempted.
4. Each question carries **4 marks**.

Section I

1. Match the Column I (number) with Column II (number of significant figures) and choose the correct answer from the options given below.

	Column I		Column II
A.	959	P.	3
B.	0.001486	Q.	4
C.	2.6000	R.	5
D.	8.00165	S.	6

(a) A → P, B → S, C → R, D → Q
(b) A → P, B → S, C → Q, D → R
(c) A → Q, B → S, C → R, D → P
(d) A → P, B → Q, C → R, D → S

2. If the value of Stefan's constant in CGS system is $\sigma = 5.67 \times 10^{-5}$ erg $s^{-1} cm^{-2} K^{-4}$. Its numerical value in SI system is
(a) 5.67×10^{-2}
(b) 5.67×10^{-10}
(c) 5.67×10^{-8}
(d) 5.67

3. Displacement travelled by a particle along a straight line with uniform acceleration a in nth second is given by $s_n = u + \frac{a}{2}(2n-1)$, where u = initial velocity.
The equation is
(a) only numerically correct
(b) dimensionally incorrect
(c) Both numerically and dimensionally correct
(d) numerically correct but dimensionally incorrect

4. A physical equation is given by $\phi = \frac{Ma}{\alpha}\sqrt{1+\frac{2\alpha l}{Ma}}$, where M represents mass, a represents acceleration, l represent length, then SI unit of ϕ should be
(a) m/s (b) m/s^2 (c) m (d) s^{-1}

5. A metal wire has mass (12 ± 0.012) g, radius (0.4 + 0.002) mm and length (20 + 0.01) cm. The maximum percentage error in the measurement of its density is
(a) 0.2% (b) 0.5% (c) 1.15% (d) 0.25%

6. A particle is moving in YZ-plane such that its position, velocity and acceleration are given by
$$\mathbf{r} = y\hat{\mathbf{j}} + z\hat{\mathbf{k}},\ \mathbf{v} = v_y\hat{\mathbf{j}} + v_z\hat{\mathbf{k}},\ \mathbf{a} = a_y\hat{\mathbf{j}} + a_z\hat{\mathbf{k}}$$
If the particle is speeding down, then which of the following condition is correct?
(a) $yv_y + zv_z < 0$ (b) $yv_y + zv_z > 0$
(c) $a_yv_y + a_zv_z < 0$ (d) $a_yv_y + a_zv_z > 0$

7. A ball is thrown vertically upwards with a speed of 40 m/s from the top of a tower and another ball is thrown horizontally with same speed simultaneously. If the time difference between them in reaching the ground is 6 s, then height of the tower is (Take, $g = 10\ m/s^2$)
(a) 80 m (b) 45 m (c) 12.5 m (d) zero

8. Assertion (A) Distance between two balls, dropped one after other from a high tower, increases linearly with time.
Reason (R) Relative acceleration of balls is zero.
In the light of the above statements, choose the most appropriate answer from the options given below:
(a) Both A and R are true but R is not the correct explanation of A.
(b) A is true but R is false.

(c) A is false but R is true.
(d) Both A and R are true and R is the correct explanation of A.

9. The equation of motion of a projectile is given as

$$y = 3x - \frac{x^2}{20}$$

where, x and y are in metres. Initial velocity and maximum height attained by particle are respectively

(a) 10 m/s, 4.5 m (b) 20 m/s, 15 m
(c) 10 m/s, 45 m (d) $10\sqrt{10}$ m/s, 45 m

10. Consider $\hat{\mathbf{a}}$, $\hat{\mathbf{b}}$ and $\hat{\mathbf{c}}$ as the unit vectors which are lying in the same plane. It is given that $|\hat{\mathbf{a}} \times \hat{\mathbf{b}}| = \frac{1}{2}$ and $\hat{\mathbf{b}} \cdot \hat{\mathbf{c}} = -\frac{3}{5}$, then angle between $\hat{\mathbf{a}}$ and $\hat{\mathbf{c}}$ cannot be

(a) 97° (b) 113°
(c) 157° (d) None of these

11. A spring of force constant k is cut into two pieces such that one piece is three times the length of the other. The longer piece will have a force constant of

(a) $\frac{3k}{4}$ (b) $\frac{4k}{3}$
(c) $4k$ (d) $9k$

12. A block of mass m is placed on a rough inclined plane of inclination θ. Its downward motion can be prevented by applying an upward pull F and it can be made to slide upwards by applying a force $2F$. The coefficient of friction between the block and the inclined plane is

(a) $\frac{1}{3}\tan\theta$ (b) $\frac{\tan\theta}{2}$
c) $\tan\theta$ (d) $2\cot\theta$

13. A block of mass 2 kg is placed on a rough horizontal surface. A force is applied on the block at some angle. The minimum value of force applied on block to just slide down is 12 N. If the applied force is increased to double the minimum value in same direction, then acceleration of block is ($g = 10 \text{ m/s}^2$)

(a) 2.5 m/s^2 (b) 5 m/s^2 (c) 7.5 m/s^2 (d) 9.3 m/s^2

14. A block of mass 4 kg is resting on a weighing machine. A water jet is released and falls on the top surface of the block of 120 kg/min with a speed of 4 m/s. Assuming that block does not absorb water, then reading of weighing machine will be

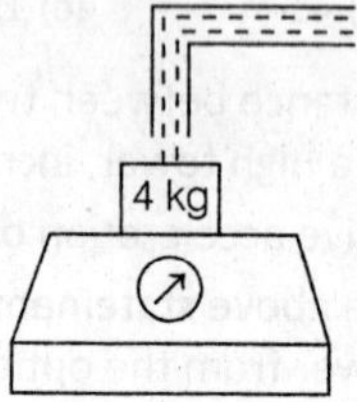

(a) 4 kg (b) 4.8 kg
(c) 3.6 kg (d) 484 kg

15. A lift is accelerating up with acceleration $\frac{g}{2}$ as shown in the following figure. The reading of the spring balance is

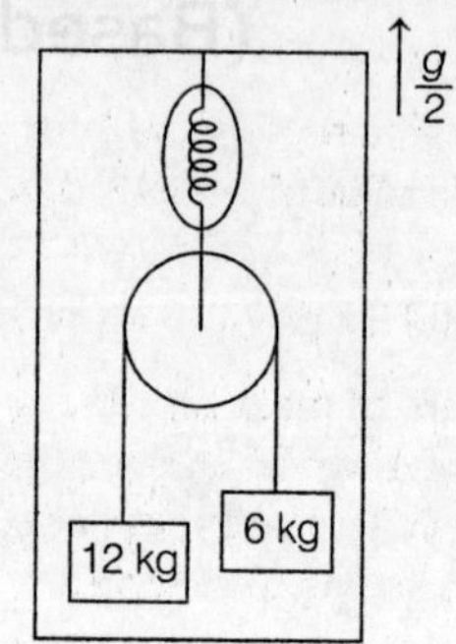

(a) 16 kg (b) 18 kg
(c) 24 kg (d) 36 kg

16. A force F acting on a particle varies with the position x as shown in the following figure. The work done by this force in displacing the particle from $x = -2$ m to $x = 0$ m is

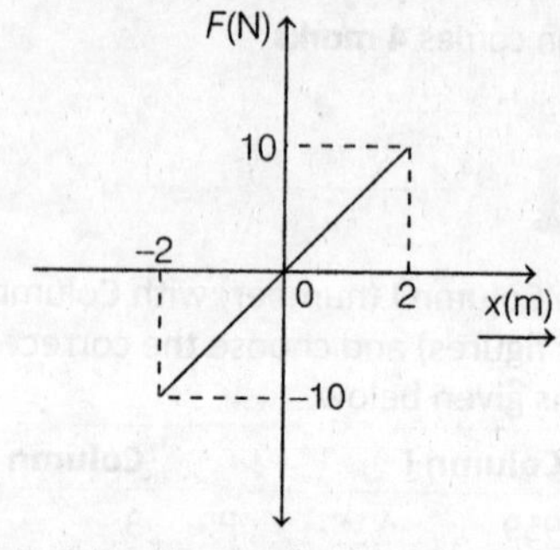

(a) −10 J (b) 20 J (c) −5 J (d) 10 J

17. Two bodies of masses 4 kg and 16 kg are moving with equal kinetic energies. The ratio of magnitudes of their momenta is

(a) 1 : 4 (b) 1 : 2
(c) 3 : 1 (d) 2 : 1

18. The potential energy of a spring increases by 15 J, when stretched by 3 cm. If it is stretched by 4 cm, then increase in potential energy is

(a) 20 J (b) $\frac{40}{3}$ J (c) 27 J (d) $\frac{80}{3}$ J

19. The angle between the force, $\mathbf{F} = 2\hat{\mathbf{i}} - 3\hat{\mathbf{j}} + 4\hat{\mathbf{k}}$ and displacement, $\mathbf{d} = 3\hat{\mathbf{i}} - 4\hat{\mathbf{j}} - 4.5\,\hat{\mathbf{k}}$ is

(a) 60° (b) 30°
(c) 90° (d) 180°

20. A uniform chain of length L and mass M is lying on a smooth table and one-third of its length is hanging vertically down over the edge of the table. The work required to pull the hanging part on the table is

(a) MgL (b) $\frac{MgL}{3}$
(c) $\frac{MgL}{9}$ (d) $\frac{MgL}{18}$

21. A flywheel of moment of inertia 2 kg-m^2 is rotated at a speed of 25 rad/s. A tangential force at the rim stops the wheel in 10 s. Average torque of the force is

(a) 5 N-m (b) 10 N-m (c) 15 N-m (d) 2.5 N-m

22. Wheel of an engine revolves with an angular speed of 120 rev/min. If radius of wheel is 2 m, then its linear velocity is

(a) 16 π m/s (b) 8 π m/s (c) 4 π m/s (d) 2 π m/s

23. A uniform sphere of mass 1 kg and radius 10 cm rolls without slipping down an inclined plane at an angle of 30° to the horizontal. The kinetic energy of the sphere after 2 s from the beginning of motion is

(a) 35.7 J (b) 40.4 J (c) 36.4 J (d) 56.8 J

24. Two thin uniform rings made of some material and of radii *R* and 4*R* are joined as shown below. The mass of smaller ring is *M*. The moment of inertia about an axis passing through the centre of mass of system of rings and perpendicular to the plane is

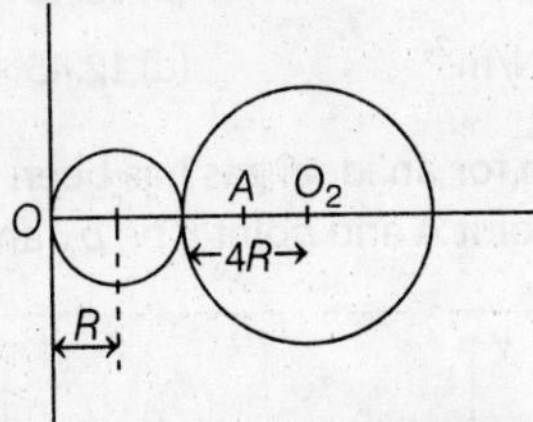

(a) 60 MR^2 (b) 85 MR^2
(c) 55 MR^2 (d) 20 MR^2

25. A ring of mass 2 kg and radius 1 m is rolling on a surface with an instantaneous angular position $\theta(t) = (2t^3 - 4t^2 + 4)$ rad. Torque on the wheel after 10 s is

(a) 36 N-m (b) 44 N-m
(c) 224 N-m (d) 112 N-m

26. Two objects attract each other with a gravitational force of magnitude 1.67×10^{-9} N, when separated by 20 cm. If the total mass of objects is 2.5 kg, then the mass of objects are, respectively

(a) 1 kg, 1.5 kg (b) 0.5 kg, 2 kg
(c) 0.7 kg, 1.8 kg (d) 0.1 kg, 2.4 kg

27. An object is projected vertically upwards from the surface of the Earth of radius *R* with a speed equal to one-third of escape velocity. The maximum height attained by it from the surface of the earth is

(a) $\frac{R}{2}$ (b) $\frac{3R}{8}$ (c) $\frac{R}{8}$ (d) $\frac{2R}{9}$

28. The escape velocity for a planet is v_e. A particle starts from rest at a large distance from the planet, reaches the planet only under gravitational attraction and passes through a smooth tunnel through its centre. The speed of particle at the centre of the planet is

(a) $v_e\sqrt{\frac{3}{2}}$ (b) $\frac{v_e}{\sqrt{2}}$ (c) v_e (d) $\frac{v_e}{\sqrt{3}}$

29. According to Kepler, the law of area can be understand as a consequence of conservation of

(a) linear momentum (b) angular momentum
(c) mass (d) energy

30. The figure shows an elliptical orbit of a planet about the sun *S*. If t_1 is the time for planet to traverse *BAC* and t_2 is the time to traverse *CPB*, then

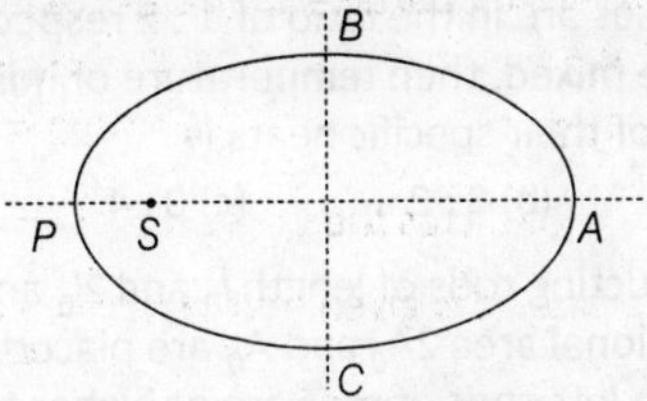

(a) $t_1 < t_2$ (b) $t_1 > t_2$
(c) $t_1 = t_2$ (d) Cannot be predicted

31. Statement I Leaves and small insects can float on surface of water as their weight is balanced by upthrust.

Statement II Archimedes' principle is applicable only an objects which are submerged fully inside water.

In light of above statements, choose the most appropriate answer from the options given below:

(a) Both Statement I and Statement II are incorrect.
(b) Statement I is correct and Statement II is incorrect.
(c) Statement I is incorrect and Statement II is correct.
(d) Both Statement I and Statement II are correct.

32. If radius of the body is increased to double keeping all the parameters constant, then its terminal velocity will

(a) increase to double
(b) increase to four times
(c) decrease to half
(d) decrease to one-fourth

33. The temperature of sun is 5500 K and it emits a maximum intensity radiation in the yellow region (5.5×10^{-7} m). The maximum radiation from a furnace occurs at wavelength 11×10^{-7} m. The temperature of the furnace is

(a) 5500 K (b) 4600 K
(c) 2750 K (d) 8250 K

34. A force of 100 N is applied at one end of a wire of length 1 m and having area of cross-section 1 cm^2. The other end of the wire is rigidly fixed. If coefficient of linear expansion of the wire $\alpha = 8 \times 10^{-6}$/°C and Young's modulus, $Y = 4.4 \times 10^{11}$ N/m^2 and its temperature is increased by 10°C, then the increase in the tension in the wire will be

(a) 1.5 kN (b) 3.5 kN
(c) 2.5 kN (d) 4.5 kN

35. When 27 mercury drops coalesce to form one mercury drop, the energy changes by a factor of

(a) 9 (b) 3
(c) 6 (d) 12

Section II

36. 2 g of ice at 0°C is mixed with 1 g of steam at 100°C. After thermal equilibrium is achieved, the temperature of the mixture is

(a) 0°C (b) 10°C (c) 55°C (d) 100°C

37. Two liquids A and B are at temperature 30°C and 50°C and their masses are in the ratio of 1 : 2 respectively. Both liquids are mixed, then temperature of mixture is 42°C. The ratio of their specific heats is

(a) 2 : 3 (b) 3 : 2 (c) 3 : 4 (d) 4 : 3

38. Two conducting rods of length l_0 and $2l_0$ and of cross-sectional area $2A_0$ and A_0 are placed as shown in the figure. The left ends of rods are at higher temperature and right ends of rods are at lower temperature. The equivalent thermal conductivity of the arrangement, is

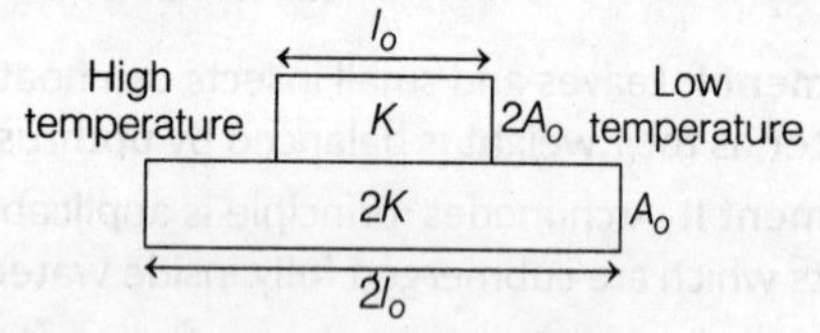

(a) $\frac{4}{3}K$ (b) $\frac{3}{2}K$ (c) $\frac{6}{5}K$ (d) $\frac{6}{3}K$

39. Three liquids A, B and C having same specific heats have masses m, $2m$ and $3m$, respectively. Their temperature are θ, 2θ and 3θ respectively. For temperature of mixture, match the following two columns and choose the correct answer from options given below :

	Column I		Column II
A.	When A and B are mixed	P.	$\frac{5}{2}\theta$
B.	When A and C are mixed	Q.	$\frac{5}{3}\theta$
C.	When B and C are mixed	R.	$\frac{7}{3}\theta$
D.	When A, B and C all are mixed	S.	$\frac{13}{5}\theta$

(a) A → Q, B → S, C → P, D → R
(b) A → R, B → P, C → S, D → Q
(c) A → Q, B → P, C → S, D → R
(d) A → R, B → Q, C → S, D → P

40. Heat is being supplied at a constant rate to a solid metallic cube. The temperature of material is changing with heat input as shown in the following figure. The slope of E represent

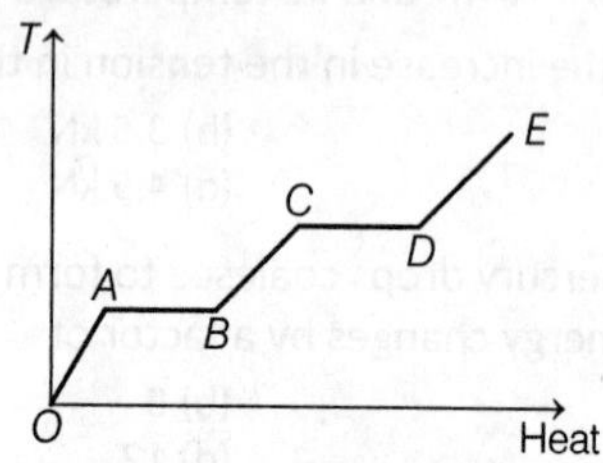

(a) latent heat of liquid
(b) latent heat of vaporisation
(c) heat capacity of vapour
(d) inverse of heat capacity of vapour

41. How much degree of freedom each atom has in a crystalline solids?

(a) 3 (b) 4
(c) 5 (d) 6

42. One mole of an ideal gas undergoes a process where molar specific heat capacity is $4R$ and which work done per mole is given by $dW = 2RdT$. Ratio of C_p and C_V of gas for the process is

(a) 1 (b) $\frac{5}{3}$ (c) $\frac{3}{2}$ (d) $\frac{7}{5}$

43. A cubical vessels of side 0.2 m contains 2 mole of helium and one mole of oxygen gas at 400 K temperature. The pressure of the mixture of gas is ($R = 8.3 \text{ J mol}^{-1}\text{ K}^{-1}$)

(a) 10^6 N/m^2 (b) 12.45×10^5 N/m^2
(c) 16.6×10^5 N/m^2 (d) 12.45×10^6 N/m^2

44. The V-T graph for an ideal gas has been plotted. The pressure of point A and point B be p_A and p_B respectively, then

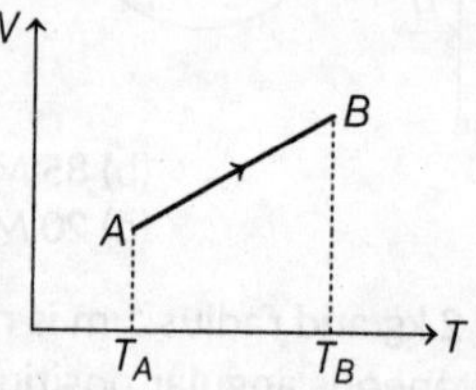

(a) $p_A > p_B$ (b) $p_A = p_B$
(c) $p_A < p_B$ (d) Cannot be concluded

45. An ideal gas is enclosed by a closed vessel which is moving with constant velocity v. If the vessel is suddenly stopped, then rise in the temperature of gas is
(M is molecular weight of the gas and $\gamma = \frac{C_P}{C_V}$)

(a) $\frac{Mv^2(\gamma-1)}{2R}$ (b) $\frac{Mv^2(\gamma+1)}{2R}$ (c) $\frac{Mv^2}{2R\gamma}$ (d) $\frac{Mv^2}{2R(\gamma+1)}$

46. Equation of a wave travelling along + x-direction is given as $y = p\sin(2\pi qt - 2\pi rx)$. If the maximum velocity of particle is two times the velocity of wave, then correct relation is

(a) $p\pi = \frac{1}{r}$ (b) $pqr < 1$
(c) $pq > 1$ (d) All are correct

47. A vibrating tuning fork of frequency 1280 Hz is held above a tube filled with water. If the water level is lowered, then consecutive maxima in intensity are observed at intervals of about ($v_{\text{sound}} = 330$ m/s)

(a) 12.9 cm (b) 19.4 cm
(c) 25.8 cm (d) 51.7 cm

48. Longitudinal waves with frequency 180 Hz are formed in a liquid with density 1.2 g/cm^3. The wavelength of the wave is 8 m. The bulk modulus of the liquid is

(a) 1.72×10^6 N/m^2 (b) 7.86×10^8 N/m^2
(c) 2.48×10^9 N/m^2 (d) 5×10^{10} N/m^2

49. A 2 kg collar is attached to a spring of spring constant 200 Nm^{-1}. It slides without friction over a horizontal rod. The collar is displaced from its equilibrium position by 5 cm and released. The maximum speed of the collar is

(a) 5 cm/s (b) 10 cm/s (c) 0.5 m/s (d) 10 m/s

50. One end of a horizontal rope is attached to a prong of an electrically driven tuning fork that vibrates at 80 Hz. The other end passes over a pulley and supports a 2 kg mass. The linear mass density of the rope is 0.05 kg/m. If the mass is increased to 4 kg, then change in the wavelength is ($g = 9.8$ m/s^2)

(a) 1.75 m
(b) 2.53 m
(c) 0.253 m
(d) 0.175 m

Answers

1 (d)	2 (c)	3 (c)	4 (c)	5 (c)	6 (c)	7 (b)	8 (c)	9 (d)	10 (b)
11 (b)	12 (a)	13 (c)	14 (b)	15 (c)	16 (a)	17 (b)	18 (d)	19 (c)	20 (d)
21 (a)	22 (b)	23 (a)	24 (b)	25 (c)	26 (b)	27 (c)	28 (a)	29 (b)	30 (b)
31 (a)	32 (b)	33 (c)	34 (b)	35 (a)	36 (d)	37 (d)	38 (c)	39 (c)	40 (d)
41 (d)	42 (c)	43 (b)	44 (a)	45 (a)	46 (a)	47 (a)	48 (c)	49 (c)	50 (d)

See detailed explanations on page no. 231

Part Test 02

(Based on Complete Class 12th Syllabus)

NEET

PHYSICS

Instructions

1. This question paper contains 50 Multiple Choice Questions of Physics, divided into two Sections; **Section I** and **Section II**.
2. Section I contains **35 questions** and all questions are compulsory.
3. Section II contains **15 questions** out of which **only 10 questions** are to be attempted.
4. Each question carries **4 marks**.

Section I

1. Two charged particles are placed in vacuum at a distance r. If a medium of dielectric constant K is filled between them, for what distance electrostatic force between charges is same?

(a) $\sqrt{Kr}$ (b) Kr (c) $\frac{r}{\sqrt{K}}$ (d) $\frac{r}{K}$

2. An electron is added into a system of two protons from infinity, the electrostatic potential energy of the system

(a) becomes zero (b) increases
(c) decreases (d) cannot be negative

3. The charge stored by a capacitor of capacitance 2μF in the figure is

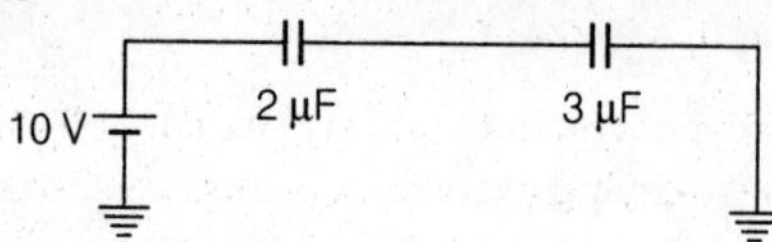

(a) 8μC (b) 12μC (c) (24 / 5)μC (d) 20μC

4. Two point charges q_1 and q_2 are kept at some distance along the line joining these two charges. The variation of electric field with distance has been shown in the figure below.

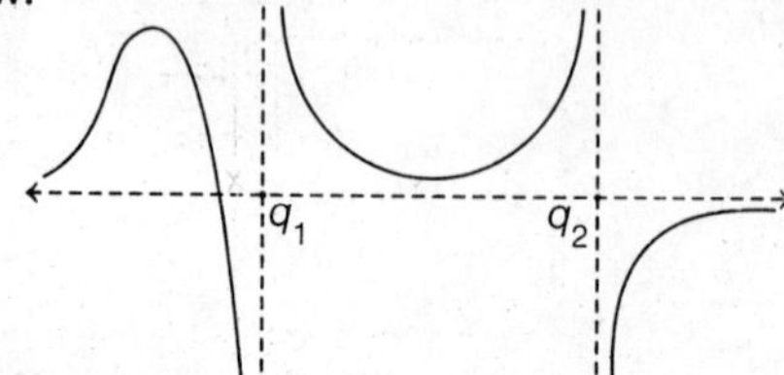

If rightwards is taken as positive and leftward as negative, then predict the nature of charges q_1 and q_2, respectively

(a) positive, positive (b) positive, negative
(c) negative, positive (d) negative, negative

5. The variation of potential with position x from origin along X-axis is shown in figure. In which region, magnitude of electric field is maximum?

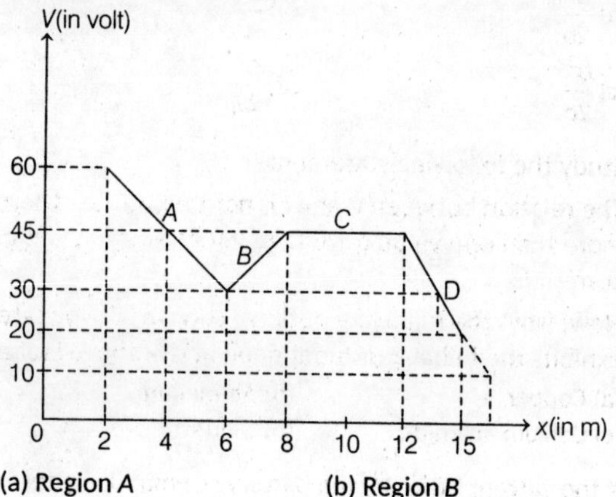

(a) Region A (b) Region B
(c) Region C (d) Region D

6. An air filled parallel plate capacitor has a capacitance of 4 μF. The separation between the plates is tripled and interspace between the plates is filled with dielectric medium. If the capacitance is increased by 20 μF, the dielectric constant of medium is

(a) 2 (b) 15 (c) 18 (d) $\frac{5}{3}$

7. Consider the circuit shown below, if the power dissipated in each resistor R_1, R_2 and R_3 are equal, then ratio the $R_1 : R_2 : R_3$ is

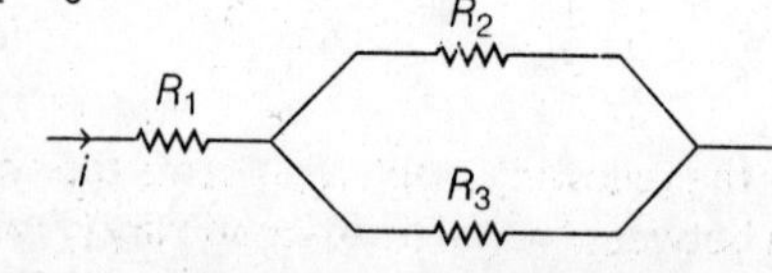

(a) 1 : 1 : 1 (b) 4 : 4 : 1 (c) 4 : 1 : 1 (d) 1 : 4 : 4

8. An aluminium wire of diameter 0.8 mm is carrying a current of I A. If electron field inside the wire is 0.55 V/m, then the value of I is (Assume, resistivity of wire $= 2.75 \times 10^{-8}$ Ω-m)

(a) 10.05 A (b) 9.06 A
(c) 9.66 A (d) 10.58 A

9. 100 identical cells of emf 4 V each, are kept in box in series arrangement. If net emf across the box is 360 V, then the number of cells with reversed polarity in the box is

(a) 10 (b) 5 (c) 40 (d) 20

10. In a discharge tube of cross-section area A, the number density of positive ion and negative ion are $2n$ and n, respectively. If positive and negative ions are moving in opposite direction with velocity v and $2v$ respectively, then electric current in tube is
(Charge on positive ion $= + e$, charge on negative ion $= - e$)

(a) zero (b) $neAv$ (c) $2neAv$ (d) $4neAv$

11. The charge flowing through a conducting wire is given as $q = at - bt^2$, where a and b both are positive constants. The amount of charge flown through the wire is

(a) $\frac{a^2}{2b}$ (b) $\frac{a^2}{4b}$
(c) $\frac{b^2}{2a}$ (d) $\frac{b^2}{4a}$

12. Study the following statement.
The relation between V and I is not unique, i.e., there are more than one value of voltage V for the same value of current I.
Now, from the following options, choose which material exhibits the behaviour mentioned in the above statement.

(a) Copper (b) Aluminium
(c) Gallium arsenide (d) Diode

13. If the current flown by the battery of emf 50 V is zero, then find the ratio of currents I_1 and I_2 in the circuit shown below.

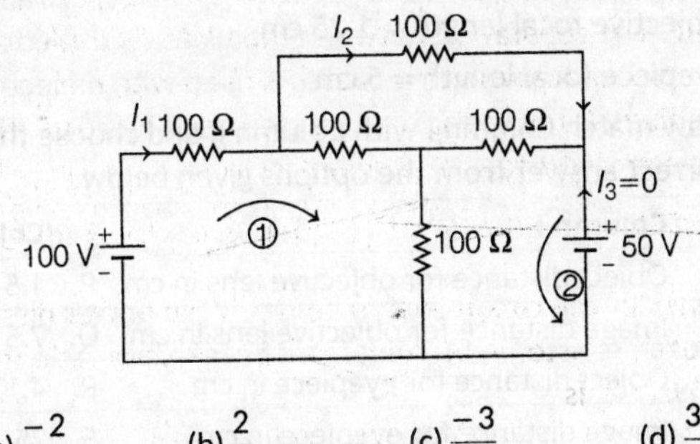

(a) $\frac{-2}{1}$ (b) $\frac{2}{1}$ (c) $\frac{-3}{1}$ (d) $\frac{3}{1}$

14. Which of the following graph represents the correct variation between magnetic susceptibility (χ) and temperature (T) for ferromagnetic materials?

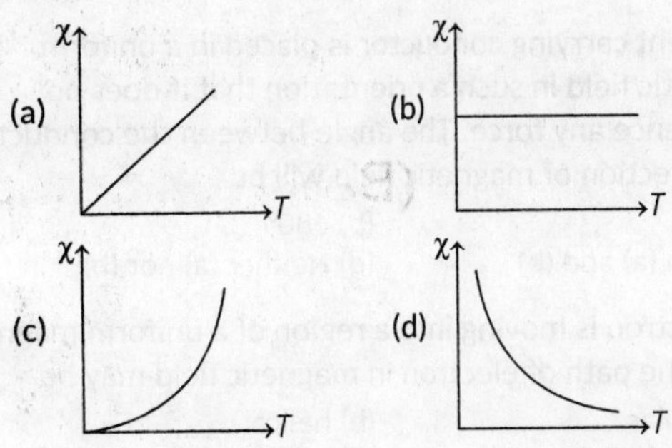

15. An α-particle and a proton enter into a region of uniform magnetic field perpendicular to it with same magnitude of velocity, then

(a) both particles will move on circular path with same time period
(b) both particles will move on circular path and time period of α-particle will be double to that of proton
(c) both particles will move on circular path and time period of α-particle will be half to that of proton
(d) None of the above

16. Consider a solenoid and a toroid both with same number of turns per unit length and same diameter.
Now, match Column I with Column II and choose the correct answer from the options given below.

	Column I		Column II
A.	Magnetic dipole moment per unit volume of solenoid	P.	$\frac{\mu_0}{4\pi} \cdot \frac{2M}{r^3}$
B.	Potential energy of a toroid placed in an external field	Q.	$MB(\cos\theta_1 - \cos\theta_2)$
C.	Work done in rotating solenoid by angle θ_1 to θ_2	R.	zero
D.	Field of solenoid on axis at a distance r from centre	S.	nI

(a) A → P, B → Q, C → R, D → S
(b) A → S, B → R, C → Q, D → P
(c) A → S, B → P, C → Q, D → R
(d) A → R, B → Q, C → P, D → S

17. If the radius of current carrying circular coil is increased to four times keeping the same current, then magnetic field strength at its centre will be

(a) increased to four times (b) decreased to $\frac{1}{4}$ times
(c) increased to double (d) decreased to half

18. Magnetic field strength at the centre O shown below is

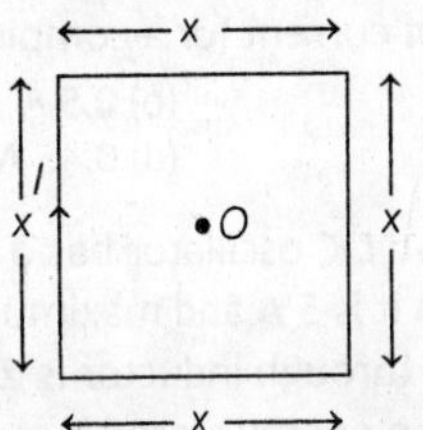

(a) $\frac{2\mu_0 I}{\pi x}$ (b) $\frac{2\sqrt{2}\mu_0 I}{\pi x}$ (c) $\frac{\sqrt{2}\mu_0 I}{\pi x}$ (d) $\frac{4\mu_0 I}{\pi x}$

19. A current carrying conductor is placed in a uniform magnetic field in such a orientation that it does not experience any force. The angle between the conductor and direction of magnetic field will be

(a) 0° (b) 180°
(c) Both (a) and (b) (d) Neither (a) nor (b)

20. An electron is moving into a region of a uniform magnetic field. The path of electron in magnetic field may be

(a) circular (b) helical
(c) straight line (d) All of these

21. A square loop of side 5 cm and resistance 1Ω is placed vertically in the East-West plane. A uniform magnetic field of 0.2 T is set-up across the plane in the North-East direction. The magnetic field is decreased to zero in 0.2 s at a steady rate, the charge flown through the cross-section of area of wire of loop during this time interval is

(a) 1.25 mC (b) 0.25 mC (c) 0.5 mC (d) 2.5 mC

22. The phase difference between capacitive and inductive reactance is

(a) zero
(b) $\frac{\pi}{2}$
(c) π
(d) may be any thing between $\frac{\pi}{2}$ to π

23. Two different *L-C-R* series circuits as are subjected with same input AC sinusoidal voltages. The graph between average power *P* and angular frequency ω has been shown in the figure below.

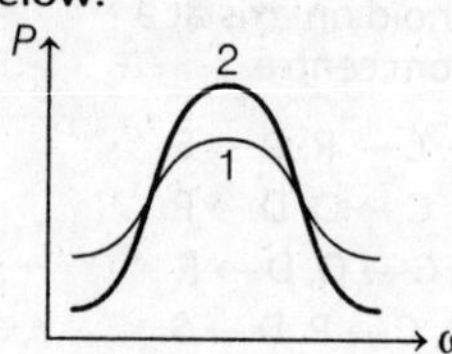

Both circuits have same values of *L* and *C* but have different values of *R*. The values of resistance *R* and quality factor *Q* for graph 1 as compared to 2 are respectively

(a) low, low (b) high, low
(c) low, high (d) high, high

24. In an *R-L-C* series circuit, $R = 10\,\Omega$, $X_L = 20\,\Omega$ and $X_C = 10\,\Omega$. If the source voltage $V = 20\sin(314\,t)$ V, then average value of current for a complete cycle is

(a) 0 (b) 0.5 A
(c) 2 A (d) 0.45 A

25. An inductor in an *L-C* oscillator has a maximum current flowing through it is 5 A and maximum energy of 160 μJ. If current flowing through inductor is 2 A and stored energy in it is 10 μJ, then energy stored by capacitor is

(a) 10 μJ (b) 150 μJ
(c) 160 μJ (d) 170 μJ

26. A rectangular loop of area *A* is placed in *YZ*-plane. A time varying magnetic field of strength $\mathbf{B} = \alpha t\hat{\mathbf{i}} + \beta t^2\hat{\mathbf{j}} + \gamma\hat{\mathbf{k}}$, where α, β and γ are the constants, is applied across it. If the magnitude of induced emf at $t = 1$ s is 2 V, then at $t = 4$ s, induced emf is

(a) 2 V (b) 8 V
(c) 16 V (d) depends on *A*, α, β and γ

27. Arrange the following electromagnetic radiations in order of increasing frequency.

(i) Blue light (ii) Yellow light
(iii) Infrared (iv) Radiowave

(a) (i), (ii), (iii), (iv) (b) (iv), (iii), (ii), (i)
(c) (iv), (ii), (i), (iii) (d) (ii), (i), (iv), (iii)

28. An electromagnetic wave is travelling through a material medium which has relative permittivity 1.5 and relative permeability 6. The speed of wave in medium is

(a) 10^8 m/s (b) 2.45×10^8 m/s
(c) 1.22×10^8 m/s (d) 3×10^8 m/s

29. A plane EM wave is propagating along *y*-direction. It can have components of electric field *E* and magnetic field *B* along

(a) *X*-axis and *Y*-axis (b) *Y*-axis and *Z*-axis
(c) *Z*-axis and *Z*-axis (d) *X*-axis and *Z*-axis

30. In an oscillator, a charged particle oscillates about its mean position with a frequency of 10^8 Hz. The frequency of the electromagnetic waves produced by the oscillator is

(a) 10^8 Hz (b) $\frac{1}{2} \times 10^8$ Hz
(c) 2×10^8 Hz (d) can be anything

31. In a plane EM wave, the magnetic field oscillates sinusoidally at a frequency of 6×10^{10} Hz and it's amplitude is 2×10^{-7} T, then the wavelength of the wave, is

(a) 5 mm (b) 10 mm (c) 50 mm (d) 100 mm

32. A compound microscope is used to obtain an angular magnification of 30.
Objective focal length = 1.25 cm
Eyepiece focal length = 5 cm
Now match Column I with Column II and choose the correct answer from the options given below.

Column I	Column II
A. Object distance for objective lens in cm	P. 1.5
B. Image distance for objective lens in cm	Q. 7.5
C. Object distance for eyepiece in cm	R. 4.17
D. Image distance for eyepiece in cm	S. 25

(a) A → P, B → Q, C → R, D → S
(b) A → Q, B → P, C → R, D → S
(c) A → R, B → Q, C → P, D → S
(d) A → R, B → P, C → Q, D → S

33. Assertion (A) Size of objective is kept smaller than eyepiece in a compound microscope.

Reason (R) For better resolution a large objective is required.

In the light of the above statements, choose the most appropriate answer from the options given below:

(a) Both A and R are true but R is not the correct explanation of A.

(b) A is true but R is false.

(c) A is false but R is true.

(d) Both A and R are true and R is the correct explanation of A.

34. A telescope has a focal length of 30 cm and eyepiece has a focal length of 3 cm. It is focussed on an object at 2m. For final image at infinity, distance of objective and eyepiece must be around

(a) 10 cm (b) 20 cm
(c) 30 cm (d) 40 cm

35. A particle *A* has momentum *p*, while another particle *B* has a momentum 2*p*. The momentum of the particles increase with time but their ratio always remains 1 : 2. The de-Broglie wavelength of the particles (that of *A* to that of *B*)

(a) increases with time

(b) decreases with time

(c) remains same and equal to 1 : 2

(d) remains same and equal to 2 : 1

Section II

36. In a photon-particle collision such as photoelectron collision

I. Total energy is conserved.

II. Total momentum is conserved.

III. The number of photons may or may not be conserved.

The correct statement(s) is/are

(a) I, III (b) Only III
(c) I, II (d) I, II and III

37. A proton, a neutron, an electron and an α-particle have same kinetic energy, then the relation between their de-Broglie wavelengths is

(a) $\lambda_p = \lambda_n > \lambda_e > \lambda_\alpha$

(b) $\lambda_\alpha < \lambda_p = \lambda_n < \lambda_e$

(c) $\lambda_e < \lambda_p = \lambda_n > \lambda_\alpha$

(d) $\lambda_e = \lambda_p = \lambda_n = \lambda_\alpha$

38. An X-ray tube operates at the voltage of 10 kV. If specific charge of electron is 1.8×10^{11} C/kg, then the ratio of the de-Broglie wavelength of the incident electrons to the shortest wavelength of X-rays produced is

(a) 1 : 10 (b) $1 : 10\sqrt{2}$
(c) $10\sqrt{2} : 1$ (d) 10 : 1

39. A particle of mass *m* is dropped from a height *H* under the action of gravity. The de-Broglie wavelength of the particle just before striking the ground, is directly proportional to

(a) H (b) $\sqrt{H}$ (c) $\frac{1}{\sqrt{H}}$ (d) $H\sqrt{H}$

40. In photoelectric effect experiment, when the wavelength λ of incident photon is halved, the velocity of the most energetic electron is doubled. The work function of the metal is

(a) $\frac{hc}{4\lambda}$ (b) $\frac{hc}{3\lambda}$ (c) $\frac{hc}{2\lambda}$ (d) $\frac{2}{3}\frac{hc}{\lambda}$

41. The half-life of ${}^{238}_{92}$U undergoing α-decay is 4.5×10^9 years. The activity of 2 g sample of ${}^{238}_{92}$U will be

(a) 1.23×10^3 Bq (b) 1.23×10^4 Bq
(c) 2.46×10^3 Bq (d) 2.46×10^4 Bq

42. Statement I de-Broglie's hypothesis states that, wavelength associated with electrons is $\lambda = \frac{h}{mv}$, which gave an explanation for Bohr's quantised orbits by bringing in the wave particle duality.

Statement II Bohr's model is applicable only to hydrogenic (single electron) atoms.

In light of above statements, choose the most appropriate answer from the options given below:

(a) Both Statement I and Statement II are incorrect.

(b) Statement I is correct and Statement II is incorrect.

(c) Statement I is incorrect and Statement II is correct.

(d) Both Statement I and Statement II are correct.

43. An electron is moving towards a stationary α-particle with a kinetic energy of 4 eV. If the electron is captured by the α-particle to form He^+ ion in first excited state, then wavelength of emitted photon, is
(Assume that initially both are separated by a large distance)

(a) 227.48 Å (b) 211.9 Å (c) 703.12 Å (d) 1672.29 Å

44. An electron is revolving in a circular orbit of radius *r* under the action of a uniform magnetic field *B*. Assuming that, Bohr's postulate regarding the quantisation of angular momentum is applicable to this electron. The kinetic energy of the electron in *n*th orbit, is

(a) $\frac{nhBe}{4\pi m}$ (b) $\frac{nhBe}{2\pi m}$ (c) $\frac{n^2hBe}{4\pi^2 m}$ (d) $\frac{2nhBe}{\pi m}$

45. A hydrogen like atom of atomic number *Z* is in an excited state of quantum number 2*n*. It can emit a photon of maximum energy 204 eV. If it makes a transition to quantum state *n*, a photon of energy 40.8 eV is emitted, then values of *Z* and *n* respectively, are
(Take, ground state energy of hydrogen atom equal to – 13.6 eV)

(a) 4, 2 (b) 2, 4 (c) 3, 4 (d) 4, 1

46. Which among the following is used in unbiased condition for its proper operation?

(a) Zener diode (b) Photodiode

(c) LED (d) Solar cell

47. The values of potential barrier for silicon and germanium are respectively

(a) 0.2 V and 0.7 V

(b) 0.7 V and 0.2 V

(c) 3 V and 0.7 V

(d) 0.7 V and 0.7 V

48. Amongst the following option, which electrical device is used as a voltage regulator?

(a) Thermistor

(b) Photodiode

(c) *n-p-n* transistor in common emitter mode

(d) Zener diode

49. Which of following graphs shows correct *I-V* characteristics of solar cell?

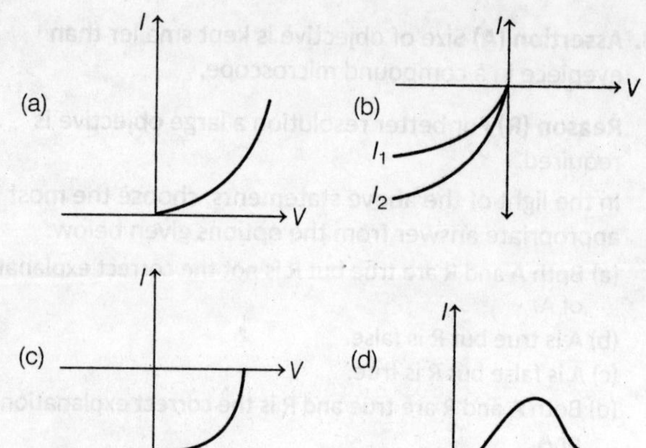

50. With increasing biasing voltage of a photodiode, the photocurrent magnitude

(a) increases initially and after attaining certain value, it decreases

(b) increases initially and saturates finally

(c) remains constant

(d) increases linearly

Answers

1 (c)	2 (c)	3 (b)	4 (c)	5 (d)	6 (c)	7 (d)	8 (a)	9 (b)	10 (d)
11 (b)	12 (c)	13 (d)	14 (d)	15 (b)	16 (b)	17 (b)	18 (b)	19 (c)	20 (d)
21 (c)	22 (c)	23 (b)	24 (a)	25 (b)	26 (a)	27 (b)	28 (a)	29 (d)	30 (a)
31 (a)	32 (a)	33 (a)	34 (d)	35 (d)	36 (d)	37 (b)	38 (a)	39 (c)	40 (d)
41 (d)	42 (d)	43 (c)	44 (a)	45 (a)	46 (d)	47 (b)	48 (d)	49 (c)	50 (b)

See detailed explanations on page no. 237

The Knockouts

10 Full Syllabus Mock Tests for NEET

Mock Tests given here will help you to be acquainted with Pattern & Level of NEET. Practicing these tests in systematic manner will ensure your good score in the Exam.

Knockout 01

NEET

PHYSICS

Instructions

1. This question paper contains 50 Multiple Choice Questions of Physics, divided into two Sections; **Section I** and **Section II**.
2. Section I contains **35 questions** and all questions are compulsory.
3. Section II contains **15 questions** out of which **only 10 questions** are to be attempted.
4. Each question carries **4 marks**.

Section I

1. Escape velocity v of a rocket of mass m which is situated at mid-point of line joining two planets each of mass M at a distance r from each other is

(a) $v = 2\sqrt{\frac{2GM}{r}}$ (b) $v = \sqrt{\frac{2GM}{r}}$

(c) $v = \sqrt{\frac{GM}{2r}}$ (d) $v = \frac{1}{2}\sqrt{\frac{GM}{2r}}$

2. An electron travels with velocity, $\mathbf{v} = 60\,\hat{i}$ m/s through a point in space, where $\mathbf{B} = 0.1\,\hat{j}$ T. The force on the electron at this point is $\mathbf{F} = (9.6 \times 10^{-19}\,\hat{i} - 9.6 \times 10^{-19}\hat{k})$ N The electric field $\mathbf{E}$ is given by

(a) $-6\,\hat{i}$ N/C (b) $(6\hat{i} - 12\hat{k})$ N/C

(c) $(-12\hat{i} + 6\hat{k})$ N/C (d) $(-6\hat{i} - 6\hat{j} + 6\hat{k})$ N/C

3. Angle between two unit vectors $\hat{a}$ and $\hat{b}$ is θ. A unit vector along angle bisector of $\hat{a}$ and $\hat{b}$ is

(a) $\frac{\hat{a}+\hat{b}}{2\cos\frac{\theta}{2}}$ (b) $\frac{\hat{a}-\hat{b}}{2\cos\frac{\theta}{2}}$ (c) $\frac{\hat{a}+\hat{b}}{4\cos\frac{\theta}{2}}$ (d) $\frac{\hat{a}-\hat{b}}{4\cos\frac{\theta}{2}}$

4. A student applies a potential difference $V = (4.0 \pm 0.1)$ V across a resistor of resistance $R = (10.0 \pm 0.3)\,\Omega$ for a time $t = (50 \pm 1)$s. Student calculates dissipated energy E using formula,

$$E = \frac{V^2 \times t}{R} = \frac{(4.0)^2 \times 50}{10.0} = 80 \text{ J}$$

what is the absolute uncertainty in the calculated energy value?

(a) 1.5 J (b) 3 J (c) 6 J (d) 8 J

5. A particle moves in a straight line and its position x at time t is given by $x^2 = 4 + t$. The acceleration of the particle is given by

(a) $\frac{1}{x^3}$ (b) $-\frac{2}{x^3}$ (c) $\frac{1}{4x^3}$ (d) $-\frac{1}{4x^3}$

6. If the coefficient of volume expansion of brass is $6 \times 10^{-5}\,{}^\circ\text{C}^{-1}$, then fractional change in its density for a 60°C rise in temperature will be

(a) 2×10^{-6} (b) 10^{-6}

(c) 3.6×10^{-5} (d) -3.6×10^{-3}

7. A variable frequency of AC source is connected to a capacitor. If the frequency of AC source is decreased, then displacement current will

(a) decrease

(b) increase

(c) remain same

(d) depend on the shape of AC waveform

8. Heat required to complete following cycle $ABCDA$ with an ideal monoatomic gas will be

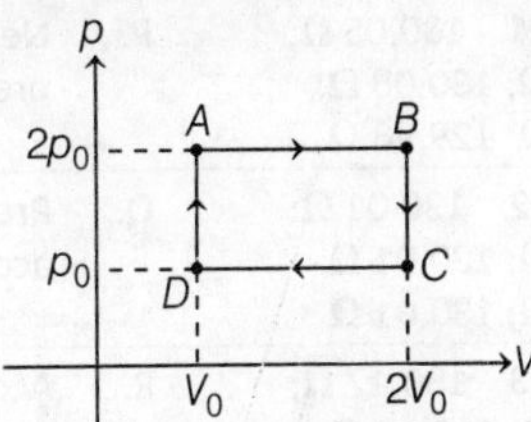

(a) p_0V_0 (b) $\frac{13}{2}p_0V_0$

(c) $\frac{11}{2}p_0V_0$ (d) $4p_0V_0$

9. In the circuit shown below, assume that diode have 20 Ω resistance in forward bias. When V_i increases from 8 V to 12 V, then change in the current is

V_i —200 Ω— diode — + 10 V

(a) 9 mA (b) 50 mA (c) 47 mA (d) 40 mA

10. If λ_1, λ_2 and λ_3 are the wavelengths of the waves giving resonance to the fundamental, first and second overtone modes, respectively in a string fixed at both ends. The ratio of the wavelengths $\lambda_1 : \lambda_2 : \lambda_3$ is

(a) 1 : 2 : 3 (b) 1 : 3 : 5 (c) 6 : 3 : 2 (d) 15 : 5 : 3

11. The drift velocity of free electrons in a conducting wire is the order of 10^{-4} m/s. Yet, the bulb glows very quickly after the switch is put ON because

(a) the random speed of electrons is very high of order of 10^6 m/s
(b) the electrons transfer their energy very quickly through collisions
(c) electric field is set-up in the wire with a speed of light producing a current through each cross-section, almost instantaneously
(d) All of the above

12. Statement I Ratio of gravitational potential on surface and at centre of a hollow shell is infinity.

Statement II Ratio of gravitational potential on surface and at centre of a solid sphere is $\frac{2}{3}$.

In the light of the above statements, choose the most appropriate answer from the options given below.

(a) Both Statement I and Statement II are incorrect.
(b) Statement I is correct and Statement II is incorrect.
(c) Statement I is incorrect and Statement II is correct.
(d) Both Statement I and Statement II are correct.

13. A short bar magnet of magnetic moment of 0.15 J/T is placed in a uniform magnetic field of 0.4 T. The potential energy of the magnet in unstable equilibrium is

(a) 6×10^{-4} J (b) -6×10^{-2} J (c) 6×10^{-2} J (d) -6×10^{-4} J

14. In an experiment, four students measure resistance of a wire using a meter bridge. Resistance of wire is 130 Ω with an accuracy of 0.1 Ω. Now, match data collected given in Column I with its nature given in Column II.

	Column I		Column II
A.	**Student 1** 130.05 Ω; 130.03 Ω; 130.08 Ω; 130.06 Ω; 129.98 Ω	P.	Neither accurate nor precise.
B.	**Student 2** 130.01 Ω; 130.02 Ω; 130.01 Ω; 130.02 Ω; 130.01 Ω	Q.	Precise but not accurate
C.	**Student 3** 130.17 Ω; 130.18 Ω; 130.17 Ω; 130.19 Ω; 130.17 Ω	R.	Accurate and precise
D.	**Student 4** 129.19 Ω; 130.24 Ω; 130.19 Ω; 130.26 Ω; 129.28 Ω	S.	Accurate but not precise

Choose the correct answer from options given below.

(a) A → P, B → Q, C → R, D → S
(b) A → Q, B → P, C → R, D → S
(c) A → S, B → R, C → Q, D → P
(d) A → S, B → Q, C → R, D → P

15. A voltmeter with resistance 500 Ω is used to measure the emf of a cell of internal resistance 4 Ω. The percentage error in the reading of the voltmeter will be

(a) 0.2% (b) 0.8%
(c) 1.4% (d) 2.2%

16. For a cell, *V-I* graph is

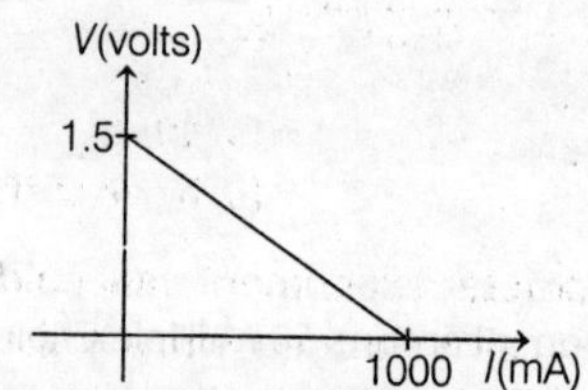

Which of the following options gives correct value of emf of cell and its internal resistance?

(a) 1.5 V, 1.0 Ω (b) 1.5 V, 2.0 Ω
(c) 1.0 V, 1.5 Ω (d) 1.5 V, 1.5 Ω

17. In a single slit diffraction, if the width of the slit is made half as compared to the original width, then

(a) the size of the central diffraction band reduces to half of the initial size
(b) the intensity of the central diffraction band becomes four times
(c) the size of the central diffraction band becomes four times
(d) the intensity of the central diffraction band becomes one-fourth of the initial

18. Assertion (A) Two parallel current carrying wires having current in same direction attracts when they carry currents parallel to each othe : (in same sense).

Reason (R) If we hold conductor in right hand such that thumb points in direction of current, then fingers curl along the conductor to give direction of field.

In the light of the above statements, choose the most appropriate answer from the options given below.

(a) Both A and R are true but R is not the correct explanation of A.
(b) A is true but R is false.
(c) A is false but R is true.
(d) Both A and R are true and R is the correct explanation of A.

19. An electromagnetic wave of frequency $\nu = 3$ MHz passes from vacuum into a dielectric medium with permittivity $\varepsilon = 4$. Then,

(a) wavelength is doubled and frequency remains unchanged
(b) wavelength is doubled and frequency is halved
(c) wavelength is halved and frequency remains same
(d) wavelength and frequency both remain same

20. A point charge $q = 6\,\mu C$ is moving with velocity $v = 5 \times 10^4\,\hat{i}\,ms^{-1}$. Magnitude of magnetic field at origin (in T) when charge reach at point P(3m, 4m, 0) will be

(a) $9.6 \times 10^{-1}\,\hat{k}$ (b) $9.6 \times 10^{-10}\,\hat{k}$
(c) $9.6 \times 10^{-10}\,\hat{j}$ (d) zero

21. What should be the value of distance d, so that final image is formed on the object itself?

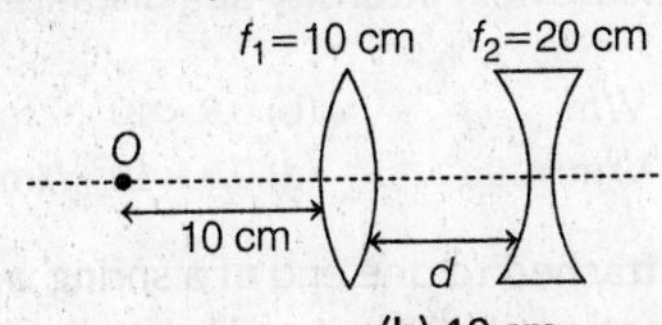

(a) 5 cm (b) 10 cm
(c) 20 cm (d) None of these

22. In a potentiometer experiment, null point with a cell is at 52 cm. When cell is shunted with a resistance of 5 Ω, balance point is obtained at 40 cm. Internal resistance of cell will be

(a) 1 Ω (b) 1.5 Ω (c) 2 Ω (d) 2.5 Ω

23. A non-conducting solid sphere of radius 20 cm has a uniform charge density throughout its volume. If the ratio of potential at its centre to a point P inside the sphere which is at a distance r from the centre is 4 : 3, then value of r is

(a) 17.32 cm (b) 16.67 cm (c) 17.72 cm (d) 23.09 cm

24. The pressure of a real gas in a container is given as $p = \frac{XT}{2V - b} - \frac{a}{b^2}$, where V is volume and T is temperature.
The dimensional formulae of X and b are respectively

(a) $[ML^2T^{-2}K^{-1}]$, $[ML^5T^{-2}]$ (b) $[M^1L^2T^{-2}K^{-1}]$, $[L^3]$
(c) $[ML^{-2}T^{-2}K^{-1}]$, $[L^3]$ (d) $[M^{-1}L^{-2}T^2K]$, $[L^6]$

25. In the following CE, *n-p-n* configuration, current gain $\beta = 90$ has been used. The output voltage (V_o) of the amplifier is ($V_{BE} = 0$)

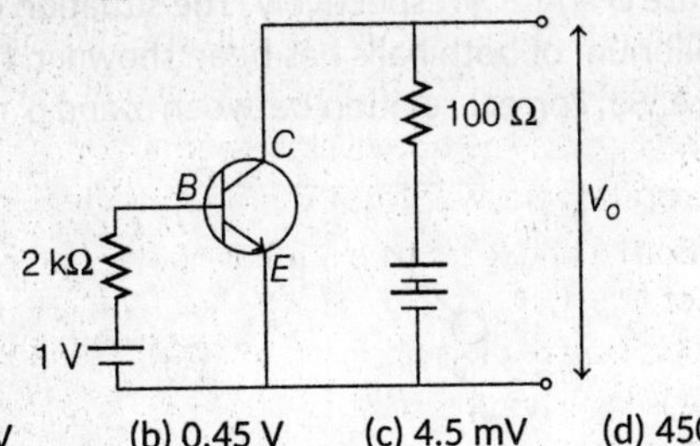

(a) 4.5 V (b) 0.45 V (c) 4.5 mV (d) 450 V

26. An L-C oscillator cannot have

(a) very low frequency
(b) very high frequency
(c) frequency of range 100 Hz to 500 Hz
(d) frequency same as input AC frequency

27. The ratio of minimum wavelengths of Balmer and Paschen series of hydrogen atom will be

(a) 1 : 4 (b) 4 : 9 (c) 9 : 4 (d) 4 : 1

28. The moment of inertia of a solid hemisphere about its diameter is
(Here, m = mass of solid hemisphere, R = radius)

(a) $\frac{1}{5}MR^2$ (b) $\frac{2}{5}MR^2$ (c) $\frac{1}{3}MR^2$ (d) $\frac{2}{3}MR^2$

29. The stress *versus* strain graphs for wires of two materials A and B are as shown in the figure. If Y_A and Y_B are the Young's modulii of the materials, then

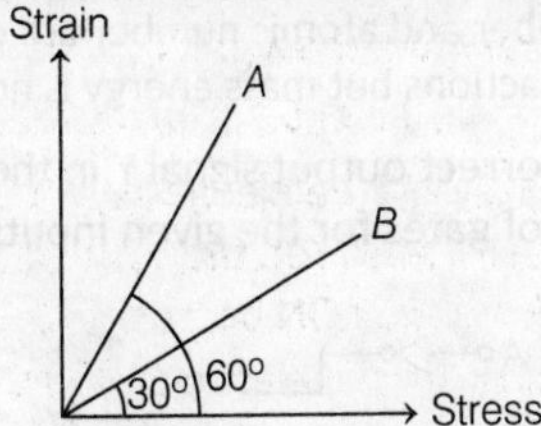

(a) $Y_B = 2Y_A$ (b) $Y_A = Y_B$ (c) $Y_B = 3Y_A$ (d) $Y_A = 3Y_B$

30. 100 g of ice at 0°C is mixed with 100 g of water at 80°C. The final temperature of the mixture is
(Given, latent heat of fusion of ice, L_f = 80 cal/g and specific heat capacity of water, S_{water} = 1 cal/g-°C)

(a) 0°C (b) 20°C (c) 40°C (d) 60°C

31. A piston is slowly pushed into a closed metal cylinder containing an ideal gas. Which of the following statements is incorrect regarding the gas?

(a) The pressure of the gas increases.
(b) The number of the molecules per unit volume increases.
(c) The average speed of gas molecules increases.
(d) The frequency of collision of the gas molecules with the piston increases.

32. Light of intensity 10^{-5} W/m^2 falls on sodium photocell of surface area 2 cm^2 and work function 2 eV.
Assume that only top 5-layers of sodium absorb the incident energy and effective atomic area of sodium atom is 10^{-20} m^2. The time required for photo emission considering wave picture of light will be nearly

(a) 10.5 s (b) 0.5 s
(c) 0.5 h (d) 0.5 yr

33. Ratio of mass of an ideal moderator and mass of a neutron is about

(a) nearly 2.50 (b) nearly 0.50
(c) nearly 1.00 (d) nearly 0.10

34. In an L-R series circuit, resistance is R and inductive reactance $X_L = 3R$. When a capacitor is added in a circuit such that $X_C = 2R$.
The ratio of initial and final power factors of circuit is

(a) $\sqrt{3}$ (b) $\sqrt{5}$
(c) $1/\sqrt{3}$ (d) $1/\sqrt{5}$

35. If the frequency of incident photon on metal surface is doubled, then stopping potential will become

(a) doubled (b) less than double
(c) more than double (d) less than existing value

Section II

36. Choose the correct statement.

(a) Binding energy per nucleon decreases in α-decay and β-decay.

(b) By emission of one α and four β-particles, isobars are produced.

(c) Mass of products formed is less than the original mass in nuclear fission and nuclear fusion reactions.

(d) Mass number and atomic number are conserved in all nuclear reactions but mass energy is not.

37. Identify the correct output signal Y in the given combination of gates for the given inputs A and B shown in the figure.

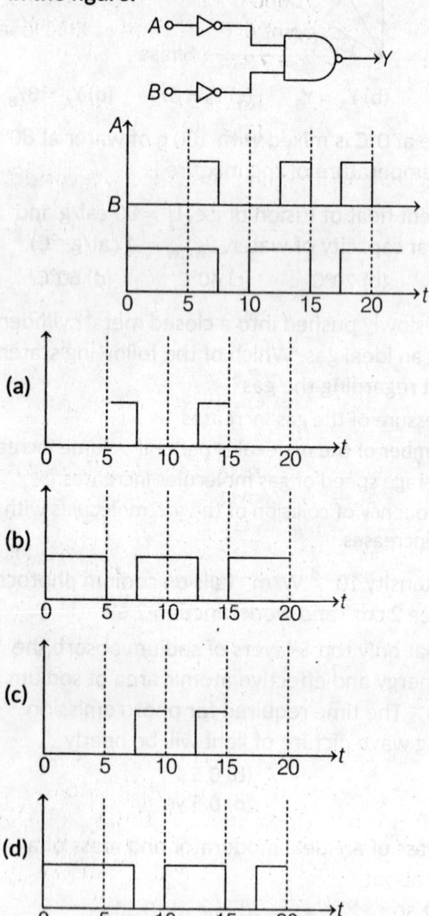

38. In YDSE, monochromatic light falls on a screen 1.80 m from two slits separated by 2.08 mm. The first and second order bright fringes are separated by 0.553 mm. The wavelength of light used is

(a) 520 nm (b) 639 nm
(c) 715 nm (d) None of these

39. Two identical discs are placed on a vertical axis one above the other at certain distance. The bottom disc is rotating with constant angular velocity and its rotational kinetic energy K_0. The upper disc is initially at rest. If this disc is released, then it sticks to the lower disc. The change in the rotational kinetic energy of the system after the collision, is (Assume the initial distance between the discs is negligible)

(a) $\frac{K_0}{2}$ (b) $-\frac{K_0}{2}$
(c) $\frac{K_0}{4}$ (d) $-\frac{K_0}{4}$

40. Infinite long wire have a linear charge density of 0.2 C/m. Find the electric field intensity at a distance of 2m from wire.

(a) 1.8×10^9 V/m (b) 0.9×10^9 V/m
(c) 2.7×10^9 V/m (d) 0.3×10^5 V/m

41. A block is attached to one end of a spring which executes harmonic motion about an equilibrium position with an amplitude A. Its speed as it passes through the equilibrium position is v. If spring is extended to $2A$ and released, then the speed of the block passing through the equilibrium position will be

(a) $2v$ (b) $4v$
(c) $\sqrt{3}v$ (d) $3v$

42. The three wire loops shown in the figure below have same width and vertical edge lengths of L, $2L$ and $3L$. They will move with the same speed into a region of uniform magnetic field **B** directed out of the page. Rank them according to the maximum magnitude of the induced emf, greatest to least.

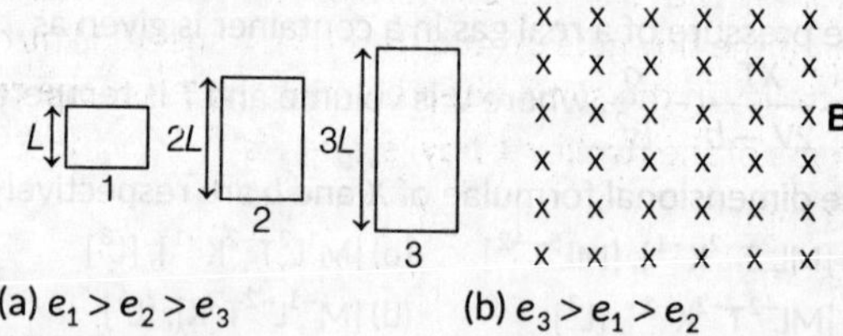

(a) $e_1 > e_2 > e_3$ (b) $e_3 > e_1 > e_2$
(c) $e_3 > e_2 > e_1$ (d) $e_2 > e_3 > e_1$

43. Two pith balls with mass m are suspended from insulating threads. The charges on the left pith ball and right pith ball are Q and $2Q$, respectively. The situation of equilibrium of both balls has been shown in the following figure. So, correct relation between α and β is

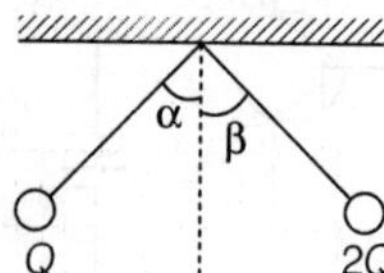

(a) $\alpha = \beta$ (b) $\alpha > \beta$
(c) $\alpha < \beta$ (d) None of these

44. A resistance of 10 Ω draws power 150 W when connected to an AC source. If an inductor is now placed in series with the resistance, such that the impedance of the circuit becomes 20Ω, the power drawn and inductive reactance are respectively

(a) 37.5 W, 10Ω (b) 37.5 W, $10\sqrt{3}$ Ω
(c) 75 W, 10Ω (d) 75 W, $10\sqrt{3}$ Ω

45. A block of mass m slides down on an inclined plane of slope angle θ with constant velocity. If block is then projected up the same plane with an initial velocity v_0. The distance travelled by block along the incline in upward motion before coming to rest, is

(a) $\frac{v_0^2}{2g\sin\theta}$ (b) $\frac{v_0^2}{4g\sin\theta}$

(c) $\frac{v_0^2}{4g}$ (d) Need more information

46. The trajectory of a stone that has been launched from ground has been shown in figure given below. It flies just over the wall and lands 30 m from the wall in 1 s. If the time of flight of the stone is 8 s, then its projection velocity is

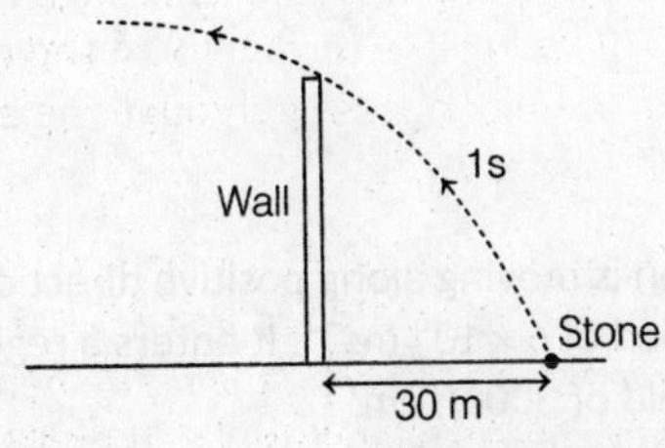

(a) 30 m/s (b) 40 m/s

(c) 50 m/s (d) $10\sqrt{3}$ m/s

47. A boy sits stationary at one end of a long trolley moving uniformly with a speed 20 km/h on a smooth horizontal floor. If the boy gets up and runs with a speed 3 km/h on the trolley in the same direction, then speed of the centre of mass of the (trolley + boy) system is

(a) 3 km/h (b) 17 km/h

(c) 20 km/h (d) 23 km/h

48. The equivalent capacitance of the arrangement shown in the figure below is $\frac{3\varepsilon_0 A}{d}$. The value of K_3 is

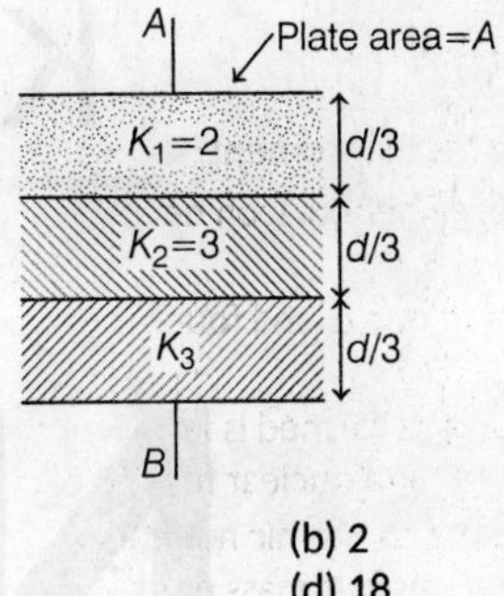

(a) 1 (b) 2

(c) 3 (d) 18

49. A ball of mass 0.5 kg is thrown vertically upwards with a speed u from a tower of height 80 m. The time taken by the particle to hit the ground is 4 times the time taken by it to reach the highest point of its path. The initial kinetic energy of ball is (Take, $g = 9.8\,\text{m/s}^2$)

(a) 14 J (b) 24.5 J

(c) 39.2 J (d) 49 J

50. Match Column I with Column II and select the correct answer from the options given below.

	Column I (Position of the object)		Column II (Magnification)
A.	An object is placed at centre of curvature before a concave mirror	P.	Magnification is ∞
B.	An object is placed at focus before a concave mirror	Q.	Magnification is +1
C.	An object is placed at centre of curvature before a convex mirror	R.	Magnification is −1
		S.	Magnification is 0.33

(a) A → R, B → P, C → S

(b) A → R, B → Q, C → P

(c) A → Q, B → P, C → S

(d) A → P, B → R, C → Q

Answers

1. (a)	2. (a)	3. (a)	4. (d)	5. (d)	6. (d)	7. (a)	8. (b)	9. (a)	10. (c)
11. (c)	12. (c)	13. (c)	14. (c)	15. (b)	16. (d)	17. (d)	18. (d)	19. (c)	20. (b)
21. (b)	22. (b)	23. (a)	24. (b)	25. (a)	26. (a)	27. (b)	28. (b)	29. (c)	30. (a)
31. (a)	32. (d)	33. (c)	34. (b)	35. (c)	36. (c)	37. (d)	38. (b)	39. (b)	40. (a)
41. (a)	42. (c)	43. (a)	44. (b)	45. (b)	46. (c)	47. (c)	48. (b)	49. (d)	50. (a)

See detailed explanations on page no. 243

Knockout 02

NEET

PHYSICS

Instructions See Knockout 01

Section I

1. If momentum p, area A and time t are taken as fundamental quantities, then the dimensional formula for energy is
(a) $[p^2AT^{-2}]$
(b) $[pA^{-1}T^{-2}]$
(c) $[pA^{1/2}T^{-1}]$
(d) $[p^{1/2}AT^{-1}]$

2. The magnetic field $B(x,t)$ of a plane electromagnetic wave travelling through vacuum is given by

$$B(x, t) = 9 \times 10^{-6} \sin(3.25 \times 10^4 x + \omega t) \text{ T}$$

The frequency and peak value of electric field are respectively.
(a) 1.55×10^{12} Hz, 3×10^{-13} V/m
(b) 1.55×10^4 Hz, 3.81 kV/m
(c) 1.55×10^{12} Hz, 2.7 kV/m
(d) 1.55×10^{12} Hz, data insufficient

3. **Statement I** In adiabatic expansion, temperature of gas always decreases.
Statement II In adiabatic process, exchange of heat is zero.
In light of above statements, choose the most appropriate answer from the options given below:
(a) Both Statement I and Statement II are incorrect.
(b) Statement I is correct and Statement II is incorrect.
(c) Statement I is incorrect and Statement II is correct.
(d) Both Statement I and Statement II are correct.

4. At any instant, the ratio of amounts of two radioactive substances in a sample is 2 : 1. If their half-lives are 12 h and 16 h respectively, then after 2 days, the ratio of amount of substances left is
(a) 1 : 1 (b) 2 : 1 (c) 1 : 4 (d) 1 : 2

5. An electron is moving along positive direction of X-axis with a speed of 6×10^6 ms^{-1}. It enters a region of uniform electric field of 300 V/cm $\cdot \hat{\mathbf{j}}$.
Magnitude and direction of magnetic field needed to keep electron moving in x-direction will be
(a) 5×10^{-4} T along $-z$-direction
(b) 5×10^{-3} T along $+z$-direction
(c) 5×10^{-3} T along $-y$-direction
(d) 5×10^{-4} T along $+y$-direction

6. When p-n junction diode is forward biased, then
(a) both the depletion region and barrier height are reduced
(b) the depletion region is widened and barrier height is reduced
(c) the depletion region is reduced and barrier height is increased
(d) both the depletion region and barrier height are increased

7. A 27 mW laser beam has an area of 20 mm^2. Magnitude of maximum electric field in laser is
(Take $\varepsilon_0 = 9 \times 10^{-12}$ SI unit and $c = 3 \times 10^8$ m/s)
(a) 1 kV/m (b) 0.7 kV/m (c) 2 kV/m (d) 1.4 kV/m

8. Choose the correct statement from the following options.
(a) Natural convection takes place due to gravity.
(b) Warming a room by a heat blower is not an example of natural convection.
(c) A normal body can never radiate energy more than a perfectly black body.
(d) Emissivity of any body is always greater than the absorptivity.

9. If the resultant of two forces of magnitudes P and $2P$ is perpendicular to **P**, then the angle between the forces is
(a) $\frac{2\pi}{3}$ (b) $\frac{5\pi}{6}$ (c) $\frac{3\pi}{4}$ (d) $\frac{\pi}{3}$

10. Temperature of a body can be related to kinetic energy of molecules of body. This statement explains which of the given principle in physics?

(a) Unification
(b) Reduction
(c) Comparison
(d) Bifurcation

11. A spring of stiffness constant k and natural length l is cut into two parts $\frac{3l}{4}$ and $\frac{l}{4}$, respectively and an arrangement is made as shown below. If the mass is slightly displaced and then, released. The time period of oscillations is

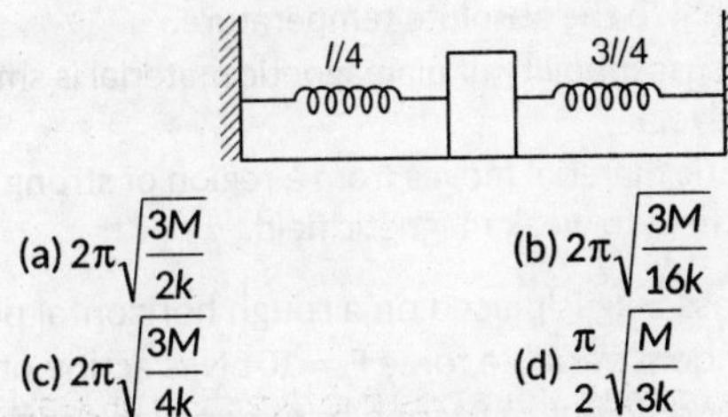

(a) $2\pi\sqrt{\frac{3M}{2k}}$
(b) $2\pi\sqrt{\frac{3M}{16k}}$
(c) $2\pi\sqrt{\frac{3M}{4k}}$
(d) $\frac{\pi}{2}\sqrt{\frac{M}{3k}}$

12. An object is placed at a distance of 12 cm from a convex lens. When convex mirror of focal length 15 cm is placed on other side of lens at a distance of 8 cm, image coincides with object.

On removing convex mirror distance of image and object is around

(a) 20 cm
(b) 60 cm
(c) 50 cm
(d) 28 cm

13. A source of 6.6 kW produces 10^{20} photons per second, then source is

(a) an incandescent bulb
(b) a red LED
(c) coolidge tube
(d) a hot iron rod

14. A hydrogen atom emits a photon as it transits from $n = 5$ to $n = 1$ state. Recoil speed of hydrogen atom will be

(a) 4.17 m/s
(b) 2.19 m/s
(c) 3.25 m/s
(d) 4.34 m/s

15. In the figure shown below, box of two inputs A and B consists arrangement of logic gate(s). The input waveform A and B and output waveform (Y) has been shown. The Boolean output Y is

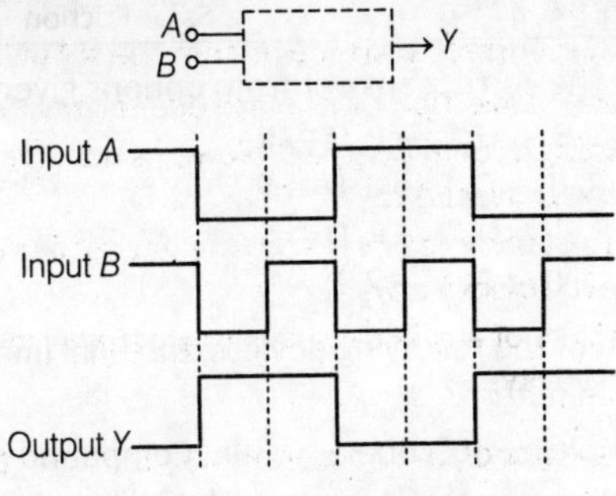

(a) $\overline{A}$
(b) $A \cdot (A + B)$
(c) $\overline{A + B}$
(d) $\overline{A}\,\overline{B} + AB$

16. The potential energy of a particle oscillating along X-axis is given by $U = 20 + (x - 1)^2$, where U is in joules and x in metres. Total mechanical energy of the particle is 36 J. The maximum kinetic energy of the particle is

(a) 24 J
(b) 36 J
(c) 16 J
(d) 20 J

17. A particle is projected from ground. The graph between its vertical velocity v_y and time t is shown in the figure. The maximum height attained by particle is (Take, $g = 10$ m/s^2)

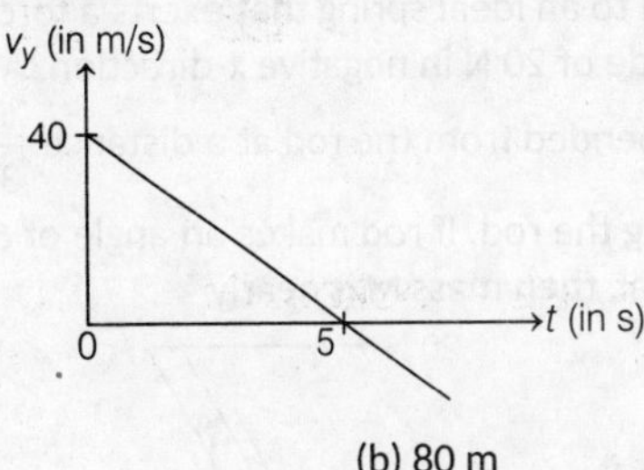

(a) 40 m
(b) 80 m
(c) 100 m
(d) 200 m

18. A measurement taken from an instrument having lower least count increases which of these?

(a) Accuracy of measurement
(b) Precision of measurement
(c) Significant digits in measurement
(d) Value of measured quantity

19. Four plates of equal area A are separated by equal distances d and are arranged as shown in the following figure. The equivalent capacitance is

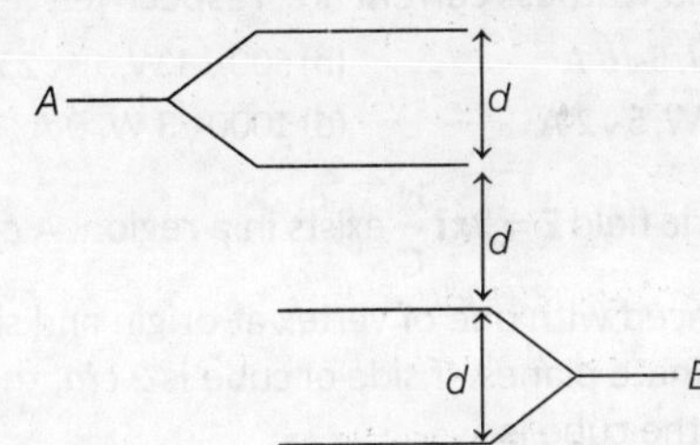

(a) $\frac{\varepsilon_0 A}{d}$
(b) $\frac{3}{2}\frac{\varepsilon_0 A}{d}$
(c) $\frac{2\varepsilon_0 A}{d}$
(d) $3\frac{\varepsilon_0 A}{d}$

20. A satellite revolving around the earth in an orbit of radius R is taken to a orbit of radius $1.02R$. Percentage increase in time period of rotation of satellite is around

(a) 1%
(b) 2%
(c) 3%
(d) 4%

21. Assertion (A) A geostationary satellite can be parked only in an equatorial orbit.

Reason (R) In an equatorial orbit, gravitational force pulls the orbit towards the centre of the orbit.

In the light of the above statements, choose the most appropriate answer from the options given below.

(a) Both A and R are true but R is not the correct explanation of A.
(b) A is true but R is false.
(c) A is false but R is true.
(d) Both A and R are true and R is the correct explanation of A.

22. A massless rod of length L is held in equilibrium as shown in the following figure, which lower end is placed on a rough horizontal surface. The upper end of the rod is attached to an ideal spring that exerts a force of magnitude of 20 N in negative x-direction. A block of mass M is suspended from the rod at a distance $\frac{2L}{3}$ from bottom end along the rod. If rod makes an angle of 60° with horizontal, then mass M is nearly

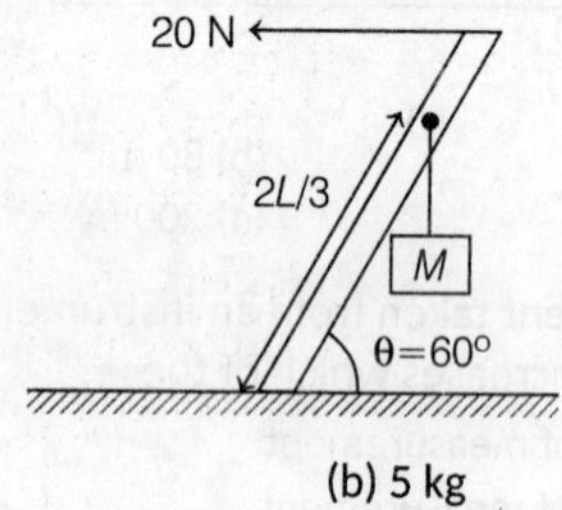

(a) 2.5 kg (b) 5 kg
(c) 0 kg (d) 7 kg

23. In an AC circuit, the instantaneous voltage and current are given by $V = 100\sin(100\pi t)$ V and $i = 20\cos\left(100\pi t - \frac{\pi}{6}\right)$ A. In one cycle of AC, the average power consumed by the circuit and wattless current are, respectively

(a) 500 W, $5\sqrt{6}$ A (b) $500\sqrt{3}$ W, $10\sqrt{2}$ A
(c) 1000 W, $5\sqrt{2}$ A (d) $1000\sqrt{3}$ W, 0 A

24. An electric field $\mathbf{E} = 2x\hat{\mathbf{i}}\,\frac{\text{N}}{\text{C}}$ exists in a region. A cubical metal box is placed with one of vertex at origin and sides parallel to coordinate planes. If side of cube is 2 cm, then net flux through the cube is

(a) $4\times10^{-2}\,\frac{\text{N}}{\text{C}}\,\text{cm}^2$ (b) $8\times10^{-2}\,\frac{\text{N}}{\text{C}}\,\text{cm}^2$
(c) $0.5\times10^{-2}\,\frac{\text{N}}{\text{C}}\,\text{cm}^2$ (d) zero

25. Two identical loops of silver and copper are subjected to a non-uniform magnetic field which is perpendicular to the plane of loops. The magnetic field is changing with constant rate. Which of the following statement(s) is/are true regarding the induced emf?

(a) Induced emf and induced current are same in both loops.
(b) Induced emf remains same but induced current changes in both loops.
(c) Induced emf changes but induced current remains same in both loops.
(d) Induced emf will be more in copper loop.

26. The moment of inertia of a body about the given axis is 10 kg-m^2. Initially, the body is at rest. In order to produce a rotational kinetic energy of 980 J, an angular acceleration of 28 rad/s^2 must be applied about that axis for duration of

(a) 0.5 s (b) 2 s
(c) 4 s (d) None of these

27. Which of the following is not a characteristic of diamagnetic materials?

(a) The diamagnetic materials are repelled by a magnetic field.
(b) Susceptibility of diamagnetic materials is inversely proportional to the absolute temperature.
(c) Magnetic susceptibility of diamagnetic material is small and negative.
(d) Diamagnetic material moves from a region of strong magnetic field to weak magnetic field.

28. A block of mass 5 kg is placed on a rough horizontal plane. A time dependent variable force $F = 10t$ N is acting on the block. If the coefficient of friction between block and surface is 0.2, then work done by friction force in initial 4 s is (Take, $g = 10$ m/s^2)

(a) 90 N (b) – 90 N
(c) – 202.5 N (d) None of these

29. A non-conducting rod AB of length L has linear charge density λ that varies as $\lambda = \frac{\lambda_0}{L}x$, where x is distance from end A and λ_0 is constant over its length. The rod is rotated about an axis passing through its end A with constant angular velocity ω. The magnetic moment of the rod is

(a) $\frac{\lambda_0\omega L^2}{3}$ (b) $\frac{\lambda_0\omega L^2}{6}$ (c) $\frac{\lambda_0\omega L^3}{8}$ (d) $\frac{\lambda_0\omega L^3}{16}$

30. Let q_1 and q_2 are values of charges obtained an two neutral bodies due to same charging process. Now, match Column I and Column II correctly.

	Column I		Column II
A.	$q_1 + q_2 = 0$	P.	Induction
B.	$q_1 - q_2 = 0$	Q.	Conduction
C.	$q_1 \geq -q_2$	R.	Photo emission
D.	$q_1 > 0, q_2 > 0$	S.	Friction

Choose the correct answer from options given below:

(a) A → S, B → Q, C → P, D → R
(b) A → R, B → Q, C → S, D → P
(c) A → P, B → Q, C → R, D → S
(d) A → Q, B → P, C → R, D → S

31. In which of the following devices, the final image formed is erect in nature?

I. Simple microscope II. Compound microscope
III. Astronomical telescope IV. Galilean telescope

(a) I and IV only (b) I and III only
(c) II and IV only (d) I, II, III and IV

32. A straight wire carrying a current of 12 A is bent into a semi-circular loop of radius 2.0 cm. What will be magnetic field at the centre of the semi-circular loop?

(a) $\mathbf{B} = 1.9 \times 10^{-4}$ T, ⊙

(b) $\mathbf{B} = 1.9 \times 10^{4}$ T, ⊙

(c) $\mathbf{B} = 1.9 \times 10^{-4}$ T, ⊗

(d) $\mathbf{B} = 1.9 \times 10^{4}$ T, ⊗

33. A charge passing through a resistor is varying with time as shown in the figure. The amount of heat generated H in time t as a function of time is best represented by

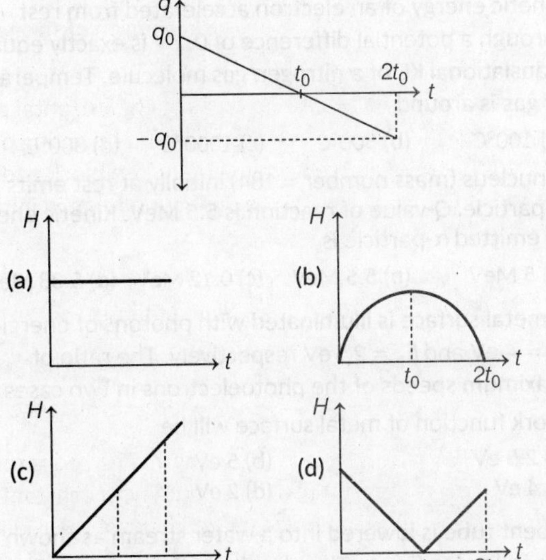

34. The intensity of light through each slit in Young's double slit experiment is I_0. The minimum separation between the two points on the screen, where intensities are $2I_0$ and I_0 is (Here, β is fringe width)

(a) $\frac{\beta}{4}$ (b) $\frac{\beta}{3}$

(c) $\frac{\beta}{6}$ (d) $\frac{\beta}{12}$

35. Four rods of different masses and lengths are arranged in XY-plane as shown in the following figure. The centre of mass of such arrangement lies in which of the following mentioned regions?

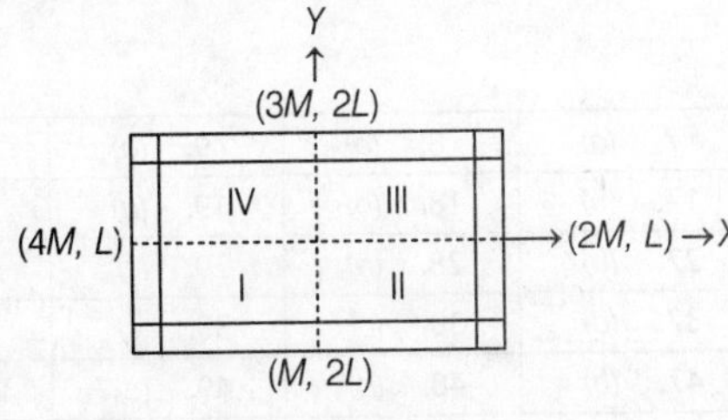

(a) I (b) II (c) III (d) IV

Section II

36. The relation between R and r (internal resistance of the battery) for which the power consumed in the external part of the circuit is maximum?

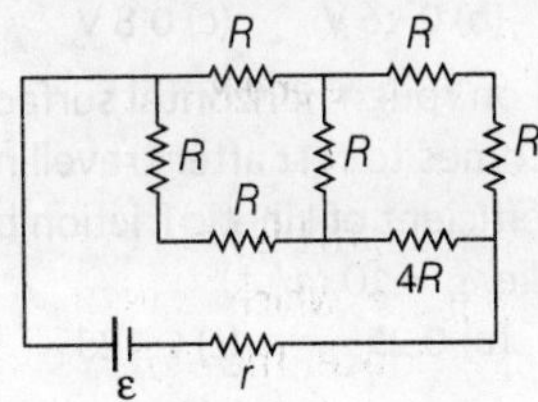

(a) $R = r$ (b) $R = \frac{r}{2}$ (c) $R = 2r$ (d) $R = \frac{3}{2}r$

37. Current density at a section of a wire is $\mathbf{J} = (2 \times 10^4)\,\hat{\mathbf{j}}\,\frac{\text{A}}{\text{m}^2}$.

Area vector of wire at this section is $\mathbf{A} = (2\hat{\mathbf{i}} + 3\hat{\mathbf{j}})\ \text{cm}^2$.

Charge that flows through this cross-section in 2 s is

(a) 12 μC (b) 12 nC

(c) 12 mC (d) 12 C

38. If an uncharged capacitor is being charged by a constant current, then which graph represents correct variation in change in voltage across the capacitor with time t?

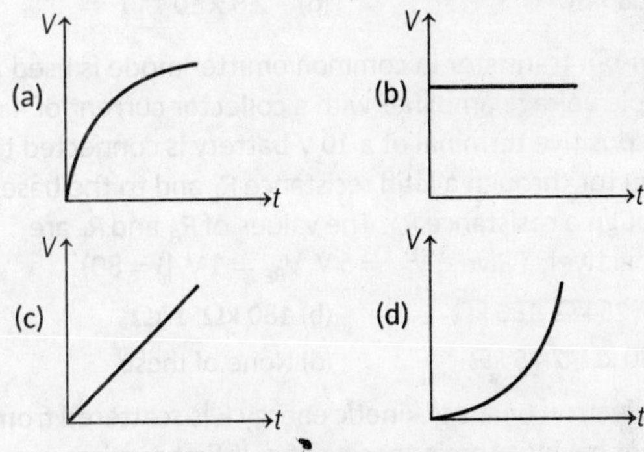

39. A town has a demand of 800 kW power at 220 V is situated at a distance of 15 km away from an hydroelectric power plant generating 440 V.

Resistance of the two wire line transmitting power is 0.5 Ω per km. Town gets power from the line through a 4000 V – 220 V step down transformer at a sub-station at town.

Using above information match entries of Column I and Column II correctly.

	Column I		Column II
A.	Line current (in A)	P.	7
B.	Line power loss (in kW)	Q.	1400
C.	Power supplied by plant (in kW)	R.	600
D.	Voltage of line at plant (in kV)	S.	200

Choose the correct answer from options given below:

(a) A → P, B → Q C → R, D → S

(b) A → Q, B → P, C → R, D → S

(c) A → S, B → R, C → Q, D → P

(d) A → R, B → S, C → P, D → Q

40. A potentiometer wire *AB* of length 100 cm has resistance of 10 Ω. It is connected in series with a resistance $R = 40\ \Omega$ and a battery of emf 2 V and negligible internal resistance. If a source of unknown emf *E* is balanced by 40 cm length of the potentiometer wire, the value of *E* is

(a) 0.08 V (b) 0.16 V (c) 0.8 V (d) 1.6 V

41. A block slides on rough horizontal surface with a velocity of 20 m/s. It comes to rest after travelling a distance of 80 m. The coefficient of kinetic friction between block and surface is (Take, $g = 10\ m/s^2$)

(a) 0.20 (b) 0.25 (c) 0.125 (d) 0.05

42. From top of tower, two particles are simultaneously projected horizontally in opposite directions. If 30 m/s and 40 m/s are the initial velocities, then the time after which their velocities are mutually perpendicular is given by (Take, $g = 10\ m/s^2$)

(a) 5 s (b) $\sqrt{21}$ s (c) $2\sqrt{3}$ s (d) $2\sqrt{7}$ s

43. An electric dipole with dipole moment $\mathbf{p} = (3\hat{i} + 4\hat{j}) \times 10^{-30}$ C-m is placed in an electric field $\mathbf{E} = 4000\ \hat{i}$ N/C. The dipole is rotated very slowly until its electric dipole moment becomes $(-4\hat{i} + 3\hat{j}) \times 10^{-30}$ C-m. The work done by external torque is equal to

(a) -4×10^{-28} J (b) 4×10^{-28} J

(c) 2.8×10^{-26} J (d) -2.8×10^{-26} J

44. An *n-p-n* transistor in common emitter mode is used as a simple voltage amplifier with a collector current of 4 mA. The positive terminal of a 10 V battery is connected to the collector through a load resistance R_L and to the base through a resistance R_B. The values of R_B and R_L are respectively (Given, $V_{CE} = 6$ V, $V_{BE} = 1$ V, $\beta = 80$)

(a) 2.25 kΩ, 180 kΩ (b) 180 kΩ, 1 kΩ

(c) 80 kΩ, 2.25 kΩ (d) None of these

45. An electron beam of kinetic energy *E* is scattered from a target having atomic spacing of *d*. If first maxima occurs at angle θ, then correct relation is

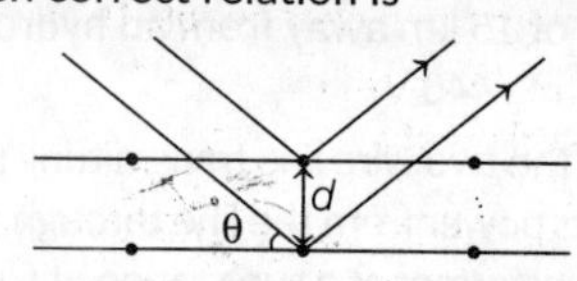

(a) $d\sin\theta = \frac{h}{\sqrt{2Em}}$ (b) $2d\sin\theta = \frac{h}{\sqrt{2Em}}$

(c) $2d\sin\theta = \frac{h}{\sqrt{Em}}$ (d) $d\sin\theta = \frac{h}{\sqrt{Em}}$

46. An ideal liquid flows through the horizontal pipe *AB*, which is of uniform cross-section. The vertical pipes 1, 2 and 3 are equispaced. The liquid levels in these pipes are at heights h_1, h_2 and h_3, respectively above *AB*. Liquid flows from *A* to *B* in *AB*. Then, correct relation is

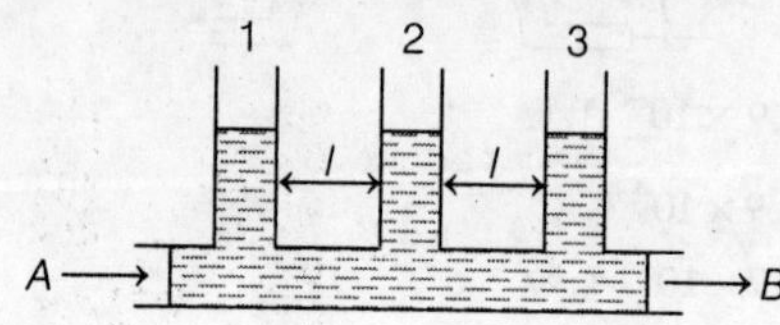

(a) $h_1 = h_2 = h_3$ (b) $h_2 = \frac{1}{2}(h_1 + h_3)$

(c) $h_2 > \frac{1}{2}(h_1 + h_3)$ (d) $h_2 < \frac{1}{2}(h_1 + h_3)$

47. Kinetic energy of an electron accelerated from rest through a potential difference of 0.1 V is exactly equals to translational KE of a nitrogen gas molecule. Temperature of gas is around

(a) 100°C (b) 500°C (c) 1000°C (d) 300°C

48. A nucleus (mass number = 184) initially at rest emits an α-particle. *Q*-value of reaction is 5.5 MeV. Kinetic energy of emitted α-particle is

(a) 5 MeV (b) 5.5 MeV (c) 0.12 MeV (d) 5.38 MeV

49. A metal surface is illuminated with photons of energies $E_1 = 4$ eV and $E_2 = 2.5$ eV respectively. The ratio of maximum speeds of the photoelectrons in two cases is 2. Work function of metal surface will be

(a) 2.5 eV (b) 5 eV

(c) 4 eV (d) 2 eV

50. A bent tube is lowered into a water stream as shown in the following figure. The velocity of the stream relative to the tube is 2.5 m/s. The closed upper end of the tube located at the height 12 cm has a small orifice. The height *h* up to which water jet spurt is ($g = 9.8\ m/s^2$)

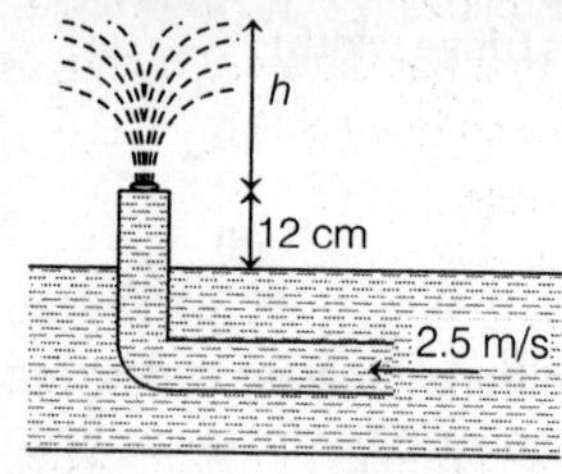

(a) 0.32 m (b) 0.2 m

(c) 0.44 m (d) 0 m

Answers

1. (c)	2. (c)	3. (d)	4. (a)	5. (b)	6. (a)	7. (a)	8. (a)	9. (a)	10. (b)
11. (b)	12. (c)	13. (c)	14. (a)	15. (a)	16. (c)	17. (b)	18. (b)	19. (a)	20. (c)
21. (d)	22. (b)	23. (a)	24. (d)	25. (b)	26. (a)	27. (b)	28. (b)	29. (c)	30. (a)
31. (a)	32. (c)	33. (c)	34. (d)	35. (a)	36. (b)	37. (d)	38. (c)	39. (c)	40. (b)
41. (b)	42. (c)	43. (c)	44. (b)	45. (b)	46. (a)	47. (b)	48. (d)	49. (d)	50. (b)

See detailed explanations on page no. 247

Knockout 03

NEET

PHYSICS

Instructions See Knockout 01

Section I

1. An ideal gas of given mass is kept at constant pressure. By what percentage should the pressure be increased, so as to decrease its volume by 5%?

(a) 2.5% (b) 3.6%
(c) 5% (d) 5.26%

2. Which one of the following statement is true?

(a) The energy gap between conduction band and valence band is very small for insulators.
(b) The resistivity of a semiconductor increases with temperature.
(c) Semiconductors have negative temperature coefficient of resistivity.
(d) Carbon is a semiconductor.

3. Which of the following cannot be changed by an ideal transformer that has different number of turns in its primary and secondary coils?

(a) Resistive loads
(b) Electric current
(c) Electric power
(d) Electric potential difference or voltage

4. The length and breadth of a rectangular sheet are 16.2 cm and 10.1 cm, respectively. The area of the sheet in appropriate significant figures and error is

(a) $(163.62\pm3)\ cm^2$ (b) $(163.6\pm2.6)\ cm^2$
(c) $(163.6\pm2.6)\ cm^2$ (d) $(164\pm3)\ cm^2$

5. Two liquids are at temperatures 20°C and 40°C. When same amount of mass of both of them is mixed, the temperature of the mixture is 32°C. The ratio of their specific heats is

(a) 4 : 3 (b) 2 : 5
(c) 3 : 2 (d) 2 : 3

6. The transistors provide good power amplification when they are used in

(a) common collector configuration
(b) common emitter configuration
(c) common base configuration
(d) depend on type of transistor either *n-p-n* or *p-n-p*

7. A projectile is projected with initial velocity $(10\hat{i} + 15\hat{j})$ m/s from a height 20 m from ground. The velocity of the projectile just before hitting the ground is ($g = 10\ m/s^2$)

(a) $(10\hat{i} - 15\hat{j})$ m/s (b) $(-10\hat{i} + 15\hat{j})$ m/s
(c) $(25\hat{i} - 15\hat{j})$ m/s (d) $(10\hat{i} - 25\hat{j})$ m/s

8. If two soap bubbles of different radii are connected by a tube, then

(a) air flows from the smaller bubble to the bigger bubble
(b) air flows from bigger bubble to the smaller bubble till the sizes are interchanged
(c) air flows from the bigger bubble to the smaller bubble till the sizes becomes equal
(d) there is no flow of air

9. The electric field lines due to positive charge has been shown in the following figure. If a small negative charge is released at point *B*, then the difference of potential energy of negative charge between the points *B* and *A* is

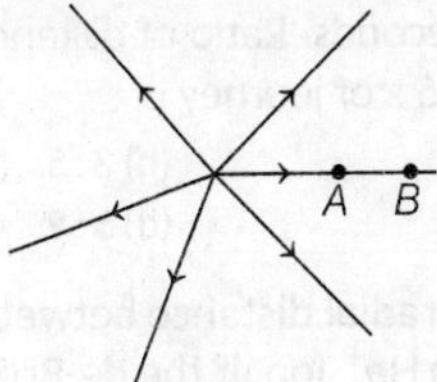

(a) positive
(b) negative
(c) zero
(d) either positive or negative

10. Two infinitely long straight conductors are laid along X and Y-axes as shown below.

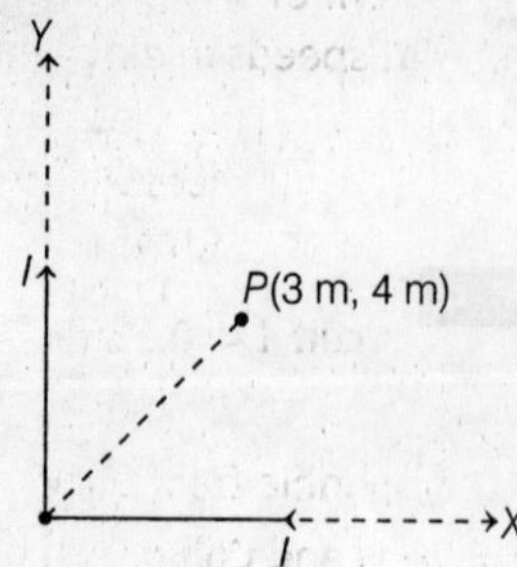

Both wires carry I current. Find magnitude of magnetic field (in tesla) at point P(3 m, 4 m).

(a) $\frac{\mu_0 I}{4\pi}$ (b) $\frac{4}{5}\cdot\frac{\mu_0 I}{4\pi}$

(c) $\frac{3}{5}\cdot\frac{\mu_0 I}{4\pi}$ (d) $\frac{9}{15}\cdot\frac{\mu_0 I}{4\pi}$

11. A thin lens made of glass $\left(n_g = \frac{3}{2}\right)$ of focal length f_1 in air. This lens when dipped in a liquid of refractive index $\frac{7}{5}$, focal length of lens will become f_2. Ratio of $\frac{f_2}{f_1}$ will be

(a) 1
(b) 5
(c) 7
(d) 9

12. If E and B are the electric field and magnetic field at any instant in an electromagnetic wave, then rate of flow of energy across a unit area at any instant is given as

(a) EB (b) $\frac{EB}{\mu_0}$

(c) $\frac{EB}{\sqrt{\mu_0 \varepsilon_0}}$ (d) $\frac{EB}{c^2}$

13. A particle is at height h from the surface of the earth. If it is fired with a velocity greater than escape velocity parallel to the surface of earth, then trajectory of the projectile is

(a) straight line (b) parabolic
(c) elliptical (d) hyperbolic

14. Position of a particle moving along X-axis is $x = (t^3 - 6t^2 + 9t)$ m where t is in seconds. Ratio of distance and displacement of particle in first 5 s of journey is

(a) 1 : 1 (b) 3 : 5
(c) 7 : 5 (d) 5 : 9

15. The minimum radial distance between first orbit and second orbit in He^+ ion, if the de-Broglie wavelength of an electron in first orbit is λ, will be

(a) 2λ (b) $\frac{2\lambda}{\pi}$

(c) $\frac{\lambda}{2\pi}$ (d) $\frac{\lambda}{4\pi}$

16. If a container filled with liquid is heated, the level of liquid in container

(a) increases
(b) decreases
(c) remains same
(d) depends on coefficient of volume expansion of container and liquid

17. Assertion (A) Gravitational potential inside a hollow spherical shell is zero

Reason (R) Gravitational field inside a spherical shell is zero

In the light of the above statements, choose the most appropriate answer from the options given below:

(a) Both A and R are true but R is not the correct explanation of A.
(b) A is true but R is false.
(c) A is false but R is true.
(d) Both A and R are true and R is the correct explanation of A.

18. A charge q is enclosed by an imaginary Gaussian surface.

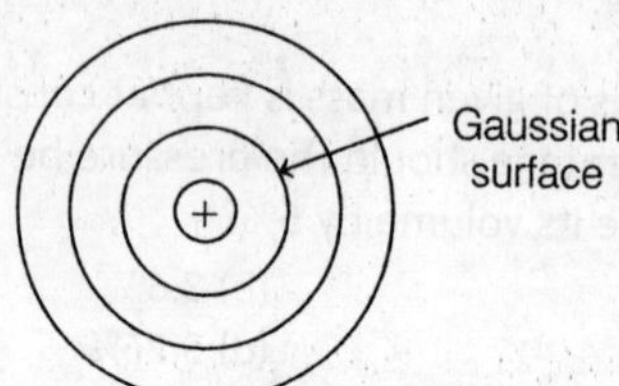

If the radius of Gaussian surface is increasing at a rate $\frac{dr}{dt} = \alpha$, then flux linked with surface is

(a) increasing at a rate, $\frac{d\phi}{dt} = \alpha$

(b) decreasing at a rate, $\frac{d\phi}{dt} = -\alpha$

(c) decreasing at a rate, $\frac{d\phi}{dt} = \frac{1}{k}$

(d) $\frac{q}{\varepsilon_0}$

19. A particle is executing SHM about origin. It has time period 8 s and amplitude 6 cm. At $t = 0$, particle is at right extreme position, then displacement at $t = 10$ s, is

(a) 0 cm (b) -3 cm
(c) $+3$ cm (d) $+2$ cm

20. If width of one slit in YDSE is slightly increased, then

(a) maximum intensity will decrease and minimum intensity will increase
(b) maximum intensity will increase and minimum intensity will decrease
(c) both maximum and minimum intensities will increase
(d) both maximum and minimum intensities will decrease

21. A battery of emf $E_1 = 9$ V and internal resistance $r_1 = 0.02\Omega$ is connected to a second battery of emf $E_2 = 12$ V and internal resistance $r_2 = 0.04\ \Omega$. Batteries are connected to form a closed loop such that their like terminals are connected together.

Now match Column I and Column II correctly.

	Column I		Column II
A.	Net emf of combination (in volts)	P.	100
B.	Current in circuit (in ampere)	Q.	50
C.	Rate of heat produced in cell of emf E_2 (in watts)	R.	10
D.	Potential difference between terminals of cell of emf E_1 (in volt)	S.	3

Choose the correct answer from options given below.

(a) A → Q, B → P, C → R, D → S
(b) A → S, B → P, C → R, D → Q
(c) A → S, B → R, C → Q, D → P
(d) A → S, B → Q, C → P, D → R

22. The initial mass of a rocket is 2000 kg. If the fuel is burning at the rate of 60 kg/s and gases come out at a speed of 400 m/s relative to rocket, then acceleration of rocket is (Take, $g = 10\ m/s^2$)

(a) $12\ m/s^2$ (b) $2\ m/s^2$
(c) $22\ m/s^2$ (d) zero

23. In the given circuit, the correct waveform depicting voltage across resistance V_R with time t, is

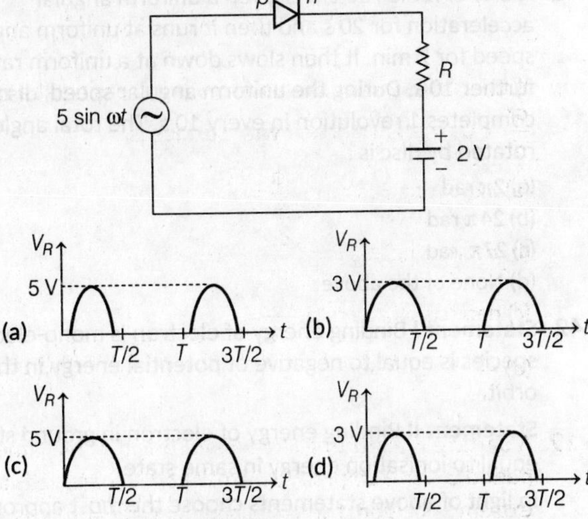

24. Two non-ideal batteries are connected in parallel. Consider the following statements.

Statement I The equivalent emf is smaller than either of the two emf's.

Statement II The equivalent internal resistance is smaller than either of the two internal resistances.

In light of above statements choose the most appropriate answer from the options given below:

(a) Both Statement I and Statement II are incorrect.
(b) Statement I is correct and Statement II is incorrect.
(c) Statement I is incorrect and Statement II is correct.
(d) Both Statement I and Statement II are correct.

25. A copper wire of diameter 20 mm is connected with another copper wire of diameter 4 mm. Through combination, a current of 5A flows when connected in a circuit. Ratio of drift speeds in different sections of composite wire is

(a) 1 : 1 (b) 1 : 2
(c) 1 : 4 (d) 4 : 1

26. Consider an L-C-R circuit, $L = 0.12\mu$, $C = 480 \times 10^{-9}$ F, $R = 23\ \Omega$

Supply is a 230 V, variable frequency AC.

Now match Column I and Column 2 correctly and choose the correct answer from the options given below.

	Column I		Column II
A.	Source frequency for maximum current (in Hz)	P.	around 664
B.	Maximum power used by circuit used (in kW)	Q.	around 2.3
C.	Half power frequency of source (in Hz)	R.	around 679
D.	Q-factor of circuit	S.	around 22

Choose the correct answer from options given below.

(a) A → P, B → Q, C → R, D → S
(b) A → Q, B → S, C → P, D → R
(c) A → S, B → R, C → Q, D → P
(d) A → R, B → P, C → S, D → Q

27. Amongst the following options, which combination is true in case of inelastic collision?

	Total energy	Kinetic energy	Momentum
(a)	not conserved	not conserved	conserved
(b)	conserved	conserved	not conserved
(c)	conserved	not conserved	conserved
(d)	conserved	conserved	conserved

28. An aluminium slab of thickness equals to the one-third distance between the plates of capacitor is inserted between the plates. The ratio of capacitances after and before the insertion of slab is

(a) 1 : 3 (b) 3 : 1
(c) 2 : 3 (d) 3 : 2

29. In a photoelectric experiment, a light of wavelength 4000 Å is used with metal cathode having work function 1.1 eV. If the wavelength of incident light is changed to 6200 Å, then change in the stopping potential is (Take, $hc = 12400$ eV-Å)

(a) 0.9 V (b) 1.1 V
(c) 2 V (d) 3.1 V

30. If dimensional formula of critical velocity v_c of a liquid flowing through a tube is expressed as $[\eta^\alpha \rho^\beta r^\gamma]$, where η, ρ, r are the coefficient of viscosity of liquid, density of liquid and radius of the tube respectively, then $\alpha + \beta + \gamma$ is

(a) 0 (b) 1
(c) − 1 (d) 2

31. A metal wire of mass density 5×10^{-4} kg/m is stretched by a tension force of 80 N is fixed at both ends. If it resonates at frequency 450 Hz and 500 Hz consecutively, then length of the wire is

(a) 2.5 m (b) 4 m (c) 4.6 m (d) 6 m

32. A charged shell has a potential of 5V at its centre. Radius of shell is 1 m. Potential at a point at a distance of 1 m from its surface is

(a) 2.5 V (b) 5 V (c) 7.5 V (d) 1.25 V

33. Three long straight wires parallel and equally spaced carrying equal amount of currents as shown in the figure. If net magnetic force experienced by wire A, B and C due to the other are F_A, F_B and F_C respectively, then

A B C

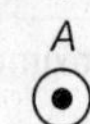 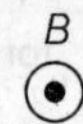 ⊗

(a) $F_A > F_B > F_C$ (b) $F_B > F_C > F_A$

(c) $F_C > F_A > F_B$ (d) $F_A = F_B = F_C$

34. Moment of inertia of a uniform quarter disc of mass M and radius R about an axis passing through its centre and perpendicular to plane is

(a) $\frac{MR^2}{2}$ (b) $\frac{MR^2}{4}$ (c) $\frac{MR^2}{8}$ (d) $\frac{MR^2}{16}$

35. A rigid rod of length 1m hinged from lower end and free to rotate in vertical plane about horizontal axis. It is released from rest from vertical position, then the velocity of free end when rod again becomes vertical is nearly

(a) 13.3 m/s (b) 7.7 m/s (c) 5.4 m/s (d) 3.8 m/s

Section II

36. An inductor coil stores 24 mJ of magnetic field energy and dissipates energy at the rate 160 W when a current of 4 A is passed through it. If inductor coil is connected across an ideal battery, then time constant of the circuit is

(a) 0.3 ms (b) 3.33×10^3 s

(c) 30 ms (d) 15 ms

37. An aeroplane is flying horizontally with constant speed u at height h from the surface of the earth. At some instant, a person is standing on ground just below it. At that instant, aeroplane drops a food packet which has to be catched by man. What should be the minimum acceleration, so that man just catches the food packet?

(a) $2u\sqrt{\frac{g}{h}}$ (b) $\frac{u}{2}\sqrt{\frac{g}{h}}$ (c) $u\sqrt{\frac{2g}{h}}$ (d) $u\sqrt{\frac{g}{2h}}$

38. An α-particle enters in a region of uniform magnetic field. If the velocity makes an angle 37° with the magnetic field and pitch of the helical path followed by α-particle is P, then radius of helix is

(a) $\frac{P}{\pi}$ (b) $\frac{3P}{8\pi}$ (c) $\frac{2P}{3\pi}$ (d) $\frac{3P}{4\pi}$

39. A rod of length l is placed along the Y-axis. Its lower end is at origin. If it is charged non-uniformly such that the linear charge density on rod varies as $\lambda = \lambda_0\left(\frac{y}{l}\right)$, where λ_0 is a positive constant, then total charge on the rod is

(a) $\frac{\lambda_0 l}{2}$ (b) $\lambda_0 l$

(c) $\lambda_0 l^2$ (d) $2\lambda_0 l$

40. For a long solenoid, if the product of total number of turns and cross-sectional area of solenoid is kept constant, then which of the following graph represent the variation of self-inductance L and volume V?

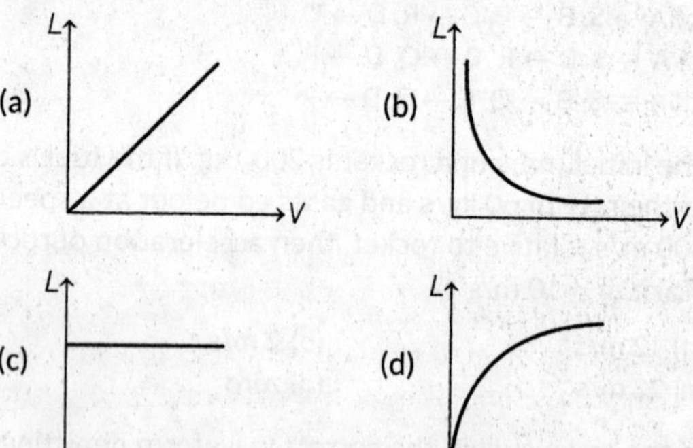

41. A disc of radius 50 cm is given a uniform angular acceleration for 20 s and then it runs at uniform angular speed for 2 min. It then slows down at a uniform rate for further 10 s. During the uniform angular speed, disc completes 1 revolution in every 10 s. The total angle rotated by disc is

(a) 2π rad

(b) 24π rad

(c) 27π rad

(d) None of the above

42. Statement I Binding energy of electron is mono-electronic species is equal to negative of potential energy in that orbit.

Statement II Binding energy of electron in ground state is equal to ionisation energy in same state.

In light of above statements choose the most appropriate answer from the options given below:

(a) Both Statement I and Statement II are incorrect.

(b) Statement I is correct and Statement II is incorrect.

(c) Statement I is incorrect and Statement II is correct.

(d) Both Statement I and Statement II are correct.

43. About 5% of power of a 100 W light bulb is converted to visible radiation. Average intensity of light at a distance of 1 m from the bulb is nearly

(a) 1 W/m^2

(b) 0.5 W/m^2

(c) 0.4 W/m^2

(d) 0.2 W/m^2

44. Two light waves having same wavelength of 550 nm are travelling through vacuum are in phase initially.

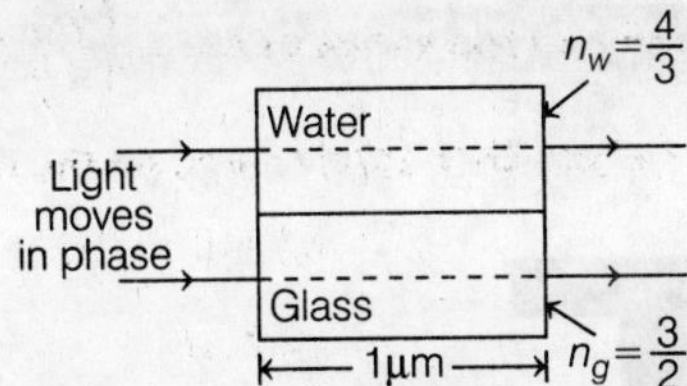

They pass through 1 μm blocks of water and glass, respectively as shown above. Phase difference between waves as they emerge out is

(a) 0.4 π rad
(b) 0.5 π rad
(c) 0.7 π rad
(d) 0.6 π rad

45. Minimum wavelength of X-rays produced by 30 kV electrons is around

(a) 0.002 nm (b) 0.001 nm
(c) 0.041 nm (d) 0.1 nm

46. A germanium crystal is doped with arsenic atoms and indium atoms simultaneously. Number of arsenic atoms used $= 5 \times 10^{22}$ per m^3 and number of indium atoms used $= 5 \times 10^{20}$ per m^3, then resulting crystal is a

(a) *p-n* junction
(b) *p*-type semiconductor
(c) *n*-type semiconductor
(d) Depends on number of germanium atoms in given sample.

47. A thin equiconvex lens of glass has radii of curvature of each surface 30 cm. The lens has different medium on its left and right side of refractive indices 1.2 and 1.6, respectively. If the refractive index of the glass is 1.5, then focal length of this lens for parallel beam incident from left is

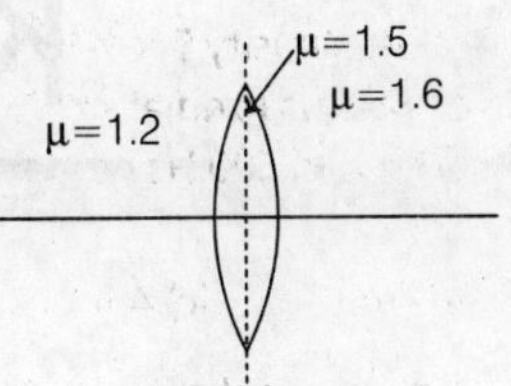

(a) 30 cm (b) 60 cm
(c) 120 cm (d) 240 cm

48. The de-Broglie wavelength of electron in second excited state of He^+ ion, when radius of final orbit of hydrogen atoms is 0.53 Å, is

(a) 3.328 Å (b) 9.98 Å
(c) 5 Å (d) 0.176 Å

49. While executing simple harmonic motion, at a certain instant of time the displacement, velocity and acceleration of a particle are y, α and β, respectively. Then according to dimensional formula analysis, which of the following expression for amplitude may be correct?

(a) $y\sqrt{\frac{\alpha^2 - \beta^2}{\beta}}$
(b) $\sqrt{\frac{y(\alpha^2 - \beta y)}{\beta}}$
(c) $\sqrt{\frac{\beta(\beta y - \alpha^2)}{y}}$
(d) $\frac{y}{\beta}\sqrt{\beta y - \alpha^2}$

50. In a certain thermodynamic process, pressure of a gas depends ($p = kV^3$) on its volume and work done by gas when its temperature changes from 100°C to 300°C will be

(a) 50 *nR* (b) 20 *nR*
(c) 100 *nR* (d) 10 *nR*

Answers

1. (d)	2. (c)	3. (c)	4. (d)	5. (d)	6. (b)	7. (d)	8. (a)	9. (a)	10. (a)
11. (c)	12. (b)	13. (d)	14. (c)	15. (c)	16. (d)	17. (c)	18. (d)	19. (a)	20. (c)
21. (d)	22. (b)	23. (d)	24. (d)	25. (d)	26. (a)	27. (c)	28. (d)	29. (b)	30. (c)
31. (b)	32. (a)	33. (b)	34. (a)	35. (b)	36. (a)	37. (c)	38. (b)	39. (a)	40. (b)
41. (c)	42. (c)	43. (c)	44. (d)	45. (c)	46. (c)	47. (d)	48. (c)	49. (b)	50. (a)

See detailed explanations on page no. 252

Knockout 04

NEET

PHYSICS

Instructions See Knockout 01

Section I

1. A uniform rod of mass 1.5 kg is hanged with one end attached to ceiling. The rod is 60 cm long and have 100 cm^2 area of cross-section.If the Young's modulus of the material of rod is $1.2 \times 10^{11} N/m^2$, then elongation of the rod due to its weight is

(a) $3.67 \times 10^{-9} m$ (b) $7.35 \times 10^{-11} m$
(c) $1.47 \times 10^{-10} m$ (d) $7.35 \times 10^{-9} m$

2. While measuring acceleration due to gravity by a simple pendulum, a student makes a positive error of 2% in the length of the pendulum and negative error of 1% in the value of time period. The percentage error in the measurement of g will be

(a) 0 (b) 4% (c) 3% (d) 1%

3. Two persons A and B perform same amount of work in moving a body through same distance d with application of forces acting at angles 45° and 60°, respectively with the direction of displacement. The ratio of force applied by person A to the force applied by person B is

(a) 1 : 1 (b) $1 : \sqrt{2}$ (c) $\sqrt{2} : 1$ (d) $\sqrt{3} : 2$

4. In a common emitter transistor amplifier $\beta = 60$, output resistance $R_{out} = 5 \text{ k}\Omega$ and input resistance R_{in} of transistor is 500 Ω. The voltage amplification of amplifier is

(a) 300 (b) 460 (c) 560 (d) 600

5. Assertion (A) Distance of earth and sun is 1 parsec.

Reason (R) Parsec is unit of distance.

In the light of the above statements, choose the most appropriate answer from the options given below:

(a) Both A and R are true but R is not the correct explanation of A.
(b) A is true but R is false.
(c) A is false but R is true.
(d) Both A and R are true and R is the correct explanation of A.

6. A carnot engine is working within – 5°C and 45°C temperature limit. If the engine produces output power 25 W, then at what rate heat is given to engine?

(a) 25.7 W (b) 159 W
(c) 198.75 W (d) 50 W

7. A bar magnet is oscillating in earth's magnetic field with a period T. What happens to its period of motion, if its mass is quadrupled?

(a) Motion remains simple harmonic with new period = $T/2$
(b) Motion remains simple harmonic with new period = $2T$
(c) Motion remains simple harmonic with new period = $4T$
(d) None of the above

8. The de-Broglie wavelength for a proton with a kinetic energy of 8 GeV is

(a) 3.205 Å (b) 6.41 Å
(c) 13.732 nm (d) 0.3205 fm

9. Statement I The resistance of p-n junction diode decreases when forward biased and increases when reverse biased.

Statement II In forward biased, the potential barrier is supported by the battery and in reverse biased, potential barrier is opposed by battery.

In light of above statements choose the most appropriate answer from the options given below:

(a) Both Statement I and Statement II are incorrect.
(b) Statement I is correct and Statement II is incorrect.
(c) Statement I is incorrect and Statement II is correct.
(d) Both Statement I and Statement II are correct.

10. The heat given to a body to raise its temperature is given by $Q = ms\,\Delta\theta$, where Q = heat given, m = mass of body, s = specific heat and $\Delta\theta$ = change in temperature. The dimensional formula of specific heat is

(a) $[M^1L^2T^{-2}K^{-1}]$ (b) $[M^0L^2T^{-2}K^0]$
(c) $[M^0L^1T^{-2}K^{-2}]$ (d) $[M^0L^2T^{-2}K^{-1}]$

11. Six identical charged particles are placed on the vertices of a regular hexagon of side 0.9 m. One of the charged particle is released from hexagon. When it reaches infinity, another particle adjacent to the first particle is released. If the difference of kinetic energies of both the particles at infinity is 90 mJ, then magnitude of the charge is

(a) 3 μC (b) 2 μC (c) 0.284 C (d) 0.1 C

12. The angle between two vectors **P** and **Q** is 60°. If $|\mathbf{P} + 2\mathbf{Q}| = |3\mathbf{P} - 2\mathbf{Q}|$ and $\frac{\mathbf{P}}{4}$ is a unit vector, then magnitude of **Q** is

(a) 2 (b) 4 (c) 8 (d) $2\sqrt{3}$

13. Select incorrect statement regarding the shape of the wavefront.

(a) Light diverging from a point source, have spherical wavefront.

(b) Light emerging out of a convex lens when a point source is placed at its focus, have plane wavefront.

(c) The portion of the wavefront of light from a distance star intercepted by earth, is plane.

(d) Light reflecting from a concave mirror when a plane wave is incident on the concave mirror, have plane wavefront.

14. A cubical block of density 400 kg / m^3 and weight 80 N is floating on liquid of density 1200 kg / m^3 as shown in the figure. If the container starts moving with an upward acceleration of 2 m/s^2, then buoyant force acting on the block is

[Take, acceleration due to gravity, $g = 10$ m/s^2)

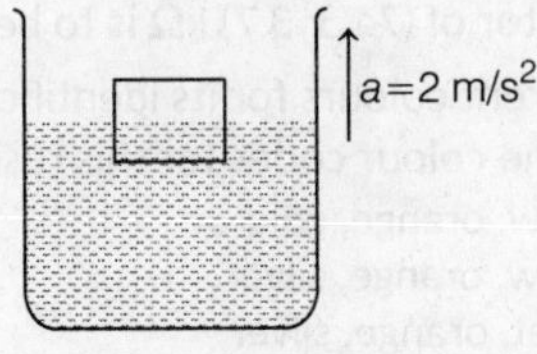

(a) 640 N (b) 64 N

(c) 80 N (d) 96 N

15. The straight wire *AB* carries a current *I*. The ends of the wire subtend angles θ_1 and θ_2 at the point *P* as shown in figure. The magnetic field at the point *P* is

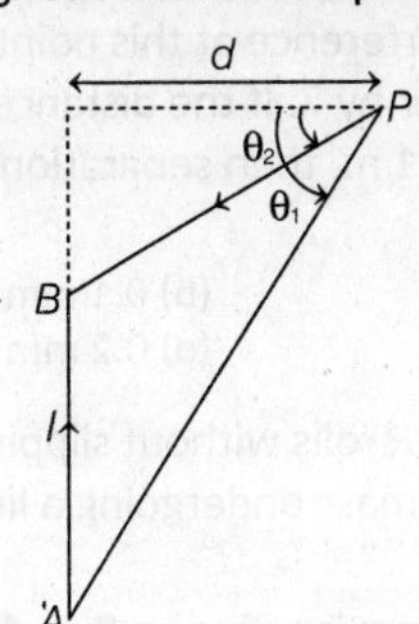

(a) $\frac{\mu_0 I}{4\pi d}(\sin\theta_1 - \sin\theta_2)$ (b) $\frac{\mu_0 I}{4\pi d}(\sin\theta_1 + \sin\theta_2)$

(c) $\frac{\mu_0 I}{4\pi d}(\cos\theta_1 - \cos\theta_2)$ (d) $\frac{\mu_0 I}{4\pi d}(\cos\theta_1 + \cos\theta_2)$

16. An object of mass *m* is kept at a point on the line joining the centres of two planets of masses M_1, M_2 and radii R_1, R_2, respectively. Centres of the planets are separated by a distance *r*. If the object is $\frac{r}{3}$ distance away from the centre of planet having mass M_1, then what minimum velocity should be given to the object, so that it can just overcome the gravitational force of mass of two planets?

(a) $\sqrt{\frac{3G}{r}(2M_1 + M_2)}$ (b) $\sqrt{\frac{3G}{2r}(2M_1 + M_2)}$

(c) $\sqrt{\frac{3G}{r}(M_1 + 2M_2)}$ (d) $\sqrt{\frac{3G}{r}(M_1 + M_2)}$

17. A mass of 50 kg is placed at the centre of uniform spherical shell of mass 100 kg and radius 50 m. The gravitational potential at a point 25 m from the centre will be

(a) 4G J/kg (b) –4G J/kg (c) 3G J/kg (d) –5G J/kg

18. A particle is moving along the curved path with acceleration $-5\hat{j}$ m/s^2. At an instant, its velocity is $(8\hat{i} - 6\hat{j})$ m/s^2. The tangential acceleration vector at this instant is given by

(a) $(24\hat{i} - 18\hat{j})$ m/s^2 (b) $(26\hat{i} + 18\hat{j})$ m/s^2

(c) $(-24\hat{i} + 18\hat{j})$ m/s^2 (d) $(-26\hat{i} - 18\hat{j})$ m/s^2

19. A series *R-L-C* circuit is subjected to a AC of voltage 220 V and 50 Hz frequency. The circuit contains a resistor $R = 10\ \text{k}\Omega$, an inductor of inductance 2.5 H and an unknown capacitor. What value of capacitance should be taken, so that power consumption in circuit can be maximum?

(a) 4 μF (b) 40 μF (c) 25 μF (d) 400 μF

20. Match the following Column I and Column II.

	Column I (Physical system)		Column II (Types of equilibrium)
A.	*m*	P.	In stable equilibrium
B.	*l*, *l* — Uniform *L*-shaped rod	Q.	In unstable equilibrium
C.	*M*, μ=0.75, 37°	R.	In neutral equilibrium
D.	*m*	S.	Not in equilibrium

Choose correct answer from options given below :
(a) A → R, B → P, C → S, D → Q
(b) A → P, B → S, C → R, D → Q
(c) A → Q, B → P, C → R, D → S
(d) A → P, B → Q, C → R, D → S

21. A 5.80 μF parallel plate air capacitor has a plate separation of 5 mm and is charged to a potential difference of 400 V. The energy density in the region between the plates is
(a) 2.83×10^{-2} J/m^3
(b) 2.83 J/m^3
(c) 2.83×10^{-4} J/m^3
(d) 2.83×10^{6} J/m^3

22. There are two identical containers A and B. Container A contains 5 moles of H_2 and B contains 10 moles of O_2 at same temperature.
Now match Column I and Column II assuming real gas behaviour.

	Column I		Column II
A.	Container A	P.	Pressure is more
B.	Container B	Q.	rms speed is more
C.	More number of moles	R.	Average thermal energies are same
D.	Smaller molecular mass	S.	Internal energy is more

Choose the correct answer from options given below.
(a) A → P, B → Q, C → R, D → S
(b) A → P, B → R, C → Q, D → S
(c) A → P, B → S, C → R, D → Q
(d) A → Q, B → P, C → S, D → Q

23. In photoelectric experiment, a light of wavelength 4800 nm is incident on a metal surface of work function 1.67 eV, then photoelectrons are emitted. A fastest photoelectron combines with an excited He^{+2} ion in its third excited state to form He^{+} ion. What is energy of photon emitted by de-excitation of He^{+} ion?
(a) 4.5 eV (b) 4.3 eV (c) 6.9 eV (d) 0.9 eV

24. **Assertion (A)** In an uniform electric field, a free dipole cannot have zero potential energy.
Reason (R) A free dipole can take position of stable or unstable equilibrium in an uniform eletric field.
In the light of the above statements, choose the most appropriate answer from the options given below:
(a) Both A and R are true but R is not the correct explanation of A.
(b) A is true but R is false.
(c) A is false but R is true.
(d) Both A and R are true and R is the correct explanation of A.

25. If the intensity of laser beam is 2×10^7 W/cm^2, then amplitude of magnetic field in the beam is
(a) 41 mT (b) 29 mT (c) 501 T (d) 708 T

26. The displacement time equations of two particles A and B executing SHM are given as
$$x_A = 4\sin\left(\omega t + \frac{\pi}{4}\right) + 3\cos\left(\omega t - \frac{\pi}{4}\right)\text{ m}$$
$$x_B = 5\sqrt{2}(\sin 2\pi t + \cos 2\pi t)\text{ m}$$
The ratio of amplitudes of particles A and B is
(a) 1 (b) $\frac{1}{2}$ (c) $\frac{1}{\sqrt{3}}$ (d) $\frac{7}{10}$

27. The device Klystron is used for generation of
(a) X-rays (b) cathode rays
(c) microwaves (d) radiowaves

28. Which of the following component(s), thermistor can have?
(a) A low resistance at high temperature
(b) A high resistance at high temperature
(c) Zero resistance at 0°C
(d) Either (a) or (b)

29. The output of an AC generator is given by $e = e_0 \sin\left(\omega t - \frac{\pi}{4}\right)$ and current is given by $i = i_0 \sin\left(\omega t - \frac{3\pi}{4}\right)$. The circuit contains a single element other than the generator. It is
(a) capacitor (b) resistor
(c) inductor (d) Need more information

30. A carbon resistor of (74 ± 3.7) kΩ is to be marked with bands of different colours for its identification. The sequence of the colour codes for this resistor will be
(a) violet, yellow, orange, gold
(b) violet, yellow, orange, silver
(c) yellow, violet, orange, silver
(d) green, orange, violet, gold

31. A parallel beam of light of all wavelengths greater than 3000 Å falls on a double slit in a YDSE. It was found that wavelengths 3600 Å and 6000 Å are absent at a distance of 31.5 mm from the position of the central maximum and orders of the interference at this point for the two wavelengths differ by 7. If the distance between the slits and the screen is 1 m, then separation between the two slits is
(a) 0.08 mm (b) 0.1 mm
(c) 0.13 mm (d) 0.2 mm

32. A wheel of radius R rolls without slipping on a flat surface, with its centre of mass undergoing a linear deceleration α. Then,
(a) a non-zero torque is acting on the wheel about its CM
(b) the net torque acting on the wheel may be zero or non-zero
(c) the net torque acting on the wheel is zero
(d) the net torque acting on the wheel cannot be calculated as the data is insufficient.

33. Consider arrangement given below

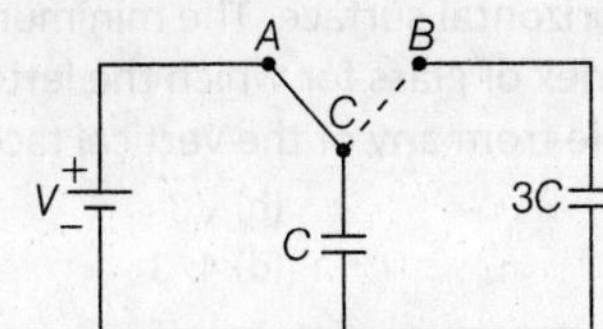

When C and A are in contact, charge on capacitor of capacity C is q. Energy dissipated when C is connected to B will be

(a) $\frac{3}{4}\frac{q^2}{C}$ (b) $\frac{5}{8}\frac{q^2}{C}$

(c) $\frac{1}{8}\frac{q^2}{C}$ (d) $\frac{3}{8}\frac{q^2}{C}$

34. In a helium ion, if potential energy of electron in ground state is assumed to be zero, then its energy in first excited state is equal to

(a) 13.6 eV (b) 27.2 eV

(c) 54.4 eV (d) 95.2 eV

35. Magnetic field in a region is changing at a constant rate. As a result, an induced electric field appears in the region which give rise to an emf. Induced electric field lines are

(a) open curves

(b) closed loops

(c) can be open or closed depending on magnetic field

(d) no field lines are produced

Section II

36. A radioactive nucleus A decays first into B and then into C.

$$A \longrightarrow B \longrightarrow C$$

The half-life for the first process is 30 s and that for the second is 60 s. The effective mean life of the nucleus is

(a) 20 s

(b) 28.9 s

(c) 45 s

(d) 64.9 s

37. In context of diamagnetic material, the correct graphs for intensity of magnetisation *versus* magnetic field strength and susceptibility *versus* temperature are

(i) 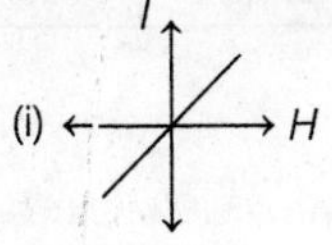

(ii) 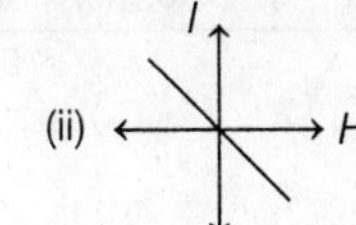

(iii) 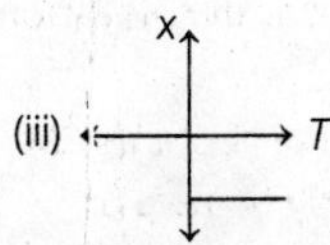

(iv) 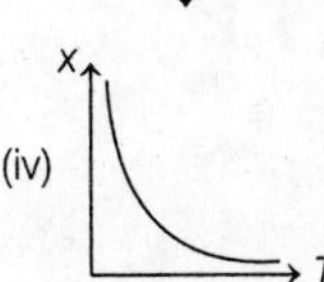

(a) (i) and (iii) (b) (ii) and (iv)

(c) (i) and (iv) (d) (ii) and (iii)

38. Two concentric spherical shells (radii r and R) are given a total charge Q, such that their surface charge densities are equal.

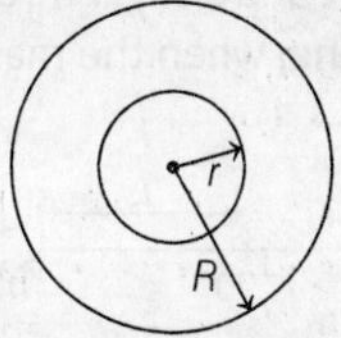

Electrical potential at centre of arrangement of shells will be $\left(K = \frac{1}{4\pi\varepsilon_0}\right)$

(a) $K \cdot \frac{R+r}{2(R^2+r^2)} \cdot Q$ (b) $K \cdot \frac{2R+r}{(R^2+r^2)} \cdot Q$

(c) $K \cdot \frac{(R+2r)}{2(R^2+r^2)} \cdot Q$ (d) $K \cdot \frac{R+r}{R^2+r^2} \cdot Q$

39. An unknown resistance R is connected to left gap of a meter bridge and another unknown resistance S is connected to right gap, such that the balance point from left end is at 30 cm. If now a resistance of 2 Ω is connected in parallel with S, the null point occurs at 40 cm. The value of S is

(a) 1.1 Ω (b) 2 Ω

(c) 3.2 Ω (d) 4 Ω

40. An electric bulb is rated at 220 V and 100 W. Power consumed by bulb when operated at 110 W will be

(a) 50 W (b) 75 W

(c) 100 W (d) 25 W

41. A series R-L-C circuit has $L = 12$ mH, $C = 1.6\,\mu$F and $R = 1.5\,\Omega$. At what time, amplitude of charge oscillations is 50% of its initial value?

(a) 50 ms (b) 25 ms

(c) 11 ms (d) 5 ms

42. A particle is projected with initial speed of 30 m/s making an angle 60° with horizontal. The velocity of particle when its velocity makes angle of 30° with horizontal, is

(a) 10 m/s (b) $10\sqrt{2}$ m/s

(c) $10\sqrt{3}$ m/s (d) 20 m/s

43. A particle starts moving in a circular path of radius R with an initial angular velocity ω_0 rad/s and angular retardation α rad/s^2. The acceleration of the particle will be directed along its velocity after time

(a) $\frac{\omega_0}{\alpha}$ (b) $\frac{2\omega_0}{\alpha}$

(c) $\frac{\omega_0}{2\alpha}$ (d) Not possible

44. Which of the following transitions of He^+ ion will give rise to spectral line which has same wavelength as the spectral line in hydrogen atom?

(a) $n = 4$ to $n = 2$ (b) $n = 6$ to $n = 5$

(c) $n = 6$ to $n = 3$ (d) None of these

45. A mass m is attached to a string of length L which makes $90°$ angle with the vertical as shown in figure. The mass is released from rest and swings through a circular arc. The tension in the string, when the mass reaches the bottom of the arc is

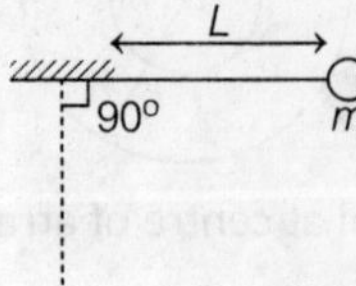

(a) zero (b) mg
(c) $2mg$ (d) $3mg$

46. A 0.124 m long pencil is oriented perpendicular to the principal axis of a concave spherical mirror that has a radius of curvature of 0.3 m. If the pencil is 0.018 m from the mirror, then height of image is
(a) 2.13 cm (b) 16.5 cm
(c) 9.3 cm (d) 1.6 cm

47. Inside a solenoid of radius 0.5 m, magnetic field is changing at a rate of 50×10^{-6} T/s. Acceleration of an electron placed at a distance of 0.3 m from axis of solenoid will be
(a) 1.3×10^{6} ms^{-2}
(b) 2.6×10^{6} m/s^{2}
(c) 1.3×10^{9} ms^{-2}
(d) 2.6×10^{9} m/s^{2}

48. A particle is executing SHM on a straight line starting from its mean position. It passes through the mean position at successive intervals 1.5 s and 3 s with a speed of 1.57 m/s. The amplitude of the motion is
(a) 0.5 m (b) 0.75 m
(c) 1 m (d) 1.5 m

49. A rectangular block of glass is placed on a printed page lying on a horizontal surface. The minimum value of the refractive index of glass for which the letters on the page are not visible from any of the vertical faces of the block is
(a) 2 (b) $\sqrt{3}$
(c) $\sqrt{2}$ (d) 4/3

50. Given diagram shows a p-n junction immediately after formation of the junction.

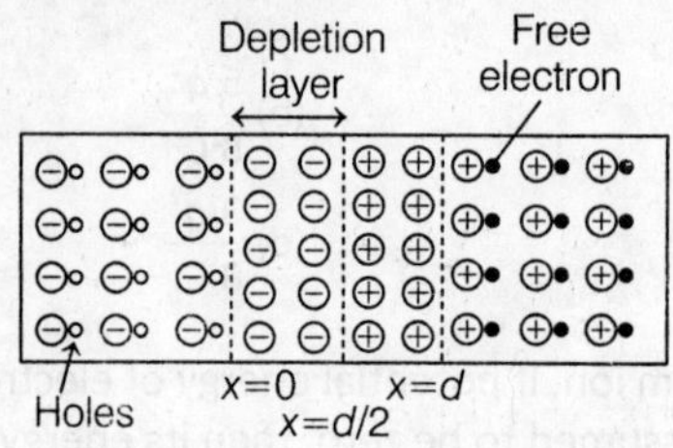

If a graph between charge density and distance from $x = 0$ to $x = d$ is plotted, then it is best represented as

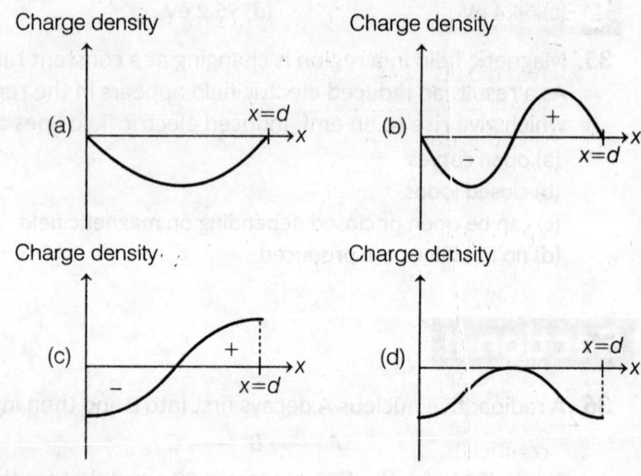

Answers

1. (a)	2. (b)	3. (b)	4. (d)	5. (c)	6. (b)	7. (b)	8. (d)	9. (b)	10. (d)
11. (a)	12. (c)	13. (d)	14. (d)	15. (a)	16. (a)	17. (b)	18. (a)	19. (a)	20. (b)
21. (c)	22. (d)	23. (b)	24. (d)	25. (b)	26. (d)	27. (c)	28. (d)	29. (c)	30. (a)
31. (d)	32. (a)	33. (d)	34. (d)	35. (a)	36. (b)	37. (d)	38. (d)	39. (a)	40. (d)
41. (c)	42. (c)	43. (a)	44. (a)	45. (d)	46. (b)	47. (a)	48. (b)	49. (c)	50. (b)

See detailed explanations on page no. 258

Knockout 05

NEET

PHYSICS

Instructions See Knockout 01

Section I

1. Two diodes of silicon and germanium are connected in series as shown below. The current flowing through the circuit will be around

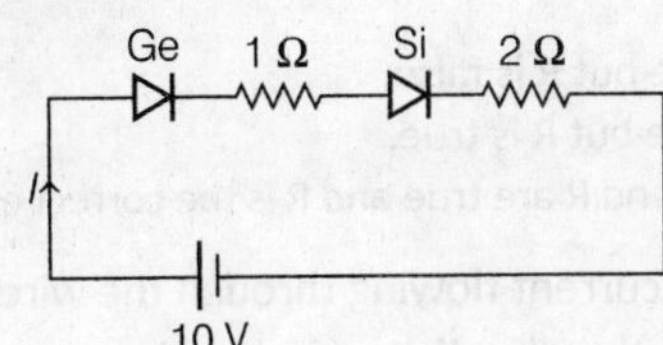

(a) 0 (b) 3 A (c) 4 A (d) 3.5 A

2. A car turns on a banked road of radius 300 m. If the coefficient of friction between the tyres and the road is 0.3, then maximum speed of the car on the turn is [Take, $g = 10 \text{ m/s}^2$]

(a) 10 m/s (b) 30 m/s
(c) 40 m/s (d) 50 m/s

3. A thin convex lens of glass $\left(n_g = \frac{3}{2}\right)$ has power of 2 D.

When immersed in two different liquids of refractive indices $n_1 = \frac{4}{3}$ and $n_2 = \frac{5}{3}$, its power is P_1 and P_2. Then, $P_1 - P_2$ (in D) will be

(a) $\frac{9}{10}$ (b) $\frac{1}{10}$
(c) $\frac{5}{3}$ (d) $\frac{7}{4}$

4. Side of a cube measured using a vernier calliper is, $L = (30.0 \pm 0.1)$ mm. Percentage uncertainty in volume is about

(a) 0.1% (b) 0.3%
(c) 1% (d) 3%

5. If the number of turns of a current carrying solenoid is decreased to half of its previous value, then its self-inductance is

(a) increased to double
(b) decreased to one-fourth
(c) increased to four times
(d) decreased to half

6. A system consisting of two masses connected by a massless rod lies along the X-axis. A 0.4 kg mass is at a distance $x = 2$ m while a 0.6 kg mass is at a distance $x = 7$ m. The x-coordinate of the centre of mass is

(a) 5 m (b) 3.5 m
(c) 4.5 m (d) 4 m

7. In the following circuit diagram, potential difference across 4 μF capacitor is

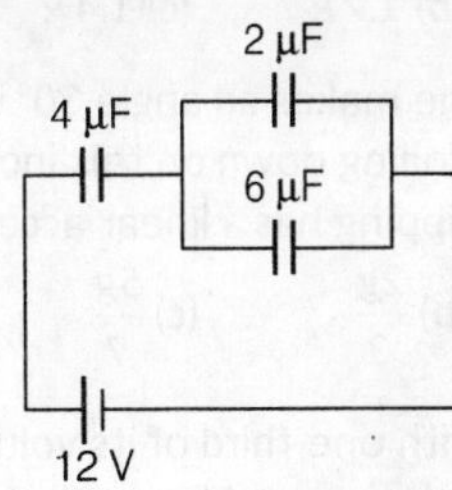

(a) 19 V (b) 14 V
(c) 16 V (d) 8 V

8. A particle is moving in XOY-plane with velocity, $\mathbf{v} = k(y\hat{\mathbf{i}} + x\hat{\mathbf{j}})$, where k is a constant.

Equation of trajectory of particle will be

(a) $x^2 + y^2 =$ constant
(b) $xy =$ constant
(c) $\frac{x^2}{y^2} =$ constant
(d) $x^2 - y^2 =$ constant

9. **Statement I** When lengths of 123 cm and 5.35 cm are added, reported length (sum) is found to be 128 cm instead of 128.35 cm.

Statement II If length of a room is 13.8 m and width is 9m then recorded area of room is 100 m^2

In light of above statements, choose the most appropriate answer from the options given below:

(a) Both Statement I and Statement II are incorrect.
(b) Statement I is correct and Statement II is incorrect.
(c) Statement I is incorrect and Statement II is correct.
(d) Both Statement I and Statement II are correct.

10. A spring is vibrating with frequency n under some mass. It is cut into two equal parts and same mass is suspended from one part, then the new frequency of vibration is

(a) n (b) $\frac{n}{\sqrt{2}}$ (c) $\frac{n}{2}$ (d) $n\sqrt{2}$

11. A planet goes around sun in an elliptical orbit, if it has

I. a constant velocity of revolution
II. least velocity when it is nearest to sun
III. to follow a trajectory that its areal velocity remains constant with time
IV. a variable orbital angular momentum

Correct statement(s) is/are

(a) Only III (b) I and IV (c) II and III (d) Only IV

12. A light wave is incident normally over single slit of width 3 μm. The angular position of third dark fringe from the central maxima is 30°, then the wavelength of light is

(a) 4000 Å (b) 4500 Å (c) 5000 Å (d) 6000 Å

13. Two moles of oxygen is mixed with eight mole of helium. The effective specific heat of the mixture at constant volume will be

(a) 2.5 R (b) 1.7 R (c) 1.4 R (d) 1.8 R

14. An inclined plane makes an angle 30° with the horizontal. A solid sphere rolling down on this inclined plane from rest, without slipping has a linear acceleration equal to

(a) $\frac{g}{3}$ (b) $\frac{2g}{3}$ (c) $\frac{5g}{7}$ (d) $\frac{5g}{14}$

15. A body floats with one-third of its volume outside water and 3/4 of its volume outside another liquid. The density of liquid is

(a) $\frac{9}{4}$ g/cc (b) $\frac{4}{9}$ g/cc (c) $\frac{8}{3}$ g/cc (d) $\frac{3}{8}$ g/cc

16. The ratio of product of velocity and time period of electron orbiting in second and third stable orbits is

(a) $\frac{16}{81}$ (b) $\frac{2}{3}$ (c) $\frac{8}{27}$ (d) $\frac{4}{9}$

17. Electric field in a region is $\mathbf{E} = (20x + 10)\,\hat{\mathbf{i}}$ N/C, where x is in metres. Find potential difference $[V_1(x=1) - V_2(x=-5)]$.

(a) −48 V (b) −520 V
(c) 180 V (d) 320 V

18. The moment of a force, $F = 4\hat{i} + 5\hat{j} - 6\hat{k}$ acting at (2, 0, − 3) about the point (2, − 2, − 2) is given by

(a) $-4\hat{i} - \hat{j} - 8\hat{k}$ (b) $-7\hat{i} - 4\hat{j} - 8\hat{k}$
(c) $-7\hat{i} - 8\hat{j} - 4\hat{k}$ (d) $-8\hat{i} - 4\hat{j} - 7\hat{k}$

19. In forward biasing of a p-n junction,

(a) electrons move from lower to higher energy level
(b) electrons move from higher to lower energy level
(c) holes in valence band move from higher energy level to lower energy level
(d) None of the above

20. A rectangular film of liquid is extended from (4 cm × 2 cm) to (5 cm × 4 cm). If the work done is 6×10^{-4} J, then the value of the surface tension of the liquid is

(a) 0.25 N/m (b) 0.50 N/m
(c) 0.75 N/m (d) 1.25 N/m

21. **Assertion** In photon-electron collision, the total energy and momentum remains conserved.

Reason Photon-electron collision is an inelastic collision.

In the light of the above statements, choose the most appropriate answer from the options given below:

(a) Both A and R are true but R is not the correct explanation of A.
(b) A is true but R is false.
(c) A is false but R is true.
(d) Both A and R are true and R is the correct explanation of A.

22. When the current flowing through the wire PQ is increasing, the direction of induced current in the closed loop X will be

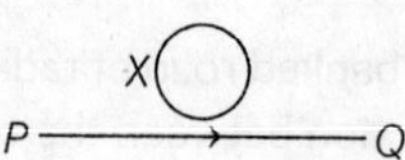

(a) clockwise (b) anti-clockwise
(c) zero (d) None of these

23. A conducting wire is stretched by applying a deforming force, so that its diameter decreases to 40% of original value. The percentage change in its resistance will be

(a) 0.9% (b) 0.12%
(c) 1.6% (d) 0.5%

24. In Young's double slit experiment, if the distance between the slits and screen is increased to double and distance between the slits is decreased to half, then fringe width is

(a) increased to four times (b) decreased to one-third
(c) decreased to half (d) decreased to one-fourth

25. At a place in magnetic meridian, the angle of dip is found to be 45°. So, the horizontal component of earth's magnetic field

(a) is equal to vertical component of earth's magnetic field
(b) is greater than the vertical component of earth's magnetic field
(c) is less than the vertical component of earth's magnetic field
(d) None of the above

26. A train is approaching the platform with a speed of 4 m/s. Another train is leaving the platform with the same speed. The velocity of sound is 320 m/s. If both the trains sound their whistles at frequency 280 Hz, the number of beats heard per second will be

(a) 5 (b) 6 (c) 7 (d) 8

27. A particle moves in XOY-plane, its position, velocity and acceleration are $\mathbf{r} = x\hat{\mathbf{i}} + y\hat{\mathbf{j}}$, $\mathbf{v} = v_x\hat{\mathbf{i}} + v_y\hat{\mathbf{j}}$ and $\mathbf{a} = a_x\hat{\mathbf{i}} + a_y\hat{\mathbf{j}}$, respectively.

If particle is slowing down, then choose the correct option.

(a) $xv_x + yv_y < 0$ (b) $xv_x + yv_y > 0$
(c) $a_xv_x + a_yv_y < 0$ (d) $a_xv_x + a_yv_y > 0$

28. A thin glass prism placed in air produces deviation of 10° in a light ray. If the prism is immersed in water of refractive index $\frac{4}{3}$, then what will be the deviation produced by it?

(Take, ${}_a\mu_g = 1.5$)

(a) 1.5° (b) 4.5° (c) 7.5° (d) 2.5°

29.

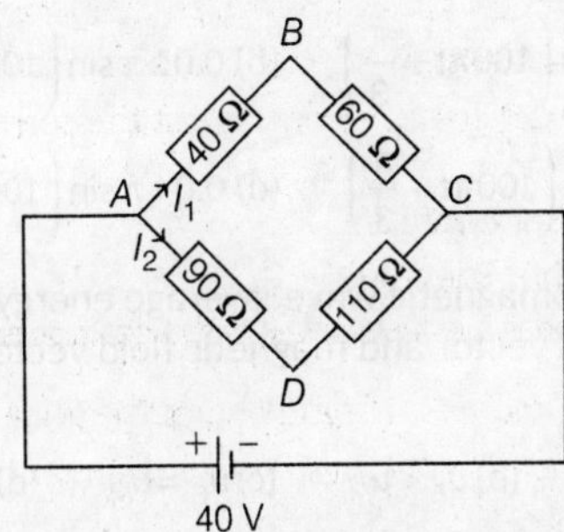

In above circuit, potential drop $V_B - V_D$ (in V) is

(a) 0 (b) 2 (c) 3 (d) 4

30. A constant magnetic field of 1 T exists in region

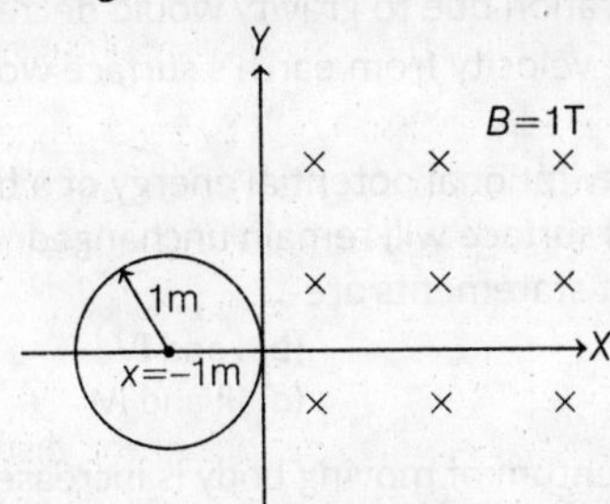

At $t = 0$, centre of a conducting ring of radius 1 m is at $x = -1$ m and ring is moving with a constant velocity of $v = 1\hat{\mathbf{i}}$ m/s. Value of induced emf in ring at $t = 1$ s will be

(a) 1 V (b) 1.5 V
(c) 2 V (d) 0

31. A current flowing through a conductor at any instant t is given as, $i = (2t + 1)$ A. The amount of charge flowing through the cross-section of wire in time interval, $t = 0$ s to $t = 4$ s is

(a) 10 C (b) 15 C (c) 20 C (d) 25 C

32. A proton and an α-particle, both are accelerated from rest with same energy. The ratio of de-Broglie wavelength of α-particle to that of proton is

(a) 1 : 4 (b) 4 : 1 (c) 1 : 2 (d) 2 : 1

33. An ideal refrigerator has a freezer at a temperature of −13°C. The coefficient of performance of the engine is 5. The temperature of the air (to which heat is rejected) will be

(a) 312 K (b) 325 K (c) 225 K (d) 286 K

34. In given circuit,

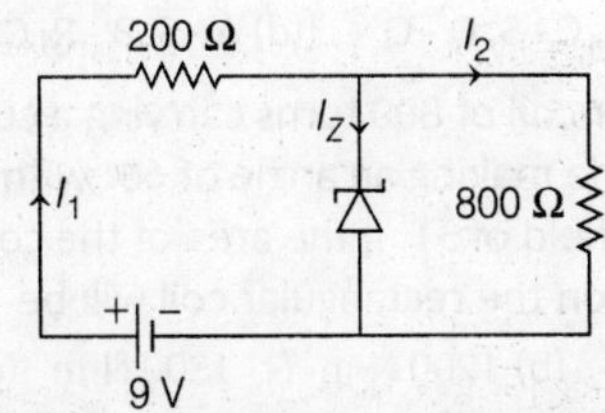

Reverse breakdown voltage of Zener diode is 5.6 V. Current through diode will be

(a) 0 (b) 10 mA (c) 17 mA (d) 7 mA

35. If area (A), time (T) and momentum (p) are taken to be fundamental quantities, then energy has the dimensional formula

(a) $[A^{1/2}T^{-1}p^{1}]$ (b) $[A^{-1/2}Tp^{-2}]$
(c) $[A^{1/2}T^{1}p^{-1}]$ (d) $[A^{-1/2}T^{-1/2}p^{1/2}]$

Section II

36. A battery of emf E is connected across a conductor AB of variable cross-section (as shown).

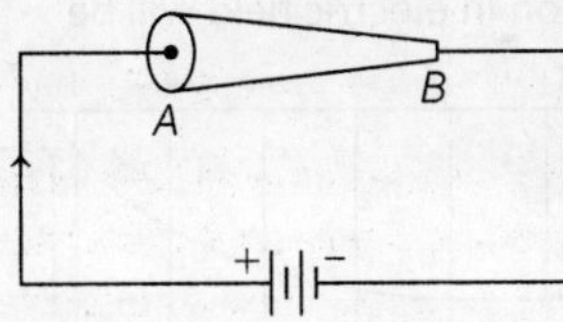

As, we move from A to B

(a) drift velocity increases (b) current increases
(c) electric field decreases (d) electric potential increases

37. A wire of resistance R is bend to form a square $ABCD$. Effective resistance between points E and C (E is mid-point of CD) is

(a) $\frac{7}{64}R$ (b) $\frac{3}{4}R$ (c) R (d) $\frac{1}{16}R$

38. Radioactive material A has decay constant 8λ and material B has decay constant λ. Initially, they have same number of nuclei. After what time, the ratio of number of nuclei of material A to that of B will be $\frac{1}{e}$?

(a) $\frac{1}{\lambda}$ (b) $\frac{1}{7\lambda}$ (c) $\frac{1}{8\lambda}$ (d) $\frac{1}{9\lambda}$

39. Match the following Column I with Column II and choose the correct answer from options given below.

	Column I		Column II
A.	$_8O^{16}$ and $_8O^{15}$	P.	Isobars
B.	$_6C^{14}$ and $_7N^{14}$	Q.	Isomers
C.	$_7N^{14}$ and $_8O^{15}$	R.	Isotopes
D.	A nucleus in its ground state and the identical nucleus in metastable excited state	S.	Isotones

(a) A - R, B - P, C - S, D - Q (b) A - R, B - S, C - P, D - Q
(c) A - P, B - R, C - S, D - Q (d) A - S, B - R, C - S, D - P

40. A rectangular coil of 800 turns carrying a current of 10 A when its plane making an angle of 60° with the direction of magnetic field of 5T. If the area of the coil is 800 cm^2, then torque on the rectangular coil will be

(a) 1600 N-m (b) 1200 N-m (c) 1300 N-m (d) 1400 N-m

41. In Column I, some famous numbers associated with electromagnetic radiations are given and in Column II, names of part of spectrum to which they belong. Match entries of Column I and Column II correctly and choose the correct answer from options given below.

	Column I		Column II
A.	21 cm	P.	X-rays
B.	1057 Hz	Q.	Microwaves
C.	2.7 λ	R.	Short-waves
D.	14.4 eV	S.	Radio waves

(a) A - P, B - Q, C - R, D - S (b) A - Q, B - R, C - P, D - S
(c) A - S, B - R, C - Q, D - P (d) A - S, B - P, C - R, D - Q

42. An electron enters into an electric field E as shown below. Path of electron in electric field will be

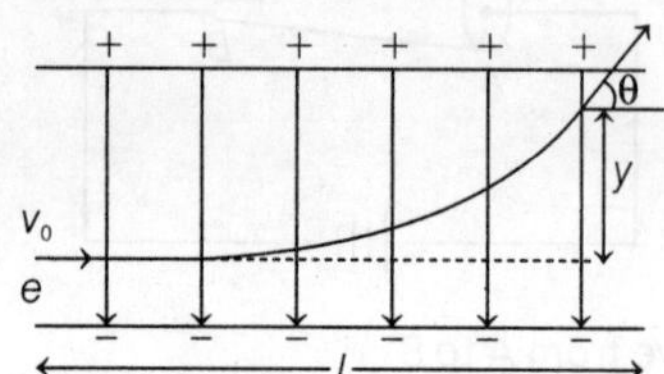

(a) elliptical (b) parabolic (c) circular (d) None of these

43. Certain quantity of water cools from 70°C to 60°C in the first 5 min and to 54°C in the next 5 min. The temperature of the surrounding is

(a) 45°C (b) 39°C (c) 56°C (d) 52°C

44. A stone is thrown up vertically upward with velocity u_0. It reaches a maximum height upto h. If one wishes to triple the maximum height, then the ball should be thrown with velocity

(a) $\sqrt{2}u_0$ (b) $\sqrt{3}u_0$ (c) $\sqrt{\frac{2}{3}}u_0$ (d) $\frac{\sqrt{3}}{2}u_0$

45. A current carrying wire of length l is bent first in the shape of square and then in the shape of circle, then the ratio of their magnetic moment is

(a) $\pi:2$ (b) $\pi:1$ (c) $\pi:3$ (d) $\pi:4$

46. Eight small liquid drops of potential 16 V each are combined to form a single large drop. The potential of large drop is

(a) 32 V (b) 16 V (c) 48 V (d) 64 V

47. When an alternating voltage source $V = 100\sin\left(100\pi t + \frac{\pi}{6}\right)$ is applied to a pure capacitor of 1 μF, then the instantaneous value of current through capacitor is

(a) $0.01\,\pi\sin\left(100\pi t + \frac{\pi}{3}\right)$ (b) $0.01\,\pi\sin\left(100\pi t + \frac{\pi}{6}\right)$

(c) $0.04\,\pi\sin\left(100\pi t + \frac{\pi}{3}\right)$ (d) $0.04\,\pi\sin\left(100\pi t + \frac{\pi}{6}\right)$

48. In an electromagnetic wave, average energy density of electric field vector and magnetic field vector are u_E and u_M, then

(a) $u_E > u_M$ (b) $u_E < u_M$ (c) $u_E = u_M$ (d) $u_E = \frac{1}{u_M}$

49. If both the mass and radius of earth decrease by 1%, then the value of

I. acceleration due to gravity would increase by 1%
II. acceleration due to gravity would decrease by 1%
III. escape velocity from earth's surface would decrease by 1%
IV. the gravitational potential energy of a body on earth's surface will remain unchanged

Correct statements are

(a) I and III (b) I and IV
(c) II and IV (d) III and IV

50. If the momentum of moving body is increased to 100%, then percentage increase in its kinetic energy is

(a) 50% (b) 100% (c) 200% (d) 300%

Answers

1. (b)	2. (b)	3. (a)	4. (c)	5. (b)	6. (a)	7. (d)	8. (d)	9. (d)	10. (d)
11. (a)	12. (c)	13. (b)	14. (d)	15. (c)	16. (d)	17. (c)	18. (b)	19. (b)	20. (a)
21. (b)	22. (a)	23. (c)	24. (a)	25. (a)	26. (c)	27. (c)	28. (d)	29. (b)	30. (c)
31. (c)	32. (c)	33. (a)	34. (b)	35. (a)	36. (a)	37. (a)	38. (b)	39. (a)	40. (a)
41. (c)	42. (b)	43. (a)	44. (b)	45. (d)	46. (d)	47. (a)	48. (c)	49. (b)	50. (d)

See detailed explanations on page no. 263

Knockout 06

NEET

PHYSICS

Instructions See Knockout 01

Section I

1. Young's double slit experiment is performed in a medium of refractive index of 1.33. The maximum intensity is I_0. The intensity at a point on the screen, where path difference between the light coming out from slits is $\frac{\lambda}{4}$, is

(a) 0 (b) $\frac{I_0}{2}$ (c) $\frac{3I_0}{8}$ (d) $\frac{2I_0}{3}$

2. Match Column I (lengths given) with Column II (their values).

	Column I		Column II
A.	1 fermi	P.	1.5×10^{11} m
B.	1 astronomical unit	Q.	10^{-15} m
C.	1 light year	R.	9.46×10^{15} m
D.	1 persec	S.	3.08×10^{16} m

Choose the correct answer from the options given below:

(a) $A \to Q, B \to P, C \to R, D \to S$

(b) $A \to R, B \to S, C \to Q, D \to P$

(c) $A \to P, B \to Q, C \to S, D \to R$

(d) $A \to S, B \to R, C \to P, D \to Q$

3. If a equiconvex lens is made of number of layers of different refractive index for a given wavelength as shown in the figure, then number of images formed for an object kept in front is

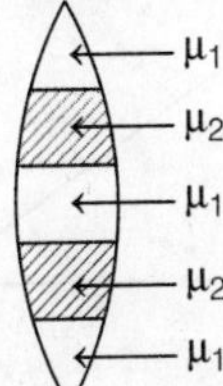

(a) only 1 (b) 2 (c) 2.5 (d) 5

4. A student records the mass of an object five times. The readings are 2.46 kg, 2.47 kg, 2.42 kg, 2.41 kg and 2.44 kg. The mean mass with error is

(a) 2.44 ± 0.01 kg

(b) 2.44 ± 0.02 kg

(c) 2.44 ± 0.03 kg

(d) 2.44 ± 0.04 kg

5. A ball is thrown vertically upwards with a velocity u from the balloon descending with velocity v (constant). The ball will pass by the balloon after time

(a) $\frac{|u-v|}{2g}$

(b) $\frac{u+v}{2g}$

(c) $\frac{2|u-v|}{g}$

(d) $\frac{2(u+v)}{g}$

6. A helium balloon rises in air. Its speed increases as it gains height. Now, choose the correct statement.

(a) Potential energy of air is converted into potential energy of balloon.

(b) Potential energy of air is converted into kinetic energy of balloon.

(c) Potential energy of air is converted into potential and kinetic energy of balloon.

(d) Potential energy of air remains constant.

7. Choose the correct statement from the following options.

(a) Photoelectric effect experiment proves the particle nature of light.

(b) Davisson and Germer experiment demonstrates the particle nature of electrons.

(c) X-rays can be deflected by electric or magnetic fields.

(d) Cathode rays are a part of electromagnetic waves.

8. The output of the given arrangement of logic gates for $A = 0, B = 1$ and $A = 1, B = 1$ will be

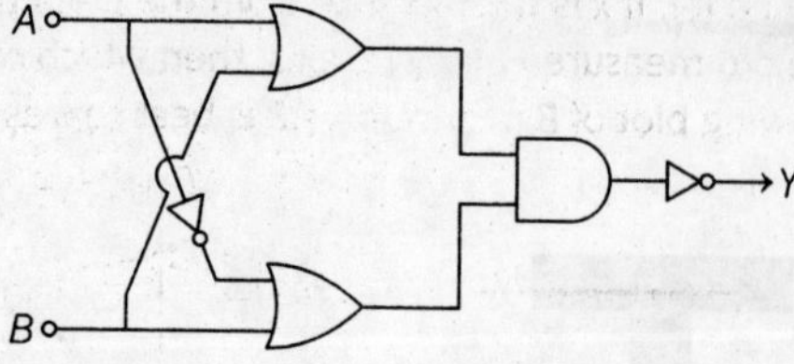

(a) (0, 0) (b) (0, 1)
(c) (1,1) (d) (1, 0)

9. A particle is moving in XY-plane, such that its position co-ordinates at time t are given by $x = 3t$ and $y = 3t(1 - 4t)$. The time at which velocity vector makes an angle of 45° with acceleration vector, is

(a) 4 s (b) $\frac{1}{4}$ s
(c) 45 s (d) $\frac{1}{3}$ s

10. Which of these graphs correctly shows change of kinetic energy (K) of a small steel ball in a deep water lake?

(a) 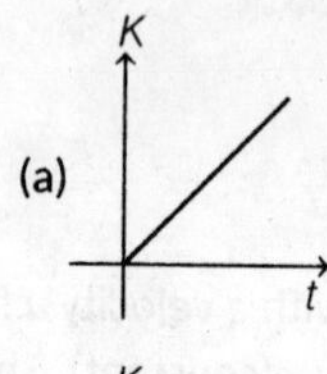

(b) 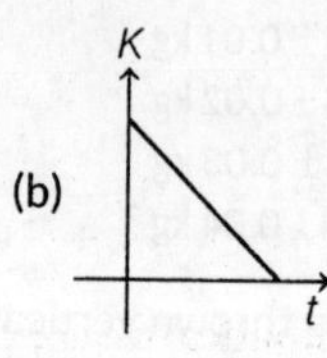

(c) 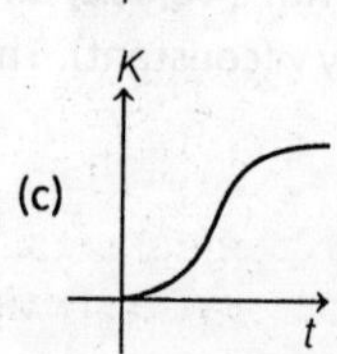

(d) 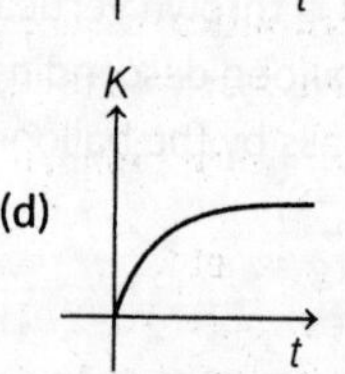

11. In a single slit diffraction observed by using yellow light ($\lambda = 600$ nm). Now in same set-up, if X-rays are used, then

(a) central maxima will be more narrower
(b) more fringes appear
(c) less fringes appear
(d) no diffraction will be observed

12. The potential energy of a particle of mass m moving along positive X-axis is given by

$$U(x) = \begin{cases} E_0; & 0 \le x \le 1 \\ 0; & x > 1 \end{cases}$$

If λ_1 and λ_2 are the de-Broglie wavelengths of the particle, when $0 \le x \le 1$ and $x > 1$, respectively. If the total energy of particle is $2E_0$, then ratio $\frac{\lambda_1}{\lambda_2}$ is

(a) 1 : 1 (b) $\sqrt{2} : 1$
(c) $1 : \sqrt{2}$ (d) None of these

13. A disc rolls without slipping and climbs on a rough inclined surface and come back as shown in the figure. During the motion on inclined surface,

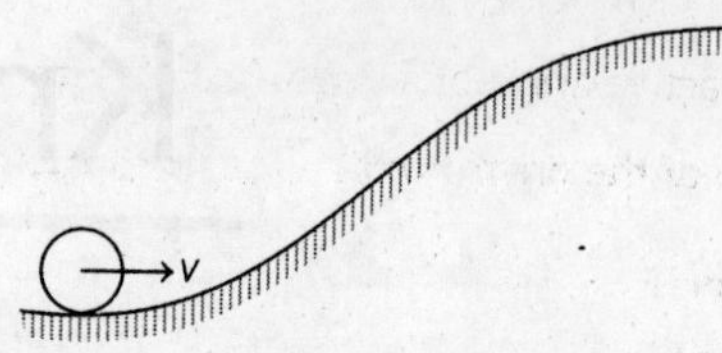

(a) friction is downward during the upward journey
(b) friction is upward during the upward journey
(c) friction is zero
(d) information is insufficient to determine the direction

14. **Statement I** Without any external force, there is no change in velocity.

Statement II Force = mass × acceleration in all reference frames.

In light of above statements, choose the most appropriate answer from the options given below:

(a) Both Statement I and Statement II are incorrect.
(b) Statement I is correct and Statement II is incorrect.
(c) Statement I is incorrect and Statement II is correct.
(d) Both Statement I and Statement II are correct.

15. The activity of a radioactive substance decays from 8000 becquerel to 4000 becquerel in 5 days. The activity of the substance after the next 10 days will be

(a) 500 becquerel (b) 1000 becquerel
(c) 1500 becquerel (d) 2000 becquerel

16. Attaching two rheostat in series in a potentiometer, circuit can

(a) decrease sensitivity of potentiometer by increasing its potential gradient
(b) increase sensitivity of potentiometer by increasing its potential gradient
(c) increase sensitivity of potentiometer by decreasing its potential gradient
(d) None of the above

17. In a plane electromagnetic wave, the electric field oscillate sinusoidally at a frequency of 2×10^{10} Hz and amplitude 48 V/m. The wavelength of the wave is

(a) 24×10^{-10} m (b) 1.5×10^{-2} m
(c) 4.16×10^{8} m (d) 3×10^{8} m

18. Two point charges Q_1 and Q_2 are placed on two vertices of a right angle triangle as shown in figure. The resultant electric field at point O is perpendicular to the hypotenuse, then ratio of $\frac{Q_1}{Q_2}$ is equal to

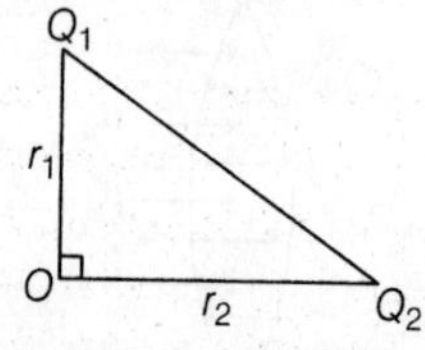

(a) $\frac{r_1}{r_2}$ (b) $\frac{r_2}{r_1}$ (c) $\frac{r_1^2}{r_2^2}$ (d) $\frac{r_2^3}{r_1^3}$

19. The refractive angle of a prism is A. If refractive index of material of the prism is $\cot\left(\frac{A}{2}\right)$, then angle of minimum deviation is

(a) $180° - A$ (b) $180° - 2A$
(c) $2A$ (d) $90° - A$

20. Electric field associated with an electromagnetic wave in a medium of refractive index $\frac{3}{2}$ is

$$E = 40\cos(kz - 6\times10^{8}t)$$

By how many degrees phase of wave changes when it travels $\left(\frac{\pi}{2}\right)$ m?

(a) 90° (b) 180°
(c) 270° (d) 360°

21. Two imaginary spherical surfaces of radii R and $2R$ respectively, surrounded a positive point charge Q located at the centre of the concentric spheres. When compared to the number of field lines N_1 going through the sphere of radius R, the number of electric field lines N_2 going through the sphere of radius $2R$ is

(a) $N_2 = \frac{N_1}{4}$ (b) $N_2 = \frac{N_1}{2}$
(c) $N_2 = 2N_1$ (d) $N_2 = N_1$

22. A coil of area 10 cm^2 and 10 turns is in magnetic field directed perpendicular to the plane and changing at a rate of 10^8 G/s. The resistance of coil is 20 Ω. The current in the coil will be

(a) 0.5 A (b) 5×10^{-3} A
(c) 0.05 A (d) 5 A

23. Four different configurations of charges has been shown in the figure. The increasing order of electrostatic potential energies of the given system of charges is

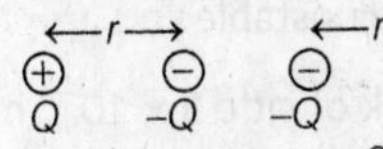

(a) $U_1 = U_4 < U_2 < U_3$ (b) $U_2 = U_4 < U_3 < U_1$
(c) $U_2 = U_3 < U_1 < U_4$ (d) $U_3 < U_1 < U_2 < U_4$

24. **Statement I** In nuclear reactor, heavy water or graphite can be used as moderator.

Statement II When a light object collides with a heavy object, nearly whole of kinetic energy is given to heavier object.

In light of above statements choose the most appropriate answer from the options given below:

(a) Both Statement I and Statement II are incorrect.
(b) Statement I is correct and Statement II is incorrect.
(c) Statement I is incorrect and Statement II is correct.
(d) Both Statement I and Statement II are correct.

25. A very long straight semi-infinite solenoid has radius R, number of turns per unit length n and current flowing through it I. If x is the distance from the one end of the solenoid measured along its axis, then which of the following plot of B and ratio x / R is best represented?

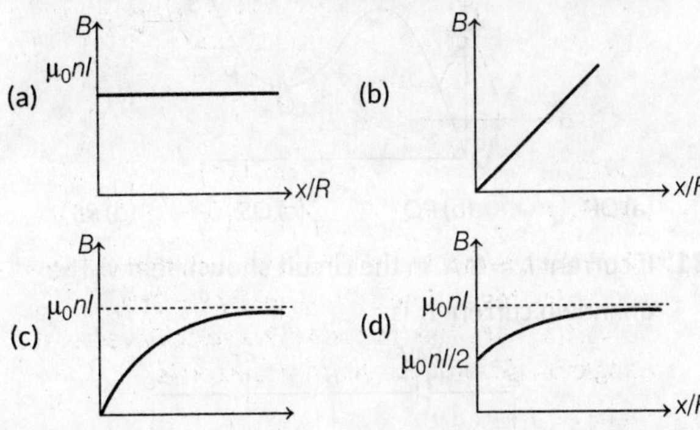

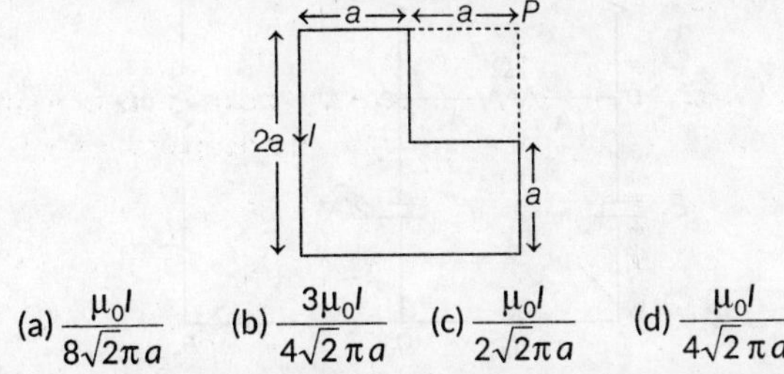

26. The magnetic field B at the point P shown in the figure is

(a) $\frac{\mu_0 I}{8\sqrt{2}\pi a}$ (b) $\frac{3\mu_0 I}{4\sqrt{2}\pi a}$ (c) $\frac{\mu_0 I}{2\sqrt{2}\pi a}$ (d) $\frac{\mu_0 I}{4\sqrt{2}\pi a}$

27. A hypothetical planet of mass m is moving around a massive star whose potential energy is given as $U = -\frac{1}{2}mb^2r^2$, where b is a constant and r is the distance of the planet from star. It is assumed that Bohr model of quantisation of angular momentum is valid, then which of these are correct for planet's nth orbit?

(a) $r_n \propto n$ (b) $v_n \propto n$ (c) $r_n \propto \sqrt{n}$ (d) $v_n \propto \frac{1}{\sqrt{n}}$

28. An ammeter has range (0-1)A. Its internal resistance is 0.81 Ω. If its range has to be increased to 10 A, the value of the required shunt is

(a) 0.09 Ω (b) 0.03 Ω (c) 0.3 Ω (d) 0.9 Ω

29. **Assertion (A)** A rolling body (pure rolling over a horizontal surface) stops after sometime due to dissipation of energy as work done against friction.

Reason (R) Point of contact of a rolling body has a zero relative velocity with respect to ground.

In the light of the above statements, choose the most appropriate answer from the options given below:

(a) Both A and R are true but R is not the correct explanation of A.
(b) A is true but R is false.
(c) A is false but R is true.
(d) Both A and R are true and R is the correct explanation of A.

30. The graph between current I and voltage V has been shown in figure given below, so which portion of the graph shows the negative dynamic resistance?

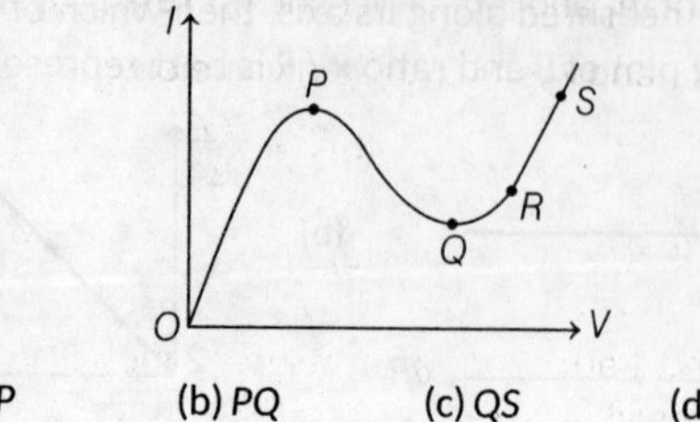

(a) OP (b) PQ (c) QS (d) RS

31. If current $I_3 = 8$ A in the circuit shown below. The unknown current I_4 is

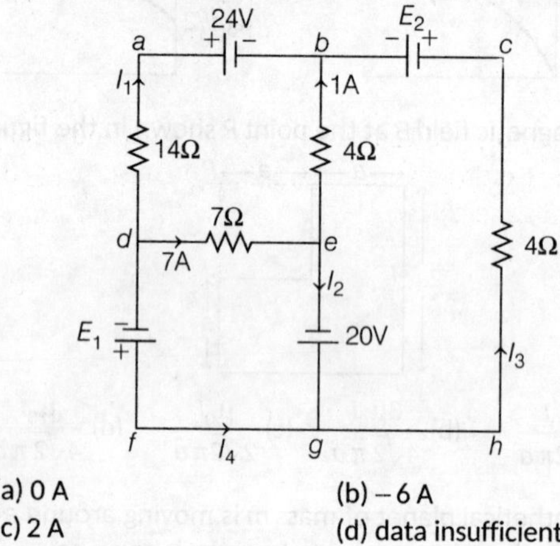

(a) 0 A (b) – 6 A
(c) 2 A (d) data insufficient

32. Current in an AC circuit is $I = 100 \sin 200\,\pi t$ ampere. Now match column I and column II.

	Column I		Column II
A.	Time after which current is zero	P.	$\frac{1}{1200}$ s
B.	Time after which current reaches rms value	Q.	$\frac{1}{600}$ s
C.	Time after which current is half of its maximum value	R.	$\frac{1}{800}$ s
D.	Time after which current becomes 0.86 times of its maximum value	S.	$\frac{1}{200}$ s

Choose the correct answers from the options given below:
(a) A → S, B → R, C → P, D → Q
(b) A → P, B → S, C → Q, D → R
(c) A → S, B → R, C → Q, D → P
(d) A → P, B → R, C → S, D → Q

33. Two identical circular loops A and B of copper wire are lying on a table without touching each other. Loop A carriers a current which is increasing with time, then the loop B
(a) remains uneffected
(b) attracted by loop A
(c) repelled by loop A
(d) rotates about its centre of mass

34. Which of the following equations can be derived using method of dimensional analysis?
(a) $N = N_0 \cdot e^{-\lambda t}$ (b) $y = A\sin(\omega t + kx)$
(c) $E = \frac{1}{2}mv^2 + \frac{1}{2}I\omega^2$ (d) None of these

35. The equation of a transverse wave propagating in a string is given by $y = 0.02\sin(x + 30t)$, where x and y are in metres and t is in seconds. If linear density of the string is 1.3×10^{-4} kg/m, then the tension in the string is
(a) 0.12 N (b) 1.2 N (c) 12 N (d) 120 N

Section II

36. The potential energy of a particle of mass 0.5 kg in motion along the X-axis is given by $U = 2(1 - \cos 5x)$ J, where x is in metres. The time period of small oscillations is
(a) $\frac{\pi}{\sqrt{5}}$ s (b) $\sqrt{5}\,\pi$s (c) $\frac{\pi}{5}$ s (d) $\frac{\pi}{10}$ s

37. A uniformly charged ring of radius R and charge $+Q$ is placed in XZ-plane. A point charge $+q$ of mass m is placed at a point P on axis of ring. Charge is located at $y = \frac{R}{\sqrt{2}}$. It is found that, point charge remains at rest at point P. Then, equilibrium of point charge

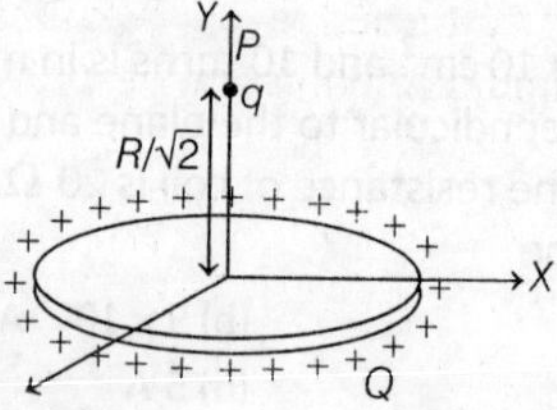

(a) at point P, stable
(b) at point P, unstable
(c) at point P, neutral
(d) above point P, stable and below unstable

38. The bottom end of a cubical block of side 5×10^{-2} m is fixed. A force of 10^5N tangential to the top face displaces it by 1.2×10^{-4} m. The rigidity modulus is
(a) 6×10^{-10} Nm^{-2} (b) 6×10^{-9} Nm^{-2}
(c) 1.67×10^{10} Nm^{-2} (d) 10^{11} Nm^{-2}

39. Two resistors of resistances, $R_1 = 10 \pm 0.2\ \Omega$ and $R_2 = 20 \pm 0.1\Omega$ are connected in series. The equivalent resistance with limit of possible percentage error is
(a) $(30\pm0.3)\ \Omega$ (b) $(6.67\pm0.67)\Omega$
(c) $(6.67\pm0.1)\Omega$ (d) $(6.67\pm0.08)\Omega$

40. A large glass surface is 2 mm thick. The outside temperature is – 20°C and the inside temperature is 25°C. If the thermal conductivity of glass is 0.8 W/m-K, then the temperature at the mid-point of the window is
(a) 0°C (b) 2.5°C (c) –2.5 °C (d) 22.5°C

41. Assertion (A) Magnetism of earth is not due to iron or ferromagnetic deposits in core.

Reason (R) A ferromagnetic substance becomes paramagnetic above curie temperature.

In the light of the above statements, choose the most appropriate answer from the options given below:

(a) Both A and R are true but R is not the correct explanation of A.
(b) A is true but R is false.
(c) A is false but R is true.
(d) Both A and R are true and R is the correct explanation of A.

42. If the earth shrinks to n times of its radius without changing its mass, then duration of the day will be

(a) nT (b) $\frac{T}{n}$ (c) n^2T (d) $\frac{T}{n^2}$

(where, T = duration of day before shrinking)

43. A particle moves in a straight line, its angular momentum with respect to a choosen origin is

(a) a constant
(b) keeps on increasing with time
(c) first increases then decreases
(d) keeps on decreasing

44. A solid sphere of mass M is rolling with a velocity v on a smooth horizontal surface and strikes a massless spring of force constant k attached to a massless smooth platform, then the maximum compression of spring is

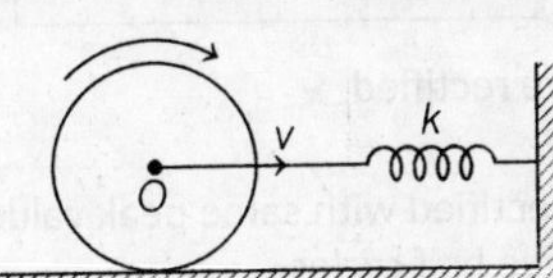

(a) $v\sqrt{\frac{7M}{5k}}$ (b) $v\sqrt{\frac{2M}{3k}}$ (c) $v\sqrt{\frac{M}{5k}}$ (d) $v\sqrt{\frac{5M}{3k}}$

45. A water drop in air refracts the light rays as

(a) 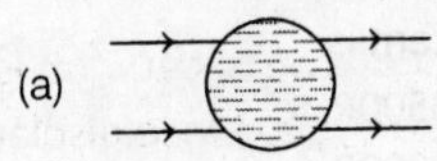 (b) 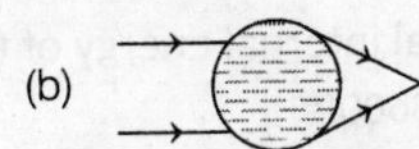

(c) 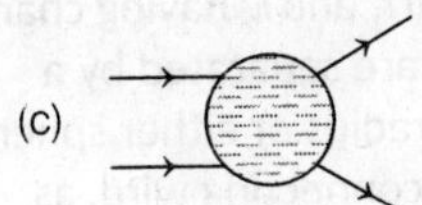 (d) 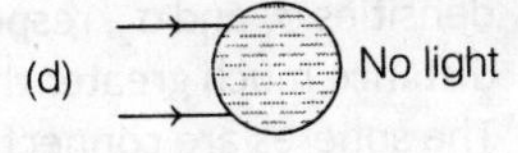

46. Two balls of masses m_1 and m_2 are moving with velocities $v_1\hat{i}$ and $v_2\hat{i}$ undergoes a collinear collision. After collision, velocities of m_1 and m_2 are $v_3\hat{i}$ and $v_4\hat{i}$ respectively. If $m_2 = 0.5m_1$ and $v_3 = 0.5v_1$, then value of v_1 is

(a) $v_4 + v_2$ (b) $v_4 - \frac{v_2}{4}$
(c) $v_4 - \frac{v_2}{2}$ (d) $v_4 - v_2$

47. At 42°C and 1 atmospheric pressure, 2 moles of helium gas is enclosed in a cubical vessel of 1 m side. Assuming that the molecules are moving with root mean square speed, then the number of collision per second which the molecules make with the vessel wall is

(a) 1.72×10^{23} (b) 1.72×10^{24}
(c) 5.43×10^{27} (d) 5.43×10^{26}

48. The p-V graph of three different gases A, B and C during adiabatic expansion has been plotted. The gases A, B and C can be respectively,

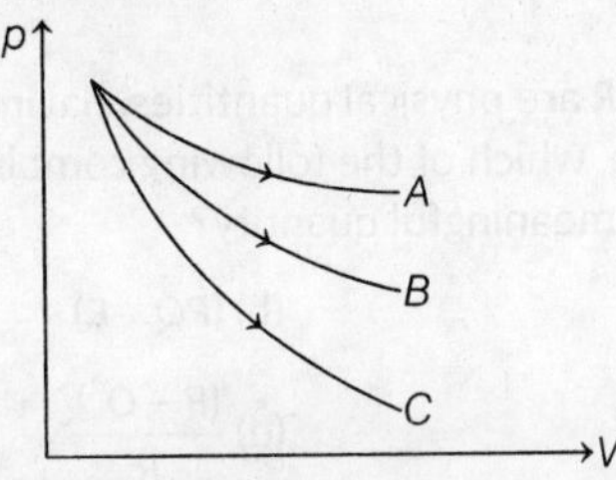

(a) monoatomic, diatomic, polyatomic
(b) polyatomic, diatomic, monoatomic
(c) diatomic, triatomic (linear), triatomic (non-linear)
(d) monoatomic, triatomic (linear), triatomic (non-linear)

49. A boy riding a bike with a speed of 5 m/s towards east direction observes raindrops falling vertically downwards. On increasing the speed of 15 m/s, rain appears to fall making an angle at 45° of the vertical. The magnitude of velocity of rain w.r.t. ground is

(a) 5 m/s (b) $5\sqrt{5}$ m/s
(c) 25 m/s (d) 10 m/s

50. A 50 Hz, 10 V source is connected to a resistance of 40 Ω, an inductance of 191 mH and a capacitance of 106 μF in series. The time in which the resistor having heat capacity 6 J/°C gets heated by 80°C is

(a) 4 s (b) 6 s (c) 12 s (d) 480 s

Answers

1. (b)	2. (a)	3. (b)	4. (b)	5. (d)	6. (c)	7. (a)	8. (a)	9. (b)	10. (d)
11. (d)	12. (b)	13. (b)	14. (b)	15. (b)	16. (c)	17. (b)	18. (a)	19. (b)	20. (c)
21. (d)	22. (d)	23. (a)	24. (b)	25. (d)	26. (d)	27. (c)	28. (a)	29. (c)	30. (b)
31. (c)	32. (a)	33. (c)	34. (d)	35. (a)	36. (c)	37. (d)	38. (c)	39. (c)	40. (b)
41. (d)	42. (d)	43. (a)	44. (a)	45. (b)	46. (d)	47. (c)	48. (b)	49. (b)	50. (b)

See detailed explanations on page no. 268

Knockout 07

NEET

PHYSICS

Instructions See Knockout 01

Section I

1. If P, Q and R are physical quantities, having different dimensions, which of the following combinations can never be a meaningful quantity?

(a) $\frac{P-Q}{R}$ (b) $(PQ-R)$

(c) $\frac{PQ}{R}$ (d) $\frac{(P-Q^2)}{R}$

2. For a transistor, to operate in saturation mode, emitter-base bias and collector-base bias should be

(a) forward and reverse biased, respectively

(b) forward and forward biased, respectively

(c) reverse and reverse biased, respectively

(d) reverse and forward biased, respectively

3. Two identical particles each of mass m kg are moving with velocities $2\hat{\mathbf{i}}$ m/s and $-2\hat{\mathbf{j}}$ m/s collides at $t = 0$ s. Collision is completely inelastic. Loss of energy in collision in joules is

(a) m (b) $3m$

(c) 0 (d) $2m$

4. The binding energy of ${}_1^2\text{H}$ is 1.15 MeV per nucleon, an alpha particle ${}_2^4\text{He}$ has a binding energy of 7.1 MeV per nucleon. The Q-value of the following reaction is

$${}_1^2\text{H} + {}_1^2\text{H} \rightarrow {}_2^4\text{He} + Q$$

(a) 5.95 MeV (b) 23.8 MeV

(c) 26.1 MeV (d) 28.9 MeV

5. In a YDSE, the coherent sources are at distance d from each other and screen is placed at a distance D from the slits. If mth bright fringe is formed on the screen is exactly opposite to a slit, then value of m must be (λ is the wavelength used in experiment)

(a) $\frac{d^2}{4\lambda D}$ (b) $\frac{d^2}{2\lambda D}$ (c) $\frac{d^2}{\lambda D}$ (d) $\frac{2\lambda^2}{\lambda D}$

6. In the circuit given below, V_{in} is the sinusoidal voltage source. The voltage drop across $R\,[R_1 \neq R_2]$

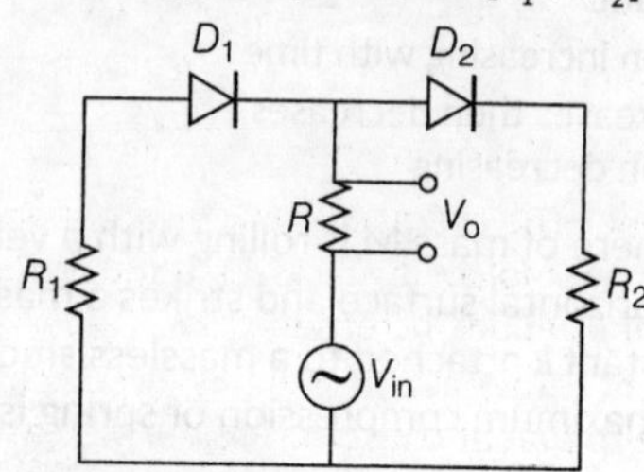

(a) is half wave rectified

(b) is pure DC

(c) full wave rectified with same peak values in the positive and negative half cycles

(d) full wave rectified with different peak values in the positive and negative half cycles

7. A cylinder contains 3 moles of oxygen and 1 mole of argon gas at room temperature of 27°C.

Total internal energy of the system is

(a) 3600R (b) 5500R

(c) 2700R (d) 3200R

8. Two spherical conductors of radii r_1 and r_2 having charge densities σ_1 and σ_2, respectively are separated by a distance much greater than the radius of either sphere. The spheres are connected by a connecting wire, as shown in the following figure. If there is no flow of charge through connecting wire, then true condition is

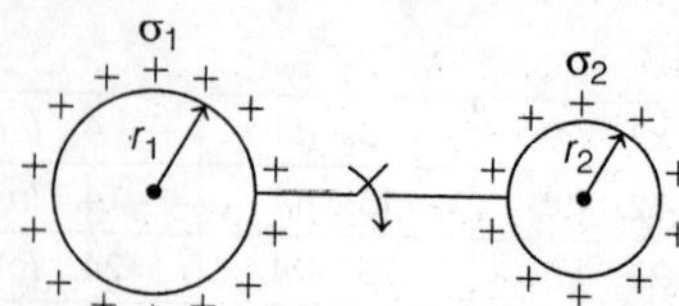

(a) $\frac{\sigma_1}{r_1} = \frac{\sigma_2}{r_2}$ (b) $\sigma_1 = \sigma_2$ (c) $\sigma_1 r_1 = \sigma_2 r_2$ (d) $\frac{\sigma_1}{r_1^2} = \frac{\sigma_2}{r_2^2}$

9. When the surface area of liquid is increased, the molecules from the interior of the liquid rises to the surface. In this process,

I. molecule do work against the downward cohesive force

II. potential energy of molecule increases

III. internal energy of molecule increases

Correct statements are

(a) I, II (b) I, III

(c) II, III (d) I, II, III

10. If the elastic limit of a typical rock on the top of mountain is 3.43×10^8 Nm^{-2} and material density is 3×10^3 kg/m^3, then maximum height of rock is ($g = 9.8$ m/s^2)

(a) 1.167 km (b) 5.83 km

(c) 11.667 km (d) 23.33 km

11. A body cools from $5T$ to $2T$ in 5 min. The room temperature is T. Assume that Newton's law of cooling is applicable. The temperature of the body at the end of next 5 min is

(a) $\frac{T}{3}$ (b) $\frac{2T}{3}$ (c) $\frac{5T}{4}$ (d) T

12. Consider the following two statements.

Statement I The average kinetic energy per degree of freedom per molecule at a given temperature increases as degree of freedom increases.

Statement II The ratio of molar specific heat at constant pressure to that at constant volume increases as the atomicity increases.

In light of above statements, choose the most appropriate answer from the options given below:

(a) Both Statement I and Statement II are incorrect.

(b) Statement I is correct and Statement II is incorrect.

(c) Statement I is incorrect and Statement II is correct.

(d) Both Statement I and Statement II are correct.

13. Mass of a box is 2.3 kg, if you added two stones of mass 2.15 g and 12.39 g to box. Total mass you now have in correct number of significant figures will be

(a) 2.3 kg (b) 2.31 kg

(c) 2.314 kg (d) 2.3145 kg

14. Experimental observations of time period of a pendulum are 2.63 s; 2.56 s; 2.42 s; 2.71 s; 2.80 s

Then, reported value of time period will be

(a) $(2.62 + 0.11)$ s

(b) $(2.62 - 0.11)$ s

(c) (2.62 ± 0.11) s

(d) All of the above

15. Dimensions of gyromagnetic ratio are

(a) [MLTA]

(b) $[M^{-1}LTA]$

(c) $[ML^0TA]$

(d) $[M^{-1}L^0TA]$

16. A potentiometer circuit shown in the figure is set-up to measure emf of a cell E. As the point P moves from X to Y, the galvanometer G shows deflection always in one direction but the deflection continuously until Y is reached. In order to obtain balance point between X and Y, it is necessary to

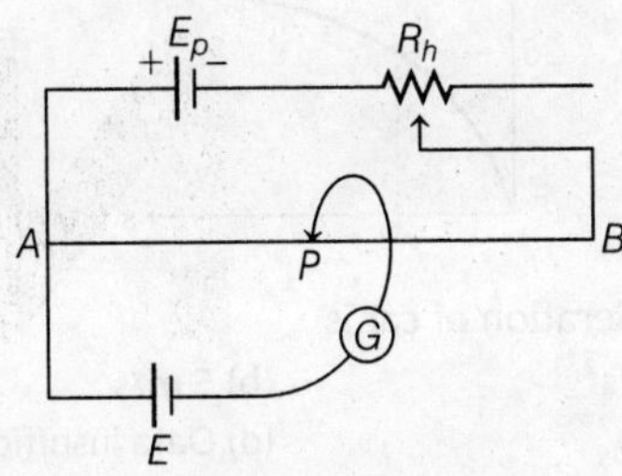

(a) decrease the rheostat resistance R_h

(b) increase the rheostat resistance R_h

(c) reverse the terminals of battery of emf E_P

(d) reverse the terminals of cell of emf E

17.

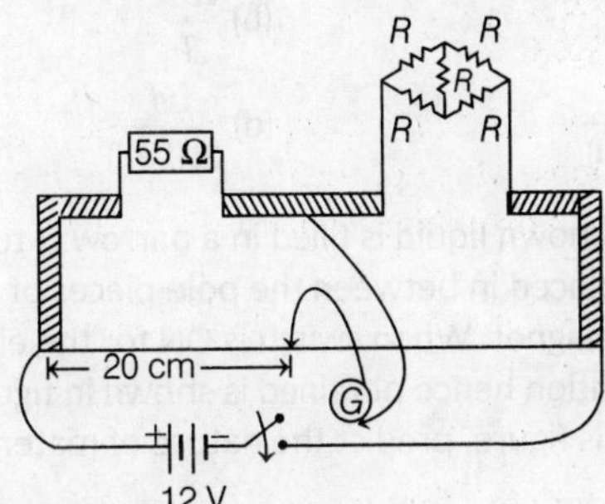

In above arrangement, value of R is

(a) 110 Ω

(b) 220 Ω

(c) 55 Ω

(d) 72 Ω

(balance length is 20 cm)

18. An object is thrown vertically downward from a height above earth's surface. It travels h_1 height in first t s and h_2 height in next t s. The time t is given by (in second)

(a) $\sqrt{\frac{h_2 - h_1}{g}}$

(b) $\sqrt{\frac{h_1 + h_2}{g}}$

(c) $\sqrt{\frac{2(h_2 - h_1)}{g}}$

(d) depends on initial velocity

19. An alpha particle of energy $\frac{1}{2}mv^2$ bombards a heavy nuclear target of charge Ze, then the minimum distance of closest approach is proportional to

(a) $\frac{1}{Ze}$ (b) v^2

(c) $\frac{1}{m}$ (d) $\frac{1}{v^4}$

20. A car accelerates from rest with uniform acceleration. The graph between its velocity and displacement has been plotted

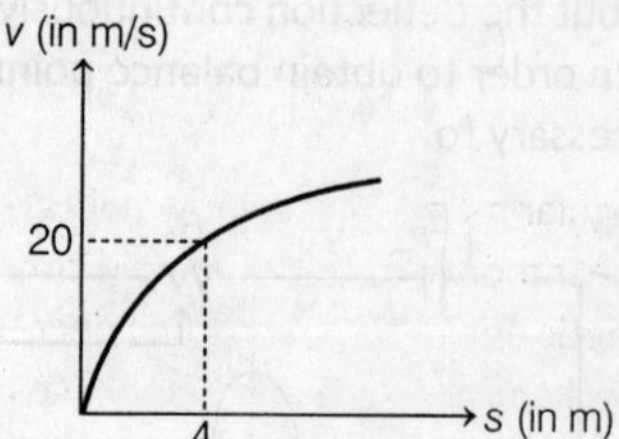

The acceleration of car is

(a) 2.5 m/s^2 (b) 5 m/s^2
(c) 50 m/s^2 (d) Data insufficient

21. An open organ pipe of length L is sounded together with another open organ pipe of length $(L + l)$ in their fundamental modes. If speed of sound in air is v, then number of beats heard per second is

(a) $\frac{vl}{4L^2}$ (b) $\frac{vL^2}{2l}$
(c) $\frac{vl^2}{2(L+l)}$ (d) $\frac{vl}{2L(L+l)}$

22. If an unknown liquid is filled in a narrow U-tube and one limb is placed in between the pole pieces of an electromagnet. When switch is ON for the electromagnet, the situation hence obtained is shown in figure below. From this figure, predict the nature of material

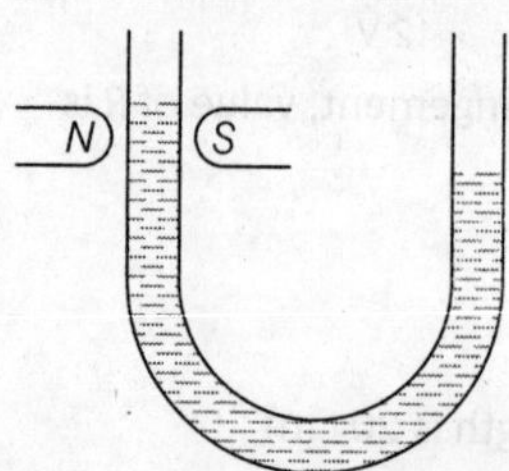

(a) Paramagnetic (b) Ferromagnetic
(c) Diamagnetic (d) Can be (a) or (b)

23. Radiowaves of constant amplitude can be produced by using

(a) LED (b) rectifier
(c) logic gates (d) oscillator

24. Consider the following two statements.

Statement I A dead beat galvanometer contains a coil wrapped with aluminium plate.

Statement II Eddy currents dissipates oscillation energy as heat.

In light of above statements, choose the most appropriate answer from the options given below:

(a) Both Statement I and Statement II are incorrect.
(b) Statement I is correct and Statement II is incorrect.
(c) Statement I is incorrect and Statement II is correct.
(d) Both Statement I and Statement II are correct.

25. Assertion (A) When certain mass of wood and same mass of metal left in sun for sometime, iron piece is hotter to touch.

Reason (R) Iron absorbs more heat than wood.

In the light of the above statements, choose the most appropriate answer from the the options given below:

(a) Both A and R are true but R is not the correct explanation of A.
(b) A is true but R is false.
(c) A is false but R is true.
(d) Both A and R are true and R is the correct explanation of A.

26. A ball of mass m strikes a rough horizontal surface with speed u at an angle θ with the normal and it rebounds with the speed v at angle ϕ with the normal. If the ball remain in contact for time Δt, then average normal force on the ball due to horizontal surface is

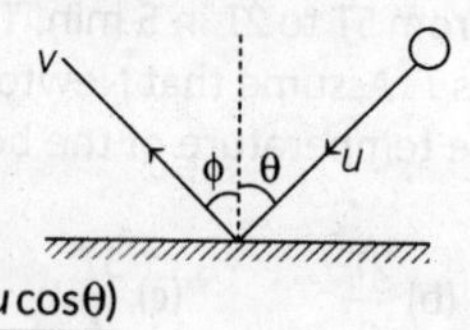

(a) $\frac{m(v\cos\phi - u\cos\theta)}{\Delta t}$
(b) $\frac{m(v\sin\phi - u\sin\theta)}{\Delta t}$
(c) $\frac{m(v\cos\phi + u\cos\theta)}{\Delta t}$
(d) $\frac{m(v\sin\phi + u\sin\theta)}{\Delta t}$

27. Match the Column I (planar loops of different shapes) with Column II (direction of induced current).

Column I	Column II
A. (loop with corners d, a, c, b)	P. *b a c b*
B. (loop with corners a, b, c)	Q. *c d a b c*
C. (loop with points a, b, c, d)	R. *b c d a b*

Choose the correct answers from the options given below:

(a) A $\rightarrow$ R, B $\rightarrow$ P, C $\rightarrow$ Q
(b) A $\rightarrow$ Q, B $\rightarrow$ P, C $\rightarrow$ R
(c) A $\rightarrow$ P, B $\rightarrow$ Q, C $\rightarrow$ R
(d) A $\rightarrow$ P, B $\rightarrow$ R, C $\rightarrow$ Q

28. The magnetic flux (ϕ) linked with a conducting coil depends on time t as $\phi = 4t^n - 3^n$, where n is a positive constant.
If the magnitude of emf induced in the coil is e, then which of the following is incorrect about induced emf e?
(a) If $n = 1$, then e is constant.
(b) If $n > 1$, then e increases with time.
(c) If $n > 1$, then e decreases with time.
(d) If $0 < n < 1$, then e decreases with time.

29. Four gases hydrogen, oxygen, nitrogen and helium are at temperatures T, $2T$, $3T$ and $4T$, respectively. The correct increasing order of the de-Broglie wavelengths of their molecules is
(a) hydrogen, helium, nitrogen, oxygen
(b) oxygen, nitrogen, hydrogen, helium
(c) oxygen, nitrogen, helium, hydrogen
(d) nitrogen, oxygen, helium, hydrogen

30. The radius of the circle, the periodic revolution, the initial position and sense of revolution are indicated in the given figure. The simple harmonic motion of X-projection of the radius vector of the revolving particle P, is

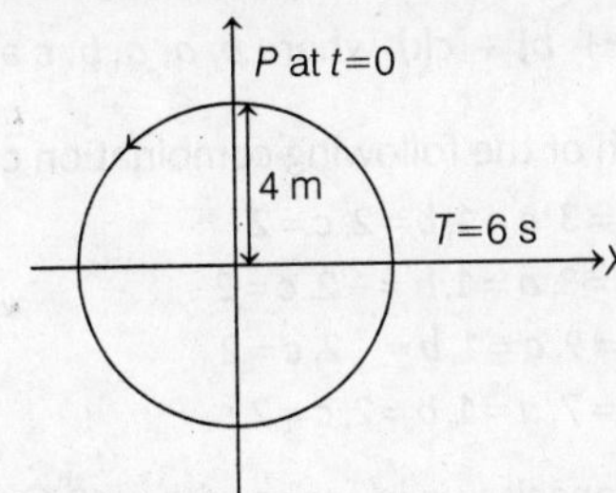

(a) $x = 4\sin\left(\frac{\pi}{3}t + \pi\right)$ (b) $x = 4\cos\left(\frac{\pi}{3}t + \pi\right)$
(c) $x = 4\sin\left(\frac{2\pi}{3}t - \pi\right)$ (d) $x = 4\cos\left(\frac{2\pi}{3} - \pi\right)$

31. Two Identical small conducting spheres having charges q_1 and q_2 (with $q_2 << q_1$). The spheres are placed at a certain distance. The electrostatic force between them is F_1. The spheres are made to touch each other and then placed at same distance. Now force acting between them is F_2.
Then, $\frac{F_1}{F_2}$ is
(a) $\frac{q_1}{4q_2}$ (b) $\frac{4q_1}{q_2}$
(c) $\frac{4q_2}{q_1}$ (d) $\frac{q_1}{q_2}$

32. A convex lens of focal length 30 cm is used to see an image over a screen. Distance between object and screen is
(a) 100 cm (b) 95 cm
(c) 115 cm (d) 125 cm

33. A smooth tube of certain mass closed at both ends is rotated in a gravity free space and released. The two balls shown in the figure move towards the ends of the tube and remains at rest there. For this whole system, which statement is incorrect?

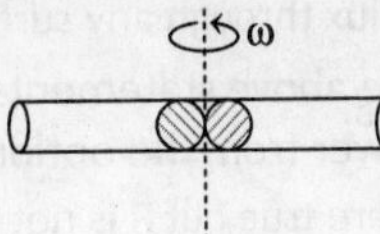

(a) Total angular momentum will remain conserved.
(b) Total linear momentum will remain conserved.
(c) Total kinetic energy of system will decrease.
(d) Total mechanical energy will remain cosntant.

34. Two quarter rings of masses m and $2m$ and radii $2r$ and r respectively, are placed in the first and third quadrant of a cartesian co-ordinate system with centre at origin as shown in the following figure.

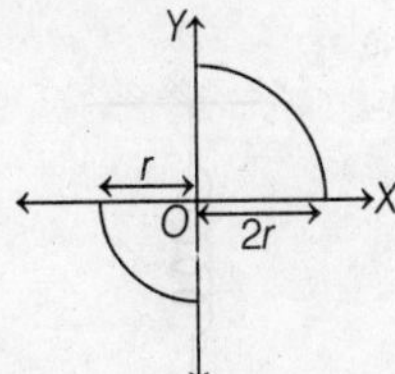

The co-ordinates of centre of mass of system is
(a) (0, 0) (b) $\left(\frac{2}{3\pi}r, \frac{2r}{3\pi}\right)$ (c) $\left(\frac{4r}{3\pi}, \frac{4r}{3\pi}\right)$ (d) $\left(-\frac{4r}{3\pi}, -\frac{4r}{3\pi}\right)$

35. Two bodies of mass m each are revolving around a planet of mass M in a circular orbit of radius r. The position of bodies during the motion remains along the diameter. The orbital speed of bodies is
(a) $\sqrt{\frac{G}{r}(M+m)}$ (b) $\sqrt{\frac{G}{4r}(m+4M)}$
(c) $\sqrt{\frac{G}{2r}(2M+m)}$ (d) $\sqrt{\frac{G}{4r}(4M+m)}$

Section II

36. Three thin dielectric slabs of dielectric constants K_1, K_2 and K_3 are inserted between the plates of a parallel plate capacitor as shown in the following figure. The variation of electric field between the plates with distance x is shown below.

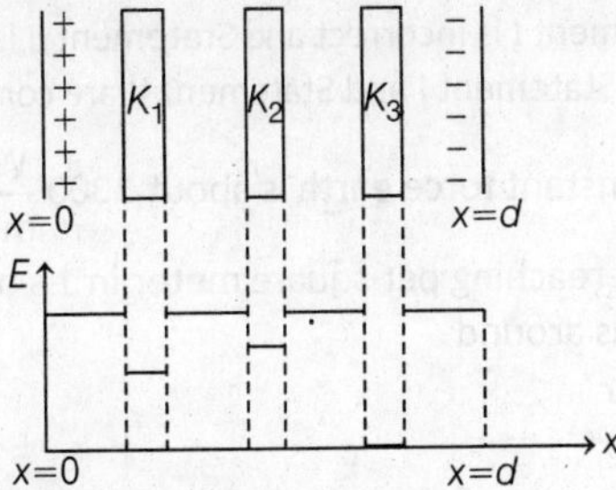

Then, correct relation is
(a) $K_1 > K_2 > K_3$ (b) $K_1 > K_3 > K_2$
(c) $K_3 > K_1 > K_2$ (d) $K_2 > K_1 > K_3$

37. Assertion (A) If only electric dipoles exists in nature, then Gauss' law is not valid.

Reason (R) Net flux through any surface is then always zero.

In the light of the above statements, choose the most appropriate answer from the options given below:

(a) Both A and R are true but R is not the correct explanation of A.

(b) A is true but R is false.

(c) A is false but R is true.

(d) Both A and R are true and R is the correct explanation of A.

38. In the figure shown, block attached with the spring is at equilibrium position and at rest. If it is displaced by a distance $\frac{mg}{3k}$ downward and released, then

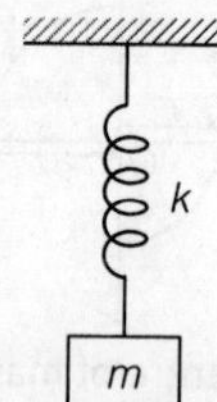

(a) just after released net force acting on block is $\frac{mg}{3}$ downward

(b) the work done by external source is $\frac{m^2g^2}{3k}$

(c) change in spring potential energy is $\frac{7}{18}\frac{m^2g^2}{k}$

(d) All are correct

39. Consider the following two statements.

Statement I In an L-R circuit, current and voltage are just out of phase.

Statement II Time lag between maximum current and maximum voltage in an L-R circuit $\tau = \frac{\phi}{\omega}$, where ϕ is phase difference and ω is angular frequency.

In the light of above statements, choose the most appropriate answer from the options given below:

(a) Both Statement I and Statement II are incorrect.

(b) Statement I is correct and Statement II is incorrect.

(c) Statement I is incorrect and Statement II is correct.

(d) Both Statement I and Statement II are correct.

40. Solar constant force earth is about 1300 $\frac{W}{m^2}$. Number of photons reaching per square meter in 1 s of earth's surface is around

(a) 4×10^{19}

(b) 4×10^{16}

(c) 4×10^{21}

(d) Data insufficient

41. In a certain process pV^n = constant, the heat Q given to a monoatomic gas leads to a change in internal energy of a gas which is equal to $\frac{Q}{4}$. The value of n is

(a) $\frac{7}{9}$ (b) 2 (c) $\frac{3}{5}$ (d) $\frac{6}{7}$

42. A lift is accelerating upwards with uniform acceleration a. A uniform string of length L and mass m supports a small block of mass M that hangs from the ceiling of the lift. The tension at a distance l from the ceiling is T. The value of a is

(a) $\frac{T}{M+m-\frac{ml}{L}} - g$ (b) $\frac{T}{2M+m-\frac{ml}{L}} + g$

(c) $\frac{T}{M+\frac{ml}{L}} - g$ (d) $\frac{T}{2M-m+\frac{ml}{L}} - g$

43. If two vectors are given by $\mathbf{A} = \hat{\mathbf{i}} + 2\hat{\mathbf{j}} + 2\hat{\mathbf{k}}$ and $\mathbf{B} = 3\hat{\mathbf{i}} + 6\hat{\mathbf{j}} + 2\hat{\mathbf{k}}$. Another vector **C** has the same magnitude as B but has the same direction as **A**. If $\mathbf{C} = \frac{p}{q}(a\hat{\mathbf{i}} + b\hat{\mathbf{j}} + c\hat{\mathbf{k}})$, where p, q, a, b, c are integers, then which of the following combination can represent **C**?

(a) $p=7, q=3, a=1, b=2, c=2$

(b) $p=7, q=3, a=1, b=-2, c=2$

(c) $p=7, q=9, a=1, b=-2, c=2$

(d) $p=9, q=7, a=1, b=2, c=2$

44. A 100 μF capacitor is in series with a 40 Ω resistance. It is connected with a supply of 110 V and 60 Hz. Time lag between maximum current and maximum voltage is

(a) 1 ms (b) 2 ms

(c) 3 ms (d) None of these

45. Potential energy of a satellite of mass m in a circular orbit is $U = -x$. Escape speed of satellite in this orbit is

(a) $v_e = \sqrt{\frac{2x}{m}}$ (b) $v_e = \sqrt{\frac{x}{2m}}$ (c) $v_e = \sqrt{\frac{x}{m}}$ (d) $v_e = 2\sqrt{\frac{x}{m}}$

46. A system of three charges is shown below.

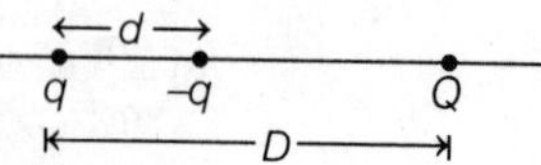

Now, $-q$ charge is shifted near Q charge as shown.

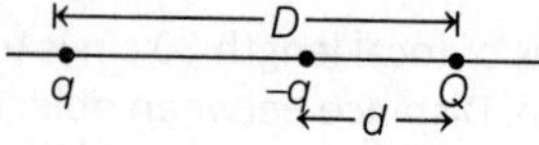

Work done in the process is (Take, $Q = 2q$ and $D = 3d$)

(a) $\frac{kq^2}{d}$ (b) $\frac{-kq^2}{d}$ (c) $\frac{-kq^2}{2d}$ (d) $\frac{kq^2}{2d}$

47. In a YDSE, a beam of electrons is used. If speed of electrons is made 4 times, then central bright fringe width becomes

(a) 4 times
(b) 2 times
(c) $\frac{1}{2}$ times
(d) No fringes are obtained with electrons

48. A resistor of resistance $r/2$ and n resistors of resistance r are connected to a battery. If internal resistance of the battery is negligible. At what value of n would the amount of power consumed by all resistors of resistance r be the largest?

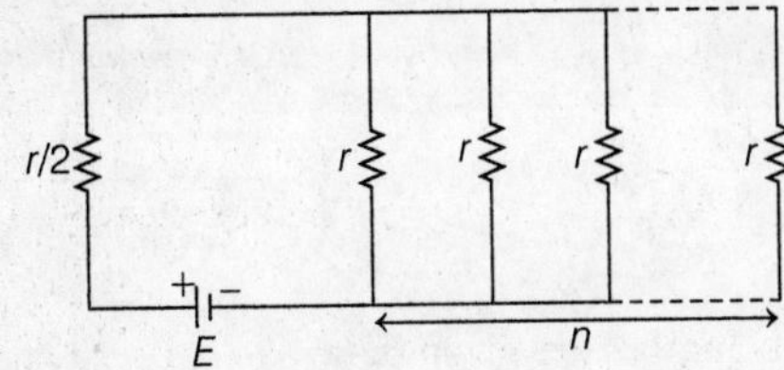

(a) 1
(b) 2
(c) 3
(d) 4

49. Angle of incidence (i) for a light incident on a prism and deviation (δ) produced by the prism is plotted as shown in the following figure.

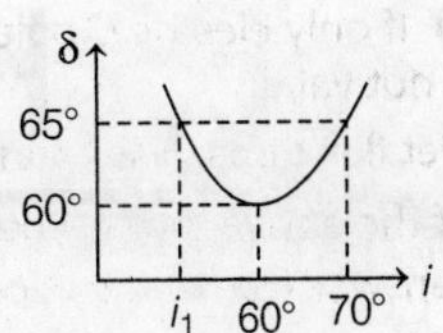

I. The angle of prism is 60°.
II. Refractive index of the prism is $\sqrt{2}$.
III. The value of i_1 is 55°.

The correct statements are

(a) Only I
(b) Only III
(c) I and III
(d) I, II, III

50. In Column I, first and last member of radioactive decay series are given and in Column II, number of lost particles is given. Match entries of Column I and Column II correctly.

	Column I		Column II
A	$^{232}_{90}Th \rightarrow ^{208}_{82}Pb$	P.	$\alpha = 8, \beta = 5$
B	$^{237}_{93}N_p \rightarrow ^{209}_{83}Bi$	Q.	$\alpha = 8, \beta = 6$
C	$^{238}_{92}U \rightarrow ^{206}_{82}Pb$	R.	$\alpha = 6, \beta = 4$
D	$^{227}_{89}Ac \rightarrow ^{207}_{82}Pb$	S	$\alpha = 7, \beta = 4$

(a) A → P, B → Q, C → R, D → S
(b) A → R, B → P, C → Q, D → S
(c) A → P, B → R, C → S, D → Q
(d) A → Q, B → S, C → R, D → P

Answers

1. *(a)*	2. *(b)*	3. *(d)*	4. *(b)*	5. *(b)*	6. *(d)*	7. *(c)*	8. *(c)*	9. *(a)*	10. *(c)*
11. *(c)*	12. *(a)*	13. *(a)*	14. *(c)*	15. *(d)*	16. *(a)*	17. *(b)*	18. *(a)*	19. *(c)*	20. *(c)*
21. *(d)*	22. *(a)*	23. *(d)*	24. *(a)*	25. *(b)*	26. *(a)*	27. *(a)*	28. *(d)*	29. *(d)*	30. *(a)*
31. *(c)*	32. *(d)*	33. *(c)*	34. *(a)*	35. *(d)*	36. *(c)*	37. *(d)*	38. *(c)*	39. *(c)*	40. *(c)*
41. *(a)*	42. *(a)*	43. *(a)*	44. *(d)*	45. *(c)*	46. *(d)*	47. *(a)*	48. *(b)*	49. *(c)*	50. *(b)*

See detailed explanations on page no. 273

Knockout 08

NEET

PHYSICS

Instructions See Knockout 01

Section I

1. Two polaroids are kept perpendicular to each other. If $(n-2)$ more polaroids are inserted between them with their axes equally inclined, then intensity of transmitted light I after emerging from fourth polaroid is

(a) $\frac{27}{128}I_0$ (b) $\frac{27}{32}I_0$ (c) $\frac{273}{256}I_0$ (d) zero

2. A bubble under water oscillates with period T, which is directly proportional to $p^{-5/6}\,d^{1/2}\,E^{\gamma}$, where p is pressure, d is density and E is energy. The value of γ is

(a) $\frac{1}{3}$ (b) $\frac{1}{5}$ (c) $\frac{1}{6}$ (d) $\frac{1}{7}$

3. A metal sheet with two rectangular shaped holes is shown in the figure.

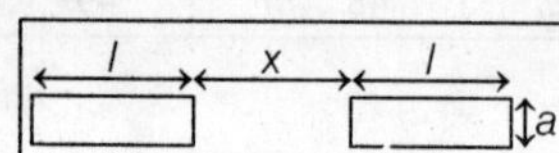

If the temperature of the metal sheet is increased, then

(a) l, x and a increase

(b) l and a increase but x decreases

(c) l increases but x and a decrease

(d) l, x and a will decrease

4. A small loop Q is kept coaxially with a bigger loop.

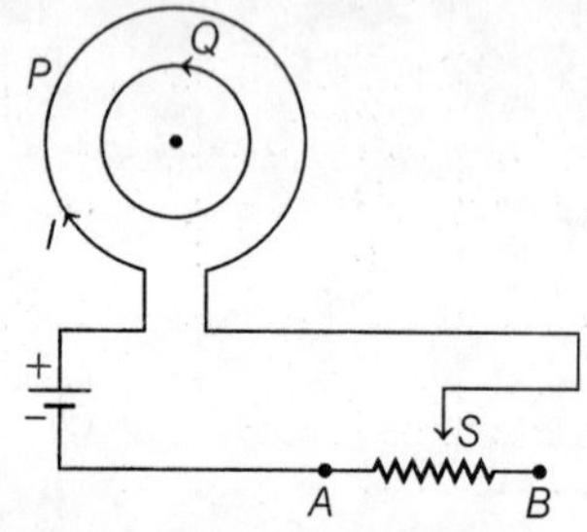

As slider S moves from B to A, then current in Q

(a) is zero

(b) flows clockwise

(c) flows anti-clockwise

(d) initially clockwise then anti-clockwise

5. The value of current I_0 for the circuit shown in figure below is (Assume that diodes are ideal)

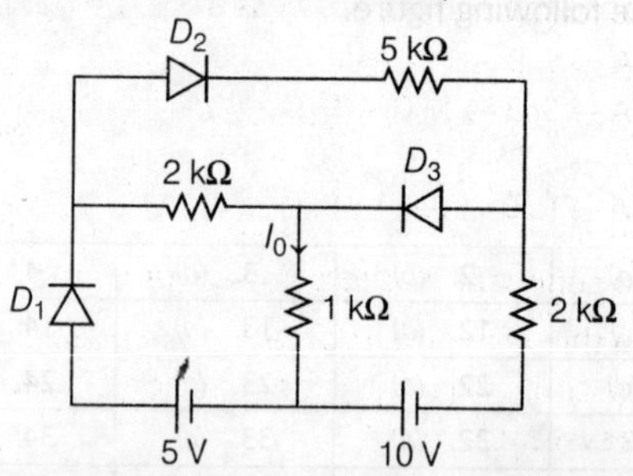

(a) 1 mA (b) 0.66 mA (c) 1.25 mA (d) 1.66 mA

6. A particle is projected from ground at an angle θ with the vertical such that its horizontal range R is related to its time of flight T as $R = 10\frac{\sqrt{3}}{2}T^2$. The value of projection angle θ is (Take, $g = 10\ \text{m/s}^2$)

(a) 30° (b) 45°

(c) 60° (d) None of these

7. A wheel of radius r consists of a thin uniform rim of mass m and six thin spokes of mass m. The moment of inertia of the wheel about axis passing through point P and perpendicular to the plane is

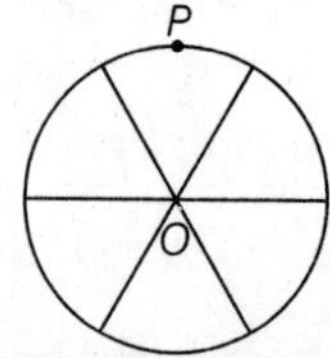

(a) $3mr^2$ (b) $4mr^2$ (c) $6mr^2$ (d) $10\,mr^2$

8. van der Waals' gas equation is

$$\left(p+\frac{a}{V^2}\right)(V-b)=RT$$

here, p = pressure
V = volume
R = molar gas constant
T = absolute temperature

Dimensions of a. b are

(a) $[ML^6T^{-2}]$ (b) $[ML^5T^{-2}]$ (c) $[ML^8T^{-2}]$ (d) $[M^2L^5T^{-2}]$

9. A DC battery of 2 V emf and internal resistance 1 Ω connected through the external load. Current of 1 A is flowing through the external load. If this type of battery are connected twice in series, then the value of current through same load is

(a) 1.33 A (b) 2.7 A (c) 0.67 A (d) 1.11 A

10. Consider a satellite in an orbit of radius r, match Column I (quantity) and Column II (proportionality).

	Column I		Column II
A.	Linear momentum	P.	r^{-1}
B.	Time period	Q.	$r^{1/2}$
C.	Angular momentum	R.	$r^{3/2}$
D.	Energy	S.	$r^{-1/2}$

Choose the correct answers from the options given below:

(a) A → S, B → P, C → R, D → Q
(b) A → S, B → R, C → P, D → Q
(c) A → S, B → R, C → Q, D → P
(d) A → R, B → S, C → P, D → Q

11. Two conducting spheres of radius R_1 and R_2 are connected by a thin wire. The separation between the spheres is very large compared to their dimensions. The capacitance of this system is

(a) $4\pi\varepsilon_0 R_1 R_2$ (b) $2\pi\varepsilon_0(R_1+R_2)$
(c) $4\pi\varepsilon_0(R_1+R_2)$ (d) None of these

12. Position of a particle is

$$x=t^3-6t^2+9t$$

Ratio of distance and displacement of body in first five seconds will be

(a) 1 (b) 2 (c) $\frac{3}{7}$ (d) $\frac{7}{5}$

13. A particle when hung from a spring streches it by 1 cm at earth's surface. Radius of earth is 6400 km. At a place 800 km above earth's surface, stretch of spring will be

(a) 1 cm (b) 8 cm (c) 0.1 cm (d) 0.79 cm

14. An EM wave of wavelength λ is incident on a photosensitive surface of negligible work function. If the photoelectrons emitted from the surface have the de-Broglie wavelength λ_0, then λ is equal to

(a) $\lambda_0\sqrt{\frac{2mc}{h}}$ (b) $\lambda_0^2\left(\frac{2mc}{h}\right)$ (c) $\sqrt{\lambda_0\frac{h}{2mc}}$ (d) $\lambda_0\left(\frac{2mc}{h}\right)^2$

15. A bead of mass m enters at end A of a U-shaped wire and leaves from B and friction is zero. Magnitude of force exerted by bead on wire is

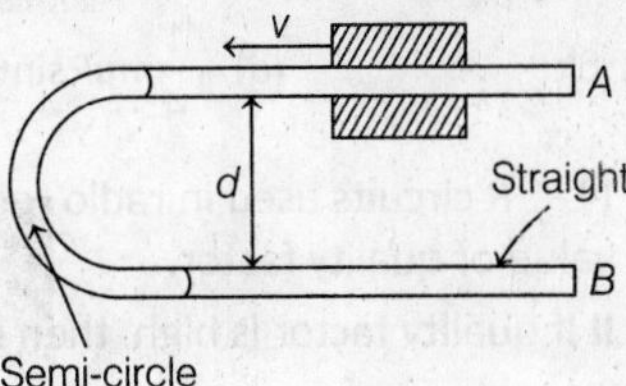

(a) Zero (b) $\frac{4mv^2}{\pi d}$
(c) $\frac{2mv^2}{\pi d}$ (d) Depends on mass of wire

16. Four moles of an ideal gas is taken through the process ABC as shown in the following figure. The total work done by the gas is

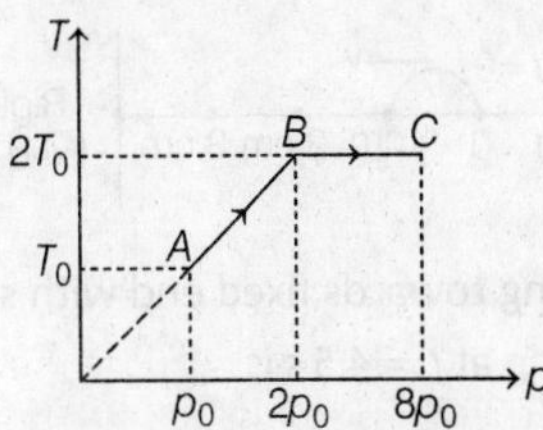

(a) $8RT_0\ln 2$ (b) $-8RT_0\ln 2$ (c) $16RT_0\ln 2$ (d) $-16RT_0\ln 2$

17. A particle of mass m is executing SHM according to the equation $y=4\sin\left(4t+\frac{\pi}{3}\right)$ cm, where t is in seconds and has time period T. The ratio of kinetic energy to total energy at $t=\frac{T}{4}$ is

(a) 1 : 4 (b) 3 : 4
(c) 1 : 2 (d) 3 : 8

18. Assertion (A) Potential of a dipole falls as $\frac{1}{r^2}$.

Reason (R) Electric potential at a point on equatorial line of electric dipole is zero.

In the light of the above statements, choose the most appropriate answer from the options given below:

(a) Both A and R are true but R is not the correct explanation of A.
(b) A is true but R is false.
(c) A is false but R is true.
(d) Both A and R are true and R is the correct explanation of A.

19. Trajectory of a particle of mass m projected with velocity u at an angle θ with ground, is shown below.

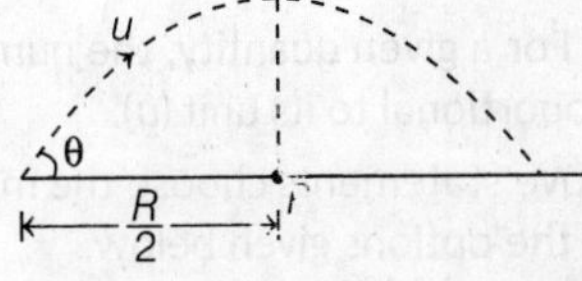

Angular momentum of particle about P, mid point of range R of particle is

(a) $\frac{1}{4}muR\cos\theta\hat{k}$ (b) $-\frac{1}{4}muR\cos\theta\hat{k}$

(c) $\frac{1}{4}muR\sin\theta\hat{k}$ (d) $-\frac{1}{4}muR\sin\theta\hat{k}$

20. Statement I *L-C-R* circuits used in radio receivers must have a low value of quality factor.

Statement II If quality factor is high, then resonance is much sharper.

In light of above statements choose the most appropriate answer from the options given below:

(a) Both Statement I and Statement II are incorrect.
(b) Statement I is correct and Statement II is incorrect.
(c) Statement I is incorrect and Statement II is correct.
(d) Both Statement I and Statement II are correct.

21. A wave pulse on a string at $t = 0$ is as shown.

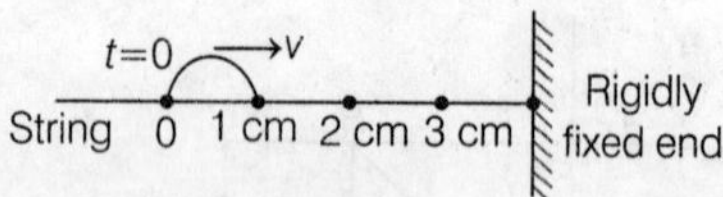

Pulse is moving towards fixed end with speed $v = 1$ cm/s. Wave on string at $t = 4.5$ s is

(a) 

(b)

(c)

(d)

22. An ideal gas $\left(\frac{C_p}{C_V} = \gamma\right)$ undergoes following cyclic process.

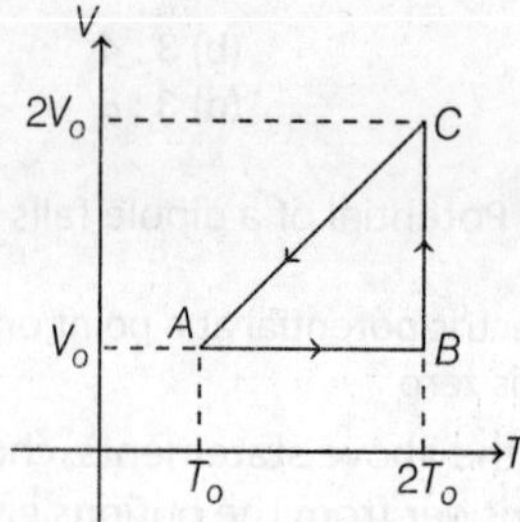

Cycle efficiency is

(a) $\frac{2\ln 2 - 1}{\left[\frac{\gamma}{(\gamma-1)}\right]}$ (b) $\frac{1 - 2\ln 2}{\left[\frac{\gamma}{(\gamma-1)}\right]}$ (c) $\frac{2\ln 2 + 1}{\left[\frac{\gamma}{(\gamma-1)}\right]}$ (d) $\frac{2\ln 2 - 1}{\left[\frac{\gamma}{(\gamma+1)}\right]}$

23. Consider the following two statements.

Statement I Sum of 12.0 + 0.038 will not have three significant figures.

Statement II For a given quantity, the numerical value (n) is directly proportional to its unit (u).

In light of above statements choose the most appropriate answer from the options given below:

(a) Both Statement I and Statement II are incorrect.
(b) Statement I is correct and Statement II is incorrect.
(c) Statement I is incorrect and Statement II is correct.
(d) Both Statement I and Statement II are correct.

24. Plates of an isolated charged capacitor are pulled apart to make separation double. Energy density of field becomes

(a) double (b) half
(c) same (d) four times

25. In YDSE, ratio of intensity at centre of bright fringe to the intensity at a point (1/4) th of distance between two fringes from the centre is

(a) 2 (b) $\frac{1}{2}$
(c) 4 (d) 16

26. The circuit diagram of a potentiometer experiment has been shown in the figure below. A cell of emf ε_2 is connected in secondary circuit to measure its emf. When the galvanometer shows no deflection, the length of potentiometer wire from point P is l.

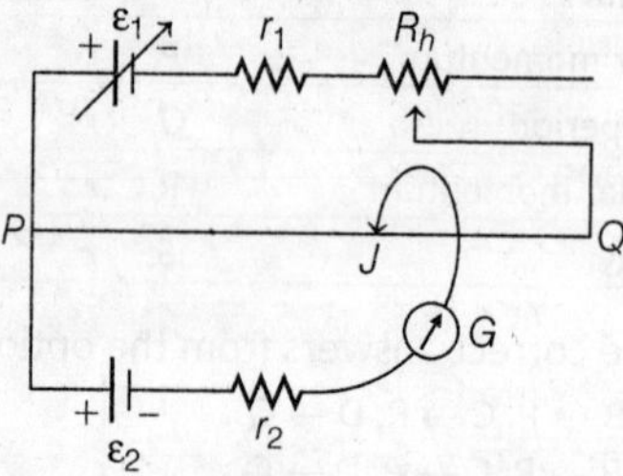

If the value of cell of emf ε_1 is increased, then

(a) potential gradient will remain unchanged
(b) balancing length will increase
(c) balancing length will decrease
(d) balancing length will not change

27. If kinetic energy, potential energy, vibrational energy and total energy of a gas are denoted by E_K, E_P, E_V and E_T respectively, then which of these energy(s) is zero at 0 K temperature?

(a) E_K only (b) E_K and E_V
(c) E_K, E_V, E_T (d) All

28. An EM wave propagates in a medium whose electric field vector is given as $E = 150\sin(18\times10^8 t - 8x)$ V/m. The medium may be

(a) air
(b) water
(c) glass
(d) diamond

29. While examing the magnetic properties of substances, it is found that a hydrogen atom is paramagnetic. The hydrogen molecule is

(a) diamagnetic
(b) paramagnetic
(c) ferromagnetic
(d) may be anything depends upon temperature

30. When a 20 Ω resistor is connected in parallel with a moving coil galvanometer, then its deflection reduces from 75 divisions to 25 divisions, then the resistance of galvanometer is

(a) 10 Ω (b) 20 Ω (c) 40 Ω (d) 60 Ω

31. A conducting triangular frame made of thin wire is kept in XY-plane as shown in the following figure. If a space magnetic field is applied as $\mathbf{B} = 4x^2\hat{\mathbf{i}}$ T, where x is in metre, then emf induced in the loop, is

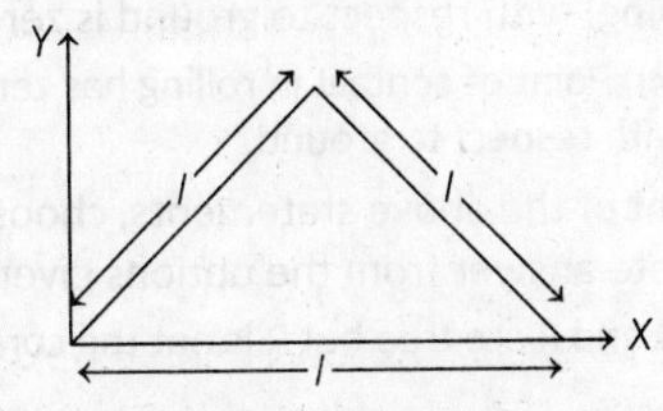

(a) $\sqrt{3}l^2$ (b) $\frac{\sqrt{3}}{2}l^2$ (c) $\frac{1}{2}l^2$ (d) zero

32. A cell of 6 V is connected across a resistance wire of 6Ω. Number of electrons per unit volume of resistance wire are 10^{29} m^{-3}, length of wire is 10 cm and area of cross-section is 1 mm^2.

Time taken to lost energy by the electrons is

(a) 10^{-9}s (b) 10^{-10} s (c) 10^{-15} s (d) 10^{-17} s

33. The electric potential V is given as a function of distance as $V = (10x^2 + 5x + 2)$ V, where x is in metre. The difference of electrostatic potential energy of a charge $+2\,\mu$C at $x = 1$ m and $x = 2$ m is

(a) 7μJ (b) 3.5 μJ (c) 70 μJ (d) 35 μJ

34. To decrease cut off wavelength of continuous X-rays by 25%, potential difference of a coolidge tube must be

(a) increased by 34% (b) decreased by 34%
(c) increased by 25% (d) decreased by 25%

35. In an experiment, photoelectric cut-off voltage is 1.5 V. Maximum KE of emitted electrons is

(a) 1.6×10^{-19} J (b) 1.5×10^{-19} J
(c) 2.4×10^{-19} J (d) zero

Section II

36. Which among the following graphs shows the correct variation of photoelectric current with intensity of light for a given frequency?

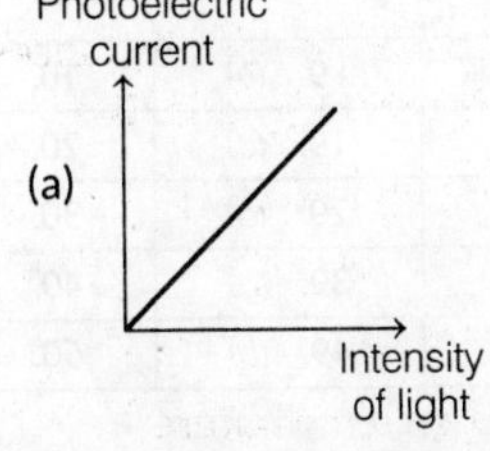

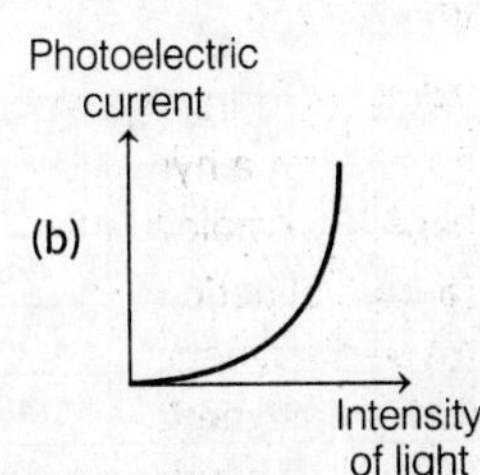

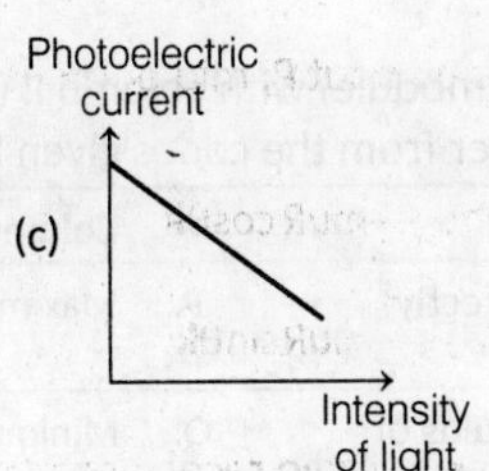

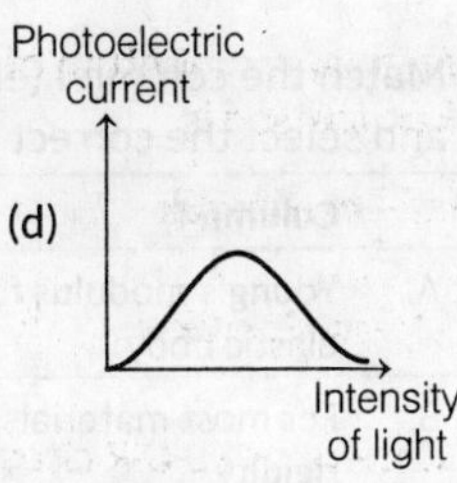

37. In an LED, electrons moves from

(a) lower levels to higher in conduction band
(b) lower levels to higher in valance band
(c) conduction to valance band
(d) valance to conduction band

38. Samples of two radioactive nuclides A and B are taken. λ_A and λ_B are the disintegration constants of sample A and B, respectively. In which of the following cases, the two samples can simultaneously have the same decay rate at any time?

(a) Initial rate of decay of A is twice the initial rate of decay of B and $\lambda_A = \lambda_B$
(b) Initial rate of decay of A is twice the initial rate of decay of B and $\lambda_A > \lambda_B$
(c) Initial rate of decay of B is twice the initial rate of decay of A and $\lambda_A > \lambda_B$
(d) $\frac{\lambda_A}{\lambda_B} = \frac{N_B}{N_A}$

39. The kinetic energy of a particle moving in a straight line is varying with time as $K = 20t^2$. The force acting on the particle is

(a) constant (b) increasing
(c) decreasing
(d) first increases and then decreases

40. Two balls of equal masses m_1 and m_2 are placed in smooth X-Y plane along the Y-axis. Ball of mass m_1 is given velocity and it moves towards another ball and collides elastically. The situation of collision has been shown in figure below in which both balls move at angle θ_1 and θ_2 respectively from Y-axis. The correct relation is

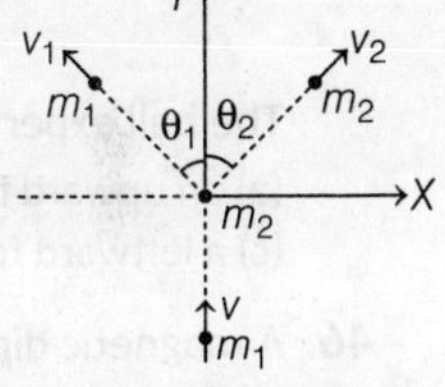

(a) $\theta_1 + \theta_2 = 90°$ (b) $|\theta_1 - \theta_2| = 90°$
(c) $\frac{\theta_1 + \theta_2}{2} = 90°$ (d) $\theta_1 = \theta_2$

41. If $\mathbf{E}_1$ and $\mathbf{E}_2$ be respective electric fields at equipotential position and axial position of electric dipole at same distance, then

(a) $\mathbf{E}_1 \cdot \mathbf{E}_2 = 0$ (b) $|\mathbf{E}_1 + \mathbf{E}_2| = 0$
(c) $|\mathbf{E}_1 \times \mathbf{E}_2| = 0$ (d) $|\mathbf{E}_1 - \mathbf{E}_2| = 0$

42. A metallic rod of length l is tied to an string of length $2l$ and is rotated with constant angular speed ω in region of a perpendicular magnetic field of strength B. Induced emf in rod is

(a) $\frac{7}{2}Bl^2\omega$ (b) $\frac{5}{3}Bl^2\omega$ (c) $\frac{5}{2}Bl^2\omega$ (d) $\frac{3}{5}Bl^2\omega$

43. Match the column I (elastic module) with column II (value) and select the correct answer from the codes given below.

	Column I		Column II
A.	Young's modulus for perfectly elastic body	P.	Maximum
B.	For most materials, modulus of rigidity	Q.	Minimum
C.	Bulk modulus for solid	R.	Y/3
D.	Bulk modulus for gas	S.	Infinite

(a) A → S, B → P, C → R, D → Q
(b) A → S, B → R, C → P, D → Q
(c) A → P, B → Q, C → S, D → R
(d) A → R, B → S, C → P, D → Q

44. Two particles *A* and *B* are on same horizontal line in a gravity free space. Distance between particles at $t = 0$ is 2m. Now *A* is launched at an angle of 60° with horizontal with a speed of 10 m/s and *B* is launched at an angle of 30° with a velocity *v*. If horizontal distance between particles is always 2m, find angular speed of *B* with respect to *A*.

(a) $10\sqrt{3}$ rad s^{-1} (b) $\frac{10}{\sqrt{3}}$ rad s^{-1}
(c) $5\sqrt{3}$ rad s^{-1} (d) $\frac{5}{\sqrt{3}}$ rad s^{-1}

45. A ball is moving in a straight line through a fluid which is spinning around its own centre of mass as shown below.

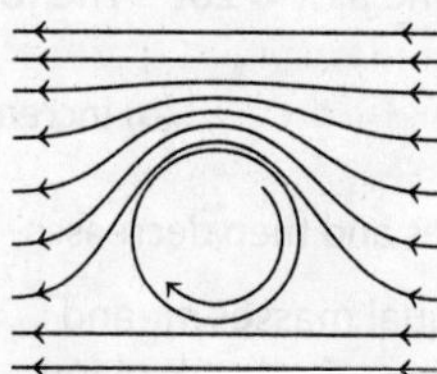

The ball experiences
(a) an upward force (b) a downward force
(c) a leftward force (d) a rightward force

46. A magnetic dipole of moment *M* is placed in external uniform magnetic field *B*. If magnetic dipole is rotated from field direction to a position θ very slowly, then work done by external source is

(a) $2MB\sin\theta$ (b) $2MB\sin\frac{\theta}{2}$
(c) $MB\cos^2\frac{\theta}{2}$ (d) $2MB\sin^2\frac{\theta}{2}$

47. Which among the following statement(s) is/are correct?
I. Energy released per fusion is much greater than energy released per fission.
II. For pair production, minimum, energy of photon should be 0.51 MeV.
III. In pair annihilation, the energy released is in form of one gamma photon.

(a) Only I (b) Only II (c) I, III (d) I, II, III

48. Assertion (A) Acceleration of lowest point of a rolling disc (pure rolling) with respect to ground is zero.
Reason (R) Point of contact in rolling has zero relative velocity with respect to ground.
In the light of the above statements, choose the most appropriate answer from the options given below:
(a) Both A and R are true but R is not the correct explanation of A.
(b) A is true but R is false.
(c) A is false but R is true.
(d) Both A and R are true and R is the correct explanation of A.

49. Magnetic field of an electromagnetic wave,
$B = 8 \times 10^{-6} \cdot \sin(5000\,\pi x - 3 \times 10^{11}\pi t)$ T.
Electric field of wave is
(a) $8 \times 10^{-6}\sin(5000\,\pi x - 3 \times 10^{11}\pi t)$
(b) $480\sin(5000\,\pi x - 3 \times 10^{11}\pi t)$
(c) $480\sin(5000\pi y - 3 \times 10^{11}\pi t)$
(d) $8 \times 10^{-6}\sin(5000\,\pi z - 3 \times 10^{11}\pi t)$

50. An object *O* and Mirror *M* are moving with the velocities shown in the figure. The velocity of the image of the object in the mirror is

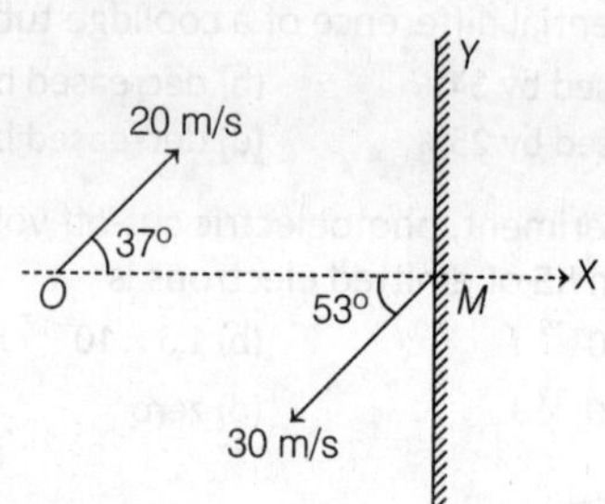

(a) $(-34\hat{i} + 12\hat{j})$ m/s (b) $(-34\hat{i} + 16\hat{j})$ m/s
(c) $(-52\hat{i} + 12\hat{j})$ m/s (d) $(52\hat{i} + 12\hat{j})$ m/s

Answers

1. (a)	2. (a)	3. (a)	4. (c)	5. (d)	6. (a)	7. (d)	8. (c)	9. (a)	10. (c)
11. (c)	12. (d)	13. (d)	14. (b)	15. (b)	16. (d)	17. (a)	18. (a)	19. (d)	20. (c)
21. (d)	22. (a)	23. (a)	24. (c)	25. (a)	26. (b)	27. (a)	28. (b)	29. (a)	30. (c)
31. (d)	32. (d)	33. (c)	34. (a)	35. (c)	36. (a)	37. (c)	38. (d)	39. (a)	40. (a)
41. (c)	42. (c)	43. (b)	44. (d)	45. (a)	46. (d)	47. (a)	48. (b)	49. (b)	50. (c)

See detailed explanations on page no. 278

Knockout 09

NEET

PHYSICS

Instructions See Knockout 01

Section I

1. Conservation of mechanical energy holds true when on system
(a) only conservative forces act
(b) only non-conservative forces act
(c) total work done of non-conservative force is zero
(d) total work done of both conservative and non-conservative forces is zero

2. A certain gas obeys the equation of state, $U = \dfrac{as^7}{V^4N^4}$. Here, U represents the internal energy of gas, s the entropy, V the volume and N the fixed number of particles of the gas, then unit of a is
(a) $J^6m^{12}K^7$
(b) $kg^{-6}s^{12}K^7$
(c) $kg^6m^{12}K^7$
(d) $kg^5m^{-12}s^{-2}K^{-6}$

3. Select the correct option about harmonic progressive wave.
(a) All particles have same phase at given instant of time.
(b) All particles have different amplitudes.
(c) All particles have different phase at a given instant of time.
(d) All particles have same momentum at a given instant of time.

4. Colour code for a resistance of 470 Ω with an uncertainty of 10% will be
(Y : Yellow, V = Violet, B = Blue, G = Gold, S = Silver)
(a) YVBG (b) VBYG (c) VBYS (d) YVBS

5. A particle is projected with some initial velocity at an angle θ with the horizontal from the ground. If the particle remains in air for 4 s, then its maximum possible horizontal range is (Take, $g = 10\ m/s^2$)
(a) 40 m (b) 60 m
(c) 80 m (d) 100 m

6. **Statement I** Newton's laws are not valid in non-inertial frame of reference.
Statement II A non-inertial frame has a non-zero velocity.
In light of above statements choose the most appropriate answer from the options given below:
(a) Both Statement I and Statement II are incorrect.
(b) Statement I is correct and Statement II is incorrect.
(c) Statement I is incorrect and Statement II is correct.
(d) Both Statement I and Statement II are correct.

7. A body starts from rest with uniform acceleration. The velocity of the body after t_0 s is v_0. The displacement of the body in last three seconds is
(a) $\dfrac{3v_0}{2}(t_0 - 3)$ (b) $\dfrac{3v_0}{2}(t_0 + 3)$
(c) $3v_0\left(1 - \dfrac{3}{2t_0}\right)$ (d) $3v_0\left(1 + \dfrac{3}{2t_0}\right)$

8. In a potentiometer arrangement, a cell of emf 2.25 V gives a balance point at 45 cm length of the wire. If the cell is replaced by another cell and the balance point shifts to 99 cm, then the emf of the second cell is
(a) 4.25 V (b) 4.34 V (c) 4.55 V (d) 4.95 V

9. In the circuit shown below, the rms value of current is 5 A. The power factor of circuit lies between

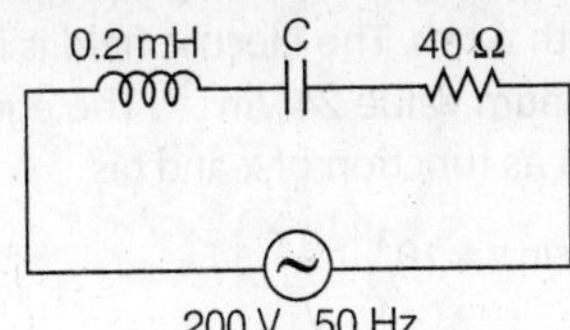

(a) 0 to $\dfrac{1}{\sqrt{2}}$
(b) $\dfrac{1}{\sqrt{2}}$ to 1
(c) unity
(d) depends on the value of C

10. A body is released from a point distance r from the centre of Earth. If R is the radius of the Earth and $r > R$, then the velocity of the body at the time of striking the Earth will be

(a) $\sqrt{2gr}$ (b) $\sqrt{2gR}$ (c) $\sqrt{\frac{2gRr}{r-R}}$ (d) $\sqrt{\frac{2gR(r-R)}{r}}$

11. Three identical metal rods A, B and C are placed end to end and a temperature difference is maintained between their ends. If the thermal conductivity of $B\,(K_B)$ is twice that of $C(K_C)$ and half that of $A(K_A)$, then the effective thermal conductivity of the arrangement is

(a) $\frac{K_A}{7}$ (b) $\frac{6}{7}K_B$ (c) $\frac{7}{3}K_B$ (d) $7K_C$

12. A carnot heat engine with efficiency of 1/10 is used as a refrigerator. If the work done on the system is 20 J, the amount of energy absorbed from the reservoir at lower temperature is

(a) 200 J (b) 180 J
(c) 198 J (d) 2 J

13. A square loop of side 15 cm carrying a steady current of 2 A is placed with its one side parallel to a long straight conductor carrying a current of 5 A as shown in the following figure. The correct statement related to net force experienced by the loop due to wire is

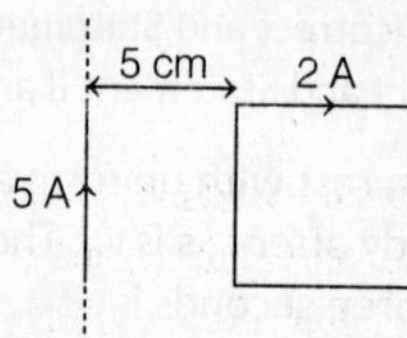

(a) repulsive in nature having magnitude equal to 37.5×10^{-7} N
(b) repulsive in nature having magnitude equal to 5×10^{-7} N
(c) attractive in nature having magnitude equal to 5×10^{-7} N
(d) attractive in nature having magnitude equal to 7.0×10^{-7} N

14. A transformer with efficiency of 90% works at 10 kW and 2000 V. If the secondary voltage is 100 V, then the primary and secondary currents are, respectively

(a) 5 A, 90 A (b) 4.5 A, 100 A
(c) 5 A, 50 A (d) 10 A, 45 A

15. A plane electron magnetic wave propagating in z-direction has wavelength 6 μm. The electric field is in x-direction and has maximum value 24 Vm^{-1}. The equation for the magnetic field as function of x and t is

(a) $2.33 \times 10^{-8} \sin \pi \times 10^{3}\left(t - \frac{x}{c}\right)$ T

(b) $8 \times 10^{-8} \sin \pi \times 10^{14}\left(t - \frac{x}{c}\right)$ T

(c) $8 \times 10^{-8} \sin \pi \times 10^{3}\left(1 - \frac{x}{c}\right)$ T

(d) $2.33 \times 10^{-8} \sin \pi \times 10^{14}\left(t - \frac{x}{c}\right)$ T

16. A ray of light is incident normally on the prism ($\mu = \frac{3}{2}$) immersed in a liquid of unknown refractive index as shown in the following figure. The largest value for the angle θ, so that ray is totally reflected at the face AC is 37°. The value of μ is

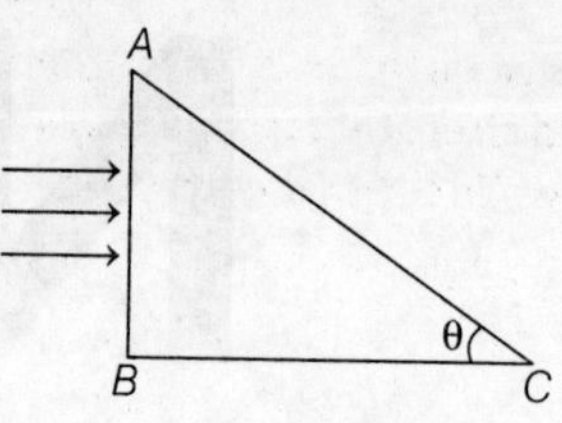

(a) 1.2 (b) 1.3
(c) 1.33 (d) None of these

17. The de-Broglie wavelength of a particle moving with a velocity 2.5×10^{8} ms^{-1} is equal to the wavelength of a photon. The ratio of kinetic energy of the particle to the energy of the photon is (velocity of light is 3×10^{8} m/s)

(a) 3 : 4 (b) 5 : 12 (c) 5 : 6 (d) 3 : 8

18. When a charged particle enters perpendicularly in a uniform magnetic field, then which of following quantities do not vary or change?

I. Kinetic energy
II. Momentum
III. Velocity

(a) Only II (b) Only I (c) I, III (d) I, II and III

19. Assertion (A) A magnetron can produce electromagnetic waves which are able to melt metals.

Reason (R) Metal containers are not used in microwave ovens because of danger of getting a shock from accumulated charges.

In the light of the above statements, choose the most appropriate answer from the options given below:

(a) Both A and R are true but R is not the correct explanation of A.
(b) A is true but R is false.
(c) A is false but R is true.
(d) Both A and R are true and R is the correct explanation of A.

20. Eight capacitors of capacitance C_1 are connected in series with a battery of 4 V, are charged. Now, five capacitors of capacitance C_2 are connected in parallel with a battery of 1 V. If the energy stored in both types of arrangement is same, then

(a) $C_1 = 20C_2$ (b) $C_2 = 10C_1$ (c) $5C_1 = 4C_2$ (d) $2C_1 = 5C_2$

21. A block of mass m is given an initial velocity v over a rough surface, then time taken by block to stop is

(a) directly proportional to mass of block
(b) inversely proportional to mass of block
(c) inversely proportional to square of mass
(d) independent of mass of block

22. Which of these increases with number of significant digits in a measured value?

(a) Accuracy
(b) Precision
(c) Order of magnitude
(d) Both (a) and (c)

23. The graph between intensity of magnetisation I and magnetic field strength H is for an unknown substance is found as shown in the figure, then the substance is

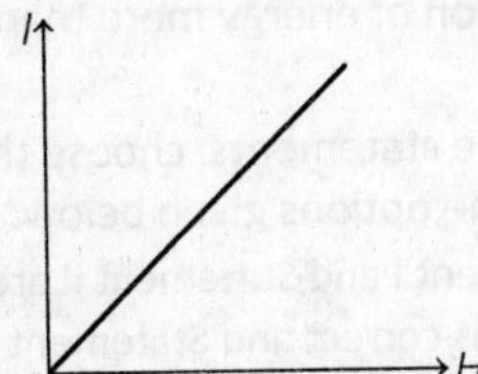

(a) diamagnetic (b) paramagnetic
(c) ferromagnetic (d) Both (a) and (b)

24. A conducting coil of resistance 120 Ω, 300 turns and area of 4×10^{-2} m^2 lies with its plane normal to a uniform magnetic field of 0.3 T. If coil is rotated from perpendicular position to parallel position to magnetic field in 0.5 s, then average power produced is

(a) 216 mW (b) 432 mW
(c) 324 mW (d) 894 mW

25. A cable that can support a maximum load of 320 kg is cut into two equal parts. The maximum load that can be supported by either part is

(a) 80 kg (b) 160 kg
(c) 320 kg (d) 640 kg

26. The de-Broglie wavelength of electron in first excited state of He^+ ion is

(a) 0.53 Å (b) 1.06 Å
(c) 2.12 Å (d) 3.33 Å

27. Resolution limit of our eye is around 1 min. Two persons at a distance of 3 m from each other can be distinguished from a maximum distance of

(a) 10 km
(b) 15 km
(c) 20 km
(d) 30 km

28. Consider hydrogen (H), deuterium (D), singly ionised helium atom (He^+) and doubly ionized lithium (Li^{++}).

In $n = 2$ to $n = 1$ transition let wavelengths emitted are $\lambda_1, \lambda_2, \lambda_3$ and λ_4 respectively, then correct relation is

(a) $\lambda_1 = \lambda_2 = 4\lambda_3 = 9\lambda_4$
(b) $4\lambda_1 = 2\lambda_2 = 2\lambda_3 = \lambda_4$
(c) $\lambda_1 = 2\lambda_2 = 2\sqrt{2}\lambda_3 = 3\sqrt{2}\lambda_4$
(d) $\lambda_1 = \lambda_2 = 2\lambda_3 = 3\lambda_4$

29. Match the Column I (graph) with Column II (relation) and select the correct answer from the codes given below.

Column I	Column II
A. 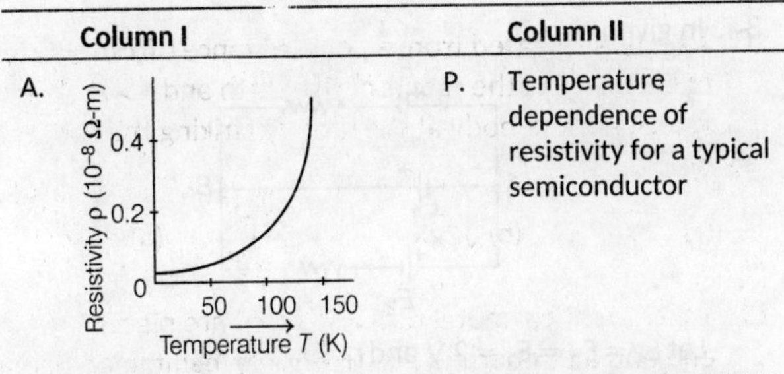	P. Temperature dependence of resistivity for a typical semiconductor
B. 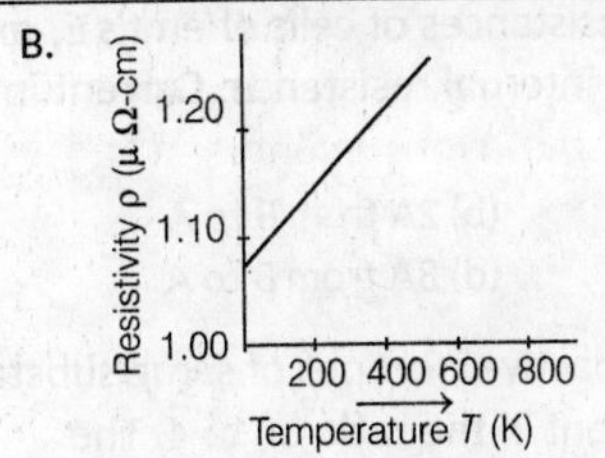	Q. Resistivity ρ of copper as a function of temperature T
C. 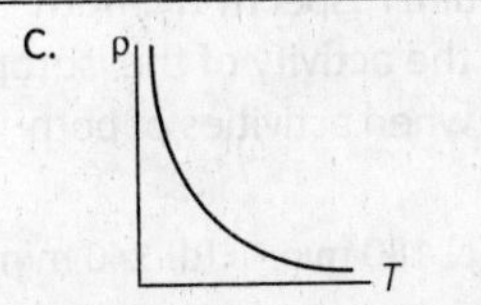	R. Resistivity ρ of nichrome as a function of absolute temperature T.

Choose the correct answers from the options given below:

(a) A → R, B → Q, C → P
(b) A → Q, B → P, C → R
(c) A → Q, B → R, C → P
(d) A → R, B → P, C → Q

30. A particle of mass 4 kg starts its motion from rest with a constant acceleration 1 m/s^2. In the system, there is another particle of same mass which is moving with a constant velocity of 2 m/s. Which among the following is not possible value of the speed of centre of mass after 2 s?

(a) 0.5 m/s (b) 1 m/s (c) 2 m/s (d) 4 m/s

31. The time period of particle executing SHM is doubled by keeping maximum velocity constant, then

(a) amplitude becomes half
(b) maximum acceleration becomes double
(c) total energy becomes four times
(d) total energy becomes double

32. A planet moves around sun. Its closest distance from sun is d_1 and at this point speed is v_1. At farthest point from sun, its distance is d_2, speed of planet at farthest point will be

(a) $\frac{d_1^2 v_1}{d_2^2}$ (b) $\frac{d_2 v_1}{d_1}$
(c) $\frac{d_1 v_1}{d_2}$ (d) $\frac{d_2^2 v_1}{d_1}$

33. A dipole is placed parallel to an electric field. Let W is work done in rotating the dipole by 60°.
Then, work done in rotating dipole by 180° will be

(a) $2W$ (b) $3W$
(c) $4W$ (d) $0.5W$

34. In given circuit,

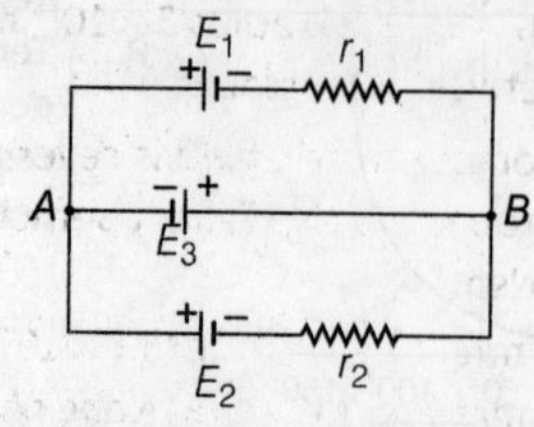

Let $E_1 = E_2 = E_3 = 2$ V and $r_1 = r_2 = 4\ \Omega$.
r_1 and r_2 are internal resistances of cells of emf's E_1 and E_2. Cell of emf E_3 has zero internal resistance. Current in branch AB is

(a) Zero (b) 2A from B to A
(c) 2A from A to B (d) 3A from B to A

35. The nuclei of two radioactive isotopes of same substance X^{234} and X^{236} are present in the ratio of 1 : 4. The half-lives are 60 min and 30 min, respectively. Both isotopes decay α-particles. If the activity of the isotope X^{236} is 4×10^6 dps. The time, when activities of both isotopes becomes same is

(a) 60 min (b) 120 min (c) 180 min (d) 240 min

Section II

36. A metallic rod has mass m, length l and cross-sectional area A. If a block of mass M is suspended at the lower end of rod suspended vertically. The stress in rod at $\frac{L}{3}$ distance form its lower end is

(a) $\frac{Mg}{A}$ (b) $\frac{\left(M+\frac{m}{3}\right)g}{A}$

(c) $\frac{\left(M+\frac{gm}{3}\right)g}{A}$ (d) $\frac{(M+m)g}{A}$

37. In the circuit shown below, diode has potential barrier of 0.5 V across it. A current greater than 10 mA produces large amount of heat and damages diode. If diode is to be operated at 5 mA, the required series resistance R is (the internal resistance of battery)

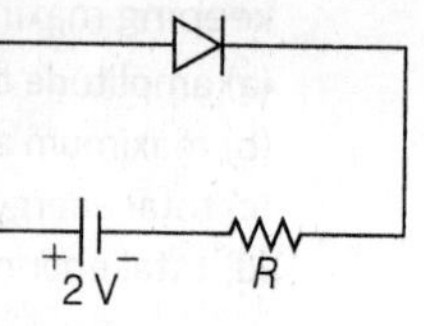

(a) 300 Ω (b) 300 kΩ (c) 200 kΩ (d) 3 kΩ

38. Output Y from input $A = 0$ and $B = 1$ is

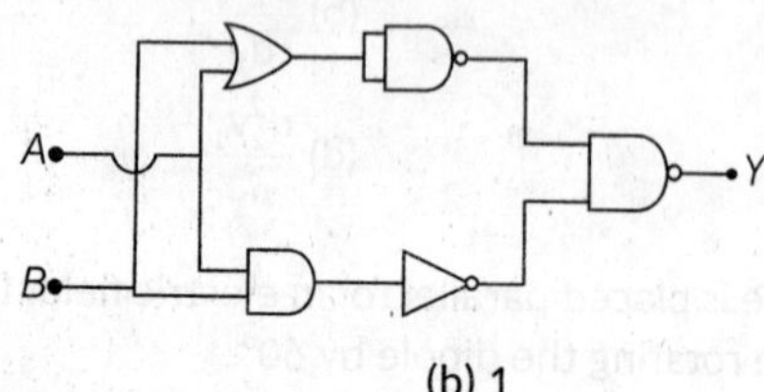

(a) 0 (b) 1
(c) fluctuates between 0 and 1
(d) gate does not work

39. A gas is heated at constant pressure. Fraction of heat that can be used to do external work is $\left(\gamma = \frac{C_p}{C_V}\right)$

(a) $\frac{1}{\gamma}$ (b) $1 - \frac{1}{\gamma}$ (c) $1 - \frac{1}{\gamma^2}$ (d) $\gamma - 1$

40. Statement I A photon of energy 10.21 eV is not absorbed by a H_2 electron.

Statement II An electron of H_2 atom in ground state must absorbs a photon of energy more than or equals to 10.2 eV.

In light of above statements, choose the most appropriate answer from the options given below:

(a) Both Statement I and Statement II are incorrect.
(b) Statement I is correct and Statement II is incorrect.
(c) Statement I is incorrect and Statement II is correct.
(d) Both Statement I and Statement II are correct.

41. Match the column and choose correct options from codes given below.

	Column I		Column II
A.	Mobility	P.	mVA^{-1}
B.	Resistivity	Q.	$m^2V^{-1}s^{-1}$
C.	Conductance	R.	$J^{-1}A^2s$
D.	Current density	S.	$m^{-2}A$

(a) $A \to Q$, $B \to P$, $C \to R$, $D \to S$
(b) $A \to P$, $B \to Q$, $C \to R$, $D \to S$
(c) $A \to Q$, $B \to P$, $C \to S$, $D \to R$
(d) $A \to Q$, $B \to R$, $C \to S$, $D \to P$

42. Which of the following phenomenon cannot explained by Huygens' principle of secondary wavelets?

(a) Diffraction (b) Polarisation
(c) Reflection (d) Refraction

43. A particle is moving on circular path of radius 2 m with uniform speed 10 m/s. At $t = 0$ s, the particle is at point P as shown in the following figure. The direction of acceleration vector at $t = \frac{3\pi}{10}$ s is

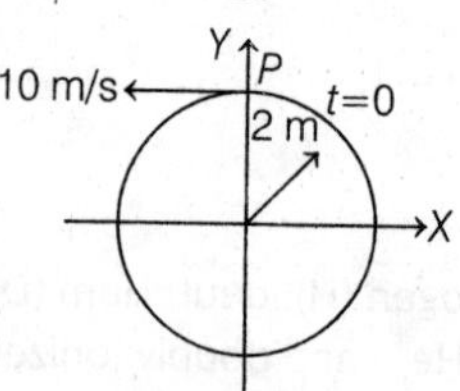

(a) along $\hat{i}$ (b) along $(-\hat{i})$ (c) along $\hat{j}$ (d) along $\left(\frac{\hat{i}-\hat{j}}{\sqrt{2}}\right)$

44. A hollow sphere of mass 3 kg and radius 50 cm rolls down without slipping on inclined plane of height 20 m. When it reaches at the bottom, its rotational kinetic energy is $(g = 10\ m/s^2)$

(a) 600 J (b) 240 J (c) 360 J (d) 171.4 J

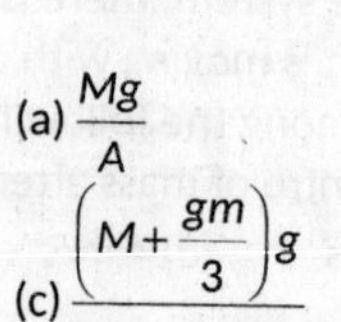

45. A galvanometer of resistance 1.8 Ω is converted into an ammeter of range 0 to 1 A. Full scale deflection current is 0.1 A. Resistance needed for the purpose is

(a) 0.2 Ω in series (b) 0.2 Ω in parallel
(c) 0.5 Ω in series (d) 0.5 Ω in parallel

46. A telescope has an objective lens of focal length 100 cm and an eye piece with focal length 2 cm. If this telescope is used to see a 50 m tall building at a distance of 1 km, the height of the image of the building formed by the objective lens is

(a) 1 cm (b) 2 cm (c) 5 cm (d) 10 cm

47. Assertion (A) The average time of collisions τ decreases with increasing temperature.

Reason (R) At increased temperature, average speed of the electrons, which act as the carriers of current increases, resulting in more frequent collisions.

In the light of the above statements, choose the most appropriate answer from the options given below:

(a) Both A and R are true but R is not the correct explanation of A.
(b) A is true but R is false.
(c) A is false but R is true.
(d) Both A and R are true and R is the correct explanation of A.

48. Two oppositely charged horizontal parallel plates are kept at a distance of 1.5 cm and electric field between them is 10^5 Vm^{-1} in vertically downward direction. An oil drop of mass 4.9×10^{-15} kg and radius 5×10^{-5} m is placed stationary between the plates.

If the direction of electric field is reversed, then terminal velocity of drop is nearly (Take, coefficient of viscosity $= 1.8 \times 10^{-5}$ Nsm^{-2})

(a) 3.7×10^{-6} m/s (b) 5.7×10^{-6} m/s
(c) 4.7×10^{-5} m/s (d) None of these

49. A wire A carrying current $3I$ and other wire B carrying $5I$ in same direction produce a magnetic field B at the mid-point as shown in the following figure. When current flowing through wire B is made zero, then magnetic field at same point is

A B
$3I\uparrow$ • $\uparrow 5I$

(a) $\frac{3}{5}B$ (b) $\frac{3}{8}B$ (c) $\frac{2}{3}B$ (d) $\frac{3}{2}B$

50. A photon of wavelength 4400 Å is passing through vacuum. The effective mass and momentum of the photon are respectively

(a) 5×10^{-36} kg , 1.5×10^{-27} kg-m/s
(b) 5×10^{-35} kg, 1.5×10^{-26} kg-m/s
(c) Zero, 1.5×10^{-26} kg-m/s
(d) 5×10^{-36} kg, 1.67×10^{-43} kg-m/s

Answers

1. (c)	2. (b)	3. (c)	4. (d)	5. (c)	6. (b)	7. (c)	8. (d)	9. (c)	10. (d)
11. (b)	12. (b)	13. (c)	14. (a)	15. (b)	16. (a)	17. (b)	18. (b)	19. (a)	20. (d)
21. (d)	22. (b)	23. (b)	24. (b)	25. (c)	26. (d)	27. (a)	28. (a)	29. (c)	30. (d)
31. (b)	32. (c)	33. (c)	34. (c)	35. (c)	36. (b)	37. (a)	38. (b)	39. (b)	40. (d)
41. (a)	42. (b)	43. (b)	44. (b)	45. (b)	46. (c)	47. (d)	48. (b)	49. (b)	50. (a)

See detailed explanations on page no. 282

Knockout 10

NEET

PHYSICS

Instructions See Knockout 01

Section I

1. Force between two atoms of a gas is given by

$$F = \alpha\beta \cdot \exp\left(\frac{-x^2}{\alpha k_B T}\right)$$

where, x = distance between atoms,
k_B = Boltzmann's constant,
T = absolute temperature of gas sample
and α, β = gas constants.
Dimensions of constant β are

(a) $[MLT^{-2}]$
(b) $[M^0L^2T^{-4}]$
(c) $[M^2LT^{-4}]$
(d) $[M^2L^2T^{-2}]$

2. Let A and B are two quantities and let $[A] = [M^{\alpha}L^{\beta}T^{\gamma}]$ and $[B] = [M^{\beta}L^{\gamma}T^{\alpha}]$

Then, which of these functions have a finite value?

(a) $A \times B$
(b) $A + B$
(c) $A - B$
(d) All of these

3. Which of the following is a wrong description about the binding energy of a stable nucleus?

(a) It is the energy required to break a nucleus into its constituent nucleons.
(b) It is the energy released, when free nucleons combine to form a nucleus.
(c) It is the sum of rest mass energies of its nucleons minus the rest mass energy of the nucleus.
(d) It is the sum of kinetic energy of all the nucleons in the nucleus.

4. If C_p and C_V represent the specific heats of a gas at constant pressure and volume respectively, then which among the following relation is incorrect for ratio $\frac{C_p}{C_V}$?

(R is gas constant).

(a) $1+\frac{R}{C_V}$
(b) $\frac{1}{1-\frac{R}{C_p}}$
(c) $\frac{C_p - R}{C_V + R}$
(d) $\frac{C_p}{C_p - R}$

5. Match Column I (device) with Column II (process on which function of device is based).

	Column I		Column II
A.	Bimetallic strip	P.	Radiation
B.	Steam engine	Q.	Energy conversion
C.	Incandescent lamp	R.	Melting
D.	Electric fuse	S.	Thermal expansion

(a) A → S, B → Q, C → P, D → R
(b) A → R, B → Q, C → S, D → P
(c) A → P, B → Q, C → R, D → S
(d) A → S, B → Q, C → P, D → R

6. An ideal gas undergoes a process such that pT^2 = a constant, coefficient of volume expansion of gas is

(a) $\frac{1}{T}$
(b) $\frac{2}{T}$
(c) $\frac{3}{T}$
(d) $\frac{4}{T}$

7. To eliminate end error in a meter bridge experiment,

(a) resistance box must be connected in left gap
(b) resistance box must be connected in right gap
(c) resistance box must be connected first in left and then in right gap
(d) ends of connecting rises are connected properly

8. On increasing the temperature, the elasticity of the material in general

(a) increases
(b) decreases
(c) remains same
(d) may increase or decrease depends on the nature of material

9. When a planet revolves around the sun in elliptical orbits, then which among the following quantities does not remain constant?

(a) Angular momentum (b) Binding energy
(c) Total energy (d) Angular speed

10. The maximum number of possible interference maxima for slit separation equal to thrice the wavelength in YDSE is

(a) 3 (b) 4 (c) 7 (d) 8

11. A particle is attached to one end of a string whose other end is fixed at point O in the vertical plane. The particle is released from rest, when the string is horizontal. Then, the angle made by the string with the vertical, when the net acceleration of particle is horizontal is

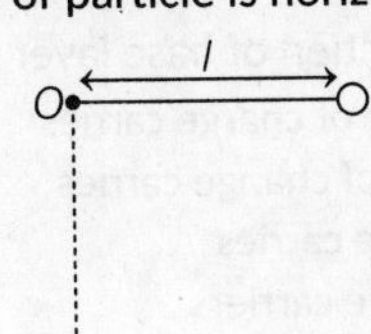

(a) $\tan^{-1}(2)$ (b) $\tan^{-1}(\sqrt{2})$
(c) $\tan^{-1}\left(\frac{1}{2}\right)$ (d) $\tan^{-1}\left(\frac{1}{\sqrt{2}}\right)$

12. A frog can jump maximum horizontal distance of 30 cm. If it spends negligible time on ground, then the horizontal distance covered by it in 10 s is

(a) 3.06 m (b) 6.12 m (c) 12.24 m (d) 18.37 m

13. Six 1.1 V cells with internal resistance 3 Ω each are connected in three parallel branches of two cell each. If the resistance of external circuit is 2 Ω, then power consumed by external circuit is

(a) 0.66 W (b) 0.88 W
(c) 0.605 W (d) 0.871 W

14. A square loop *PQRS* is placed in *XY*- plane with its centre at the origin and carrying a current *I* along the direction shown. If it is placed in a magnetic field, $\mathbf{B} = B_0(\hat{\mathbf{i}} - \hat{\mathbf{j}})$ and loop is released from rest, then loop will rotate about an axis along

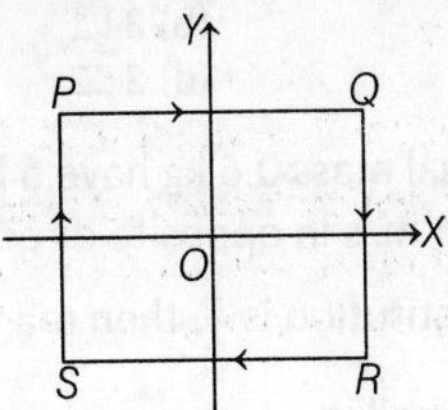

(a) *X*-axis (b) *Z*-axis
(c) *PR* (d) *QS*

15. Assertion (A) Only polar dielectrics can be used in a capacitor.

Reason (R) Capacity of a capacitor increases when a polar dielectric is placed between plates of a capacitor.

In the light of the above statements, choose the most appropriate answer from the options given below:

(a) Both A and R are true but R is not the correct explanation of A.
(b) A is true but R is false.
(c) A is false but R is true.
(d) Both A and R are true and R is the correct explanation of A.

16. If vector **a** is represented as $\mathbf{a} = m\mathbf{b} + \mathbf{c}$, where **b** and **c** are non-zero vectors. The value of scalar *m* is

(a) $\frac{\mathbf{a}\cdot\mathbf{b} - \mathbf{b}\cdot\mathbf{c}}{b^2}$ (b) $\frac{\mathbf{c}\cdot\mathbf{b} - \mathbf{a}\cdot\mathbf{c}}{a^2}$ (c) $\frac{\mathbf{c}\cdot\mathbf{a} - \mathbf{b}\cdot\mathbf{c}}{c^2}$ (d) $\frac{\mathbf{a}\cdot\mathbf{b} - \mathbf{b}\cdot\mathbf{c}}{a^2}$

17. Statement I In two concentric readings of a meter bridge experiment, null point cannot be obtained at same length.

Statement II Temperature coefficient of meter bridge wire and wires of resistance box may be different.

In light of above statements, choose the most appropriate answer from the options given below:

(a) Both Statement I and Statement II are incorrect.
(b) Statement I is correct and Statement II is incorrect.
(c) Statement I is incorrect and Statement II is correct.
(d) Both Statement I and Statement II are correct.

18. Statement I Reflecting type telescopes gives much sharp image than refracting type telescopes.

Statement II Dust trapped between tube of telescope makes image dull.

In light of above statements, choose the most appropriate answer from the options given below:

(a) Both Statement I and Statement II are incorrect.
(b) Statement I is correct and Statement II is incorrect.
(c) Statement I is incorrect and Statement II is correct.
(d) Both Statement I and Statement II are correct.

19. Two thin parallel infinite line charge having charge densities $+\lambda$ each and a semi-circular ring of the same charge, density are arranged with separation as shown in the figure below. The net electric field at point O is

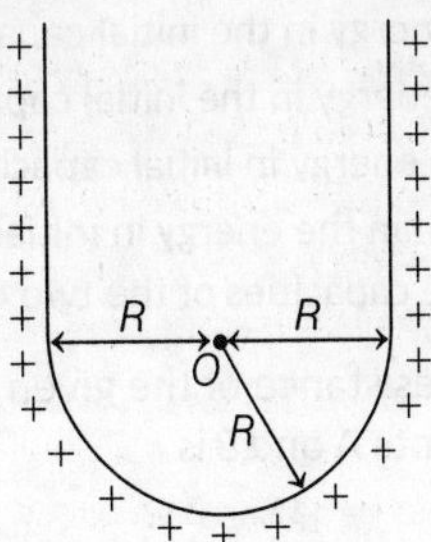

(a) 0 (b) $\frac{\lambda}{2\pi\varepsilon_0 R}$ (c) $\frac{\lambda}{\pi\varepsilon_0 R}$ (d) $\frac{\sqrt{2}\,\lambda}{\pi\varepsilon_0 R}$

20. A monochromatic light is passing through three mediums I, II and III. The correct relation between the refractive indices of these mediums in the descending is

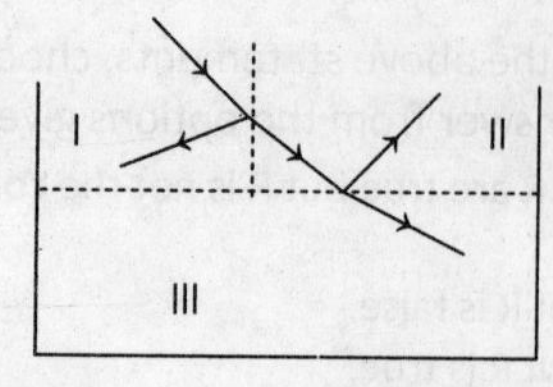

(a) I, II, III
(b) II, I, III
(c) III, II, I
(d) None of these

21. The magnetic field at the origin due to the current flowing in the wire *ABCD* as shown in figure below is

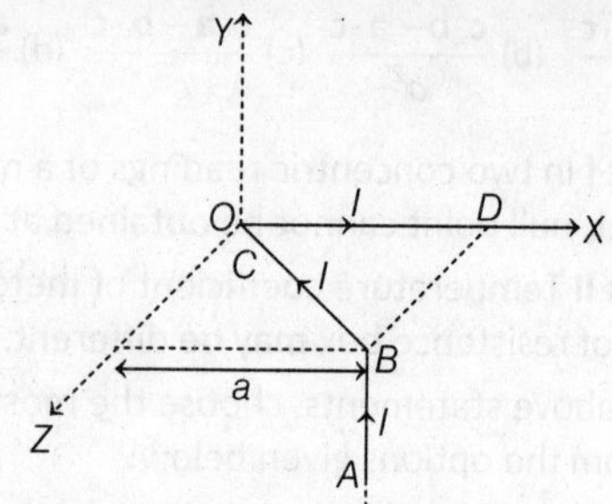

(a) $-\frac{\mu_0 I}{8\pi a}(\hat{i}+\hat{k})$
(b) $\frac{\mu_0 I}{2\pi a}(\hat{i}+\hat{k})$
(c) $\frac{\mu_0 I}{8\pi a}(-\hat{i}+\hat{k})$
(d) $\frac{\mu_0 I}{4\pi a\sqrt{2}}(\hat{i}+\hat{k})$

22. Statement I More fuel is needed by a rocket to go to moon from earth than its return journey.

Statement II Distance of zero gravitational potential point is less from moon than earth.

In the light of above statements, choose the most appropriate answer from the options given below:

(a) Both Statement I and Statement II are incorrect.
(b) Statement I is correct and Statement II is incorrect.
(c) Statement I is incorrect and Statement II is correct.
(d) Both Statement I and Statement II are correct.

23. If an uncharged capacitor is connected across another charged capacitor, then the energy stored in the combination can be

(a) equal to the energy in the initial capacitor
(b) less than the energy in the initial capacitor
(c) more than the energy in initial capacitor
(d) more or less than the energy in initial capacitor depending on the relative capacities of the two capacitors

24. The equivalent resistance of the given electrical network between the points *A* and *B* is

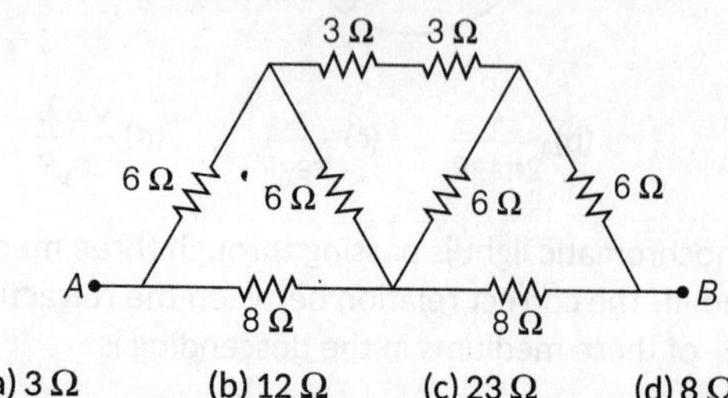

(a) 3 Ω
(b) 12 Ω
(c) 23 Ω
(d) 8 Ω

25. In a thermal power plant, electric power is produced at 4000 V. A step-up transformer with number of turns of primary to that in the secondary is 1 : 10. If power is to be supplied at 200 V, the ratio of number of turns of primary to that of secondary in the step-down transformer is

(a) 200 : 1
(b) 150 : 1
(c) 100 : 1
(d) 50 : 1

26. The linear velocity of a particle executing circular motion, varies with time as $\mathbf{v} = (4t\hat{i} + t^2\hat{j})$ m/s, where *t* is in second. The tangential acceleration of particle at *t* = 2 s, is

(a) $\frac{3}{\sqrt{5}}$ m/s²
(b) $\frac{4}{\sqrt{5}}$ m/s²
(c) $\frac{6}{\sqrt{5}}$ m/s²
(d) $\frac{12}{\sqrt{5}}$ m/s²

27. In a transistor, junction of base layer is to

(a) increase number of charge carries
(b) reduce number of change carries
(c) accelerate charge carries
(d) decelerate charge carriers

28. In an experiment of resonance tube for finding speed of sound, tuning fork of frequency 480 Hz is used. Resonance occurs at two successive lengths of air column $l_1 = 30$ cm and $l_2 = 70$ cm. Speed of sound obtained will be

(a) 332 m/s
(b) 340 m/s
(c) 384 m/s
(d) 379 m/s

29. Three identical rods of mass *m* and length *l* each are joined in such a way that, they form a shape *T* as shown in the following figure. The moment of inertia about axes passing through points *A* and *B* and perpendicular to plane of rods are I_A and I_B respectively, then $\frac{I_A}{I_B}$ is

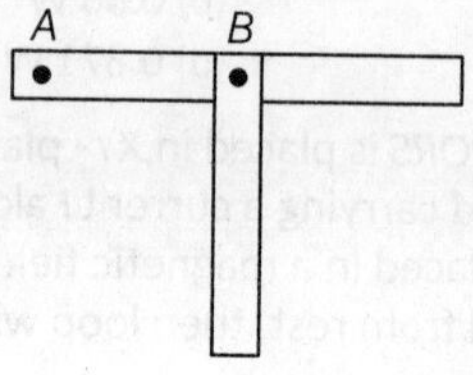

(a) 4 : 1
(b) 3 : 1
(c) 4 : 3
(d) 3 : 2

30. Two balls of equal mass 0.6 kg have a head on collision with 3 m/s and 6 m/s in opposite direction. If the coefficient of restitution is $\frac{1}{2}$, then magnitude of impulse exerted by each ball is

(a) 4.05 N-s
(b) 2.4 N-s
(c) 6.5 N-s
(d) 2.0 N-s

31. Two blocks *A* and *B* of masses *m* and 3*m*, respectively are connected by a massless spring of force constant *k*. A force *F* is applied on the block of mass *m*. At the instant shown, the acceleration of block of mass 3*m* is *a* leftwards. Then, acceleration of block of mass *m* at that instant is

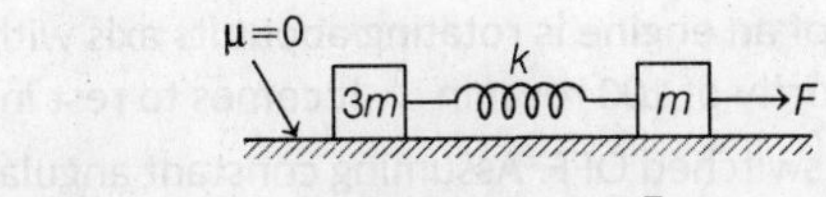

(a) $\frac{F}{m}-3a$ (b) $\frac{F}{m}+3a$ (c) $\frac{F}{3m}+a$ (d) $\frac{F}{3m}-a$

32. A parallel plate capacitor has plate area A and distance between them is d. It is connected to a battery of emf ε. After sometime, battery is disconnected and separation between plates is made 2 times of initial distance. The work done by external source is

(a) $\frac{\varepsilon_0 A\varepsilon^2}{d}$ (b) $\frac{2\varepsilon_0 A\varepsilon^2}{d}$ (c) $\frac{\varepsilon_0 A\varepsilon^2}{2d}$ (d) $\frac{3\varepsilon_0 A\varepsilon^2}{2d}$

33. A laser with an average power output of 16 mW puts out a narrow beam 4.00 mm in diameter. If the rms fields are $\frac{1}{\sqrt{2}}$ times their maximum values, then rms values of E and B in the beam, respectively are

(a) 978.48 V/m, 3.252 μT (b) 978.48 V/m, 3.252 mT
(c) 692 V/m, 2.3 μT (d) 692 V/m, 2.3 mT

34. A graph of the square of the velocity against the square of the acceleration of a given simple harmonic motion is

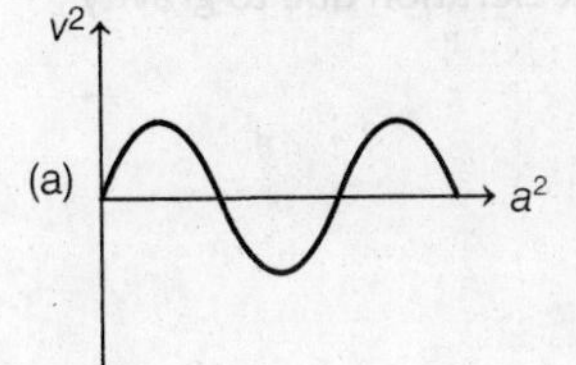

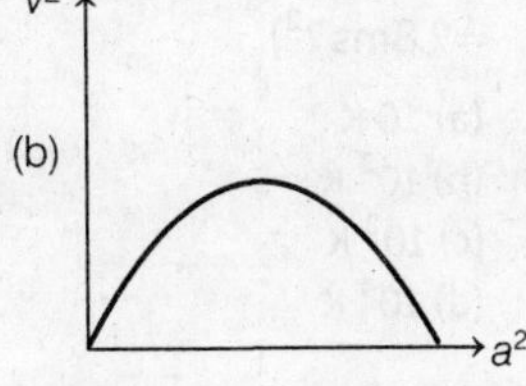

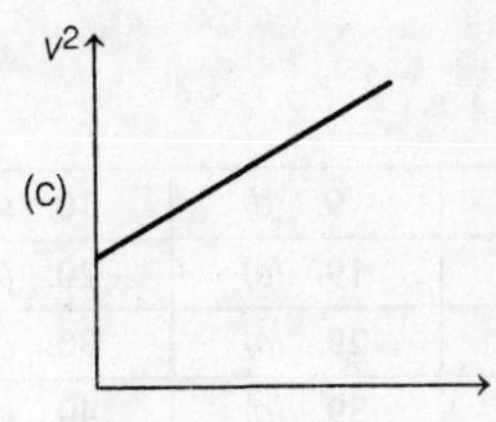

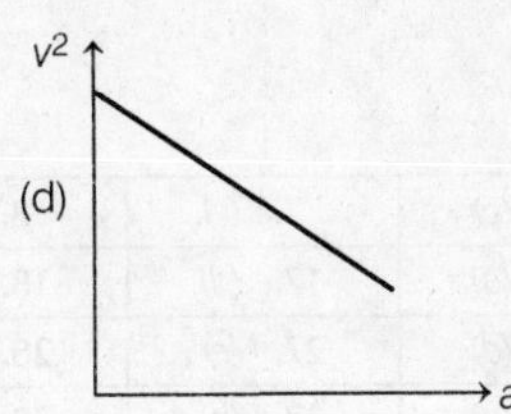

35. Which of the following waves are used to detect fault or crack on bridges?

(a) Microwaves (b) Infrared waves
(c) X-rays (d) Gamma rays

Section II

36. The ratio of wavelengths of 1st line of Lyman series to that of 1st line of Balmer series is k. The correct answer that replace the value of k is

(a) 3 : 8 (b) 5 : 27
(c) 7 : 31 (d) 2 : 27

37. The equivalent output of the given logic circuit is

(a) NOR gate (b) NAND gate
(c) OR gate (d) AND gate

38. In an L-R circuit, a sinusoidal voltage $V = V_0 \sin\omega t$ is applied. $L = 35$ mH, $R = 11\Omega$, $V_{rms} = 220$ V, $\frac{\omega}{2\pi} = 50$ Hz and $\pi = \frac{22}{7}$. Now, match Column I and Column II.

	Column I		Column II
A.	Inductive reactance (in ohms)	P.	15.56
B.	Impedence (in ohms)	Q.	20.00
C.	Voltage amplitude (in volts)	R.	11.00
D.	Current amplitude (in amperes)	S.	311.10

(a) A → P, B → Q, C → R, D → S
(b) A → Q, B → R, C → S, D → P
(c) A → P, B → Q, C → S, D → R
(d) A → R, B → P, C → S, D → Q

39. Assertion (A) To measure a large quantity, we use a larger unit.

Reason (R) Physical quantities are generally described in terms of small numeric values.

In the light of the above statements, choose the most appropriate answer from the options given below:

(a) Both A and R are true but R is not the correct explanation of A.
(b) A is true but R is false.
(c) A is false but R is true.
(d) Both A and R are true and R is the correct explanation of A.

40. If the accelerating voltage of electron is multiplied by constant five, then new de-Broglie wavelength

(a) increases 1.8 times (b) decreases 0.4 times
(c) decreases 0.44 times (d) increases 0.4 times

41. Which of the following material is ferromagnetic in nature?

(a) Aluminium (b) Copper
(c) Cobalt (d) Silver

42. An L-C oscillator has, $L = 27$ mH and $C = 60$ μF. The value of angular frequency of oscillation that can be generated by using it is

(a) $\frac{1211}{\sqrt{5}}$ rad/s (b) $\frac{1111}{\sqrt{2}}$ rad/s
(c) 1111 rad/s (d) 1211 rad/s

43. For common emitter transistor amplifier, parameters are given as $\beta = 50$, $R_C = 4$ kΩ, $V_C = 8$ V, $R_B = 2$ kΩ. The value of input voltage is (Symbols have their usual meaning)

(a) 20 mV (b) 60 mV
(c) 80 mV (d) 20 mV

44. The ratio of peak induced emf in a coil having 100 turns and operating with 50 Hz to that of induced emf of another coil having 50 turns and operating with 300 Hz in same magnetic field is

(a) 5 : 6 (b) 1 : 3
(c) 1 : 6 (d) None of these

45. A voltmeter has resistance 300 Ω. The operating range of voltmeter is 5 V. If it is to be converted into an ammeter of 5 A, then value of required resistance is

(a) 6.3 Ω (b) 1.5 Ω (c) 11 Ω (d) 1 Ω

46. In a nuclear reaction in a star, three α-particles undergo fusion in a single reaction to form ${}^{12}_{6}C$ nucleus.

$$3\,{}^{4}_{2}He \longrightarrow {}^{12}_{6}C + Q$$

The *Q*-value of this reaction (in MeV) is

(Take, $m({}^{4}_{2}He) = 4.002604\text{ u}$, $m({}^{12}_{6}C) = 12.000000\text{ u}$ and $1\text{u} = \frac{931\text{ MeV}}{c^2}$)

(a) 7.81 (b) 7.27 (c) 2.79 (d) 72.7

47. Which of the following graphs cannot possibly represent one-dimensional motion of a particle?

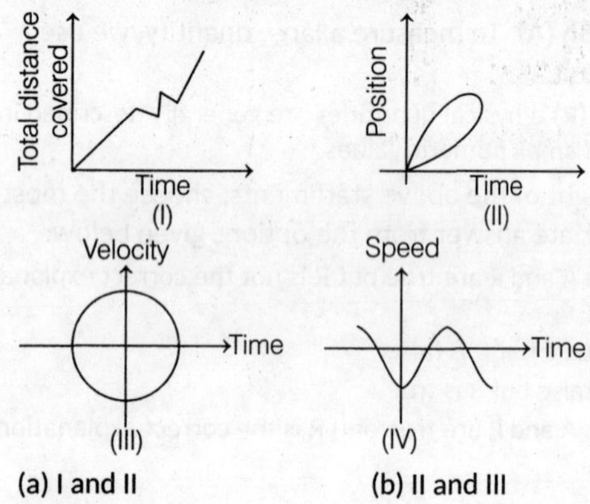

(a) I and II (b) II and III
(c) II and IV (d) All of these

48. The motor of an engine is rotating about its axis with an angular velocity of 100 rev min^{-1}. It comes to rest in 15 s after being switched OFF. Assuming constant angular deceleration, what are the number of revolutions made by it before coming to rest?

(a) 12.5
(b) 40
(c) 32.6
(d) 15.6

49. A body of mass 4*m* is lying in *XY*-plane at rest. It suddenly explodes into three pieces. Two pieces each of mass *m* move perpendicular to each other with equal speeds *v*. The total kinetic energy generated due to explosion is

(a) mv^2
(b) $(3/2)mv^2$
(c) $2mv^2$
(d) $4mv^2$

50. At what temperature, hydrogen molecules will escape from the earth's surface?

(Take, radius of earth $= 6.4 \times 10^6$ m, mass of hydrogen molecule $= 0.34 \times 10^{-26}$ kg, Boltzmann constant $= 1.38 \times 10^{-23}\text{ JK}^{-1}$ and acceleration due to gravity $= 9.8\text{ms}^{-2}$)

(a) 10 K
(b) 10^2 K
(c) 10^3 K
(d) 10^4 K

Answers

1. (c)	2. (a)	3. (d)	4. (c)	5. (a)	6. (c)	7. (c)	8. (b)	9. (d)	10. (c)
11. (b)	12. (c)	13. (c)	14. (d)	15. (c)	16. (a)	17. (d)	18. (c)	19. (a)	20. (a)
21. (c)	22. (b)	23. (b)	24. (d)	25. (a)	26. (d)	27. (c)	28. (c)	29. (a)	30. (a)
31. (b)	32. (c)	33. (c)	34. (d)	35. (c)	36. (b)	37. (b)	38. (d)	39. (b)	40. (c)
41. (c)	42. (b)	43. (c)	44. (d)	45. (d)	46. (b)	47. (d)	48. (a)	49. (b)	50. (d)

See detailed explanations on page no. 287

The Real Nuts

Past Years' NEET Question Papers

Now you are ready for exam, so attempt these Past Exams' Papers and compare your score the with the Cut Off Score of that year.

The Real Nuts

NEET

(Real Nut 1 - 2020 Solved Paper)

PHYSICS

Instructions

1. This question paper contains of 45 Multiple Choice Questions of Physics.
2. All questions are compulsory.
3. Each question carries **4 marks**.

1. The phase difference between displacement and acceleration of a particle in a simple harmonic motion is

(a) $\frac{3\pi}{2}$ rad (b) $\frac{\pi}{2}$ rad

(c) zero (d) π rad

2. A long solenoid of 50 cm length having 100 turns carries a current of 2.5 A. The magnetic field at the centre of solenoid is

(Take, $\mu_0 = 4\pi \times 10^{-7}$ T-m A^{-1})

(a) 3.14×10^{-4} T (b) 6.28×10^{-5} T

(c) 3.14×10^{-5} T (d) 6.28×10^{-4} T

3. Two bodies of mass 4 kg and 6 kg are tied to the ends of a massless string. The string passes over a pulley which is frictionless (see figure). The acceleration of the system in terms of acceleration due to gravity g is

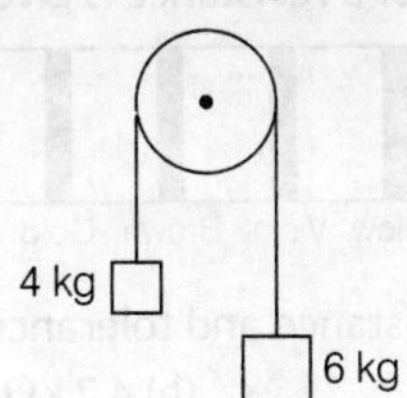

(a) $g/2$ (b) $g/5$

(c) $g/10$ (d) g

4. The ratio of contributions made by the electric field and magnetic field components, to the intensity of an electromagnetic wave is (where, c = speed of electromagnetic waves)

(a) $1:1$ (b) $1:c$

(c) $1:c^2$ (d) $c:1$

5. In a certain region of space with volume 0.2 m^3, the electric potential is found to be 5 V throughout. The magnitude of electric field in this region is

(a) 0.5 N/C (b) 1 N/C (c) 5 N/C (d) zero

6. The average thermal energy for a monoatomic gas is (where, k_B is Boltzmann constant and T is absolute temperature)

(a) $\frac{3}{2}k_BT$ (b) $\frac{5}{2}k_BT$

(c) $\frac{7}{2}k_BT$ (d) $\frac{1}{2}k_BT$

7. Find the torque about the origin when a force of $3\hat{j}$ N acts on the particle whose position vector is $2\hat{k}$ m.

(a) $6\hat{j}$ N-m (b) $-6\hat{i}$ N-m

(c) $6\hat{k}$ N-m (d) $6\hat{i}$ N-m

8. The mean free path λ for a gas, with molecular diameter d and number density n can be expressed as

(a) $\frac{1}{\sqrt{2}\,n\pi d^2}$ (b) $\frac{1}{\sqrt{2}\,n^2\pi d^2}$

(c) $\frac{1}{\sqrt{2}\,n^2\pi^2 d^2}$ (d) $\frac{1}{\sqrt{2}\,n\pi d}$

9. The energy equivalent of 0.5 g of a substance is

(a) 4.5×10^{13} J (b) 1.5×10^{13} J

(c) 0.5×10^{13} J (d) 4.5×10^{16} J

10. A screw gauge has least count of 0.01 mm and there are 50 divisions in its circular scale. The pitch of the screw gauge is

(a) 0.25 mm (b) 0.5 mm

(c) 1.0 mm (d) 0.01 mm

11. Two cylinders *A* and *B* of equal capacity are connected to each other *via* a stop cock. *A* contains an ideal gas at standard temperature and pressure. *B* is completely evacuated. The entire system is thermally insulated. The stop cock is suddenly opened. The process is

(a) adiabatic (b) isochoric
(c) isobaric (d) isothermal

12. A cylinder contains hydrogen gas at pressure of 249 kPa and temperature 27°C. Its density is ($R = 8.3$ J mol^{-1} K^{-1})

(a) 0.2 kg/m^3 (b) 0.1 kg/m^3
(c) 0.02 kg/m^3 (d) 0.5 kg/m^3

13. When a uranium isotope ${}^{235}_{92}U$ is bombarded with a neutron, it generates ${}^{89}_{36}Kr$, three neutrons and

(a) ${}^{91}_{40}Zr$ (b) ${}^{101}_{36}Kr$ (c) ${}^{103}_{36}Kr$ (d) ${}^{144}_{56}Ba$

14. A charged particle having drift velocity of 7.5×10^{-4} ms^{-1} in an electric field of 3×10^{-10} Vm^{-1}, has a mobility (in $m^2V^{-1}s^{-1}$) of

(a) 2.5×10^6 (b) 2.5×10^{-6}
(c) 2.25×10^{-15} (d) 2.25×10^{15}

15. Taking into account of the significant figures, what is the value of 9.99 m − 0.0099 m?

(a) 9.98 m (b) 9.980 m (c) 9.9 m (d) 9.9801 m

16. An iron rod of susceptibility 599 is subjected to a magnetising field of 1200 Am^{-1}. The permeability of the material of the rod is

(Take, $\mu_0 = 4\pi \times 10^{-7}$ T-m A^{-1})

(a) 8.0×10^{-5} T-m A^{-1} (b) $2.4\pi \times 10^{-5}$ T-m A^{-1}
(c) $2.4\pi \times 10^{-7}$ T-m A^{-1} (d) $2.4\pi \times 10^{-4}$ T-m A^{-1}

17. A spherical conductor of radius 10 cm has a charge of 3.2×10^{-7} C distributed uniformly. What is the magnitude of electric field at a point 15 cm from the centre of the sphere? $\left(\frac{1}{4\pi\varepsilon_0} = 9 \times 10^9 \text{ N-m}^2/\text{C}^2\right)$

(a) 1.28×10^5 N/C (b) 1.28×10^6 N/C
(c) 1.28×10^7 N/C (d) 1.28×10^4 N/C

18. A series *L-C-R* circuit is connected to an AC voltage source. When *L* is removed from the circuit, the phase difference between current and voltage is $\frac{\pi}{3}$. If instead C is removed from the circuit, the phase difference is again $\frac{\pi}{3}$ between current and voltage. The power factor of the circuit is

(a) 0.5 (b) 1.0 (c) −1.0 (d) zero

19. A capillary tube of radius *r* is immersed in water and water rises in it to a height *h*. The mass of the water in the capillary tube is 5 g. Another capillary tube of radius 2*r* is immersed in water. The mass of water that will rise in this tube is

(a) 5.0 g (b) 10.0 g (c) 20.0 g (d) 2.5 g

20. In Young's double slit experiment, if the separation between coherent sources is halved and the distance of the screen from the coherent sources is doubled, then the fringe width becomes

(a) half (b) four times
(c) one-fourth (d) double

21. For the logic circuit shown below, the truth table is

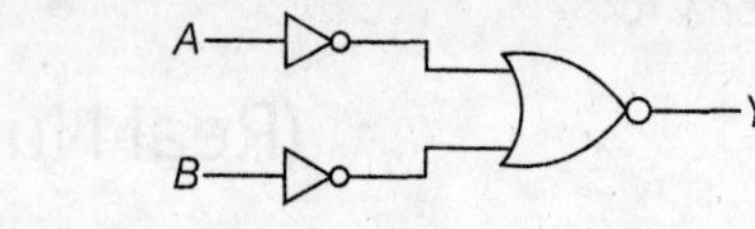

(a)

A	B	Y
0	0	0
0	1	1
1	0	1
1	1	1

(b)

A	B	Y
0	0	1
0	1	1
1	0	1
1	1	0

(c)

A	B	Y
0	0	1
0	1	0
1	0	0
1	1	0

(d)

A	B	Y
0	0	0
0	1	0
1	0	0
1	1	1

22. The colour code of a resistance is given below.

The values of resistance and tolerance respectively, are

(a) 47 kΩ, 10% (b) 4.7 kΩ, 5%
(c) 470 Ω, 5% (d) 470 kΩ, 5%

23. The capacitance of a parallel plate capacitor with air as medium is 6 μF. With the introduction of a dielectric medium, the capacitance becomes 30 μF. The permittivity of the medium is ($\varepsilon_0 = 8.85 \times 10^{-12}$ $C^2N^{-1}m^{-2}$)

(a) 1.77×10^{-12} $C^2N^{-1}m^{-2}$
(b) 0.44×10^{-10} $C^2N^{-1}m^{-2}$
(c) 5.00 $C^2N^{-1}m^{-2}$
(d) 0.44×10^{-13} $C^2N^{-1}m^{-2}$

24. A ball is thrown vertically downward with a velocity of 20 m/s from the top of a tower. It hits the ground after sometime with a velocity of 80 m/s. The height of the tower is ($g = 10\ m/s^2$)

(a) 340 m (b) 320 m
(c) 300 m (d) 360 m

25. A body weights 72 N on the surface of the earth. What is the gravitational force on it, at a height equal to half of radius of the earth?

(a) 32 N (b) 30 N
(c) 24 N (d) 48 N

26. Two particles of mass 5 kg and 10 kg respectively are attached to the two ends of a rigid rod of length 1 m with negligible mass. The centre of mass of the system from the 5 kg particle is nearly at a distance of

(a) 50 cm (b) 67 cm (c) 80 cm (d) 33 cm

27. The increase in the width of the depletion region in a *p-n* junction diode is due to

(a) reverse bias only
(b) both forward bias and reverse bias
(c) increase in forward current
(d) forward bias only

28. Light of frequency 1.5 times the threshold frequency is incident on a photosensitive material. What will be the photoelectric current, if the frequency is halved and intensity is doubled?

(a) Four times
(b) One-fourth
(c) Zero
(d) Doubled

29. Assuming that, light of wavelength 600 nm is coming from a star. The limit of resolution of telescope whose objective has a diameter of 2 m is

(a) 1.83×10^{-7} rad (b) 7.32×10^{-7} rad
(c) 6.00×10^{-7} rad (d) 3.66×10^{-7} rad

30. A resistance wire connected in the left gap of a metre bridge balances a 10 Ω resistance in the right gap at a point which divides the bridge wire in the ratio 3 : 2. If the length of the resistance wire is 1.5 m, then the length of 1 Ω of the resistance wire is

(a) 1.0×10^{-1} m
(b) 1.5×10^{-1} m
(c) 1.5×10^{-2} m
(d) 1.0×10^{-2} m

31. Light with an average flux of 20 W/cm^2 falls on a non-reflecting surface at normal incidence having surface area 20 cm^2. The energy received by the surface during time span of 1 min is

(a) 12×10^3 J (b) 24×10^3 J
(c) 48×10^3 J (d) 10×10^3 J

32. A ray is incident at an angle of incidence *i* on one surface of a small angle prism (with angle of prism *A*) and emerges normally from the opposite surface. If the refractive index of the material of the prism is μ, then the angle of incidence is nearly equal to

(a) $\frac{2A}{\mu}$ (b) μA
(c) $\frac{\mu A}{2}$ (d) $\frac{A}{2\mu}$

33. A 40 μF capacitor is connected to a 200 V, 50 Hz AC supply. The rms value of the current in the circuit is, nearly

(a) 2.05 A
(b) 2.5 A
(c) 25.1 A
(d) 1.7 A

34. Dimensions of stress are

(a) $[ML^2T^{-2}]$
(b) $[ML^0T^{-2}]$
(c) $[ML^{-1}T^{-2}]$
(d) $[MLT^{-2}]$

35. The Brewster's angle i_b for an interface should be

(a) $30° < i_b < 45°$
(b) $45° < i_b < 90°$
(c) $i_b = 90°$
(d) $0° < i_b < 30°$

36. A wire of length *L*, area of cross-section *A* is hanging from a fixed support. The length of the wire changes to L_1 when mass M is suspended from its free end. The expression for Young's modulus is

(a) $\frac{Mg(L_1 - L)}{AL}$ (b) $\frac{MgL}{AL_1}$
(c) $\frac{MgL}{A(L_1 - L)}$ (d) $\frac{MgL_1}{AL}$

37. A short electric dipole has a dipole moment of 16×10^{-9} C-m. The electric potential due to the dipole at a point at a distance of 0.6 m from the centre of the dipole, situated on a line making an angle of 60° with the dipole axis is $\left(\frac{1}{4\pi\varepsilon_0} = 9 \times 10^9\ N\text{-}m^2/C^2\right)$

(a) 200 V (b) 400 V
(c) zero (d) 50 V

38. In a guitar, two strings *A* and *B* made of same material are slightly out of tune and produce beats of frequency 6 Hz. When tension in *B* is slightly decreased, the beat frequency increases to 7 Hz. If the frequency of *A* is 530 Hz, the original frequency of *B* will be

(a) 524 Hz
(b) 536 Hz
(c) 537 Hz
(d) 523 Hz

39. An electron is accelerated from rest through a potential difference of *V* volt. If the de-Broglie wavelength of the electron is 1.227×10^{-2} nm, the potential difference is

(a) 10^2 V (b) 10^3 V
(c) 10^4 V (d) 10 V

40. The solids which have the negative temperature coefficient of resistance are

(a) insulators only
(b) semiconductors only
(c) insulators and semiconductors
(d) metals

41. The energy required to break one bond in DNA is 10^{-20} J. This value (in eV) is nearly

(a) 0.6 (b) 0.06
(c) 0.006 (d) 6

42. The quantities of heat required to raise the temperature of two solid copper spheres of radii r_1 and r_2 ($r_1 = 1.5\, r_2$) through 1 K are in the ratio

(a) $\frac{9}{4}$
(b) $\frac{3}{2}$
(c) $\frac{5}{3}$
(d) $\frac{27}{8}$

43. Which of the following graph represents the variation of resistivity (ρ) with temperature (*T*) for copper?

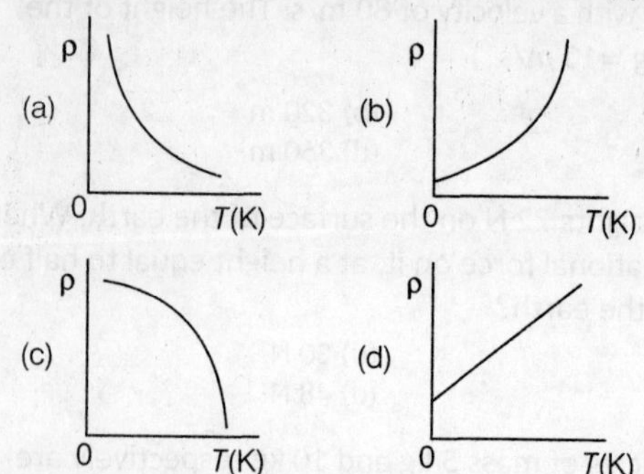

44. For transistor action, which of the following statement is correct?

(a) Base, emitter and collector regions should have same size.
(b) Both emitter junction as well as the collector junction are forward biased.
(c) The base region must be very thin and lightly doped.
(d) Base, emitter and collector regions should have same dopping concentrations.

45. For which one of the following, Bohr model is not valid?

(a) Singly ionised helium atom (He^+)
(b) Deuteron atom
(c) Singly ionised neon atom (Ne^+)
(d) Hydrogen atom

Answers

1	(d)	2	(d)	3	(b)	4	(d)	5	(d)	6	(a)	7	(b)	8	(a)	9	(a)	10	(b)
11	(a)	12	(a)	13	(d)	14	(a)	15	(a)	16	(d)	17	(a)	18	(b)	19	(d)	20	(b)
21	(d)	22	(c)	23	(b)	24	(c)	25	(a)	26	(b)	27	(a)	28	(c)	29	(d)	30	(a)
31	(b)	32	(b)	33	(b)	34	(c)	35	(b)	36	(c)	37	(a)	38	(a)	39	(c)	40	(c)
41	(b)	42	(d)	43	(b)	44	(c)	45	(c)										

See detailed explanations on page no. 294

The Real Nuts

NEET

(Real Nut 2 - 2021 Solved Paper)

PHYSICS

Instructions

1. This question paper contains of 50 Multiple Choice Questions of Physics, divided into two Sections; **Section I** and **Section II**.
2. Section I contains **35 questions** and all questions are compulsory.
3. Section II contains **15 questions** out of which **only 10 questions** are to be attempted.
4. Each question carries **4 marks**.

Section I

1. An inductor of inductance L, a capacitor of capacitance C and a resistor of resistance R are connected in series to an AC source of potential difference V volts as shown in the following figure.

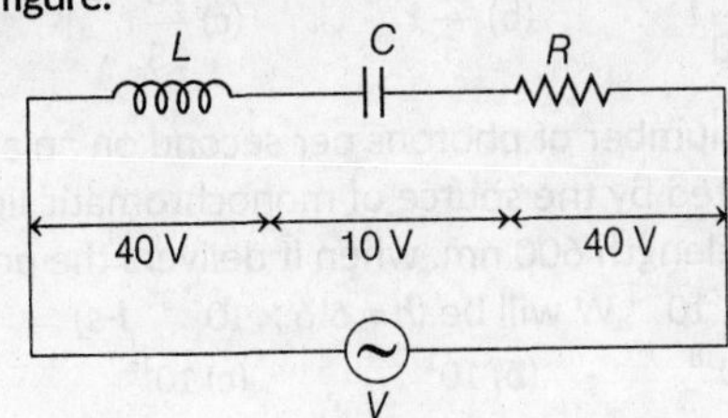

Potential difference across L, C and R is 40 V, 10 V and 40 V, respectively. The amplitude of current flowing through L-C-R series circuit is $10\sqrt{2}$ A. The impedance of the circuit is

(a) $4\sqrt{2}\ \Omega$ (b) $5\sqrt{2}\ \Omega$
(c) $4\ \Omega$ (d) $5\ \Omega$

2. Find the value of the angle of emergence from the prism. Refractive index of the glass is $\sqrt{3}$.

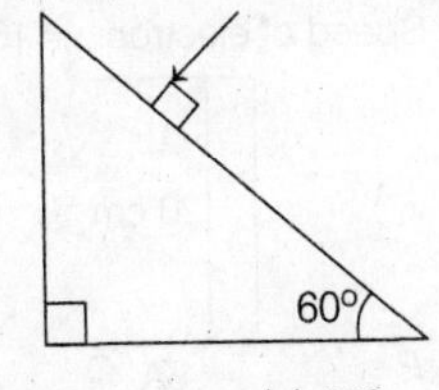

(a) 60° (b) 30° (c) 45° (d) 90°

3. A dipole is placed in an electric field as shown below. In which direction will it move?

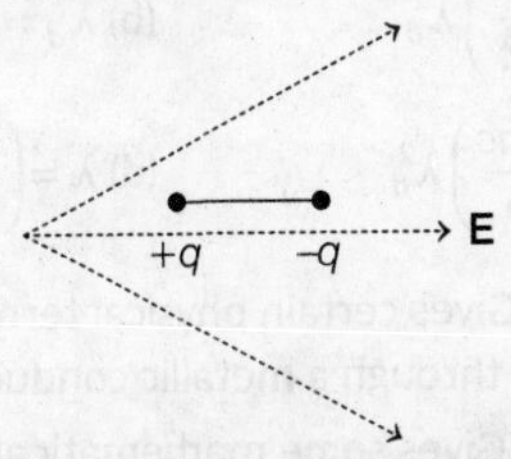

(a) Towards the left as its potential energy will increase
(b) Towards the right as its potential energy will decrease
(c) Towards the left as its potential energy will decrease
(d) Towards the right as its potential energy will increase

4. A capacitor of capacitance C, is connected across an AC source of voltage V, given by

$$V = V_0 \sin \omega t$$

The displacement current between the plates of the capacitor, would then be given by

(a) $I_d = V_0 \omega C \cos \omega t$

(b) $I_d = \dfrac{V_0}{\omega C} \cos \omega t$

(c) $I_d = \dfrac{V_0}{\omega C} \sin \omega t$

(d) $I_d = V_0 \omega C \sin \omega t$

5. A thick current carrying cable of radius R carries current I uniformly distributed across its cross-section. The variation of magnetic field B due to the cable with the distance r from the axis of the cable is represented by

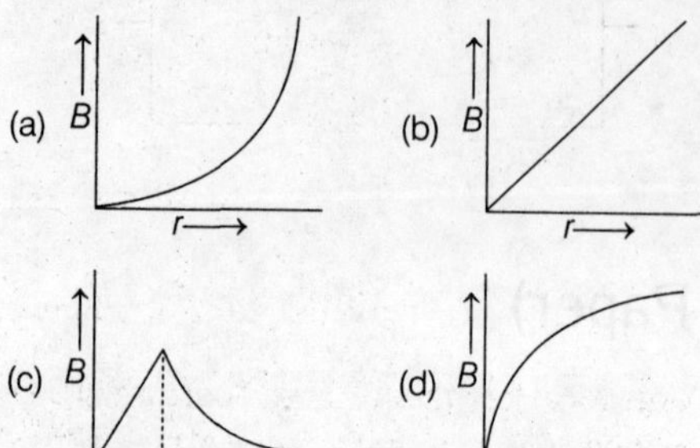

6. A convex lens A of focal length 20 cm and a concave lens B of focal length 5 cm are kept along the same axis with a distance d between them. If a parallel beam of light falling on A leaves B as a parallel beam, then the distance d (in cm) will be
(a) 25 (b) 15
(c) 50 (d) 30

7. An electromagnetic wave of wavelength λ is incident on a photosensitive surface of negligible work function. If m is the mass of photoelectron emitted from the surface, has de-Broglie wavelength λ_d, then
(a) $\lambda = \left(\frac{2m}{hc}\right)\lambda_d^2$ (b) $\lambda_d = \left(\frac{2mc}{h}\right)\lambda^2$
(c) $\lambda = \left(\frac{2mc}{h}\right)\lambda_d^2$ (d) $\lambda = \left(\frac{2h}{mc}\right)\lambda_d^2$

8. **Column I** Gives certain physical terms associated with flow of current through a metallic conductor.
Column II Gives some mathematical relations involving electrical quantities. Match Column I and Column II with appropriate relations.

Column I		Column II
A. Drift velocity	1.	$\frac{m}{ne^2\rho}$
B. Electrical resistivity	2.	nev_d
C. Relaxation period	3.	$\frac{eE}{m}\tau$
D. Current density	4.	$\frac{E}{J}$

Codes

	A	B	C	D
(a)	3	4	1	2
(b)	3	4	2	1
(c)	3	1	4	2
(d)	3	2	4	1

9. A radioactive nucleus ${}_Z^AX$ undergoes spontaneous decay in the sequence
${}_Z^AX \longrightarrow {}_{Z-1}B \longrightarrow {}_{Z-3}C \longrightarrow {}_{Z-2}D$, where Z is the atomic number of element X. The possible decay particles in the sequence are
(a) α, β^-, β^+ (b) α, β^+, β^- (c) β^+, α, β^- (d) β^-, α, β^+

10. The effective resistance of a parallel connection that consists of four wires of equal length, equal area of cross-section and same material is 0.25 Ω. What will be the effective resistance, if they are connected in series?
(a) 0.25 Ω (b) 0.5 Ω (c) 1 Ω (d) 4 Ω

11. A particle is released from height S from the surface of the earth. At a certain height, its kinetic energy is three times its potential energy. The height from the surface of earth and the speed of the particle at that instant are respectively
(a) $\frac{S}{4}, \frac{3gS}{2}$ (b) $\frac{S}{4}, \frac{\sqrt{3gS}}{2}$ (c) $\frac{S}{2}, \frac{\sqrt{3gS}}{2}$ (d) $\frac{S}{4}, \sqrt{\frac{3gS}{2}}$

12. The half-life of a radioactive nuclide is 100 h. The fraction of original activity that will remain after 150 h would be
(a) $\frac{1}{2}$ (b) $\frac{1}{2\sqrt{2}}$ (c) $\frac{2}{3}$ (d) $\frac{2}{3\sqrt{2}}$

13. A cup of coffee cools from 90°C to 80°C in t minutes, when the room temperature is 20°C. The time taken by a similar cup of coffee to cool from 80°C to 60°C at a room temperature at 20°C, is
(a) $\frac{13}{10}t$ (b) $\frac{13}{5}t$ (c) $\frac{10}{13}t$ (d) $\frac{5}{13}t$

14. The number of photons per second on an average emitted by the source of monochromatic light of wavelength 600 nm, when it delivers the power of 3.3×10^{-3} W will be ($h = 6.6 \times 10^{-34}$ J-s)
(a) 10^{18} (b) 10^{17} (c) 10^{16} (d) 10^{15}

15. A body is executing simple harmonic motion with frequency n, the frequency of its potential energy is
(a) n (b) $2n$ (c) $3n$ (d) $4n$

16. An infinitely long straight conductor carries a current of 5 A as shown below. An electron is moving with a speed of 10^5 m/s parallel to the conductor. The perpendicular distance between the electron and the conductor is 20 cm at an instant. Calculate the magnitude of the force experienced by the electron at that instant.

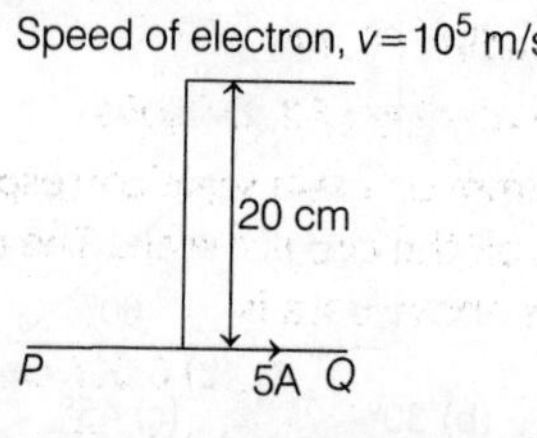

(a) 4×10^{-20} N (b) $8\pi \times 10^{-20}$ N
(c) $4\pi \times 10^{-20}$ N (d) 8×10^{-20} N

17. If force $[F]$, acceleration $[a]$ and time $[T]$ are chosen as the fundamental physical quantities. Find the dimensions of energy.

(a) [F a T]
(b) $[F\,a\,T^2]$
(c) $[F\,a\,T^{-1}]$
(d) $[F\,a^{-1}\,T]$

18. Match Column I with Column II and choose the correct match from the given choices.

Column I	Column II
A. Root mean square speed of gas molecules	1. $\frac{1}{3}nm\bar{v}^2$
B. Pressure exerted by ideal gas	2. $\sqrt{\frac{3RT}{M}}$
C. Average kinetic energy of a molecule	3. $\frac{5}{2}RT$
D. Total internal energy of 1 mole of a diatomic gas	4. $\frac{3}{2}k_BT$

Codes

	A	B	C	D
(a)	3	1	4	2
(b)	2	3	4	1
(c)	2	1	4	3
(d)	3	2	1	4

19. A small block slides down on a smooth inclined plane, starting from rest at time $t = 0$. Let s_n be the distance travelled by the block in the interval $t = n - 1$ to $t = n$. Then, the ratio $\frac{s_n}{s_{n+1}}$ is

(a) $\frac{2n-1}{2n}$
(b) $\frac{2n-1}{2n+1}$
(c) $\frac{2n+1}{2n-1}$
(d) $\frac{2n}{2n-1}$

20. A nucleus with mass number 240 breaks into two fragments each of mass number 120, the binding energy per nucleon of unfragmented nuclei is 7.6 MeV, while that of fragments is 8.5 MeV. The total gain in the binding energy in the process is

(a) 0.9 MeV (b) 9.4 MeV (c) 804 MeV (d) 216 MeV

21. A screw gauge gives the following readings when used to measure the diameter of a wire

Main scale reading : 0 mm

Circular scale reading : 52 divisions

Given that, 1 mm on main scale corresponds to 100 divisions on the circular scale. The diameter of the wire from the above data is

(a) 0.52 cm
(b) 0.026 cm
(c) 0.26 cm
(d) 0.052 cm

22. The equivalent capacitance of the combination shown in the figure is

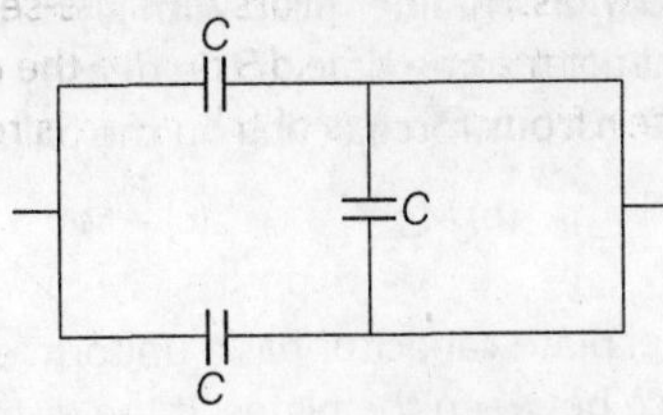

(a) 3C
(b) 2C
(c) $\frac{C}{2}$
(d) $\frac{3C}{2}$

23. A lens of large focal length and large aperture is best suited as an objective of an astronomical telescope, since

(a) a large aperture contributes to the quality and visibility of the images
(b) a large area of the objective ensures better light gathering power
(c) a large aperture provides a better resolution
(d) All of the above

24. Two charged spherical conductors of radii R_1 and R_2 are connected by a wire. Then, the ratio of surface charge densities of the spheres (σ_1 / σ_2) is

(a) $\frac{R_1}{R_2}$
(b) $\frac{R_2}{R_1}$
(c) $\sqrt{\left(\frac{R_1}{R_2}\right)}$
(d) $\frac{R_1^2}{R_2^2}$

25. A spring is stretched by 5 cm by a force 10 N. The time period of the oscillations when a mass of 2 kg is suspended by it is

(a) 0.0628 s
(b) 6.28 s
(c) 3.14 s
(d) 0.628 s

26. For a plane electromagnetic wave propagating in *x*-direction, which one of the following combination gives the correct possible directions for electric field (*E*) and magnetic field (*B*) respectively?

(a) $\hat{j}+\hat{k}, \hat{j}+\hat{k}$
(b) $-\hat{j}+\hat{k}, -\hat{j}-\hat{k}$
(c) $\hat{j}+\hat{k}, -\hat{j}-\hat{k}$
(d) $-\hat{j}+\hat{k}, -\hat{j}+\hat{k}$

27. The escape velocity from the earth's surface is *v*. The escape velocity from the surface of another planet having a radius, four times that of earth and same mass density is

(a) *v*
(b) 2 *v*
(c) 3 *v*
(d) 4 *v*

28. In a potentiometer circuit, a cell of emf 1.5 V gives balance point at 36 cm length of wire. If another cell of emf 2.5 V replaces the first cell, then at what length of the wire, the balance point occurs?

(a) 60 cm
(b) 21.6 cm
(c) 64 cm
(d) 62 cm

29. The velocity of a small ball of mass M and density d when dropped in a container filled with glycerine becomes constant after some time. If the density of glycerine is $d/2$, then the viscous force acting on the ball will be

(a) $\frac{Mg}{2}$ (b) Mg (c) $\frac{3}{2}Mg$ (d) $2Mg$

30. A parallel plate capacitor has a uniform electric field **E** in the space between the plates. If the distance between the plates is d and the area of each plate is A, the energy stored in the capacitor is (ε_0 = permittivity of free space)

(a) $\frac{1}{2}\varepsilon_0 E^2$ (b) $\varepsilon_0 EAd$

(c) $\frac{1}{2}\varepsilon_0 E^2 Ad$ (d) $\frac{E^2 Ad}{\varepsilon_0}$

31. The electron concentration in an n-type semiconductor is the same as hole concentration in a p-type semiconductor. An external field (electric) is applied across each of them. Compare the currents in them.

(a) Current in n-type = Current in p-type
(b) Current in p-type > Current in n-type
(c) Current in n-type > Current in p-type
(d) No current will flow in p-type. Current will only flow in n-type

32. Consider the following statements (A) and (B) and identify the correct answer.

(A) A Zener diode is connected in reverse bias, when used as a voltage regulator.
(B) The potential barrier of p-n junction lies between 0.1 V to 0.3 V.

(a) A and B both are correct.
(b) A and B both are incorrect.
(c) A is correct and B is incorrect.
(d) A is incorrect but B is correct.

33. Polar molecules are the molecules

(a) having zero dipole moment
(b) acquire a dipole moment only in the presence of electric field due to displacement of charges.
(c) acquire a dipole moment only when magnetic field is absent
(d) having a permanent electric dipole moment

34. If E and G respectively denote energy and gravitational constant, then $\frac{E}{G}$ has the dimensions of

(a) $[M^2L^{-1}T^0]$ (b) $[ML^{-1}T^{-1}]$
(c) $[ML^0T^0]$ (d) $[M^2L^{-2}T^{-1}]$

35. Water falls from a height of 60 m at the rate of 15 kg/s to operate a turbine. The losses due to frictional force are 10% of the input energy. How much power is generated by the turbine? ($g = 10$ m/s^2)

(a) 10.2 kW (b) 8.1 kW (c) 12.3 kW (d) 7.0 kW

Section II

36. A car starts from rest and accelerates at 5 m/s^2. At $t = 4$ s, a ball is dropped out of a window by a person sitting in the car. What is the velocity and acceleration of the ball at $t = 6$ s? (Take, $g = 10$ m/s^2)

(a) 20 m/s, 5 m/s^2
(b) 20 m/s, 0
(c) $20\sqrt{2}$ m/s, 0
(d) $20\sqrt{2}$ m/s, 10 m/s^2

37. For the given circuit, the input digital signals are applied at the terminals A, B and C. What would be the output at the terminal?

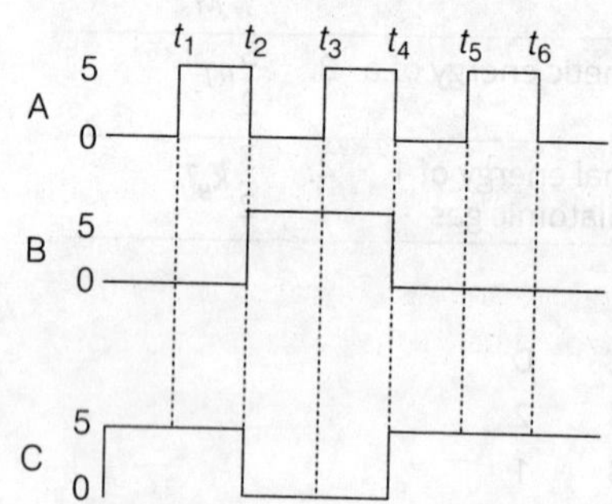

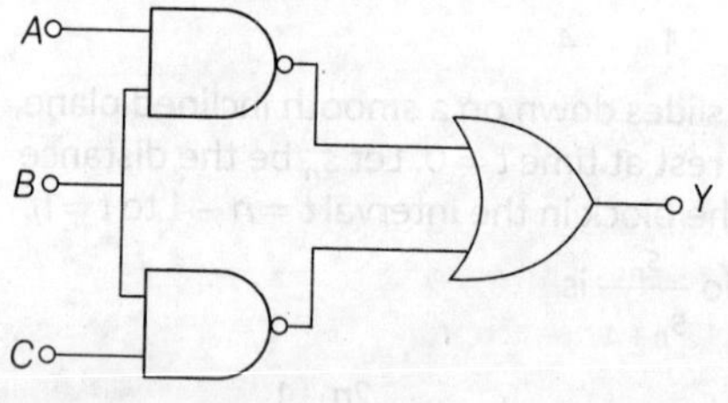

(a) 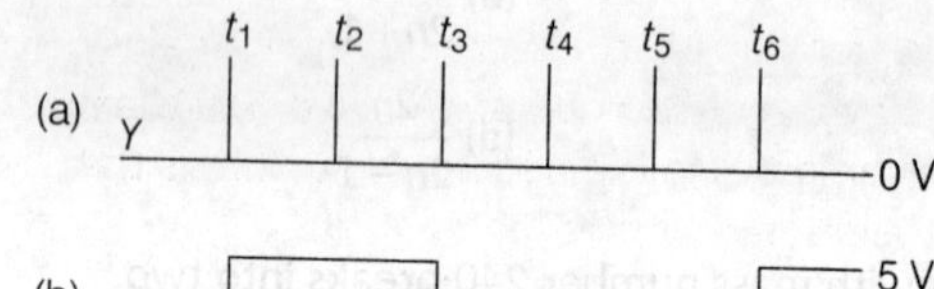

(b) 

(c) 5 V

(d) 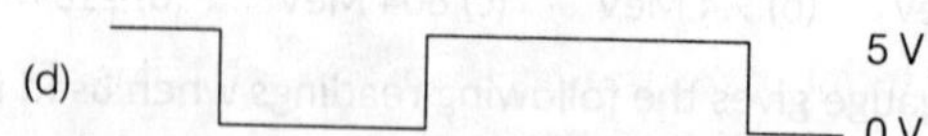

38. A ball of mass 0.15 kg is dropped from a height 10 m, strikes the ground and rebounds to the same height. The magnitude of impulse imparted to the ball is nearly ($g = 10$ m/s^2)

(a) 0
(b) 4.2 kg-m/s
(c) 2.1 kg-m/s
(d) 1.4 kg-m/s

39. A uniform rod of length 200 cm and mass 500 g is balanced on a wedge placed at 40 cm mark. A mass of 2 kg is suspended from the rod at 20 cm and another unknown mass m is suspended from the rod at 160 cm mark as shown in the following figure. Find the value of m such that the rod is in equilibrium. ($g = 10\ m/s^2$)

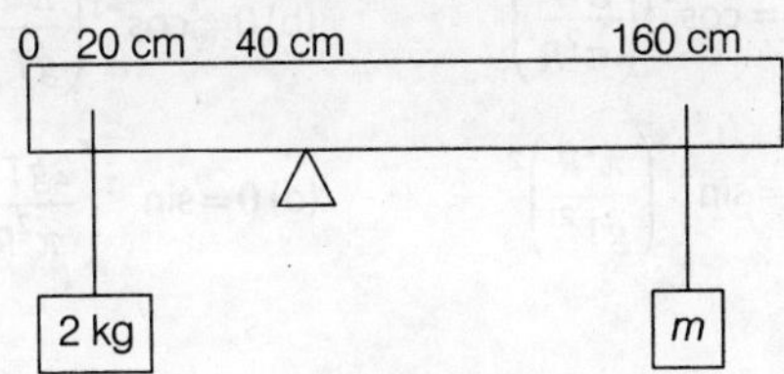

(a) $\frac{1}{2}$ kg (b) $\frac{1}{3}$ kg
(c) $\frac{1}{6}$ kg (d) $\frac{1}{12}$ kg

40. A point object is placed at a distance of 60 cm from a convex lens of focal length 30 cm. If a plane mirror were put perpendicular to the principal axis of the lens and at a distance of 40 cm from it, the final image would be formed at a distance of

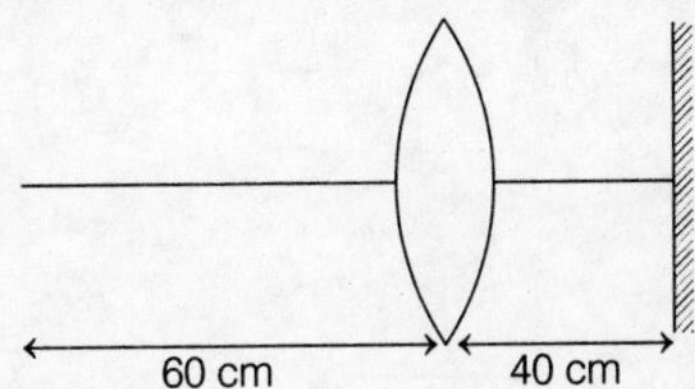

(a) 20 cm from the lens, it would be a real image
(b) 30 cm from the lens, it would be a real image
(c) 30 cm from the plane mirror, it would be a virtual image
(d) 20 cm from the plane mirror, it would be a virtual image

41. A step down transformer connected to an AC mains supply of 220 V is made to operate at 11 V, 44 W lamp. Ignoring power losses in the transformer, what is the current in the primary circuit ?

(a) 0.2 A (b) 0.4 A
(c) 2 A (d) 4 A

42. Three resistors having resistances r_1, r_2 and r_3 are connected as shown in the given circuit. The ratio $\frac{i_3}{i_1}$ of currents in terms of resistances used in the circuit is

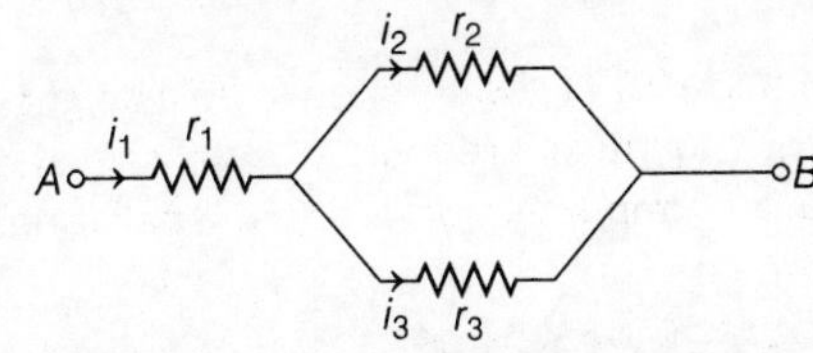

(a) $\frac{r_1}{r_2+r_3}$ (b) $\frac{r_2}{r_2+r_3}$ (c) $\frac{r_1}{r_1+r_2}$ (d) $\frac{r_2}{r_1+r_3}$

43. In the product

$$\mathbf{F} = q(\mathbf{v} \times \mathbf{B})$$
$$= q\mathbf{v} \times (B\hat{i} + B\hat{j} + B_0\hat{k})$$

For $q = 1$ and $\mathbf{v} = 2\hat{i} + 4\hat{j} + 6\hat{k}$ and

$\mathbf{F} = 4\hat{i} - 20\hat{j} + 12\hat{k}$

What will be the complete expression for **B**?

(a) $-8\hat{i} - 8\hat{j} - 6\hat{k}$ (b) $-6\hat{i} - 6\hat{j} - 8\hat{k}$
(c) $8\hat{i} + 8\hat{j} - 6\hat{k}$ (d) $6\hat{i} + 6\hat{j} - 8\hat{k}$

44. A particle of mass m is projected with a velocity, $v = kv_e (k < 1)$ from the surface of the earth.
(Here, v_e = escape velocity)
The maximum height above the surface reached by the particle is

(a) $R\left(\frac{k}{1-k}\right)^2$ (b) $R\left(\frac{k}{1+k}\right)^2$
(c) $\frac{R^2k}{1+k}$ (d) $\frac{Rk^2}{1-k^2}$

45. Twenty seven drops of same size are charged at 220 V each. They combine to form a bigger drop. Calculate the potential of the bigger drop.

(a) 660 V (b) 1320 V
(c) 1520 V (d) 1980 V

46. A series L-C-R circuit containing 5.0 H inductor, 80 μF capacitor and 40 Ω resistor is connected to 230 V variable frequency AC source. The angular frequencies of the source at which power transferred to the circuit is half the power at the resonant angular frequency are likely to be

(a) 25 rad/s and 75 rad/s (b) 50 rad/s and 25 rad/s
(c) 46 rad/s and 54 rad/s (d) 42 rad/s and 58 rad/s

47. A uniform conducting wire of length $12a$ and resistance R is wound up as a current (I) carrying coil in the shape of
1. an equilateral triangle of side a.
2. a square of side a.
The magnetic dipole moments of the coil in each case respectively are

(a) $\sqrt{3}\,Ia^2$ and $3\,Ia^2$ b) $3\,Ia^2$ and Ia^2
(c) $3\,Ia^2$ and $4\,Ia^2$ (d) $4\,Ia^2$ and $3\,Ia^2$

48. From a circular ring of mass M and radius R, an arc corresponding to a 90° sector is removed. The moment of inertia of the remaining part of the ring about an axis passing through the centre of the ring and perpendicular to the plane of the ring is K times MR^2. Then, the value of K is

(a) $\frac{3}{4}$ (b) $\frac{7}{8}$
(c) $\frac{1}{4}$ (d) $\frac{1}{8}$

49. Two conducting circular loops of radii R_1 and R_2 are placed in the same plane with their centres coinciding. If $R_1 >> R_2$, the mutual inductance M between them will be directly proportional to

(a) $\frac{R_1}{R_2}$ (b) $\frac{R_2}{R_1}$

(c) $\frac{R_1^2}{R_2}$ (d) $\frac{R_2^2}{R_1}$

50. A particle moving in a circle of radius R with a uniform speed takes a time T to complete one revolution. If this particle were projected with the same speed at an angle θ to the horizontal, the maximum height attained by it equals $4R$. The angle of projection θ is then given by

(a) $\theta = \cos^{-1}\left(\frac{gT^2}{\pi^2 R}\right)^{\frac{1}{2}}$ (b) $\theta = \cos^{-1}\left(\frac{\pi^2 R}{gT^2}\right)^{\frac{1}{2}}$

(c) $\theta = \sin^{-1}\left(\frac{\pi^2 R}{gT^2}\right)^{\frac{1}{2}}$ (d) $\theta = \sin^{-1}\left(\frac{2gT^2}{\pi^2 R}\right)^{\frac{1}{2}}$

Answers

1 (d)	2 (a)	3 (b)	4 (a)	5 (c)	6 (b)	7 (c)	8 (a)	9 (c)	10 (d)
11 (d)	12 (b)	13 (b)	14 (c)	15 (b)	16 (d)	17 (b)	18 (c)	19 (b)	20 (d)
21 (d)	22 (b)	23 (d)	24 (b)	25 (d)	26 (b)	27 (d)	28 (a)	29 (a)	30 (c)
31 (c)	32 (c)	33 (d)	34 (a)	35 (b)	36 (d)	37 (c)	38 (b)	39 (d)	40 (d)
41 (a)	42 (b)	43 (b)	44 (d)	45 (d)	46 (c)	47 (a)	48 (a)	49 (d)	50 (d)

See detailed explanations on page no. 297

The Real Nuts

NEET

(Real Nut 3 - 2022 Solved Paper)

PHYSICS

Instructions

1. This question paper contains of 50 Multiple Choice Questions of Physics, divided into two Sections; **Section I** and **Section II**.
2. Section I contains **35 questions** and all questions are compulsory.
3. Section II contains **15 questions** out of which **only 10 questions** are to be attempted.
4. Each question carries **4 marks**.

Section I

1. If a soap bubble expands, the pressure inside the bubble
(a) increases
(b) remains the same
(c) is equal to the atmospheric pressure
(d) decreases.

2. The graph which shows the variation of the de-Broglie wavelength (λ) of a particle and its associated momentum (p) is

(a) 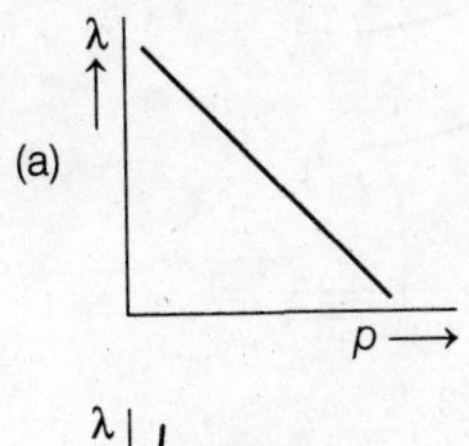

(b) 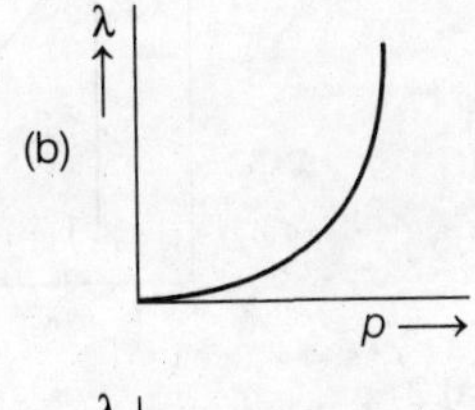

(c) 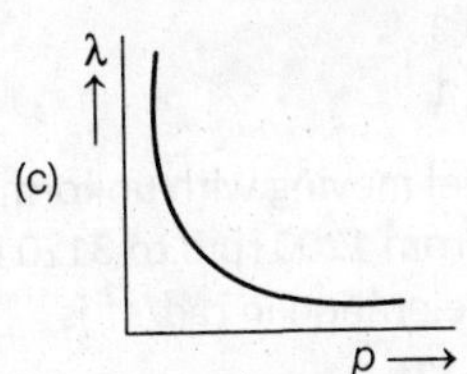

(d) 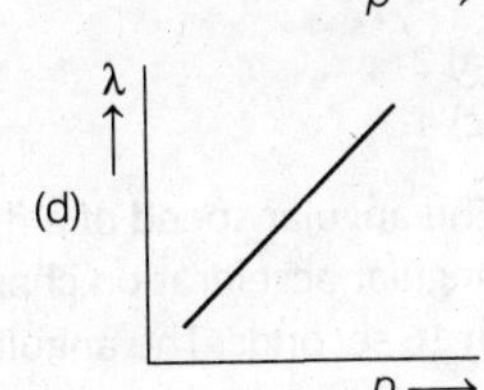

3. A body of mass 60 g experiences a gravitational force of 3.0 N, when placed at a particular point. The magnitude of the gravitational field intensity at that point is
(a) 50 N/kg (b) 20 N/kg
(c) 180 N/kg (d) 0.05 N/kg

4. Given below are two statements
Statement I Biot-Savart's law gives us the expression for the magnetic field strength of an infinitesimal current element (Idl) of a current carrying conductor only.
Statement II Biot-Savart's law is analogous to Coulomb's inverse square law of charge q, with the former being related to the field produced by a scalar source, Idl while the latter being produced by a vector source, q. In light of above statements choose the most appropriate answer from the options given below
(a) Both Statement I and Statement II are incorrect.
(b) Statement I is correct and Statement II is incorrect.
(c) Statement I is incorrect and Statement II is correct.
(d) Both Statement I and Statement II are correct.

5. The ratio of the distances travelled by a freely falling body in the 1st, 2nd, 3rd and 4th second
(a) 1 : 4 : 9 : 16 (b) 1 : 3 : 5 : 7
(c) 1 : 1 : 1 : 1 (d) 1 : 2 : 3 : 4

6. In half wave rectification, if the input frequency is 60 Hz, then the output frequency would be
(a) 30 Hz (b) 60 Hz
(c) 120 Hz (d) zero

7. A spherical ball is dropped in a long column of a highly viscous liquid. The curve in the graph shown, which represents the speed of the ball (v) as a function of time (t) is

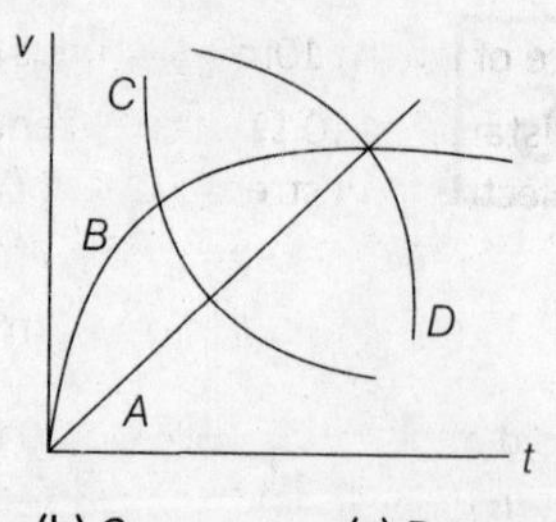

(a) *B* (b) *C* (c) *D* (d) *A*

8. The angle between the electric lines of force and the equipotential surface is

(a) 45° (b) 90° (c) 180° (d) 0°

9. As the temperature increases, the electrical resistance

(a) decreases for both conductors and semiconductors.

(b) increases for conductors but decreases for semiconductors.

(c) decreases for conductors but increases for semiconductors.

(d) increases for both conductors and semiconductors.

10. In the given nuclear reaction, the element *X* is

$$^{22}_{11}\text{Na} \longrightarrow X + e^{+} + \nu$$

(a) $^{23}_{10}$Ne (b) $^{22}_{10}$Ne (c) $^{22}_{12}$Mg (d) $^{23}_{11}$Na

11. Let T_1 and T_2 be the energy of an electron in the first and second excited states of hydrogen atom, respectively. According to the Bohr's model of an atom, the ratio of $T_1 : T_2$ is:

(a) 4 : 1 (b) 4 : 9 (c) 9 : 4 (d) 1 : 4

12. The ratio of the radius of gyration of a thin uniform disc about an axis passing through its centre and normal to its plane to the radius of gyration of the disc about its diameter is

(a) $\sqrt{2}:1$ (b) 4 : 1 (c) $1:\sqrt{2}$ (d) 2 : 1

13. When light propagates through a material medium of relative permittivity ϵ_r and relative permeability μ_r, the velocity of light, *v* is given by (*c*-velocity of light in vacuum)

(a) $v = \sqrt{\frac{\mu_r}{\varepsilon_r}}$ (b) $v = \sqrt{\frac{\varepsilon_r}{\mu_r}}$

(c) $v = \frac{c}{\sqrt{\varepsilon_r \mu_r}}$ (d) $v = c$

14. The energy that will be ideally radiated by a 100 kW transmitter in 1 hour is :

(a) 36×10^4 J (b) 36×10^5 J (c) 1×10^5 J (d) 36×10^7 J

15. An electric lift with a maximum load of 2000 kg (lift + passengers) is moving up with a constant speed of 1.5 ms^{-1}. The frictional force opposing the motion is 3000 N. The minimum power delivered by the motor to the lift in watts is ($g = 10$ ms^{-2})

(a) 20000 (b) 34500

(c) 23500 (d) 23000

16. Two resistors of resistance, 100 Ω and 200 Ω are connected in parallel in an electrical circuit, The ratio of the thermal energy developed in 100 Ω to that in 200 Ω in a given time is

(a) 2 : 1

(b) 1 : 4

(c) 4 : 1

(d) 1 : 2

17. The peak voltage of the AC source is equal to

(a) the rms value of the AC source

(b) $\sqrt{2}$ times the rms value of the AC source

(c) $1/\sqrt{2}$ times the rms value of the AC source.

(d) the value of voltage supplied to the circuit.

18. A shell of mass *m* is at rest initially. It explodes into three fragments having mass in the ratio 2 : 2 : 1. If the fragments having equal mass fly off along mutually perpendicular directions with speed *v*, the speed of the third (lighter) fragment is

(a) $\sqrt{2}\,v$ (b) $2\sqrt{2}\,v$

(c) $3\sqrt{2}\,v$ (d) *v*

19. If the initial tension on a stretched string is doubled, then the ratio of the initial and final speeds of a transverse wave along the string is

(a) $\sqrt{2}:1$ (b) $1:\sqrt{2}$

(c) 1 : 2 (d) 1 : 1

20. An ideal gas undergoes four different processes from the same initial state as shown in the figure below. Those processes are adiabatic, isothermal, isobaric and isochoric. The curve which represents the adiabatic process among 1, 2, 3 and 4 is

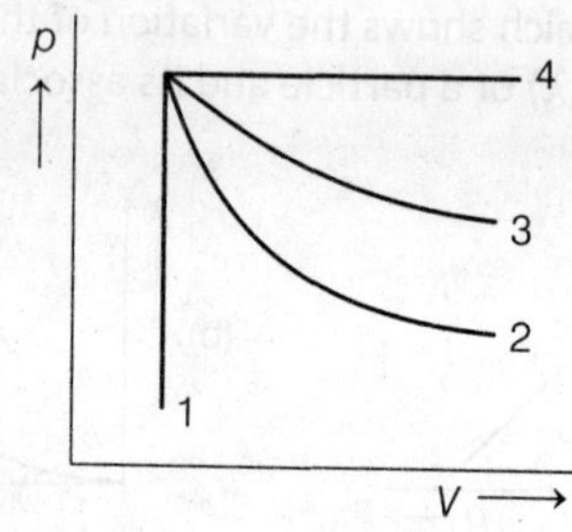

(a) 2 (b) 3

(c) 4 (d) 1

21. The angular speed of a fly wheel moving with uniform angular acceleration changes from 1200 rpm to 3120 rpm in 16 seconds. The angular acceleration in rad/s^2 is

(a) 4π (b) 12π

(c) 104π (d) 2π

22. Plane angle and solid angle have

(a) Dimensions but no units

(b) No units and no dimensions

(c) Both units and dimensions

(d) Units but no dimensions

23.

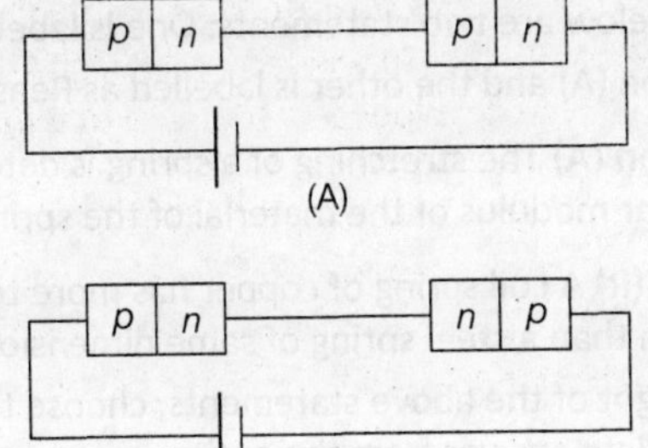

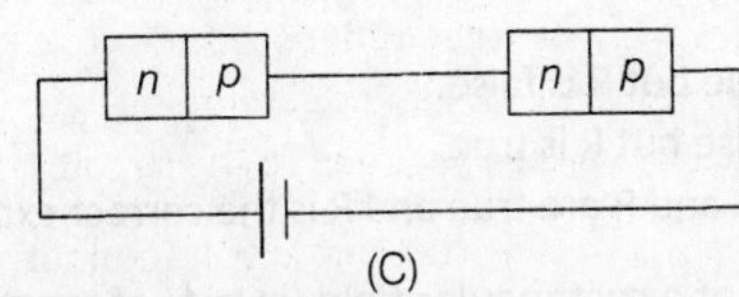

In the given circuits (A), (B) and (C) the potential drop across the two *p-n* junctions are equal in

(a) Circuit (B) only
(b) Circuit (C) only
(c) Both circuits (A) and (C)
(d) Circuit (A) only

24. In a Young's double slit experiment, a student observes 8 fringes in a certain segment of screen when a monochromatic light of 600 nm wavelength is used. If the wavelength of light is changed to 400 nm, then the number of fringes he would observe in the same region of the screen is

(a) 8 (b) 9
(c) 12 (d) 6

25. When two monochromatic lights of frequency, ν and $\frac{\nu}{2}$ are incident on a photoelectric metal, their stopping potential becomes $\frac{V_s}{2}$ and V_s respectively.

The threshold frequency for this metal is :

(a) 3ν (b) $\frac{2}{3}\nu$
(c) $\frac{3}{2}\nu$ (d) 2ν

26. A square loop of side 1 m and resistance 1 Ω placed in a magnetic field of 0.5 T. If the plane of loop is perpendicular to the direction of magnetic field, the magnetic flux through the loop is

(a) 0.5 Wb (b) 1 Wb
(c) zero Wb (d) 2 Wb

27. Two hollow conducting spheres of radii R_1 and $R_2 (R_1 > R_2)$ have equal charges. The potential would be

(a) more on smaller sphere
(b) equal on both the spheres
(c) dependent on the material property of the sphere
(d) more on bigger sphere

28. A Copper wire of length 10m and radius $(10^{-2}/\sqrt{\pi})$ m has electrical resistance of 10 Ω. The current density in the wire for an electric field strength of 10 (V / m) is

(a) 10^6 A/m^2 (b) 10^{-5} A/m^2
(c) 10^5 A/m^2 (d) 10^4 A/m^2

29. A long solenoid of radius 1 mm has 100 turns per mm. If 1A current flows in the solenoid, the magnetic field strength at the centre of the solenoid is

(a) 12.56×10^{-2} T (b) 12.56×10^{-4} T
(c) 6.28×10^{-4} T (d) 6.28×10^{-2} T

30. Two objects of mass 10 kg and 20 kg, respectively are connected to the two ends of a rigid rod of length 10 m with negligible mass. The distance of the center of mass of the system from the 10 kg mass is

(a) $\frac{20}{3}$ m (b) 10 m
(c) 5 m (d) $\frac{10}{3}$ m

31. A light ray falls on a glass surface of refractive index $\sqrt{3}$ at an angle 60°. The angle between the refracted and reflected rays would be

(a) 60° (b) 90°
(c) 120° (d) 30°

32. The dimensions $[MLT^{-2}A^{-2}]$ belong to the

(a) self inductance
(b) magnetic permeability
(c) electric permittivity
(d) magnetic flux

33. The displacement-time graph of two moving particles make angles of 30° and 45° with the X-axis as shown in the figure. The ratio of their respective velocity is

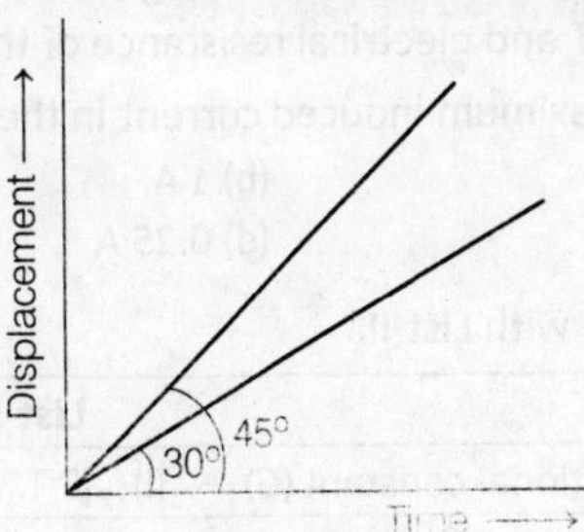

(a) 1 : 1 (b) 1 : 2
(c) 1: $\sqrt{3}$ (d) $\sqrt{3}$:1

34. A biconvex lens has radii of curvature, 20cm each. If the refractive index of the material of the lens is 1.5, the power of the lens is

(a) + 20 D
(b) + 5 D
(c) infinity
(d) + 2 D

35. Match List - I with List - II

List-I (Electromagnetic waves)	List-II (Wavelength)
(A) AM radio waves	(i) 10^{-10}m
(B) Microwaves	(ii) 10^2m
(C) Infrared radiations	(iii) 10^{-2}m
(D) X-rays	(iv) 10^{-4}m

Choose the correct answer from the options given below

(a) (A) - (iii), (B) - (ii), (C) - (i), (D) - (iv)
(b) (A) - (iii), (B) - (iv), (C) - (ii), (D) - (i)
(c) (A) - (ii), (B) - (iii), (C) - (iv), (D) - (i)
(d) (A) - (iv), (B) - (iii), (C) - (ii), (D) - (i)

Section II

36. A nucleus of mass number 189 splits into two nuclei having mass number 125 and 64. The ratio of radius of two daughter nuclei, respectively is:

(a) 4 : 5 (b) 5 : 4
(c) 25 : 16 (d) 1 : 1

37. Two transparent media A and B are separated by a plane boundary. The speed of light in those media are 1.5×10^8 m/s and $2.0 \times 10^8 \mathrm{m/s}$, respectively. The critical angle for a ray of light for these two media is

(a) $\sin^{-1}(0.750)$
(b) $\tan^{-1}(0.500)$
(c) $\tan^{-1}(0.750)$
(d) $\sin^{-1}(0.500)$

38. A big circular coil of 1000 turns and average radius 10m is rotating about its horizontal diameter at $2\ \mathrm{rad\ s^{-1}}$. If the vertical component of earth's magnetic field at that place is 2×10^{-5}T and electrical resistance of the coil is 12.56 Ω, then the maximum induced current in the coil will be

(a) 1.5 A (b) 1 A
(c) 2 A (d) 0.25 A

39. Match List-I with List-II.

List-I	List-II
(A) Gravitational constant (G)	(i) $[L^2T^{-2}]$
(B) Gravitational potential energy	(ii) $[M^{-1}L^3T^{-2}]$
(C) Gravitational potential	(iii) $[LT^{-2}]$
(D) Gravitational intensity	(iv) $[ML^2T^{-2}]$

Choose the correct answer from the options given below

(a) (A) - (ii), (B) - (iv), (C) - (i), (D) - (iii)
(b) (A) - (ii), (B) - (iv), (C) - (iii), (D) - (i)
(c) (A) - (iv), (B) - (ii), (C) - (i), (D) - (iii)
(d) (A) - (ii), (B) - (i), (C) - (iv), (D) - (iii)

40. Given below are two statements: One is labelled as Assertion (A) and the other is labelled as Reason (R)

Assertion (A) The stretching of a spring is determined by the shear modulus of the material of the spring.

Reason (R) A coil spring of copper has more tensile strength than a steel spring of same dimensions.

In the light of the above statements, choose the most appropriate answer from the options given below

(a) Both A and R are true but R is not the correct explanation of A.
(b) A is true but R is false.
(c) A is false but R is true.
(d) Both A and R are true and R is the correct explanation of A.

41. The area of a rectangular field (in m^2) of length 55.3m and breadth 25m after rounding off the value for correct significant digits is

(a) 1382 (b) 1382.5
(c) 14×10^2 (d) 138×10^1

42.

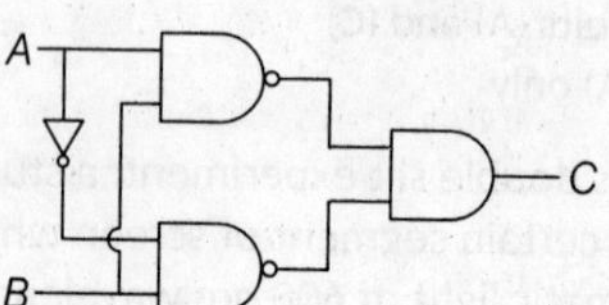

The truth table for the given logic circuit is

(a)

A	B	C
0	0	1
0	1	0
1	0	0
1	1	1

(b)

A	B	C
0	0	1
0	1	0
1	0	1
1	1	0

(c)

A	B	C
0	0	0
0	1	1
1	0	0
1	1	1

(d)

A	B	C
0	0	0
0	1	1
1	0	1
1	1	0

43. The volume occupied by the molecules contained in 4.5 kg water at STP, if the intermolecular forces vanish away is

(a) $5.6 \times 10^3\ m^3$ (b) $5.6 \times 10^{-3}\ m^3$

(c) $5.6\ m^3$ (d) $5.6 \times 10^6\ m^3$

44. A wheatstone bridge is used to determine the value of unknown resistance X by adjusting the variable resistance Y as shown in the figure. For the most precise measurement of X, the resistances P and Q

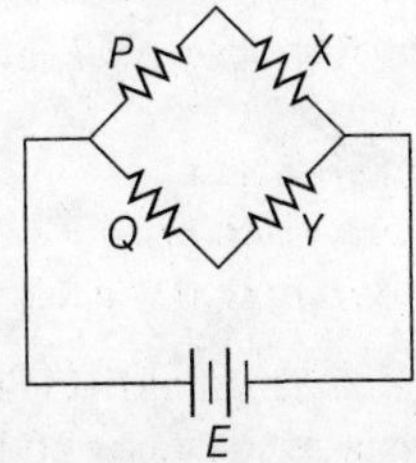

(a) should be approximately equal and are small

(b) should be very large and unequal

(c) do not play any significant role

(d) should be approximately equal to $2X$

45. A series L-C-R circuit with inductance 10 H, capacitance 10 μF, resistance 50Ω is connected to an AC source of voltage, $V = 200 \sin(100\, t)$ volt. If the resonant frequency of the LCR circuit is ν_0 and the frequency of the AC source is ν, then

(a) $\nu_0 = \nu = \frac{50}{\pi}$ Hz (b) $\nu_0 = \frac{50}{\pi}$ Hz, $\nu = 50$ Hz

(c) $\nu = 100$ Hz ; $\nu_0 = \frac{100}{\pi}$ Hz (d) $\nu_0 = \nu = 50$ Hz

46. A capacitor of capacitance $C = 900$ pF is charged fully by 100 V battery B as shown in figure (a). Then, it is disconnected from the battery and connected to another uncharged capacitor of capacitance $C = 900$ pF as shown in figure (b). The electrostatic energy stored by the system (b) is

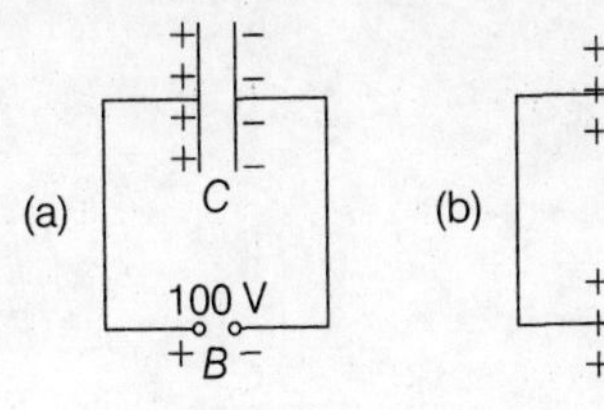

(a) 3.25×10^{-6} J (b) 2.25×10^{-6} J

(c) 1.5×10^{-6} J (d) 4.5×10^{-6} J

47. Two point charges $-q$ and $+q$ are placed at a distance of L, as shown in the figure.

$-q$ ← L → $+q$

The magnitude of electric field intensity at a distance $R(R >> L)$ varies as

(a) $\frac{1}{R^3}$ (b) $\frac{1}{R^4}$

(c) $\frac{1}{R^6}$ (d) $\frac{1}{R^2}$

48. A ball is projected with a velocity, 10 ms^{-1}, at an angle of 60° with the vertical direction. Its speed at the highest point of its trajectory will be

(a) $5\sqrt{3}\ ms^{-1}$

(b) $5\ ms^{-1}$

(c) $10\ ms^{-1}$

(d) zero

49. From Ampere's circuital law for a long straight wire of circular cross-section carrying a steady current, the variation of magnetic field in the inside and outside region of the wire is :

(a) a linearly increasing function of distance upto the boundary of the wire and then linearly decreasing for the outside region.

(b) a linearly increasing function of distance r upto the boundary of the wire and then decreasing one with $1/r$ dependence for the outside region.

(c) a linearly decreasing function of distance upto the boundary of the wire and then a linearly increasing one for the outside region.

(d) uniform and remains constant for both the regions.

50. Two pendulums of length 121 cm and 100 cm start vibrating in phase. At some instant, the two are at their mean position in the same phase. The minimum number of vibrations of the shorter pendulum after which the two are again in phase at the mean position is

(a) 9 (b) 10

(c) 8 (d) 11

Answers

1. (d)	2. (c)	3. (a)	4. (b)	5. (b)	6. (b)	7. (a)	8. (b)	9. (b)	10. (b)
11. (c)	12. (a)	13. (c)	14. (d)	15. (b)	16. (a)	17. (b)	18. (b)	19. (b)	20. (a)
21. (a)	22. (d)	23. (c)	24. (c)	25. (*)	26. (a)	27. (a)	28. (c)	29. (a)	30. (a)
31. (b)	32. (b)	33. (c)	34. (b)	35. (c)	36. (b)	37. (a)	38. (b)	39. (a)	40. (b)
41. (c)	42. (*)	43. (c)	44. (a)	45. (a)	46. (b)	47. (a)	48. (b)	49. (b)	50. (d)

Note *(*) None of the option is correct.*

See detailed explanations on page no. 305

Explanations

Qualifiers, Part Tests, Knockouts and Real Nuts

QUALIFIERS

Qualifier 1 (Physical World & Measurement)

1. (*c*) As we know that, luminous flux,

$$\phi = \frac{\text{total light energy emitted by a source}}{\text{time}}$$

$$[\text{Luminous flux}] = \frac{[\text{Energy}]}{[\text{Time}]}$$

$$[\phi] = \frac{[ML^2T^{-2}]}{[T]} = [ML^2T^{-3}]$$

2. (*c*) The unit ohm is the ratio of unit of voltage to unit of current.

$$\text{ohm} = \frac{\text{volt}}{\text{ampere}} = \frac{\text{volt-ampere}}{(\text{ampere})^2}$$

$$= \frac{\text{watt}}{(\text{ampere})^2} = \frac{\text{Js}^{-1}}{(\text{A})^2}$$

$$= \frac{\text{Js}}{s^2A^2} = \frac{\text{Js}}{(\text{A-s})^2}$$

$$\text{Unit of ohm} = \frac{\text{Unit of } h}{\text{Unit of (charge)}^2} = \frac{h}{e^2}$$

3. (*c*) As we know that, exponentials are always dimensionless, so

$$[\alpha x] = [M^0L^0T^0]$$

or $[\alpha][x] = [M^0L^0T^0]$

or $[\alpha][L] = [M^0L^0T^0]$

or $[\alpha] = [M^0L^{-1}T^0]$

4. (*d*) According to the principle of homogeneity, each term in an expression should have same dimensional formula.

$\Rightarrow \quad [p] = [\alpha V^2]$

or $\quad [\alpha] = \frac{[p]}{[V]^2} = \frac{[ML^{-1}T^{-2}]}{[L^3]^2}$

$$= [ML^{-7}T^{-2}]$$

5. (*c*) As we know that, dimensional formula of area $[A] = [L^2]$, velocity $[v] = [LT^{-1}]$ and density $[\rho] = [ML^{-3}]$.

Let power of dimensions of force are *a* in area, *b* in velocity and *c* in density, then

$$[F] = [A]^a [v]^b [\rho]^c$$

$$[M^1L^1T^{-2}] = [L^2]^a [LT^{-1}]^b [M^1L^{-3}]^c$$

$$[M^1L^1T^{-2}] = [M^c L^{2a+b-3c} T^{-b}]$$

On comparing both sides, we get

$$c = 1, -b = -2 \text{ or } b = 2$$

and $\quad 2a + b - 3c = 1$

$\Rightarrow \quad 2 \times a + 2 - 3 \times 1 = 1$

$\Rightarrow \quad 2a = 2$

$\Rightarrow \quad a = 1$

Therefore, $[F] = [A]^1 [v]^2 [\rho]^1 = Av^2\rho$

6. (*b*) Given equation,

$$F = \frac{\alpha}{\beta + \sqrt{\rho}}$$

$\Rightarrow \quad F\beta + F\sqrt{\rho} = \alpha$

$\therefore \quad [F\beta] = [F\sqrt{\rho}] = [\alpha]$

From $[\alpha] = [F\sqrt{\rho}] = [F][\rho]^{\frac{1}{2}}$

$$= [M^1L^1T^{-2}][M^{\frac{1}{2}}L^{-\frac{3}{2}}]$$

$$[\alpha] = \left[M^{\frac{3}{2}}L^{-\frac{1}{2}}T^{-2}\right]$$

Similarly, from $[F\beta] = [F\sqrt{\rho}]$

or $\quad [\beta] = [\rho]^{\frac{1}{2}}$

$$[\beta] = \left[M^{\frac{1}{2}}L^{-\frac{3}{2}}\right]$$

7. (*b*) A is true but R is false.

$$\left(p + \frac{a}{V^2}\right)(V - b) = \text{constant}$$

As we can add (or subtract) physical quantities of same dimensions,

$$[p] = \left[\frac{a}{V^2}\right] \Rightarrow [a] = [p][V^2]$$

Also, $[V] = [b]$

So, $[a] \cdot [b] = [p][V^2] \cdot [V]$

$$= [p][V^3] = \frac{[F]}{[L^2]} \cdot [L^3]^3$$

$$= [F] \cdot [L^7]$$

So, unit of $a \cdot b = \text{N-m}^7$.

Any two physical quantities can be multiplied or divided irrespective of their dimensions. Hence, reason is not correct.

8. (*c*) Let power of dimensions of surface tension be *a* in *K*, *b* in *v*, *c* in *T*, then

$$[\text{Surface tension}] = [K]^a [v]^b [T]^c$$

$$[M^1L^0T^{-2}] = [M^1L^2T^{-2}]^a [LT^{-1}]^b [T]^c$$

$$[M^1L^0T^{-2}] = [M^a L^{2a+b} T^{-2a-b+c}]$$

On comparing both sides of the above equation, we get

$$a = 1$$

$$2a + b = 0$$

$$2 \times 1 + b = 0 \quad \text{or} \quad b = -2$$

and $\quad -2a - b + c = -2$

$$-2 \times 1 - (-2) + c = -2$$

$$c = -2$$

Hence, [surface tension]

$$= [Kv^{-2}T^{-2}]$$

9. (*c*) According to the principle of homogeneity of dimensions, only those terms can be added or subtracted, which have same dimensional formula but we can multiply or divide the physical quantities which have different dimensional formulae and gives new physical quantity with non-zero dimensions.

In the question, it is given that *P* and *Q* have different dimensional formula. So, both quantities cannot be added (i.e. $P + Q$) but dividing *P* and *Q*, we can have new physical quantity.

Also we know that, exponents and trigonometric angles are dimensionless. So, given term $\frac{P}{Q}$ must be a dimensionless quantity which is not possible as *P* and *Q* have different dimensional formula.

10. (*b*) The dimensional formulae of the given physical quantities are as follows

$$[P] = [M^1L^2T^{-3}]$$

$$[c] = [LT^{-1}]$$

$$[G] = [M^{-1}L^3T^{-2}]$$

$$[R] = [L]$$

$$[\omega] = [T^{-1}]$$

Given expression, $P = kc^xG^yM^2R^4\omega^6$

The dimensional formula of both sides should be identical in accordance with principle of homogeneity,

i.e., $\quad [P] = [kc^xG^yM^2R^4\omega^6]$

or $\quad [P] = [k][c]^x [G]^y [M]^2 [R^4][\omega]^6$

or $[M^1L^2T^{-3}] = [M^0L^0T^0][LT^{-1}]^x [M^{-1}L^3T^{-2}]^y [M]^2[L]^4[T^{-1}]^6$

or $[M^1L^2T^{-3}]$

$$= [M^{2-y}L^{x+3y+4}T^{-x-2y-6}]$$

Comparing the powers on both sides, we get

$$2-y=1 \text{ or } y=1$$

or $x+3y+4=2$

or $x+3\times1+4=2$

or $x=-5$

$\therefore$ Sum, $x+y=-5+1$

$x+y=-4$

11. (*d*) As given, $X=\varepsilon_0 L\dfrac{\Delta V}{\Delta t}$

According to the principle of homogeneity, for the equation to be correct, the dimensional formula of both sides should be same, i.e.

Dimensional formula of $X=$ Dimensional formula of $\varepsilon_0 L\dfrac{\Delta V}{\Delta t}$

or $[X]=\left[\varepsilon_0 L\dfrac{\Delta V}{\Delta t}\right]$

$$=\frac{[\varepsilon_0][L][\Delta V]}{[\Delta t]} \quad \text{... (i)}$$

As we know that,

$[\varepsilon_0]=[M^{-1}L^{-3}T^4A^2]$

$[L]=[L^1]$

$[\Delta V]=[M^1L^2T^{-3}A^{-1}]$

$[\Delta t]=[T]$

Putting all values, in Eq. (i), we get

$$[X]=\frac{[M^{-1}L^{-3}T^4A^2][L][M^1L^2T^{-3}A^{-1}]}{[T]}$$

$=[M^0L^0T^0A]$

which is equivalent to dimensional formula of current.

12. (*d*) The dimensional formulae of physical quantities given in options are as follows :

[Reynolds number] = $[M^0L^0T^0]$ and

[Friction coefficient] = $[M^0L^0T^0]$

[Latent heat] = $[M^0L^2T^{-2}]$ and

[Gravitational potential] = $[M^0L^2T^{-2}]$

[Activity] = $[T^{-1}]$ and [Frequency] = $[T^{-1}]$

[Planck's constant] = $[M^1L^2T^{-1}]$

[Torque] = $[M^1L^2T^{-2}]$

It is clear that the dimensional formulae of Planck's constant and torque are different.

13. (*c*) We have, $[c]=[LT^{-1}]$

$[G]=[M^{-1}L^3T^{-2}]$

and $[h]=[ML^2T^{-1}]$

Now, mass, $m\propto c^xG^yh^z$

Then,

$$[M]=[LT^{-1}]^x\cdot[M^{-1}L^3T^{-2}]^y\cdot[ML^2T^{-1}]^z$$

Equating powers of similar quantities on both sides, we have

$$x=\frac{1}{2},\ y=-\frac{1}{2} \text{ and } z=\frac{1}{2}$$

$$\therefore \quad m\propto c^{\frac{1}{2}}G^{-\frac{1}{2}}h^{\frac{1}{2}}$$

Similarly, for length,

$$l\propto c^{-\frac{3}{2}}\cdot G^{\frac{1}{2}}\cdot h^{\frac{1}{2}}$$

time, $t\propto c^{-\frac{5}{2}}G^{\frac{1}{2}}h^{\frac{1}{2}}$

and density, $d\propto c^5G^{-2}h^{-1}$

14. (*a*) $\dfrac{1}{\sqrt{LC}}=\omega$

$=$ Angular frequency $=[T^{-1}]$

$\eta A\left(\dfrac{\Delta v}{\Delta x}\right)=F=\text{Force}=[MLT^{-2}]$

$\dfrac{1}{\sqrt{\varepsilon_0\mu_0}}=c=\text{Speed of light}=[LT^{-1}]$

$\dfrac{1}{2}CV^2=U=\text{Energy}=[ML^2T^{-2}]$

15. (*b*) A measurement is said to be more accurate when it has a lesser value of relative error. However, a measurement is said to be more precise when it has a lesser value of absolute error, i.e. is measured by an instrument that has a smaller least count.

From both statements, we conclude that a most precise measurement may be most accurate but not necessarily and *vice-versa* is not true.

16. (*b*) Given that, $x=\dfrac{a^m}{b^n}$

If the relative error in measurement of a and b are $\pm\dfrac{\Delta a}{a}$ and $\pm\dfrac{\Delta b}{b}$, respectively.

Then, on solving the above expression, we get

$$\frac{\Delta x}{x}=m\left(\pm\frac{\Delta a}{a}\right)+n\left(\pm\frac{\Delta b}{b}\right)$$

where, m and n may be any real number (positive, negative rational or irrational).

The value of Δa and Δb should not be comparable to their respective quantity or we can say that $\dfrac{\Delta a}{a}$ and $\dfrac{\Delta b}{b}$ should be very small. Thus, the above relation is valid when $\Delta a << a$ and $\Delta b << b$.

Here, the value of Δa and Δb denotes change in quantities a and b but absolute error is always taken as positive because error cannot be negative.

17. (*c*) Given, $x=\dfrac{a\sqrt{b}}{c^{3/2}d^4}$

Maximum percentage error in x,

$$\frac{\Delta x}{x}\times100=\frac{\Delta a}{a}\times100+\frac{1}{2}\frac{\Delta b}{b}\times100+\frac{3}{2}\frac{\Delta c}{c}\times100+\frac{4\Delta d}{d}\times100 \quad \text{...(i)}$$

Given that, $\dfrac{\Delta a}{a}\times100=2\%$

$\dfrac{\Delta b}{b}\times100=3\%$

$\dfrac{\Delta c}{c}\times100=1\%$

$\dfrac{\Delta d}{d}\times100=0.5\%$

Substituting given values in Eq. (i), we get

$$\frac{\Delta x}{x}\times100=2\%+\frac{1}{2}\times3\%+\frac{3}{2}\times1\%+4\times0.5\%$$

$$\frac{\Delta x}{x}\times100=7\%$$

18. (*d*) As we know that,

$$\text{error}\propto\frac{1}{\text{number of observations}}$$

Here, number of observations are made four times, thus possible error is reduced to one-fourth.

19. (*c*) Given that, $\dfrac{\Delta A}{A}\times100=1\%$,

$\dfrac{\Delta B}{B}\times100=1.5\%$, $\dfrac{\Delta C}{C}\times100=3\%$,

Assume physical quantity X depends on A, B and C as $X=A^\alpha B^\beta C^\gamma$

Then, relative error in measurement of X can be written as

$$\frac{\Delta X}{X}=\left|\alpha\frac{\Delta A}{A}\right|+\left|\beta\frac{\Delta B}{B}\right|+\left|\gamma\frac{\Delta C}{C}\right|$$

or percentage error in X,

$$\frac{\Delta X}{X}\times100=|\alpha|\frac{\Delta A}{A}\times100+|\beta|\frac{\Delta B}{B}\times100+|\gamma|\frac{\Delta C}{C}\times100$$

Given that, $\dfrac{\Delta X}{X}\times100=6\%$

$\Rightarrow 6\%=|\alpha|(1\%)+|\beta|(1.5\%)+|\gamma|(3\%)$

or $6 = |\alpha| + |\beta| \times \frac{3}{2} + |\gamma| 3$

or $2|\alpha| + 3|\beta| + 6|\gamma| = 12$

For option (a), $|\alpha| = 2, |\beta| = 1, |\gamma| = \frac{1}{2}$

$2|\alpha| + 3|\beta| + 6|\gamma|$

$= 2\times 2 + 3\times 1 + 6\times \frac{1}{2} = 10$

does not satisfy the condition.

For option (b), $|\alpha| = 2, |\beta| = \frac{1}{2}, |\gamma| = 3$

$\therefore\ 2|\alpha| + 3|\beta| + 6|\gamma|$

$= 2\times 2 + 3\times \frac{1}{2} + 6\times 3 = 23.5$

does not satisfy the condition.

For option (c), $|\alpha| = \frac{3}{2}, |\beta| = 1, |\gamma| = 1$

$2|\alpha| + 3|\beta| + 6|\gamma|$

$= 2\times \frac{3}{2} + 3\times 1 + 6\times 1 = 12$

satisfy the condition.

For option (d), $|\alpha| = 1, |\beta| = 2, |\gamma| = 1$

$2|\alpha| + 3|\beta| + 6|\gamma|$

$= 2\times 1 + 3\times 2 + 6\times 1$

$= 14$

does not satisfy the condition.

Among all given options, only option (c) satisfy the derived condition.

20. (*b*) All the non-zero digits are significant and the trailing zero (zero to the right of the last non-zero digit) in a number with a decimal point are significant, so 20.000 has 5 significant figures.

When the number is expressed in exponential form, the exponential term does not affect the number of significant figure. So, 6.23×10^1 has 3 significant figures.

21. (*b*) The number of significant figures of a measurement cannot be increased by changing the unit. Thus, for the given measurement of state highway in km and metre, the number of significant figures will be same and equal to 3.

22. (*b*) Given that, initial temperature, $T_i = (30.4 \pm 0.2)°C$

Final temperature, $T_f = (51.5 \pm 0.4)°C$

$\therefore$ Rise in temperature,

$T = T_f - T_i = 51.5 - 30.4$

$T = 21.1°C$

$\Delta T = \pm(\Delta T_i + \Delta T_f)$

$= \pm(0.2 + 0.4)$

$= \pm 0.6°C$

$\therefore$ Rise in temperature $= (21.1 \pm 0.6)°C$

23. (*d*) Here, $A = (1.0 \pm 0.2)$m

$B = (2.0 \pm 0.2)$m

Let $X = (AB)^{\frac{1}{2}}$

$\Rightarrow\ X = (1\times 2)^{\frac{1}{2}} = 1.414$m

Rounding off to two significant digits,

$X = 1.4$m

Now, $\frac{\Delta X}{X} = \frac{1}{2}\left[\frac{\Delta A}{A} + \frac{\Delta B}{B}\right]$

$= \frac{1}{2}\left[\frac{0.2}{1.0} + \frac{0.2}{2.0}\right]$

$\frac{\Delta X}{X} = 0.15$

or $\Delta X = 0.15X$

$= (0.15)(1.414)$

$= 0.2121$

Rounding off to one significant digit,

$\Delta X = 0.2$m

Hence, $(AB)^{\frac{1}{2}} = (1.4 \pm 0.2)$m

24. (*a*) From the given figure,

Least Count (LC) of vernier calliper

$= \frac{1}{10} = 0.1$ mm

Here, vernier scale is on the left hand side from main scale, so zero error will be negative.

$\therefore$ Zero error = (Number of divisions on vernier scale – Number of divisions that coincides with a main scale division) × LC

$= -(10 - 4) \times 0.1$

$\Rightarrow$ Zero error = – 0.6 mm

As, zero correction = – zero error

$= -(-0.6)$ mm

$= 0.6$ mm

25. (*b*) We know that,

Reading of micrometer = Reading of main scale + Reading of thimble scale

As per the figure given in the question, on main scale, each division is equal to $\frac{1}{2} = 0.5$ mm. So, main scale reading

= number of division on main scale × reading of each division

$= 6 \times 0.5 = 3$ mm

The main scale line is coinciding with 30 on thimble scale.

$\therefore$ Reading of thimble scale = Number of divisions × Reading of each division

$= 30 \times 0.01 = 0.3$ mm

$\therefore$ Reading of micrometer

$= 3$ mm $+ 0.3$ mm

$= 3.30$ mm

Qualifier 2 (Kinematics)

1. (*c*) Displacement vectors according to the figure given in the question is as follows

$\mathbf{OA} = 4\hat{i}$ m $\Rightarrow$ $\mathbf{AB} = 3\hat{j}$ m

$\mathbf{BC} = 5\cos 53°\,\hat{i} + 5\sin 53°\,\hat{j}$

$= 5\times\frac{3}{5}\hat{i} + 5\times\frac{4}{5}\hat{j}$

$\mathbf{BC} = (3\hat{i} + 4\hat{j})$m

Total displacement = **OA** + **AB** + **BC**

$= 4\hat{i}$m $+ 3\hat{j}$m $+ (3\hat{i} + 4\hat{j})$m

$= (7\hat{i} + 7\hat{j})$ m

Magnitude $= \sqrt{7^2 + 7^2} = 7\sqrt{2}$ m

2. (*d*) At $t = 0$, packet will have only velocity of aeroplane and its acceleration $a = g$, $u_x = 30$ m/s

At $t = 3$ s, vertical velocity,

$v_y = u_y + gt = 0 + 10 \times 4 = 40$ m/s

$\therefore$ Velocity, $\mathbf{v} = (30\hat{i} + 40\hat{j})$ m/s

Magnitude, $|\mathbf{v}| = \sqrt{(30)^2 + (40)^2} = 50$ m/s

At $t = 3$ s, only gravity is acting on packet, so acceleration is equal to the acceleration due to gravity (i.e. *g*)

$a = 10$ m/s^2

3. (*c*) A is false but R is true. Coordinates of first projectile as seen from second projectile are

$x = x_1 - x_2 = u_1 \cos\alpha \cdot t - u_2 \cos\beta \cdot t$

$= (u_1 \cos\alpha - u_2 \cos\beta)\cdot t$

and $y = y_1 - y_2 = (u_1 \sin\alpha \cdot t - \frac{1}{2}gt^2)$

$- (u_2 \sin\beta \cdot t - \frac{1}{2}gt^2)$

or $y = (u_1 \sin\alpha - u_2 \sin\beta)t$

So, $\frac{y}{x} = \frac{(u_1 \sin\alpha - u_2 \sin\beta)t}{(u_1 \cos\alpha - u_2 \cos\beta)t}$

$\Rightarrow \frac{y}{x}$ = a constant (Let *m*) $\Rightarrow y = mx$

This is the equation of a straight line.

R is correct as both projectiles are accelerated by gravitational force, so for both

$a_x = 0$

and $a_y = g$

4. (*b*) According to the question, the trajectory of the ball is shown below.

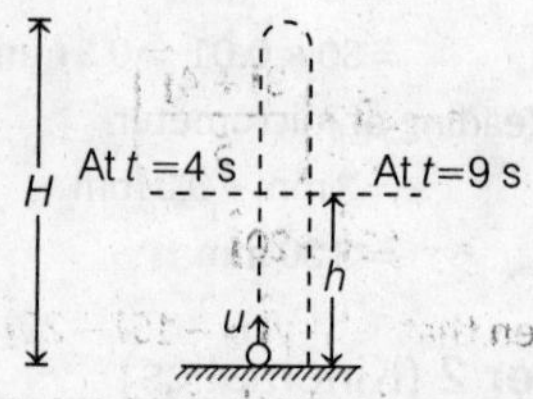

Total time taken by ball from point to reach again at point

$=(9-4)s=5$ s

So, time taken by ball from point to reach at the maximum height is

$=\frac{5}{2}=2.5$ s (half of the total time)

Since, it is given that during upward motion, ball is passing through point, then total time taken by the ball from ground to reach at the maximum height will be $4+2.5=6.5$ s

Using equation of motion,

$$s=ut+\frac{1}{2}at^2$$

$$H=0\times6.5+\frac{1}{2}\times10(6.5)^2$$

$$H=5(6.5)^2 \quad ...(i)$$

Similarly, $H-h=0\times2.5+\frac{1}{2}\times10\times(2.5)^2$

$$H-h=5(2.5)^2 \quad ...(ii)$$

Subtracting Eq. (i) from Eq. (ii), we get

$$H-(H-h)=5(6.5)^2-5(2.5)^2$$

$$=5\times36$$

$$h=180 \text{ m}$$

5. (*d*) Given that, initial velocity,

$$u=120 \text{ m/s}$$

Retardation due to air resistance,

$$a=2 \text{ m/s}^2$$

During upward motion, both gravity and air resistance will act in downward direction.

$$a_{net}=a+g$$

$$=2+10=12 \text{ (downward)}$$

Let the time of ascent be t_1, then

From first equation of motion,

$$v=u+at$$

$$0=120+(-12)\times t_1$$

$$t_1=10 \text{ s}$$

Maximum height attained by the ball,

$$H=\frac{u^2}{2a_{net}}$$

$$=\frac{120\times120}{2\times12}=600 \text{ m}$$

During downward motion, air resistance will act opposite to motion and gravity will act downward.

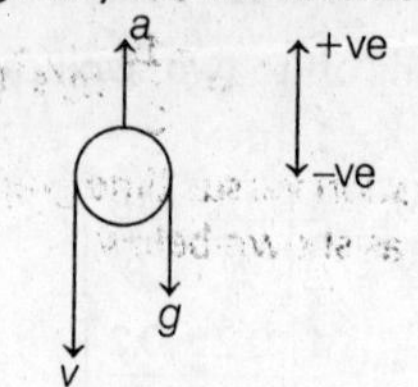

$$a_{net}=g-a$$

$$=10-2=8 \text{ m/s}^2 \text{ (downward)}$$

Let the time of descent be t_2, then from second equation of motion,

$$s=ut+\frac{1}{2}at^2$$

$$-600=0\times t_2+\frac{1}{2}\times(-8)\times(t_2^2)$$

$$-600=0-4t_2^2$$

$$t_2^2=\frac{600}{4}=150 \text{ s}$$

$$t_2=\sqrt{150}=5\sqrt{6} \text{ s}$$

Total time, $t=t_1+t_2$

$$=(10+5\sqrt{6}) \text{ s}$$

6. (*a*) According to question, drawing the situation

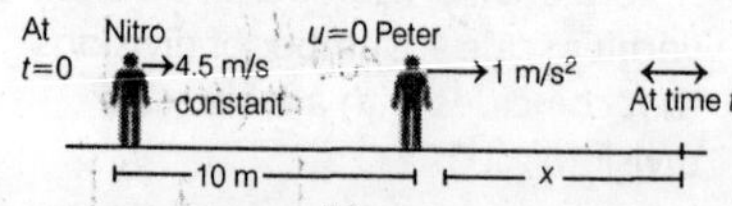

Let at time t, Peter has travelled a distance x and to catch Peter, Nitro has to move $(10+x)$ distance.

For Peter, using 2nd equation of motion

$$s=ut+\frac{1}{2}at^2$$

$$x=0\times t+\frac{1}{2}\times1\times t^2$$

$$x=\frac{t^2}{2} \quad ...(i)$$

For Nitro, using 2nd equation of motion

$$10+x=4.5t$$

$$10+\frac{t^2}{2}=4.5t \quad \text{[from Eq. (i)]}$$

or $\quad t^2-9t+20=0$

or $\quad t^2-5t-4t+20=0$

or $\quad (t-5)-4(t-5)=0$

or $\quad (t-5)(t-4)=0$

or $\quad t=4 \text{ s}, t=5 \text{ s}$

There are the values of time, when the position of both persons are same. For $t\le4$ s, the velocity of Nitro is greater than that of Peter, so distance will decrease continuously and at $t=4$ s, Nitro will catch Peter but at $t=5$ s, Peter will be crossing as velocity becomes greater than that of Nitro.

Alternate Method

This kind of problem is also solved by using the concept of relative motion. Let observe the motion of Peter in frame of Nitro. So, the velocity and acceleration of Nitro will be subtracted from velocity and acceleration of Peter, respectively.

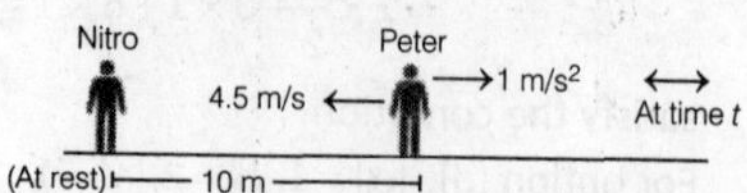

Using 2nd equation of motion,

$$s=ut+\frac{1}{2}at^2$$

Here, $u=-4.5$ m/s

$$a=+1 \text{ m/s}^2$$

$$s=-10 \text{ m}$$

(As Peter has travelled initial distance between them, i.e. 10 m)

$$-10=(-4.5)t+\frac{1}{2}\times(+1)\times t^2$$

$$\frac{t^2}{2}-4.5t+10=0$$

$$t^2-9t+20=0$$

On solving, we get $t=4$ s and 5 s.

7. (*c*) During the whole motion of ball, acceleration is directed vertically downward and equal to 9.8 m/s^2.

Maximum height attained by the ball after rebound, $H_{max}=\frac{u^2}{2g}$

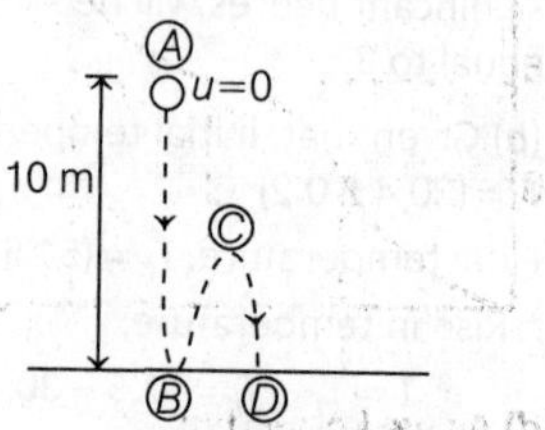

Here, $u=7$ m/s and $g=9.8$ m/s^2

$$\therefore \quad H_{max}=\frac{(7)^2}{2\times9.8}=2.5 \text{ m}$$

First, we will draw displacement-time graphs.

For A to B Acceleration is negative and magnitude of velocity is increasing.

For B to C Acceleration is negative and magnitude of velocity is decreasing

For C to D Acceleration is negative and magnitude of velocity is increasing.

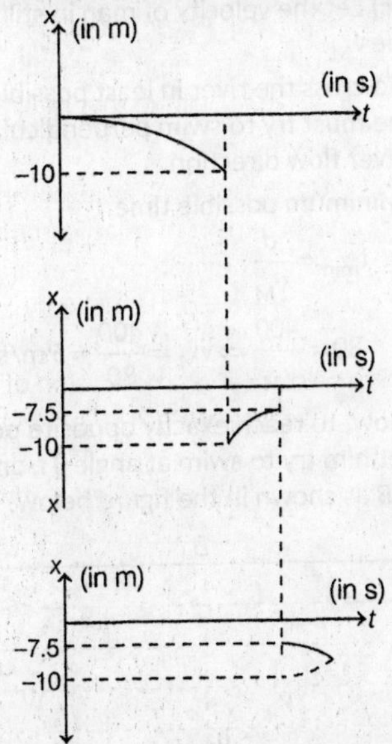

Overall displacement-time graph is as follows:

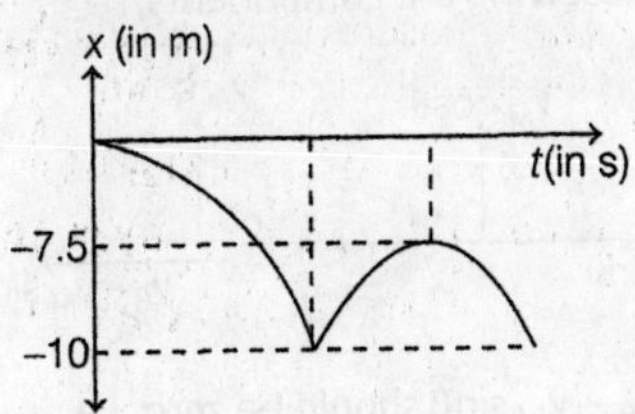

As distance cannot be negative and cannot decrease, so we have to take a mirror image of displacement-time graph at the instant when velocity goes zero to negative.

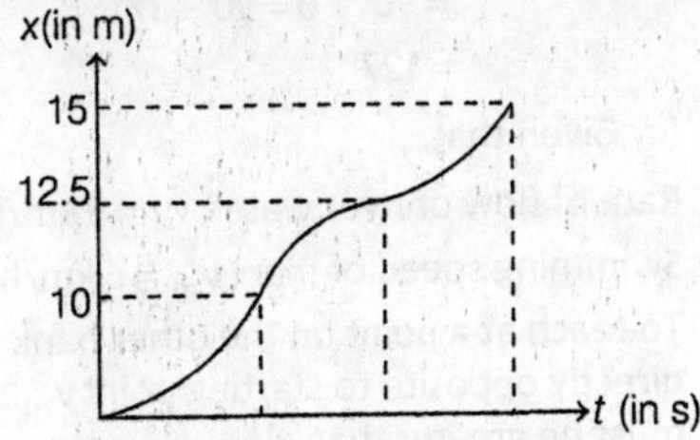

8. (*d*) As we know that,

Acceleration = Slope of *v*-*t* graph

$$= \frac{v_f - v_i}{t_f - t_i}$$

For $0 < t \le 2$ s, $a = \frac{10-0}{2-0} = 5\text{ m/s}^2$ (constant)

For $2 < t < 7$ s, $a = \frac{10-10}{7-2} = 0\text{ m/s}^2$

For $7 < t < 10$ s, $a = \frac{0-10}{10-7}$

$$= \frac{-10}{3}\text{ m/s}^2 \text{ (constant)}$$

Acceleration *versus* time graph is plotted as shown below

9. (*a*) Given that, velocity,

$$v = \frac{400}{10+t}\text{ m/s}$$

$$5 = \frac{400}{10+t} \quad (\because v = 5\text{ m/s})$$

$$50 + 5t = 400 \Rightarrow 5t = 350$$

or $t = \frac{350}{5} = 70$ s

Acceleration, $a = \frac{dv}{dt} = \frac{d}{dt}\left(\frac{400}{10+t}\right)$

$$= 400\frac{d}{dt}\left(\frac{1}{10+t}\right)$$

$$= 400\left\{-\frac{1}{(10+t)^2}\right\}$$

$$a = -\frac{400}{(10+t)^2}$$

At $t = 70$ s, $a = -\frac{400}{(10+70)^2} = -\frac{400}{(80)^2}$

$$a = -\frac{1}{16}\text{ m/s}^2$$

10. (*c*) Given that, $\mathbf{a} = 3\hat{\mathbf{i}} + 4\hat{\mathbf{j}}$

$$a = \sqrt{3^2 + 4^2} = 5$$

$$\hat{\mathbf{a}} = \frac{\mathbf{a}}{a} = \frac{3\hat{\mathbf{i}} + 4\hat{\mathbf{j}}}{5}$$

$$\mathbf{b} = 7\hat{\mathbf{i}} + 24\hat{\mathbf{j}},$$

$$b = \sqrt{7^2 + 24^2} = 25$$

Let the vector be **c** having the same magnitude as **b** and opposite direction as **a**, so it can be written as

$$\mathbf{c} = b(-\hat{\mathbf{a}})$$

$$= -25 \times \left(\frac{3\hat{\mathbf{i}} + 4\hat{\mathbf{j}}}{5}\right)$$

$$= -15\hat{\mathbf{i}} - 20\hat{\mathbf{j}}$$

Given that, $x\hat{\mathbf{i}} + y\hat{\mathbf{j}} = -15\hat{\mathbf{i}} - 20\hat{\mathbf{j}}$

On comparing both sides, we get

$$x = -15, y = -20$$

$$\therefore \quad \frac{x+y}{5} = \frac{-15 + (-20)}{5}$$

$$= -7$$

11. (*a*) Co-ordinates of points *A*, *E* and *G* of the given cube is shown as follows:

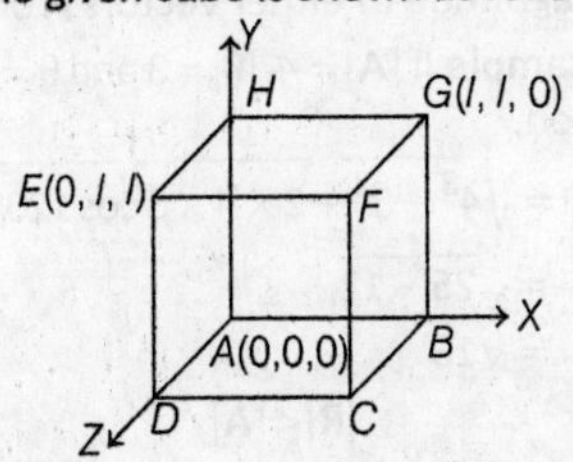

Here,

$$\mathbf{AE} = (0-0)\hat{\mathbf{i}} + (l-0)\hat{\mathbf{j}} + (l-0)\hat{\mathbf{k}}$$

$$\mathbf{AE} = l\hat{\mathbf{j}} + l\hat{\mathbf{k}}$$

$$\mathbf{AG} = (l-0)\hat{\mathbf{i}} + (l-0)\hat{\mathbf{j}} + (0-0)\hat{\mathbf{k}}$$

$$\mathbf{AG} = l\hat{\mathbf{i}} + l\hat{\mathbf{j}}$$

$$|\mathbf{AE}| = AE = \sqrt{l^2 + l^2} = \sqrt{2}l$$

$$|\mathbf{AG}| = AG = \sqrt{l^2 + l^2} = \sqrt{2}l$$

Angle, $\theta = \cos^{-1}\left(\frac{\mathbf{AE} \cdot \mathbf{AG}}{AE \cdot AG}\right)$

$$= \cos^{-1}\left(\frac{(l\hat{\mathbf{j}} + l\hat{\mathbf{k}}) \cdot (l\hat{\mathbf{i}} + l\hat{\mathbf{j}})}{\sqrt{2}l \times \sqrt{2}l}\right)$$

$$= \cos^{-1}\left(\frac{l \times l + 0}{2l^2}\right) = \cos^{-1}\left(\frac{1}{2}\right)$$

$$\theta = 60°$$

12. (*b*)

A. All the vectors are arranged in same order and making a closed triangle so, $\mathbf{a} + \mathbf{b} + \mathbf{c} = 0$ or $\mathbf{a} + \mathbf{b} = -\mathbf{c}$

B. **a** and **b** are in same order and **c** is arranged in opposite order, so **c** is resultant at **a** and **b**.
i.e., $\mathbf{a} + \mathbf{b} = \mathbf{c}$

C. Here, **c** and **b** are connected in same order and **a** is arranged in opposite order, thus **a** is resultant of **c** and **b**
i.e., $\mathbf{c} + \mathbf{b} = \mathbf{a}$ or $\mathbf{a} - (\mathbf{b} + \mathbf{c}) = 0$

D. Similarly, **c** and **a** are in same order and **b** is in opposite order, so **b** is resultant vector
$\mathbf{c} + \mathbf{a} = \mathbf{b}$ or $\mathbf{b} - \mathbf{c} = \mathbf{a}$

13. (c) In case of vector addition,

$$|\mathbf{A}+\mathbf{B}| = \sqrt{A^2+B^2+2AB\cos\theta} \quad ...(i)$$

In case of vector subtraction,

$$|\mathbf{A}-\mathbf{B}| = \sqrt{A^2+B^2-2AB\cos\theta}$$

If $\theta = 90°$, then $|\mathbf{A}+\mathbf{B}| = \sqrt{A^2+B^2}$

$$|\mathbf{A}-\mathbf{B}| = \sqrt{A^2+B^2}$$

It is clear that $|\mathbf{A}+\mathbf{B}| = |\mathbf{A}-\mathbf{B}|$

So, statement I is incorrect.

If θ is an obtuse angle, then magnitude of resultant vector **R** will be less than magnitude of either vectors **A** or **B**.

Example If $|\mathbf{A}| = 4$, $|\mathbf{B}| = 3$ and $\theta = 120°$, then,

$$|\mathbf{R}| = \sqrt{4^3+3^2+2\times4\times3\cos120°}$$

$$= \sqrt{25-12}$$

$$= \sqrt{13}$$

$\therefore \qquad |\mathbf{R}| < |\mathbf{A}|$

If the vectors are in opposite directions and are equal in magnitude, then also the magnitude of **R** will be less than the magnitude of either vectors **A** or **B**.

Example if $|\mathbf{A}| = |\mathbf{B}|$ and $\theta = 180°$ then,

$$|\mathbf{R}| = \sqrt{A^2+A^2-2A^2\cos180°}$$

$$|\mathbf{R}| = \sqrt{2A^2-2A^2}$$

$$|\mathbf{R}| = 0 \Rightarrow |\mathbf{R}| < |\mathbf{A}| \text{ or } |\mathbf{B}|$$

So, statement II is correct.

14. (*a*) Using parallelogram law,

$$R^2 = a^2+b^2+2ab\cos\theta$$

$$\Rightarrow (\sqrt{7}b)^2 = a^2+b^2+2ab\cos60°$$

On dividing the above equation by a^2 and solving, we get

$$\Rightarrow 6\left(\frac{b}{a}\right)^2 - \left(\frac{b}{a}\right) - 1 = 0$$

$$\Rightarrow \frac{b}{a} = \frac{1\pm\sqrt{1+24}}{2\times6} = \frac{1\pm5}{12}$$

As magnitudes of vectors must be positive, so

$$\frac{b}{a} = \frac{1+5}{12} = \frac{1}{2}$$

15. (a) Position of particle,

$$\mathbf{r} = 6t\,\hat{\mathbf{i}} - 2t^2\,\hat{\mathbf{j}} + 4\mathbf{k}$$

So, velocity,

$$\mathbf{v} = \frac{d\mathbf{r}}{dt} = 6\hat{\mathbf{i}} - 4t\,\hat{\mathbf{j}}$$

and acceleration,

$$\mathbf{a} = \frac{d\mathbf{v}}{dt} = -4\hat{\mathbf{j}}\ \text{m/s}^2$$

Magnitude of velocity at $t = 2$ s,

$$|\mathbf{v}|_{t=2} = \sqrt{6^2+(4\times2)^2}$$

$$= 10 \text{ m/s}$$

Magnitude of acceleration at $t = 2$ s,

$$|\mathbf{a}| = 4 \text{ m/s}^2$$

$$\therefore \quad \text{Ratio} = \frac{10}{4} = \frac{5}{2}$$

16. (*b*) Given that, velocity of boy, $\mathbf{v}_b = 5\hat{\mathbf{i}}$ m/s

Let velocity of rain w.r.t. ground

$$\mathbf{v}_r = v_x\hat{\mathbf{i}} + v_y\hat{\mathbf{j}} \text{ m/s}$$

Velocity of rain w.r.t. boy

$$\mathbf{v}_{rb} = \mathbf{v}_r + (-\mathbf{v}_b)$$

$$= v_x\hat{\mathbf{i}} + v_y\hat{\mathbf{j}} - 5\hat{\mathbf{i}}$$

$$= (v_x-5)\hat{\mathbf{i}} + v_y\hat{\mathbf{j}}$$

It is in vertical direction, so $(v_x - 5)$ must be zero.

or $\qquad v_x = 5$ m/s $\qquad$ ...(i)

On increasing the speed of boy, velocity of rain w.r.t. boy becomes

$$\mathbf{v}'_{rb} = (v_x-15)\hat{\mathbf{i}} + v_y\hat{\mathbf{j}}$$

$$\therefore \quad \tan\theta = \tan45° = \frac{v_x-15}{v_y}$$

$$1 = \frac{v_x-15}{v_y} \quad \text{or} \quad 1 = \frac{5-15}{v_y}$$

or $\qquad v_y = -10$ m/s

$\therefore$ Velocity of rain w.r.t. ground,

$$\mathbf{v}_r = (5\hat{\mathbf{i}} - 10\hat{\mathbf{j}}) \text{ m/s}$$

Magnitude of velocity of rain,

$$\mathbf{v}_r = \sqrt{5^2+(-10)^2} = \sqrt{25+100}$$

$$= \sqrt{125}$$

$$= 5\sqrt{5} \text{ m/s}$$

17. (c) Given that, both make an angle 37° with the banks, then drawing the situation

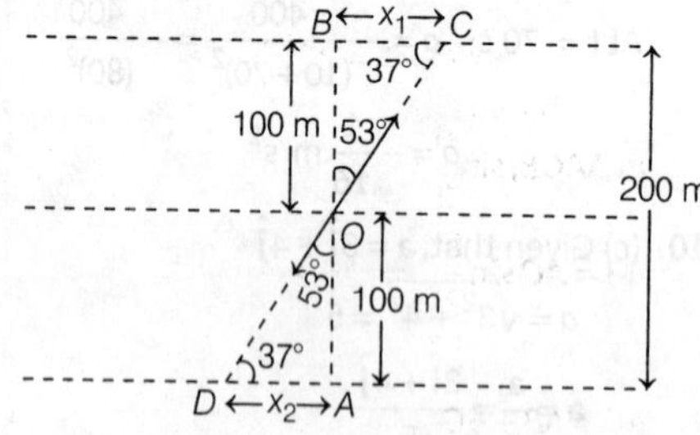

In ΔOBC, $\tan53° = \dfrac{x_1}{100}$

or $\qquad x_1 = 100\tan53°$

In ΔOAD, $\tan53° = \dfrac{x_2}{100}$

or $\qquad x_2 = 100\tan53°$

Distance between them along the river,

$$x_1 + x_2 = 100\tan53° + 100\tan53°$$

$$= 200\tan53°$$

$$= 200\times\frac{4}{3}$$

$$x_1 + x_2 = \frac{800}{3} \text{ m}$$

18. (c) Let the velocity of man in still water be v_M.

To cross the river in least possible time, he must try to swim perpendicular to river flow direction.

Minimum possible time,

$$t_{min} = \frac{d}{v_M}$$

$$80 = \frac{400}{v_M} \Rightarrow v_M = \frac{400}{80} = 5 \text{ m/s}$$

Now, to reach exactly opposite point, let him try to swim at angle θ from line AB as shown in the figure below.

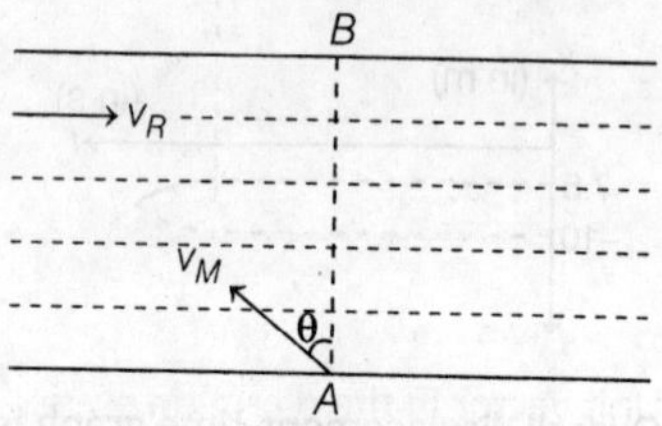

Resolving the components,

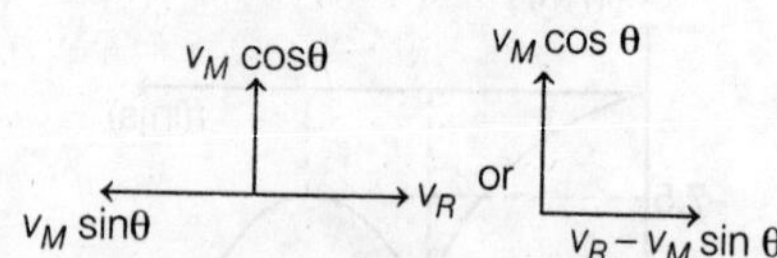

$v_R - v_M\sin\theta$ should be zero, i.e.

$$v_R - v_M\sin\theta = 0$$

$$\sin\theta = \frac{v_R}{v_M} = \frac{3}{5}$$

$$\Rightarrow \qquad \theta = 37°$$

Direction from the flow of river

$$= 90° + \theta = 90° + 37°$$

$$= 127°$$

19. (*d*) Given that,

Rate of flow of river water, $v_r = 8$ km/h

Swimming speed of man, $v_m = 6$ km/h

To reach at a point on the other bank directly opposite to starting point v_m must be greater than v_r

i.e., $\qquad v_m > v_r$

But in the question $v_m < v_r$

So, man cannot reach to the desired point directly by swimming.

20. (*d*)

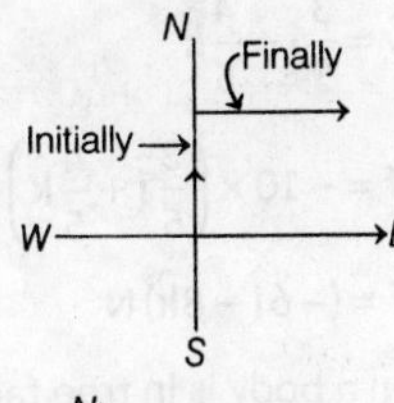

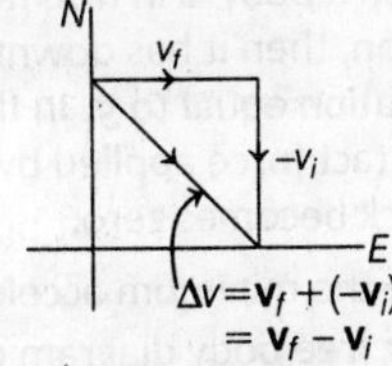

$\Delta v = v_f + (-v_i)$
$= v_f - v_i$

Now, $\Delta v = v_f - v_i = 10\sqrt{2}\,\hat{i} - 10\sqrt{2}\,\hat{j}$

$|\Delta \mathbf{v}| = \sqrt{(10\sqrt{2})^2 + (10\sqrt{2})^2} = 20\text{ m/s}$

So, $|\mathbf{a}| = \dfrac{|\Delta \mathbf{v}|}{\Delta t} = \dfrac{20}{2} = 10\text{ m/s}^2$, due *S-E*

21. (*c*) According to the question, the situation is as shown in the figure below

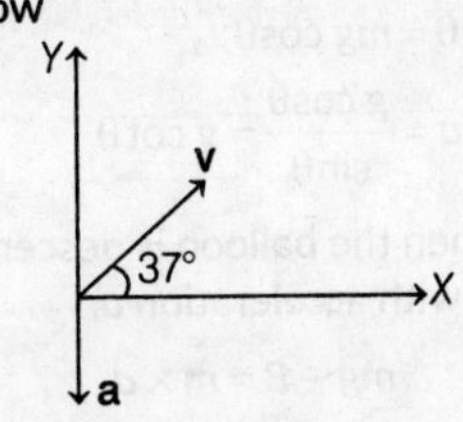

Unit vector in the direction of velocity,

$\hat{\mathbf{v}} = \cos\theta\,\hat{i} + \sin\theta\,\hat{j}$

$= \cos 37°\,\hat{i} + \sin 37°\,\hat{j}$

$= \dfrac{4}{5}\hat{i} + \dfrac{3}{5}\hat{j}$

Acceleration, $\mathbf{a} = -10\hat{j}\text{ m/s}^2$

Component of acceleration **a** in the direction of **v** is given as

$(\mathbf{a}\cdot\hat{\mathbf{v}}) = (-10\hat{j})\cdot\left(\dfrac{4}{5}\hat{i} + \dfrac{3}{5}\hat{j}\right)$

$= (-10)\left(+\dfrac{3}{5}\right) = -6\text{ m/s}^2$

22. (*b*) Given that, $u = 25\text{ m/s}, \theta = 53°$

Maximum height, $H = \dfrac{u^2 \sin^2\theta}{2g}$

$= \dfrac{(25)^2 \times \sin^2 53°}{2\times 10}$

$H = \dfrac{25\times 25\times 4\times 4}{2\times 10\times 5\times 5} = 20\text{ m}$

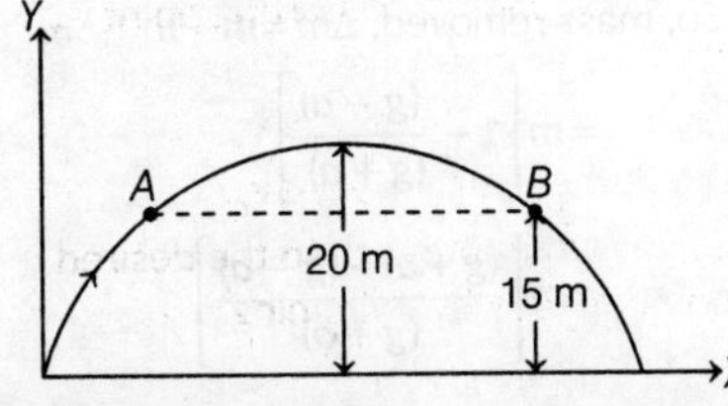

From the relation, $8H = gT^2$

Here, *H* is maximum height attained by projectile which have time of flight *T*. Similarly, we can assume another projectile motion from *A* to *B* and let the time taken to reach from *A* to *B* be t_{AB},

then $8(H-h) = gt_{AB}^2$

or $t_{AB} = \sqrt{\dfrac{8(H-h)}{g}} = \sqrt{\dfrac{8\times(20-15)}{10}}$

$= \sqrt{\dfrac{8\times 5}{10}} = 2\text{ s}$

23. (*a*) Given that, $\theta = 60°$

$x = 10\sqrt{3}\text{ m}, y = 15\text{ m}$

$g = 10\text{ m/s}^2$

From the equation of trajectory,

$y = x\tan\theta - \dfrac{gx^2}{2u^2\cos^2\theta}$

$15 = (10\sqrt{3})\tan 60° - \dfrac{10\times(10\sqrt{3})^2}{2u^2\cos^2 60°}$

$15 = 10\sqrt{3}\times\sqrt{3} - \dfrac{10\times 300}{2u^2\times\dfrac{1}{4}}$

$15 = 30 - \dfrac{6000}{u^2}$

or $\dfrac{6000}{u^2} = 15 \Rightarrow u^2 = \dfrac{6000}{15} = 400$

or $u = \sqrt{400} = 20\text{ m/s}$

24. (*d*) The figure is shown as below

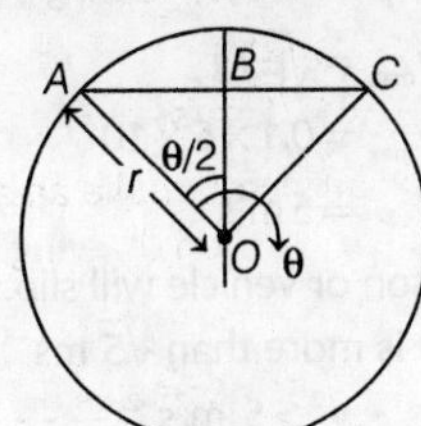

In $\Delta AOB, \sin\dfrac{\theta}{2} = \dfrac{AB}{AO}$

$AB = AO\sin\dfrac{\theta}{2} \Rightarrow AB = r\sin\dfrac{\theta}{2}$

$(\because AO = r)$

$AC = AB + BC$

$AC = r\sin\dfrac{\theta}{2} + r\sin\dfrac{\theta}{2}$ $(\because AB = BC)$

$AC = 2r\sin\dfrac{\theta}{2}$

So, the magnitude of the corresponding linear displacement will be $2r\sin\dfrac{\theta}{2}$.

25. (*c*) ΔOAB is equilateral triangle.

$\therefore$ Magnitude of displacement = 10 m

Change in speed = 0 m/s

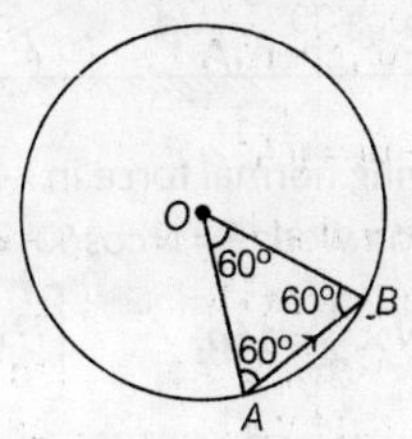

Change in velocity. $\Delta \mathbf{v} = \mathbf{v}_A - \mathbf{v}_B$

$|\Delta \mathbf{v}| = \sqrt{v_A^2 + v_B^2 - 2v_Av_B\cos 60°}$

$= \sqrt{v^2 + v^2 - 2v^2\times\dfrac{1}{2}}$

$= v = 10\text{ m/s}$

Arc length, $AB = r\theta = 10\times\dfrac{\pi}{3}$

$\therefore$ Distance $= \dfrac{10}{3}\pi\text{ m}$

Qualifier 3 (Laws of Motion)

1. (*a*) For bullet,

$v^2 - u^2 = 2as$

Here, $u = 10\text{ m/s}$

$s = 50\text{ cm}$

$= 50\times 10^{-2}\text{ m} = 0.50\text{ m}$

$\Rightarrow 0 - (10)^2 = 2(a)(0.50)$

$\Rightarrow a = -100\text{ m/s}^2$

Force $= ma = 0.1\times(-100)$

$= -10\text{ N}$

So, magnitude of retarding force is 10 N.

2. (*b*) Impulse = Force × Time

= Change in momentum

So, at $t = 0$s,

Impulse, $\Delta p = m(v-u) = m\cdot\dfrac{d}{dt}(x_f - x_i)$

$= m\cdot\dfrac{d}{dt}\left(\dfrac{3}{4}t - 0\right) = m\left(\dfrac{3}{4}\right)$

$= 4\times\dfrac{3}{4} = 3\text{ N-s}$ $(\because m = 4\text{ kg})$

Similarly, at $t = 4$s,

Impulse, $\Delta p = -3\text{ N-s}$

3. (*b*) As, $F = \dfrac{\Delta p}{\Delta t}$

$\Rightarrow \Delta p = F\times\Delta t$ = constant, if both *F* and Δt are same.

Direction of change in momentum is the direction of acceleration while direction of momentum as that of velocity. So, both may be different.

4. (*a*) FBD of wedge is

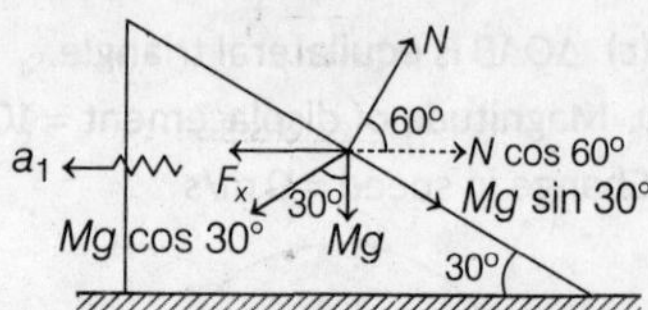

Resolving normal force in x-direction,

Force on wedge $= N\cos 60° = Ma_1$

$\Rightarrow \quad N \times \frac{1}{2} = 16a_1 \qquad \left[\because \cos 60° = \frac{1}{2}\right]$

$N = 32a_1$

Now, $\quad N = 8g\cos 30° - 8a_1 \sin 30°$

$\Rightarrow \quad 32a_1 = 8g\frac{\sqrt{3}}{2} - 8a_1 \times \frac{1}{2}$

$\Rightarrow \quad a_1 = \frac{\sqrt{3}}{9}\cdot g$

Now, resolving forces along the inclined plane,

$mg\sin 30° + ma_1\cos 30° = ma_2$

$8g \times \frac{1}{2} + 8 \times \frac{\sqrt{3}}{9} \times g \times \frac{\sqrt{3}}{2} = 8a_2$

or $\quad a_2 = \frac{2g}{3}$

So, $\quad \frac{a_1}{a_2} = \frac{\sqrt{3}}{9} \times \frac{3}{2} = \frac{1}{2\sqrt{3}}$

5. (*c*) Elevator moving with constant speed,

Force $= mg = 600$ N

Elevator moving with constant acceleration of $3\ \text{ms}^{-2}$

(i) Up $\Rightarrow F = m(g+a) = 60 \times 13 = 780$ N

(ii) Down $\Rightarrow F = m(g-a)$

$= 60 \times 7 = 420$ N

Cable breaks $\Rightarrow F = (g-g) \times m = 0$

So, A $\rightarrow$ P, B $\rightarrow$ Q, C $\rightarrow$ R, D $\rightarrow$ S.

6. (*c*) Given that, mass of boy, $m = 45$ kg

As boy is standing stationary w.r.t. the conveyor belt, so

Acceleration of boy = Acceleration of belt

$\therefore$ Acceleration of boy, $a = 2\ \text{m/s}^2$

$\therefore$ Net force on boy will be equal to the force applied by conveyor belt.

i.e. Net force on boy, $F = ma = 45 \times 2$

$F = 90$ N

7. (*c*) Let at some instant (particle crossing X-axis) velocity is $v\hat{i}$, then

Initial velocity $= v\hat{i}$

After covering $\frac{1}{4}$th of circle,

Final velocity $= v\hat{j}$

So, change in momentum,

$\Delta \mathbf{p} = m(v\hat{j} - v\hat{i}) = mv(\hat{j} - \hat{i})$

$= m(\hat{j} - \hat{i}) \qquad (\because v = 1\ \text{m/s})$

Magnitude of change in momentum

$= |\Delta \mathbf{p}| = m\sqrt{1^2 + 1^2}$

$= \sqrt{2}\,m$

8. (*b*) Given, $u = 30\sqrt{2}$ m/s

Distance = s metre

Let a be the acceleration of the bullet.

According to the first condition, ($v = 0$)

Using, $v^2 = u^2 - 2as$

$0 = 900 \times 2 - 2as$

$\Rightarrow \quad a = \frac{900}{s}\ \text{m/s}^2$

For second condition,

$v^2 = u^2 - 2as = (30\sqrt{2})^2 - 2 \times \frac{900}{s} \times \frac{s}{2}$

$\Rightarrow v^2 = 1800 - 900$

$\Rightarrow \ v = \sqrt{900}$

$= 30$ m/s

9. (*b*) We know that,

$\tan\theta = \frac{v^2}{rg} \qquad \text{... (i)}$

and $\qquad F = \mu_s mg \qquad \text{... (ii)}$

From Eqs. (i) and (ii) for maximum speed of vehicle,

$\mu_s mg \geq \frac{mv_{max}^2}{r}$

(v_{max} = maximum velocity of vehicle)

(where, $\mu_s = 0.1$, $r = 5$ m, $g = 10\ \text{ms}^{-2}$)

$v_{max} = \sqrt{\mu_s rg}$

$v_{max}^2 = 0.1 \times 5 \times 10$

$= 5\ \text{m}^2\text{s}^{-2}$

So, person or vehicle will slip, if the velocity is more than $\sqrt{5}\ \text{ms}^{-1}$.

or $\qquad v^2 > 5\ \text{m}^2\text{s}^{-2}$

10. (*d*) Magnitude of friction force acting on the block,

$f = \mu N$ or $\mu mg \quad (\because N = mg)$

$= 0.5 \times 2 \times 10$

$= 10$ N

Kinetic friction will act on the block opposite to the motion.

$\therefore$ $\mathbf{f} = f(-\hat{\mathbf{v}})$, where $\hat{\mathbf{v}}$ is unit vector along velocity.

$\hat{\mathbf{v}} = \frac{\mathbf{v}}{v} = \frac{15\hat{i} + 20\hat{k}}{\sqrt{(15)^2 + (20)^2}}$

$= \frac{15\hat{i} + 20\hat{k}}{25}$

$\hat{\mathbf{v}} = \frac{3}{5}\hat{i} + \frac{4}{5}\hat{k}$

$\therefore \qquad \mathbf{f} = -10 \times \left(\frac{3}{5}\hat{i} + \frac{4}{5}\hat{k}\right)$

$\mathbf{f} = (-6\hat{i} - 8\hat{k})$ N

11. (*c*) When a body is in free fall condition, then it has downward acceleration equal to g. In this case, the contact force applied by wedge on the block becomes zero.

Let a be the minimum acceleration and drawing free body diagram of block in wedge frame.

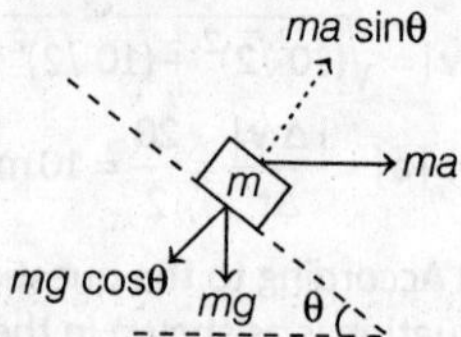

$ma\sin\theta = mg\cos\theta$

or $\quad a = \frac{g\cos\theta}{\sin\theta} = g\cot\theta$

12. (*a*) When the balloon is descending down with acceleration a.

So, $\qquad mg - B = m \times a \qquad \text{... (i)}$

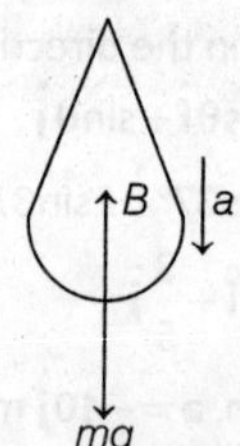

[where, B = Buoyant force]

Here, we should assume that while removing same mass, the volume of balloon and hence buoyant force will not be changed.

Let the new mass of the balloon is m', so mass removed $= m - m'$

$B - m'g = m' \times a \qquad \text{... (ii)}$

On solving Eqs. (i) and (ii), we get

$mg - m'g = ma + m'a$

$\Rightarrow \qquad m(g-a) = m'(g+a)$

$m' = \frac{m(g-a)}{g+a}$

So, mass removed, $\Delta m = m - m'$

$= m\left[1 - \frac{(g-a)}{(g+a)}\right]$

$= m\left[\frac{(g+a) - (g-a)}{(g+a)}\right]$

$$= m\left[\frac{g+a-g+a}{g+a}\right] = \frac{2ma}{g+a}$$

13. (*a*) From FBD of man,

Using $F_{net} = Ma$,

$$Ma = Mg - N$$

$$M\left(\frac{Mg}{M+m}\right) = Mg - N \quad \left[\because a = \frac{Mg}{M+m}\right]$$

or $$N = Mg\left(\frac{M+m-M}{M+m}\right)$$

$$= \frac{Mmg}{M+m}$$

Reading of weighing machine,

$$= \frac{Mm}{M+m}$$

14. (*b*) Acceleration of system,

$$a = \frac{180-60}{2+3+7}$$

$$= \frac{120}{12} = 10 \text{ m/s}^2 \quad \text{(leftward)}$$

Let contact force between 2 kg and 3 kg be N_1 and that of between 3 kg and 7 kg be N_2.

Drawing FBD,

$$2 \times a = N_1 - 60$$

or $$2 \times 10 = N_1 - 60$$

or $$N_1 = 80 \text{ N}$$

$$3 \times a = N_2 - N_1$$

$$3 \times 10 = N_2 - 80$$

$\Rightarrow$ $$N_2 = 110 \text{ N}$$

So, ratio $= \dfrac{N_1}{N_2} = \dfrac{80}{110}$

or $$\frac{N_1}{N_2} = \frac{8}{11} \text{ or } 8:11$$

15. (*c*) Spring force, $F = -kx$

When x is positive, F is negative (i.e. in opposite direction to that of displacement).

When x is negative, F will be positive.

So, A is false but R is true.

16. (*d*) According to the question,

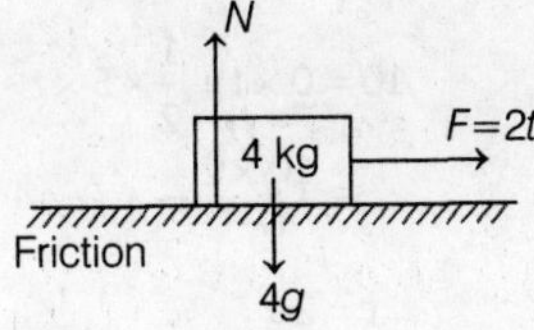

Motion of block will start when $F \geq$ friction (static)

For just starting motion,

$$F = \text{Friction (static)}$$

$$2t = \mu_s(4 \times g) \quad (\because f_s = \mu_s mg)$$

$$t = 2\mu_s g$$

When motion starts, the friction force will be kinetic in nature which is less than static friction force here.

$\therefore$ Acceleration,

$$a = \frac{F - \text{Kinetic friction}}{m}$$

$$= \frac{2t - \mu_k \times 4 \times g}{4}$$

$$= \frac{t}{2} - \mu_k g$$

Acceleration of block when motion starts (i.e. at $t = 2\mu_s g$)

$$a = \frac{2\mu_s g}{2} - \mu_k g$$

$$= (\mu_s - \mu_k)g$$

$$a \neq 0 \quad (\text{As } \mu_s > \mu_k)$$

The graph between acceleration and time t is shown below.

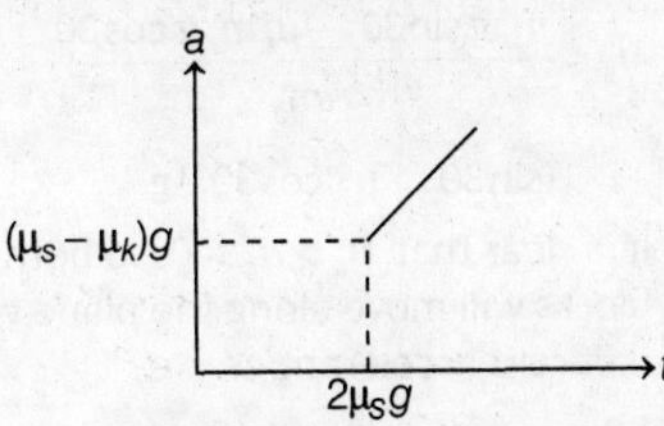

17. (*c*) Let the acceleration of blocks be a

Given that, for block B,

$$u = 0$$

$$s = 2.5 \text{ m}$$

$$t = 2 \text{ s}$$

From second equation of motion,

$$s = ut + \frac{1}{2}at^2$$

$$2.5 = 0 \times t + \frac{1}{2} \times a \times (2)^2$$

or $$a = \frac{2 \times 2.5}{(2)^2}$$

or $$a = \frac{5}{4} \text{ m/s}^2$$

Acceleration of blocks is given as

$$a = \frac{m_1 - m_2}{m_1 + m_2} g$$

Here, $m_1 = 2$ kg, $m_2 = M$ kg, $g = 10 \text{ m/s}^2$

$$\frac{5}{4} = \frac{2-M}{2+M} \times 10$$

$$5(2+M) = 40(2-M)$$

$$10 + 5M = 80 - 40M$$

$$5M + 40M = 80 - 10$$

$$45M = 70$$

$$M = \frac{14}{9} \text{ kg}$$

18. (*b*) Acceleration of each block,

$$a = \frac{\text{Net pulling force}}{\text{Total mass}}$$

$$= \frac{F - 12g - 8g - Mg}{12+8+M}$$

$$= \frac{F - (12+8+M)g}{20+M} \quad \text{... (i)}$$

From FBD of 8 kg block,

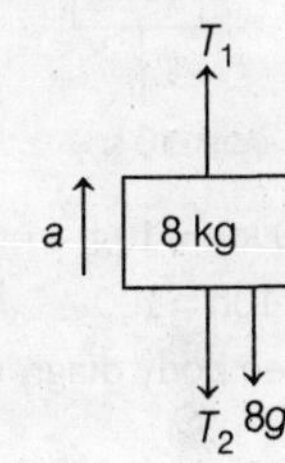

$$8 \times a = T_1 - T_2 - 8g$$

Given that, $T_1 - T_2 = 80$ N ... (ii)

$$8 \times a = 80 - 8 \times 10 = 0$$

$$a = 0$$

From FBD of M kg block,

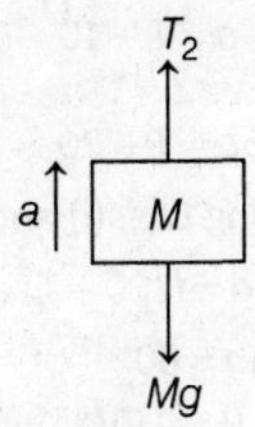

$$M \times a = T_2 - Mg$$

$$M \times 0 = T_2 - Mg \quad (\because a = 0)$$

$$T_2 = Mg \text{ or } 10M \quad \text{... (iii)}$$

Putting the value of T_2 in Eq. (ii), we get

$$T_1 - Mg = 80$$

or $\quad T_1 = 80 + 10M \quad \text{... (iv)}$

Dividing Eq. (iv) by Eq. (iii), we get

$$\frac{T_1}{T_2} = \frac{80 + 10M}{10M}$$

Given, $\quad \frac{T_1}{T_2} = \frac{3}{1}$

$$\frac{3}{1} = \frac{80 + 10M}{10M}$$

or $\quad 3M = 8 + M$

or $\quad 2M = 8$

or $\quad M = 4\text{ kg}$

Putting the values of a and M in Eq. (i), we get

$$0 = \frac{F - (12 + 8 + 4) \times 10}{20 + 4}$$

$$F = (12 + 8 + 4) \times 10$$

$$= 24 \times 10$$

$$= 240\text{ N}$$

19. (*b*) Acceleration,

$$a = \frac{\text{Net pulling force}}{\text{Total mass}}$$

From FBD of 10 kg,

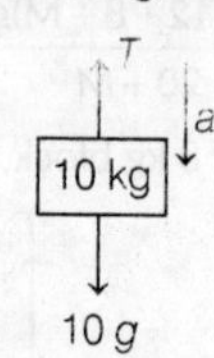

$$10 \times a = 10g - T$$

or $\quad 10a = 100 - T \quad \text{... (i)}$

From Free body diagram of 6 kg,

$$6 \times a = T + 10 - 6g \sin 30^\circ$$

or $\quad 6 \times a = T + 10 - 6 \times 10 \times \frac{1}{2}$

or $\quad 6a = T - 20 \quad \text{...(ii)}$

On adding Eqs. (i) and (ii), we get

$$10a + 6a = (100 - T) + (T - 20)$$

$$16a = 80$$

$\Rightarrow \quad a = 5\text{ m/s}^2$

When system is released from rest, the block of 10 kg will cover height of 10 m before reaching on the ground.

Using 2nd equation of motion,

$$s = ut + \frac{1}{2}at^2$$

$$10 = 0 \times t + \frac{1}{2} \times 5 \times t^2$$

or $\quad t^2 = \frac{10 \times 2}{5} = 4$

or $\quad t = 2\text{ s}$

20. (*c*) Angle of inclination, $\theta = 30^\circ$

or $\tan\theta = \tan 30^\circ$

$$= \frac{1}{\sqrt{3}} = 0.866$$

Here, $\tan\theta > \mu_B > \mu_A$, so friction force acting on both blocks is not sufficient to prevent motion of blocks and nature of frictional force will be kinetic.

Friction force on block A,

$$f_A = \mu_A m_A g \cos 30^\circ$$
$$= 0.6 g \cos 30^\circ$$

Friction force on block B,

$$f_B = \mu_B m_B g \cos 30^\circ$$
$$= 0.8 g \cos 30^\circ$$

Here, first assumption will consider that both are not in contact, then acceleration of block A,

$$a_A = \frac{\text{net force}}{\text{mass}}$$

$$= \frac{m_A g \sin 30^\circ - \mu_A m_A g \cos 30^\circ}{m_A}$$

$$= (\sin 30^\circ - \mu_A \cos 30^\circ) g$$

Similarly, acceleration of block B,

$$a_B = \frac{m_B g \sin 30^\circ - \mu_B m_A g \cos 30^\circ}{m_B}$$

$$= (\sin 30^\circ - \mu_B \cos 30^\circ) g$$

It is clear that, $a_A > a_B > 0$, so both blocks will move along the plane with different accelerations.

21. (*d*) Here, we will consider two cases

Case (I) When $\tan\theta < \mu$: In this case, block will remain at rest

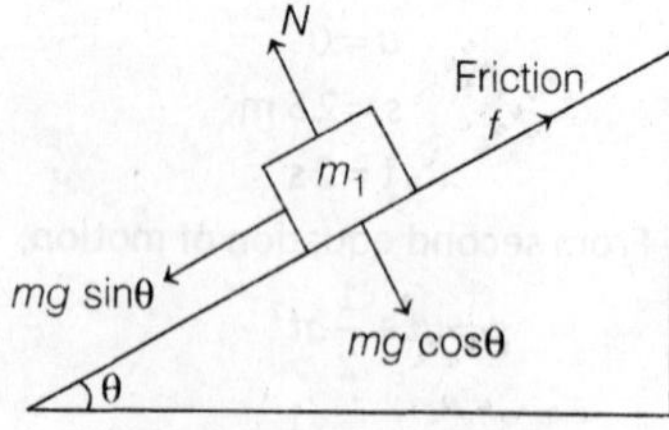

Normal reaction, $N = mg\cos\theta$

Friction force, $\quad f = mg\sin\theta$

Contact force,

$$F_c = \sqrt{N^2 + f^2}$$

$$= \sqrt{(mg\cos\theta)^2 + (mg\sin\theta)^2}$$

$$= mg \text{ (constant)}$$

Case (II) When $\tan\theta \geq \mu$: In this case, block will move down the plane and frictional force will be kinetic in nature.

Normal reaction, $N = mg\cos\theta$

Friction force, $f = \mu N = \mu mg\cos\theta$

Contact force, $F_c = \sqrt{N^2 + f^2}$

$$= \sqrt{(mg\cos\theta)^2 + (\mu mg\cos\theta)^2}$$

$$= mg\cos\theta\sqrt{1 + \mu^2}$$

If θ is increased, then $\cos\theta$ decreases and contact force F_c decreases.

At $\theta = 90^\circ$, $F_c = 0$

The variation between F_c and θ can be shown as

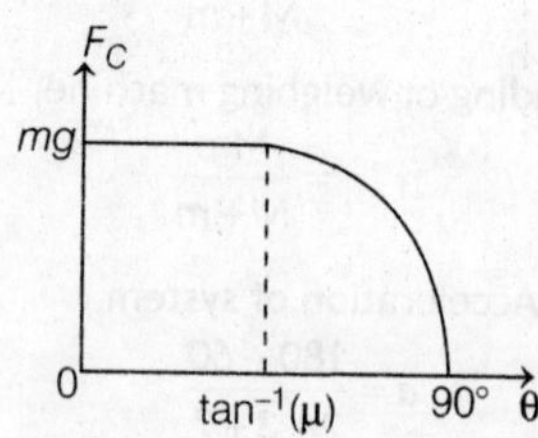

22. (*c*) Normal reaction on block is

$$N = mg\cos\theta$$

Ratio of normal reaction force on block at angular positions of 45° and 30° is,

$$\text{Ratio} = \frac{N_1}{N_2} = \frac{mg\cos\theta_1}{mg\cos\theta_2}$$

$$= \frac{\cos\theta_1}{\cos\theta_2} = \frac{\cos 45^\circ}{\cos 30^\circ}$$

$$= \frac{\frac{1}{\sqrt{2}}}{\frac{\sqrt{3}}{2}} = \frac{\sqrt{2}}{\sqrt{3}}$$

23. (*c*) Just after release, the elongation in spring is zero, so spring force will also be zero. The one end of spring is connected to string, so tension in string is also zero.

FBD of blocks just after release

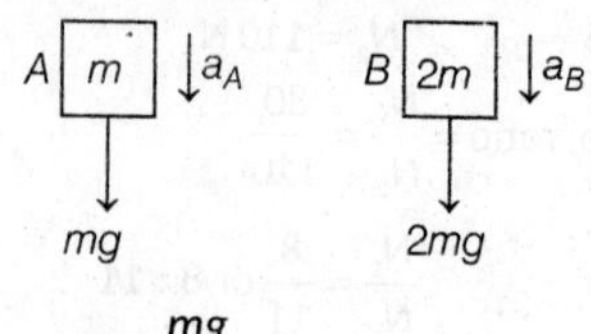

$$a_A = \frac{mg}{m}$$

and $\quad a_B = \frac{2mg}{2m}$

$$a_A = g \text{ and } a_B = g$$

Both acceleration of blocks are equal to g downward.

24. (*b*) For a level road, maximum speed for safe turning,

$$v_1 = \sqrt{\mu_s Rg} = \sqrt{0.2\, Rg} = 0.45\sqrt{Rg}$$

As $\mu_s = 0.2$.

On a banked road ($\theta = 30°$), keeping all other parameters same, maximum permissible speed for safe turn,

$$v_2 = \sqrt{Rg \cdot \tan\theta} = \left(\frac{1}{\sqrt{3}}\right)^{\frac{1}{2}} \times \sqrt{Rg}$$

$\therefore \quad \tan 30° = \frac{1}{\sqrt{3}}$

or $\quad v_2 = 0.58\sqrt{Rg}$

Percentage increase in maximum

$$\text{speed} = \frac{v_2 - v_1}{v_1} \times 100 = \frac{0.58 - 0.45}{0.45} \times 100 \approx 29\ \%$$

25. (*d*) Let the tension in string connected to M be T_1 and that of T_2 in string connected to 6 kg.

FBD of M

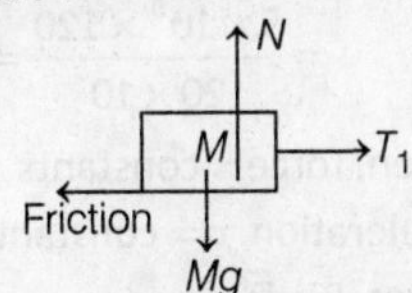

$N = Mg$

To prevent the motion of M, the friction $\geq T_1$

or $\quad \mu N \geq T_1$

For minimum value of M,

$$\mu N = T_1$$
$$\mu Mg = T_1 \quad \ldots \text{(i)}$$

Drawing the free body diagram of knot

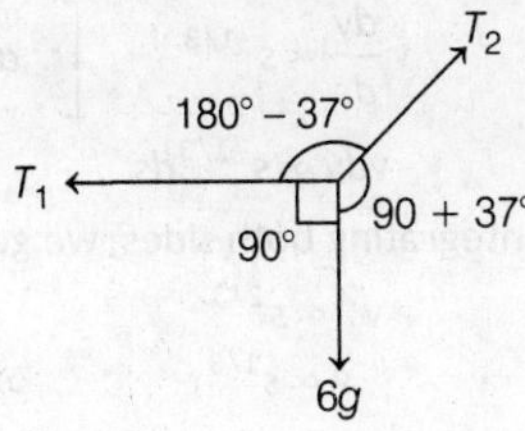

Using Lami's theorem,

$$\frac{T_1}{\sin(90° + 37°)} = \frac{T_2}{\sin 90°} = \frac{6g}{\sin(180° - 37°)}$$

or $\quad \frac{T_1}{\cos 37°} = \frac{T_2}{1} = \frac{6g}{\sin 37°}$

or $\quad T_1 = 6g\frac{\cos 37°}{\sin 37°}$

$\Rightarrow \quad T_1 = 6 \times 10 \times \cot 37° = 6 \times 10 \times \frac{4}{3}$

$$T_1 = 80\text{ N}$$

From Eq. (i), $\mu Mg = 80$

$$0.5 \times M \times 10 = 80$$
$$M = 16\text{ kg}$$

Qualifier 4 (Work, Energy and Power)

1. (*b*) Due to viscous and buoyant forces of air, acceleration of drop keeps on reducing as viscous force increases with speed.

2. (*d*) When a body moves along a circular path with a uniform speed, there is no change in its kinetic energy. By work-energy theorem, the work done by the centripetal force is zero.

3. (*a*) Here, $\quad F = 3y^2 - 4y + 5$

We know that, work done by variable force,

$$dW = F dy$$

$\Rightarrow \quad \int_0^W dW = \int_0^4 F dy$

$\Rightarrow \quad W = \int_0^4 (3y^2 - 4y + 5)\, dy$

$$= \left[3 \cdot \frac{y^3}{3} - 4 \cdot \frac{y^2}{2} + 5y\right]_0^4$$
$$= [y^3 - 2y^2 + 5y]_0^4$$
$$= [4^3 - 2 \times 4^2 + 5 \times 4 - 0]$$
$$= 64 - 32 + 20$$
$$= 52\text{ J}$$

4. (*c*) Displacement of body,

$$\Delta \mathbf{r} = \mathbf{r}_2 - \mathbf{r}_1 = (2\hat{i} - \hat{j} + 2\hat{k}) - (\hat{i} + \hat{j} - \hat{k}) = \hat{i} - 2\hat{j} + 3\hat{k}$$

$\therefore$ Work done, $W = F \cdot \Delta r$

$$= (3\hat{i} - \hat{j} + \hat{k}) \cdot (\hat{i} - 2\hat{j} + 3\hat{k})$$
$$= 3(1) + (-1)(-2) + 1(3)$$
$$= 3 + 2 + 3$$
$$= 8\text{ J}$$

5. (*d*) Area of displacement *versus* force graph gives the amount of work done.

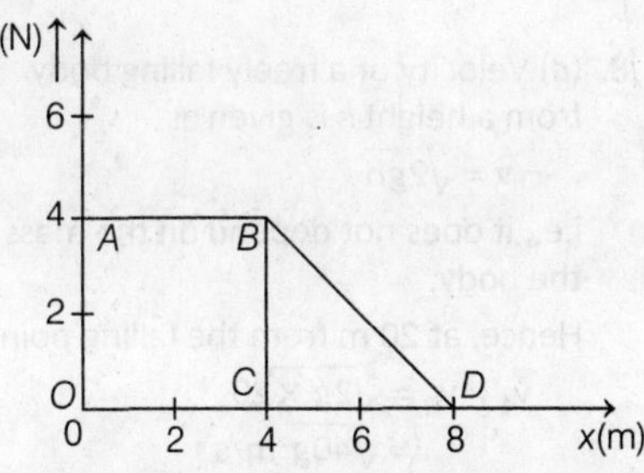

Work done from $x = 0$ to $x = 8$ m is given as

W = area of region $ODBA$

= area of $\square\, OCBA$ + area of ΔCBD

$$= (OC \times BC) + \frac{1}{2} \times CD \times BC$$
$$= 4 \times 4 + \frac{1}{2} \times (8 - 4) \times 4$$
$$= 16 + \frac{1}{2} \times 4 \times 4 = 24\text{ J}$$

6. (*c*) Here,

$$m = 1\text{ kg}, v = a\,x^{3/2}, a = 4\text{ m/s}^2$$

Work done, $W = ?$

We know that,

$$\text{Acceleration, } a' = \frac{dv}{dt} = \frac{d}{dt} \cdot ax^{3/2} = \frac{d}{dt} \cdot 4x^{3/2}$$

$\Rightarrow \quad a' = 4 \times \frac{3}{2} \cdot x^{1/2}\frac{dx}{dt}$

$$= 6x^{1/2} \cdot v = 6x^{1/2} \times ax^{3/2} = 6x^{1/2} \times 4x^{3/2} = 24x^2$$

$\therefore$ Force, $F = ma' = 1 \times 24x^2 = 24x^2$

$\therefore$ Work done, $W = \int_0^1 F dx$

$$= \int_0^1 24x^2 dx = 24\left[\frac{x^3}{3}\right]_0^1$$
$$= 8[x^3]_0^1 = 8 \times 1^3 - 8 \times 0 = 8\text{ J}$$

7. (*c*) According to given graph,

Initial velocity of car, $v_i = 10$ m/s

Final velocity of car, $v_f = 0$ m/s

$\therefore$ According to work-energy theorem,

Work done on the car

= Change in kinetic energy of car

$$= \frac{1}{2}m(v_f^2 - v_i^2) = \frac{1}{2} \times 100 \times (0^2 - 10^2) = \frac{1}{2} \times 100 \times (-100) = -5 \times 10^3\text{ J}$$

8. (*a*) Velocity of a freely falling body from a height h is given as

$$v = \sqrt{2gh}$$

i.e., it does not depend on the mass of the body.

Hence, at 20 m from the falling point,

$$v_1 = v_2 = \sqrt{2g \times 20}$$
$$= \sqrt{40g} \text{ m/s}$$

Thus, $\frac{K_1}{K_2} = \frac{\frac{1}{2}m_1 v_1^2}{\frac{1}{2}m_2 v_2^2}$

$$= \frac{m_1}{m_2} \cdot \frac{40g}{40g} = \frac{m_1}{m_2} = \frac{8}{4} = \frac{2}{1}$$

$\Rightarrow K_1 : K_2 = 2:1$

9. (*a*) If F be the force resisting the motion, then power required to move the car,

$$P = F \cdot v$$

$\Rightarrow \quad F = \frac{P}{v} = \frac{5000}{25} = 200 \text{ N}$

10. (*b*) Given, initial kinetic energy,

$$K_1 = K$$

Final kinetic energy, $K_2 = 4K$

We know that,

Momentum (p) and kinetic energy (K) are related as,

$$p = \sqrt{2mK}$$

$\Rightarrow \quad p \propto \sqrt{K}$

$\Rightarrow \quad \frac{p_2}{p_1} = \sqrt{\frac{K_2}{K_1}} = \sqrt{\frac{4K}{K}} = 2$

$\Rightarrow \quad p_2 = 2p_1$

$\therefore$ Percentage increase in momentum of body

$$= \frac{p_2 - p_1}{p_1} \times 100$$
$$= \frac{2p_1 - p_1}{p_1} \times 100$$
$$= 1 \times 100 = 100\%$$

11. (*a*) Here, displacement,

$$x = 2t^3 + 5t + 2$$

$\therefore$ Speed, $v = \frac{dx}{dt}$

$$v = 6t^2 + 5$$

Initial speed (at $t = 0$),

$$v_i = 6 \times 0^2 + 5$$
$$= 5 \text{ m/s}$$

Final speed (at $t = 1$ s),

$$v_f = 6 \times 1^2 + 5$$
$$= 11 \text{ m/s}$$

$\therefore$ Increase in KE $= \frac{1}{2}m(v_f^2 - v_i^2)$

$$= \frac{1}{2} \times 4 \times (11^2 - 5^2)$$
$$= 2 \times 96 = 192 \text{ J}$$

12. (*a*) According to work-energy theorem,

Work done, W = Change in KE of vehicle

$\Rightarrow \quad W = K_f - K_i$

$\Rightarrow \quad Fdx = K_f - \frac{1}{2}mv_i^2$

$\Rightarrow \quad Fdx = K_f - \frac{1}{2} \times 75 \times 20^2$

$\Rightarrow \quad Fdx = K_f - 15000$

$\Rightarrow \quad \int_{10}^{20} (-0.2x)\,dx = K_f - 15000$

$\Rightarrow \quad \left[-0.2 \cdot \frac{x^2}{2}\right]_{10}^{20} = K_f - 15000$

$$[-0.1x^2]_{10}^{20} = K_f - 15000$$

$\Rightarrow -0.1 \times 20^2 + 0.1 \times 10^2 = K_f - 15000$

$\Rightarrow \quad -40 + 10 = K_f - 15000$

$\Rightarrow \quad K_f = 14970 \text{ J}$

$$= 14.97 \times 10^3 \text{ J}$$
$$= 14.97 \text{ kJ}$$
$$\simeq 15 \text{ kJ}$$

13. (*c*) Let the ball is dropped from height h.

$\therefore$ Initial potential energy,

$$U_i = mgh$$

Potential energy after first bounce,

$$U_f = mg \times 60\% \text{ of } h$$
$$= mg\,(0.6\,h)$$
$$= 0.6\,mgh$$

Loss in potential energy in each bounce

$$= mgh - 0.6mgh$$
$$= 0.4\,mgh$$

$\therefore$ Fraction of potential energy lost in each bounce $= \frac{0.4mgh}{mgh} = 0.4$

14. (*c*) According to first given situation,

$$W = \frac{1}{2}m(10^2 - 0^2)$$

$$W = 50m \quad \text{...(i)}$$

According to second given situation,

$$W' = \frac{1}{2}m(20^2 - 10^2)$$

$$W' = \frac{1}{2}m \times 300 = 150m \quad \text{...(ii)}$$

From Eqs. (i) and (ii),

It can be seen that, $W' = 3W$

15. (*d*) Since, body moves on a circular path.

$\therefore$ Centripetal force, $F = \frac{k}{r^2}$

$\Rightarrow \quad \frac{mv^2}{r} = \frac{k}{r^2}$

$\Rightarrow \quad mv^2 = \frac{k}{r} \quad \text{...(i)}$

$\therefore$ Kinetic energy of the body,

$$E_K = \frac{1}{2}mv^2 = \frac{1}{2}\left(\frac{k}{r}\right) \quad \text{[from Eq. (i)]}$$

$$E_K = \frac{k}{2r} \quad \text{...(ii)}$$

Potential energy, $U = \int_r^\infty -Fdr$

$$= \int_r^\infty -\frac{k}{r^2}\,dr = \left[\frac{k}{r}\right]_r^\infty$$

$$= \frac{k}{\infty} - \frac{k}{r} = \frac{-k}{r}$$

Total energy $= E_K + U$

$$= \frac{k}{2r} - \frac{k}{r} = \frac{-k}{2r}$$

16. (*c*) We know that,

$$P = \frac{W}{t}$$

$\Rightarrow \quad P = \frac{mgh}{t} \quad [\because W = mgh]$

$\Rightarrow \quad m = \frac{Pt}{hg}$

$$= \frac{5 \times 10^3 \times 120}{20 \times 10} = 3000 \text{ kg}$$

17. (*c*) Given, force = constants

$\therefore$ Acceleration, a = constant

$\therefore$ Power, $P = Fv$

$$P = Fat \quad [\because v = at]$$

Since, F and a are constants.

$\therefore \quad P \propto t$

So, correct graph is shown is option (c).

18. (*c*) Since,

$$F \propto s^{-1/3} \quad \text{...(i)}$$

$\Rightarrow \quad ma \propto s^{-1/3}$

$\Rightarrow \quad a \propto s^{-1/3}$

$\Rightarrow \quad v\frac{dv}{ds} \propto s^{-1/3} \quad \left[\because a = v\frac{dv}{ds}\right]$

$\Rightarrow \quad vdv \propto s^{-1/3}ds$

By integrating both sides, we get

$$v^2 \propto s^{2/3}$$

or $\quad v \propto s^{1/3} \quad \text{...(ii)}$

Now, power, $P \propto F \cdot v$

$$P \propto s^{-1/3} \cdot s^{1/3}$$

[from Eqs. (i) and (ii)]

$$P \propto s^0$$

19. (*c*) Energy available, $E = mc^2$

$$= 1 \times 10^{-12} \times (3 \times 10^8)^2$$
$$= 9 \times 10^4 \text{ J}$$

Time for which bulb can glow $= \frac{E}{P}$

$$= \frac{9 \times 10^4}{10^3} = 90\text{ s}$$

$$= \frac{90}{60}\text{ min} = 1.5\text{ min}$$

So, A is incorrect. R is correct as every chemical reaction follows law of conservation of mass.

20. (*b*) According to given situation, the given collision is head-on-collision. Thus, according to the law of conservation of linear momentum,

$$m_1u_1 + m_2u_2 = m_1v_1 + m_2v_2$$

Here, $m_1 = M, m_2 = 4M, u_1 = v, u_2 = 0$

and $\quad v_1 = 0$

$\therefore \quad Mv + 4M \times 0 = 0 + 4Mv_2$

$\Rightarrow \quad Mv = 4Mv_2$

$\Rightarrow \quad v_2 = \frac{v}{4} \qquad \text{...(i)}$

$\therefore$ Coefficient of restitution,

$$e = \frac{\text{Relative velocity of separation after collision}}{\text{Relative velocity of approach}}$$

$$= \frac{v_2 - v_1}{u_2 - u_1}$$

$$= \frac{\frac{v}{4} - 0}{0 - v} \qquad \text{[from Eq. (i)]}$$

$$= -\frac{1}{4} = -0.25$$

21. (*a*) The given situation is shown below

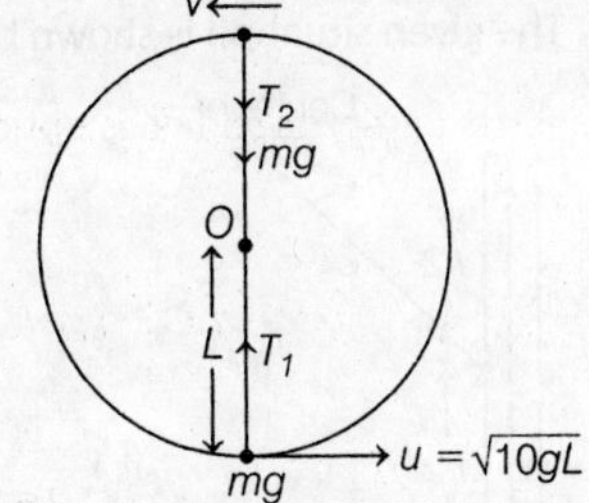

At the lowest position,

$$T_1 - mg = \frac{mu^2}{L}$$

$$= \frac{m}{L} \times 10\,gL$$

$$= 10\,mg$$

$\Rightarrow \quad T_1 = 11\,mg \qquad \text{...(i)}$

At highest position, $v^2 = u^2 - 2gh$

$$= u^2 - 2g \times 2L$$

$$= 10gL - 4gL$$

$\Rightarrow \quad v^2 = 6gL \qquad \text{...(ii)}$

Also, $T_2 + mg = \frac{mv^2}{L}$

$$= \frac{m}{L} \times 6gL \quad \text{[From Eq. (ii)]}$$

$\Rightarrow \quad T_2 + mg = 6mg$

$\Rightarrow \quad T_2 = 5mg \qquad \text{...(iii)}$

In lower vertical circle, situation is shown below

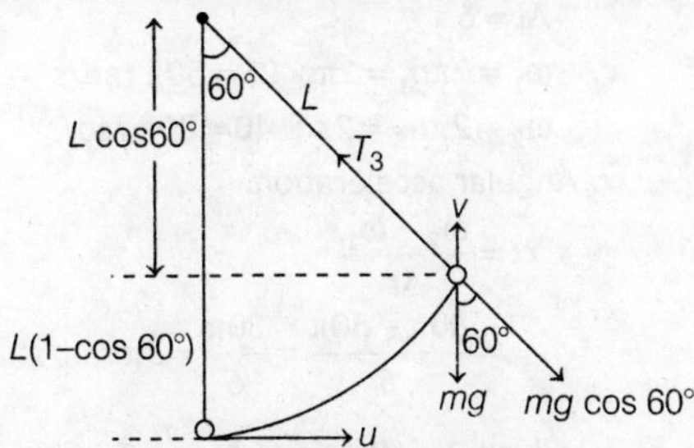

In this situation, we can write

$$v^2 = u^2 - 2gh$$

$$= u^2 - 2gL(1 - \cos 60^\circ)$$

$$v^2 = 10gL - 2gL\left(1 - \frac{1}{2}\right) = 9gL$$

Also, $T_3 - mg\cos 60^\circ - \frac{mv^2}{}$

$\Rightarrow \quad T_3 - \frac{mg}{2} = \frac{m}{L} \cdot 9gL = 9mg$

$\Rightarrow \quad T_3 = 9mg + \frac{mg}{2} = \frac{19}{2}mg$

In upper vertical circle, situation is shown below

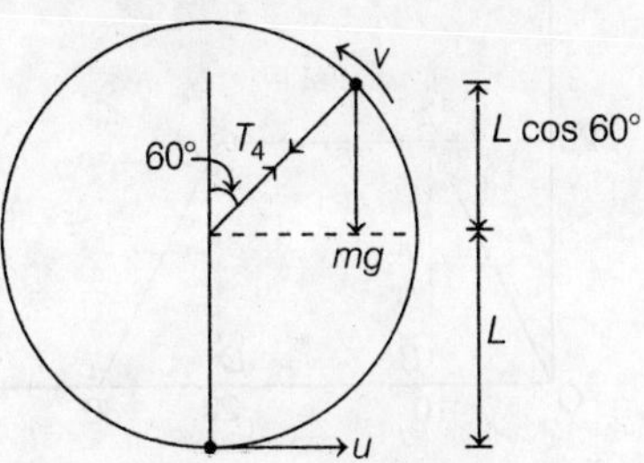

In this situation, we can write

$$v^2 = u^2 - 2gh$$

$$= 10gL - 2gL(1 + \cos 60^\circ)$$

$$v^2 = 7gL$$

Also, $T_4 + mg\cos 60^\circ = \frac{mv^2}{L}$

$\Rightarrow \quad T_4 + \frac{mg}{2} = \frac{m}{L} \times 7gL$

$\Rightarrow \quad T_4 = \frac{13mg}{2}$

22. (*a*) Loss of energy of block = Work done against friction + Energy stored in spring

Let x = Spring's full compression,

then $\mu_k(mg)(BC + x) = \frac{1}{2}mv^2 - \frac{1}{2}kx^2$

V=0
A B C x D

$\Rightarrow 0.2(0.5)(10)(1.14 + x) = \frac{1}{2}(0.5)(3^2) - \frac{1}{2}(4)(x^2)$

$\Rightarrow \quad 2(1.14 + x) = 0.5 \times 9 - 4x^2$

$\Rightarrow \quad 2.28 + 2x = 4.5 - 4x^2$

or $2x^2 + x - 0.61 = 0$

$\Rightarrow \quad x = 0.3\text{ m}$

So, distance covered by block

$$= AB + BC + x$$

$$= 2 + 1.14 + 0.3$$

$$= 3.44\text{ m}$$

23. (*b*) In elastic collision, when balls are in contact, only some part of total energy is converted into potential energy. All energy losses follow the law of conservation of energy.

24. (*b*) Conservation of momentum gives

$$mu = (m + m)v$$

$$u = 2v \text{ or } v = \frac{u}{2}$$

Loss of energy $= \frac{1}{2}mu^2 - \frac{1}{2}(2m)v^2$

$$= \frac{1}{2}mu^2 - m \cdot \left(\frac{u}{2}\right)^2$$

$$= \frac{1}{2}mu^2 - \frac{1}{4}mu^2$$

$$= \frac{1}{4}mu^2$$

$$\therefore \text{ Loss } \frac{\frac{1}{2}mu^2 - \frac{1}{4}mu^2}{\frac{1}{2}mu^2} \times 100 = 50\%$$

25. (*c*) (A → S, B → Q,R, C → T, D → P)

As, $F = -\frac{dU}{dx}$

So, F is maximum at point C.

Force acting towards left at points A, E and F.

Force acting towards right at point C.

Stable equilibrium, at D.

Unstable equilibrium at G.

Qualifier 5 (Motion of System of Particles and Rigid Body)

1. (*c*) Given, $m_1 = 4$ kg and $m_2 = 5$ kg

$$\mathbf{r}_1 = -\hat{\mathbf{i}} + \hat{\mathbf{j}} + 2\hat{\mathbf{k}},\ \mathbf{r}_2 = 4\hat{\mathbf{i}} - 3\hat{\mathbf{j}} + \hat{\mathbf{k}}$$

If **r** be the position vector of centre of mass, then

$$\mathbf{r} = \frac{m_1\mathbf{r}_1 + m_2\mathbf{r}_2}{m_1 + m_2}$$

$$= \frac{4(-\hat{\mathbf{i}} + \hat{\mathbf{j}} + 2\hat{\mathbf{k}}) + 5(4\hat{\mathbf{i}} - 3\hat{\mathbf{j}} + \hat{\mathbf{k}})}{4+5}$$

$$= \frac{1}{9}(16\hat{\mathbf{i}} - 11\hat{\mathbf{j}} + 13\hat{\mathbf{k}})$$

2. (*c*) The given situation is shown below

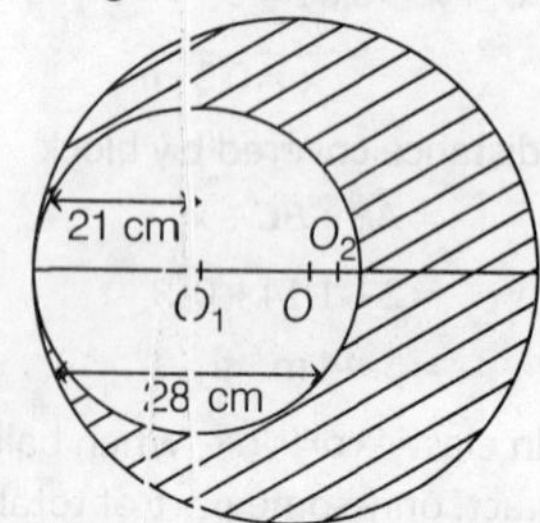

O_2 is the final position of centre of mass of remaining body and O is the centre of circular plate. Let m be the mass per unit area of the plate.

$\therefore$ Mass of the original plate,

$$M = \pi(28)^2 = 784\,\pi m$$

Mass of removed portion,

$$M_1 = \pi(21)^2 m = 441\pi m$$

Mass of the shaded portion,

$$M_2 = M - M_1$$
$$= \pi[784 - 441]m = 343\,\pi m$$

According to principle of moment,

Moment of M_1 about O_1 = Moment of M_2 about O_2

or $M_1 \times O_1O = M_2 \times O_2O$

$$O_2O = \frac{M_1}{M_2} \times O_1O$$

$$= \frac{441\,\pi m}{343\,\pi m}(28-21) = 9 \text{ cm}$$

3. (*d*) Here, $\omega = 1 + t$

$$\Rightarrow \quad \frac{d\theta}{dt} = 1 + t$$

$$\int d\theta = \int_1^2 (1+t)\,dt$$

$$\theta = \left[t + \frac{t^2}{2}\right]_1^2$$

$$\Rightarrow \quad \theta = \frac{5}{2} \text{ rad}$$

Distance moved by bicycle $= \theta R$

$$= \frac{5}{2} \times 1 \qquad [\because R = 1 \text{ m}]$$

$$= 2.5 \text{ m}$$

4. (*c*) Given, $n_2 = 2400 \text{ rpm} = \frac{2400}{60}$ rps

$$= 40 \text{ rps}$$

$$n_1 = 1500 \text{ rpm} = \frac{1500}{60} = 25 \text{ rps}$$

$$\Delta t = 6 \text{ s}$$

$$\therefore \quad \omega_1 = 2\pi n_1 = 2\pi \times 25 = 50\pi \text{ rad/s}$$

$$\omega_2 = 2\pi n_2 = 2\pi \times 40 = 80\pi \text{ rad/s}$$

$\therefore$ Angular acceleration,

$$\alpha = \frac{\omega_2 - \omega_1}{\Delta t}$$

$$= \frac{80\pi - 50\pi}{6} = \frac{30\pi}{6} = 5\pi \text{ rad/s}^2$$

5. (*c*) Given, $T_1 = 8$ s, $r_1 = r$, $r_2 = \frac{r}{4}$, $T_2 = ?$

By the conservation of angular momentum,

$$I_1\omega_1 = I_2\omega_2$$

$$\Rightarrow \quad mr_1^2 \cdot \frac{2\pi}{T_1} = mr_2^2 \cdot \frac{2\pi}{T_2}$$

$$\Rightarrow \quad r^2 \cdot \frac{2\pi}{8} = \left(\frac{r}{4}\right)^2 \frac{2\pi}{T_2}$$

$$T_2 = \frac{1}{2} \text{ s} = 0.5 \text{ s}$$

6. (*b*) The area of angular velocity *versus* time graph gives the angular displacement θ.

ω (rad s^{-1})

20, A, C, O, B, D, E, 10, 20, 30, t(s)

$\therefore \quad \theta$ = Area of trapezium *OACE*

$$= \frac{1}{2}(AC + OE) \times AB$$

$$\theta = \frac{1}{2}(10 + 30) \times 20 = 400 \text{ rad}$$

7. (*c*) A is false but R is true.

R is true as when

$$\tau_{ext} = 0;\ I_1\omega_1 = I_2\omega_2$$

But $KE = \frac{1}{2}I\omega^2$

So, final $KE = \frac{1}{2}I_2 \times (\omega_2^2)$

$$= \frac{1}{2}I_2 \times \left(\frac{I_1}{I_2} \times \omega_1\right)^2$$

$$= \frac{I_1}{I_2} \times \frac{1}{2}I_1\omega_1^2$$

So, final KE $\neq$ Initial KE if $I_1 \neq I_2$

8. (*c*) Equation of line,

$$y = 2x + 2 \Rightarrow 2x - y + 2 = 0$$

$\therefore$ Length of perpendicular from origin on this line,

$$r = 0 - 0 + \frac{2}{\sqrt{2^2 + (-1)^2}}$$

$$= \frac{2}{\sqrt{5}}$$

$\therefore$ Angular momentum, $L = mvr$

$$= 2 \times \frac{1}{\sqrt{5}} \times \frac{2}{\sqrt{5}} = \frac{4}{5}$$

$$= 0.8 \text{ unit}$$

9. (*d*) Given, $\theta(t) = 3t^3 - 3t^2 + 6t + 1$

According to question,

torque $\tau = 0$

$$\Rightarrow \quad I\alpha = 0$$

$$\Rightarrow \quad \alpha = 0$$

$$\Rightarrow \quad \frac{d^2\theta(t)}{dt^2} = 0$$

$$\Rightarrow \quad \frac{d}{dt}\left[\frac{d}{dt}\theta(t)\right] = 0$$

$$\Rightarrow \quad \frac{d}{dt}\left[\frac{d}{dt}(3t^3 - 3t^2 + 6t + 1)\right] = 0$$

$$\Rightarrow \quad \frac{d}{dt}(9t^2 - 6t + 6) = 0$$

$$\Rightarrow \quad 18t - 6 = 0$$

$$\Rightarrow \quad t = \frac{1}{3} \text{ s}$$

10. (*d*) The given situation is shown below

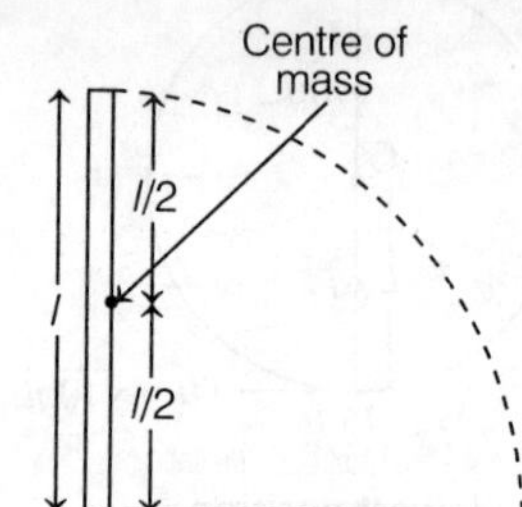

By the law of conservation of energy,

Loss in potential energy = Gain in rotational kinetic energy

$$\Rightarrow \quad \frac{mgl}{2} = \frac{1}{2}I\omega^2$$

$$\Rightarrow \quad \frac{mgl}{2} = \frac{1}{2} \cdot \frac{ml^2}{3} \cdot \left(\frac{v}{l}\right)^2 \qquad \left[\because I = \frac{ml^2}{3} \text{ and } \omega = \frac{v}{l}\right]$$

$$\Rightarrow v^2 = 3gl$$

$$\Rightarrow \quad v = \sqrt{3gl}$$

11. (*b*) A → S, B → R, C → Q, D → P

Moment of inertia of spherical shell about its diameter having mass M and radius R,

$$I_1 = \frac{2}{3}MR^2$$

Spherical shell

Moment of inertia of spherical shell about a tangential axis,

$$I_2 = \frac{2}{3}MR^2 + MR^2$$

(Using parallel axes theorem)

$$\Rightarrow \quad I_2 = \frac{5}{3}MR^2$$

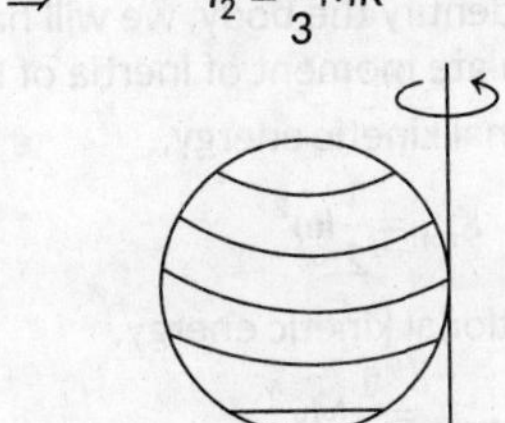

Spherical shell

Moment of inertia of solid sphere about its diametric axis,

$$I_3 = \frac{2}{5}MR^2$$

Solid sphere

Moment of inertia of solid sphere about its tangential axis,

$$I_4 = \frac{2}{5}MR^2 + MR^2 = \frac{7}{5}MR^2$$

(Using parallel axes theorem)

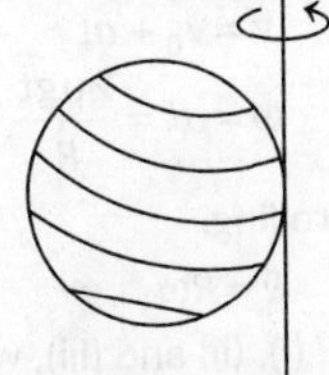

Solid sphere

12. (*c*) The given situation is shown below

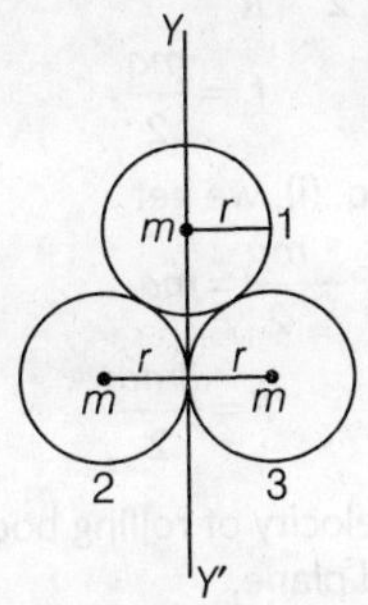

The total moment of inertia of the given system is given as

$$I = I_1 + I_2 + I_3 \quad \text{... (i)}$$

where, $I_1 = \frac{2}{3}mr^2$

$$I_2 = I_3 = \frac{2}{3}mr^2 + mr^2$$

(Applying parallel axes theorem)

$$\Rightarrow \quad I_2 = I_3 = \frac{5}{3}mr^2$$

From Eq. (i), we have

$$I = \frac{2}{3}mr^2 + \frac{5}{3}mr^2 + \frac{5}{3}mr^2$$

$$= \frac{12}{3}mr^2 = 4mr^2$$

13. (*b*) We know that, moment of inertia of a rod about an axis passing through an end

$$= \frac{ML^2}{3}$$

(using perpendicular axes theorem)

$$I_{\text{given system}} = \frac{ML^2}{3} + \frac{ML^2}{3}$$

$$= \frac{2ML^2}{3}$$

14. (*b*) Given, radius of gyration, $K = 1$ m

Mass, $m = 2$ kg

$$\omega = 4 \text{ rad/s}$$

Moment of inertia, $I = mK^2$

$$= 2 \times 1^2 = 2 \text{ kg-m}^2$$

Kinetic energy of rotation,

$$K = \frac{1}{2}I\omega^2$$

$$= \frac{1}{2} \times 2 \times 4^2$$

$$= 16 \text{ J}$$

15. (*d*) Given, moment of inertia,

$$I = 0.2 \text{ kg-m}^2$$

Rotational kinetic energy, $K_r = 1000$ J

Angular acceleration, $\alpha = 10 \text{ rad/s}^2$

$$\omega_0 = 0, \; t = ?$$

We know that, rotational kinetic energy,

$$K_r = \frac{1}{2}I\omega^2$$

$$\Rightarrow \quad \omega = \sqrt{\frac{2K_r}{I}}$$

$$= \sqrt{\frac{2 \times 1000}{0.2}}$$

$$= 100 \text{ rad/s}$$

Now, from the equation of rotational motion,

$$\omega = \omega_0 + \alpha t$$

$$\Rightarrow \quad t = \frac{\omega - \omega_0}{\alpha}$$

$$= \frac{100 - 0}{10}$$

$$= 10 \text{ s}$$

16. (*b*) Rotational kinetic energy,

$$E = \frac{1}{2}I\omega^2$$

$$= \frac{1}{2I} \cdot (I\omega)^2$$

$$= \frac{L^2}{2I}$$

[∵ Angular momentum, $L = I\omega$]

$$\Rightarrow \quad L^2 = 2IE$$

$$\Rightarrow \quad L = \sqrt{2IE}$$

$$L \propto \sqrt{E}$$

$$\Rightarrow \quad \frac{L_2}{L_1} = \sqrt{\frac{E_2}{E_1}} \quad \text{... (i)}$$

Since, $E_2 = E_1 + 300\%$ of E_1

$$= E_1 + 3E_1 = 4E_1$$

From Eq. (i), we get

$$\frac{L_2}{L_1} = \sqrt{\frac{4E_1}{E_1}} = 2$$

$$\Rightarrow \quad L_2 = 2L_1$$

∴ % increase in angular momentum

$$= \frac{L_2 - L_1}{L_1} \times 100$$

$$= \frac{2L_1 - L_1}{L_1} \times 100$$

$$= 100\%$$

17. (*a*) We know that, $\tau = I\alpha = RF$

Here, $R = \frac{d}{2} = \frac{4}{2} = 2\text{m}$

$$F = (20t - 5t^2) \text{ N},$$

$$I = 10 \text{ kg-m}^2$$

From $I\alpha = RF$

$\therefore \quad 10\alpha = 2(20t - 5t^2)$

$\Rightarrow \quad \alpha = 4t - t^2$

$\frac{d\omega}{dt} = 4t - t^2$

$\Rightarrow \quad \int d\omega = \int (4t - t^2)dt = 2t^2 - \frac{t^3}{3}$

$\Rightarrow \quad \omega = \frac{d\theta}{dt} = 2t^2 - \frac{t^3}{3}$

$\Rightarrow \quad \int d\theta = \int\left(2t^2 - \frac{t^3}{3}\right)dt$

$\Rightarrow \quad \theta = \frac{2t^3}{3} - \frac{t^4}{12}$

When $t = 6$ s, then $\theta = 36$ rad

$\Rightarrow \quad 2\pi n = 36$

$\Rightarrow \quad n = \frac{36}{2\pi} < 6$

18. (*a*) A → Q, B → P, C → S, D → R

$\because \quad v_A = 0, v_B = v\sqrt{2}, v_C = 2v, v_D = v$

19. (*d*) Given, $I = 5$ kg-m^2, $\omega_0 = 40$ rad/s, $t = 5$ s and $\omega = 0$

Required average power,

$P = \frac{\omega}{t}$

$P = \frac{\tau\theta}{t}$ ...(i)

From the first equation of rotational motion, we have

$\omega = \omega_0 + \alpha t$

$0 = 40 - \alpha(5)$

$\Rightarrow \quad \alpha = \frac{40}{5} = 8$ rad/s^2

$\therefore \quad \theta = \omega_0 t - \frac{1}{2}\alpha t^2$

$= 40 \times 5 - \frac{1}{2} \times 8 \times 5^2$

$= 200 - 100$

$= 100$ rad

From Eq. (i), $P = \frac{\tau\theta}{t} = \frac{I\alpha\theta}{t}$ $[\because \tau = I\alpha]$

$\Rightarrow \quad P = \frac{5 \times 8 \times 100}{5} = 800$ W

20. (*b*) The given situation is shown below

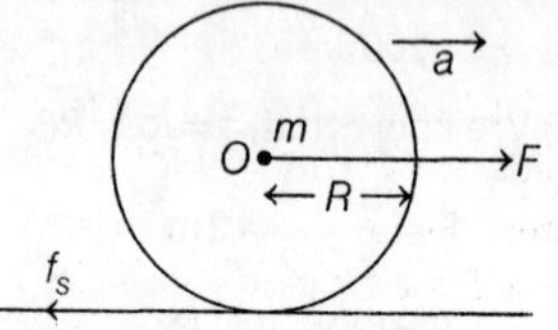

According to Newton's law of motion,

$F - f_s = ma$ ...(i)

Torque, $\tau = I\alpha = f_s R$

$\Rightarrow \quad \frac{mR^2}{2} \cdot \frac{a}{R} = f_s R$

$\Rightarrow \quad f_s = \frac{ma}{2}$

From Eq. (i), we get

$F - \frac{ma}{2} = ma$

$\Rightarrow \quad F = \frac{3ma}{2}$

21. (*b*) $\because$ Velocity of rolling body on an inclined plane,

$v = \sqrt{\frac{2gh}{1 + \frac{K^2}{R^2}}}$

For a ring, $K^2 = R^2$

$\therefore \quad v_r = \sqrt{\frac{2gh}{1 + K^2/R^2}}$

$= \sqrt{\frac{2gh}{1+1}}$

$\Rightarrow \quad v_r = \sqrt{gh}$

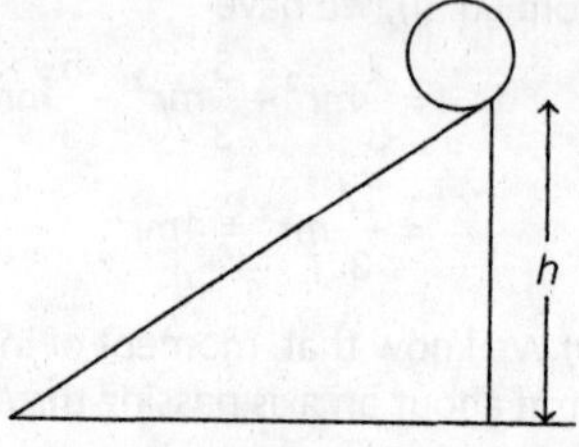

For a disc, $K^2 = \frac{R^2}{2}$

$\therefore \quad v_d = \sqrt{\frac{2gh}{1 + 1/2}} = \sqrt{\frac{4gh}{3}}$

Hence, $v_d > v_r$

22. (*a*) Acceleration of centre of mass of the rolling body on an inclined plane without slipping is given by

$a = \frac{g\sin\theta}{1 + \left(\frac{I}{MR^2}\right)}$

Given, $\theta = 60°$

For hollow sphere, $I = \frac{2}{3}MR^2$

$\therefore \quad a = \frac{g\sin 60°}{1 + \left(\frac{\frac{2}{3}MR^2}{MR^2}\right)}$

$= \frac{\sqrt{3}g/2}{5/3} = \frac{3\sqrt{3}g}{10}$

23. (*b*) We know that, kinetic energy of a rotating body,

$K = \frac{1}{2}I\omega^2$

For a ring, $K_r = \frac{1}{2}I_r\omega_r^2$

$= \frac{1}{2} \cdot \frac{1}{2}mr^2\omega_r^2$

$\Rightarrow \quad K_r = \frac{1}{4}mr^2\omega_r^2$

For a solid sphere, $K_s = \frac{1}{2}I_s\omega_s^2$

$= \frac{1}{2} \cdot \frac{2}{5}mr^2 \cdot (2\omega_r)^2 \quad [\because \omega_s = 2\omega_r]$

$= \frac{4}{5}mr^2\omega_r^2$

$\therefore \quad \frac{K_r}{K_s} = \frac{\frac{1}{4}mr^2\omega_r^2}{\frac{4}{5}mr^2\omega_r^2} = \frac{5}{16}$

or $\quad 5:16$

24. (*b*) To identify the body, we will have to calculate moment of inertia of body.

Rotational kinetic energy,

$K_{rot} = \frac{1}{2}I\omega^2$

Translational kinetic energy,

$K_{trans} = \frac{1}{2}Mv^2$

$\therefore \quad K_{total} = K_{rot} + K_{trans}$

$K_{total} = \frac{1}{2}I\omega^2 + \frac{1}{2}Mv^2$

But, $\quad \frac{K_{rot}}{K_{total}} = \frac{2}{5}$

$\Rightarrow \quad \frac{\frac{1}{2}I\omega^2}{\frac{1}{2}I\omega^2 + \frac{1}{2}Mv^2} = \frac{2}{5}$

$\Rightarrow \quad \frac{\frac{1}{2}I\omega^2}{\frac{1}{2}I\omega^2 + \frac{1}{2}M\omega^2R^2} = \frac{2}{5} \quad [\because v = R\omega]$

$\Rightarrow \quad I = \frac{2}{3}MR^2$

which is the moment of inertia of hollow sphere.

25. (*c*) Let v = linear velocity and ω = angular velocity at time t,

then $\quad v = v_0 + at$ ...(i)

$\omega = \alpha t = \frac{2\mu g t}{R}$ ...(ii)

For pure rolling,

$v = R\omega$ ...(iii)

From Eqs. (i), (ii) and (iii), we get

$t = \frac{v_0}{3\mu g}$

Qualifier 6 (Gravitation)

1. (*b*) Gravitational force has a range of millions of kilometres but it is also the weakest of all field forces.

2. (*a*) Both A and R are true but R is not the correct explanation of A.
As gravitational force on planet is always directed towards sun, its tangential component is always zero. Hence there is no torque on planet and so its angular momentum remains constant. Now areal speed of planet is

$$\frac{\Delta A}{\Delta t} = \frac{1}{2}(\mathbf{r} \times \mathbf{v})$$
$$= \frac{\mathbf{r} \times \mathbf{p}}{2m} = \frac{\mathbf{L}}{2m} = \text{a constant}$$

3. (*d*) According to Kepler's third law, the time period *T* of revolution is directly proportional to 3/2 power of semi-major axis.

i.e. $T \propto (a)^{3/2}$

or $\frac{T_A}{T_B} = \left(\frac{a_A}{a_B}\right)^{3/2} = \left(\frac{2}{1}\right)^{3/2}$

$\Rightarrow \frac{T_A}{T_B} = 2\sqrt{2}$

4. (*c*) The situation given in the question is shown below

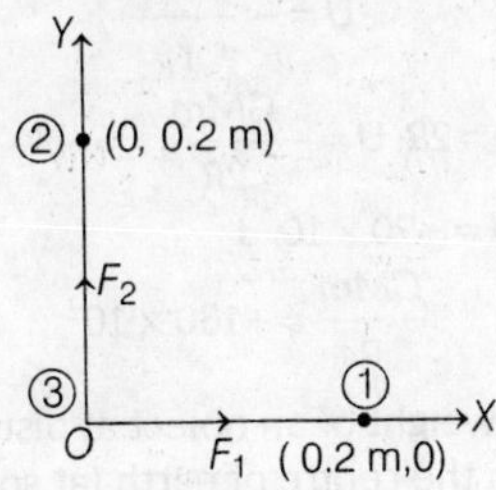

The gravitational force between two point masses is given as

$$F = \frac{Gm_1m_2}{r^2}$$

Force on mass placed at origin, due to mass 1,

$$F_1 = \frac{Gm_1m_2}{r^2}$$
$$= \frac{6.67 \times 10^{-11} \times (2)(2)}{(0.2)^2}$$
$$F_1 = 6.67 \times 10^{-9}\ \text{N}$$

and due to mass 2,

$$F_2 = \frac{Gm_1m_2}{r^2}$$
$$F_2 = \frac{6.67 \times 10^{-11} \times (2)(2)}{(0.2)^2}$$
$$= 6.67 \times 10^{-9}\ \text{N}$$

From the figure, the net force on mass 3,

$$\hat{\mathbf{F}} = \hat{\mathbf{F}}_1 + \hat{\mathbf{F}}_2$$
$$= 6.67 \times 10^{-9}\,(\hat{\mathbf{i}}) + 6.67 \times 10^{-9}\,(\hat{\mathbf{j}})$$
$$= 6.67 \times 10^{-9}\,(\hat{\mathbf{i}} + \hat{\mathbf{j}})\ \text{N}$$

5. (*d*) The situation given in the question is shown below.

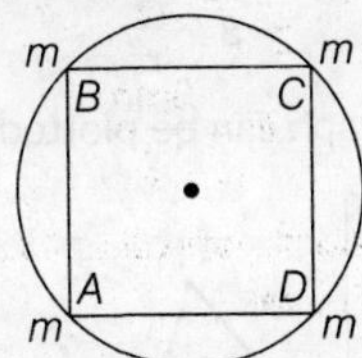

Gravitational force is a vector quantity. So, net force at fourth point mass placed at *D* point is the vector sum of three forces exerted by three point masses *A*, *B* and *C*.

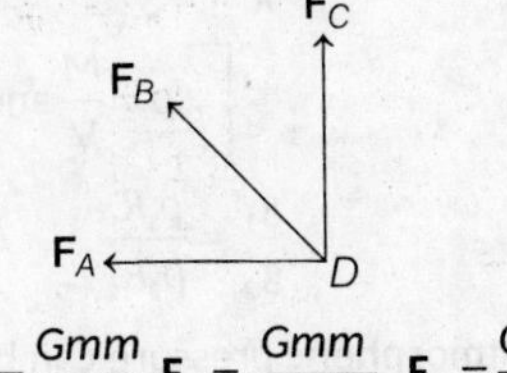

$$\mathbf{F}_A = \frac{Gmm}{a^2}, \mathbf{F}_B = \frac{Gmm}{(\sqrt{2}a)^2}, \mathbf{F}_C = \frac{Gmm}{a^2}$$

Resultant of $\mathbf{F}_A$ and $\mathbf{F}_C$,

$$\mathbf{F}_{AC} = \sqrt{\mathbf{F}_A^2 + \mathbf{F}_C^2 + 2F_AF_C \cos 90^\circ}$$
$$\left[\because \mathbf{F}_{\text{Resultant}} = \sqrt{F_1^2 + F_2^2 + 2F_1F_2 \cos\theta}\right]$$
$$= \sqrt{\left(\frac{Gmm}{a^2}\right)^2 + \left(\frac{Gmm}{a^2}\right)^2 + 0}$$
$$F_{AC} = \frac{\sqrt{2}Gm^2}{a^2}$$

The resultant force F_{AC} is in the direction of F_B,

$$\therefore \quad \mathbf{F}_{\text{net}} = \mathbf{F}_{AC} + \mathbf{F}_B$$
$$= \frac{\sqrt{2}Gm^2}{a^2} + \frac{Gm^2}{2a^2}$$
$$= \frac{Gm^2}{a^2}\left(\sqrt{2} + \frac{1}{2}\right)$$

(towards centre of square)

Now, due to this net force, point mass placed at *D* will continue to move in a circular path. Let velocity be *v*, then we can write

$$\frac{mv^2}{r} = \frac{Gm^2}{a^2}\left(\sqrt{2} + \frac{1}{2}\right)$$
$$\because \quad r = \frac{a}{\sqrt{2}}$$
$$\therefore \quad \frac{mv^2}{a/\sqrt{2}} = \frac{Gm^2}{a^2}\left(\sqrt{2} + \frac{1}{2}\right)$$
$$v = \sqrt{\frac{Gm}{a}\left(1 + \frac{1}{2\sqrt{2}}\right)}$$

6. (*b*) Given that, gravitational force,

$$F \propto r^n$$

or $F = kr^n$

where, *k* is constant.

Now, this force provides the necessary centripetal force.

$\therefore \quad \frac{mv^2}{r} = kr^n$

or $v^2 \propto r^{n+1}$

or $v \propto r^{\frac{n+1}{2}}$

The time period is given as

$$T = \frac{2\pi r}{v}$$

or $T \propto \frac{r}{v}$

or $T \propto \frac{r}{r^{\frac{n+1}{2}}}$

or $T \propto r^{\frac{1}{2} - \frac{n}{2}}$

or $T \propto r^{\frac{1-n}{2}}$

7. (*b*) If both mass and radius of the earth decrease by 1%, then the value of acceleration due to gravity,

$$g' = \frac{G(0.99M_e)}{(0.99R_e)^2}$$
$$\approx 1.01\frac{GM_e}{R_e^2} = 1.01\,g$$

So, *g* would increase by

$$(1.01 - 1) \times 100\% = 1\%$$

New escape velocity would be

$$v_e' = \sqrt{\frac{2 \times 0.99M_eG}{0.99R_e}}$$
$$= \sqrt{\frac{2GM_e}{R_e}} = v_e$$

So, it will remain unchanged.

Also, gravitational potential energy

$$= -\frac{Gm(0.99M_e)}{0.99R_e}$$
$$= -\frac{GM_em}{R_e}$$

Hence, it will also remain same.

8. (*b*) To calculate the force of attraction on the point mass *m*, we should calculate the force due to the solid sphere and subtract from the force which the mass of the hollow sphere would have exerted on *m*, i.e.

$$F = \frac{GMM}{x^2} - \frac{GMM'}{y^2} \quad \text{...(i)}$$
$$\left[\because x = \frac{R}{4},\ x + y = \frac{R}{2}\right]$$

Since, mass, $M = \left(\frac{4}{3}\right)\pi R^3 \rho$

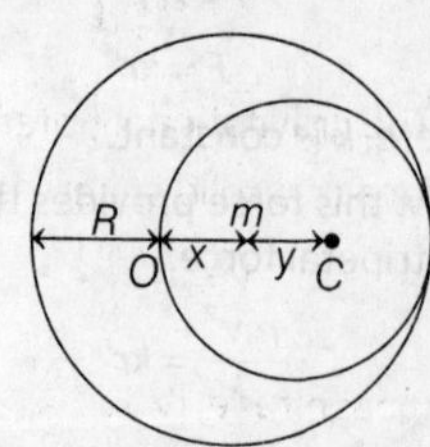

and $M' = \frac{4}{3}\pi\left(\frac{R}{2}\right)^3 \rho = \frac{M}{8}$

$\therefore \quad M' = \frac{M}{8}$

From Eq. (i); we get

$$F = \frac{GMm}{\left(\frac{R}{4}\right)^2} - \frac{Gm\left(\frac{M}{8}\right)}{\left(\frac{R}{4}\right)^2}$$

$$= \frac{14GmM}{R^2}$$

9. (*d*) The weight of an object at height h is given as

$$w = \frac{GMm}{(R+h)^2} \quad \text{...(i)}$$

where, M is mass of earth and R is radius of earth.

At $h = R$, $w = 50$ N.

From Eq. (i), we get

$$50 = \frac{GMm}{(R+R)^2}$$

or $$50 = \frac{GMm}{4R^2}$$

or $$200 = \frac{GMm}{R^2} \quad \text{...(ii)}$$

This is also the weight of object on surface of earth. Weight of object at depth d is given as

$$w' = \frac{GMm}{R^2}\left(1 - \frac{d}{R}\right)$$

At $d = \frac{R}{2}$, $w' = \frac{GMm}{R^2}\left(1 - \frac{R/2}{R}\right)$

$$w' = \frac{GMm}{2R^2} \quad \text{...(iii)}$$

From Eqs. (ii) and (iii), we get

$$\frac{200}{w'} = 2$$

or $$w' = \frac{200}{2} = 100 \text{ N}$$

$\therefore$ Ratio of weight $\frac{w}{w'} = \frac{200}{100} = \frac{2}{1}$

10. (*c*) The variation of acceleration due to gravity g from the centre of earth at a distance r is given as

$$g = \begin{cases} \frac{GMr}{R^3}; & r < R \\ \frac{GM}{r^2}: & r \geq R \end{cases}$$

Since, M and R are constants, so

$$g \propto r \quad (\text{for } r < R)$$

and $$g \propto \frac{1}{r^2} \quad (\text{for } r \geq R)$$

Thus, graph can be plotted as

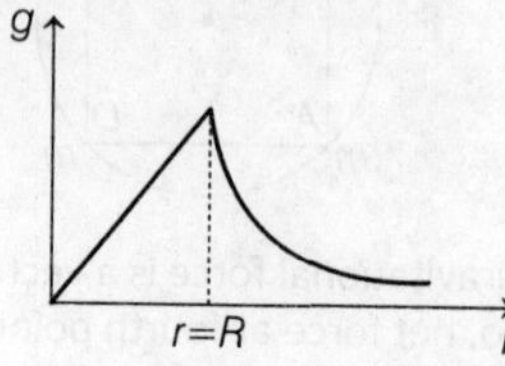

11. (*d*) Acceleration due to gravity,

$$g = \frac{GM}{R^2} = \frac{4}{3}\pi\rho GR$$

$$\left[\because \rho = \frac{M}{V} \text{ and } V = \frac{4}{3}\pi R^3\right]$$

$\therefore$ $$\frac{g_1}{g_2} = \frac{\rho_1 R_1}{\rho_2 R_2} \quad \text{...(i)}$$

Atmospheric pressure can be given by

$$p = \frac{w}{S} \quad \text{...(ii)}$$

where, w = weight of atmosphere and S = surface area of the planet.

From $w = mg$, we get

$$\frac{m_1}{m_2} = \frac{w_1 g_2}{w_2 g_1}$$

$\therefore$ $$\frac{m_1}{m_2} = \frac{p_1 S_1 g_2}{p_2 S_2 g_1} \quad [\text{from Eq. (ii)}]$$

$$= \frac{p_1 \cdot (4\pi R_1^2)}{p_2 (4\pi R_2^2)} \cdot \frac{\rho_2 R_2}{\rho_1 R_1} \quad [\text{from Eq. (i)}]$$

$\therefore$ $$\frac{m_1}{m_2} = \frac{p_1 R_1 \rho_2}{p_2 R_2 \rho_1}$$

12. (*a*) The work done by an external agent to lift object from surface to a height very slowly is equal to change in its gravitational potential energy, i.e.

$$W = \Delta U$$

or $$W = U_f - U_i$$

or $$= -\frac{GMm}{R+h} - \left(-\frac{GMm}{R}\right)$$

$$= \frac{GMm}{R} - \frac{GMm}{R+h}$$

Given that,

$$m = 2 \text{ kg}, \ h = 4R$$

$\therefore$ $$W = \frac{GM \times 2}{R} - \frac{GM \times 2}{R + 4R}$$

$$= 2GM\left(\frac{1}{R} - \frac{1}{5R}\right)$$

$\therefore$ $$W = \frac{8}{5}\frac{GM}{R}$$

13. (*b*) Let the acceleration due to gravity on the surface of planet be g, then gravitational potential difference between a point at height h and surface is given as

$$V_h - V_{\text{surface}} = \frac{W_{\text{ext}}}{m}$$

$\because$ $$W_{\text{ext}} = mgh \quad \text{...(i)}$$

$\therefore$ $$V_h - V_{\text{surface}} = gh \quad \text{...(ii)}$$

Given that, $V_h - V_{\text{surface}} = 4$ J/kg

and $h = 20$ m

From Eq. (ii), we get

$$4 = g \times 20$$

or $$g = \frac{4}{20} = \frac{1}{5} \text{ m/s}^2$$

From Eq. (i), we get

$$W_{\text{ext}} = 2 \times \frac{1}{5} \times 5 \quad [\because m = 2 \text{ kg}]$$

$$= 2 \text{ J}$$

14. (*b*) The gravitational potential energy of an object at a distance r from centre is given as

$$U = -\frac{GMm}{r}$$

At $r = 2R$, $U = -\frac{GMm}{2R}$

$\because$ $U = -90 \times 10^7$ J

$\therefore$ $$\frac{GMm}{R} = +180 \times 10^7$$

The weight of an object at distance r from the centre of earth (at some height) is given as

$$w = \frac{GMm}{r^2}$$

At $r = 3R$,

$$w = \frac{GMm}{(3R)^2}$$

$$= \frac{GMm}{9R^2} = \frac{1}{9R}\left(\frac{GMm}{R}\right)$$

$$= \frac{1}{9 \times 6.4 \times 10^6}(180 \times 10^7)$$

$$[\because R = 6400 \text{ km}]$$

$$w = 31.25 \text{ N}$$

15. (*d*) Let v be the speed of the projectile at highest point and r_{max} its distance from the centre of the earth.

Applying conservation of angular momentum and mechanical energy,

$$mv_0 R \sin\theta = mvr_{max} \sin 90^\circ$$

$\therefore$ At maximum separation, $r_{max} \perp v$

$$v_0 \sin\theta = v r_{max} \quad ...(i)$$

and $$\frac{1}{2}mv_0^2 - \frac{GMm}{R} = \frac{1}{2}mv^2 - \frac{GMm}{r_{max}}$$

or $$v_0^2 - v^2 = 2GM\left(\frac{1}{R} - \frac{1}{r_{max}}\right) \quad ...(ii)$$

Solving Eqs. (i) and (ii) with given data, we get

$$r_{max} = \frac{3R}{2}$$

16. (*c*) The total energy of planet of mass m revolving around the sun of mass m in elliptical orbit whose semi-major axis (let a) is given as

$$E = -\frac{GMm}{2a}$$

It does not change with the change of position of planet as the planet moves from A to B. It comes closer to the sun and then its speed increases. With increase in speed, its kinetic energy and magnitude of linear momentum increases.

The torque about the centre of sun of planet is zero as gravitational force acting on planet is directed towards centre of sun, due to which its angular momentum remains conserved.

17. (*b*) The energies of a satellite of mass m revolving around the earth in orbit of radius r is given as

Kinetic energy, $K = +\frac{GMm}{2r}$

Potential energy, $U = -\frac{GMm}{r}$

Total energy, $E = -\frac{GMm}{2r}$

where, M is mass of earth.

So, $\frac{E}{K} = -1$ and $\frac{E}{U} = \frac{1}{2}$

$\therefore \quad x = -1$ and $y = \frac{1}{2}$

Hence, ratio, $\left|\frac{x}{y}\right| = \left|\frac{-1}{1/2}\right| = 2:1$

18. (*c*) Energy in orbit of radius $2R$,

$$E_i = -\frac{GMm}{2(2R)} = -\frac{GMm}{4R}$$

Energy in orbit of radius $4R$,

$$E_f = -\frac{GMm}{2(4R)} = -\frac{GMm}{8R}$$

Kinetic energy in orbit of radius $2R$,

$$K_i = -E_i = \frac{GMm}{4R} = \frac{-E}{2}$$

Kinetic energy in orbit of radius $4R$,

$$K_f = -E_f = \frac{GMm}{8R} = \frac{-E}{4}$$

So, $$\Delta K = K_f - K_i = \frac{E}{4}$$

19. (*c*) Binding energy is equal to negative of total energy and equal to kinetic energy in that orbit.

$\therefore$ $$E = \frac{1}{2}mv^2$$

or $$v = \sqrt{\frac{2E}{m}}$$

Given that, $E = 4 \times 10^6$ J, $m = 800$ kg

$\therefore$ $$v = \sqrt{\frac{2 \times 4 \times 10^6}{800}}$$

$$v = 10^2 \text{ m/s} = 100 \text{ m/s}$$

20. (*b*) Let their velocities are v_1 and v_2 at distance $\frac{d_0}{2}$.

$\frac{v_1}{m} \rightarrow \quad \leftarrow \frac{v_2}{2m}$

$\bullet m \longleftarrow d_0 \longrightarrow \bullet 2m \qquad \longleftarrow \frac{d_0}{2} \longrightarrow$

From conservation of linear momentum,

$$p_i = p_f$$
$$0 = mv_1 - 2mv_2$$

or $$v_1 = 2v_2 \quad ...(i)$$

From conservation of mechanical energy,

$$E_i = E_f$$
$$K_i + U_i = K_f + U_f$$

or $$0 + \left(\frac{-Gm(2m)}{d_0}\right) = \frac{1}{2}mv_1^2 + \frac{1}{2}(2m)v_2^2 + \left(-\frac{Gm(2m)}{\frac{d_0}{2}}\right)$$

or $$-\frac{2Gm^2}{d_0} = \frac{1}{2}mv_1^2 + mv_2^2 - \frac{4Gm^2}{d_0}$$

or $$v_1^2 + 2v_2^2 = \frac{4Gm}{d_0} \quad ...(ii)$$

On solving Eqs. (i) and (ii), we get

$$v_1 = 2\sqrt{\frac{2Gm}{3d_0}}$$

and $$v_2 = \sqrt{\frac{2Gm}{3d_0}}$$

21. (*b*) The gravitational potential on the surface of a solid sphere is given as

$$V = -\frac{GM}{R}$$

and magnitude, $|V| = \frac{GM}{R}$

Here, radius, $R = y$, $|V| = x$

$\therefore$ $$x = \frac{GM}{y}$$

$\Rightarrow$ $$GM = xy \quad ...(i)$$

For outside point, field intensity

$$E = \frac{GM}{r^2}$$

At $r = 2y$, $E = \frac{GM}{(2y)^2} = \frac{xy}{(2y)^2} = \frac{x}{4y}$ [Using Eq. (i)]

The magnitude of gravitational potential due to a solid sphere at a point inside it, is given as

$$|V| = \frac{GM}{2R^3}[3R^2 - r^2]$$

Here, $R = y$, $r = \frac{y}{2}$ and $GM = xy$

$$|V| = \frac{xy}{2y^3}\left[3(y)^2 - \left(\frac{y}{2}\right)^2\right] = \frac{11}{8}x$$

The field at a point inside it in solid sphere is given as

$$E = \frac{GMr}{R^3}$$

At $r = \frac{y}{2}$ $\quad E = \frac{(xy)(y/2)}{(y)^3} = \frac{x}{2y}$

For outside point, the magnitude of gravitational potential due to a solid sphere is given as

$$|V| = \frac{GM}{r}$$

At $r = 2y$, $|V| = \frac{Gm}{2y} = \frac{xy}{2y}$

$$|V| = \frac{x}{2}$$

Thus, correct match is A $\rightarrow$ (R), B $\rightarrow$ (S), C $\rightarrow$ (P), D $\rightarrow$ (Q)

22. (*a*) The energies of a satellite revolving around earth in circular orbit are given as

Potential energy, $U = -\frac{GMm}{r}$

Kinetic energy, $K = \frac{GMm}{2r}$

Total energy, $E = -\dfrac{GMm}{2r}$

where, M is mass of earth, m is mass of satellite and r is radius of circular orbit.

$$K - E = \frac{GMm}{2r} - \left(-\frac{GMm}{2r}\right) = +\frac{GMm}{r}$$

$$E + K = -\frac{GMm}{2r} + \frac{GMm}{2r} = 0$$

Thus, graph can be plotted as

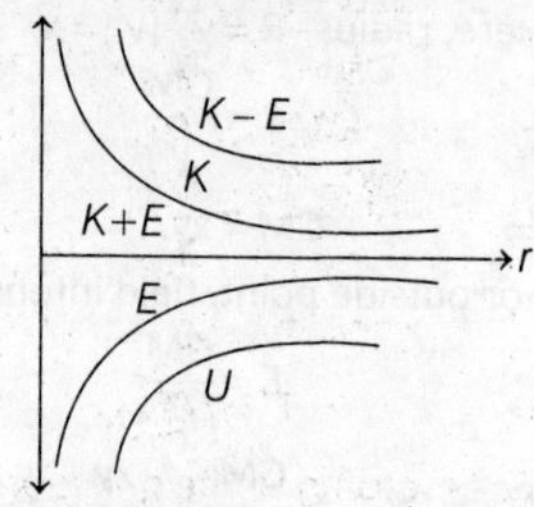

From the graph, it is clear that I, II and III denote K, E, U, respectively.

23. (*b*) The time period T of a planet revolving around sun is given as

$$T \propto (r)^{3/2} \quad \text{...(i)}$$

where, r is mean radius.

or $\quad y \propto x$

Thus, graph between T and $(r)^{3/2}$ is a straight line passing through origin.

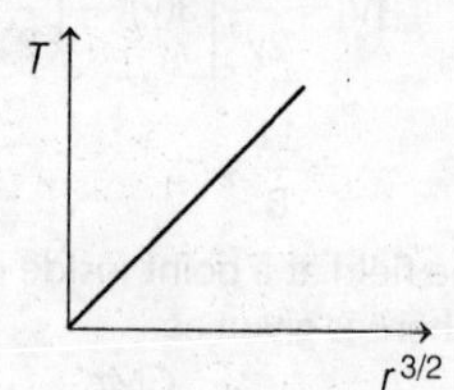

24. (*a*) Let the minimum velocity given to object from the centre of planet be $v_{\min}$. When it just overcomes with gravitational pull of earth, its velocity becomes zero.

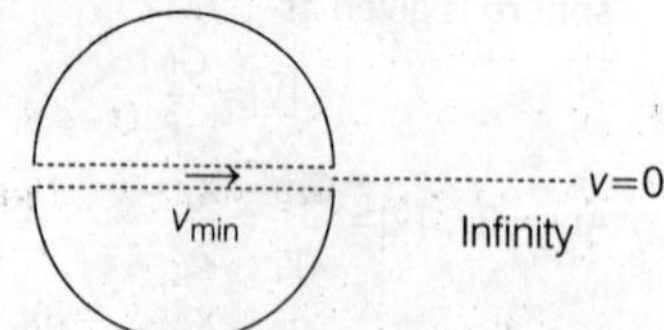

Using principle of conservation of mechanical energy,

$$ME_i = ME_f$$

$$KE_i + PE_i = KE_f + PE_f$$

$$\frac{1}{2}mv_{\min}^2 + m\left(-\frac{3GM}{2R}\right) = \frac{1}{2}m(0)^2 + m \times (0)$$

$$\frac{1}{2}mv_{\min}^2 - \frac{3}{2}\frac{GM}{R} = 0$$

or $\quad v_{\min}^2 = \dfrac{3GM}{R}$

Given that, $v_{\min} = v$

$$v^2 = \frac{3GM}{R} \quad \text{...(i)}$$

Change in potential energy,

$$\Delta U = U_f - U_i$$

$$= 0 - \left(-\frac{3}{2}\frac{GM}{R}\right) \times m$$

$$= \frac{3}{2}\frac{GMm}{R}$$

$$= \frac{m}{2}\left(\frac{3GM}{R}\right)$$

Using Eq. (i), we get

$$\Delta U = \frac{m}{2}(v^2)$$

or $\quad = \dfrac{1}{2}mv^2$

25. (*d*) Time period of geostationary satellite = Time period of spinning of earth

$$= 24 \text{ h} = 24 \times 60 \times 60 = 86400 \text{ s}$$

Also, using

$$m\omega^2(R+h) = \frac{GMm}{(R+h)^2}$$

We have, $\quad (R+h)^3 = \dfrac{GMT^2}{4\pi^2}$

$$h \approx 36000 \text{ km}$$

and $\quad v = \omega(R+h) = 3070$ m/s

Qualifier 7 (Properties of Bulk Matter)

1. (*c*) Given, stress $= 5 \times 10^9$ N/m^2

$$l_1 = l, l_2 = 2l_1 = 2l$$

$\therefore$ Change in length, $\Delta l = l_2 - l_1$

$$= 2l - l = l$$

$\therefore$ Young's modulus, $Y = \dfrac{\text{Stress}}{\text{Strain}}$

$$= \frac{5 \times 10^9}{\left(\frac{\Delta l}{l}\right)} = \frac{5 \times 10^9}{\left(\frac{l}{l}\right)}$$

$$= 5 \times 10^9 \text{ N/m}^2$$

2. (*d*) We know that, elastic potential energy per unit volume is

$$U = \frac{1}{2} \times \frac{(\text{stress})^2}{Y}$$

$\Rightarrow \quad U \propto (\text{stress})^2$

$$\therefore \quad \frac{U_1}{U_2} = \frac{(\text{stress})_1^2}{(\text{stress})_2^2}$$

$$\frac{U_1}{U_2} = \frac{(F_1/A_1)^2}{(F_2/A_2)^2} = \left(\frac{F_1}{F_2}\right)^2 \cdot \left(\frac{A_2}{A_1}\right)^2$$

As, both the wires are stretched by the same load, therefore

$$\frac{U_1}{U_2} = \left(\frac{A_2}{A_1}\right)^2 = \left(\frac{d_2^2}{d_1^2}\right)^2 = \left(\frac{2}{1}\right)^4 = \frac{16}{1}$$

$\Rightarrow \quad U_1 : U_2 = 16 : 1$

3. (*b*) Given, Poisson's ratio, $\sigma = 0.2$

Longitudinal strain, $\dfrac{\Delta L}{L} = 3 \times 10^{-3}$

$\therefore$ Poisson's ratio, $\sigma = \dfrac{-\Delta D/D}{\Delta L/L}$

$$= \frac{-\Delta R/R}{\Delta L/L}$$

$$\Rightarrow \quad \frac{\Delta R}{R} = -\sigma \times \frac{\Delta L}{L}$$

$$= -0.2 \times 3 \times 10^{-3}$$

$$= -0.6 \times 10^{-3}$$

Volume, $V = \pi R^2 L$

$\therefore$ Percentage change in its volume,

$$\frac{\Delta V}{V} \times 100 = \left(2\frac{\Delta R}{R} + \frac{\Delta L}{L}\right) \times 100$$

$$= [2 \times (-0.6 \times 10^{-3}) + 3 \times 10^{-3}] \times 100$$

$$= 0.18\%$$

4. (*b*) Given, $\Delta l_s - \Delta l_b = \Delta l$

Let $\quad l_s = l$, $l_b = (l-5)$ cm

$$\alpha_s = 12 \times 10^{-6}/°\text{C},$$

$$\alpha_b = 18 \times 10^{-6}/°\text{C}$$

We know that, $\Delta l_s = l_s \alpha_s t_1$

$$\Rightarrow \quad \alpha_s = \frac{\Delta l_s}{l_s \times t_1}$$

$$\Rightarrow \quad 12 \times 10^{-6} = \frac{\Delta l}{l \times t} \quad \text{... (i)}$$

Similarly, $\Delta l_b = l_b \alpha_b t_2$

$$\Rightarrow \quad \alpha_b = \frac{\Delta l_b}{l_b \times t_2}$$

$$\Rightarrow \quad 18 \times 10^{-6} = \frac{\Delta l}{(l-5) \times t} \quad \text{... (ii)}$$

Dividing Eq. (i) by Eq. (ii), we get

$$\frac{12 \times 10^{-6}}{18 \times 10^{-6}} = \frac{\Delta l/(l \times t)}{\Delta l/[(l-5) \times t]}$$

$$\Rightarrow \quad \frac{2}{3} = \frac{l-5}{l}$$

$$\Rightarrow \quad l = 15 \text{ cm}$$

$$\therefore \quad l_b = l - 5 = 15 - 5$$

$$= 10 \text{ cm}$$

5. (c) Let r be the radius of each drop. The terminal velocity of the drop is given as

$$v = \frac{2r^2(\rho - \sigma) g}{9\eta} \quad \text{... (i)}$$

where, ρ is density of drop and σ is density of water.

When two drops are coalesced to form a new big drop of radius R, then

$$R = 2^{1/3} \cdot r$$

∴ New terminal velocity of coalesced drop,

$$v' = \frac{2}{9}\left[\frac{(2^{1/3}r)^2(\rho - \sigma)g}{\eta}\right] \quad \text{... (ii)}$$

From Eqs. (i) and (ii), we get

$$\frac{v'}{v} = 2^{2/3}$$

$$\Rightarrow \quad v' = 2^{2/3} v = 4^{1/3} v$$

6. (b) Given, $h = 45$ m

Velocity of efflux,

$$v = \sqrt{2gh}$$
$$= \sqrt{2 \times 10 \times 45}$$
$$= \sqrt{900} = 30 \text{ m/s}$$

7. (c) Given, density of first liquid, $\rho_1 = \rho$

Density of second liquid, $\rho_2 = 4\rho$

Volume of first liquid, $V_1 = 2V$

Volume of second liquid, $V_2 = V$

Density of the mixture is given as

$$\rho_{\text{mix}} = \frac{\rho_1 V_1 + \rho_2 V_2}{V_1 + V_2}$$
$$= \frac{\rho \cdot 2V + 4\rho \cdot V}{2V + V} = \frac{6\rho V}{3V} = 2\rho$$

8. (b) By Bernoulli's theorem,

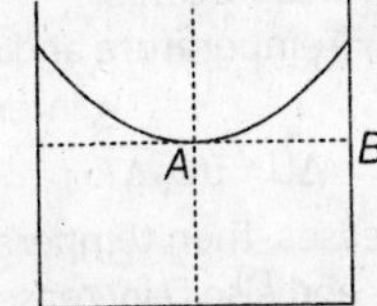

$$p_A + \frac{1}{2}\rho v_A^2 = p_B + \frac{1}{2}\rho v_B^2$$

$$\Rightarrow p_A - p_B = h\rho g = \frac{1}{2}\rho r^2 \omega^2$$

or $$h = \frac{r^2 \omega^2}{2g}$$

9. (c) We know that liquid film has two surfaces, hence increase in surface area,

$$\Delta A = 2[(20 \times 25) - (10 \times 20)] \times 10^{-4}$$
$$= 2(300) \times 10^{-4} = 6 \times 10^{-2} \text{ m}^2$$

Since, $W = T\Delta A$

$$\Rightarrow \quad T = \frac{W}{\Delta A} = \frac{5 \times 10^{-3}}{6 \times 10^{-2}}$$
$$= 0.083 \text{ N/m}$$

10. (b) For liquids, which wet the walls of a vessel, the angle of contact is acute. The liquid that wets the solid surface has concave meniscus because adhesive force is greater than the cohesive force.

11. (c) We know that, rise of liquid in capillary tube is given as

$$h = \frac{2T \cos\theta}{r\rho g}$$

$$\therefore \quad hr = \frac{2T \cos\theta}{\rho g} = \text{constant}$$

$$\Rightarrow \quad hr = \text{constant}$$

$$\Rightarrow \quad h_1 r_1 = h_2 r_2$$

$$\Rightarrow \quad h_2 = \frac{h_1 r_1}{r_2} = 2 \times \frac{r_1}{r_1/2} \quad \left(\because r_2 = \frac{r_1}{2}\right)$$
$$= 4 \text{ cm}$$

12. (b) Volume of liquid flowing through capillary tube per second is given by Poiseuille's formula as

$$V = \frac{\pi p r^4}{8\eta l} \quad \text{... (i)}$$

$$\Rightarrow \quad \frac{V_2}{V_1} = \left(\frac{r_2}{r_1}\right)^4$$

$$\Rightarrow \quad V_2 = V_1\left(\frac{r_1 + 10\% \text{ of } r_1}{r_1}\right)^4$$

$$= V_1 \left(\frac{\frac{11 r_1}{10}}{r_1}\right)^4 = V_1 (1.1)^4$$

$$\Rightarrow \quad V_2 = 1.4641 V_1$$

∴ Percentage change of flow of liquid

$$= \frac{V_2 - V_1}{V_1} \times 100$$
$$= \frac{1.4641 V_1 - V_1}{V_1} \times 100$$
$$= 46.41\% \simeq 46\%$$

13. (b) Given, surface tension of water, $T = 7.2 \times 10^{-2}$ N/m

Radius of air bubble, $R = 0.1$ mm $= 10^{-4}$ m

The excess pressure inside the air bubble is given by

$$p_2 - p_1 = \frac{2T}{R}$$

∴ Pressure inside the air bubble,

$$p_2 = p_1 + \frac{2T}{R}$$
$$= (1.013 \times 10^5) + \frac{2 \times 7.2 \times 10^{-2}}{10^{-4}}$$
$$= 1.027 \times 10^5 \text{ Nm}^{-2}$$
$$\simeq 10^5 \text{ N/m}^2$$

14. (d) The given situation is shown in the following figure.

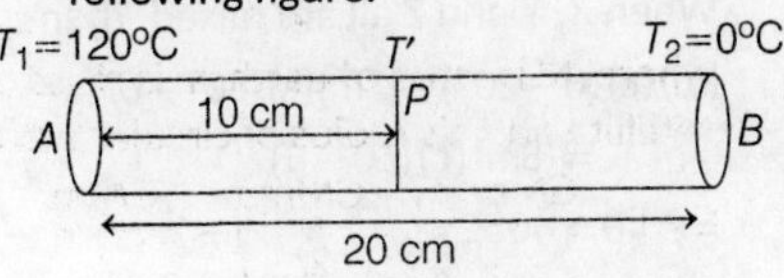

Heat current is same in the rod AB.

$$\therefore \quad \frac{120 - T'}{R_{AP}} = \frac{120 - 0}{R_{AB}}$$

$$\Rightarrow \quad \frac{120 - T'}{\frac{l_{AP}}{KA}} = \frac{120}{\frac{l_{AB}}{KA}}$$

$$\Rightarrow \quad \frac{120 - T'}{l_{AP}} = \frac{120}{2 l_{AP}}$$

$$\Rightarrow \quad 120 - T' = 60$$

$$\Rightarrow \quad T' = 60°\text{C}$$

15. (b) According to the question, conversion of energy takes place. Energy gained by the ice during its fall from height h is given by

$$E = mgh$$

As given, only one-quarter of its energy is absorbed by the ice.

So, $$\frac{mgh}{4} = mL_f$$

$$\Rightarrow \quad h = \frac{mL_f \times 4}{mg} = \frac{L_f \times 4}{g}$$
$$= \frac{3.4 \times 10^5 \times 4}{10}$$
$$= 1.36 \times 10^5 \text{ m}$$

16. (a) Slope of heating curve (ΔT *versus* ΔQ)

$$= \frac{dy}{dx} = \frac{\Delta T}{\Delta Q} = \frac{\Delta T}{mc\Delta T} = \frac{1}{mc}$$

or slope $\propto \dfrac{1}{\text{specific heat}}$

Also during melting or boiling,

$$\Delta T = 0$$

So, slope = 0

17. (a) A → R, B → S, C → Q, D → P

When X and Y are mixed together, then

$$mc(\theta - 20°) = (2m)(c)(40° - \theta)$$

$$\Rightarrow \quad \theta = \frac{100}{3} = 33.3°\text{C}$$

When X and Z are mixed together, then

$$(m)(c)(\theta - 20°) = (3m)(c)(60° - \theta)$$

$$\Rightarrow \quad \theta = 50°\text{ C}$$

When Y and Z are mixed together, then

$$(2m)(c)(\theta - 40°) = (3m)(c)(60° - \theta)$$

$\Rightarrow \quad \theta = 52°\,C$

When X, Y and Z all are mixed, then

$$(m)(c)(\theta - 20°) + (2m)(c)(60° - \theta) = (3m)(c)(60 - \theta)$$

$\Rightarrow \quad \theta = 40°\,C$

18. (*b*) Given, $T_1 = 227°C = (273 + 227)\,K = 500\,K$

$T_2 = (527 + 273)K = 800\,K$

$E_1 = 8\,cal\,cm^{-2}\,s^{-1}$

According to Stefan's law,

$$E = \sigma T^4$$

$$\Rightarrow \quad \frac{E_2}{E_1} = \left(\frac{T_2}{T_1}\right)^4$$

$$\Rightarrow \quad E_2 = E_1\left(\frac{T_2}{T_1}\right)^4 = 8\left(\frac{800}{500}\right)^4$$

$$\therefore \quad E_2 = 8\left(\frac{8}{5}\right)^4 cal\,cm^{-2}s^{-1}$$

19. (*a*) Given, mass of the steam,

$m_s = 10\,g$

Mass of ice, $m_i = 5\,g$

Temperature,

$\Delta T = T_2 - T_1 = 100 - 0 = 100°C$

Heat required to melt ice at 0°C,

$Q_1 = m_i L_f = 5 \times 80 = 400\,cal$

Heat required to raise the temperature of water from 0° to 100°C, $Q_2 = m_i C_w = 5 \times 100 = 500\,cal$

Ice can absorb maximum heat to reach at boiling point.

i.e. $Q_1 + Q_2 = 400 + 500 = 900\,cal$

Heat rejected by steam on complete condensation,

$Q_3 = m_s L_v = 10 \times 54 = 540\,cal$

The heat rejected can melt the ice completely but cannot raise the temperature of water from 0° to 100°C as there is deficiency of heat

$= Q_1 + Q_2 - Q_3 = 900 - 540 = 360\,cal$

$\therefore$ Resulting temperature $= 100°C - \dfrac{\text{Deficiency of heat}}{\text{Thermal capacity of system}}$

$$= 100°C - \frac{360}{6\,g \times 1\,cal\,g^{-1}\,°C^{-1}}$$

$$= 100 - \frac{360}{6} = 40°C$$

20. (*a*) Given, $b = 2.8 \times 10^{-3}$ m-K

$\lambda_m = 2.8\,\mu m = 2.8 \times 10^{-6}\,m$

According to Wien's displacement law,

$\lambda_m T = b$

$$\Rightarrow \quad T = \frac{b}{\lambda_m} = \frac{2.8 \times 10^{-3}}{2.8 \times 10^{-6}} = 10^3 = 1000\,K$$

21. (*b*) Let, θ = temperature at C.

Then, Heat flow from A to C = Heat flow from C to B + Heat flow from C to D

$$\Rightarrow \quad \frac{kA}{l}(T_A - \theta) = \frac{kA}{l}(\theta - T_B) + \frac{kA}{l}(\theta - T_C)$$

$$\Rightarrow \quad 3\theta = T_A + T_B + T_C$$

$$\text{or} \quad \theta = \frac{T_A + T_B + T_C}{3} = 30°$$

$$\theta = 30°\,C$$

Hence, no heat flow from B to C.

22. (*b*) According to Newton's law of cooling,

$$\frac{T_1 - T_2}{t} = k\left[\frac{T_1 + T_2}{2} - T_0\right] \quad \text{... (i)}$$

According to first condition,

$T_1 = 80°C$, $T_2 = 64°C$, $t = 5$ min

From Eq. (i), we get

$$\frac{80° - 64°}{5} = k\left(\frac{80° + 64°}{2} - T_0\right)$$

$$\Rightarrow \quad k = \frac{3.2}{72 - T_0} \quad \text{... (ii)}$$

According to second condition,

$$\frac{64° - 52°}{10} = k\left(\frac{64° + 52°}{2} - T_0\right)$$

$$\Rightarrow \quad 1.2 = \frac{3.2}{72 - T_0}(58 - T_0) \quad \text{[from Eq. (ii)]}$$

$$\Rightarrow \quad T_0 = 49.6°C \simeq 49.5°\,C$$

23. (*d*) Energy radiated,

$$E = \sigma A T^4 \cdot t$$

$$E = \sigma 4\pi R^2 T^4 t$$

For spheres,

$$\frac{E_1}{E_2} = \frac{R_1^2 T_1^4}{R_2^2 T_2^4} = \left(\frac{R_1}{R_2}\right)^2 \cdot \left(\frac{T_1}{T_2}\right)^4$$

$$\Rightarrow \quad \frac{E_1}{E_2} = \left(\frac{1}{2}\right)^2 \cdot \left(\frac{2}{1}\right)^4 = 4$$

or $E_1 : E_2 = 4 : 1$

24. (*d*) As $\lambda_{max} \propto \dfrac{1}{T}$ or $T \propto \dfrac{1}{\lambda_{max}}$

Since, wavelength of blue light is less than wavelength of red light, hence a blue star is hotter than a red star.

So, both statements I and II are correct.

25. (*d*) Conduction in solids at low and moderate temperatures : Phenon vibration

Conduction in solids at high temperatures : Phenon vibration and drift of electron

Conduction in gases : Molecular collisions

Conduction in liquids : Drift of electron and molecular collisions

Qualifier 8 (Thermodynamics)

1. (*b*) A is true but R is false.

We know that, kinetic energy, $K \propto T$, where T is temperature.

When a matter sample absorbs heat, both molecular (or atomic) separation and molecular (or atomic) vibration changes.

So, heat is absorbed both as KE and PE of molecules (or atoms).

2. (*a*) If a system is in thermodynamic equilibrium with its surroundings, it means that its thermodynamic state variables will not change with time, which is possible only when the temperature of the system and surroundings is same.

3. (*d*) The thermodynamic state variables are of two types : extensive and intensive. Extensive variables indicate the size of the system, while pressure and temperature are intensive variables.

4. (*d*) In isobaric process,

Volume $\propto$ Temperature and change in internal energy

$$\Delta U = \mu C_V \Delta T$$

As V increases, then temperature increases and also U increases.

In isochoric process, V is constant, then

$$W = 0$$

From first law of thermodynamics,

$$\Delta Q = \Delta U + W$$

$$\Delta Q = \Delta U \neq 0$$

The process cannot be isochoric.

In the isothermal process, temperature is kept constant. So, change in temperature, when work is done on the system is zero. The internal energy of the system depends on temperature. So, change in potential energy is zero.

But in cyclic process, system returns to its initial state or we can say initial and final temperatures of the gas are same. Then,

$$\Delta U = 0$$

Therefore, there are two possibilities if for a process $\Delta U = 0$, then it may be isothermal or cyclic but in question process is given non-cyclic, then process has to be isothermal.

5. (*b*) When volume of gas increases, the work done on the gas is negative and *vice-versa*.

In case (i), volume of gas is increasing, work done on the gas is negative.

In case (ii), the value $\frac{1}{V}$ is decreasing, it means that volume of gas V increases and the work done on gas is negative. We also know that, work done by gas in clockwise direction is negative and *vice-versa*.

In case (iii), ideal gas is taken through cyclic process in anti-clockwise direction, so work done on the gas is positive.

In case (iv), the given *p*-*V* graph is the combination of two cyclic processes i.e. one is in clockwise direction and other is in anti-clockwise direction.

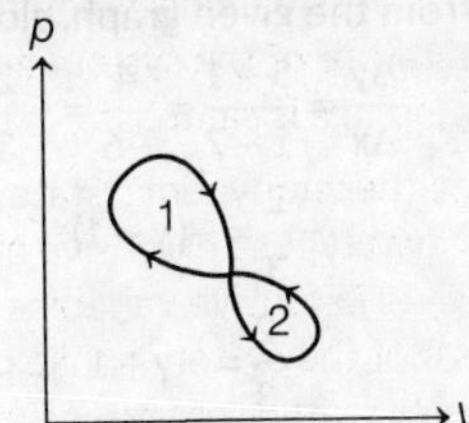

$$W_{\text{on gas}} = W_1 + W_2$$

W_1 is negative (clockwise direction)

W_2 is positive (anti-clockwise direction)

$$|W_1| > |W_2|$$

$$\therefore \quad (W_{\text{on gas}})_{(\text{iv})} < 0$$

6. (*c*) At constant pressure, $T \propto V$

As gas expands, then V increases. Therefore, T also increases and ΔT is positive.

In the expression $Q = \mu C_V \Delta T$, Q is positive.

Change in internal energy,

$$\Delta U = \mu C_V \Delta T$$

As $\Delta T > 0$

$$\Rightarrow \quad \Delta U > 0$$

Internal energy increases.

Since, volume of the gas is increasing, then $\Delta V > 0$ at constant pressure,

$$W = p\Delta V$$

$$W > 0$$

Work done by the gas is positive.

The given process is isobaric process and for such process, molar heat capacity is given as

$$C_p > \frac{\gamma}{\gamma - 1} R$$

Here, $\gamma > 1$.

So, $C_p > 0$ which is not equal to zero.

7. (*a*) In adiabatic process, heat transfer to the thermodynamic system is zero i.e., $\Delta Q = 0$

Hence, by first law of thermodynamics

$$\Delta Q = \Delta U + W$$

$$\Delta U + \Delta W = 0 \quad [\because \Delta Q = 0]$$

$$\therefore \quad \Delta W = -\Delta U$$

So, work done is equal to the negative of change in internal energy. Since, the internal energy is a function of thermodynamic state of the system. It does not depend on the path. Therefore, work done is also independent of path in adiabatic process.

In expansion, W is positive. So, ΔU is negative.

Hence, temperature of gas decreases.

State equations of adiabatic process are

$$pV^{\gamma} = \text{constant}$$

$$TV^{\gamma-1} = \text{constant}$$

$$p^{1-\gamma}T^{\gamma} = \text{constant}$$

From above, it is clear that all three thermodynamic variables depend on each other. If a single variable is changed, then remaining two variables will also be changed.

8. (*b*) As, initial state = final state

$\therefore$ Process is cyclic.

and so $\Delta U = 0$

9. (*c*) The *p*-*V* graph of all given processes in doubling the volumes shown in the graph given below

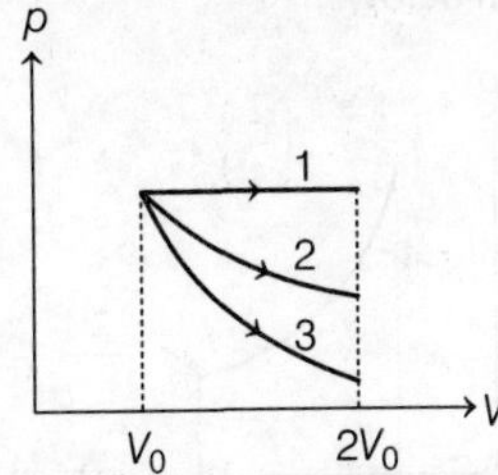

Here, process-1 is isobaric, process-2 is isothermal and process-3 is adiabatic.

The minimum area of *p*-*V* graph on *V* axis is for process-3.

10. (*d*) As, for diatomic gas, $\gamma = \frac{7}{5}$

Heat given at constant pressure,

$$\Delta Q_p = \mu C_p \Delta T$$

At constant pressure, work done

$$W = p[V_2 - V_1]$$

$$= p\Delta V$$

$$= \mu R \Delta T \quad (\because p\Delta V = \mu R \Delta T)$$

$$\text{Ratio } \frac{W}{\Delta Q_p} = \frac{\mu R \Delta T}{\mu C_p \Delta T} = \frac{R}{C_p}$$

$$= \frac{R}{\left(\frac{\gamma}{\gamma - 1}\right) R} \quad \left(\because C_p = \frac{\gamma}{\gamma - 1} R\right)$$

$$= \left(\frac{\gamma - 1}{\gamma}\right) = \frac{\frac{7}{5} - 1}{\frac{7}{5}} = \frac{\frac{2}{5}}{\frac{7}{5}} = \frac{2}{7}$$

11. (*a*) From the figure,

At point *A*, $p_A = p_0$, $V_A = 2V_0$

At point *B*, $p_B = p_0$, $V_B = V_0$

At point *C*, $p_C = 2p_0$, $V_C = V_0$

Ideal gas equation for point *A*,

$$p_A V_A = \mu R T_A$$

$$p_0(2V_0) = \mu R T_A$$

$$\text{or} \quad T_A = \frac{2p_0V_0}{\mu R} \quad \text{...(i)}$$

Ideal gas equation for point *C*,

$$p_C V_C = \mu R T_C$$

$$2p_0V_0 = \mu R T_C$$

$$\text{or} \quad T_C = \frac{2p_0V_0}{\mu R} \quad \text{...(ii)}$$

From Eqs. (i) and (ii), we get

$$T_A = T_C$$

$$\text{or} \quad \Delta T = 0$$

$\therefore$ Change in internal energy for process *ABC*,

$$\Delta U_{ABC} = \mu R \Delta T$$

$$\Delta U_{ABC} = \mu R(0) = 0$$

12. (*c*) As we know, ideal gas equation is given as

$$pV = \mu RT$$

$$\text{or} \quad T = \frac{pV}{\mu R}$$

From the given diagram,

Temperature at point *A*,

$$T_A = \frac{p_A V_A}{\mu R} = \frac{(2p_0)(V_0)}{2R} = \frac{p_0V_0}{R}$$

Temperature at point *B*,

$$T_B = \frac{p_B V_B}{\mu R} = \frac{(2p_0)(2V_0)}{2R}$$

$$= \frac{2p_0V_0}{R}$$

Temperature at point C,

$$T_C = \frac{p_C V_C}{\mu R} = \frac{(p_0)(2V_0)}{2R} = \frac{p_0 V_0}{R}$$

Temperature at point D,

$$T_D = \frac{p_D V_D}{\mu R} = \frac{p_0 V_0}{2R} = \frac{p_0 V_0}{2R}$$

The change in internal energy of gas,

$\Delta U = \mu C_V \Delta T$

If ΔT is positive, then ΔU will increase.

Among all given processes, temperature increases for AB and DA processes.

Thus, in processes AB and DA, the internal energy of gas increases.

13. (*c*) Given that, for polytropic process

$$pV^{\alpha} = \text{constant}$$

or $\quad p_A V_A^{\alpha} = p_B V_B^{\alpha}$

From the given graph, we can write

$$(2p_0)(V_0)^{\alpha} = p_0(2V_0)^{\alpha}$$

or $\quad \dfrac{(2V_0)^{\alpha}}{V_0^{\alpha}} = \dfrac{2p_0}{p_0}$

or $\quad 2^{\alpha} = 2$

or $\quad \alpha = 1$

14. (*c*) Given, initial temperature, $T_i = T_0$

Final temperature, $T_f = 2T_0$

Change in temperature,

$$\Delta T = T_f - T_i = 2T_0 - T_0$$
$$\Delta T = T_0$$

For isochoric process,

$$Q_1 = \mu C_V \Delta T$$
$$Q_1 = \mu \times \frac{3}{2} R \times T_0$$

(For monoatomic gas, $C_V = \frac{3}{2}R$)

$$Q_1 = \frac{3}{2}\mu R T_0 \qquad \text{...(i)}$$

For isobaric process,

$$Q_2 = \mu C_p \Delta T = \mu \times \frac{5}{2} R \times T_0$$
$$= \frac{5}{2}\mu R T_0 \qquad \text{...(ii)}$$

($\because C_V = \frac{5}{2}R$ for monoatomic gas)

For adiabatic process,

$$Q_3 = 0 \qquad \text{...(iii)}$$

From Eqs. (i), (ii) and (iii), we get

$$Q_2 > Q_1 > Q_3$$

15. (*b*) As given, $p_i = p_0$ (let)

$$p_f = 8p_0$$
$$V_i = V_0$$
$$V_f = \frac{3}{4}V_0$$
$$T_i = T$$

For adiabatic process,

$$p_i V_i^{\gamma} = p_f V_f^{\gamma}$$
$$p_0 V_0^{\gamma} = 8p_0\left(\frac{3}{4}V_0\right)^{\gamma}$$
$$1 = 8\left(\frac{3}{4}\right)^{\gamma} \qquad \text{...(i)}$$

Also, from $T_i V_i^{\gamma-1} = T_f V_f^{\gamma-1}$

$$TV_0^{\gamma-1} = T_2\left(\frac{3}{4}V_0\right)^{\gamma-1} \qquad \text{...(ii)}$$

Multiplying by V_0 on both sides of Eq. (ii), we get

$$TV_0^{\gamma} = T_2\left(\frac{3}{4}V_0\right)^{\gamma-1} V_0$$

Multiplying the above equation by $\left(\frac{3}{4}\right)$, we get

or $\quad \dfrac{3}{4}TV_0^{\gamma} = T_2\left(\dfrac{3}{4}V_0\right)^{\gamma-1}\left(\dfrac{3}{4}V_0\right)$

or $\quad TV_0^{\gamma} = \dfrac{4}{3}T_2\left(\dfrac{3}{4}V_0\right)^{\gamma}$

or $\quad T = \dfrac{4}{3}\left(\dfrac{3}{4}\right)^{\gamma} T_2 \qquad \text{...(iii)}$

On dividing Eq. (i) by Eq. (iii), we get

$$\frac{1}{T} = \frac{8\left(\frac{3}{4}\right)^{\gamma}}{\frac{4}{3}\left(\frac{3}{4}\right)^{\gamma} T_2}$$

$$\frac{1}{T} = \frac{6}{T_2} \text{ or } T_2 = 6T$$

16. (*d*) At first, the gas undergoes isothermal expansion from V_0 to $2V_0$. For such a process, the equation of gas will be

$$pV = \text{constant}$$

This means pressure is inversely proportional to volume. Thus, p-V curve for such a process will be as shown below

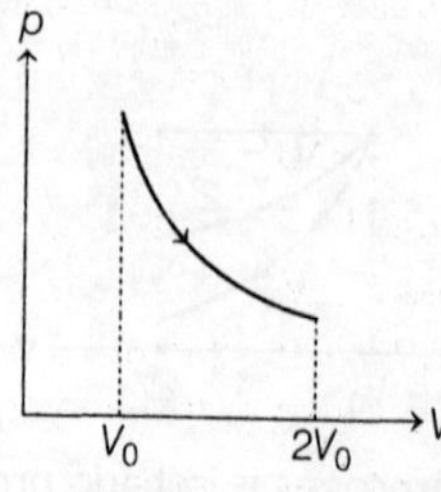

After that, its volume is decreased or reduced from $2V_0$ to V_0 at constant pressure. Thus, the final p-V curve for this ideal gas will be as shown below

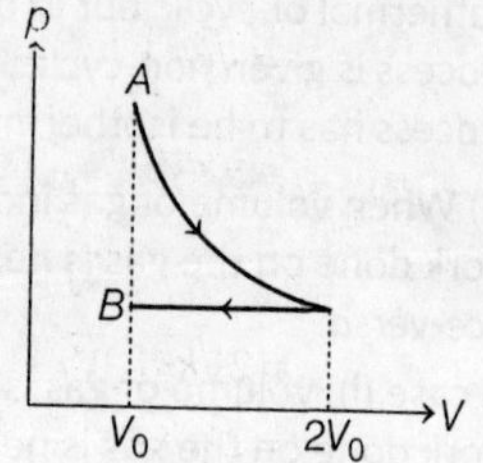

Thus, the graph given in option (d) is correctly representing the given situation.

17. (*a*) For adiabatic process,

$$TV^{\gamma-1} = \text{constant}$$

Take log on both sides, we get

$$\log TV^{\gamma-1} = \log \text{constant}$$
$$\log T + \log V^{\gamma-1} = \text{constant}$$
$$(\because \log mn = \log m + \log n)$$

or $\log T + (\gamma - 1)\log V = \text{constant}$

The above equation represents a straight line equation whose slope is equal to $-(\gamma - 1)$.

As from the given graph, slope

$$\frac{\Delta y}{\Delta x} = \frac{5-1}{1-7} = \frac{4}{-6} = -\frac{2}{3}$$

$\therefore \quad -\dfrac{2}{3} = -(\gamma - 1)$

or $\quad -\dfrac{2}{3} = -\gamma + 1$

or $\quad -\gamma = -\dfrac{2}{3} - 1$

or $\quad \gamma = \dfrac{5}{3}$

The value of γ for monoatomic gas is $\dfrac{5}{3}$.

18. (*b*) Given, $pT = \text{constant} = k$ (let).... (i)

or $\quad pT = p_1T_1 = p_2T_2 = k$

From ideal gas equation,

$$pV = \mu RT$$

or $\quad T = \dfrac{pV}{R} \qquad (\because \mu = 1)$

From Eq. (i), we get

$$p\left(\frac{pV}{R}\right) = k$$

or $\quad p^2V = kR$

or $\quad p = \sqrt{\dfrac{kR}{V}}$

As, work done by gas,

$$W = \int_{V_1}^{V_2} p\,dV$$

$$W_0 = \int_{V_1}^{V_2} \sqrt{\frac{kr}{V}}dV$$
$$= \sqrt{kR}\int_{V_1}^{V_2} \frac{dV}{\sqrt{V}}$$
$$= \sqrt{kR}[2\sqrt{V}]_{V_1}^{V_2}$$
$$(\because \int x^n dx = \frac{x^{n+1}}{n+1} + C)$$
$$= 2\sqrt{kR}[\sqrt{V_2} - \sqrt{V_1}]$$
$$= 2[\sqrt{kRV_2} - \sqrt{kRV_1}]$$
$$= 2[\sqrt{p_2T_2RV_2} - \sqrt{p_1T_1RV_1}]$$
$$= 2[\sqrt{p_2V_2RT_2} - \sqrt{p_1V_1RT_1}]$$
$$= 2[\sqrt{(RT_2)RT_2} - \sqrt{(RT_1)(RT_1)}]$$
$$= 2[RT_2 - RT_1]$$
$$W_0 = 2R(T_2 - T_1) \quad \text{...(ii)}$$

For first case,

$$T_1 = T_0, T_2 = 2T_0$$
$$W_0 = 2R[2T_0 - T_0]$$
$$W_0 = 2RT_0$$

For second case,

$$T_1 = 2T_0, T_2 = 3T_0$$
$$W = 2R(3T_0 - 2T_0) = 2RT_0$$
$$W = W_0$$

19. (*a*) The work done by a gas in a thermodynamic process is equal to area of *pV* diagram under the *X*-axis

For diagram (i),

$$W_1 = \pi\left(\frac{3V_0 - V_0}{2}\right)\left(\frac{3p_0 - p_0}{2}\right)$$
$$= \pi p_0V_0 = 3.14 p_0V_0$$

For diagram (ii), W_2 = Area of trapezium

$$= \frac{1}{2} \times (3V_0 - V_0) \times (p_0 + 2p_0)$$
$$= 3p_0V_0$$

For diagram (iii), W_3 = Area of rectangle

$$= (3V_0 - V_0)(2p_0 - p_0) = 2p_0V_0$$

It is clear that,

$$W_1 > W_2 > W_3$$

20. (*c*) From the second law of thermodynamics, change in entropy,

$$\Delta s = \frac{\Delta Q}{T}$$

For adiabatic process, $\Delta Q = 0$

$$\Rightarrow \quad \Delta s = 0$$

Thus, change in entropy is zero. So, entropy will remain same.

21. (*c*) The work done by a gas in cyclic process is equal to the area enclosed by *pV* indicator diagram,

W = Area of square *XYZH*

$$= (3 \times 10^5 - 1 \times 10^5) \times (3 - 1)\ \frac{\text{N}}{\text{m}^2} \times \text{m}^3$$
$$= 2 \times 2 \times 10^5 \text{ N-m}$$
$$= 4 \times 10^5 \text{ J} \quad (\because 1\text{ J} = 1 \text{ N-m})$$

Only in process *XY* and *HX*, heat is given,

Heat given in *XY* process,

$$Q_{XY} = \mu C_p \Delta T$$
$$(\because XY \text{ is isobaric process})$$
$$= \mu \times \frac{5}{2}R \times \Delta T$$
$$= \frac{5}{2}\mu R\Delta T = \frac{5}{2}p\Delta V$$
$$= \frac{5}{2} \times 3 \times 10^5 \times (3 - 1)$$
$$Q_{XY} = 15 \times 10^5 \text{ J}$$

Heat given in *HZ* process,

$$Q_{WZ} = \mu C_V \Delta T$$
$$(\because HZ \text{ process is isochoric})$$
$$= \mu \times \frac{3}{2}R \times \Delta T \quad \left(\because C_V = \frac{3}{2}R\right)$$
$$= \frac{3}{2}\mu R\Delta T = \frac{3}{2}(\Delta p)V$$
$$= \frac{3}{2} \times (3 \times 10^5 - 1 \times 10^5) \times 1$$
$$= \frac{3}{2} \times 2 \times 10^5$$
$$Q_{HX} = 3 \times 10^5 \text{ J}$$

$$\text{Efficiency, } \eta = \frac{\text{Work done}}{\text{Heat given}} = \frac{W}{Q_{XY} + Q_{HX}}$$
$$= \frac{4 \times 10^5}{15 \times 10^5 + 3 \times 10^5} = 0.222$$

or $\eta = 22.2\%$

22. (*a*) We have,

$$C = \frac{\Delta Q}{n\Delta T}$$

Process A $\Delta Q = 0$ as gas is compressed fast.

$$\therefore \quad C = 0$$

Process B $\Delta Q \neq 0,\ \Delta T = 0$

$$\therefore \quad C = \frac{\Delta Q}{n \times 0} = \infty$$

Process C $\Delta Q \neq 0, \Delta T < 0$

$$\Rightarrow \quad C = \frac{\Delta Q}{n\Delta T} < 0$$

23. (*a*) **Process 1** $\Delta Q - \Delta W = \Delta U$

$$\Rightarrow \quad 35 - (-15) = \Delta U$$

or $\Delta U = 50$ unit

Hence, $\Delta U = Z = 50$ unit

Process 2 $\Delta Q - \Delta U = \Delta W$

or $\Delta W = -15 - (-20) = 5$ unit

i.e. $\Delta W = Y = 5$ unit

Process 3 $\Delta Q = \Delta U + \Delta W$

$$= 20 + (-20)$$
$$= 0 \text{ unit}$$

i.e. $X = \Delta Q = 0$ unit

24. (*b*) Let the efficiency of engines *A* and *B* be η_A and η_B respectively, we have

$$\frac{\eta_A}{\eta_B} = \frac{3}{2}$$

The efficiency of carnot engine is given as

$$\eta = 1 - \frac{T_L}{T_H} \quad \text{...(i)}$$

The efficiency of engine *A* is more than that of engine *B*, it means the working temperature of engine *A* is more than that of engine *B*. So, we may write

$$T_A = T + 50 \text{ and } T_B = T$$

($\because$ Sink temperature, $T_0 = 300$ K)

From Eq. (i), we get

$$\eta_A = 1 - \frac{T + 50}{300} \quad \text{...(ii)}$$

and
$$\eta_B = 1 - \frac{T}{300} \quad \text{...(iii)}$$

On dividing Eq. (ii) by Eq. (iii), we get

$$\frac{\eta_A}{\eta_B} = \frac{1 - \frac{T+50}{300}}{1 - \frac{T}{300}}$$
$$\frac{3}{2} = \frac{300 - T - 50}{300 - T}$$
$$\frac{3}{2} = \frac{250 - T}{300 - T}$$
$$900 - 3T = 500 - 2T$$
$$T = 900 - 500$$
$$T = 400 \text{ K}$$
$$\therefore \quad T_A = 400 + 50$$
$$= 450 \text{ K}$$
$$T_B = 400 \text{ K}$$

25. (*b*) Given that, $T_H = 27°$C or 300 K

$$T_L = 5°\text{C or } 278 \text{ K}$$

Coefficient of performance,

$$\beta = \frac{T_H}{T_H - T_L}$$
$$\beta = \frac{300}{300 - 278} = \frac{300}{22}$$

Heat extracted from water at 5°C to convert into ice at 0°C,

$$Q = mL_f + ms_w\Delta\theta$$
$$= 50 \times 3.4 \times 10^5 + 50 \times 4.2 \times 10^3 \times (5 - 0)$$
$$= 1.7 \times 10^7 + 0.1 \times 10^7$$
$$= 1.8 \times 10^7 \text{ J}$$
$$\because \quad \beta = \frac{\text{Heat extracted}}{\text{Work done}} = \frac{Q}{W}$$

or
$$W = \frac{Q}{\beta} = \frac{1.8 \times 10^7}{\frac{300}{22}} = 1.32 \times 10^6 \text{ J}$$

Qualifier 9 (Behaviour of Perfect Gase & Kinetic Theory)

1. (c) **From Boyle's law** $pV = \text{constant}$
($T = \text{constant}$)

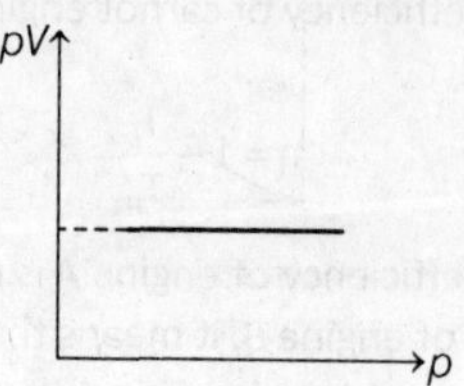

From Charles' law For constant pressure and given mass of the gas,

$$V \propto T$$

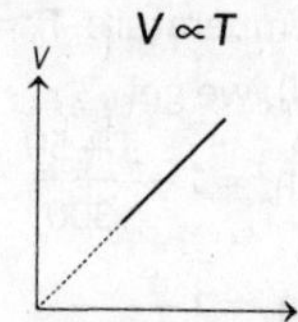

From Gay Lussac's law If V is kept constant of given mass of gas,

$$p \propto T \text{ or } \frac{p}{T} = \text{constant}$$

p/T
T

Hence, $A \to Q$, $B \to P$, $C \to R$

2. (b) According to given situation,
$$\rho_A = 1.5\rho_B$$
$$p_A = 2p_B$$
According to ideal gas equation, we have
$$\text{Pressure, } p = \frac{\rho RT}{M}$$
where, M is molecular weight of an ideal gas.
$$\Rightarrow \quad M = \frac{\rho RT}{p}$$
where, R and T are constants.
$$\text{So,} \quad M \propto \frac{\rho}{p} \Rightarrow \frac{M_A}{M_B} = \frac{\rho_A}{\rho_B} \times \frac{p_B}{p_A}$$
$$= 1.5 \times \frac{1}{2} = 0.75 = \frac{3}{4}$$

3. (a) A gas that satisfies equation $pV = \mu RT$ exactly at all pressures and temperatures is defined to be an ideal gas. An ideal gas is a simple theoretical model of gas. No real gas is truly ideal. The given figure shows departures from ideal gas behaviour for a real gas at three different temperatures. All curves approach the ideal gas behaviour for low pressures and high temperatures. At low pressures or high temperatures, the molecules are far apart and molecular interactions are negligible, hence the gas behaves like an ideal one. So, the term $\frac{pV}{T}$ becomes constant.

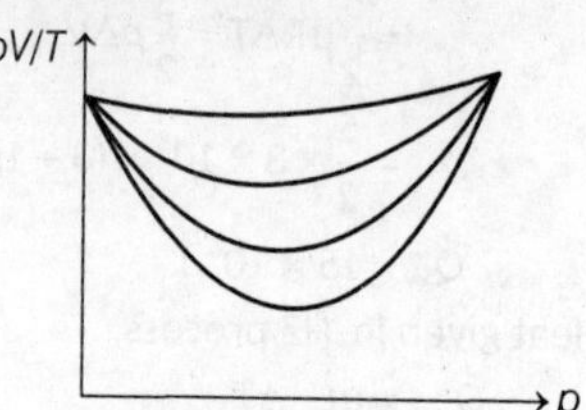

For real gas, if we decrease the temperature from high temperature, then graph deviates from the ideal gas behaviour. More the temperature more the deviation.

It is concluded that $T_3 < T_2 < T_1$.

4. (c) From the ideal gas equation,
$$p = \left(\frac{\mu R}{V}\right)T = \left(\frac{mR}{MV}\right)T \quad \left(\because \mu = \frac{m}{M}\right) \quad \text{... (i)}$$
The constant volumes are straight lines with slope $\frac{mR}{MV}$. The slope of lines is proportional to the mass of the gas.

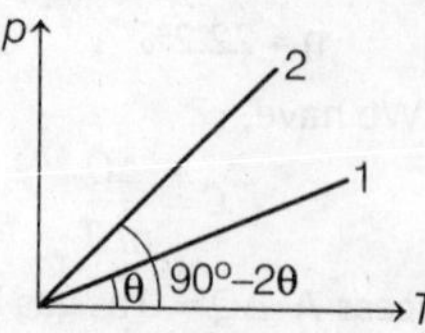

From Eq. (i),
$$\frac{(\text{slope})_1}{(\text{slope})_2} = \frac{m_1}{m_2} = \frac{\tan\theta}{\tan(90° - 2\theta)}$$
$$= \frac{\tan\theta}{\cot 2\theta}$$
$$\frac{(\text{Slope})_1}{(\text{Slope})_2} = \tan\theta \tan 2\theta$$
$$\left(\because \cot x = \frac{1}{\tan x}\right)$$

5. (a) From ideal gas equation,
$$pV = nkT$$
$$\text{or} \quad n = \frac{pV}{kT}$$
Here, $p = 761$ mm of Hg or 1.01×10^5 N/m²
$$V = 500 \text{ cm}^3$$
$$\text{or} \quad 500 \times 10^{-6} \text{ m}^3$$
$$k = 1.38 \times 10^{-23} \text{ J/K}$$
$$T = 98.6° \text{ F or } 37°\text{C}$$
$$T = 310 \text{ K}$$
(normal body temperature)

Putting all the values, we get
$$n = \frac{1.01 \times 10^5 \times 500 \times 10^{-6}}{1.38 \times 10^{-23} \times 310}$$
$$= 1.19 \times 10^{22}$$
$$n \simeq 1.2 \times 10^{22}$$

6. (b) As partial pressure of a gas in a mixture is the pressure, it would exert for the same volume and temperature, if it alone occupied the vessel.
Therefore, for same V and T, let p_1 and p_2 be partial pressures.
From ideal gas equations,
$$p_1V = \mu_1 RT$$
$$\text{and} \quad p_2V = \mu_2 RT$$
Here, 1 and 2 refer to helium gas and nitrogen gas, respectively.
$$\text{Now,} \quad \frac{p_1}{p_2} = \frac{\mu_1}{\mu_2} \text{ or } \frac{\mu_1}{\mu_2} = \frac{p_1}{p_2} = \frac{5}{3}$$
$$\therefore \quad \frac{\mu_1}{\mu_2} = \frac{5}{3} \quad \left(\because \frac{p_1}{p_2} = \frac{5}{3}\right)$$

7. (d) Saturated vapours does not follow gas law as the pressure is independent of volume, whereas unsaturated vapour obeys gas law.

8. (a) Both A and R are true but R is not the correct explanation of A.
$$\text{As} \quad pV = nRT$$
$$\Rightarrow \quad p \propto T$$
Hence, when temperature of a gas is increased to 3 times, then its pressure also increase 3 times.
Also, pressure of N molecules of an ideal gas contained in volume V is,
$$p = \frac{2}{3}\frac{N}{V}\left(\frac{1}{2}m\bar{v}^2\right)$$

9. (b) Given, mass, $m = 1$ kg
Density, $\rho = 4$ kgm⁻³
$$\therefore \text{ Volume, } V = \frac{\text{Mass}}{\text{Density}} = \frac{1}{4} \text{ m}^3$$
Pressure, $p = 8 \times 10^4$ Nm⁻²
Thermal energy corresponds to internal energy, i.e. internal energy of diatomic gas,
$$E = \frac{5}{2}k_BNT = \frac{5}{2}p \times V \quad (\because pV = k_BNT)$$
$$= \frac{5}{2} \times 8 \times 10^4 \times \frac{1}{4}$$
$$= 5 \times 10^4 \text{ J}$$

10. (d) Rms speed of atoms, $v_{rms} = \sqrt{\frac{3RT}{M_w}}$
Here, $T = 27°\text{C}$ or 300 K

$M_w = 36$ g or 36×10^{-3} kg

$R = 8.31$ J/kg-K

$\therefore \; v_{rms} = \sqrt{\dfrac{3 \times 8.31 \times 300}{36 \times 10^{-3}}}$

$= 455.8$ m/s

As, pressure = force per unit area

or pressure = rate of change in momentum per unit area

= (Number of molecules striking) × (Rate of change in momentum of one atom per unit area)

$= N \times \dfrac{m[v_{rms} - (-v_{rms})]}{At}$

[Here, m is mass of one atom of Ar]

$\Rightarrow \quad p = \left(\dfrac{N}{At}\right) 2mv_{rms}$

$= n2mv_{rms}$

(Here, n = number of atoms striking per unit area per second)

or $\quad n = \dfrac{p}{2mv_{rms}}$

Given, $p = 2$ atm or $2 \times 1.01 \times 10^5$ Pa

$m = \dfrac{36}{6.023 \times 10^{23}}$ g or 5.977×10^{-26} kg

$n = \dfrac{2 \times 1.01 \times 10^5}{2 \times 5.977 \times 10^{-26} \times 455.8}$

$n = 3.7 \times 10^{27}$

11. (*d*) With increase in temperature, the curve between n *versus* v shift towards right and becomes broader because with temperature increase, molecular speed increases.

From given graph at temperature T_3, curve is broadest and at T_2, it is steepest.

$\therefore \quad T_3 > T_1 > T_2$

12. (*d*) For a gas,

$C_V = \dfrac{f}{2} R$

and $\quad C_p = \left(1 + \dfrac{f}{2}\right) R$

$\gamma = \dfrac{C_p}{C_V} = 1 + \dfrac{2}{f}$

If atomicity increases, then degree of freedom also increases, therefore C_p and C_V increase but γ decreases.

13. (*b*) Given that, $V = 67.2$ L

$\Delta T = 30°C$

$C_V = \dfrac{3}{2} R$ or $\dfrac{3}{2} \times 8.31$ (for helium)

Number of moles, $\mu = \dfrac{V}{22.4} = \dfrac{67.2}{22.4}$

$\therefore$ Heat given at constant volume,

$Q = \mu C_V \Delta T$

$= \dfrac{67.2}{22.4} \times \dfrac{3}{2} \times 8.31 \times 30$

$= 1121.85$ J

14. (*b*) $\because$ CO is a diatomic gas.

For diatomic gas,

$C_p = \dfrac{7}{2} R$

$C_V = \dfrac{5}{2} R$

$\therefore \quad \gamma = \dfrac{C_p}{C_V}$

$= \dfrac{7R/2}{5R/2} = 1.40$

15. (*a*) Let unknown rms speed be $(v_{rms})_2$ at

$T_2 = 227°C = 500$ K

and at $T_1 = 127°C = 400$ K

$(v_{rms})_1 = 200$ m/s

$\therefore$ Using the relation $v_{rms} \propto \sqrt{T}$, we can write,

$\dfrac{(v_{rms})_2}{(v_{rms})_1} = \sqrt{\dfrac{T_2}{T_1}}$ ... (i)

Substituting these given values in Eq. (i), we get

$(v_{rms})_2 = \sqrt{\dfrac{500}{400}} \times 200$ m/s

$\therefore \; (v_{rms})_2 = \dfrac{1}{2}\sqrt{5} \times 200$ m/s

$= 100\sqrt{5}$ m/s

16. (*c*) Given, $n = 2.7 \times 10^{25}$ m^{-3}

and $\quad r = 10^{-10}$ m

So, diameter, $d = 2 \times 10^{-10}$ m

$\because$ Mean free path, $\lambda = \dfrac{1}{\sqrt{2}\pi n d^2}$

On putting given values, we get

$\lambda = \dfrac{1}{\sqrt{2} \times 3.14 \times 2.7 \times 10^{25} \times (2 \times 10^{-10})^2}$

$= 2.05 \times 10^{-7}$ m

17. (*c*) If volume is kept constant, then $\dfrac{p}{T}$ is constant. Thus, λ will not depend on p and T, i.e. $\lambda \propto (T)^0$ or $\lambda \propto (p)^0$.

18. (*c*) At high temperatures (greater than 250 K), heat capacity is nearly constant and equals to 3R. At low temperatures, the heat capacities decrease. At $T = 0$ K. C tends to zero. The correct variation of heat capacity with temperature is shown in the figure given below

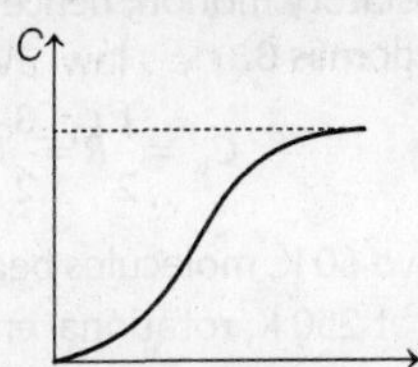

19. (*d*) Translational kinetic energy of diatomic gas at temperature T,

$KE_{trans} = \dfrac{3\mu}{2} RT$

Potential energy of an ideal gas is equal to zero, i.e. $U = 0$

Ratio, $\dfrac{KE_{trans}}{U} = \dfrac{\dfrac{3\mu RT}{2}}{0}$

$\dfrac{KE_{trans}}{U} = \infty$

which is not defined.

20. (*b*) As given that, an unknown gas is monoatomic and molar specific heat at constant volume is $C_V = \dfrac{f}{2} R$, where f is degree of freedom.

For monoatomic gas, $f = 3$

As, $\quad C_V = M_w c_V$

$\therefore \quad M_w c_V = \dfrac{f}{2} R$

or $\quad M_w = \dfrac{fR}{2c_V} = \dfrac{3 \times 2}{2 \times 0.15}$

($\because R = 2$ cal/mol-K and $c_V = 0.15$ cal/g-K)

$= 20$ g/mol

21. (*a*) Now, in given case,

For gas A, $C_p = 29$, $C_V = 22$

For gas B, $C_p = 30$, $C_V = 21$

By using,

$\gamma = \dfrac{C_p}{C_V} = 1 + \dfrac{2}{f}$

For gas A,

$1 + \dfrac{2}{f} = \dfrac{29}{22} \approx 1.3$

$\Rightarrow \quad f = 6.67 \approx 7$

So, gas A has vibrational mode of degree of freedom.

For gas B,

$1 + \dfrac{2}{f} = \dfrac{30}{21} \approx 1.4 \Rightarrow f = 5$

Hence, gas B does not have any vibrational mode of degree of freedom.

22. (*b*) At about 60 K or less, temperature is low and gas molecules have only translatory motion, hence its degree of freedom is 3.

So, $C_V = \frac{f}{2}R = \frac{3}{2}R$

Above 60 K, molecules begin to rotate and at 250 K, rotational energy attains its classical value. At 250 K, gas molecules have 3 translatory and 2 rotatory degrees of freedom. i.e. $f = 5$

So, $C_V = \frac{5}{2}R$.

At 280 K, H_2 gas molecules do not begin to vibrate because is too low temperature.

23. (*c*) KE per mole $= \frac{f}{2}RT$

$f = 3$: Monoatomic

$f = 5$: Diatomic

$f = 6$: Triatomic linear

$f = 7$: Triatomic non-linear

$\therefore$ KE per mole for

Monoatomic $= \frac{3}{2}RT = 1.5\,RT$

Diatomic $= \frac{5}{2}RT = 2.5\,RT$

Triatomic linear $= \frac{6}{2}RT = 3\,RT$

Triatomic non-linear $= \frac{7}{2}RT = 3.5\,RT$

24. (*b*) Ratio of rms to mean speed of molecules $= \frac{5.45}{5} = 1.09$

25. (*b*) van der Waals' equation for real gas of μ moles,

$$\left(p + \frac{\mu^2 a}{V^2}\right)(V - \mu b) = \mu RT$$

$$p = \frac{\mu Rt}{V - \mu b} - \frac{\mu^2 a}{V^2} \quad \text{... (i)}$$

Given equation can be written as

$$p = \frac{2RT}{V - 2b} - \frac{a}{4b^2} \quad \text{... (ii)}$$

Comparing both Eqs. (i) and (ii), we get

$$\mu = \frac{1}{2}$$

$$\because \quad \mu = \frac{m}{M}$$

$\therefore$ Mass of gas, $m = \mu M$

$$= \frac{1}{2} \times 44 \quad (\because M \text{ for } CO_2 = 44\text{ g})$$

$$= 22\text{ g}$$

Qualifier 10 (Oscillations and Waves)

1. (*a*) Force = Mass × Acceleration

$$= m(-\omega^2 x)$$

$$= -m\omega^2 A\sin(\omega t + \phi)$$

Force is periodic as $\sin(\omega t + \phi)$ is periodic.

2. (*c*) As given, displacement

$$x = (\sin\omega t - \cos\omega t)$$

Multiplying and dividing by $\sqrt{2}$ in RHS, we get

$$x = \frac{\sqrt{2}}{\sqrt{2}}(\sin\omega t - \cos\omega t)$$

$$= \sqrt{2}\left(\sin\omega t \times \frac{1}{\sqrt{2}} - \cos\omega t \times \frac{1}{\sqrt{2}}\right)$$

$$= \sqrt{2}\left[\sin\omega t \cos\frac{\pi}{4} - \cos\omega t \sin\frac{\pi}{4}\right]$$

$$= \sqrt{2}\left[\sin\left(\omega t - \frac{\pi}{4}\right)\right]$$

$$[\because \sin(A - B) = \sin A\cos B - \cos A\sin B]$$

Comparing the above equation with the general equation for the displacement of a particle executing SHM is $x = A\sin(\omega t + \phi)$, we get

Phase, $\phi = \omega t - \frac{\pi}{4}$

Initial phase, $\phi = \omega \times 0 - \frac{\pi}{4}$

$$\phi = -\frac{\pi}{4}$$

Amplitude, $A = \sqrt{2}$ m

3. (*c*) The average potential energy of a block for one complete period is given as

$$U_{av} = \frac{1}{4}m\omega^2 A^2$$

Also, average kinetic energy,

$$K_{avg} = \frac{1}{4}m\omega^2 A^2$$

It means both energies are equal for one time period and it is independent of x. So,for all values of x, average value of both energies are equal.

4. (*a*) Given that, relative density of simple pendulum, $\rho = 4$

Relative density of non-viscous fluid, $\sigma = 2$

Length, $l = 1$ m

As time period, $T = 2\pi\sqrt{\dfrac{l}{g\left(1 - \dfrac{\sigma}{\rho}\right)}}$

$$= 2 \times 3.14\sqrt{\frac{1}{9.8\left(1 - \frac{2}{4}\right)}}$$

$$= 2.83\text{ s}$$

5. (*b*) In series combination, equivalent spring constant k_{eq} is given as,

$$k_{eq} = \frac{k_1 k_2}{k_1 + k_2}$$

If $k_1 = k_2 = k$, then $k_{eq} = \frac{k \times k}{k + k} = \frac{k}{2}$

In parallel combination, equivalent spring constant k_{eq} is given as

$$k_{eq} = k_1 + k_2 + k_3 + \ldots + k_n$$

Now, let us solve first equivalent spring constant of given arrangement.

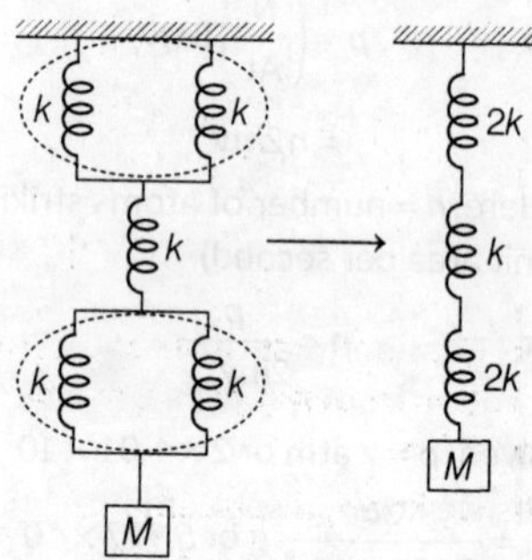

Since, three springs are connected in series and in series, equivalent spring constant is given as

$$\frac{1}{k_{eq}} = \frac{1}{2k} + \frac{1}{k} + \frac{1}{2k}$$

$$\frac{1}{k_{eq}} = \frac{2}{k}$$

or $\quad k_{eq} = \frac{k}{2}$

Time period of spring-block system,

$$T = 2\pi\sqrt{\frac{M}{k_{eq}}}$$

$$= 2\pi\sqrt{\frac{M}{k/2}}$$

$$= 2\sqrt{2}\,\pi\sqrt{\frac{M}{k}}$$

6. (*c*) Let the spring constant of original spring and length be k and l_0, respectively.

Initially, time period of spring-block system, $\quad T_0 = 2\pi\sqrt{\frac{m}{k}} \quad \text{... (i)}$

Length of smaller part of spring,

$$l_1 = \frac{3}{3 + 5}l_0 = \frac{3}{8}l_0$$

Length of longer part of spring,

$$l_2 = \frac{5}{3+5} l_0 = \frac{5}{8} l_0$$

If the spring constant of smaller part of spring is k_1, then we know that for a part of spring

$$k \times l = \text{constant}$$

or $k_1 l_1 = k \times l_0$

or $k_1 \times \frac{3l_0}{8} = k \times l_0$

or $k_1 = \frac{8}{3} k$ ... (ii)

As time period, $T = 2\pi\sqrt{\frac{m}{k_1}}$

$$= 2\pi\sqrt{\frac{m}{\frac{8}{3}k}} \quad [\because \text{using Eq. (ii)}]$$

$$= \sqrt{\frac{3}{8}}\, 2\pi\sqrt{\frac{m}{k}}$$

$$= \sqrt{\frac{3}{8}}\, T_0 \quad [\text{from Eq. (i)}]$$

7. (*c*) Consider that the block starts its motion from negative extreme position.

As we know, displacement

$$x = A\sin(\omega t + \theta) \quad \text{... (i)}$$

At $t = 0, x = -A$

$\therefore$ $-A = A\sin(\omega \times 0 + \theta)$

or $\sin\theta = -1$

or $\sin\theta = \sin\frac{3\pi}{2}$

or $\theta = \frac{3\pi}{2}$

Given that, $A = 8$ cm, $T = 2$s

$$\omega = \frac{2\pi}{T} = \frac{2\pi}{2} = \pi \text{ rad/s}$$

Putting the values of A, ω, θ in Eq. (i), we get

$$x = 8\sin\left(\pi t + \frac{3\pi}{2}\right) \text{cm}$$

or $x = -8\cos\pi t$ cm ... (ii)

3 cm

At $t=0$ Negative extremity | At t | $x=0$ Mean position | Positive extremity

At time t, position of block

$$= -8 + 3 = -5 \text{ cm}$$

From Eq. (ii), we get $-5 = -8\cos\pi t$

or $\cos\pi t = \frac{5}{8} = 0.9$

$\therefore$ $t = \frac{0.9}{\pi} = \frac{0.9}{3.14}$

$$= 0.286 \text{ s}$$

8. (*a*)

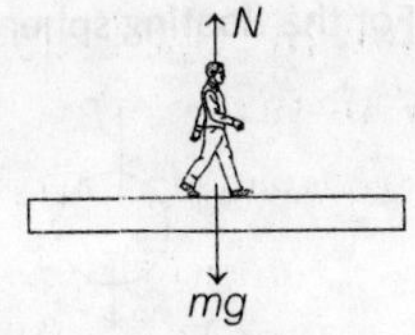

As platform moves from top extreme position.

From given FBD, we have

$$mg - N = ma \text{ or } N = m(g - a)$$

In this case, N decreases as a increases. At the extreme position, acceleration is maximum ($= \omega^2 A$). So N is minimum when the block is about to leave but still in contact with platform, then N becomes zero.

$\therefore$ $0 = m(g - \omega^2 A)$

or $g - \omega^2 A = 0$

or $\omega^2 = \frac{g}{A}$

or $\omega = \sqrt{\frac{g}{A}}$

$$= \sqrt{\frac{9.8}{5}}$$

$$= 1.4 \text{ rad/s}$$

9. (*a*) According to question,

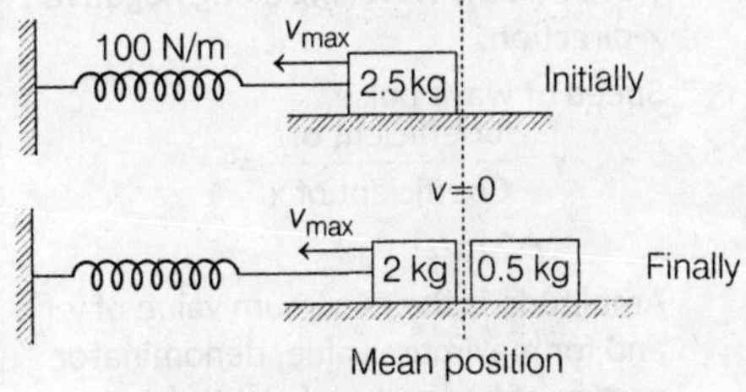

When block passes through mean position, then external force acting on the block is zero. So, using the principle of conservation of momentum

$$\mathbf{p}_i = \mathbf{p}_f$$

$$mv_{max} = m'v'_{max}$$

where, v'_{max} is new maximum velocity of the block of mass 2 kg.

or $v'_{max} = \frac{mv_{max}}{m'}$ or $v'_{max} = \frac{m}{m'} A\sqrt{\frac{k}{m}}$

Here, $m = 2.5$ kg, $m' = 2$ kg

$k = 100$ N/m, $A = 1$ m

$\therefore$ $v'_{max} = \frac{2.5}{2} \times 1 \times \sqrt{\frac{100}{2.5}}$

$$= 7.9 \text{ m/s}$$

10. (*a*) As given, $x(t) = 20\sin\frac{\pi}{3}(15t + 0.5)$ cm

$\Rightarrow$ $x(t) = 20\sin\left(5\pi t + \frac{\pi}{6}\right)$ cm

$\therefore$ Amplitude, $A_x = 20$ cm

Time period, $T_x = \frac{2\pi}{\omega_x} = \frac{2\pi}{5\pi} = \frac{2}{5}$ s

Also, $y(t) = 8[\sin 10\pi t + 0.75\cos 10\pi t]$ cm

$= 8\sin 10\pi t + 6\cos 10\pi t$

$$= \frac{\sqrt{8^2+6^2}}{\sqrt{8^2+6^2}}[8\sin 10\pi t + 6\cos 10\pi t]$$

$$= 10\left[\sin 10\pi t \times \frac{8}{10} + \cos 10\pi t \times \frac{6}{10}\right]$$

$$= 10\left[\sin 10\pi t \times \frac{4}{5} + \cos 10\pi t \times \frac{3}{5}\right]$$

$$= 10[\sin 10\pi t \cos 37^\circ + \cos 10\pi t \sin 37^\circ]$$

$y(t) = 10\sin(10\pi t + 37^\circ)$ cm

$[\because \sin(A+B) = \sin A\cos B + \cos A\sin B]$

$\therefore$ Amplitude, $A_y = 10$ cm

Time period, $T_y = \frac{2\pi}{\omega_y} = \frac{2\pi}{10\pi} = \frac{1}{5}$ s

Ratio, $\frac{A_x}{A_y} = \frac{20}{10} = \frac{2}{1}$

and $\frac{T_x}{T_y} = \frac{2/5}{1/5} = \frac{2}{1}$

11. (*b*) Given, $U = 4 + (x-1)^2$ J

As force, $F = -\frac{dU}{dx}$

$$= -\frac{d}{dx}[4 + (x-1)^2]$$

$$= -(0 + 2(x-1))$$

$$= -2(x-1)$$

Acceleration, $a = \frac{F}{m} = \frac{-2(x-1)}{2}$

$(\because m = 2 \text{ kg})$

$$a = -(x-1)$$

On comparing with standard equation of SHM,

$$a = -\omega^2(x - x_0)$$

We get

$$\omega^2 = 1 \text{ or } \omega = 1 \text{ rad/s}$$

At $x = 1$ m,

Minimum potential energy,

$$U_{min} = 4 + (0)^2$$

$$= 4 \text{ J}$$

At mean position, potential energy is minimum and kinetic energy is maximum and sum of both energies is equals to total mechanical energy. So, we may write

$$TE = U_{min} + KE_{max}$$

$$KE_{max} = TE - U_{min}$$

$$= 20 - 4$$

$$= 16 \text{ J}$$

Maximum kinetic energy of a particle in SHM is given as

$$KE_{max} = -\frac{1}{2}m\omega^2A^2$$

Putting the values of KE_{max}, m and ω^2 in the above expression, we get

$$16 = \frac{1}{2} \times 2 \times 1^2 \times A^2$$

$$A^2 = 16$$

or $A = 4$ m

12. (b) A.

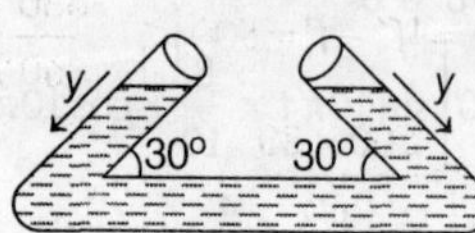

The restoring force, $F = -pA$

$$= -[\rho g(2y\sin 30°)]A$$

$$F = \rho gA(-y)$$

$\therefore$ $a = \frac{F}{m} = \frac{\rho gA}{m}(-y)$

Thus, $T = 2\pi\sqrt{\frac{m}{\rho gA}}$

B.

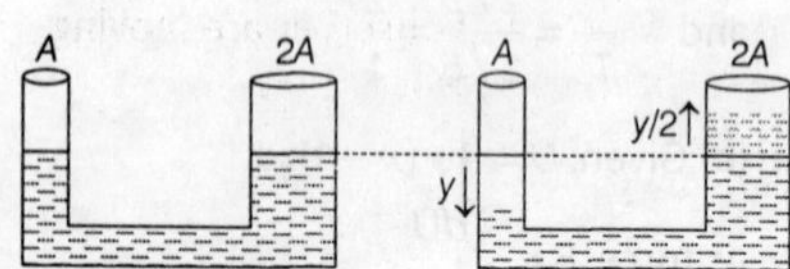

Suppose the liquid in left side limb is displaced slightly by y, the liquid in right limb will increase by $\frac{y}{2}$. The restoring force,

$$F = -pA = -\rho g\left(\frac{3y}{2}\right) \times 2A$$

$$F = 3\rho gA(-y)$$

or $a = \frac{F}{m} = 3\rho gA(-y)/m$

On comparing with, $a = -\omega^2 y$, we get

$$\omega = \sqrt{\frac{3\rho gA}{m}}$$

or $T = 2\pi\sqrt{\frac{m}{3\rho gA}}$

C.

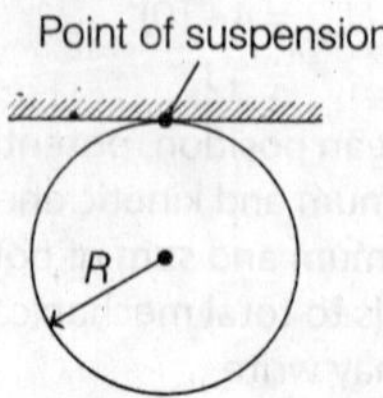

Point of suspension, $T = 2\pi\sqrt{\frac{I_{suspension}}{mgd}}$

$$= 2\pi\sqrt{\frac{mR^2 + mR^2}{mgR}} = 2\pi\sqrt{\frac{2R}{g}}$$

D. For the floating sphere,

$$mg = B \Rightarrow mg = \left(\frac{V}{2}\right)\rho g$$

$$\Rightarrow mg = \left(\frac{2}{3}\pi R^3\right)\rho g$$

$$\therefore m = \frac{2\pi R^3 \rho}{3}$$

The time period of oscillation is given by

$$T = 2\pi\sqrt{\frac{m}{A\rho g}}$$

$$= 2\pi\sqrt{\frac{2\pi R^3\rho/3}{(\pi R^2)\rho g}} \quad [\because A = \pi R^2]$$

$$= 2\pi\sqrt{\frac{2R}{3g}}$$

Thus, the correct match code is A → Q, B → P, C → S, D → R

13. (c) The given equation is similar to the standard function of wave $y = f(ax + bt)$ travelling in negative x-direction. Thus, wave pulse is travelling along negative x-direction.

Speed of wave pulse,

$$v = \frac{\text{Coefficient of } t}{\text{Coefficient of } x} = \frac{2}{1}$$

$$= 2 \text{ m/s}$$

Amplitude is the maximum value of y and for maximum value, denominator part must be least, so $(x + 2t)^2$ has to be zero.

$$A = \frac{20}{3 + 0^2} = \frac{20}{3} \text{ m}$$

14. (a) As, maximum velocity of particle,

$$v_{max} = a\omega$$

$\Rightarrow$ $\omega = \frac{v_{max}}{a}$

or $A = \frac{40 \text{ cm/s}}{10 \text{ cm}} = 4 \text{ s}^{-1}$

Similarly, wave velocity, $v = \frac{\omega}{k}$

or $k = \frac{\omega}{v}$

$\Rightarrow$ $B = \frac{A}{v} = \frac{4}{2}$

$$= 2 \text{ m/s}$$

15. (b) Equation for a travelling wave is given as

$$y = 4\cos 2\pi(5t - 0.0040x + 0.25)$$

$$= 4\cos(10\pi t - 0.008\pi x + 0.5\pi)$$

where, propagation constant,

$$k = 0.008\pi \text{ cm}^{-1}$$

Amplitude, $a = 4$ cm

Angular frequency, $\omega = 20\pi$ rad/s

Phase difference is given by the relation,

$$\Delta\phi = k\Delta x$$

For $\Delta x = 2$ m or 200 cm,

$$\Delta\phi = 0.008\pi \times 200$$

$$= 1.6\pi \text{ rad}$$

16. (b) Given that,

$$y = 0.04\sin\left(\frac{\pi}{3}x\right)\cos(60\pi t)$$

So, wavelength, $\lambda = \frac{2\pi}{k} = \frac{2\pi}{\pi/3} = 6$ m

Frequency, $f = \frac{\omega}{2\pi} = \frac{60\pi}{2\pi} = 30$ Hz

Speed, $v = f\lambda$

$$= (30)(6)$$

$$= 180 \text{ m/s}$$

The speed of a wave in a string is given by

$$v = \sqrt{\frac{T}{\mu}}$$

or $T = v^2 \times \mu$

or $T = \frac{v^2 m}{l} \quad \left(\because \mu = \frac{m}{l}\right)$

$$= \frac{(180)^2 \times 2 \times 10^{-2}}{2}$$

$$T = 324 \text{ N}$$

17. (d) When the rod is clamped at its middle, a node (N) is formed at its centre and anti-nodes (A) are formed at its two ends as shown in the following figure.

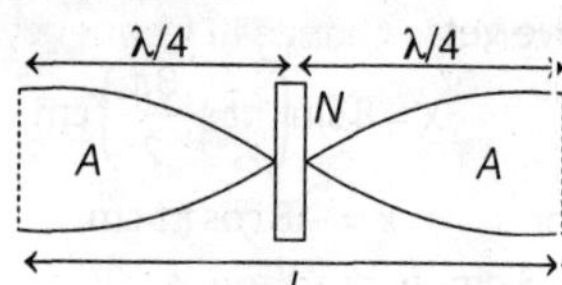

The distance between two successive antinodes is $\frac{\lambda}{4} + \frac{\lambda}{4} = \frac{\lambda}{2}$

$\therefore$ $l = \frac{\lambda}{2}$

or $\lambda = 2l = 2 \times 2 = 4$ m

The speed of sound in steel is given by the relation,

$$v = f\lambda = 2000 \times 4$$

$$= 8000 \text{ m/s}$$

or $= 8$ km/s

18. (*d*) Given, length of the pipe, $l = 20$ cm or 0.2 m

Source frequency = nth normal mode of frequency, $f_n = 1650$ Hz

Speed of sound, $v = 330$ m/s

In pipe is open at both ends, the nth mode of vibration frequency is given by the relation

$$f_n = \frac{nv}{2l}$$

or $$n = \frac{2f_n l}{v}$$

$$= \frac{2 \times 1650 \times 0.2}{330}$$

$\therefore$ $$f_n = 2$$

19. (*a*) As, frequency of sound wave is given as

$$n = \frac{v}{\lambda}$$

where, v is speed of sound.

Beat, $$n = n_1 - n_2$$

$$n = \frac{v}{\lambda_1} - \frac{v}{\lambda_2}$$

$$n = v\left(\frac{1}{\lambda_1} - \frac{1}{\lambda_2}\right)$$

or $$v = \frac{n\lambda_1\lambda_2}{\lambda_2 - \lambda_1}$$

Here, $n = 9$ beats/s, $\lambda_1 = 4$ m and $\lambda_2 = 4.5$ m

$\Rightarrow$ $$v = \frac{9 \times 4 \times 4.5}{4.5 - 4} = 324 \text{ m/s}$$

20. (*a*) Given that, frequency, $f = 300$ Hz

Change in frequency, $\Delta f = 3$ beats/s

Fractional change in frequency,

$$\frac{\Delta f}{f} = \frac{3}{300}$$

Percentage change in frequency,

$$\frac{\Delta f}{f} \times 100 = \frac{3}{300} \times 100$$

$$= 1\%$$

As we know that frequency of oscillation in air columns

$$f \propto \frac{1}{\text{Length of air column}}$$

$\Rightarrow$ $l \propto \frac{1}{f}$ or f^{-1}

If the change in frequency is very small, then we can write

$$\frac{\Delta l}{l} \times 100 = \frac{\Delta f}{f} \times 100$$

$$\frac{\Delta l}{l} \times 100 = 1\%$$

21. (*d*) A standing wave is as shown below.

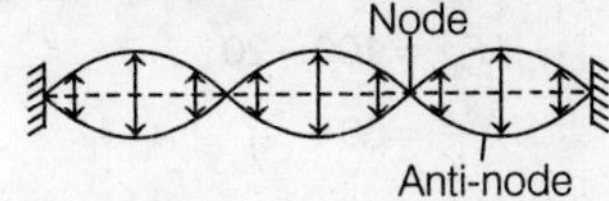

As all particles vibrate together, they cross mean position simultaneously. In stationary wave, a node is place of zero amplitude and an anti-node is a place of maximum amplitude and velocity is directly proportional to amplitude, hence velocity is maximum the position of anti-node and zero at node.

22. (*b*) Let L_0 be the length of the pipe at T_0, then its length at temperature T is

$$L = L_0[1 + \alpha(T - T_0)]$$

where, α is coefficient of linear expansion.

The speed of sound at temperature T is given as

$$v = \sqrt{\frac{\gamma RT}{m}}$$

We have to find the temperature T_0 at which $f(T_0) = f(T)$

For small temperature difference,

$$T = T_0$$

$$\frac{v'}{2L} = \frac{v}{2L_0}$$

$$\frac{\sqrt{\frac{\gamma RT}{m}}}{2L_0[1 + \alpha(T - T_0)]} = \frac{\sqrt{\frac{\gamma RT_0}{m}}}{2L_0}$$

or $$\sqrt{\frac{T}{T_0}} = 1 + \alpha(T - T_0)$$

or $$\left[1 + \left(\frac{T - T_0}{T_0}\right)\right]^{1/2} = 1 + \alpha(T - T_0)$$

For small $(T - T_0)$, by using binomial approximation, we can write

$$1 + \frac{1}{2}\left(\frac{T - T_0}{T_0}\right) = 1 + \alpha(T - T_0)$$

$$[\because (1 + x)^n = 1 + nx]$$

$$\frac{1}{2}\left(\frac{T - T_0}{T_0}\right) = \alpha(T - T_0)$$

$$(T - T_0) = 2\alpha T_0(T - T_0)$$

or $$1 = 2\alpha T_0$$

or $$T_0 = \frac{1}{2\alpha}$$

Given, $\alpha = 4 \times 10^{-3}$ per °C

$\therefore$ $$T_0 = \frac{1}{2 \times 4 \times 10^{-3}}$$

$$= 125°\text{C}$$

23. (*b*) Source moving away, $f' = f\left(\frac{v}{v + v_s}\right)$

$$= 500\left(\frac{330}{330 + 30}\right)$$

$$= \frac{500 \times 330}{360}$$

$$\Delta f = |f' - f| = 500\left(1 - \frac{330}{360}\right)$$

$$= \frac{500 \times 30}{360}$$

$$\approx 42 \text{ Hz}$$

When both source and observer are moving towards each other, then

$$\Delta f = f - f' = \left|1 - \left(\frac{v + v_0}{v - v_s}\right)\right| f$$

$$= \left|\frac{-2v_s}{v - v_s}\right| \cdot f \quad (\text{As } v_0 = v_s)$$

$$= \frac{2 \times 30}{300} \times 500 = 100 \text{ Hz}$$

When source and observer are moving away from each other, then

$$\Delta f = \left(\frac{2v_s}{v + v_s}\right) \cdot f$$

$$= \frac{2 \times 30}{360} \times 500$$

$$= 83 \text{ Hz}$$

24. (*d*) Given, speed of source, $v_s = 0$ m/s

Speed of observer, $v_0 = 25$ m/s

Let the original frequency of sound be f.

Case I When observer is approaching source of sound, the apparent frequency is given as

$$f_a = \left(\frac{v + v_0}{v}\right) f$$

or $$f_a = \left(1 + \frac{v_0}{v}\right) f$$

or $$\frac{v_0}{v} = \frac{f_a}{f} - 1 \quad \text{... (i)}$$

Case II When the observer is receding the source, the apparent frequency is given as

$$f_a' = \left(\frac{v - v_0}{v}\right) f$$

or $$\frac{f_a'}{f} = 1 - \frac{v_0}{v}$$

or $$\frac{v_0}{v} = 1 - \frac{f_a'}{f} \quad \text{... (ii)}$$

From Eqs. (i) and (ii), we get

$$\frac{f_a}{f} - 1 = 1 - \frac{f_a'}{f}$$

or $f = \dfrac{f_a + f_a'}{2}$

Here, $f_a = 540$ Hz

and $f_a' = 420$ Hz

$\therefore f = \dfrac{540 + 420}{2}$

$= 480$ Hz

25. (*a*) According to the question, the situation is as shown in the figure below

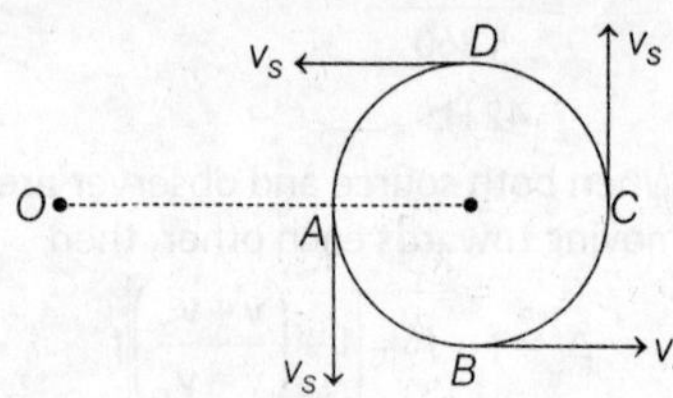

Apparent frequency will be minimum when the source is at *B* and moving away from the observer, i.e.

$$f_{\min} = \left(\frac{v}{v + v_s}\right) f \quad \text{... (i)}$$

Here, $v = 330$ m/s, $v_s = 20$ m/s and $f = 400$ Hz

$$\therefore \quad f_{\min} = \frac{330}{330 + 20} \times 400$$

$= 377.14$ Hz

Frequency will be maximum when source is at point *D* and approaching the observer, i.e.

$$f_{\max} = \frac{v}{v - v_s} \times f \quad \text{... (ii)}$$

$$= \frac{330}{330 - 20} \times 400$$

$= 425.8$ Hz

Further when source is at *A* and *C* points, angle between the velocity of source and line joining the source and observer is 90°, i.e.

$$v_s \cos\theta = v_s \cos 90° = 0$$

So, there will be no change in the apparent frequency.

From Eqs. (i) and (ii), we see that $f_{\min}$ and $f_{\max}$ does not depend on the radius. It means on changing the value of radius, $f_{\min}$ and $f_{\max}$ will not change.

Qualifier 11 (Electrostatics)

1. (*b*) Let the magnitude of electrostatic force be F_0 in air.

The net electrostatic force between the both charges in medium is equal to $\dfrac{F_0}{K}$, where *K* is dielectric constant.

Given, $F_0 = 100$ N

$F_{\text{net}} = F_0 -$ decrease in force

$F_{\text{net}} = 100 - 20$

$\dfrac{F_0}{K} = 80$

or $\dfrac{100}{K} = 80$

or $K = \dfrac{100}{80} = \dfrac{5}{4} = 1.25$

2. (*d*) Electric field due to a dipole along the axis of electric dipole is

$$\mathbf{E} = \frac{1}{4\pi\varepsilon_0}\frac{2\mathbf{p}}{r^3} \quad \text{... (i)}$$

Along the perpendicular bisector at a distance 2*r*, electric field due to electric dipole is given as

$$\mathbf{E}' = \frac{1}{4\pi\varepsilon_0} \cdot \frac{\mathbf{p}}{(2r)^3} \quad \text{... (ii)}$$

Dividing Eq. (ii) by Eq. (i), we get

$$\frac{\mathbf{E}'}{\mathbf{E}} = \frac{1}{16}$$

$$\Rightarrow \quad \mathbf{E}' = \frac{\mathbf{E}}{16}$$

3. (*d*) **Gauss' law** The net electric flux (due to the charges enclosed by the surface as well as the charges outside it) through any imaginary closed surface (called gaussian surface) of any arbitrary shape is equal to the total charge enclosed by the surface divided by ε_0.

$$\phi = \frac{\Sigma q_{\text{enclosed}}}{\varepsilon_0} \quad \text{... (i)}$$

$\therefore$ The above law is true for any closed surface irrespective of its shape.

The derivation of this law can be obtained from Coulomb's law and we know that, Coulomb's law follows inverse square law. Thus, Gauss' law is also based on the inverse square dependence on distance contained in the Coulomb's law. Any violation of Gauss' law will indicate departure from the inverse square law.

4. (*c*) Electric field at shaded surface ($x = 2a$),

$$\mathbf{E} = \frac{E_0(2a)}{a}\hat{\mathbf{i}} \qquad \left[\because \mathbf{E} = \frac{E_0 x}{a}\hat{\mathbf{i}}\right]$$

$$\mathbf{E} = 2E_0\hat{\mathbf{i}}$$

Area of surface, $\mathbf{A} = (2a)^2\hat{\mathbf{i}}$

$$\mathbf{A} = 4a^2\hat{\mathbf{i}}$$

Electric flux, $\phi = \mathbf{E} \cdot \mathbf{A}$

$= (2E_0\hat{\mathbf{i}}) \cdot (4a^2\hat{\mathbf{i}})$

$= 8E_0 a^2$

5. (*c*) The torque on an electric dipole **p** in uniform electric field **E** is given as

$$\boldsymbol{\tau} = \mathbf{p} \times \mathbf{E}$$

or $\tau = pE\sin\theta$, where θ is angle between **p** and **E**

For case (I), $\theta = 90°$, $\tau_I = pE\sin 90° = pE$

For case (II), $\theta = 0°$, $\tau_{II} = pE\sin 0° = 0$

For case (III), $0 < \theta < 90°$, $\tau_{III} = pE\sin\theta < pE$

For case (IV), $\theta = 180°$, $\tau_{IV} = pE\sin 180° = 0$ (as, $\sin 180° = 0$)

6. (*c*) The electric field due to a uniformly charged insulating sphere at distance *r* from its centre is

$$E = \frac{\rho}{3\varepsilon_0} r$$

(where, ρ is volume charge density)

$\Rightarrow \quad E \propto r$

$\therefore$ The graph between *E* and *r* is straight line, whose slope is equal to $\dfrac{\rho}{3\varepsilon_0}$

From figure, slope

$$= \frac{\Delta y}{\Delta x} = \frac{(6-3)\times 10^4}{(8-4)\times 10^{-3}}$$

$$\text{Slope} = \frac{3\times 10^4}{4\times 10^{-3}}$$

$$\Rightarrow \quad \frac{\rho}{3\varepsilon_0} = \frac{3}{4}\times 10^7$$

$$\frac{\rho}{3\times 8.85\times 10^{-12}} = \frac{3}{4}\times 10^7$$

or $\rho = \dfrac{3}{4}\times 3\times 8.85\times 10^{-5}$

$\rho = 19.91\times 10^{-5}$

$\simeq 2\times 10^{-4}$ C/m³

7. (*d*) The potential energy of a dipole system is the sum of internal and external potential energy.

$$\Rightarrow U_{\text{system}} = U_{\text{internal}} + U_{\text{external}}$$

$$= \frac{K(q)(-q)}{l} + (-\mathbf{p}\cdot\mathbf{E})$$

$$= \frac{-Kq^2}{l} - pE\cos\theta$$

8. (*c*) Work, $W =$ Change in kinetic energy + Change in potential energy

or $W = \Delta\text{KE} + \Delta U$

Since, it is rotating very slowly $\Delta\text{KE} = 0$

$W = 0 + \Delta U$

$= U_f - U_i$

$= -pE\cos\theta_f - (-pE\cos\theta_i)$

$= -pE\cos\theta_f + pE\cos\theta_i$

$= pE(\cos\theta_i - \cos\theta_f)$

$= pE(\cos 0° - \cos 180°)$

$= pE(1 - (-1)) = 2pE$

9. (*d*) The electric field due to an infinite long conducting charged sheet, which have charge on one side is $E = \frac{\sigma}{2\varepsilon_0}$

(where, σ is surface charge density)

The direction of field due to charged sheets in given question can be shown as

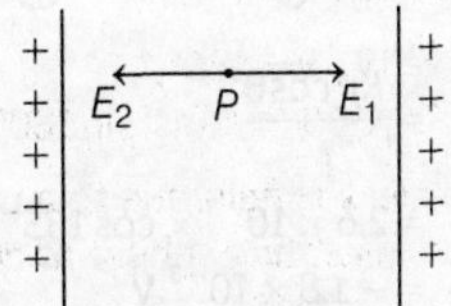

$$E_1 = E_2 = \frac{\sigma}{2\varepsilon_0}$$

Electric field at point P, $E_P = E_1 - E_2$

$$= \frac{\sigma}{2\varepsilon_0} - \frac{\sigma}{2\varepsilon_0}$$

$$E_P = 0$$

Hence, electric field at point *P* does not depend on the position of point *P* and charge density σ.

10. (*c*) FBD for pendulum bob is as follows

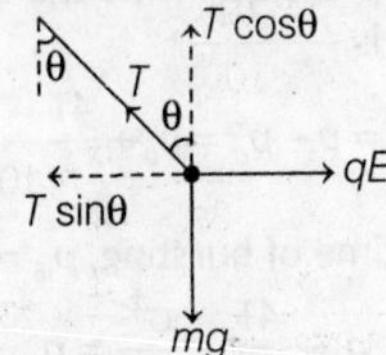

In equilibrium,

$$T\sin\theta = qE \quad \text{... (i)}$$

and $$T\cos\theta = mg \quad \text{... (ii)}$$

From Eqs. (i) and (ii), we get

$$\tan\theta = \frac{qE}{mg} \text{ or } E = \frac{mg}{q}\tan\theta$$

As *m*, *g*, and *q* are constants.

$$\therefore \quad E \propto \tan\theta$$

11. (*c*) Volume of *n*-drops = Volume of single bigger drop

$$n \times \frac{4}{3}\pi r^3 = \frac{4}{3}\pi R^3$$

$$\Rightarrow \quad R = (n)^{\frac{1}{3}} r$$

As, we know that, potential at surface of spherical charged drop is given as

$$V = \frac{1}{4\pi\varepsilon_0} \cdot \frac{\text{Charge}}{\text{Radius}}$$

or $$V \propto \frac{\text{Charge}}{\text{Radius}}$$

or $$\frac{V_2}{V_1} = \frac{Q_2}{Q_1} \cdot \frac{R_1}{R_2}$$

Given that, $V_1 = 1$ V,

and $V_2 = 100$ V

$$\frac{100}{1} = \frac{nQ}{Q} \cdot \frac{r}{(n)^{\frac{1}{3}} r}$$

or $$100 = (n)^{\frac{2}{3}}$$

or $$n = 1000$$

12. (*b*) Let the minimum potential point *P* be at *x* distance away from 9 μC.

$$\underset{9\,\mu C}{\bullet} \xleftarrow{x} \underset{P}{} \xrightarrow{(1-x)} \underset{16\,\mu C}{\bullet}$$

The potential due to a point charge *q* at a distance *r* is given as

$$V = \frac{Kq}{r}$$

So, potential at point *P* of given system of charge can be written as,

$$V_P = \frac{K \times 9 \times 10^{-6}}{x} + \frac{K \times 16 \times 10^{-6}}{1-x}$$

$$= K \times 10^{-6}\left(\frac{9}{x} + \frac{16}{1-x}\right)$$

To find the distance from the charges where, *V* is minimum $\frac{dV_P}{dx} = 0$

$$\frac{dV_P}{dx} = K \times 10^{-6}\left(-\frac{9}{x^2} + \frac{16}{(1-x)^2}\right) = 0$$

or $$-\frac{9}{x^2} + \frac{16}{(1-x)^2} = 0$$

$$\Rightarrow \quad \left(\frac{3}{x}\right)^2 = \left(\frac{4}{1-x}\right)^2$$

$$\Rightarrow \quad \frac{3}{x} = \frac{4}{1-x}$$

$$\Rightarrow \quad 3 - 3x = 4x$$

or $$x = \frac{3}{7}\text{ m}$$

13. (*d*) Let the charges on inner shell and outer shell be Q_1 and Q_2, respectively.

According to the question,

Potential of inner sphere,

$$\frac{KQ_1}{R_1} + \frac{KQ_2}{R_2} = 30 \quad \text{... (i)}$$

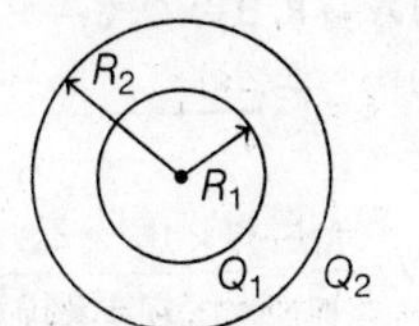

and potential of outer sphere,

$$\frac{KQ_1}{R_2} + \frac{KQ_2}{R_2} = 20 \quad \text{... (ii)}$$

Subtracting Eq. (i) from Eq. (ii), we get

$$\frac{KQ_1}{R_2} - \frac{KQ_1}{R_1} = -10 \quad \text{... (iii)}$$

When outer shell is grounded.

Let Q_3 be the charge on outer sphere,

$$V_{\text{outer}} = \frac{KQ_1}{R_2} + \frac{KQ_3}{R_2} = 0$$

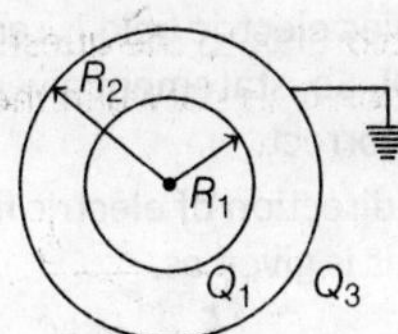

or $$Q_3 = -Q_1 \quad \text{...(iv)}$$

Now, $$V_{\text{inner}} = \frac{KQ_1}{R_1} + \frac{KQ_3}{R_2}$$

$$= \frac{KQ_1}{R_1} - \frac{KQ_1}{R_2} \quad \text{[using Eq. (iv)]}$$

$$= +10\text{ V} \quad \text{[From Eq. (iii)]}$$

14. (*b*) Given, force *F* = 480 dyne

$$= 480 \times 10^{-5}\text{ N}$$

Charge, $q = 8\,\mu C = 8 \times 10^{-6}$ C

distance, $d = 3.2$ cm $= 3.2 \times 10^{-2}$ m

As we know,

$$\text{Electric field, } E = \frac{\text{Force}}{\text{Charge}}$$

$$= \frac{480 \times 10^{-5}}{8 \times 10^{-6}}$$

$$= 600\text{ N/C}$$

Potential difference between two points (say *A* and *B*) along the electric field is given by

$$V_A - V_B = Ed$$

$$= 600 \times 3.2 \times 10^{-2}$$

$$= 19.2\text{ V}$$

$$\approx 18.6\text{ V}$$

15. (*b*) A is true but R is false, we cannot use $F = QE = Q \cdot \frac{\sigma}{\varepsilon_0}$

or $$F = Q \cdot \frac{Q}{\varepsilon_0 A} = \frac{Q^2}{\varepsilon_0 A}$$

The electric field at any plate due to other plate is

$$\frac{1}{2}E = \frac{1}{2}\frac{\sigma}{\varepsilon_0}$$

16. (*d*) Given, potential,

$$V = 3x^2 + (y^3 - 1)$$

When $V = 0$

$$\Rightarrow \quad 3x^2 + (y^3 - 1) = 0$$

or $$3x^2 + y^3 = 1 \quad \text{... (i)}$$

There can be many combination of *x* and *y*, which can satisfy the above equation, so statement given in option (a) is incorrect.

As, $\mathbf{E} = -\frac{\partial V}{\partial x}\hat{\mathbf{i}} - \frac{\partial V}{\partial y}\hat{\mathbf{j}}$

$\Rightarrow \quad = -6x\hat{\mathbf{i}} - 3y^2\hat{\mathbf{j}}$ [using Eq. (i)]

From above, **E** is zero at (0, 0) and this implies electric field is zero at point (0, 0). So, statement given in option (b) is incorrect.

The direction of electric field from X-axis is given as,

$$\tan\alpha = \frac{E_y}{E_x} = \frac{-3y^2}{-6x} = \frac{y^2}{2x}$$

Now, If we change values of x and y, then value of $\tan\alpha$ will also be changed and the direction of electric field also changes. Thus, the direction of electric field is not same in space, so statement given in option (c) is incorrect.

α depends on value of x and y, so direction changes

At $(1\text{ m}, \sqrt{2}\text{ m})$, electric field,

$$\mathbf{E} = -6 \times 1\hat{\mathbf{i}} - 3 \times (\sqrt{2})^2\hat{\mathbf{j}}$$

$$= -6\hat{\mathbf{i}} - 6\hat{\mathbf{j}} \text{ V/m}$$

or $|\mathbf{E}| = E = 6\sqrt{2}$ V/m

Electric force on charge q,

$$F = qE = 2\sqrt{2} \times 10^{-6} \times 6\sqrt{2}$$

$$= 24 \times 10^{-6} \text{ N}$$

Therefore, statement given in option (d) is correct.

17. (*d*) From the graph, it is clear that, potential difference across capacitor C_2 is maximum and that for C_1 is minimum.

i.e. $\quad V_2 > V_3 > V_1 \quad$ ...(i)

As we know that, in series, charge on each capacitor remain same.

$$Q = CV = \text{constant}$$

or $\quad C \propto \frac{1}{V}$

$\therefore \quad C_1 > C_3 > C_2 \quad$ [using Eq. (i)]

18. (*c*) Given, charge

$q = 50\mu\text{C} = 50 \times 10^{-6}$ C

Dielectric constant, $K = 5$

As we know that, induced charge on surface of dielectric slab is given by

$$q_{\text{induced}} = -q\left(1 - \frac{1}{K}\right)$$

or $\quad q_A = -50 \times 10^{-6} \times \left(1 - \frac{1}{5}\right)$

$$= -40 \times 10^{-6} \text{ C}$$

$$= -40\mu\text{C}$$

19. (*d*) Initial charge on left plate, $Q = 2\mu$C

Final charge on left plate, i.e. after switch is ON,

$$Q' = CV = 10^{-6} \times 10 \text{ C}$$

$$= 10\mu\text{C}$$

Charge flown by the battery,

$$\Delta Q = Q' - Q$$

$$= 10 - 2 = 8\mu\text{C}$$

Work done by battery,

$$W_{\text{battery}} = (\Delta Q)V$$

$$= (8 \times 10^{-6}) \times 10$$

$$= 80 \times 10^{-6}$$

$$= 80\mu\text{J}$$

20. (*a*) Let the surface charge density on plate be $+\sigma$ and $-\sigma$.

Force on right side plate,

$F = q \times$ Electric field of left plate

$$= (\sigma \times A) \times \left(\frac{\sigma}{2\varepsilon_0}\right)$$

$$F = \frac{\sigma^2 A}{2\varepsilon_0}$$

Tension in string, $T = mg$

FBD of right side plate,

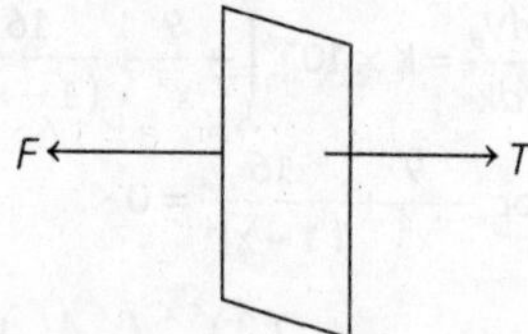

At stationary position, $F = T$

or $\quad \frac{\sigma^2 A}{2\varepsilon_0} = Mg$

or $\quad \sigma = \sqrt{\frac{2Mg\varepsilon_0}{A}}$

As we know that, electric field between the plates, $E = \frac{\sigma}{\varepsilon_0}$

or $\quad E = \frac{\sqrt{\frac{2Mg\varepsilon_0}{A}}}{\varepsilon_0} = \sqrt{\frac{2Mg}{A\varepsilon_0}}$

21. (*a*) A → R, B → Q, C → P

(A)

$$V = \frac{Kp}{r^3} = \frac{9 \times 10^9 \times 4.8 \times 10^{-30}}{(4.1 \times 10^{-9})^2}$$

$$= 2.6 \times 10^{-3} \text{ V}$$

(B)

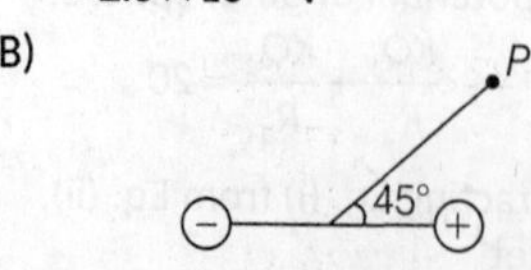

$$V' = \frac{Kp\cos\theta}{r^3} = v\cos\theta$$

$$= 2.6 \times 10^{-3} \times \cos 45°$$

$$= 1.8 \times 10^{-3} \text{ V}$$

(C)

$$V'' = \frac{Kp\cos\theta}{r^2}$$

$$= 2.6 \times 10^{-3} \times \cos 135°$$

$$= -1.8 \times 10^{-3} \text{ V}$$

22. (*a*) Force $= p\left(\frac{dE}{dx}\right)\cos\theta$

$$= p \cdot \frac{d}{dx}\frac{KQ}{x^2} \cdot \cos 0° = \frac{2KQp}{x^3}$$

23. (*a*) Pressure inside soap bubble is

$p = p_0 + \frac{4T}{r}$ (acting increased). Due to charging, electrostatic pressure is

$p_\sigma = \frac{\sigma^2}{2\varepsilon_0}$ (acting outward)

So, net pressure inside the charged bubble is

$$p_{\text{net}} = p - p_\sigma = p_0 + \frac{4T}{r} - \frac{\sigma^2}{2\varepsilon_0}$$

At the time of bursting, $p_{\text{in}} = p_{\text{out}}$,

$$p_0 + \frac{4T}{r} - \frac{\sigma^2}{2\varepsilon_0} = p_0$$

$\Rightarrow \quad \frac{4T}{r} = \frac{\sigma^2}{2\varepsilon_0} = \frac{(\varepsilon_0 V/r)^2}{2\varepsilon_0}$

$\Rightarrow \quad \frac{4T}{r} = \frac{\varepsilon_0 V^2}{2r^2}$

or $\quad V = \sqrt{\frac{8Tr}{\varepsilon_0}}$

24. (*c*)

A. When S is open, then

$$C_{\text{eq}} = \frac{C_1 C_2}{C_1 + C_2} = \frac{(2\mu\text{F})(3\mu\text{F})}{(2\mu\text{F} + 3\mu\text{F})} = \frac{6}{5}\mu\text{F}$$

Charge q on both the capacitors will be the same (as these are in series), i.e.

$$q = C_{\text{eq}} V = \left(\frac{6}{5}\mu\text{F}\right)(30 + 60) \text{ V} = 108\,\mu\text{C}$$

B. Charge on C_2, i.e. $q_2 = C_2 V_2 = (3\,\mu\text{F})(60 \text{ V}) = 180\,\mu\text{C}$

C. When S is closed, charge on C_1, i.e. $q_1 = C_1 V_1 = (2\mu\text{F})(30\text{V}) = 60\,\mu\text{C}$

D. Charge on C_1 and C_2 $= 60\,\mu\text{C} + 180\,\mu\text{C} = 240\,\mu\text{C}$

Hence, A → P, B → S, C → R and D → Q.

25. (*c*) Energy density in air gap, $u_0 = \frac{1}{2}\varepsilon_0 E_0^2$

Energy density in the dielectric

$$= \frac{1}{2}\varepsilon_0 K E^2$$

$$= \frac{1}{K}\cdot\frac{1}{2}\varepsilon_0 E_0^2 \quad \left(E = \frac{E_0}{K}\right)$$

$$= \frac{1}{K}\cdot u_0$$

So, energy stored = energy density × volume

So, ratio, $\frac{U_{\text{dielectric}}}{U_{\text{total}}}$

$$= \frac{\frac{1}{K}\cdot u_0 \cdot A \cdot t}{u_0 \cdot A(d-t) + \frac{1}{K}u_0 A t} = \frac{1}{2} \quad \text{(given)}$$

$$\Rightarrow \frac{t}{t + K(d-t)} = \frac{1}{2} \quad (\because K = 3)$$

$$\Rightarrow 2t = 3d - 2t$$

$$\Rightarrow 4t = 3d$$

or $$t = \frac{3}{4}d$$

Qualifier 12 (Current Electricity)

1. (*b*) Given that, relaxation time,

$$\tau = 16.2 \times 10^{-12} \text{s}$$

Electric charge, $e = 1.6 \times 10^{-19}$ C

Mass of electron, $m_e = 9.1 \times 10^{-31}$ kg

As we know that, mobility, $\mu = \frac{e\tau}{m}$

Substituting the given values, we get

$$\Rightarrow \mu = \frac{1.6 \times 10^{-19} \times 16.2 \times 10^{-12}}{9.1 \times 10^{-31}}$$

$$= 2.84 \text{ m}^2\text{V}^{-1}\text{s}^{-1}$$

2. (*a*) As given current,

$$I = (100 + 8t) \text{ A} \quad \text{... (i)}$$

$\therefore$ Net charge, $q = \int I dt$

$$q = \int_0^{10} (100 + 8t)\, dt \quad \text{[using Eq. (i)]}$$

$$= \int_0^{10} 100\, dt + \int_0^{10} 8t\, dt$$

$$= 100\int_0^{10} dt + 8\int_0^{10} t\, dt$$

$$= 100[t]_0^{10} + 8\left[\frac{t^2}{2}\right]_0^{10}$$

$$= 100[10 - 0] + 4[(10)^2 - 0^2]$$

$$= 1000 + 4 \times 100$$

$$\Rightarrow q = 1400$$

Average value of current, $I_{\text{avg}} = \frac{q}{t}$

Here, $t = 10$ s

$$= \frac{1400}{10}$$

$$I_{\text{avg}} = 140 \text{ A}$$

3. (*b*) In a conductor, free electrons move with drift velocity.

So, total momentum of free electrons,

p = (mass of free electron) × velocity

$$= Mv_d$$

$$= (Nm)v_d$$

(where, N is total number of free electrons)

$$= Nm \times \frac{i}{neA} \quad \left(\because v_d = \frac{i}{neA}\right)$$

$$= nVm \times \frac{i}{neA} \quad (\because N = nV)$$

$$= Vm\frac{i}{eA} \times \frac{l}{l} \quad (\because A \times l = V)$$

$$p = \frac{mil}{e}$$

4. (*a*) Given that, electron density,

$$n = 8 \times 10^{22} \text{ m}^{-3}$$

Collision time, $\tau = 4 \times 10^{-11}$ s

Mass of ion, $m = 2.56 \times 10^{-26}$ kg

Charge on electron, $e = 1.6 \times 10^{-19}$ C

As, resistivity, $\rho = \frac{ne^2\tau}{m}$

$$= \frac{8 \times 10^{22} \times (1.6 \times 10^{-19})^2 \times 4 \times 10^{-11}}{2.56 \times 10^{-26}}$$

$$\rho = 3.2 \ \Omega\text{-m}$$

5. (*d*) Let us calculate the value of resistance of carbon resistor optionwise.

According to the colour coding of carbon resistors, for

Option(a)

Brown,	Red,	Brown,	No colour
↓	↓	↓	↓
1	2	10^1	20%

$\therefore R = 12 \times 10^1 \pm 20\%$

or $120 \pm 20\%$ → 96 Ω to 144 Ω

Option (b)

Red,	Red,	Black,	No colour
↓	↓	↓	↓
2	2	10^0	20%

$\therefore R = 22 \times 10^0 \pm 20\%$ Ω

or $22 \pm 20\%$ → 17.6 Ω to 26.4 Ω

Option (c)

Red,	Black,	Red,	No colour
↓	↓	↓	↓
2	0	10^2	20%

$\therefore R = 20 \times 10^2 \pm 20\%$

or $2000 \pm 20\%$ → 1600 Ω to 2400 Ω

Option (d)

Red,	Red,	Red,	No colour
↓	↓	↓	↓
2	2	10^2	20%

$\therefore R = 22 \times 10^2 \pm 20\%$

or $2200 \pm 20\%$ → 1760 Ω to 2640 Ω

The given value of resistance 1760 Ω to 2640 Ω is correct for option (d).

6. (*c*) Let at temperature T_0, resistivities of the given two materials be ρ_1 and ρ_2 and at temperature T, resistivities are ρ_1' and ρ_2', respectively.

So, we have, for material-1,

$$\rho_1' = \rho_1[1 + \alpha_1(T - T_0)]$$

or $$\rho_1' - \rho_1 = \rho_1\alpha_1(T - T_0)$$

or $$\Delta\rho_1 = \rho_1\alpha_1(T - T_0) \quad \text{... (i)}$$

Similarly, for material-2,

$$\rho_2' = \rho_2[1 + \alpha_2(T - T_0)]$$

$$\rho_2' - \rho_2 = \rho_2\alpha_2(T - T_0)$$

or $$\Delta\rho_2 = \rho_2\alpha_2(T - T_0) \quad \text{... (ii)}$$

As it is given in the question that, resistivity of the new material does not change with temperature, it means Sum of change in resistivity should be zero.

$\therefore$ Adding Eqs. (i) and (ii), we get

$$\Delta\rho_1 + \Delta\rho_2 = \rho_1\alpha_1(T - T_0) + \rho_2\alpha_2(T - T_0)$$

$$0 = (\rho_1\alpha_1 + \rho_2\alpha_2)(T - T_0)$$

or $\rho_1\alpha_1 + \rho_2\alpha_2 = 0$ or $\alpha_1 = \frac{-\rho_2}{\rho_1}\alpha_2$

Here, materials are different, so $\rho_1 \neq \rho_2$. Thus, $|\alpha_1| \neq |\alpha_2|$, but they must be of opposite sign.

7. (*b*) In parallel connection, equivalent resistance of n equal resistor of resistance R each, is

$$R_{\text{eq}} = \frac{R}{n}$$

As, current, $I = \frac{E}{R_{\text{eq}} + r} = \frac{E}{\frac{R}{n} + r}$

(where, r is internal resistance of battery)

Here, $r = R$

$$\Rightarrow \quad I = \frac{E}{\frac{R}{n} + R} \Rightarrow I = \frac{nE}{(n+1)R} \quad \text{... (i)}$$

In series connection, equivalent resistance of n equal resistors is

$$R'_{eq} = nR$$

and total emf $= nE$

As, current, $I' = \dfrac{nE}{nR + r}$

$$= \frac{nE}{nR + R} \quad (\text{As, } r = R)$$

$$\frac{I}{6} = \frac{nE}{(n+1)R} \quad \text{... (ii)}$$

$$\left[\because \text{ given, } I' = \frac{I}{6}\right]$$

On comparing Eqs. (i) and (ii), we get

$$n = 6$$

8. (*a*) In absence of voltmeter (actual potential difference), the circuit is as shown below

200 Ω 100 Ω
V_1 V_2
12 V

$$V_1 = \frac{R_1}{R_1 + R_2} \times V$$

$$= \frac{200}{200 + 100} \times 12 = 8\text{ V}$$

In presence of voltmeter (measured potential difference), the circuit is as shown below

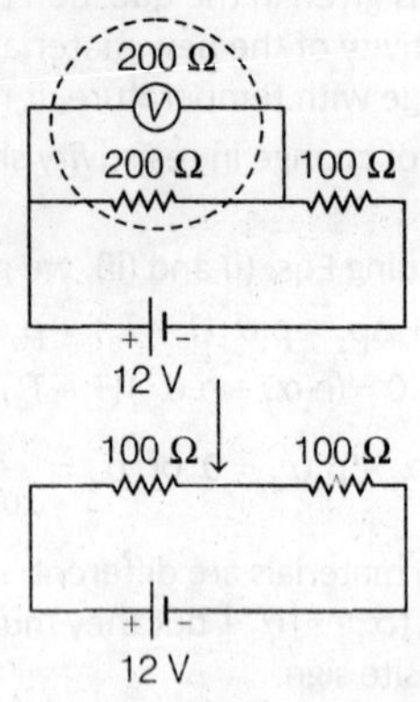

$$V_1' = \frac{100}{100 + 100} \times 12 = 6\text{ V}$$

$$\therefore \text{ Percentage change} = \frac{V_1 - V_1'}{V_1} \times 100$$

$$= \frac{8 - 6}{8} \times 100$$

$$= 25\%$$

9. (*d*) First we shall find the equivalent resistance R' of 10 Ω, 10 Ω, and 20 Ω resistor. Since, all are connected in parallel.

$$\Rightarrow \quad \frac{1}{R'} = \frac{1}{10} + \frac{1}{10} + \frac{1}{20}$$

$$\frac{1}{R'} = \frac{2 + 2 + 1}{20} = \frac{5}{20} = \frac{1}{4}$$

or $\quad R' = 4\ \Omega$

Now, the circuit, can be redrawn as

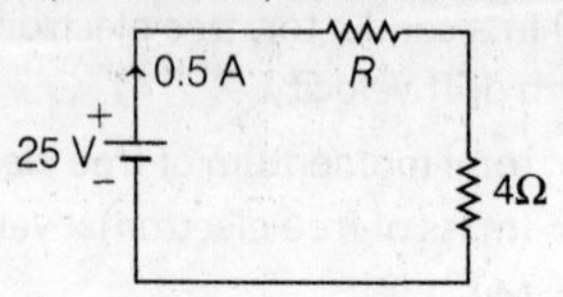

Using Ohm's law, $i = \dfrac{25}{R + 4}$

$$0.5 = \frac{25}{R + 4}$$

$$0.5R + 2 = 25$$

$$0.5R = 23$$

or $\quad R = \dfrac{23}{0.5} = 46\ \Omega$

Current through 20 Ω resistor

$$= \frac{5}{20 + 5} \times 0.5 = 0.1\text{ A}$$

and potential difference across middle resistor = potential difference across 20 Ω

$$= 20 \times 0.1 = 2\text{ V}$$

10. (*c*) To find the current flown by the battery, we will reduce the given circuit as

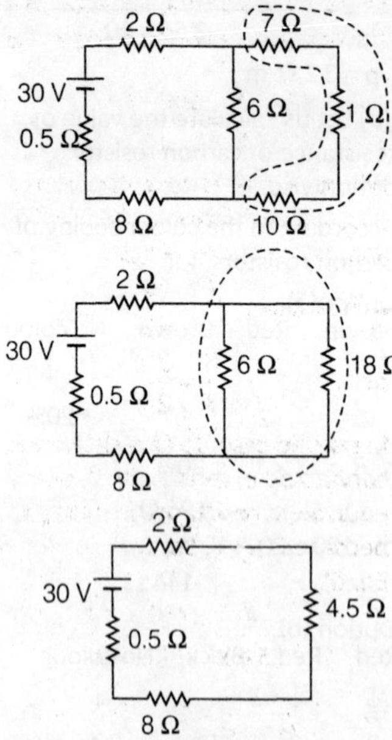

Equivalent resistance,

$$R_{eq} = 0.5 + 8 + 2 + 4.5 = 15\ \Omega$$

Current through battery,

$$I = \frac{E}{R_{eq}} = \frac{30}{15} = 2\text{ A}$$

From the given figure,

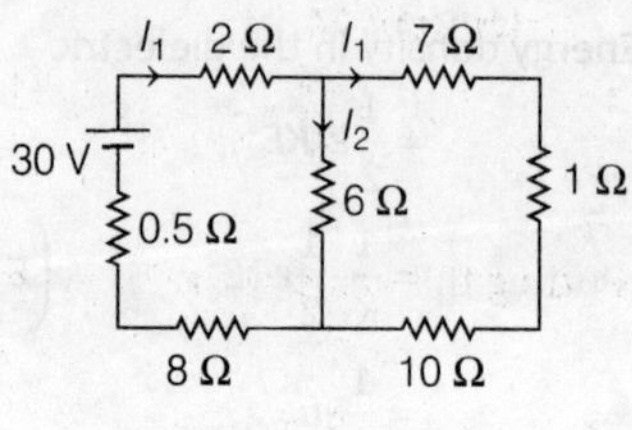

$$I_1 = \frac{R_2}{R_1 + R_2} \times I$$

$$= \frac{6}{(7 + 1 + 10) + 6} \times 2$$

$$I_1 = 0.5\text{ A}$$

$$I_2 = I - I_1 = 2 - 0.5$$

$$I_2 = 1.5\text{ A}$$

Power supplied by battery,

$$P_{battery} = V \cdot I = 30 \times 2 = 60\text{ W}$$

Power consumed by 2 Ω resistor,

$$P_{2\Omega} = I^2R = (2)^2 \times 2 = 8\text{ W}$$

Power consumed by 6 Ω resistor,

$$P_{6\Omega} = I_2^2R = (1.5)^2 \times 6$$

$$= 13.5\text{ W}$$

Power consumed by 7 Ω resistor,

$$P_{7\Omega} = I_1^2R = (0.5)^2 \times 7$$

$$= 1.75\text{ W}$$

The correct match code is

A → S, B → P, C → Q, D → R

11. (*a*) The cell equation of a battery in discharging mode is given as

$$V = E - Ir$$

Comparing this equation with the equation of straight line, i.e.,

$$y = c + mx$$

We get the slope of V-I graph is equal to negative of internal resistance of cell, i.e.

$$r = -\text{ slope of the } V\text{-}I \text{ graph}$$

$$r = -\frac{20 - 0}{0 - (4)} = 5\ \Omega$$

12. (*b*) Given that, internal resistance,

$$r = 0.5\ \Omega$$

External resistance, $R = 3\ \Omega$

Let for maximum current, n number of row and m number of cells are required in each row.

Total number of cells $= m \times n = 24$ ... (i)

For maximum current, $R = \dfrac{m}{n} r$

$$3 = \frac{m}{n} \times 0.5$$

$$\frac{m}{n} = 6$$

or $\quad m = 6n \quad$ ... (ii)

From Eq. (i),

$$(6n)(n)=24$$

$$n^2=\frac{24}{6}=4$$

$$\Rightarrow \quad n=2$$

Putting this value in Eq. (ii), we get

$$m=6\times 2$$

$$\Rightarrow \quad m=12$$

13. (c) Cell equation in discharging mode,

$$V=E-Ir$$

$$20=E-4r \quad \dots (i)$$

Cell equation in charging mode

$$V=E+Ir$$

$$25=E+Ir \quad (\because I=1\text{ A})$$

$$25=E+r \quad \dots (ii)$$

On subtracting Eq. (ii) from Eq. (i), we get

$$-5=-5r$$

or $r=1\,\Omega$

Putting the value of r in Eq. (i), we get

$$20=E-4\times 1$$

or $E=20+4$

$$E=24\text{ V}$$

14. (d) $V=IR$

So, when ammeter has very low resistance ($R\approx 0$), then there is no potential drop across ammeter.

15. (b) When capacitor is fully charged, circuit is reduced to as shown below.

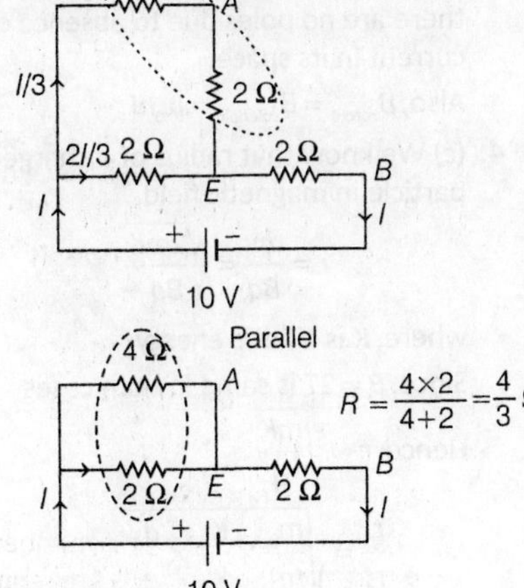

So, total resistance is

$$R_{eq}=\frac{4}{3}+2$$

$$=\frac{10}{3}\,\Omega$$

Current in circuit, $I=\frac{V}{R_{eq}}=\frac{10}{10/3}=3\text{ A}$

Hence, potential difference across capacitor = potential difference across AEB

$$=2I/3+2\times I=2\times\frac{3}{3}+2\times 3=8\text{ V}$$

16. (d) The given circuit can be redrawn as,

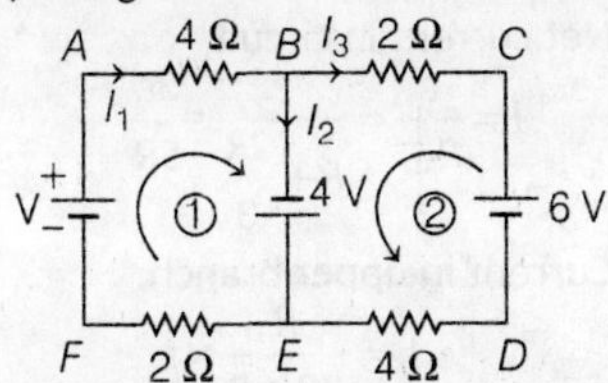

At junction B, $I_1=I_2+I_3 \quad \dots (i)$

Applying KVL in loop ① as shown the direction

$$2-4I_1+4-2I_1=0$$

or $6I_1=6$ or $I_1=1\text{ A}$

Applying KVL in loop ② as shown the direction

$$6+2I_3+4+4I_3=0$$

$$6I_3=-10$$

or $I_3=-\frac{5}{3}\text{ A}$

From Eq. (i), we get

$$I_2=I_1-I_3$$

$$=1-\left(-\frac{5}{3}\right)=\frac{8}{3}\text{ A}$$

So, $\frac{I_1}{I_2}=\frac{1}{8/3}=\frac{3}{8}$

17. (a) At the balancing situation of bridge, the relation between X and Y is given as

$$\frac{X}{Y}=\frac{100-l}{l} \quad \dots (i)$$

where, X is resistance connected in left gap, Y is resistance connected in right gap, l is balancing length.

In first case, $\frac{X}{Y}=\frac{60}{40}$

or $\frac{X}{Y}=\frac{3}{2} \quad \dots (ii)$

In second case, 15 Ω resistance is connected in series with Y, then equivalent resistance in right gap becomes $15+Y$. So, we can write from Eq. (i),

$$\frac{X}{15+Y}=\frac{(60-10)}{40+10}$$

$$\Rightarrow \quad \frac{X}{15+Y}=1 \quad \dots (iii)$$

On solving Eqs. (ii) and (iii), we get

$$X=45\,\Omega \quad \text{and} \quad Y=30\,\Omega$$

18. (a) In given circuit, Wheatstone bridge is balanced,

As, $\frac{P}{Q}=\frac{R}{S}$

$$\Rightarrow \quad \frac{40}{10}=\frac{60}{15}=4$$

Hence, $V_{AB}=V_{AD}$

$$\Rightarrow \quad 40I_1=60I_2 \text{ or } I_1=1.5I_2$$

Power branch $AB=I_1^2R$

$$=(1.5I_2)^2\times 40=90I_2^2$$

Power branch $BC=I_1^2R=(1.5I_2)^2\times 10$

$$=22.5I_2^2$$

Power branch $AD=I_2^2R=60I_2^2$

Power branch $DC=I_2^2R=15I_2^2$

19. (b) Let the potential gradient of wire of potentiometer be x.

When switch S is open, no current will flow through R and emf of cell ε_2 is balanced on wire of potentiometer. So, we can write

$$\varepsilon_2=x\,(AP) \text{ or } \varepsilon_2=x\times 70 \quad \dots (i)$$

When switch S is open, R is in circuit. At balance condition, current in secondary circuit of potentiometer,

$$I=\frac{\varepsilon_2}{R+r}$$

where, r is internal resistance of cell. In this case, voltage across R (i.e. IR) is balanced over wire of potentiometer. Thus,

$$IR=x\,(AQ)$$

$$\frac{\varepsilon_2}{R+r}\cdot R=x\times 60$$

$$\frac{\varepsilon_2}{6+r}\times 6=x\times 60 \quad \dots (ii)$$

$$(\because R=6\,\Omega)$$

On dividing Eq. (i) by Eq. (ii), we get

$$\frac{\varepsilon_2}{\frac{\varepsilon_2}{6+r}\times 6}=\frac{x\times 70}{x\times 60}$$

$$\frac{6+r}{6}=\frac{7}{6}\Rightarrow 1+\frac{r}{6}=\frac{7}{6}$$

or $\frac{r}{6}=\frac{7}{6}-1$

or $\frac{r}{6}=\frac{1}{6}$

$$r=1\,\Omega$$

20. (c) A is false but R is true.

As emf or input voltage is mainted by source, an increase of resistance decreases the current. This will slow down heat production rate.

21. (b) When current flow through potentiometer wire is reduced, potential drop per unit length will be small and we are able to balance a small potential drop.

Statement II is incorrect as sensitivity of a potentiometer is inversely proportional to its potential gradient.

22. (a) Resistance of bulb-1,

$$R_1 = \frac{V_{\text{rated}}^2}{P_{\text{rated}}} = \frac{(100)^2}{100} = 100\,\Omega$$

Resistance of bulb-2,

$$R_2 = \frac{V_{\text{rated}}^2}{P_{\text{rated}}} = \frac{(100)^2}{200} = 50\,\Omega$$

Let us find the voltage across each bulbs,

$$V_1 = \frac{R_1}{R_1+R_2} \times 200 = \left(\frac{100}{100+50}\right) \times 200 = 133\text{ V}$$

Similarly, $V_2 = 200 - V_1 = 200 - 133 = 67\text{ V}$

For bulb-1, voltage supply is greater than its rated voltage, so bulb will get fused and circuit will become open. So, no current will pass through either of the bulb.

Therefore, power consumption in circuit will be zero.

23. (d) Given that, all bulbs are identical, so resistance of each bulb will be same.

As, power, $P = I^2R$

where, R is constant.

or $P \propto I^2$

Let emf of battery be ε, so, the given circuit can be redrawn as,

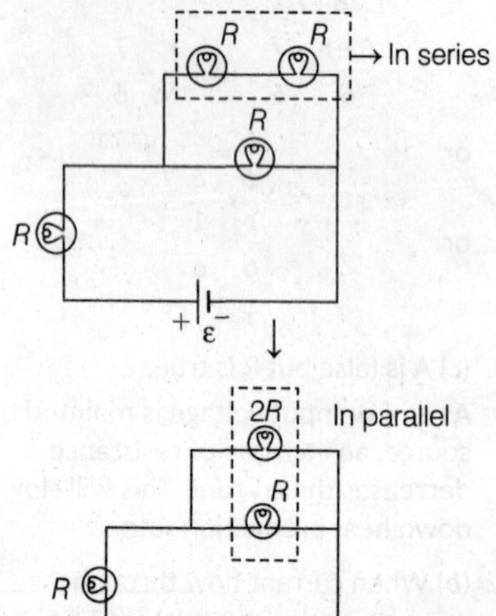

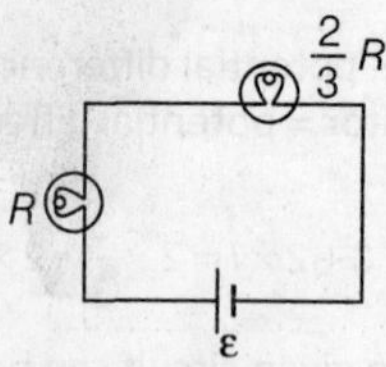

Net current in circuit,

$$I = \frac{\varepsilon}{R_{\text{net}}} = \frac{\varepsilon}{R + \frac{2R}{3}} = \frac{3\varepsilon}{5R}$$

Current in upper branch,

$$I_1 = \frac{R}{2R+R} \times I$$

$$I_1 = \frac{R}{3R} \times \frac{3\varepsilon}{5R}$$

$$I_1 = \frac{\varepsilon}{5R}$$

and $I_2 = I - I_1 = \frac{3\varepsilon}{5R} - \frac{\varepsilon}{5R} = \frac{2\varepsilon}{5R}$

Power consumption of B_1, $P_1 = I^2R$

$$= \left(\frac{3\varepsilon}{5R}\right)^2 \times R = \frac{9\varepsilon^2}{25R}$$

Power consumption of B_2,

$$P_2 = I_1^2 \times R = \left(\frac{\varepsilon}{5R}\right)^2 \times R = \frac{\varepsilon^2}{25R}$$

Power consumption of B_3,

$$P_3 = P_2 = \frac{\varepsilon^2}{25R}$$

Power consumption of B_4, $P_4 = I_2^2R$

$$= \left(\frac{2\varepsilon}{5R}\right)^2 \times R$$

$$P_4 = \frac{4\varepsilon^2}{25R}$$

$\Rightarrow P_1 > P_4 > P_2 = P_3$

As, brightness of bulb $\propto$ power consumption

So, correct order of bulb brightness $B_1 > B_4 > B_2 = B_3$

24. (c) Power dissipated in appliance is

$$P = \frac{V^2}{R} = \frac{(300)^2}{20} = 4.5\text{ kW}$$

So, heat generated is more than heat dissipated (2 kW). Hence, option (c) is correct.

25. (b) Using, $R = \rho\frac{l}{A}$, resistance of nichrome (ribbon B) is less, so rate of heat (I^2R) is higher. So, B is good choice.

Qualifier 13 (Magnetic Effects of Current and Magnetism)

1. (c) Here, $B = 2 \times 10^{-3}$ T

radius, $r = 20\text{ cm} = 0.2\text{ m}$

$e = 1.6 \times 10^{-19}$ C

$m = 9.1 \times 10^{-31}$ kg

We know that, radius of circular path,

$$r = \frac{mv}{Bq}$$

$$\Rightarrow v = \frac{rBq}{m} = \frac{rBe}{m} \quad [\because q = e]$$

$$v = \frac{0.2 \times 2 \times 10^{-3} \times 1.6 \times 10^{-19}}{9.1 \times 10^{-31}} = 7 \times 10^7\text{ m/s}$$

2. (b) We know that, radius of circular path of a charged particle in magnetic field is given by

$$r = \frac{mv}{Bq}$$

$$r = \frac{p}{Bq} \quad [\text{momentum, } p = mv]$$

$$p = qBr$$

$$\therefore \text{Energy, } E = \frac{p^2}{2m} = \frac{q^2B^2r^2}{2m}$$

3. (a) Both A and R are true but R is not the correct explanation of A.

At any point in the empty space surrounded by toroid will have zero magnetic field, hence for a toroid, magnetic dipole moment is zero as there are no poles due to absence of current in its space.

Also, $B_{\text{toroid}} = B_{\text{solenoid}} = \mu_0 nI$

4. (c) We know that radius of a charged particle in magnetic field,

$$r = \frac{mv}{Bq} = \frac{\sqrt{2mK}}{Bq}$$

where, K is kinetic energy.

Since, $B = 2$T is same in both cases

Hence, $r \propto \sqrt{\frac{mK}{q}}$

$$\therefore \frac{r_p}{r_d} = \sqrt{\frac{m_p}{m_d} \times \frac{K_p}{K_d} \times \frac{q_d}{q_p}}$$

$$\Rightarrow \frac{2}{1} = \sqrt{\frac{m_p}{2m_p} \times \frac{K_p}{K_d} \times \frac{q_p}{q_p}}$$

$$\Rightarrow 2 = \sqrt{\frac{K_p}{2K_d}}$$

$$\Rightarrow 8K_d = K_p \Rightarrow K_p = 8K_d = 8 \times 100 = 800\text{ keV}$$

5. (*d*) We know that, angular momentum of revolving electron with speed v in Bohr's orbit of radius r is given as

$$L = mvr \quad \text{... (i)}$$

Current associated with revolving electron in Bohr's orbit,

$$I = \frac{e}{T} = \frac{e}{2\pi r / v} = \frac{ev}{2\pi r}$$

$\therefore$ Magnetic dipole moment,

$$\mu = I \cdot A = \frac{ev}{2\pi r} \times \pi r^2 = \frac{evr}{2} \quad \text{... (ii)}$$

From Eqs. (i) and (ii), we get

$$\therefore \quad \frac{L}{\mu} = \frac{mvr}{evr/2} = \frac{2m}{e}$$

6. (*c*) When a charged particle moves perpendicular to uniform magnetic field, according to Fleming's left hand rule, magnetic force on charged particle acts perpendicular to its direction of motion, hence charged particle follows a curved path in magnetic field. The particle continues to follow this curved path until it forms a complete circle. Intensity of magnetisation of a bulk material is given by magnetic dipole moment developed per unit volume when it is placed in magnetic field.

7. (*b*) The correct pairs are given as A $\rightarrow$ R, B $\rightarrow$ P, C $\rightarrow$ Q, D $\rightarrow$ S.

A. Magnetic field at point P due to a straight current carrying wire is given by

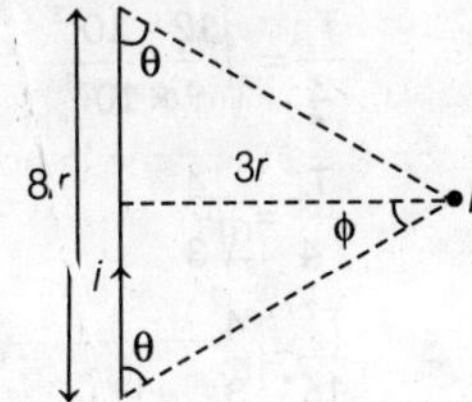

$$B_P = \frac{\mu_0 i}{4\pi d}(\cos\theta_1 + \cos\theta_2)$$

where, $d = 3r$, $\theta_1 = \theta_2 = \theta$

$$\therefore \quad B_P = \frac{\mu_0 i}{6\pi r}\cos\theta$$

From the figure, $\cos\theta = \frac{4}{5}$

$$\therefore \quad B_P = \frac{2\mu_0 i}{15\pi r}$$

B.

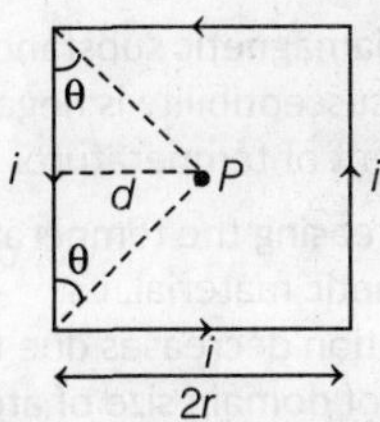

Magnetic field at point P due to one side of square is given by

$$B_P = \frac{\mu_0 i}{4\pi d}(\cos\theta + \cos\theta)$$

(Here, $\theta = 45°$ from geometry)

$$= \frac{\mu_0 i}{4\pi r} \cdot 2 \cdot \left(\frac{1}{\sqrt{2}}\right) \quad (\because d = r)$$

$$\Rightarrow \quad = \frac{\mu_0 i}{2\sqrt{2}\pi r}$$

Magnetic field at point P due to square box

$$B_P = 4B = 4 \times \frac{\mu_0 i}{2\sqrt{2}\,\pi r} = \frac{\sqrt{2}\mu_0 i}{\pi r}$$

C.

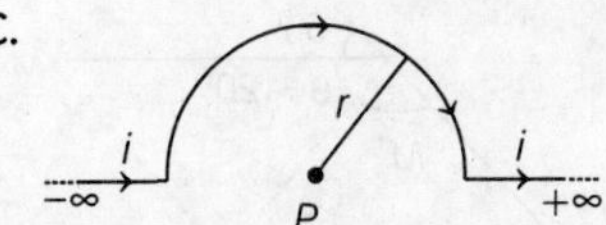

Magnetic field at point P due to straight wire will cancel out each other. Thus, magnetic field due to a semi-circular wire is given by

$$B_P = \frac{\mu_0 i}{4r}$$

D.

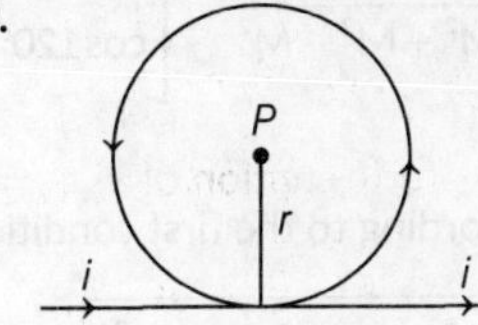

Magnetic field due to a straight wire,

$$B_S = \frac{\mu_0 i}{2\pi r}$$

Magnetic field due to circular wire,

$$B_C = \frac{\mu_0 i}{2r}$$

$$B_P = B_S + B_C = \frac{\mu_0 i}{2\pi r} + \frac{\mu_0 i}{2r} = \frac{\mu_0 i}{2\pi r}(1 + \pi)$$

8. (*b*) The given situation is shown below.

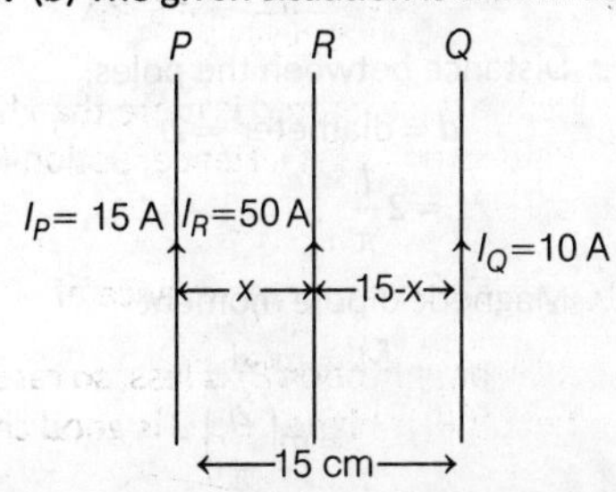

Since, wire R is placed, so that it experiences no force, $\frac{F_{PR}}{l} = \frac{F_{RQ}}{l}$

$$\Rightarrow \quad \frac{\mu_0 I_P I_R}{2\pi x} = \frac{\mu_0 I_R I_Q}{2\pi(15 - x)}$$

$$\Rightarrow \quad \frac{I_P}{x} = \frac{I_Q}{15 - x}$$

$$\Rightarrow \quad \frac{15}{x} = \frac{10}{15 - x}$$

$$\Rightarrow \quad 225 - 15x = 10x$$

$$\Rightarrow \quad 25x = 225$$

$$x = 9 \text{ cm}$$

9. (*b*) Two parallel current carrying conductors having currents in same direction attract each other, while having currents in opposite direction repel each other.

10. (*a*) Given, $G = 12\,\Omega$

$$I_G = 2.5 \times 10^{-3} \text{ A}$$

and $V = 10$ V

For ammeter, shunt resistance

$$S = \frac{GI_G}{I - I_G} = \frac{12 \times 2.5 \times 10^{-3}}{7.5 - (2.5 \times 10^{-3})} = 4 \times 10^{-3}\,\Omega$$

Now, resistance of ammeter

$$R_A = \frac{SG}{S + G} = \frac{4 \times 10^{-3} \times 12}{4 \times 10^{-3} + 12}$$

$$\Rightarrow \quad = 4 \times 10^{-3}\,\Omega$$

For a galvanometer as voltmeter.

Resistance,

$$R = \frac{V}{I_G} - G = \frac{10}{2.5 \times 10^{-3}} - 12 = 3988\,\Omega$$

$\therefore$ Voltmeter's resistance,

$$R_V = R + G = 4000\,\Omega = 4 \times 10^3\,\Omega$$

$$\therefore \quad \frac{R_A}{R_V} = \frac{4 \times 10^{-3}}{4 \times 10^3} = 10^{-6}$$

11. (*a*) Given, $R_1 = 11$ cm, $R_2 = 12$ cm

$I = 0.7$ A, $B = 2.5$ T, $N = 1000$

Mean radius of the toroid,

$$R = \frac{R_1 + R_2}{2} = \frac{11 + 12}{2} = 11.5 \text{ cm} = 11.5 \times 10^{-2} \text{ m}$$

As we know, $B = \mu H = \mu n I \quad [\because H = nI]$

$$\Rightarrow \quad B = \mu_r \mu_0 n I \quad [\mu = \mu_r \mu_0]$$

$$\Rightarrow \quad \mu_r = \frac{B}{\mu_0 n I} = \frac{B}{\mu_0 (N/2\pi R) I}$$

$$= \frac{2.5 \times 2\pi(11.5 \times 10^{-2})}{4\pi \times 10^{-7} \times 1000 \times 0.7} = 2055$$

12. (*a*) Given, $N = 500$ turns, $I = 2\text{ mA}$
$$= 2\times10^{-3}\text{ A},\ B=\sqrt{3}\text{ T}$$
$\theta = 30°$, $l = 2\text{ cm} = 2\times10^{-2}\text{ m}$,
$b = 1\text{ cm} = 10^{-2}\text{ m}$

Area of the coil, $A = l\times b$
$$= 2\times10^{-2}\times10^{-2} = 2\times10^{-4}\text{ m}^2$$

Angle made by normal of rectangular coil with the direction of magnetic field,
$$\alpha = 90° - \theta = 90° - 30° = 60°$$
$\therefore$ Torque, $\tau = NIAB\sin\alpha$
$$= 500\times2\times10^{-3}\times2\times10^{-4}\times\sqrt{3}\times\sin60°$$
$$= 1000\times10^{-3}\times2\times10^{-4}\times\sqrt{3}\times\frac{\sqrt{3}}{2}$$
$$= 3\times10^{-4}\text{ N-m}$$

13. (*b*) The given ammeter can be regarded as the galvanometer
$\therefore$ $I_g = 1\text{ A}, R_g = 0.8\Omega$

Total current, $I = 5\text{ A}$

$\therefore$ The required value of shunt resistance,
$$R_s = \left(\frac{I_g}{I - I_g}\right)\times R_g$$
$$= \left(\frac{1}{5-1}\right)\times0.8$$
$$= 0.2\,\Omega$$

14. (*d*) Sensitivity of a moving coil galvanometer is given by
$$S = \frac{\theta}{i} = \frac{NBA}{C}$$
Since, $S\propto N$, $S\propto B$ and $S\propto A$.
Hence, option (d) is correct.

15. (*a*) The correct match is given as
A → Q, B → R, C → P, D → S

A. Diamagnetic materials have small but negative value of magnetic susceptibility. It is independent of temperature.

B. Ferromagnetic materials have large value of magnetic susceptibility, which decreases with increases in temperature.

C. Paramagnetic materials have small value of magnetic susceptibility, which decreases $\left(\chi\propto\frac{1}{T}\right)$, with increases in temperature.

D. Anti-ferromagnetic materials have positive value of magnetic susceptibility, which first increases with temperature and after a critical temperature starts decreasing.

16. (*c*) For a diamagnetic substance, magnetic susceptibility is negative and independent of temperature.

17. (*b*) On increasing the temperature of a ferromagnetic material, its magnetisation decreases due to reduction of domain size of atoms having dipole moment in same direction. Above Curie temperature, a ferromagnetic substance becomes paramagnetic substance.

18. (*b*) Magnetic dipole moment of each bar magnet is shown below.

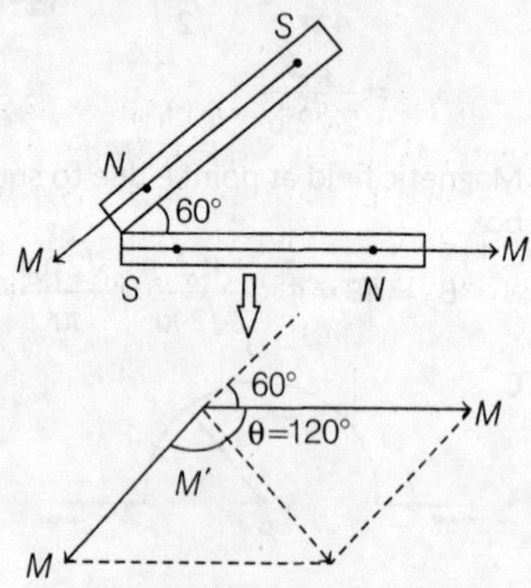

$\therefore$ Resultant magnetic dipole moment of the system is given as
$$M' = \sqrt{M_1^2 + M_2^2 + 2M_1M_2\cos\theta}$$
$$= \sqrt{M^2 + M^2 + 2M\cdot M\cdot\cos120°}$$
$$= \sqrt{M^2 + M^2 - M^2}\qquad\left[\cos120° = -\frac{1}{2}\right]$$
$$= M$$

19. (*b*) According to the first condition,

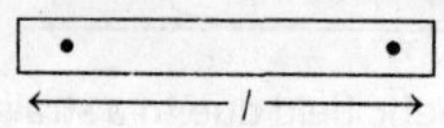

$$M = ml \qquad \text{... (i)}$$
When magnet is bent into semi-circle of radius r, then $l = \pi r$
$$\Rightarrow \qquad r = \frac{l}{\pi}$$

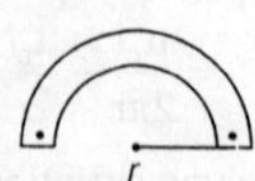

$\therefore$ Distance between the poles,
$$d = \text{diameter} = 2r$$
$$= 2\frac{l}{\pi}$$
$\therefore$ Magnetic dipole moment
$$M' = m\cdot d$$
$$= m\left(\frac{2l}{\pi}\right)$$
$$= \frac{2}{\pi}\cdot ml$$
$$= \frac{2M}{\pi}$$

20. (*b*) Work done in rotating the magnetic dipole in uniform magnetic field B from θ_1 to θ_2 is given by
$$W = -MB(\cos\theta_2 - \cos\theta_1)$$
In case-I,
$$W_1 = -MB(\cos90° - \cos0°) = MB$$
$$\Rightarrow \qquad W_1 = MB \qquad \text{...(i)}$$
In case-II, $W_2 = -MB(\cos60° - \cos0°)$
$$= -MB\left(\frac{1}{2} - 1\right)$$
$$\Rightarrow \qquad W_2 = \frac{MB}{2} \qquad \text{... (ii)}$$
From Eqs. (i) and (ii), we have
$$W_2 = \frac{W_1}{2}$$
$$\Rightarrow \qquad W_1 = 2W_2$$
$$= nW_2 \text{ (given)}$$
$$\therefore \qquad n = 2$$

21. (*a*) Given, $(B_H)_1 = 12\text{ mT}$
$$= 12\times10^{-3}\text{ T}$$
$$(B_H)_2 = 9\text{ mT} = 9\times10^{-3}\text{ T}$$
$$T_1 = 4\text{ s}$$
We know that, time-period of vibrational magnetometer.
$$T = 2\pi\sqrt{\frac{I}{MB_H}}$$
$$\Rightarrow \qquad T\propto\frac{1}{\sqrt{B_H}}$$
$$\Rightarrow \qquad \frac{T_2}{T_1} = \sqrt{\frac{(B_H)_1}{(B_H)_2}}$$
$$\Rightarrow \qquad \frac{T_2}{4} = \sqrt{\frac{12\times10^{-3}}{9\times10^{-3}}}$$
$$\Rightarrow \qquad \frac{T_2}{4} = \sqrt{\frac{4}{3}}$$
$$\Rightarrow \qquad \frac{T_2^2}{16} = \frac{4}{3}$$
$$T_2^2 = \frac{64}{3}$$
$$T_2 = \frac{8}{\sqrt{3}}\text{ s}$$

22. (*d*) Given, $B_V = B_H$
If δ be the angle of dip, then
$$\tan\delta = \frac{B_V}{B_H}$$

$$= \frac{B_V}{B_V} \quad [\because B_V = B_H]$$
$$= 1$$
$$\tan\delta = \tan 45°$$
$$\Rightarrow \quad \delta = 45°$$

23. (*d*) Given, $B_H = 0.8$ G

$$\delta = 60°$$
$$\therefore \quad B_H = B\cos\delta$$
$$\therefore \quad B = \frac{B_H}{\cos\delta} = \frac{0.8}{\cos 60°}$$
$$= \frac{0.8}{1/2} = 1.6 \text{ G}$$

24. (*b*) As, $M \propto \frac{B_0}{T}$

$$\text{So,} \quad \frac{M_1}{M_2} = \frac{B_1}{B_2} \times \frac{T_2}{T_1}$$
$$\Rightarrow \quad \frac{6}{M_2} = \frac{0.4}{0.3} \times \frac{24}{4}$$
$$\text{or} \quad M = 0{\cdot}75 \text{ A/m}$$

25. (*c*) Area of *B* - *H* curve = Energy loss as heat per unit volume of a sample in one cycle of magnetisation and demagnetisation.

Qualifier 14 (Electromagnetic Induction & Alternating Current)

1. (*c*) Given that, $\phi = (6t^3 - 18t^2)$ mT, $N = 40$ and $R = 5\,\Omega$

Magnitude of induced emf, $|e| = N\left|\frac{d\phi_B}{dt}\right|$

$$|e| = 40\frac{d}{dt}(6t^3 - 18t^2) \times 10^{-3}$$
$$= 40(18t^2 - 36t) \times 10^{-3}$$
$$= 40 \times 18(t^2 - 2t) \times 10^{-3}$$
$$= 720(t^2 - 2t) \times 10^{-3}$$

Current through coil,

$$I = \frac{|e|}{R} = \frac{720(t^2 - 2t)}{5} \times 10^{-3}$$
$$= 144(t^2 - 2t) \times 10^{-3}$$

For current to be maximum,

$$\frac{di}{dt} = 0$$
$$\frac{d}{dt}144(t^2 - 2t) = 0$$
$$144(2t - 2) = 0$$
$$\text{or} \quad 2t - 2 = 0 \quad \text{or} \quad t = 1\text{s}$$

i.e. at $t = 1$ s current is maximum. This maximum current is

$$|I_{max}| = |144(t^2 - 2t) \times 10^{-3}|$$
$$|I_{max}| = |144(1^2 - 2 \times 1) \times 10^{-3}|$$
$$= 0.144 \text{ A}$$

2. (*b*) Due to time varrying magnitude, AC cannot be measured by instruments based on magnetic effect.

Hence, ammeter based on galvanometer cannot be used to measure AC.

A hot wire ammeter measures the rms value of alternating current. So, it can be used to measure the direct current of constant value because that constant value will be equal to the rms value of alternating current.

3. (*b*) Current *I* is given as

$$I = (t^2 - 1)\text{ A}$$
$$\text{or} \quad I = (t + 1)(t - 1)\text{ A}$$

For $0 < t \leq 1$, current *I* is negative and magnitude of *I* decreases. During this time period, *I* will produce ⊙ magnetic field passing through the loop. As current *I* increases, so ⊙ magnetic field will also increase.

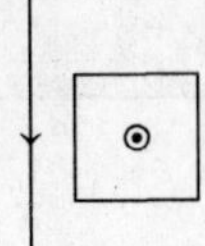

Therefore, induced current should produce cross magnetic field. For producing cross magnetic field in the loop, induced current from our side should be anti-clockwise.

For $t > 1$ s, current *I* will produce ⊗ magnetic field passing through the loop. Current *I* is increasing, so dot magnetic field will also increase. Therefore, induced current should produce cross magnetic field. For producing cross magnetic field in the loop, induced current from our side should be anti-clockwise.

4. (*b*) Let the required magnetic field be *B*.

The peak voltage induced in magnetic field in coil is given as

$$E_0 = NA\omega B$$
$$\text{or } B = \frac{E_0}{NA\omega}$$
$$= \frac{100}{3000 \times 20 \times 10^{-4} \times 400}$$
$$= \frac{1}{24} = 0.041 \text{ T}$$
$$= 41 \text{ mT}$$

5. (*a*) When a conductor is moving through a uniform magnetic field with certain velocity in a perpendicular magnetic field, free electrons present in the conductor experience a magnetic force which is given as,

$$\mathbf{F}_m = q(\mathbf{v} \times \mathbf{B})$$

Due to the action of this force, the positive charge will move in the direction of $(\mathbf{v} \times \mathbf{B})$ and negative charge will move opposite to $(\mathbf{v} \times \mathbf{B})$. The direction of velocities of points *P* and *Q* is as shown in the following figure.

The direction of velocity of upper half part of rod is rightwards, so free electrons present in upper half part experience force according to right hand thumb rule towards point *O* about which rod is being rotated, leaving a net positive charge at the upper end.

Similarly, the direction of velocity of lower half part of rod is leftwards, so direction of $\mathbf{v} \times \mathbf{B}$ is downwards. The force experienced by positive charge is towards lower end, whereas electrons experiences force towards point *O*. Thus, the accumulation of charges can be shown as follows :

6. (*d*) Initial magnetic flux through the coil, $\phi_i = B_H A\cos\theta$

$$= 3 \times 10^{-5} \times \pi(0.2)^2 \times \cos 0°$$
$$= 1.2\pi \times 10^{-6} = 1.2\pi\mu \text{ Wb}$$

Final magnetic flux after the rotation,

$$\phi_f = 3 \times 10^{-5} \times \pi \times (0.2)^2 \times \cos 180°$$
$$= -1.2\pi\mu \text{ Wb}$$

$$\text{Induced emf, } e = -\frac{\Delta\phi}{\Delta t} = \frac{\phi_i - \phi_f}{\Delta t}$$
$$= \frac{1.2\pi\mu - (-1.2\pi\mu)}{0.5}$$
$$= 4.8\pi\mu \text{ V}$$

7. (*d*) Both A and R are correct and R explains A.

Lenz's law is a direct consequence of conservation of energy.

8. (*a*) Given, $L = 40$ mH

dt = net time difference

$= t_2 - t_1 = 4\text{ ms} = \Delta t$

$dI = I_2 - I_1$

$= 11 - 1 = 10\text{ A} = \Delta I$

Induced emf, $e = L\dfrac{dI}{dt}$

$= L\dfrac{\Delta I}{\Delta t} = 40 \cdot \left(\dfrac{10}{4}\right)$

$= 100$ V

9. (*c*) When the total flux associated with one coil links with the other, i.e. a case of maximum flux linkage, then

$\therefore \quad M_{max} = \sqrt{L_1 L_2}$

Given, $L_1 = 2$ mH, $L_2 = 8$ mH

$\therefore \quad M_{max} = \sqrt{2 \times 8} = \sqrt{16} = 4$ mH

10. (*c*) Let the instantaneous current be *i*.

Applying KVL from *P* to *Q*,

$V_P - iX_L - iX_C = V_Q$

or $\quad V_P - V_Q = i(X_L + X_C)$

or $\quad i = \dfrac{V_P - V_Q}{X_L + X_C}$

Given that,

$V_P - V_Q = 30$ V

$X_L = 2\,\Omega, X_C = 8\,\Omega$

$i = \dfrac{V_P - V_Q}{X_L + X_C}$

$i = \dfrac{30}{2+8} = 3$ A

At same instant, voltage across resistor,

$V_R = iR = 3 \times 8 = 24$ V

Impedance of circuit,

$Z = \sqrt{R^2 + (X_C - X_L)^2}$

$= \sqrt{8^2 + (8-2)^2}$

$= \sqrt{64 + 36}$

$= 10\,\Omega$

$\therefore$ Instantaneous source voltage, $V = iZ$

$V = 3 \times 10$

$= 30$ V

11. (*d*) The frequency of DC current is zero, so the resistance offered by inductor is $X_L = \omega L = 0$. Thus, when a DC current is applied across inductor, it behaves as an short-circuit and a very large amount (infinite) of current flows through it. Thus, resulting current wave equation can be written as

$I = \infty + I(V_1) - I(V_2)$

where, $I(V_1)$ and $I(V_2)$ are currents due to $V_1 = 100 \sin 157\,t$ and $V_2 = 75 \sin 942\,t$

Hence, $\quad I = \infty$.

12. (*b*) As voltage across inductor is given as

$V_L = \dfrac{LdI}{dt}$

or $\quad dI = \dfrac{1}{L}V_L dt$

Integrating on both sides within limit, we get

$\int_0^I dI = \dfrac{1}{L}\int_0^t V_L dt$

$[I]_0^I = \dfrac{1}{L}\int_0^t V_L dt$

$[I - 0] = \dfrac{1}{L} \times$ Area under V_L *versus* *t* graph

Area of V_L and *t* graph from $t = 0$ to $t = 3$ s.

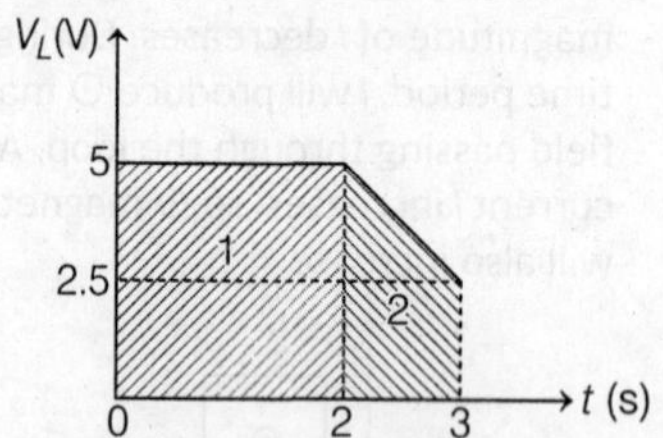

$A = A_1 + A_2$

$= \dfrac{1}{2} \times 2 \times 5 + \dfrac{1}{2} \times (5 + 2.5) \times 1$

$= 5 + 3.75$

$= 8.75$

$\therefore I = \dfrac{1}{0.6} \times 8.75 \quad [\because \text{Given, } L = 0.6\text{ H}]$

$= 14.58$ A

13. (*c*)

For *R*-*L* circuit, $V = \sqrt{V_R^2 + V_L^2}$

or $\quad V_L = \sqrt{V^2 - V_R^2}$

$= \sqrt{(100)^2 - (60)^2}$

$= \sqrt{10000 - 3600}$

$= \sqrt{6400} = 80$ V

Power rating of bulb, $P = VI$

or $\quad I = \dfrac{P}{V} = \dfrac{10}{60} = \dfrac{1}{6}$ A

Voltage across inductor, $V_L = IX_L$

or $\quad X_L = \dfrac{V_L}{I}$

$= \dfrac{80}{1/6} = 480\,\Omega$

$2\pi f L = 480$

or $\quad 2\pi \times 50\,L = 480$

$\Rightarrow \quad L = \dfrac{480}{100\pi} = 1.528$ H

14. (d) Bandwidth of the system is the range of frequencies for which the total power is more than the half of maximum power. It is represented by $\Delta\omega$.

$\Delta\omega = \omega_2 - \omega_1 = \dfrac{R}{L}$

or $\quad 2\pi\Delta f = \dfrac{R}{L}$

or $\quad \Delta f = \dfrac{R}{2\pi L}$

15. (*d*) Sharpness of an *L*-*C*-*R* series resonant circuit can be measured using the quality factor.

Here, $\quad X_L \neq X_C$

It means the circuit is not in resonance, therefore quality factor cannot be defined.

16. (*c*) Let the resistance of choke coil be *R*.

Given that, $f_1 = 180$ Hz, $\cos\phi = 0.5$ and $f_2 = 60$ Hz

Power factor, $\cos\phi = \dfrac{R}{Z}$

where, *Z* is impedance of choke coil

or $\quad R = Z\cos\phi$

or $\quad R = Z \times 0.5$ or $\dfrac{Z}{2}$

But $\quad Z = \sqrt{R^2 + (\omega L)^2}$

or $\quad \omega L = \sqrt{Z^2 - R^2}$

or $\quad 2\pi f_1 L = \sqrt{Z^2 - \left(\dfrac{Z}{2}\right)^2} \quad [\because \omega = 2\pi f]$

or $\quad 2\pi \times 180 L = \dfrac{\sqrt{3}}{2}Z$

or $\quad L = \dfrac{\sqrt{3}Z}{720\pi}$

When frequency is changed to ω_2, then new inductive reactance,

$X_L' = \omega_2 L = 2\pi f_2 L$

$= 2\pi \times 60 \times \dfrac{\sqrt{3}Z}{720\pi}$

$= \dfrac{Z}{2\sqrt{3}}$

New impedance, $Z' = \sqrt{R^2 + (X_L')^2}$

$= \sqrt{\left(\dfrac{Z}{2}\right)^2 + \left(\dfrac{Z}{2\sqrt{3}}\right)^2}$

$= \sqrt{\dfrac{Z^2}{4} + \dfrac{Z^2}{12}} = \dfrac{Z}{\sqrt{3}}$

$\therefore$ New power factor, $\cos\phi_2 = \dfrac{R}{Z'}$

$$\cos\phi_2 = \frac{\frac{Z}{2}}{\frac{Z}{\sqrt{3}}}$$

$$\cos\phi_2 = \frac{\sqrt{3}}{2} = 0.866$$

17. (*d*) Given that, $V = 200 \sin\left(\omega t + \dfrac{\pi}{3}\right)$ V

$$I = 5\sqrt{2}\cos\left(\omega t - \frac{\pi}{6}\right) \text{A}$$

or $\quad I = 5\sqrt{2}\sin\left(\dfrac{\pi}{2} + \omega t - \dfrac{\pi}{6}\right)$

$$= 5\sqrt{2}\sin\left(\omega t + \frac{\pi}{3}\right) \text{A}$$

$$\left[\because \sin\left(\frac{\pi}{2} + \theta\right) = \cos\theta\right]$$

Phase difference between voltage and current,

$$\phi = \left(\omega t + \frac{\pi}{3}\right) - \left(\omega t + \frac{\pi}{3}\right)$$

$$= 0$$

Power consumption ,

$$P = V_{rms} I_{rms} \cos\phi$$

$$= \left(\frac{200}{\sqrt{2}}\right)\left(\frac{5\sqrt{2}}{\sqrt{2}}\right)\cos 0^\circ$$

$$= 100\sqrt{2} \times 5 \times 1$$

$$= 500\sqrt{2} \text{ W}$$

18. (*d*) Consider a circuit with inductor L and capacitor C connected in series with an alternating potential V. If V_L and V_c are the potential difference across inductor and capacitor, respectively, then

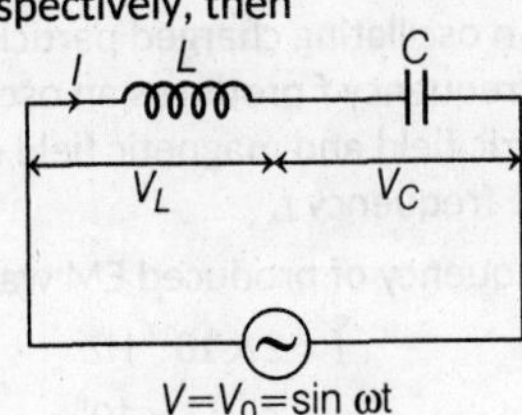

Supply voltage, $V = V_L - V_c$

$$= IX_L - IX_C$$

[As V_L and V_c are in opposite phases with each other]

$$= I(X_L - X_C)$$

Impedance, $z = \dfrac{V}{I} = \dfrac{I(X_L - X_C)}{I}$

$$= X_L - X_C$$

$$= \omega L - \frac{1}{\omega C}$$

When $\omega = 0$,

$$Z = 0L - \frac{1}{0 \times C} = -\infty$$

When $\omega = \dfrac{1}{\sqrt{LC}}$,

$$Z = \frac{1}{\sqrt{LC}} \times L - \frac{\sqrt{LC}}{C} = \sqrt{\frac{L}{C}} - \sqrt{\frac{L}{C}}$$

$$Z = 0$$

When $\omega = \infty$,

$$Z = \infty \times L - \frac{1}{\infty \times C}$$

$$= \infty - 0 = \infty$$

Thus, graph between Z and ω can be plotted as

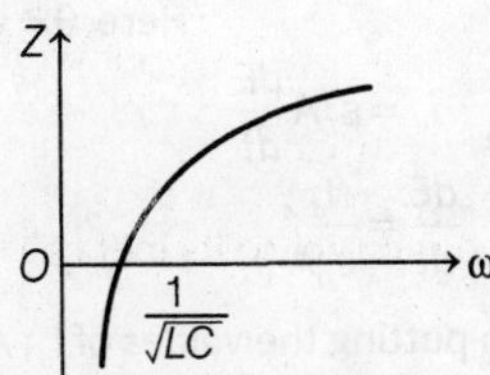

19. (*c*)

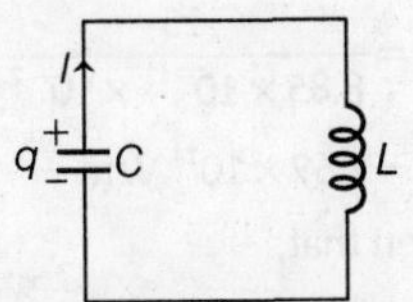

Given that, both capacitor and inductor have same amount of energy,

$$U_C = U_L$$

$$\frac{q^2}{2C} = \frac{1}{2}LI^2$$

$$\frac{q_0^2\cos^2\omega t}{2C} = \frac{1}{2}L(q_0^2\omega^2\sin^2\omega t)$$

$$\left[\because I = \frac{dq}{dt} = \frac{d}{dt}q_0\cos\omega t = -\omega q_0\sin\omega t\right]$$

or $\quad \cos^2\omega t = LC\omega^2\sin^2\omega t$

or $\quad \cos^2\omega t = \dfrac{1}{\omega^2} \times \omega^2\sin^2\omega t$

$$\left[\because \omega = \frac{1}{\sqrt{LC}} \Rightarrow LC = \frac{1}{\omega^2}\right]$$

or $\quad \cot^2\omega t = 1$

or $\quad \cot\omega t = 1$

or $\quad \omega t = \dfrac{\pi}{4}, \dfrac{3\pi}{4}, \dfrac{5\pi}{4}, \ldots\ldots$

or $\quad t = \dfrac{\pi}{4\omega}, \dfrac{3\pi}{4\omega}, \dfrac{5\pi}{4\omega}$

$$t = \frac{\pi}{4}\sqrt{LC}, \frac{3}{4}\pi\sqrt{LC}, \frac{5\pi}{4}\sqrt{LC}$$

20. (*c*) In a resistive circuit, current and voltages are in phase i.e. $\phi = 0$. In a capacitive or inductive circuit, current and voltages are 90° out of phase. In an L-C-R circuit, $\phi = \tan^{-1}\dfrac{X_L - X_C}{R}$.

When $X_L = 2X_C$ and $R = X_C$, then

$$\phi = \tan^{-1}\left[\frac{2X_C - X_C}{X_C}\right] = \tan^{-1}(1) = 45^\circ$$

Similarly, when $X_L = 2X_C$ and $R = \sqrt{3}X_C$, then $\phi = \tan^{-1}\dfrac{1}{\sqrt{3}} = 30^\circ$.

21. (*a*) At very high frequencies,

$$X_L = 2\pi f L = \infty$$

Here, inductor behaves like a open switch at very high frequency.

So, given circuit will be

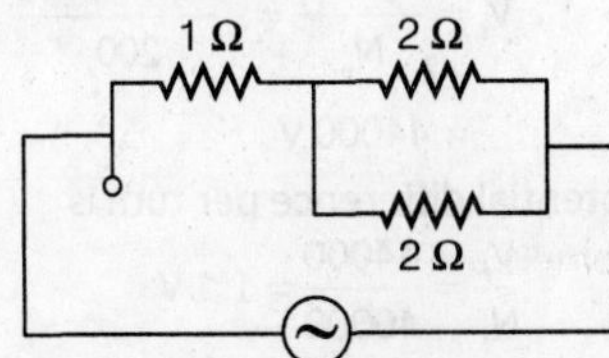

So, effective impedance

$$= [1\,\Omega \text{ in series with } (2\Omega \,||\, 2\Omega)]$$

$$= 2\,\Omega$$

22. (*c*) At $t = 0$, inductor is open circuited,

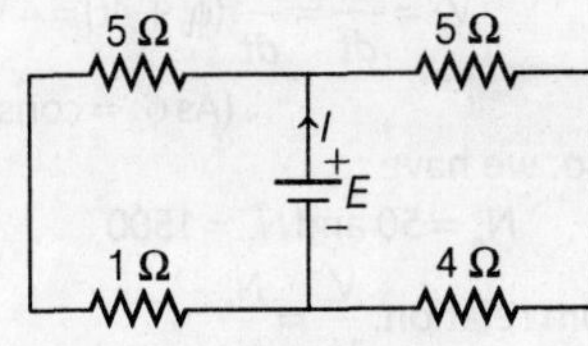

So, $\quad I_1 = \dfrac{E}{R_{eq}} = \dfrac{5}{18}E$

At $t = \infty$, inductor is short circuited,

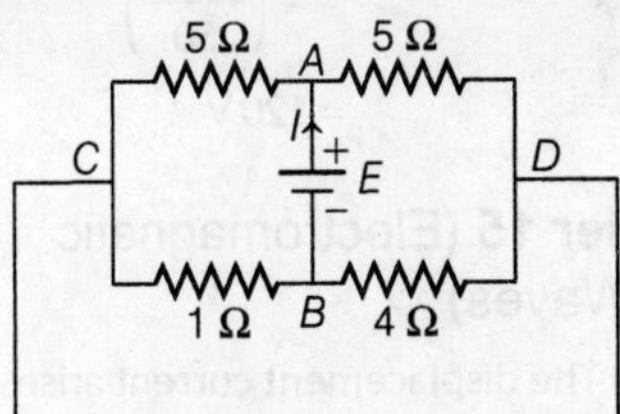

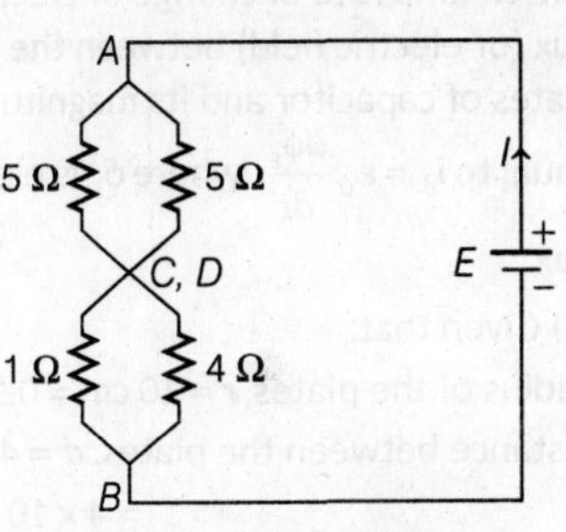

So, $\quad I_2 = \dfrac{E}{\left(\dfrac{33}{10}\right)} = \dfrac{10E}{33}$

Ratio $\frac{I_1}{I_2}=\frac{5/18}{10/33}=\frac{33\times 5}{10\times 18}=\frac{33}{36}$

23. (*a*) Flux $=BA=(a+bt)(\pi r^2)$

Flux at $t=0$ is $=a\pi r^2$

Induced emf, $\varepsilon=\frac{-d\phi_B}{dt}=-\pi br^2$

Induced current, $I=\frac{\varepsilon}{R}=\frac{-\pi br^2}{R}$

Power dissipated, $P=\varepsilon I=\frac{\pi^2b^2r^4}{R}$

24. (*a*) From transformer ratio,

$$\frac{V_s}{V_p}=\frac{N_s}{N_p}$$

$\Rightarrow$ $V_s=\frac{V_p\times N_s}{N_p}=\frac{220\times 40000}{200}$

$=44000$ V

Potential difference per turn is

$\frac{V_s}{N_s}=\frac{44000}{40000}=1.1$ V

25. (*b*) The magnetic flux linked with the primary coil is given by

$$\phi=\phi_0+4t$$

So, voltage across primary coil,

$$V_p=\frac{d\phi}{dt}=\frac{d}{dt}(\phi_0+4t)=4\text{ V}$$

(As $\phi_0=$ constant)

Also, we have

$N_p=50$ and $N_s=1500$

From relation, $\frac{V_s}{V_p}=\frac{N_s}{N_p}$

$\Rightarrow$ $V_s=V_p\frac{N_s}{N_p}$

$=4\left(\frac{1500}{50}\right)$

$=120$ V

Qualifier 15 (Electromagnetic Waves)

1. (*a*) The displacement current arises due to time rate of change of electric flux (or electric field) between the two plates of capacitor and its magnitude is equal to $i_d=\varepsilon_0\frac{d\phi_E}{dt}$, where ϕ_E is electric flux.

2. (*b*) Given that,

Radius of the plates, $r=10$ cm $=0.1$ m

Distance between the plates, $d=4$ cm $=4\times 10^{-2}$ m

Charging current, $i_c=0.2$ A

As we know that, during charging of a capacitor, the displacement current between the plates is equal to the conduction current in connecting wire. i.e.

Displacement current $(i_d)=$ Conduction current $(i_c)=0.2$ A

3. (*c*) As given,

Area of each plate, $A=10^{-12}\text{m}^2$

Displacement current, $i_d=15$ A

The displacement current across the plates,

$i_d=\varepsilon_0\frac{d\phi_E}{dt}$, where, ϕ_E is electric flux

$=\varepsilon_0\frac{d}{dt}(EA)$ $[\because \phi=\mathbf{E}\cdot\mathbf{A}=EA\cos\theta$

Here, $\theta=0°\Rightarrow\phi=EA]$

$$i_d=\varepsilon_0 A\frac{dE}{dt}$$

or $\frac{dE}{dt}=\frac{I_d}{\varepsilon_0 A}$

On putting the values of I_d, A and ε_0 in the above equation, we get

$$\frac{dE}{dt}=\frac{15}{8.85\times 10^{-12}\times 10^{-2}}$$

$=1.69\times 10^{14}$ V/m

4. (*a*) Given that,

Side, $a=8$ cm $=8\times 10^{-2}$ m

Distance, $d=2$ cm $=2\times 10^{-2}$ m

Charging current, $i=0.5$ A

Area of each conducting plate, $A=a^2$

$A=(8\times 10^{-2})^2$

$A=64\times 10^{-4}\text{m}^2$

As, capacitance, $C=\frac{\varepsilon_0 A}{d}$

Substituting the given values, we get

$$C=\frac{8.85\times 10^{-12}\times 64\times 10^{-4}}{2\times 10^{-2}}$$

or $C=2.832\times 10^{-12}$ F

Charging current, $i=\frac{dq}{dt}$

$$i=\frac{d}{dt}(CV)$$

$$i=C\frac{dV}{dt}$$

or $\frac{dV}{dt}=\frac{i}{C}=\frac{0.5}{2.832\times 10^{-12}}$

$\frac{dV}{dt}=17.65\times 10^{10}$ V/s

5. (*b*) The correct match is given as

A → S, B → R, C → Q, D → P

According to Gauss's law,

$$\oint\mathbf{E}\cdot d\mathbf{S}=\oint_s\frac{\rho}{\varepsilon_0}\cdot dS$$

$[\because E=\frac{\rho}{\varepsilon_0}$, $\rho=$ surface charge density]

According to Faraday's law of electromagnetic induction,

$$\oint\mathbf{E}\cdot d\mathbf{l}=\frac{-d\phi}{dt}=\frac{-d}{dt}\oint_s\mathbf{B}\cdot d\mathbf{S}$$

$\therefore$ $\phi=\oint\mathbf{B}\cdot d\mathbf{S}$

According to Ampere-Maxwell's law,

$$\oint\mathbf{B}\cdot d\mathbf{l}=\mu_0\left(I+\varepsilon_0\frac{d\phi_E}{dt}\right)$$

According to Ampere's circuital law,

$$\oint\mathbf{B}\cdot d\mathbf{l}=\mu_0 I$$

6. (*a*) The angular frequency of produced EM wave,

$$\omega=\frac{1}{\sqrt{LC}}=\frac{1}{\sqrt{5\times 10^{-4}\times 8\times 10^{-11}}}$$

$=5\times 10^{7}$ rad/s

7. (*d*) The speed of EM wave in a medium is given by

$$v=\frac{c}{\sqrt{\mu_r\varepsilon_r}}\quad\text{... (i)}$$

where, μ_r and ε_r are relative permeability and relative permittivity of the medium, respectively

From Eq. (i), we get $v^2=\frac{c^2}{\mu_r\varepsilon_r}$

So, $\varepsilon_r=\frac{c^2}{v^2\mu_r}=\frac{(3\times 10^8)^2}{(6\times 10^7)^2\times 5}$

$\varepsilon_r=5$

8. (*b*) An oscillating charged particle of the frequency *f* produces an oscillating electric field and magnetic field of same frequency *f*.

$\therefore$ Frequency of produced EM wave,

$f=2\times 10^{10}$ Hz

Wavelength, $\lambda=\frac{c}{f}=\frac{3\times 10^8}{2\times 10^{10}}$

$=1.5\times 10^{-2}$ m

$\lambda=1.5$ cm

This wavelength lies in microwave region.

9. (*c*) Given that, $E=E_0\sin(px+qt)$

and $B=B_0\sin(px+qt)$

Speed of wave, $v=\dfrac{\text{Coefficient of } t}{\text{Coefficient of } \omega}$

$$v=\frac{q}{p} \quad \text{... (i)}$$

Also, $$v=\frac{E_0}{B_0} \quad \text{... (ii)}$$

On equating both Eqs. (i) and (ii), we get

$$\frac{q}{p}=\frac{E_0}{B_0}$$

or $$pE_0=qB_0 \quad \text{...(i)}$$

Also, $E_{rms}=\dfrac{E_0}{\sqrt{2}}$ and $B_{rms}=\dfrac{B_0}{\sqrt{2}}$ ...(ii)

From Eqs. (i) and (ii), we get

$$p\times\sqrt{2}\,E_{rms}=q\times\sqrt{2}\,B_{rms}$$

or $pE_{rms}=qB_{rms}$

10. (*c*) As we know, magnitude of magnetic field, $B=\dfrac{|\mathbf{E}|}{c}$

Substituting the given values, we get

$$B=\frac{8}{3\times10^8}$$

$$B=2.33\times10^{-8}\text{T}$$

If the direction of magnetic field is $\hat{\mathbf{n}}$, then direction of propagation of wave is along $\hat{\mathbf{E}}\times\hat{\mathbf{B}}$

$$\hat{\mathbf{j}}=\hat{\mathbf{k}}\times\hat{\mathbf{n}}$$

$$\Rightarrow \quad \hat{\mathbf{n}}=\hat{\mathbf{i}} \qquad [\because \hat{\mathbf{k}}\times\hat{\mathbf{i}}=\hat{\mathbf{j}}]$$

$\therefore$ Magnetic field, $\mathbf{B}=2.33\times10^{-8}\,\hat{\mathbf{i}}$ T

11. (*c*) Given, equation of magnetic field,

$B_x=6\times10^{-8}\sin(2\times10^3y-3\times10^{10}t)$ T

The coefficient of y and t are of opposite nature and phase contains term y. Therefore, EM wave is propagating in $+y$ direction.

If amplitude of electric field is E_0, so we can write

$$E_0=B_0c$$

where, B_0 is the amplitude of magnetic field and c is the speed of light in vacuum.

$$\Rightarrow \quad E_0=6\times10^{-8}\times3\times10^8$$

$$E_0=18\text{ V/m}$$

As we know, in an EM wave, the phase of electric field and magnetic field component are same, therefore

$E=18\sin(2\times10^3y-3\times10^{10}t)$ V/m

12. (*c*) Speed of EM wave is given by

$$v=\frac{\omega}{k}$$

As electric field in air is

$$E_1=E_{01}\sin\left[\frac{\pi v x}{c}-\pi v t\right]$$

$\therefore$ Speed in air $=\dfrac{\pi v}{\left(\dfrac{\pi v}{c}\right)}=c=\dfrac{1}{\sqrt{\mu_0\varepsilon_0}}$ ... (i)

Also, speed in medium,

$$v=\frac{1}{\sqrt{\mu_0\mu_r\varepsilon_r\varepsilon_0}} \quad \text{... (ii)}$$

where, μ_r and ε_r are the relative permeability and relative permittivity of the medium, respectively.

In medium,

$$E_2=E_{02}\sin[k(2x-ct)]$$

$\therefore$ Speed in medium $=\dfrac{kc}{2k}=\dfrac{c}{2}$

Also, $$\frac{c}{2}=\frac{1}{\sqrt{\mu_0\mu_r\varepsilon_r\varepsilon_0}} \quad \text{... (iii)}$$

As the medium is non-magnetic medium

$\therefore \quad \mu_{medium}=\mu_{air}$ or $\mu_r=1$

From Eq (iii), $$\frac{c}{2}=\frac{1}{\sqrt{\mu_0\varepsilon_r\varepsilon_0}} \quad \text{... (iv)}$$

On dividing Eqs. (i) and (iv), we get

$$2=\sqrt{\varepsilon_r}$$

or $$\varepsilon_r=4$$

13. (*a*) Given, equation,

$$E_y=200\sin\omega\left(t-\frac{x}{c}\right)\text{V/m}$$

Amplitude of electric field,

$$E_0=200\text{ V/m}$$

As, amplitude of magnetic field, $B_0=\dfrac{E_0}{c}$

$$=\frac{200}{3\times10^8} \qquad (\because c=3\times10^8\text{ m/s})$$

$$B_0=6.67\times10^{-7}\text{ T}$$

Maximum magnetic force, $F_{B\max}=B_0qv$

Here, $q=2\mu\text{C}=2\times10^{-6}$ C, $v=400$ m/s

Substituting the given values, we get

$$\Rightarrow F_{B\max}=6.67\times10^{-7}\times2\times10^{-6}\times400$$

$$F_{B\max}=5.33\times10^{-10}\text{ N}$$

14. (*c*) When a wave is reflected from denser medium, the type of wave does not change but only its phase changes by 180° or π radian.

Thus, for the reflected wave, $\hat{\mathbf{i}}=-\hat{\mathbf{i}}$ and $\hat{\mathbf{k}}=-\hat{\mathbf{k}}$ and additional phase of π in the incident wave.

Thus, reflected wave is given as

$$\mathbf{E}_r=(-\hat{\mathbf{k}})\,40\cos[k(-x)-6\times10^8t+\pi]$$

$$=-\hat{\mathbf{k}}\,40\cos[\pi-(kx+6\times10^8t)]$$

$$=-\hat{\mathbf{k}}\,40[(-\cos(kx+6\times10^8t)]$$

$$[\because \cos(\pi-\theta)=-\cos\theta]$$

$$=\hat{\mathbf{k}}\,40\cos(kx+6\times10^8t)\text{ V/m}$$

15. (*d*) From option (d),

$$\mathbf{a}\cdot\mathbf{B}=(\hat{\mathbf{i}}-2\hat{\mathbf{j}}+5\hat{\mathbf{k}})\cdot(7\hat{\mathbf{i}}+16\hat{\mathbf{j}}+5\hat{\mathbf{k}})$$

$$=1\times7+(-2)\times16+5\times5=0$$

and $$\mathbf{b}\cdot\mathbf{B}=(3\hat{\mathbf{i}}-\hat{\mathbf{j}}-\hat{\mathbf{k}})\cdot(7\hat{\mathbf{i}}+16\hat{\mathbf{j}}+5\hat{\mathbf{k}})$$

$$=3\times7+(-1)\times16+(-1)\times5=0$$

Thus, the direction of magnetic field given in option (d) is correct.

16. (*a*) The wavelength of an EM wave,

$$\lambda=\frac{c}{v} \quad \text{... (i)}$$

where, c is speed of wave in vacuum and v is speed of wave in medium.

As we know that, speed of wave in a medium is always less than its speed in vacuum

$$v<c \text{ or } \frac{c}{v}>1$$

From Eq. (i), $\lambda>1$ m

17. (*d*) Given that,

Amplitude of electric field, $E_0=80$ N/C

Frequency, $f=30$ MHz or 30×10^6 Hz

As, electromagnetic wave is travelling in positive x-direction.

So, we can write, the general equation of magnetic field of wave as

$$B=B_0\sin(\omega t-kx) \quad \text{... (i)}$$

where, B_0 is amplitude of magnetic field,

and k is wave constant ω is angular frequency.

$$\because \quad B_0=\frac{E_0}{c}=\frac{80}{3\times10^8}$$

$$=2.67\times10^{-7}\text{T}$$

and $$\omega=2\pi f$$

$$=2\pi\times30\times10^6$$

$$=6\pi\times10^7\text{ rad/s}$$

and $$k=\frac{\omega}{c}$$

$$k=\frac{6\pi\times10^7}{3\times10^8}=0.6\text{ m}^{-1}$$

Substituting the values of B_0, ω and k in Eq. (i), we get

$$B=2.67\times10^{-7}\sin\{6\pi\times10^7(\text{rad/s})t-0.6(\text{m}^{-1})x\}\text{ T}$$

18. (*b*) Given electric field equation,

$$E(x,t)=0.1\sin\pi(3\times10^4x-7.5\times10^{14}t)\text{ V/m}$$

On comparing with standard equation of electric field of EM wave, we get

$$\omega=7.5\times10^{14}\text{ rad/s}$$

$$k=3\times10^4\text{ cm}^{-1}$$

or $$3\times10^6\text{ m}^{-1}$$

The speed of wave in medium, $v = \frac{\omega}{k}$

$$= \frac{7.5 \times 10^{14}}{3 \times 10^{6}}$$

$$v = 2.5 \times 10^8 \text{ m/s}$$

From the definition of refractive index,

$$\mu = \frac{c}{v} = \frac{3 \times 10^8}{2.5 \times 10^8} \quad [\because c = 3 \times 10^8 \text{ m/s}]$$

$$= 1.2$$

19. (*b*) A point source radiates light in all directions uniformly as spheres.

At a distance of 3 m, the surface area of the surrounding sphere is $A = 4\pi r^2$

$$= 4\pi(3)^2$$

$$\Rightarrow \quad A = 113.04 \text{ m}^2$$

Then, intensity of the bulb/source at 3 m is

$$I = \frac{\text{Power } (P)}{\text{Area } (A)} = \frac{60 \times 0.05}{113.04}$$

[$\because$ Given, useful power $P = 5\%$ of 60 W $= 0.05 \times 60$ W]

$$\Rightarrow \quad I = 0.0265 \text{ W/m}^2 \quad \text{... (i)}$$

As, the total intensity is the sum of individual intensity of electric field and magnetic field. Since, both the field intensities are equal in magnitude, so the electric field intensity

$$I_E = \frac{\text{Total Intensity}}{2}$$

$$\Rightarrow \frac{1}{2}\varepsilon_0 E_{\text{rms}}^2 c = \frac{0.0265}{2} \quad [\because \text{Using Eq (i)}]$$

or $\quad E_{\text{rms}} = \sqrt{\dfrac{0.0265}{\varepsilon_0 \times c}}$

$$= \sqrt{\frac{0.0265}{8.85 \times 10^{-12} \times 3 \times 10^8}}$$

$$= 3.16 \text{ V/m.}$$

Maximum value of electric field,

$$E_m = \sqrt{2} \times E_{\text{rms}}$$

$$= \sqrt{2} \times 3.16$$

$$= 4.46 \text{ V/m}$$

20. (*c*) Given that,

Intensity, $I = 5.9 \times 10^{-4}$ W/m^2

Speed of light, $c = 3 \times 10^8$ m/s

The intensity in EM wave due to its electric field component is half of total intensity.

i.e., $I_E = \frac{I}{2}$

$\because I_E = \frac{1}{2}\varepsilon_0 E^2 c$, where E is rms value of electric field

or $\quad \frac{I}{2} = \frac{1}{2}\varepsilon_0 E^2 c \quad$ or $E = \sqrt{\frac{I}{\varepsilon_0 c}}$

Substituting the given values, we get

$$E = \sqrt{\frac{5.9 \times 10^{-4}}{8.85 \times 10^{-12} \times 3 \times 10^8}}$$

$$= 0.471 \text{ V/m}$$

21. (*c*) Electric and magnetic field component of electromagnetic wave, both vibrates perpendicular to each other and also perpendicular to the direction propagation of electromagnetic wave.

Since, electromagnetic wave carries both energy and radiation pressure, hence it exerts radiation pressure.

22. (*c*) Given expression of electromagnetic wave,

$$\mathbf{E} = E_0 \hat{\mathbf{n}} \sin[\omega t + (6y - 8z)] \quad \text{... (i)}$$

$$\Rightarrow \mathbf{E} = E_0 \hat{\mathbf{n}} \sin[\omega t - (8z - 6y)] \quad \text{... (ii)}$$

Comparing Eq. (ii) with Eq. (i), we get

$$\mathbf{k} \cdot \hat{\mathbf{r}} = 8z - 6y \quad \text{... (iii)}$$

Here, $\hat{\mathbf{r}} = x\hat{\mathbf{i}} + y\hat{\mathbf{j}} + z\hat{\mathbf{k}}$

and $\mathbf{k} = k_x \hat{\mathbf{i}} + k_y \hat{\mathbf{j}} + k_z \hat{\mathbf{k}}$

$$\therefore \quad \mathbf{k} \cdot \hat{\mathbf{r}} = xk_x + yk_y + zk_z \quad \text{... (iv)}$$

From Eqs. (iii) and (iv), we get

$xk_x = \text{zero} \Rightarrow k_x = 0$

$$yk_y = -6y$$

$$\Rightarrow \quad k_y = -6$$

$$zk_z = 8z$$

$$\Rightarrow \quad k_z = 8$$

Hence, $\mathbf{k} = -6\hat{\mathbf{j}} + 8\hat{\mathbf{k}}$

So, direction of propagation

$$\hat{\mathbf{s}} = \hat{\mathbf{k}} = \frac{\mathbf{k}}{|k|}$$

$$= \frac{-6\hat{\mathbf{j}} + 8\hat{\mathbf{k}}}{\sqrt{6^2 + 8^2}}$$

$$= \frac{-6\hat{\mathbf{j}} + 8\hat{\mathbf{k}}}{10}$$

$$= \frac{-3\hat{\mathbf{j}} + 4\hat{\mathbf{k}}}{5}$$

23. (*b*) Water molecules resonates at about 3 GHz and oscillation energy is converted into heat warms up food.

24. (*c*) A. Microwaves have short wavelength than radiowaves and its application is found in measurement of speed of vehicle.

B. Ground wave propagation is a type of radio propagation which is also known as a surface wave propagation. These waves propagate over the earth's surface in low and medium frequencies. These wave have the tendency to bend around the corners or obstructions during propagation, which makes them more efficient and also, these are not affected by the change in atmospheric conditions for this purpose radiowaves are used.

C. From night vision goggles to heat seeking missiles, the military relies on infrared technology. In war zones, infrared light can also help save lives by detecting land mines and can be used to uncover evidence of war cranes. Thus, it is clear that infrared waves for military purpose.

D. Ultraviolet sterilization is the newest technology that uses short wavelength UV light to kill or inactivate viruses or bacteria by destroying nucleic acids and prevents harmful micro-organism sustainable.

The correct match code is

A $\rightarrow$ Q, B $\rightarrow$ P, C $\rightarrow$ S, D $\rightarrow$ R

25. (*a*) An electron experiences both electric and magnetic forces.

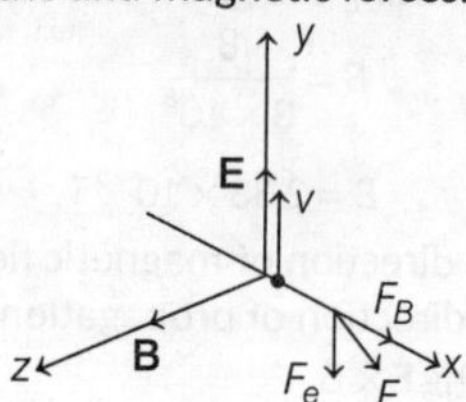

Magnetic force, $F_B = q(\mathbf{v} \times \mathbf{B})$

$$= qv\hat{\mathbf{j}} \times B\hat{\mathbf{k}} = qvB_0\hat{\mathbf{i}}$$

Electric force, $F_e = q\mathbf{E} = qE_0\hat{\mathbf{j}}$

As both electric and magnetic forces are perpendicular, total force,

$$F = \sqrt{F_B^2 + F_e^2}$$

Now given, $E_0 = 800$ V/m

$$B_0 = \frac{E_0}{c} = \frac{800}{3 \times 10^8} \text{ T}$$

Force magnitudes are,

$$F_e = qE_0 = (1.6 \times 10^{-19})(800)$$

$$= 1.28 \times 10^{-16} \text{ N}$$

and $\quad F_B = qvB_0$

$$= 1.6 \times 10^{-19} \times 3 \times 10^7 \times \frac{800}{3 \times 10^8}$$

$$= 1.6 \times 10^{-19} \times 80$$

$$= 1.28 \times 10^{-17} \text{ N}$$

So, total force is

$$F = \sqrt{F_e^2 + F_B^2}$$

$$= \sqrt{(1.28 \times 10^{-16})^2 + (1.28 \times 10^{-17})^2}$$

$$= 1.28 \times 10^{-17} \times \sqrt{100 + 1}$$

$$= \sqrt{101} \times 1.28 \times 10^{-17} \text{ N}$$

$$\approx 1.28 \times 10^{-16} \text{ N}$$

Qualifier 16. (Optics)

1. (*c*)

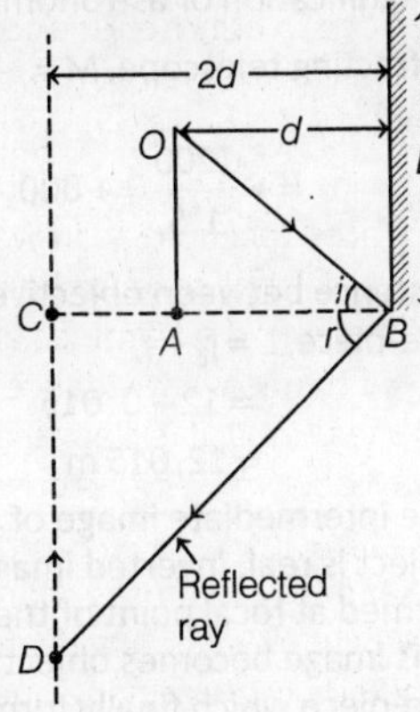

Here given, $AB = d$, $CB = 2d$, $AO = \frac{L}{2}$

In similar triangles ΔAOB and ΔCDB,

$$\frac{AB}{CB} = \frac{AO}{CD}$$

$$CD = \frac{AO \times CB}{AB}$$

$$= \frac{\frac{L}{2} \times 2d}{d}$$

$$\Rightarrow \quad L = 5\text{ m}$$

So, distance upto which image of bulb can be seen $= 5 + 5 = 10$ m

Time for which image can be observed

$$= \frac{\text{Distance}}{\text{Speed}} = \frac{10\text{ m}}{0.5\text{ m/s}}$$

$= 20$ s

2. (*a*) Both A and R are correct and R does not explains A.

To produce clear spectrum from prism, a wide angle prism is preferred because path length through the glass of the prism is greater, therefore spreading of different colours is greater.

Angular dispersion = Separation of extreme colours

$$\theta = (\mu_V - \mu_R)A$$

3. (*d*) As we know that, magnification,

$$m = -\frac{v}{u}$$

or $$m = \frac{-f}{u-f}$$

If the change in u and v are very small, then we can write

$$dv = -\frac{v^2}{u^2} \cdot du$$

$$dv = -\left(\frac{-f}{u-f}\right)^2 du \quad \text{...(i)}$$

Given that, $f = 4$ cm, $u = 6$ cm

$du = 1$ cm

On putting the values in Eq. (i), we get

$$dv = -\left(\frac{-4}{6-4}\right)^2 \times 1$$

$$dv = -4\text{ cm}$$

or $$|dv| = 4\text{ cm}$$

4. (*b*) As we know that,

$$\frac{\text{Real depth}(D_R)}{\text{Apparent depth}(D_A)} = \frac{\mu_2}{\mu_1}$$

or Real depth $= \frac{\mu_2}{\mu_1}$ (Apparent depth)

or change in $D_R = \frac{\mu_2}{\mu_1}$ (change in D_A)

$$\therefore \quad \Delta D_R = \frac{\mu_2}{\mu_1} \Delta D_A$$

Volume, $V = \pi R^2 D$

$$\Delta V_R = \frac{\mu_2}{\mu_1} \Delta V_A$$

or $$\frac{\Delta V_R}{\Delta t} = \frac{\mu_2}{\mu_1} \frac{\Delta V_A}{\Delta t}$$

$$\frac{\Delta V_R}{\Delta t} = \frac{\mu_2}{\mu_1} \cdot \pi R^2 \frac{\Delta D_A}{\Delta t}$$

Given that, drained out rate,

$$\frac{\Delta D_A}{\Delta t} = x\text{ cm/min}$$

$\therefore$ Amount of water drained,

$$\frac{\Delta V_R}{\Delta t} = \frac{\mu_2}{\mu_1} \cdot \pi R^2 \cdot x$$

5. (*a*) Let the maximum value of angle of incidence be θ, so that a ray of light can be propagated through the fibre as shown below.

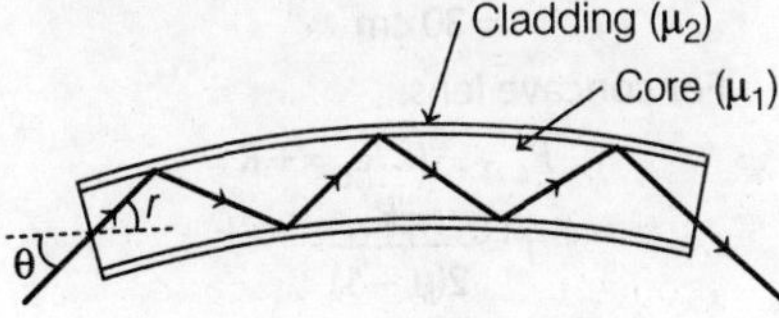

By Snell's law, $\frac{\sin\theta}{\sin r} = \mu_1$

or $$\sin\theta = \mu_1 \sin r \quad \text{...(i)}$$

From the geometry of the figure, angle of incidence

$$i = 90° - r$$

For total internal reflection taking place, $90° - r > C$.

Here, C is critical angle

or $\sin(90° - r) > \sin C$

$$\cos r > \frac{\mu_2}{\mu_1} \quad \text{...(ii)} \quad \left[\because C = \sin^{-1}\left(\frac{\mu_2}{\mu_1}\right)\right]$$

Using Eq. (i),

$$\sin\theta_{max} = \mu_1\sqrt{1 - \cos^2 r}$$

$$= \mu_1\sqrt{1 - \left(\frac{\mu_2}{\mu_1}\right)^2} \quad \text{[from Eq. (ii)]}$$

$$\sin\theta_{max} = \sqrt{\mu_1^2 - \mu_2^2}$$

or $$\theta_{max} = \sin^{-1}(\sqrt{\mu_1^2 - \mu_2^2})$$

6. (*b*) In the given case, the light gets refracted twice from air to ice at A and from ice to glass at B as shown below.

At A, air - ice interface

Applying Snell's law, $\frac{\sin i_1}{\sin r_1} = {}^{air}n_{ice} = \frac{n_{ice}}{n_{air}}$

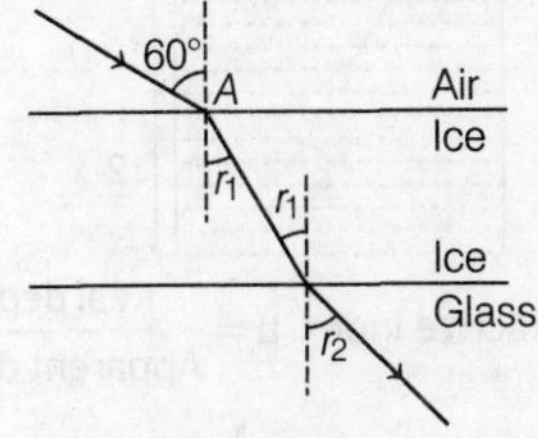

$$\Rightarrow \quad \frac{\sin 60°}{\sin r_1} = \frac{n_{ice}}{1} \quad \text{...(i)}$$

$$\Rightarrow \sin r_1 = \frac{\sin 60°}{n_{ice}} = \frac{\sqrt{3}/2}{4/3} = \frac{3\sqrt{3}}{8}$$

Similarly, at B, ice - glass interface

Applying Snell's law,

$$\frac{\sin r_1}{\sin r_2} = {}^{ice}n_{glass} = \frac{n_{glass}}{n_{ice}} \quad \text{...(ii)}$$

On multiplying Eqs. (i) and (ii), we get

$$\frac{\sin 60°}{\sin r_1} \times \frac{\sin r_1}{\sin r_2} = \frac{n_{ice}}{1} \times \frac{n_{glass}}{n_{ice}}$$

$$\Rightarrow \quad \frac{\sin 60°}{\sin r_2} = n_{glass}$$

$$\Rightarrow \quad \sin r_2 = \frac{\sin 60°}{n_{glass}} = \frac{\sqrt{3}/2}{3/2} = \frac{1}{\sqrt{3}}$$

Also, refractive index of ice w.r.t. glass,

$${}^{glass}n_{ice} = \frac{{}^{air}n_{ice}}{{}^{air}n_{glass}} = \frac{4/3}{3/2} = \frac{8}{9}$$

Hence, A → Q, B → P and C → R.

7. (*d*) Given that, focal length, $f = -40$ cm

(focal length of convex lens is negative)

Beam converges at point 20 cm. Without convex lens, it mean

$u = +20$ cm

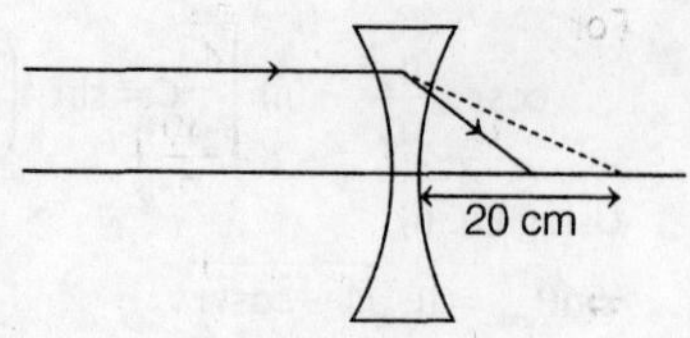

From lens formula, $\frac{1}{v}-\frac{1}{u}=\frac{1}{f}$

or $\frac{1}{v}=\frac{1}{u}+\frac{1}{f}$

$=\frac{1}{20}+\frac{1}{(-40)}$

$\frac{1}{v}=+\frac{1}{40}$, $v=40$ cm

8. (*d*) Suppose the bubble is at a distance *x* from the top face of the cube. We know that

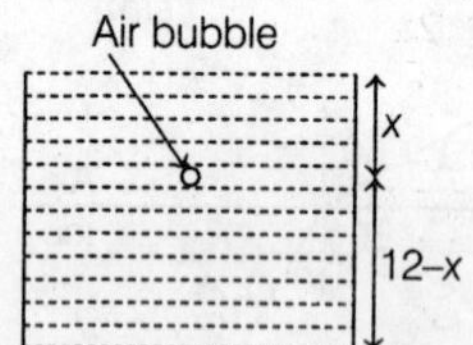

Refractive index, $\mu=\frac{\text{Real depth}}{\text{Apparent depth}}$

or $\mu=\frac{x}{3}$ ...(i)

and $\mu=\frac{12-x}{5}$ ...(ii)

On solving Eqs. (i) and (ii), we get

$x=\frac{9}{2}=4.5$ cm

Putting the value of *x* in Eq. (i), we get

$\mu=1.5$

9. (*b*) Suppose the object is placed at *O*, at a height *x* from the surface of the liquid. For the observer at the position of the mirror inside transparent liquid, the apparent distance of the object becomes $=\mu x+h$

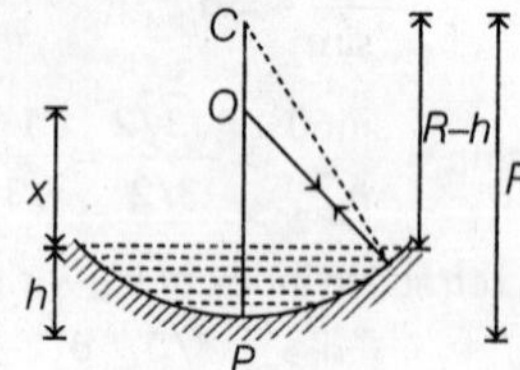

The image will form on the object itself when mirror forms virtual image at *C*. i.e. at a distance *R* from *P*. Thus,

$\mu x+h=R$

or $\mu=\frac{R-h}{x}$ ...(i)

Given that, $R=15$ cm, $h=3$ cm, $x=9$ cm.
On putting the value in Eq. (i), we get

$\mu=\frac{15-3}{9}=\frac{12}{9}$

$\mu=\frac{4}{3}=1.33$

10. (*c*) The ray is incident on face *AC* at an angle α. After reflection, it is incident on face *BC*, at an angle β. Thus,

$\angle\alpha+\angle\beta=90°$

As $\beta<\alpha$, so the ray if totally reflected from face *BC*, must be reflected from *AC*. Also for this angle, β should be greater than critical angle θ_c. For minimum value of μ, β can be infinitesimally than θ_c, So, $\beta=\theta_c$ (critical angle).

We know that, $\mu=\frac{1}{\sin\theta_c}=\frac{1}{\sin\beta}$ $[\because \theta_c=\beta]$

For $\alpha=\beta$, $\beta=45°$

$\therefore\ \mu_{min}=\frac{1}{\sin 45°}$

$=\frac{1}{1/\sqrt{2}}=\sqrt{2}$

11. (*b*) $\frac{1}{f}=(\mu-1)\left(\frac{1}{R_1}-\frac{1}{R_2}\right)$

For convex lens,

$R_1=R, R_2=-R$

$\therefore\ \frac{1}{f}=(\mu-1)\left(\frac{1}{R}-\frac{1}{(-R)}\right)$

$=\frac{(\mu-1)\times 2}{R}$

or $f=\frac{R}{2(\mu-1)}$

$=\frac{30}{2(1.5-1)}$

or $f=\frac{30}{2\times 0.5}$

$=30$ cm

For concave lens,

$R_1=-R, R_2=+R$

$\therefore\ f=\frac{-R}{2(\mu-1)}$

$=-30$ cm

For plano-convex lens,

$R_1=\infty, R_2=-R$

$\therefore\ f=\frac{R}{\mu-1}=60$ cm

For plano-concave lens,

$R_1=-R, R_2=\infty$

$\Rightarrow\ f=-60$ cm

12. (*c*) Given that, focal length of objective, $f_o=12$ m

Focal length of eye-piece, $f_e=1.5$ cm

Magnification of astronomical refracting telescope, $M=+\frac{f_o}{f_e}$

$=+\frac{1200}{1.5}=+800$

Distance between objective and eye-piece, $L=f_o+f_e$

$=12+0.015$

$=12.015$ m

The intermediate image of a distant object is real, inverted image and formed at focal point of the objective. This image becomes object for eye-piece which finally forms virtual and inverted image. Thus, statement given in option (c) is incorrect.

Objective lens is of large aperture or of focal length commonly 50 to 100 cm, while eye-piece is of small aperture or focal length commonly 2 to 5 cm.

13. (*b*) Given that, focal length of objective, $f_o=50$ cm

Focal length of eye-piece, $f_e=4$ cm

Magnification of simple telescope,

$M=\frac{f_o}{f_e}=\frac{50}{4}=12.5$

If α and β are the angles subtended by object and image, then we can write,

magnification, $M=\frac{\beta}{\alpha}$

Given, $\alpha=2°$

$\therefore\ 12.5=\frac{\beta}{2°}$

or $\beta=25°$

14. (*a*) Given that, focal length of objective, $f_o=4$ cm

Focal length of eye-piece, $f_e=5$ cm

Length of tube, $L=20$ cm

When the final image is formed at infinity, then $L=v_o+f_o=20$ cm

or $v_o+4=20$ cm

or $v_o=16$ cm

For objective lens, using lens equation

$\frac{1}{v_o}-\frac{1}{u_o}=\frac{1}{f_o}$

$\Rightarrow\ \frac{1}{16}-\frac{1}{u_o}=\frac{1}{4}$

$\Rightarrow\ \frac{1}{u_o}=\frac{1}{16}-\frac{1}{4}=\frac{1-4}{16}$

$\Rightarrow\ \frac{1}{u_o}=\frac{-3}{16}$

or $u_o=-\frac{16}{3}=-5.33$ cm

15. (*a*) The magnification of astronomical telescope is given by

$$m = -\frac{f_o}{f_e}\left(1+\frac{f_e}{D}\right)$$

where, f_o is focal length of objective, f_e is focal length of eye-piece and D is least distance of distinct vision.
From the formula, it is clear that, f_e should be least and f_o should be greatest.
Thus the correct values for the largest magnification, f_o and f_e should be +200 cm and +10 cm, respectively.

16. (*d*) As $I \propto A^2 \Rightarrow \frac{I_1}{I_2} = \left(\frac{A_1}{A_2}\right)^2 = \left(\frac{2}{1}\right)^2$

or $\frac{I_1}{I_2} = \frac{4}{1}$

$\Rightarrow \sqrt{\frac{I_1}{I_2}} = \frac{2}{1}$

Now, $I_{max} = (\sqrt{I_1}+\sqrt{I_2})^2 = I_2\left(\sqrt{\frac{I_1}{I_2}}+1\right)^2$

and $I_{min} = (\sqrt{I_1}-\sqrt{I_2})^2 = I_2\left(\sqrt{\frac{I_1}{I_2}}-1\right)^2$

So, $\frac{I_{max}-I_{min}}{I_{max}+I_{min}} = \frac{\frac{I_{max}}{I_{min}}-1}{\frac{I_{max}}{I_{min}}+1}$

$$= \frac{\left(\sqrt{\frac{I_1}{I_2}}+1\right)^2 - 1}{\left(\sqrt{\frac{I_1}{I_2}}-1\right)^2 + 1}$$

$$= \frac{(2+1)^2-1}{(2-1)^2+1} = \frac{8}{2} = \frac{4}{1}$$

17. (*c*) Angular width, $\theta = \frac{\lambda_0}{\mu d}$

If λ_0 and d are constants, then $\theta \propto \frac{1}{\mu}$

The above dependancy is similar to $y \propto \frac{1}{x}$, which have variation according to rectangular hyperbola. The variation between θ and μ can be shown as

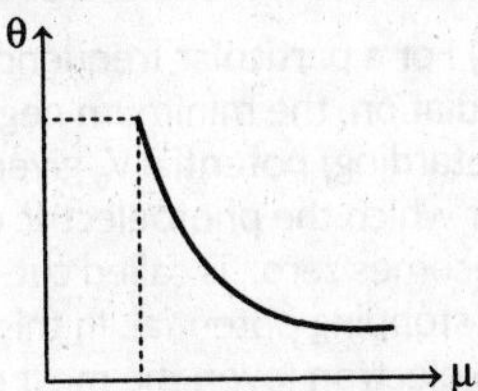

18. (*a*) Given that, $\lambda_1 = 5800\,Å$, $\lambda_2 = \lambda$ (Let)
The distance between consecutive dark fringes and bright fringes are same and equal to

$$\beta = \frac{\lambda D}{d} \quad ...(i)$$

So, $\beta_1 = 7.25$ mm
and $\beta_2 = 5.075$ mm
For a particular YDSE, d and D are same.
So, we can write from Eq. (i),

$$\beta \propto \lambda \quad \text{or} \quad \frac{\beta_1}{\beta_2} = \frac{\lambda_1}{\lambda_2}$$

or $\lambda_2 = \left(\frac{\beta_2}{\beta_1}\right)\lambda_1$

$= \left(\frac{5.075}{7.25}\right)\times 5800$

$\lambda_2 = 4060\,Å$

19. (*c*) Given that, distance between the slits, $d = 0.24$ mm or 0.24×10^{-3} m
Distance between screen to slits,

$D = 0.8$ m

The position of nth dark fringe from central point is given as

$$(y_n)_{dark} = \frac{(2n-1)\lambda D}{2d}$$

and the position of mth bright fringe from central point is given as

$$(y_m)_{bright} = \frac{m\lambda D}{d}$$

For $n = 9, m = 6$, i.e. distance between ninth dark fringe to sixth bright fringe,

$$\Delta y = (y_9)_{dark} - (y_6)_{bright}$$

$$\Delta y = \frac{(2n-1)\lambda D}{2d} - \frac{m\lambda D}{d}$$

$$\Delta y = \left[\left(n-\frac{1}{2}\right)-m\right]\frac{\lambda D}{d}$$

$$5.4\times10^{-3} = \frac{\left[\left(9-\frac{1}{2}\right)-6\right]\times\lambda\times0.8}{0.24\times10^{-3}}$$

$$5.4\times10^{-3} = \frac{2.5\times\lambda\times0.8}{0.24\times10^{-3}}$$

or $\lambda = 6480\,Å$

20. (*b*) The resultant intensity at a point P, where the phase difference between the light is $\Delta\phi$, can be expressed as

$$I_P = I_{max}\cos^2\left(\frac{\Delta\phi}{2}\right)$$

Here, $I_P = I = I_{max}\cos^2(\pi)$
$I = I_{max}$

For $I_P = \frac{I}{4}$ or $\frac{I_{max}}{4}$

$\frac{I_{max}}{4} = I_{max}\cos^2\left(\frac{\Delta\phi}{2}\right)$

$\Rightarrow \cos^2\left(\frac{\Delta\phi}{2}\right) = \frac{1}{4}$

$\Rightarrow \cos\left(\frac{\Delta\phi}{2}\right) = \pm\frac{1}{2}$

$\Rightarrow \cos\frac{\Delta\phi}{2} = \cos 60°$

or $\cos 120°$

$\frac{\Delta\phi}{2} = 60°$ or $120°$

$\Rightarrow \Delta\phi = 120°$ or $240°$

$\Rightarrow \Delta\phi = \frac{2\pi}{3}, \frac{4\pi}{3}$

If $\Delta\phi = \frac{2\pi}{3}$,

$\frac{\lambda}{2\pi}\times\Delta\phi = \frac{\lambda}{2\pi}\times\frac{2\pi}{3} = \frac{\lambda}{3}$

and if $\Delta\phi = \frac{4\pi}{3}$,

$\Delta x = \frac{\lambda}{2\pi}\times\Delta x = \frac{\lambda}{2\pi}\times\frac{4\pi}{3}$

$= \frac{2\lambda}{3}$

The correct values of path difference S are $\frac{\lambda}{3}$ and $\frac{2\lambda}{3}$.

21. (*b*) Given that, wavelength,
$\lambda = 6000\,Å$
$= 6\times10^{-7}$ m
Width of slit, $a = 0.24$ mm
or 2.4×10^{-4} m
Distance of slit to screen, $D = 1$ m
The width of central maxima is given as

$$\text{width} = \frac{2D\lambda}{a}$$

$$= \frac{2\times1\times6\times10^{-7}}{2.4\times10^{-4}}$$

$= 5\times10^{-3}$ m

width = 0.5 cm

The width of first secondary maxima is equal to half that of central maxima, i.e.

$$\Rightarrow \text{width}_{first} = \frac{(\text{width})_{central}}{2}$$

$$= \frac{0.5}{2} = 0.25 \text{ cm}$$

22. (*d*) The light intensity distribution for a single slit diffraction pattern at angle θ is expressed as

$$I = I_0\left[\frac{\sin\left(\frac{\pi a\sin\theta}{\lambda}\right)}{\left(\frac{\pi a\sin\theta}{\lambda}\right)}\right]^2$$

where, I_0 is at $\theta = 0$ (the central maximum)

a is width of slit

λ is wavelength of the light used

From above expression, we see that minima occurs when $\frac{\pi a\sin\theta}{\lambda} = m\pi$ or

$$\sin\theta = \frac{m\lambda}{a}$$

where $m = \pm 1, \pm 2, \pm 3.....$

For first secondary maxima, $m = 1$,

$$\sin\theta = \frac{\lambda}{a}$$

For second secondary maxima, $m = 2$,

$$\sin\theta = \frac{2\lambda}{a}$$

Thus, the graph between I and $\sin\theta$ can be plotted as

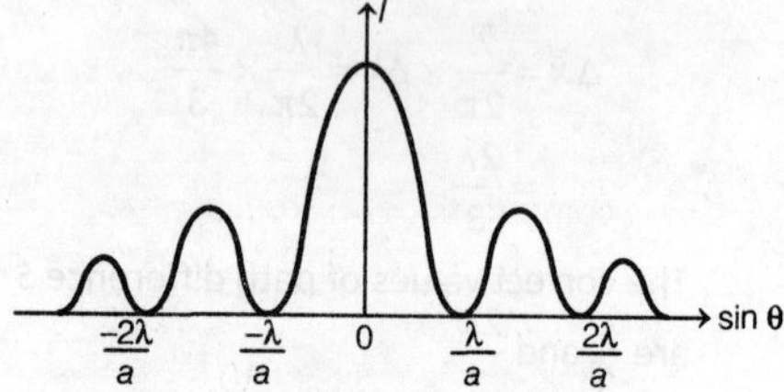

23. (*a*) Let the intensity of unpolarised beam $= I$

As we know that, when unpolarised light is passed through a polaroid P, the intensity of polarised light becomes $\frac{I}{2}$.

Case (i) When beam of intensity $\frac{I}{2}$ is placed through P_2, its intensity becomes,

$$I' = \left(\frac{I}{2}\right)\cos^2\phi$$

[$\because$ using Malus law]

where, ϕ is angle between P_1 and P_2.

According to question, no light is emitted from the second polaroid, i.e. $I' = 0$

$$\Rightarrow \quad \left(\frac{I}{2}\right)\cos^2\phi = 0$$

or $\quad \cos\phi = 0$

or $\quad \cos\phi = \cos 90°$

or $\quad \phi = 90°$

Case (ii) When a third identical polaroid whose polarisation axis makes an angle θ with the polarisation axis of first polaroid, is placed between these polaroids, then

Intensity of light when it is passed through P_2 becomes $\frac{I_0}{2}\cos^2\theta$.

Now, angle between P_2 and $P_3 = 90° - \theta$

So, $\quad I' = \left\{\left(\frac{I}{2}\right)\cos^2\theta\right\}\cos^2(90° - \theta)$

$$= \frac{I}{2}\cos^2\theta\sin^2\theta$$

$$= \frac{I}{2\times 4}(2\sin\theta\cos\theta)^2 = \frac{I}{8}\sin^2 2\theta$$

24. (*c*) The angle of polarisation (θ_p) is given as

$$\theta_p = \tan^{-1}(\mu)$$

For option (a)

$$\theta_p = \tan^{-1}\left(\frac{\sqrt{3}}{1}\right) = 60°$$

But incidence angle is 30°, so reflected and refracted rays are not perpendicular.

For option (b)

$$\theta_p = \tan^{-1}\left(\frac{4/3}{1}\right) = 53°$$

Again, incidence angle is not equal to angle of polarisation, so reflected and refracted rays are not perpendicular.

For option (c) From the figure

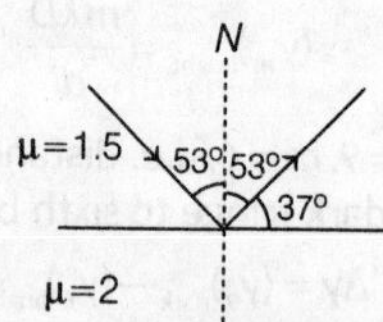

Angle of incidence $= 90° - 37° = 53°$

Angle of polarisation, $\theta_p = \tan^{-1}\left(\frac{\mu_2}{\mu_1}\right)$

$$= \tan^{-1}\left(\frac{2}{1.5}\right) = \tan^{-1}\left(\frac{4}{3}\right)$$

$$\theta_p = 53°$$

Here, angle of incidence = angle of polarisation

Hence, the angle between reflected ray and refracted ray is 90°.

For option (d) Incidence angle = 45°

Angle of polarisation, $\theta_p = \tan^{-1}(\sqrt{2})$

$$\theta_p = 54.74°$$

As the angle of incidence is not equal to angle of polarisation, so reflected ray and refracted ray will not be perpendicular.

25. (*b*) For sustained interference, the positions of maxima and minima of intensity on the observation screen do not change with time and interfering waves should be in the same sate of polarisation.

Qualifier 17 (Dual Nature of Matter and Radiation)

1. (*d*) Both A and R are correct and R is correct explanation of A.

$$2\pi r = \frac{nh}{p} = n\lambda$$

$$\Rightarrow \quad mvr = L = \frac{nh}{2\pi}$$

$$\therefore \quad L = \frac{h}{2\pi}, \frac{2h}{2\pi}, \frac{3h}{2\pi} ...\text{etc.}$$

2. (*d*) As saturation current for b and c is same

$$\therefore \quad I_b = I_c$$

Also, stopping potential for a and b is same, so $f_a = f_b$.

3. (*c*) We use,

$$eV_0 = k_{max} = hf - \phi_0$$

When f increases, V_0 increases also, k_{max} also increases. When ϕ_0 is decreased, then V_0 and k_{max} increases. When intensity of incident radiation is increased, then due to increasing the number of incident photons, more number of photoelectrons are emitted, hence saturation current increases. Photoelectric current does not depend on the distance of cathode and anode, hence no change occurs in voltmeter and ammeter readings.

4. (*c*) Wavelength of IR > 5200 Å and wavelength of UV < 5200 Å.

For photoemission, incident wavelength must be smaller than threshold wavelength.

5. (*d*) Low energy electrons lost due to collision from gas atoms in a photoelectric experiment.

Hence, photoelectric experiment is carried keeping cathode and anode in an evacuated glass tube. For photoelectric emission, frequency of incident radiation must be greater than or equal to threshold frequency.

6. (*d*) For a particular frequency of incident radiation, the minimum negative (retarding) potential V_0 given to plate A for which the photoelectric current becomes zero, is called cut-off potential or stopping potential. In this condition, no electron (even the most energetic electron) reaches to plate A.

7. (*d*) Given that, $1.5\,eV \le \phi \le 2.5\,eV$,

where, ϕ is work function of the metal.

Wavelength corresponding to minimum and maximum values of work function are

$$\lambda_{max} = \frac{hc}{\phi_{min}}$$

$$= \frac{6.62 \times 10^{-34} \times 3 \times 10^{8}}{1.5 \times 1.6 \times 10^{-19}}$$

$= 8.275 \times 10^{-7}$ m or 827.5 nm

Similarly, $\lambda_{min} = \dfrac{hc}{\phi_{max}}$

$$= \frac{6.62 \times 10^{-34} \times 3 \times 10^{8}}{2.5 \times 1.6 \times 10^{-19}}$$

$= 4.965 \times 10^{-7}$ or 496.5 nm

So, clearly, wavelength range would be $496.5\text{ nm} \le \lambda \le 827.5\text{ nm}$

The wavelength greater than 827.5 nm is not suitable for photoelectric effect.

8. (*b*) Force on a surface due to radiation is given as

$$F = \frac{P(1+\alpha)\cos\theta}{c} \quad \text{... (i)}$$

where, P is the power, θ is angle of incidence, c is speed of light and α is coefficient of reflection.

Power, $P = \dfrac{\text{Energy}}{\text{Time}} = \dfrac{N\left(\dfrac{hc}{\lambda}\right)}{t}$

$P = n\dfrac{hc}{\lambda}$, where n is number of photons incident per second.

From Eq. (i), $F = \dfrac{nhc(1+\alpha)\cos\theta}{\lambda\, c}$

$$F = \frac{nh}{\lambda}(1+\alpha)\cos\theta$$

or $\quad n = \dfrac{F\lambda}{h(1+\alpha)\cos 60°}$ ... (ii)

$[\because \theta = 60°]$

Here, $F = 10^{-6}$N, $\lambda = 600$ nm or 6×10^{-7} m

$h = 6.62 \times 10^{-34}$ J-s, $\alpha = 0.4$

Putting all the values in Eq. (ii), we get

$$n = \frac{10^{-6} \times 6 \times 10^{-7}}{6.62 \times 10^{-34} \times (1+0.4) \times \frac{1}{2}}$$

$= 1.29 \times 10^{21}$ photons per second

9. (*c*) From Einstein's photoelectric equation,

$$\phi = \phi_0 + eV_0$$

[here, V_0 = stopping potential]

$\Rightarrow \quad hf = \phi_0 + eV_0$ ... (i)

From graph, take point $B(5.5 \times 10^{14}$ Hz, 0 V)

On satisfying Eq. (i) with point B, we get

$$6.62 \times 10^{-34} \times 5.5 \times 10^{14} = \phi_0 + 1.6 \times 10^{-19} \times 0$$

$$36.41 \times 10^{-20} = \phi_0 + 0$$

$$\phi_0 = 36.41 \times 10^{-20}\text{ J}$$

$$= \frac{36.41 \times 10^{-20}}{1.6 \times 10^{-19}}\text{ eV}$$

$= 22.75 \times 10^{-1}$ eV

$= 2.275$ eV

$\simeq 2.27$ eV

10. (*b*) From Einstein's photoelectric equation,

$$KE_{max} = h\nu - \phi \quad \text{... (i)}$$

For case (i), $KE_{max} = 0.8$ eV

$\therefore \quad h\nu - \phi = 0.8$ ... (ii)

For case (ii), $KE_{max} = 1.2$ eV

and incident energy is increased by 40%, then

$h\nu' = h\nu + 40\%$ of $h\nu$

$= h\nu + 0.4h\nu$

$= 1.4h\nu$

From Eq. (i), we get

$1.4h\nu - \phi = 1.2$ ... (iii)

On solving Eqs. (ii) and (iii), we get

$$\phi = 0.2\text{ eV}$$

11. (*a*) Momentum, $p = \dfrac{h}{\dfrac{c}{f}}$

$$p = \frac{hf}{c}$$

or $\quad f = \dfrac{pc}{h}$ ... (i)

Here, $h = 6.62 \times 10^{-34}$ J-s

$c = 3 \times 10^{8}$ m/s,

$p = 1.65 \times 10^{-29}$ kg-ms^{-1}

Putting these values in Eq. (i), we get

$$f = \frac{1.65 \times 10^{-29} \times 3 \times 10^{8}}{6.62 \times 10^{-34}}$$

$= 7.47 \times 10^{12}$ Hz

12. (*d*) On comparing with standard equation of electromagnetic wave, $E = E_0 \sin(\omega t - kx)$, we get

$\omega = 1.5 \times 10^{15}$ rad/s

or $\quad f = \dfrac{\omega}{2\pi}$

$$= \frac{1.5 \times 10^{15}}{2 \times 3.14}$$

$= 2.355 \times 10^{14}$ Hz

Energy of photons, $E = hf$

$= 6.62 \times 10^{-34} \times 2.355 \times 10^{14}$

$= 15.59 \times 10^{-20}$ J

or $\quad = \dfrac{15.59 \times 10^{-20}}{1.6 \times 10^{-19}}$ eV

$(\because 1\text{ eV} = 1.6 \times 10^{-19}\text{ J})$

$= 0.974$ eV

Since, the energy of incident photon is less than minimum amount of energy to emit the electron from the metal surface (i.e., work function). Thus, no photoemission can take place and there will be no maximum kinetic energy associated with the particle.

13. (*c*) Energy of photon, $E = \dfrac{hc}{\lambda}$

Here, $h = 6.62 \times 10^{-34}$ J-s,

$c = 3 \times 10^{8}$ m/s,

$\lambda = 520$ nm or 520×10^{-9} m

$$\therefore \quad E = \frac{6.62 \times 10^{-34} \times 3 \times 10^{8}}{520 \times 10^{-9}}$$

$= 3.82 \times 10^{-19}$ J

or $\quad = \dfrac{3.82 \times 10^{-19}}{1.6 \times 10^{-19}}$ eV $= 2.387$ eV

$\because$ Momentum of photon, $p = mc$

or $\quad \dfrac{h}{\lambda} = mc \quad$ or $\quad m = \dfrac{h}{\lambda c}$

$$= \frac{6.62 \times 10^{-34}}{520 \times 10^{-9} \times 3 \times 10^{8}}$$

$m = 4.24 \times 10^{-36}$ kg

14. (*b*) Given, threshold frequency of A is given by

$\nu_{OA} = 5 \times 10^{14}$ Hz

and for B, $\nu_{OB} = 10 \times 10^{14}$ Hz

We know that, work function, $\phi = h\nu_0$

or $\phi \propto \nu_0$

So, from the graph given in the question

$$\frac{\phi_A}{\phi_B} = \frac{5 \times 10^{14}}{10 \times 10^{14}} = \frac{1}{2} < 1$$

$\Rightarrow \quad \phi_A < \phi_B$

As we know that, slope of stopping potential (V_s) and incident frequency (ν) graph is equal to $\dfrac{h}{e}$.

For metal A,

$$\text{slope} = \frac{h_A}{e} = \frac{3-0}{10 \times 10^{14} - 5 \times 10^{14}}$$

or $\quad h_A = \dfrac{3}{5 \times 10^{14}} \times e$ ... (i)

For metal B,

$$\text{slope} = \frac{h_B}{e} = \frac{3.5-0}{15 \times 10^{14} - 10 \times 10^{14}}$$

$$h_B = \frac{3.5}{5 \times 10^{14}} \times e \quad \text{... (ii)}$$

From Eqs. (i) and (ii), we get

$$h_A < h_B$$

Since, the value of h obtained from experiment for metals A and B is different. Hence, experiment is not consistent with theory.

15. (*b*) Given that, power, $P = 60$ W

Wavelength, $\lambda = 662$ nm or 6.62×10^{-7} m

Energy of a photon is given as

$$E = \frac{hc}{\lambda} = \frac{6.62 \times 10^{-34} \times 3 \times 10^{8}}{6.62 \times 10^{-7}}$$

$(\because$ Given, $h = 6.62 \times 10^{-34}$ J-s)

$$= 3 \times 10^{-19} \text{ J}$$

Let n be the rate at which the photons are incidenting to the sphere, then

$$n = \frac{\text{Energy radiated per second}}{\text{Energy of each photon}}$$

$$= \frac{\text{Power}}{\text{Energy on one photon}} = \frac{60}{3 \times 10^{-19}}$$

$$h = 2 \times 10^{20} \text{ photon/s}$$

16. (*c*) From the Einstein's photoelectric equation,

$E = \phi + eV$, where ϕ is work function and V cut-off voltage.

$$\because \quad E = h\nu$$

$$\therefore \quad h\nu = \phi + eV \quad \text{or} \quad eV = h\nu - \phi$$

or $$V = \frac{h\nu}{e} - \frac{\phi}{e}$$

Comparing the above equation with the general equation for straight line i.e. $y = mx + c$, it is clear that slope of cut-off voltage (V) and frequency (ν) graph is equal to $\frac{h}{e}$.

i.e., $$\text{Slope} = \frac{h}{e}$$

Given that, slope $= 4.13 \times 10^{-15}$

$$\Rightarrow \quad 4.13 \times 10^{-15} = \frac{h}{e}$$

or $$h = 4.13 \times 10^{-15} \times e$$

$$= 4.13 \times 10^{-15} \times 1.6 \times 10^{-19}$$

$$= 6.608 \times 10^{-34}$$

$$\simeq 6.61 \times 10^{-34} \text{ J-s}$$

17. (*c*) Photocell is a device which converts light energy into electrical energy.

18. (*d*) Given that, potential difference,

$$V = 41.4 \text{ kV} \quad \text{or} \quad V = 41.4 \times 10^{3} \text{ V}$$

Kinetic energy of electron which are accelerated through this potential difference,

Kinetic energy = Charge × potential difference

$$= 1.6 \times 10^{-19} \times 41.4 \times 10^{3}$$

$$= 66.24 \times 10^{-16} \text{ J}$$

When all energies of electron is converted in production of X-rays, the frequency will be maximum

i.e., frequency, $\nu = \frac{E}{h}$ $\quad (\because E = h\nu)$

$$= \frac{66.24 \times 10^{-16}}{6.62 \times 10^{-34}}$$

$$= 1 \times 10^{19} \text{ Hz}$$

19. (*d*) Given that, change in de-Broglie wavelength,

$\frac{\Delta\lambda}{\lambda} \times 100 = 0.25\%$ and change in momentum, $\Delta p = p$

The change in wavelength is very small, so we may replace the symbol Δ by d

$$\therefore \quad \frac{d\lambda}{\lambda} \times 100 = 0.25\%$$

or $$\frac{d\lambda}{\lambda} = \frac{0.25}{100} \quad \text{...(i)}$$

As we know that, momentum, $p = \frac{h}{\lambda}$

On differentiating above equation, we get

$$\frac{dp}{d\lambda} = -\frac{h}{\lambda^2}$$

$$\left(\because \frac{d}{dx}\left(\frac{1}{x}\right) = -\frac{1}{x^2}\right)$$

$$\frac{dp}{d\lambda} = -\frac{h}{\lambda} \cdot \frac{1}{\lambda}$$

or $$\frac{|dp|}{d\lambda} = \frac{h}{\lambda} \cdot \frac{1}{\lambda}$$

or $$|dp| = \frac{d\lambda}{\lambda} \cdot \frac{h}{\lambda}$$

or $$|dp| = \frac{d\lambda}{\lambda} \cdot p_i \quad (\text{As}, |dp| = \Delta p)$$

or $$p = \left(\frac{0.25}{100}\right) p_i \quad [\text{using Eq. (i)}]$$

or $$p_i = \frac{100}{0.25} p$$

or $$= 400p$$

20. (*b*) The de-Broglie wavelength of a charged particle of charge q and mass m accelerated through a potential difference V is given as

$$\lambda = \frac{h}{\sqrt{2\,qVm}},$$

where, h is Planck's constant.

A. For helium ion, $q = 1.6 \times 10^{-19}$ C and $m = 4 \times 1.67 \times 10^{-27}$ kg

$$\therefore \lambda_{He^+} = \frac{6.62 \times 10^{-34}}{\sqrt{2 \times (1.6 \times 10^{-19}) \times 64 \times (4 \times 1.6 \times 10^{-27})}}$$

$$= 0.0178 \text{ Å}$$

B. For deutron ion, $q = 1.6 \times 10^{-19}$,

$$m = 2 \times 1.67 \times 10^{-27} \text{ kg}$$

$$\therefore \lambda_{H^+} = \frac{6.62 \times 10^{-34}}{\sqrt{2 \times (1.6 \times 10^{-19}) \times 64 \times (2 \times 1.67 \times 10^{-27})}}$$

$$= 0.02525 \text{ Å}$$

C. For α-particle (He^{++})

$$m = 4 \times 1.67 \times 10^{-27}$$

$$q = 2 \times 1.6 \times 10^{-19} \text{ C}$$

$$\therefore \lambda_\alpha = \frac{6.62 \times 10^{-34}}{\sqrt{2 \times 2 \times 1.6 \times 10^{-19} \times 64 \times 4 \times 1.67 \times 10^{-27}}}$$

$$= 0.0126 \times 10^{-10} \text{ m}$$

$$= 0.0126 \text{ Å}$$

21. (*b*) Initially,

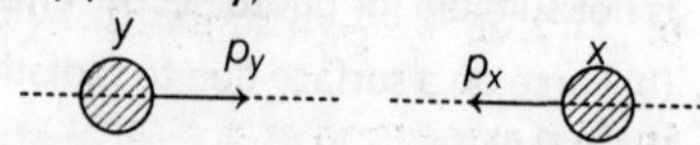

We have, de-Broglie wavelengths associated with particles are

$$\lambda_x = \frac{h}{p_x} \text{ and } \lambda_y = \frac{h}{p_y}$$

$$\Rightarrow \quad p_x = \frac{h}{\lambda_x} \text{ and } p_y = \frac{h}{\lambda_y}$$

Finally, particles collided to form a single particle.

As we know that, linear momentum is conserved in collision.

So, $\mathbf{p}_p = |\mathbf{p}_x - \mathbf{p}_y| \Rightarrow \mathbf{p}_p = \left|\frac{h}{\lambda_x} - \frac{h}{\lambda_y}\right|$

So, de-Broglie wavelength of combined particle is

$$\lambda_p = \frac{h}{|\mathbf{p}_p|} = \frac{h}{\left|\frac{h}{\lambda_x} - \frac{h}{\lambda_y}\right|} = \frac{h}{\left|\frac{h\lambda_y - h\lambda_x}{\lambda_x\lambda_y}\right|}$$

$$= \frac{\lambda_x\lambda_y}{|\lambda_x - \lambda_y|}$$

22. (*c*) As we know that, de-Broglie wavelength.

$\lambda = \frac{h}{\sqrt{2mE}}$, where h is Planck's constant and E is the energy of the particle

or $$\lambda \propto \frac{1}{\sqrt{E}}$$

or $$\frac{\lambda_2}{\lambda_1} = \sqrt{\frac{E_1}{E_2}}$$

Substituting the given values, we get

$$\frac{0.6\times10^{-10}}{1.2\times10^{-10}}=\sqrt{\frac{E_1}{E_2}}$$

or $\sqrt{\frac{E_1}{E_2}}=\frac{1}{2}$

or $\frac{E_1}{E_2}=\frac{1}{4}$ or $E_2=4E_1$

Hence, added energy, $\Delta E=E_2-E_1$

$$=4E_1-E_1$$

$$\Delta E=3E_1$$

Percentage of energy,

$$\frac{\Delta E}{E_1}\times100=\frac{3E_1}{E_1}\times100=300\%$$

23. (*d*) The de-Broglie wavelength in terms of kinetic energy *E* of the particle is given as

$$\lambda=\frac{h}{\sqrt{2mE}} \text{ or } =\frac{h}{\sqrt{2m}\sqrt{E}}$$

or $\lambda\sqrt{E}=\frac{h}{\sqrt{2m}}=\text{constant}$ ...(i)

Eq. (i) is in the form of yx = constant, which is again the equation of a rectangular hyperbola.

∴ The graph between λ and $\sqrt{E}$ can be plotted as

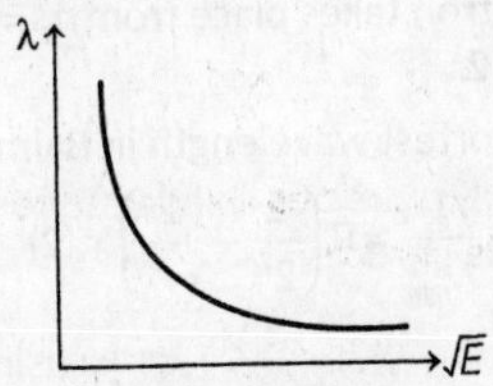

24. (*d*) Intensity of scattered beam of electrons was found to be maximum, when angle of scattering is 50°.

Here, $\theta+\phi+\theta=180°$, i.e. $\theta=65°$

($\because \phi=50°$)

25. (*a*) Given that, wavelength, $\lambda=1.2$ Å

Distance, $d=2.4$ Å

For second maxima, $n=2$

For N_1 crystal, by using Bragg's equation, we can write

$$2d\sin\theta=n\lambda$$

$$2\times3\times\sin\theta=2\times1.5$$

$$\sin\theta=\frac{1}{2}$$

or $\theta=30°$

Qualifier 18 (Atoms and Nuclei)

1. (*a*) At distance of minimum separation, Kinetic Energy [KE] = Potential Energy [PE].

$$\Rightarrow \quad KE=\frac{k\,Ze\cdot2e}{r}$$

where, $k=9\times10^9$ N-m^{2}C^{-2}

$Z=79$, $e=1.6\times10^{-19}$ C

and $r=4\times10^{-14}$ m

or $KE=\frac{9\times10^9\times79\times2\times(1.6\times10^{-19})^2}{4\times10^{-14}}$ J

$$=\frac{9\times10^9\times79\times2\,(1.6\times10^{-19})^2}{4\times10^{-14}\times1.6\times10^{-19}} \text{ eV}$$

$$=5.68 \text{ MeV}$$

2. (*a*) In Bohr's model, there was a drawback about the Bohr's assumption regarding stationary orbits which is again of Heisenberg uncertainty principle. Also, this model only specifies the magnitude of angular momentum but nothing about its directions. Since, we know that, angular momentum is a vector quantity. Thus, Bohr's model does not give correct values of angular momentum of revolving electron.

3. (*d*) The total energy of an electron in hydrogen and hydrogen like atom is given as

$$E=-13.6\frac{Z^2}{n^2}$$

or $E\propto-\frac{Z^2}{n^2}$

where, *Z* is atomic number and *n* is principal quantum number. If *n* is increased, then *E* increases.

The time period of revolution of electron around nucleus is directly proportional to $\frac{n^3}{Z^2}$, i.e. $T\propto\frac{n^3}{Z^2}$

So, on increasing the value of *n*, time period increases.

The angular speed of electron around a nucleus is directly proportional to $\frac{Z^2}{n^3}$,

i.e. $\omega\propto\frac{Z^2}{n^3}$. So, if *n* is increased, then angular speed decreases.

4. (*b*) Given that, energy of electron in *n*th orbit is

$$E_n=\frac{-20}{n^2} \text{ eV}$$

For $n=1$, $E_1=-\frac{20}{(1)^2}=-20$ eV

For $n=2$, $E_2=-\frac{20}{(2)^2}=-5$ eV

For $n=3$, $E_3=\frac{-20}{(3)^2}=-2.22$ eV

For $n=4$, $E_4=\frac{-20}{(4)^2}=-1.25$ eV

As we know that, the potential difference through which an electron should be accelerated to acquire the value of excitation energy is the excitation potential.

For second excitation state, $n=3$

The energy required to reach the electron from $n=1$ to $n=3$ is

$$\Delta E=E_3-E_1$$

$$=-2.22-(-20)$$

$$=17.78 \text{ eV}$$

Thus, excitation potential,

$$V=\frac{\text{Energy difference}}{e}$$

$$=\frac{17.78}{e}\text{ eV}$$

$$=17.78 \text{ V}$$

5. (*b*) The potential energy of electron is given as

$$U_n=-27.2\times\frac{Z^2}{n^2}\text{ eV}$$

For He^+ ion first excited state, $Z=2$, $n=2$

$$U_2=-27.2\times\frac{2^2}{2^2}$$

$$=-27.2 \text{ eV}$$

If the potential energy of electron in He^+ ion in first excited state is to be zero, then we have to increase it by 27.2 eV. It implies that we have increased it by 27.2 eV in all states.

$\because \quad U_1=-27.2\times\frac{(2)^2}{(1)^2}$

$$=-108.8 \text{ eV}$$

Net potential energy,

$$U_1'=-108.8+27.2$$

$$=-81.6 \text{ eV}$$

Kinetic energy in ground state,

$$K_n=+13.6\times\frac{Z^2}{n^2}$$

For $n=1$, $K_1=13.6\times\frac{(2)^2}{(1)^2}$

$$K_1=54.4 \text{ eV}$$

Therefore, total energy,

$$E'=U_1'+K_1=-81.6+54.4$$

$$=-27.2 \text{ eV}$$

6. (*b*) For a hydrogen like monoelectronic species, the difference in energy is given as,

$$\Delta E=-13.6\left[\frac{1}{n^2}-\frac{1}{m^2}\right]Z^2\text{eV}$$

If electron is removed from its first excited state, then $n = \infty$ and $m = 2$

$$\therefore \quad \Delta E = -13.6\left[\frac{1}{\infty^2} - \frac{1}{2^2}\right]Z^2$$

$$\Delta E = 3.4\, Z^2 \text{eV}$$

Given that, $\Delta E = 30.6$ eV

$$30.6 \text{ eV} = 3.4\, Z^2 \text{eV}$$

or $\quad Z^2 = \frac{30.6}{3.4} = 9$

or $\quad Z = 3$

The radius is given as $r = 0.53 \times \frac{n^2}{Z}$ Å

Putting the values of n and Z in above expression, we get

$$r = 0.53 \times \frac{(2)^2}{3}$$

$$= 0.706 \text{ Å}$$

7. (*c*) As we know that, In Bohr model of the hydrogen atom.

Radius of orbit, $r \propto n^2$

Velocity of electron, $v \propto \frac{1}{n}$

Total energy of electron in orbit, $E \propto \frac{1}{n^2}$

Option (a), $v^2 r \propto \left(\frac{1}{n}\right)^2 (n^2)$

$$v^2 r \propto n^0$$

Option (b), $rE \propto (n^2)\left(\frac{1}{n^2}\right)$

$$rE \propto n^0$$

Option (c), $\frac{v}{E} \propto \frac{\left(\frac{1}{n}\right)}{\left(\frac{1}{n^2}\right)}$

$$\frac{v}{E} \propto n$$

Option (d), $\frac{r}{E} \propto \frac{n^2}{\left(\frac{1}{n^2}\right)}$

$$\frac{r}{E} \propto n^4$$

8. (*b*) In Paschen, Brackett and Pfund series, emission lies in infrared region.

Photons absorbed by a metal surface may give rise to photoemission.

Fast electron on scattering gives X-rays.

Proton decay is

$$_1^1n \rightarrow {}_1^0p + {}_{-1}\beta^0 + \nu$$

9. (*a*) For absorption spectrum, atom must be in ground state. The given energy level diagram is shown below.

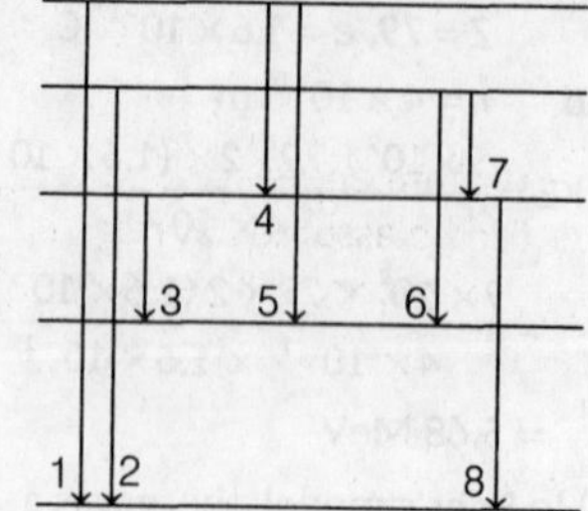

The spectral lines 3, 4, 5, 6, 7 will not occur in the absorption spectrum. They are the transitions from the higher excited energy state to lower excited energy state but not to the ground energy state. The transitions from the excited energy state to the ground energy state will occur in the absorption spectrum. Thus, lines 1, 4 and 8 will be in absorption spectrum.

10. (*c*) The minimum wavelength corresponding to the maximum energy of the X-rays is equal to the maximum kinetic energy qV or eV of the striking electrons. Thus,

$$\frac{hc}{\lambda_{min}} = eV \text{ or } \lambda_{min} = \frac{hc}{eV}$$

where, V is applied potential difference.

$$\Rightarrow \quad \lambda_{min} \propto \frac{1}{V}$$

$\therefore$ If V is decreased, then λ_{min} increases.

The variation of intensity of X-ray at various accelerating voltages applied to X-ray tube has been shown below.

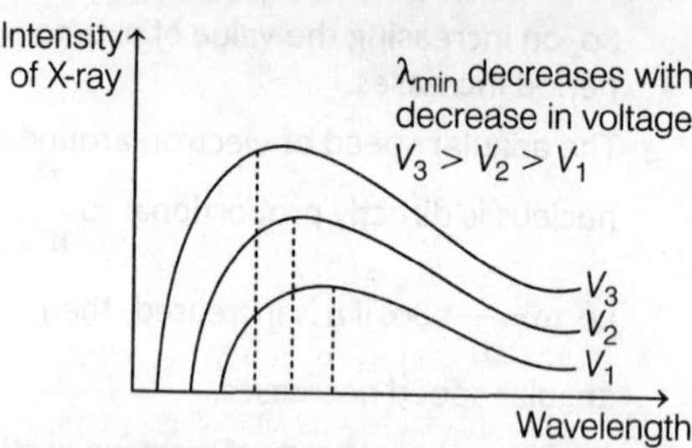

From the above graph, it is clear that the wavelengths at which the intensity is maximum, depends on the accelerating voltage. It is shorter for higher voltage and *vice-versa*.

11. (*b*) The frequency of proton emitted, when an electron makes a transition from orbit n to m is given by

$$\nu = Rc\left(\frac{1}{m^2} - \frac{1}{n^2}\right) \quad \text{... (i)}$$

When the transition takes place from $n = 4$ to $m = 3$, the frequency of Paschen series will be minimum.

$$\therefore \quad (\nu_P)_{min} = Rc\left(\frac{1}{3^2} - \frac{1}{4^2}\right) \quad \text{... (ii)}$$

[$\because$ using Eq. (i)]

When the transition takes place from $n = 5$ to $m = 4$, the frequency of Brackett series will be minimum.

$$\therefore \quad (\nu_B)_{min} = Rc\left(\frac{1}{4^2} - \frac{1}{5^2}\right) \quad \text{... (iii)}$$

[$\because$ using Eq. (i)]

On dividing Eq. (ii) by Eq. (iii), we get

$$\frac{(\nu_P)_{min}}{(\nu_B)_{min}} = \frac{\frac{1}{3^2} - \frac{1}{4^2}}{\frac{1}{4^2} - \frac{1}{5^2}}$$

or $\quad = \frac{175}{81}$

12. (*a*) Wavelength of photon emitted due to transition of electron is

$$\frac{1}{\lambda} = R\left(\frac{1}{n_1^2} - \frac{1}{n_2^2}\right)Z^2 \quad \text{... (i)}$$

For He^+ ion, $Z = 2$

In Balmer series, shortest wavelength is emitted when the transition of electron takes place from $n_2 = \infty$ to $n_1 = 2$.

$\therefore$ Shortest wavelength in Balmer series,

$$\frac{1}{\lambda_{min}} = R\left(\frac{1}{2^2} - \frac{1}{\infty^2}\right) \times (2)^2$$

[$\because$ using Eq. (i)]

or $\quad \frac{1}{\lambda_{min}} = R\left(\frac{1}{4} - 0\right) \times 4$

or $\quad \lambda_{min} = \frac{1}{R}$

13. (*c*) Given that, $m(p) = 1.007$ amu, $m(n) = 1.008$ amu

Binding energy per nucleon of $_{26}^{56}Fe = 8.6$ MeV

$\therefore$ Binding energy of nucleus of $_{26}^{56}Fe$,

$$BE = 8.6 \times 56$$

$$= 481.6 \text{ MeV}$$

The mass of a nucleus is given by

$$M(N, Z) = Nm_n + Zm_p - \frac{BE}{c^2}$$

For iron, $N = 30$, $Z = 26$, $m(30, 26)$

$$= \left[30 \times 1.008 + 26 \times 1.007 - \frac{481.6}{931.5}\right] \text{amu}$$

$$= (30.24 + 26.182 - 0.517) \text{ MeV}$$

$$M(30, 26) = 55.905 \text{ amu}$$

14. (*c*) A is false but R is true.
An electron can absorb energy greater than 13.6 eV.
Atom is then ionised and electron carries excess energy as kinetic energy.

15. (*d*) If N be the number of nuclei present in a radioactive substance at any instant t. Let dN be the number of nuclei that disintegrates in short interval dt.
Then, the rate of disintegration $-\frac{dN}{dt}$ is proportional to N

i.e., $\frac{dN}{dt} \propto N$

or $-\frac{dN}{dt} = \lambda N$

or $\frac{dN}{dt} = -\lambda N$

The above expression is similar to $y = mx$, which is the equation of a straight line passing through origin and having slope negative. So, the variation between $\frac{dN}{dt}$ *versus* N can be represented as

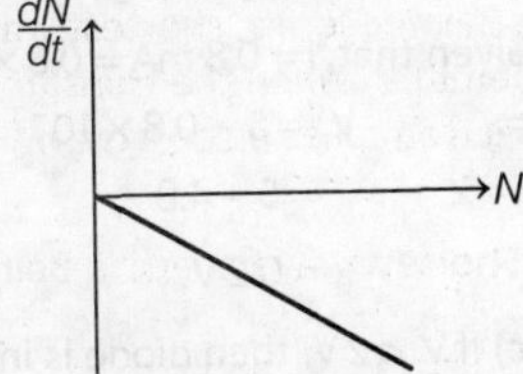

16. (*a*) In a nuclear reaction, atomic mass number and atomic number remains conserved.
For reaction I Let atomic mass number A and atomic number Z for X. So, we can write

$$6 + A = 7 + 1 \Rightarrow A = 2$$
$$3 + Z = 4 + 0 \Rightarrow Z = 1$$

$\therefore$ X is ${}^{2}_{1}H$.

For reaction II $35 + A = 32 + 4 \Rightarrow A = 1$
$17 + Z = 16 + 2 \Rightarrow Z = 1$
$\therefore$ Y is ${}^{1}_{1}H$

For reaction III $79 + 2 = A + 2 \times 1$
$\Rightarrow \quad A = 79$
$35 + 1 = Z + 2 \times 0$
$\Rightarrow \quad Z = 36$

$\therefore$ Z is ${}^{79}_{36}Kr$

17. (*b*) Given that, $m({}^{176}Lu) = 175.942694$ u
$m({}^{176}Hf) = 175.941420$ u

Mass defect,
$\Delta m = m({}^{176}Lu) - m({}^{176}Hf)$
$= 175.942694 - 175.941420$
$\Delta m = 0.001274$ u

Energy released, $\Delta E = \Delta m \times 931.5$ MeV
$= 0.001274 \times 931.5$
$= 1.182$ MeV

For maximum energy of β-particle, all other can be assumed at rest and maximum energy will be equal to released energy.

$\therefore \quad KE_{max} = \Delta E$
$= 1.182$ MeV

18. (*a*) Initially activity is N_0 and at $t = 10$ s it is $\frac{N_0}{e^2}$

The activity at time t is given as

$$N = N_0 e^{-\lambda t}$$
$$\Rightarrow \quad \frac{N_0}{e^2} = N_0 e^{-\lambda \times 10}$$

or $\quad e^{-\lambda \times 10} = e^{-2}$

On comparing the power on both sides, we get

$$10\lambda = 2$$
$$\therefore \quad \lambda = \frac{2}{10} = \frac{1}{5} s^{-1}$$

Time at which the activity reduces to half its value is the half life i.e.,

$$t_{half} = \frac{\ln 2}{\lambda}$$
$$= \frac{\ln 2}{1/5}$$
$$= 5 \ln 2$$
$$= 5 \log_e 2 \text{ s}$$

19. (*b*) Let N be the number of nuclei present at any time t, then activity, $R = \lambda N$, where λ is decay constant.
As, $R_1 = N_1 \lambda$ and $R_2 = N_2 \lambda$
Mean life, $T = \frac{1}{\lambda}$

$$\therefore \quad R_1 - R_2 = (N_1 - N_2)\lambda$$
$$R_1 - R_2 = (N_1 - N_2)\frac{1}{T}$$

or $\quad N_1 - N_2 = (R_1 - R_2)T$

So, number of nuclei disintegrated in time duration t to $3t$ is equal to $(R_1 - R_2)T$.

20. (*b*) Given that, mass of nucleus,

$$m = 48 \text{ amu}$$
$$= 48 \times 1.67 \times 10^{-27}$$
$$= 8 \times 10^{-26} \text{ kg}$$

Energy of photon, $E = 7$ MeV
$= 7 \times 1.6 \times 10^{-13}$
$(\because 1 \text{ MeV} = 1.6 \times 10^{-13} \text{ J})$
$= 1.12 \times 10^{-12}$ J

Let the recoil energy of the nucleus be KE, then using conservation of momentum,
Momentum of photon = Photon of nucleus

$$\frac{E}{c} = \sqrt{2(KE)m} \quad \text{or} \quad KE = \frac{E^2}{2mc^2}$$

Substituting the given values, we get

$$= \frac{(1.12 \times 10^{-12})^2}{2 \times 8 \times 10^{-26} \times (3 \times 10^8)^2}$$
$$KE = 8.71 \times 10^{-17} \text{ J}$$
$$= \frac{8.71 \times 10^{-17}}{1.6 \times 10^{-19}} \text{ eV}$$
$$= 0.55 \times 10^3 \text{ eV}$$
$$= 0.55 \text{ keV}$$

21. (*b*) Given that, initially both radioactive substance A and B have same number of nucleus. Let it be N_0.
Decay constant for A, $\lambda_A = 4\lambda$
Decay constant for B, $\lambda_B = \lambda$
At time t, according to Rutherford and Soddy decay law, number of nuclei,
$N = N_0 e^{-\lambda t}$

For A, $\quad N_A = N_0 e^{-\lambda_1 t}$
$= N_0 e^{-4\lambda \times \frac{2}{3\lambda}} \quad \left(\because t = \frac{2}{3\lambda}\right)$
$= N_0 e^{-\frac{8}{3}} \quad$ ... (i)

For B, $\quad N_B = N_0 e^{-\lambda_2 t}$
$= N_0 e^{-\lambda \times \frac{2}{3\lambda}}$
$= N_0 e^{-\frac{2}{3}} \quad$ ... (ii)

On dividing Eq. (i) by Eq. (ii), we get

$$\frac{N_A}{N_B} = \frac{N_0 e^{-\frac{8}{3}}}{N_0 e^{-\frac{2}{3}}} = \frac{e^{-\frac{8}{3}}}{e^{-\frac{2}{3}}}$$
$$= e^{-\frac{8}{3} + \frac{2}{3}} = e^{-2}$$
$$= \frac{1}{e^2}$$

22. (*a*) Both statements I and II are incorrect.
A good moderator thermalise or slow down fast neutrons. For efficient KE transfer between a fast neutron and moderator molecule, both must have nearby masses.
It is not necessary that moderator could have large value of specific heat. Specific heat of D_2O is less than that of helium, but D_2O is used as moderator in nuclear reactor.
Moderator molecules collides among themselves and converts KE into heat.

23. (c) Initially at $t = 0$,

$$\left(\frac{dN_0}{dt}\right)_A = \left(\frac{dN_0}{dt}\right)_B$$

[From figure]

So, $(N_0)_A = (N_0)_B$

It means that initially both samples has equal number of radioactive nuclei.

Let us consider an instant from figure,

$$\left(\frac{dN_0}{dt}\right)_B > \left(\frac{dN_0}{dt}\right)_A$$

$$\lambda_A N_A = \lambda_B N_B \quad \left[\because -\frac{dN}{dt} = \lambda N\right]$$

$$N_A > N_B$$

$\Rightarrow$ $\lambda_A < \lambda_B$

or $\frac{\ln 2}{t_A} < \frac{\ln 2}{t_B}$ $\left[\because \lambda = \frac{\ln 2}{t_{half}}\right]$

or $t_A > t_B$

24. (b) By emitting one α-particle, atomic number decreases by 2 and mass number decreases by 4.

By emitting one β-particle atomic number increases by 1.

For *A* and *C* to be isotopes, $Z_A = Z_C$

$$A = A - m \times 2 + n \times 1$$

$$A = A - 2m + n$$

or $n = 2m$

If $m = 1$ and $n = 2$, then it satisfy above condition.

Thus, statement given in option (b) is correct.

The given equation can be written as

$${}^{A}_{Z}A \longrightarrow {}^{A-m\times 4}_{Z-m\times 2}B \times m\alpha$$

$${}^{A-m\times 4}_{Z-m\times 2}B \longrightarrow {}^{A-m\times 4}_{Z-m\times 2+n\times 1}C + n\beta$$

For *A* and *C* to be isobars, it means

Mass number of *A* = Mass number of *B*

$$A = (A - m \times 4)$$

$\Rightarrow$ $m = 0$

Thus, statement given in option (c) is incorrect.

For *A* and *B* to be isotone, number of neutrons in *A* should be equal to number of neutron in *B*

$$N_A = N_B$$

$$A - Z = (A - m \times 4) - (Z - m \times 2)$$

$$A - Z = A - Z - 2 \times m$$

or $2m = 0$

or $m = 0$

Thus, statement given in option (d) is incorrect.

25. (c) In any nuclear reaction, mass number and charge number are conserved.

Qualifier 19 (Electronic Devices)

1. (b) For a semiconductor, the energy gap between conduction band and valence band is comparatively small and its value is less than 3 eV as shown below

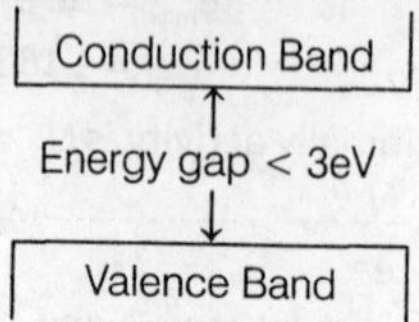

2. (a) Given that pure semiconductor is doped by pentavalent atom of 4 ppm.

$\therefore$ Number of donor atom,

$$N_D = \frac{2 \times 10^{27}}{4 \times 10^6}$$

$$N_D = 0.5 \times 10^{21} \text{ per m}^3$$

$\therefore$ Concentration of electron, $n_e = N_D$

$$n_e = 0.5 \times 10^{21} \text{ per m}^3$$

If n_h is the concentration of holes, then by using mass action law, we can write

$$n_e n_h = n_i^2$$

or $n_h = \frac{n_i^2}{n_e} = \frac{(10^{16})^2}{0.5 \times 10^{21}}$

$$n_h = 2 \times 10^{11} \text{ per m}^3$$

3. (d) Depletion width of a *p-n* junction diode decreases with increase in doping. As, increase in carrier concentration leads to more recombination of majority charge carriers with oppositely charged ions of their depletion regions leading to a decrease in depletion width.

4. (c) A is false but R is true.

When current flows from *p* to *n*-side, electrons diffuse from *n* to *p*-side i.e. from conduction band to valence band and the released energy appears in form of heat.

5. (c) After formation of depletion layer, a potential difference across the layer and internal electric field *E* directed from *n*-side to *p*-side throughout the layer.

As we move rightwards from $x = 0$, the number of negatively charged ions starts increasing and it contributes in increasing the electric field.

When we enter in the region of positively charged ions, the number of positively charged ions decreases and it leads to decrease in magnitude of electric field without change in direction. Thus, variation of electric field across the depletion layer can be plotted as

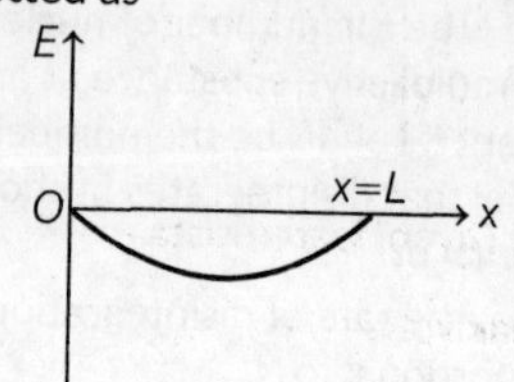

6. (a) Let potential barrier of the diode in forward biasing be V_T and *I* be the current flowing in the circuit given in the question.

Using KVL in loop *ABCDA*,

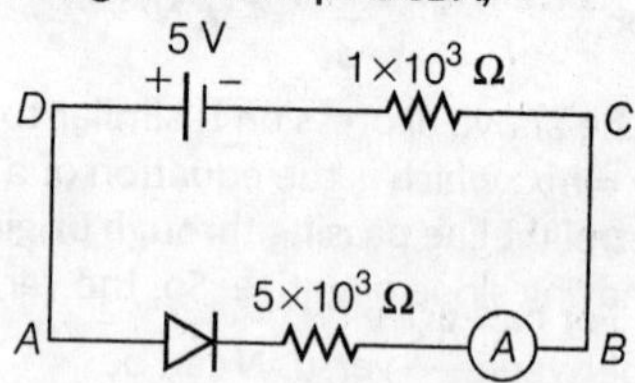

$$5 - V_T - I \times 5 \times 10^3 - I \times 1 \times 10^3 = 0$$

or $V_T = 5 - I \times 6 \times 10^3$

Given that, $I = 0.8 \text{ mA} = 0.8 \times 10^{-3}$ A

$\Rightarrow$ $V_T = 5 - 0.8 \times 10^{-3} \times 6 \times 10^3$

$$= 5 - 4.8$$

$$= 0.2 \text{ V}$$

7. (c) If $V_i < 2$ V, then diode is in reverse bias and diode will not conduct. In this case, circuit will act as an open circuit.

$\therefore$ Circuit diagram can be shown as

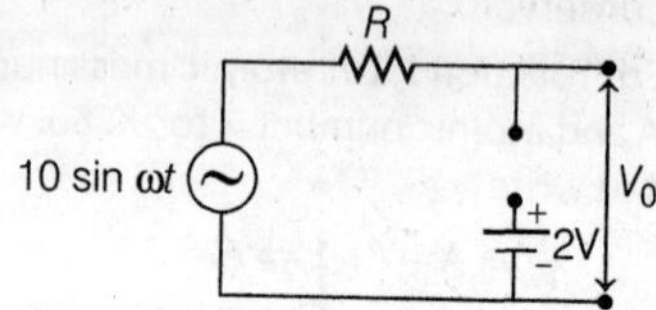

Using KVL, $10\sin\omega t - iR - V_0 = 0$

$$10\sin\omega t - 0 \times R - V_0 = 0$$

or $V_0 = 10\sin\omega t$

If $V_i > 2$ V, then diode is in forward bias and diode will conduct. In this case, diode may be replaced by a short circuit as it is ideal.

The circuit diagram can be shown as

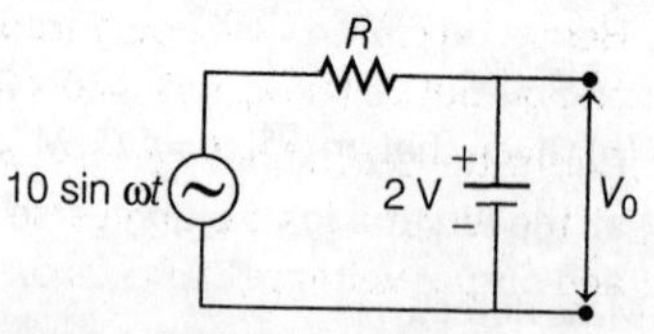

It is clear that, $V_0 = 2$ V

The output waveform can be plotted as

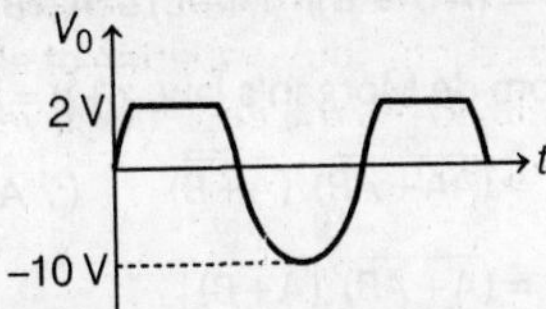

8. (*a*) Given, load resistance, $R_L = 2k\Omega$

Peak voltage, $V_{peak} = 100\text{ V}$

Output DC voltage,

$$V_{DC} = \frac{V_{peak}}{\pi} = \frac{100}{3.14}$$

$$= 31.84\text{ V}$$

As we know that, ripple factor,

$$r = \frac{(V_{ripple})_{rms}}{V_{DC}}$$

or $(V_{ripple})_{rms} = rV_{DC}$

For half-wave rectifier, $r = 1.21$

$\therefore \quad (V_{ripple})_{rms} = 1.21 \times 31.84$

$$= 38.5\text{ V}$$

9. (*a*) Given, peak voltage, $V_{peak} = 10\text{ V}$

The DC component of the output voltage is given as

$$V_{DC} = \frac{V_{peak}}{\pi}$$

$$= \frac{10}{\pi}\text{ V}$$

10. (*a*) First let us connect input and output according to situation in given question.

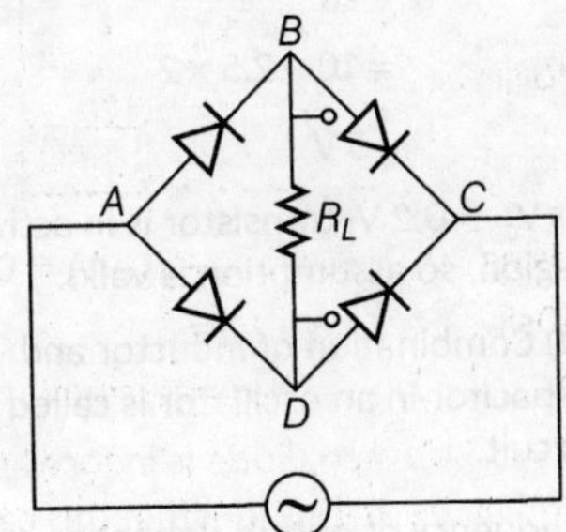

During the first half cycle, $V_A > V_C$, so all the four diodes are in forward bias. Hence, no current will flow through R_L and output will be $V_0 = IR_L = 0 \times R_L = 0$

During the second half cycle, $V_C > V_A$ so all the four diodes are in reverse bias and output voltage will be zero.

11. (*a*) From given figure, diodes D_1 and D_3 are in forward bias and diode D_2 in reverse bias. These can be replaced by their internal resistance in accordance with their biasing.

The circuit can be redrawn

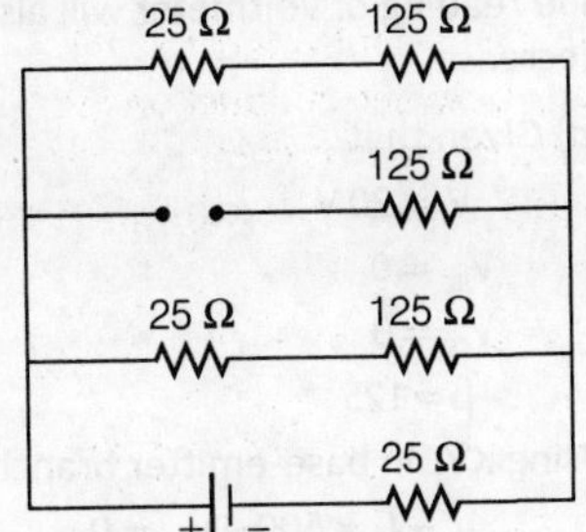

Equivalent resistance,

$$R_{eq} = \frac{(25 + 125)}{2} + 25 = 100\ \Omega$$

Given that, $I = 50\text{ mA} = 5 \times 10^{-2}\text{ A}$

$\therefore \quad \varepsilon = IR_{eq}$

$$= 5 \times 10^{-2} \times 100$$

$$= 5\text{ V}$$

12. (*d*) To understand the given situation let us take an example of *p*-type semiconductor.

Without illumination,

number of holes $(n_h) >>$ number of electron (n_e) ...(i)

This is because holes are the majority charge carriers in *p*-type semiconductor.

On illumination, let Δn_e and Δn_h are the excess electrons and holes generated.

$$\Delta n_e = \Delta n_h \quad \text{... (ii)}$$

From Eqs. (i) and (ii), we get

$$\frac{\Delta n_e}{n_e} >> \frac{\Delta n_h}{n_h}$$

From above, it can be concluded that the fractional change due to illumination on the minority carrier dominated reverse bias current, is more easily measurable than the fractional change in the forward bias current.

13. (*b*) For voltage regulation, circuit can be drawn as

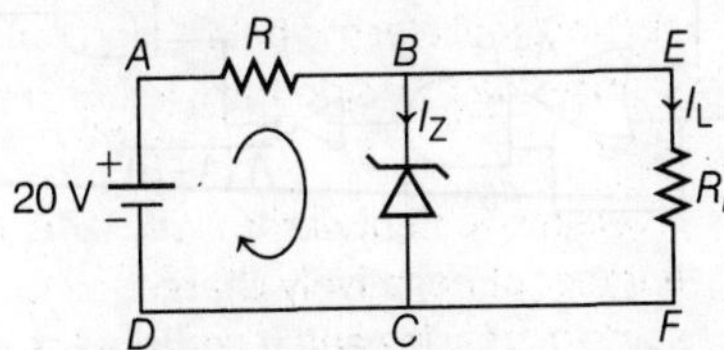

Given that, load current, $I_L = 12\text{ mA}$

Current through zener diode, $I_Z = 25\text{ mA}$

Current through series resistor R,

$$I = I_L + I_Z = 12 + 25$$

$$I = 37\text{ mA}$$

Breakdown voltage of zener diode,

$$V_Z = 12\text{ V}$$

Using KVL in loop *ABCDA*

$$+20 - IR - V_Z = 0$$

$$20 - 37 \times 10^{-3} \times R - 12 = 0$$

or $\quad 37 \times 10^{-3} R = 8$

or $\quad R = \dfrac{8}{37 \times 10^{-3}} = 216.2\ \Omega$

14. (*c*) From the given figure of transfer characteristics of transistor, the mode of operation are as follows

For $0 < V_i < 0.7\text{ V} \rightarrow$ In cut-off mode

For $0.7\text{ V} < V_i < 2\text{ V} \rightarrow$ In active mode

For $V_i > 2\text{V} \rightarrow$ In saturation mode

We know that in saturation mode transistor works as switch which is in ON mode.

15. (*d*) Given, resistance across load,

$$R_L = 800\ \Omega$$

Voltage drop across load, $V_L = 0.8\text{ V}$

Input resistance of the circuit,

$$R_i = 192\ \Omega$$

Collector current is given by

$$I_C = \frac{V_L}{R_L} = \frac{0.8}{800} = \frac{8}{8000} = 1\text{ mA}$$

$\therefore$ Current amplification,

$$\alpha = \frac{\text{Output current}}{\text{Input current}}$$

$$0.96 = \frac{I_C}{I_B}$$

or $\quad I_B = \dfrac{I_C}{0.96}$

$$I_B = \frac{1 \times 10^{-3}}{0.96}$$

$\therefore$ Voltage gain,

$$A_V = \frac{V_L}{V_{in}} = \frac{V_L}{I_B R_i} = \frac{0.8}{\frac{1 \times 10^{-3}}{0.96} \times 192}$$

$$= 4$$

And power gain, $A_P = \alpha^2 \dfrac{R_L}{R_i}$

$$= (0.96)^2 \times \frac{800}{192}$$

$$= 3.84$$

16. (*a*) As given,

$$V_{CE} = 7\text{ V}$$

$$R_C = 2\text{k}\Omega$$

$$= 2 \times 10^3\ \Omega$$

$$V_{BE} = 0$$

Collector current to base current ratio,

$$\beta = 100$$

Using KVL in battery connected collector - emitter loop,

$$V - I_C R_C - V_{CE} = 0$$

or $$I_C = \frac{V - V_{CE}}{R_C} = \frac{15-7}{2 \times 10^3}$$

$$= 4 \times 10^{-3} \text{ A} = 4 \text{ mA}$$

As, base current, $I_B = \frac{I_C}{\beta}$

$$= \frac{4 \text{ mA}}{100} = 40 \mu\text{A}$$

17. (*a*) **For solar cell**

$$E_g \sim 1.1 \text{ to } 1.5 \text{ eV}$$

For LED

$$E_g \sim 1.8 \text{ to } 2.8 \text{ eV}$$

For rectifier diode

$$E_g \sim 0.75 \text{ to } 1.1 \text{ eV}$$

For optical link

$$E_g \approx 1 \text{ eV}$$

18. (*d*) Let the emfs of battery be V_1 and V_2

From given figure,

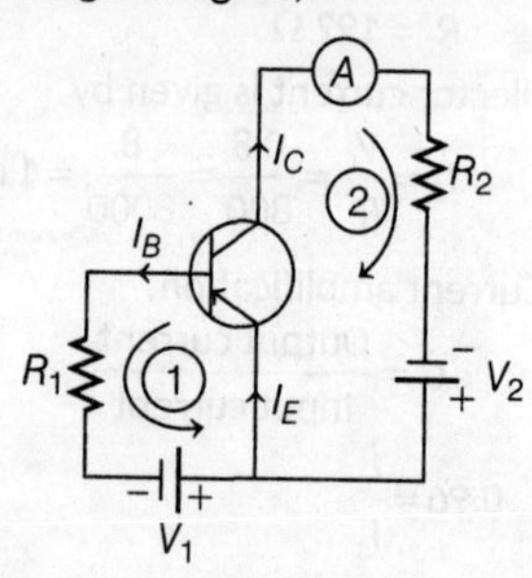

Applying KVL in loop (1) along the direction shown,

$$V_1 - V_{EB} - I_B R_1 = 0$$

$\Rightarrow$ $$I_B = \frac{V_1 - V_{EB}}{R_1} \quad \text{... (i)}$$

Similarly applying KVL in loop (2)

$$V_2 - V_{EC} - I_E R_2 = 0$$

$\Rightarrow$ $$I_E = \frac{V_2 - V_{EC}}{R_2} \quad \text{... (ii)}$$

For a transistor,

$\because$ $$I_C = \beta I_B \quad \text{... (iii)}$$

where, β is gain constant.

From Eq. (i), if R_1 is increased, then I_B decreases and from Eq (iii), if their is decrease in I_B, I_C will also decrease.

The reading of ammeter which is equal to I_B, also decreases.

Reading of voltmeter $= I_C R_2$

As R_1 is increased, then I_C decreases and reading of voltmeter will also decrease.

19. (*a*) Given that,

$$V_i = 20 \text{ V}$$

$$V_{BE} = 0$$

$$V_{CE} = 0$$

$\Rightarrow$ $$\beta = 125$$

Using KVL in base-emitter branch,

$$V_i - I_B \times 500 - V_{BE} = 0$$

or $$I_B = \frac{V_i - V_{BE}}{R_B} = \frac{20-0}{500 \times 10^3}$$

$$(\because R_B = 500 \text{ k}\Omega)$$

$$= 40 \mu\text{A}$$

Using kΩ in collector-emitter branch,

$$20 - I_C R_C - V_{CE} = 0$$

or $$I_C = \frac{20 - V_{CE}}{R_C}$$

$$= \frac{20-0}{4 \times 10^3} \quad (\because R_C = 4 \text{ k}\Omega)$$

$$= 5 \text{ mA}$$

20. (*c*) In cascaded system, overall voltage gain is the product of individual voltage gain. So, we can write

$$A = A_1 A_2$$

or $\log_{10} A = \log_{10} A_1 + \log_{10} A_2$

or $20 \log_{10} A = 20 \log_{10} A_1 + 20 \log_{10} A_2$

Given that, $20 \log_{10} A_1 = 20$,

$$20 \log_{10} A_2 = 20$$

$\therefore$ Gain (in dB) $= 20 + 20$

$$= 40 \text{ dB}$$

21. (*b*) From the given voltage waveforms, it is clear that output Y is low, if both A and B are high, otherwise Y is high. This is the output of NAND gate.

22. (*d*) From the given figure,

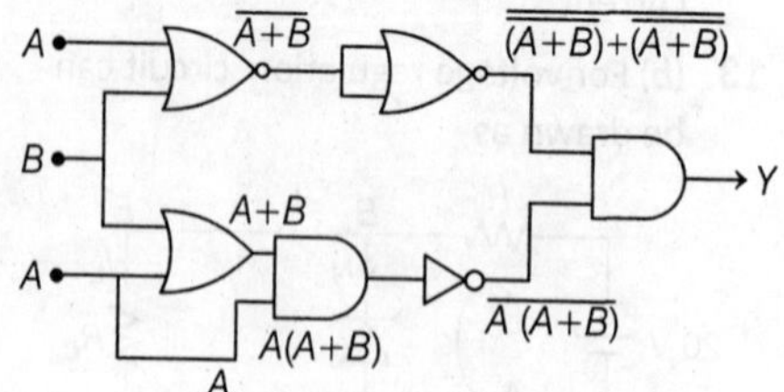

The output,

$$Y = (\overline{A(A+B)}) \cdot (\overline{(\overline{A+B}) + (\overline{A+B})})$$

From de Morgan's law, $\overline{x+y} = \bar{x} \cdot \bar{y}$

$$= (\overline{AA + AB}) \cdot (\overline{\overline{A+B}}) \quad (\because A + A = A)$$

$$= (\overline{A + AB}) \cdot (A+B)$$

$$= (\overline{A(1+B)}) \cdot (A+B)$$

$$= (\overline{A \cdot 1}) \cdot (A+B)$$

$$= \bar{A} \cdot (A+B)$$

$$= \bar{A}A + \bar{A}B \quad (\because A \cdot \bar{A} = 0)$$

$$= 0 + \bar{A}B$$

$$Y = \bar{A} \cdot B$$

The above boolean expression does not correspond to that of OR, AND, NAND gate boolean expressions.

23. (*a*) In an *n-p-n* CE amplifier, there is a phase difference of π rad in input and output voltages.

24. (*a*) As $V_{BB} > 0.7$ V, transistor is ON and $V_{BE} = 0.7$ V.

Applying KVL to input loop,

$$2.7 - I_B \times 80 - 0.7 = 0$$

$\Rightarrow$ $$I_B = 0.025 \text{ mA}$$

Assuming active state,

$$I_C = \beta I_B$$

$$= 100 \times 0.025$$

$$= 2.5 \text{ mA}$$

Applying KVL to output loop,

$$V_{CE} = V_{CC} - I_C R_C$$

$$= 10 - 2.5 \times 2$$

$$= 5 \text{ V}$$

As $V_{CE} > 0.2$ V, transistor is in active region, so assumption is valid.

25. (*d*) Combination of inductor and capacitor in an oscillator is called tank circuit.

Frequency of output voltage $= \frac{1}{2\pi\sqrt{LC}}$

Hence, frequency of out voltage depends on the value of inductance (L) and capacitance (C) used in tank circuit.

PART TESTS

Part Test 1

1. (*d*)

A. All non-zero digits are significant, so 959 has 3 significant figures.

B. If the number is less than 1, the zeros on the right of decimal point and to the left of the first non-zero digit are not significant. So, in 0.001486, underlined zero(s) are not significant and it has 4 significant figures.

C. The trailing zero(s) in a number with decimal points are significant, so in 2.6000, there are 5 significant figures.

D. All the zero(s) between two non-zero digits are significant, no matter where the decimal point is. Thus, 8.00165 has 6 significant figures.

The correct matching sequence is

$$A \to P, B \to Q, C \to R, D \to S.$$

2. (*c*) Let the numerical value of Stefan's constant in SI system be n_2, and n_1 in the CGS system.

$$\therefore \quad n_2 = n_1 \left[\frac{M_1}{M_2}\right]^a \left[\frac{L_1}{L_2}\right]^b \left[\frac{T_1}{T_2}\right]^c$$

For Stefan's constant, $a = 1, b = 0, c = -3$

$$n_2 = 5.67 \times 10^{-5} \left[\frac{1\text{ g}}{1\text{ kg}}\right]^1 \left[\frac{1\text{ cm}}{1\text{ m}}\right]^0 \left[\frac{1\text{s}}{1\text{s}}\right]^{-3}$$

$$= 5.67 \times 10^{-5} \left[\frac{1\text{ g}}{1000\text{ g}}\right]^1$$

$$= 5.67 \times 10^{-8}$$

3. (*c*) While deriving the given equation, u is multiplied by time duration and a is multiplied by square of time duration but in final result, it does not appear because time interval is 1 s. Hence, it is both numerically as well as dimensionally correct. So, option (c) is correct.

4. (*c*) According to principle of homogeneity, only those terms can be added which have same dimensional formula. So, dimensions of terms 1 and $\frac{2\alpha l}{Ma}$ should be same.

$$\left[\frac{2\alpha l}{Ma}\right] = [1]$$

$$\frac{[\alpha l]}{[Ma]} = [M^0L^0T^0]$$

or $\quad \frac{[\alpha]}{[Ma]} = \frac{1}{[l]} = [L^{-1}]$

Also, $\quad [\phi] = \frac{[Ma]}{[\alpha]} = [l]$

$$[\phi] = [L]$$

Therefore, unit of ϕ should be metre (m).

5. (*c*) Given, mass $= (12 \pm 0.012)$g

Radius $= (0.4 + 0.002)$ mm

Length $= (20 + 0.01)$ cm

Relative error in mass

$$= \frac{\Delta M}{M} = \frac{0.012}{12} = 0.001$$

Relative error in radius

$$= \frac{\Delta r}{r} = \frac{0.002}{0.4} = 0.005$$

Relative error in length

$$= \frac{\Delta l}{l} = \frac{0.01}{20} = 0.0005$$

As, density, $\rho = \frac{\text{mass}}{\text{volume}}$

$$= \frac{M}{A \times l} = \frac{M}{\pi r^2 \times l}$$

or maximum relative error in density,

$$\frac{\Delta\rho}{\rho} = \frac{\Delta M}{M} + \frac{2\Delta r}{r} + \frac{\Delta l}{l}$$

$$= 0.001 + 2 \times 0.005 + 0.0005$$
$$= 0.0115$$

Maximum percentage error in density

$$= \frac{\Delta\rho}{\rho} \times 100$$

$$= 0.0115 \times 100$$
$$= 1.15\%$$

6. (*c*) For any particle to be speeding down, the dot product of acceleration and velocity must be negative,

i.e. $\quad \mathbf{a} \cdot \mathbf{v} < 0$

Here, $\quad \mathbf{a} = a_y\hat{\mathbf{j}} + a_z\hat{\mathbf{k}}$

$$\mathbf{v} = v_y\hat{\mathbf{j}} + v_z\hat{\mathbf{k}}$$

$$\therefore \quad (a_y\hat{\mathbf{j}} + a_z\hat{\mathbf{k}}) \cdot (v_y\hat{\mathbf{j}} + v_z\hat{\mathbf{k}}) < 0$$

$$a_yv_y + a_zv_z < 0$$

7. (*b*) Let the height of tower be h. For first ball, $u = 40$ m/s, $g = -10$ m/s^2 and time taken by ball is t_1, then using second equation of motion,

$$s = ut + \frac{1}{2}gt^2$$

$$-h = 40 \times t_1 + \frac{1}{2} \times (-10)t_1^2$$

or $\quad 5t_1^2 - 40t_1 - h = 0$

or $\quad t_1^2 - 8t_1 - \frac{h}{5} = 0$

$$t_1 = \frac{-(-8) \pm \sqrt{(-8)^2 - 4(1)\left(\frac{-h}{5}\right)}}{2(1)}$$

$$t_1 = 4 + \sqrt{16 + \frac{h}{5}} \text{ or } 4 - \sqrt{16 + \frac{h}{5}}$$

As t cannot be negative, so

$$t_1 = 4 + \sqrt{16 + \frac{h}{5}}$$

For second ball, let the time taken by ball to reach at the ground be t_2, then

$$t_2 = \sqrt{\frac{2h}{g}} = \sqrt{\frac{2h}{10}} = \sqrt{\frac{h}{5}}$$

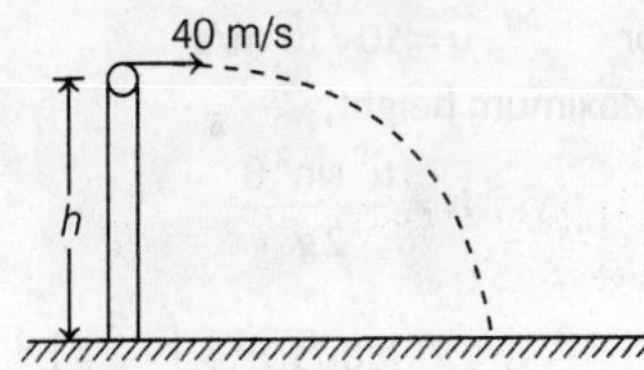

According to question, $t_1 - t_2 = 6$ s

$$\left(4 + \sqrt{16 + \frac{h}{5}}\right) - \left(\sqrt{\frac{h}{5}}\right) = 6$$

or $\quad \sqrt{16 + \frac{h}{5}} = \sqrt{\frac{h}{5}} + 6 - 4$

or $\quad \sqrt{16 + \frac{h}{5}} = \sqrt{\frac{h}{5}} + 2$

On squaring both sides, we get

$$\left(\sqrt{16 + \frac{h}{5}}\right)^2 = \left(\sqrt{\frac{h}{5}} + 2\right)^2$$

$$\left(\sqrt{16 + \frac{h}{5}}\right)^2 = \left(\sqrt{\frac{h}{5}}\right)^2 + (2)^2 + 2 \times 2 \times \sqrt{\frac{h}{5}}$$

$$16 + \frac{h}{5} = \frac{h}{5} + 4 + 4\sqrt{\frac{h}{5}}$$

or $\quad 12 = 4\sqrt{\frac{h}{5}}$

or $\quad 3 = \sqrt{\frac{h}{5}}$ or $h = 45$ m

8. (c) A is false but R is true.

Positions of balls are

$x_1 = -gt_1^2$ and $x_2 = -gt_2^2$

(As they are thrown one after other, so time values are not same for both)

Hence, relative position or distance between particles,

$\Delta x = x_2 - x_1 = g(t_1^2 - t_2^2)$

This is not a linear relation.

9. (d) Given, trajectory equation,

$y = 3x - \frac{x^2}{20}$ or $y = 3x\left(1 - \frac{x}{60}\right)$

Now, comparing this equation from standard equation of projectile motion,

i.e. $\quad y = x\tan\theta\left(1 - \frac{x}{R}\right)$

Here, $\tan\theta = 3$ and $R = 60$ m

or $\quad \sin\theta = \frac{3}{\sqrt{10}}$ and $\cos\theta = \frac{1}{\sqrt{10}}$

As, range, $R = \frac{2u^2\sin\theta\cos\theta}{g}$

$60 = \frac{2u^2 \times \frac{3}{\sqrt{10}} \times \frac{1}{\sqrt{10}}}{10}$

or $\quad u^2 = 1000$

or $\quad u = 10\sqrt{10}$ m/s

Maximum height,

$H = \frac{u^2\sin^2\theta}{2g}$

$= \frac{(10\sqrt{10})^2 \times \left(\frac{3}{\sqrt{10}}\right)^2}{2 \times 10}$

$= \frac{1000 \times \frac{9}{10}}{2 \times 10} = 45$ m

10. (b) Given, $|\hat{\mathbf{a}}| = |\hat{\mathbf{b}}| = |\hat{\mathbf{c}}| = 1$

$|\hat{\mathbf{a}} \times \hat{\mathbf{b}}| = |\hat{\mathbf{a}}||\hat{\mathbf{b}}|\sin\theta_1$

$\frac{1}{2} = 1 \times 1 \sin\theta_1$

$\Rightarrow \quad \sin\theta_1 = \frac{1}{2}$

$\Rightarrow \quad \theta_1 = 30°$

$\hat{\mathbf{b}} \cdot \hat{\mathbf{c}} = |\hat{\mathbf{b}}||\hat{\mathbf{c}}|\cos\theta_2$

$-\frac{3}{5} = 1 \times 1 \cos\theta_2$

$\Rightarrow \quad \cos\theta_2 = -\frac{3}{5}$

$\Rightarrow \quad \theta_2 = 127°$

These are following possibility according to orientation of vectors

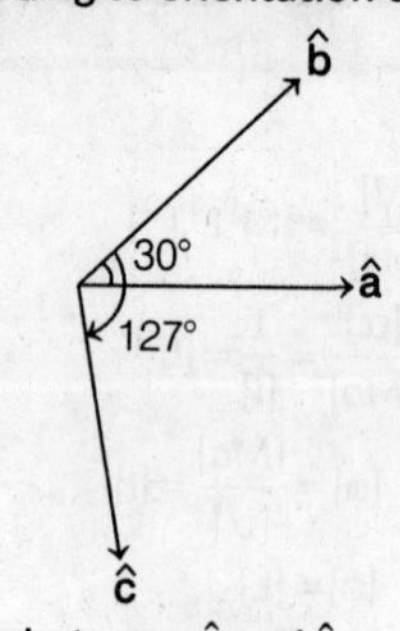

Angle between $\hat{\mathbf{a}}$ and $\hat{\mathbf{c}}$

$= 127° - 30° = 97°$

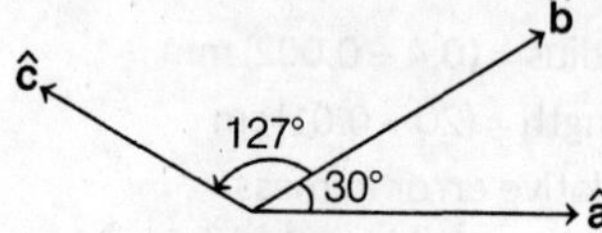

Angle between $\hat{\mathbf{a}}$ and $\hat{\mathbf{c}}$

$= 127° + 30° = 157°$

11. (b) Length of the spring $= l$

Force constant of the spring $= k$

$\therefore$ Ratio in which spring is cut $= 1:3$

Length of larger piece $= 3l/(3+1)$

$= 3l/4$

Force constant of larger piece $= k'$

$\therefore$ Force constant $\propto \frac{1}{\text{Length of spring}}$

$\frac{k}{k'} = \frac{3l/4}{l}$

$\frac{k}{k'} = \frac{3}{4} \Rightarrow k' = (4/3)k$

12. (a) On applying a pull of F upwards, it remains at rest.

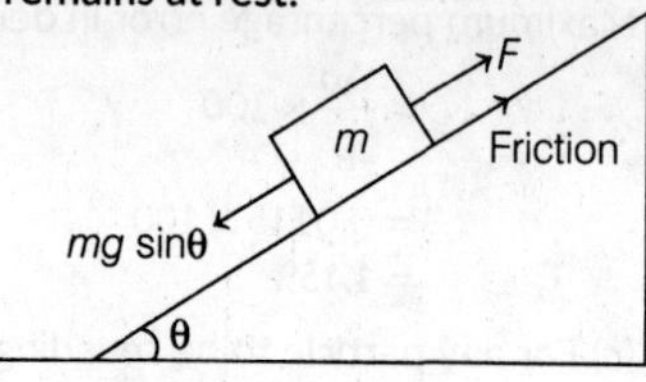

$\therefore F = mg\sin\theta - \text{Friction}$

$= mg\sin\theta - \mu N$

$= mg\sin\theta - \mu mg\cos\theta \quad$ ...(i)

$(\because N = mg\cos\theta)$

If $2F$ force is applied upwards, then block is about to slide. In this condition, frictional force will act down the plane.

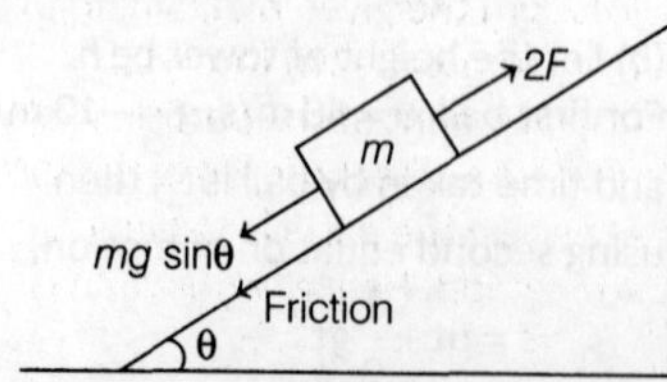

$2F = mg\sin\theta + \text{Friction}$

$2F = mg\sin\theta + \mu mg\cos\theta$

or $F = \frac{mg\sin\theta + \mu mg\cos\theta}{2} \quad$ ...(ii)

On equating Eqs. (i) and (ii), we get

$mg\sin\theta - \mu mg\cos\theta = \frac{mg\sin\theta + \mu mg\cos\theta}{2}$

$2mg\sin\theta - 2\mu mg\cos\theta = mg\sin\theta + \mu mg\cos\theta$

or $\quad 3\mu mg\cos\theta = mg\sin\theta$

or $\quad 3\mu\cos\theta = \sin\theta$

or $\quad \mu = \frac{1}{3} \cdot \frac{\sin\theta}{\cos\theta}$ or $\mu = \frac{\tan\theta}{3}$

13. (c) Let the applied force F be at an angle ϕ with horizontal.

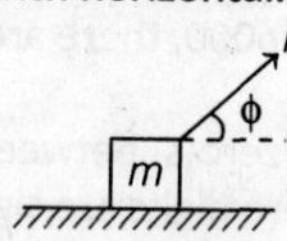

The value of minimum force is given as

$F_{\min} = \frac{\mu mg}{\sqrt{1+\mu^2}} \quad$ ... (i)

and direction, $\phi = \tan^{-1}(\mu) \quad$ ...(ii)

Given, $\quad F_{\min} = 12$ N, $m = 2$ kg, $g = 10$ m/s^2

Putting the values in Eq. (i), we get

$12 = \frac{\mu \times 2 \times 10}{\sqrt{1+\mu^2}}$

or $\quad 0.6 = \frac{\mu}{\sqrt{1+\mu^2}}$

$(0.6)^2 = \frac{\mu^2}{1+\mu^2}$

or $\quad 0.36 = \frac{\mu^2}{1+\mu^2}$

$0.36 + 0.36\mu^2 = \mu^2$

or $\mu^2 - 0.36\mu^2 = 0.36$

or $\quad 0.64\mu^2 = 0.36$

or $\quad \mu^2 = \frac{0.36}{0.64}$

or $\quad \mu = \sqrt{\frac{0.36}{0.64}} = \frac{0.6}{0.8} = \frac{3}{4}$

From Eq. (ii), $\phi = \tan^{-1}\left(\frac{3}{4}\right) = 37°$

Now, $2F_{\min}$ is applied on block.

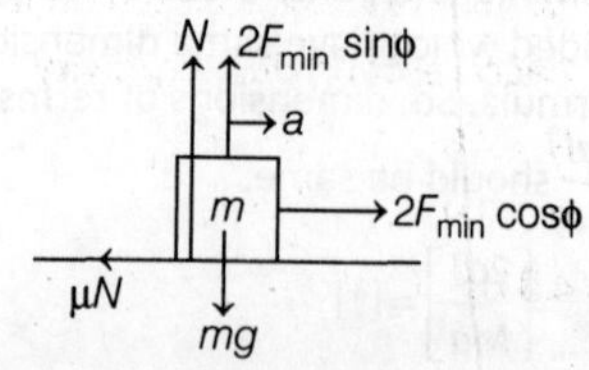

In y-direction,

$$N+2F_{min}\sin\phi=mg$$
$$N=mg-2F_{min}\sin\phi$$

In x-direction,

$$ma=2F_{min}\cos\phi-\mu N$$
$$ma=2F_{min}\cos\phi-\mu(mg-2F_{min}\sin\phi)$$
$$ma=[2F_{min}\cos\phi-\mu mg+2\mu F_{min}\sin\phi]$$
$$ma=2F_{min}(\cos\phi+\mu\sin\phi)-\mu mg$$

or $a=\frac{2F_{min}}{m}(\cos\phi+\mu\sin\phi)-\mu g$

Putting the values, we get

$$a=\frac{2\times12}{2}\left(\cos37^\circ+\frac{3}{4}\sin37^\circ\right)-\frac{3}{4}\times10$$
$$=12\left(\frac{4}{5}+\frac{3}{4}\times\frac{3}{5}\right)-\frac{15}{2}$$
$$=12\left(\frac{4}{5}+\frac{9}{20}\right)-\frac{15}{2}$$
$$=12\times\left(\frac{25}{20}\right)-\frac{15}{2}$$
$$=15-\frac{15}{2}$$
$$a=\frac{15}{2}\text{ m/s}^2=7.5\text{ m/s}^2$$

14. (*b*) Here, due to water jet, a thrust force will also act on the block whose magnitude is equal to $v\frac{dm}{dt}$ and direction of block is vertically downwards.

Drawing FBD of block,

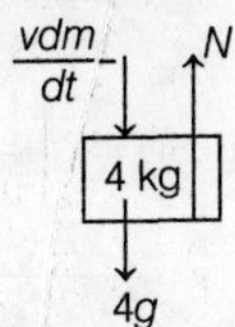

At equilibrium,

$$N=\frac{vdm}{dt}+4g$$

Here, $v=4$ m/s, $\frac{dm}{dt}=120$ kg/min or 2 kg/s

and $g=10\text{ m/s}^2$

$\therefore$ $N=4\times(2)+4\times10$

$N=8+40=48$ N

Now, reading of weighing machine

$$=\frac{\text{Normal reaction exerted on it}}{\text{Acceleration due to gravity}}$$
$$=\frac{N}{g}=\frac{48}{10}$$
$$=4.8\text{ kg}$$

15. (*c*) Let the tension in string be T and acceleration of block be a w.r.t. lift. From FBD of 6 kg block in lift.

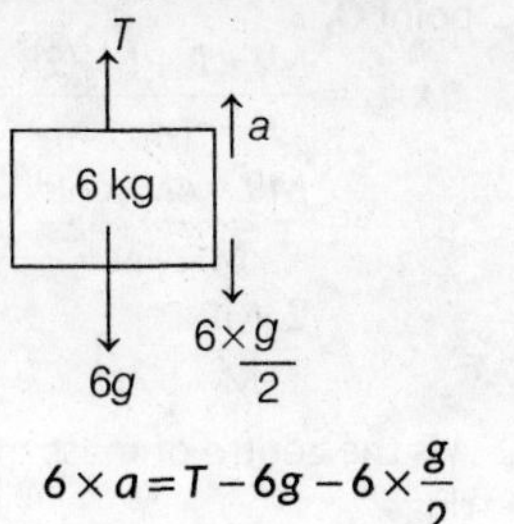

$$6\times a=T-6g-6\times\frac{g}{2}$$
$$6\times a=T-9g \quad \text{... (i)}$$

Similarly,

$$12\times a=12g+12\times\frac{g}{2}-T$$
$$12a=18g-T \quad \text{... (ii)}$$

On adding Eqs. (i) and (ii), we get

$$6a+12a=18g-9g$$

or $18a=9g$

or $a=\frac{9g}{18}=\frac{9\times10}{18}=5\text{ m/s}^2$

Putting this value in Eq. (i), we get

$$6\times5=T-9\times10$$

$\Rightarrow$ $T=30+90=120$ N

Spring force, $T'=T+T=2T$

or $=2\times120=240\text{ N}=240$ N

As we know that, spring balance always measure tension force across its one end.

FBD of pulley,

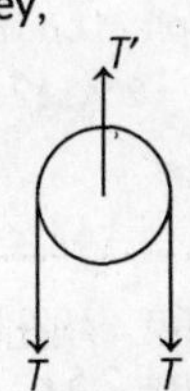

Reading of spring balance

$$=\frac{\text{Spring force}}{g}$$
$$=\frac{240}{10}=24\text{ kg}$$

16. (*a*) From the given diagram, it is clear that from $x=-2$ m to $x=0$, displacement of the particle is along positive x-direction, while the force acting on the particle is along negative x-direction. Hence, work done is negative and is given by the area under F-x graph.

$$W=-\frac{1}{2}\times2\times10=-10\text{ J}$$

17. (*b*) Given, $m_1=4$ kg, $m_2=16$ kg

$$K_1=K_2=K$$

We know that, kinetic energy and momentum are related as

$$p=\sqrt{2mK}$$
$$\frac{p_1}{p_2}=\sqrt{\frac{m_1}{m_2}}\cdot\sqrt{\frac{K_1}{K_2}}$$
$$=\sqrt{\frac{4}{16}}\cdot\sqrt{\frac{K}{K}}=\frac{1}{2}$$

$\Rightarrow$ $p_1:p_2=1:2$

18. (*d*) We know that, potential energy of a spring is given as

$$U=\frac{1}{2}kx^2\Rightarrow U\propto x^2\Rightarrow\frac{U_2}{U_1}=\left(\frac{x_2}{x_1}\right)^2$$

Given, $U_1=15$ J, $x_1=3$ cm, $x_2=4$ cm

$$\therefore\quad\frac{U_2}{15}=\left(\frac{4}{3}\right)^2$$
$$\Rightarrow\quad U_2=\frac{16}{9}\times15=\frac{80}{3}\text{ J}$$

19. (*c*) We know that,

Work done, $W=\mathbf{F}\cdot\mathbf{d}$

$$=(2\hat{\mathbf{i}}-3\hat{\mathbf{j}}+4\hat{\mathbf{k}})\cdot(3\hat{\mathbf{i}}-4\hat{\mathbf{j}}-4.5\hat{\mathbf{k}})$$
$$=2\times3+(-3)(-4)+(4)(-4.5)$$
$$=6+12-18=0$$

$\therefore$ $\mathbf{F}\perp\mathbf{d}$

i.e., $\theta=90^\circ$

20. (*d*) The given situation is shown below.

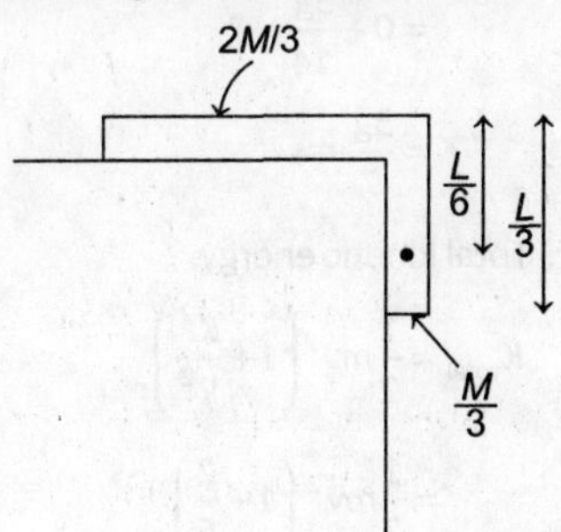

Centre of mass of hanging part of chain will be $\frac{L}{6}$ below the table surface.

Mass of hanging part $=\frac{1}{3}\times$ total mass of the chain

$$m'=\frac{M}{3}$$

$\therefore$ Required work done $= W = m'g\frac{L}{6}$

$$= \frac{M}{3} \cdot g \cdot \frac{L}{6} = \frac{MgL}{18}$$

21. (*a*) Given, $I = 2$ kg-m^2, $\omega = 25$ rad/s and $t = 10$ s

Average torque of the force,

$$\tau = I\alpha = I \cdot \frac{\omega}{t} = 2 \times \frac{25}{10} = 5 \text{ N-m}$$

22. (*b*) Given, angular frequency,

$$f = 120 \text{ rev/min} = \frac{120}{60} \text{ rev/min} = 2 \text{ rev/s}$$

$\therefore$ Angular velocity of wheel,

$$\omega = 2\pi f = 2\pi \times 2 = 4\pi \text{ rad/s}$$

$\because$ Radius of wheel, $R = 2$ m

$\therefore$ Linear velocity of wheel,

$$v = \omega R = 4\pi \times 2 = 8\pi \text{ m/s}$$

23. (*a*) Given, $M = 1$ kg, $R = 10$ cm $= 0.1$ m, $\theta = 30°$, $t = 2$ s

For pure rolling,

$$a = \frac{g\sin\theta}{1 + \frac{K^2}{R^2}} = \frac{g\sin 30°}{1 + \frac{2}{5}} = \frac{5g}{14}$$

Linear velocity of sphere after $t = 2$ s,

$$v = u + at = 0 + \frac{5g}{14} \times 2 = \frac{5g}{7} \text{ ms}^{-1}$$

$\therefore$ Total kinetic energy,

$$K_{\text{total}} = \frac{1}{2}mv^2\left(1 + \frac{K^2}{R^2}\right) = \frac{1}{2}mv^2\left(1 + \frac{2}{5}\right) = \frac{7}{10}mv^2$$

$$= \frac{7}{10} \times 1 \times \left(\frac{5g}{7}\right)^2 = \frac{7}{10} \times \frac{25}{49} \times 10^2 = 35.7 \text{ J}$$

24. (*b*) Given, $M_1 = M$ and $M_2 = 4M$

Location of centre of mass from point O.

$$x_{CM} = \frac{M_1 \times R + M_2(2R + 4R)}{M_1 + M_2} = \frac{MR + 4M \times 6R}{M + 4M} = \frac{25MR}{5M} = 5R$$

A is the centre of mass of system of rings.

$$\therefore \quad I_A = I_1 + I_2 = \{MR^2 + M(5R - R)^2\} + \{4M(4R)^2 + 4M(6R - 5R)^2\}$$

$$= MR^2(1 + 16) + MR^2(64 + 4) = 85MR^2$$

25. (*c*) Given, mass of ring, $m = 2$ kg

Radius, $r = 1$ m

$$\theta(t) = (2t^3 - 4t^2 + 4) \text{ rad}$$

$\therefore$ Instantaneous angular acceleration of ring,

$$\alpha = \frac{d^2\theta(t)}{dt^2} = \frac{d}{dt}\left[\frac{d}{dt}(2t^3 - 4t^2 + 4)\right] = \frac{d}{dt}(6t^2 - 8t) = 12t - 8$$

Angular acceleration, at $t = 10$ s,

$$\alpha = 12 \times 10 - 8 = 112 \text{ rad/s}^2$$

Moment of inertia of ring,

$I = mR^2 = 2 \times 1^2 = 2$ kg-m^2

$\therefore$ Torque applied on the ring,

$$\tau = I\alpha = 2 \times 112 = 224 \text{ N-m}$$

26. (*b*) Given,

$$F = 1.67 \times 10^{-9} \text{ N}$$

$$r = 20 \text{ cm or } 0.2 \text{ m}$$

Total mass, $m = 2.5$ kg

Let the mass of objects be m kg and $(2.5 - m)$ kg.

The force of gravitation between two objects of masses m_1 and m_2 placed at a distance r is given as

$$F = \frac{Gm_1m_2}{r^2}$$

or $$m_1m_2 = \frac{Fr^2}{G}$$

On substituting the given values, we get

$$m \times (2.5 - m) = \frac{1.67 \times 10^{-9} \times (0.2)^2}{6.67 \times 10^{-11}}$$

$$m \times (2.5 - m) = 1$$

$$2.5m - m^2 = 1$$

or $m^2 - 2.5m + 1 = 0$

or $2m^2 - 5m + 2 = 0$

or $2m^2 - 4m - m + 2 = 0$

or $2m(m - 2) - 1(m - 2) = 0$

or $(2m - 1)(m - 2) = 0$

or $(2m - 1) = 0$

or $(m - 2) = 0$

$m = \frac{1}{2}$ kg or 0.5 kg

or $m = 2$ kg

27. (*c*) The maximum height attained by an object thrown vertically upwards, with initial velocity u from the surface of earth is given as

$$h_{\text{max}} = \frac{u^2}{2g - \frac{u^2}{R}} \quad \text{...(i)}$$

where, g is acceleration due to gravity on surface of earth and R is the radius of earth

The escape velocity, v_e is given as

$$v_e = \sqrt{2gR}$$

Given, $$u = \frac{v_e}{3} = \frac{\sqrt{2gR}}{3}$$

From Eq. (i),

$$h_{\text{max}} = \frac{\left(\frac{\sqrt{2gR}}{3}\right)^2}{2g - \left(\frac{\sqrt{2gR}}{3}\right)^2 \times \frac{1}{R}} = \frac{\frac{2gR}{9}}{2g - \frac{2gR}{9R}} = \frac{R}{8}$$

28. (*a*) The escape velocity for a planet of mass M and radius R is

$$v_e = \sqrt{\frac{2GM}{R}} \quad \text{...(i)}$$

Within the planet, the gravitational potential at a distance r from the center is given as

$$V = -\frac{GM}{2R^3}(3R^2 - r^2)$$

At the centre of earth, $r = 0$

So, potential, $V_C = -\dfrac{3GM}{2R}$

At very large distance, potential, $V_\infty = 0$

Using conservation of mechanical energy principle.

Gain in kinetic energy = Decrease in potential energy

$$K_f - K_i = U_i - U_f$$

$$\frac{1}{2}mv^2 - 0 = 0 - \left(-\frac{3GM}{2R}\right) \times m \qquad [\because U = V \times m]$$

$$\frac{1}{2}mv^2 = \frac{3GMm}{2R}$$

or $$v^2 = \frac{3GM}{R}$$

or $$v^2 = \frac{3}{2}\frac{2GM}{R}$$

From Eq. (i),

$$v^2 = \frac{3}{2}v_e^2$$

or $$v = \sqrt{\frac{3}{2}}\,v_e$$

29. (*b*) According to Kepler's second law of area, the radius vector drawn from the sun to planet sweeps out equal areas in equal intervals of time, i.e. the areal velocity of a planet around the sun is constant. The linear speed of a planet is greater when it is closer to the sun than its linear speed when away from the sun.

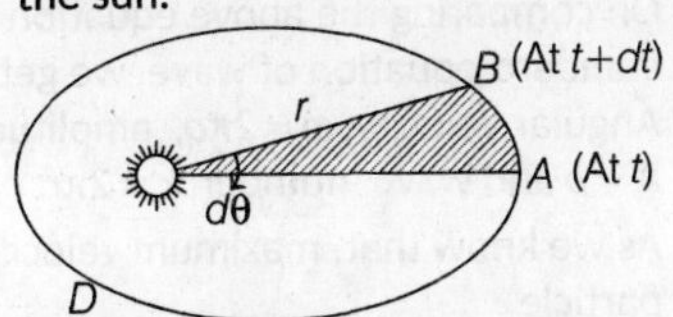

Consider a small wedge of the orbit traced out in time dt, so the area of the wedge,

$$dA = \frac{1}{2}(r)(r d\theta)$$

and the rate at which area is swept out on the orbit,

$$\frac{dA}{dt} = \frac{1}{2}(r)\left(r\frac{d\theta}{dt}\right)$$

or $$\frac{dA}{dt} = \frac{1}{2}rv\theta \qquad \text{...(i)}$$

From the definition of angular momentum, $\tau = m(\mathbf{r} \times \mathbf{v})$

or $$L = mrv \sin\theta$$

If θ is very very small, then $L = mrv\theta$

or $$rv\theta = \frac{L}{m}$$

From Eq. (i), we get

$$\frac{dA}{dt} = \frac{L}{2m}$$

Equal areas in equal times means the rate at which area is swept out on the orbit $\left(\dfrac{dA}{dt}\right)$ is constant.

The rate at which a planet sweeps out area on its orbit is equal to one half its angular momentum divided by its mass. Thus, angular momentum is conserved.

30. (*b*) According to Kepler's second law,

$$\frac{\Delta A}{\Delta t} = \text{constant}$$

or $$\frac{\Delta A_1}{\Delta t_1} = \frac{\Delta A_2}{\Delta t_2} \qquad \text{...(i)}$$

From the given figure,

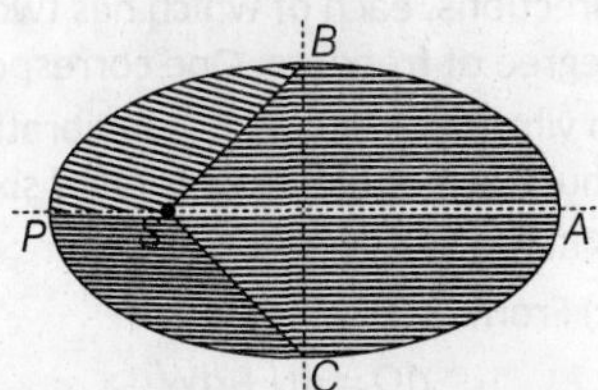

Area of $SBAC$ > Area of $SCPB$

From Eq. (i), $t_1 > t_2$

31. (*a*) Both Statement I and Statement II are incorrect.

Small objects float on surface of a fluid due to surface tension.

Archimedes' principle is applicable on bodies which are wholly or partially submerged in a fluid.

32. (*b*) Terminal velocity,

$$v = \frac{2r^2(\rho - \sigma)g}{9\eta}$$

$\Rightarrow$ $$v \propto r^2$$

$\Rightarrow$ $$\frac{v_2}{v_1} = \left(\frac{r_2}{r_1}\right)^2 = \left(\frac{2r_1}{r_1}\right)^2 = 4$$

$\Rightarrow$ $$v_2 = 4v_1$$

33. (*c*) Given, $T_1 = 5500$ K,

$\lambda_{m_2} = 11 \times 10^{-7}$ m

$\lambda_{m_1} = 5.5 \times 10^{-7}$ m, $T_2 = ?$

According to the Wien's displacement law,

$$\lambda_{m_1}T_1 = \lambda_{m_2}T_2$$

$\Rightarrow$ $$T_2 = \frac{\lambda_{m_1}T_1}{\lambda_{m_2}}$$

$$= \frac{5.5 \times 10^{-7} \times 5500}{11 \times 10^{-7}}$$

$$= 2750 \text{ K}$$

34. (*b*) Given, $Y = 4.4 \times 10^{11}$ N/m^2

$$A = 1 \text{ cm}^2 = 10^{-4} \text{ m}^2$$

$$\Delta\theta = 10°\text{C}$$

We know that, increase in tension of wire due to increase in temperature $(\Delta\theta)$.

i.e. $T = YA\alpha\,\Delta\theta$

$$= 4.4 \times 10^{11} \times 10^{-4} \times 8 \times 10^{-6} \times 10$$

$$= 3.52 \times 10^3 \text{ N}$$

$$\approx 3.5 \text{ kN}$$

35. (*a*) As volume remains constant, therefore

$$R = n^{1/3}r \qquad \text{... (i)}$$

where, R = radius of big drop and r = radius of small drop.

$$\therefore \frac{\text{Energy of big drop}}{\text{Energy of small drop}} = \frac{4\pi R^2 T}{4\pi r^2 T}$$

$$= \frac{R^2}{r^2}$$

$$= \frac{(n^{1/3}r)^2}{r^2} \qquad \text{[from Eq. (i)]}$$

$$= n^{2/3} = (27)^{2/3}$$

$$= (3^3)^{2/3} = 3^2 = 9$$

36. (*d*) Heat taken by 2 g ice in transforming from ice at 0°C to water 100°C,

$$Q = mL + ms\Delta\theta$$

$$= 2 \times 80 + 2 \times 1 \times 100$$

$$= 360 \text{ cal}$$

Mass of steam condensed to give this much heat is

$$m = \frac{Q}{L}$$

$$= \frac{360}{540} = \frac{2}{3} \text{ g}$$

This is less than 2 g or total mass of steam. Therefore, whole steam is not condensed and mixture temperature is 100°C.

37. (*d*) Given, $T_A = 30°$C, $T_B = 50°$C,

$$T_0 = 42°\text{C}$$

$$\frac{m_A}{m_B} = \frac{1}{2}$$

or $$m_A = m \text{ and } m_B = 2m$$

Let the specific heats of liquid A and B be s_A and s_B respectively, then from the principle of calorimetry

Heat gaining by liquid A = Heat lost by liquid B

$$m_B s_B \Delta T_B = -m_A s_A \Delta T_A$$

Putting the values in above equation, we get

$$(2m)(s_B)(50-42) = m(s_A)(42-30)$$

$$16 s_B = 12 s_A$$

$$\frac{s_A}{s_B} = \frac{16}{12} = \frac{4}{3}$$

38. (c) Both the conducting rods are in parallel.

$$\therefore \quad H_{net} = H_1 + H_2$$

$$\frac{\Delta T}{R_{eq}} = \frac{\Delta T}{R_1} + \frac{\Delta T}{R_2} \quad \left(\because H = \frac{\Delta T}{R}\right)$$

$$\frac{T_H - T_L}{R_{eq}} = \frac{T_H - T_L}{\frac{l_0}{K(2A_0)}} + \frac{T_H - T_L}{\frac{2l_0}{2K(A_0)}} \quad \left(\because R = \frac{l}{KA}\right)$$

$$\frac{1}{R_{eq}} = \frac{2KA_0}{l_0} + \frac{KA_0}{l_0} \Rightarrow \frac{1}{R_{eq}} = \frac{3KA_0}{l_0}$$

If both rods are replaced by an arrangement which have same dimensions and same material, then we can write

$$\frac{K_{eq}(2A_0)}{l_0} + \frac{K_{eq}(A_0)}{2l_0} = \frac{3KA_0}{l_0}$$

$$\frac{5}{2}K_{eq}\frac{A_0}{l_0} = \frac{3KA_0}{l_0}$$

or $$K_{eq} = \frac{6}{5}K$$

39. (c) A. When A and B are mixed, from the principle of calorimetry

Heat lost by hot body = Heat gained by cold body

$$2m(s)(2\theta - \theta') = ms(\theta' - \theta)$$

On solving, we get

$$\theta' = \frac{5}{3}\theta$$

B. When A and C are mixed, then

$$3m(s)(3\theta - \theta') = ms(\theta' - \theta)$$

On solving, we get

$$\theta' = \frac{5}{2}\theta$$

C. When B and C are mixed, then

$$2m(s)(\theta' - 2\theta) = 3ms(3\theta - \theta')$$

On solving, we get

$$\theta' = \frac{13}{5}\theta$$

D. When A, B and C all are mixed,

$$ms(\theta' - \theta) + 2ms(\theta' - 2\theta) + 3ms(\theta' - 3\theta) = 0$$

On solving, we get

$$\theta' = \frac{7}{3}\theta$$

The column match is

A → Q, B → P, C → S, D → R

40. (d) Heat given, $dQ = mS$

or $$\frac{dT}{dQ} = \frac{1}{ms}$$

or $$\frac{dT}{dQ} = \frac{1}{C}$$

$$\text{Slope} = \frac{1}{C}$$

So, the slope of the given graph is equal to inverse of heat capacity of vapour.

41. (d) Each atom in a lattice can vibrate along three mutually perpendicular directions, each of which has two degree of freedom. One corresponding to vibrations KE and other vibration PE. Thus, each atom has a total of six degrees of freedom.

42. (c) From first law,

$$dQ = dU + dW$$

$$\Rightarrow \quad n \cdot CdT = n \cdot C_V dT + n \cdot 2RdT$$

$$\Rightarrow \quad C = C_V + 2R$$

$$\Rightarrow \quad 4R = C_V + 2R$$

$$\Rightarrow \quad C_V = 2R$$

Also, $$C_V = \frac{R}{\gamma - 1}$$

So, $$\frac{R}{\gamma - 1} = 2R$$

or $$\gamma - 1 = \frac{1}{2} \Rightarrow \gamma = \frac{3}{2}$$

43. (b) For helium gas,

$$p_1 V = \mu_1 RT$$

or $$p_1 = \frac{\mu_1 RT}{V}$$

Here, $\mu_1 = 2, T = 400\text{ K}$, $V = (0.2)^3$ or $8 \times 10^{-3}\text{ m}^3$

$$p_1 = \frac{2 \times 8.3 \times 400}{8 \times 10^{-3}}$$

$$= 8.3 \times 10^5\text{ N/m}^2$$

For oxygen gas,

$$p_2 V = \mu_2 RT$$

or $$p_2 = \frac{\mu_2 RT}{V}$$

Here, $\mu_2 = 1, T = 400\text{ K}$, $V = 8 \times 10^{-3}\text{ m}^3$

$$p_2 = \frac{1 \times 8.3 \times 400}{8 \times 10^{-3}}$$

$$= 4.15 \times 10^5\text{ N/m}^2$$

∴ Pressure of the mixture, $p = p_1 + p_2$

$$= 8.3 \times 10^5 + 4.15 \times 10^5$$

$$= 12.45 \times 10^5\text{ N/m}^2$$

44. (a) From the given graph, we find that V and T are related as $V = aT - b$, where a and b both are positive constants.

From ideal gas equation, $pV = \mu RT$,

then $p(aT - b) = \mu RT$

or $$p = \frac{\mu RT}{aT - b}$$

From the graph, $T_B > T_A$, therefore $p_B < p_A$.

45. (a) If m is the total mass of the gas, then the kinetic energy is $\frac{1}{2}mv^2$.

When the vessel is suddenly stopped, the total kinetic energy will decrease and hence the temperature of the gas.

Hence, loss in kinetic energy,

$$\frac{1}{2}mv^2 = \mu C_V \Delta T$$

$$\Rightarrow \quad \frac{1}{2}mv^2 = \frac{m}{M}C_V \Delta T$$

$$\Rightarrow \quad \Delta T = \frac{Mv^2(\gamma - 1)}{2R}$$

46. (a) Given that, $y = p\sin(2\pi qt - 2\pi rx)$

On comparing the above equation with standard equation of wave, we get Angular velocity, $\omega = 2\pi q$, amplitude, $A = p$ and wave number, $k = 2\pi r$.

As we know that, maximum velocity of particle,

$$v_{max} = \omega A$$

$$v_{max} = 2\pi qp$$

Wave velocity, $v = \frac{\omega}{k} = \frac{2\pi q}{2\pi r}$ or $\frac{q}{r}$

Given, $$v_{max} = 2v$$

$$2\pi qp = \frac{2q}{r}$$

$$p\pi = \frac{1}{r}$$

47. (a) Given, $f = 1280\text{ Hz}$

$$v_{sound} = 330\text{ m/s}$$

The distance between consecutive maxima in intensity is $x = \frac{\lambda}{2}$ ... (i)

$$\because \quad v = f \times \lambda$$

[where, v is speed of sound, λ is wavelength of wave] or $\lambda = \frac{v}{f}$

From Eq. (i), $x = \frac{v}{2f} = \frac{330}{2 \times 1280}$

$= 12.9$ cm

48. (*c*) Given, density, $\rho = 1.2$ gm/cm^3 or 1200 kg/m^3

Frequency, $f = 180$ Hz

Wavelength, $\lambda = 8$ m

We know that,

Speed of sound, $v = f\lambda$

and $v = \sqrt{\frac{B}{\rho}}$, where B is bulk modulus

or $f\lambda = \sqrt{\frac{B}{\rho}}$

or $B = \rho(f\lambda)^2$

$= 1200\,(180 \times 8)^2$

$= 2.48 \times 10^9$ N/m^2

49. (*c*) Given, mass, $m = 2$ kg

Spring constant, $k = 2000$ Nm^{-1}

Amplitude, A

= Displacement from mean position

$\Rightarrow A = 5$ cm or 0.05 m

Angular frequency, $\omega = \sqrt{\frac{k}{m}} = \sqrt{\frac{200}{2}}$

$= 10$ rad/s

Maximum speed, $v_{max} = \omega A$

$= 10 \times 0.05$

$= 0.5$ m/s

50. (*d*) Given, frequency, $f = 80$ Hz

Mass, $m = 2$ kg

Linear mass density, $\mu = 0.05$ kg/m

Increased value of mass, $m' = 4$ kg

Wavelength, $\lambda = \frac{1}{f}\sqrt{\frac{mg}{\mu}}$

Change in wavelength, $\Delta\lambda = \lambda' - \lambda$

$= \frac{1}{f}\sqrt{\frac{m'g}{\mu}} - \frac{1}{f}\sqrt{\frac{mg}{\mu}}$

$\Delta\lambda = \frac{1}{f}\sqrt{\frac{g}{\mu}}\,(\sqrt{m'} - \sqrt{m})$

Putting all values, we get

$\Delta\lambda = \frac{1}{80} \times \sqrt{\frac{9.8}{0.05}}\,(\sqrt{4} - \sqrt{1})$

$= \frac{1}{80} \times \sqrt{196}\,(2 - 1)$

$= \frac{14}{80} = 0.175$ m

Part Test 2

1. (*c*) When charges are placed in vacuum, electrostatic force between the charges q_1 and q_2,

$$F = \frac{1}{4\pi\varepsilon_0} \cdot \frac{q_1 q_2}{r^2} \quad \text{... (i)}$$

When dielectric medium is filled between them and let the distance between them is r', then electrostatic force,

$$F' = \frac{1}{4\pi\varepsilon_0 K} \cdot \frac{q_1 q_2}{r'^2} \quad \text{... (ii)}$$

where, K is dielectric strength.

According to the question, $F = F'$

$$\Rightarrow \frac{1}{4\pi\varepsilon_0} \cdot \frac{q_1 q_2}{r^2} = \frac{1}{4\pi\varepsilon_0 K} \cdot \frac{q_1 q_2}{r'^2}$$

[from Eqs. (i) and (ii)]

$$r'^2 = \frac{r^2}{K}$$

or $r' = \frac{r}{\sqrt{K}}$

2. (*c*) When electron is brought from infinity, it experiences a force of attraction exerted by proton and work done by electrostatic force is positive. In this case, electrostatic force is internal force and we know that, when internal force does work, the potential energy of the system decreases.

$\because \quad W_{system} = -\Delta U$

3. (*b*) The given circuit diagram can be redrawn as

[Circuit: 10 V battery in series with 2 μF capacitor (V_1) and 3 μF capacitor (V_2); 0 V, 0 V]

Let the potential difference across capacitors of capacitance 2μF and 3μF be V_1 and V_2, respectively.

$$V_1 = \frac{C_2}{C_1 + C_2} \times V$$

Here, $C_1 = 2\,\mu$F, $C_2 = 3\,\mu$F and $V = 10$ V

$\therefore \quad V_1 = \frac{3}{2+3} \times 10$

$= 6$ V

$\therefore$ The charge on capacitor of 2μF capacitance, $Q_1 = C_1 V_1$

$= 2 \times 10^{-6} \times 6$

$Q_1 = 12 \times 10^{-6}$ or 12μC

4. (*c*) As, we know that, the direction of electric field due to a positive point charge is always away from it and that due to negative charge, is towards the charge.

In the given figure, the electric field due to q_1 is towards left. So, nature of charge is negative and field due to q_2 is towards right, so it is positive.

5. (*d*) As we know, electric field,

$$E = -\frac{dV}{dx} \text{ or } -\frac{\Delta V}{\Delta x}$$

For region A, $E_A = -\frac{30 - 60}{6 - 2} = +7.5$ V/m

For region B, $E_B = -\frac{45 - 30}{8 - 6} = -7.5$ V/m

For region C, $E_C = 0$

For region D, $E_D = -\frac{20 - 45}{15 - 12}$

$= +8.33$ V/m

6. (*c*) The capacitance of parallel plate capacitor is given as

$$C = \frac{\varepsilon_r \varepsilon_0 A}{d} \quad \text{... (i)}$$

where, ε_0 is permittivity of medium in between plates and ε_r is relative permittivity of medium in between plates.

A is area of plates of capacitor and d is distance between the plates of capacitor.

Given that, $C = 4\,\mu$F

For air, $\varepsilon_r = 1$

$\therefore \quad 4 = \frac{\varepsilon_0 A}{d} \quad$ ... (ii)

[using Eq.(i)]

Now, distance is tripled and dielectric medium is filled in between region of plates.

Then, $d' = 3d$, $C' = 4 + 20 = 24\,\mu$F

$\therefore \quad 24 = \frac{K\varepsilon_0 A}{3d} \quad$ ... (iii)

On dividing Eq. (ii) by Eq. (iii), we get

$\frac{4}{24} = \frac{3}{K}$ or $K = 18$

7. (*d*) As it is given that, power dissipation in each resistor is equal. i.e.,

$$P_{R_1} = P_{R_2} = P_{R_3}$$

In parallel arrangement, voltage remains same (say V).

Since, R_2 and R_3 are in parallel connection, so we can write

$$\frac{V^2}{R_2} = \frac{V^2}{R_3}$$

or $R_2 = R_3$

$\therefore$ Same current will flow through R_2 and R_3 as shown below

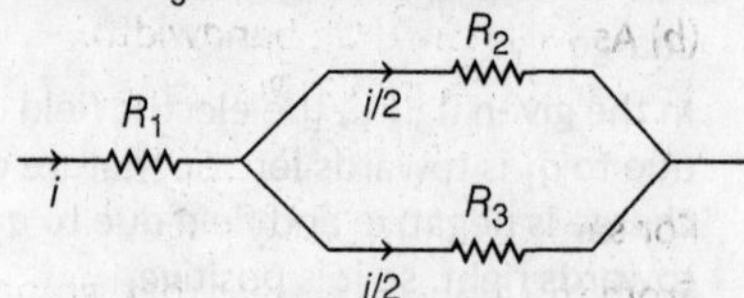

Since, current through R_1 will be doubled, so R_1 should be 1/4 th of R_2 or R_3.

For same power, as $P = i^2R$.

$\therefore$ Ratio, $R_1 : R_2 : R_3 = \frac{1}{4} : 1 : 1$

or $R_1 : R_2 : R_3 = 1 : 4 : 4$

8. (*a*) Given, diameter,

$$d = 0.8 \text{ mm or } 0.8 \times 10^{-3} \text{m}$$

Electric field, $E = 0.55$ V/m

Resistivity, $\rho = 2.75 \times 10^{-8}$ Ω-m

As, current density, $J = \frac{E}{\rho}$ ...(i)

and $J = \frac{I}{A}$ ...(ii)

From Eqs. (i) and (ii), we get

$\therefore$ $I = \frac{E}{\rho} \times A$

$$= \frac{0.55}{2.75 \times 10^{-8}} \times \frac{\pi \times (0.8 \times 10^{-3})^2}{4}$$

$$\left(\because A = \frac{\pi d^2}{4}\right)$$

$I = 10.05$ A

9. (*b*) Let m is the number of cells are in reversed polarity.

Equivalent emf, $E_{\text{net}} = (n - 2m)E$

Given that, $E_{\text{net}} = 360$ V

$n = 100$

$E = 4$ V

$\therefore$ $360 = (100 - 2 \times m) \times 4$

$90 = 100 - 2m$

or $2m = 100 - 90$

or $2m = 10$

or $m = 5$

10. (*d*) In a discharge tube, current is due to both positive and negative ions present in it.

$\therefore$ $I_{\text{total}} = I_+ + I_-$

$= (2n) eAv + neA(2v)$

$(\because I = neAv_d)$

$= 4neAv$

11. (*b*) Given, $q = at - bt^2$

Instantaneous current, $I = \frac{dq}{dt}$

$$= \frac{d}{dt}(at - bt^2)$$

or $I = a - 2bt$

Charge will flow till current becomes zero i.e.

$I = 0$

$a - 2bt = 0$

or $t = \frac{a}{2b}$

It means charge will flow from $t = 0$ to $t = \frac{a}{2b}$.

At $t = 0, q_i = a \times 0 - b \times 0^2 = 0$

At $t = \frac{a}{2b}$,

$$q_f = a \times \frac{a}{2b} - b \times \left(\frac{a}{2b}\right)^2$$

$\Rightarrow$ $q_f = \frac{a^2}{4b}$

Net charge flown, $\Delta q = q_f - q_i$

$$= \frac{a^2}{4b} - 0$$

$$= \frac{a^2}{4b}$$

12. (*c*) We know that, metallic conductors follow Ohm's law, it means the graph between I and V is straight line passing through origin. So, there is only one value of V for corresponding current.

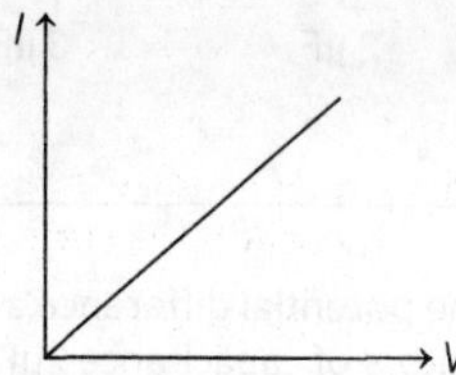

Diode does not follow Ohm's law as its I-V graph is non-linear in nature as shown below.

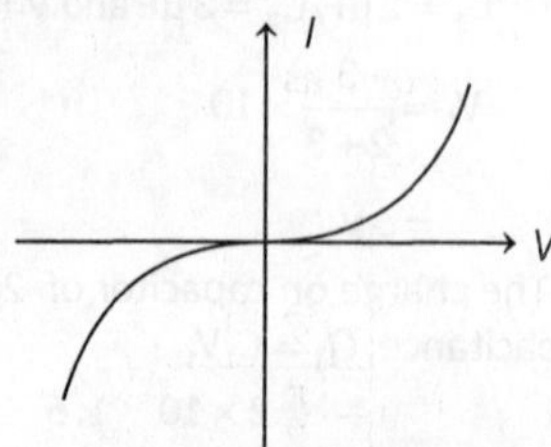

From above, it is clear that there is only one value V for each corresponding value of current.

Now, the I-V graph for gallium arsenide has been shown in the figure below.

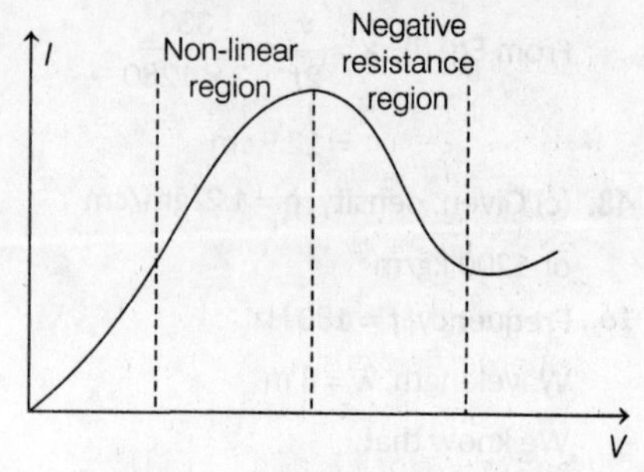

From the above mentioned graph, the relation between V and I is not unique i.e. there is more than one value of V for the same value of current I.

13. (*d*) The currents in the given figure can be shown as

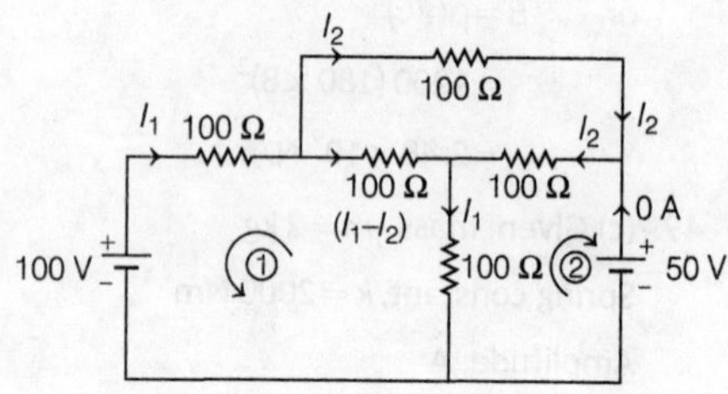

Using Kirchhoff's loop law in loop ① along the direction shown.

$100 - 100I_1 - 100(I_1 - I_2) - 100I_1 = 0$

$100 - 100I_1 - 100I_1 + 100I_2 - 100I_1 = 0$

$300I_1 - 100I_2 = 100$

or $3I_1 - I_2 = 1$ ... (i)

Using KVL in loop ②,

$50 - 100I_2 - 100I_1 = 0$

or $100I_1 + 100I_2 = 50$

or $2I_1 + 2I_2 = 1$ ... (ii)

On solving Eqs. (i) and (ii), we get

$$I_1 = \frac{3}{8}, I_2 = \frac{1}{8}$$

Ratio, $\frac{I_1}{I_2} = \frac{3/8}{1/8} = \frac{3}{1}$

14. (*d*) When temperature of ferromagnetic material increases, its magnetic susceptibility decreases and it is converted into paramagnetic at curie temperature. Hence, graph shown in option (d) is correct.

15. (*b*) Mass of α-particle, $m_\alpha = 4m_p$

Charge on α-particle, $q_\alpha = 2q_p$

Since, α-particle and proton, both enters into magnetic field in perpendicular direction, hence both will move on circular path in magnetic field.

We know that, time period of charged particle in magnetic field B having charge q and mass m,

$$T = \frac{2\pi m}{Bq} \Rightarrow T \propto \frac{m}{q}$$

$$\Rightarrow \quad \frac{T_\alpha}{T_p} = \frac{m_\alpha}{m_p} \cdot \frac{q_p}{q_\alpha} = \frac{4m_p}{m_p} \times \frac{q_p}{2q_p} = 2$$

$$\Rightarrow \quad T_\alpha = 2T_p$$

16. (*b*) Potential energy of a toroid in an external field is always zero. As,

$$U = -\mathbf{M} \cdot \mathbf{B}$$

and $M = 0$ for a toroid.

17. (*b*) Magnetic field strength at the centre of current carrying circular coil,

$$B = \frac{\mu_0 I}{2r}$$

For same value of I,

$$B \propto \frac{1}{r}$$

$$\Rightarrow \quad \frac{B_2}{B_1} = \frac{r_1}{r_2} = \frac{r_1}{4r_1} \quad (\because r_2 = 4r_1)$$

$$= \frac{1}{4}$$

$$\Rightarrow \quad B_2 = \frac{B_1}{4}$$

18. (*b*) The situation is shown below

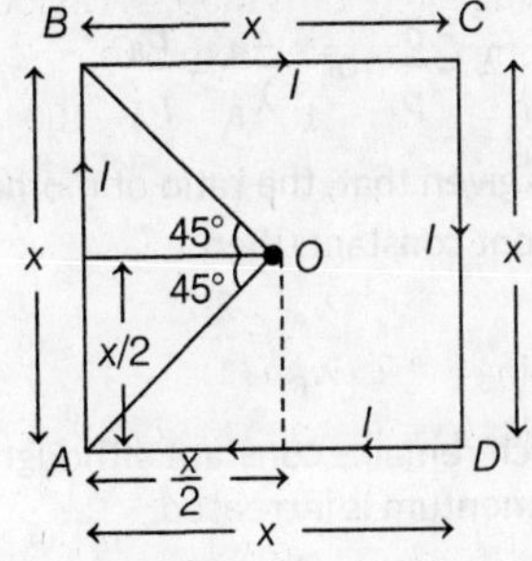

Here, $\theta_1 = \theta_2 = 45°$

Magnetic field at O due to current carrying wire AB,

$$B_1 = \frac{\mu_0}{4\pi} \frac{I}{\left(\frac{x}{2}\right)} (\sin 45° + \sin 45°)$$

$$= \frac{\mu_0}{2\pi} \cdot \frac{I}{x}\left[\frac{1}{\sqrt{2}} + \frac{1}{\sqrt{2}}\right]$$

$$= \frac{\mu_0}{2\pi} \cdot \frac{I}{x} (\sqrt{2})$$

Total magnetic field at O due to whole loop.

$$B = 4B_1$$

$$= 4 \times \frac{\mu_0}{2\pi} \cdot \frac{I}{x} \cdot \sqrt{2}$$

$$= \frac{2\sqrt{2}\mu_0 I}{\pi x}$$

19. (*c*) Force experienced by a current carrying conductor placed in uniform magnetic field B is given as

$$F = BIl \sin\theta \quad \text{...(i)}$$

where, θ is the angle between the conductor and direction of magnetic field.

If $\theta = 0°$ or $180°$, then from Eq. (i),

$$F = 0$$

20. (*d*) If electrons enter into uniform magnetic field with any angle except 0°, 90° or 180°, then its path will be helical.

Similarly, for 0° or 180°, its path will be straight line and if $\theta = 90°$, then its path will be circular.

21. (*c*) Given that, side, $a = 5$ cm or 5×10^{-2} m

Area, $A = a^2 = (5 \times 10^{-2})^2$

$$= 25 \times 10^{-4} \text{ m}^2$$

Resistance, $R = 1\,\Omega$

Magnetic field, $B = 0.2$ T

The loop is in East-West plane and magnetic field is in the North-East direction, therefore angle between **B** and **A** is 0°.

Initial magnetic flux, $\phi_i = BA\cos\theta$

$$= 0.2 \times 25 \times 10^{-4} \times \cos 0°$$

$$= 5 \times 10^{-4} \text{ Wb}$$

Final magnetic flux, $\phi_f = BA\cos\theta$

$$\phi_f = 0 \times (A\cos\theta) = 0$$

The charge flow, $\Delta q = -\frac{\Delta\phi_B}{R} = -\frac{\phi_f - \phi_i}{R}$

$$= \frac{\phi_i - \phi_f}{R} = \frac{5 \times 10^{-4} - 0}{1}$$

$$= 0.5 \text{ mC}$$

22. (*c*) When an AC voltage is applied across a capacitor, the current leads voltage by a phase of $\frac{\pi}{2}$.

Similarly, when AC inductor is subjected to same AC voltage, the current flowing through it lags voltage by a phase of $\frac{\pi}{2}$. The phase diagram can be shown as

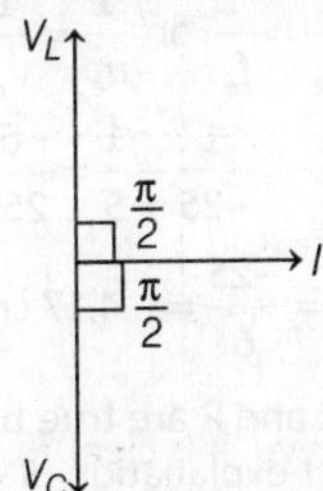

From the phasor diagram, it is clear that phase difference between V_L and V_C is π.

23. (*b*) As we know that, bandwidth,

$$\Delta w = \frac{R}{L} \quad \text{... (i)}$$

For same value of L, $\Delta w \propto R$

From the graph, it is clear that, graph 2 has less bandwidth as compared to 1.

i.e. $\Delta w_2 < \Delta w_1$

$\therefore$ From Eq. (i), $\frac{R_2}{L} < \frac{R_1}{L}$

or $\quad R_2 < R_1$ or $R_1 > R_2$

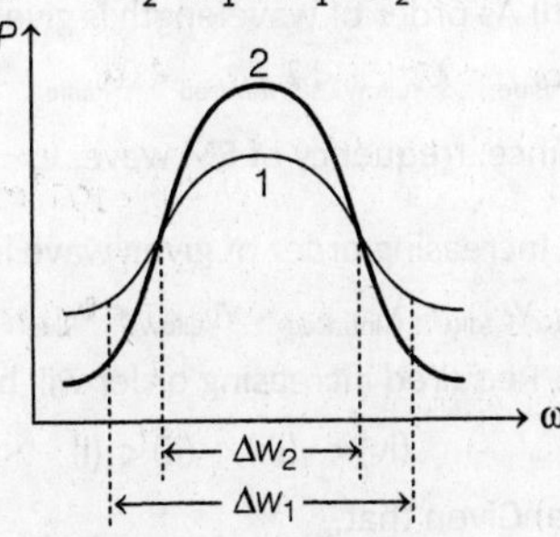

Also, ϕ-factor, $Q = \frac{1}{R}\sqrt{\frac{L}{C}}$

For same values of L and C, $Q \propto \frac{1}{R}$

$$R_2 < R_1$$

$$\therefore \quad \frac{1}{R_2} > \frac{1}{R_1}$$

$$\therefore \quad Q_2 > Q_1 \text{ or } Q_1 < Q_2$$

24. (*a*) Given, $R = 10\,\Omega$, $X_L = 20\,\Omega$, $X_C = 10\,\Omega$ and $V = 20\sin(314t)$ V

Since, the nature of source voltage is AC sinusoidal and the average value of current for complete cycle is zero.

25. (*b*) In *L-C* oscillator, the energy stored is transformed from capacitor-to-inductor and inductor-to-capacitor back.

Given that, maximum energy,

$$U_m = 160\,\mu\text{J}$$

when $I = 5$ A, energy stored by inductor $U_L = 10\,\mu\text{J}$

So, at same instant of time the energy stored by capacitor is

$$U_c = U_m - U_L$$

$$= 160 - 10$$

$$= 150\,\mu\text{J}$$

26. (*a*) Given that, magnetic field,

$$\mathbf{B} = \alpha t\hat{\mathbf{i}} + \beta t^2\hat{\mathbf{j}} + \gamma\hat{\mathbf{k}}$$

Area vector, $\mathbf{A} = A\hat{\mathbf{i}}$

($\because$ loop is placed in *YZ*-plane)

Magnetic flux associated to loop,

$$\phi = \mathbf{B} \cdot \mathbf{A}$$

$$= (\alpha t\hat{\mathbf{i}} + \beta t^2\hat{\mathbf{j}} + \gamma\hat{\mathbf{k}}) \cdot (A\hat{\mathbf{i}})$$

$$= A\alpha t$$

Magnitude of induced emf, $|e| = \left|\frac{d\phi}{dt}\right|$

$$= \left|\frac{d}{dt}(A\alpha t)\right|$$

$$= A\alpha \text{ (constant)}$$

At $t = 1$ s, $|e| = A\alpha = 2$ V

and at $t = 4$ s, $|e| = A\alpha = 2$ V

27. (*b*) As order of wavelength is given by,

$$\lambda_{Blue} < \lambda_{Yellow} < \lambda_{Infrared} < \lambda_{Radio}$$

Since, frequency of EM wave, $\nu \propto \frac{1}{\lambda}$

∴ Increasing order of given wave is

$$\nu_{Radio} < \nu_{Infrared} < \nu_{Yellow} < \nu_{Blue}$$

∴ Required increasing order will be

(iv) < (iii) < (ii) < (i)

28. (*a*) Given that,

Relative permittivity, $\varepsilon_r = 1.5$

Relative permeability, $\mu_r = 6$

The speed of EM wave in a material medium is given as

$$v = \frac{c}{\sqrt{\varepsilon_r \mu_r}}$$

where, c is speed of light in vacuum/air.

Substituting the given values, we get

$$v = \frac{3 \times 10^8}{\sqrt{1.5 \times 6}}$$

$$= \frac{3 \times 10^8}{\sqrt{9}}$$

$$= \frac{3 \times 10^8}{3}$$

$$= 10^8 \text{ m/s}$$

29. (*d*) Electric field **E**, magnetic field **B** and direction of propagation of wave, all are mutually perpendicular to each other.

Given that, EM wave is propagating along y-direction, so **E** and **B** will be perpendicular to that, this means they will be along X-axis and Z-axis.

30. (*a*) When an oscillating charged particle of the frequency f is oscillating in an oscillator, this particle produces an oscillating electric field of same frequency f. Now, this oscillating electric field becomes a source of oscillating magnetic field. This oscillating magnetic field again becomes a source of oscillating electric field and so on thereby, producing an electromagnetic wave, which has the frequency equals to the frequency of oscillating charged particle.

31. (*a*) Given that,

Frequency, $f = 6 \times 10^{10}$ Hz

Amplitude of magnetic field,

$$B = 2 \times 10^{-7} \text{ T}$$

Speed of EM wave, $c = 3 \times 10^8$ m/s

From the relation, $c = f \times \lambda$

Wavelength, $\lambda = \frac{c}{f}$

$$= \frac{3 \times 10^8}{6 \times 10^{10}}$$

$$= 5 \times 10^{-3} \text{ m}$$

or $= 5$ mm

32. (*a*) In a compound microscope preferred position of final image is at least distance of distinct vision.

So, $v_e = 25$ cm

Angular magnification of eyepiece,

$$m_e = 1 + \frac{D}{f_e} = 1 + \frac{25}{5} = 6$$

Magnification of objective,

$$m_o = \frac{m}{m_e} = \frac{30}{6} = 5$$

For objective,

$$\frac{v_o}{u_o} = -5 \Rightarrow v_o = -5u_o$$

Also for objective,

$$u_o = -x \Rightarrow u_o = -5(-x) = 5x$$

Now,

$$\frac{1}{f_o} = \frac{1}{v_o} - \frac{1}{u_o} = \frac{1}{5x} - \left(\frac{1}{-x}\right)$$

$$\Rightarrow \frac{1}{1.25} = \frac{6}{5x} \quad \text{or} \quad x = 1.5 \text{ cm}$$

So, $u_o = -1.5$ cm

$$v_o = -5u_o = -5(-1.5)$$

$$= 7.5 \text{ cm}$$

For eyepiece,

$$\frac{1}{v_e} - \frac{1}{u_e} = \frac{1}{f_e} \quad \text{or} \quad \frac{1}{u_e} = \frac{1}{v_e} - \frac{1}{f_e}$$

$$\Rightarrow \frac{1}{u_e} = \frac{1}{-25} - \frac{1}{5} = \frac{-6}{25}$$

or $u_e = \frac{-25}{6} = -4.17$ cm

33. (*a*) Both A and R are true but R is not the correct explanation of A.

In a compound microscope as object to be viewed are small, so we need a smaller objective to keep field of vision smaller.

Also resolution is directly proportional to diameter of objective.

34. (*d*) For final image at infinity image of objective must be formed at focal point of eyepiece.

Now for objective,

$$\frac{1}{v_o} - \frac{1}{u_o} = \frac{1}{f_o}$$

Here, $u_o = -2$ m, $f_o = +30$ cm

$= -200$ cm

So, $v_o = 35.5$ cm

Now, distance of objective and eyepiece

$$= v_o + f_e = 38.5 \text{ cm} \simeq 40 \text{ cm}$$

35. (*d*) As, given

Momentum of particle A, $p_A = p$

Momentum of particle B, $p_B = 2p$

The ratio of momentum at every instant of time

$$\frac{p_A}{p_B} = \frac{1}{2} \text{ or } \frac{p_B}{p_A} = \frac{2}{1}$$

We know that, de-Broglie wavelength,

$$\lambda = \frac{h}{p} \quad \text{or} \quad \frac{\lambda_A}{\lambda_B} = \frac{p_B}{p_A}$$

It is given that, the ratio of momentum is kept constant, then

$$\frac{\lambda_A}{\lambda_B} = \frac{2}{1}$$

which remains constant although momentum is increased.

36. (*d*) In a photon-particle collision, such as photoelectron collision, the total energy and total momentum are conserved. However, the number of photons may or may not be conserved. The photon may be absorbed or a new photon may be created.

As, in the case of Compton effect, when a photon with some energy collides with a stationary electron, some of the energy and momentum is transferred to the electron.

Thus, all the given statements are true.

37. (*b*) We know that, the relation between de-Broglie wavelength λ and kinetic energy K of a particle is given by

$$\lambda = \frac{h}{\sqrt{2mK}}$$

Here, for the given value of kinetic energy, $\frac{h}{\sqrt{2K}}$ is a constant.

Thus, $\lambda \propto \frac{1}{\sqrt{m}}$

$\therefore \lambda_p : \lambda_n : \lambda_e : \lambda_\alpha$

$= \frac{1}{\sqrt{m_p}} : \frac{1}{\sqrt{m_n}} : \frac{1}{\sqrt{m_e}} : \frac{1}{\sqrt{m_\alpha}}$

Since, $m_p = m_n$, hence $\lambda_p = \lambda_n$

and $m_\alpha = m_p$, therefore $\lambda_\alpha < \lambda_p$

and $m_e < m_n$, therefore $\lambda_e > \lambda_n$

Thus, correct sequence is

$\lambda_\alpha < \lambda_p = \lambda_n < \lambda_e$

38. (*a*) de-Broglie wavelength when a charge q is accelerated by a potential difference of V volts, is

$$\lambda_d = \frac{h}{\sqrt{2qVm}} \quad \text{... (i)}$$

For cut off wavelength of X-rays, we have

$$qV = \frac{hc}{\lambda_m}$$

or $$\lambda_m = \frac{hc}{qV} \quad \text{... (ii)}$$

From Eqs. (i) and (ii), we get

$$\frac{\lambda_d}{\lambda_m} = \frac{\sqrt{\frac{qV}{2m}}}{c} \quad \text{... (iii)}$$

Given that, for electron, specific charge,

$$\frac{q}{m} = 1.8 \times 10^{11} \text{ C/kg}$$

Potential difference, $V = 10$ kV or 10^4 V

Putting these values in Eq. (iii), we get

$$\frac{\lambda_d}{\lambda_m} = \frac{\sqrt{\frac{1.8 \times 10^{11} \times 10^4}{2}}}{3 \times 10^8}$$

$$= 0.1 \text{ or } 1 : 10$$

39. (*c*) Velocity of a particle falling through a height H is given as

$$v = \sqrt{2gH}$$

We know that, de-Broglie wavelength,

$\lambda = \frac{h}{mv}$, where h is Planck's constant

$$\lambda = \frac{h}{m\sqrt{2gH}}$$

$$= \frac{h}{m\sqrt{2g}\sqrt{H}}$$

Here, $\frac{h}{m\sqrt{2g}}$ is a constant.

$$\therefore \quad \lambda \propto \frac{1}{\sqrt{H}}$$

40. (*d*) Let the work function of the metal be ϕ.

Case (i) When photon of wavelength λ is incident on metal surface, the velocity of most energetic photoelectron v, then

From Einstein's photoelectric equation,

$$E = \phi + \text{KE}_{max}$$

$$\frac{hc}{\lambda} = \phi + \frac{1}{2}mv^2 \quad \text{... (i)}$$

Case (ii) When wavelength of photon is halved $\left(\lambda' = \frac{\lambda}{2}\right)$, the velocity of most energetic photoelectron becomes double.

Again by using Einstein's photoelectric equation,

$$\frac{hc}{\lambda/2} = \phi + \frac{1}{2}m(2v)^2$$

$$\Rightarrow \quad \frac{2hc}{\lambda} = \phi + 4 \cdot \frac{1}{2}mv^2 \quad \text{... (ii)}$$

Multiplying Eq (i). by 4 and then subtracting from Eq. (ii), we get

$$\frac{2hc}{\lambda} = 3\phi$$

or $$\phi = \frac{2}{3}\frac{hc}{\lambda}$$

41. (*d*) Given that, half-life of $^{238}_{92}$U,

$$T_{1/2} = 4.5 \times 10^9 \text{ years}$$

$$= 4.5 \times 10^9 \times 3.16 \times 10^7 \text{ s}$$

$$(\because 1 \text{ year} = 3.16 \times 10^7 \text{ s})$$

$$= 1.42 \times 10^{17} \text{ s}$$

Number of atoms in 2 g sample of $^{238}_{92}$U

is $N = \frac{m}{m_W} \times N_A$

$$N = \frac{2}{238} \times 6.023 \times 10^{23}$$

or $$N = 50.6 \times 10^{20} \text{ atoms}$$

As, the activity of radioactive sample,

$$R = \lambda N$$

$$= \frac{0.693}{T_{1/2}} N$$

$$\left(\because \text{Decay constant, } \lambda = \frac{0.693}{T_{1/2}}\right)$$

$$= \frac{0.693}{1.42 \times 10^{17}} \times 50.6 \times 10^{20}$$

$$= 2.46 \times 10^4 \text{ decay/s}$$

$$= 2.46 \times 10^4 \text{ Bq}$$

42. (*d*) According to de-Broglie hypothesis, a stationary orbit is that which contains an integral number of de-Broglie standing waves associated with the revolving electron.

For an electron revolving in nth circular orbit of radius r_n,

Total distance covered = Circumference of the orbit $= 2\pi r_n$

$\therefore$ For the permissible orbit, $2\pi r_n = n\lambda$

According to de-Broglie wavelength,

$$\lambda = \frac{h}{mv_n}$$

where, v_n is the speed of electron revolving in nth orbit.

$$\therefore \quad 2\pi r_n = \frac{nh}{mv_n} \quad \text{or} \quad mv_n r_n = \frac{nh}{2\pi}$$

i.e. Angular momentum of electron revolving in nth orbit must be an integral multiple of $\frac{h}{2\pi}$, which is the quantum condition proposed by Bohr's in second postulate.

Bohr's atomic model is applicable only to a single electron atoms or ions and this electron can be in any excited state.

43. (*c*) Energy of electron in first excited state at He$^+$ ion, $E_2 = -13.6 \times \frac{(Z)^2}{(n)^2}$ eV

Here, $Z = 2, n = 2$

$$\therefore \quad E_2 = -13.6 \frac{(2)^2}{(2)^2}$$

$$= -13.6 \text{ eV}$$

Therefore, energy of photon released during formation of He$^+$ ion,

$$\Delta E = E' - E_2 = 4 - (-13.6)$$

$$= 17.6 \text{ eV} \quad (\because \text{given, } E' = 4 \text{ eV})$$

As, wavelength of emitted photon,

$$\lambda = \frac{12375}{\Delta E} \Rightarrow = \frac{12375}{17.6}$$

$$= 703.12 \text{ Å}$$

44. (*a*) When charge particle is moving in a circular path in presence of magnetic field, its radius is given by

$$r = \frac{mv}{qB}$$

$$= \frac{mv}{eB} \quad \text{... (i)}$$

$$(\because q = e)$$

According to Bohr quantisation of angular momentum,

$$mvr = \frac{nh}{2\pi} \quad \text{... (ii)}$$

From Eqs. (i) and (ii), we get

$$v = \sqrt{\frac{nhBe}{2\pi m^2}}$$

As, kinetic energy of revolving electron,

$$K = \frac{1}{2}mv^2$$

$$\Rightarrow \quad = \frac{1}{2}m\left(\sqrt{\frac{nhBe}{2\pi m^2}}\right)^2$$

$$= \frac{nhBe}{4\pi m}$$

45. (*a*) The energy of electron in *n*th orbit of hydrogen like atom is given as

$$E_n = -13.6\frac{Z^2}{n^2}\text{ eV}$$

The electron is in quantum state of quantum number $2n$, so the maximum energy that can emit electron in the form of photon, if transition takes place from $2n$ to 1 will be

Difference of energy,

$$E_{2n} - E_1 = \left[-13.6\frac{Z^2}{(2n)^2}\right] - \left[-13.6\frac{Z^2}{(1)^2}\right]$$

$$E_{2n} - E_1 = 13.6\,Z^2\left(1 - \frac{1}{4n^2}\right)\text{eV}$$

Given, $E_{2n} - E_1 = 204$ eV

$$204 = 13.6\,Z^2\left(1 - \frac{1}{4n^2}\right)$$

or $$1 - \frac{1}{4n^2} = \frac{15}{Z^2} \quad \text{... (i)}$$

Further, $E_{2n} - E_n = 40.8$ eV

$$-13.6\frac{Z^2}{(2n)^2} - \left(-13.6\frac{Z^2}{n^2}\right) = 40.8$$

$$13.6\,Z^2\left(\frac{1}{n^2} - \frac{1}{4n^2}\right) = 40.8$$

or $$13.6 \times Z^2 \times \frac{3}{4n^2} = 40.8$$

$$\frac{Z^2}{n^2} = 4 \quad \text{... (ii)}$$

On solving Eqs. (i) and (ii), we get

$$Z = 4, n = 2$$

46. (*d*) A solar cell is basically a *p-n* junction, which generates emf when solar radiation falls on the *p-n* junction. The difference between a photodiode, LED or zener diode with a solar cell is that, no external bias is applied across the solar cell. The junction area of a solar cell is kept much larger.

47. (*b*) The *p-n* junction diode does not allow the current to flow through its junction, if the applied voltage is less than the barrier voltage. The barrier potential for germanium *p-n* diode and silicon diode is 0.2 V and 0.7 V, respectively.

48. (*d*) Zener diode is a reverse biased heavily doped *p-n* junction diode. It is operated in breakdown region. It is designed to operate in the reverse breakdown voltage continuously without being damaged. When the applied reverse voltage (V_Z) reaches the breakdown voltage (V_Z) of the zener diode, there is a large change in the current. So, after the breakdown voltage V_Z, a large change in the current can be produced by almost insignificant change in the reverse bias voltage, i.e., zener voltage remains constant even though the current through the zener diode varies over a wide range.

Due to this, zener diode is joined in reverse bias to the fluctuating DC input voltage through a resistance *R*. Thus, it is used as a voltage stabiliser (voltage regulator).

49. (*c*) The *I-V* characteristics of solar cell is drawn in the fourth quadrant of the coordinate axis because a solar cell does not draw current but supplies the same to the load. Therefore, the *I - V* characteristics of solar cell has been shown below in figure

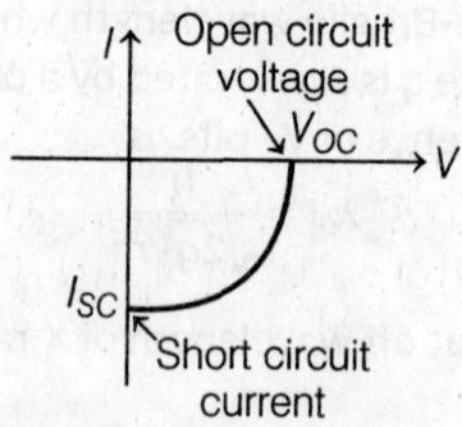

50. (*b*) The *I-V* characteristic curve for a photodiode is shown below.

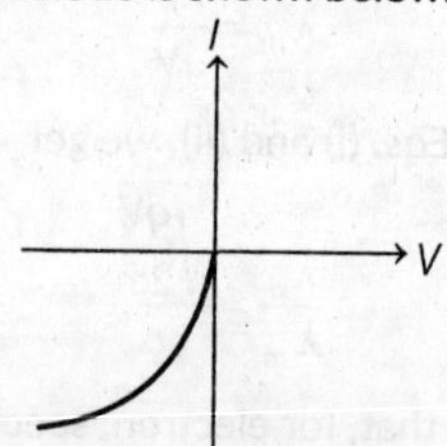

With increasing biasing voltage of a photodiode, the photocurrent first increases and then becomes saturated. i.e. After certain potential, electron-hole pair production will be nearly constant.

KNOCKOUTS

Knockout 1

1. (*a*)

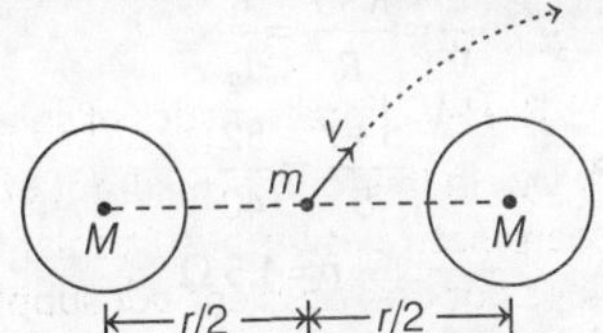

Total initial energy of rocket

$$= \frac{1}{2}mv^2 - 2\left(\frac{GMm}{r/2}\right)$$

Final energy of rocket = 0

Conservation of energy gives

$$\frac{1}{2}mv^2 - \frac{4GMm}{r} = 0$$

$$\frac{1}{2}mv^2 = \frac{4GMm}{r}$$

$$v^2 = \frac{8GM}{r} \text{ or } v = 2\sqrt{\frac{2GM}{r}}$$

2. (*a*) Net force on a charged particle in electric field and magnetic field is given by

$$\mathbf{F} = q(\mathbf{v}\times\mathbf{B} + \mathbf{E})$$

or $\mathbf{E} = \frac{\mathbf{F}}{q} - \mathbf{v}\times\mathbf{B}$

$$= \frac{9.6\times10^{-19}(\hat{\mathbf{i}} - \hat{\mathbf{k}})}{-1.6\times10^{-19}} - (60\hat{\mathbf{i}})\times(0.1\,\hat{\mathbf{j}})$$

$$= -6(\hat{\mathbf{i}} - \hat{\mathbf{k}}) - 6(\hat{\mathbf{i}}\times\hat{\mathbf{j}})$$

$$= -6\hat{\mathbf{i}} + 6\hat{\mathbf{k}} - 6\hat{\mathbf{k}} \qquad (\because \hat{\mathbf{i}}\times\hat{\mathbf{j}} = \hat{\mathbf{k}})$$

$$\mathbf{E} = -6\hat{\mathbf{i}} \text{ N/C}$$

3. (*a*) A vector along angle bisector of $\hat{\mathbf{a}}$ and $\hat{\mathbf{b}}$ is $\hat{\mathbf{a}} + \hat{\mathbf{b}}$ (using parallelogram law).

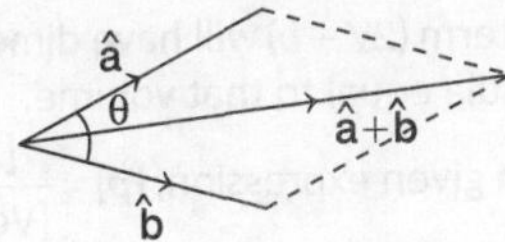

Also magnitude of $\hat{\mathbf{a}} + \hat{\mathbf{b}}$ is

$$R = \sqrt{(\hat{\mathbf{a}})^2 + (\hat{\mathbf{b}})^2 + 2\hat{\mathbf{a}}\hat{\mathbf{b}}\cos\theta}$$

$$= \sqrt{1 + 1 + 2\cos\theta}$$

$$= \sqrt{2(1+\cos\theta)}$$

$$= \sqrt{4\cos^2\frac{\theta}{2}} = 2\cos\frac{\theta}{2}$$

So, unit vector $= \frac{\hat{\mathbf{a}}+\hat{\mathbf{b}}}{R} = \frac{\hat{\mathbf{a}}+\hat{\mathbf{b}}}{2\cos\frac{\theta}{2}}$.

4. (*d*) $E = \frac{V^2 \times t}{R}$

$\Rightarrow$ Fractional uncertainty in energy is

$$\frac{\Delta E}{E} = 2\frac{\Delta V}{V} + \frac{\Delta t}{t} + \frac{\Delta R}{R}$$

$\Rightarrow$ Absolute uncertainty in energy will be,

$$\Delta E = E\left(\frac{2\Delta V}{V} + \frac{\Delta t}{t} + \frac{\Delta R}{R}\right)$$

Substituting given values, we get

$$\Delta E = 80\left(2\times\frac{0.1}{4.0} + \frac{1}{50} + \frac{0.3}{10.0}\right)$$

$$= 0.1\times80 = 8\text{ J}$$

5. (*d*) Given that, $x^2 = 4 + t$ or $x = \sqrt{4+t}$

We know that velocity,

$$v = \frac{dx}{dt} = \frac{d}{dt}(\sqrt{4+t})$$

$$v = \frac{1}{2\sqrt{4+t}} = \frac{1}{2x}$$

$$\left[\because \frac{d}{dx}(ax+b)^n = na(ax+b)^{n-1}\right]$$

Also, acceleration, $a = v\frac{dv}{dx}$

$$= \frac{1}{2x}\frac{d}{dx}\left(\frac{1}{2x}\right) = \frac{1}{2x}\left(-\frac{1}{2x^2}\right)$$

$$a = -\frac{1}{4x^3}$$

6. (*d*) Density at temperature T,

$$\rho = \rho_0(1 - \alpha\Delta T)$$

$$\rho = \rho_0 - \rho_0\,\alpha\,\Delta T$$

$$\Rightarrow \frac{\rho - \rho_0}{\rho_0} = -\alpha\Delta T$$

$\therefore$ Fractional change in density,

$$\frac{\Delta\rho}{\rho_0} = -\alpha\Delta T = -6\times10^{-5}\times60$$

$$\frac{\Delta\rho}{\rho_0} = -3.6\times10^{-3}$$

Negative sign indicates that density decreases with rise in temperature.

7. (*a*) As we know,

Capacitive reactance, $X_C = \frac{1}{\omega C}$ or $\frac{1}{2\pi fC}$

with decrease in frequency, X_C will increase, so current flowing through capacitor will decrease.

Also, in the case of a capacitor,

Displacement current = Conduction current

i.e. $i_d = i_c$

As, i_c has decreased on decreasing frequency, so i_d will also decrease.

8. (*b*) Heat is supplied in process D to A at constant volume and in process A to B at constant pressure.

$\therefore$ Heat supplied,

$$Q = nC_V(\Delta T)_{DA} + nC_p(\Delta T)_{AB}$$

For an ideal monoatomic gas,

$$C_V = \frac{3}{2}R \text{ and } C_p = \frac{5}{2}R$$

$$\Rightarrow \quad Q = \frac{3}{2}nR\Delta T + \frac{5}{2}nR\Delta T$$

$$[\because nR\Delta T = p\Delta V]$$

$$= \frac{3}{2}(p_0V_0) + 5(p_0V_0) = \frac{13}{2}p_0V_0$$

9. (*a*) Diode will be in forward bias when V_i becomes 10 V and it conducts till V_i is 12 V.

Total circuit resistance

$$= 200 + 20 = 220\,\Omega$$

When V_i = 8V, then diode will not conduct due to its reverse biasing.

Thus, initial current, $I_1 = 0$.

When V_i = 12V, then diode will be in forward bias with effective voltage,

$V' = 12 - 10 = 2$V

$\therefore$ Maximum current, $I_2 = \frac{V'}{R} = \frac{2}{220}$

$$= 0.009\text{A} = 9\text{ mA}$$

$\therefore$ Change in current, $\Delta I = I_2 - I_1 = 9$ mA

10. (*c*) Let f_1, f_2 and f_3 be the fundamentals, first and second overtone modes, frequencies, respectively.

As we know that, for a string fixed at both ends,

$$f_1 : f_2 : f_3 = 1 : 2 : 3 \qquad \text{...(i)}$$

Also, wavelength,

$\lambda = \frac{v}{f}$, where v is the speed of wave.

or $\lambda \propto \frac{1}{f}$

$\therefore \lambda_1 : \lambda_2 : \lambda_3 = 1 : \frac{1}{2} : \frac{1}{3}$ [from Eq. (i)]

or $\lambda_1 : \lambda_2 : \lambda_3 = 6 : 3 : 2$

11. (*c*) When electric field is applied, the random motion of all free electrons converted into unidirectional within very short duration of time of order 10^{-9} s.

Thus, a current through each cross-section is produced almost instantaneously.

Hence, the bulb glows very quickly.

12. (c) At surface of a hollow shell gravitational potential, $V_{surface} = \frac{-GM}{R}$

and as field inside shell is zero,

$V_{centre} = -\frac{GM}{R}$

So, ratio $\frac{V_{surface}}{V_{centre}} = 1.$

Statement II is correct.

13. (c) Magnetic potential of a bar magnet in external magnetic field is given by

$$U = -MB\cos\theta$$

Here, $M = 0.15$ J/T, $B = 0.4$ T,

and $\theta = 180°$ as magnet is in unstable equilibrium.

$$\therefore \quad U = -0.15 \times 0.4 \times \cos 180°$$
$$= -0.15 \times 0.4 \times (-1)$$
$$= 6 \times 10^{-2} \text{ J}$$

14. (c) Accurate values are closed to true value of quantity.

Precise values are nearly reproducible, i.e. they are closed to each other.

So, correct answer is

A → S, B → R, C → Q, D → P

15. (b) Let the emf of cell be E.

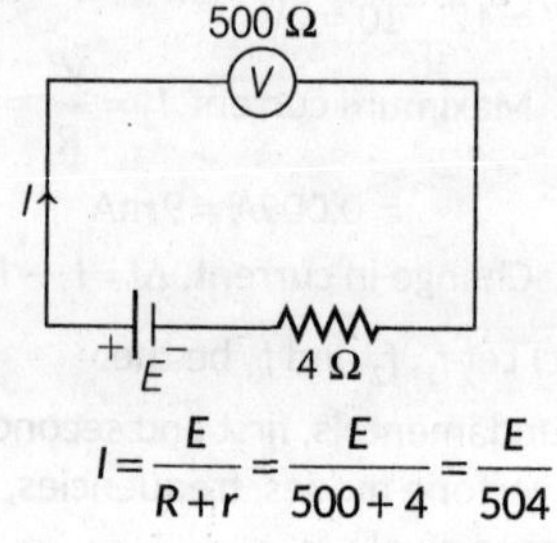

$$I = \frac{E}{R+r} = \frac{E}{500+4} = \frac{E}{504}$$

Reading of voltmeter, $V = E - I \times r$

$$= E - \frac{E}{504} \times 4 = \frac{500}{504} \cdot E$$

$$\% \text{ Error} = \frac{\text{Absolute error}}{\text{Actual value}} \times 100$$

$$= \left(\frac{E - \frac{500}{504}E}{E} \right) \times 100$$

$$= 0.8\%$$

16. (d) From graph, $V = 1.5$ V at $I = 0$

∴ EMF of cell = 1.5 V

At $V = 0$, $I = 1000$ mA = 1 A

Now using, $E - V = Ir$

We have, $1.5 - 0 = 1 \times r$

$$\Rightarrow \quad r = 1.5\,\Omega$$

17. (d) The size of central diffraction pattern $= \frac{2D\lambda}{a}$

where, a is the width of the slit.

For same D and λ,

size of diffraction pattern $\propto \frac{1}{a}$

If the width of the single slit is made half as compared to the original width, then the size of the central diffraction pattern becomes double.

Now, on reducing the width of the slit to half, amplitude will also become half.

As, intensity ∝ (amplitude)^2

It means the intensity of the central diffraction band becomes one-fourth of the initial.

18. (d) Both A and R are true and R is the correct explanation of A.

I_1 ↑ × × B_1 ∘ ∘ B_2 ↑ I_2

When two parallel current carrying conductors have currents in same direction, then magnetic field lines are anti-parallel. If first conductor creates a South pole, then second creates a North pole, hence they attract to each other.

19. (c) Refractive index of medium,

$$\mu = \sqrt{\frac{\varepsilon}{\varepsilon_0}} = \sqrt{\frac{4}{1}} = 2$$

So, wavelength in medium,

$$\lambda' = \frac{\lambda}{\mu} = \frac{\lambda}{2}$$

and frequency does not changes in refraction.

20. (b) $\mathbf{B} = \frac{\mu_0}{4\pi}\left(\frac{q\mathbf{v} \times \mathbf{r}}{r}\right)$

Here, $\mathbf{r} = 3\hat{\mathbf{i}} + 4\hat{\mathbf{j}}$

$$\mathbf{v} = 5 \times 10^4\,\hat{\mathbf{i}},\ q = 6 \times 10^{-6}\text{ C}$$

So, $\mathbf{B} = \frac{4\pi \times 10^{-7}}{4\pi}$

$$\times \frac{6 \times 10^{-6}[5 \times 10^4\,\hat{\mathbf{i}}\,(3\hat{\mathbf{i}} + 4\hat{\mathbf{j}})]}{5}$$

$$= 9.6 \times 10^{-10}\,\hat{\mathbf{k}}\text{ T}$$

21. (b) Since, the object is placed at focus of convex lens. So, after refracting through convex lens, all rays will be parallel and these will pass through concave lens. The concave lens will diverge these rays and a virtual image will be formed at its focus which is 20 cm left from concave lens.

So, to form final image on the object itself,

$$20 = 10 + d \quad \text{or} \quad d = 10\text{cm}$$

22. (b) For experiment of finding internal resistance,

$$\frac{E}{V} = \frac{R+r}{R} = \frac{l_1}{l_2}$$

$$\Rightarrow \quad \frac{5+r}{5} = \frac{52}{40}$$

$$\Rightarrow \quad r = 1.5\,\Omega$$

23. (a) As we know that, for a non-conducting solid sphere,

Electric potential at centre,

$$V_{centre} = \frac{3}{2}\frac{KQ}{R}$$

Electric potential at r distance from centre inside a point,

$$V_{inside} = \frac{KQ}{2R^3}[3R^2 - r^2]$$

$$\Rightarrow \quad \frac{V_{centre}}{V_{inside}} = \frac{3R^2}{3R^2 - r^2}$$

$$\frac{4}{3} = \frac{3R^2}{3R^2 - r^2}$$

$$\left[\because \text{Given, } \frac{V_{centre}}{V_{inside}} = \frac{4}{3}\right]$$

$$r = \frac{\sqrt{3}}{2}R$$

$$= \frac{\sqrt{3}}{2} \times 20 \quad (\because R = 20\text{ cm})$$

$$= 17.32\text{ cm}$$

24. (b) According to principle of homogeneity, we can add or subtract only those physical quantities which have same dimensional formula.

i.e. $[2V] = [b]$

or $[b] = [V] = [L^3]$

The term $(2V - b)$ will have dimensional formula equal to that volume.

From given expression, $[p] = \frac{[X][T]}{[\text{Volume}]}$

or $[X] = \frac{[p][\text{Volume}]}{[T]}$

$$= \frac{[ML^{-1}T^{-2}]}{[K]}[L^3]$$

$$[X] = [ML^2T^{-2}K^{-1}]$$

25. (a) Base current,

$$I_B = \frac{V_{in} - V_{BE}}{R_B}$$

$$I_B = \frac{1-0}{2\text{k}\Omega} = 0.5 \times 10^{-3}\text{ A}$$

$\because$ Current gain, $\beta = \frac{I_C}{I_B}$ or $I_C = \beta I_B$

$= 90 \times 0.5 \times 10^{-3}$

$I_C = 45 \times 10^{-3}$ A

$\therefore$ Output voltage, $V_{out} = I_C \times R_{out}$

$= 45 \times 10^{-3} \times 100$

$V_{out} = 4.5$ V

26. (*a*) Frequency of an *L-C* oscillatory circuit,

$$f = \frac{1}{2\pi\sqrt{LC}} \text{ Hz}$$

Now to have very low frequency, a large value of inductance and capacitance is needed. This is not practically desirable as a large inductor and capacitor needs large power to operate.

27. (*b*) Minimum wavelength for Balmer series,

$$\frac{1}{\lambda_{\min B}} = R\left(\frac{1}{2^2} - \frac{1}{\infty^2}\right)$$

$$\frac{1}{\lambda_{\min B}} = \frac{R}{4} \text{ or } \lambda_{\min B} = \frac{4}{R} \quad \text{... (i)}$$

Similarly for Paschen series,

$$\frac{1}{\lambda_{\min P}} = R\left(\frac{1}{3^2} - \frac{1}{\infty^2}\right)$$

$$\frac{1}{\lambda_{\min P}} = \frac{R}{9} \text{ or } \lambda_{\min P} = \frac{9}{R} \quad \text{... (ii)}$$

From Eqs. (i) and (ii), we get

$$\frac{\lambda_{\min B}}{\lambda_{\min P}} = \frac{4}{9} = 4:9$$

28. (*b*) The total moment of inertia of a solid sphere is the sum of that of two hemispheres about diagonal. From symmetry, both solid hemispheres will have same moment of inertia *I*.

$\therefore \quad 2I = \frac{2}{5}(2M)R^2$

or $\quad I = \frac{2}{5}MR^2$

29. (*c*) As we know,

Slope of strain - stress curve $= \frac{1}{Y}$

where, *Y* is Young's modulus.

or $\quad \frac{(\text{Slope})_A}{(\text{Slope})_B} = \frac{Y_B}{Y_A}$

$\Rightarrow \quad \frac{\sqrt{3}}{\frac{1}{\sqrt{3}}} = \frac{Y_B}{Y_A}$

or $\quad Y_B = 3Y_A$

30. (*a*) Let the final temperature of mixture be *T*°C.

From calorimetry principle,

Heat given by 100 g of water = Heat taken by 100 g of ice

$$m_1 S_{water}(\Delta T_1) = m_2 L_f + m_2 S_{water} \Delta T_2$$

Substituting the given values, we get

$$100 \times 1 \times (80 - T) = 100 \times 80 + 100 \times 1 \times (T - 0)$$

$\Rightarrow \quad 80 - T = 80 + T$

$\Rightarrow \quad 2T = 0$

$\Rightarrow \quad T = 0$°C

31. (*a*) In given situation, process will be isothermal.

So, $p_1V_1 = p_2V_2$

$\because \quad V_1 > V_2 \Rightarrow p_1 < p_2$

32. (*d*) Intensity = Energy per unit area per unit time

Now, given energy needed for emission $\phi_0 = 2 \text{ eV} = 2 \times 1.6 \times 10^{-19}$ J

Intensity $= 10^{-5}$ Wm^{-2}

Area of atom $= 10^{-20}$ m^2

Now, number of atoms in top 5-layers,

$$N = \frac{5 \times \text{Area of surface}}{\text{Area of 1 atom}} = \frac{5 \times 2 \times 10^{-4}}{10^{-20}} = 10^{17}$$

Hence, time needed for photoemission,

$$t = \frac{\phi_0}{\text{Energy available for each electron}}$$

$$\Rightarrow t = \frac{\phi_0}{\left(\frac{I \times A}{N}\right)} = \frac{\phi_0 \times N}{I \times A}$$

$$= \frac{2 \times 1.6 \times 10^{-19} \times 10^{17}}{10^{-5} \times 2 \times 10^{-4}}$$

$= 1.6 \times 10^7$ s

≈ 0.5 yr

33. (*c*) For effective kinetic energy transfer between fast neutrons and moderator molecules, their masses must be nearly equal. So, ratio is unity.

34. (*b*) Power factor, $\cos\phi = \frac{R}{Z}$

$$\therefore \frac{\cos\phi_1}{\cos\phi_2} = \frac{R/Z_1}{R/Z_2} = \frac{Z_2}{Z_1}$$

$$= \frac{\sqrt{X_L^2 + R^2}}{\sqrt{(X_L - X_C)^2 + R^2}}$$

$$= \frac{\sqrt{(3R)^2 + R^2}}{\sqrt{(3R - 2R)^2 + R^2}}$$

$$= \frac{\sqrt{10}}{\sqrt{2}} = \sqrt{5}$$

35. (*c*) According to Einstein's photoelectric equation,

$$hf = W_0 + eV_0 \quad \text{... (i)}$$

If frequency is doubled, then

$$h(2f) = W_0 + eV_0'$$

or $\quad 2hf = W_0 + eV_0' \quad$ ...(ii)

Substituting *hf* from Eq. (i) in Eq. (ii), we have,

or $\quad V_0' = 2V_0 + \frac{W_0}{e}$

or $\quad V_0' > 2V_0$

36. (*c*) Statement given in option (c) is correct but rest are incorrect.

37. (*d*) Given circuit can be shown as below

Output, $Y = \overline{(\overline{A})(\overline{B})} = \overline{\overline{A}} + \overline{\overline{B}} = A + B$

The truth table will be

A	B	Y=A+B
0	0	0
0	1	1
1	0	1
1	1	1

The corresponding input and output waveforms are shown below.

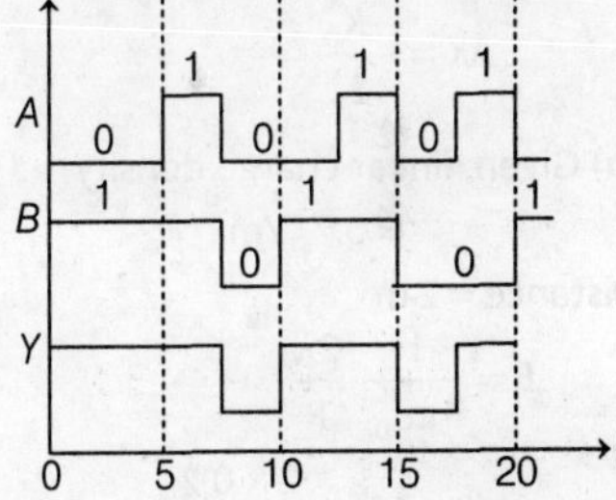

38. (*b*) Position of first bright fringe,

$$y_1 = \frac{\lambda D}{d}$$

Position of second bright fringe,

$$y_2 = \frac{2\lambda D}{d}$$

$$y_2 - y_1 = \frac{2\lambda D}{d} - \frac{\lambda D}{d}$$

$$y_2 - y_1 = \frac{\lambda D}{d}$$

or $\quad \lambda = \frac{(y_2 - y_1)d}{D}$

Substituting given values, we have

$$\lambda = \frac{0.553 \times 10^{-3} \times 2.08 \times 10^{-3}}{1.8}$$

$$= 639 \times 10^{-9} \text{ m}$$

or $\lambda = 639$ nm

39. (*b*) Initial rotational kinetic energy,

$$K_0 = \frac{1}{2} I\omega^2$$

Since, there is no external torque acting about vertical axis, so we can use conservation of angular momentum,

$$J_i = J_f$$

$$\omega_0 = I_1\omega_1 + I_2\omega_2$$

When both sides stick together, they will move with same angular velocity ω.

$\therefore$ $I\omega_0 = I\omega + I\omega$

or $\omega = \frac{\omega_0}{2}$ ...(i)

Final rotational kinetic energy,

$$K_f = K_1 + K_2$$

$$= \frac{1}{2} I\omega^2 + \frac{1}{2} I\omega^2 = I\omega^2$$

$$= I \times \left(\frac{\omega_0}{2}\right)^2 \quad \text{[using Eq. (i)]}$$

$$= \frac{1}{4} I\omega_0^2 = \frac{K_0}{2}$$

Change in rotational kinetic energy,

$$\Delta K = K_f - K_i$$

$$= \frac{K_0}{2} - K_0$$

$$\Delta K = \frac{-K_0}{2}$$

40. (*a*) Given, linear charge density

$= 0.2$ C/m

Distance $= 2$ m

$\because$ $E = \frac{1}{4\pi\varepsilon_0} \cdot \frac{2\lambda}{R}$

$$= 9 \times 10^9 \times \frac{2 \times 0.2}{2}$$

$$= 1.8 \times 10^9 \text{ V/m}$$

41. (*a*) In SHM, speed of the block at equilibrium position is given by

$v = A\omega$, where $\omega = \sqrt{\frac{k}{m}}$ ... (i)

If spring is extended to $2A$, then new amplitude, $A' = 2A$ and new velocity

$$v' = A'\omega'$$

$v' = (2A)\omega$ ... (ii)

$(\because \omega' = \omega = \sqrt{\frac{k}{m}})$

From Eqs. (i) and (ii), we get

$$\frac{v}{v'} = \frac{1}{2}$$

or $v' = 2v$

42. (*c*) Given that all are moving with same speed, let it be v.

As, $e = Blv$

Here, B and v are constants.

$\Rightarrow$ $e \propto l$ or vertical height

As, if the perpendicular length of a loop is more, so its induced emf will also be more.

$\therefore$ Correct order for the induced emf for the given loops is $e_3 > e_2 > e_1$.

43. (*a*) FBD for pith ball with charge Q is as follows

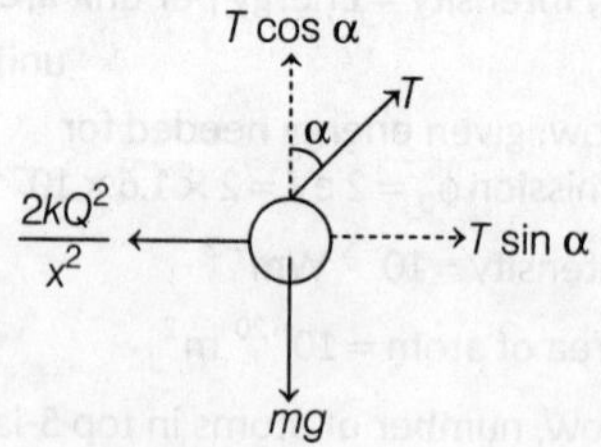

In equilibrium,

$$\Sigma F_x = 0$$

and $\Sigma F_y = 0$

$\Rightarrow$ $T\sin\alpha = \frac{2kQ^2}{x^2}$ ... (i)

$T\cos\alpha = mg$ ... (ii)

From Eqs. (i) and (ii), we get

$$\tan\alpha = \frac{\frac{2kQ^2}{x^2}}{mg}$$

or $\tan\alpha = \frac{2kQ^2}{mg\,x^2}$ ... (iii)

Similarly, FBD for pith ball with charge $2Q$ is as follows

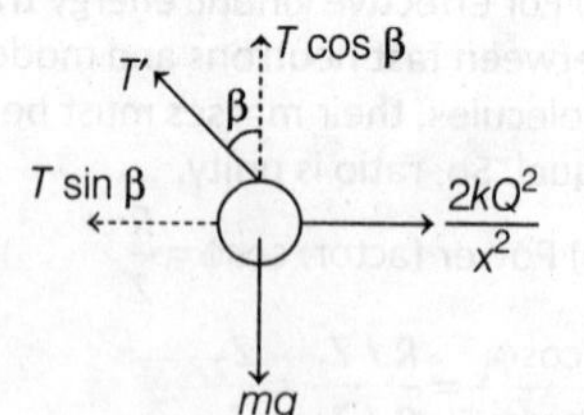

So, $\tan\beta = \frac{2kQ^2}{mgx^2}$ ... (iv)

From Eqs. (iii) and (iv), we get

$$\tan\alpha = \tan\beta$$

or $\alpha = \beta$

44. (*b*) When a resistor is connected to an AC source. The power drawn will be

$$P = V_{rms} I_{rms}$$

For resistance, $I_{rms} = \frac{V_{rms}}{R}$

$\therefore$ $P = V_{rms} \cdot \frac{V_{rms}}{R}$

or $V_{rms}^2 = PR$ ... (i)

Now, an inductor is connected in series with resistor, so the power will be

$P' = V_{rms} I_{rms} \cos\phi$, where $\cos\phi$ is the power factor of circuit.

$$P' = V_{rms}\left(\frac{V_{rms}}{Z}\right)\left(\frac{R}{Z}\right)$$

$\Rightarrow$ $P' = V_{rms}^2 \frac{R}{Z^2}$

From Eq. (i), we get

$$P' = (PR)\frac{R}{Z^2}$$

$\Rightarrow$ $P' = \frac{PR^2}{Z^2}$

Here, $P = 150$ W,

$R = 10\ \Omega$, $Z = 20\ \Omega$

$\therefore$ $P' = 150 \times \frac{(10)^2}{(20)^2} = 37.5$ W

And inductive reactance,

$$X_L = \sqrt{Z^2 - R^2}$$

$$= \sqrt{(20)^2 - (10)^2} = 10\sqrt{3}\ \Omega$$

45. (*b*) As, acceleration is zero in downward motion.

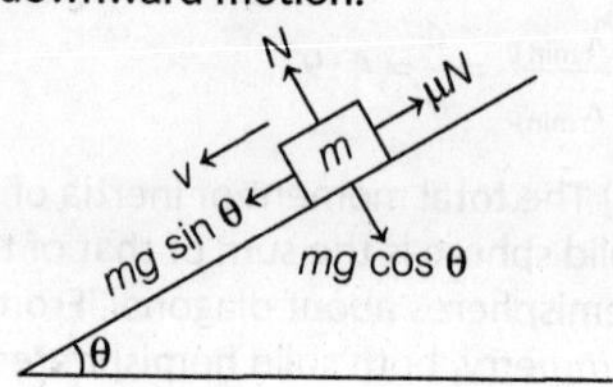

$\therefore$ $mg\sin\theta = \mu N$

$mg\sin\theta = \mu mg\cos\theta$

$(\because N = mg\cos\theta)$

or $\mu = \tan\theta$ ... (i)

When it is projected upward with a velocity v_0, it will be retarded by both $mg\sin\theta$ component and frictional force.

$\Rightarrow$ $ma = -(mg\sin\theta + f)$

$ma = -(mg\sin\theta + \mu N)$

$ma = -(mg\sin\theta + mg\sin\theta)$

[$\because$ using Eq. (i)]

$\Rightarrow a = -2g\sin\theta$, here negative sign implies that the block is stopped by retardation.

Now, using 3rd equation of motion along the plane,

$$v^2 = u^2 + 2as$$

$$0^2 = v_0^2 + 2(-2g\sin\theta)s$$

or $$s = \frac{v_0^2}{4g\sin\theta}$$

46. (*c*) Let u be the projection velocity of stone, where u_x and u_y be the horizontal and vertical components of u, respectively.

Horizontal distance, $x = u_x t$

or $$u_x = \frac{x}{t} = \frac{30}{1} = 30 \text{ m/s}$$

We also know that, time of flight, $T = \frac{2u_y}{g}$, where u_y is the vertical component of initial velocity.

or $$u_y = \frac{T \times g}{2} = \frac{8 \times 10}{2}$$

$$u_y = 40 \text{ m/s}$$

∴ Projection velocity,

$$u = \sqrt{u_x^2 + u_y^2} = \sqrt{(30)^2 + (40)^2}$$

$$u = 50 \text{ m/s}$$

47. (*c*) As, $F_{\text{external}} = 0$

⇒ $$a_{CM} = 0$$

∴ $$v_{CM} = \text{constant}$$

48. (*b*) The capacitance of a parallel plate capacitor is given as $C = \frac{\varepsilon_0 A}{d}$

The given arrangement can be treated as

A, A; $K_1=2$, d/3, C_1; $K_2=3$, d/3, C_2; K_3, d/3, C_3; B, B

Here, $$C_1 = \frac{2\varepsilon_0 A}{d/3} = \frac{6\varepsilon_0 A}{d}$$

$$C_2 = \frac{3\varepsilon_0 A}{d/3} = \frac{9\varepsilon_0 A}{d}$$

$$C_3 = \frac{K_3\varepsilon_0 A}{d/3} = \frac{3K_3\varepsilon_0 A}{d}$$

Since, C_1, C_2 and C_3 are in series,

$$\frac{1}{C_{eq}} = \frac{1}{C_1} + \frac{1}{C_2} + \frac{1}{C_3}$$

$$\frac{d}{3\varepsilon_0 A} = \frac{d}{6\varepsilon_0 A} + \frac{d}{9\varepsilon_0 A} + \frac{d}{3K_3\varepsilon_0 A}$$

$$1 = \frac{1}{2} + \frac{1}{3} + \frac{1}{3K_3}$$

or $$\frac{1}{3K_3} = \frac{1}{6} \text{ or } K_3 = 2$$

49. (*d*) As given, initial velocity $= u$

Acceleration due to gravity,

$$g = 9.8 \text{ m/s}^2$$

Time to reach at highest point,

$$t = \frac{u}{g} \text{ or } u = tg \quad \text{...(i)}$$

According to question,

Time taken by ball to reach ground,

$$t' = 4t \quad \text{...(ii)}$$

B, u, A, g, H, C

For A to C,

Using 2nd equation of motion,

$$s = ut + \frac{1}{2}gt^2$$

⇒ $$-H = u \times t' + \frac{1}{2}(-g)(t'^2)$$

⇒ $$-80 = (tg) \times (4t) - \frac{g(4t)^2}{2}$$

[using Eqs. (i) and (ii)]

⇒ $$-80 = 4gt^2 - 8gt^2$$

or $$4gt^2 = 80$$

or $$4 \times 9.8t^2 = 80$$

$$t^2 = \frac{80}{9.8 \times 4}$$

or $$t = \frac{10}{7} \text{ s}$$

and $$u = tg$$

$$u = \frac{10}{7} \cdot 9.8$$

$$= 14 \text{ m/s}^2$$

Initial kinetic energy,

$$K = \frac{1}{2}mu^2$$

$$= \frac{1}{2} \times 0.5 \times (14)^2$$

$$K = 49 \text{ J}$$

50. (*a*) When object is at C, its image is real of same size and is at C

∴ $$m = -1$$

When object is at focus, its image formed at ∞

∴ $$m = \infty$$

For a convex mirror, magnification is always less than 1.

∴ $$m = 0.33$$

Knockout 2

1. (*c*) Let energy E in terms of momentum p, area A and time t is,

$$[E] = [p^x A^y t^z]$$

⇒ $$[ML^2T^{-2}] = [MLT^{-1}]^x [L^2]^y [T]^z$$

$$[ML^2T^{-2}] = [M]^x [L]^{x+2y} [T]^{-x+z}$$

Equating powers of same physical quantity, we have

$$x = 1, x + 2y = 2$$

and $$-x + z = -2$$

So, $x = 1, y = \frac{1}{2}, z = -1$

Hence, $[E] = [pA^{1/2}T^{-1}]$

2. (*c*) Given that, $B(x, t) = 9 \times 10^{-6} \sin(3.25 \times 10^4 x + \omega t)$ T

On comparing with standard equation of plane electromagnetic wave which is $B(x, t) = B_0 \sin(kx + \omega t)$, we get

$$k = 3.25 \times 10^4 \text{ rad/m}$$

Wavelength,

$$\lambda = \frac{2\pi}{k} = \frac{2 \times 3.14}{3.25 \times 10^4}$$

$$= 1.932 \times 10^{-4} \text{ m}$$

As we know that, in vacuum speed of electromagnetic wave,

$$c = 3 \times 10^8 \text{ m/s}$$

∴ Frequency, $$f = \frac{c}{\lambda} = \frac{3 \times 10^8}{1.932 \times 10^{-4}}$$

$$= 1.55 \times 10^{12} \text{ Hz}$$

Peak value of electric field,

$$E_0 = c \times B_0$$

$$= 3 \times 10^8 \times 9 \times 10^{-6}$$

$$= 2.7 \text{ kV/m}$$

3. (*d*) ∴ From first law of thermodynamics,

$$\Delta Q = \Delta U + W$$

In adiabatic process, $\Delta Q = 0$,

$$\Delta U + W = 0$$

or $$\Delta U = -W$$

In expansion, W is positive, so ΔU is negative.

So, internal energy and temperature decreases.

4. (*a*) Let at given instant, amount of radioactive substance be N_{0A} and N_{0B} respectively, then $\frac{N_{0A}}{N_{0B}} = \frac{2}{1}$

For radioactive substance *A*,

Number of half-lives, $n_1 = \frac{48}{12} = 4$

$$N_A = N_{0A}\left(\frac{1}{2}\right)^{n_1}$$

$$= N_{0A}\left(\frac{1}{2}\right)^4 \quad \text{... (i)}$$

For radioactive substance *B*,

Number of half-lives, $n_2 = \frac{48}{16} = 3$

$$N_B = N_{0B}\left(\frac{1}{2}\right)^{n_2}$$

$$= N_{0B}\left(\frac{1}{2}\right)^3 \quad \text{... (ii)}$$

On dividing Eq. (i) by Eq. (ii), we get

$$\frac{N_A}{N_B} = \frac{N_{0A}}{N_{0B}} \times \frac{1}{2}$$

$$\frac{N_A}{N_B} = 2 \times \frac{1}{2} = 1 \text{ or } 1:1$$

5. (*b*) Magnetic force must be opposite to electric force. For this by left hand rule, magnetic field must be in $+z$-direction. Magnitude of magnetic field,

$$B = \frac{E}{v}$$

$$= \frac{3 \times 10^4}{6 \times 10^6} = 5 \times 10^{-3} \text{ T}$$

6. (*a*) In forward bias, the applied voltage is opposite to the junction barrier potential. Due to this, effective potential barrier and depletion region decreases.

7. (*a*) $\text{Intensity} = \frac{\text{Energy}}{\text{Area} \times \text{Time}}$

$$\Rightarrow \frac{1}{2} c\varepsilon_0 E^2 = \frac{P}{A}$$

$$\Rightarrow E = \sqrt{\frac{2P}{Ac\varepsilon_0}}$$

$$= \sqrt{\frac{2 \times 27 \times 10^{-3}}{20 \times 10^{-6} \times 3 \times 10^8 \times 9 \times 10^{-12}}}$$

$$= 1 \times 10^3 \text{ V/m} = 1 \text{ kV/m}$$

8. (*a*) Statement given in option (a) is correct but rest statements are incorrect.

The convection process of heat transfer can be natural or forced. In natural convection, heat is transferred due to gravity, while in forced convection, some external source is needed to do that like in case of warming a room by a heat blower.

A normal body can radiate energy more than a perfectly black body. The emissivity of a body always lies between 0 to 1. So, it cannot be greater than the absorptivity.

9. (*a*) For two vectors **A** and **B**,

$$\tan\alpha = \frac{B\sin\theta}{A + B\cos\theta}$$

where, θ is the angle between vectors **A** and **B** and α is the angle between **B** and resultant of **A** and **B**.

Condition given is,

$$\alpha = 90^\circ, \; A = P, B = 2P$$

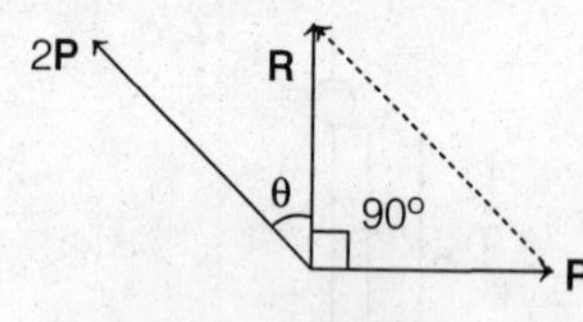

$$\Rightarrow \tan 90^\circ = \frac{2P\sin\theta}{P + 2P\cos\theta}$$

$$\frac{1}{0} = \frac{2P\sin\theta}{P + 2P\cos\theta}$$

$$P + 2P\cos\theta = 0$$

$$\text{or} \quad \cos\theta = -\frac{1}{2} = \cos\frac{2\pi}{3}$$

$$\text{or} \quad \theta = \frac{2\pi}{3}$$

10. (*b*) A large problem or a system of complex equations can be broken into smaller parts, this is called reduction. For example, temperature can be related to KE of molecules.

11. (*b*) As we know that,

$$\text{Spring constant, } k \propto \frac{1}{\text{Natural length}}$$

As, spring is cut into two parts of length $\frac{3l}{4}$ and $\frac{l}{4}$, so $k_1 = \frac{4k}{3}$ and $k_2 = 4k$.

The given system of spring is arranged in parallel combination,

$$\text{So,} \quad k_{eq} = k_1 + k_2$$

$$= \frac{4k}{3} + 4k$$

$$= \frac{16k}{3}$$

$$\therefore \text{Time period, } T = 2\pi\sqrt{\frac{M}{k_{eq}}}$$

$$= 2\pi\sqrt{\frac{3M}{16k}}$$

12. (*c*) Initially image coincides with object. This is possible when rays incident over mirror are reflected back on their path.

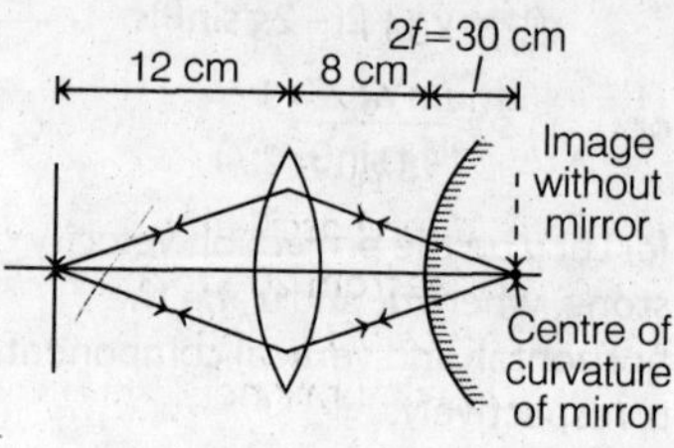

Hence, light rays must be incident towards centre of curvature of mirror.

So, distance of object and its image after removing mirror will be

$$\text{Distance} = 12 \text{ cm} + 8 \text{ cm} + 30 \text{ cm}$$

$$= 50 \text{ cm}$$

13. (*c*) Power of source = Energy of 1 photon × Total number of photons

$$\Rightarrow 6.6 \times 10^3 = hf \times 10^{20}$$

$$\Rightarrow \quad f = \text{frequency of source}$$

$$\Rightarrow \quad f = \frac{6.6 \times 10^3}{6.6 \times 10^{-34} \times 10^{20}}$$

$$= 10^{17} \text{ Hz}$$

So, source is emitting X-rays and it is a coolidge tube.

14. (*a*) Wavelength of emitted photon,

$$\frac{1}{\lambda} = R\left(\frac{1}{n_f^2} - \frac{1}{n_i^2}\right) \quad \text{...(i)}$$

and if recoil speed is v, then from

$$\lambda = \frac{h}{p} = \frac{h}{mv}$$

$$\text{We have, } v = \frac{h}{m} \cdot \frac{1}{\lambda} \quad \text{...(ii)}$$

From Eqs. (i) and (ii), we get

$$v = \frac{h}{m} \cdot R \cdot \left(\frac{1}{n_f^2} - \frac{1}{n_i^2}\right)$$

$$= \frac{6.6 \times 10^{-34}}{9.1 \times 10^{-31}} \times 1.1 \times 10^7 \times \left(\frac{1}{1} - \frac{1}{25}\right)$$

$$= 4.17 \text{ ms}^{-1}$$

15. (*a*) Making truth table by observing the given waveforms

A	B	Y
0	0	1
0	1	1
1	0	0
1	1	0

It is clear that, *Y* is complement of *A*

So, $Y = \overline{A}$

16. (c) Given,

$$U = 20 + (x-1)^2 \text{ J}$$

$$U_{max} = 36 \text{ J}$$

U is minimum at $x = 1$ m

$$U_{min} = 20 \text{ J}$$

It means, during oscillation potential energy varies from 20 J to 36 J. Hence, the difference of U_{max} and U_{min} will be equal to maximum kinetic energy.

$$K_{max} = U_{max} - U_{min}$$

$$K_{max} = (36 - 20) \text{ J}$$

$$K_{max} = 16 \text{ J}$$

17. (b) From the graph, it is clear that, component of initial vertical velocity,

$$u_y = 40 \text{ m/s}$$

So, maximum height,

$$H = \frac{u_y^2}{2g} = \frac{(40)^2}{2 \times 10} = 80 \text{ m}$$

18. (b) Precision increases with decrease in value of least count.

Precision is the closeness of a measure with actual value of quantity.

19. (a) The given system of plates, with respective charges on them can be drawn as follows.

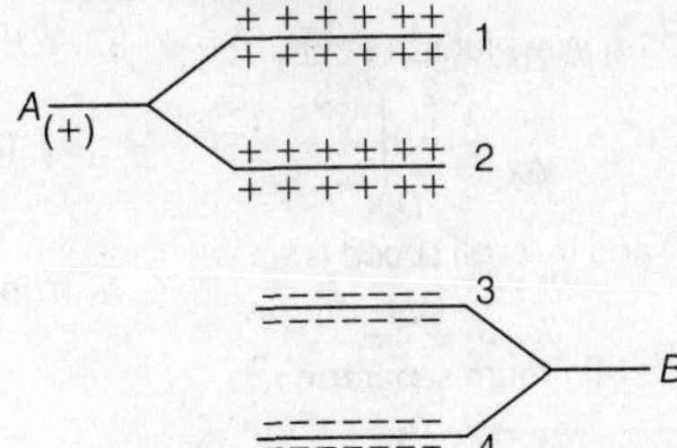

From the above figure, we can say that, there is only one capacitor between (2, 3),

So, $C_{eq} = \frac{\varepsilon_0 A}{d}$.

20. (c) For a satellite, $T^2 \propto R^3$

or $T \propto R^{3/2}$

$$\Rightarrow \frac{dT}{T} = \frac{3}{2}\left(\frac{dR}{R}\right)$$

$$\Rightarrow \frac{dT}{T} = \frac{3}{2}\left(\frac{1.02R - R}{R}\right) = 0.03$$

So, % change in time period

$$= \frac{dT}{T} \times 100 = 3\%$$

21. (d) If orbit is not in equatorial plane then gravitational force pulls satellite towards centre of earth, (which is not orbit's centre). So, gravity pulls satellite out of orbit and motion of satellite around earth is not possible.

22. (b) FBD of the given rod is as shown below,

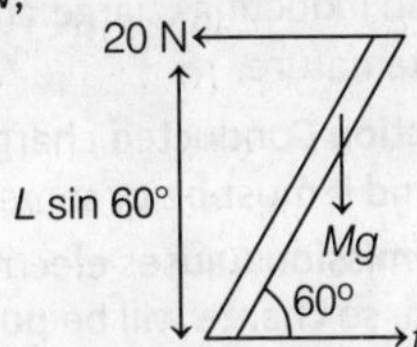

For rotational equilibrium, $\Sigma\tau = 0$.

Taking moments about bottom of rod we have,

$$20 \times L \sin 60° = Mg \times \frac{2L}{3} \cos 60°$$

$$\Rightarrow 20 \times L \times \frac{\sqrt{3}}{2} = M \times 10 \times \frac{2L}{3} \times \frac{1}{2}$$

$$\Rightarrow M = 3\sqrt{3} \text{ kg} = 3 \times 1.7 \approx 5 \text{ kg}$$

23. (a) Given that, $V = 100 \sin(100\pi t)$ V

and $i = 20 \cos\left(100\pi t - \frac{\pi}{6}\right)$ A

$$= 20 \sin\left(100\pi t - \frac{\pi}{6} + \frac{\pi}{2}\right) \text{A}$$

$$= 20 \sin\left(100\pi t + \frac{\pi}{3}\right) \text{A}$$

Phase difference, $\phi = \frac{\pi}{3}$

Average power consumption,

$$P = V_{rms}\, i_{rms} \cos\phi = V_{rms} \cdot i_{rms} \cos\frac{\pi}{3}$$

$$= \left(\frac{100}{\sqrt{2}}\right)\left(\frac{20}{\sqrt{2}}\right) \times \frac{1}{2}$$

$$= 500 \text{ W}$$

Wattless current $= i_{rms} \sin\phi$

$$= \left(\frac{20}{\sqrt{2}}\right) \times \left(\sin\frac{\pi}{3}\right) = 5\sqrt{6} \text{ A}$$

24. (d) No field exists inside a metallic cavity.

∴ Net flux through metal cube will be zero.

25. (b) Induced emf generated in a loop is given by

$$e = -\frac{d\phi}{dt} = -A\frac{dB}{dt}$$

So, induced emf is same in both loops.

However, induced current is given by

$$i = \frac{|e|}{R}$$

For same induced emf, $i \propto \frac{1}{R}$

So, it will depend upon the value of resistance, so lower the resistance, higher will be the current. Therefore, induced current is different in both the loops.

26. (a) Let angular acceleration is applied for t seconds.

Given that, $\omega_i = 0$

$$\alpha = 28 \text{ rad/s}^2$$

$$I = 10 \text{ kg-m}^2$$

∵ Kinetic energy, KE $= \frac{1}{2}I\omega^2$

or $\omega = \sqrt{\frac{2\text{KE}}{I}}$

$$= \sqrt{\frac{2 \times 980}{10}} = 14 \text{ rad/s}$$

From first equation of rotational motion,

$$\omega_f = \omega_i + \alpha t$$

$$14 = 0 + 28 \times t \qquad (\because \omega_f = \omega)$$

$$t = 0.5 \text{ s}$$

27. (b) The diamagnetism is temperature independent, i.e. susceptibility is constant and does not vary with temperature.

28. (b) Maximum friction force,

$$f = \mu N \text{ or } \mu mg$$

$$= 0.2 \times 5 \times 10$$

$$= 10 \text{ N}$$

Motion of block will start, when frictional force becomes equal to applied force, i.e.

$$F = f$$

$$10t = 10$$

or $t = 1$ s

The motion of block will start at $t = 1$ s.

Let acceleration of block for $t \geq 1$ s be a,

$$a = \frac{F - t}{m} = \frac{10t - 10}{5} = (2t - 2) \text{ m/s}^2$$

If velocity at any time t be v, then

$$\frac{dv}{dt} = 2(t-1)$$

or $\int_0^v dv = \int_{t=1}^{t} 2(t-1)\, dt$

$$\Rightarrow [v]_0^v = 2\left[\frac{(t-1)^2}{2}\right]_{t=1}^{t}$$

$$\Rightarrow v - 0 = [(t-1)^2 - (1-1)^2]$$

$$\Rightarrow v = (t-1)^2 \text{ m/s}$$

$$\Rightarrow \frac{dx}{dt} = (t-1)^2$$

$$\Rightarrow dx = (t-1)^2 dt$$

Integrating on both sides of the above equation, we get

$$\int_0^x dx = \int_1^t (t-1)^2\, dt$$

$$\Rightarrow \quad [x]_0^x = \left[\frac{(t-1)^3}{3}\right]_1^t$$

$$\Rightarrow \quad [x-0] = \left[\frac{(t-1)^3}{3} - \frac{(1-1)^3}{3}\right]$$

$$\Rightarrow \quad x = \frac{(t-1)^3}{3}\ \text{m}$$

At $t = 4$ s, $x = \frac{(4-1)^3}{3} = 9$ m

Work done by friction,

$$W_{friction} = \mathbf{f}_{friction} \cdot \mathbf{x}$$
$$= fx \cos 180^\circ$$
$$= (10) \times (9) \times (-1)$$
$$W_{friction} = -90\ \text{N}$$

29. (c) Let us consider a small element of charge dq of length dx at distance x from end A as shown below.

Charge on small element,

$$dq = \lambda dx = \frac{\lambda_0}{L} x\, dx \qquad \text{...(i)}$$

From the relation,

Gyromagnetic ratio

$$= \frac{\text{Angular momentum}}{\text{Magnetic moment}}$$
$$= \frac{2 \times \text{Mass}}{\text{Charge}}$$

Magnetic moment due to rotation of small element,

$$dM = (dL)\left(\frac{dq}{2 \times dm}\right)$$

$$dM = (dI\omega)\left(\frac{dq}{2 \times dm}\right) \qquad (\because L = I\omega)$$

$$dM = (dm)x^2\omega \times \frac{\frac{\lambda_0}{L} x\, dx}{2 \times dm} \qquad (\because I = mx^2)$$

[using Eq. (i)]

$$dM = \frac{\lambda_0 \omega}{2L} x^3 dx$$

Magnetic moment due to rotation of rod,

$$M = \int_0^L dM = \int_0^L \frac{\lambda_0 \omega}{2L} x^3 dx$$

$$= \frac{\lambda_0 \omega}{2L}\left[\frac{x^4}{4}\right]_0^L$$

$$= \frac{\lambda_0 \omega}{2L}\left[\frac{L^4}{4} - \frac{0^4}{4}\right]$$

$$M = \frac{\lambda_0 \omega L^3}{8}$$

30. (a) **Induction** Induced charge may be less than inducting charge and is of opposite nature.

Conduction Conducted charge may be equal and it must be of same sign.

Photoemission Causes electrons ejection, so charge will be positive.

Friction $q_1 + q_2 = 0$, following conservation of charge.

31. (a)

I. In simple microscope, when an object is placed between pole and focus of lens, a virtual, erect and magnified image is formed.

IV. In Galilean telescope, a convergent lens is used as the objective and a divergent lens as the eye piece. The objective lens forms a real and inverted image (let say P'Q') but the divergent lens comes in between. This intermediate image acts as virtual object for eye piece. The final image (let say P''Q'') is erect and magnified.

32. (a) Given, current, $I = 12$ A,

radius, $R = 2\ \text{cm} = 2 \times 10^{-2}$ m

Magnetic field at the centre of current carrying circular loop,

$$B_c = \frac{\mu_0 I}{2R} = \frac{\mu_0}{2\pi} \cdot \frac{\pi I}{R}$$

Magnetic field at the centre of semi-circular loop,

$$B = \frac{B_c}{2} = \frac{\mu_0}{4\pi} \frac{\pi I}{R}$$
$$= 10^{-7} \times \frac{3.14 \times 12}{2 \times 10^{-2}}$$
$$= 1.9 \times 10^{-4}\ \text{T}$$

Thus, **B** is 1.9×10^{-4} T normal to the plane of the paper going into it, i.e. ⊗.

33. (c) Current, $I =$ Slope of q-t graph

$$= \frac{y_2 - y_1}{x_2 - x_1} = \frac{q_0 - 0}{0 - t_0} = -\frac{q_0}{t_0}$$

Heat produced,

$$H = I^2 Rt \quad \text{or} \quad H = \frac{q_0^2 R}{t_0^2} t$$

or $\quad H \propto t$

So, the graph between H and t should be straight line passing through the origin.

34. (d) Intensity at any point is given by

$$I = I_{max} \cos^2 \frac{\phi}{2} = 4I_0 \cos^2 \frac{\phi}{2}$$

Let the phase difference at the point where, intensity is $2I_0$ be ϕ_1,

$$2I_0 = 4I_0 \cos^2 \frac{\phi_1}{2}$$

or $\cos^2 \frac{\phi_1}{2} = \frac{1}{2}$

or $\cos \frac{\phi_1}{2} = \frac{1}{\sqrt{2}}$

or $\frac{\phi_1}{2} = \frac{\pi}{4}$

or $\phi_1 = \frac{\pi}{2}$

Path difference, $\Delta x_1 = \frac{\lambda}{2\pi} \times \phi_1 = \frac{\lambda}{4}$

Let position of that point be y_1 from central maxima, then

$$\Delta x_1 = \frac{y_1 d}{D}$$

or $\quad y_1 = \frac{D \Delta x_1}{d} = \frac{\lambda D}{4d} \qquad \text{... (i)}$

Similarly, for a point where, intensity is I_0, phase difference be ϕ_2.

$$\Rightarrow \quad I_0 = 4I_0 \cos^2 \frac{\phi_2}{2}$$

or $\cos^2 \frac{\phi_2}{2} = \frac{1}{4}$ or $\cos \frac{\phi_2}{2} = \frac{1}{2}$

$$\phi_2 = \frac{2\pi}{3}$$

Corresponding path difference,

$$\Delta x_2 = \frac{\lambda}{2\pi} \times \frac{2\pi}{3} = \frac{\lambda}{3}$$

$$\Delta x_2 = \frac{y_2 d}{D}$$

or $y_2 = \frac{D \Delta x_2}{d} = \frac{\lambda D}{3d} \qquad \text{... (ii)}$

∴ Minimum separation,

$$\Delta y = y_2 - y_1$$
$$= \frac{\lambda D}{3d} - \frac{\lambda D}{4d} = \frac{1}{12}\left(\frac{\lambda D}{d}\right)$$
$$= \frac{\beta}{12} \qquad \left(\because \beta = \frac{D\lambda}{d}\right)$$

35. (a) Co-ordinates of centre of mass of all four rods w.r.t. origin are as shown below

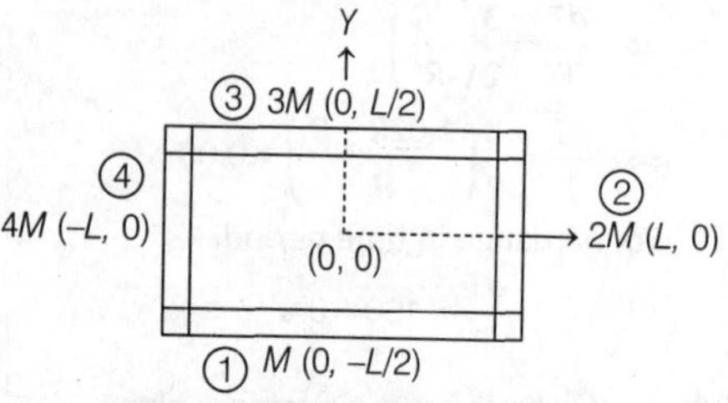

For system of rods,

$$X_{CM} = \frac{m_1 x_1 + m_2 x_2 + m_3 x_3 + m_4 x_4}{m_1 + m_2 + m_3 + m_4}$$
$$= \frac{-2}{10} L = \frac{-L}{5}$$

and similarly $Y_{CM} = \frac{-L}{10}$

It is clear that both X and Y co-ordinates of centre of mass are negative, so it lies in 3rd quadrant (or I region).

36. (*b*) The given circuit can be redrawn as

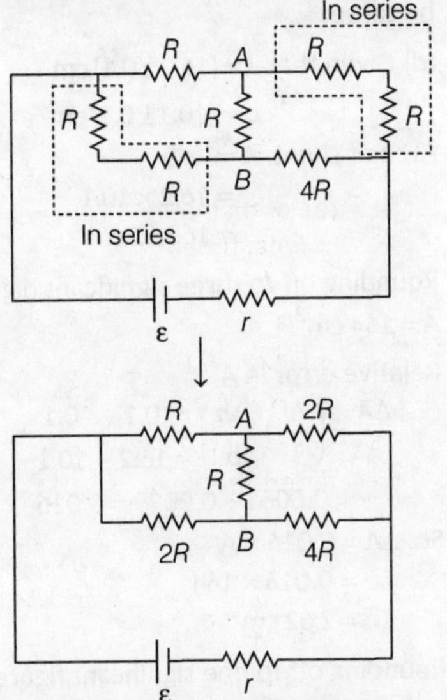

This represents a balanced Wheatstone bridge, so current will not flow through resistor R across the branch AB. It can be removed from circuit.

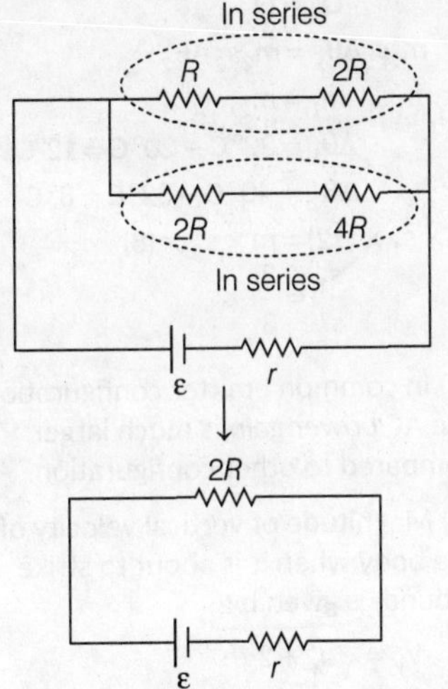

For maximum power transfer to the load, the load resistance must be equal to internal resistance of the battery,

$$2R = r \text{ or } R = \frac{r}{2}$$

37. (*d*) Current,

$$I = \mathbf{J} \cdot \mathbf{A}$$
$$= (2 \times 10^4 \hat{\mathbf{j}}) \cdot (2\hat{\mathbf{i}} + 3\hat{\mathbf{j}}) \times 10^{-4}$$
$$= 6 \times 10^4 \times 10^{-4} = 6 \text{ A}$$

Charge, $Q = I \times t = 6 \times 2 = 12$ C

38. (*c*) Given that, $i =$ constant

Let at any instant of time, charge on capacitor be q.

$$\frac{dq}{dt} = \text{constant}$$

or $\frac{d(CV)}{dt} = k \quad (\because q = CV)$

or $C\frac{dV}{dt} = k$

or $dV = \frac{k}{C} dt$

Integrating on both sides, we get

$$\int_0^V dV = \frac{k}{C}\int_0^t dt$$
$$[V]_0^V = \frac{k}{C}[t]_0^t$$
$$V - 0 = \frac{k}{C}[t - 0]$$

or $V = \frac{k}{C} t$

or $V \propto t$, i.e. graph is straight line passing through origin.

39. (*c*) Power needed at town = 800 kW

RMS line current,

$$I = \frac{P}{V} = \frac{800 \times 10^3}{4000} = 200 \text{ A}$$

Line loss $= I^2R = (200)^2 \times 15 \times (0.5 + 0.5)$

$$= 600 \text{ kW}$$

Power supplied by plant

$$= 600 + 800 = 1400 \text{ kW}$$

Voltage drop in line

$$= IR = 200 \times 15$$
$$= 3000 \text{ V}$$

So, total voltage supplied by plant

$$= 4000 + 3000$$
$$= 7000 \text{ V} = 7 \text{ kV}$$

40. (*b*) Current in primary circuit,

$$i = \frac{E}{R + R'} = \frac{2}{40 + 10} = 0.04 \text{ A}$$

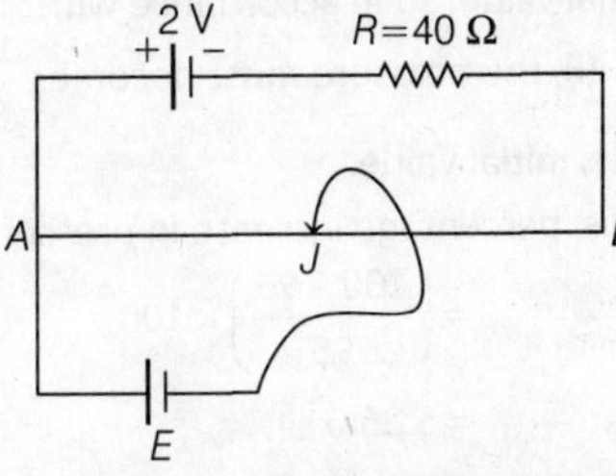

Resistance per unit length of potentiometer $= \frac{R}{L} = \frac{10}{100} = 0.10$ Ω/cm

Resistance of 40 cm length of wire of potentiometer,

$$R'' = \frac{R}{L} \times 40$$
$$= 0.10 \times 40$$
$$= 4 \Omega$$

$\therefore \quad E = i \times R''$
$$= 0.04 \times 4$$
$$= 0.16 \text{ V}$$

41. (*b*) Friction force, $F = \mu N$

and acceleration, $a = \frac{-F}{m} = -\frac{\mu mg}{m}$

$$a = -\mu g = -10\mu$$

Using third equation of motion,

$$v^2 = u^2 + 2as$$

or $0^2 = (20)^2 + 2(-10\mu)80$

or $\mu = \frac{(20)^2}{2 \times 10 \times 80} = \frac{1}{4}$

or $\mu = 0.25$

42. (*c*) Let the projection velocities of particles be u_1 and u_2.

Velocities after t s are

$$\mathbf{v}_1 = u_1\hat{\mathbf{i}} - gt\hat{\mathbf{j}}$$

and $\mathbf{v}_2 = -u_2\hat{\mathbf{i}} - gt\hat{\mathbf{j}}$

When velocities becomes perpendicular, i.e.

$$\mathbf{v}_1 \cdot \mathbf{v}_2 = 0$$
$$(u_1\hat{\mathbf{i}} - gt\hat{\mathbf{j}}) \cdot (-u_2\hat{\mathbf{i}} - gt\hat{\mathbf{j}}) = 0$$
$$-u_1u_2 + g^2t^2 = 0$$

or $g^2t^2 = u_1u_2$

or $t = \frac{\sqrt{u_1u_2}}{g}$

Here, $u_1 = 30$ m/s, $u_2 = 40$ m/s, $g = 10$ m/s^2

$$t = \frac{\sqrt{30 \times 40}}{10}$$
$$t = 2\sqrt{3} \text{ s}$$

43. (*c*) Work done on dipole by external torque,

$$W = \Delta U = U_f - U_i$$
$$= (-\mathbf{p}_f \cdot \mathbf{E}) - (-\mathbf{p}_i \cdot \mathbf{E})$$
$$= (\mathbf{p}_i - \mathbf{p}_f) \cdot \mathbf{E}$$
$$= [(3\hat{\mathbf{i}} + 4\hat{\mathbf{j}}) - (-4\hat{\mathbf{i}} + 3\hat{\mathbf{j}})] \times 10^{-30} \cdot 4000\hat{\mathbf{i}}$$
$$= (7\hat{\mathbf{i}} + \hat{\mathbf{j}}) \times 10^{-30} \cdot 4000\hat{\mathbf{i}}$$
$$= 2.8 \times 10^{-26} \text{ J}$$

44. (*b*) The circuit of common emitter mode is as shown below

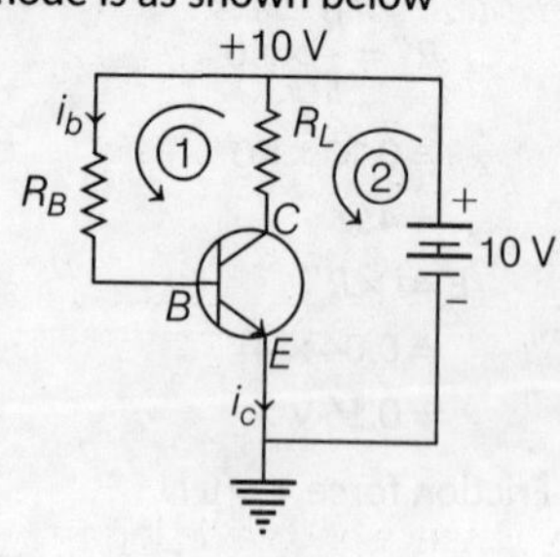

Current gain, $\beta = \frac{i_c}{i_b}$

or $\quad i_b = \frac{i_c}{\beta} = \frac{4 \times 10^{-3}}{80} = 50\ \mu A$

Applying KVL in outer loop, we have

$$+10\ V - i_b \cdot R_B - V_{BE} = 0$$

or $\quad R_B = \frac{10 - V_{BE}}{i_b} = \frac{10 - 1}{50 \times 10^{-6}} = 180\ k\Omega$

Further, using KVL in loop (2), we have

$$+10 - i_c R_L - V_{CE} = 0$$

or $\quad R_L = \frac{10 - V_{CE}}{i_c} = \frac{10 - 6}{4 \times 10^{-3}}$

$$= \frac{4}{4} \times 10^3$$

$$R_L = 1\ k\Omega$$

45. (*b*) For first maxima,

$$2d \sin\theta = \lambda = \frac{h}{p}$$

As $p = \sqrt{2Em}$, we have

$$2d \sin\theta = \frac{h}{\sqrt{2Em}}$$

46. (*a*) As, we know that, the cross-sectional area of vertical pipes 1, 2 and 3 is constant.

∴ By equation of continuity,

$\Rightarrow A \times v = \text{constant}$

$\Rightarrow \quad v = \text{constant}$

⇒ So, pressure is same at all points. Hence, height of liquid will also be same.

47. (*b*) $eV = \frac{3}{2} k_B T$

$$\Rightarrow T = \frac{2eV}{3k_B} = \frac{2 \times 1.6 \times 10^{-19} \times 0.1}{3 \times 1.38 \times 10^{-23}}$$

$$\Rightarrow T = 773\ K = (773 - 273)^\circ C = 500^\circ C$$

48. (*d*) $X_Z^{184} \rightarrow Y_{Z-2}^{180} + \alpha + Q$

Also, $p_\alpha = p_y = \sqrt{2m_\alpha E_\alpha} = \sqrt{2m_y E_y}$

$\Rightarrow \quad E_\alpha = \frac{180}{4} E_y = 45 E_y$

So, $5.5 = E_y + E_\alpha = \frac{E_\alpha}{45} + E_\alpha$

or $\quad 5.5 = E_\alpha \left(\frac{46}{45}\right)$

$\Rightarrow \quad E_\alpha = \frac{5.5 \times 45}{46} = 5.38\ \text{MeV}$

49. (*d*) As $KE = hf - \phi_0$

$\Rightarrow \quad \frac{1}{2} m v_1^2 = 4 - \phi_0$

and $\quad \frac{1}{2} m v_2^2 = 2.5 - \phi_0$

$\therefore \quad \frac{v_1^2}{v_2^2} = \frac{4 - \phi_0}{2.5 - \phi_0}$

or $\quad 4 = \frac{4 - \phi_0}{2.5 - \phi_0} \quad \left(\text{as}, \frac{v_1}{v_2} = 2\right)$

So, $\quad \phi_0 = 2\ eV$

50. (*b*) Using Bernoulli's equation,

$(KE)_{\text{lowered end}}$ = Pressure energy + KE

or $\quad \frac{1}{2} \rho v^2 = h_0 \rho g + \frac{1}{2} \rho v_1^2 \quad$ ...(i)

The kinetic energy at the opening is converted into the potential energy.

Thus, $\quad \frac{1}{2} \rho v_1^2 = \rho g h \quad$ ...(ii)

From Eqs. (i) and (ii), we get

$$h = \frac{v^2}{2g} - h_0$$

Here, $v = 2.5$ m/s and $h_0 = 12$ cm or 0.12 m and $g = 9.8\ m/s^2$

$$h = \frac{(2.5)^2}{2 \times 9.8} - 0.12$$

$$= 0.318 - 0.12 = 0.198\ m$$

$$h \simeq 0.2\ m$$

Knockout 3

1. (*d*) As we know, ideal gas equation is given as $pV = \mu RT$

When temperature T is kept constant,

$pV = \text{constant} \quad$ ... (i)

If volume is decreased by 5%, this means its volume becomes $\frac{95}{100}$ of the initial value, so in accordance with Eq. (i), the pressure must becomes $\frac{100}{95}$ of its initial value.

Thus, percentage increase in pressure

$$= \left(\frac{100 - 95}{95}\right) \times 100$$

$$= 5.26\%$$

2. (*c*) When temperature of semiconductor is increased, its resistivity decreases as more number of free electrons are available in lattice. So, temperature coefficient of semiconductor is negative.

3. (*c*) If a transformer is ideal, it means there is no loss of power due to flux leakage, hysteresis, eddy currents and heating of coils. So, power transferred through primary coil to secondary will be same.

4. (*d*) Given that, $l = (16.2 \pm 0.1)$ cm

$b = (10.1 \pm 0.1)$ cm

Area of sheet, $A = l \times b$

$= 16.2 \times 10.1$

$= 163.62\ cm^2$

Rounding off to three significant digits, $A = 164\ cm^2$

Relative error in A,

$$\frac{\Delta A}{A} = \left(\frac{\Delta l}{l} + \frac{\Delta b}{b}\right) = \frac{0.1}{16.2} + \frac{0.1}{10.1}$$

$$= 0.0061 + 0.0099 = 0.016$$

So, $\Delta A = 0.016 \times A$

$= 0.016 \times 164$

$= 2.62\ cm^2$

Rounding off to one significant figure,

$$\Delta A = 3\ cm^2$$

$$\therefore \quad A = (164 \pm 3)\ cm^2$$

5. (*d*) Let the specific heat capacities of liquids be s_1 and s_2, then according to the principle of calorimetry,

$$Q_1 = Q_2$$

$$m_1 s_1 \Delta\theta_1 = m_2 s_2 \Delta\theta_2$$

Here, $\quad m_1 = m_2$,

$\Delta\theta_1 = 32^\circ C - 20^\circ C = 12^\circ C$

$\Delta\theta_2 = 40^\circ C - 32^\circ C = 8^\circ C$

$m \times s_1 \times (12) = m \times s_2 \times (8)$

or $\quad \frac{s_1}{s_2} = \frac{2}{3}$

6. (*b*) In common emitter configuration, the AC power gain is much larger compared to other configuration.

7. (*d*) Magnitude of vertical velocity of the body when it is about to strike ground, is given by

$$v_y = \sqrt{u_y^2 + 2gh}$$

$$= \sqrt{(15)^2 + 2 \times 10 \times 20}$$

$$= \sqrt{225 + 400} = \sqrt{625}$$

$$v_y = 25\ m/s$$

As we know that, in projectile motion, horizontal velocity never changes, so striking velocity, $\mathbf{v} = v_x(\hat{i}) + v_y(-\hat{j})$

Here, $v_x = u_x = 10$ m/s, $v_y = 25$ m/s

$$\mathbf{v} = (10\hat{i} - 25\hat{j})\ m/s$$

8. (*a*) Excess pressure in a bubble,

$$\Delta p = \frac{2T}{r} \text{ or } \Delta p \propto \frac{1}{r}$$

So, pressure in smaller bubble is greater than pressure in bigger bubble, therefore air will flow from the smaller bubble to the bigger bubble.

9. (*a*) $U_B - U_A = (V_B - V_A) \cdot q'$

$$= \left(\frac{kq}{r_B} - \frac{kq}{r_A}\right) \cdot q' = \text{a positive number}$$

Here, q' is negative, also $V_B - V_A$ is also negative. So, product is positive.

10. (*a*) Magnetic field of wire along *X*-axis,

$$B_x = \frac{\mu_0 I}{4\pi(r)} \cdot (\sin\theta_1 + \sin\theta_2)$$

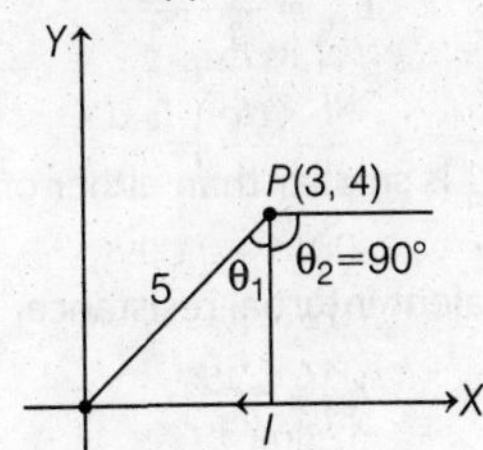

Here, $r = 4$ m

$$\theta_2 = 90°, \sin\theta_1 = \frac{3}{5}$$

$$\text{So, } B_x = \frac{\mu_0 I}{4\pi(4)} \times \left(\frac{3}{5} + 1\right)$$

Similarly, magnetic field due to wire along *Y*-axis,

$$B_y = \frac{\mu_0 I}{4\pi(3)} \cdot \left(\frac{4}{5} + 1\right)$$

Both B_x and B_y are along *Z*-axis, so

$$B_{\text{Total}} = B_x + B_y$$

$$= \frac{\mu_0 I}{4\pi}\left(\frac{8}{20} + \frac{9}{15}\right)$$

$$= \frac{\mu_0 I}{4\pi}\left(\frac{60}{60}\right)$$

$$= \frac{\mu_0 I}{4\pi} \text{ T}$$

11. (c) We have, $\frac{1}{f_1} = \left(\frac{n_g}{n_a} - 1\right)\left(\frac{1}{R_1} - \frac{1}{R_2}\right)$

$$\Rightarrow \frac{1}{f_1} = \left(\frac{3}{2} - 1\right)\left(\frac{1}{R_1} - \frac{1}{R_2}\right)$$

$$\text{or } \frac{1}{f_1} = \frac{1}{2}\left(\frac{1}{R_1} - \frac{1}{R_2}\right) \quad \text{...(i)}$$

$$\text{and } \frac{1}{f_2} = \left(\frac{n_g}{n_l} - 1\right)\left(\frac{1}{R_1} - \frac{1}{R_2}\right)$$

$$\Rightarrow \frac{1}{f_2} = \left(\frac{3/2}{7/5} - 1\right)\left(\frac{1}{R_1} - \frac{1}{R_2}\right)$$

$$\Rightarrow \frac{1}{f_2} = \frac{1}{14}\left(\frac{1}{R_1} - \frac{1}{R_2}\right) \quad \text{...(ii)}$$

From Eqs. (i) and (ii), we get

$$\frac{f_2}{f_1} = 7$$

12. (*b*) The rate of flow of energy in an electromagnetic wave is described by Poynting vector **s** which is defined by the expression,

$$\mathbf{s} = \frac{1}{\mu_0}(\mathbf{E} \times \mathbf{B})$$

Its magnitude *s* is related to the rate at which energy is transported by a wave across a unit area at any instant.

Since, **E** and **B** are mutually perpendicular.

Hence, $|\mathbf{E} \times \mathbf{B}| = EB$

$$\text{Thus, } s = \frac{EB}{\mu_0}$$

13. (*d*) According to question,

If $v \le v_e$, then trajectory will be parabolic.

But $v > v_e$, then it escapes the gravitational field to the earth in a hyperbolic path.

14. (c) At $t = 0$,

$$x_i = 0^3 - 6 \times 0^2 + 9 \times 0 = 0 \text{ m}$$

At $t = 5$s, $x_f = 5^3 - 6 \times 5^2 + 9 \times 5 = 20$ m

So displacement of particle in first 5 s,

$$s = x_f - x_i = 20 - 0 = 20 \text{ m}$$

Now, velocity of particle is

$$v = \frac{dx}{dt} = 3t^2 - 12t + 9$$

$$= 3(t-1)(t-3)$$

Velocity changes its sign as shown below

Sign of *v* :

⊕		⊖		⊕	
t = 0s	t = 1s, v = 0		t = 3s, v = 0		t = 5s

So, particle moves in forward direction from $t = 0$ to $t = 1$s. It turns back and moves in negative direction from $t = 1$s to $t = 3$s.

It again moves from $t = 3$s to $t = 5$s in positive direction. Also at $t = 3$s, position of particle is,

$$x = 3^3 - 6 \times 3^2 + 9 \times 3 = 0 \text{m}$$

Hence, particle moves as

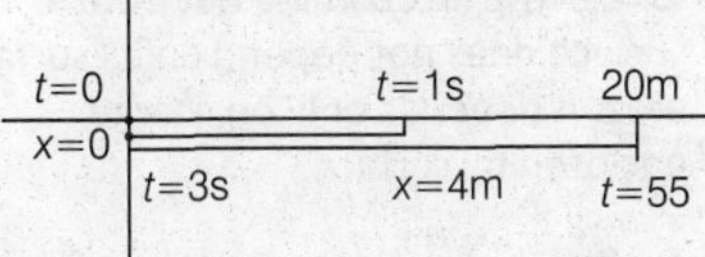

So, distance of particle in first 5 s

$$D = 4 + 4 + 20 = 28 \text{ m}$$

Hence, ratio is $\frac{28}{20} = \frac{7}{5}$.

15. (*c*) By de-Broglie hypothesis,

$$2\pi r_n = n\lambda$$

For first orbit, $n = 1, r = r_1$, then

$$2\pi r_1 = \lambda \text{ or } r_1 = \frac{\lambda}{2\pi}$$

For second orbit, $n = 2, r = r_2$, then

$$2\pi r_2 = 2\lambda$$

$$\text{or} \quad r_2 = \frac{2\lambda}{2\pi}$$

Minimum radial distance between first orbit and second orbit is

$$r_2 - r_1 = \frac{2\lambda}{2\pi} - \frac{\lambda}{2\pi}$$

$$\Rightarrow r_2 - r_1 = \frac{\lambda}{2\pi}$$

16. (*d*) When the liquid is heated, the container will also expand along with liquid.

Thus, apparent expansion coefficient of liquid is $\gamma_a = \gamma_l - \gamma_s$

where, γ_l = coefficient of real expansion of a liquid and

γ_s = coefficient of cubical expansion of the container.

If $\gamma_l > \gamma_s$, then $\gamma_a > 0$ and level of liquid will rise.

If $\gamma_l = \gamma_s$, then $\gamma_a = 0$ and level of liquid will not change.

If $\gamma_l < \gamma_s$ then $\gamma_a < 0$, hence level of liquid will fall.

Thus, there are three possibilities as mentioned above. All these will depend upon the coefficients of volume expansion of container and liquid.

17. (*c*) A is false but R is true.

Gravitational potential gradient = − Gravitational field

$$\Rightarrow \frac{d}{dx}V_g = -E_g$$

As inside a shell, field $E_g = 0$

$$\Rightarrow \quad \frac{dV_g}{dx} = 0$$

or $\quad V_g = \text{constant}$

$\therefore$ For a shell, $V_g(\text{surface}) = V_g(\text{inside})$

18. (*d*) Electric flux coming out from a surface does not depend on its surface area. It depends only on charge enclosed by surface.

As, flux, $\phi = \frac{q}{\varepsilon_0}$

19. (*a*) As given, time period, $t = 8$ s and amplitude, $A = 6$ cm

The time taken by a particle executing SHM from either extreme position to mean position and mean position to either extreme position is $t/4$, here $t = 2$ s.

According to question situation,

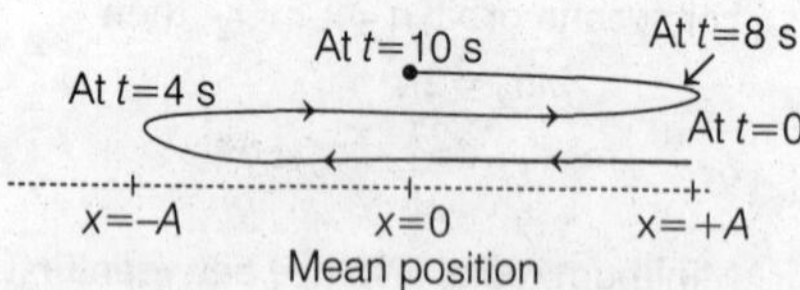

Thus, displacement of particle at $t = 10$ s is $x = 0$ cm.

20. (*c*) If the intensities of light coming out from slits are I_1 and I_2 respectively, then

$$I_{max} = (\sqrt{I_1} + \sqrt{I_2})^2 \quad \text{... (i)}$$

and $\quad I_{min} = (\sqrt{I_1} - \sqrt{I_2})^2 \quad$ ... (ii)

When $\quad I_1 = I_2 = I_0$ (Let)

then $\quad I_{max} = (\sqrt{I_0} + \sqrt{I_0})^2 = 4I_0$

and $\quad I_{min} = (\sqrt{I_0} - \sqrt{I_0})^2 = 0$

When width of one slit is slightly increased, then intensity due to that slit becomes greater than I_0. In that case, we can see that

$I_{max} > 4I_0$ [using Eq. (i)]

and $I_{min} > 0$ [using Eq. (ii)]

Thus, both maximum and minimum intensities will increase.

21. (*d*) Circuit given is;

$E_1 = 9$V, $r_1 = 0.02\ \Omega$

$E_2 = 12$V, $r_2 = 0.04\ \Omega$

Net emf, $E_{net} = 12 - 9 = 3$ V

Current in circuit,

$$I = \frac{E_{net}}{R_{total}} = \frac{12-9}{0.02+0.04} = 50 \text{ A}$$

Heat produced per second in cell of emf $E_2 = I^2 r_2$

$$= 50 \times 50 \times 0.04 = 100 \text{ W}$$

Potential drop across cell 1 is, (+ sign as cell is charging)

$$V_1 = E_1 + Ir_1 = 9 + 50 \times 0.02 = 10 \text{ V}$$

22. (*b*) Given that,

Initial mass, $m_0 = 2000$ kg

Rate of fuel consumption, $\frac{dm}{dt} = 60$ kg/s

Relative velocity of gas, $v_r = 400$ m/s

The free body diagram of the rocket is as shown below

In equilibrium, $\Sigma F_y = 0$

$\Rightarrow \quad m_0 a = F_T - m_0 g$

or $\quad a = \frac{F_T}{m_0} - g$

$$= \frac{v_r\left(\frac{dm}{dt}\right)}{m_0} - g = \frac{400 \times 60}{2000} - 10 = 12 - 10$$

$$a = 2 \text{ m/s}^2$$

23. (*d*) For positive half cycle when $V_i > 2$ V, diode is in forward bias and current will flow from the diode.

Voltage across resistance, $V_R = V_i - 2$

$$V_R = 5\sin\omega t - 2 = 3 \text{ V}$$

$[\because \sin \omega t = 1(\text{max})]$

For negative half cycle, diode is in reverse bias, so no current will flow through diode.

Voltage across resistance, $V_R = 0$ V

So, the input and output waveform for the given circuit is as shown below.

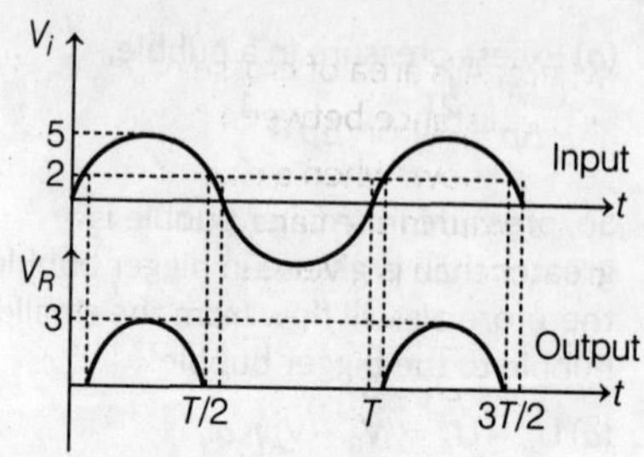

24. (*d*) Consider that there are two batteries of emf's E_1 and E_2 which have internal resistances r_1 and r_2. When the batteries are connected in parallel, equivalent emf is given by

$$E_{eq} = \frac{\frac{E_1}{r_1} + \frac{E_2}{r_2}}{\frac{1}{r_1} + \frac{1}{r_2}}$$

So, E_{eq} is smaller than either of the two emf's.

Equivalent internal resistance,

$$r_{eq} = \frac{r_1 r_2}{r_1 + r_2}$$

which is less than both r_1 and r_2.

Hence, both statements I and II are correct.

25. (*d*) As $v_d = \frac{I}{neA}$

$$\frac{v_{d_1}}{v_{d_2}} = \frac{A_2}{A_1} = \frac{d_2^2}{d_1^2} = \frac{4^2}{2^2}$$

or $\quad v_{d_1} : v_{d_2} :: 4 : 1$

26. (*a*) (A) Resonance occurs at frequency $f = \frac{\omega_R}{2\pi} = 663.48 \text{ Hz} \simeq 664 \text{ Hz}$

(B) $P_{max} = \frac{1}{2}(I_0)^2_{max} R = 2299.3$ W $= 2.3$ kW

(C) $\Delta\omega = \frac{R}{2L}$ and half power frequencies are $\omega_R \pm \Delta\omega$ $= 678.74$ Hz and 648.22 Hz

(D) Q-factor $= \frac{\omega_R L}{R} = 21.74 \simeq 22$

27. (*c*) In inelastic collision, linear momentum is conserved but part of kinetic energy of colliding particles is lost. Total energy is always conserved.

28. (*d*) According to question, thickness of the slab, $t = \frac{d}{3}$

Capacitance of the capacitor before the insertion of the slab, $C = \frac{\varepsilon_0 A}{d}$ ...(i) where, A is area of cross-section and d is the distance between the plates.

As we know, when a slab of thickness t is inserted in the capacitor, its capacitance is given as

$$C' = \frac{\varepsilon_0 A}{d - t + \frac{t}{K}}$$

$$= \frac{\varepsilon_0 A}{d - \frac{d}{3} + \frac{t}{\infty}} \text{ (for conductor, } K = \infty)$$

$$= \frac{3}{2}\frac{\varepsilon_0 A}{d}$$

$$\therefore \text{ Ratio } \frac{C'}{C} = \frac{3}{2} \qquad [\because \text{ from Eq. (i)}]$$

29. (*b*) From photoelectric equation, for wavelength λ_1

$$eV_s = \frac{hc}{\lambda_1} - \phi$$

$$\Rightarrow \quad eV_s = \frac{12400}{4000} - 1.1$$

or $\quad V_s = 2\text{ V}$

Now, when wavelength λ_2 is used, let stopping potential becomes V_s'

$$\Rightarrow \quad eV_s' = \frac{12400}{6200} - 1.1$$

$$V_s' = 0.9\text{ V}$$

Change in stopping potential,

$$V_s - V_s' = 2 - 0.9 = 1.1\text{ V}$$

30. (*c*) According to the question,

$$[v_c] = [\eta^\alpha \rho^\beta r^\gamma] \qquad \text{... (i)}$$

As we know that, $[v_c] = [M^0LT^{-1}]$

$$[\eta] = [ML^{-1}T^{-1}]$$

$$[\rho] = [ML^{-3}]$$

$$[r] = [L]$$

Substituting the dimensions of above mentioned quantities in Eq. (i), we get

$$[M^0LT^{-1}] = [ML^{-1}T^{-1}]^\alpha [M^1L^{-3}]^\beta [L]^\gamma$$

$$[M^0LT^{-1}] = [M^{\alpha+\beta}L^{-\alpha-3\beta+\gamma}T^{-\alpha}]$$

On comparing the powers of M, L and T on both sides, we get

$$\alpha + \beta = 0$$

$$-\alpha - 3\beta + \gamma = 1$$

$$-\alpha = -1$$

On solving above equations, we get

$$\alpha = 1, \beta = -1, \gamma = -1$$

Thus, $\alpha + \beta + \gamma = 1 + (-1) + (-1) = -1$

31. (*b*) For a string or wire,

frequency of nth harmonic, $f_n = \dfrac{nv}{2l}$

As per given condition,

or $\quad 450 = \dfrac{nv}{2l} \qquad$ ... (i)

and $\quad 500 = \dfrac{(n+1)v}{2l} \qquad$ ... (ii)

On dividing Eq. (i) by Eq. (ii), we get

$$\frac{450}{500} = \frac{n}{n+1}$$

or $\quad n = 9$

As, $\quad l = \dfrac{nv}{2f_n}$

$\because \quad v = \sqrt{\dfrac{T}{\mu}}$

where, T is the tension in the string and μ is the linear mass density.

$$\therefore \quad l = \frac{n}{2f_n} \times \sqrt{\frac{T}{\mu}}$$

$$= \frac{9}{2 \times 450} \times \sqrt{\frac{80}{5 \times 10^{-4}}}$$

$$l = 4\text{ m}$$

32. (*a*) $V_{\text{centre}} = V_{\text{surface}} = \dfrac{kQ}{R} = 5$

So, $kQ = 5 \times R = 5 \times 1 = 5$

Now at a point 1 m from surface, potential will be

$$V = \frac{kQ}{r}, \text{ here } r = 2\text{ m}$$

So, $V = \dfrac{kQ}{2} = \dfrac{5}{2} = 2.5\text{ V}$

33. (*b*) Magnetic field due to a long straight current carrying wire at distance d is given by

$$B = \frac{\mu_0 I_1}{2\pi d}$$

Magnetic force per unit length experienced by other long straight wire carrying current I_2 is given as

$$\frac{F}{L} = \frac{\mu_0 I_1 I_2}{2\pi d}$$

$B_C = \dfrac{\mu_0 I}{2\pi(2d)}$, $B_A = \dfrac{\mu_0 I}{2\pi d}$, $B_A = \dfrac{\mu_0 I}{2\pi(2d)}$, $B_C = \dfrac{\mu_0 I}{2\pi d}$, $B_B = \dfrac{\mu_0 I}{2\pi d}$

A ←d→ B ←d→ C

$B_B = \dfrac{\mu_0 I}{2\pi d}$

So, we have

$$\frac{F_A}{l} = IB_{\text{net A}} = I \times \left(\frac{\mu_0 I}{2\pi d} - \frac{\mu_0 I}{4\pi d}\right) = \frac{\mu_0 I^2}{4\pi d}$$

$$\frac{F_B}{l} = IB_{\text{net B}} = I \times \left(\frac{\mu_0 I}{2\pi d} + \frac{\mu_0 I}{2\pi d}\right) = \frac{\mu_0 I^2}{\pi d}$$

$$\frac{F_C}{l} = IB_{\text{net C}} = I \times \left(\frac{\mu_0 I}{2\pi d} + \frac{\mu_0 I}{4\pi d}\right) = \frac{3\mu_0 I^2}{4\pi d}$$

Clear that, $\dfrac{F_B}{l} > \dfrac{F_C}{l} > \dfrac{F_A}{l}$

or $\quad F_B > F_C > F_A$

34. (*a*) Given that uniform quarter disc has mass M and radius R. Let the complete disc is of same density and radius.

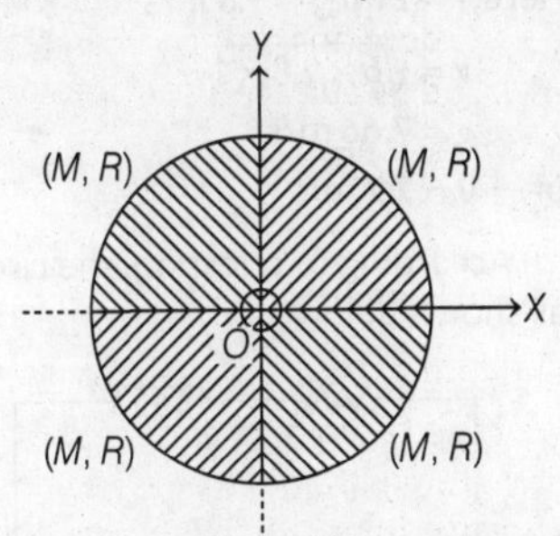

As we know that, moment of inertia of disc about axis passing through its centre and perpendicular to its plane is equal to $\dfrac{mR^2}{2}$.

If the moment of inertia due to quarter ring is I, then all other three parts will also be having moment of inertia I. So, we can write

$$I + I + I + I = \frac{(\text{Mass of disc})R^2}{2}$$

$$4I = \frac{(4M)R^2}{2}$$

or $\quad I = \dfrac{MR^2}{2}$

35. (*b*) Let angular speed of rod when it becomes vertical again be ω.

The given condition in the question is as shown below.

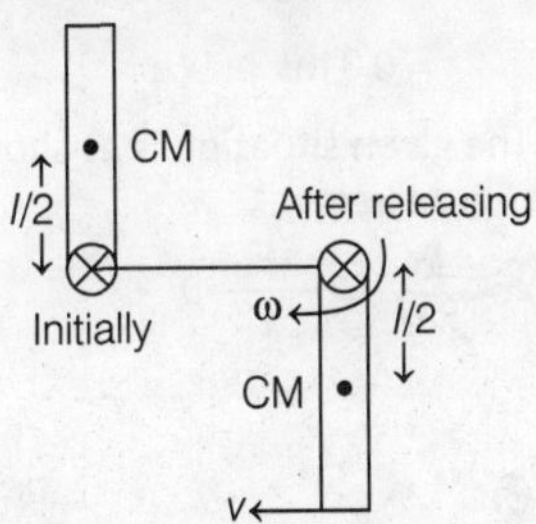

Using principle of mechanical energy conservation,

$$KE_i + U_i = KE_f + U_f$$

or $\quad KE_f - KE_i = U_i - U_f$

or $\quad \dfrac{1}{2}I\omega^2 - 0 = mg\,\Delta h_{CM}$

or $\quad \dfrac{1}{2}\left(\dfrac{ml^2}{3}\right)\omega^2 = mg\left[\dfrac{l}{2} - \left(-\dfrac{l}{2}\right)\right]$ or mgl

$$\frac{ml^2}{6}\omega^2 = mgl$$

or $\omega = \sqrt{\frac{6g}{l}}$

Velocity of free end, $v = l\omega$

$$v = l\sqrt{\frac{6g}{l}} = \sqrt{6gl}$$

Here, $l = 1$ m, $g = 9.8$ m/s^2

$$v = \sqrt{6 \times 9.8 \times 1}$$

$$v = 7.66 \text{ m/s}$$

or $v \approx 7.7$ m/s

36. (*a*) According to question, the circuit is as shown below.

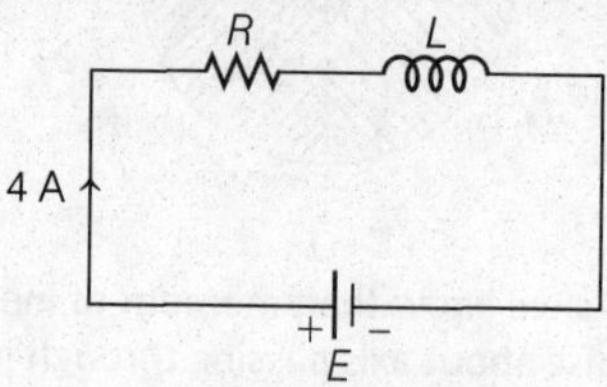

Given, $U = 24 \text{ mJ} = 24 \times 10^{-3}$ J

$$P = 160 \text{ W}$$

Energy stored by inductor, $U = \frac{1}{2}LI^2$

or $$L = \frac{2U}{I^2} = \frac{2 \times 24 \times 10^{-3}}{(4)^2}$$

$$L = 3 \times 10^{-3} \text{ H}$$

Power dissipation, $P = I^2 R$

or $$R = \frac{P}{I^2} = \frac{160}{(4)^2}$$

$$R = 10\,\Omega$$

Time constant of *L*-*R* circuit is given by

$$\tau = \frac{L}{R} = \frac{3 \times 10^{-3}}{10}$$

$$= 0.3 \times 10^{-3}$$

$$= 0.3 \text{ ms}$$

37. (*c*) The given situation is as shown in the figure below.

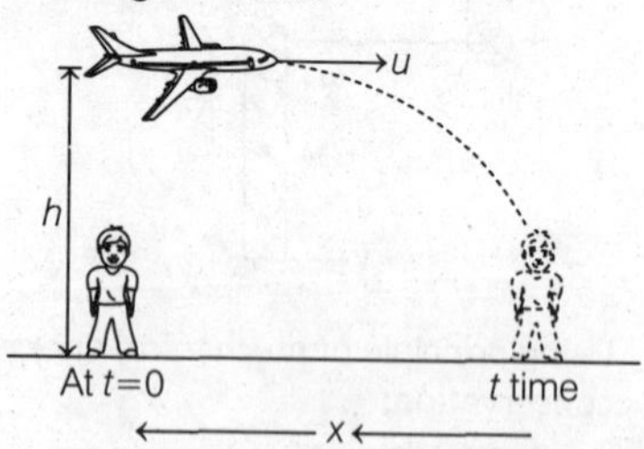

Time taken by the food packet to reach at ground,

$$t = \sqrt{\frac{2h}{g}} \quad \text{... (i)}$$

and horizontal distance covered,

$$x = u \times t \quad \text{... (ii)}$$

Let the man has acceleration $a_{\min}$,

then $$x = \frac{1}{2}a_{\min}t^2 \quad \text{... (iii)}$$

From Eqs. (ii) and (iii), we get

$$ut = \frac{1}{2}a_{\min}t^2$$

or $$a_{\min} = \frac{2u}{t} = \frac{2u}{\sqrt{\frac{2h}{g}}} \quad \text{[using Eq. (i)]}$$

$$a_{\min} = u\sqrt{\frac{2g}{h}}$$

38. (*b*) Let the magnitude of velocity of the α-particle be *u*. As the α-particle enters in magnetic field by making angle 37°. So, it has two components of velocity. One which is parallel to magnetic field and second which is perpendicular to it. So, we can write

$$v_{\perp} = u\sin 37°$$

$$v_{\parallel} = u\cos 37°$$

As, pitch of the helix is product of velocity component along the magnetic field and time period *T* i.e.

Pitch, $P = (v_{\parallel})T$

$$= (u\cos 37°)\left(\frac{2\pi m}{qB}\right) \quad \left(\because T = \frac{2\pi m}{qB}\right)$$

$$P = \frac{2\pi mu\cos 37°}{qB} \quad \text{... (i)}$$

Radius of helix, $R = \frac{mv_{\perp}}{qB}$

$$R = \frac{mu\sin 37°}{qB} \quad \text{... (ii)}$$

On dividing Eq. (i) by Eq. (ii), we get

$$\frac{P}{R} = \frac{2\pi\cos 37°}{\sin 37°} = 2\pi\cot 37°$$

$$= 2\pi \times \frac{4}{3}$$

$$\Rightarrow \frac{P}{R} = \frac{8\pi}{3}$$

or $$R = \frac{3P}{8\pi}$$

39. (*a*) According to given question, consider a small element on charged rod at *y* distance from origin.

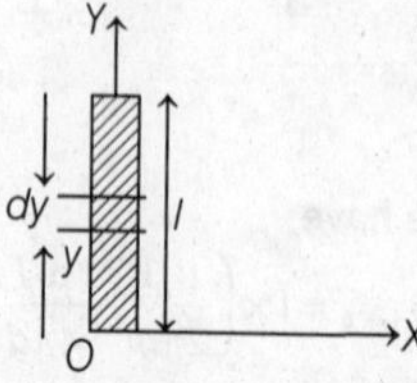

Charge on small element, dq = (linear charge density) × (length)

$$\Rightarrow dq = \lambda\,dy$$

$$dq = \lambda_0 \frac{y}{l} \cdot dy$$

Total charge on rod, $q = \int_0^l dq$

$$= \int_0^l \frac{\lambda_0 y}{l}dy$$

$$= \frac{\lambda_0}{l}\int_0^l y\,dy$$

$$= \frac{\lambda_0}{l}\left[\frac{y^2}{2}\right]_0^l$$

$$= \frac{\lambda_0}{l}\left[\frac{l^2}{2} - \frac{0^2}{2}\right] = \frac{\lambda_0 l}{2}$$

40. (*b*) The self-inductance of a long solenoid is given as

$$L = \frac{\mu_0 N^2 A}{l} \quad \text{... (i)}$$

$$= \frac{\mu_0 N^2 A}{l \times A} \times A$$

$$= \frac{\mu_0 (NA)^2}{V} \quad [\because V = l \times A]$$

or $$L \propto \frac{1}{V} \quad [\because NA = \text{constant}]$$

This means, inductance is inversely proportional to volume *V*.

So, the graph between *L* and *V* will be a rectangular hyperbola.

41. (*c*) In this problem, first we shall find angular velocity during uniform motion, $\omega = \frac{\theta}{t}$

Given that, disc completes 1 revolution or 2π rad in every 10 s.

$$\omega = \frac{2\pi}{10} = \frac{\pi}{5} \text{ rad/s}$$

Now, during acceleration motion, Angular acceleration,

$$\alpha_1 = \frac{\omega_f - \omega_i}{t}$$

$$\alpha_1 = \frac{\frac{\pi}{5} - 0}{20}$$

$$= \frac{\pi}{100} \text{ rad/s}^2$$

Angular displacement covered,

$$\theta_1 = \omega_i t + \frac{1}{2}\alpha t^2$$

$$= 0 \times 20 + \frac{1}{2} \times \frac{\pi}{100} \times (20)^2$$

$$\theta_1 = 2\pi \text{ rad}$$

During uniform circular motion, Angle covered, $\theta_2 = \omega \times t$

$$\theta_2 = \frac{\pi}{5} \times 120 = 24\,\pi \text{ rad}$$

During slow down motion,

Angular acceleration, $\alpha_2 = \dfrac{\omega_f - \omega_i}{t}$

$= \dfrac{0 - \dfrac{\pi}{5}}{10}$

$\alpha_2 = -\dfrac{\pi}{50}\ \text{rad/s}^2$

Angular displacement,

$\theta_3 = \omega_i t + \dfrac{1}{2}\alpha t^2$

$= \dfrac{\pi}{5} \times 10 + \dfrac{1}{2} \times \left(-\dfrac{\pi}{50}\right) \times (10)^2$

$\theta_3 = 2\pi - \pi = \pi$ rad

Total angular displacement during complete motion, $\theta = \theta_1 + \theta_2 + \theta_3$

$= 2\pi + 24\pi + \pi$

$\theta = 27\pi$ rad

42. (*c*) Binding energy,

$BE = -$ (Total energy)

$= \dfrac{13.6Z^2}{n^2}$ eV ... (i)

Thus, statement I is incorrect.

Also, $E_{\text{ionisation}} = E_\infty - E_n$

$= 0 - \left[-13.6\dfrac{Z^2}{n^2}\right]$

$E_{\text{ionisation}} = 13.6\dfrac{Z^2}{n^2}$ ... (ii)

From Eqs. (i) and (ii), we get

$E_{\text{ionisation}} = BE$

Therefore, statement II is correct.

43. (*c*) Power available as light,

$P = \dfrac{5}{100} \times 100 = 5$ W

Intensity, $I = \dfrac{P}{4\pi d^2}$

$= \dfrac{5}{4\pi \times 1^2}$

$= 0.398\ \text{W/m}^2$

$\approx 0.4\ \text{W/m}^2$

44. (*d*) Wavelength in water and glass will be

$\lambda_w = \dfrac{\lambda}{n_w} = \dfrac{550}{4/3}$

and $\lambda_g = \dfrac{\lambda}{n_g} = \dfrac{550}{3/2}$

Number of waves occuring in 1 μm length of medium will be

N_1 (in water) $= \dfrac{1 \times 10^{-6}}{\lambda_w}$

$= \dfrac{10^9 \times 4 \times 10^{-6}}{550 \times 3}$

$= 2.4$

and N_2 (in glass) $= \dfrac{10^9 \times 3 \times 10^{-6}}{550 \times 2}$

$= 2.7$

Difference in number of waves

$= \Delta N = (2.7 - 2.4)$

$= 0.3$

So, phase difference between waves is

$\Delta\phi = 0.3 \times 2\pi$

$= 0.6\pi$ rad

45. (*c*) Using $hf = E$

$\Rightarrow \dfrac{hc}{\lambda} = E$

So, wavelength (minimum),

$\lambda = \dfrac{hc}{E}$

$= \dfrac{1240\ \text{eV}}{30 \times 1000\ \text{eV}}$

$= 0.0413$ nm

46. (*c*) Arsenic is pentavalent while indium is trivalent.

Also, n(As) > n(In), so resulting crystal is n-type.

For a p-n junction, we have to doped different regions of crystal.

47. (*d*) From the lens Makers formula, we know that,

$\dfrac{\mu_2}{v} - \dfrac{\mu_1}{u} = \dfrac{\mu_0 - \mu_1}{R_1} + \dfrac{\mu_2 - \mu_1}{R_2}$

It is given that light is coming parallel to each other, then image will be formed at focus.

$\therefore$ $u = \infty, v = f$

Here $\mu_0 = 1.5, \mu_1 = 1.2, \mu_2 = 1.6,$

$R_1 = +30$ cm, $R_2 = -30$ cm

$\dfrac{1.6}{f} = \dfrac{1.5 - 1.2}{30} + \dfrac{1.6 - 1.5}{-30}$

$\dfrac{1.6}{f} = \dfrac{0.3}{30} - \dfrac{0.1}{30}$

$f = 240$ cm

48. (*c*) In general, the radius of a mono-electron species in nth orbit is given as

$r_n = a_0 \times \dfrac{n^2}{Z}$

where, a_0 is the radius of first orbit in hydrogen atom.

$\therefore$ $r = 0.53 \times \dfrac{n^2}{Z}$ Å

For second excited state of He^+ ion,

$Z = 2, n = 3$

$r_3 = 0.53 \times \dfrac{(3)^2}{2}$

$(r_3)_{He} = 0.53 \times \dfrac{9}{2}$ Å ...(i)

From Bohr's quantisation of angular momentum,

$mvr = \dfrac{nh}{2\pi}$

$mv\left(0.53 \times \dfrac{9}{2}\right) = \dfrac{3h}{2\pi}$ [using Eq. (i)]

$\dfrac{h}{mv} = 0.53 \times 3 \times \pi$

$\lambda = 4.99$ Å $\left(\because \lambda = \dfrac{h}{mv}\right)$

or $\lambda = 5$ Å

49. (*b*) Displacement, $[y] = [L]$

Velocity, $[\alpha] = [LT^{-1}]$

Acceleration, $[\beta] = [LT^{-2}]$

Amplitude, $[A] = [L]$

Now, dimensional formula of

$\sqrt{\dfrac{y(\alpha^2 - \beta y)}{\beta}} = \dfrac{[y]^{\frac{1}{2}}(\alpha^2 - \beta y)^{\frac{1}{2}}}{[\beta]^{\frac{1}{2}}}$

$= \dfrac{[L]^{\frac{1}{2}}[L^2T^{-2}]^{\frac{1}{2}}}{[LT^{-2}]^{\frac{1}{2}}}$

$= [L]$

The physical equation is correct as dimensional formula is equal to that of amplitude.

50. (*a*) By gas equation,

$pV = nRT$

$\Rightarrow kV^3 \cdot V = nRT$ $[\because p = kV^3$ (given)]

or $kV^4 = nRT$

Differentiating with respect to T, we have

$4kV^3 \cdot \dfrac{dV}{dT} = nR$

$\Rightarrow kV^3 \cdot dV = \dfrac{nR}{4} \cdot dT$

or $p\Delta V = \dfrac{nR}{4} \cdot \Delta T$

Hence, work done

$= p\Delta V = \dfrac{nR}{4}(300 - 100)$

$= 50\,nR$

Knockout 4

1. (*a*) Elongation produced in the rod is given as

$$\Delta l = \frac{wl}{2YA} = \frac{mgl}{2YA}$$

Putting all the given values, we get

$$\Delta l = \frac{1.5 \times 9.8 \times 0.6}{2 \times 1.2 \times 10^{11} \times 10^{-2}}$$

$$= 3.675 \times 10^{-9} \text{ m}$$

2. (*b*) We know that,

$$T = 2\pi\sqrt{\frac{L}{g}}$$

or $g = \frac{4\pi^2 L}{T^2}$ or $g = 4\pi^2 LT^{-2}$

Maximum percentage error in the measurement of *g*,

$$\frac{\Delta g}{g} \times 100 = \frac{\Delta L}{L} \times 100 + 2\frac{\Delta T}{T} \times 100$$

$$= 2\% + 2 \times 1\%$$

$$= 4\%$$

3. (*b*) $\because W_A = W_B$

$$\Rightarrow \quad F_A d\cos\theta_A = F_B d\cos\theta_B$$

or $\frac{F_A}{F_B} = \frac{\cos\theta_B}{\cos\theta_A}$

$$= \frac{\cos 60°}{\cos 45°}$$

$$= \frac{\frac{1}{2}}{\frac{1}{\sqrt{2}}} = 1 : \sqrt{2}$$

4. (*d*) Voltage amplification,

$$A_V = \beta \times \frac{R_{\text{out}}}{R_{\text{in}}}$$

$$= 60 \times \frac{5 \times 10^3}{500}$$

$$= 600$$

5. (*c*) A is incorrect but R is correct.

Following diagram, illustrates 1 parsec.

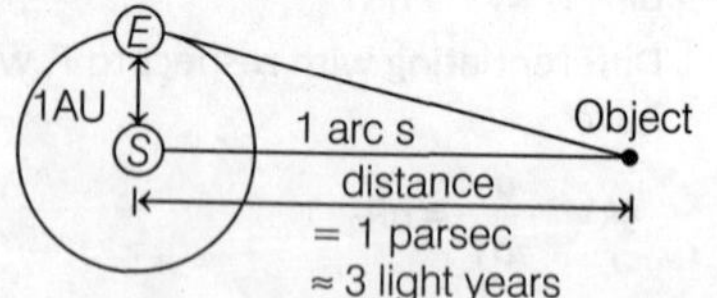

6. (*b*) According to question,

$$T_L = 273 + (-5) = 268 \text{ K}$$

$$T_H = 273 + 45$$

$$= 318 \text{ K}$$

Efficiency of carnot cycle,

$$\eta = 1 - \frac{T_L}{T_H}$$

$$= 1 - \frac{268}{318} = \frac{50}{318}$$

As, we know that, efficiency, $\eta = \frac{W}{Q_{\text{in}}}$

$$\therefore \quad Q_{\text{in}} = \frac{W}{\eta}$$

$$= \frac{25 \times 318}{50}$$

$$= 159 \text{ W}$$

7. (*b*) The time period of a bar magnet in a magnetic field is given by $T = 2\pi\sqrt{\frac{I}{MB}}$

where, I = moment of inertia,

M = moment of magnet

and B = magnetic field.

$$\therefore \quad T \propto \sqrt{I} \propto \sqrt{m}$$

Therefore, *T* becomes twice as mass becomes four times.

8. (*d*) Given,

Kinetic energy of proton, KE = 8 GeV

or $\text{KE} = 8 \times 10^9 \times 1.6 \times 10^{-19}$

$\text{KE} = 12.8 \times 10^{-10}$ J

$(\because 1 \text{ eV} = 1.6 \times 10^{-19} \text{ J})$

de-Broglie wavelength is given by

$$\lambda = \frac{h}{\sqrt{2(\text{KE})m}}$$

$$= \frac{6.626 \times 10^{-34}}{\sqrt{2 \times 12.8 \times 10^{-10} \times 1.67 \times 10^{-27}}}$$

$$= 3.205 \times 10^{-16} \text{ m}$$

or $\lambda = 0.3205$ fm

9. (*b*) When *p-n* junction is forward biased, the width of depletion layer decreases and the barrier potential is opposed by the forward biased. In other words, potential barrier decreases. Hence, the diffusion of holes and electrons through the junction increases. Due to this, the diode current increases and hence resistance decreases.

When *p-n* junction is reversed biased, the barrier potential is supported and the width of depletion layer increases. As a result of this, the diode current becomes almost zero, as there is no diffusion of majority carrier (electrons and holes) through the junction. Hence, the resistance of the junction diode increases, when reverse biased.

10. (*d*) $\because \quad Q = ms\Delta\theta$

$$\Rightarrow \quad s = \frac{Q}{m\Delta\theta}$$

or $[s] = \frac{[Q]}{[m][\Delta\theta]} = \frac{[ML^2T^{-2}]}{[M][K]}$

$$[s] = [M^0L^2T^{-2}K^{-1}]$$

11. (*a*) The difference of kinetic energies will be equal to electrostatic potential energy of both the charged particles initially.

$$\therefore \text{KE} = \text{PE} = \frac{1}{4\pi\varepsilon_0} \cdot \frac{q_1 q_2}{a},$$

where q_1 and q_2 are the charges of two particles and a is the distance between them.

Here, $q_1 = q_2 = q$ (Let)

$$\Rightarrow \quad K = \frac{1}{4\pi\varepsilon_0} \cdot \frac{q^2}{a}$$

or $q = \sqrt{4\pi\varepsilon_0 aK}$

Given, $a = 0.9$ m,

$K = 90$ mJ or 9×10^{-2} J

$$q = \sqrt{\frac{1}{9 \times 10^9} \times 0.9 \times 9 \times 10^{-2}}$$

$$= 3 \times 10^{-6} \text{ or } 3\,\mu\text{C}$$

12. (*c*) Given, angle between **P** and **Q** is 60°. So, angle between **P** and 2**Q** vectors will also be 60° and angle between 3**P** and −2**Q** vectors will be 180° − 60° = 120°.

Also, $\frac{\mathbf{P}}{4}$ is a unit vector, so $\frac{|\mathbf{P}|}{4} = 1$

or $|\mathbf{P}| = 4$

Here,

$$|\mathbf{P} + 2\mathbf{Q}| = |3\mathbf{P} - 2\mathbf{Q}|$$

or $|\mathbf{P} + 2\mathbf{Q}| = |3\mathbf{P} + (-2\mathbf{Q})|$

Squaring on both sides, we get

$$(\mathbf{P})^2 + (2\mathbf{Q})^2 + 2\mathbf{P} \cdot 2\mathbf{Q}$$

$$= (3\mathbf{P})^2 + (-2\mathbf{Q})^2 + 2 \cdot 3\mathbf{P} \cdot -2\mathbf{Q}$$

$$P^2 + (2Q)^2 + 2(P)(2Q)\cos 60°$$

$$= (3P)^2 + (2Q)^2 - 2(3P)(2Q)\cos 120°$$

$$P^2 + 4Q^2 + 4PQ \times \frac{1}{2}$$

$$= 9P^2 + 4Q^2 - 12PQ\left(-\frac{1}{2}\right)$$

$$P^2 + 2PQ = 9P^2 + 6PQ$$

$$8P^2 + 4PQ = 0$$

$$4P(2P + Q) = 0$$

So, either $P = 0$

Not possible, as $|\mathbf{P}| = 4$

or $2P + Q = 0$

$$Q = -2P = -8$$

$$\therefore \quad |Q| = 8$$

13. (*d*) When a plane wavefront is incident on concave mirror, then after reflection, the shape of the wavefront is spherical in nature as shown below.

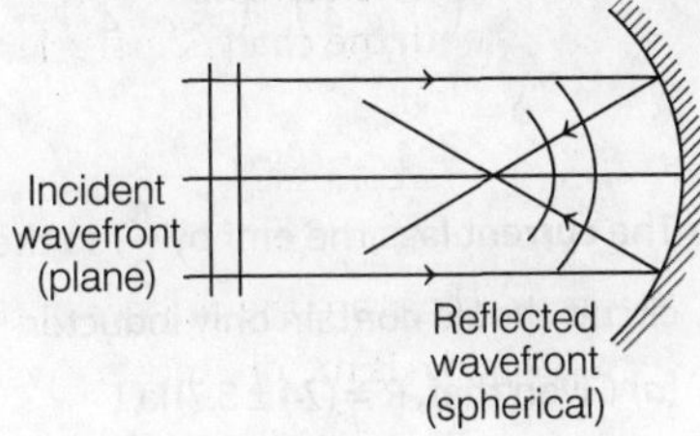

14. (*d*) Buoyant force in a non-inertial frame is given by

$$B = V_i \rho_l g_{eff} \quad \text{... (i)}$$

Here, V_i = volume of block immersed in liquid,

ρ_l = density of liquid and

g_{eff} = effective gravity

(Here, $g_{eff} = g + a$)

Also, $V_i = \frac{\rho_{block}}{\rho_l} \times V_{block}$

$\Rightarrow \quad V_i = \frac{M_{block}}{\rho_l}$

$\therefore$ Eq. (i) can be written as

$$B = \frac{M_{block}}{\rho_l} \times \rho_l \times g_{eff}$$
$$= M_{block} \times g_{eff}$$
$$= \left(\frac{W_{block}}{g}\right) \times g_{eff}$$

Substituting the given values, we get

$$B = \left(\frac{80}{10}\right) \times (10 + 2)$$
$$= 96 \text{ N}$$

15. (*a*) The magnetic field at a point *P* due to a current carrying straight wire, such that the ends of the wires, makes angle α and β (see figure) is given by

$$B = \frac{\mu_0 I}{4\pi d}(\sin\alpha - \sin\beta)$$

where, *d* is the distance between the point *P* and wire.

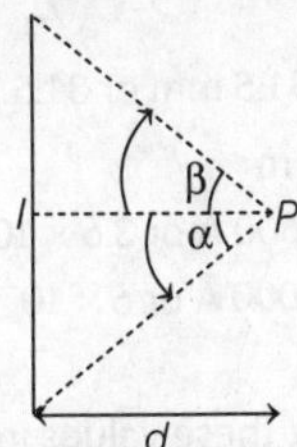

In the given problem,

$\alpha = \theta_1$ and $\beta = \theta_2$

$\therefore \quad B = \frac{\mu_0 I}{4\pi d}(\sin\theta_1 - \sin\theta_2)$

16. (*a*) Let the object has been given velocity *u*.

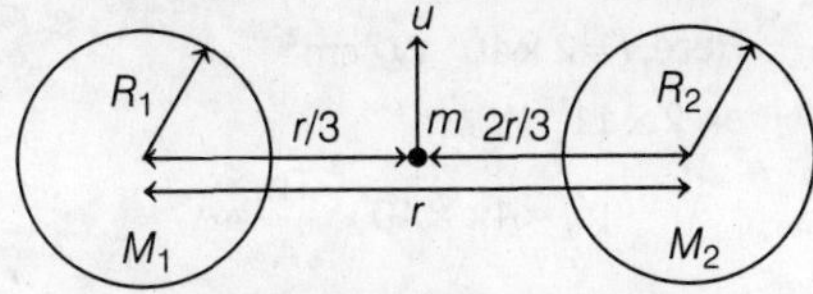

Using principle of conservation of mechanical energy,

$$KE_i + U_i = KE_f + U_f$$

$$\frac{1}{2}mu^2 + \left(-\frac{GM_1 m}{\frac{r}{3}} - \frac{GM_2 m}{\frac{2r}{3}}\right) = 0 + 0$$

$$\frac{1}{2}mu^2 - \frac{3Gm}{r}\left(M_1 + \frac{M_2}{2}\right) = 0$$

or $\quad u^2 = \frac{3G}{r}(2M_1 + M_2)$

or $\quad u = \sqrt{\frac{3G}{r}(2M_1 + M_2)}$

17. (*b*) Gravitational potential at point *P* = Gravitational potential due to shell + Gravitational potential due to mass at centre

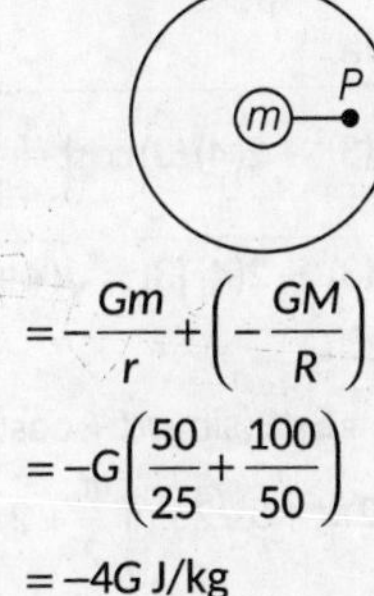

$$= -\frac{Gm}{r} + \left(-\frac{GM}{R}\right)$$
$$= -G\left(\frac{50}{25} + \frac{100}{50}\right)$$
$$= -4G \text{ J/kg}$$

18. (*a*) Given, acceleration, $\mathbf{a} = -5\hat{\mathbf{j}}$ m/s^2

Velocity, $\mathbf{v} = (8\hat{\mathbf{i}} - 6\hat{\mathbf{j}})$ m/s^2

Unit vector along velocity vector,

$$\hat{\mathbf{v}} = \frac{\mathbf{v}}{|\mathbf{v}|}$$
$$= \frac{8\hat{\mathbf{i}} - 6\hat{\mathbf{j}}}{\sqrt{(8)^2 + (6)^2}}$$
$$= \frac{4}{5}\hat{\mathbf{i}} - \frac{3}{5}\hat{\mathbf{j}}$$

As, we know that, tangential acceleration vector is the component of acceleration vector along the velocity vector which is given as

$$\mathbf{a}_t = (\mathbf{a} \cdot \mathbf{v})\hat{\mathbf{v}}$$
$$= (-5\hat{\mathbf{j}}) \cdot (8\hat{\mathbf{i}} - 6\hat{\mathbf{j}})\left(\frac{4}{5}\hat{\mathbf{i}} - \frac{3}{5}\hat{\mathbf{j}}\right)$$
$$= 30\left(\frac{4}{5}\hat{\mathbf{i}} - \frac{3}{5}\hat{\mathbf{j}}\right)$$
$$= (24\hat{\mathbf{i}} - 18\hat{\mathbf{j}}) \text{ m/s}^2$$

19. (*a*) Power consumption in series *R-L-C* circuit is maximum at resonance,

$$X_L = X_C$$
$$\frac{1}{\omega L} = \omega C$$

or $\quad C = \frac{1}{\omega^2 L} = \frac{1}{(2\pi f)^2 \times L}$

Here, $f = 50$ Hz, $L = 2.5$ H

$$C = \frac{1}{(2 \times 3.14 \times 50)^2 \times 2.5}$$
$$= 4.05 \times 10^{-6} \simeq 4\ \mu\text{F}$$

20. (*b*) A $\rightarrow$ When mass is displaced slightly either left or right from its equilibrium position, it has tendency to come back towards the equilibrium position, so it is in stable equilibrium.

B $\rightarrow$ Taking torque about pivot point,

$$\tau = mg \times 0 + mg \times \frac{l}{2}$$
$$\tau \neq 0$$

So, uniform L-shaped rod is not in equilibrium.

C $\rightarrow$ Here, $\mu = \tan\theta$

$\Rightarrow$ Net force on block is zero

$$F_{net} = 0$$

So, block is in equilibrium.

If the block is displaced from equilibrium position, then it will remain at rest or will stay at displaced position, so it is in neutral equilibrium.

D $\rightarrow$ When mass is displaced, then it will continuously move in same direction and it will not come back towards the equilibrium position. So, equilibrium is unstable.

21. (*c*) The energy density in the region between the plates is given by

$$u = \frac{1}{2}\varepsilon_0 E^2$$
$$= \frac{1}{2}\varepsilon_0\left(\frac{V}{d}\right)^2 \quad \left(\because E = \frac{V}{d}\right)$$

$$\Rightarrow \quad u = \frac{1}{2} \times 8.85 \times 10^{-12} \times \left(\frac{400}{5 \times 10^{-3}}\right)^2$$
$$= 283.2 \times 10^{-12} \times 10^6$$
$$= 283.2 \times 10^{-6}$$
$$= 2.83 \times 10^{-4} \text{ J/m}^3$$

22. (*d*) Since, $v_{rms} = \sqrt{\frac{3RT}{M}}, \Rightarrow v_{rms} \propto \frac{1}{\sqrt{M}}$

As in A, H_2 has lower molecular mass, RMS speed of H_2 is more and thermal energy same. As in *B*, pressure is more so internal energy is more.

23. (*b*) Energy of light incident on metal surface,

$$E=\frac{12375}{\lambda}=\frac{12375}{480}=2.57\text{ eV}$$

Maximum kinetic energy of photon in accordance with Einstein's photoelectric equation,

KE_{max} = Incident energy − Work function

$=E-\phi$, where ϕ is work function.

$\Rightarrow KE_{max}=2.57-1.67$

$=0.9$ eV

Now, energy of electron in third excited state, i.e. $n=4$ in He^+ ion

$$E_n=-13.6\times\frac{Z^2}{n^2}\text{ eV}$$

For He^+, $Z=2$

$$\Rightarrow E_4=-13.6\times\frac{(2)^2}{(4)^2}$$

$E_4=-3.4$ eV

From energy conservation,

Kinetic energy of photoelectron = Total energy of electron in He^+ + Energy of emitted photon

$KE_{max}=E_4+E'$

or $E'=KE_{max}-E_4$

$=0.9-(-3.4)$

$=4.3$ eV

24. (*d*) Both A and R are true and R explains assertion.

As a free dipole can take stable equilibrium position or unstable equilibrium position ($F_{net}=0$).

Angle of **p** and **E** is either 0° or 180°.

Hence potential energy is,

$U=\mathbf{p}\cdot\mathbf{E}$

$=-pE\cos\theta$

This is always a non-zero value.

25. (*b*) As we know that, electric field and magnetic field both contribute equally to the intensity of an electromagnetic wave. i.e.

$$I_E=I_B=\frac{I}{2} \quad \text{... (i)}$$

where, I is the total intensity of the electromagnetic wave.

Also, $I_B=\frac{1}{2}\frac{B^2}{\mu_0}c$

where, B is the magnitude of magnetic field.

$$\Rightarrow B=\sqrt{\frac{2\mu_0 I_B}{c}}$$

$$=\sqrt{\frac{2\times\mu_0}{c}\times\frac{I}{2}} \quad \text{[using Eq. (i)]}$$

$$=\sqrt{\frac{\mu_0 I}{c}}$$

Here, $I=2\times10^7$ W/cm²

or 2×11^{11} W/m²

$\mu_0=4\pi\times10^{-7}\frac{\text{Tm}}{\text{A}}$

$c=3\times10^8$ m/s

Substituting these values in the above equation, we get

$$\Rightarrow B=\sqrt{\frac{4\pi\times10^{-7}\times2\times10^7}{3\times10^8}}$$

$B\simeq29\times10^{-3}$ T or 29 mT

26. (*d*) Given that,

$$x_A=4\sin\left(\omega t+\frac{\pi}{4}\right)+3\cos\left(\omega t-\frac{\pi}{4}\right)\text{m}$$

or

$$x_A=4\sin\left(\omega t+\frac{\pi}{4}\right)+3\sin\left(\frac{\pi}{2}+\omega t-\frac{\pi}{4}\right)$$

$$=4\sin\left(\omega t+\frac{\pi}{4}\right)+3\sin\left(\omega t+\frac{\pi}{4}\right)$$

$$\left[\because \sin\left(\frac{\pi}{2}+\theta\right)=\cos\theta\right]$$

∴ Amplitude,

$$A_1=\sqrt{(4)^2+(3)^2+2(4)(3)\cos\left(\frac{\pi}{4}-\frac{\pi}{4}\right)}$$

$$=\sqrt{(4)^2+(3)^2+2(4)(3)}=\sqrt{(4+3)^2}$$

$=7$ m

Similarly, $x_B=5\sqrt{2}(\sin2\pi t+\cos2\pi t)$

$$x_B=5\sqrt{2}\sin2\pi t+5\sqrt{2}\sin\left(\frac{\pi}{2}+2\pi t\right)$$

So phase, $\phi=\left(\frac{\pi}{2}+2\pi t\right)-2\pi t=\frac{\pi}{2}$

and amplitude,

$$A_2=\sqrt{(5\sqrt{2})^2+(5\sqrt{2})^2+2(5\sqrt{2})(5\sqrt{2})\cos\frac{\pi}{2}}$$

$=10$ m

∴ Ratio, $\frac{A_1}{A_2}=\frac{7}{10}$

27. (*c*) Microwaves may be generated by the oscillations of electrons in a device called Klystron.

28. (*d*) A negative temperature coefficient thermistor has a low resistance at high temperature.

While a thermistor with a positive temperature coefficient has a high resistance at a high temperature.

29. (*c*) Given that, emf, $e=e_0\sin\left(\omega t-\frac{\pi}{4}\right)$

Current, $i=i_0\sin\left(\omega t-\frac{3\pi}{4}\right)$

Phase difference,

$$\phi=\left(\omega t-\frac{\pi}{4}\right)-\left(\omega t-\frac{3\pi}{4}\right)$$

$$\phi=\frac{\pi}{2}$$

The current lags the emf by $\frac{\pi}{2}$, so the circuit should contain only inductor.

30. (*a*) Given that, $R=(74\pm3.7)\text{k}\Omega$

$=(74\pm3.7)\times10^3$

$=74+10^3\pm5\%$

From the carbon resistor, coding sequence is

First significant figure → colour-1 → violet

Second significant figure → colour-2 → yellow

Decimal multiplier → colour-3 → orange

Tolerance → colour-4 → gold

31. (*d*) Given that,

At $x=31.5$ mm, wavelengths 3600 Å and 6000 Å are absent, it means they are producing minima.

Let the slit separation be d.

As we know, path difference for minima is given as by $\frac{xd}{D}=\left(n_1+\frac{1}{2}\right)\lambda_1$

and $\frac{xd}{D\lambda_1}=n_1+\frac{1}{2}$ ... (i)

Similarly, for λ_2, path difference

or $\frac{xd}{D\lambda_2}=n_2+\frac{1}{2}$ ... (ii)

Subtracting Eq. (ii) from Eq. (i), we get

$$\frac{xd}{D}\left(\frac{1}{\lambda_1}-\frac{1}{\lambda_2}\right)=n_1-n_2$$

or

$$d=\frac{D(n_1-n_2)}{x\left(\frac{1}{\lambda_1}-\frac{1}{\lambda_2}\right)}$$

Given, $x=31.5$ mm or 31.5×10^{-3}m

$D=1$ m

$\lambda_1=3600$ Å or 3.6×10^{-7}m

$\lambda_2=6000$ Å or 6×10^{-7}m

$n_1-n_2=7$

Substituting these values in the above relation, we get

$$d=\frac{1\times7}{31.5\times10^{-3}\left(\frac{1}{3.6\times10^{-7}}-\frac{1}{6\times10^{-7}}\right)}$$

$d=0.2$ mm

32. (*a*) The wheel rolling without slipping on a flat surface is as shown below.

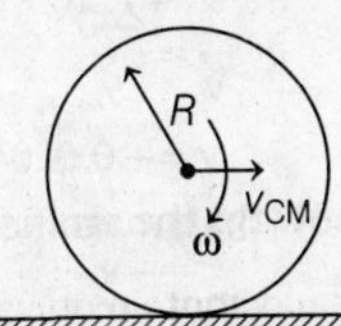

Since, it is decelerating, so net force on it will be non-zero,

$$\mathbf{F}_{net} = \mathbf{F}_0 \text{ or } \mathbf{a}_{CM} \neq 0$$

From the condition of pure rolling motion, we know that

$$a_{CM} = \alpha R \text{ or } \alpha = \frac{a_{CM}}{R} \neq 0$$

Also, $\tau = I\alpha \Rightarrow \tau \neq 0$

33. (*d*) When A and C are connected,

energy stored, $U_1 = \frac{1}{2}CV^2$

and charge, $q = CV$

When *B* and *C* are connected, common potential, $V' = \frac{\text{Total charge}}{\text{Total capacity}} = \frac{CV}{4C}$

$$\Rightarrow \quad V' = \frac{V}{4}$$

Final stored energy,

$$U_2 = \frac{1}{2}(C_{eq})V'^2$$

$$= \frac{1}{2} \times 4C \times \left(\frac{V}{4}\right)^2 = \frac{1}{8}CV^2$$

Loss of energy $= U_1 - U_2$

$$= \frac{1}{2}CV^2 - \frac{1}{8}CV^2$$

$$= \frac{3}{8}CV^2 = \frac{3}{8}\frac{q^2}{C}$$

34. (*d*) Potential energy of a He^+ ion in ground state is

$$U_1 = 2E_1 = 2\left(-13.6\frac{Z^2}{n^2}\right)$$

$\because \quad n = 1$ and $Z = 2$

$\Rightarrow \quad U_1 = -108.8$ eV

But PE in ground state is given zero. So, we have to increase PE (and total energy) by 108.8 eV.

Hence, for given He^+ ion, energy of first excited state ($n = 2$) will be

$$E(n=2) = -13.6\frac{Z^2}{n^2} + 108.8$$

$$= -13.6 \times \frac{4}{4} + 108.8$$

$$= 95.2 \text{ eV}$$

35. (*a*) Induced electric field lines are open loops. It emerges from positive charge and going to infinity and it enter into negative charge coming from infinity.

36. (*b*) When a nucleus decays in two, then decay constant is given as

$$\lambda_{eff} = \lambda_1 + \lambda_2$$

$$\because \quad \lambda = \frac{\ln 2}{T}$$

$$\therefore \quad \lambda_{eff} = \frac{\ln 2}{T_1} + \frac{\ln 2}{T_2} = \ln 2\left(\frac{1}{T_1} + \frac{1}{T_2}\right)$$

Here, $T_1 = 30$s, $T_2 = 60$ s and $\ln 2 = 0.693$

$$\lambda_{eff} = 0.693 \times \left(\frac{1}{30} + \frac{1}{60}\right)$$

$$= 0.693 \times \left(\frac{2+1}{60}\right) = 0.693 \times \frac{1}{20}$$

Effective mean life, $T_{mean} = \frac{1}{\lambda_{eff}}$

$$= \frac{1}{0.693 \times \frac{1}{20}} = \frac{20}{0.693}$$

$$T_{mean} = 28.86 \text{ s} \simeq 28.9 \text{ s}$$

37. (*d*) The susceptibility χ of diamagnetic material is always small and negative. It is constant and does not vary with field or temperature. Its variation is shown below.

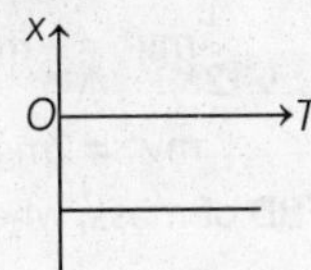

The intensity of magnetisation varies as

$$-I \propto H$$

where, H = magnetic field strength.

So, for a diamagnetic material,

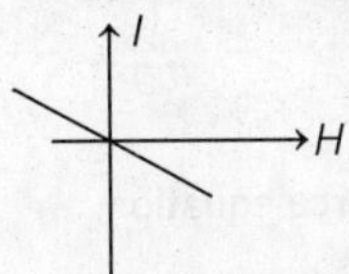

38. (*d*) Charge densities are equal

$$\therefore \quad \frac{Q_1}{4\pi r^2} = \frac{Q_2}{4\pi R^2}$$

$$\Rightarrow \quad \frac{Q_1}{r^2} = \frac{Q_2}{R^2}$$

Also, $Q_1 + Q_2 = Q$

So, $Q_1 = \frac{Qr^2}{(r^2 + R^2)}$

and $Q_2 = \frac{QR^2}{(r^2 + R^2)}$

$$\text{Potential at centre} = \frac{KQ_1}{r} + \frac{KQ_2}{R}$$

$$= K \cdot \frac{r + R}{(r^2 + R^2)} \cdot Q$$

39. (*a*) At balanced condition in a meter bridge, unknown resistance *S* is given by

$$S = \frac{100 - l}{l} \times R$$

where, R = unknown resistance,

l = balance length from left end.

When $l = 30$ cm,

$$S = \frac{100 - 30}{30} \times R$$

$$= \frac{7}{3}R \quad \text{... (i)}$$

Now, resistance of 2 Ω is connected in parallel with *S*, then equivalent of *S* and 2 Ω when balanced length is 40 cm, will be

$$\Rightarrow \quad \frac{2S}{2+S} = \frac{100 - 40}{40} \times R$$

$$\frac{2S}{2+S} = \frac{3}{2}R \quad \text{... (ii)}$$

Dividing Eq. (i) by Eq. (ii), we get

$$\frac{S}{\frac{2S}{2+S}} = \frac{\frac{7}{3}R}{\frac{3}{2}R}$$

$$\frac{2+S}{2} = \frac{14}{9}$$

$$18 + 9S = 28$$

$$9S = 28 - 18 = 10$$

or $\quad S = \frac{10}{9} = 1.1\,\Omega$

40. (*d*) $P_{rated} = \frac{V_{rated}^2}{R}$

or $\quad R = \frac{(220)^2}{100}$

Now, power consumed

$$= \frac{V^2}{R} = \frac{(110)^2 \times 100}{(220)^2} = 25 \text{ W}$$

41. (*c*) $Qe^{-\frac{Rt}{2L}} = 0.50\,Q$

$$\Rightarrow \quad -\frac{Rt}{2L} = \log 0.5$$

$$\Rightarrow \quad \frac{Rt}{L} = \log 2$$

$$\Rightarrow \quad t = \frac{\log 2 \times 2 \times 12 \times 10^{-3}}{1.5}$$

$$= 11 \text{ ms}$$

42. (*c*) Given that,

Initial speed, $u = 30$ m/s

Projection angle, $\theta = 60°$

Let at an instant when velocity vector makes an angle 30° be *v*. We know that, in projectile motion, horizontal component of velocities are equal.

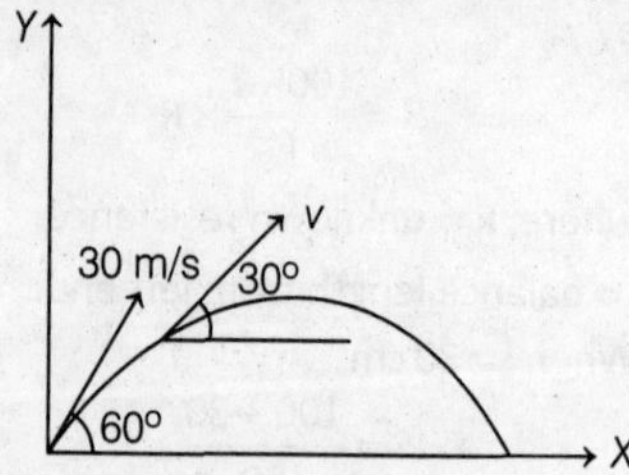

$$\Rightarrow \quad v\cos 30° = 30\cos 60°$$

$$v \times \frac{\sqrt{3}}{2} = 30 \times \frac{1}{2}$$

$$v = \frac{30}{\sqrt{3}}$$

or $\quad v = 10\sqrt{3}$ m/s

43. (*a*) In circular motion, a particle have two accelerations, centripetal and tangential acceleration.

Centripetal acceleration acts towards centre of the circular path and tangential acceleration acts either along velocity or opposite to velocity.

If the particle has acceleration along its velocity, it means its centripetal acceleration should be zero at that instant or angular velocity $\omega = 0$.

Using first equation of motion,

$$\omega_f = \omega_i + \alpha t$$

$$0 = \omega_0 + (-\alpha)t$$

or $\quad t = \dfrac{\omega_0}{\alpha}$

44. (*a*) Let the transition of electron in hydrogen atom ($Z = 1$) gives wavelength λ_1 for transition from n_2 to n_1, then

$$\frac{1}{\lambda} = RZ^2\left(\frac{1}{m^2} - \frac{1}{n^2}\right)$$

Here, $\lambda = \lambda_1, Z = 1, m = n_1, n = n_2$

$$\frac{1}{\lambda_1} = R(1)^2\left(\frac{1}{n_1^2} - \frac{1}{n_2^2}\right)$$

$$= R\left(\frac{1}{n_1^2} - \frac{1}{n_2^2}\right)$$

Now, if electron makes transition in He^+ ion from n_4 to n_3 and gives wavelength λ_2, then

$$\frac{1}{\lambda_2} = R(2)^2\left(\frac{1}{n_3^2} - \frac{1}{n_4^2}\right)$$

$$= R\left[\frac{1}{\left(\frac{n_3}{2}\right)^2} - \frac{1}{\left(\frac{n_4}{3}\right)^2}\right]$$

Given that, $\lambda_1 = \lambda_2$

$$\Rightarrow R\left(\frac{1}{n_1^2} - \frac{1}{n_2^2}\right) = R\left[\frac{1}{\left(\frac{n_3}{2}\right)^2} - \frac{1}{\left(\frac{n_4}{2}\right)^2}\right]$$

On comparing both sides, we get

$$n_1 = \frac{n_3}{2}$$

and $\quad n_2 = \dfrac{n_4}{2}$

The value of n_1, n_2, n_3 and n_4 must be an integer, as they denote principal quantum number.

If $n_3 = 2$ and $n_4 = 4$, then the given condition is satisfied.

45. (*d*) Let the velocity of mass at bottom of the arc be v.

Using mechanical energy conservation principle,

$$\Delta ME = 0$$

$\Rightarrow \quad \Delta KE + \Delta U = 0$

or $\quad \Delta KE = -\Delta U$

$$\frac{1}{2}mv^2 - 0 = -mg\Delta h$$

$$\frac{1}{2}mv^2 = -mg(0 - L)$$

or $\quad mv^2 = 2mgL \quad$ ...(i)

Drawing FBD of mass, when it is at bottom.

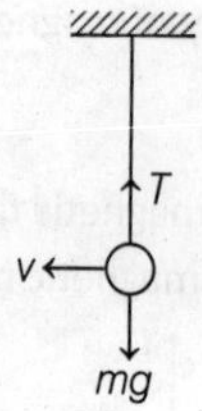

Using force equation,

$$\frac{mv^2}{L} = T - mg$$

or $\quad T = \dfrac{mv^2}{L} + mg$

$$= \frac{2mgL}{L} + mg \quad \text{[using Eq. (i)]}$$

$$= 3mg$$

46. (*b*) Given that,

Height of object, $h_o = 0.124$ m

Radius of curvature, $R = -0.3$ m

Position of object from mirror, $u = -0.018$ m

Using mirror formula,

$$\frac{1}{v} + \frac{1}{u} = \frac{2}{R}$$

or $\quad \dfrac{1}{v} + \dfrac{1}{-0.018} = \dfrac{2}{-0.3}$

or $\quad \dfrac{1}{v} = \dfrac{440}{9}$

or $\quad v = +0.0204$ m

As we know that, magnification,

$$m = \frac{-v}{u}$$

$$= -\frac{0.024}{0.018}$$

$$= \frac{4}{3}$$

Also, $m = \dfrac{\text{Height of image}}{\text{Height of object}}$

or Height of image $= m \times$ Height of object

$$= \frac{4}{3} \times 0.124$$

$$h_i = 0.165 \text{ m}$$

or $\quad h_i = 16.5$ cm

47. (*a*) Acceleration of electron,

$$a = \frac{eE}{m} = \frac{e}{m}\cdot\frac{r}{2}\left(\frac{dB}{dt}\right)$$

$$= \left(\frac{1.6 \times 10^{-19} \times 0.3 \times 50 \times 10^{-6}}{2 \times 9.1 \times 10^{-31}}\right)$$

$$= 1.3 \times 10^6 \text{ m/s}^2$$

48. (*b*) Given that, particle is starting from mean position, then initial phase, $\phi = 0$.

Let the particle's mean position be at origin as shown below

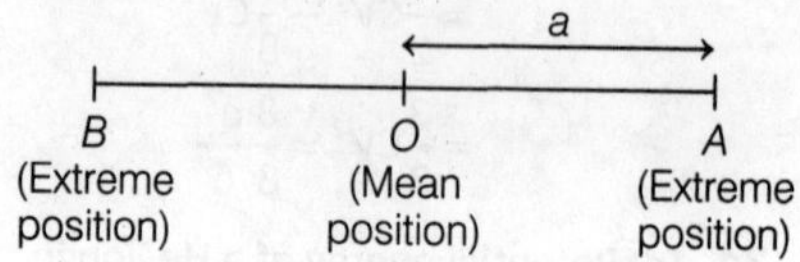

Time period for one complete oscillation, $T = (t_{OA} + t_{AO}) + (t_{OB} + t_{BO})$

$$= t + t$$

$$T = 2t$$

$\because \quad T = \dfrac{2\pi}{\omega}$

$\Rightarrow \quad 2t = \dfrac{2\pi}{\omega}$

or $\quad \omega = \pi/t \quad$ ... (i)

As we know, displacement time equation for a particle executing SHM is given as

$$x = a\sin\omega t$$

Velocity, $v = \dfrac{dx}{dt} = \dfrac{d}{dt}(a\sin\omega t)$

where, a is the amplitude.

$$v = a\omega\cos\omega t$$

$$= a\omega\cos\frac{\pi}{t}\times t \quad [\because \text{using Eq. (i)}]$$

$$= a\omega\cos\pi = -a\omega \quad (\because \cos\pi = -1)$$

or $v = -\dfrac{a\pi}{t}$ or $|v| = \dfrac{a\pi}{t}$

Amplitude, $a = \dfrac{|v|\times t}{\pi}$

$$= \frac{1.57\times 1.5}{3.14} = 0.75 \text{ m}$$

49. (*c*) The situation is shown in the figure given below

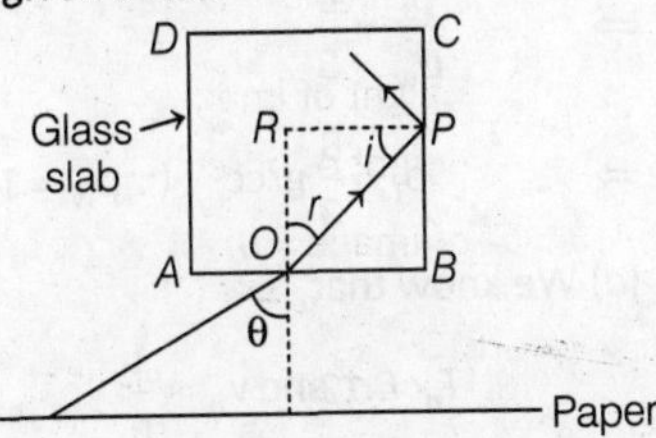

Light will not emerge out from the vertical face *BC* only, if

$$i > \theta_C$$

or $\sin i > \sin\theta_C$

or $\sin i > \dfrac{1}{\mu}$ ... (i)

$$\left(\because \sin\theta_C = \frac{1}{\mu}\right)$$

Applying Snell's law at *O*,

$$\mu_1 \sin i = \mu_2 \sin r$$

$\Rightarrow$ $1\times\sin\theta = \mu\times\sin r$

In ΔOPR, $r + i = 90°$

or $r = 90° - i$

So, $\sin r = \sin\theta = \sin(90° - i)$

$$= \mu\cos i$$

or $\cos i = \dfrac{\sin\theta}{\mu}$

So, $\sin i = \sqrt{1-\cos i}$

$$= \sqrt{1-\left(\frac{\sin\theta}{\mu}\right)^2} \quad \text{... (ii)}$$

Putting the value of $\sin i$ from Eq. (ii) in Eq. (i), we have

$$\sqrt{1-\frac{\sin^2\theta}{\mu^2}} > \frac{1}{\mu}$$

i.e. $\mu^2 > 1+\sin^2\theta$

As, $(\sin^2\theta)_{max} = 1$, so $\mu^2 > 2$,

i.e. $\mu > \sqrt{2}$

$$\mu_{min} = \sqrt{2}$$

50. (*b*) The depletion layer consists of immobile positive and negative ions which have no free electrons and holes.

At $x = 0$, number of negatively charged immobile ions increases, as we move rightwards, so charge density increases but after some distance, it starts to decrease and at $x = \dfrac{d}{2}$, it becomes zero and the corresponding charge density becomes zero.

Now, from $x = \dfrac{d}{2}$, number of positively charged immobile ions increasing and reaches its maximum value, then at some distance, it decreases and at $x = d$, it becomes zero.

Thus, the variation of charge density and distance is best represented as in option (b).

Knockout 5

1. (*b*) We know that, barrier potential of Ge, $V_{B_1} = 0.3$ V

and barrier potential of Si, $V_{B_2} = 0.7$ V

Redrawing the given figure as

0.3 V 1 Ω 0.7 V 2 Ω

I

10 V

Applying KVL, we get

$$10 - 0.3 - I\times 1 - 0.7 - 2\times I = 0$$

$\Rightarrow$ $3I = 9 \Rightarrow I = 3$ A

2. (*b*) Given, $r = 300$ m, $\mu = 0.3$, $g = 10 \text{ m/s}^2$

If *v* is the velocity of the vehicle while turning on the road, then

$$\frac{mv^2}{r} \le \mu mg$$

$\Rightarrow$ $v \le \sqrt{\mu rg}$

$\Rightarrow$ $v_{max} = \sqrt{\mu rg}$

$$= \sqrt{0.3\times 300\times 10}$$

$$= 30 \text{ m/s}$$

3. (*a*) We have,

$$P_{air} = \frac{1}{f} = (n_g - 1)\left(\frac{1}{R_1} - \frac{1}{R_2}\right)$$

$$= \left(\frac{3}{2} - 1\right)\left(\frac{1}{R_1} - \frac{1}{R_2}\right)$$

$\Rightarrow$ $2 = \dfrac{1}{2}\left(\dfrac{1}{R_1} - \dfrac{1}{R_2}\right)$

or $\dfrac{1}{R_1} - \dfrac{1}{R_2} = 4$

Now, when lens is dipped in liquid,

In liquid 1, $P_1 = \left(\dfrac{n_g}{n_1} - 1\right)\left(\dfrac{1}{R_1} - \dfrac{1}{R_2}\right)$

or $P_1 = \left(\dfrac{3/2}{4/3} - 1\right)\times 4 = \dfrac{1}{2}$

and similarly, $P_2 = \left(\dfrac{3/2}{5/3} - 1\right)\times 4 = -\dfrac{2}{5}$

So, $P_1 - P_2 = \dfrac{1}{2} - \left(-\dfrac{2}{5}\right)$

$$= \frac{5+4}{10} = \frac{9}{10}$$

4. (*c*) Volume, $V = L^3$

Percentage uncertainty in volume is

$$\frac{\Delta V}{V}\times 100 = \frac{3\Delta L}{L}\times 100$$

$$= \frac{3\times 0.1\times 100}{30}$$

$$= \frac{30}{30} = 1\%$$

5. (*b*) We know that, self-inductance of a long current carrying solenoid is given as

$$L = \frac{\mu_0 N^2 A}{l}$$

$\Rightarrow$ $L \propto N^2$

$\Rightarrow$ $\dfrac{L_2}{L_1} = \left(\dfrac{N_2}{N_1}\right)^2$

$$= \left(\frac{\frac{N_1}{2}}{N_1}\right)^2 \quad \left[\because N_2 = \frac{N_1}{2}\right]$$

$$= \left(\frac{1}{2}\right)^2 = \frac{1}{4}$$

$\Rightarrow$ $L_2 = \dfrac{L_1}{4}$

6. (*a*) The *x*-coordinate of centre of mass is given by

$$x = \frac{m_1x_1 + m_2x_2}{m_1 + m_2}$$

Here, $m_1 = 0.4$ kg, $x_1 = 2$ m, $m_2 = 0.6$ kg, $x_2 = 7$ m

Hence, $x = \dfrac{0.4\times 2 + 0.6\times 7}{0.4 + 0.6}$

$$= \frac{5}{1} = 5 \text{ m}$$

7. (*d*) Equivalent capacitance of the given circuit diagram,

$$C_{eq} = \frac{(2+6)\times 4}{2+6+4}$$

$$= \frac{32}{12} = \frac{8}{3}\mu\text{F}$$

Charge flowing through 4 μF capacitor

$$q = C_{eq}\cdot V$$

$$= \frac{8}{3}\times 10^{-6}\times 12 = 32\,\mu\text{C}$$

$\therefore$ Potential difference across $4\,\mu C$ capacitor,

$$V = \frac{q}{C} = \frac{32}{4} = 8\text{ V}$$

8. (*d*) For the particle, let position is given by $\mathbf{r} = x\hat{\mathbf{i}} + y\hat{\mathbf{j}}$, then velocity will be

$$\mathbf{v} = \frac{d\mathbf{r}}{dt} = \frac{dx}{dt}\hat{\mathbf{i}} + \frac{dy}{dt}\hat{\mathbf{j}}$$

But given velocity is

$$\mathbf{v} = ky\hat{\mathbf{i}} + kx\hat{\mathbf{j}}$$

So, $\frac{dx}{dt} = ky$ and $\frac{dy}{dt} = kx$

$\therefore \quad \frac{dx}{y} = kdt$ and $\frac{dy}{x} = kdt$

$\Rightarrow \quad \frac{dx}{y} = \frac{dy}{x}$

or $\quad x\,dx = y\,dy$

Integrating, we have

$$\frac{x^2}{2} = \frac{y^2}{2} + \text{constant}$$

$\Rightarrow x^2 - y^2 = \text{constant}$

9. (*d*) Both Statement I and Statement II are correct.

In a sum, we take least number of decimal places as that in any of term in the sum.

Hence, $123 + 5.35 = 128.35 = 128$

(in three significant figures)

In a product (or ratio), the number of significant figures in final product (or ratio) are same as the number of significant figures in least accurate measurement.

So, 13.8 m $\rightarrow$ 3 significant figures

$\times$ 9.0 m $\rightarrow$ 1 significant figure

$= 124.2\text{ m}^2 \leftarrow$ This is actual product.

$= 100\text{ m}^2 \leftarrow$ Only one siginificant figure is reported.

10. (*d*) We know that, time period of vibrating string,

$$T = 2\pi\sqrt{\frac{m}{k}}$$

$\Rightarrow \quad \frac{1}{n} = 2\pi\sqrt{\frac{m}{k}} \qquad \left(\because T = \frac{1}{n}\right)$

$\Rightarrow \quad n \propto \sqrt{k} \qquad \text{...(i)}$

Also for a spring,

$$k \propto \frac{1}{x} \qquad \text{...(ii)}$$

From Eqs. (i) and (ii), we get

$$n \propto \frac{1}{\sqrt{x}} \Rightarrow \frac{n_2}{n_1} = \sqrt{\frac{x_1}{x_2}}$$

$$= \sqrt{\frac{x_1}{x_1/2}} \qquad \left(\because x_2 = \frac{x_1}{2}\right)$$

$$= \sqrt{2} \Rightarrow n_2 = \sqrt{2}n_1$$

$$= \sqrt{2}n \qquad (\because n_1 = n)$$

11. (*a*) From Kepler's law, areal velocity remains constant in an elliptical orbit. i.e. angular velocity remains constant.

Also, its linear velocity continuously changes and becomes maximum when it is nearest to the sun.

12. (*c*) Given, $a = 3\,\mu\text{m} = 3 \times 10^{-6}$ m

$$\theta = 30^\circ$$

We know that, for nth dark fringe in single slit,

$$a\sin\theta = n\lambda$$

For third dark fringe, $n = 3$

$\therefore \quad a\sin\theta = 3\lambda$

$\Rightarrow \quad 3 \times 10^{-6} \times \sin 30^\circ = 3\lambda$

$\Rightarrow \quad \lambda = 10^{-6}\sin 30^\circ$

$= 0.5 \times 10^{-6}$ m

$= 5000 \times 10^{-10}$ m

$= 5000$ Å

13. (*b*) For the mixture of gases, specific heat at constant volume is given as

$$C_V = \frac{n_1(C_V)_1 + n_2(C_V)_2}{n_1 + n_2}$$

$$= \frac{2 \times \frac{5R}{2} + 8 \times \frac{3R}{2}}{2 + 8}$$

$$= \frac{17R}{10} = 1.7\,R$$

14. (*d*) On inclined plane, when solid sphere rolls down without slipping with linear acceleration a, then

$$a = \frac{g\sin\theta}{1 + \frac{I}{MR^2}}$$

For solid sphere,

$$I = \frac{2MR^2}{5}$$

$$\therefore \quad a = \frac{g\sin\theta}{1 + \left(\frac{\frac{2}{5}MR^2}{MR^2}\right)}$$

$$= \frac{g\sin 30^\circ}{1 + \frac{2}{5}} = \frac{g \times \frac{1}{2}}{\frac{7}{5}} = \frac{5g}{14}$$

15. (*c*) Let V be the volume of body and its density is ρ, then by law of floatation in water

$$V_{\rho g} = \frac{2}{3}V \times \rho_w g \qquad \text{...(i)}$$

[$\because \frac{2}{3}V$ is immersed in water of density ρ_w]

Similarly, in a liquid,

$$V_{\rho g} = \frac{1}{4}V \times \rho_l g \qquad \text{...(ii)}$$

[$\because$ mass is same in both the cases]

From Eqs. (i) and (ii), we get

$$\frac{2}{3}V\rho_w g = \frac{1}{4}V\rho_l g$$

$\Rightarrow \quad \frac{\rho_l}{\rho_w} = \left(\frac{2}{3}\right) \times \left(\frac{4}{1}\right)$

$\Rightarrow \quad \frac{\rho_l}{\rho_w} = \frac{8}{3}$

$\Rightarrow \quad \rho_l = \frac{8}{3}$ g/cc $\quad (\because \rho_w = 1$ g/cc$)$

16. (*d*) We know that,

$$T_n \propto n^3 \text{ and } v_n \propto \frac{1}{n}$$

$$T_n \times v_n \propto n^3 \times \frac{1}{n}$$

$\Rightarrow \quad T_n \times v_n \propto n^2$

$\Rightarrow \quad \frac{T_2 v_2}{T_3 v_3} = \frac{2^2}{3^2} = \frac{4}{9}$

17. (*c*) From $\frac{dV}{dx} = -\mathbf{E}$

$\Rightarrow \quad \int_1^2 dV = -\int_1^{-5}(\mathbf{E} \cdot d\mathbf{x})$

$\Rightarrow \quad V_2 - V_1 = -\left[\int_1^{-5}(20x + 10)\,\hat{\mathbf{i}} \cdot dx\hat{\mathbf{i}}\right]$

$\Rightarrow \quad V_1 - V_2 = \int_1^{-5}(20x + 10)\,dx$

$\Rightarrow \quad V_1 - V_2 = \left[20\frac{x^2}{2} + 10x\right]_1^{-5}$

$= 180$ V

18. (*b*) Given, $\mathbf{F} = 4\hat{\mathbf{i}} + 5\hat{\mathbf{j}} - 6\hat{\mathbf{k}}$

$$\mathbf{r}_1 = 2\hat{\mathbf{i}} + 0\hat{\mathbf{j}} - 3\hat{\mathbf{k}}$$

$$\mathbf{r}_2 = 2\hat{\mathbf{i}} - 2\hat{\mathbf{j}} - 2\hat{\mathbf{k}}$$

Moment of force $= \mathbf{r} \times \mathbf{F}$

$= (\mathbf{r}_1 - \mathbf{r}_2) \times \mathbf{F}$

$= [(2\hat{\mathbf{i}} + 0\hat{\mathbf{j}} - 3\hat{\mathbf{k}}) - (2\hat{\mathbf{i}} - 2\hat{\mathbf{j}} - 2\hat{\mathbf{k}})] \times [4\hat{\mathbf{i}} + 5\hat{\mathbf{j}} - 6\hat{\mathbf{k}}]$

$= (0\hat{\mathbf{i}} + 2\hat{\mathbf{j}} - 1\hat{\mathbf{k}}) \times (4\hat{\mathbf{i}} + 5\hat{\mathbf{j}} - 6\hat{\mathbf{k}})$

$$= \begin{vmatrix} \hat{\mathbf{i}} & \hat{\mathbf{j}} & \hat{\mathbf{k}} \\ 0 & 2 & -1 \\ 4 & 5 & -6 \end{vmatrix}$$

$= -7\hat{\mathbf{i}} - 4\hat{\mathbf{j}} - 8\hat{\mathbf{k}}$

19. (*b*) When a p-n junction is connected in forward bias, an electric field exists which causes electrons to move from *n* to *p* side (forward current).

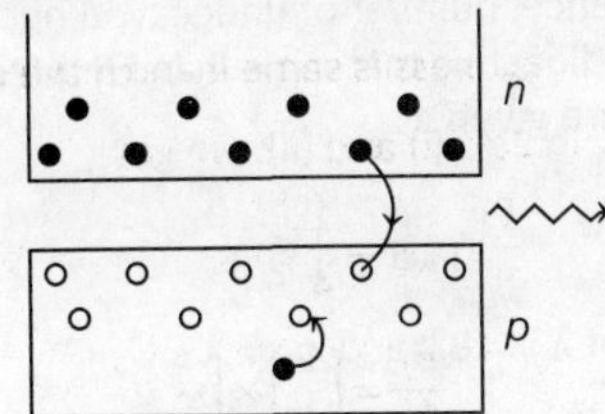

As electrons are in conduction band and holes are in valence band, thus electrons move from higher to lower energy levels.

20. (*a*) Increase in surface energy
= Work done
= Increase in surface area × Surface tension

$\Rightarrow \quad W = \Delta A \times T$

$\Rightarrow 6\times 10^{-4} = 2(5\times 4 - 4\times 2)\times 10^{-4}\times T$

$\Rightarrow \quad T = \dfrac{6\times 10^{-4}}{24\times 10^{-4}}$

$T = \dfrac{1}{4}$ N/m

$= 0.25$ N/m

21. (*b*) In photon-electron collision, the total energy and momentum remains conserved because such type of collision is elastic in nature.

Hence, A is true but R is false.

22. (*a*) According to Fleming's right hand rule, the magnetic field due to current carrying wire *PQ* acts on the loop in a direction perpendicular to the plane of paper and outwards. By Lenz's law, the induced current should oppose the increase of flux i.e. it will produce inward flux. So, the induced current in the loop *X* flows in the clockwise direction.

23. (*c*) On stretching, volume of wire remains constant.

So, $V = Al$ or $l = \dfrac{V}{A}$

$\therefore \quad R = \rho\cdot\dfrac{l}{A} = \dfrac{\rho V}{A^2}$

$= \dfrac{\rho V}{\dfrac{\pi^2 D^4}{16}}$

$= \dfrac{16\rho V}{\pi^2 D^4}$

$\therefore \quad \dfrac{\Delta R}{R} = -4\dfrac{\Delta D}{D}$

$= -4(-0.4) = 1.6\%$

24. (*a*) We know that, fringe width

$\beta = \dfrac{D\lambda}{d}$

$\Rightarrow \quad \beta \propto \dfrac{D}{d}$

$\Rightarrow \quad \dfrac{\beta_2}{\beta_1} = \dfrac{D_2}{D_1}\times\dfrac{d_1}{d_2}$

(Here, $D_2 = 2D_1$ and $d_2 = \dfrac{d_1}{2}$)

$\therefore \quad \dfrac{\beta_2}{\beta_1} = \dfrac{2D_1}{D_1}\times\dfrac{d_1}{d_1/2} = 4$

$\Rightarrow \quad \beta_2 = 4\beta_1$

25. (*a*) Given, $\delta = 45°$

We know that,

$\tan\delta = \dfrac{B_V}{B_H}$

$\Rightarrow \quad \tan 45° = \dfrac{B_V}{B_H}$

$\Rightarrow \quad 1 = \dfrac{B_V}{B_H}$

$\Rightarrow \quad B_V = B_H$

or $\quad B_H = B_V$

26. (*c*) For the first train (according to Doppler's effect),

$f_1 = \dfrac{v}{v - v_s}\times f$

$= \dfrac{320}{320-4}\times 280$

$= \dfrac{320}{316}\times 280$ Hz ...(i)

Similarly, for the second train

$f_2 = \dfrac{v}{v + v_s}\times f$

$= \dfrac{320}{320+4}\times 280$

$= \dfrac{320}{324}\times 280$ ...(ii)

From Eqs. (i) and (ii), number of beats is given as

$f_1 - f_2 = 320\times 280\left(\dfrac{1}{316} - \dfrac{1}{324}\right)$

$= \dfrac{320\times 280}{316\times 324}\times 8$

$= 7$

27. (*c*) For slowing of a particle, **a** and **v** must be inclined at an obtuse angle.

$\Rightarrow \quad \mathbf{a}\cdot\mathbf{v} < 0$

$\Rightarrow (a_x\hat{\mathbf{i}} + a_y\hat{\mathbf{j}})\cdot(v_x\hat{\mathbf{i}} + v_y\hat{\mathbf{j}}) < 0$

$\Rightarrow \quad a_x v_x + a_y v_y < 0$

28. (*d*) When prism is placed in air, then deviation produced by it

$\delta_{air} = ({}_a\mu_g - 1)A = (1.5 - 10)A = \dfrac{A}{2}$

$\Rightarrow \quad \delta_{air} = \dfrac{A}{2} = 10°$ (given)

When prism is placed in water, deviation produced by it.

$\delta_w = ({}_w\mu_g - 1)A = \left(\dfrac{{}_a\mu_g}{{}_a\mu_w} - 1\right)A$

$= \left(\dfrac{1.5}{4/3} - 1\right)A$

$= \dfrac{0.5}{4}A$

$= 0.25\times\dfrac{A}{2}$

$\Rightarrow \quad \delta_w = 0.25\times\delta_{air}$

$= 0.25\times 10°$

$= 2.5°$

29. (*b*) Current I_1 through path *ABC*

$= \dfrac{V_{AC}}{R_{AB} + R_{BC}} = \dfrac{40}{100}$

$= \dfrac{2}{5}$ A

Current, $I_2 = \dfrac{V_{AC}}{R_{AD} + R_{DC}}$

$= \dfrac{40}{200} = \dfrac{1}{5}$ A

Now, for path *BA*,

$V_A - V_B = I_1\times 40 = 16$ V

And for path *AD*, $V_A - V_D = I_2\times 90$

$= 18$ V

So, $V_B - V_D = (V_A - V_D) - (V_A - V_B)$

$= 2$ V

30. (*c*) Induced emf $= Blv = B\times 2R\times v$

$= 1\times 2\times 1\times 1$

$= 2$ V

31. (*c*) Let *dQ* be the charge flowing through the conductor in small interval of time *dt*, then

$dQ = Idt \quad \left(\because I = \dfrac{dQ}{dt}\right)$

$\int_0^Q dQ = \int_0^4 (2t+1)dt$

$\Rightarrow \quad Q = \left[2\dfrac{t^2}{2} + t\right]_0^4$

$\Rightarrow \quad Q = [t^2 + t]_0^4$

$\Rightarrow \quad Q = 4^2 + 4 - 0$

$\Rightarrow \quad Q = 20$ C

32. (*c*) de-Broglie wavelength of a moving particle in terms of kinetic energy is given as

$\lambda = \dfrac{h}{\sqrt{2mK}}$

For proton,

$$\lambda_p = \frac{h}{\sqrt{2m_pK_p}}$$

For α-particle,

$$\lambda_\alpha = \frac{h}{\sqrt{2m_\alpha K_\alpha}}$$

$$\therefore \quad \frac{\lambda_p}{\lambda_\alpha} = \sqrt{\frac{m_\alpha K_\alpha}{m_pK_p}}$$

$$\frac{\lambda_p}{\lambda_\alpha} = \sqrt{\frac{4m_pK_p}{m_pK_p}} \quad \left(\because K_p = K_\alpha \text{ and } m_\alpha = 4m_p\right)$$

$$\frac{\lambda_p}{\lambda_\alpha} = \sqrt{\frac{4}{1}} = \frac{2}{1}$$

$$\Rightarrow \frac{\lambda_\alpha}{\lambda_p} = \frac{1}{2}$$

$$\Rightarrow \lambda_\alpha : \lambda_p = 1:2$$

33. (*a*) Given, the temperature of freezer

$$T_2 = -13°\text{C}$$
$$= -13 + 273 = 260\text{K}$$

Coefficient of performance, $\beta = 5$

If T_1 be the temperature of air(sink), then we know that

$$\beta = \frac{T_2}{T_1 - T_2}$$

$$\Rightarrow \quad 5 = \frac{260}{T_1 - 260}$$

$$\Rightarrow \quad T_1 - 260 = \frac{260}{5} = 52$$

$$\Rightarrow \quad T_1 = 312\text{ K}$$

34. (*b*) Potential drop across 800 Ω resistor is equals to potential drop of Zener diode.

$$\Rightarrow \quad 800 \times I_2 = 5.6$$

or $\quad I_2 = 7\text{ mA}$

Now, potential drop across 200 Ω resistor = 9 − 5.6 = 3.4 V

Current, $I_1 = \frac{V}{R}$

$$= \frac{3.4}{200} = 17\text{ mA}$$

So, diode current,

$$I_Z = I_1 - I_2$$
$$= 17\text{ mA} - 7\text{ mA}$$
$$= 10\text{ mA}$$

35. (*a*) Let energy,

$$E \propto A^aT^bp^c = kA^aT^bp^c$$

where, *k* is dimensionless constant.

$$\Rightarrow [\text{M}^1\text{L}^2\text{T}^{-2}] = [\text{L}^2]^a[\text{T}]^b[\text{MLT}^{-1}]^c$$

$$\Rightarrow [\text{ML}^2\text{T}^{-2}] = [\text{L}^{2a+c}\text{T}^{b-c}\text{M}^c]$$

$$\Rightarrow [\text{ML}^2\text{T}^{-2}] = [\text{M}^c\text{L}^{2a+c}\text{T}^{b-c}]$$

On comparing the exponents of M, L and T both sides, we have

$$c = 1, 2a + c = 2$$
$$2a = 2 - c$$
$$= 2 - 1 = 1$$

$$\Rightarrow \quad a = \frac{1}{2}$$

and $\quad b - c = -2$

$$\Rightarrow \quad b - 1 = -2$$

$$\Rightarrow \quad b = -1$$

$$\therefore \quad [E] = [\text{A}^{1/2}\text{T}^{-1}\text{p}^1]$$

36. (*a*) As, $I = nev_dA$

$$\Rightarrow \quad v_d = \frac{I}{neA}$$

or $\quad v_d \propto \frac{1}{A}$

So, drift velocity increases as we move from *A* to *B*.

Current remains constant, while potential decreases and field increases.

37. (*a*)

Let the side length of square be *a*, then resistance per unit length of wire will be $\frac{R}{4a}$.

Now, between *E* and *C*, we have two resistances in parallel.

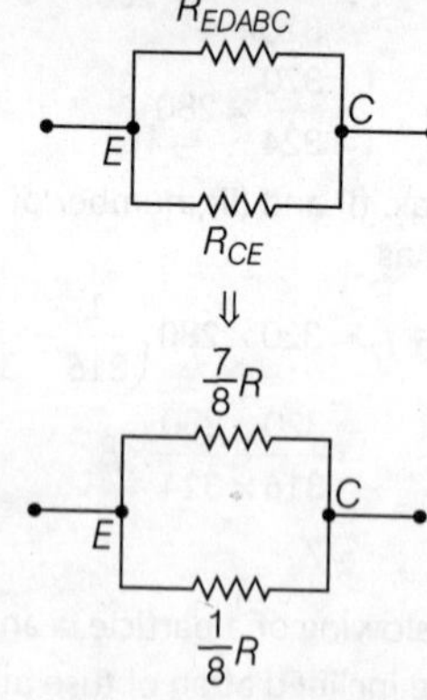

$$\text{So, } R_{EC} = \frac{R_1R_2}{R_1 + R_2} = \frac{7/8R \times \frac{1}{8}R}{\left(\frac{7}{8}R + \frac{1}{8}R\right)}$$

$$= \frac{7}{64}R$$

38. (*b*) Suppose N_0 be the initial number of nuclei in each of radioactive materials *A* and *B*.

Hence, number of undecayed nuclei in radioactive materials *A* and *B* after time *t* are given as

$$N_A = N_0e^{-\lambda_At}$$
$$N_B = N_0e^{-\lambda_Bt}$$

But $\lambda_A = 8\lambda$ and $\lambda_B = \lambda$

$$\therefore \quad N_A = N_0e^{-8\lambda t} \quad \text{...(i)}$$

and $\quad N_B = N_0e^{-\lambda t} \quad$ ...(ii)

From Eqs. (i) and (ii), we have

$$\frac{N_A}{N_B} = \frac{N_0e^{-8\lambda t}}{N_0e^{-\lambda t}}$$

$$\Rightarrow \quad \frac{N_A}{N_B} = e^{-7\lambda t}$$

$$\frac{1}{e} = e^{-7\lambda t} \quad \left(\because \frac{N_A}{N_B} = \frac{1}{e} \text{ given}\right)$$

$$\Rightarrow \quad e^{-1} = e^{-7\lambda t}$$

$$\Rightarrow \quad 7\lambda t = 1$$

$$\Rightarrow \quad t = \frac{1}{7\lambda}$$

39. (*a*) ${}_8\text{O}^{16}$ and ${}_8\text{O}^{15}$ have same atomic numbers but different atomic masses, hence these are isotopes.

${}_6\text{C}^{14}$ and ${}_7\text{N}^{14}$ have same mass number but different atomic number, hence these are isobars.

${}_7\text{N}^{14}$ and ${}_8\text{O}^{15}$ have same number of neutrons in the nucleus, hence these are isotones.

A nucleus in its ground state and the identical nucleus in metastable excited state are called isomers.

40. (*a*) Torque, $\tau = NIAB\sin\theta$

$$= 800 \times 10 \times 8 \times 10^{-2} \times 5 \times \sin(90° - 60°)$$
$$= 3.2 \times 10^3 \times \sin 30°$$
$$= 3.2 \times 10^3 \times \frac{1}{2}$$
$$= 1.6 \times 10^3 \text{ N-m}$$
$$= 1600 \text{ N-m}$$

41. (*c*) 21 cm is wavelength of radio waves 1057 Hz is frequency of short waves, 2.7 λ gives wavelength of 0.11 cm which is microwaves, 14.4 eV corresponds to photon energy of X-rays.

42. (*b*) Equation of motion of electron along vertical direction,

$$y = 0 \times t + \frac{1}{2}a_yt^2$$

$$= \frac{1}{2}\left(\frac{eE}{m}\right) \cdot t^2 \quad \left[\because a_y = a = \frac{eE}{m}\right]$$

$$=\frac{1}{2}\cdot\frac{eE}{m}\left(\frac{l}{v_0}\right)^2 \qquad \left[\because t=\frac{l}{v_0}\right]$$

$$=\frac{1}{2}\frac{eE}{mv_0^2}\cdot l^2$$

$$\Rightarrow \quad y=\frac{eE}{2mv_0^2}l^2$$

This equation is in the form of $y=ax^2$, which represents the equation of parabola. Hence, path of electron in electric field is parabolic.

43. (*a*) According to Newton's law of cooling,

$$\frac{T_1-T_2}{\Delta t}=k\left[\frac{T_1+T_2}{2}-T_0\right]$$

According to first condition,

$$\frac{70-60}{5}=k\left[\frac{70+60}{2}-T_0\right]$$

$$\Rightarrow \quad 2=k(65-T_0) \qquad \text{...(i)}$$

According to second condition,

$$\frac{60-54}{5+5}=k\left[\frac{60+54}{2}-T_0\right]$$

$$\Rightarrow \quad \frac{3}{5}=k(57-T_0) \qquad \text{...(ii)}$$

From Eqs. (i) and (ii), we get

$$\frac{2}{(3/5)}=\frac{65-T_0}{57-T_0}$$

$$\Rightarrow \quad T_0=45°\text{C}$$

44. (*b*) At maximum height, $v=0$

Initial speed of stone, $u=u_0$

By the third equation of motion,

$$v^2=u^2-2gh$$

$$0=u_0^2-2gh$$

$$\Rightarrow \quad u_0=\sqrt{2gh} \qquad \text{...(i)}$$

When, $h'=3h$, then

$$0=(u_0')^2-2g(3h)$$

$$\Rightarrow \quad (u_0')^2=6gh$$

$$u_0'=\sqrt{6gh}$$

$$=\sqrt{3}\sqrt{2gh}$$

$$=\sqrt{3}u_0 \qquad \text{[from Eq. (i)]}$$

45. (*d*) Length of wire $=l$

Case I For square shape,

Length of side $=\frac{l}{4}$

$$\therefore \text{Area, } A_1=\left(\frac{l}{4}\right)^2=\frac{l^2}{16}$$

$\therefore$ Magnetic moment,

$$M_1=IA_1=\frac{I\cdot l^2}{16}$$

Case II For circular shape,

$$l=2\pi r_2$$

$$\Rightarrow \quad r_2=\frac{l}{2\pi} \qquad \text{...(i)}$$

$\therefore$ Magnetic moment,

$$M_2=IA_2=I\cdot\pi r_2^2$$

$$=I\cdot\pi\left(\frac{l}{2\pi}\right)^2 \qquad \text{[using Eq. (i)]}$$

$$=I\pi\frac{l^2}{4\pi^2}$$

$$M_2=\frac{Il^2}{4\pi}$$

$$\therefore \quad \frac{M_1}{M_2}=\frac{\frac{Il^2}{16}}{\frac{Il^2}{4\pi}}=\frac{\pi}{4}$$

$$\therefore \quad M_1:M_2=\pi:4$$

46. (*d*) Volume of 8 drops = Volume of a large drop

$$\Rightarrow \quad 8\times\frac{4}{3}\pi r^3=\frac{4}{3}\pi R^3$$

$$\Rightarrow \quad 2r=R \qquad \text{...(i)}$$

According to conservation of charge,

$$Q=8q \qquad \text{...(ii)}$$

Potential of each small drop,

$$V=\frac{1}{4\pi\varepsilon_0}\cdot\frac{q}{r}$$

$$\Rightarrow \quad 16=\frac{1}{4\pi\varepsilon_0}\cdot\frac{q}{r}$$

$$\Rightarrow \quad \frac{1}{4\pi\varepsilon_0}\cdot\frac{q}{r}=16 \qquad \text{...(iii)}$$

Potential of a large drop,

$$V'=\frac{1}{4\pi\varepsilon_0}\cdot\frac{Q}{R}$$

$$=\frac{1}{4\pi\varepsilon_0}\cdot\frac{8q}{2r}$$

[from Eqs. (i) and (ii)]

$$=4\times\frac{1}{4\pi\varepsilon_0}\cdot\frac{q}{r}$$

$$=4\times16 \qquad \text{[from Eq. (iii)]}$$

$$=64\text{ V}$$

47. (*a*) $V=100\sin\left(100\pi t+\frac{\pi}{6}\right)$

$$\therefore \quad \phi_1=\frac{\pi}{6}$$

Since, alternating current leads $\frac{\pi}{2}$ angle from alternating voltage in purely capacitive circuit, hence phase angle of alternating current,

$$\phi_2=\frac{\pi}{2}-\phi_1=\frac{\pi}{2}-\frac{\pi}{6}=\frac{\pi}{3}$$

$\therefore$ Instantaneous value of alternative current

$$i=i_0\sin(100\pi t+\phi_2)$$

$$=V_0\omega C\sin\left(100\pi t+\frac{\pi}{3}\right)$$

$$=100\times100\pi\times1\times10^{-6}\sin\left(100\pi t+\frac{\pi}{3}\right)$$

$$=0.01\pi\sin\left(100\pi t+\frac{\pi}{3}\right)$$

48. (*c*) In an electromagnetic wave, energy is equally shared between electric and magnetic fields.

So, $u_M=u_E$

49. (*b*) If both the mass and radius of the earth decrease by 1%, then the value of acceleration due to gravity,

$$g'=\frac{G(0.99M_e)}{(0.99R_e)^2}$$

$$\approx1.01\frac{GM_e}{R_e^2}=1.01g$$

So, g would increase by

$$(1.01-1)\times100\%=1\%$$

New escape velocity would be

$$v_e'=\sqrt{\frac{2\times0.99M_eG}{0.99R_e}}$$

$$v_e'=\sqrt{\frac{2GM_e}{R_e}}=v_e$$

So, it will remain unchanged.

Also, gravitational potential energy

$$=-\frac{Gm(0.99M_e)}{0.99R_e}$$

$$=-\frac{GM_em}{R_e}$$

Hence, it also will remain same.

50. (*d*) Given, $p_1=p, E_1=E$

$$p_2=p+100\%\text{ of }p$$

$$=2p$$

We know that, kinetic energy (E) and momentum (p) are related as

$$E=\frac{p^2}{2m}$$

$$\therefore \quad \frac{E_2}{E_1}=\left(\frac{p_2}{p_1}\right)^2=\left(\frac{2p}{p}\right)^2=4$$

$$\Rightarrow \quad E_2=4E_1=4E$$

$\therefore$ Percentage increase in KE

$$=\frac{E_2-E_1}{E_1}\times100$$

$$=\frac{4E-E}{E}\times100$$

$$=3\times100=300\%$$

Knockout 6

1. (*b*) Given that, path difference, $\Delta x = \frac{\lambda}{4}$

Phase difference,

$$\phi = \left(\frac{2\pi}{\lambda}\right) \times \text{(Path difference)}$$

$$= \frac{2\pi}{\lambda} \times \frac{\lambda}{4}$$

$$= \frac{\pi}{2} \quad \text{...(i)}$$

It is given that, maximum intensity is I_0. So, intensity at a point on the screen, where phase difference ϕ is given by

$$I = I_0 \cos^2\left(\frac{\phi}{2}\right)$$

$$= I_0 \times \cos^2\left(\frac{\frac{\pi}{2}}{2}\right) \quad [\because \text{using Eq.(i)}]$$

$$= I_0 \times \left(\frac{1}{\sqrt{2}}\right)^2$$

$$= \frac{I_0}{2}$$

2. (*a*) 1 fermi $= 10^{-15}$ m

1 astronomical unit $= 1.5 \times 10^{11}$ m

1 light year $= 9.46 \times 10^{15}$ m

1 parsec $= 3.08 \times 10^{16}$ m

3. (*b*) Given materials of μ_1 and μ_2 refractive indices are used to form lens. So, corresponding to these, there are two focal lengths of lens. Thus, the number of images formed will be 2.

4. (*b*) As we know, mean reading of mass,

$$M_{mean} = \frac{M_1 + M_2 + M_3 + M_4 + M_5}{5}$$

$$= \frac{2.46 + 2.47 + 2.42 + 2.41 + 2.44}{5}$$

$M_{mean} = 2.44$ kg

Also, absolute error in reading of M_1,

$|\Delta M_1| = |\text{Mean} - M_1|$

$|\Delta M_1| = |2.44 - 2.46| = 0.02$ kg

Similarly,

$|\Delta M_2| = |2.44 - 2.47| = 0.03$ kg

$|\Delta M_3| = |2.44 - 2.42| = 0.02$ kg

$|\Delta M_4| = |2.44 - 2.41| = 0.03$ kg

$|\Delta M_5| = |2.44 - 2.44| = 0$ kg

$\therefore$ Mean absolute error,

$$\Delta M_{mean} = \frac{|\Delta M_1| + |\Delta M_2| + |\Delta M_3| + |\Delta M_4| + |\Delta M_5|}{5}$$

$$= \frac{0.02 + 0.03 + 0.02 + 0.03 + 0}{5}$$

$\Delta M_{mean} = 0.02$ kg

$\Rightarrow$ Reading of mass with error $= 2.44 \pm 0.02$ kg

5. (*d*) Consider the motion of ball in frame of balloon, so various parameters of ball in frame of balloon are as follows

$(u+v)$ ↑, g ↓

Initial velocity, $\mathbf{u} = \mathbf{u}_{ball} - \mathbf{u}_{balloon}$

$$= u - (-v)$$

$$= u + v$$

Acceleration of ball, $\mathbf{a} = \mathbf{a}_{ball} - \mathbf{a}_{balloon}$

$$= -g - (0)$$

$$\mathbf{a} = -g$$

Let t be the time, when ball pass by the balloon.

From 2nd equation of motion,

$$s = ut + \frac{1}{2}at^2$$

$$0 = (u+v) \times t + \frac{1}{2}(-g)t^2$$

or $$t = \frac{2(u+v)}{g}$$

6. (*c*) As, balloon goes up, an equal volume of air comes down, PE of air = (PE + KE) of balloon.

7. (*a*) From the given options, statement in option (a) is correct but rest are incorrect. They can be corrected as, Davisson and Germer experiment demonstrated the wave nature of electrons.

Since, X-rays contains no charge (or they are chargeless), so cannot deflected by electric or magnetic fields. Cathode rays are stream of electrons, they are not electromagnetic waves.

8. (*a*) For $A = 0, B = 1, Y = 0$

For $A = 1, B = 1, Y = 0$

9. (*b*) As, position vector, $\mathbf{r} = x\hat{\mathbf{i}} + y\hat{\mathbf{j}}$

$$= 3t\hat{\mathbf{i}} + 3t(1 - 4t)\hat{\mathbf{j}}$$

$$\mathbf{r} = 3t\hat{\mathbf{i}} + (3t - 12t^2)\hat{\mathbf{j}}$$

Velocity vector,

$$\mathbf{v} = \frac{d\mathbf{r}}{dt} = \frac{d}{dt}[3t\hat{\mathbf{i}} + (3t - 12t^2)\hat{\mathbf{j}}]$$

$$= 3\hat{\mathbf{i}} + (3 - 24t)\hat{\mathbf{j}}$$

Acceleration vector,

$$\mathbf{a} = \frac{d\mathbf{v}}{dt} = \frac{d}{dt}[3\hat{\mathbf{i}} + (3 - 24t)\hat{\mathbf{j}}]$$

$$= -24\hat{\mathbf{j}} \text{ m/s}^2$$

Let the time, when **v** makes angle 45° with **a** be t.

As, we know,

$\cos\theta = \frac{\mathbf{v} \cdot \mathbf{a}}{va}$, where θ is the angle between **a** and **v**.

$$\Rightarrow \cos 45° = \frac{[3\hat{\mathbf{i}} + (3 - 24t)\hat{\mathbf{j}}] \cdot [-24\hat{\mathbf{j}}]}{\sqrt{3^2 + (3 - 24t)^2} \cdot 24}$$

$$\frac{1}{\sqrt{2}} = -\frac{(3 - 24t)}{\sqrt{9 + (3 - 24t)^2}}$$

or $$\frac{1}{2} = \frac{(3 - 24t)^2}{9 + (3 - 24t)^2}$$

or $$9 + (3 - 24t)^2 = 2(3 - 24t)^2$$

or $$9 = (3 - 24t)^2$$

or $$(3 - 24t) = \pm 3$$

Taking positive sign,

$$3 - 24t = +3 \text{ or } t = 0 \text{ (not possible)}$$

Taking negative sign,

$$3 - 24t = -3 \text{ or } t = \frac{6}{24} = \frac{1}{4} \text{ s}$$

10. (*d*) As ball drops in water, its velocity increases till it reaches terminal velocity. So, KE first increases, then it becomes constant.

11. (*d*) As, $\lambda_{X\text{-rays}} = 1$ to 100 Å.

So, slit width ~ 600 nm = 6000 Å is very wide for X-rays. As diffraction is only observed when slit width is order of wavelength, so no diffraction pattern appears on screen.

12. (*b*) Kinetic energy in the region, when $0 \le x \le 1$ is $2E_0 - E_0 = E_0$ and if $x > 1$ kinetic energy is equal to total energy i.e., $2E_0$ as potential energy is zero.

As we know that, de-Broglie wavelength $\propto \frac{1}{\sqrt{\text{kinetic energy}}}$

$$\therefore \quad \frac{\lambda_1}{\lambda_2} = \sqrt{\frac{KE_2}{KE_1}}$$

$$\frac{\lambda_1}{\lambda_2} = \sqrt{\frac{2E_0}{E_0}}$$

$$\frac{\lambda_1}{\lambda_2} = \frac{\sqrt{2}}{1}$$

13. (*b*)

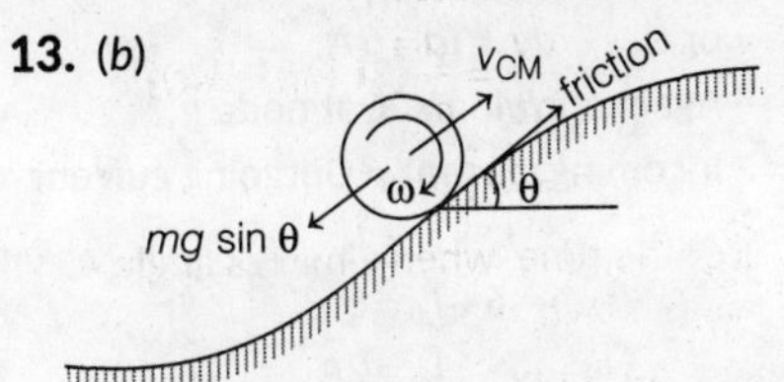

During the upward motion, the component of mg parallel to the plane is $mg\sin\theta$, which is in the direction opposite to motion that decreases the velocity of centre of mass.

Also, for pure rolling, the relation $v_{CM} = \omega R$ must be obeyed. Therefore, ω must decrease. Here, only friction can provide a torque about the centre. Torque due to friction must be opposite to ω.

Therefore, friction force will act up the plane during upward journey.

14. (*b*) Statement I is correct but Statement II is incorrect.

In an accelerating frame, we also have a pseudo force.

Hence in an accelerating frame, $F_{\text{applied}} + F_{\text{pseudo}} = m \times a_{\text{body}}$.

15. (*b*) Given that, activity decreases from 8000 becquerel to 4000 becquerel in 5 days.

So, we can say,

Half-life = 5 days ...(i)

Given, $t = 10$ days $= 2 \times 5$ days

$t = 2 \times$ half-life [∵ using Eq. (i)]

Activity after 2 half-life

$$= N\left(\frac{1}{2}\right)^{t/T_{1/2}} = 4000\left(\frac{1}{2}\right)^2$$

$$= 4000 \times \frac{1}{4} = 1000 \text{ becquerel}$$

16. (*c*) A high resistance in series with potentiometer wire increases sensitivity by decreasing potential drop per unit length of wire.

17. (*b*) Here, speed of electromagnetic wave in vacuum/air, $c = 3 \times 10^8$ m/s

Frequency, $f = 2 \times 10^{10}$ Hz

As we know, wavelength,

$$\lambda = \frac{c}{f} = \frac{3 \times 10^8}{2 \times 10^{10}}$$

$$= 1.5 \times 10^{-2} \text{ m}$$

18. (*a*) Let electric fields produced by charges Q_1 and Q_2 at point O be E_1 and E_2, respectively. Also, drawing perpendicular to hypotenuse that passes through point O as shown in the following figure.

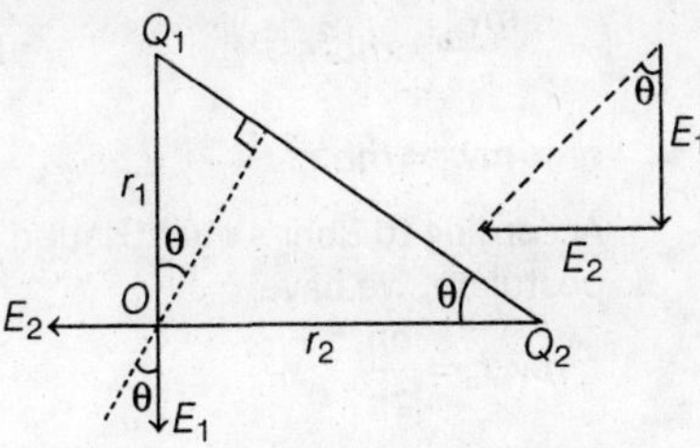

If the resultant electric field at point O is perpendicular to hypotenuse which means resultant of E_1 and E_2 must be along it.

$$\therefore \quad \tan\theta = \frac{E_2}{E_1} = \frac{\frac{kQ_2}{r_2^2}}{\frac{kQ_1}{r_1^2}} = \frac{Q_2}{Q_1} \cdot \frac{r_1^2}{r_2^2} \quad \text{...(i)}$$

In ΔOAB, $\tan\theta = \frac{r_1}{r_2}$ ...(ii)

From Eqs. (i) and (ii), we get

$$\frac{Q_2}{Q_1} \cdot \frac{r_1^2}{r_2^2} = \frac{r_1}{r_2}$$

or $$\frac{Q_1}{Q_2} = \frac{r_1}{r_2}$$

19. (*b*) Given that, $\mu = \cot\left(\frac{A}{2}\right)$

or $$\mu = \frac{\cos\left(\frac{A}{2}\right)}{\sin\left(\frac{A}{2}\right)} \quad \text{...(i)}$$

and we know that, refractive index,

$$\mu = \frac{\sin\left(\frac{A+\delta_m}{2}\right)}{\sin\left(\frac{A}{2}\right)} \quad \text{... (ii)}$$

On equating both Eqs. (i) and (ii), we get

$$\frac{\cos\left(\frac{A}{2}\right)}{\sin\left(\frac{A}{2}\right)} = \frac{\sin\left(\frac{A+\delta_m}{2}\right)}{\sin\left(\frac{A}{2}\right)}$$

$$\Rightarrow \quad \cos\left(\frac{A}{2}\right) = \sin\left(\frac{A+\delta_m}{2}\right)$$

$$\Rightarrow \sin\left(90° - \frac{A}{2}\right) = \sin\left(\frac{A+\delta_m}{2}\right)$$

$$\Rightarrow \quad 90° - \frac{A}{2} = \frac{A+\delta_m}{2}$$

$$\Rightarrow \quad 180° - A = A + \delta_m$$

$$\Rightarrow \quad \delta_m = 180° - 2A$$

20. (*c*) Wave speed in medium, $v = \frac{c}{n}$

$$= \frac{3 \times 10^8}{3/2}$$

$$= 2 \times 10^8 \text{ m/s}$$

Now, wave speed, $v = \frac{\omega}{k}$

$$\Rightarrow \quad 2 \times 10^8 = \frac{6 \times 10^8}{k}$$

or $$k = 3 \text{ rad m}^{-1}$$

So, a phase change of 3 rad occurs in 1 m length.

$\therefore$ Phase change in $\frac{\pi}{2}$ m $= 3 \times \frac{180}{\pi} \times \frac{\pi}{2}$

$$= 270°$$

21. (*d*) Number of field lines flux is proportional to charge enclosed.

$$N \propto q_{\text{enc}}$$

Given that, for two spherical surfaces, charge enclosed is same. So, number of field lines will also be same, i.e.

$$N_1 = N_2$$

22. (*d*) Given, area of coil, $A = 10 \text{ cm}^2$

$$= 10^{-3} \text{ m}^2$$

Number of turns, $N = 10$

$$\frac{dB}{dt} = 10^8 \text{ G/s} = 10^4 \text{ T/s}$$

Induced emf, $e = NA\frac{dB}{dt}$

$$= 10 \times 10^{-3} \times 10^4$$

$$\Rightarrow \quad e = 10^2$$

Current, $i = \frac{e}{R} = \frac{10^2}{20} = 5$ A

23. (*a*) The electrostatic potential energy U between two point charges q_1 and q_2 are placed at a distance r is given by

$$U = \frac{1}{4\pi\varepsilon_0} \cdot \frac{q_1 q_2}{r}$$

For the given configurations, expression of electrostatic potential energy are as follows

$$U_1 = \frac{1}{4\pi\varepsilon_0} \cdot \frac{Q(-Q)}{r} = -\frac{Q^2}{4\pi\varepsilon_0 r}$$

$$U_2 = \frac{1}{4\pi\varepsilon_0} \cdot \frac{(-Q)(-Q)}{r} = \frac{Q^2}{4\pi\varepsilon_0 r}$$

$$U_3 = \frac{1}{4\pi\varepsilon_0} \cdot \frac{(-Q)(-2Q)}{r} = \frac{2Q^2}{4\pi\varepsilon_0 r}$$

$$U_4 = \frac{1}{4\pi\varepsilon_0} \cdot \frac{Q(-2Q)}{2r} = -\frac{Q^2}{4\pi\varepsilon_0 r}$$

It is clear that, $U_1 = U_4 < U_2 < U_3$

24. (*b*) Heavy water or graphite are used as moderator in nuclear reactor.

When a light object collides with a heavy object, light object recoils with nearly same kinetic energy and no energy is given to heavier object. i.e. its whole kinetic energy is transformed to heavy object.

25. (d) The value of B near end is $\frac{\mu_0 nI}{2}$ and increases to $\mu_0 nI$.

So, graph between B and $\frac{x}{R}$ may be plotted as

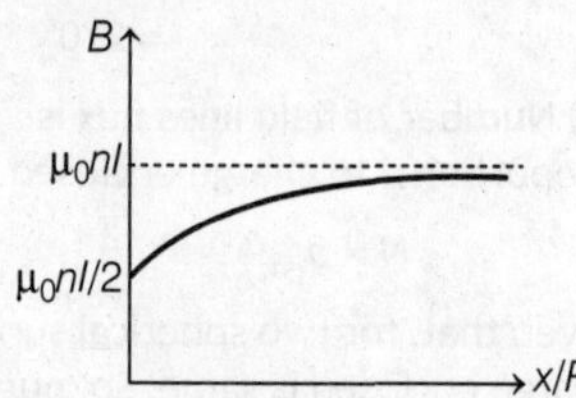

26. (d) Magnetic field at point P due to SM and OQ is zero. Similarly, **B** due to QR and RS are equal and outwards. **B** due to MN and NO are equal and inwards.

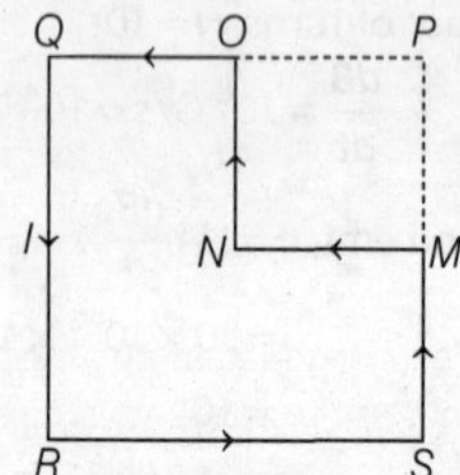

$\therefore$ **B** due to QR and RS,

$$\mathbf{B}_1 = 2\left[\frac{\mu_0}{4\pi}\frac{I}{2a}(\sin 0° + \sin 45°)\right]$$

$$\mathbf{B}_1 = \frac{\mu_0 I}{4\sqrt{2}\pi a}\odot$$

B due to MN and NO,

$$\mathbf{B}_2 = 2\left[\frac{\mu_0}{4\pi}\cdot\frac{I}{a}(\sin 0° + \sin 45°)\right]$$

$$\mathbf{B}_2 = \frac{\mu_0 I}{2\sqrt{2}\pi a}\otimes$$

Net magnetic field at point P,

$$\mathbf{B}_{net} = \mathbf{B}_1 + \mathbf{B}_2$$

or $\mathbf{B}_{net} = \frac{\mu_0 I}{4\sqrt{2}\pi a}\odot + \frac{\mu_0 I}{2\sqrt{2}\pi a}\otimes$

or $\mathbf{B}_{net} = \frac{\mu_0 I}{4\sqrt{2}\pi a}\otimes$

27. (c) In the given situation, the centripetal force on electron in nth orbit is given by

$$F = -\frac{dU}{dr} = -\frac{d}{dr}\left(-\frac{1}{2}mb^2r_n^2\right)$$

$$\Rightarrow F = mb^2 r_n$$

If in nth orbit speed of electron is v_n, then the centripetal force is

$$\frac{mv_n^2}{r_n} = mb^2 r_n \qquad (r = r_n)$$

or $mv_n^2 = mb^2 r_n^2$ ... (i)

According to Bohr's quantisation postulate, we have

$$mv_n r_n = \frac{nh}{2\pi} \quad \text{... (ii)}$$

Solving Eqs. (i) and (ii), we get

$$r_n = \left(\frac{nh}{2\pi mb}\right)^{\frac{1}{2}} \text{ or } r_n \propto \sqrt{n}$$

and $v_n = \left(\frac{nhb}{2\pi m}\right)^{\frac{1}{2}}$ or $v_n \propto \sqrt{n}$

28. (a) Let the required shunt be S,

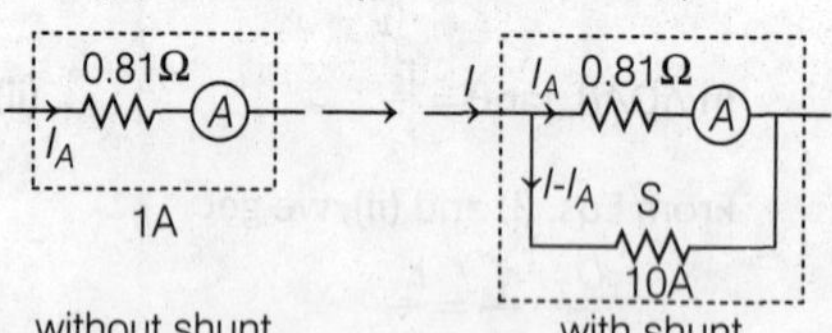

Applying KVL in the above circuit of ammeter and shunt, we get

$$(I - I_A)\times S = I_A \times 0.81$$

or $S = \frac{I_A}{I - I_A}\times 0.81$

Here, $I_A = 1$ A, $I = 10$ A

$$S = \frac{1}{10-1}\times 0.81$$

$$S = 0.09\,\Omega$$

29. (c) A is false but R is true.

A rolling body stops due to torque of normal reaction which provides a negative angular acceleration about centre of rotation.

In pure rolling motion, point of contact of a rolling body has a zero relative velocity with respect to ground.

30. (b) Dynamic resistance, $R = \frac{\Delta V}{\Delta I}$

Here, slope $= \tan\theta = \frac{\Delta I}{\Delta V} = \frac{1}{R}$

If we draw the tangents for given regions (see figure), then we find,

For region PQ, $90° < \theta < 180°$

$\Rightarrow \quad \tan\theta_2 = -$ ve

$\Rightarrow \quad R = -$ ve

31. (c) Applying KCL at node e,

Incoming current = Outgoing current

$$7 = 1 + I_2$$

or $I_2 = 6$ A

Again applying KCL at node g,

Incoming current = Outgoing current

$$I_2 + I_4 = I_3$$
$$6 + I_4 = 8$$
$$I_4 = 2\text{A}$$

32. (a) Given $\omega = 200\pi$

$$\therefore \quad T = \frac{2\pi}{\omega} = \frac{2\pi}{200\pi} = \frac{1}{100}\text{ s}$$

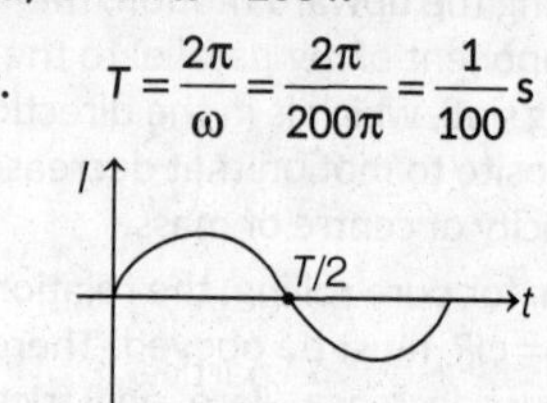

Current is zero after $\frac{T}{2}$ second.

$\therefore \quad I = 0 \Rightarrow t = \frac{T}{2} = \frac{1}{200}$ s

Current reaches rms value

$\Rightarrow \quad I_{rms} = 100\sin 200\pi t$

$\Rightarrow \quad \frac{100}{\sqrt{2}} = 100\sin 200\pi t$

$\Rightarrow \quad 200\pi t = \frac{\pi}{4}$

$\Rightarrow \quad t = \frac{1}{800}$ s

Current reaches $\frac{1}{2}$ of maximum value

$\Rightarrow \quad 200\pi t = \frac{\pi}{6}$

or $\quad t = \frac{1}{1200}$ s

Current reaches 0.86 value of maximum

$\Rightarrow \quad I_0 \times \frac{\sqrt{3}}{2} = I_0 \sin\omega t$

or $\quad 200\pi t = \frac{\pi}{3}$

$\Rightarrow \quad t = \frac{1}{600}$ s

33. (c) Following Lenz's law, induced emf in B opposes the change which produces it. So, B repels A.

34. (d) None of the given relations in **(a)**, **(b)** and **(c)** can be derived using dimensional analysis. Method of dimensions cannot be used to derive exponential, logarithmic, trigonometric or product of power functions.

35. (a) For transverse wave, velocity.

$$v = \frac{\text{Coefficient of } t}{\text{Coefficient of } x} = \frac{\omega}{k}$$

Velocity of wave in string, $v = \sqrt{\frac{T}{\mu}}$

where, T is tension and μ is linear density.

or $\sqrt{\frac{T}{\mu}} = \frac{\omega}{k}$

or $T = \mu\left(\frac{\omega}{k}\right)^2$

$= (1.3 \times 10^{-4}) \times \left(\frac{30}{1}\right)^2$

$T = 0.12\ \text{N}$

36. (*c*) Force acting on particle, $F = -\frac{dU}{dx}$

$= -\frac{d}{dx} 2(1 - \cos 5x)$

$= -2\frac{d}{dx}(1 - \cos 5x)$

$F = -2[0 + 5\sin 5x]$

or $F = -10\sin 5x$ N

For small oscillations means small values of x,

$\sin 5x \simeq 5x$

$F = -10 \times 5x$

$F = -50x$ ...(i)

Force on spring mass system is

$F = -kx$ ... (ii)

On comparing Eqs. (i) and (ii), we get

$k = 50$

As, time period, $T = 2\pi\sqrt{\frac{m}{k}} = 2\pi\sqrt{\frac{0.5}{50}}$

$T = \frac{\pi}{5}$ s

37. (*d*) Electric field is maximum at

$y = \pm\frac{R}{\sqrt{2}}$

If point charge is shifted above point P $\left(y > \frac{R}{\sqrt{2}}\right)$, then electric field will decrease and in this case, weight will be greater than electric force and net force will be downward. So, point charge move towards equilibrium position. Hence, stable equilibrium lies above point P.

Now, if we displace point charge slightly downwards $\left(y < \frac{R}{\sqrt{2}}\right)$, then again electric field of ring will also decrease slightly and electric force will decrease slightly. Net force on point charge is downward and point charge will continue to move in the direction of net force (i.e., downwards), so it will not return to equilibrium position. Hence, below point P equilibrium is unstable.

38. (*c*) After applying tangential force, let top face makes angle θ (angular displacement) as shown in the figure below.

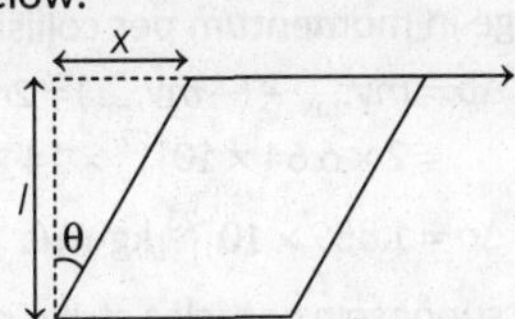

$\theta \simeq \tan\theta = \frac{x}{l} = \frac{1.2 \times 10^{-4}}{5 \times 10^{-2}}$

$\theta = 2.4 \times 10^{-3}$ rad

Rigidity modulus, $\eta = \frac{F/A}{\theta} = \frac{F}{A\theta}$

$\eta = \frac{10^5}{(5 \times 10^{-2})^2 \times 2.4 \times 10^{-3}}$

$\eta = 1.67 \times 10^{10}\ \text{Nm}^{-2}$

39. (*c*) Given that, $R_1 = (10 \pm 0.2)\,\Omega$

$R_2 = (20 \pm 0.1)\,\Omega$

The equivalent resistance of parallel combination,

$R = \frac{R_1 R_2}{R_1 + R_2} = \frac{10 \times 20}{10 + 20}$

$= 6.67\,\Omega$

Then, from $\frac{1}{R} = \frac{1}{R_1} + \frac{1}{R_2}$

or $R^{-1} = R_1^{-1} + R_2^{-1}$

Differentiating above equation, we get

$(-1)R^{-1-1}dR = (-1)R_1^{-1-1}dR_1 + (-1)R_2^{-1-1}dR_2$

$-\frac{dR}{R^2} = -\frac{dR_1}{R_1^2} - \frac{dR_2}{R_2^2}$

Here, dR, dR_1 and dR_2 can be replaced by ΔR, ΔR_1 and ΔR_2, respectively.

$\frac{\Delta R}{R^2} = \frac{\Delta R_1}{R_1^2} + \frac{\Delta R_2}{R_2^2}$

or $\Delta R = R^2\left[\frac{\Delta R_1}{R_1^2} + \frac{\Delta R_2}{R_2^2}\right]$

$= (6.67)^2\left[\frac{0.2}{(10)^2} + \frac{0.1}{(20)^2}\right]$

$= 0.1001\,\Omega$

So, $R = (6.67 \pm 0.1001)\,\Omega$

Here, ΔR is expressed as 0.1 instead of 0.1001 in confirmity with the rules of significant figure,

$R = (6.67 \pm 0.1)\,\Omega$

40. (*b*) The given situation is as shown in the figure below

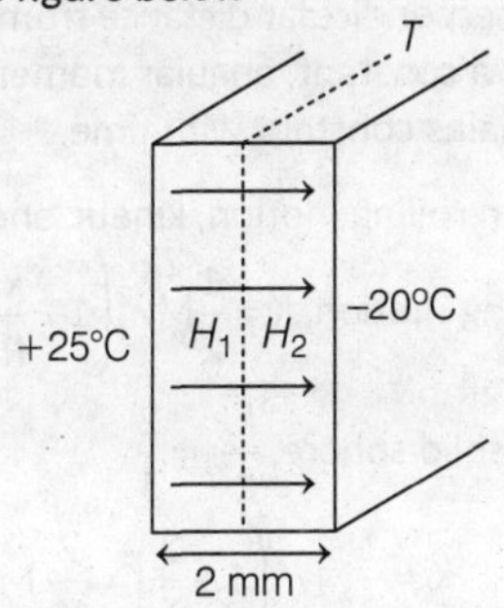

Let the temperature of mid-point be T°C.

At steady state, rate of heat transfer from inside to outside will be same.

$H_1 = H_2$

$\frac{K_1 A_1 \Delta T_1}{l_1} = \frac{K_2 A_2 \Delta T_2}{l_2}$ ...(i)

Here, $K_1 = K_2$, $A_1 = A_2$

and $l_1 = l_2 = 1$ mm

So, from Eq. (i),

$\Delta T_1 = \Delta T_2$

$25 - T = T - (-20)$

$2T = 25 - 20$

or $T = \frac{5}{2} = 2.5$°C

41. (*d*) If core contains large amounts of ferromagnetic substances, then also they are not cause of earth's magnetism, because due to high temperatures, at core ferromagnetic substances loses their ferromagnetism. Hence, above curie temperature, a ferromagnetic substance becomes paramagnetic.

42. (*d*) Using conservation of angular momentum,

Initial angular momentum of the system = Final angular momentum of the system

$L_i = L_f$

$I_i\omega_i = I_f\omega_f$

Since, earth is spherical in nature, so its moment of inertia, $I = \frac{2}{5}MR^2$

$\Rightarrow \frac{2}{5}MR^2\omega_i = \frac{2}{5}M\left(\frac{R}{n}\right)^2\omega_f$

or $\omega_f = n^2\omega_i$ or $\frac{2\pi}{T_f} = n^2\frac{2\pi}{T_i}$

$\Rightarrow \frac{1}{T_f} = \frac{n^2}{T_i} \Rightarrow T_f = \frac{T_i}{n^2}$

$\Rightarrow T_f = \frac{T}{n^2}$ (here, $T_i = T$)

43. (*a*) Angular momentum $\mathbf{L} = mv\,(r_\perp)$

As perpendicular distance from origin $r_\perp$ is a constant, angular momentum remains constant with time.

44. (*a*) In rolling motion, kinetic energy in rolling motion, $K = \frac{1}{2}Mv^2\left(1+\frac{k^2}{R^2}\right)$

For solid sphere, $\frac{k^2}{R^2} = \frac{2}{5}$

$$K = \frac{1}{2}Mv^2\left(1+\frac{2}{5}\right) = \frac{7}{10}Mv^2$$

At the maximum compression of spring, sphere will come to rest.

Using mechanical energy conservation,

$$ME_i = ME_f$$

$$KE_i + U_i = KE_f + U_f$$

$$\frac{7}{10}Mv^2 + 0 = 0 + \frac{1}{2}kx_{max}^2$$

or $\quad x_{max}^2 = \frac{7}{5}\frac{Mv^2}{k}$

or $\quad x_{max} = v\sqrt{\frac{7M}{5k}}$

45. (*b*) The refractive index of air is lesser than the refractive index of water, i.e., $\mu_{air} < \mu_{water}$.

Initially the path of ray is

As, we know, when the ray goes from rarer to denser medium, it bends towards the normal. However, when the ray goes from denser to rarer medium, it bends away from the normal.

⇒ For water interface, the path of the rays are as follows

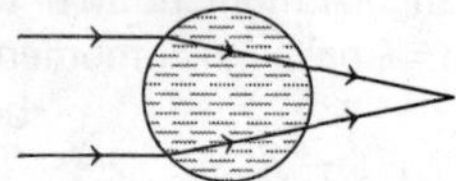

From the above diagram, it can be concluded that water drop is converging the light at a point.

46. (*d*) $m_1v_1\hat{\mathbf{i}} + m_2v_2\hat{\mathbf{i}} = m_1v_3\hat{\mathbf{i}} + m_2v_4\hat{\mathbf{i}}$

$$2mv_1\hat{\mathbf{i}} + mv_2\hat{\mathbf{i}} = 2m\left(\frac{v_1}{2}\right)\hat{\mathbf{i}} + mv_4\hat{\mathbf{i}}$$

⇒ $\quad v_4 = v_1 + v_2$

or $\quad v_1 = v_4 - v_2$

47. (c) Mass of one helium atom,

$$m = \frac{M}{N_A} = \frac{4}{6.023\times10^{23}}\text{ g}$$

$$= 6.64\times10^{-24}\text{ g}$$

$$m = 6.64\times10^{-27}\text{ kg}$$

Root mean square speed,

$$v_{rms} = \sqrt{\frac{3kT}{m}} = \sqrt{\frac{3\times1.38\times10^{-23}\times315}{6.64\times10^{-27}}}$$

$$v_{rms} = 14\times10^2\text{ m/s}$$

Change in momentum per collision,

$$\Delta p = mv_{rms} - (-mv_{rms}) = 2mv_{rms}$$

$$= 2\times6.64\times10^{-27}\times14\times10^2$$

$$\Delta p = 1.859\times10^{-23}\text{ kg-m/s}$$

Now, suppose *n* particles strike per second, so net force,

$$F = n(\Delta p)$$

and pressure, $p = \frac{F}{A} = \frac{n(\Delta p)}{A}$

or $\quad n = \frac{p\times A}{\Delta p}$

Here, $p = 1\text{ atm} = 1.01\times10^5$ Pa,

$$A = 1\text{ m}\times1\text{ m} = 1\text{ m}^2$$

$$n = \frac{1.01\times10^5\times(1)^2}{1.859\times10^{-23}}$$

$$= 5.43\times10^{27}\text{ per s}$$

48. (*b*) For an adiabatic process,

$$pV^\gamma = \text{constant}$$

Differentiating above expression,

$$\gamma pV^{\gamma-1}dV + V^\gamma dp = 0$$

⇒ $\quad V^\gamma dp = -\gamma pV^{\gamma-1}dV$

⇒ $\quad \frac{dp}{dV} = -\frac{\gamma pV^{\gamma-1}}{V^\gamma} = -\gamma\left(\frac{p}{V}\right)$

∴ Slope of adiabatic curve,

$$\left[\frac{dp}{dV}\right]_{adiabatic} = -\frac{\gamma p}{V}$$

So, slope of *p* - *V* graph is more for gas which higher value of γ.

As, we know that,

$$\gamma_{monoatomic} > \gamma_{diatomic} > \gamma_{polyatomic}$$

So, $(\text{slope})_{monoatomic} > (\text{slope})_{diatomic} > (\text{slope})_{polyatomic}$

From the graph, it is clear that $(\text{slope})_C > (\text{slope})_B > (\text{slope})_A$

Hence, $A \to$ Polyatomic, $B \to$ Diatomic, $C \to$ Monoatomic

Note For linear arrangement of triatomic gas, $\gamma = \frac{9}{7}$ and for non-linear arrangement, it is $\frac{4}{3}$.

49. (*b*) Given that, velocity of boy,

$$\mathbf{v}_L = 5\hat{\mathbf{i}}\text{ m/s}$$

Let velocity of rain w.r.t. ground,

$$\mathbf{v}_r = v_x\hat{\mathbf{i}} + v_y\hat{\mathbf{j}}\text{ m/s}$$

Velocity of rain w.r.t boy,

$$\mathbf{v}_{rb} = \mathbf{v}_r + (-\mathbf{v}_b) = v_x\hat{\mathbf{i}} + v_y\hat{\mathbf{j}} - 5\hat{\mathbf{i}}$$

$$= (v_x - 5)\hat{\mathbf{i}} + v_y\hat{\mathbf{j}}$$

It is in vertical direction.

So, $(v_x - 5)$ must be zero or $v_x = 5$ ... (i)

On increasing the speed of boy, velocity of rain w.r.t. boy becomes $(v_x - 15)\,\hat{\mathbf{i}} + v_y\hat{\mathbf{j}}$

$$\tan\theta = \tan45° = \frac{v_x - 15}{v_y}$$

$$1 = \frac{v_x - 15}{v_y}$$

or $\quad 1 = \frac{5-15}{v_y}$

or $\quad v_y = -10$

∴ Velocity of rain w.r.t. ground,

$$\mathbf{v}_r = (5\hat{\mathbf{i}} - 10\hat{\mathbf{j}})\text{ m/s}$$

Magnitude of velocity of rain,

$$v_r = \sqrt{5^2 + (-10)^2} = \sqrt{25+100}$$

$$= \sqrt{125} \Rightarrow v_r = 5\sqrt{5}\text{ m/s}$$

50. (*b*) Inductive reactance, $X_L = \omega L$

$$= 2\times\pi\times50\times(191\times10^{-3}) = 60\ \Omega$$

Capacitive reactance, $X_C = \frac{1}{\omega C}$

$$= \frac{1}{2\times\pi\times50\times106\times10^{-6}} = 30\ \Omega$$

Impedance of series *R*-*L*-*C* circuit is given as

$$Z = \sqrt{R^2 + \left(\omega L - \frac{1}{\omega C}\right)^2}$$

$$= \sqrt{(40)^2 + (60-30)^2}$$

$$Z = \sqrt{40^2 + 30^2} = 50\ \Omega$$

Power dissipated in circuit is given as

$$P = V_{rms}\times I_{rms}\times\cos\phi$$

$$= V_{rms}\times\left(\frac{V_{rms}}{Z}\right)\times R$$

$$P = \frac{V_{rms}^2\times R}{Z} = \frac{(10)^2\times40}{50} = 80\text{ W}$$

Heat produced in resistance to raise its temperature by 20°C is given as

H = (heat capacity) × (temperature difference)

$$H = 6\times80 = 480\text{ J}$$

Let this much amount of heat is produced in *t* s, then $Pt = 480$

or $\quad t = \frac{480}{80} = 6\text{ s}$

Knockout 7

1. (*a*) Physical quantities having different dimensions cannot be added or subtracted. As, P, Q and R are physical quantities having different dimension, therefore they can neither be added nor be subtracted.

   Thus, (a) can never be a meaningful quantity.

2. (*b*) In saturation mode, maximum collector current flows and transistor acts as a closed switch from collector to emitter terminal. In this mode, emitter-base bias is forward biased and collector-base bias is also forward biased.

3. (*d*) Momentum is conserved, so

$$m2\hat{\mathbf{i}} - m2\hat{\mathbf{j}} = 2m\mathbf{v}$$

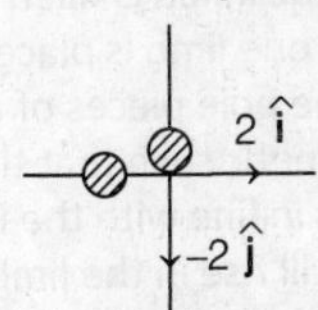

Before collision

or $\quad \mathbf{v} = \hat{\mathbf{i}} - \hat{\mathbf{j}}$ or $|\mathbf{v}| = \sqrt{2}$ m/s

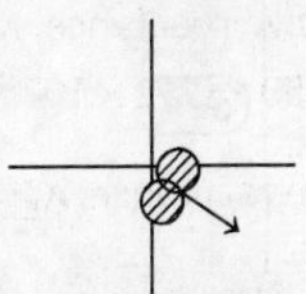

After collision

Initial kinetic energy, K_i

$$= \frac{1}{2}m(2)^2 + \frac{1}{2}m(2)^2 = 4m$$

Final kinetic energy, K_f

$$= \frac{1}{2}(2m)(\sqrt{2})^2 = 2m$$

Hence, energy loss $= K_i - K_f = 2m$

4. (*b*) As we know that,

   Binding energy of ${}_1^2\text{H}$,

$$(\text{BE})_{\text{H}} = 2 \times 1.15 = 2.3 \text{ MeV}$$

   Binding energy of ${}_2^4\text{He}$,

$$(\text{BE})_{\text{He}} = 4 \times 7.1 \text{ MeV} = 28.4 \text{ MeV}$$

$$\text{Q-value} = \Sigma\text{BE}_{\text{product}} - \Sigma\text{BE}_{\text{reactant}}$$
$$= 28.4 - (2.3 + 2.3)$$
$$= 23.8 \text{ MeV}$$

5. (*b*) The YDSE set-up is shown below

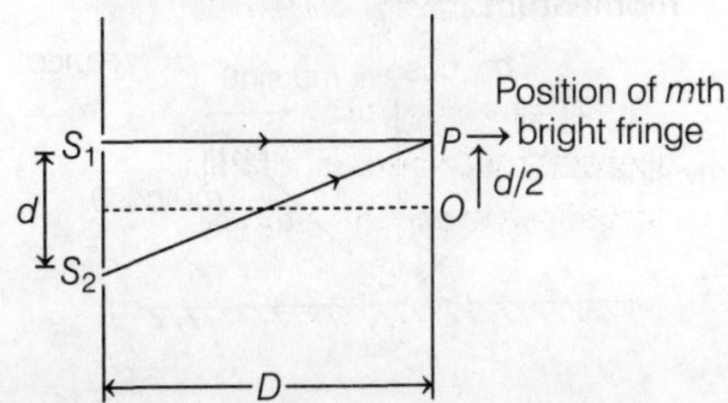

Given that *m*th bright fringe is exactly opposite to the one slit. It means the position of *m*th bright fringe from central point O, i.e., $m\beta$ is equal to $\frac{d}{2}$.

$$m\beta = \frac{d}{2}, \text{ here } \beta = \text{fringe width}$$

$$m\left(\frac{\lambda D}{d}\right) = \frac{d}{2} \quad \text{or} \quad m = \frac{d^2}{2\lambda D}$$

6. (*d*) Given that, $R_1 \neq R_2$

   For the first half cycle, $D_1 \rightarrow$ forward bias and $D_2 \rightarrow$ reverse bias.

   For the next half cycle, $D_1 \rightarrow$ reverse bias and $D_2 \rightarrow$ forward bias.

   In both the half cycle, voltage will appear across load resistance R but due to the different values of R_1 and R_2 peak of both the half cycle will have different peak values. Thus, voltage drop across R is not full wave rectified.

7. (*c*) Internal energy of a gas at T kelvin is

$$U = n\frac{f}{2}RT$$

$\therefore$ Internal energy of O_2 molecules

$$= U_1 = 3 \times \frac{5}{2}R \times 300$$

or $\quad U_1 = 2250R$

and Internal energy of Ar molecules

$$= U_2 = 1 \times \frac{3}{2} \times R \times 300$$
$$= 450R$$

Total internal energy $= U_1 + U_2 = 2700R$

8. (*c*) If there is no flow of charge through connecting wire, i.e. both spheres are at same potentials

$$V_1 = V_2$$
$$\frac{Kq_1}{r_1} = \frac{Kq_2}{r_2}$$
$$\frac{K \times (\sigma_1 \times 4\pi r_1^2)}{r_1} = \frac{K \times (\sigma_2 \times 4\pi r_2^2)}{r_2}$$

or $\quad \sigma_1 r_1 = \sigma_2 r_2$

9. (*a*) When the surface area of liquid is increased, the molecules from the interior of the liquid rise to the surface. As these molecules reach near the surface, work is done against the downward cohesive force. This work is stored in the molecules in the form of potential energy. Thus, the potential energy of the molecules lying in the surface is greater than that of the molecules in the interior of the liquid. As a result, its potential energy increases and internal energy decreases.

10. (*c*) The stress at the base of the mountain $= h\rho g$

    The stress must be less than the elastic limits, otherwise the rock begins to fall down.

    Stress $\leq$ Elastic limit

$$h\rho g \leq \text{Elastic limit}$$
$$h \leq \frac{\text{Elastic Limit}}{\rho g}$$

For maximum value of h,

$$h_{\max} = \frac{\text{Elastic limit}}{\rho g} = \frac{3.43 \times 10^8}{3 \times 10^3 \times 9.8}$$
$$h_{\max} = 1.1667 \times 10^4 \text{ m}$$
$$h_{\max} = 11.667 \text{ km}$$

11. (*c*) According to the Newton's law of cooling, if a body is cooled from T_1 to T_2 temperature in t time, then relation is given as

$$\frac{T_1 - T_2}{t} = K\left[\frac{T_1 + T_2}{2} - T_0\right] \quad \text{...(i)}$$

where, T_0 is the temperature of surrounding and K is constant.

Given that, body cools from $5T$ to $2T$ in 5 min. Then

From Eq. (i), we can write

$$\frac{5T - 2T}{5} = K\left[\frac{5T + 2T}{2} - T\right]$$
$$\frac{3T}{5} = K[2.5T]$$

or $\quad K = \frac{6}{25} \text{ min}^{-1}$

Let the temperature of body in next 5 min be T', then again from Eq. (i), we can write

$$\frac{2T - T'}{5} = \frac{6}{25}\left[\frac{2T + T'}{2} - T\right]$$
$$5(2T - T') = 6\left[\frac{2T + T' - 2T}{2}\right]$$
$$10T - 5T' = 3[T']$$
$$10T - 5T' = 3T'$$
$$8T' = 10T$$

or $\quad T' = \frac{10T}{8} = \frac{5}{4}T$

12. (*a*) The average kinetic energy of per molecules of a gas is given as

$$K_{\text{avg}} = \frac{1}{2}kT$$

$\therefore$ It is independent of degree of freedom

As we know that, $\gamma = \frac{C_p}{C_v}$ and value of γ decreases as atomicity of gas increases, hence $\frac{C_p}{C_V}$ decreases as atomicity increases.

13. (*a*) Total mass $= 2.3$ kg

$$+\ 0.00215 \text{ kg}$$
$$+\ 0.01239 \text{ kg}$$
$$= 2.31454$$

As least number of significant figure in quantities added will be 2.3 kg.

14. (*c*) True value or average value

$$= \frac{2.63 + 2.56 + 2.42 + 2.71 + 2.80}{5}$$
$$= 2.62 \text{ s}$$

Errors $\Delta T_1 = 2.63 - 2.62 = 0.01$

$\Delta T_2 = 0.06, \Delta T_3 = 0.20$

$\Delta T_4 = 0.09, \Delta T_5 = 0.18$

$\therefore$ Mean error $= \frac{\Sigma \Delta T}{5} = \frac{0.84}{5} = 0.11$ s

Reported value $= (2.62 \pm 0.11)$ s

15. (*d*) Gyromagnetic ratio is the ratio of magnetic moment and angular momentum

Gyromagnetic ratio

$$= \frac{\text{m}}{\text{L}} = \frac{e}{2m_e} \text{ (for electron)}$$

So, dimensions of gyromagnetic ratio

$$= \frac{[e]}{[m]} = \frac{[It]}{[m]} = [M^{-1}L^0T^1A^1]$$

16. (*a*) If the value of R_h is increased, then voltage across the wire *AB* is increased and balance point may be obtained on wire *AB*. If the current further increases in this situation, then balance point cannot be obtained.

Hence, in order to obtain balance point between *X* and *Y*, it is necessary to decrease the value of R_h.

17. (*b*) At balance, we have

$$\frac{55}{20} = \frac{R}{(100 - 20)}$$

$\Rightarrow$ $R = 220\,\Omega$

18. (*a*) Let the initial velocity of throw be *u*. Object travels h_1 height in *t* second.

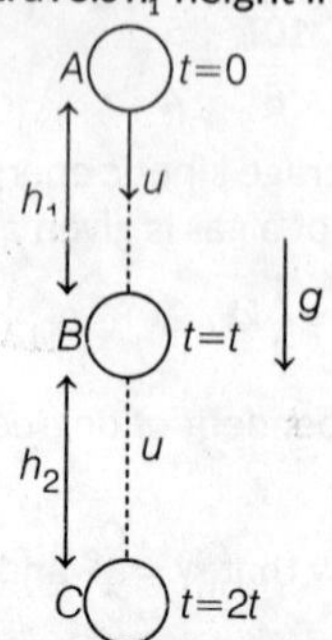

A to *B* using second equation of motion,

$$s = ut + \frac{1}{2}at^2$$
$$h_1 = ut + \frac{1}{2}gt^2 \quad \text{...(i)}$$

A to *C* using second equation of motion,

$$h_1 + h_2 = u(t + t) + \frac{1}{2}g(t + t)^2$$
$$h_1 + h_2 = 2ut + \frac{1}{2} \times g\, 4t^2 \quad \text{...(ii)}$$

Subtracting Eq. (i) from Eq. (ii), we get

$$h_2 = ut + \frac{1}{2}3gt^2$$
$$h_2 = ut + \frac{1}{2}gt^2 + \frac{1}{2}2gt^2$$
$$h_2 = h_1 + gt^2 \quad [\because \text{from Eq. (i)}]$$

or $gt^2 = h_2 - h_1$

or $t = \sqrt{\frac{h_2 - h_1}{g}}$ second

19. (*c*) At closest point,

Decrease in kinetic energy of α-particle = Increase in potential energy

$$\frac{1}{2}mv^2 - 0 = \frac{K(Ze)(2e)}{r_{min}} - 0$$

[r_{min} = minimum distance between two nuclei]

or $r_{min} = \frac{4KZe^2}{mv^2}$

From above it is clear that,

$$r_{min} \propto Ze^2$$
$$r_{min} \propto \frac{1}{v^2}$$
$$r_{min} \propto \frac{1}{m}$$

20. (*c*) As car starts from rest, then initial velocity is zero and let uniform acceleration be *a*.

Using third equation of motion,

$$v^2 = u^2 + 2as$$
$$v^2 = 0^2 + 2as$$

or $v^2 = 2as \quad \text{...(i)}$

From the graph, when $s = 4$ m, then $v = 20$ m/s

Putting these values in Eq. (i), we get

$$(20)^2 = 2 \times a \times (4)$$
$$20 \times 20 = 8a$$

or $a = \frac{400}{8}$

$$a = 50 \text{ m/s}^2$$

21. (*d*) The frequency of an organ pipe with length *L* is

$f_1 = \frac{v}{2L}$, where *v* is the speed of sound

The frequency of an open organ pipe with length $(L + l)$ is

$$f_2 = \frac{v}{2(L + l)}$$

Number of beats heard per second,

$$\Delta f = f_1 - f_2 = \frac{v}{2L} - \frac{v}{2(L + l)}$$
$$= \frac{v}{2}\left[\frac{1}{L} - \frac{1}{L + l}\right] = \frac{v}{2}\left[\frac{L + l - L}{L(L + l)}\right]$$
$$\Delta f = \frac{vl}{2L(L + l)}$$

22. (*a*) Paramagnetic substances when placed in a magnetic field, acquire a feeble magnetisation in the same sense as the applied magnetic field. These substances are attracted towards magnetic field. When a paramagnetic liquid is filled in a narrow U-tube and one limb is placed in between the pole pieces of an electromagnetic such that the level of the liquid is in line with the field, then the liquid will rise in the limb as the field is switched ON. The situation is shown below in the figure.

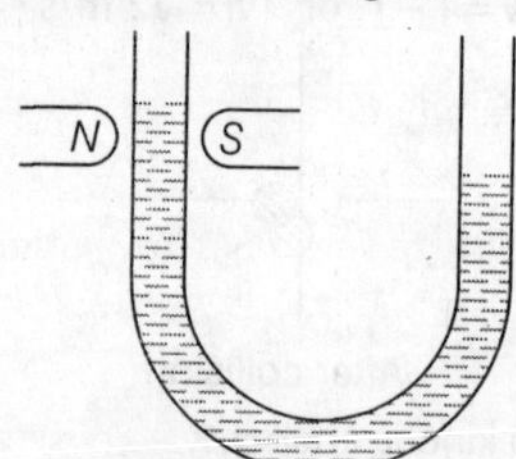

23. (*d*) Radiowaves are produced by oscillating charge particles between plates of capacitor in *L-C* circuit.

24. (*a*) Damping in a galvanometer can be achieved by putting an aluminium plate with coil. Eddy current will be induced in plate. This will dissipates oscillation energy or heat.

25. (*b*) A is true but R is false.

Wood absorbs more heat but as iron is more conductive, it appears hot due to large rate of heat conduction.

26. (*a*) As normal force of surface acts in perpendicular direction, so it changes only perpendicular component of momentum.

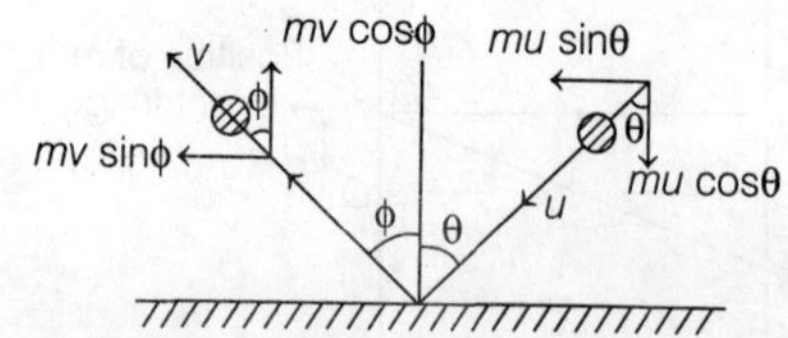

Horizontal component of momentum remains constant, so force

$$= \frac{\Delta p}{\Delta t} = \frac{p_f - p_i}{\Delta t}$$

$$= \frac{mv\cos\phi - mu\cos\theta}{\Delta t}$$

27. (*a*)

A. The magnetic flux through the rectangular loop *abcd* increases, due to the motion of the loop into the region of magnetic field. Thus, the induced current must flow along the path *bcdab*, so that it opposes the increasing flux.

B. Due to the outward motion, magnetic flux through the triangular loop *abc* decreases. Thus, the induced current must flow along *bacb*, so as to oppose the change in flux.

C. As the magnetic flux decreases due to the motion of the irregular shaped loop *abcd* out of the region of magnetic field, the induced current flows along *cdabc*, so as to oppose the change in flux.

Hence, A → R, B → P and C → Q.

28. (*d*) Given that,

$$\phi = 4t^n - 3^n \quad \text{...(i)}$$

According to Faraday's law, induced emf $= -\frac{d\phi}{dt}$

Magnitude of induced emf, $e = \left| -\frac{d\phi}{dt} \right|$

Differentiating Eq. (i) with respect to time, we get

$$\frac{d\phi}{dt} = \frac{d}{dt}(4t^n - 3^n)$$

$$= 4nt^{n-1} - 0 \quad (\text{As } 3^n \text{ is constant})$$

$$\frac{d\phi}{dt} = 4nt^{n-1}$$

or $e = \left| -\frac{d\phi}{dt} \right| = 4nt^{n-1}$

If $n = 1$, $e = 4(1)t^{1-1} = 4$ constant.

So, option (a) is correct.

If $n > 1$, $e = 4nt^{n-1}$

Let $n = 2$, $e = 8t$, i.e. $e \propto t$

With increase in time *t*, *e* also increases, so option (b) is correct and option (c) is correct.

If $n < 1$, $e = 4nt^{n-1}$

Let $n = 0.5$, $e = 4 \times 0.5t^{0.5-1}$

$$e = \frac{2}{\sqrt{t}} \text{ or } e \propto \frac{1}{\sqrt{t}}$$

On increasing *t*, the value of *e* decreases.

29. (*d*) As we know,

$$(m)_{H_2} = 2 \text{ amu}, (m)_{O_2} = 32 \text{ amu}$$
$$(m)_{N_2} = 28 \text{ amu}, (m)_{He} = 4 \text{ amu}$$

Also, $T_{H_2} = T$, $T_{O_2} = 2T$, $T_{N_2} = 3T$, $T_{He} = 4T$

The kinetic energy of a gas molecules is $\frac{3}{2}k_B T$.

de-Broglie wavelength of a gas molecule,

$$\lambda = \frac{h}{\sqrt{3mk_B T}}$$

or $$\lambda \propto \frac{1}{\sqrt{mT}}$$

i.e. λ will be greater for the smaller the value of mT.

According to the given question,

$$(mT)_{H_2} = 2 \times T = 2T$$
$$(mT)_{O_2} = 32 \times 2T = 64T$$
$$(mT)_{N_2} = 28 \times 3T = 84T$$
$$(mT)_{He} = 4 \times 4T = 16T$$

Thus, $(mT)_{N_2} > (mT)_{O_2} > (mT)_{He} > (mT)_{H_2}$

$$\lambda_{N_2} < \lambda_{O_2} < \lambda_{He} < \lambda_{H_2}$$

30. (*a*) Let the displacement-time equation of simple harmonic motion is given as

$$x = A\sin(\omega t + \phi) \quad \text{...(i)}$$

From given figure, $A = 4$ m

$$T = 6 \text{ s}$$

$$\therefore \quad \omega = \frac{2\pi}{T} = \frac{2\pi}{6} = \frac{\pi}{3} \text{ rad/s}$$

Initially (at $t = 0$), $x = 0$

From Eq. (i), $0 = A\sin(\omega \times 0 + \phi)$

$$A\sin\phi = 0$$

or $$\sin\phi = 0$$

$$\Rightarrow \quad \phi = 0, \pi, 2\pi$$

ϕ cannot be zero as particle is going away from mean position to the left extreme position.

$$\phi = \pi$$

Equation, $x = 4\sin\left(\frac{\pi}{3}t + \pi\right)$ m

31. (*c*) Let both spheres are placed at *d* distance.

$$\therefore \quad F_1 = \frac{1}{4\pi\varepsilon_0} \cdot \frac{q_1 q_2}{d^2} \quad \text{...(i)}$$

As we know after touching, both spheres acquire the same charge and equal to half of the total charge.

New charges on spheres,

$$q_1' = q_2' = \frac{q_1 + q_2}{2}$$

Given that, $q_1 >> q_2$

$$q_1' = q_2' = \frac{q_1}{2}$$

$$F_2 = \frac{1}{4\pi\varepsilon_0} \cdot \frac{q_1' q_2'}{d^2}$$

$$= \frac{1}{4\pi\varepsilon_0} \cdot \frac{\left(\frac{q_1}{2}\right)^2}{d^2}$$

$$F_2 = \frac{1}{4} \cdot \frac{1}{4\pi\varepsilon_0} \cdot \frac{q_1^2}{d^2} \quad \text{...(ii)}$$

On dividing Eqs. (i) and (ii), we get

$$\frac{F_1}{F_2} = \frac{4q_2}{q_1}$$

32. (*d*) Minimum distance of a real image from object in case of a convex lens is $4f$. So, screen must be at a distance greater than 4×30 or 120 cm.

33. (*c*) The net external torque acting on the system is zero.

Thus, angular momentum remains conserved i.e.

$$J_i = J_F$$

or $$I_i\omega_i = I_f\omega_f \quad \text{...(i)}$$

When the system rotates, then due to the centrifugal force, balls will move away from the centre of rod.

Therefore, moment of inertia of system, the given axis increases.

i.e. $$I_f > I_i$$

$$\Rightarrow \quad \frac{I_f}{I_i} > 1$$

From Eq. (i), we get

$$\omega_f = \frac{\omega_i}{\left(\frac{I_f}{I_i}\right)}$$

$$\omega_f < \omega_i$$

Thus, angular velocity (ω) will decrease, so that angular momentum remains constant.

As $F_{net} = 0$

⇒ Linear momentum will remain conserved.

So, statement given in option (b) is correct.

When $F_{net} = 0$ and $\tau_{net} = 0$, then by energy conservation principle,

$$\omega = \int \tau_{ext}\, d\theta + \int F_{net} = 0$$

$$\omega = 0$$

$$\Delta ME = 0$$

$$ME = \text{constant}$$

Thus, statement given in option (d) is correct.

As the tube remains horizontal, so potential energy will not change, so we can write

$$\Delta ME = \Delta U + \Delta K$$
$$\Delta K = \Delta ME - \Delta U = 0 - 0$$
$$\Delta K = 0$$

Kinetic energy will remain conserved. Thus, statement given in option (c) is incorrect.

34. (*a*) The centre of mass of a quarter ring of radius *r* from its centre is

$$r_{CM} = \frac{R\sin\frac{\theta}{2}}{\frac{\theta}{2}},$$

($\because$ for quarter ring, $\theta = 90°$)

$$r_{CM} = \frac{r\sin\left(\frac{\pi}{4}\right)}{\frac{\pi}{4}} = \frac{2\sqrt{2}}{\pi}r$$

The centre of mass lies on the line of bisector.

Thus, co-ordinates of centre of mass can be given as

$$r_1 = \frac{2\sqrt{2}}{\pi}(2r)[\cos 45\hat{i} + \sin 45\hat{j}]$$
$$r_2 = \frac{2\sqrt{2}}{\pi}r[-\cos 45\hat{i} - \sin 45\hat{j}]$$

The centre of mass of the system is given

$$r_{CM} = \frac{m_1 r_1 + m_2 r_2}{m_1 + m_2}$$

here, $m_1 = m, m_2 = 2m$

$$r_{CM} = \frac{m \times \frac{2\sqrt{2}}{\pi} \times 2r[\cos 45\hat{i} + \sin 45\hat{j}] + 2m \times \frac{2\sqrt{2}}{\pi} \times r[-\cos 45\hat{i} - \sin 45\hat{j}]}{m + 2m}$$

$$r_{CM} = \frac{m \times \frac{2\sqrt{2}}{\pi} \times r[2\cos 45\hat{i} + 2\sin 45\hat{i} - 2\cos 45\hat{i} - 2\sin 45\hat{j}]}{3m}$$

$$r_{CM} = \frac{m \times 2\sqrt{2}}{\pi} \times \frac{r}{3m} \times (0)$$

$$r_{CM} = 0 = 0\hat{i} + 0\hat{j}$$

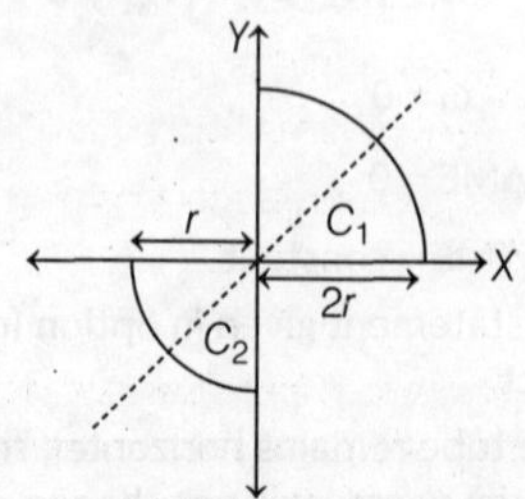

Thus, co-ordinate of centre of mass of system is (0, 0).

35. (*d*) Let the velocity of each particle in circular path be v_0. According to the question, situation is drawn below

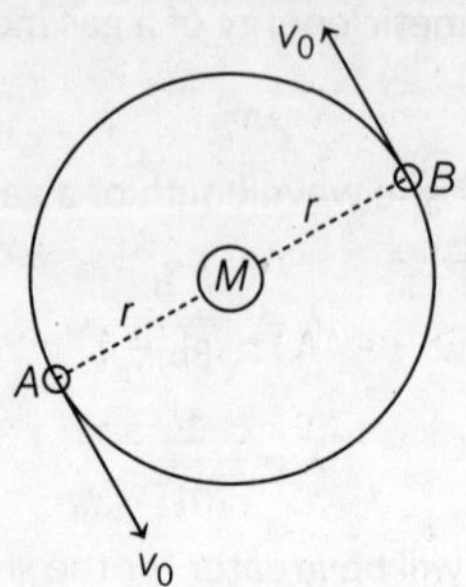

While revolving in circular path, the necessary centripetal force is provided by gravitational force of planet and other force of mass *m*.

The FBD of body *A* is as follows

m → GMm/r^2, $Gmm/(2r)^2$ (A)

$$F_{net} = \frac{Gmm}{(2r)^2} + \frac{GMm}{r^2}$$
$$\frac{mv^2}{r} = \frac{Gm}{r^2}\left[\frac{m}{4} + M\right]$$
$$\Rightarrow \quad v^2 = \frac{G}{r}\left[M + \frac{m}{4}\right]$$
$$\Rightarrow \quad v = \sqrt{\frac{G}{4r}(4M + m)}$$

36. (*c*) If the electric field between the plates of parallel plate capacitor in air is E_0, then net electric field in dielectric medium of dielectric constant *K*, will be $\frac{E_0}{K}$

or we can say that, $E_{medium} \propto \frac{1}{K}$ ...(i)

Given, electric field is minimum for medium-3 and greatest for medium-2.

$$E_3 < E_1 < E_2$$

From Eq. (i), we get

$$\frac{1}{K_3} < \frac{1}{K_1} < \frac{1}{K_2}$$

or $\quad K_3 > K_1 > K_2$

37. (*d*) Both A and R are correct and R explains A.

As only dipoles exist, $q_{net} = +q - q = 0$

$\therefore$ According to Gauss's law,

$$\phi_E = \frac{q_{net}}{\varepsilon_0} = \frac{0}{\varepsilon_0} = 0$$

38. (*c*) Let x_0 be the elongation in spring in mean position, then

At equilibrium, $kx_0 = mg$

or $\quad x_0 = \frac{mg}{k}$

FBD of the block is as follows:

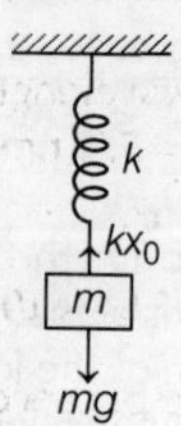

When block is elongated $\frac{mg}{3k}$ downward, then

FBD of block is follows

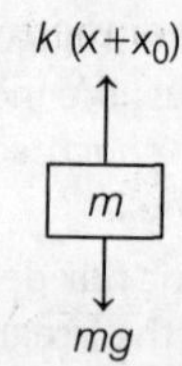

Net force, $F = k(x + x_0) - mg$ (upwards)

$$F = k\left[\frac{mg}{k} + \frac{mg}{3k}\right] - mg \text{ (upwards)}$$
$$= mg + \frac{mg}{3} - mg$$
$$F = \frac{mg}{3} \text{ (upwards)}$$

Change in potential energy of spring,

$$\Delta U = \frac{1}{2}k(x_f^2 - x_i^2)$$
$$\Delta U = \frac{1}{2}k[(x + x_0)^2 - x_0]^2$$
$$\Delta U = \frac{k}{2}\left[\left(\frac{mg}{k} + \frac{mg}{3k}\right)^2 - \left(\frac{mg}{k}\right)^2\right]$$
$$= \frac{k}{2} \times \frac{m^2g^2}{k^2} \times \frac{7}{9}$$
$$\Delta U = \frac{7}{18}\frac{m^2g^2}{k}$$

Work done by external source,

$$W = \Delta K + \Delta U$$
$$W_{ext} = 0 + \frac{7}{18}\frac{m^2g^2}{k} - mg \times x$$
$$W_{ext} = \frac{7}{18}\frac{m^2g^2}{k} - mg \times \frac{mg}{3k}$$
$$W_{ext} = \frac{m^2g^2}{18k}$$

39. (*c*) Statement I is incorrect but Statement II is correct.

As phase difference is given by $\tan\phi = \frac{X_L}{R}$.

In L-R circuit, voltage leads by current by an angle of $\tan^{-1}\left(\frac{X_L}{R}\right)$.

Time lag in L-R circuit, $t = \frac{1}{\omega}\tan^{-1}\frac{L}{R}$

40. (*c*) Average wavelength of photons (sunlight), $\lambda = 550$ nm

So, photon flux,

$$n = \frac{P}{E} = \frac{P\lambda}{hc} \approx 3.84 \times 10^{21} \text{ photons per}$$

square metre per second

$$\approx 4 \times 10^{21}$$

41. (*a*) Given, change in internal energy,

$$\Delta U = \frac{Q}{4}$$

From first law of thermodynamics,

$$\Delta Q = \Delta U + \Delta W$$

$$Q = \frac{Q}{4} + W$$

$$W = \frac{3Q}{4} = \frac{R}{1-n}\Delta T \quad \text{...(i)}$$

$$\Delta U = \frac{Q}{4} = \frac{3}{2}R\Delta T \quad \text{...(ii)}$$

$\therefore$ Gas is monoatomic.

From Eqs. (i) and (ii), we get

$$\frac{9}{2}R = \frac{R}{1-n}$$

or $\quad 1 - n = \frac{2}{9} \Rightarrow n = \frac{7}{9}$

42. (*a*) Let the mass of string of length l be m_1 and that of length $(L-l)$ be m_2

$$m_1 = \frac{\text{Length of part}}{\text{Total length of string}} \times \text{Mass of string}$$

$$m_1 = \frac{l}{L} \times m$$

$$m_2 = m - m_1$$

$$= m - \frac{l}{L} \times m$$

$$m_2 = \left(\frac{L-l}{L}\right)m \quad \text{...(i)}$$

The FBD of string and small block is as follows.

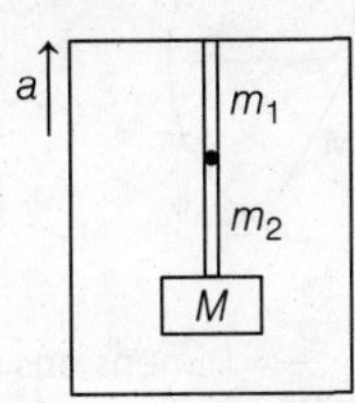

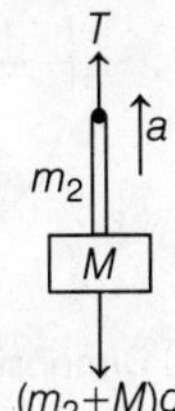

From force equation,

$$(m_2 + M)a = T - (m_2 + M)g$$

or $\quad a = \frac{T}{m_2 + m} - g$

$$a = \frac{T}{\left(\frac{L-l}{L}\right)m + M} - g \quad \text{[using Eq. (i)]}$$

$$a = \frac{T}{\left(1 - \frac{l}{L}\right)m + M} - g$$

or $\quad a = \frac{T}{M + m - \frac{ml}{L}} - g$

43. (*a*) Given that $\mathbf{A} = \hat{\mathbf{i}} + 2\hat{\mathbf{j}} + 2\hat{\mathbf{k}}$

Magnitude, $|\mathbf{A}| = \sqrt{1^2 + 2^2 = 2^2} = 3$

Unit vector along direction of **A**,

$$\mathbf{A} = \frac{\mathbf{A}}{|\mathbf{A}|} = \frac{\hat{\mathbf{i}} + 2\hat{\mathbf{j}} + 2\hat{\mathbf{k}}}{3}$$

and $\quad \mathbf{B} = 3\hat{\mathbf{i}} + 6\hat{\mathbf{j}} + 2\hat{\mathbf{k}}$

Magnitude of **B**,

$$|\mathbf{B}| = \sqrt{3^2 + 6^2 + 2^2} = \sqrt{49}$$

$$|\mathbf{B}| = 7$$

The vector C has same magnitude as **B** but has the same direction as **A**. Thus **C** can be written as

$$\mathbf{C} = |B|\,\mathbf{A}$$

or $\quad \mathbf{C} = 7 \times \left(\frac{\hat{\mathbf{i}} + 2\hat{\mathbf{j}} + 2\hat{\mathbf{k}}}{3}\right)$

or $\quad \mathbf{C} = \frac{7}{3}(\hat{\mathbf{i}} + 2\hat{\mathbf{j}} + 2\hat{\mathbf{k}}) \quad \text{...(i)}$

Given, $\mathbf{C} = \frac{p}{q}(a\hat{\mathbf{i}} + b\hat{\mathbf{j}} + c\hat{\mathbf{k}}) \quad \text{...(ii)}$

On Comparing Eqs. (i) and (ii), we get

$$p = 7, q = 3, a = 1, b = 2, c = 2$$

44. (*d*) Time lag,

$$\tau = \frac{\phi}{\omega} = \frac{33.56\,\pi}{180 \times 120\,\pi}$$

$$= 1.55 \times 10^{-3} \text{ s}$$

$$= 1.55 \text{ ms}$$

45. (*c*) As, $U = -x$, $K = \frac{x}{2}$

$\therefore$ Total energy of satellite $= U + K$

$$= -x + \frac{x}{2} = \frac{-x}{2}$$

$\therefore$ Energy needed to escape $= \frac{x}{2}$

If escape speed is v_e

Then, $\frac{1}{2}mv_e^2 = \frac{x}{2}$ or $v_e = \sqrt{\frac{x}{m}}$

46. (*d*) Work done

$$= -q(V_f - V_i)$$

$$= -q\left[\frac{kq}{d} + \frac{kQ}{2d} - \frac{kq}{2d} - \frac{kQ}{d}\right]$$

$$= -q\left[\frac{kq}{d} + \frac{2kq}{2d} - \frac{kq}{2d} - \frac{2kq}{d}\right]$$

$$= -q\frac{kq}{d}\left(1 + 1 - \frac{1}{2} - 2\right)$$

$$= \frac{kq^2}{2d}$$

47. (*a*) The fringe width,

$$\beta = \frac{D\lambda}{d} \Rightarrow \beta \propto \lambda$$

We have

$$v = n\lambda \quad \text{or} \quad \lambda \propto v$$

So, $\beta \propto v$

$$\Rightarrow \quad \frac{\beta_1}{\beta_2} = \frac{v_1}{v_2} = \frac{v_1}{4v_1} \quad [\text{Given } v_2 = 4v_1]$$

$$\beta_2 = 4\beta_1$$

If speed of electrons is made 4 times, then central bright fringe width become 4 times.

48. (*b*) The equivalent resistance of n resistors connected in parallel is given as

$$\frac{1}{R_{eq}} = \frac{1}{R_1} + \frac{1}{R_2} + \frac{1}{R_3} + \text{........}$$

$$\frac{1}{R_{eq}} = \frac{1}{r} + \frac{1}{r} + \frac{1}{r} + \ldots$$

$$\frac{1}{R_{eq}} = \frac{n}{r} \Rightarrow R_{eq} = \frac{r}{n}$$

The given circuit diagram may be redrawn as

$r/2$ $\quad E \quad$ r/n

According to maximum power transfer theorem, the power consumed by all resistors of resistance r will be largest if the equivalent of all resistors $\left(i.e.\frac{r}{n}\right)$ is equal to $\frac{r}{2}$.

$$\frac{r}{2} = \frac{r}{n} \Rightarrow n = 2$$

49. (*c*) Angle of deviation in a prism is given by

$$\delta = i + e - A \quad \text{...(i)}$$

where, i = angle of incidence,

e = angle of emergence

and $\quad A$ = angle of prism.

For minimum deviation, $i = e$

So, minimum deviation from Eq. (i) can be written as

$$\delta_m = 2i - A \quad \text{...(ii)}$$

From the graph, it is clear that minimum deviation is 60° and corresponding angle of incidence is $i = 60°$

$\therefore$ From Eq. (ii),

$$60° = 2 \times 60° - A$$

or $60° = 120° - A$

or $A = 120° - 60°$

$$A = 60°$$

The refractive index of the prism is given by

$$\mu = \frac{\sin\left(\frac{A+\delta_m}{2}\right)}{\sin\frac{A}{2}}$$

Putting the values of A and δ_m in above expression, we get

$$\mu = \frac{\sin\left(\frac{60°+60°}{2}\right)}{\sin\left(\frac{60°}{2}\right)} = \frac{\sin 60°}{\sin 30°} = \frac{\sqrt{3}/2}{1/2}$$

$$\mu = \sqrt{3}$$

Thus, refractive index of the given graph of the prism is $\sqrt{3}$. So, statement II is incorrect.

And for deviation, $\delta_1 = 65°$, we get from Eq. (i)

$$\delta_1 = i_1 + e - A$$

Substituting the values, we get

$$65° = i_1 + 70° - 60°$$

$$\Rightarrow \quad i_1 = 55°$$

Thus, statement III is correct.

50. (*b*) $^{232}_{90}\text{Th} \xrightarrow{6\alpha,\ 4\beta} {}^{208}_{82}\text{Pb}$

$$^{237}_{93}\text{Np} \xrightarrow{8\alpha,\ 5\beta} {}^{209}_{83}\text{Bi}$$

$$^{238}_{92}\text{U} \xrightarrow{8\alpha,\ 6\beta} {}^{206}_{82}\text{Pb}$$

$$^{227}_{89}\text{Ac} \xrightarrow{7\alpha,\ 4\beta} {}^{207}_{82}\text{Pb}$$

Knockout 8

1. (*a*)

30° 30° 30° I_0 P_1 P_2 P_3 P_4 $\theta_{14} = 90°$

Intensity after polaroid P_1

$= \frac{I_0}{2}$, where I_0 = incident intensity.

Intensity after polaroid P_2

$$= \frac{I_0}{2} \times \cos^2 30° \text{ (Malus' law)}$$

$$= \frac{I_0}{2}\left(\frac{\sqrt{3}}{2}\right)^2 = \frac{3}{8} I_0$$

Intensity after polaroid P_3

$$= \frac{3}{8} I_0 \times \cos^2 30° = \frac{9}{32} I_0$$

Intensity after polaroid P_4

$$= \frac{9}{32} I_0 \times \cos^2 30° = \frac{27}{128} I_0$$

2. (*a*) According to question,

$$T \propto p^{-5/6} d^{1/2} E^{\gamma}$$

Dimensional formula of LHS = Dimensional formula of RHS

$$[T] = [p^{-5/6}][d^{1/2}][E^{\gamma}] \quad \text{...(i)}$$

Putting dimensions of all quantities in Eq. (i), we get

$$[M^0L^0T^1] = [M^1L^{-1}T^{-2}]^{-5/6} [M^1L^{-3}]^{1/2} [M^1L^2T^{-2}]^{\gamma}$$

$$[M^0L^0T^1] = [M^{-\frac{5}{6}+\frac{1}{2}+\gamma} L^{\frac{5}{6}-\frac{3}{2}+2\gamma} T^{\frac{5}{3}-2\gamma}]$$

On comparing both sides, we get

$$-\frac{5}{6} + \frac{1}{2} + \gamma = 0 \text{ or } \gamma = \frac{5}{6} - \frac{1}{2} = \frac{1}{3}$$

3. (*a*) On increasing the temperature, inter-molecular spacing increases and arrangement can be treated as photographic enlargement. Hence, all parameters will increase with increase in temperature.

4. (*c*) Following Lenz's law, as current increases in coil *P*, an anti-clockwise current flows in *Q*.

5. (*d*) The potential at *P* terminal is higher that of *N* terminal for D_1 and D_2 diodes connected in circuit. Both diodes are in forward bias, similarly diode D_3 is in reverse bias as its *P* terminal has lower potential than *N* terminal. The diodes D_1 and D_2 can be replaced by short-circuit, where D_3 is replaced by an open circuit.

5 kΩ Short-circuit 2 kΩ I_0 Open circuit Short-circuit 1 kΩ 2 kΩ 5 V 10 V

Using the KVL in loop along the direction shown,

$$5 - 2 \times 10^3 I_0 - 1 \times 10^3 I_0 = 0$$

$$3 \times 10^3 I_0 = 5$$

$$\Rightarrow \quad I_0 = 1.66 \times 10^{-3} \text{ A} = 1.66 \text{ mA}$$

6. (*a*) As we know that,

$$\text{Horizontal range} = \frac{2u^2 \sin\theta \cos\theta}{g}$$

where, *u* is projection speed and θ is angle of projection.

$$\text{Time of flight, } T = \frac{2u\sin\theta}{g}$$

$$\text{Given that, } R = \frac{10\sqrt{3}}{2} T^2$$

Putting the values of *R* and *T*, we get

$$\frac{2u^2 \sin\theta\cos\theta}{g} = \frac{10\sqrt{3}}{2}\left(\frac{2u\sin\theta}{g}\right)^2$$

we get $\cot\theta = \sqrt{3}$

$$\Rightarrow \quad \theta = 30°$$

7. (*d*) The moment of inertia of the wheel about its axis, $I_1 = mr^2$

The moment of inertia of every spoke,

$$I_2 = \frac{mr^2}{3}$$

[considering as a rod and axis is passing through one end]

So, total moment of inertia of wheel about its axis (i.e. passing through centre and perpendicular to its plane),

$$I_C = I_1 + 6I_2 = mr^2 + 6 \times \frac{1}{3} mr^2$$

$$I_C = 3mr^2 \quad [\because \text{Number of spokes} = 6]$$

If moment of inertia of wheel passing through point *P* and perpendicular to the plane is I_P, then using parallel axes theorem, we can write

$$I = I_{CM} + Md^2$$

$$M = 6m + m = 7m, \ d = r$$

$$I_P = I_C + (7m)r^2 = 3mr^2 + 7mr^2$$

$$I_P = 10mr^2$$

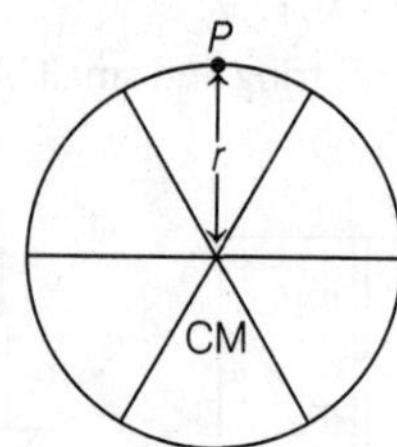

8. (*c*) Dimensions of $\frac{a}{V^2}$ = Dimensions of pressure

$\Rightarrow$ Dimensions of $a = [pV^2]$

$$= [ML^{-1}T^{-2}][L^3]^2$$

$$= [ML^5T^{-2}]$$

Dimensions of $b=[V]=L^3$

Dimensions of $ab=[ML^8T^{-2}]$

9. *(a)* Given that, $\varepsilon=2\text{ V}, r=1\ \Omega, I=1\text{ A}$

Let external resistance be R.

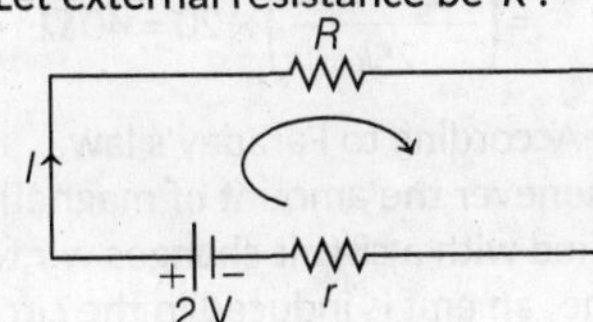

we have, $I=\dfrac{2}{R+r}$ or $1=\dfrac{2}{R+1}$

or $R+1=2 \Rightarrow R=1\Omega$

Now, two identical batteries are connected, then circuit

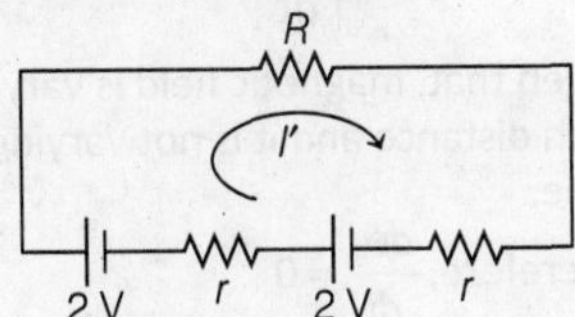

Let I' = current, then

or $I'=\dfrac{4}{(2r+R)}$

Putting the value of R and r, we get

$$I'=\frac{4}{2\times1+1}=\frac{4}{2+1}=\frac{4}{3}$$

$$I'=1.33\text{ A}$$

10. (c) $A\rightarrow S, B\rightarrow R, C\rightarrow Q, D\rightarrow P$

Energy = KE + PE $\propto \dfrac{1}{r}$

Angular momentum $L\propto\sqrt{r}$

Linear momentum $p\propto\dfrac{1}{\sqrt{r}}$

Time period $T\propto r^{3/2}$

11. (c) Total capacitance, $C=C_1+C_2$

$$=4\pi\varepsilon_0R_1+4\pi\varepsilon_0R_2$$
$$=4\pi\varepsilon_0(R_1+R_2)$$

12. *(d)* $x=t^3-6t^2+9t$

Velocity, $v=3t^2-12t+9$

or $=3(t-1)(t-3)$

So, velocity changes sign at $t=1$ and $t=3$ s

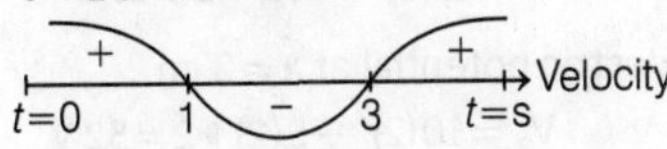

Hence, particle moves are

t=0 t=1 s t=5 s x t=2 s

Position at $t=0$, $x=0$ m

Position at $t=1$ s, $x=4$ m

Position at $t=3$ s, $x=0$ m

Position at $t=5$ s, $x=20$ m

so, distance of particle at $t=5$ s is

$$d=4+4+20=28\text{ m}$$

Displacement of particle at $t=5$ s is $x=20$ m.

$$\text{Ratio}=\frac{d}{x}=\frac{28}{20}=\frac{7}{5}$$

13. *(d)* $\dfrac{kx_1}{kx_2}=\dfrac{F_1}{F_2}=\left(\dfrac{r_2}{r_1}\right)^2$

$$\Rightarrow \frac{x_1}{x_2}=\left(\frac{800+6400}{6400}\right)^2$$

$$\Rightarrow x_2=\frac{64}{81}x_1=\frac{64}{81}=0.79\text{ cm}$$

14. *(b)* Kinetic energy of emitted photoelectron is

$$\frac{1}{2}mv^2=\frac{hc}{\lambda}$$

As work function is negligible

or $\dfrac{p^2}{2m}=\dfrac{hc}{\lambda}$ or $p=\sqrt{\dfrac{2mhc}{\lambda}}$

∴ de-Broglie wavelength associated to photoelectron,

$$\lambda_0=\frac{h}{p}=\frac{h}{\sqrt{\dfrac{2mhc}{\lambda}}}=\sqrt{\frac{h\lambda}{2mc}}$$

or $\lambda=\lambda_0^2\left(\dfrac{2mc}{h}\right)$

15. *(b)* Change in momentum of wire = – Change in momentum of bead = $2mv$

Time taken by bead to turn

$$=\frac{\pi(d/2)}{v}=\frac{\pi d}{2v}$$

Force = Rate of momentum change

$$=\frac{4mv^2}{\pi d}$$

16. *(d)* From the given figure, A to B process,

$$T\propto p$$

or $p\propto T$

⇒ Volume is constant and process is isochoric and in isochoric process, work done by gas is always zero.

$$W_{AB}=0$$

B to C is an isothermal process and work done by the gas is

$$W_{BC}=\mu RT\ln\frac{p_i}{p_f},$$

Given that, $\mu=4, T_{BC}=2T_0, p_i=2p_0$ and $p_f=8p_0$

$$\therefore \quad W_{BC}=4R(2T_0)\ln\frac{2p_0}{8p_0}$$

$$=8RT_0\ln\left(\frac{1}{4}\right)=8RT_0\ln(2)^{-2}$$

$$=-16RT_0\ln2$$

∴ Total work done for the process ABC,

$$W_{ABC}=W_{AB}+W_{BC}$$
$$=-16RT_0\ln2$$

17. *(a)* Now, kinetic energy,

$$K=\frac{1}{2}k(A^2-y^2)$$

Total energy, $E=\dfrac{1}{2}kA^2$

Thus, ratio, $\dfrac{K}{E}=\dfrac{A^2-y^2}{A^2}=1-\left(\dfrac{y}{A}\right)^2$

$$=1-\left(\frac{\sqrt{3}A/2}{A}\right)^2=1-\frac{3}{4}$$

$$=\frac{1}{4}$$

18. *(a)* Both A and R are true and R is the correct explanation of A.

Electric potential due to electric dipole,

$$V=\frac{1}{4\pi\varepsilon_0}\cdot\frac{p\cos\theta}{r^2}$$

i.e. $V\propto\dfrac{1}{r^2}$

At equatorial position,

$$\theta=90^\circ \Rightarrow \cos90^\circ=0$$

∴ $V=0$

19. *(d)* $\mathbf{L}=m(\mathbf{r}\times\mathbf{v})$

$$=m(H\hat{j})\times(u\cos\theta\hat{i})$$
$$=-mHu\cos\theta\hat{k}$$
$$=-\frac{mR\tan\theta}{4}\cdot u\cos\theta\hat{k}$$
$$=-\frac{muR}{4}\cdot\sin\theta\hat{k}$$

20. (c) A high Q factor implies a small bandwidth $(2\Delta w)$, so resonance is much sharper.

Therefore, for sharp resonance, the value of quality factor must be high.

Hence, statement I is incorrect.

21. *(d)* At $t=4.5$ s, wave is reflected from a rigid end, so a crest is reflected as a trough.

22. *(a)* $W_{CA}=p_B\Delta V=nR\Delta T=-nRT_0$

$$W_{BC}=2nRT_0\ln2$$

$$\Delta Q_{AB}=nC_V\Delta T=\frac{n\gamma RT_0}{\gamma-1}$$

$$\text{Cycle efficiency}=\frac{2\ln2-1}{\left[\dfrac{\gamma}{(\gamma-1)}\right]}$$

23. (*a*) The significant figures in 12.0 is 3 and in 0.038 is 3.

The addition of these two numbers with correct significant figures will be 12.0 i.e. 3 significant figures instead of 12.038. Thus, statement I is incorrect.

Also, for a physical quantity, the product of numerical value (n) and its unit (u) is always constant.

i.e. $n \times u =$ constant

or $\quad n \propto \frac{1}{u}$

Thus, given statement II is incorrect.

24. (*c*) Initially, charge $= Q$

where, $C =$ capacitance $= \frac{\varepsilon_0 A}{d}$

Energy density, $u = \frac{U}{V}$

Energy, $U = \frac{Q^2}{2C}$

Finally, charge remains same, so $Q' = Q$.

$$C' = \frac{\varepsilon_0 A}{2d} = \frac{C}{2}$$

Energy, $U' = \frac{q'^2}{2C'} = \frac{Q^2}{2 \times \frac{C}{2}}$

or $\quad U' = \frac{Q^2}{C} = 2U$

Volume, $V' = A \times 2d = 2V$

Again, new energy density,

$$u' = \frac{U'}{V'} = \frac{2U}{2V} = \frac{U}{V} = u$$

Hence, energy density remains same.

25. (*a*) $I_{max} = 4I_0$

Phase difference between two points seperated by a distance equal to one quarter of the distance between two sucessive fringes is $\Delta\phi = \frac{1}{4} \times 2\pi = \frac{\pi}{2}$

$\therefore \quad I = 4I_0 \cos^2\left(\frac{\pi/2}{2}\right) = 2I_0$

Hence, ratio $= \frac{4I_0}{2I_0} = 2$

26. (*b*) Let the resistance of potentiometer wire be R_p and at zero deflection, the potential gradient x is given as

$$x = \frac{\text{Potential across the potentiometer wire}}{\text{Length of potentiometer wire}}$$

$$= \frac{V_{PQ}}{L} \quad \text{...(i)}$$

At zero deflection, current,

$$I = \frac{\varepsilon_1}{r_1 + R_h + R_{pd}}$$

and $\quad x = I \cdot \rho = \frac{\varepsilon_1}{r_1 + R_h + R_{pd}} \cdot \rho$

where, ρ is resistance per unit length of potentiometer

$$\varepsilon_2 = xl \quad \text{...(ii)}$$

where l is balance length. If ε_1 is increased, then x will also increase and from Eq. (ii) l decreases as ε_2 remain same.

27. (*a*) The kinetic energy of an ideal gas molecules at T temperature is given as,

$E_K = \frac{3}{2} k_B T$, where k_B is Boltzmann's constant.

If $T = 0\text{K}$, then $E_K = \frac{3}{2} k_B \times 0$

$$E_K = 0$$

The potential energy of gas molecules will depend on its configuration. It is completely independent of temperature. The vibrational energy are significant at higher temperature. At very low temperatures, the value of vibrational kinetic energy is almost zero and at 0 K temperature, it is equal to zero.

28. (*b*) Speed of propagation of EM wave,

$$v = \frac{\omega}{k} = \frac{18 \times 10^8}{8} = 2.25 \times 10^8 \text{ m/s}$$

The refractive index of medium is given as

$$\mu = \frac{\text{Speed of EM wave in vacuum}}{\text{Speed of EM wave in medium}}$$

$$= \frac{3 \times 10^8}{2.25 \times 10^8} = \frac{4}{3}$$

The refractive index of water is $\frac{4}{3}$.

29. (*a*) In case of hydrogen molecule, there is no unpaired electron. Thus the net magnetic moment is zero although each atom of hydrogen has a permanent magnetic moment.

30. (*c*) Let the initial full scale deflection in galvanometer is I_g and final full scale deflection is I'_g, we can write

$$I_g = 75\,k \text{ and } I_g' = 25\,k$$

where, k is the figure of merit of galvanometer.

According to the question, the circuit arrangement can be shown as

I_g G I_g $(I_g - I_g')$ S

where, S is the resistance connected in parallel.

In parallel voltage across,

G = Voltage across S

$$I_g' G = (I_g - I_g') S \text{ or } G = \frac{(I_g - I_g')}{I_g'} S$$

$$= \left(\frac{75k - 25k}{25k}\right) \times 20 = 40\,\Omega$$

31. (*d*) According to Faraday's law, whenever the amount of magnetic flux linked with a circuit changes w.r.t. time, an emf is induced in the circuit.

The magnitude of the induced emf in a circuit is equal to the time rate of change of magnetic flux through the circuit.

$$\text{Induced emf} = \left|\frac{d\phi_B}{dt}\right| \quad \text{...(i)}$$

Given that, magnetic field is varying with distance and it is not varying w.r.t. time.

Therefore, $\frac{d\phi_B}{dt} = 0$

From Eq. (i), $e = 0$

No emf is induced in triangular loop.

32. (*d*) $I = \frac{V}{R} = \frac{6}{6} = 1\text{ A}$

Here, $v_d = \frac{I}{neA}$

$$= \frac{1}{10^{29} \times 1.6 \times 10^{-19} \times 10^{-6}} = \frac{10^{-4}}{1.6} \frac{\text{m}}{\text{s}}$$

Energy of electrons,

$$\text{KE} = \frac{1}{2} m v_d^2 \times n \times Al$$

$$= \frac{1}{2} \times 9.1 \times 10^{-31} \times \frac{10^{-8}}{2.56} \times 10^{29} \times 10^{-6} \times 10^{-1}$$

$$= 2 \times 10^{-17}\text{ J}$$

Heat is lost at rate $P = I^2 R = 1^2 \times 6$

$\therefore$ All energies are lost in time,

$$t = \frac{2 \times 10^{-17}}{6} \approx 10^{-17}\text{ s}$$

33. (*c*) Given that, electric potential,

$$V = 10x^2 + 5x + 2\text{ V}$$

Electric potential at $x = 1$ m,

$$V_1 = 10(1)^2 + 5(1) + 2 = 17\text{ V}$$

Electric potential at $x = 2$ m,

$$V_2 = 10(2)^2 + 5(2) + 2 = 52\text{ V}$$

The electrostatic potential energy of a charge q in a electric field is given as $U = qV$, where V is the electric potential at that point.

Difference, $\Delta U = U_2 - U_1$

$$= qV_2 - qV_1$$

$$= q(V_2 - V_1)$$

$$= 2 \times 10^{-6} \times (52 - 17)$$
$$= 70 \times 10^{-6}\ \text{J}$$
$$\Rightarrow \quad \Delta U = 70\ \mu\text{J}$$

34. (*a*) $\lambda = \dfrac{hc}{eV} \Rightarrow \dfrac{\lambda_1}{\lambda_2} = \dfrac{V_2}{V_1} \Rightarrow$ If $\lambda_2 = \dfrac{3}{4}\lambda_1$

Then, $V_2 = \dfrac{4}{3} V_1$

$\therefore$ An increase of $\dfrac{100}{3}\% \approx 34\%$

35. (*c*) $KE_{max} = eV_0 = (1.6 \times 10^{-19} \times 1.5)$ J
$$= 2.4 \times 10^{-19}\ \text{J}$$

36. (*a*) The photoelectric current is directly proportional to the intensity of light incident on the surface of metal.

37. (*c*) In a forward biased *p-n* junction, electrons moves from conduction to valence band under an electric impulse.

38. (*d*) Total decay rate of a sample is
$$R = -\frac{dN}{dt}$$

As, rate of change of N is $\dfrac{dN}{dt} = -\lambda N$
$$\Rightarrow \quad R = \lambda N$$

So, in order to have the same decay rate for both the samples A and B, we have
$$\lambda_A N_A = \lambda_B N_B$$
$$\frac{\lambda_A}{\lambda_B} = \frac{N_B}{N_A}$$

39. (*a*) Given that, kinetic energy, $K = 20t^2$
$$\therefore \quad K = \frac{1}{2}mv^2 \Rightarrow \frac{1}{2}mv^2 = 20t^2$$

or $\quad v^2 = \dfrac{40}{m}t^2$ or $v = \sqrt{\dfrac{40}{m}}\, t$

Acceleration, $a = \dfrac{dv}{dt} = \dfrac{d}{dt}\left(\sqrt{\dfrac{40}{m}}\, t\right)$
$$a = \sqrt{\frac{40}{m}}$$

Force, $F = ma = m\sqrt{\dfrac{40}{m}}$, $F = \sqrt{40m}$

which is constant.

40. (*a*) When two masses undergo a elastic collision with one of them at rest, then after the collision, they will move at right angles to each other.

i.e. $\quad \theta_1 + \theta_2 = 90°$

41. (*c*) Both the fields are anti-parallel to each other, so angle between them $\theta = 180°$.
$$\mathbf{E}_1 \times \mathbf{E}_2 = \mathbf{E}_1\mathbf{E}_2 \sin 180°$$
$$\mathbf{E}_1 \times \mathbf{E}_2 = 0$$
and $\quad |\mathbf{E}_1 \times \mathbf{E}_2| = 0$

42. (c) Induced emf $= \displaystyle\int_{2l}^{3l} \omega x B \cdot dx$

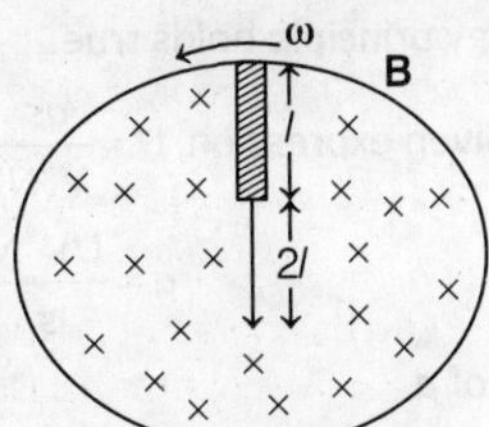

$$= \frac{B\omega}{2}[(3l)^2 - (2l)^2] = \frac{5}{2}Bl^2\omega$$

43. (*b*) A $\rightarrow$ Young's modulus for elastic body,
$$Y = \frac{\text{Stress}}{\text{Strain}}$$

For perfectly elastic body, strain is zero
$$\therefore \quad Y = \frac{\text{Stress}}{0} = \infty$$

B $\rightarrow$ For most materials, modulus of rigidity G is less than its Young's modulus Y and it is equal to 1/3 times of Young's modulus.

C $\rightarrow$ Bulk modulus *B* is the ratio of hydraulic stress to the corresponding hydraulic strain.

$\therefore \quad B = \dfrac{-\Delta p}{\left(\dfrac{\Delta V}{V}\right)}$, where Δp is change in pressure and ΔV is change in volume.

The value of ΔV is maximum for gas and minimum for solids. Bulk modulus for solids is much larger than for liquids.

D $\rightarrow$ Bulk modulus of liquids is greater than the bulk modulus for gases (air).

Thus, correct match code is

A $\rightarrow$ S, B $\rightarrow$ R, C $\rightarrow$ P, D $\rightarrow$ Q.

44. (*d*) As horizontal distance is constant,
$$v\cos 30° = u\cos 60°$$
$$\Rightarrow \quad v = 10 \times \frac{1}{2} \times \frac{2}{\sqrt{3}} = \frac{10}{\sqrt{3}}\ \frac{\text{m}}{\text{s}}$$

Now, perpendicular velocity components of *A* and *B* are
$$(v_\perp)_A = u\sin 60° = 10 \times \frac{\sqrt{3}}{2} = 5\sqrt{3}\ \text{ms}^{-1}$$
and $(v_\perp)_B = v\sin 30°$
$$= \frac{10}{\sqrt{3}} \times \frac{1}{2} = \frac{5}{\sqrt{3}}\ \text{ms}^{-1}$$

v_{relative} (*B* w.r.t. *A*) $= v_{BA}$
$$= v_B - v_A = \frac{5}{\sqrt{3}} - 5\sqrt{3}$$
$$= \frac{-10}{\sqrt{3}}\ \text{ms}^{-1}$$

So, $\omega_{BA} = \dfrac{v_{BA}}{d} = \dfrac{-10/\sqrt{3}}{2}$
$$= \frac{-5}{\sqrt{3}}\ \frac{\text{rad}}{\text{s}}$$
$$\therefore \quad |\omega_{BA}| = \frac{5}{\sqrt{3}}\ \text{rad/s}$$

45. (*a*) A ball which is spinning drags the fluid along with it. The given figure shows the streamlines of fluid and spinning at the same line.

The ball is moving forward and relative to it, the fluid is moving backwards. Therefore, the velocity of the fluid above to the ball is larger and below is smaller. This difference in the velocity of fluid result in pressure difference between the lower and upper faces and there is a net upward force on the ball.

46. (*d*) The potential energy of dipole at position θ is given as
$$U = -\mathbf{M} \cdot \mathbf{B} \quad \text{or} \quad -MB\cos\theta$$

and work done in rotating dipole from position θ_1 to θ_2 is
$$W = \Delta U = U_2 - U_1$$
$$= -MB\cos\theta_2 - (-MB\cos\theta_1)$$
$$= MB\cos\theta_1 - MB\cos\theta_2$$

Given that,
$$\theta_1 = 0°, \theta_2 = \theta$$
$$W = MB[\cos 0° - \cos\theta]$$
$$= MB[1 - \cos\theta]$$
$$\because \quad 1 - \cos 2\theta = 2\sin^2\theta$$
$$\therefore \quad = MB[2\sin^2\theta/2]$$
$$= 2MB\sin^2(\theta/2)$$

47. (*a*) I. Energy released per nucleon in fission is approximately 0.85 MeV, whereas energy released per nucleon in fusion is 6 MeV, which is much larger.

II. A photon of energy more than 1.02 MeV, when interact with a nucleus produces pair of electron (e^-) and positron (e^+). The energy equivalent to rest mass of e^- (or e^+) = 0.51 MeV.

The energy equivalent to rest mass of pair $(e^{-1} + e^+) = 1.02$ MeV

For pair production, energy of photon $\geq$ 1.02 MeV and if energy of γ-photon is less than 1.02 MeV and if energy γ-photon is less 1.02 MeV, then pair will not produce.

III. When electron and positron combined, they annihilate to each other and only energy is released in the form of two γ-photons. If the energy of electron and positron are negligible, then energy of each γ-photon is 0.51 MeV.

Thus among given statements, only I is correct.

48. (*b*) A is true but R is false.

$v_P = 0$ but P has a centeripetal acceleration as disc is rotating. Linear acceleration with respect to ground is zero.

49. (*b*) Using, $\frac{E_0}{B_0} = v = \frac{\omega}{k}$

$\therefore \quad E_0 = \frac{\omega}{k} \times B_0$

$= \frac{3 \times 10^{11} \pi}{5000 \pi} \times 8 \times 10^{-6}$

$= 480$ N/C

So, correct option is (b).

50. (*c*) Velocity components normal to mirror and parallel to mirror are shown in figure.

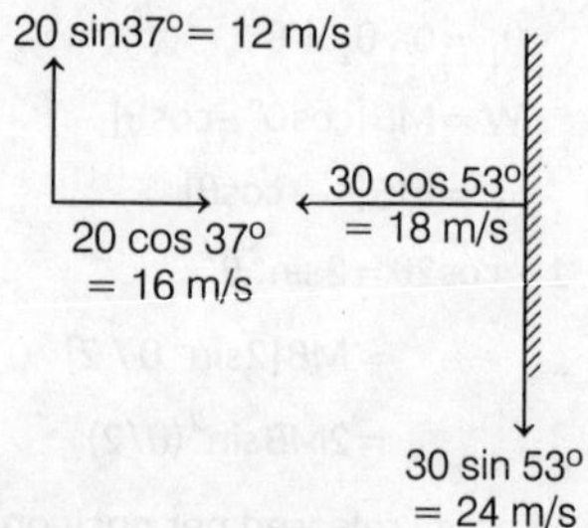

Now, horizontal velocity of image with respect to ground

$= 16 + (2 \times 18) = 52$ m/s

Vertical velocity of image = 12 m/s

$v_{image} = (-52\hat{i} + 12\hat{j})$ m/s

Knockout 9

1. (*c*) From the work-energy theorem,

$W_{conservative} + W_{non\text{-}conservative} = \Delta KE$

$-\Delta U + W_{non\text{-}conservative} = \Delta KE$

$W_{non\text{-}conservative} = \Delta KE + \Delta U$

or $\quad W_{non\text{-}conservative} = \Delta ME$

If total work done by all non-conservative forces is zero,

i.e. $W_{non\text{-}conservative} = 0$

then, $\quad \Delta ME = 0$

Mechanical energy of the system remains constant, then mechanical energy principle holds true.

2. (*b*) Given expression, $U = \frac{as^7}{V^4N^2}$

or $\quad a = \frac{UV^4N^2}{s^7}$

Unit of a

$= \frac{\text{Unit of } U \times (\text{Unit of } V)^4 \times (\text{Unit of } N)^2}{(\text{Unit of } s)^7}$

$= \frac{J \times (m^3)^4 \times (\text{Unit of } N)^2}{(JK^{-1})^7}$

Unit of $a = J^{-6} m^{12} K^7$

$= (\text{kg-m}^2 s^{-2})^{-6} m^{12} K^7$

Unit of $a = \text{kg}^{-6} m^0 s^{12} K^7$

3. (*c*) During propagation of a plane progressive mechanical wave, all the particles are vibrating with different phases. Rest statements are incorrect.

4. (*d*) Number for the colour code of carbon resistor is given as

Yellow – 4

Violet – 7

Multiplier $= 10^1$; Brown – 1

Tolerence = 10% ; Silver

$\because R = 470 + 10\% = 47 \times 10^1 + 10\%$

= YVBS

5. (*c*) As given, time of flight, $T = 4$ s

$g = 10 \text{ m/s}^2$

From the relation, $8H = gT^2$

or $\quad H = \frac{gT^2}{8}$

$= \frac{10 \times (4)^2}{8}$

$= 20$ m

Now, from the relation, $4H = R\tan\theta$

or $\quad R = \frac{4H}{\tan\theta}$

For maximum horizontal range, projection angle θ should be 45°.

$\therefore \quad R = \frac{4H}{\tan 45^\circ}$

$= \frac{4 \times 20}{1}$

$= 80$ m

6. (*b*) A non-inertial frame has a non-zero acceleration, so equation in a non-inertial frame is,

$F_{applied} + F_{pseudo} = ma$

Hence, Newton's laws are not valid.

7. (*c*) Let a be the uniform acceleration from 1st equation of motion, $v = u + at$

$v_0 = 0 + at_0$

or $\quad a = \frac{v_0}{t_0}$

Displacement after time t_0, using 2nd equation of motion,

$s = ut + \frac{1}{2}at^2$

$= \frac{1}{2}\left(\frac{v_0}{t_0}\right)t_0^2 \quad (\because u = 0)$

Displacement travelled in initial $(t_0 - 3)$ s,

$s' = \frac{1}{2}\left(\frac{v_0}{t_0}\right)(t_0 - 3)^2$

$\therefore$ Displacement of the body in last three seconds,

$\Delta s = s - s'$

$= \frac{1}{2}\left(\frac{v_0}{t_0}\right)t_0^2 - \frac{1}{2}\left(\frac{v_0}{t_0}\right)(t_0 - 3)^2$

$= \frac{1}{2}\left(\frac{v_0}{t_0}\right)[t_0^2 - (t_0 - 3)^2]$

$= \frac{1}{2}\left(\frac{v_0}{t_0}\right)(t_0 + t_0 - 3)(t_0 - t_0 + 3)$

$= 3v_0\left(1 - \frac{3}{2t_0}\right)$

8. (*d*) Let the potential gradient of potentiometer be K.

In case (i), balance length, $l_1 = 45$ cm

$E_1 = xl_1$

$2.25 = x \times 45 \text{ cm} \quad$ ... (i)

In case (ii), balance length,

$l_2 = 99$ cm

$E_2 = x \times 99 \text{ cm} \quad$ ... (ii)

Dividing Eq. (i) by Eq. (ii), we get

$\frac{2.25}{E_2} = \frac{45}{99}$

$E_2 = 4.95$ V

9. (*c*) Given that, $V_{rms} = 200$ V

$I_{rms} = 5$ A

$R = 40\,\Omega$

Voltage across resistor, $V_R = IR$

$= 5 \times 40$

$= 200$ V

It is clear that, voltage across resistor is equal to input voltage which is possible only in condition of resonance and in resonance, the current is always in the same phase of voltage. So, phase difference is 0 and power factor is unity.

10. (*d*) ME at striking point = ME at distance *r* from the centre

$$-\frac{GMm}{R}+\frac{1}{2}mv^2=-\frac{GMm}{r}+0$$

or $$\frac{v^2}{2}=\frac{GM}{R}-\frac{GM}{r}$$

$$\frac{v^2}{2}=GM\left(\frac{1}{R}-\frac{1}{r}\right)$$

$$\frac{v^2}{2}=gR^2\left(\frac{r-R}{Rr}\right)\left(\because g=\frac{GM}{R^2}\right)$$

$$v=\sqrt{\frac{2gR(r-R)}{r}}$$

11. (*b*) Let the length and area of cross-section of rods be *l* and A, respectively.

Thermal resistance of rod-A, $R_A=\frac{l}{K_A A}$

Thermal resistance of rod-B, $R_B=\frac{l}{K_B A}$

Thermal resistance of rod-C, $R_C=\frac{l}{K_C A}$

Like electrical equivalent circuit, thermal resistance in series are added. In question, rods are joined end to end i.e. arrangement in series,

$$R_s=R_A+R_B+R_C$$

$$\frac{3l}{K_{eff}A}=\frac{l}{K_A A}+\frac{l}{K_B A}+\frac{l}{K_C A}$$

or $$\frac{3}{K_{eff}}=\frac{1}{K_A}+\frac{1}{K_B}+\frac{1}{K_C}$$

Here, $K_A=2K_B$ and $K_C=\frac{K_B}{2}$

$$\therefore \frac{3}{K_{eff}}=\frac{1}{2K_B}+\frac{1}{K_B}+\frac{2}{K_B}$$

$$=\frac{1+2+4}{2K_B}$$

$$=\frac{7}{2K_B}$$

or $$K_{eff}=\frac{6}{7}K_B$$

12. (*b*) Coefficient of performance of a refrigerator is

$$\beta=\frac{1-\eta}{\eta}=\frac{1-\frac{1}{10}}{\frac{1}{10}}=\frac{\frac{9}{10}}{\frac{1}{10}}=9$$

Also, $$\beta=\frac{Q_L}{W}$$

or $$Q_L=\beta W=9\times 20$$

$$=180\text{ J}$$

13. (*c*) From the given figure

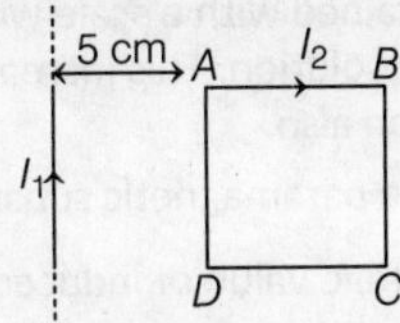

Force experienced by *AB* and *CD* are equal and opposite, so the contribution in the net force experienced by loop is only due to *AD* and *BC*.

Magnetic field at the location of *AD* is

$$B_1=\frac{\mu_0 I_1}{2\pi d}$$

Here, $I_1=2\text{A}$, $d=5$ cm or 5×10^{-2}m

$$B_1=\frac{4\pi\times10^{-7}\times2}{2\pi\times5\times10^{-2}}$$

$$=8\times10^{-6}\text{ T}$$

Magnetic force experienced by *AD* is

$$F_1=I_1B_1l$$

or $$F_1=5\times8\times10^{-6}\times0.15$$

$$=6\times10^{-6}\text{ N towards wire}$$

Magnetic field at the location of *BC* is

$$B_2=\frac{\mu_0 I_1}{2\pi d}$$

Here, $I_1=2\text{A}$, $d=20$ cm or 0.2 m

$$B_2=\frac{4\pi\times10^{-7}\times2}{2\pi\times0.2}$$

$$=2\times10^{-6}\text{ T}$$

Magnetic force experienced by *BC* is

$$F_2=I_1B_2l$$

$$=5\times2\times10^{-6}\times0.15$$

$$=1.5\times10^{-6}\text{ N (away from wire)}$$

Net force experienced by loop is

$$F=F_1-F_2$$

$$=2\times10^{-6}-1.5\times10^{-6}$$

$$=0.5\times10^{-6}$$

$$=5\times10^{-7}\text{ N}$$

(towards the wire or attractive)

14. (*a*) Efficiency of a transformer,

$$\eta=\frac{\text{Output power }(P_{out})}{\text{Input power }(P_{in})}$$

$$=\frac{V_sI_s}{V_pI_p} \quad ...\text{(i)}$$

From Eq. (i),

$$0.9=\frac{P_{out}}{10\times10^3} \quad (\because P_{in}=10\text{ kW})$$

$$\therefore P_{out}=0.9\times10\times10^3$$

$$=9000\text{ W}$$

Secondary side current,

$$I_s=\frac{\text{Output power}}{\text{Secondary side voltage}}$$

$$=\frac{9000}{100}=90\text{ A}$$

Also, primary side current,

$$I_p=\frac{\text{Input power}}{\text{Primary side voltage}}$$

$$=\frac{10\times10^3}{2000}=5\text{ A}$$

15. (*b*) Angular frequency, $\omega=2\pi f$

$$=\frac{2\pi c}{\lambda}$$

$$=\frac{2\pi\times3\times10^8}{6\times10^{-6}}$$

$$\omega=\pi\times10^{14}\text{ rad/s} \quad ...\text{(i)}$$

The maximum value of magnetic field is given as

$$B_0=\frac{E_0}{c}=\frac{24}{3\times10^8}=8\times10^{-8}\text{ T}$$

The equation for the magnetic field is

$$B_y=B_0\sin\omega\left(t-\frac{x}{c}\right)$$

$$=8\times10^{-8}\sin\pi\times10^{14}\left(t-\frac{x}{c}\right)\text{T}$$

[using Eq (i)]

16. (*a*) The rays will totally reflected, if the angle of incidence at surface *AC* is greater than the critical angle.

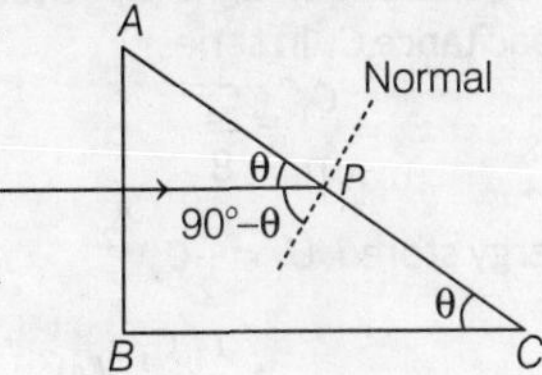

Here, (90°−θ) is the critical angle. For total internal reflection at point *P* and largest value at θ, angle of incidence should be 90°−θ. Angle of reflection is 37°C.

From Snell's law,

$$\mu_g\times\sin(90°-\theta)=\mu_L\times\sin90°$$

or $$\mu_g\times\sin(90-37°)=\mu_L\times1$$

or $$\mu_L=\mu_g\times\cos37°$$

$$=\frac{3}{2}\times\frac{4}{5}=\frac{12}{10}=1.2$$

17. (*b*) de-Broglie wavelength of particle moving with speed of *v*,

$$\lambda=\frac{h}{mv} \quad ...\text{(i)}$$

The energy of a photon of this wavelength,

$$E = \frac{hc}{\lambda} = \frac{hc}{\frac{h}{mv}} \quad \text{[from Eq. (i)]}$$

$$= mvc \quad \text{... (ii)}$$

Kinetic energy of the particle,

$$K = \frac{1}{2}mv^2 \quad \text{... (iii)}$$

On dividing Eq. (iii) by Eq. (ii), we get

$$\frac{K}{E} = \frac{\frac{1}{2}mv^2}{mvc} = \frac{v}{2c}$$

Given that, $v = 2.5 \times 10^8$ m/s,

$$c = 3 \times 10^8 \text{ m/s}$$

$$\frac{K}{E} = \frac{2.5 \times 10^8}{2 \times 3 \times 10^8} = \frac{2.5}{6} = \frac{5}{12}$$

18. (*b*) When a charged particle is projected perpendicular to a magnetic field,

(i) its path is circular in a plane perpendicular to the plane of magnetic field.

(ii) the speed and kinetic energy of the particle remains constant.

(iii) the velocity and momentum of the particle changes only in direction.

19. (*a*) Both A and R are true but R does not explain A. Magnetron valves are used to produce microwaves in an microwave oven.

20. (*d*) Equivalent of eight capacitors of capacitance C_1 in series,

$$C_s = \frac{C_1}{n} = \frac{C_1}{8}$$

Energy stored, $U_1 = \frac{1}{2}C_sV^2$

$$= \frac{1}{2}\left(\frac{C_1}{8}\right)(4)^2$$

Equivalent of five capacitors of capacitance C_2 in parallel,

$$C_p = nC_2 = 5C_2$$

Energy stored, $U_2 = \frac{1}{2}C_pV_2$

$$= \frac{1}{2}(5C_2)(1)^2 = \frac{5}{2}C_2$$

According to question, $U_1 = U_2$

$$C_1 = \frac{5}{2}C_2$$

or $\quad 2C_1 = 5C_2$

21. (*d*) Force on block = Force of friction

$\Rightarrow \quad F = ma$

or $\quad \mu mg = ma$ or $a = \mu g$

Time taken by block to come to rest,

$$t = \frac{u}{\mu g} \quad \text{[from } v = u + at\text{]}$$

22. (*b*) Larger number of significant figures are obtained with a scale which has more resolution. This increases precision also.

23. (*b*) For a paramagnetic substance, $I \propto H$

24. (*b*) Average value of induced emf,

$$\varepsilon = -\frac{N\Delta\phi}{\Delta t} = \frac{N(\phi_1 - \phi_2)}{\Delta t}$$

$$= \frac{NBA\cos\theta_1 - NBA\cos\theta_2}{\Delta t}$$

$$= \frac{NBA[\cos\theta_1 - \cos\theta_2]}{\Delta t}$$

$$= \frac{300 \times 0.3 \times 4 \times 10^{-2}[\cos 0° - \cos 90°]}{0.5}$$

$$= 7.2 \text{ V}$$

Average power induced,

$$P_{avg} = \frac{\varepsilon^2}{R}$$

$$= \frac{(7.2)^2}{120}$$

$$= 432 \text{ mW}$$

25. (*c*) Maximum load that can be supported by cable is 320 kg, so for either part, it is also 320 kg.

26. (*d*) For $Z = 2$, $n = 2$

$$r_2 = \frac{0.53n^2}{Z} = 0.53 \times \frac{(2)^2}{2}$$

$$= 1.06 \text{ Å}$$

According to Bohr's theory, only those orbitals are permitted to electrons for which circumference is integer multiple to wavelength i.e.

$2\pi r = n\lambda$ (where, λ is de-Broglie wave length)

$$\lambda = \frac{2\pi r}{n} = \frac{2 \times 3.14 \times 1.06}{2}$$

($\because n = 2$, for first excited state)

$$= 3.328 \text{ Å}$$

27. (*a*)

Using $s = r\theta$ or $r = \frac{s}{\theta}$

Here $s = 3\text{m}, \theta = 1' = \frac{1}{60} \times \frac{\pi}{180}$ rad

So, $r = \frac{3}{\left(\frac{1}{60} \times \frac{\pi}{180}\right)}$

$$= \frac{3 \times 60 \times 180}{\pi}$$

$$\approx 10 \text{ km}$$

28. (*a*) For same initial and final states ($n_1 = 2$ and $n_2 = 1$),

$$E \propto Z^2 \text{ or } \frac{hc}{\lambda} \propto Z^2$$

$$\Leftrightarrow \; hc = \lambda Z^2$$

or $\lambda Z^2 =$ constant

$$\therefore \lambda_1 Z_1^2 = \lambda_2 Z_2^2 = \lambda_3 Z_3^2 = \lambda_4 Z_4^2$$

or $\lambda_1 \times 1^2 = \lambda_2 \times 1^2 = \lambda_3 \times 2^2 = \lambda_4 \times 3^2$

29. (*a*)

A $\rightarrow$ The relation of resistivity of a metal (like copper) with temperature is $\rho_T = \rho_0[1 + \alpha(T - T_0)]$.

It implies that a graph of ρ_T plotted against T would be a straight line. At temperature much lower than 0°C, the graph, however deviates considerably from a straight line as shown.

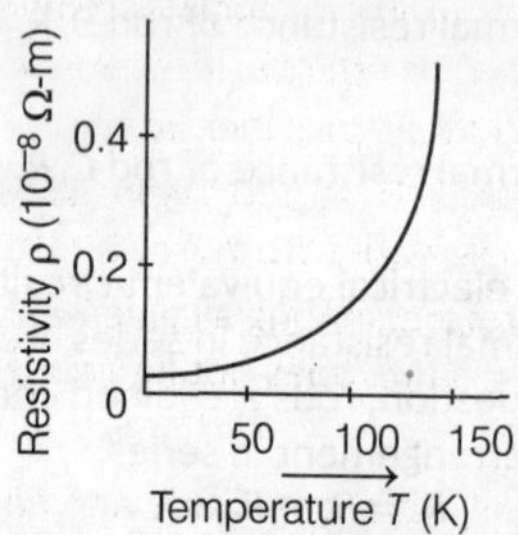

B $\rightarrow$ Some materials like nichrome, exhibit a very weak dependence of resistivity with temperature as shown

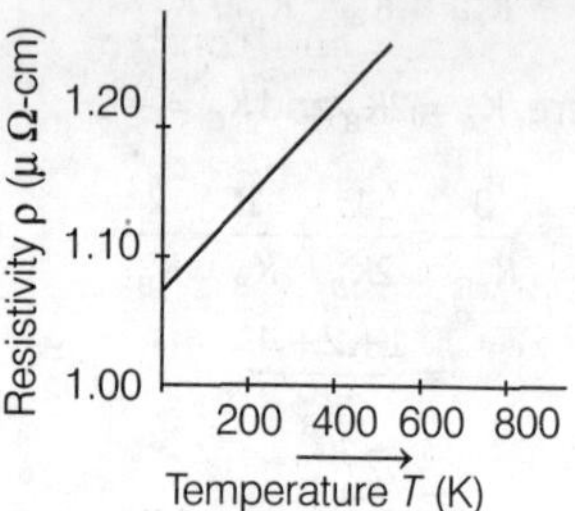

C $\rightarrow$ Unlike metals, the resistivites of semiconductors decreases with increasing temperatures.Its dependence is as shown

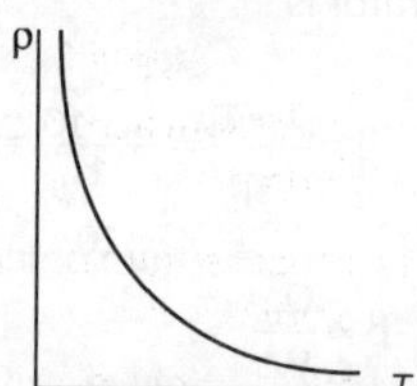

Hence, A $\rightarrow$ Q, B $\rightarrow$ R and C $\rightarrow$ P.

30. (*d*) Given that, $m_1 = 4$ kg, $u_1 = 0$ m/s, $a_1 = 1$ m/s^2, $m_2 = 4$ kg, $u_2 = 2$ m/s, $a_2 = 0$ m/s^2

Initial velocity of CM,

$$\mathbf{u}_{CM} = \frac{m_1\mathbf{u}_1 + m_2\mathbf{u}_2}{m_1 + m_2} = \frac{4\times 0 + 4\times 2}{4+4}$$

$$u_{CM} = 1 \text{ m/s}$$

Here, first we will assume that u_{CM} and a_{CM} are in same direction, then velocity of cm at $t = 2$ s

$$v_{CM} = u_{CM} + a_{CM}t = 1 + 0.5\times 2$$

$$v_{CM} = 2 \text{ m/s}$$

In second case, we will assume that $\mathbf{u}_{CM}$ and a_{CM} both are in opposite direction , then velocity to CM at $t = 2$ s

$$v_{CM} = 1 + (-0.5)\times 2$$

$$v_{CM} = 1 - 1 = 0 \text{ m/s}$$

In this problem, angle between $\mathbf{u}_{CM}$ and $\mathbf{a}_{CM}$ is not specified. So, we have to consider all possible situations.

For angle 0° to 180°, velocity of centre of mass varies from 0 m/s to 2 m/s.

Therefore, among all given options, $v_{CM} = 4$ m/s does not lie between the range.

31. (*b*) Let initial amplitude and time period be A and T, respectively and final be $A'$and T'

Given, $T' = 2T$

As, maximum velocity,

$$v_{max} = A\omega = \text{constant}$$

$$A'\omega' = A\omega \quad \text{...(i)}$$

or $A'\times\frac{2\pi}{T'} = A\times\frac{2\pi}{T}$

or $A'\times\frac{2\pi}{2T} = A\times\frac{2\pi}{T}$

or $A' = 2A$ ...(ii)

It means, amplitude becomes double.

Maximum acceleration, $a_{max} = \omega^2 A$

$$a'_{max} = \omega'^2 A' = \omega^2 2A = 2\omega^2 A = 2a_{max}$$

[using Eqs. (i) and (ii)]

It means, maximum acceleration becomes double.

32. (*c*) Angular momentum of planet remains constant,

so $mv_1 d_1 = mv_2 d_2$

or $v_2 = v_1 d_1 / d_2$

33. (*c*) We have,

$$W = pE(\cos\theta_1 - \cos\theta_2) = pE(\cos 0° - \cos 60°) = pE\left(1 - \frac{1}{2}\right) = \frac{1}{2}pE$$

Now, $W' = pE(\cos 0° - \cos 180°) = 2pE = 2(2W) = 4W$

34. (*c*) Circuit is equivalent to,

$$E_{eq} = \frac{E_1 r_2 + E_2 r_1}{r_1 + r_2} = \frac{2\times 4 + 2\times 4}{4+4} = 2\text{ V}$$

$$R_{eq} = \frac{4}{2} = 2\Omega$$

$\therefore$ Current, $I = \frac{2+2}{2} = 2$ A

Current is from A to B.

35. (*c*) Let the number of nuclei of X^{234} and X^{236} be N_{0_1} and N_{0_2}, respectively.

Given, $\frac{N_{0_1}}{N_{0_2}} = \frac{1}{4}$

Half-life of two isotopes are

$(t_{1/2})_1 = 60$ min, $(t_{1/2})_2 = 30$ min

Initial activity of isotope X^{234} i.e.

$(R_0)_2 = 4\times 10^6$ dps

As we know that, activity of radioactive substance is

$$R = \lambda N$$

and decay constant, $\lambda = \frac{0.693}{t_{1/2}}$,

where, $t_{1/2}$ = half-life

$$R = \frac{0.693}{t_{1/2}}N$$

or $\frac{(R_0)_1}{(R_0)_2} = \frac{(t_{1/2})_2}{(t_{1/2})_1}\cdot\frac{N_{0_1}}{N_{0_2}}$

$$\frac{R_0}{4\times 10^6} = \frac{30}{60}\times\frac{1}{4}$$

$$(R_0) = 0.5\times 10^6 \text{ dps}$$

Let their activities become equal after time t,

$$R_1 = R_2$$

As we know that, activity after h half-life,

$$R = R_0\left(\frac{1}{2}\right)^n$$

We have, $n_1 = \frac{t}{(t_{1/2})_1} = \frac{t}{60}$

$n_2 = \frac{t}{(t_{1/2})_2} = \frac{t}{30}$

$$\therefore\ 0.5\times 10^6\left(\frac{1}{2}\right)^{\frac{t}{60}} = 4\times 10^6\left(\frac{1}{2}\right)^{\frac{t}{30}}$$

$$\left(\frac{1}{2}\right)^{\frac{t}{30}-\frac{t}{60}} = \frac{1}{8}$$

or $\left(\frac{1}{2}\right)^{\frac{t}{60}} = \left(\frac{1}{2}\right)^3$

On comparing both sides, we get

$$\frac{t}{60} = 3$$

$$t = 180 \text{ min}$$

36. (*b*) According to question,

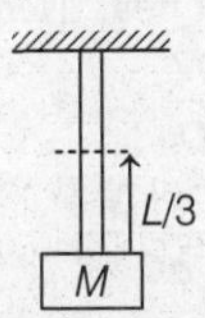

Mass of rod of length $\frac{L}{3}$,

$$m_1 = \frac{\text{Length of part of rod}}{\text{Length of rod}}\times\text{Mass of rod} = \frac{L/3}{L}\times m = \frac{m}{3}$$

The block and part of rod has total mass $(M + \frac{m}{3})$ can be treated as a single block as shown below

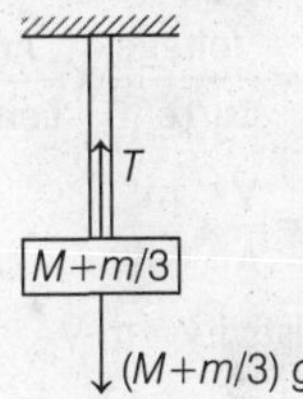

Since, block is at rest, $T = \left(M + \frac{m}{3}\right)g$

$$\therefore\ \text{Stress} = \frac{\text{Tension}}{\text{Area}} = \frac{\left(M+\frac{m}{3}\right)g}{A}$$

37. (*a*) Given that, current, $I = 5$ mA $= 5\times 10^{-3}$ A

Potential barrier, $V_T = 0.5$ V

Here, $V > V_T$, diode is in forward bias and in forward bias, it allows the current.

$$\therefore\ I = \frac{V - V_T}{R}$$

or $R = \frac{V - V_T}{I} = \frac{2 - 0.5}{5\times 10^{-3}} = \frac{1.5}{5\times 10^{-3}} = 300\,\Omega$

38. (*b*)

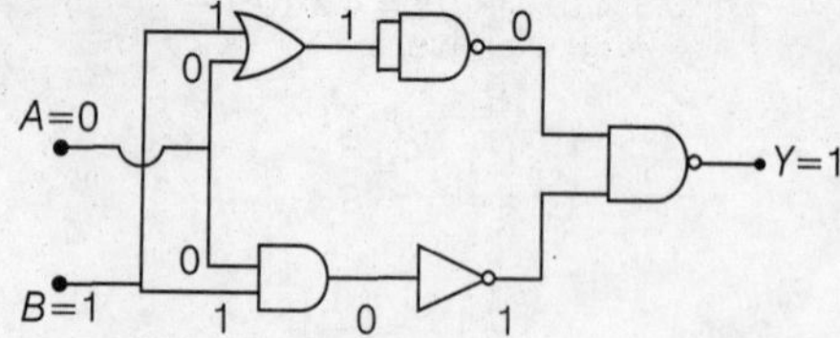

Outputs are shown above.

39. (*b*) In constant pressure process,

$$\Delta Q = nC_p\Delta T$$

and $\Delta U = nC_V\Delta T$

$\therefore$ Fraction of heat used in work done

$$= \frac{\Delta W}{\Delta Q}$$

$$= \frac{\Delta Q - \Delta U}{\Delta Q}$$

$$= 1 - \frac{C_V}{C_p} = 1 - \frac{1}{\gamma}$$

40. (*d*) Both statement I and II are correct. Energy to reach first excited state is 10.2 eV.

41. (*a*) Mobility $= \frac{\text{Drift velocity}}{\text{Electric field}}$

$$= \frac{\text{m/s}}{\text{V/m}}$$

Unit of mobility $= \text{m}^2\ \text{V}^{-1}\ \text{s}^{-1}$

Resistivity $= \frac{\text{Voltage}}{\text{Current}} \times \frac{\text{Area}}{\text{Length}}$

$$= \frac{\text{V}}{\text{A}} \times \frac{\text{m}^2}{\text{m}}$$

Unit of resistivity = m-VA^{-1}

Conductance $= \frac{1}{\text{Resistance}}$

$$= \frac{\text{Current}}{\text{Voltage}}$$

$$= \frac{\text{A}}{\text{J/C}}$$

$$= \frac{\text{A}\cdot\text{C}}{\text{J}} \quad (\because \text{Coulomb} = \text{A-s})$$

$$= \frac{\text{A(A-s)}}{\text{J}}$$

Unit of conductance = $\text{J}^{-1}\text{A}^2\text{- s}$

Current density $= \frac{\text{Current}}{\text{Area}}$

$$= \frac{\text{A}}{\text{m}^2}$$

Unit of current density $= \text{m}^{-2}\text{A}$

The correct code is

A $\rightarrow$ Q, B $\rightarrow$ P, C $\rightarrow$ R, D $\rightarrow$ S

42. (*b*) Huygens' principle can explain diffraction, reflection and refraction.

43. (*b*) Angular displacement in $\frac{3\pi}{10}$ s,

$$\omega = \frac{v}{r} = \frac{10}{2} = 5 \text{ rad/s}$$

$$\theta = \omega t$$

$$= 5 \times \frac{3\pi}{10} = \frac{3\pi}{2} \text{ rad}$$

After travelling $\frac{3\pi}{2}$ rad angular displacement, the position of particle will be at point Q, as shown in the figure.

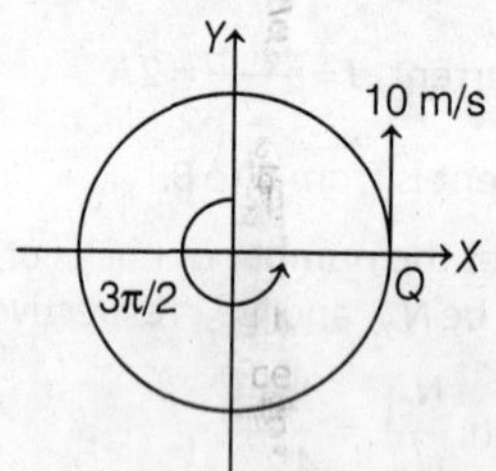

While revolving in circular path, particle have centripetal acceleration only (when speed is constant) which acts towards the centre of circular path. Thus, $t = \frac{3\pi}{5}$ s, the direction of particle is along negative X-axis.

44. (*b*) For hollow sphere, $\frac{K^2}{R^2} = \frac{2}{3}$

As we know that, ratio of rotational kinetic energy K_R to total kinetic energy

$$= \frac{\frac{K^2}{R^2}}{1 + \frac{K^2}{R^2}}$$

$$\Rightarrow \quad \frac{K_R}{K_T} = \frac{\frac{K^2}{R^2}}{1 + \frac{K^2}{R^2}}$$

or $$K_R = \left(\frac{\frac{K^2}{R^2}}{1 + \frac{K^2}{R^2}}\right) \times K_T$$

As $K_T = mgh = 600$ J

$$\therefore \text{ Ratio} = \frac{\frac{2}{3}}{1 + \frac{2}{3}} \times 600 = 240 \text{ J}$$

45. (*b*)

$I = 1$ A, $I_g = 0.1$ A, $G = 1.8\,\Omega$

Now, $I_g G = (I - I_g)S$

$\Rightarrow 0.1 \times 1.8 = (1 - 0.1) \times S$

$$\Rightarrow \quad S = \frac{0.1 \times 1.8}{0.9} = 0.2\,\Omega$$

46. (*c*) For objective lens, $f_0 = +100$ cm

Position of object, $u_0 = -1$ km or 10^5 cm

From lens formula, $\frac{1}{v_0} - \frac{1}{u_0} = \frac{1}{f_0}$

or $$\frac{1}{v_0} = \frac{1}{f_0} + \frac{1}{u_0}$$

$$= \frac{1}{100} - \frac{1}{10^5}$$

$$\frac{1}{v_0} = \frac{999}{10^5}$$

or $$v_0 = \frac{10^5}{999} \text{ cm}$$

Magnification due to objective lens,

$$m = \frac{\text{Size of image}}{\text{Size of object}} = \frac{|v_0|}{|u_0|}$$

or Size of image = Size of object $\times \frac{|v_0|}{|u_0|}$

$$= (50 \times 100 \text{ cm}) \times \frac{\frac{10^5}{999}}{10^5}$$

Size of image $\simeq 5$ cm

47. (*d*) With increase in temperature, average speed of the electrons, which acts as the carriers of current increases, resulting in more frequent collisions.

Thus, the average time of collisions τ decreases with increasing temperature.

Therefore, Assertion and Reason are correct and Reason is the correct explanation of Assertion.

48. (*b*) Given that, the distance between plates, $d = 1.5$ cm or 1.5×10^{-2} m

Electric field, $E = 10^5 \text{Vm}^{-1}$

Mass, $m = 4.9 \times 10^{-15}$ kg

Radius, $r = 5 \times 10^{-5}$ m

Coefficient of viscosity,

$$\eta = 1.8 \times 10^{-5} \text{ Nsm}^{-2}$$

In first case, it is given that, oil drop is at rest from FBD of drop,

$$qE = mg \quad \text{...(i)}$$

or $$q = \frac{mg}{E}$$

(viscous force will be zero as oil drop is at rest)

Now, the direction of electric field is reversed, then electric force on drop will be vertically downwards and viscous force will act opposite to motion i.e. vertically upwards.
Now, from FBD of drop,
when drop is acquired terminal velocity, the net force acting ball will become zero.

$\therefore$ $mg + qE =$ Viscous force

$$mg + qE = 6\pi r \eta v_T$$

$$2mg = 6\pi r\eta v_T \quad \text{[from Eq.(i)]}$$

$$v_T = \frac{mg}{3\pi r\eta}$$

Putting the values, we get

$$v_T = \frac{4.9\times10^{-15}\times9.8}{3\times3.14\times5\times10^{-5}\times1.8\times10^{-5}}$$

$$= 5.66\times10^{-6}\ \text{m/s}$$

$$\approx 5.7\times10^{-6}\ \text{m/s}$$

49. (*b*) Magnetic field due to wire-A at mid-point,

$$B_A = \frac{\mu_0(3I)}{2\pi(d/2)} = \frac{3\mu_0 I}{\pi d}$$

Magnetic field due to wire-B at mid-point,

$$B_B = \frac{\mu_0(5I)}{2\pi(d/2)} = \frac{5\mu_0 I}{\pi d}$$

Net magnetic field at mid-point,

$$\mathbf{B}_{\text{net}} = \mathbf{B}_A + \mathbf{B}_B$$

$$B = \frac{3\mu_0 I}{\pi d} + \frac{5\mu_0 I}{\pi d}$$

or $$B = \frac{8\mu_0 I}{\pi d} \quad \text{... (i)}$$

Now, current flowing through wire-B is made zero, then field will be due to wire-A,

$$\therefore \quad B_A = \frac{3\mu_0 I}{\pi d} \quad \text{...(ii)}$$

On dividing Eqs. (i) and (ii), we get

$$\frac{B}{B_A} = \frac{8}{3}$$

or $$B_A = \frac{3}{8}B$$

50. (*a*) Momentum of photon,

$$p = \frac{h}{\lambda} = \frac{6.6\times10^{-34}}{4.4\times10^{-7}}$$

$$= 1.5\times10^{-27}\ \text{kg-m/s}$$

Effective mass of photon,

$$m = \frac{p}{c} = \frac{1.5\times10^{-27}}{3\times10^{8}}$$

$$= 5\times10^{-36}\ \text{kg}$$

Knockout 10

1. (*c*) Given, $F = \alpha\beta\cdot\exp\left(\frac{-x^2}{\alpha k_B T}\right)$

As exponent term is dimensionless, we have

$$\left[\frac{-x^2}{\alpha k_B T}\right] \equiv [M^0L^0T^0]$$

$\Rightarrow$ Dimensions of $[\alpha] \equiv$ Dimensions of $\left[\frac{x^2}{k_B T}\right]$

$$[\alpha] \equiv \frac{[L^2]}{[ML^2T^{-2}]},$$

as $\quad k_B T =$ energy

or $\quad [\alpha] = [M^{-1}L^0T^2]$

Now, dimensions of force, F
= dimensions of $\alpha\times$ dimensions of β

$\Rightarrow$ Dimensions of $\beta = \frac{\text{Dimensions of } F}{\text{Dimensions of } \alpha}$

$$= \frac{[MLT^{-2}]}{[M^{-1}L^0T^2]} = [M^2LT^{-4}]$$

2. (*a*) Only $A\times B$ has physical meaning.
Two similar quantities can be added or subtracted.

3. (*d*) Binding energy is the amount of energy given to a nucleus, so that it can break into its constituent nucleons or energy released, when a nucleus is formed.
Binding energy is the amount of energy equivalent to mass defect.

4. (*c*) Substituting $C_p - C_V = R$ and checking, we have

$$\frac{C_p - R}{C_V + R} = \frac{\frac{\gamma R}{\gamma-1} - R}{\frac{R}{\gamma-1} + R} = \frac{R\left(\frac{\gamma}{\gamma-1} - 1\right)}{R\left(\frac{1}{\gamma-1} + 1\right)}$$

$$= \frac{\gamma-(\gamma-1)}{1+(\gamma-1)} = \frac{\gamma-\gamma+1}{\gamma}$$

$$\frac{C_p - R}{C_V + R} = \frac{1}{\gamma}$$

So, option (c) is incorrect and options (a), (b) and (d) are correct.

5. (*a*) A $\rightarrow$ S, B $\rightarrow$ Q, C $\rightarrow$ P, D $\rightarrow$ R
Electric fuse melts at high current.
Steam engine converts heat into work.
Bimetallic strip bends due to unequal expansion of strips.
Incandescent lamp emits the radiation.

6. (*c*) $pT^2 =$ constant (C)

$$\Rightarrow \quad \frac{nRT}{V}\cdot T^2 = C$$

$$\Rightarrow \quad T^3\cdot V^{-1} = C$$

Differentiating, we get

$$\Rightarrow \quad \frac{3T^2}{V}\cdot dT - \frac{T^3}{V^2}\cdot dV = 0$$

$$\Rightarrow \quad 3dT = \frac{T}{V}dV$$

or $$dV = \frac{3}{T}\cdot V\cdot dT$$

Comparing with $dV = V\cdot\gamma\, dT$, we get coefficient of volumetric expansion,

$$\gamma = \frac{3}{T}$$

7. (*c*) To eliminate end error, we put resistance box in left and right gaps and then average value of both observations is taken.

8. (*b*) When temperature of the material is increased, then due to the weakening of inter-molecular force, the elastic properties in general decrease, it means elastic constant decreases.

9. (*d*) In an elliptical orbit, speed as well as angular speed vary, so kinetic energy also varies.

10. (*c*) In YDSE,

$$d\sin\theta = n\lambda$$

or $$\sin\theta = \frac{n\lambda}{d}$$

Given that, $d = 3\lambda$

$\therefore$ $$\sin\theta = \frac{n\lambda}{3\lambda}$$

$$\sin\theta = \frac{n}{3}$$

For $n = 0$, $\sin\theta = 0$, $\theta = 0°$ (possible)

For $n = 1$, $\sin\theta = \frac{1}{3}$, $\theta = \sin^{-1}\left(\frac{1}{3}\right)$ (possible)

For $n = 2$, $\sin\theta = \frac{2}{3}$, $\theta = \sin^{-1}\left(\frac{2}{3}\right)$ (possible)

For $n = 3$, $\sin\theta = 1$, $\theta = 90°$ (possible)

Thus, there is a central maximum ($\theta = 0°$) and two for each $\theta = 30°$, $\theta = \sin^{-1}\left(\frac{2}{3}\right)$ and $\theta = 90°$, so total number of maxima are 7.

11. (*b*) Let the angle made by the string with vertical be θ as shown below

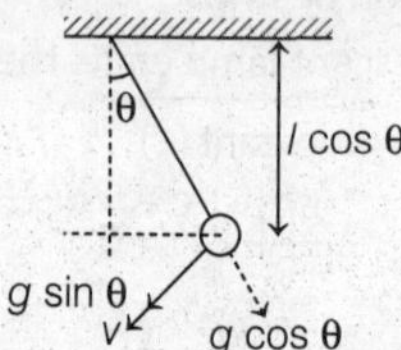

Using conservation mechanical energy principle,

Decrease in potential energy = Increase in kinetic energy

$$+mgl\cos\theta = \frac{1}{2}mv^2$$

or $$v^2 = 2\,gl\cos\theta$$

Tangential acceleration, $a_t = g\sin\theta$

Centripetal acceleration,

$$a_c = \frac{v^2}{R} = \frac{2gl\cos\theta}{l} = 2g\cos\theta$$

The acceleration diagram of particle is as follows

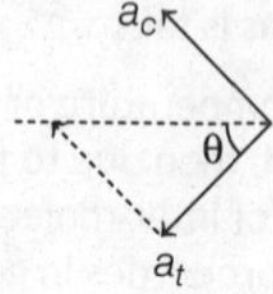

Given that, net acceleration is toward horizontal,

$\therefore$ $$\tan\theta = \frac{a_c}{a_t} = \frac{2g\cos\theta}{g\sin\theta}$$

$$\tan\theta = 2\cot\theta = \frac{2}{\tan\theta}$$

or $\tan^2\theta = 2$

or $\tan\theta = \sqrt{2}$

$\Rightarrow$ $\theta = \tan^{-1}(\sqrt{2})$

12. (*c*) Horizontal distance travelled by frog will be maximum, if it makes an jump at angle, $\theta = 45°$. From the horizontal and maximum range,

$$R_{max} = \frac{u^2}{g} \quad \ldots \text{(i)}$$

$\therefore$ From Eq. (i), $0.3 = \frac{u^2}{10}$

or $u = \sqrt{3}$ m/s

Horizontal component of velocity of frog, $u_x = u\cos\theta$

$$= \sqrt{3}\cos 45° = \sqrt{\frac{3}{2}} \text{ m/s}$$

Total distance covered by it in 10 s,

$$x = u_x t$$

$$= \sqrt{\frac{3}{2}} \times 10$$

$$= 1.224 \times 10$$

$$= 12.24 \text{ m}$$

13. (*c*) According to the given question, the circuit is as shown below.

In series combination of two cell, the equivalent emf and internal resistance is given as

$$E_{eq} = E_1 + E_2 \text{ and } r_{eq} = r_1 + r_2$$

So, the given circuit can be redrawn as

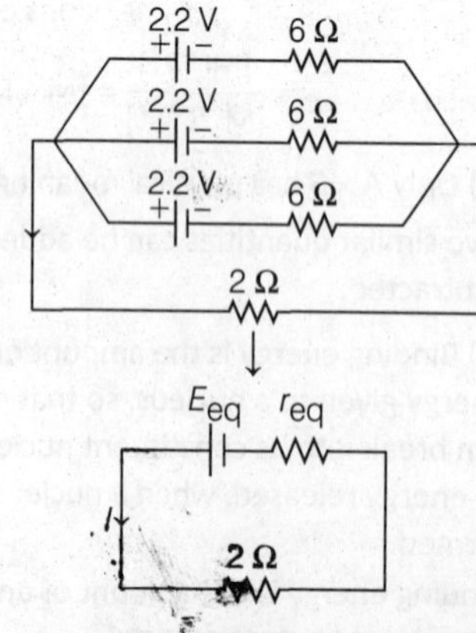

Here, equivalent emf,

$$E_{eq} = \frac{\frac{E_1}{r_1} + \frac{E_2}{r_2} + \frac{E_3}{r_3}}{\frac{1}{r_1} + \frac{1}{r_2} + \frac{1}{r_3}}$$

$$= \frac{\frac{2.2}{6} + \frac{2.2}{6} + \frac{2.2}{6}}{\frac{1}{6} + \frac{1}{6} + \frac{1}{6}} = 2.2 \text{ V}$$

$$r_{eq} = \frac{r}{3} = \frac{6}{3} = 2\,\Omega$$

[As, all are connected in parallel]

Current *I* through external resistance,

$$I = \frac{E_{eq}}{r_{eq} + R} = \frac{2.2}{2+2} = 0.55 \text{ A}$$

Power delivered to external resistance,

$$P = I^2R = (0.55)^2 \times 2 = 0.605 \text{ W}$$

14. (*d*) The magnetic moment of a current carrying loop is given as $M = IA\,\hat{\mathbf{n}}$

where, *I* is current flowing through the loop, *A* is the area of loop and $\hat{\mathbf{n}}$ is unit vector and its direction is determined by right hand thumb rule.

For the given figure, $\mathbf{M} = IA(-\hat{\mathbf{k}})$

[As, the current is flowing in clockwise direction]

Given, magnetic field, $\mathbf{B} = B_0(\hat{\mathbf{i}} - \hat{\mathbf{j}})$

Torque, $\tau = \mathbf{M} \times \mathbf{B}$

$$= IA(-\hat{\mathbf{k}}) \times B_0(\hat{\mathbf{i}} - \hat{\mathbf{j}})$$

$$= IAB_0[(-\hat{\mathbf{k}}) \times \hat{\mathbf{i}} + \hat{\mathbf{k}} \times \hat{\mathbf{j}}]$$

$$= IAB_0[-\hat{\mathbf{j}} - \hat{\mathbf{i}}]$$

Thus, the direction of torque is along $(-\hat{\mathbf{i}} - \hat{\mathbf{j}})$ and from figure, this direction is along *Q* to *S*. So, loop will rotate about an axis along *QS*.

15. (*c*) A is false but R is true.

We can use either a polar or a non-polar dielectric to increase capacity.

$$C = \frac{\varepsilon_0 A}{d} \times K$$

16. (*a*) Given that, $\mathbf{a} = m\mathbf{b} + \mathbf{c}$

Taking dot product with $\mathbf{b}$ on both sides on the above equation, we get

$$\mathbf{a} \cdot \mathbf{b} = (m\mathbf{b} + \mathbf{c}) \cdot \mathbf{b}$$

$$\mathbf{a} \cdot \mathbf{b} = m(\mathbf{b} \cdot \mathbf{b}) + \mathbf{c} \cdot \mathbf{b}$$

$\because$ $\mathbf{b} \cdot \mathbf{b} = b^2$

$\therefore$ $\mathbf{a} \cdot \mathbf{b} = mb^2 + \mathbf{c} \cdot \mathbf{b}$

or $mb^2 = \mathbf{a} \cdot \mathbf{b} - \mathbf{c} \cdot \mathbf{b}$

or $\quad m = \dfrac{\mathbf{a}\cdot\mathbf{b} - \mathbf{c}\cdot\mathbf{b}}{b^2}$

or $\quad m = \dfrac{\mathbf{a}\cdot\mathbf{b} - \mathbf{b}\cdot\mathbf{c}}{b^2} \quad (\because \mathbf{c}\cdot\mathbf{b} = \mathbf{b}\cdot\mathbf{c})$

17. (*d*) Both Statement I and Statement II are correct.

While doing experiment, temperature of all resistance wires increases, so two consecutive values of balance lengths is not same.

18. (*c*) Reflecting type telescope has lenses which have chromatic aberration defect, this causes dullness of image.

19. (*a*) We know that, the electric field vector due to a semi-infinite line charge sheets separated by a distance *d* vector is given as

$$\mathbf{E} = \frac{\lambda}{4\pi\varepsilon_0 d}\hat{\mathbf{a}} + \frac{\lambda}{4\pi\varepsilon_0 d}\hat{\mathbf{b}}$$

where, $\hat{\mathbf{a}}$ and $\hat{\mathbf{b}}$ are unit vectors and λ is the surface charge density.

Also, the electric field vector due to a semi-circular ring is

$\mathbf{E} = \dfrac{\lambda}{2\pi\varepsilon_0 R}\hat{\mathbf{c}}$, where $\hat{\mathbf{c}}$ is unit vector along angle bi-section.

According to question, the direction of field at point O for each part is as shown below.

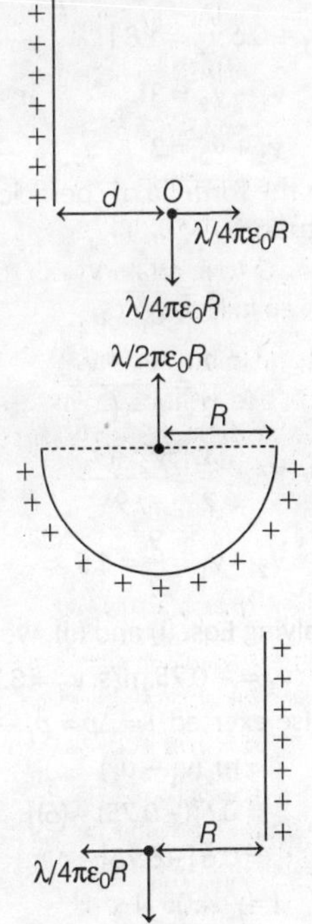

In simplified form at point O, we get

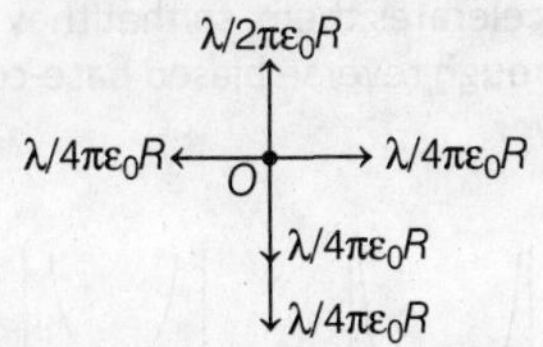

Net electric field at point O, $E = 0$

20. (*a*) Using Snell's law at the boundary of I and II medium.

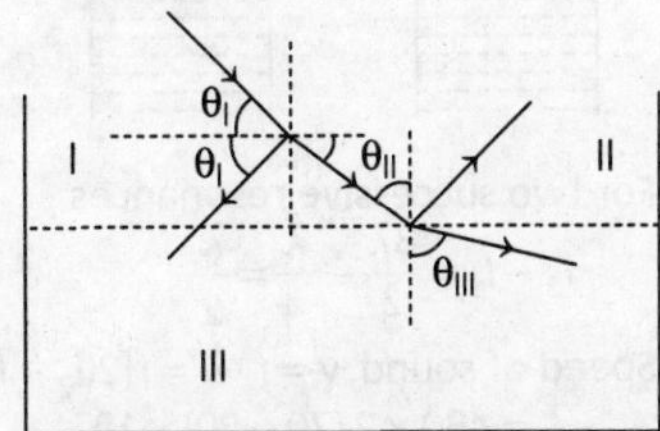

$\mu_I \sin\theta_I = \mu_{II}\sin\theta_{II}$, where θ_I is angle of incidence and θ_{II} is angle of refraction.

From figure, $\theta_I < \theta_{II}$

$\Rightarrow \quad \sin\theta_I < \sin\theta_{II}$

$\therefore \quad \mu_I > \mu_{II} \quad$ ... (i)

Similarly, for the boundary of II and III medium using Snell's law,

$$\mu_{II}\sin\theta_{II} = \mu_{III}\sin\theta_{III}$$

From figure, $\theta_{II} < \theta_{III}$

$\Rightarrow \quad \sin\theta_{II} < \sin\theta_{III}$

$\therefore \quad \mu_{II} > \mu_{III} \quad$ ... (ii)

From Eqs. (i) and (ii), we get

$$\mu_I > \mu_{II} > \mu_{III}$$

21. (*c*) From the given figure, it is clear that, magnetic field at origin due to two parts (i.e. *BC* and *CD*) of wire will be zero, as point O is lying the wires. Magnetic field is only due to section parallel to *Y*-axis i.e. *AB* is given as

$$\mathbf{B} = \frac{\mu_0 I}{4\pi d}\hat{\mathbf{r}}$$

where, $\hat{\mathbf{r}}$ is determined by right hand rule.

$$\therefore \mathbf{B} = \frac{\mu_0 I}{4\pi(a\sqrt{2})}[\cos 45°(-\hat{\mathbf{i}}) + \cos 45°\hat{\mathbf{k}}]$$

$$= \frac{\mu_0 I}{4\sqrt{2}\pi a}\left[-\frac{1}{\sqrt{2}}\hat{\mathbf{i}} + \frac{1}{\sqrt{2}}\hat{\mathbf{k}}\right]$$

$$\mathbf{B} = \frac{\mu_0 I}{8\pi a}[-\hat{\mathbf{i}} + \hat{\mathbf{k}}]$$

22. (*b*) Statement I is correct but Statement II is incorrect.

There is no zero potential point between moon and earth as gravitational potentials of moon and earth are always having same (negative) sign.

23. (*b*) There is always loss of energy when two capacitors share charge. This is due to

(i) loss of energy in form of radiation due to acceleration of charges.

(ii) dipoles re-alignment

24. (*d*) The given network is symmetrical about the dotted line which is perpendicular to *AB* as shown in given figure below. As we know that, point lying on this line is not electrically connected and behave as a false junction and it can be lift off.

So, the given circuit can be redrawn as

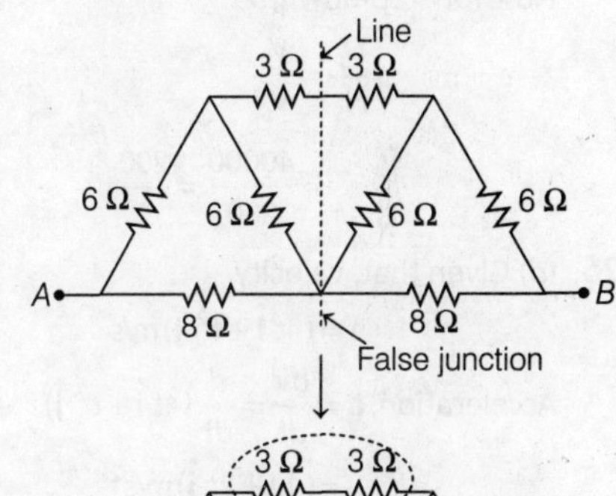

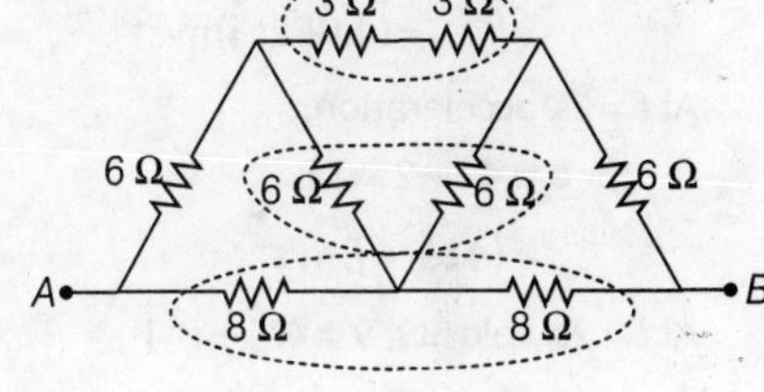

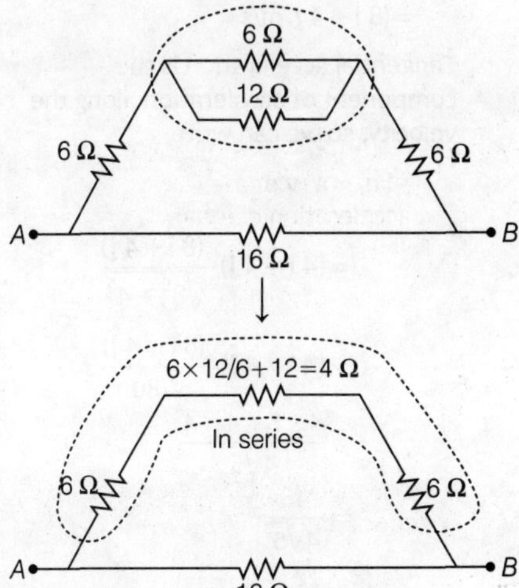

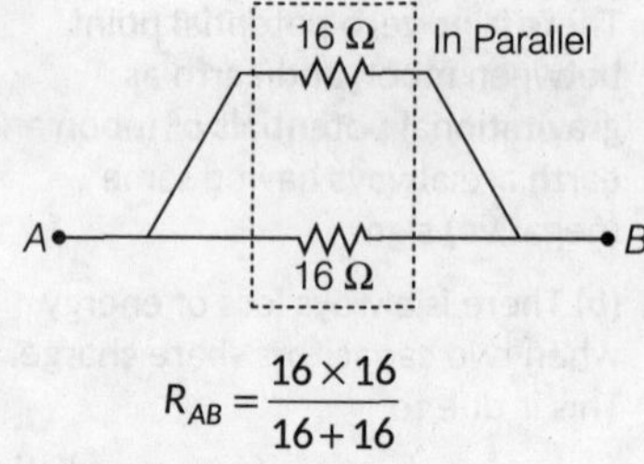

$$R_{AB}=\frac{16\times16}{16+16}$$

[∵ In parallel combination of two resistance, $R_{eq}=\frac{R_1R_2}{R_1+R_2}$]

$$R_{AB}=8\,\Omega$$

25. (*a*) During step-up,

$$\frac{N_P}{N_S}=\frac{V_P}{V_S}$$

$$\Rightarrow \quad \frac{1}{10}=\frac{4000}{V_S}$$

$$\Rightarrow \quad V_S=40000\text{ V}$$

Now for step-down,

$$\frac{N_P}{N_S}=\frac{V_P}{V_S}$$

$$=\frac{40000}{200}=\frac{200}{1}$$

26. (*d*) Given that, velocity,

$$\mathbf{v}=(4t\,\hat{\mathbf{i}}+t^2\,\hat{\mathbf{j}})\text{m/s}$$

Acceleration, $\mathbf{a}=\frac{d\mathbf{v}}{dt}=\frac{d}{dt}(4t\,\hat{\mathbf{i}}+t^2\,\hat{\mathbf{j}})$

$$=(4\,\hat{\mathbf{i}}+2t\,\hat{\mathbf{j}})\text{m/s}^2$$

At $t=2$s, acceleration,

$$\mathbf{a}=4\,\hat{\mathbf{i}}+2\times2\,\hat{\mathbf{j}}$$

$$=(4\,\hat{\mathbf{i}}+4\,\hat{\mathbf{j}})\text{m/s}^2$$

At $t=2$s, velocity, $\mathbf{v}=4t\,\hat{\mathbf{i}}+t^2\,\hat{\mathbf{j}}$

$$=4\times2\,\hat{\mathbf{i}}+(2)^2\,\hat{\mathbf{j}}$$

$$=(8\,\hat{\mathbf{i}}+4\,\hat{\mathbf{j}})\text{m/s}$$

Tangential acceleration is the component of acceleration along the velocity, so we can write,

$$a_t=\mathbf{a}\cdot\mathbf{v}\text{ or }\mathbf{a}\cdot\frac{\mathbf{v}}{v}$$

$$=(4\,\hat{\mathbf{i}}+4\,\hat{\mathbf{j}})\cdot\frac{(8\,\hat{\mathbf{i}}+4\,\hat{\mathbf{j}})}{\sqrt{8^2+4^2}}$$

$$=(4\,\hat{\mathbf{i}}+4\,\hat{\mathbf{j}})\cdot\frac{(8\,\hat{\mathbf{i}}+4\,\hat{\mathbf{j}})}{\sqrt{80}}$$

$$=\frac{4\times8+4\times4}{4\sqrt5}$$

$$=\frac{48}{4\sqrt5}$$

$$a_t=\frac{12}{\sqrt5}\text{m/s}^2$$

27. (*c*) Base attracts charge carriers and accelerates them, so that they pass through reverse biased base-collector layer.

28. (*c*)

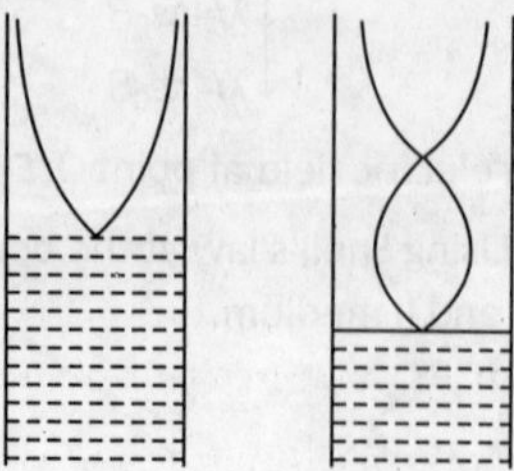

For two successive resonances

$$l_2-l_1=\frac{3\lambda}{4}-\frac{\lambda}{4}=\frac{\lambda}{2}$$

Speed of sound, $v=f\cdot\lambda=f[2(l_2-l_1)]$

$$=480\times2\,(70-30)\times10^{-2}$$

$$=384\text{ m/s}$$

29. (*a*) The moment of inertia of rod about an axis passing through its one end and perpendicular to it, is $I=\frac{ML^2}{3}$.

where, M is mass of rod and L is length.

From given diagram,

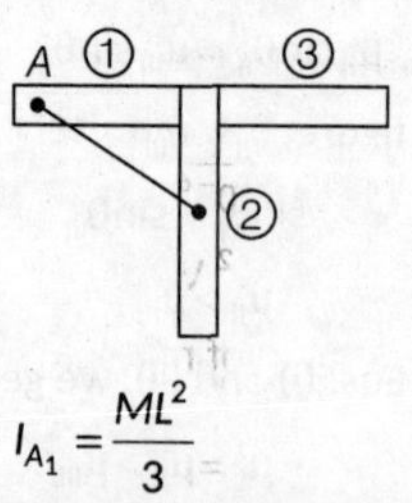

$$I_{A_1}=\frac{ML^2}{3}$$

[using parallel axes theorem]

$$I_{A_2}=I_{CM}+Md^2$$

$$=\frac{ML^2}{12}+M\left[\sqrt{L^2+\left(\frac{L}{2}\right)^2}\right]^2$$

$$=\frac{4}{3}ML^2$$

Similarly, $I_{A_3}=I_{CM}+Md^2$

$$=\frac{ML^2}{12}+M\left(\frac{3L}{2}\right)^2=\frac{7}{3}ML^2$$

Total moment of inertia about point A of given arrangement,

$$I_A=I_{A_1}+I_{A_2}+I_{A_3}$$

$$=\frac{ML^2}{3}+\frac{4}{3}ML^2+\frac{7}{3}ML^2$$

$$=4ML^2$$

Similarly, point B is located at one end for each rod, so we can write,

$$I_B=I_{B_1}+I_{B_2}+I_{B_3}$$

$$=\frac{ML^2}{3}+\frac{ML^2}{3}+\frac{ML^2}{3}$$

$$=ML^2$$

Thus, ratio, $\frac{I_A}{I_B}=\frac{4ML^2}{ML^2}=4$

30. (*a*) The situation given in the question has been shown as

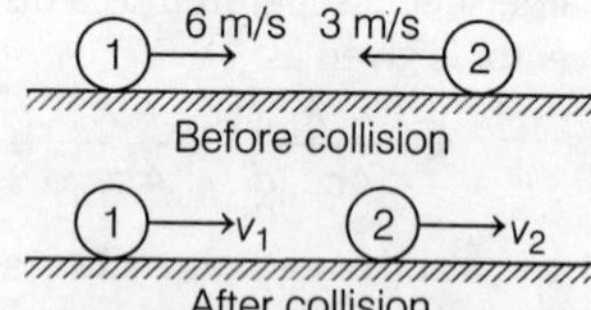

Using conservation of linear momentum,

$$\mathbf{p}_i=\mathbf{p}_f$$

$$m_1\mathbf{u}_1+m_2\mathbf{u}_2=m_1\mathbf{v}_1+m_2\mathbf{v}_2$$

Here, $m_1=0.6$ kg, $m_2=0.6$ kg,

$\mathbf{u}_1=6\hat{\mathbf{i}}$ m/s, $\mathbf{u}_2=-3\hat{\mathbf{i}}$ m/s

$$0.6\times6\,\hat{\mathbf{i}}+0.6\times(-3\hat{\mathbf{i}})=0.6\times\mathbf{v}_1+0.6\,\mathbf{v}_2$$

$$0.6\,\mathbf{v}_1+0.6\,\mathbf{v}_2=1.8\,\hat{\mathbf{i}}$$

$$\mathbf{v}_1+\mathbf{v}_2=3\hat{\mathbf{i}}$$

or $\quad v_1+v_2=3 \quad$ ...(i)

From the formula of coefficient of restitution,

$$e=\frac{v_2-v_1}{u_1-u_2}$$

$$\frac{1}{2}=\frac{v_2-v_1}{6-(-3)}$$

$$\frac{1}{2}=\frac{v_2-v_1}{9}$$

$$v_2-v_1=\frac{9}{2}=4.5 \quad \text{... (ii)}$$

On solving Eqs. (i) and (ii), we get

$$v_1=-0.75\text{ m/s}, v_2=3.75\text{ m/s}$$

Impulse exerted, $I=\Delta p=p_f-p_i$

$$=m_1(v_1-u_1)$$

$$=0.6[(-0.75)-(6)]$$

$$=0.6[-6.75]$$

$$I=-4.05\text{ N-s}$$

or $\quad |I|=4.05$ N-s

31. (*b*) Let the acceleration of centre of system of two block be a_{CM}.

The acceleration of centre of mass of two block system is given as

$$\mathbf{a}_{CM} = \frac{m_1\mathbf{a}_1 + m_2\mathbf{a}_2}{m_1 + m_2} \quad \text{... (i)}$$

Here, $m_1 = m$ and $m_2 = 3m$

$\mathbf{a}_1 = a'\hat{\mathbf{i}}$ (Let) and $\mathbf{a}_2 = -a\,\hat{\mathbf{i}}$

$$\mathbf{a}_{CM} = \frac{\text{Net force}}{\text{Total mass}} = \frac{F-0}{3m+m}\hat{\mathbf{i}} = \frac{F}{4m}\mathbf{i}$$

From Eq. (i),

$$\frac{F}{4m}\hat{\mathbf{i}} = \frac{m\times(a'\hat{\mathbf{i}}) + 3m\times(-a\,\hat{\mathbf{i}})}{4m}$$

$$F\,\hat{\mathbf{i}} = m(a' - 3a)\,\hat{\mathbf{i}}$$

or $\quad F = m(a' - 3a)$

or $\quad \dfrac{F}{m} = a' - 3a$

or $\quad a' = \dfrac{F}{m} + 3a$

32. (*c*) The capacitance of a parallel plate capacitor is as follows

$$C = \frac{\varepsilon_0 A}{d} \quad \text{... (i)}$$

where, A is area of plate, d is separation between plates and ε_0 is the permittivity of free space.

The potential energy stored by a capacitor, $U = \dfrac{Q^2}{2C}$

Initially, the capacitor is charged through a potential difference ε, then energy,

$$U_i = \frac{Q^2}{2C} = \frac{(C\varepsilon)^2}{2C} = \frac{1}{2}C\varepsilon^2 \quad [\because Q = CV]$$

Now, battery is disconnected and distance between the plates is doubled, then charge on capacitor will remain same but

$$\because \quad C \propto \frac{1}{d}$$

So, capacitance will be halved, i.e.,

$$C_f = \frac{C}{2}$$

$\therefore$ Final energy, $U_f = \dfrac{Q^2}{2C_f}$

$$U_f = \frac{(C\varepsilon)^2}{2\dfrac{C}{2}} = C\varepsilon^2$$

Work done by external source to pull plates,

$$W = \Delta U = U_f - U_i$$

$$= C\varepsilon^2 - \frac{1}{2}C\varepsilon^2$$

$$= \frac{1}{2}C\varepsilon^2 = \frac{1}{2}\left(\frac{\varepsilon_0 A}{d}\right)\varepsilon^2 \quad \text{[using Eq. (i)]}$$

or $\quad = \dfrac{\varepsilon_0 A\varepsilon^2}{2d}$

33. (*c*) Given that, average power of beam, $P_{avg} = 16$ mW or 16×10^{-3} W

Diameter, $d = 4$ mm or 4×10^{-3}m

or radius, $R = 2\times10^{-3}$m

Area, $A = \pi R^2 = 3.14\times(2\times10^{-3})^2$

$A = 12.56\times10^{-6}$ m^2

As, average intensity,

$$I_{avg} = \frac{P_{avg}}{A}$$

and $\quad I_{avg} = c\varepsilon_0 E_{rms}^2$

$$\therefore \quad c\varepsilon_0 E_{rms}^2 = \frac{P_{avg}}{A}$$

$$\therefore \quad E_{rms} = \sqrt{\frac{P_{avg}}{Ac\varepsilon_0}}$$

Putting the given values in above expression, we get

$$E_{rms} = \sqrt{\frac{16\times10^{-3}}{12.56\times10^{-6}\times3\times10^{8}\times8.85\times10^{-12}}}$$

$$E_{rms} = 6.92\times10^{2}\text{ V/m}$$

and rms value of magnetic field,

$$B_{rms} = \frac{E_{rms}}{c} = \frac{6.92\times10^2}{3\times10^8}$$

$$= 2.3\times10^{-6}\text{ T}$$

$$= 2.3\,\mu\text{T}$$

34. (*d*) From the relation between velocity v and displacement x,

$$v = \omega\sqrt{(A^2 - x^2)}$$

Squaring on both sides, we get

$$v^2 = \omega^2(A^2 - x^2) \quad \text{... (i)}$$

and we know that, $a = -\omega^2 x$

or $\quad a^2 = (-\omega^2 x)^2$

$$= \omega^4 x^2 \quad \text{...(ii)}$$

From the Eqs. (i) and (ii), we get

$$v^2 = -\frac{a^2}{\omega^2} + \omega^2 A^2$$

The above equation is similar to a straight line equation,

$$y = mx + C$$

The line has positive slope and negative intercept on Y-axis.

The graph between v^2 and a^2 can be drawn as

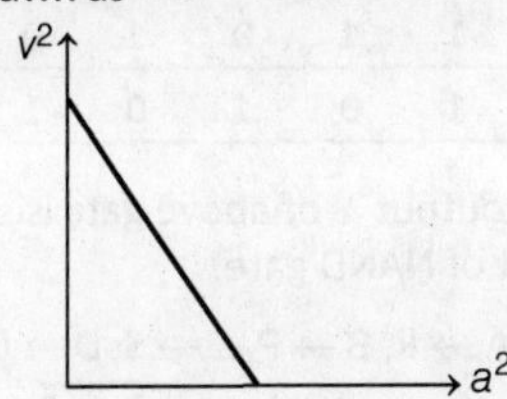

35. (*c*) X-rays are used to check cracks and welding defects.

36. (*b*) As, we know that, wavelength corresponding to transition, $n = n_1$ to $n = n_2$ is given by the following expression,

$$\frac{1}{\lambda} = RZ^2\left(\frac{1}{n_2^2} - \frac{1}{n_1^2}\right) \quad \text{... (i)}$$

For 1st line of Lyman series;

$$n_1 = 2, n_2 = 1$$

$$\therefore \quad \frac{1}{\lambda_L} = RZ^2\left(\frac{1}{1^2} - \frac{1}{2^2}\right) \quad [\because \text{Using Eq. (i)}]$$

$$\frac{1}{\lambda_L} = RZ^2\left(1 - \frac{1}{4}\right)$$

$$\frac{1}{\lambda_L} = \frac{3}{4}RZ^2$$

or $\quad \lambda_L = \dfrac{4}{3RZ^2} \quad \text{... (ii)}$

Similarly, for 1st line of Balmer series,

$$n_1 = 2, n_3 = 3$$

$$\therefore \quad \frac{1}{\lambda_B} = RZ^2\left[\frac{1}{2^2} - \frac{1}{3^2}\right] \quad [\because \text{using Eq. (i)}]$$

$$= RZ^2\left[\frac{1}{4} - \frac{1}{9}\right]$$

$$= RZ^2\left[\frac{9-4}{36}\right]$$

$$\frac{1}{\lambda_B} = \frac{5}{36}RZ^2$$

or $\quad \lambda_B = \dfrac{36}{5RZ^2} \quad \text{... (iii)}$

On dividing Eq. (ii) by Eq. (iii), we get

$$\frac{\lambda_L}{\lambda_B} = \frac{\dfrac{4}{3RZ^2}}{\dfrac{36}{5RZ^2}} = \frac{5}{27}$$

37. (*b*) Truth table for given gate combination is

A, B, Y_1, Y_2, Y_3, Y_4

A	B	Y_1	Y_2	Y_3	Y_4	Y
0	0	1	0	1	0	1
1	0	1	0	1	0	1
0	1	1	0	1	0	1
1	1	0	1	0	1	0

So, output Y of above gate is same as that of NAND gate.

38. (*d*) $A \to R, B \to P, C \to S, D \to Q$

$X_L = L\omega = 11\,\Omega, Z = \sqrt{R^2 + X_L^2} = 11\sqrt{2}$

$V_{max} = \sqrt{2} \times V_{rms} = 220\sqrt{2}$

$I_{max} = V_{max}/Z = 20\text{ A}$

39. (*b*) A is true but R is false.

For case of measurement and not having need of a very small error, large physical quantities are expressed in terms of larger units.

40. (*c*) The de-Broglie wavelength of a charged particle is given as

$$\lambda = \frac{h}{\sqrt{2mqV}}$$

where, *m* is mass of electron, *q* is charge on electron and *V* is accelerating potential.

For electron *h*, *m* and *q* are constant,

$$\lambda \propto \frac{1}{\sqrt{V}}$$

At two accelerating potentials,

$$\frac{\lambda'}{\lambda} = \sqrt{\frac{V}{V'}} \quad \text{... (i)}$$

When accelerating potential is made five times, then $V' = 5V$

Putting the value of V' in Eq. (i), we get

$$\frac{\lambda'}{\lambda} = \sqrt{\frac{V}{5V}} = \frac{1}{\sqrt{5}}$$

or $\lambda' = \frac{\lambda}{\sqrt{5}}$

or $= \frac{\lambda}{2.23} = 0.44\,\lambda$ (decrease)

41. (*c*) Ferromagnetism is a mechanism through which certain materials form permanent magnets with the aid of a strong magnetic field and these materials can be permanently magnetised.

Examples of ferromagnetic materials are as follows

1. Cobalt
2. MnSb
3. Iron
4. Nickel
5. $Nd_2Fe_{14}B$
6. CrO_2 (Chromium dioxide)

42. (*b*) The angular frequency of a *L*-*C* oscillator is given as

$$\omega = \frac{1}{\sqrt{LC}} \quad \text{... (i)}$$

Given, $L = 27\text{ mH or } 27 \times 10^{-3}\text{H}$

$C = 60\,\mu\text{F or } 60 \times 10^{-6}\text{F}$

Putting the values of *L* and *C* in the expression of ω, we get

$$\omega = \frac{1}{\sqrt{27 \times 10^{-3} \times 60 \times 10^{-6}}}$$

$$= \frac{1}{9\sqrt{2} \times 10^{-4}} = \frac{10{,}000}{9\sqrt{2}}$$

$$\omega \simeq \frac{1111}{\sqrt{2}}\text{ rad/s}$$

43. (*c*) For the common emitter amplifier,

Collector current, $I_C = \frac{V_C}{R_C}$

where, V_C is collector voltage and R_C is collector resistance.

$\therefore \quad I_C = \frac{8}{4 \times 10^3} = 2 \times 10^{-3}\text{ A}$

Current amplification factor, $\beta = \frac{I_C}{I_B}$

or $I_B = \frac{I_C}{\beta} = \frac{2 \times 10^{-3}}{50}$

$= 40 \times 10^{-6}\text{ A}$

$\therefore$ Input voltage, $V_B = I_B R_B$

$= (40 \times 10^{-6}) \times (2 \times 10^3)$

$= 80 \times 10^{-3}\text{ V}$

$= 80\text{ mV}$

44. (*d*) When a coil of area *A* having number of turns *N* is rotated with uniform angular speed ω in magnetic field *B*, then peak induced emf is given as

$$\varepsilon = NAB\omega \text{ or } NAB(2\pi f) \quad \text{... (i)}$$

Given that, for coil-1, $N_1 = 100$,

$f_1 = 50\text{ Hz}$

For coil-2, $N_2 = 50, f_2 = 300\text{ Hz}$

$\therefore \quad \varepsilon_1 = 100 \times A_1 \times B \times 2\,\pi \times 50$ ... (ii)

and $\varepsilon_2 = 50 \times A_2 \times B \times 2\pi \times 300$ ... (iii)

[using Eq. (i)]

On dividing Eq. (ii) by Eq. (iii), we get

$$\frac{\varepsilon_1}{\varepsilon_2} = \frac{100 \times A_1 \times B \times 2\,\pi \times 50}{50 \times A_2 \times B \times 2\,\pi \times 300}$$

$$\frac{\varepsilon_1}{\varepsilon_2} = \frac{A_1}{3A_2}$$

Ratio of ε_1 and ε_2 depends on areas of the coil. Without any information of area, it cannot be calculated.

45. (*d*) If I_g is the current for full scale deflection in voltmeter, then we can write,

$$I_g = \frac{\text{Voltage range of voltmeter}}{\text{Resistance of voltmeter}}$$

$$I_g = \frac{V}{R_V} \quad \text{... (i)}$$

Given that, $V = 5\text{ V}$,

$R_V = 300\,\Omega$

From Eq. (i), $I_g = \frac{5}{300} = \frac{1}{60}\text{ A}$

On adding a small value resistance *S* in parallel to voltmeter, the arrangement will be converted into an ammeter.

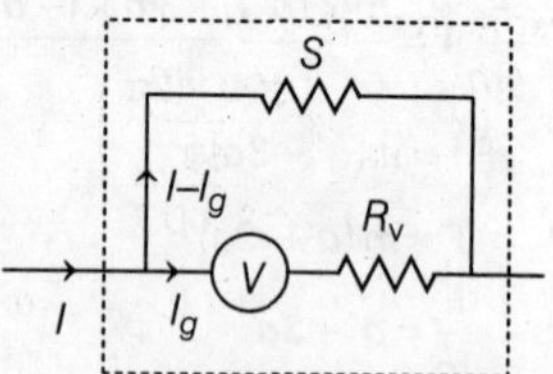

Using current division rule,

$$I_g = \frac{S}{R_V + S} \times I$$

or $\frac{I_g}{I} = \frac{S}{R_V + S}$ ... (ii)

Substituting the values in Eq. (ii), we get

$$\frac{\frac{1}{60}}{5} = \frac{S}{300 + S} \quad [\because I = 5\text{ A}]$$

$$\frac{1}{300} = \frac{S}{300 + S}$$

$300 + S = 300\,S$

$299\,S = 300$

or $S = \frac{300}{299}$

or $S = 1.003\,\Omega$

or $S \simeq 1\,\Omega$

46. (*b*) Mass defect,

$\Delta m = 3m(\text{He}) - m(\text{C})$

$= 12.007812 - 12.000000$

$= 0.007812\text{ u}$

$\therefore$ Q-value $= \Delta m \times 931\text{ MeV}$

$= 0.007812 \times 931$

$= 7.27$

47. (*d*) Graph (I) does not represent the one-dimensional motion because total distance covered by a particle always increases with time.

Graphs (II) and (III) do not represent the one-dimensional motion, because at a particular time, there cannot be two values of position or velocity. Graph (IV) is not possible, because speed can never be negative.

48. (*a*) Given, $\omega = 0, \omega_0 = 100 \text{ rev min}^{-1}$ and $t = 15$ s

From equation of angular motion,

$$0 = \omega_0 - \alpha t$$

$$\Rightarrow \quad \alpha = \frac{\omega_0}{t}$$

$$= \frac{(100 \times 2\pi)/60}{15}$$

$$= 0.69 \text{ rad s}^{-2}$$

Now, angle rotated before coming to rest is given by

$$\theta = \frac{\omega_0^2}{2\alpha} = \frac{\left(\frac{100 \times 2\pi}{60}\right)^2}{2 \times 0.7}$$

$$(\because \omega^2 = \omega_0^2 - 2\alpha\theta)$$

$$= 78.25 \text{ rad}$$

$\therefore$ Number of revolutions $= \frac{\theta}{2\pi} = 12.5$

49. (*b*) The situation is shown below.

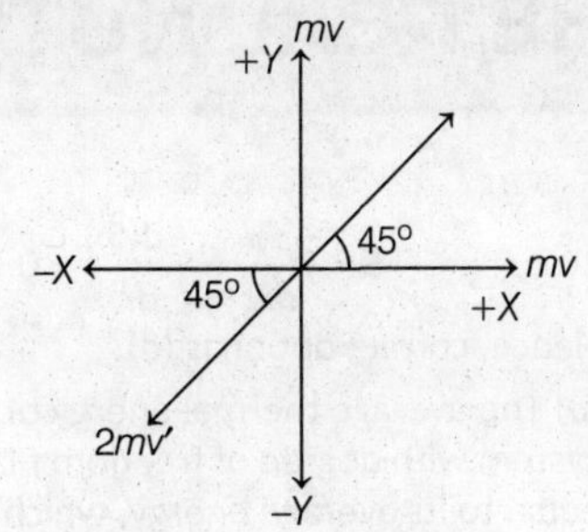

According to question, the third part of mass 2*m* will move as shown in the above figure, because the total momentum of the system after explosion must remain zero. Let the velocity of third part be v', then from the conservation of momentum,

$\sqrt{2}\, mv$ = Resultant moments of two small masses

$$\Rightarrow \sqrt{2}\,(mv) = (2m) \times v'$$

$$\Rightarrow \quad v' = \frac{v}{\sqrt{2}} \quad \text{...(i)}$$

So, total kinetic energy generated by the explosion

$$= \frac{1}{2}mv^2 + \frac{1}{2}mv^2 + \frac{1}{2}(2m)v'^2$$

$$= mv^2 + m \times \left(\frac{v}{\sqrt{2}}\right)^2 \quad \text{[using Eq. (i)]}$$

$$= mv^2 + \frac{mv^2}{2} = \frac{3}{2}mv^2$$

50. (*d*) A gas molecule escapes atmosphere of a planet when its rms speed exceeds escape speed.

In critical condition, $v_{rms} = v_{escape}$

$$\text{or} \quad \sqrt{\frac{3kT}{m}} = \sqrt{2gR_e}$$

$$\Rightarrow \quad T = \frac{2gR_e m}{3k}$$

$$\Rightarrow T = \frac{2 \times 9.8 \times 6.4 \times 10^6 \times 0.34 \times 10^{-26}}{3(1.38 \times 10^{-23})} \quad \text{(given)}$$

$$= 10^4 \text{ K}$$

Therefore, 10^4 K is the temperature at which hydrogen molecules will escape from Earth's surface.

THE REAL NUTS

The Real Nut 1

1. *(d)* In SHM, equation of displacement of a particle is $y = a\sin\omega t$ and equation of acceleration of a particle is $A = -a\omega^2 \sin\omega t$

$$= a\omega^2 \sin(\omega t + \pi)$$

$\therefore$ Phase difference between displacement and acceleration of a particle is

$$= (\omega t + \pi) - \omega t = \pi \text{ rad}$$

Hence, correct option is (d).

2. *(d)* Given, $l = 50$ cm = 0.5 m, $N = 100$ turns and $i = 2.5$ A

$\therefore$ Magnetic field at the centre of solenoid is

$$= \mu_0 ni = \mu_0 \left(\frac{N}{l}\right) \cdot i$$

$$= 4\pi \times 10^{-7} \times \frac{100}{0.5} \times 2.5$$

$$= 6.28 \times 10^{-4} \text{ T}$$

Hence, correct option is (d).

3. *(b)* Given, $m_1 = 4$ kg, $m_2 = 6$ kg and $a = ?$

From the free body diagram, the relation for acceleration of the given system can be given as

$$a = \left(\frac{m_2 - m_1}{m_1 + m_2}\right) \cdot g$$

$$= \left(\frac{6-4}{4+6}\right) \times g = \frac{g}{5}$$

Hence, correct option is (b).

4. *(d)* We know that,

$$\frac{E_0}{B_0} = c$$

where, E_0 and B_0 are the peak values of electric field and magnetic field, respectively.

$\therefore \quad E_0 : B_0 = c : 1$

Hence, correct option is (d).

5. *(d)* Given, volume, $V = 0.2\text{ m}^3$

Electric potential = 5 V (Constant)

Electric field = ?

We know that, for constant electric potential, the value of electric field is zero.

i.e. $\quad E = \dfrac{-dV}{dr} = \dfrac{-d(5)}{dr} = 0$

Hence, correct option is (d).

6. *(a)* The average thermal energy of a system with degree of freedom f is equal to its average energy, which is given as

$$= \frac{f}{2} k_B \cdot T$$

For monoatomic gas, $f = 3$

$\therefore$ Average thermal energy $= \dfrac{3}{2} k_B \cdot T$

Hence, correct option is (a).

7. *(b)* Given, position vector, $\mathbf{r} = 2\hat{\mathbf{k}}$ m

Force, $\mathbf{F} = 3\hat{\mathbf{j}}$ N

As, torque, $\tau = \mathbf{r} \times \mathbf{F} = 2\hat{\mathbf{k}} \times 3\hat{\mathbf{j}} = 6(-\hat{\mathbf{i}})$

$= -6\hat{\mathbf{i}}$ N-m

Hence, correct option is (b).

8. *(a)* The mean free path λ for a gas, with molecular diameter d and number density n is given by the relation

$$\lambda = \frac{1}{\sqrt{2}\, n\pi d^2}$$

Hence, correct option is (a).

9. *(a)* Given, $m = 0.5\text{ g} = 0.5 \times 10^{-3}$ kg

Relation for energy equivalent of mass is

$$E = mc^2$$

where, c is speed of light.

$$= 0.5 \times 10^{-3} \times (3 \times 10^8)^2 \quad (\because c = 3 \times 10^8)$$

$$= 4.5 \times 10^{13}\text{ J}$$

Hence, correct option is (a).

10. *(b)* Given, least count = 0.01 mm

Number of divisions on circular scale = 50

Pitch of the screw gauge = least count × number of divisions on circular scale

$= 0.01 \times 50 = 0.5$ mm

Hence, correct option is (b).

11. *(a)* Since, the entire system is thermally insulated. Thus, there will be no transfer of heat between the system and the surrounding. Hence, when the stop cock is suddenly opened, a sudden process of expansion takes place with no heat transfer. Thus, the given process is adiabatic, as it is a process that occurs without transferring heat or mass between a thermodynamic system and its surrounding.

Hence, correct option is (a).

12. *(a)* Given, pressure, $p = 249$ kPa

$= 249 \times 10^3$ Pa

Temperature, $T = 27°$C

$= (273 + 27)\text{K} = 300$ K

Density, $\rho = ?$

As, from ideal gas equation,

$$pV = nRT$$

$$\Rightarrow \quad pV = \frac{m}{M} RT \quad \left[\text{as } n = \frac{m}{M}\right]$$

$$\Rightarrow \quad pVM = mRT$$

$$\Rightarrow \quad pM = \frac{m}{V} RT = \rho RT \quad \left[\text{as } \frac{m}{V} = \rho\right]$$

$$\Rightarrow \quad \rho = \frac{pM}{RT}$$

$$= \frac{249 \times 10^3 \times 2 \times 10^{-3}}{8.3 \times 300}$$

[$\because$ for hydrogen gas, $M = 2$ g $= 2 \times 10^{-3}$ kg]

$$\Rightarrow \quad \rho = 0.2\text{ kg/m}^3$$

Hence, correct option is (a).

13. *(d)* Here,

$${}^{235}_{92}\text{U} + {}^{1}_{0}n \longrightarrow {}^{89}_{36}\text{Kr} + {}^{A}_{Z}\text{X} + 3({}^{1}_{0}n)$$

According to the law of conservation of energy,

(Atomic number)$_{\text{Reactant}}$ = (Atomic number)$_{\text{Product}}$

$$92 + 0 = 36 + Z$$

$$\Rightarrow \quad Z = 92 - 36 = 56$$

Similarly,

(Atomic masses)$_{\text{Reactant}}$ = (Atomic masses)$_{\text{Product}}$

$$235 + 1 = 89 + A + 3 \times 1$$

$$\Rightarrow \quad A = 144$$

$\therefore$ Other element is $^{144}_{56}$Ba.

Hence, correct option is (d).

14. *(a)* Given, drift velocity, $v_d = 7.5 \times 10^{-4}$ m/s

Electric field, $E = 3 \times 10^{-10}$ Vm^{-1}

Mobility, $\mu = ?$

As, $\mu = \frac{v_d}{E} = \frac{7.5 \times 10^{-4}}{3 \times 10^{-10}}$

$= 2.5 \times 10^6 m^2V^{-1}s^{-1}$

Hence, correct option is (a).

15. *(a)* The difference between 9.99 m and 0.0099 m is

$= 9.99 - 0.0099 = 9.9801$ m

Taking significant figures into account, as both the values has two significant figures after decimal.

So, their difference will also have two significant figures after decimal, i.e. 9.98 m.

Hence, correct option is (a).

16. *(d)* Given, susceptibility, $\chi = 599$

Magnetic field, $B = 1200$ Am^{-1}

Permeability of the material of the rod = ?

As, $\mu_m = \mu_0(1+\chi)$

$= 4\pi \times 10^{-7}(1+599)$

$= 2.4\pi \times 10^{-4}$ T-mA^{-1}

Hence, correct option is (d).

17. *(a)* Given, radius, $r = 10$ cm $= 10 \times 10^{-2}$ m

Charge, $q = 3.2 \times 10^{-7}$ C

Electric field, $E = ?$

Electric field at a point (x = 15 cm) from the centre of the sphere is

$$E = \frac{1}{4\pi\varepsilon_0} \cdot \frac{q}{x^2}$$

$$= 9 \times 10^9 \times \frac{3.2 \times 10^{-7}}{(15 \times 10^{-2})^2}$$

$$= 1.28 \times 10^5 \text{ N/C}$$

Hence, correct option is (a).

18. *(b)* For *L-C-R* circuit, phase difference,

$$\phi = \tan^{-1}\left(\frac{X_L - X_C}{R}\right)$$

When *L* is removed, then $X_L = 0$

$$\therefore \quad \phi = \tan^{-1}\left(\frac{-X_C}{R}\right)$$

$$\Rightarrow \quad \tan\phi = \left|\frac{X_C}{R}\right| \quad \text{...(i)}$$

When *C* is removed, then $X_C = 0$

$$\therefore \quad \phi = \tan^{-1}\left(\frac{X_L}{R}\right)$$

$$\Rightarrow \quad \tan\phi = \frac{X_L}{R} \quad \text{...(ii)}$$

From Eqs. (i) and (ii), we get

$$X_L = X_C$$

$\therefore$ Impedance, $Z = \sqrt{R^2 + (X_L - X_C)^2}$

$= R$

Power factor, $\cos\phi = \frac{R}{Z} = \frac{R}{R} = 1$

Hence, correct option is (b).

19. *(d)* Relation for the height of water in capillary tube is

$$h = \frac{2S\cos\theta}{\rho g r}$$

$$\Rightarrow \quad h \propto \frac{1}{r}$$

$$\Rightarrow \quad \frac{h_1}{h_2} = \frac{r_2}{r_1} = \frac{2r}{r} = 2$$

As $\quad m = A \cdot h \cdot \rho$

$$\therefore \quad \frac{m_2}{m_1} = \frac{Ah_2\rho}{Ah_1\rho} = \frac{h_2}{h_1} = \frac{1}{2}$$

$$\Rightarrow \quad m_2 = \frac{m_1}{2} = \frac{5}{2} = 2.5 \text{ g}$$

Hence, correct option is (d).

20. *(b)* Fringe width, $\beta = \frac{\lambda D}{d}$

$$\therefore \quad \frac{\beta_2}{\beta_1} = \frac{\frac{\lambda_2 D_2}{d_2}}{\frac{\lambda_1 D_1}{d_1}}$$

[As $\lambda_1 = \lambda_2, D_2 = 2D_1$ and $d_2 = \frac{d_1}{2}$]

$$\Rightarrow \quad \frac{\beta_2}{\beta_1} = \frac{2D_1}{\left(\frac{d_1}{2}\right)} \times \frac{d_1}{D_1} = 4$$

$$\Rightarrow \quad \beta_2 = 4\beta_1$$

i.e. Fringe width becomes four times.

Hence, correct option is (b).

21. *(d)* Given, logic circuit is

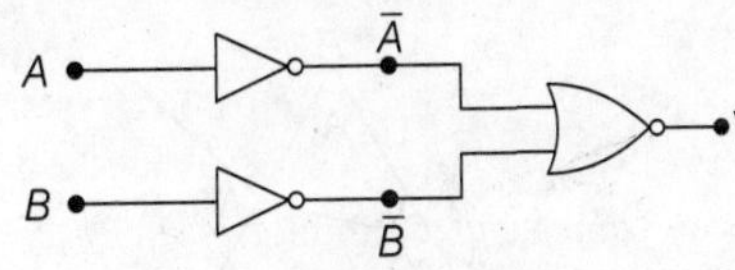

$$Y = \overline{\overline{A} + \overline{B}} = \overline{\overline{A}} \cdot \overline{\overline{B}}$$

[using de-Morgan's theorem, $\overline{x+y} = \overline{x} \cdot \overline{y}$]

$= A \cdot B \quad [\because \overline{\overline{x}} = x]$

Truth table for above given logic circuit is

A	B	$\overline{A}$	$\overline{B}$	$Y = A \cdot B$
0	0	1	1	0
0	1	1	0	0
1	0	0	1	0
1	1	0	0	1

$\Rightarrow$

A	B	Y
0	0	0
0	1	0
1	0	0
1	1	1

Hence, correct option is (d).

22. *(c)* According to the carbon colour code for resistors,

Code of yellow = 4

Code of violet = 7

Code of brown, i.e., multiplier = 10^1

Code of gold, i.e., tolerance = $\pm 5\%$

Hence, resistance of resistor

$= 47 \times 10^1 \Omega$, 5%

$= 470 \Omega$, 5%

Hence, correct option is (c).

23. *(b)* Given, $C_0 = 6\mu$F

$C_m = 30\mu$F

As, dielectric constant

$$K = \varepsilon_r = \frac{C_m}{C_0} = \frac{30}{6} = 5$$

Permittivity of the medium,

$$\varepsilon_m = K \times \varepsilon_0 = 5 \times \varepsilon_0$$

$$= 5 \times 8.85 \times 10^{-12}$$

$$= 0.44 \times 10^{-10} C^2N^{-1}m^{-2}$$

Hence, correct option is (b).

24. *(c)* Given, $u = 20$ m/s, $v = 80$ m/s, $g = 10$ ms^{-2} and $h = ?$

From kinematic equation of motion,

$$v^2 = u^2 + 2gh$$

$$\Rightarrow \quad h = \frac{v^2 - u^2}{2g}$$

$$= \frac{(80)^2 - (20)^2}{2 \times 10}$$

$$= 300 \text{ m}$$

Hence, correct option is (c).

25. *(a)* Given, $w = mg = 72$ N (on the surface of earth).

At a height equal to half of radius of the earth, $\left(\text{i.e. } h=\frac{R}{2}\right)$

Acceleration due to gravity,

$$g'=g\left(\frac{R}{R+h}\right)^2=g\left(\frac{R}{R+R/2}\right)^2$$

$$=g\left(\frac{4R^2}{9R^2}\right)$$

$$\Rightarrow \quad g'=\frac{4}{9}g$$

$$\Rightarrow \quad mg'=\frac{4}{9}mg=\frac{4}{9}\times 72=32\text{N}$$

$$w'=32\text{ N}$$

Hence, correct option is (a).

26. (b) Given, $m_1=5$ kg, $m_2=10$ kg and

$$r=1\text{ m}=100\text{ cm}$$

Let the centre of mass lies at origin O.

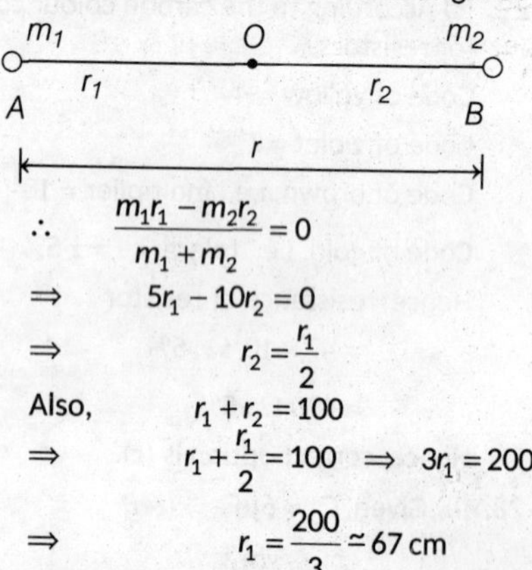

$$\therefore \quad \frac{m_1r_1-m_2r_2}{m_1+m_2}=0$$

$$\Rightarrow \quad 5r_1-10r_2=0$$

$$\Rightarrow \quad r_2=\frac{r_1}{2}$$

Also, $\quad r_1+r_2=100$

$$\Rightarrow \quad r_1+\frac{r_1}{2}=100 \Rightarrow 3r_1=200$$

$$\Rightarrow \quad r_1=\frac{200}{3}\simeq 67\text{ cm}$$

Hence, correct option is (b).

27. (a) Under reverse bias condition, the holes of p-side are attracted towards the negative terminal of the battery and electrons of the n-side are attracted towards the positive terminal of the battery. This increases the width of the depletion layer.

However, in the case of forward biasing, the width of the depletion layer decreases.

Hence, correct option is (a).

28. (c) Initially, frequency of light, $\nu=1.5\nu_0$

But when the frequency of incident light is halved, then

$$\nu'=\frac{\nu}{2}=\frac{1.5\nu_0}{2}=0.75\nu_0$$

$$\Rightarrow \quad \nu'<\nu_0$$

Thus, it becomes less than the threshold frequency. In that case, no photoelectric effect takes place. Hence, photoelectric current becomes zero.

Hence, correct option is (c).

29. (d) Given, light of wavelength,

$$\lambda=600\text{ nm}=600\times10^{-9}\text{ m}$$

Diameter, $d=2$ m

As, limit of resolution of telescope,

$$d\theta=\frac{1.22\lambda}{d}$$

$$=\frac{1.22\times600\times10^{-9}}{2}$$

$$=3.66\times10^{-7}\text{ rad}$$

Hence, correct option is (d).

30. (a) According to the question, the metre bridge is shown below,

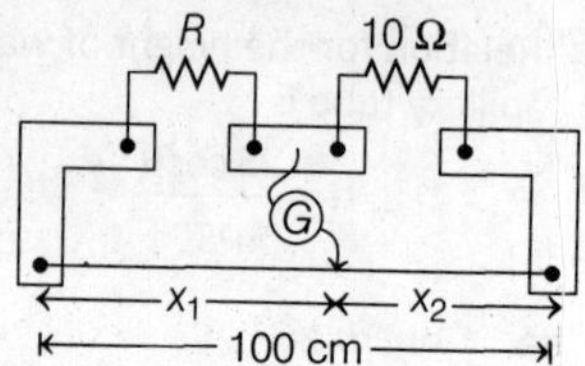

Given, $\frac{X_1}{X_2}=\frac{3}{2}$

At balance condition in metre bridge,

$$\frac{R}{10}=\frac{X_1}{X_2}$$

$$\Rightarrow \quad R=\frac{X_1}{X_2}\times10=\frac{3}{2}\times10=15\,\Omega$$

Now, length of given wire whose resistance 15 Ω is 1.5 m.

Therefore, length of 1Ω resistance wire is

$$=\frac{1.5}{15}=\frac{1}{10}=0.1=1\times10^{-1}\text{ m}$$

Hence, correct option is (a).

31. (b) Given, average flux $=20$ W/cm^2

Surface area $=20$ cm^2

Time $=1$ min $=60$ s

For non-reflecting surface,

energy received = average flux × surface area × time

$$=20\times20\times60=24\times10^3\text{ J}$$

32. (b) According to the question, the ray diagram can be shown as

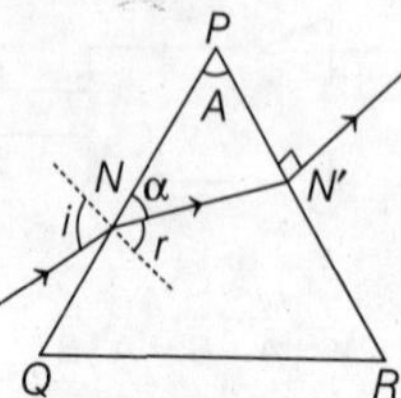

From figure in $\Delta PNN'$,

$$A+\alpha+90^\circ=180^\circ$$

$$\Rightarrow \quad \alpha=90^\circ-A \quad \text{...(i)}$$

Also, $\quad r+\alpha=90^\circ$

$$\Rightarrow \quad r=90^\circ-\alpha$$

$$=90^\circ-(90^\circ-A)=A$$

[∵ from Eq. (i)]

$$\Rightarrow \quad r=A \quad \text{...(ii)}$$

From Snell's law,

$$\mu_1\sin i=\mu_2\sin r$$

$\Rightarrow \sin i=\mu\sin A$ (here, $\mu_1=1$ and $\mu_2=\mu$)

For small angle, $\sin\theta\simeq\theta$

$$\Rightarrow \quad i=\mu A \quad [\because \text{from Eq. (ii)}]$$

Hence, correct option is (b).

33. (b) Given, $C=40\,\mu\text{F}=40\times10^{-6}$ F

$$V_{rms}=200\text{ V}$$

$$\nu=50\text{ Hz}$$

As, $\quad X_C=\frac{1}{2\pi\nu C}=\frac{1}{2\pi\times50\times40\times10^{-6}}$

$$=\frac{10^6}{100\pi\times40}=\frac{250}{\pi}\Omega$$

$$\therefore \quad I_{rms}=\frac{V_{rms}}{X_C}=\frac{200}{\left(\frac{250}{\pi}\right)}$$

$$=2.5\text{ A}$$

Hence, correct option is (b).

34. (c) ∵ Stress $=\frac{\text{Force}}{\text{Area}}$

∴ Dimensions of stress $=\frac{[\text{MLT}^{-2}]}{[\text{L}^2]}$

$$=[\text{ML}^{-1}\text{T}^{-2}]$$

Hence, correct option is (c).

35. (b) The Brewster's angle i_b for an interface should lie between 45° to 90°, i.e. $45^\circ<i_b<90^\circ$.

Hence, correct option is (b).

36. (c) Here, change in length, $\Delta L=(L_1-L)$

Area $=A$

Force, $F=Mg$

Young's modulus,

$$Y=\frac{\text{Normal stress}}{\text{Longitudinal strain}}$$

$$\Rightarrow Y=\frac{(F/A)}{\left(\frac{\Delta L}{L}\right)}=\frac{\frac{Mg}{A}}{\left(\frac{L_1-L}{L}\right)}=\frac{MgL}{A(L_1-L)}$$

Hence, correct option is (c).

37. (a) Given, electric dipole moment,

$$p=16\times10^{-9}\text{ C-m}$$

Distance, $r=0.6$ m

Angle, $\theta=60^\circ$

$$\Rightarrow \cos60^\circ=\frac{1}{2}$$

Electric potential at a point which is at a distance r at some angle θ from electric dipole is

$$V = \frac{p\cos\theta}{4\pi\varepsilon_0 r^2}$$

$$= \frac{9\times10^9\times16\times10^{-9}\times\frac{1}{2}}{(0.6)^2}$$

$$= 2\times10^2 = 200\text{ V}$$

Hence, correct option is (a).

38. (*a*) In case of beats formation, unknown frequency $(\nu_B) = \nu_A \pm$ beats where, $\nu_A = 530$ Hz and beats $= 6$ Hz.

$\Rightarrow \quad \nu_B = 530 \pm 6 = 536$ or 524 Hz

When tension in *B* is slightly decreased, then beat frequency increases to 7 Hz. This is possible, if we take original frequency of *B* as 524 Hz.

Hence, correct option is (a).

39. (*c*) Given, $\lambda = 1.227\times10^{-2}$ nm

$= 1.227\times10^{-11}$ m

Potential difference, $V = ?$

Relation for de-Broglie wavelength for moving electron is

$$\lambda = \frac{12.27}{\sqrt{V}}\text{ Å}$$

$$\Rightarrow \quad \sqrt{V} = \frac{12.27}{\lambda}\times10^{-10}$$

$$= \frac{12.27\times10^{-10}}{1.227\times10^{-11}} = 10^2$$

$$\Rightarrow \quad V = 10^4\text{ V}$$

Hence, correct option is (c).

40. (*c*) Insulators and semiconductors are those solids, which have negative temperature coefficient of resistance. As, when temperature increases resistance decreases in both insulator and semiconductor.

Hence, correct option is (c).

41. (*b*) Given, $E = 10^{-20}$ J

In terms of eV, we get

$$E = \frac{10^{-20}}{1.6\times10^{-19}}\text{ eV}$$

$$= 0.06\text{ eV}$$

Hence, correct option is (b).

42. (*d*) Since, heat required, $Q = mc\Delta T$

$$= \left(\frac{4}{3}\pi r^3\cdot\rho\right)c\Delta T$$

$[\because m = V_{\text{sphere}}\,\rho]$

Since, π, ρ, c and T are constants.

$$\Rightarrow \quad Q \propto r^3$$

or

$$\frac{Q_1}{Q_2} = \frac{r_1^3}{r_2^3}$$

$$= \left(\frac{r_1}{r_2}\right)^3 = \left(\frac{1.5r_2}{r_2}\right)^3$$

$$= \frac{27}{8}$$

Hence, correct option is (d).

43. (*b*) Resistivity of copper (a metal) as a function of temperature increases with the increase in temperature as shown below,

For copper at 0 K, value of resistivity is $1.7\times10^{-8}\ \Omega$-m.

Hence, correct option is (b).

44. (*c*) In case of transistor action, base region is thin and lightly doped. While, emitter region is heavily doped and collector region is moderately doped. Also, the size of collector is slightly more than the size of emitter.

Hence, option (c) is correct.

45. (c) Since, Bohr's model is valid for hydrogen and hydrogen like atoms He^+, deuteron, etc. So, it is not valid for singly ionised neon atom (Ne^+).

Hence, correct option is (c).

The Real Nuts 2

1. (*d*) Given,

$V_L = 40$ V, $V_C = 10$ V

and $V_R = 40$ V

The amplitude of the current flowing in the *L-C-R* series circuit,

$$I_0 = 10\sqrt{2}\text{ A} \quad \text{...(i)}$$

We know that, rms current in the *L-C-R* series circuit,

$$I_{\text{rms}} = \frac{I_0}{\sqrt{2}}$$

$$I_{\text{rms}} = \frac{10\sqrt{2}}{\sqrt{2}} \quad \text{[from Eq. (i)]}$$

$$\Rightarrow \quad I_{\text{rms}} = 10\text{ A}$$

$$\therefore \quad V_{\text{rms}} = \sqrt{V_R^2 + (V_L - V_C)^2}$$

$$\Rightarrow \quad V_{\text{rms}} = \sqrt{(40)^2 + (40-10)^2}$$

$$\Rightarrow \quad V_{\text{rms}} = 50\text{ V}$$

The impedance of the *L-C-R* series circuit,

$$Z = \frac{V_{\text{rms}}}{I_{\text{rms}}}$$

$$\Rightarrow \quad Z = \frac{50\text{ V}}{10\text{ A}} \text{ or } Z = 5\Omega$$

2. (*a*) Given, the refractive index of the glass, $n_2 = \sqrt{3}$

The refractive index of the air, $n_1 = 1$

The path of ray incident on the prism is as shown below.

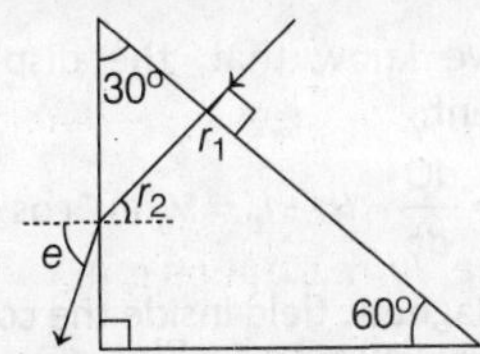

From the given figure, $r_1 = 0°$

As $\quad A = r_1 + r_2$

where, *A* is the angle of prism.

$$30° = 0° + r_2$$

$$\Rightarrow \quad r_2 = 30°$$

Using the Snell's law, in glass and air interference,

$$n_2\sin\theta_2 = n_1\sin\theta_1$$

$$\Rightarrow \quad n_2\sin r_2 = n_1\sin e$$

$$\Rightarrow \quad \sqrt{3}\sin 30° = 1\times\sin e$$

$$\Rightarrow \quad \sin e = \frac{\sqrt{3}}{2}$$

$$\Rightarrow \quad \sin e = \sin 60°$$

$$\Rightarrow \quad e = 60°$$

3. (*b*) We know that, the direction of electric dipole moment is from negative charge to positive charge.

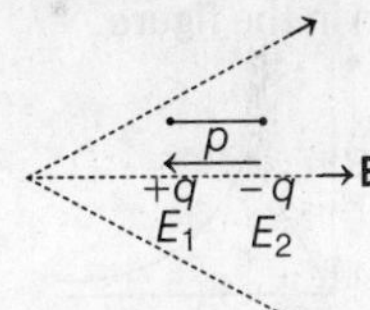

The strength of the electric field at $+q$ is greater than that at $-q$ charge, i.e. $|E_1| > |E_2|$.

So, the net force on the dipole act towards the right side.

We know that, a system always moves to decrease its potential energy.

So, the given dipole will move towards right side as its potential energy will decrease.

4. (*a*) Given, AC source voltage,

$$V = V_0\sin\omega t \quad \text{...(i)}$$

We know that,

$$Q = CV \quad \text{...(ii)}$$

Here, *Q* is the charge on the capacitor.

C is the capacitance of the capacitor, V is the AC source voltage.

On differentiating Eq. (ii) w.r.t. time, we get

$$\frac{dQ}{dt}=\frac{d(CV)}{dt}$$

$$\Rightarrow \quad \frac{dQ}{dt}=\frac{Cd(V_0 \sin \omega t)}{dt} \quad \text{[from Eq. (i)]}$$

$$\Rightarrow \quad \frac{dQ}{dt}=C\omega V_0 \cos \omega t$$

As we know that, the displacement current,

$$I_d=\frac{dQ}{dt} \Rightarrow I_d=V_0\, \omega C \cos \omega t$$

5. (*c*) Magnetic field inside the conducting cylindrical cable,

$$B=\frac{\mu_0 I}{2\pi R^2}r$$

Here, R is the radius of the cylindrical cable,

r is the distance from the axis of the cylinder,

I is the current in the cylindrical cable.

$$\Rightarrow \quad B \propto r$$

$\therefore$ The graph of magnetic field B with r is a straight line passing through origin.

For a point outside the cylinder,

$$B=\frac{\mu_0 I}{2\pi r} \Rightarrow B \propto \frac{1}{r}$$

The graph of magnetic field B with r is a rectangular hyperbola.

$\therefore$ The variation of the magnetic field B due to the cable with the distance r from the axis of the cylindrical cable is as shown in the figure.

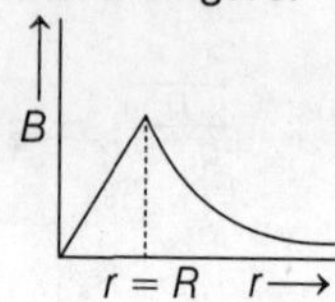

6. (*b*) Given, the focal length of convex lens A,

$$f_1=+20 \text{ cm}$$

The focal length of concave lens B,

$$f_2=-5 \text{ cm}$$

The convex lens is the converging lens and the concave lens is the diverging lens.

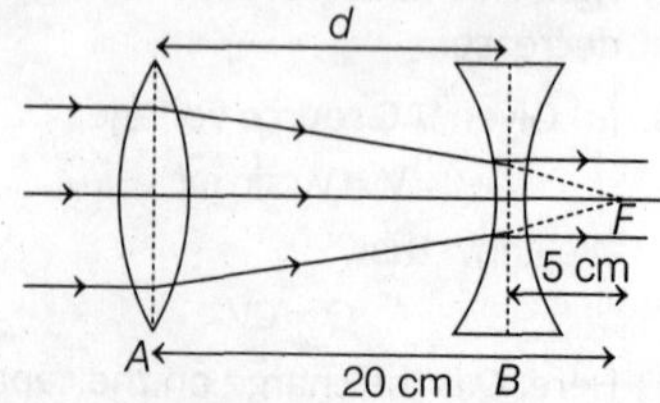

When the parallel beam of light passes through the convex lens, it converges at the focal point F and the distance between lens A to F point is 20 cm.

Now, after emerging from the lens B, the beam is still parallel in nature. So, the net focal length of the lens A and B will be infinite.

As we know,

$$\frac{1}{f}=\frac{1}{f_1}+\frac{1}{f_2}-\frac{d}{f_1 f_2}$$

$$\Rightarrow \quad \frac{1}{\infty}=\frac{1}{20}-\frac{1}{5}+\frac{d}{20\times 5}$$

$$\Rightarrow \quad \frac{3}{20}=\frac{d}{20\times 5}$$

or $\quad d=3\times 5=15$ cm

7. (*c*) We know that, de-Broglie wavelength,

$$\lambda_d=\frac{h}{mv}$$

Kinetic energy of the photoelectrons,

$$KE=\frac{1}{2}mv^2$$

$$\Rightarrow \quad v=\sqrt{\frac{2\times KE}{m}}$$

Here, m is the mass of photoelectrons.

Substituting the value of v in de-Broglie wavelength equation, we get

$$\lambda_d=\frac{h}{\sqrt{2mKE}} \quad \text{.... (i)}$$

Since, work-function of photosensitive surface is negligible, hence the kinetic energy of photoelectron is equal to the energy of the photon of electromagnetic wave,

$$KE=\frac{1}{2}mv^2=\frac{hc}{\lambda}$$

Substituting the value of KE in Eq. (i), we get

$$\lambda_d=\frac{h}{\sqrt{2m\left(\frac{hc}{\lambda}\right)}}$$

Squaring both sides of the above equation, we get

$$\lambda_d^2=\frac{h^2}{2m\left(\frac{hc}{\lambda}\right)}$$

$$\Rightarrow \quad \lambda=\left(\frac{2mc}{h}\right)\times \lambda_d^2$$

8. (*a*) As we know that, the expression of the drift velocity,

$$v_d=\frac{eE}{m}\tau$$

Here, e is the electric charge, E is the electric field, m is the mass of an electron and τ is the relaxation time.

Consider the conductor having length l, area of the cross-section A and the charge density n.

Electrical resistivity, $\rho=\frac{m}{ne^2\tau}$

Rearranging the above expression

Relaxation period, $\tau=\frac{m}{ne^2\rho}$

As we know that, the expression of current density,

$$J=\frac{I}{A}=\frac{neAv_d}{A}=nev_d$$

Again, $\frac{E}{J}=\frac{E}{\sigma E}=\frac{1}{\sigma}=\rho$

$\therefore$ Electrical resistivity, $\rho=\frac{E}{J}$

The correct match is A$\to$3, B$\to$4, C$\to$1, D$\to$2.

9. (*c*) As we know that, in α-decay, the atomic number is decreased by 2 units.

$$X_Z^A \longrightarrow {}_{Z-2}^{A-4}Y+{}_2^4\text{He}$$

In β^+-decay, the atomic number is decreased by 1 unit.

$$X_Z^A \longrightarrow {}_{Z-1}^{A}Y+{}_{+1}^{0}e+\bar{\nu}$$

In β^--decay, the atomic number is increased by 1 unit.

$$X_Z^A \longrightarrow {}_{Z+1}^{A}Y+{}_{-1}^{0}e+\bar{\nu}$$

From the above relations, the spontaneous decay given in question can be written as

$$X_Z^A \xrightarrow{\beta^+} {}_{Z-1}B \xrightarrow{\alpha} {}_{Z-3}C \xrightarrow{\beta^-} {}_{Z-2}D$$

The possible decay particles in the sequence are β^+, α, β^-.

10. (*d*) Four resistances have equal length, equal cross-sectional area and same material.

So, $R_1=R_2=R_3=R_4=R$ (say)

Given, the effective resistance,

$$R_{eq}=0.25\,\Omega$$

For parallel arrangement,

$$\frac{1}{R_{eq}}=\frac{1}{R_1}+\frac{1}{R_2}+\frac{1}{R_3}+\frac{1}{R_4}$$

$$\Rightarrow \quad \frac{1}{R_{eq}}=\frac{1}{R}+\frac{1}{R}+\frac{1}{R}+\frac{1}{R}$$

$$\Rightarrow \quad \frac{1}{0.25\Omega}=\frac{4}{R}$$

$$\Rightarrow \quad R=1\,\Omega$$

For series combination,

$$R_{eq} = R_1 + R_2 + R_3 + R_4$$

$\Rightarrow \quad R_{eq} = R + R + R + R$

$\Rightarrow \quad R_{eq} = 4R$

$\Rightarrow \quad R_{eq} = 4(1) = 4\Omega$

11. (*d*) Let the particle at height S from the surface of the earth is as shown.

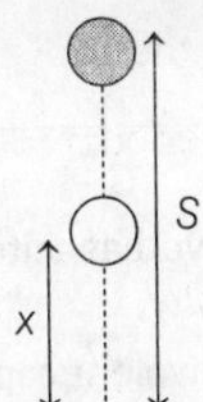

Given, at height x, kinetic energy = 3 (potential energy)

$\Rightarrow \quad KE = 3mgx$

At height S, total energy,

TE = PE + KE

TE = $mgS + 0$

$= mgS$

At height x, total energy,

TE = PE + KE

TE = $mgx + 3mgx$

$mgS = 4mgx$

$\Rightarrow \quad x = \frac{S}{4} \quad$ ...(i)

Now, we shall determine the speed of the particle at this height.

As, $\quad KE = 3 \times mgx$

$KE = 3 \times mg\frac{S}{4}$ [from Eq. (i)]

$\frac{1}{2}mv^2 = \frac{3}{4}mgS$

$\Rightarrow \quad v = \sqrt{\frac{3Sg}{2}}$

12. (*b*) Given, the half-life of a radioactive nuclide, $t_{1/2} = 100$ h

As we know that,

$$A = \frac{A_0}{2^{t/t_{1/2}}}$$

Here, A_0 is the original activity of the nuclide,

A is the activity of the nuclide after time t.

$\Rightarrow \quad \frac{A}{A_0} = 2^{-t/t_{1/2}} = 2^{\frac{150}{100}}$

$= 2^{-3/2} = \frac{1}{2\sqrt{2}}$

So, the fraction of original activity that will remain after 150 h will be $\frac{1}{2\sqrt{2}}$.

13. (*b*) **In first condition**

Given, the initial temperature of the cup of coffee ,$T_i = 90°$ C

The final temperature of the cup of coffee, $T_f = 80°$ C

The time taken to drop the temperature 90°C to 80°C is t.

The temperature of the surrounding, $T_0 = 20°$ C

Using the Newton's law of cooling,

$$\text{rate of cooling} = \frac{dT}{dt} = K\left[\frac{T_i + T_f}{2} - T_0\right]$$

Substituting the values in the above equation, we get

$$\frac{90 - 80}{t} = K\left[\frac{90 + 80}{2} - 20\right]$$

$\Rightarrow \quad \frac{10}{t} = K[65]$

$\Rightarrow \quad K = \frac{2}{13t}$

In second condition

The initial temperature of the cup of coffee,$T_i' = 80°$ C

The final temperature of the cup of coffee, $T_f' = 60°$ C

Using the Newton's law of cooling,

$$\text{rate of cooling} = \frac{dT}{dt} = K\left[\frac{T'_i + T'_f}{2} - T_0\right]$$

Substituting the values in the above equation, we get

$$\frac{80 - 60}{t_1} = \frac{2}{13t}\left[\frac{80 + 60}{2} - 20\right]$$

$\frac{20}{t_1} = \frac{2}{13t}[50]$

$\Rightarrow \quad t_1 = \frac{13}{5}t$

14. (*c*) Given, the monochromatic light of the wavelength, $\lambda = 600$ nm

The power of the source,

$$P = 3.3 \times 10^{-3} \text{ W}$$

We know that, $P = \frac{nhc}{\lambda}$

Here, P is the power of the source,

n is the number of photons per second,

h is the Planck's constant,

c is the speed of the light in vacuum,

λ is the wavelength of the monochromatic light.

Substituting the values in the above equation, we get

$$3.3 \times 10^{-3} = \frac{n \times 6.6 \times 10^{-34} \times 3 \times 10^8}{600 \times 10^{-9}}$$

$\Rightarrow \quad n = 10^{16}$

15. (*b*) In simple harmonic motion, both the kinetic energy and potential energy attains their maximum value two times in one complete oscillation. Hence, frequency of kinetic energy and potential energy is 2 for one complete oscillation. So, the frequency of the potential energy of a body executing SHM with frequency n is $2n$.

16. (*d*) Given, the current in infinitely long straight conductor, $I = 5$ A

The electron is moving with speed, $v = 10^5$ m/s

The perpendicular distance between the electron and the conductor, $r = 20$ cm $= 0.20$ m

Now, the magnetic field experience by electron due to infinitely long straight conductor,

$$B = \frac{\mu_0 I}{2\pi r}$$

$\Rightarrow \quad B = \frac{4\pi \times 10^{-7} \times 5}{2\pi\,(0.20)}$

$\Rightarrow \quad B = 5 \times 10^{-6}$ T

The magnetic force experience by an electron,

$$F = evB$$

Here, e is the charge of an electron,

v is the velocity of an electron,

B is the magnetic field experience by an electron.

Substituting the values in the above equation, we get

$$F = 1.6 \times 10^{-19} \times 10^5 \times 5 \times 10^{-6}$$

$$F = 8 \times 10^{-20} \text{ N}$$

17. (*b*) Given, fundamental physical quantities are force [F], acceleration [a] and time [T].

Now, we shall determine the dimensions of the energy.

Energy depends on force, acceleration and time as,

$$[E] = [F]^a[a]^b[T]^c$$

$\Rightarrow \quad [ML^2T^{-2}] = [MLT^{-2}]^a[LT^{-2}]^b[T]^c$

$\Rightarrow \quad [ML^2T^{-2}] = [M]^a[L]^{a+b}[T]^{-2a-2b+c}$

Comparing the powers of M, L and T on both sides, we get

$a = 1, \quad a + b = 2$ and $-2a - 2b + c = -2$

$\Rightarrow \quad 1 + b = 2$

$\Rightarrow \quad b = 1$

$\Rightarrow \quad -2(1) - 2(1) + c = -2$

$\Rightarrow \quad c = 2$

The dimensions of the energy are [F a T^2].

18. (c) We know that, the rms speed of the gas molecules,

$$v_{rms} = \sqrt{3RT/M}$$

Here, T is the temperature of the gas, R is the universal gas constant, M is the molar mass of the gas.

Pressure exerted by an ideal gas,

$$p = \frac{1}{3} nm\bar{v}^2$$

Here, n is the number of moles, m is the mass of the gas, $\bar{v}$ is the average speed of the gas molecules.

The average kinetic energy of a molecule,

$$KE_{av} = \frac{3}{2} k_B T$$

Here, k_B is the Boltzmann's constant, T is the temperature of the gas.

For diatomic gas, degree of freedom, $f = 5$

As, total internal energy of 1 mole of diatomic gas,

$$\Delta U = \frac{nfRT}{2}$$

$$\Rightarrow \quad \Delta U = \frac{1(5)RT}{2}$$

$$\Rightarrow \quad \Delta U = \frac{5RT}{2}$$

The correct match is A $\rightarrow$ 2, B $\rightarrow$ 1, C $\rightarrow$ 4 and D $\rightarrow$ 3.

19. (b) Distance covered in nth seconds is s_n.

Distance covered in $(n+1)$th seconds is s_{n+1}.

Initial velocity of small block, $u = 0$

Distance covered in nth seconds,

$$s_n = u + \frac{a}{2}(2n-1)$$

$$\Rightarrow \quad s_n = 0 + \frac{a}{2}(2n-1)$$

$$\Rightarrow \quad s_n = \frac{a}{2}(2n-1) \quad \text{...(i)}$$

Distance covered in $(n+1)$ th seconds,

$$s_{n+1} = u + \frac{a}{2}[2(n+1)-1]$$

$$\Rightarrow \quad s_{n+1} = 0 + \frac{a}{2}(2n+2-1)$$

$$\Rightarrow \quad s_{n+1} = \frac{a}{2}(2n+1) \quad \text{...(ii)}$$

On dividing Eq. (i) by Eq. (ii), we get

$$\frac{s_n}{s_{n+1}} = \frac{\frac{a}{2}(2n-1)}{\frac{a}{2}(2n+1)}$$

$$\Rightarrow \quad \frac{s_n}{s_{n+1}} = \frac{2n-1}{2n+1}$$

20. (d) A nucleus with mass number 240 breaks into two fragment each of mass number 120.

$$X^{240} \longrightarrow Y^{120} + Z^{120}$$

Given, the binding energy per nucleon of unfragmented nuclei, $X = 7.6$ MeV

The binding energy per nucleon of fragmented nuclei, $Y = Z = 8.5$ MeV

Now, we shall determine the total gain in binding energy.

Gain in binding energy = Binding energy of products − Binding energy of reactants

Gain in binding energy

$$= 2 \times 120 \times 8.5 - 240 \times 7.6$$

$$= 216 \text{ MeV}$$

21. (d) Given, the main scale reading, MSR = 0

The circular scale reading, CSR = 52 divisions

Now, we shall determine the least count of the screw gauge,

$$LC = \frac{p}{n}$$

Here, p is the pitch of the screw and n is the number of circular divisions in one complete revolution.

$$LC = \frac{1}{100} \text{ mm}$$

$$\Rightarrow \quad LC = 0.01 \text{ mm}$$

$$\Rightarrow \quad LC = 0.001 \text{ cm}$$

Thus, the least count of the screw gauge is 0.001 cm.

Therefore, diameter of the wire of screw gauge,

$$D = MSR + (CSR \times LC)$$

$$\Rightarrow \quad D = 0 + (52 \times 0.001)$$

$$\Rightarrow \quad D = 0.052 \text{ cm}$$

22. (b) Consider the nodes be A, B, E and F as shown in the following figure.

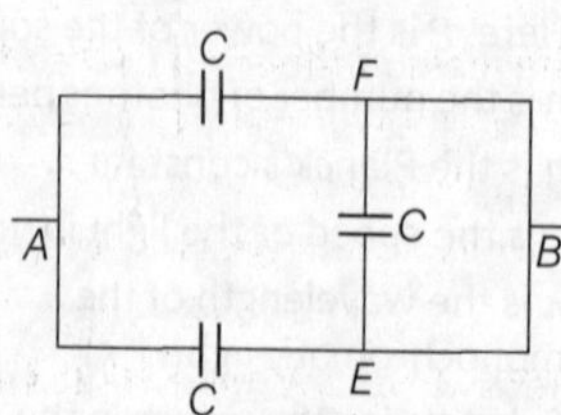

The potential at node A is equal to the potential at node B.

Similarly, the potential at node F is equal to the potential at node E.

So, there is no potential difference between the EF arms, thus no current (or charge) will flow in the circuit.

So, EF behave as an open circuit.

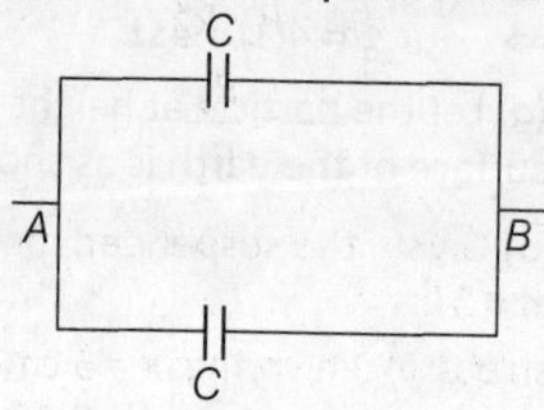

Now, the two capacitors are arranged in parallel.

The net equivalent capacitance

$$C_{eq} = C_1 + C_2$$

$$\Rightarrow \quad C_{eq} = C + C$$

$$\Rightarrow \quad C_{eq} = 2C$$

23. (d) The objective of an astronomical telescope has large focal length and large aperture. Because the lens used is convex lens and the magnification of an astronomical telescope is directly proportional to the focal length of the objective lens.

This large aperture also contributes to the better quality and visibility of the images. Thus, it provides better resolution.

Due to large focal length of the objective, it covers large area which ensures better light gathering power.

Thus, all options (a), (b) and (c) are correct.

24. (b) When two charged spherical conductors are connected by a conducting wire, the potential becomes same in both the spherical conductor, i.e.,

$V_1 = V_2$

$$\Rightarrow \quad \frac{Kq_1}{R_1} = \frac{Kq_2}{R_2}$$

$$\Rightarrow \quad \frac{q_1}{q_2} = \frac{R_1}{R_2} \quad \text{...(i)}$$

As we know that, the surface charge density of the charged spherical conductor,

$$\sigma = \frac{q}{4\pi R^2}$$

where, q is the charge on the spherical conductor, r is the radius of the spherical conductor.

$$\therefore \quad \frac{\sigma_1}{\sigma_2} = \frac{\frac{q_1}{4\pi R_1^2}}{\frac{q_2}{4\pi R_2^2}}$$

$$\Rightarrow \frac{\sigma_1}{\sigma_2} = \frac{q_1}{q_2}\frac{R_2^2}{R_1^2}$$

$$\Rightarrow \frac{\sigma_1}{\sigma_2} = \frac{R_1}{R_2}\frac{R_2^2}{R_1^2} \quad \text{[from Eq. (i)]}$$

$$\Rightarrow \frac{\sigma_1}{\sigma_2} = \frac{R_2}{R_1}$$

25. (*d*) Given, the suspended mass, $m = 2$ kg

stretching in spring, $x = 5$ cm $= 0.05$ m

The constant force applied on the spring, $F = 10$ N

As we know that, spring force,

$$F = kx$$

$$\Rightarrow 10\text{ N} = k\,(0.05\text{ m})$$

$$\Rightarrow k = 200\text{ N/m}$$

Now, time period of the oscillation,

$$T = 2\pi\sqrt{\frac{m}{k}}$$

$$\Rightarrow T = 2\pi\sqrt{\frac{2}{200}}$$

Time period, $T = 0.628$ s

26. (*b*) We know that, in electromagnetic wave, the electric field (*E*) and magnetic field (*B*) are perpendicular to each other,

$$\mathbf{E}\cdot\mathbf{B} = 0$$

Consider the option (a),

$$(\hat{\mathbf{j}}+\hat{\mathbf{k}})\cdot(\hat{\mathbf{j}}+\hat{\mathbf{k}}) = 1+1 = 2 \neq 0$$

So, it is incorrect option.

Consider the option (b),

$$(-\hat{\mathbf{j}}+\hat{\mathbf{k}})\cdot(-\hat{\mathbf{j}}-\hat{\mathbf{k}}) = 1-1 = 0$$

Hence, it satisfies the condition $\mathbf{E}\cdot\mathbf{B} = 0$

Similarly, options (c) and (d) are incorrect.

So, the correct option is (b).

27. (*d*) We know that,

escape velocity from earth's surface,

$$v_e = \sqrt{\frac{2GM_e}{R_e}}$$

where, *G* is the gravitational constant, R_e is the radius of the earth, M_e is the mass of the earth.

Also, $\text{density} = \frac{\text{mass}}{\text{volume}}$

$$\Rightarrow \text{Mass} = \text{Density} \times \text{Volume}$$

or $M_e = \rho \times V$

or $M_e = \rho \times \frac{4}{3}\pi R_e^3 \quad \left(\because V = \frac{4}{3}\pi R_e^3\right)$

Substituting the values in the escape velocity expression, we get

$$v_e = \sqrt{\frac{2G\rho \times \frac{4}{3}\pi R_e^3}{R_e}}$$

$$v_e = \sqrt{2G\rho \times \frac{4}{3}\pi R_e^2} \quad \text{...(i)}$$

Now, we shall determine the escape velocity for another planet.

Given, radius of another planet is 4 times the radius of the earth,

$$\Rightarrow v_p = \sqrt{2G\rho \times \frac{4}{3}\pi R_p^2}$$

$$v_p = \sqrt{2G\rho \times \frac{4}{3}\pi (4R_e)^2}$$

$$v_p = 4\sqrt{2G\rho \times \frac{4}{3}\pi (R_e)^2} \quad \text{...(ii)}$$

On dividing Eq. (ii) by Eq. (i), we get

$$\frac{v_p}{v_e} = \frac{4\sqrt{2G\rho \times \frac{4}{3}\pi (R_e)^2}}{\sqrt{2G\rho \times \frac{4}{3}\pi R_e^2}}$$

$$\Rightarrow v_p = 4v_e = 4v$$

28. (*a*) Given, length of balancing point,

$L_1 = 36$ cm

$E_1 = 1.5$ V

$E_2 = 2.5$ V

We know that,

$$\text{potential gradient} = \frac{E}{L}$$

$$\Rightarrow \frac{E_1}{L_1} = \frac{E_2}{L_2}$$

where, L_2 is the length of the balancing point for cell of emf E_2.

Substituting the values in the above equation, we get

$$\frac{1.5}{36} = \frac{2.5}{L_2}$$

$$\Rightarrow L_2 = 60\text{ cm}$$

29. (*a*) Given, the density of the small ball is *d*,

the mass of the small ball is *M* and the density of the glycerine is *d*/2.

As we know that,

viscous force = weight − buoyant force

$$F_v = Vd_1g - Vd_2g \quad \text{...(i)}$$

Here, *V* is the volume of submerged bodies, *g* is the acceleration due to gravity, d_1 is the density of the small ball and d_2 is the density of the glycerine.

$$d_1 = d$$

and $d_2 = d/2$

Substituting the given values in Eq. (i), we get

$$F_v = Vdg - V\frac{d}{2}g$$

$$\Rightarrow \frac{Vdg}{2} = \frac{Mg}{2} \quad (\because M = d \times V)$$

30. (*c*) We know that, capacitance of a parallel plate capacitor,

$$C = \frac{A\varepsilon_0}{d} \quad \text{...(i)}$$

The relation between the potential difference (*V*) and electric field (*E*),

$$V = Ed \quad \text{...(ii)}$$

The energy stored in the capacitor,

$$U = \frac{1}{2}CV^2$$

$$= \frac{1}{2}\left(\frac{\varepsilon_0 A}{d}\right)(Ed)^2$$

[from Eqs. (i) and (ii)]

$$= \frac{1}{2}(\varepsilon_0 A)(E)^2 d$$

or $U = \frac{1}{2}\varepsilon_0 E^2 Ad$

31. (*c*) Given, the electron concentration in *n*-type semiconductor is equal to the hole's concentration in *p*-type semiconductor.

When electric field is applied across the semiconductor, the electrons and holes will move opposite to each other. The mobility of *n*-type semiconductor is greater than the mobility of *p*-type semiconductor.

So, the current in the *n*-type semiconductor is greater than the current in the *p*-type semiconductor.

32. (*c*) Zener diode is a type of special *p-n* junction diode that operates in reverse bias. Thus, it is used as a voltage regulator. So, the statement (A) is correct.

The potential barrier of *p-n* junction for silicon is 0.6-0.7 V and for germanium is 0.2-0.35 V.

So, the statement (B) is incorrect.

33. (*d*) In polar molecules, the positive charge and negative charge do not overlap each other. So, the total charge on the polar molecule is zero. Thus, these types of molecules have permanent electric dipole moment. e.g. Water is polar molecule.

34. (*a*) The dimensions of energy

$$[E] = [F]\cdot[d]$$

$$\Rightarrow [E] = [MLT^{-2}]\,[L]$$

$$\Rightarrow [E] = [ML^2T^{-2}]$$

As we know that, the expression of gravitational force,

$$F = \frac{GM_1M_2}{r^2}$$

$$\Rightarrow \quad G = \frac{Fr^2}{M_1M_2}$$

$$\therefore \quad [G] = \frac{[F][r^2]}{[M_1][M_2]}$$

$$\Rightarrow \quad [G] = \frac{[MLT^{-2}][L^2]}{[M]\,[M]}$$

$$\Rightarrow \quad [G] = [M^{-1}L^3T^{-2}]$$

The dimensions of

$$\frac{E}{G} = \frac{[ML^2T^{-2}]}{[M^{-1}L^3T^{-2}]}$$

$$\Rightarrow \quad \left[\frac{E}{G}\right] = [M^2L^{-1}T^0]$$

35. (*b*) Given, the flow rate of the water, $\frac{m}{t}$ =15 kg/s

The height of the water fall, h = 60 m

Losses due to frictional force = 10%

The power used in the turbine

= (100 − 10) %

= 90%

The acceleration due to gravity,

$$g = 10 \text{ m/s}^2$$

We know that, power generated by the turbine

= change in potential energy = $0.90 \frac{mgh}{t}$

= 0.90 × 15 × 10 × 60

= 8100 W

= 8.1 kW

36. (*d*) Given, the initial velocity of a car,

$$u = 0$$

The acceleration of a car, $a = 5 \text{ m/s}^2$

At $t = 4$ s, $v = u + at$

$$\Rightarrow \quad v = 0 + (5)4$$

$$\Rightarrow \quad v = 20 \text{ m/s}$$

Thus, the final velocity of car at t = 4 s is 20 m/s.

At t = 4 s, the ball is dropped out of a window by a person sitting in the car.

The velocity of the ball in the x-direction,

$v_x = 20$ m/s (due to the car)

Therefore, in the y-direction, the acceleration is equal to the acceleration due to gravity,

$$a_y = g = 10 \text{ m/s}^2$$

The velocity of the ball in the y-direction,

$$v_y = u + a_y t$$

$$\Rightarrow \quad v_y = 0 + 10 \times 2 \quad (\because t = 6 - 4 = 2\text{s})$$

$$\Rightarrow \quad v_y = 20 \text{ m/s}$$

Thus, the velocity of the ball in y-direction is 20 m/s.

The net velocity at t = 6s,

$$v = \sqrt{v_x^2 + v_y^2}$$

$$\Rightarrow \quad v = \sqrt{(20)^2 + (20)^2}$$

$$\Rightarrow \quad v = 20\sqrt{2} \text{ m/s}$$

Thus, the velocity of the ball at t = 6 s is $20\sqrt{2}$ m/s.

As, there is no acceleration in the x-direction, $a_x = 0 \text{ ms}^{-2}$

In y-direction, $a_y = 10 \text{ ms}^{-2}$

Now, we shall determine the net acceleration at t = 6 s,

$$a = \sqrt{a_x^2 + a_y^2}$$

$$\Rightarrow \quad a = \sqrt{(0) + (10)^2}$$

$$\Rightarrow \quad a = 10 \text{ ms}^{-2}$$

37. (*c*) Output of the given logic circuit is given as

$$Y = \overline{AB} + \overline{BC}$$

Truth table for the given input waveforms A,B and C.

Time interval	A	B	C	AB	BC	$\overline{AB}$	$\overline{BC}$	$Y = \overline{AB} + \overline{BC}$
$0\text{-}t_1$	0	0	1	0	0	1	1	1
$t_1\text{-}t_2$	1	0	1	0	0	1	1	1
$t_2\text{-}t_3$	0	1	0	0	0	1	1	1
$t_3\text{-}t_4$	1	1	0	1	0	0	1	1
$t_4\text{-}t_5$	0	0	1	0	0	1	1	1
$t_5\text{-}t_6$	1	0	1	0	0	1	1	1

Hence, output waveform will be 5 V.

Thus, option (c) is correct.

38. (*b*) Given, the mass of the ball, m = 0.15 kg

The height from the ground,

$$h = 10 \text{ m}$$

We know that,

$$|\text{Impulse}| = m\,|\Delta \vec{v}|$$

where, $\Delta \vec{v} = \vec{v}_2 - \vec{v}_1$

Here, v_2 is velocity on reaching the height (h) and v_1 is velocity just before striking to the ground.

For case (1) Ball dropped from the 10m height and strikes to the ground.

Now, the velocity of the ball just before striking the ground is

$$v_1 = -\sqrt{2gh}$$

$$\Rightarrow \quad v_1 = -\sqrt{2(10)(10)}$$

$$\Rightarrow \quad v_1 = -10\sqrt{2} \text{ m/s}$$

For case (2) Ball rebounds to the same height.

The velocity with which the ball just reaches to the same height,

$$v_2 = \sqrt{2gh}$$

$$\Rightarrow \quad v_2 = \sqrt{2(10)(10)}$$

$$\Rightarrow \quad v_2 = 10\sqrt{2} \text{ m/s}$$

Now, magnitude of the impulse imparted to the ball,

$$|\text{Impulse}| = m\,|\Delta \vec{v}|$$

$$= 0.15\,|10\sqrt{2} - (-10\sqrt{2})|$$

$$= 0.15|2 \times 10\sqrt{2}|$$

$$= 4.2 \text{ kg - m/s}$$

39. (*d*) Given, the length of a uniform rod, L = 200 cm

The wedge is placed at the mark = 40 cm

The mass of the rod = 500 g = 0.5 kg

The mass suspended from the rod at 20 cm distance from the end, M = 2 kg

Another unknown mass suspended from the rod at 160 cm distance from the end = m

Let's draw the diagram of the uniform rod suspended with mass.

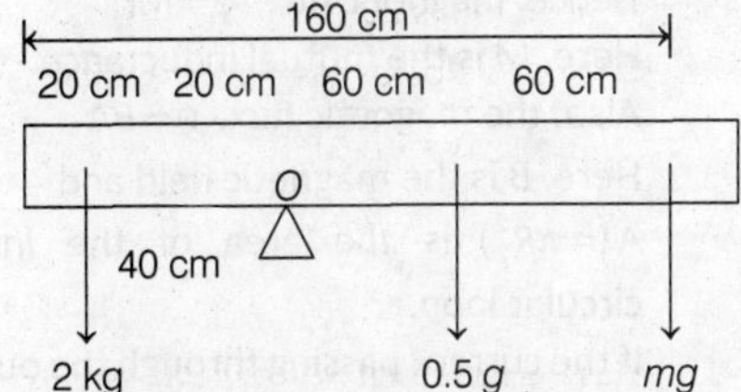

As we know in equilibrium, net moment of force is equal to zero.

$\Rightarrow 0.5\,g\,(0.60) + mg\,(1.20) - 2g\,(0.20) = 0$

$\Rightarrow \quad 0.3 + 1.20m - 0.4 = 0$

$\Rightarrow \quad 1.20m = 0.1 \Rightarrow m = \frac{1}{12}$ kg

40. (*d*) Given, the focal length of the convex lens, $f = +30$ cm

The object distance from the lens, $u = -60$ cm

The image formed by the lens be at distance v, then by using lens formula,

$$\frac{1}{f} = \frac{1}{v} - \frac{1}{u}$$

$$\frac{1}{+30} = \frac{1}{v} - \frac{1}{(-60)} \Rightarrow \frac{1}{+30} = \frac{60+v}{60v}$$

$\Rightarrow 2v = 60 + v \Rightarrow v = 60$ cm

Let's draw the ray diagram of the convex lens and mirror.

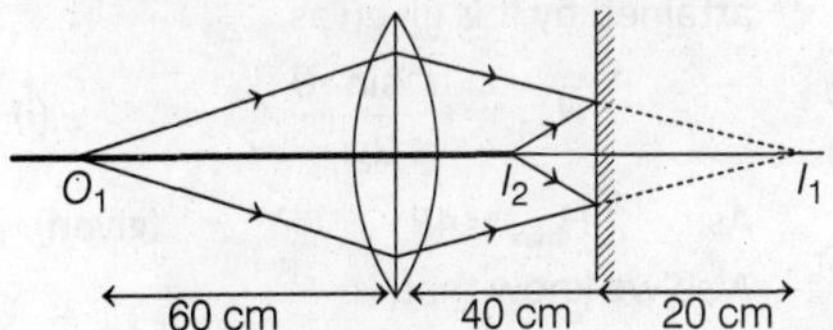

This real image will now act as a virtual object for the mirror.

Thus, a real image from the mirror is formed 20 cm in front of the mirror. Hence, at 20 cm distance from the lens. Also, this real image acts as an object for lens for final image.

Again by using lens formula,

$$\frac{1}{v} + \frac{1}{20} = \frac{1}{30}$$

or $\quad v = -60$ cm from the lens,

i.e. $60 - 40 = 20$ cm from the plane mirror and virtual in nature.

41. (*a*) Given, the main supply line voltage in transformer,

$$V = 220 \text{ V}$$

The rating of the lamp is 11 V, 44 W.

We know that,

$$P = VI_{\text{primary}} \quad \text{...(i)}$$

Here, P is the power that operates the lamp, V is the supply line voltage and I_{primary} is the primary current in the transformer.

From Eq. (i), we get

$\Rightarrow \quad 44 = I_{\text{primary}} \times 220$

$\Rightarrow \quad I_{\text{primary}} = 0.2$ A

42. (*b*) According to the given circuit diagram in question,

$$i_1 = i_2 + i_3 \quad \text{...(i)}$$

In parallel arrangement of the electrical circuit, the voltage remains same.

$\therefore \quad V = ir$ (using Ohm's law)

$\Rightarrow \quad i_2 r_2 = i_3 r_3$

$\Rightarrow \quad i_2 = \frac{i_3 r_3}{r_2}$

Substituting the value in the Eq. (i), we get

$$i_1 = \frac{i_3 r_3}{r_2} + i_3 \Rightarrow \frac{i_1}{i_3} = \frac{r_3}{r_2} + 1$$

$$\Rightarrow \frac{i_1}{i_3} = \frac{r_3 + r_2}{r_2} \Rightarrow \frac{i_3}{i_1} = \frac{r_2}{r_3 + r_2}$$

43. (*b*) Given, velocity, $\mathbf{v} = 2\hat{\mathbf{i}} + 4\hat{\mathbf{j}} + 6\hat{\mathbf{k}}$

Force, $\mathbf{F} = 4\hat{\mathbf{i}} - 20\hat{\mathbf{j}} + 12\hat{\mathbf{k}}$

As we know that,

$$\mathbf{F} = q(\mathbf{v} \times \mathbf{B})$$

Here, $q = 1$ (given)

Substituting the values in the above equation, we get

$$4\hat{\mathbf{i}} - 20\hat{\mathbf{j}} + 12\hat{\mathbf{k}} = (1)[(2\hat{\mathbf{i}} + 4\hat{\mathbf{j}} + 6\hat{\mathbf{k}}) \times (B\hat{\mathbf{i}} + B\hat{\mathbf{j}} + B_0\hat{\mathbf{k}})]$$

$$4\hat{\mathbf{i}} - 20\hat{\mathbf{j}} + 12\hat{\mathbf{k}} = \begin{vmatrix} \hat{\mathbf{i}} & \hat{\mathbf{j}} & \hat{\mathbf{k}} \\ 2 & 4 & 6 \\ B & B & B_0 \end{vmatrix}$$

$$\Rightarrow 4\hat{\mathbf{i}} - 20\hat{\mathbf{j}} + 12\hat{\mathbf{k}} = \hat{\mathbf{i}}(4B_0 - 6B) - \hat{\mathbf{j}}(2B_0 - 6B) + \hat{\mathbf{k}}(2B - 4B)$$

Comparing the LHS and RHS of the above equation, we get

$\hat{\mathbf{i}}$ terms:

$$4B_0 - 6B = 4 \quad \text{...(i)}$$

$\hat{\mathbf{j}}$ terms:

$$2B_0 - 6B = 20 \quad \text{...(ii)}$$

$\hat{\mathbf{k}}$ terms:

$$2B - 4B = 12 \Rightarrow B = -6$$

Substituting the value of B in the Eq. (ii), we get

$$2B_0 - 6(-6) = 20 \Rightarrow B_0 = -8$$

Thus, the magnetic field vector,

$$\mathbf{B} = -6\hat{\mathbf{i}} - 6\hat{\mathbf{j}} - 8\hat{\mathbf{k}}$$

44. (*d*) Given, the mass of the particle = m

The velocity of the projected particle, $v = kv_e$ $(k < 1)$

Initial energy at the time of projection

$$= \frac{1}{2}mv^2 - \frac{GMm}{R}$$

Final energy at the maximum height h from surface of the earth

$$= \frac{1}{2}mv^2 - \frac{GMm}{R+h}$$

$$= \frac{1}{2}m(0)^2 - \frac{GMm}{R+h}$$

($\because$ final velocity is zero at height h from the surface of the earth)

$$= -\frac{GMm}{R+h}$$

Using the law of conservation of energy,

initial energy at the time of projection = final energy at the maximum height h from the surface of the earth

$$\frac{1}{2}mv^2 - \frac{GMm}{R} = -\frac{GMm}{R+h} \quad \text{...(i)}$$

Substituting the value of v in the Eq. (i), we get

$$\frac{1}{2}m(kv_e)^2 - \frac{GMm}{R} = -\frac{GMm}{R+h}$$

$$\Rightarrow \frac{1}{2}mk^2\left(2\frac{GM}{R}\right) - \frac{GMm}{R} = -\frac{GMm}{R+h} \quad \left(\because v_e = \sqrt{\frac{2GM}{R}}\right)$$

$$\Rightarrow \frac{k^2}{R} - \frac{1}{R} = -\frac{1}{R+h} \Rightarrow \frac{1}{R+h} = \frac{1}{R} - \frac{k^2}{R}$$

$$\Rightarrow \frac{R}{1-k^2} = R + h \Rightarrow h = \frac{R}{1-k^2} - R$$

$$\Rightarrow \quad h = R\left(\frac{1}{1-k^2} - 1\right)$$

$$\Rightarrow \quad h = R\left(\frac{1 - 1 + k^2}{1-k^2}\right)$$

$$\Rightarrow \quad h = R\left(\frac{k^2}{1-k^2}\right)$$

45. (*d*) Given, the number of small drops, $n = 27$

Potential on each charged drop, $V = 220$ V

Consider r be the radius of the small drops and R be the radius of the bigger drop.

According to the question, 27 small drops of same size combine to form a bigger drop. So, the volume remains same, i.e.

$$V_{bigger} = 27 \times V_{small}$$

$$\Rightarrow \quad \frac{4}{3}\pi R^3 = 27 \times \frac{4}{3}\pi r^3$$

$$\Rightarrow \quad R^3 = 27 \times r^3 \Rightarrow R = 3r$$

Now, the potential of the small drop,

$$V = \frac{Kq}{r} \quad ...(i)$$

Here, q is the charge on the small drop.

The potential of the bigger drop,

$$V' = \frac{KQ}{R}$$

Here, Q is the charge on the bigger drop.

The charge on the bigger drop is 27 times the charge on the smaller drop, i.e., $Q = 27q$

So, the potential of the bigger drop,

$$V' = \frac{K \times 27q}{3r} \Rightarrow V' = 9\frac{Kq}{r}$$

$$V' = 9V \quad \text{[from Eq. (i)]}$$

$$= 9 \times 220 = 1980 \text{ V}$$

46. (*c*) Given, in the *L*-*C*-*R* series circuit, $L = 5$ H, $C = 80\,\mu$F, $R = 40\,\Omega$

Supply voltage, $V = 230$ V

We know that, resonance frequency,

$$\omega_r = \frac{1}{\sqrt{LC}}$$

Substituting the values in the above equation, we get

$$\omega_r = \frac{1}{\sqrt{5 \times 80 \times 10^{-6}}} = 50 \text{ rad/s}$$

Therefore, the angular frequencies of the source at which power transferred to the circuit is half the power at the resonant angular frequency are

$$\omega = \omega_r \pm \Delta\omega \quad ...(i)$$

We know that,

$$\Delta\omega = \frac{R}{2L} \Rightarrow \Delta\omega = \frac{40}{2(5)} \Rightarrow \Delta\omega = 4$$

Using the Eq. (i), we get

$$\omega = \omega_r \pm \Delta\omega$$

$$\omega = (50 \pm 4) \text{ rad/s}$$

So, the angular frequency is likely to be 46 rad/s and 54 rad/s.

47. (*a*) Given, the length of a uniform conducting wire, $L = 12a$

The resistance of a uniform conducting wire $= R$

We know that, magnetic dipole moment, $M = nIA$

Here, I is the current in the loop,

A is the area of the coil,

n is the number of loops.

For case (1)

An equilateral triangle of side a.

Total wire length $= n \times$ Perimeter of the triangle

$$12a = n \times 3a$$

$$\Rightarrow \quad n = 4$$

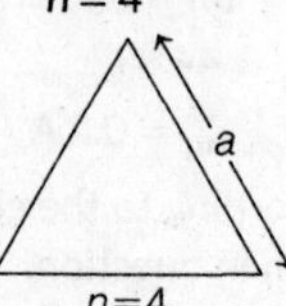

Area of the triangle, $A = \frac{\sqrt{3}}{4}a^2$

Magnetic dipole moment, $M = nIA$

$$\Rightarrow \quad M = 4I \times \frac{\sqrt{3}}{4}a^2$$

$$\Rightarrow \quad M = \sqrt{3}Ia^2$$

For case (2)

A square of side a.

Total wire length $= n \times$ Perimeter of the square

$$12a = n \times 4a$$

$$\Rightarrow \quad n = 3$$

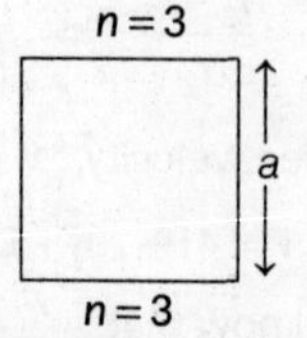

Area of the square loop, $A = a^2$

Magnetic dipole moment,

$$M = nIA$$

$$\Rightarrow \quad M = 3Ia^2$$

48. (*a*) Given, the mass of the circular ring $= M$

The radius of the circular ring $= R$

We know that, the moment of inertia of the circular ring, $I = MR^2$

An arc corresponding to a 90° sector in the circular ring is removed, means one-fourth part of circular ring is removed. Then, the remaining mass of the circular ring,

$$M' = \frac{M}{4}$$

The new moment of inertia,

$$I' = M'R^2 = \frac{MR^2}{4}$$

Now, the moment of inertia of the remaining part,

$$I'' = I - I' = MR^2 - \frac{MR^2}{4} \Rightarrow I'' = \frac{3MR^2}{4}$$

Comparing with $I'' = KMR^2$

The value of $K = 3/4$.

49. (*d*) Since, both conducting circular loops are in same plane and their centres are coinciding.

Hence, magnetic flux, $\phi = Mi \quad ...(i)$

Here, M is the mutual inductance.

Also, the magnetic flux, $\phi = BA$

Here, B is the magnetic field and $A (= \pi R_2^2)$ is the area of the inner circular loop.

If the current passing through the outer loop is i, then the magnetic field,

$$B = \frac{\mu_0 i}{2R_1}$$

Magnetic flux, $\phi = BA$

$$\Rightarrow \quad \phi = \frac{\mu_0 i}{2R_1}(\pi R_2^2) \quad ...(ii)$$

Comparing Eqs. (i) and (ii), we get

$$M = \frac{\mu_0}{2R_1}\pi R_2^2$$

Thus, the mutual inductance is directly proportional to the $\frac{R_2^2}{R_1}$

50. (*d*) Given, the radius of the circular path $= R$

The time taken by the particle to complete one revolution $= T$

When the particle is projected with the same speed (by which it is moving in circular orbit) at angle θ to the horizontal, the maximum height attained by it is given as

$$H_{max} = \frac{u^2 \sin^2\theta}{2g} \quad ...(i)$$

As, $\quad H_{max} = 4R \quad$ (given)

Also we know that,

speed of the particle in circular path,

$$u = \frac{2\pi R}{T}$$

Substituting the values of H_{max} and u in the Eq. (i), we get

$$4R = \frac{\left(\frac{2\pi R}{T}\right)^2 \sin^2\theta}{2g}$$

$$\Rightarrow \quad \sin\theta = \left(\frac{2gT^2}{\pi^2 R}\right)^{1/2}$$

$$\Rightarrow \quad \theta = \sin^{-1}\left(\frac{2gT^2}{\pi^2 R}\right)^{1/2}$$

The Real Nuts 3

1. (*d*) We know that, pressure inside the soap bubble of radius r is given as,

$$p = \frac{4T}{r}$$

where, T is surface tension.

$$\Rightarrow \quad p \propto \frac{1}{r} \quad \text{... (i)}$$

Therefore, when soap bubble expands, then its radius increases, hence from Eq. (i), pressure inside it will decrease.

2. (*c*) de-Broglie wavelength (λ) of a moving particle is given as

$$\lambda = \frac{h}{p}$$

$$\therefore \quad \lambda \propto \frac{1}{p}$$

Hence, the graph showing the variation of de-Broglie wavelength (λ) of a moving particle with its momentum (p) is shown below.

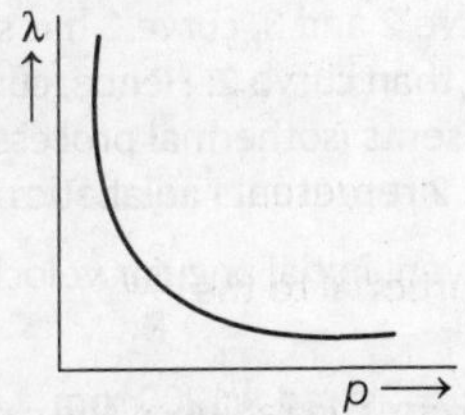

3. (*a*) Given, mass of body, $m = 60$ g

$$= 6 \times 10^{-2} \text{ kg}$$

Gravitational force, $F = 3.0$ N

Magnitude of gravitational field intensity

$$I = \frac{F}{m} = \frac{3}{6 \times 10^{-2}}$$

$$= 50 \text{ N/kg}$$

4. (*b*) According to Biot-Savart's law, magnetic field due to small current element $Id\mathbf{l}$, at a distance r from it is given as

$$dB = \frac{\mu_0 (Id\mathbf{l} \times \mathbf{r})}{4\pi r^3}$$

Thus, current element $Id\mathbf{l}$ is a vector quantity. Hence, statement-I is correct and statement-II is incorrect.

5. (*b*) Initial speed of freely falling body,

$$u = 0$$

We know that, distance travelled by freely falling body in nth second

$$s_n = u + \frac{1}{2} g(2n - 1)$$

$$= 0 + \frac{1}{2} g(2n - 1)$$

$$s_n = \frac{1}{2} g(2n - 1)$$

Distance travelled by body in first second ($n = 1$ s)

$$s_1 = \frac{1}{2} g(2 \times 1 - 1)$$

$$= \frac{g}{2}$$

Distance travelled by body in 2nd second ($n = 2$ s)

$$s_2 = \frac{1}{2} g(2 \times 2 - 1)$$

$$= \frac{3g}{2}$$

Distance travelled by body in 3rd second ($n = 3$ s)

$$s_3 = \frac{1}{2} g\,(2 \times 3 - 1)$$

$$= \frac{5g}{2}$$

Distance travelled by body in 4th second ($n = 4$ s)

$$s_4 = \frac{1}{2} g(2 \times 4 - 1)$$

$$= \frac{7g}{2}$$

$$\therefore \; s_1 : s_2 : s_3 : s_4 = \frac{g}{2} : \frac{3g}{2} : \frac{5g}{2} : \frac{7g}{2}$$

$$= 1 : 3 : 5 : 7$$

6. (*b*) In half wave rectification, input frequency,

$$f_{\text{in}} = 60 \text{ Hz}$$

Since, frequency of output voltage obtained from the half wave rectifier is same as frequency of input AC voltage.

Hence, $f_{\text{out}} = 60$ Hz

7. (*a*) When a spherical ball is dropped in a long column of a highly viscous liquid, then its velocity first increases and after sometime, it moves with constant velocity, known as terminal velocity (v). Hence, correct variation of speed of ball in liquid column with time is given as

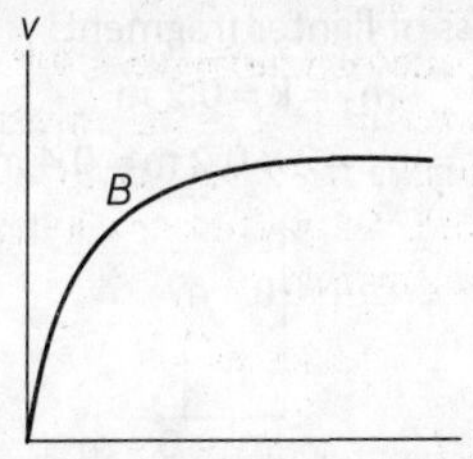

8. (*b*) Work done to move a charge (q) particle between any two points on equipotential surface is zero.

i.e. $\quad W = q(V_2 - V_1)$

$$\Rightarrow \quad \mathbf{F} \cdot d\mathbf{s} = q(V - V) \quad [\because V_1 = V_2 = V]$$

$$\Rightarrow \quad q(\mathbf{E} \cdot d\mathbf{s}) = 0 \quad [\because \mathbf{F} = \mathbf{E} \cdot d\mathbf{s})$$

$$\Rightarrow \quad \mathbf{E} \cdot d\mathbf{s} = 0$$

Therefore, $\mathbf{E} \perp d\mathbf{s}$

i.e., electric field is perpendicular to displacement vector ($d\mathbf{s}$).

Since, $d\mathbf{s}$ lies in the plane of equipotential surface.

Thus, angle between the electric lines of force and the equipotential surface is 90°.

9. (*b*) Coefficient of thermal resistance α is positive for conductor and negative for semiconductor. Thus, on increasing temperature, resistance of conductor increases and resistance of semiconductor decreases.

10. (*b*) The given nuclear reaction is represented as

$${}^{22}_{11}\text{Na} \longrightarrow {}^{M}_{Z}\text{X} + e^{+} + \nu$$

Since, atomic number and mass number are same for both side of reaction.

Hence, for atomic number,

$$11 = Z + 1 \;\Rightarrow\; Z = 10$$

For mass number,

$$22 = M$$

$$\Rightarrow \quad M = 22$$

$$\therefore \quad {}^{M}_{Z}X = {}^{22}_{10}\text{Ne}$$

11. (*c*) For the first excited state of hydrogen atom,

$$n_1 = 2$$

For the second excited state of hydrogen atom,

$$n_2 = 3$$

According to Bohr's model of H-atom, energy of an electron revolving in nth orbit.

$$E = \frac{-13.6}{n^2} \text{ eV}$$

Here, for the first excited state.

$$T_1 = E_1 = \frac{-13.6}{n_1^2}$$

$$= \frac{-13.6}{2^2} \quad [\because n_1 = 2]$$

For the second excited state,

$$T_2 = E_2 = \frac{-13.6}{n_2^2}$$

$$= \frac{-13.6}{3^2} \text{ eV} \quad [\because n_2 = 3]$$

$$\therefore \quad \frac{T_1}{T_2} = \frac{-13.6/2^2}{-13.6/3^2}$$

$$= \frac{3^2}{2^2} = \frac{9}{4}$$

$$\Rightarrow T_1 : T_2 = 9 : 4$$

12. (*a*) Radius of gyration of a body is given as

$$K = \sqrt{\frac{I}{m}}$$

where, I is moment of inertia and m is mass of body.

$$\therefore \quad \frac{K_1}{K_2} = \sqrt{\frac{I_1}{I_2}} \quad \text{... (i)}$$

I_1 = Moment of inertia of thin uniform disc about an axis passing through its centre and normal to plane.

$$= \frac{MR^2}{2}$$

(where, R = radius of disc and M = mass of disc)

I_2 = Moment of inertia of disc about its diameter.

$$= \frac{MR^2}{4}$$

∴ From Eq. (i),

$$\frac{K_1}{K_2} = \sqrt{\frac{MR^2/2}{MR^2/4}} = \sqrt{2}$$

$$\therefore \quad K_1 : K_2 = \sqrt{2} : 1$$

13. (*c*) When light (EM wave) propagates through a material medium of relative permittivity ε_r and relative permeability μ_r, then velocity of light (EM wave) is given by

$$v = \frac{c}{\sqrt{\mu_r \varepsilon_r}}$$

where, c is speed of light in vacuum.

14. (*d*) Given, power radiated by transmitter,

$$P = 100\text{ kW} = 10^5 \text{ W}$$

$$\therefore \text{ Time, } t = 1\text{ h} = 60 \times 60 \text{ s} = 3.6 \times 10^3 \text{ s}$$

∴ Energy radiated by the transmitter,

$$E = P \times t = 10^5 \times 3.6 \times 10^3 = 3.6 \times 10^8 \text{ J} = 36 \times 10^7 \text{ J}$$

15. (*b*) Given, mass (lift + passengers), $m = 2000$ kg

∴ Weight (lift + passengers),

$$w = mg = 2000\, g \text{ N}$$

$$v = 1.5 \text{ m/s}$$

Frictional force, $f = 3000$ N

Since, lift is moving with constant velocity, hence net applied force on the lift = friction force + weight.

$$F = 3000 + 2000\, g = 3000 + 2000 \times 10 = 23000 \text{ N}$$

∴ Minimum power delivered, $P = F \times v$

$$= 23000 \times 1.5 = 34500 \text{ W.}$$

16. (*a*) The given situation is shown in the following circuit diagram.

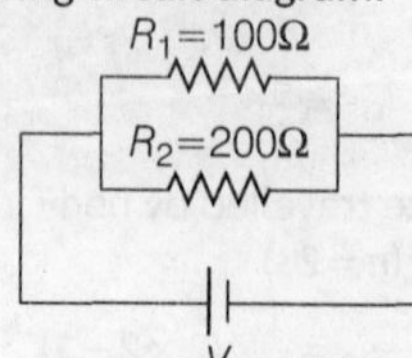

Let, these two resistors are connected with a battery of voltage V volts. We know that, in parallel combination, potential difference across each resistor is same.

Hence, potential difference across R_1, and R are given as, $V_1 = V_2 = V$ volts

If H_1 and H_2 are thermal energy produced through resistances R_1 and R_2 in time t, then

$$H_1 = \frac{V_1^2}{R_1} t = \frac{V^2 t}{100}$$

and

$$H_2 = \frac{V_2^2 t}{R_2} = \frac{V^2 t}{200}$$

Hence,

$$\frac{H_1}{H_2} = \frac{V^2 t/100}{V^2 t/200} = \frac{200}{100} = \frac{2}{1}$$

$$\Rightarrow \quad H_1 : H_2 = 2 : 1$$

17. (*b*) We know that, peak voltage (V_0) and rms voltage (V_{rms}) are related as,

$$V_0 = \sqrt{2}\, V_{rms}$$

Thus, peak voltage of the AC source is equal to $\sqrt{2}$ times the rms value of the AC source.

18. (*b*) Let total mass of the shell be m.

∴ The ratio of the masses of the fragment is 2 : 2 : 1

$$m_1 + m_2 + m_3 = m$$

$$2k + 2k + k = m \Rightarrow k = 0.2\text{ m}$$

∴ Mass of lighter fragment,

$$m_3 = k = 0.2 \text{ m}$$

$$m_1 = m_2 = 2 \times 0.2 \text{ m} = 0.4 \text{ m}$$

V_1
m_1=0.4 m
V
m_2=0.4 m
m_3=0.2 m
V_3

∴ Let the velocity of lighter fragment is v_3,

Since, $p_3 = \sqrt{p_1^2 + p_2^2}$

$$\Rightarrow \quad 0.2 m v_3 = \sqrt{(0.4mv)^2 + (0.4mv)^2}$$

$$\Rightarrow \quad v_3 = 2\sqrt{2}\, v$$

19. (*b*) We know that, velocity of transverse wave in the string, $v \propto \sqrt{T}$

Where, T is tension in the string.

$$\therefore \quad \frac{v_1}{v_2} = \sqrt{\frac{T_1}{T_2}} = \sqrt{\frac{T_1}{2T_1}} \quad [\because T_2 = 2T_1]$$

$$= \frac{1}{\sqrt{2}}$$

$$v_1 : v_2 = 1 : \sqrt{2}$$

20. (*a*) When a thermodynamic system undergoes a change in such a way that no exchange of heat takes place between it and the surrounding, the process is known as adiabatic process.

Curve 4 is isobaric process because pressure is constant.

Curve 1 is isochoric process because volume is constant.

In curve 2 and 3, curve 3 has smaller slope than curve 2. Hence, curve 3 represents isothermal process and curve 2 represents adiabatic process.

21. (*a*) Given, initial angular velocity of fly wheel,

$$\omega_0 = 2\pi \text{ rad} \times 1200 \text{ rpm} = 2\pi \text{ rad} \times \frac{1200}{60} \text{ rps} = 40\,\pi \text{ rad/s}$$

Similarly, final angular velocity of fly wheel,

$$\omega = 2\pi \text{ rad} \times 3120 \text{ rpm} = 2\pi \text{ rad} \times \frac{3120}{60} \text{ rps} = 104\,\pi \text{ rad/s}$$

Time, $t = 16$ s

If α be the angular acceleration, then using the equation of rotational motion,

$$\omega = \omega_0 + \alpha t$$

$$\Rightarrow 104\pi = 40\pi + \alpha \times 16$$

$$\Rightarrow \quad \alpha = \frac{104\,\pi - 40\,\pi}{16} = \frac{64\,\pi}{16} = 4\pi \text{ rad/s}^2$$

22. (*d*) Plane angle is measured in radian whereas solid angle is measured in steradian.

Therefore, plane angle and solid angle have units but no dimensions.

23. (c) In the circuit diagram (A) and (C), both the *p-n* junction diodes are in same biasing conditions.

So, both diodes offers equal resistances.

Since, both diodes are in series, therefore equal potential will drop across the junction.

24. (c) In Young's double slit experiment, wavelength of light used is inversely proportional to the number of fringes observed.

i.e. $\lambda_1 n_1 = \lambda_2 n_2$

$$n_2 = \frac{n_1 \lambda_1}{\lambda_2}$$

Here, $\lambda_1 = 600\ \text{nm} = 6 \times 10^{-7}\ \text{m}$

$\lambda_2 = 400\ \text{nm} = 4 \times 10^{-7}\ \text{m}$

$n_1 = 8$

$$\therefore \quad n_2 = \frac{8 \times 6 \times 10^{-7}}{4 \times 10^{-7}} = 12$$

25. (*) Using Einstein's photoelectric equation,

$$eV' = h\nu' - h\nu_0$$

when $\nu' = \nu$ and $V' = V_s$, then

$$\therefore \quad eV_s = h\nu - h\nu_0 \quad \text{... (i)}$$

Again when $\nu' = \frac{\nu}{2}$ and $V' = \frac{V_s}{2}$

$$\therefore \quad \frac{eV_s}{2} = \frac{h\nu}{2} - h\nu_0 \quad \text{... (ii)}$$

Dividing Eq. (i) by Eq. (ii), we have

$$\frac{eV_s}{eV_s/2} = \frac{h\nu - h\nu_0}{\frac{h\nu}{2} - h\nu_0}$$

$$2 = \frac{h(\nu - \nu_0)}{h\left(\frac{\nu}{2} - \nu_0\right)}$$

$$\Rightarrow \quad 2\left(\frac{\nu}{2} - \nu_0\right) = \nu - \nu_0$$

$$\nu - 2\nu_0 = \nu - \nu_0$$

$$\Rightarrow \quad \nu_0 = 0$$

Hence, question is wrong.

26. (*a*) Side of square loop, $a = 1\ \text{m}$

$\therefore$ Area of square loop, $A = a^2 = 1^2 = 1\ \text{m}^2$

Resistance of square loop, $R = 1\ \Omega$

Magnetic field, $B = 0.5\ \text{T}$

Since, plane of loop is perpendicular to the direction of magnetic field, hence angle made by the normal to the loop with the direction of magnetic field will be 0°.

i.e., $\theta = 0$

$\therefore$ Magnetic flux passing through the loop,

$$\phi = BA\cos\theta = 0.5 \times 1 \times \cos 0° = 0.5\ \text{Wb}$$

27. (*a*) Potential on the hollow conducting sphere of radius *R* due to charge *Q* is

$$V = \frac{1}{4\pi\varepsilon_0}\frac{Q}{R}$$

$$\Rightarrow \quad V \propto \frac{1}{R} \quad \text{[For same charge } Q\text{]}$$

$$\Rightarrow \quad \frac{V_1}{V_2} = \frac{R_2}{R_1}$$

Since, $R_1 > R_2$

$$\therefore \quad \frac{R_1}{R_2} > 1$$

$$\Rightarrow \quad \frac{R_2}{R_1} < 1$$

$$\therefore \quad \frac{V_1}{V_2} < 1$$

$$\therefore \quad V_1 < V_2$$

Hence, potential will more on smaller sphere.

28. (c) Given, radius, $r = \frac{10^{-2}}{\sqrt{\pi}}\ \text{m}$

$\therefore \quad R = 10\ \Omega$

$E = 10\ \text{V/m}$

$l = 10\ \text{m}$

$\therefore$ Area of cross-section of copper wire,

$$A = \pi r^2 = \pi \times \left(\frac{10^{-2}}{\sqrt{\pi}}\right)^2 = 10^{-4}\ \text{m}^2$$

$\therefore$ Current density,

$$J = \frac{i}{A} = \frac{V/R}{A} \quad \left[\because i = \frac{V}{R}\right]$$

$$= \frac{V}{RA} = \frac{El}{RA} \quad [\because V = El]$$

$$= \frac{10 \times 10}{10 \times 10^{-4}} = 10^5\ \text{A/m}^2$$

29. (*a*) Given, radius of solenoid, $r = 1\ \text{mm}$

Number of turns per mm $= \frac{100}{1\ \text{mm}}$

$\therefore$ Number of turns per metre

$$= \frac{100}{1 \times 10^{-3}\ \text{m}}$$

i.e., $n = 10^5$ turns/m

Current flowing through the solenoid,

$$I = 1\ \text{A}$$

$\therefore$ Magnetic field strength at the centre of the solenoid

$$B = \mu_0 nI = 4\pi \times 10^{-7} \times 10^5 \times 1 = 4\pi \times 10^{-2}\ \text{T} = 12.56 \times 10^{-2}\ \text{T}$$

30. (*a*) The given situation is shown below.

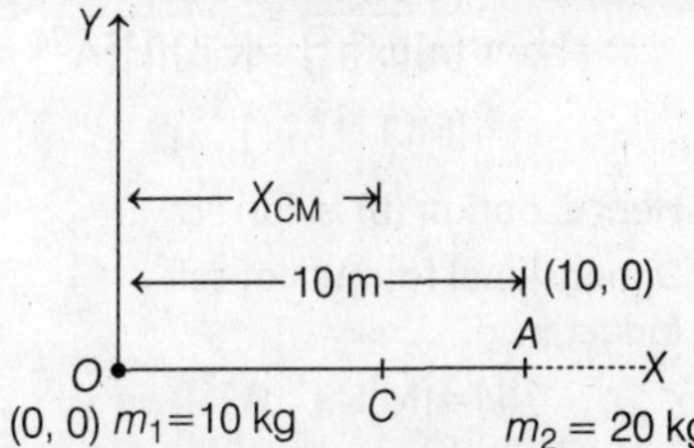

Let X_{CM} be the position of centre of mass from 10 kg mass.

$$\therefore \quad X_{CM} = \frac{m_1 x_1 + m_2 x_2}{m_1 + m_2} = \frac{10 \times 0 + 20 \times 10}{10 + 20} = \frac{200}{30} = \frac{20}{3}\ \text{m}$$

31. (*b*) Given, refractive index of glass surface

$$\mu = \sqrt{3}$$

Angle of incidence, $i = 60°$

Since, above situation follows Brewster's law because,

$$\mu = \tan i = \tan 60° = \sqrt{3}$$

Hence, angle *i* is equal to polarising angle i_p.

i.e., $i_p = i = 60°$

By snell's law

$$\mu = \frac{\sin i_p}{\sin r}$$

$$\Rightarrow \quad \tan i_p = \frac{\sin i_p}{\sin r} \quad [\text{Since, } \mu = \tan i_p]$$

$$\Rightarrow \quad \frac{\sin i_p}{\cos i_p} = \frac{\sin i_p}{\sin r}$$

$$\Rightarrow \quad \cos i_p = \sin r$$

$$\Rightarrow \quad \cos i_p = \cos(90° - r)$$

$$\Rightarrow \quad i_p = 90° - r$$

$$\Rightarrow \quad r + i_p = 90°$$

Hence, angle between the refracted and reflected rays

$$= 180° - (r + i_p) = 180° - (90°) = 90°$$

It is also called Brewster's law.

32. (*b*) We know that, magnetic field due to current carrying solenoid,

$$B = \mu_0 nI$$

$$\Rightarrow \quad \mu_0 = \frac{B}{nI} \Rightarrow [\mu_0] = \frac{[B]}{[n][I]}$$

$$= \frac{\left[\frac{F}{IL}\right]}{[n][I]} \quad \left[\because F = IBL \Rightarrow B = \frac{F}{IL}\right]$$

$$= \frac{[F]}{[n][L][I^2]} = \frac{[MLT^{-2}]}{[L^{-1}][L][A^2]}$$

$$= [MLT^{-2}A^{-2}]$$

Hence, option (b) is correct.

Dimensional formula of self inductance,

$$[L] = [M^1L^2T^{-2}A^{-2}]$$

Dimensional formula of electric permittivity,

$$[\varepsilon_0] = [M^{-1}L^{-3}T^4A^2]$$

Dimensional formula of magnetic flux,

$$[\phi] = [ML^2T^{-2}A^{-1}]$$

33. (*c*) We know that, slope of displacement-time graph for a moving object gives velocity of moving object.

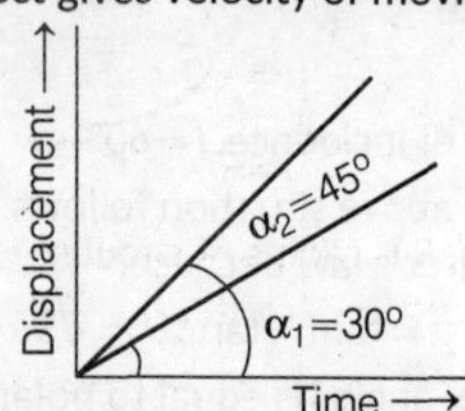

$\therefore$ Velocity of first moving particle,

$$v_1 = \tan\alpha_1$$

$$= \tan 30° = \frac{1}{\sqrt{3}}$$

Velocity of second moving particle,

$$v_2 = \tan\alpha_2 = \tan 45° = 1$$

$$\therefore \quad \frac{v_1}{v_2} = \frac{1/\sqrt{3}}{1} = \frac{1}{\sqrt{3}}$$

$$\therefore \quad v_1 : v_2 = 1 : \sqrt{3}$$

34. (*b*) For a biconvex lens,

$R_1 = +20$ cm, $R_2 = -20$ cm and $\mu = 1.5$

By using lens maker's formula, we have,

$$\frac{1}{f} = (\mu - 1)\left(\frac{1}{R_1} - \frac{1}{R_2}\right)$$

$$= (1.5 - 1)\left(\frac{1}{20} - \frac{1}{-20}\right)$$

$$= 0.5\left(\frac{2}{20}\right)$$

$$\Rightarrow \quad \frac{1}{f} = 0.5 \times \frac{1}{10}$$

$$\Rightarrow \quad f = \frac{10}{0.5}$$

$$\Rightarrow \quad f = 20 \text{ cm} = 0.2 \text{ m}$$

$\therefore$ Power of the lens, $P = \frac{1}{f}$ (in metre)

$$= \frac{1}{0.2} = +5\text{ D}$$

35. (*c*)

A. Wavelength range of AM radio waves lies between 10^2 m to 10^3 m.

B. Wavelength range of microwaves lies between 10^{-3}m to 10^{-1}m.

C. Wavelength range of infrared radiations lies between 10^{-5}m to 10^{-3}m.

D. Wavelength range of X-rays lies between 10^{-12}m to 10^{-8}m.

Therefore, correct matching pairs are (A)-(ii), (B)-(iii), (C)-(iv), (D)-(i)

36. (*b*) Given, mass number of parent nucleus, $A = 189$

Mass number of daughters nuclei,

$$A_1 = 125 \text{ and } A_2 = 64$$

We know that,

$$R = R_0(A^{1/3})$$

where, R_0 is constant.

$$\therefore \quad \frac{R_1}{R_2} = \left(\frac{A_1}{A_2}\right)^{1/3} = \left(\frac{125}{64}\right)^{1/3}$$

$$= \left[\left(\frac{5}{4}\right)^3\right]^{1/3} = \frac{5}{4}$$

$$\therefore \quad R_1 : R_2 = 5 : 4$$

37. (*a*) Given, speed of light in transparent medium A,

$$v_A = 1.5 \times 10^8 \text{ m/s}$$

Speed of light in transparent medium B,

$$v_B = 2 \times 10^8 \text{ m/s}$$

Refractive index (μ) and critical angle (i_c) are related as

$$\mu = \frac{1}{\sin i_c}$$

$$\Rightarrow \quad \sin i_c = \frac{1}{\mu} = \frac{1}{(v_B / v_A)} \quad \left[\because \mu = \frac{v_B}{v_A}\right]$$

$$= \frac{v_A}{v_B} = \frac{1.5 \times 10^8}{2 \times 10^8} = 0.750$$

$$\Rightarrow \quad i_c = \sin^{-1}(0.750)$$

38. (*b*) Given, number of turns in big circular coil, $N = 1000$

Average radius, $r = 10$ m

Vertical component of Earth's magnetic field,

$$B_V = 2 \times 10^{-5}\text{ T}$$

Resistance of coil, $R = 12.56\ \Omega$

Angular velocity, $\omega = 2$ rad/s

Maximum induced emf in the coil

$$e_{max} = NBA\omega = NB_vA\omega$$

$$= 1000 \times 2 \times 10^{-5} \times \pi(10)^2 \times 2$$

$$[\because A = \pi r^2]$$

$$e_{max} = 4\pi\text{ V}$$

$\therefore$ Maximum induced current in the coil

$$I_{max} = \frac{e_{max}}{R} = \frac{4\pi}{12 \cdot 56} = 1\text{ A}$$

39. (*a*) A. According to Newton's law of gravitation,

$$F = G\frac{m_1m_2}{r^2} \Rightarrow G = \frac{Fr^2}{m_1m_2}$$

$$\Rightarrow [G] = \frac{[F][r^2]}{[m_1][m_2]} = \frac{[MLT^{-2}][L^2]}{[M][M]}$$

$$\Rightarrow [G] = [M^{-1}L^3T^{-2}]$$

B. Gravitational potential energy,

$$U = mgh$$

$$[U] = [m][g][h]$$

$$= [M][LT^{-2}][L]$$

$$= [ML^2T^{-2}]$$

C. Gravitational potential,

$$V = -\frac{Gm}{r}$$

$$\therefore \quad [V] = \frac{[G][m]}{[r]}$$

$$= \frac{[M^{-1}L^3T^{-2}][M]}{[L]}$$

$$= [L^2T^{-2}]$$

D. Gravitational intensity,

$$I = \frac{GM}{r^2}$$

$$\therefore \quad [I] = \frac{[G][M]}{[r^2]}$$

$$= \frac{[M^{-1}L^3T^{-2}][M]}{[L^2]}$$

$$= [LT^{-2}]$$

Hence, correct matching pair is (A)-(ii), (B)-(iv), (C)-(i), (D)-(iii)

40. (*b*) When a coil spring is stretched, neither its length nor its volume changes, but there is only the change in its shape. Therefore, stretching of coil spring is determined by shear modulus.

Young's modulus of steel spring is more than Young's modulus of copper spring, therefore tensile strength of

steel spring is more than tensile strength of copper spring.
Hence, Assertion is true but Reason is false.

41. (*c*) Area = Length × Breadth

$= 55.3 \times 25 = 1382.5$

$= 13.825 \times 10^2 = 13.83 \times 10^2$

$= 13.8 \times 10^2 = 14 \times 10^2$

42. (*) The given logic circuit is represented as

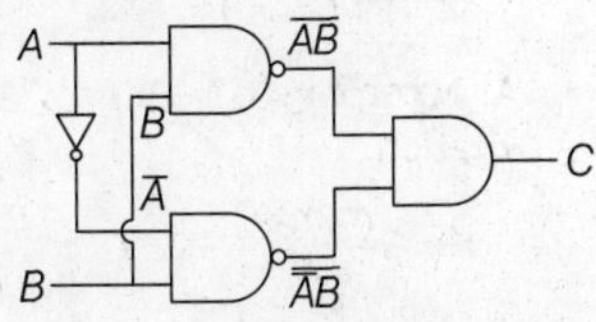

Output of logic circuit,

$$C = \overline{AB} + \overline{\overline{A}B}$$

$$= (\overline{A} + \overline{B}) + \overline{\overline{A}} + \overline{B}$$

[Using De-morgan's law $\overline{xy} = \overline{x} + \overline{y}$]

$$= \overline{A} + \overline{B} + A + \overline{B}$$

$$C = \overline{A} + A + \overline{B} = 1 + \overline{B} \qquad [\because \overline{A} + A = 1]$$

Truth table is given as

A	B	$\overline{B}$	$C = 1 + \overline{B}$
0	0	1	1
0	1	0	1
1	0	1	1
1	1	0	1

Hence, no option is correct.

43. (*c*) Molecular weight of water = 18 g

$= 1.8 \times 10^{-2}$ kg

∴ Mass of water, $M = 4.5$ kg

∴ number of moles of water,

$$n = \frac{\text{Mass of water}}{\text{Molecular weight of water}}$$

$$= \frac{4.5}{1.8 \times 10^{-2}} = 250$$

At STP, $T = 273$ K, $p = 10^5$ N/m^2

Using equation, $pV = nRT$

$$\Rightarrow \quad V = \frac{nRT}{p}$$

$$= \frac{250 \times 8.3 \times 273}{10^5}$$

$$= 5.6 \text{ m}^3$$

44. (*a*) For the most precise measurement of unknown resistance *X*, the resistances *P* and *Q* should be approximately equal and should be small so that it could decrease error in experiment.

45. (*a*) Given, In series *L*-*C*-*R* circuit,

$$L = 10 \text{ H}, C = 10 \mu\text{F} = 10^{-5} \text{ F}$$

$$R = 50 \, \Omega$$

Source voltage, $V = 200 \sin(100\,t)$ volt.

$$\omega = 100 \text{ rad/s}$$

$$\therefore \quad 2\pi\nu = 100$$

$$\Rightarrow \quad \nu = \frac{100}{2\pi} = \frac{50}{\pi} \text{ Hz}$$

Resonance frequency,

$$\nu_0 = \frac{1}{2\pi\sqrt{LC}} = \frac{1}{2\pi\sqrt{10 \times 10^{-5}}}$$

$$= \frac{1}{2\,\pi \times 10^{-2}} = \frac{50}{\pi} \text{ Hz}$$

Hence, $\nu = \nu_0 = \dfrac{50}{\pi}$ Hz

46. (*b*) The given situation is shown below.

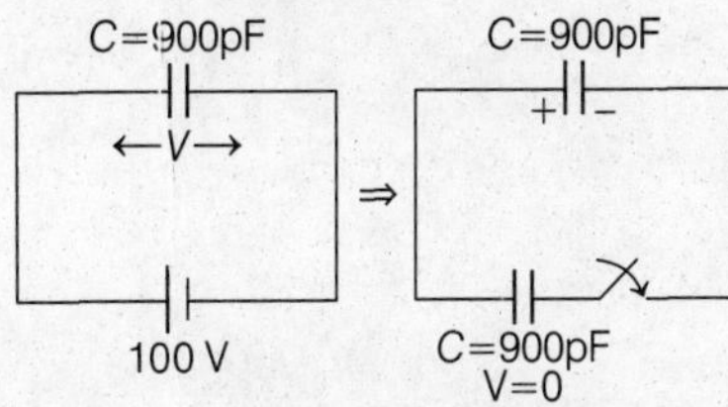

After combination,

Common potential,

$$V = \frac{C_1V_1 + C_2V_2}{C_1 + C_2}$$

$$= \frac{C \times 100 + C \times 0}{C + C} = 50 \text{ V}$$

∴ Electrostatic stored potential energy,

$$U = 2 \times \frac{1}{2} CV^2 = CV^2$$

$$= 9 \times 10^{-10} \times 50^2$$

$$= 2.25 \times 10^{-6} \text{ J}$$

47. (*a*) The arrangement of charges shown in the figure is an electric dipole. Hence, electric field at point *P* at a distance $R (R >> L)$ from the dipole is equal to electric field due to electric dipole on axial position.

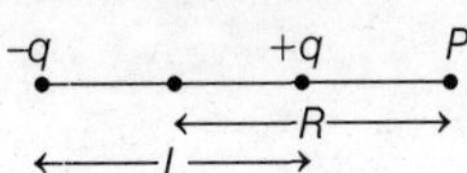

i.e., $$E = \frac{1}{4\pi\varepsilon_0} \cdot \frac{2\,p}{R^3}$$

where, $p = qL$ (Electric dipole moment)

$$\therefore \quad E \propto \frac{1}{R^3}$$

48. (*b*) Initial speed of ball, $u = 10 \text{ ms}^{-1}$

Angle of projection, $\theta = 60°$

At highest point of the trajectory of ball, its vertical component of velocity becomes zero and only horizontal component of velocity exists, which is equal to horizontal component of velocity at the time of projection.

i.e., speed of ball at highest point

$$= u\cos\theta = 10\cos 60°$$

$$= 10 \times \frac{1}{2} = 5 \text{ ms}^{-1}$$

49. (*b*) According to Ampere's circuital law, magnetic field inside the current carrying long straight wire of circular cross-section is a linearly increasing function of distance $r (r < R)$ upto the boundary of the wire and magnetic field outside the wire at distance $r (r > R)$ from its axis is decreasing one with $\frac{1}{r}$ dependence as shown in figure.

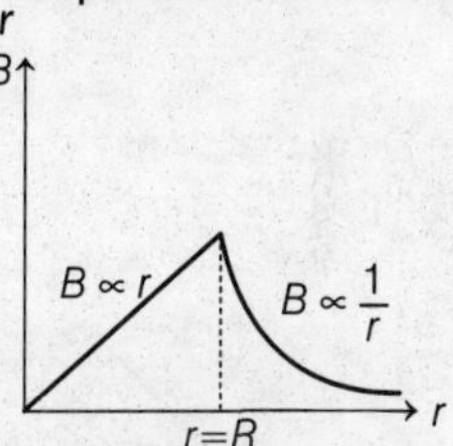

where, *R* is radius of circular cross-section of wire.

50. (*d*) Given, length of first pendulum,

$$l_1 = 121 \text{ cm} = 1.21 \text{ m}$$

length of second pendulum,

$$l_2 = 100 \text{ cm} = 1 \text{ m}$$

According to given situation, both pendulums are again in phase if vibrations made by the shorter pendulum will be known.

Let T_1 and T_2 be the time periods of longer and shorter pendulum respectively.

Since, $$T = 2\pi\sqrt{\frac{l}{g}}$$

$$\Rightarrow \quad \frac{T_1}{T_2} = \sqrt{\frac{l_1}{l_2}}$$

$$= \sqrt{\frac{1.21}{1}} = 1.1 = \frac{11}{10}$$

$$\Rightarrow \quad 10\,T_1 = 11\,T_2$$

∴ 10 vibrations of longer pendulum = 11 vibrations of shorter pendulum

∴ Minimum number of vibrations of shorter pendulum = 11